The Heath Anthology of American Literature

Volume C

Late Nineteenth Century: 1865–1910

The Heath Anthology of American Literature

Seventh Edition

Volume C
Late Nineteenth Century: 1865–1910

Paul Lauter
Trinity College
General Editor

John Alberti
Northern Kentucky University
Editor, Instructor's Guide

Mary Pat Brady
Cornell University

Kirk Curnutt
Troy University

Daniel Heath Justice
University of British Columbia

James Kyung-Jin Lee
University of California, Irvine

Richard Yarborough
University of California, Los Angeles
Associate General Editor

Wendy Martin
Claremont Graduate University

D. Quentin Miller
Suffolk University

Bethany Schneider
Bryn Mawr College

Ivy T. Schweitzer
Dartmouth College

Sandra A. Zagarell
Oberlin College

WADSWORTH
CENGAGE Learning

Australia • Brazil • Japan • Korea • Mexico • Singapore • Spain • United Kingdom • United States

The Heath Anthology of American Literature, Seventh Edition
Volume C, *Late Nineteenth Century: 1865–1910*

Edited by Paul Lauter, Richard Yarborough, John Alberti, Mary Pat Brady, Kirk Curnutt, Daniel Heath Justice, James Kyung-Jin Lee, Wendy Martin, D. Quentin Miller, Bethany Schneider, Ivy T. Schweitzer, and Sandra A. Zagarell

Editor in Chief: Lyn Uhl
Publisher: Michael Rosenberg
Senior Development Editor: Leslie Taggart
Development Editor: Laurie Dobson
Assistant Editor: Erin Bosco
Editorial Assistant: Rebecca Donahue
Media Editor: Janine Tangney
Marketing Brand Manager: Lydia LeStar
Content Project Manager: Rosemary Winfield
Art Director: Marissa Falco
Production Technology Analyst: Jeff Joubert
Print Buyer: Betsy Donaghey
Rights Acquisition Specialist: Jessica Elias
Production Service: Tania Andrabi, Cenveo Publisher Services
Text Designer: Shawn Girsberger
Cover Designer: Tani Hasegawa
Cover Image: Earnest L. Spybuck (Ernest Spybuck/Mahthela), Shawnee, Oklahoma-Pottawatomie County, 1883–1949, *Procession Before War Dance*, 1908–1910. Watercolor on paperboard, graphite, watercolor, 64 × 44 cm. National Museum of the American Indian, Washington DC. Commissioned from the artist by anthropologist Mark Raymond Harrington (1882–1971, MAI staff member) between 1908 and 1910; acquired by George Heye in 1910.
Compositor: Cenveo Publisher Services

For product information and technology assistance, contact us at **Cengage Learning Customer & Sales Support, 1-800-354-9706.**

For permission to use material from this text or product, submit all requests online at **www.cengage.com/permissions**.
Further permissions questions can be emailed to **permissionrequest@cengage.com**.

Library of Congress Control Number: 2012949135

ISBN 13: 978-1-133-31024-2
ISBN 10: 1-133-31024-9

Wadsworth
20 Channel Center Street
Boston, MA 02210
USA

Cengage Learning is a leading provider of customized learning solutions with office locations around the globe, including Singapore, the United Kingdom, Australia, Mexico, Brazil and Japan. Locate your local office at **international.cengage.com/region**.

Cengage Learning products are represented in Canada by Nelson Education, Ltd.

For your course and learning solutions, visit **www.cengage.com**.
Purchase any of our products at your local college store or at our preferred online store **www.cengagebrain.com**.

Instructors: Please visit **login.cengage.com** and log in to access instructor-specific resources.

Printed in the United States of America
3 4 5 6 7 19

CONTENTS

WRITING AND PLACE   338

IN FOCUS
The Dawes Act   552

REDEFINING THE SOUTH 601

OUTSIDE/INSIDE U.S.A.: EXPANSION AND IMMIGRATION   811

IN FOCUS
Expansion and Immigration   811

■

A SELECTION OF POETRY BY LATE-NINETEENTH- 1241
CENTURY AMERICAN WOMEN

PREFACE

The *Heath Anthology of American Literature* represents a remarkable success story. It is not the story of a book, a small board of editors, or even a few publishing houses. It is, rather, the story of the thousands of students and faculty who have in the last quarter century transformed the study of American literature.

LITERATURE AS AN INCLUSIVE CULTURAL FORM

When in 1978 we began the Reconstructing American Literature project (from which the anthology developed), the definition of what constituted American literature was very narrow in terms of the authors covered, the forms of writing included, and the ideas of literary study then dominant. Today's students would hardly recognize the anthologies or the syllabi that characterized the work of critics and teachers back in the 1950s or 1960s. That work would appear as odd today as 1900 baseball uniforms or perhaps Victorian hoop skirts—recognizable but remote from our society or culture.

The *Heath Anthology of American Literature* was part of a movement for cultural change. That movement took as its goal conceiving American literature as an inclusive cultural form, a form of creativity that spoke of and to the lives of all Americans and that spoke with many voices and in many different ways. It has always been our intent and practice to represent the writers who traditionally had constituted American literature. It was and remains our goal to be as inclusive as the limits of these five volumes permit.

A DIVERSE COMMUNITY OF SCHOLARS

Because societies and cultures change, our understanding of the meaning of *inclusive* likewise changes. As readers will see, today's seventh edition of the *Heath Anthology* differs in what we think are interesting and useful ways from the first edition of 1980 or even from the more recent sixth edition. We have updated a large number of headnotes as well as introductions. And we have made certain changes in the literary texts contained in the anthology. Many of these changes are specified below.

Most of the ideas for change originated with teachers and students who have used the anthology. The particular character of the *Heath Anthology* has always depended on the participation in the project of a wide community of scholars and teachers. Unlike other anthologies, the *Heath* includes introductory notes that have been written by scholars who specialize in a particular author. In their diverse yet consistent approaches, these headnotes illustrate for students how writing about literature is not limited to any single standard.

More important, perhaps, these contributing editors, together with readers, consultants, and users of the anthology, have provided guidance to our large and diverse editorial board as we determine the changes that will make the anthology most useful. We hope that a new generation of students and teachers will share with us their ideas about what works in the anthology and what does not, what texts and configurations might be changed, and what more we might provide so that they can make the best use of these books.

BROADENING THE "LITERARY"

What is the "best use"? The answers to that question will, of course, vary enormously depending on the students and teachers involved. One could teach a fairly traditional course using *The Heath Anthology of American Literature*, emphasizing only the writers historically considered significant. There are rich selections in these volumes of writers like Edwards, Franklin, Emerson, Hawthorne, Melville, Thoreau, Whitman, Dickinson, James, Twain, and modernists like Eliot, Fitzgerald, Hemingway, Pound, Stevens, Wharton, and the like. But we have from the beginning of this project striven to include many writers who would not have been part of such a traditional course, like Frederick Douglass, Lydia Maria Child, Frances Harper, Sarah Piatt, Charles W. Chesnutt, Mary Wilkins Freeman, Kate Chopin, José Martí, and Randolph Bourne, just to name a few from earlier times. One of the accomplishments that we are most proud of is the transformative impact of the *Heath Anthology* on the American literary canon. The inclusion of a number of important new (that is, underappreciated) authors in the *Heath* has played an important role in catalyzing a wider and deeper awareness of their significance.

Likewise, these books contain abundant selections of fiction, poetry, drama, and also nonfictional prose, polemical and historical essays, songs, chants, speeches, and the like. Another major goal of the *Heath Anthology* has been to broaden our understanding of what constitutes the "literary." On the one hand, we want to provide students with a large selection of well-known texts whose literary power and cultural relevance had been established by generations of critics and teachers—William Bradford's "Of Plymouth Plantation," Benjamin Franklin's *Autobiography*, poetry by Bradstreet and Dickinson, "Young Goodman Brown," "Self-Reliance," "Civil Disobedience," "Annabel Lee," "Daisy Miller," "The Open Boat," *The Awakening*, *The Waste Land*, "Hills Like White Elephants," "Sonny's Blues," "Howl."

At the same time, we wish to provide exemplary texts that, because of their forms or subjects, have seldom been taught and often little read. Thus, we include, for example, "sorrow songs" or spirituals, nineteenth-century folk songs and stories, *corridos* and blues lyrics, and poems written on the walls of Angel Island prison by Chinese detainees.

Likewise, we include nonfictional forms such as the spiritual autobiographies of Thomas Shepard and Elizabeth Ashbridge, sketches by Fanny Fern, polemical letters by Angelina and Sarah Grimké, columns by Finley Peter Dunne, José Martí's important "Our America," Randolph Bourne's "Trans-National America," Martin Luther King's "I Have a Dream," and chapters from Gloria Anzaldúa's *Borderlands/La Frontera*. The sixth edition extended this goal by incorporating journal entries from several members of the Lewis and Clark expedition, letters protesting Cherokee removal, "proletarian" folk songs, and graphic narratives by Art Spiegelman, Lynda Barry, and others.

The seventh edition widens the lens still further by including a broader span of written texts by Native American authors from all parts of the country, the work of many more Spanish-language writers of all centuries, including those from the period of the Mexican Revolution, Chinese American immigrants such as novelist and future actor H. T. Tsiang, and essays such as Carlos Bulosan's "The Freedom from Want" that dramatize both the allure and the pitfalls of nationalism. A section of Spoken Word poetry now concludes the anthology. It is our hope that teachers and students will be able to take advantage of what remains, by far, the most inclusive and varied anthology in the field.

LONG AND SHORT WORKS

The *Heath Anthology* has also from its beginning balanced longer complete works with shorter texts by the wide variety of authors included. Thus, this edition includes the full texts of Royall Tyler's "The Contrast," Susanna Rowson's play *Slaves in Algiers; or, A Struggle for Freedom*, Melville's "Benito Cereno" and "Billy Budd," Frederick Douglass's *Narrative*, Abraham Cahan's "The Imported Bridegroom," Kate Chopin's *The Awakening*, Nella Larsen's *Passing*, George C. Wolfe's *The Colored Museum*, and Arthur Miller's *A View From the Bridge*, among many other longer works.

HISTORICAL AND SOCIAL CONTEXTS

It has always been our view that literature, like any art form, must in part be studied in relation to the historical and social contexts from which it develops and to which it speaks. We have therefore systematically included in the volumes important historical texts ranging from the Declaration of Independence to decisive court decisions like those that enabled Indian "removal" or imposed and finally helped end racial segregation. These "In Focus" sections can be read for their own interest, since they are vivid documents in and of themselves. But they can also be read to provide contexts to the more traditionally literary texts that constitute the primary content of the anthology. With the *Heath Anthology*'s unusually wide selection, they provide instructors with broadened opportunities to help students perceive continuity and change in the literary and cultural history of what is now the United States.

Likewise, in this electronic age, we have the following electronic resources for both instructors and students:

- **Heath Anthology Premium Website for Volumes A, B, C, D, and E.** This robust Premium Website includes a wide variety of multimedia resources to help bring to life the works and time periods featured in the *Anthology*. The website can be navigated by volume and centers around thirty of the most commonly taught works for each volume.

Each is supported by reading comprehension quizzes, interactive media such as audio or video, Web links, and author biographies. In addition, the Premium Website features materials to help provide historical, social, and political context for these works, such as maps and images. A glossary of literary terms is also provided, in both list form and as interactive flashcards. A variety of eBooks are available as an optional add-on to the Premium Website, including *The Scarlet Letter* and *Adventures of Huckleberry Finn*. Access the Premium Website at www.cengagebrain.com.

- **The Heath Blog.** Available as a link from the Instructor Companion Site and from the Premium Website, the Heath Blog is dedicated to providing tools, information, and pedagogical approaches for instructors and students of American literature and culture. It provides virtual space for conversations about what choices we make when we anthologize texts, how these texts are presented and received in the classroom, and how they resonate with contemporary concerns. All users are encouraged to respond to the blog articles with their own commentary and suggestions. Instructors may access the Instructor Companion Site at www.login.cengage.com, and the Premium Website is available for students via www.cengagebrain.com.

- **Online Instructor's Manual.** The *Online Instructor's Manual*, edited by John Alberti, offers suggestions for approaching texts and authors, model assignments, and useful exam and discussion questions. This helpful resource is available on the Instructor Companion Site, which can be accessed at www.login.cengage.com.

- **Instructor Companion Site.** This password-protected website provides access to both the downloadable Online Instructor's Manual and the Heath Blog.

CHANGES IN THE SEVENTH EDITION

The seventh edition includes 176 new works across the five volumes.

WHAT IS NEW IN VOLUME A, BEGINNINGS TO 1800

Changes to Volume A, Beginnings to 1800, are relatively few but draw on the latest scholarship to update translations and headnotes as well as enrich our offerings from Native and Spanish America. As in the other volumes in the seventh edition, we have added a new "In Focus: Northern New York—Mohegan/Brotherton Tribes" section that highlights the region of Northern New York. Included in this section are writers pulled from other places in the sixth edition, such as Handsome Lake, Samson Occom, and Hendrick Aupaumut, complemented by a new excerpt from Joseph Johnson, son-in-law and close associate of Occom, capped by an introductory headnote that discusses the many interrelations among these figures across tribal affiliation and the larger cultural movements they shaped. We have added Corn

Tassel to "Native American Political Texts and Oratory" to continue integrating Native American writing and oratory throughout Volume A.

The selections from Gaspar Perez de Villagrá have been expanded and newly translated and form the hub of a group of hemispheric Spanish American writers recounting the exploration and conquest of North and South America, including new entries by Juan de Oñate, Fray Alonso Gregorio de Escobedo on the conquest of Florida, and Felipe Guaman Poma de Ayala on the conquest of Peru. Excerpts from Gaspar de Villagrá and Fray Alonso Gregorio de Escobedo are reprinted in the original Spanish.

Later in the volume, we have included two new selections from the revolutionary literature of Spanish America—a popular broadside by José Álvarez de Toledo and one of the founding documents of Latin American history, Simón Bolívar's "Letter from Jamaica," which now concludes Volume A.

The selections from New Netherland writer Adriaen van der Donck have been updated with a new translation, and we have added the entirety of Susanna Rowson's popular play *Slaves in Algiers* in the place of excerpts from her novel *Charlotte Temple*.

In the critical sections, we have added significant excerpts from Bartolomé de las Casas on the plight of the Indians, Aníbal Quijano and Immanuel Wallerstein on "Americanity," Trish Loughran on eighteenth-century print culture, and a blog post on "Decolonial Aesthetics" that reinforces the salience of colonial literature and coloniality to the present postmodern moment.

WHAT IS NEW IN VOLUME B, EARLY NINETEENTH CENTURY: 1800–1865

Volume B, Early Nineteenth Century: 1800–1865, has a newly restructured section on Native American literature, with new selections that include excerpts from Black Hawk and Mary Jemison, which frame the opening section as an exploration of complex and often misunderstood Native identities. Other Native writers, like William Appess and Jane Johnston Schoolcraft, are interspersed throughout the volume, working against the notion that Native voices precede other voices. A new "In Focus" section dedicated to the Cherokee nation and the literature surrounding Cherokee removal has been added. This enables instructors to focus on a particular Native nation, gaining a nation-specific focus that helps students understand both the Cherokee context in specific, and the larger imperative to encounter Native writing as nationally specific.

The "Cultures of Spanish America" section has been restructured and greatly expanded, with new works in English and in Spanish (with translations provided) by Victoria Moreno, José María Heredia, José María Tornel, and Vicente Pérez Rosales.

Finally, a new section focusing on "The Caribbean in the Antebellum Imagination," with works by Martin Delany, Lucy Holcombe Pickens, and Miguel Tolón, has been added.

WHAT IS NEW IN VOLUME C, LATE NINETEENTH CENTURY: 1865–1910

Thoroughly reconceived, Volume C, Late Nineteenth Century: 1865–1910, reflects even more vividly the extraordinary writing that flourished as the United States became a modern, diverse nation with an international presence. The overarching concept of this volume is that the literature written between 1865 and 1910 was so plentiful and so diverse that no single set of organizational categories does it justice. We have therefore devised several complementary categories to showcase this variety in a comprehensible manner.

Now book-ending the volume are sections on significant literary trends—"Varieties of Postwar Realism: Prose and Poetry" and literature "On the Cusp of a New Century." Of the other four sections in Volume C, one centers on Siouxian peoples ("Nation within a Nation: Lakotas/Dakotas/Nakotas"); two are organized geographically ("Writing and Place" and "Redefining the South"); and another ("Outside/Inside U.S.A.: Expansion and Immigration") foregrounds the era's cultural and political ferment with writing by or about immigrants and literature created in response to the shifting borders of the nation and to its geopolitical expansion.

All of these sections contain new material in addition to the literature of past editions. Most notably, we now feature four authors new to the *Heath Anthology*—the "Hoosier poet" James Whitcomb Riley, the witty Vermont regionalist Rowland E. Robinson, the Southern plantation tradition writer Thomas Nelson Page, and the proto-modernist poet Sadakichi Hartmann.

There are many new selections by familiar authors, among them Henry James's "The Figure in the Carpet," a section of Zitkala-Sa's "Impressions of an Indian Childhood," Mary E. Wilkins Freeman's "Old Woman Magoun," and Charles W. Chesnutt's "The Doll." We also restored the Frank Norris section.

Still further, we introduce two exciting, little-known Latino narratives—"Memories of California"/"Recuerdos de California" by Carlos F. Galán and "The Tale of a Glove"/"Historia de un guante" by N. Bolet Peraza. These selections are presented in Spanish and in English translations produced for the *Heath Anthology* by contributing editor John Alba Cutler.

In addition, Volume C now offers new or substantially revised headnotes on a number of authors included in earlier editions—Henry James, Sarah Orne Jewett, Mary E. Wilkins Freeman, Frances E. W. Harper, Alice Dunbar-Nelson, and Jack London. Finally, we also present new and revised "In Focus" sections, complete with new and updated introductory essays.

WHAT IS NEW IN VOLUME D, MODERN PERIOD: 1910–1945

Volume D, Modern Period: 1910–1945, continues to demonstrate the diversity of the literary period known as modernism by introducing readers to the array of modernisms that constitute it—the hermetic experiments of Ezra Pound and T. S. Eliot, the more commercial expression of loss and uncertainty in popular efforts by F. Scott Fitzgerald and Edna St. Vincent Millay, the ethnically complex fusion of African American and dominant-culture aesthetics that typify the Harlem Renaissance, and the political activism of the proletarian movement of the 1930s and its internal debates over the social functions of art.

Volume D continues to expand notions of both modernity and modernism by widening the scope of literary experience. Included here for the first time is a section on the literature of the Mexican Revolution, featuring Industrial Workers of the World (IWW) organizer Ricardo Flores Magón's *cri de guerre* "Land and Liberty" and a newly translated excerpt from the Spanish version of Leonor Villegas de Magnon's "La Rebelde," among others. There are two stories from Maria Cristina Mena, and a poem and two novel excerpts of H. T. Tsiang, who captures the despair of New York Chinatown like no other 1930s' writer. The famous "rent party" chapter from Wallace Thurman's *Infants of the Spring* (1932) features thinly veiled portraits of leading Harlem Renaissance writers. Also included are Meridel LeSueur's story "Annunciation" and an excerpt from her posthumously published novel, *The Girl*; Jose Garcia Villa's "Footnote to Youth" (the most famous Filipino short story of the 1930s); and a selection of poetry that expands our notions of modernist experimentation. Mexican American folklorist Jovita Gonzalez's essay "Shades of the Tenth Muses" provides a hallucinatory meditation on canon inclusion.

WHAT IS NEW IN VOLUME E, CONTEMPORARY PERIOD: 1945 TO THE PRESENT

Volume E, Contemporary Period: 1945 to the Present, has been radically restructured to reflect ongoing changes in what is considered contemporary and to make it easier for instructors and students to locate major trends and developments in the contemporary period. We have organized this section by decades, basing their placement on the date of publication rather than by the birth date of authors.

Some of the period's prolific, established authors such as Tennessee Williams, Arthur Miller, Toni Cade Bambara, Ishmael Reed, Sherman Alexie, and John Updike are represented by different works from the ones we included in previous editions.

Although we have had to reduce or cut some selections by authors previously represented in this section in the interest of limiting the volume to a reasonable length, more striking is the list of writers we have added to this volume. New authors to the seventh edition include John Cheever, Mitsuye Yamada, Kurt Vonnegut, Ralph Molina, Luís Valdez, Richard Ford, George C. Wolfe, Ann Beattie, Percival Everett, Martin Espada, Demetria Martinez, T. C. Boyle, Stephen Dunn, Natasha Trethewey, Junot Díaz, Dave Eggers, Jane Trenka, ZZ Packer, Francisco Goldman, and Manuel Munoz.

We have also added substantial new "In Focus" sections of Ojibway writings from the contemporary period, and the volume concludes with a section of "Spoken Word Poetry," which showcases some important new voices and the genre that they have helped to develop but which connects a current trend to the oral traditions that form the origin of American literature in its earliest years.

ACKNOWLEDGMENTS

We want to extend our thanks to all of the contributing editors who devoted their time and scholarship to introductory notes, choices of texts, and teaching materials. For the current edition, they include the following:

Katherine Bassard, Virginia Commonwealth University

Paula Bernat Bennett (Emerita), Southern Illinois University

Renée Bergland, Simmons College

Leah Blatt Glasser, Mount Holyoke College

David Budbill, poet and independent scholar

Raul Bueno, Dartmouth College

Keith Byerman, Indiana State University

Floyd Cheung, Smith College

Jonathan Chua, Ateneo de Manila

Hillary Chute, Harvard University

Michael C. Cohen, University of California, Los Angeles

Raúl Coronado, University of Chicago

Denise Cruz, Indiana University

Suzanne del Gizzo, Chestnut Hill College

Jared Demick, University of Connecticut

Joseph Dewey, University of Pittsburgh, Johnstown

Lyn Di Lorio, The City College of New York

Amy Doherty Mohr, Amerika Institut, Ludwig Maximilians Universität, Munich

Jennifer Emery-Peck, Oberlin College

Armando García, University of Pittsburgh

Caroline Gebhard, Tuskegee University

June Howard, University of Michigan

Caren Irr, Brandeis University

Gene Jarrett, Boston University

Ann Keniston, University of Nevada, Reno

Ryan James Kernan, Rutgers University

Kathy Knapp, University of Connecticut

Sara Kosiba, Troy University

Rodrigo Lazo, University of California, Irvine

Katherine E. Ledford, Appalachian State University

Marissa López, University of California, Los Angeles

Crystal J. Lucky, Villanova University

Manuel Martin-Rodriguez, University of California, Merced

Lauren R. Maxwell, The Citadel

Keith Mitchell, University of Massachusetts, Lowell

Charles Molesworth, City University of New York, Queens

Paula Moya, Stanford University

Viet Nguyen, University of Southern California

Ben V. Olguin, University of Texas, San Antonio

Yolana Padilla, University of Pennsylvania

Josephine Park, University of Pennsylvania

Robert Dale Parker, University of Illinois, Urbana-Champaign

Soojin Pate, Minneapolis Community and Technical College

Elizabeth Petrino, Fairfield University

Peter Reed, University of Mississippi

Domino Renee Perez, University of Texas, Austin

Ana Patricia Rodriguez, University of Maryland, College Park

Ramón Saldívar, Stanford University

James Schiff, University of Cincinnati

Lavina Dhingra, Bates College

E. Thomson Shields, East Carolina University

Susan Shillinglaw, San Jose State University

Amjrit Singh, Ohio University

Scott Slovic, University of Nevada, Reno

James Smethurst, University of Massachusetts, Amherst

Mayumi Takada, Bryn Mawr College

Justine Tally, Universidad de la Laguna

Kara Thompson, College of William and Mary

Lisa Thompson, State University of New York, Albany

Darlene Unrue, University of Nevada, Las Vegas

Joanne van der Woude, Columbia University

Ariana Vigil, University of North Carolina, Chapel Hill

Jennifer Wallach, University of North Texas

Hilary Wyss, Auburn University

Yvonne Yarbro-Bejarano, Stanford University

Thanks to Oberlin College for funding student researchers and to Amanda Shubert and Hillary Smith for the incomparable work they have done in that capacity. We also want to thank student researchers Carson Thomas and Kyle Lewis from Dartmouth College and Brandy Underwood from the University of California, Los Angeles for excellent editorial help.

We especially want to thank those who reviewed this edition:

David Anderson, University of North Texas

Craig Barrette, Brescia University

Robert Bennett, Montana State University

Brett Bodily, North Lake College

Kathryn Brewer-Strayer, Stillman College

Delmar Brewington, Piedmont Technical College

Brad Campbell, California Polytechnic State University

Beth Capo, Illinois College

Charles Cuthbertson, Southern Utah University

Joshua Dickinson, Jefferson Community College

Sharynn Owens Etheridge-Logan, Claflin University

April Gentry, Savannah State University

Wendy Gray, J. Sargeant Reynolds Community College

Deirdre Hall, University of North Carolina, Greensboro

Amy Hankins, Ottawa University

Tena Helton, University of Illinois, Springfield

Tai Houser, Broward College

Melanie Jenkins, Snow College

Bruce Johnson, Providence College

David Jones, University of Wisconsin, Eau Claire

Thomas Long, University of Connecticut

Marit MacArthur, California State University, Bakersfield

Bridget Marshall, University of Massachusetts, Lowell

John Miller, Longwood University

Keith Mitchell, University of Massachusetts, Lowell

Emmanuel Ngwang, Claflin University

Miles Orvell, Temple University

Priscilla Perkins, Roosevelt University

Jane Rosecrans, J. Sargeant Reynolds Community College

Christopher Schroeder, Northeastern Illinois University

Claudia Slate, Florida Southern College

Jimmy Smith, Union College

Blythe Tellefsen, Fullerton College

Ruthe Thompson, Southwest Minnesota State University

Stephanie Tingley, Youngstown State University

Terri Tucker, Southwest Texas Junior College

Tondalaya VanLear, Dabney S. Lancaster Community College

Trent Watts, Missouri University of Science and Technology

Michelle Weisman, College of the Ozarks

Eric Wertheimer, Arizona State University

Julie Wilhelm, Lamar University

We would like to continue to thank the many scholars who contributed to this as well as to earlier editions of this work. Their names are listed in the *Online Instructor's Manual* that accompanies this anthology.

LATE NINETEENTH CENTURY: 1865–1910

On May 1, 1893, a city spread out over a thousand acres along Lake Michigan officially opened its doors to the first of some twenty-seven and a half million people, equal to well over a third of the United States population at the time, who would visit it in the brief six months of its existence. Resplendent with white buildings designed in the classical style, whose peristyles, porticoes, and colonnades shone in the sun and in the reflected light of canals and lagoons and at night were illuminated by thousands of electric light bulbs, this spectacle was the World's Columbian Exposition, otherwise known as the Chicago World's Fair, and, most familiarly, the "White City." The largest international world's fair ever held until that time, built at a cost that today would translate into well over $300 million, it was the United States' and the world's celebration of the "discovery" of the Americas by Columbus four hundred years before. Its central core of buildings was a marvel of coordinated planning by architects, sculptors, painters, landscape gardeners, and engineers, who in less than two and a half years had transformed an area of swamp and sand into one of terraced parks, broad boulevards, and monumental buildings. Although officially commemorating the arrival of Europeans on the continent and including exhibits from countries throughout the world, the Fair was above all a spectacular statement of the United States' material and technological might on the eve of the twentieth century.

By 1893 just about all of the elements we identify with the modern United States were in place: large-scale industry and advanced technology; densely inhabited urban areas; concentrations of capital in banks, businesses, and corporations; nationwide systems of transportation and print communication; and a heterogeneous population of diverse races, classes, and ethnic groups. It was a nation that looked and was radically different from the cluster of states, primarily agrarian and increasingly riven by sectional strife, that had existed only forty years before. The launching of the Spanish-American War five years after the Fair solidified the final element, imperialistic power, that would characterize the nation in the twentieth century.

A sense of being at a historic divide, looking both back and ahead, animated the speeches given at the Fair's dedication ceremonies (held in October 1892 to mark the official date of Columbus's arrival). The opening oration swept through four hundred years of history to review Columbus's voyages; the struggles of Spain, England, and France for control of the newly discovered territories; the rise of the young American republic; and its darkest moment of threatened disunion during the years of the Civil War. That threat averted, the nation's postwar history was cast as one of steadily increasing political and material power and progress. Under the benign rule of a strong Constitution, with "the curse of slavery ... gone," and with its mills, mines, and forests producing their incomparable wealth, the United States had arrived at the moment of the Fair when it could "bask in the sunshine of ... prosperity and happiness" and proudly "bid a welcome to the world."

This mood of confidence and optimism would be shattered just five days after the Fair opened, when the stock market plunged, inaugurating a four-year depression, one of the worst the nation had ever experienced. If the Fair was proof of American progress, the Panic of 1893 revealed part of the price that progress exacted. What then did the Columbian Exposition show, not just about America's official perception of itself, but also about American realities? In its harmonies but also in its contradictions and disjunctions, both in what it included and what it ignored, the Fair tells us much about the nature of American life at the turn into the twentieth century.

For the many writers who visited the Fair and speculated about it, two impressions dominated: the esthetic unity of its central core of buildings and the awesome sense of power conveyed by its sheer size and its massive displays of technology. For William Dean Howells, one of the country's most respected and successful authors, the two impressions ideally conjoined. The Fair to him was a grand altruistic gesture. To create it, capitalists had placed themselves in the hands of artists, and "for once" American businessmen and entrepreneurs had put aside "their pitiless economic struggle, their habitual warfare" to come together in a mighty "work of peace." Howells's hopeful vision, voiced in *A Traveler from Altruria* (1894) by a visitor from a Utopian land, was one of America's money and technology put in the service of civic virtue, the nation's vast natural resources and manufactured products used for the welfare of all rather than the profit of the few. The Fair's architecture held not only esthetic but also spiritual promise.

Less sanguine was Henry Adams, for whom the Fair marked a crucial moment in that ongoing enterprise of educating himself to which he devoted his life. For him the Fair's architecture was imitative and derivative—"imported Beaux Arts"—and the Fair itself, despite any idealistic impulses in its genesis, was an "industrial, speculative growth." Like Howells, Adams was looking for some principle of meaning in American life, some way of making sense out of what seemed to be the chaos of forces, political, economic, and scientific, that had been unleashed in the post–Civil War period. He looked behind the white facades for answers. Inside the buildings "education ran riot" amidst displays of telephone and telegraph apparatus, steam engines, multiple drill presses, cable-laying devices, electric motors, transformers, convertors, and generators. The dynamo—the generator producing the electric current that powered and drove so much of the machinery and made possible the Fair's dazzling displays of incandescent lighting—became his symbol of the driving force in American life. It "gave to history a new phase," but one that Adams could not measure by the republican standards he had inherited from his presidential forebears, John and John Quincy Adams. If "Chicago asked for the first time the question whether the American people knew where they were driving," the answer was not easily arrived at. Adams feared that the uncontrolled application of new scientific discoveries would outpace and vitiate republican ideals.

Adams and Howells had focused on two aspects of the dramatic changes the United States had undergone in the second half of the nineteenth century. The very existence of the Fair testified to one of these: that by the 1890s the United States had become an urban nation. The Fair City (and it was a city, with its own transportation, sewage, police, and governmental systems) was the product of the entrepreneurial drive of Chicago, which had successfully outmaneuvered New York to get it, and Chicago in turn was the most dramatic example of postwar urban development. Little more than a fur-trapping village of about 350 people in 1830, by 1880 it had become a city of half a million people; within another ten years it had doubled its size, so that by the time of the Fair, it was the second largest city in the nation, with a population of over one million. The largest, New York, had also grown at a phenomenal rate: by 1900 it would contain almost three and a half million people. Other midwestern cities— Detroit, Columbus, Milwaukee, Minneapolis, and St. Paul—saw their populations double and triple in the postwar decades, whereas on the west coast Los Angeles went from eleven thousand inhabitants in 1880 to five times that number twenty years later. From being for more than 150 years characteristically a nation of rural dwellers, the United States had within a few short decades become distinctively urbanized. Although at the end of the nineteenth century forty percent of the American population was still rural, the trend to urbanization was irreversible.

Occurring with such rapidity, this growth had taken place with little or none of the civic planning that Howells admired in the White City. Real American cities, he knew, were the result of "the straggling and shapeless accretion of accident." At their strongest and most vivid—again, Chicago was a case in point— they manifested the nation's immense new business and commercial energy, as in the iron and steel skyscrapers of Chicago's architects Louis Sullivan, John Wellborn Root, and William LeBaron Jenney. At their worst—and the worst was widespread—they were places where what housing reformer Jacob Riis in 1890 called "the other half" lived—places of slums and overcrowding, of dirt and noise, lack of sanitation and disease, poverty, child labor, prostitution, violence, and crime. The Fair City officially ignored these urban realities, its white facades implicitly denying that not far away lay the Chicago slums, where settlement worker Jane Addams's Hull House was located among tenements crowded with Irish, Polish, Czech, Russian Jewish, and Italian immigrants, and that also within striking distance was the Union Stockyard, with its four hundred square miles of malodorous cattle pens and runways, which would be the subject of Upton Sinclair's exposé of the meat-packing industry in his novel *The Jungle* in 1906.

The Fair's much-vaunted whiteness was also a symbol of the intensified dominance in the 1890s of white Anglo-Saxon Protestantism in a nation in which African Americans, Native Americans, Mexican Americans, and other racial, ethnic, and religious groups were becoming increasingly apparent. Over the protests of some black leaders, the nation's eight to nine million African Americans were allowed no representation at the Fair's opening ceremonies, and no blacks were appointed to positions of authority on any of the Fair's various governing commissions. Frederick Douglass, present as commissioner from Haiti, not a representative of the United States, termed the Fair "a whited sepulcher." Journalist and antilynching activist Ida B. Wells-Barnett published a pamphlet, to which Douglass contributed a chapter, exposing the white supremacy that lay behind "The Reason Why the Colored American Is Not in the World's Columbia Exposition" and detailing African Americans' contributions to the United States. Other racial and ethnic groups also were excluded from the United States as the Fair represented it. Indian writer Simon Pokagon called attention to the absence of official Native American representation through his pamphlet "Red Man's Greeting." Printed on birch bark and distributed at the event, it reminded fair-goers that the exposition, and the entire city of Chicago, were built on land taken from Indians and never paid for.

The only way the Fair did officially recognize racial and ethnic variety was as something foreign to the United States. South of the main buildings, on the mile-long stretch called the Midway Plaisance, in shops, restaurants, tent shows, and miniature villages, three thousand entertainers and vendors from ethnic cultures throughout the world sold their wares, displayed native costumes, and performed dances and other ceremonies. "[O]dd bits of tribes and nationalities from every quarter of the globe" was the description in the official history of the Fair. Although the Irish Village, Japanese Bazaar, Javanese Village, German Village, and several other re-creations of "foreign" villages drew many visitors, among the greatest attractions were the Dahomey Village and the Arab section, with its "Street in Cairo," "Algerian Village," and "Persian Palace of Eros." Viewing indigenous music and dance, including "dancing girls" from Egypt and elsewhere, as spectacles, many American visitors who prized their nation's supposed homogeneity and propriety exoticized—and savored—difference as something outside U.S. borders. Professor F. W. Putnam, a Harvard professor and the Fair's "Chief of the Department of Ethnography," produced a book of portraits of the "different types of men and women" on display at the Midway Plaisance. In the introduction he captured the way the Fair's very architecture affirmed its fundamental assumption that non-Western peoples were quaint and nondeveloped, in stark contrast to the progressive modernity of the United States. Extolling the "Great Ferris Wheel" that rose in the midst of the Midway, Putnam characterized the elevated view it gave fair-goers of the Midway as at one and the same time physical and cultural: a monument to technology that embodied the superior position from which the world's most "advanced" country could survey and comprehend other cultures. "Our own crowning achievement in mechanics ... arising in the midst of this magic gathering," he proclaimed, "enabled us to view this mimic world as from another planet, and to look down upon an enchanted land filled with happy folk."

However, if the Midway in effect pinioned Jews, Arabs, Africans, and others within late-century Western ideas about the stratification of the races and peoples of the world, the Fair also became an occasion for some from supposedly "backward" countries and cultures to convey their own views of themselves—and of American culture. From September 11 to September 27, a related event, the World Parliament of Religions, was held in downtown Chicago. Featuring close to two hundred speakers representing twelve major religions, the Parliament provided a forum for various Protestant denominations and also one allowing some representative Buddhists and Hindus to explain their religions to the nearly 150,000 spectators who attended. American Protestant control of the Parliament was quickly unsettled, however, as Asian speakers galvanized attendees and the press with their faith, their profound knowledge of both their own religions and Christianity, and their attacks on Christian missionaries' lack of concern about the poverty they encountered and their cooperation with colonialism. Several Asian delegates developed enthusiastic American followings, among them Swami Vivekananda, a charismatic Hindu speaker from Calcutta. Vivekananda, an ascetic, combined religion and nationalism in a powerful repudiation of Western stereotypes of Asian men as effeminate, as Carrie Tirado Bramen explains. The Hindi-based form of celibate, virile, and self-disciplined masculinity he promoted was, in his representation of it, far superior to the sexually active, unrestrained masculinity of Western men.

Swami Vivekananda and others developed an especially large following among the American women who were the majority of the Parliament's attendees. The women's enthusiasm for the Asian religious leaders expressed a commitment to independence of thought and spiritual life that constituted one way in which many American women were beginning to assert their independence. The Fair itself officially recognized that American women were becoming less identified with domesticity and increasingly more visible as a public force. It included them in the Fair's planning to an extent unprecedented at any previous exposition, and it allotted them a "Women's Building" with its own board of managers, which housed an international display of women's achievement in art and industry. The board's chair, Mrs. Potter Palmer of Chicago, observed in her opening address that "Even more than the discovery of Columbus, which we are gathered together to celebrate, is the fact that the general government has just discovered women." Indeed, the forty-five-year-long campaign for women's political and legal rights was bearing some fruit: in the year of the Fair, Colorado became the first state to grant the vote to women, though the suffrage movement's full success came only with the passage of the Nineteenth Amendment in 1920. American women, however, as represented by the Fair, were white: African American women were kept off the board of managers despite their repeated requests for representation, and exhibits in the Women's Building included very little by or about African American women. In response to black women's pressure, however, six black women, including activist/suffragist Frances E. W. Harper and educator Anna Julia Cooper, were eventually invited to speak about African American women's circumstances and achievements at the World's Congress of Representative Women.

The energies white women were displaying at the end of the century fascinated Henry Adams, who wondered if here might be a force as significant for the nation's future as that of science and technology. However, technology made the strongest statement at the Fair, visible evidence that the overriding feature of American life, on which the cities depended for their existence and that explained their growth, was the unprecedented industrialization the nation had undergone since the end of the Civil War. Among the most important buildings at the Fair were those devoted to Manufactures, Mechanic Arts, Transportation, and Electricity, and by far the largest and most impressive of these was the Manufactures Building. In the Fair's official history, the Manufactures Building was described, in the quantitative terms Americans love to use to measure great-ness, as three times the size of St. Peter's Church in Rome, four times that of the Roman Colosseum, and big enough that six baseball games could be played on its floor at once or the entire Russian army mobilized inside it. To create such a structure, the powerful forces of the United States' economy and indus-trial machine had been marshaled.

Chief among these was the railway system. The decades before the Civil War had seen the development of steam power and the locomotive, making possible the extensive network of railroads that crisscrossed the country by the 1890s, joining all states and sections and creating national markets for agricultural pro-duce and manufactured goods. Fruits and vegetables from California, cattle from Texas, corn from Iowa, lumber from Minnesota, cotton from Georgia and Ala-bama, coal from West Virginia, and iron from Pennsylvania could all be shipped to processing and manufacturing centers, often located in cities. Chicago's extra-ordinary growth, in fact, was due to its location at the intersection of several major railroad lines that brought to it the agricultural and mineral wealth of the Midwest and that led in turn to the development of its grain, lumber, meat-packing, steel, and railroad equipment industries. By 1890 the United States had nearly half the railroad mileage in the world, and that mileage represented one-sixth of the nation's estimated wealth.

Before the Civil War, the railroads had helped to open up the Midwest, and in the postwar period they carried settlers to the Great Plains of the Dakotas, western Kansas, and Nebraska, which had been bypassed by earlier pioneers ea-ger to reach the gold fields of California and the fertile acreage of Oregon's Wil-lamette Valley. Now, tens of thousands of families moved on to the Plains, pushing the Native American inhabitants off their lands. The use on the Plains of expensive machinery—harvesters, tractors, and binders—led farmers to increase the size of their holdings. Although the small family farm that Jefferson had celebrated as the locus of the American ideal of independent self-sufficiency continued to exist, the new trend toward farming as a large-scale, mechanized operation meant that agriculture, too, had entered the modern age. The Chicago World's Fair had been the occasion, at the World's Congress Auxil-iary held in conjunction with it, for the delivery of Frederick Jackson Turner's paper "The Significance of the Frontier in American History," with its thesis that the existence of the frontier, as an area of free land beyond the line of set-tlement, had helped determine the national character and national ideals. Now, Turner announced, there was no more open land, and the frontier no longer existed.

Turner celebrated the experience of the frontier as fostering democratic institutions, but the new world of business and industry of which the railroads were both symbol and cause seemed in the postwar decades to make a mockery of many of them. The burgeoning industrial economy had entailed enormous cost in the waste and misuse of both material and moral resources. For example, the railroad companies did not hesitate to use intimidation and cutthroat com-petition to destroy rival lines or discriminatory rates and rebates to lure custom-ers. Their practices were condoned by a federal government eager to push forward America's industrial expansion and by public officials not averse to reaping from that expansion their own private gain. Whereas the Civil War had

AN IMAGE GALLERY
1865–1910

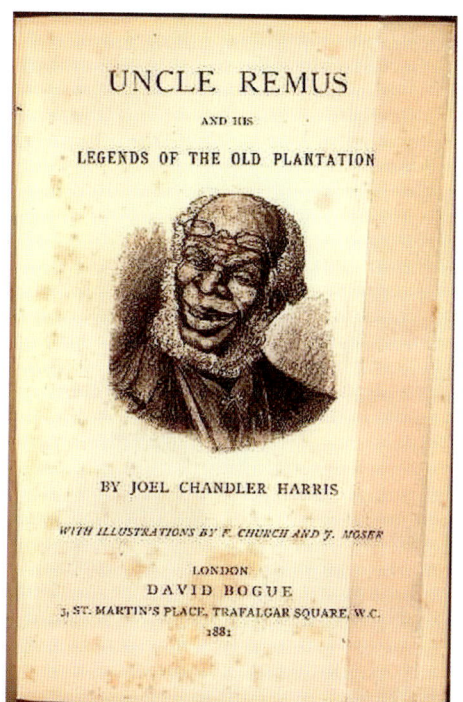

■ **TITLE PAGE FROM JOEL CHANDLER HARRIS'S** *UNCLE REMUS AND THE LEGENDS OF THE OLD PLANTATION* **(1881 edition). COVER OF CHARLES WADDELL CHESNUTT'S** *THE CONJURE WOMAN* **(c. 1899).** Joel Chandler Harris's narrator, Uncle Remus, remains one of the most controversial characters in American literature. Scholars dispute whether he is a stereotypical symbol of the Old South or a more complex storyteller who uses his tales to correct an unequal balance of power in favor of whites in postbellum Southern society. Wildly popular among readers in both the North and the South, Harris's writing exemplifies the school of literature termed the "Plantation Tradition." In addition to several of Harris's Uncle Remus tales (starting on page 695), this volume includes Thomas Nelson Page's "Marse Chan" (page 708), an especially influential plantation tradition story, as well as a cluster of African American folktales collected from a range of sources (starting on page 675). Although the illustration on the front cover of Charles Waddell Chesnutt's collection of short stories appears to capitalize on the popularity of Harris's Uncle Remus tales, Chesnutt's works directly contest the figure of Remus. Like Harris's character, Chesnutt's Uncle Julius is an elderly ex-slave who tells his captivating stories to white listeners. However, Julius is clearly an ingenious trickster who seeks to manipulate his auditors and he usually succeeds in doing so. Moreover, Chesnutt's conjure tales expose the complacent sense of racial superiority of Julius's listeners and dramatize the exploitative, dehumanizing side of slavery that was skirted, if not denied completely, in plantation tradition literature. This volume includes two of Chesnutt's conjure tales—"The Goophered Grapevine" (page 733) and "Po' Sandy" (page 742).

■ **IMMIGRANTS LANDING AT ELLIS ISLAND (c. 1900).** Opened on January 1, 1892, Ellis Island became the primary entry point for the rapidly growing number of European immigrants who sought to come to the United States in the late nineteenth and early twentieth centuries. In its first year, nearly half a million people were processed through Ellis Island; in the peak year of 1907, the number was over one million. The majority of the immigrants arrived from Italy, Russia, Hungary, Germany, and Austria, but large numbers came as well from Britain, Canada, Ireland, and Scandinavia. Located within view of the Statue of Liberty, which had been dedicated in New York Harbor in 1886, Ellis Island constituted a site charged both with the promise of new opportunity and also with a foreshadowing of the daunting and potentially traumatic challenge of cultural adjustment. Abraham Cahan's "The Imported Bridegroom" (page 898) and Mary Antin's "In the Promised Land" (page 945) both center on the experiences of immigrants from Eastern Europe. Two poems—Emma Lazarus's "The New Colossus" (page 834) and Thomas Bailey Aldrich's "Unguarded Gates" (page 834)—express contrasting attitudes towards such immigrants in the United States, and Finley Peter Dunne turns a slyly satirical eye on attempts to restrict immigration. For an unconventional, stylized look at a young Japanese woman's encounter with what she sees as a foreign and unsettling culture in this country, see Yone Noguci's "The American Diary of a Japanese Girl" (page 886).

■ **CHICAGO WORLD'S FAIR (1893).** Scheduled to commemorate the 400-year anniversary of Columbus's arrival in the Northern Hemisphere, the World's Columbian Exposition—also known as the Chicago World's Fair—was open to the public from May through October 1893. Composed of over 200 buildings occupying more than 600 acres along Lake Michigan, the Fair became an immediate sensation, with people flocking to the site from all parts of the United States and from around the world. The paid attendance totaled well over 27 million, an astounding number given that the entire U.S. population at the time of the 1890 census was approximately 63 million. This image gives some sense of the crowds that strolled the grounds of the Fair. Also on display here are the electric lights used to illuminate the area and the gigantic wheel designed by a young engineer named George Washington Ferris. Finally, the image portrays the architecture and garb that signified the presence of foreign cultures at the Fair. For countless Americans, the unusual buildings, the strikingly costumed performers, and the captivating installations from Asia, the Middle East, and elsewhere constituted an unprecedented firsthand encounter with what might today be termed "the other." Certainly lost on most viewers was the fact that the displays were often promoted for their titillating entertainment value and staged in ways that emphasized a primitive exoticism. It is no exaggeration to suggest that the Chicago World's Fair marked a watershed in mainstream America's sense of itself and of its relationship to an increasingly complex and startlingly diverse world. The introduction to this volume provides a sustained consideration of the significance of the Fair, and one finds a compelling response to the stunning, even disconcerting display of modern technology at the Chicago World's Fair (as well as at the Paris Exposition of 1900) in Henry Adams's "The Dynamo and the Virgin" (page 1061) from *The Education of Henry Adams*. Illuminating aspects of immigrant life in Chicago obscured by the Exposition's dual emphasis on progress and on those presented as "uncivilized others" are Upton Sinclair's *The Jungle* (page 469) and Finley Peter Dunn's Irish dialect sketches (starting on page 837).

■ **ISABELLA STEWART GARDNER (1888).** Although she was a prominent member of the upper-class Boston elite, Isabella Stewart Gardner (1840–1924) was also a decidedly independent spirit who challenged mainstream expectations regarding appropriate behavior for respectable, bourgeois women. With a diverse circle of friends that included the actress Sarah Bernhardt, the boxer John L. Sullivan, the philosopher George Santayana, and the writers Sarah Orne Jewett and Henry James, Gardner utilized her considerable resources to become a major art patron. Among the recipients of her support was John Singer Sargent (1856–1925), who earned $3,000 for producing this portrait of Gardner. Many of the readings in this volume reflect the sway that standards of propriety exerted in women's lives. Among these are Charlotte Perkins Gilman's "The Yellow Wallpaper" (page 1184) and "Turned" (page 1196), Henry James's "Daisy Miller" (page 195), Pauline Hopkins's *Contending Forces* (page 432) and "Talma Gordon" (page 446), Maria Guadalupe Gutierrez's "American and Filipino Women" (page 980), and Sarah Morgan Bryan Piatt's poetry (starting on page 136).

■ **YOUNG FACTORY GIRL AT A THREAD-SPINNING MACHINE IN VIVIAN COTTON MILLS, CHERRYVILLE, NORTH CAROLINA (c. 1908).** This photograph was taken by Lewis Hine, a trained sociologist who focused his camera on immigrants and children working in sweat shops and factories. In 1909 he published *Child Labor in the Carolinas* and *Day Laborers before Their Time*, two books documenting working conditions for children. His caption for this photo was "Been at it 2 years. Where will her good looks be in ten years?" The issue of labor surfaces in a range of selections in this volume. Upton Sinclair's *The Jungle* (page 469) exposes the horrors of the meat-packing industry in Chicago. Charles Chesnutt takes an imaginative look in "The Goophered Grapevine" (page 733) at the impact of slave labor on the body. Hamlin Garland's "Up the Coulé: A Story of Wisconsin" (page 485) offers a sobering view of the harsh rigors of rural farmlife. And Jack London's "South of the Slot" (page 1287) portrays the tensions that arose in the late nineteenth century as workers agitated for more just treatment.

■ **PHILLIS WHEATLEY CLUB OF BUFFALO, NEW YORK (1905).** The late nineteenth century saw the creation of a number of women's organizations as a wave of feminist activism swept the country. One of several important African American women's groups, the Phillis Wheatley Club was founded in 1895 in Nashville, Tennessee, and was dedicated to education, temperance, care for the elderly, charitable outreach, and other causes related to moral uplift. This photograph is a portrait of the Phillis Wheatley Club that had been formed in 1899 in Buffalo, New York. Standing in the back row, fourth from the left, is Mary Talbert (1866–1923), head of the club and the first black woman to win the NAACP's Spingarn Award. In 1900 Talbert and her fellow club members spearheaded a local protest against stereotypical representations of blacks at the Pan-American Exposition held in Buffalo that year. Such strategies reflected the commitment of many middle-class blacks not just to self-improvement within their communities, but also to the forthright defense of African Americans against widespread, unrelenting attacks. This commitment to social activism on the part of black women of the time emerges in a number of selections. Notable examples include works by Ida B. Wells-Barnett (page 610), Frances Ellen Watkins Harper (starting on page 781), and Anna Julia Cooper (page 793). Particularly relevant here is the excerpt from Pauline Hopkins's novel *Contending Forces* titled "The Sewing Circle" (page 432) that vividly depicts a group of middle-class African American women who gather to discuss pressing social issues.

Maurice Branger/Roger-Viollet/The Image Works

■ **MARSHALL TAYLOR (1908).** Marshall "Major" Taylor (1878–1932) was a celebrated U.S. cyclist who in 1899 became the first African American world champion in any sport. Cycling was exceedingly popular in the United States around the turn of the century, and Taylor quickly rose to the top after turning professional in 1896 at the age of eighteen. However, his success aroused considerable hostility. Not only was he banned from all-white competitions in the South, but he also was the target of cheating and even physical assault during races. Despite these obstacles, Taylor achieved worldwide renown and may well have been the most famous African American of the time after Booker T. Washington. Deeply committed to racial uplift, Taylor viewed his remarkable achievements as proof that blacks could rise through hard work, talent, and sacrifice. Such fiercely maintained faith in the possibility of social change informs texts as diverse as Charles Chesnutt's "What Is a White Man?" (page 727) and José Martí's "Nuestra America"/ "Our America" (page 1016).

Bettmann/Corbis

■ **JACK LONDON.** Said to be the highest-paid fiction writer of his day, Jack London (1876–1916) nurtured a larger-than-life persona that embodied the era's celebration of aggressive masculinity and what was known as the "vigorous" or "strenuous" life. This photograph highlights two key elements of London's life: writing and sailing. The outdoor setting of the picture as well as his clothing and pose all help to construct an image that anticipates the one that Ernest Hemingway presented to such memorable effect some years later. London plays with notions of masculinity in the story "South of the Slot" (page 1287), while similar and contrasting images of manhood appear in numerous selections in this volume, including Stephen Crane's "The Open Boat" (page 1211), Alexander Posey's "Fus Fixico's Letters" (page 558), James Whitcomb Riley's "The Old Swimmin'-Hole" (page 464), Charles Chesnutt's "The Doll" (page 771), the *corrido* "Gregorio Cortez" (page 538), and William Dean Howells's "Editha" (page 162).

■ **EMILIO AGUINALDO Y FAMY (1899).** The young, college-trained revolutionary leader who helped the Philippines to secure its independence from Spain in 1898, Emilio Aguinaldo y Famy (1869–1964) was the first president of the self-governing republic. However, he was not long in this position before coming into conflict with the United States because of an American attempt to exert control over his country. This tension led to the Philippine-American War in 1899, and hostilities between the two nations persisted well into the twentieth century, even after Aguinaldo's capture in 1901. The complex relationship of Aguinaldo and his country with the United States reveals the increasingly global reach of the American sphere of influence around the turn of the century and also the extent to which the United States was perceived both as a potentially liberating force and as an imperial power whose support sometimes came at a high price. For texts that engage the same political and cultural forces that fueled Aguinaldo's activism, see the section in this volume titled "Empire, Independence, and Self-Definition: Voices from the Philippines" (starting on page 972). The section "In Focus: Expansion and Immigration" (starting on page 811) contains selections that participate in debates at the time over the changing role of the nation in world affairs.

■ **ZITKALA-SA (1898).** Born Gertrude Bonnin (1876–1938) on the Pine Ridge Reservation in South Dakota, Zitkala-Sa (meaning "Red Bird") was a strikingly accomplished figure whose complex situation as a Native American woman at the time reflects the diverse, sometimes conflicting cultural currents that many Americans from the social margins had to negotiate. This photograph is among those that highlight Zitkala-Sa's Native heritage and, in so doing, present her as somewhat exotic, in contrast to the conventionally respectable, young bourgeois woman that we see in other portraits of her. A musician, author, and social reformer, Zitkala-Sa was a staunch advocate for Native rights and an important contributor to the Native American written literary tradition. Zitkala-Sa describes her upbringing in "Impressions of an Indian Childhood" (page 322) and details the alienation that she experienced at a Euro-American boarding school for Native children in "The School Days of an Indian Girl" (page 323). Standing Bear's "What I Am Going to Tell You Here Will Take Me until Dark" (page 519), Sarah Winnemucca (Thocmetony)'s "Life among the Piutes" (page 523), and John Milton Oskison's "The Problem of Old Harjo" (page 565) also eloquently explore questions of Native people's identities and sense of belonging.

■ **LATINO FAMILY IN LOS ANGELES (c. 1890).** This image reminds us that America has been multicultural since the outset and that perhaps no city represents this reality more dramatically than Los Angeles (Spanish for "The Angels"). Founded in 1781 by a group of almost entirely mixed-race—Indian, Spanish, and African—settlers, Los Angeles was until 1848 part of Mexico, which won its independence from Spain in 1821. Still a largely rural community in the early stages of urbanization in the late nineteenth century, Los Angeles maintained its tremendous diversity as its population began to grow, hitting just over 50,000 in 1890. The photograph of this multigenerational Mexican American family at the time is a compelling manifestation of the complex racial, ethnic, and national factors at play in the founding and expansion of the United States. It also reflects the strength of family bonds, something that several of the *corridos*, Maria Ruiz de Burton's "The Squatter and the Don" (page 573) and Carlos Galán's "Recuerdos de California, 11 June 1881"/"Memories of California, 11 June 1881" (page 1003), also take up.

demanded both massive, coordinated planning in the use of material resources and intense moral commitment and sacrifice, the postwar period saw general acceptance of a laissez-faire policy under which business, through its enormous economic power, was able to exert often corrupting pressure on government. One particularly notorious scandal erupted in 1872, when the Credit Mobilier, a construction company set up by promoters of the Union Pacific to build the transcontinental railroad at immense profit to themselves, was discovered to have bribed members of Congress and the vice president. The same year saw the conviction of "Boss" (William Marcey) Tweed, head of the infamous Tweed Ring in New York, which for years had systematically plundered the city treasury of from $75 to $200 million. The period from the 1870s to the 1890s was marked by corruption—bribery, graft, vote- and office-selling, the spoils system—at every government level, from the federal administration and Congress to the local city ward politician. "The Gilded Age," Mark Twain called it, capturing in the novel of that title (cowritten with Charles Dudley Warner in 1873) its fever of unrestrained speculation and get-rich-quick schemes, its glitter and fraudulence.

Like the railroads, other businesses and industries also consolidated on a national scale. This concentration of vast resources in the hands of a few constituted one of the most drastic changes from the prewar period. No longer an economy of small shops, local craftsmen, and artisans, nor of primarily small- or medium-sized companies producing manufactured goods, the postwar economy was characterized by the growth of giant corporations, monopolies, and trusts, such as Rockefeller's Standard Oil and Carnegie's United States Steel. Such enterprises employed hundreds, and in some cases thousands, of workers, whose traditional skills were increasingly replaced by the new machinery and who were reduced, through techniques devised by "scientific management," to performing small, unskilled, repetitive tasks. The lives of workers were increasingly separated by such experiences, often by language and religion as well, and of course by wealth, from those of company managers and owners.

With the formation of giant corporations and trusts went the making of gigantic fortunes. By 1890 one percent of American families owned over twenty-five percent of the nation's wealth. By 1893 there were over four thousand millionaires in the United States—not an inconsiderable number at a time when $700 was a comfortable, if modest, annual income. And the millionaires, or plutocrats, flaunted their wealth, spending it conspicuously, as the sociologist

---

I say that you ought to get rich, and it is your duty to get rich. How many of my pious brethren say to me, "Do you, a Christian minister, spend your time going up and down the country advising young people to get rich, to get money?" "Yes, of course I do." They say, "Isn't that awful! Why don't you preach the gospel instead of preaching about man's making money?" "Because to make money honestly is to preach the gospel. That is the reason. The men who get rich may be the most honest men you find in the community."

Russell H. Conwell, *Acres of Diamonds*, 1888

Thorstein Veblen satirically observed in his anatomy of the rich, *The Theory of the Leisure Class* (1899). They built mansions that imitated French chateaux, English castles, and Italian Renaissance palaces; bought up the art works of Europe; and, by heavily dowering their daughters, purchased titles of nobility. They also threw parties costing thousands of dollars for their friends, their horses, and their dogs. Business, *big* business, was the order of the day, and the fortunes reaped from it were justified by an ideology that drew upon the old Protestant ethic of the virtuousness of industry and of the acquisition of wealth as proof of God's favor, and also on the new social thinking, derived from Darwin's biological theories of human evolution, that defended what sociologist Herbert Spencer termed "the survival of the fittest." George F. Baer in 1902 argued that "God in His infinite wisdom has given the control of the property interests of the country" to businessmen, and the imperialist mentality that lay behind his words had also found expression in the Chicago Fair's opening dedicatory speech. Congratulating the Fair's designers and engineers, the speaker observed that "the earth and all it contains have been subservient to your will." A dramatic proof of the power of American big business occurred in the same year as the Fair, when American sugar growers in Hawaii, aided by United States gunboats and marines, overthrew the Hawaiian government, an event that led to the annexation of Hawaii five years later during the Spanish-American War.

By 1893, then, industrialization in the form of immense, privately owned corporations and trusts had established itself, and monopoly capitalism had become the American economic mode. Thus for Henry Adams 1893 meant not just the Chicago Exposition, but also the repeal of the Sherman Silver Purchase Act, a blow to the nation's debtor farmers who had wanted silver coinage in order to increase the money supply and relieve the burden of their debt, and a victory for the gold standard. Adams himself had favored silver, being "against State Street, banks, capitalism altogether," and he saw the year 1893 as symbolically marking the consolidation of power in the capitalist class. Not the farmers who supplied the raw materials nor the urban workers who supplied the physical labor and skills that ran the industrial machine, but the machine's owners—capitalists, industrialists, and bankers—would dominate in political power and significantly determine the nation's future course.

Publishing and Writing

Seen in terms of its production and distribution, literature had also become big business by the 1890s. Like telephones, tractors, or sewing machines, books and magazines were being produced on a national scale. Even before the Civil War, publishing had begun to assume many of its modern characteristics, and the postwar period saw the process accelerated. In the early decades of the nineteenth century, as in the eighteenth, publishing was still primarily local. Village printers and small shops produced newspapers, schoolbooks, religious tracts, and modest editions of novels or collections of poetry with a limited range of distribution. But by 1860, large publishing houses located in the cities could reach national markets by way of the railroads, and books and magazines could be produced more rapidly and cheaply with the new technology of steam-powered rotary presses, multiple presses, and binding machinery. National best sellers were already a phenomenon in the 1850s, as novels of domestic realism by women writers found a growing audience among the wives and daughters of the emerging middle class. (At the beginning of the postwar period in 1866, when the nation's population was thirty-six million, one such novel, Augusta Jane Evans's *St. Elmo*, reputedly reached a readership of one million in the year of its publication alone.) The steady increase in literacy in these years, with the development of a system of free public grade and high schools, kept expanding the market for printed reading matter. Publishers in turn both catered to and helped create that market, becoming increasingly aggressive in distributing and advertising their wares. Indeed, large-circulation periodical publishers found that in selling literature, especially by widely known authors, they were also able to sell the products of their advertisers, on whom they increasingly depended for revenues.

One should in fact talk of multiple markets and of different, if also often overlapping, audiences for literature. The technology of mass production and distribution meant both that something approaching a uniform national print culture was possible and also that specialized audiences could be profitably cultivated. The period therefore saw not only greater uniformity in what people read but also the development of many specialized markets. The largest audience was probably that created and served by the "story papers"—newspapers that printed romance and adventure stories in serial installments—and by the new "dime novels" that first appeared in 1860 and quickly reached circulations in the millions. Cheaper than the average novel that sold for twenty-five cents, these books, produced by Erastus Beadle and his many imitators, were like today's paperback romance novels, quickly written by a stable of writers employed by the publisher and with new titles appearing almost weekly. Read by the young and the new working class in the cities, they offered larger-than-life, simpler-than-life heroes and heroines. At a time when the frontier was closing and urban congestion was the reality of many readers' lives, they depicted stereotypically rugged and self-reliant frontiersmen and cowboys, who in their victories over stereotypically savage and treacherous Indians provided readers with the contours of a mythic American past, with elements of adventure, heroism, and spatial freedom. Later, detective stories set in the city offered new heroes in recognition of the new urban world, including its crime and violence. Consonant with the underlying mythos of individualism and self-reliance of the dime novels were the over one hundred novels produced from the 1860s through the 1890s by Horatio Alger. Their titles—*Risen from the Ranks, Strive and Succeed, Struggling Upward*—were catchy labels for their packaged messages of success achieved through a combination of industriousness, middle-class morality, and luck. That virtue and hard work brought success was a message also conveyed by the maxims and uplifting literary excerpts of the McGuffey readers, over one hundred million of which were used in the schools between 1836 and 1890 and which, like the dime novels and the Alger stories, functioned as an important part of the acculturation process for millions of immigrants, introducing them to the values of white Protestant culture.

At the same time, however, the publishing industry reflected the growing diversity of the American population. The cultures of the many peoples who comprised the nation found outlets in the approximately twelve hundred foreign

Work

Work, work, my boy, be not afraid;
    Look labor boldly in the face;
Take up the hammer or the spade,
    And blush not for your humble place.
There's glory in the shuttle's song;
    There's triumph in the anvil's stroke;
There's merit in the brave and strong,
    Who dig the mine or fell the oak.

Eliza Cook, from *McGuffey's Fifth Eclectic Reader*, 1879 edition

language periodicals that were in existence by 1896, serving immigrant groups from the Germans and Scandinavians to the Czechs and Poles, Spanish and Italians. Groups like the Germans and Scandinavians, who maintained strong connections with the old country, published works in their native languages and translated others into English. By establishing strong cultural institutions to sustain them and to aid in the translation of works into English, they both retained and modified their native cultures. In addition, there were by 1896 over 150 African American magazines and newspapers, a well-developed periodical press established by American Indians and publishing their works, newspapers in the Southwest that circulated local and international news as well as the folk songs of Mexican Americans, and several weeklies publishing news and poetry in Chinese.

On yet another level were the literary magazines—*Atlantic Monthly, Harper's Monthly,* and *Scribner's Monthly* (later the *Century*)—with an influence far greater than the modest circulations of some of them might suggest. It was in these magazines that much of the exciting and important literature of the period appeared. Mark Twain, Henry James, Stephen Crane, Charles Chesnutt, Paul Laurence Dunbar, Hamlin Garland, George Washington Cable, Sarah Orne Jewett, Mary E. Wilkins Freeman, and Abraham Cahan all published in their pages. At the center of that magazine establishment was William Dean Howells, whose career was a graph of the postwar publishing industry. Through the editorial positions he held on two of the most important magazines, Howells advanced the careers of all of those writers, disseminated his own work, and pressed his advocacy of realism as the form that literature should take.

Assistant editor and then editor in the 1860s and 1870s of the prestigious *Atlantic Monthly* in Boston, Howells moved to New York in the 1880s, signaling the shift of literary power to that metropolis. For the next thirty-five years he was associated with *Harper's Monthly,* and the literary criticism, book reviews, and social commentary with which he filled his *Atlantic* and *Harper's* editorial columns comprised the most sustained body of commentary on the postwar literary scene. When in 1892 Howells signed an agreement to write for Edward Bok's *Ladies' Home Journal,* he was still abreast of the time, for Bok's magazine heralded the advent of a new era in periodical journalism: that of the lower-priced, mass-circulated commercial magazine heavily dependent on advertising for its revenues. By then the great days of the literary magazines were ending, and a new era in American publishing had begun.

Like any label, "realism," used to describe the literature Howells wrote and encouraged others to write, obscures differences among writers to whom it is collectively applied, but it also serves to suggest certain common features of what became the distinctive form of prose fiction in the second half of the nineteenth century. Realism was the response of writers to the sweeping economic, social, and political changes of postwar life, to the recognized need to capture, report, and interpret the world of the developing cities and the declining rural regions. In order to convey the nature of an urban world of speeded-up tempos, crowded spaces, new kinds of work, and new mixtures of people, or to represent the landscapes and speech patterns, habits, and manners of the nation's rural areas, such conventions of prewar romance fiction as its often leisurely narrative pace, use of allegory and symbolism, and frequent focus on the exceptional individual no longer seemed appropriate. Rather, realists like Howells emphasized situations and characters drawn from ordinary, everyday life, and the use of authentic American speech and dialogue rather than authorial comment as primary narrative mode.

On the simplest level, realism was a matter of faithfulness to the surfaces of American life, and in its interest in accuracy it reflected the rise of science and, by the end of the nineteenth century, the social sciences, as a source of empirically derived truth, an interest that was also manifest in everything from the spate of investigative journalism to the popular fascination with the Kodak camera, invented in 1888. However, literature of course is never merely a photograph or a mirror that passively reflects external reality; like all imaginative writing, works of realism were also the products of their authors' individual perspectives conveyed through and shaped by language, literary conventions, and the literary traditions that writers inherited. For Howells and Henry James, this last included Hawthorne, especially his concern with moral ambiguities. Although they would not have been aware of this, they also built on the tradition of domestic realistic fiction developed by prewar women writers, with its interest in manners and behavior. These were as important as the French and Russian realist writers such as Balzac and Turgenev, who initially helped provide Howells with his esthetic of realism and whom he introduced to the American reading public.

Three novels that appeared in 1885 (all in the pages of *Century* magazine) suggest something of the range of realistic writing. Howells's *The Rise of Silas Lapham* was the story of a self-made American businessman encountering social situations and moral dilemmas for which his rural upbringing had scarcely prepared him. James's *The Bostonians* dealt, ambivalently, with what James saw as the most salient feature of postwar life—the changing status of women, their greater public and political visibility. And Mark Twain's *Adventures of Huckleberry Finn*, although it takes place in rural and small-town mid-America before the Civil War, dealt with issues crucial in the postwar period—racial and class divisions, the fragility of the family as an institution, social hypocrisy and pretension, and violence and crime. Among them, these three novels engaged issues central to American life in the last half of the nineteenth century: the effects of the new business economy on individual lives, the changing relationship between the sexes, and the intensification of white supremacy after the Civil War.

The 1880s were the height of realism, which could capaciously embrace everything from Twain's disreputable runaway, Huck, with his ungrammatical speech and fear of "sivilization," to Howells's decent but puzzled average Americans, to the heightened consciousness and psychological acuities of the characters who inhabited James's country houses and drawing rooms. Meanwhile, the term "realism" also encompassed the explorations of new subject matter and the perspectives of a host of other writers: the accounts of mill and factory life of Rebecca Harding Davis, Elizabeth Stuart Phelps, and Upton Sinclair; Paul Laurence Dunbar's stories of black life during and after Reconstruction; Charles Chesnutt's black dialect tales and stories of the color line and racist violence; Kate Chopin's examinations of marriage, female sexuality, and racial relations; Hamlin Garland's and Mary E. Wilkins Freeman's studies of the depredations and resilience of rural life in the Midwest and New England; and Abraham Cahan's fictions of New York Jewish ghetto life. Much of this work, given its regional focus, has been subsumed under the labels "local color" or "regional" writing—labels that at best call attention to its distinguishing concern with locale and culture, but that at worst have implied minor status for its authors. As Eric Sundquist has noted, the term "realist" has tended to be reserved for those in or nearest the seats of power in the cities, while those at a remove—midwesterners and southerners, blacks, women, immigrants—have been categorized as regionalists or local colorists. That a great deal of post–Civil War literature was regionalist in origin and emphasis should not be overlooked; regionalism was an important defining characteristic of the period's writing. In the face of the increasing homogeneity and standardization of life attendant on mass production and mass distribution of goods and entertainment, interest in preserving local and regional folkways and traditions and attention to atypical or nonnormative people was widespread. Further, as Richard Brodhead has suggested, such writing appealed to middle-class readers as a kind of cultural tourism. It complemented the development of the vacation industry in places like rural New England and Florida. Such interests helped open markets for the stories and sketches of northern New England written by Sarah Orne Jewett and by Freeman. Indeed, throughout the postwar period, numerous authors would be closely identified with the particular areas they chose to treat: Jack London with the Pacific Coast and Alaska, Cable and Chopin with Louisiana, and Twain, of course, with the Mississippi.

The city was also a region, a new space whose contours and contents were being imaginatively mapped. As Howells continued to explore this new urban space from the mid-1880s through the 1890s, however, he found it harder to accommodate it to his version of realism, which had carried with it a democratic, egalitarian faith in "the large cheerful average of health and success and happy life." The "average" he had implicitly equated with the middle class; by 1890, however, the industrial working class far outnumbered the middle class (by 1915 the poor would be sixty-five percent of the population), and the circumstances of their lives, their relative helplessness against the massed might of the industrial

> Men were nothings, mere animalcules, mere ephemerides that flut-
> tered and fell and were forgotten between dawn and dusk. Vana-
> mee had said there was no death. But for one second Presley could
> go one step further. Men were naught, death was naught, life was
> naught; FORCE only existed—FORCE that brought men into the
> world, FORCE that crowded them out of it to make way for the suc-
> ceeding generation, FORCE that made the wheat grow, FORCE that
> garnered it from the soil to give place to the succeeding crop.
>
> Frank Norris, *The Octopus*, 1901

machine, began to make a mockery of one of realism's prevailing tenets—the belief in the free moral agency of the individual, the capacity, despite adverse or countervailing pressures, to exercise choice and to a significant extent determine one's own fate that had distinguished a Silas Lapham, a Huck Finn, and the heroes and heroines of James's fictions and that had given to the great novels of realism their pivotal dramatic moments. Choice began to seem less operative than chance, as the very titles of Howells's New York novels of 1890 and 1893, *A Hazard of New Fortunes* and *The World of Chance*, recognized, and his middle-class protagonist and alter-ego, Basil March, found himself increasingly bewildered and alienated by a city he had, twenty years earlier, fondly and comfortably embraced. Increasing strife between capital and labor, which would climax in 1894 with the killing of scores of workers during the Pullman strike in Chicago, led one journalist that year to proclaim that "probably . . . in no civilized country in this century, not actually in the throes of war or open insurrection, has society been so disorganized . . . never was human life held so cheap."

As the 1890s advanced, realism darkened its hues, and a new literature by a younger generation emerged with a distinctively new emphasis. "Naturalism" is the term used to describe a dominant element of the fiction, of writers like Stephen Crane, Jack London, Frank Norris, Theodore Dreiser, Paul Laurence Dunbar, and others, where environmental forces, whether of nature, of economic and social systems, or of the city, outweigh or overwhelm human agency, the individual can exert little or no control over determining events, and the world is at worst hostile and at best indifferent to humankind. Crane's "The Open Boat" pits puny human beings against a natural force—the sea—that mocks their efforts to survive. And in Dreiser's *Sister Carrie*, personal success or failure is as much a matter of accident as of ability and will, as individuals often helplessly rise or fall within the surging, anonymous urban mass. Influenced by Darwinian ideas on the importance of environment in shaping human life and by other forms of scientific determinism, such naturalistic fiction also took issue with popular notions of heroism, including heroic interpretations of the Civil War, which had become mythologized in the fiction of southern writers and through articles on heroic battles and generals in the popular press. In *The Red Badge of Courage* or a story like "A Mystery of Heroism," Crane adopts a point of view more akin to that of the second half of the twentieth century, where courage, in the words of Michael Herr on the Vietnam War, was "only undifferentiated energy cut loose by the intensity of the moment." Ambrose Bierce's short story "Chickamauga" exposed the vainglory of war by pitting a child's pretend heroics against scenes of actual and meaningless slaughter. By the turn of the century, Crane's ironies and Bierce's cynicism were matched by the increasingly dark, even nihilistic, views of Mark Twain, whose "The War Prayer" (1905), *The Mysterious Stranger*, and other writings toward the end of his life betrayed a bitterness rooted not only in personal disappointments and family tragedies, but also in disgust at the United States' growing imperialistic stance, a bitterness anticipated in the dark doubts about human goodness that had also threaded their way through the idyllicism of *Huckleberry Finn*.

Such dark views of human nature and human possibility, however, ultimately comprise only one strand in the totality of post–Civil War realistic fiction, a body of writing that offered America a rich diversity of views of its landscapes and cityscapes, its people, their actions and their feelings, especially in narrative. The second half of the nineteenth century was above all an age of narrative prose, in which the short story and the novel predominated as literary forms, reaching out to include whole new areas of subject matter, acquiring increased formal sophistication and linguistic suppleness, and providing a legacy that later writers would inherit and develop.

Scholarly judgments of the poetry produced in the late nineteenth century were generally not favorable until recently. The early 1890s saw the deaths of most of the well-known (and long-lived) poets who had been part of the dominant New England tradition of literature at midcentury. James Russell Lowell, John Greenleaf Whittier, and Oliver Wendell Holmes all died between 1891 and 1894, although their portraits would continue to hang on schoolroom walls into the early decades of the twentieth century as the tradition they represented became enshrined as the nation's "official" culture. They would become part of what the philosopher George Santayana in 1911 called "the genteel tradition"—a literature of uplift and refinement written by latter-day New Englanders in emulation of its Transcendental past but increasingly distant from the realities of American experience and the new sources of its intellectual vitality. Walt Whitman, whose poetry had radically challenged that of the "schoolroom poets," died in 1892, and no new generation of poets had by then emerged to assume his mantle, although Edwin Arlington Robinson, working in isolation, and Paul Laurence Dunbar, writing in both black vernacular and mainstream English, were harbingers of things to come, as were numerous women poets whose substantial body of work in the postwar period has only recently begun to be systematically examined. The early 1890s also saw the first published editions of Emily Dickinson's poems, which Stephen Crane may have read and to which his own poetry bears interesting, if coincidental, resemblance. The clipped, laconic verses that Crane produced toward the end of his short life, as well as the imagist lyrics published in the 1890s by women poets, anticipated, in their ironies and understatements, one dominant mood and style of the modernists who would inaugurate a great new age of American poetry after 1912 and who would find in Dickinson and Whitman their eminent precursors.

Still, this was a flush time for the writers of verse. The explosive growth of periodicals and newspapers of all kinds in the last two decades of the nineteenth century created countless new outlets for poetry. In fact, poetry was in demand everywhere, from local papers to highbrow national magazines, and the need produced both professional and amateur poets. Much of this poetry falls into two general categories: mainstream verse in conventional English and what came to be termed "dialect poetry," an important development that paralleled the "local color" movement in fiction and is beginning to receive scholarly attention as a many-faceted cultural phenomenon. On the surface, it represented attempts to render in verse the vernacular ethnic speech of everyday Americans, and there is dialect poetry allegedly written in the voices of blacks, Chinese, Jews, Irish, Germans, rural whites, and others. Much of it was little better than doggerel, however, and it was frequently produced by writers who were not members of the groups whose language habits they were often caricaturing. Indeed, much dialect verse followed predictable formulas that had little to do with how people spoke, and it served to ridicule groups viewed as outsiders in a manner similar to that of the minstrel shows in which white men in blackface impersonated African Americans. In this way, dialect poetry reflects the complex cultural tensions resulting from the new racial and ethnic social interactions that immigration from abroad and the internal migration of certain groups spawned.

Dialect verse was exceedingly popular and, in fact, provided a medium for two men who were among the country's first poets to make their livings largely with their pens: James Whitcomb Riley and Paul Laurence Dunbar. The former wrote verse in Hoosier dialect (that of white midwestern farming folk); the latter was celebrated for his verse in southern African American dialect—though he, too, produced some Hoosier dialect poetry. While constrained by the limited conventions of dialect verse, Riley and Dunbar, along with other ambitious writers, often transcended the restrictions of the form to produce works of complexity, subtlety, and rich humanity. Dunbar, for example, produced dialect poems that subverted, usually through humor, the problematic cultural and racial assumptions that most writers of black dialect took for granted. In an important way, these accomplished dialect poets can be seen as carrying on, even if indirectly, the groundbreaking work of poets who, like Whitman, were committed to making verse out of the plain speech of plain American folk. Thus they can be seen in conjunction with the literary terrain for the modernist poetic innovators who appeared in the years just before and after World War I.

Circumstances and Literature of Women

The single most significant fact about women, especially white, middle-class women, as a group in the postwar period was their visibility, as they increasingly moved beyond domestic discourse to lay claim to the public world. The extent to which these women became the subject of attention by male writers in the period is one index to the changes taking place in their situation and status. In Daisy Miller, Isabel Archer of *The Portrait of a Lady,* and a host of other fresh, young heroines, Henry James created "the American girl," a type of the modern woman

> The woman had been set free.... One had but to pass a week in
> Florida, or on any of a hundred huge ocean steamers, or walk
> through the Place Vendome, or join a party of Cook's tourists to
> Jerusalem, to see that the woman had been set free.... Behind them,
> in every city, town and farmhouse, were myriads of new types,—or
> type-writers,—telephone and telegraph-girls, shop clerks, factory
> hands, running into millions on millions, and, as classes, unknown
> to themselves as to historians.... all these new women had been cre-
> ated since 1840; all were to show their meaning before 1940.
>
> Henry Adams, *The Education of Henry Adams*

in her independent adventurousness. And in *The Bostonians*, as suggested earlier, he directly addressed the implications of the new public roles women were assuming. Howells offered a portrait of the new professional woman in *Dr. Breen's Practice* and in Marcia Gaylord of *A Modern Instance* a woman, rare in fiction in the 1880s, of strong sexual feeling. Henry Adams wrote two novels with strong female heroines, exploring his sense of women as a potentially vital new force, and other novelists, such as Robert Herrick, would devote significant portions of their careers to studying the new, emancipated woman.

However, if the appearance of such characters was an encouraging sign, their fictional fates were not. Most often they were contained within the conventions of the traditional romantic plot, punished rather than rewarded for their forays into the world by endings that offered only a choice between a confining marriage and death—witness to their authors' ambivalence about the new freedoms women were assuming. Older attitudes toward women also persisted: woman as civilizing agent who censors man's freedom, in *Huckleberry Finn* or Crane's "The Bride Comes to Yellow Sky," or woman as helpless victim, in Crane's narrative of a young girl driven to prostitution, *Maggie: A Girl of the Streets*. Hamlin Garland approached women with much more sympathy, but his female characters were also often victims—the overworked and defeated women of isolated, impoverished midwestern farms.

Collectively, women writers told a more varied and complex story about the realities of their lives, lives that were responding to and shaped by new circumstances. Among the most important changes affecting women as a group in the second half of the nineteenth century were the increased educational and employment opportunities available to them and their increasing involvement in political and reform activity. The prewar period had seen higher education begin to open up for women, and the momentum quickened in the postwar period as the public midwestern land grant colleges admitted more women (partly due to the dearth of males as a result of the Civil War) and as private women's colleges were established. The period saw the establishment of such elite eastern institutions as Vassar, Smith, Wellesley, Bryn Mawr, and Barnard. Although serving only a limited (and privileged) group, their success nevertheless importantly demonstrated that women could be the intellectual equals of men, thus countering the still prevalent belief in women's intellectual inferiority. (A new source of resistance to women's education did arise when influential medical practitioners warned that women's development of their brains would sap reproductive and maternal energy.) Although racism operated to curtail educational opportunities, black women were attending the new coeducational and single-sex institutions established after the war, such as Howard University and Spelman College. From these and other schools came women, many of them with postgraduate training as well, who by the end of the century composed a class of professional and intellectual leaders in education, in the women's club movement, in medicine, and in the new area of work spawned by the needs of the cities—social work, including settlement house work.

Meanwhile, an expanding economy and rapid population growth were creating other forms of employment that drew ever larger numbers of women into the paid labor force. The new commercial and business world demanded higher levels of literacy of its workers, and as public elementary and high school education spread throughout the states, women were enlisted as teachers. (They could be paid less than men, and the work was seen as a suitable extension of their child-rearing capacities.) In addition, women, especially middle-and lower-middle-class white women, began entering the new business world directly, as department store clerks, telephone and telegraph operators, and "typewriters," as the earliest workers on that newly invented machine were called. Mostly young and unmarried, with incomes of their own, dressed in the slim (if still long) skirts and trim shirtwaists that had replaced the bustled and flounced, heavily layered, and cumbersome clothing of earlier decades, these women were one of the more visible manifestations of the "new woman," as the economically and socially emancipated woman at the turn of the century came to be described. Such emancipations were limited for all women, however, and sharply limited by race. As a group, women were routinely paid less than men, and only sixteen percent were in clerical, trade, or professional positions. Black women were largely confined to agricultural and domestic work, northern immigrant women to domestic work and factory labor. Many of the latter worked in the sweatshops of New York and other cities, where unsanitary and unsafe working conditions led to disasters like the Triangle Shirtwaist Company fire in 1910, in which 146 women lost their lives. Such disasters, together with the organization of unions in the clothing and other "light" industries, eventually led to successful agitation for industrial reform in hours, wages, and working conditions.

Labor legislation was but one of many reform activities in which women were involved by the turn of the century, when they were an important part of the progressive movement, helping to secure not only improved working conditions, but also better housing, sanitation, recreational, and educational facilities for the industrial class, and when they were working within the international peace movement and the suffrage movement. The woman's rights movement, the longest organized reform movement in United States history, officially dated from the Seneca Falls Convention of 1848. In abeyance during the Civil War, it resumed its work for women's rights in the postwar years and moved into a period of new activism in the 1880s and 1890s, launching state and national campaigns for women's suffrage and steadily increasing the number of its adherents. The period also saw the founding, in 1874, of what would become the largest women's organization in the world, the Woman's Christian

Temperance Union. Initially created to deal with the high degree of alcoholism in the country at the time—a condition that especially affected married women, who often still lacked legal rights to their own property and wages and were dependent on husbands for their support—the WCTU, under the charismatic leadership of Frances Willard, adopted a broad reform agenda that included not only temperance legislation, but also advocacy of the eight-hour workday, child care centers for working mothers, prison reform, and suffrage.

The woman's club movement that began in the 1870s and spread rapidly among both white and black women was by the end of the century yet another major institution through which significant numbers of women were working to educate themselves and to improve social conditions. Indeed, for black women, who were excluded on account of their race from many of the movements in which white women were active, the club movement was a crucial means of fostering racial uplift and forging connections among African Americans across the nation. It also provided the means of mounting activist responses to the racist portrayals of black women as sexually uncontrolled that pervaded both the scientific and the popular media at the time. In 1895, for instance, the National Federation of Afro-American Women formed as a direct result of a piece by a white journalist contending that black women were impure.

The quest for full legal, economic, and social equality for women would still need to be pursued in the twentieth century, and racism would remain a persistent obstacle for women of color. By 1900, however, white women of the middle and upper classes had made significant strides. The prevailing ideology of the prewar decades that had idealized the "true woman" as domestic and maternal had been largely replaced by the image of the "new woman," whose educational level, social mobility, relative economic self-sufficiency, and, by the time of World War I, greater sexual freedom had released her from much of her earlier dependency.

Post–Civil War fiction by women reflected and responded to these broad social changes. By the 1870s, women had a record of more than a half-century of substantial achievement in prose fiction; some women had established themselves as best-selling authors; some had initiated directions that realistic writing would take. In the postwar period, women writers carried further themes introduced by women before the war, and they introduced new themes and concerns. For example, women authors pioneered in writing about the conditions of industrial factory life. As early as 1861, Rebecca Harding Davis published a grim, unflinching narrative of the dehumanizing conditions of work in the iron mills of West Virginia; in 1873 Elizabeth Stuart Phelps published *The Silent Partner*, an account of the lives of the "hands" in New England textile factories and of one woman's efforts to bridge the gap between the propertied and the working classes. Work—especially the kinds available to women—became a paramount subject in the postwar decades. It was the central concern of Louisa May Alcott's novel *Work* (1873), which explored some of the options—as a domestic, a governess, a seamstress, an actress, a Civil War nurse—available to working and middle-class women in the period just preceding and immediately following the Civil War. Stemming from the prewar women's literary tradition of domestic realism, Alcott's novel focused on her heroine's pursuit of her own autonomy, the development of a strong and independent sense of self, to which rewarding work was seen as essential. This search for self-fulfilling work was seemingly encouraged by increased acceptance of women's aspirations and talents, but it was often in conflict with society's and women's own expectations and desires for marriage and motherhood. Some version of this conflict underlays a series of important postwar fictions by writers from Rebecca Harding Davis, Elizabeth Stuart Phelps, and Charlotte Perkins Gilman to Frances Ellen Watkins Harper, Pauline Hopkins, Kate Chopin, and Mary Austin.

Such fictions frequently took the romance plot beyond its conventional ending to explore the realities of women's lives after marriage, with a new emphasis on the conflicts their heroines experienced. Davis produced a number of stories in which women characters are torn by ambivalence as they try to balance their own needs for creative expression and self-fulfillment against their families' needs. In Phelps's *The Story of Avis*, the heroine's artistic talent wastes away under the incessant demands of the daily domestic routine, and in *Dr. Zay*, the question of whether marriage and the heroine's medical practice are compatible is left unanswered. In Gilman's "The Yellow Wall-Paper" and Chopin's *The Awakening*, two radical nineteenth-century fictional critiques of the effects of marriage and motherhood on middle-class white women, those institutions ultimately destroy the artist-heroines. Despite living in an age of greater economic and sexual freedom for women, Mary Austin in the early twentieth century still experienced the same conflict, which she dealt with in her autobiography, *Earth Horizon*, and her semi-autobiographical novel, *A Woman of Genius*.

Gilman's, Chopin's and Austin's frank analyses of marriage and motherhood as harmful to women's continuing development brought them censure—Chopin, for instance, wrote little after the storm of criticism that greeted *The Awakening*. Nevertheless, their writing, which by the 1890s was supported by a growing body of feminist criticism of women's role and status in society, was a logical culmination of themes introduced by prewar women writers, who had examined the stresses for women of marriage and family life, the authoritarian roles of fathers and husbands, and women's need to develop an independent sense of self while still acknowledging the claims of others and women's ties to their families. Prewar writers, by contrast, had often embraced the primacy of the values that marriage and family ideally fostered: the role women had as wives and mothers in advancing values of cooperation, connection, and responsibility to others. They saw such values, transferred to the public world, as potentially transformative, challenging and even replacing the competitiveness and materialism of capitalism. Their vision, rooted in antebellum domestic ideology, was inherited at the end of the century by Sarah Orne Jewett. Jewett's *The Country of the Pointed Firs* and "The Foreigner" depict communities of women where ties of friendship and respect for nature create the basis for living (a vision that Charlotte Perkins Gilman would also offer in her Utopian fiction *Herland* [1915]). However, Jewett's world of rural New England was nonetheless a world in economic decline, a region existing on the edges of the industrial world, and the note she struck was elegiac. Even as she wrote in the 1890s, a new cult of masculinity was emerging, partly in reaction to women's increased visibility—exemplified in the big game hunting of Theodore Roosevelt, the adventurous journalism of Rebecca Harding Davis's son Richard, the popularity of Owen Wister's novel of the West, *The Virginian* (1902), and America's imperialist expansion. Though similarly situated in declining New England rural regions, women in the stories of Mary E. Wilkins Freeman often cultivate domestic life for their own self-sustenance and even pleasure. The sometimes stark confrontations with male power and the wresting of small but suggestive victories by some of Freeman's women also testify to continuing problems of gender conflict as some women writers understood them.

Circumstances and Literature of African Americans

In the postwar period, literature by African American writers drew upon and reflected crucial realities in their lives. The most critical event, of course, had been the abolition of slavery. With the passage of the Thirteenth Amendment to the Constitution in 1865, four million black people were freed, and with emancipation came Reconstruction—the federal government's radical attempt to restructure the South. The brief period of Reconstruction (1867–1877) saw massive economic rehabilitation; the greatest black participation in local, state, and national politics before the late twentieth century; and the education of a quarter of a million black people. This last was effected especially through the efforts of the Freedman's Bureau, which established some four thousand schools staffed by black and white teachers from the North who went to the South to teach the former slaves. In the hopeful years immediately following the end of the Civil War, many important southern black colleges and universities were also established. Between 1866 and 1868 alone, Fisk, Morehouse, Howard, and Atlanta Universities and Talladega College were founded, as well as Hampton Institute, where the young, ambitious Booker T. Washington arrived in 1872, having walked and begged rides to cover the long distance from his West Virginia home.

The decade of reform ended, however, when federal troops were withdrawn from the southern states in 1877. Abandoned by the Supreme Court and the Republican party, southern blacks were disenfranchised in the ensuing decades; by

---

The nation was rushing forward with giant strides toward colossal wealth and world dominion, before the exigencies of which mere abstract ethical theories must not be permitted to stand. The same argument that justified the conquest of an inferior nation could not be denied to those who sought the suppression of an inferior race. In the South, an obscure jealousy of the negro's progress, an obscure fear of the very equality so contemptuously denied, furnished a rich soil for successful agitation. Statistics of crime, ingeniously manipulated, were made to present a fearful showing against the negro. Vital statistics were made to prove that he had degenerated from an imaginary standard of physical excellence which had existed under the benign influence of slavery. Constant lynchings emphasized his impotence and bred everywhere a growing contempt for his rights.

Charles W. Chesnutt, *The Marrow of Tradition*, 1901

1910 all eleven of the states of the former Confederacy had effectively abolished black voting rights. In addition, newly passed "Jim Crow" laws established segregation in everything from public transportation and schools to drinking fountains. Meanwhile, the Civil War had not fully dismantled the plantation system of large landholdings, and some sixty percent of southern land was owned by ten percent of whites, with the result that freed blacks, as well as poor whites, soon found themselves forced into sharecropping or tenant farming. By 1900 over three-quarters of the southern black population were tenant farmers, with black women working in the fields beside black men, as they had in the days of slavery, or hiring themselves out as domestic workers in white houses.

In these post-Reconstruction years, both illegal and legal methods of constraint and intimidation increased. Beginning with the Ku Klux Klan, first organized in 1866, white vigilante groups launched systematic campaigns of terror and violence. In the two years between 1868 and 1870, thousands of blacks were killed and tens of thousands driven from their homes, and such violence continued throughout the postwar decades. Lynchings, which often entailed torture and being burned alive, escalated in the latter part of the century. At least thirty-five hundred lynchings occurred between 1885 and 1910, with the alleged rape of white women by black men constituting the most frequent rationalization. Such intimidation and violence was not confined to the South; segregation and race riots occurred in the North as well. So virulent were attacks on the black community between 1880 and 1900 that the period has been described as "the nadir" of the free black experience.

The attacks were not only physical. Mental and psychological violence was done by the widespread propagation of negative racial stereotypes. Stereotypes are one window on relations between minority groups and the dominant culture. As cultural prescriptions for behavior, postbellum racist stereotypes denigrated blacks, limited their perceived possibilities, and denied them opportunities. The postwar period saw attacks especially on blacks' morality: men depicted as animalistic rapists and women as "Jezebels," promiscuous and lascivious. Also harmful were the stereotypes, perpetuated through such popular cultural forms as minstrel shows, of the happy darky; the loyal, self-sacrificing Mammy; and the superstitious, lazy, country folk—images that, among other purposes, served to rationalize the economic exploitation of blacks as field and domestic workers. The stereotypes were further bolstered by pseudo-scientific studies produced by white historians, sociologists, and anthropologists that appeared in the wake of Darwin's theory of evolution, claiming that blacks were nonhuman—a different species than whites—and likely doomed to extinction. Retrogressionist arguments also appeared, asserting that, once freed from the discipline of slavery, blacks had deteriorated. Such ideas—and similar ones existed to explain the alleged inferiority of women, Native Americans, Mexican Americans, Asian Americans, and the new immigrants from southern and eastern Europe—fed into and in turn were exacerbated by the imperialist and colonizing mentality that solidified in the late nineteenth century with the Spanish-American War; the annexation of Puerto Rico, Hawaii, and the Philippines; and America's growing role as a world power.

In addition, such stereotypes played a crucial role in the nostalgic depiction of prewar life that came to be known as the "plantation tradition" of writing.

Produced mainly by southern white writers like Thomas Nelson Page, this literature mythologized the South as a noble, well-ordered patriarchal world run by
kindly masters and inhabited by contented slaves. The grimmer underside of
such depictions emerged in the pro–Ku Klux Klan novels of Thomas Dixon,
whose *The Clansman* inspired one of the most important silent movies of the
newly developing film industry, D. W. Griffith's *The Birth of a Nation* (1915).
Other white southern writers, however, produced thoughtful, sensitive portrayals of black individuals as part of their interest in exploring both the
strengths and the stresses of a multicultural society. The Louisiana writers
George Washington Cable and Kate Chopin wrote of the Creoles, Acadians,
blacks, whites (Anglo-Americans), and those of mixed blood in their region,
exposing in the process the false idealization of the antebellum South and
reflecting on the actualities of racial mixing and the light it cast on white claims
to racial purity. In addition, the Georgia writer Joel Chandler Harris, through
his collections of black dialect tales and creation of the character Uncle Remus,
offered to white audiences sympathetic though patronizing and often distorted
readings of black slave culture.

For black writers, the postwar decades provided increased publishing opportunities and a larger readership. As black literacy increased, so too did the number of newspapers and magazines addressing them as an audience, among them
the *Colored American Magazine*. Some black writers published as well in the pages
of the major nationally circulated journals like the *Atlantic Monthly*, *Harper's*,
and *McClure's*. However, the new opportunities were accompanied by constraints. Although the postwar period saw growing interest in reclaiming and
preserving slave culture, especially the spirituals and work songs that had been
the slaves' major expressive outlets, the association in the public mind of dialect
and vernacular language with comic ignorance and inferiority posed a dilemma
for the black writer who wanted to represent the racial experience in the language of the rural black masses. Like others of his generation, Paul Laurence
Dunbar, one of the most popular poets in the postwar period, faced what Marcus Cunliffe has called the "double burden of racial and linguistic definition."
Throughout his career, Dunbar wrote both in the vernacular and in the more
formal and conventional language of late-nineteenth-century genteel poetry, but
influential whites like Howells wanted him to produce only "dialect" literature.
The agonized debates he conducted with himself over the use of folk language
and art forms would be repeated by other black writers in the years of the Harlem Renaissance before black vernacular became fully acceptable in literature.
Meanwhile, Charles Chesnutt, consciously trying to undermine racist preconcep-
tions, used dialect to create the sly ironies of his conjure tales, where the ex-slave
narrator, Uncle Julius, drawing upon rich black oral traditions, scores victories
over his white listeners. Moreover, through the interactive play of black and white
voices, Chesnutt explored and exposed the inequitable power relationships in both
pre– and post–Civil War society.

White mainstream literary conventions and audience expectations also
posed serious obstacles for black women writers. Chesnutt might ironically
declare that "the object of my writings would not be so much the elevation of
the colored people as the elevation of the whites," but postwar novelists like
Pauline Hopkins and Frances Harper, whose *Iola LeRoy* in 1892 culminated a

distinguished career as writer and reformer that stretched back to the pre–Civil War period, saw their mission very explicitly as one of "racial uplift"—that of improving not just the public image but also the self-image of blacks, and especially of black women, for whom the Jezebel stereotype, which blamed them for the sexual exploitation they suffered, was especially pernicious. Some heroines in *Iola LeRoy* and in Hopkins's novels, including her most important work, *Contending Forces* (1900), are pale-skinned and light-haired—physical features associated with racial and moral superiority. In creating black heroines who were thus often physically indistinguishable from whites, Harper and Hopkins reveal the power of reigning middle-class white cultural standards, but their work is centered primarily in issues crucial to black women: family stability, education and finding worthwhile employment, ending sexual exploitation, the advancement of African American community, and racial pride. By the late nineteenth century, with the growth of a substantial black middle class, especially though not exclusively in the North, African American professional women, often working through their extensive network of women's clubs and organizations, were a significant force for racial progress. Educator Anna Julia Cooper, whose feminist essays, *A Voice from the South*, appeared in 1892, proclaimed that the status of black women would be a crucial determinant of the condition of the entire race. Only the black woman can say, Cooper asserted, that "when and where I enter, in the quiet, undisputed dignity of my womanhood, without violence and without suing or special patronage, then and there the whole *Negro race enters with me.*"

By the turn of the century, the terms on which blacks could or should enter into mainstream society were in fact the subject of extensive and ongoing debate, crystallized in the opposing positions of Booker T. Washington and W.E.B. Du Bois. The dominant black political leader at the end of the nineteenth century, Washington argued for conciliating and accommodating to the white world. His famous Atlanta Exposition Speech in 1895, while promoting black pride and extolling self-help, urged blacks to eschew any hopes for social equality with whites and to limit their expectations for legal and economic advancement as well. By the turn of the century, a vocal younger generation was demanding a more militant posture, refusing to be defined as a separate underclass. Du Bois's rejoinder to Washington, *The Souls of Black Folk* (1903), articulated his demand not only for civil rights for blacks, but also for the right to equal participation in higher education and liberal learning. By the beginning of the twentieth century, in poetry, fiction, and nonfictional prose, African American writers had established the terms for many of the major issues that the rest of the century would continue to confront.

Circumstances and Literature of Native Peoples

During the four decades following the Civil War, Native peoples suffered social discontinuity on a larger scale and to a greater degree than ever before or since, as white American society penetrated and firmly rooted itself in even the remotest interior of the trans-Mississippi West. War, confinement to reservations, and the resulting poverty, disease, and dispossession through fraud contributed to many white Americans' belief that Native peoples were casualties of the sweep of the Caucasian (abetted by Western technology) across the face of the continent and that they were destined to vanish, losers in the struggle for the fittest survivors. Opposed to this view were those well-meaning reformers who believed that with certain adjustments in their way of life, "American Indians" could be saved. Thus during this period assimilation became the watchword, and federal policy drifted slowly from one of trying to defeat Native peoples in warfare to attempting to make them over in white America's image. To do so required drastic changes in Native peoples' relation to the land, new directions in their education, and a revolution in their way of life, all of which bore significantly on literary production among Native peoples.

To obtain the "proper" relation between Native peoples and land, the federal government had to undo its former policy of removal, which involved settling tribes in Indian Territory (now Oklahoma). Both before the Civil War and in the twenty years after it, removal had chilling and sometimes devastating effects on individual and tribal life, including sharp rises in mortality rates. It was not, however, until after the forced march of the Poncas in 1877 from Dakota Territory to Indian Territory that any substantial sentiment rose against the policy. In significant measure, this shift in public attitude occurred in response to the efforts of a small group of writers, both Native and white, who shaped the new public awareness of the effects of removal and contributed significantly to the development of an Indian policy reform movement that culminated in a major step toward assimilation—the General Allotment Act of 1887, or Dawes Act.

The first protest literature emerged from the Omaha Ponca Committee and the people they attracted. Consisting of Standing Bear (Ponca), Susette La Flesche (Omaha), her brother Francis La Flesche, and journalist Thomas H. Tibbles, the committee toured the East in 1879 and 1880, lecturing to inform the public about the dire effects of the Poncas' march. Capturing the public's attention, they won the support of reform and religious groups and of writers such as the aging Henry Wadsworth Longfellow, Oliver Wendell Holmes, and Helen Hunt Jackson, who took the Indians' situation to the periodical press. In 1881 Jackson published *A Century of Dishonor*, an indictment of federal Indian policy and an important step in the movement for reform. The book that captured the public imagination, however, and became a Native *Uncle Tom's Cabin*, was Jackson's popular novel, *Ramona* (1885). In the dispossession of Alisandro's people from their rancheria, readers found the archetype of dispossession of all Native peoples in the past.

The General Allotment Act of 1887 dissolved collective tribal title to the land and allotted plots to individual Natives, who received deeds just as their Euro-American counterparts did throughout the country. The balance of unallotted land, which was always sizeable, was put up for sale, with the proceeds to be held in trust for the Native nations by the U.S. government. Allotted Native people also became citizens, subject to state laws and liable to taxation. The idea that private property would serve as an effective engine of democracy was an old one. The nation's agrarian founders had believed that the best life was that of the yeoman farmer, and ownership of land had figured prominently in the definition of the good citizen. In transferring the idea to Native nations, however, reformers ran roughshod over tribal traditions, gender and family, and collective land use; they also failed to consider Natives' lack of operating capital, the poor quality of much Native land, and their lack of enough legal knowledge to prevent them from losing their land. They also failed to calculate the scale of white American land hunger. Reactionary elements and land-hungry railroads had supported the General Allotment Act for their own reasons. They viewed reservation land as a vast resource waiting to be exploited by the forces of expansionist capitalism. By 1887 Native peoples had lost all but 150 million acres of their aboriginal three-billion-acre landhold. By 1934, when the General Allotment Act was repealed, only 48 million acres, less than 1.5 percent of aboriginal America, still remained in Indian hands.

The goal of assimilation into mainstream society was pursued not just by disrupting Native peoples' communal land base and thus undermining tribal sovereignty and self-determination, but also by an educational policy that separated individuals from their tribal heritage and customs. On the reservations, education was mainly mission based, giving Natives instruction in Christian dogma and basic skills. In 1878 the government began a policy of off-reservation education by creating a number of boarding schools far from the reservations. Students were taken from their homes for a number of years, given Christian instruction, discouraged from speaking their own languages or following traditional practices, and provided with vocational training in the trades. The assumption underlying this plan was that the educated students could not return to the reservation and feel satisfied with conditions there. Rather, they were to enter mainstream America, participate in its economic system, and share its goods. Hamlin Garland and others, including the Santee Sioux writer Charles A. Eastman, believed that the transition would be easier if, like the immigrants arriving from abroad, Native peoples' names were "Americanized." In the early twentieth century, Eastman, funded by the U.S. government, assigned Anglicized names to the Sioux.

Much literary production by Native people in this period was in some way a response to these efforts at assimilation. Susette La Flesche initially believed that individual land ownership and citizenship were the only means by which Native peoples could protect themselves; later she became disillusioned and concluded that the American economic system favored the rich over the poor, no matter what their color. Her brother, Francis, however, remained faithful to his early views, while also using his knowledge of traditional Indian life in writing autobiographical works, stories, legends, and a libretto for an opera. Although Charles A. Eastman found it difficult to reconcile the Christian faith he had embraced as a teenager and the Army's massacre of Native people at Wounded Knee, he continued in his Christianity and also championed Native cultures. In the face of growing evidence that full participation in American society was not possible for Native peoples, writers such as Zitkala-Sa, who had early embraced white America's ways, became embittered, professed their "paganism," and began a revival of interest in Native peoples' cultures. Her work, and that of others in her generation, led directly to the reforms in the 1920s and 1930s that attempted to arrest many of the devastating effects of allotment and recognized the value of cultural pluralism.

Representing another development in American Indian writing are those authors from tribes in the Indian Territory (especially the Cherokees, Choctaws, and Creeks) that had been there for many years before the Civil War. Having reestablished themselves as constitutional nations following removal in the 1830s and 1840s, they had developed systems of public education, embraced modern farming and ranching techniques, and were, in most respects, on the road to assimilation well before the U.S. government promoted assimilation. The educated populations in those tribes were well read in mainstream U.S. literature, and from their ranks came a number of writers who, by the end of the nineteenth century, were adept in the rhetoric and conventions of that literature. By the late 1870s, the Cherokees, for instance, had established libraries, reading circles, and debating societies, and they subscribed to the popular magazines from the states, gaining access to the poetry and fiction of mainstream U.S. writers. In their local newspapers appeared works by writers such as Mark Twain, Josh Billings, and Joel Chandler Harris. Cherokee writers such as D. W. C. Duncan (Tooquastee), John T. Adair, D. J. Brown, and John Oskison carried on the literary tradition begun by pre–Civil War Cherokees, including Elias Boudinot and John Rollin Ridge.

Literary activity also flourished elsewhere in the Indian Territory. Writers like Carrie Le Flore followed pre–Civil War Choctaw authors such as Israel Folsom and George Harkins. In the Creek Nation, writers James Roan Gregory, Charles Gibson, and Alexander Posey emerged, as did William Jones among the Sac and Fox and Bertrand N. O. Walker (Hen-toh) among the Wyandots.

Many Native writers responded to literary movements in mainstream America. Dialect and humor became favorite forms of expression for writers such as Alexander Posey and, later, Will Rogers (Cherokee), and lesser-known writers contributed pieces to local publications after the fashion of Billings and other popular literary comedians. Posey created dialect poetry from his Creek background just as Paul Laurence Dunbar and Frances Ellen Watkins Harper did from their African American one. Walker wrote animal stories in the manner of Harris's Uncle Remus stories, and Posey, Jones, and Oskison produced a number of stories in the tradition of the regional writers.

Through the efforts of the Indian Territory writers, the La Flesches, Zitkala-Sa, and Eastman from the Great Plains, or Sarah Winnemucca of the Northern Paiutes, Native literature began to find a national market. Autobiographies were of special interest, dealing as they did with the problem of a double identity that members of other ethnic groups were struggling with at the turn of the century, as the question of what it meant to be "American" gained new urgency in a time both of increasing cultural diversity and of pressures to conform to mainstream ways. Simultaneously, the sharply increased interest in compilations of Native peoples' oral traditions and tribal lore indicated a growing awareness of the erosion of indigenous cultural life. Native writers by the end of the century created a rich corpus of writing that is taking its place both as American literature and as Native literature.

Circumstances and Literature of Latino/as

For the Latino/as of the Southwest, the fifty years after 1865 comprised a period during which their traditions and literature evolved into a distinctive culture and body of expression. The Treaty of Guadalupe Hidalgo, which ended the

Mexican War in 1848, transformed Spanish-speaking peoples from California to New Mexico into Americans only in a political sense, and a generation passed before they began to delineate new geo-cultural realities. The literature that Latino/as created includes historical and personal narratives; fiction; the *columbrista* sketch (a sketch of customs or manners); poetry; various folkloric forms such as the folktale, the legend, and the *corrido* (a type of ballad); and, occasionally, the novel.

Aside from the question of Americanization, the issues that gripped the attention of writers in more populous regions of the United States—urbanization, technological innovation, the entrenchment of industrial capitalism—were regarded with considerably less enthusiasm in the Latino/a Southwest, which remained, defiantly, a place apart. Its heritage was unique among all the regions of the United States, a *mestizo* blend of Spanish, Native, and, Mexican traditions that contrasted vividly with the English traits of the dominant culture. Additionally, the primary religious influence was Catholic, not Protestant. For many Latino/as in the last third of the nineteenth century, the fountainheads of mainstream American culture and politics—Boston, New York, Philadelphia, and Washington—seemed remote if not irrelevant. What was decidedly neither remote nor irrelevant was the physical presence of the *gringos*, arriving in the Southwest in ever larger numbers, presumably to take Latino/as land and to demolish their culture.

Among American ethnic groups, Latino/as of the Southwest occupied a curious position, being neither immigrants—the United States, after all, had absorbed them—nor a minority in many of the southwestern communities they inhabited. Latino/as took pride in the fact that they could trace a longer history in North America than Anglo-Americans: Juan de Oñate had established a permanent settlement in northern New Mexico along the Rio Grande in 1598, nine years before the founding of Jamestown and twenty-two years before Plymouth. Another factor that separated Latino/as from other ethnic groups was the proximity of their homeland. The United States and Mexico shared a border that stretched some two thousand miles from the Pacific to the Gulf of Mexico, and most Latino/as lived within easy traveling distance; many lived on or near the border itself. While ethnic Europeans mourned the decline of their traditional cultures far away from their homelands, Latino/as had easy access to theirs.

Their long presence in the Southwest and their enduring cultural vitality and pride help to explain the vehemence with which Latino/as responded to the many Anglo-Americans who came into the region with little respect for them and little interest in cultural accommodation. Numerous historical and personal narratives appeared to denounce the arrogant and bigoted *gringos*. Not surprisingly, many of the fiercest condemnations came from once-wealthy and prominent landowners who had lost the most to the acquisitive Anglos. In addition to Mariano Vallejo (represented in Volume B of this anthology), writers of such works included Ignacio Sepúlveda, Juan Bautista Alvarado, Juan Bandini, and María Arparo Ruiz de Burton.

Even as they denounced the Anglo interlopers, Latino/as recognized that their world had changed and would change still more. Here, then, were the components of a distinctive Latino/a sensibility: ethnic pride and a powerful sense of history and endurance forged within the dynamics of the border.

In the late nineteenth century, easily the most popular literary form among Latino/as was poetry, much of which appeared in the hundreds of Spanish-language newspapers that proliferated in the Southwest. Much of the poetry was lyrical, generally in the prevailing Spanish and Latin American styles, and a great deal was political, treating such issues as the quality of education available for Latino/as, the necessity of learning English, and land grant disputes. A particularly explosive issue debated in verse was the Spanish-American War of 1898. Some poets encouraged their readers to support the war effort as a show of patriotism; others maintained that the United States had done nothing to deserve Latino/a loyalty.

While the production of conventional literary works increased steadily toward the end of the nineteenth century and beyond, folkloric forms also flourished. The *corrido* ballad tradition matured around the turn of the century and thrived thereafter. The *corrido* proved to be a perfect medium for expressing both dispossession and cultural conflict with Anglos. *Corridos* were composed—usually anonymously—and sung across the Southwest, attaining epic proportions in the lower border regions of Texas. Here, in an environment of intense conflict with the Anglo community and true transculturalism, "border Mexicans" celebrated the exploits of such figures as Gregorio Cortez and Jacinto Treviño, common men who stood up to Anglo injustice with, as the saying went, pistols in their hands.

Although Latino/a literary works, including the narratives of Miguel Otero and Andrew García, occasionally appeared in English, Spanish remained the primary language of expression in both conventionally literary and folkloric forms until well into the twentieth century. Indeed, the Spanish of Latino/as had become a distinctive literary and oral idiom, incorporating English words and phrases and creating new expressions from both standard Spanish and English.

Along the central and southern East Coast of the United States, there was also ferment among Spanish-language writers and activists connected with the Antilles and more generally with the Caribbean and Latin America. Best-known of these figures among English-speakers today is Cuban revolutionary and writer José Martí. The scope of Martí's activities and accomplishments, as well as his heroism, were exceptional, but his life and work attest to the hemispheric scope of the anticolonial movements in which he took part and, in many ways, spurred. Exiled from Spanish-ruled Cuba for his political activity for much of his life, he lived and was politically active in Spain, Venezuela, Guatemala, Mexico, and the United States. His associations with and publications in Spanish-language periodicals in many countries bespeak the supranational networks among Latino/as during the late nineteenth century. Among those periodicals were *La República* (Honduras), *La Nación* (Buenos Aires), *La Opinión Pública* (Montevideo), and *La América* (New York City); in the United States he also founded and published in the Spanish-language *PATRIA* (Fatherland) and published in the English-language *Hour*. He was also chair of the Spanish-American Literary Society in New York City. As for many others in the Antillean exile community, for Martí, writing and political activity were fused. If much of his writing was political, his life itself was dedicated to Cuban independence, to democracy, and to advocating the common interests of hemispheric Spanish-speaking countries. He was the Uruguayan, Argentine, and Paraguayan consul in New York and Uruguay's representative to the International Monetary Conference in Washington in 1891. He was also tireless in organizing resistance to Spanish rule in Cuba— which, in his view, had to be part of a broad Latin-American movement for democracy and cultural self-determination—and in 1892 founded the Cuban Revolutionary Party. Joining Cubans in their war for independence from Spain shortly after it began, he was killed in it in 1895.

Martí's most famous essay, "Nuestra América" (1891), speaks in many ways to the pan-Americanism he embraced. Written in New York City, it appeared in Spanish in *Revista Ilustrada* (New York) and in *El Partido Liberal* (Mexico City). Long recognized as a pioneering expression of Latina/o self-determination and a major work of *modernismo*, it continues to be read in Spanish throughout Latin America and in the United States. That in "English" translation it also enjoys an ever-increasing non-Spanish readership reflects a deepening recognition within the United States, as elsewhere, that "America" has always signified far more than the national contours of any single country.

Circumstances and Literature of Asian Americans

At the turn of the twentieth century, Asian Americans constituted a comparatively small percentage of the population of the United States. Out of a total of fourteen million immigrant arrivals between 1860 and 1900, less than half a million were of Asian descent. Of this number, Chinese immigrants comprised roughly 260,000 but experienced discrimination out of all proportion to their modest numerical presence. Indeed, in the post–Civil War period, Sinophobia became widespread, and cities, states, and the national government passed repressive legislation. The Chinese had been the primary labor force in the building of the transcontinental railroad east from Sacramento, doing the backbreaking and dangerous work of tunneling through the Sierra Nevada and Rocky Mountains. With the railroad's completion in 1869, however, they found themselves barred from other occupations, a situation that worsened throughout the 1870s, when a nationwide depression led to a scarcity of jobs. In California they were largely confined to cooking, laundry, and domestic work; elsewhere, employers' exploitation of them as strikebreakers exacerbated hostility against them. Designed primarily to increase contributions, accounts of missionaries working in China that described the Chinese as "heathens living in darkness" served to encourage feelings of distrust and disgust among whites. By the late nineteenth century, the Chinese were contributing to American society in a variety of fields, including innovations in the Florida citrus fruit and the California wine industries; nonetheless, the prevalent stereotype saw them as "coolies," slant-eyed and idolatrous.

From the 1870s on, local and state laws in California limited not only the employment of Chinese but also their freedom to engage in their own cultural practices. Violence against them also escalated, with over a thousand killed and innumerable others driven from their homes between 1871 and 1886 in California, Washington, Wyoming, and Colorado. The repression took legal form in 1882 with the passage of the Chinese Exclusion Act, which banned the entry of all Chinese except for a few diplomats, students, teachers, merchants, and tourists. Further legislation in 1888 voided Certificates of Return, leaving twenty thousand Chinese stranded outside the United States with useless reentry permits.

Compared to the antipathy directed toward the Chinese, mainstream American attitudes toward Japanese immigrants were relatively benign for a time. Modest immigration flows, coupled with Japan's military power (manifested by its victories over China in 1872 and 1895 and over Russia in 1905), helped prevent anti-Chinese sentiment from spilling into violence and discrimination against Japanese. Still, the Gentleman's Agreement of 1908, which limited but did not completely bar Japanese immigration, portended greater restrictions on Japanese as the United States became increasingly isolationist and as racist social theory continued to fuel segregationist domestic policies.

The status of Koreans in the United States in the early twentieth century was tied closely to Japan's imperialistic drive to control Korea, which it made a protectorate in 1905 before formal annexation occurred in 1910. Upon becoming subjects of the Japanese emperor, the roughly eight thousand Koreans in the United States were directly affected by the Gentleman's Agreement. The loss of their sovereignty generated considerable nationalist sentiment among them, and in 1905 Koreans in Hawaii sent a letter to President Theodore Roosevelt asking for American intervention in the wake of the Japanese takeover of Korea. This political appeal was but one manifestation of what was to be a vibrant independence movement among Koreans in this country.

That few Asian American writers of this period came to the notice of mainstream readers should not cause us to overlook the plentiful material produced by every Asian group in the United States. Much of the writing by Koreans consisted of tracts, pamphlets, and sermons in Korean. It would take another generation for authors like Younghill Kang during the 1930s to begin expressing in English some of the aforementioned political sentiments that marked the Korean American community.

Filipino literary expression was marked by a strong nationalist strain as well, with exiles from the Philippines such as Felipe Agoncillo, Sixto Lopez, and Galicano Apacible writing to dispel American colonialist stereotypes of their people and to prove Filipino competence. Although these authors generally did not write for or about the several thousand Filipino workers in the United States, their nationalist fervor would inspire the next (the "manong") generation to focus attention on the experiences of this group.

In the late nineteenth and early twentieth centuries, native Hawaiian cultural workers (including the overthrown Queen Liliuokalani) composed poems and songs that quietly but defiantly expressed resentment against continental U.S. missionary and business interests intent on expropriating Hawaii's resources and lands. The lyrics of Kaulana na Pua, for instance, exhort the children of Hawaii to remain loyal to the land in the face of the "evil-hearted messenger" with his "greedy document of extortion," but because the song was sung in Hawaiian, its protest statement went unrecognized by the colonizers even as it spread among the colonized. Such expressions of protest would persist throughout the islands and inspire writers on the mainland in the twentieth century.

The best-known early Asian American authors were Edith and Winnifred Eaton. The Canada-raised daughters of a Chinese mother and an English father, both adopted pen names that reflected the ethnic identities they chose to assume. Under the Chinese pseudonym Sui Sin Far, Edith Eaton published short fiction in the major magazines of the day that portrayed intricacies of Chinese

Americans' lives with subtlety and respect, thereby becoming the first Chinese American to write on their behalf. Winifred Eaton, in contrast, chose a Japanese-sounding name, Onoto Watanna, under which, between 1899 and 1925, she published hundreds of stories and nearly a score of novels, mostly set in Japan. Her widely popular fiction may sometimes seem to conform to racial and sexual stereotypes of the time—noble, martial Japanese men and shy, charming Japanese young women—but it often played against or troubled the Orientalism in which it seemingly participated. Following a different course, Edith Eaton portrayed Chinese Americans facing discrimination, the anguish of being in Chinese-Caucasian marriages that predated the antimiscegenation laws that obtained in many states, the havoc that U.S. cultural conventions could create for Chinese women and men who settled in the United States, and also the imaginativeness with which people navigated the dangerous circumstances of being Chinese in the United States. In presenting in her autobiographical work a sense of her own split identity as a person living in two cultures but feeling at home in neither, she also explored a sense of dual belonging that later Asian American writers would affirm, challenge, or revise in their own contexts.

Two other writers, Yone Noguchi (Noguchi Yonejiro) and Sadakichi Hartmann, sought recognition as artists—writers whose work was of significant aesthetic merit. Each made use of Japanese forms in some of his writing; each also hoped to make Americans aware of Japanese aesthetic traditions. Noguchi, who lived in the United States between 1893 and 1903, modeled two fictional travelogues, purportedly by a wealthy young Japanese woman who visits the United States, on a Japanese genre of travel writing; while his own poetry tended towards the conventional, he urged American poets to "create a new poetics" by adapting a form of Japanese *haiku*, as Mayumi Takada tells us. Hartmann, the son of a German father and Japanese mother who came to the United States in 1882 and soon became a U.S. citizen, immersed himself in American art, publishing *A History of American Art* in 1902. A gifted and versatile writer, he wrote journalistic pieces, a play, a novel, and short stories as well as poetry, some of it influenced by Whitman, whom he revered (and visited), some of it in the Japanese *haiku* and *tanka* forms, some of it elegantly lyrical and quite sensuous.

By the early twentieth century, Asian American literature was varied and noteworthy, if not yet extensive. Whether this literature reflects on Asian Americans' lives or tropes on Japanophilia and whether it takes the form of lyric poetry, satiric travelogue, drama, essay, or fiction, Asian American literature of this period creatively mixes aesthetics, cultures, and styles. At the same time, much of it also preserves the cultural, social and racial tensions that inform it. It is distinctive in the traditions on which it draws and how it does so; its subject matter is frequently distinctive as well. For these very reasons it also shares commonalities with the vast body of U.S. literature in which diverse traditions, histories, and circumstances are complexly brought into play.

Immigration, Urban Conditions, and Reform

If the need to balance the claims of one's ethnic or racial heritage against those of the dominant culture was an imperative for African Americans, Native peoples, Latino/as, and Asian Americans, so too at the turn of the century it became the paramount literary subject for the first generation of writers to emerge from among those called the "new immigrants," the southern and eastern Europeans who entered the United States in unprecedented numbers in the decades after the Civil War. Before 1860 most immigrants had come from Great Britain, Ireland, Germany, and Scandinavia, and while their entry was steady, it was not overwhelming: five million had arrived in the forty years between 1820 and 1860. The next forty years, however, saw fourteen million new arrivals to the United States, the vast majority of whom came from Italy and Poland, Russia, Austria, Turkey, Greece, and Syria. Heavily Catholic or Jewish and non–English-speaking, they settled primarily in the cities of the Northeast and Midwest, where they frequently took the least skilled industrial jobs and were viewed by the native-born and by earlier arrivals with apprehension and distrust. Their sheer numbers radically altered the ethnic composition of the nation, and their different manners and customs, modes of dress, and religious observances were seen as threatening and disruptive to Anglo-Saxon hegemony and power. Reaction to the new immigrants took the form of expressed fears of race suicide or a dilution of "American" racial stock, which led after World War I to major legislation restricting immigration into the country.

Increased cultural diversity created increased pressure to conform, and as with American Indians, assimilation was the prescribed goal. The idea of the United States as a melting pot in which ethnic and racial differences would be dissolved into a common identity prevailed, and by the end of the century that common identity was being consciously defined as based on spoken and written English and on Anglo-Saxon cultural values. As with Native peoples, education was an essential mechanism for accomplishing the process. The public school, as Mary Antin declared, was to be "the immigrant child's road to Americanization."

The ways in which the new immigrants responded to the expectations of their newly adopted country differed from those of other minority groups, primarily because, unlike blacks, who were brought to America forcibly, or Native peoples and Latino/as, who first inhabited the land and were then subjugated by white settlers, the new immigrants largely chose to come. True, they came because conditions at home were often intolerable—wars, religious and political persecutions, crop failures and famines, overpopulation and unemployment—but they came, like Abraham Cahan in 1882 or Mary Antin's father in 1892, because they saw America as a land of economic opportunity and political freedom. The terms on which they struck their bargains with the new land, the conflicts they experienced, and the accommodations they made, therefore, bore the marks of their own unique situations.

Some immigrant groups, such as the Jews and the Germans, brought with them traditions of literacy and often cultural networks and institutions. Others, such as southern Italians, Poles, and many Irish, came from peasant stock with well-developed oral but not written literary traditions. Among the new arrivals, Jewish immigrants took quickly to print, and their autobiographies and novels expressed the eagerness to assimilate that distinguished the new immigrants as a whole from most of the other American minority populations. The immediate popularity of Mary Antin's autobiography, *The Promised Land*, which appeared in 1912 after having first been serialized in the *Atlantic Monthly*, was to a significant extent due to the glowing portrait it presented of the acculturation

process. Antin was eager to exchange her "hateful homemade European costume" for "real American machine-made garments" and her "impossible" Hebrew name, "Maryashe," for "Mary." But her truly transformative experience
came when she was enrolled in the public school—a moment of supreme fulfillment for her father as well, who through his children thus vicariously "took possession of America." More problematic was the experience recorded in the
novels of Abraham Cahan, which assessed the emotional and spiritual cost of
economic success for his immigrant heroes, a price paid in a sense of self-divi-
sion and even self-betrayal by the sundering of family, religious, and class
bonds. Like most Jewish immigrants from eastern Europe, the titular hero of
his novel *Yekl* (1896) lives both in the Old World with its biblical and Talmudic
roots and values and in the New World of hustle and competition. The claims of
the Old World, and of his own former self, he is "neither willing to banish from
his memory nor able to reconcile with the actualities of his American present."
The tensions that begin to surface in *Yekl* are more fully exposed in Cahan's *The
Rise of David Levinsky* (1917), a classic rendition of the immigrant experience.
Levinsky's rise to business success as a cloak manufacturer can be compared to
that of Howells's Silas Lapham thirty years earlier, as a measure of the more
acute degree of personal and cultural dislocation, and of the increased precari-
ousness of the self, given the greater estrangement between one's cultural origins and one's new social and economic goals.

   Antin's autobiography and Cahan's novels recognize that the success of
some is built on the deprivation of others—Antin's older sister, Frieda, who
must work in a factory if the younger children are to be educated, or the fellow
tailors whom Levinsky abandons when he rises above their ranks. For the mass
of the new immigrants, the good fortune of an Antin or a Cahan was elusive,
and the nightmare side of their American success dream was powerfully captured by socialist writer Upton Sinclair, whose hero Jurgis in *The Jungle* (1906)
is also an immigrant, for whom Chicago initially holds the promise that Boston
held for Antin or New York for Yekl and Levinsky. Jurgis's life, however, both as
factory worker and as husband, father, and provider for his extended family,
becomes a series of brutalizing defeats, as the impersonal workings of the industrial economy crush, one by one, all of his hopes and efforts to rise.

   Based on actual investigation of the filthy working conditions and contaminated products of the Chicago meat-packing industry, Sinclair's novel was one
instance of the "muckraking" literature that appeared in the 1890s and early
1900s—journalistic exposés intended to underscore and bring to public attention the plight of groups like the factory workers and the business and government practices that were often responsible for their plight. Such exposés, often
first appearing in the new mass circulation magazines such as *McClure's* and *Cosmopolitan* and later published as books, included Ida Tarbell's articles on Standard Oil, Jacob Riis's on the conditions of New York city tenements, and Lincoln
Steffens's on graft and corruption in municipal governments. In turn they were
a part of what had become by the turn of the century a groundswell of social
protest writing that also included, for example, Ray Stannard Baker's and
Charles W. Chesnutt's on race riots and Ida B. Wells's on lynching. Such writing
was indicative of the ever-deepening concern of writers, social workers, sociologists, economists, and social philosophers over the destructive effects both for

social stability and democratic ideals of the unregulated growth and periodic breakdowns of the industrial economy and of the inequities inherent in America's social and economic structures. This extensive literature of social protest, which took the form of novels, journalistic articles, and book-length scholarly analyses, addressed major social problems and offered programs for change that ranged from Utopian visions of radically restructured societies to remedies that would alleviate specific social ills.

One of the distinguishing features of realistic fiction throughout the post-war period, of course, was its awareness of and concern for the effects of the industrial economy on individual lives, social groups, and regional cultures. Indeed, much of the fiction (as well as nonfiction) of the post–Civil War period that seems most alive to us today is that dealing with the social dislocations created by America's overwhelming material progress, and such writing is often informed, at least implicitly, by political engagement. Often, therefore, writers crossed the line—an arbitrary one at best—between esthetic and political intent to produce narratives, like *The Jungle*, with a deliberate "message." Hamlin Garland, for example, always the advocate of the midwestern farmer, responded to their worsening conditions in the early 1890s—falling crop prices exacerbated by often exorbitant railroad freight and bank loan rates—by writing novels that made the case for specific legislative reforms, including the single tax on land that Henry George had proposed in *Progress and Poverty* in 1879, and other legislative remedies advocated by the Populist party, formed in the early 1890s in response to agrarian and labor needs. And in *The Octopus* (1901), Frank Norris exposed the railroads' immense power over the farmers. Other writers used the genre of the Utopian novel as a vehicle for their visions of transformed societies based on principles of social justice. The most famous and influential of these was Edward Bellamy's *Looking Backward* (1888), the first Utopia of the industrial age, which depicted the United States in the year 2000 as a nation where government ownership of the means of production and the rational, "scientific" rule of a managerial class guaranteed economic equality and happiness for all citizens. Bellamy's work, which was still selling as many as ten thousand copies a week in the early 1890s, inspired a host of successors—several hundred Utopian fictions appeared between the 1880s and the early 1900s, including Howells's *A Traveler from Altruria*, a work that, like Bellamy's, envisioned a socialist state. Many Utopias by women, including Charlotte Perkins Gilman's *Herland* (1915), addressed crucial issues of women's continuing subordination, which male writers were likely to ignore.

On balance, however, it was the conditions of urban life and of the industrial workers that increasingly catalyzed writers and reformers and that led to the outpouring of social protest literature, as well as to direct political action. The periodic breakdowns of the economy that resulted from uncontrolled industrial growth affected all groups, including farmers and the middle class; however, they had their most dramatic, because most visible and most violent, impact on the working class in the congested cities. The severe and prolonged depressions that began in 1873 and again in 1893 were especially devastating, leading to massive unemployment; in 1894 the situation reached crisis proportions, with twenty percent of the labor force out of work. With the formation of the Knights of Labor and later the Industrial Workers of the World and the

> The golf links lie so near the mill
> That almost every day
> The laboring children can look out
> And see the men at play.
>
> Sarah N. Cleghorn

American Federation of Labor, the postwar period saw the steady growth of the trade union movement, which, however, reached only a portion of workers and met with widespread employer resistance. Labor dissatisfaction therefore took the form of strikes, which management countered with armed force and violence. The extremity of the conflict between capital and labor can be read in the fact that between 1881 and 1905 the nation witnessed over thirty-six thousand strikes involving some six million workers. The Chicago Fair was bracketed by two of the most notorious: the Homestead Strike in 1892, which broke the organizing efforts of the iron and steel workers, and the Pullman strike in Chicago in 1894, in which scores of striking workers were killed when state militia and federal troops were called in and the American Railway Union, led by Eugene V. Debs, was broken. It was the specter of such industrial violence, already apparent in the 1880s, and the fear of social chaos that had led Bellamy to conceive his Utopia, where state control of the industrial machine precludes the potential anarchy of free enterprise.

Efforts to implement social change peaked in the Progressive Era, the period from the 1890s until the eve of World War I, which saw the first nationwide reform movement in modern history, when calls for social justice issued in a flood from the nation's presses. To the exposés of the muckrakers were added the investigative studies and documented reports of social workers and sociologists calling attention to the social ills of free-wheeling capitalism: the uneven and unplanned growth of the cities with their rapid influx of population, which had led to hastily built tenement housing with its attendant problems of lack of sanitation, overcrowding, dirt, and noise; the existence of a working class, and heavily immigrant, population dependent on an inadequate weekly wage and vulnerable to the erratic shifts in a profit-oriented market economy; the resulting poverty that led to long working hours, child labor, prostitution, and crime; and the rule of corrupt party bosses that blocked reform. The settlement house movement, described in Chicagoan Jane Addams's *Twenty Years at Hull House* (1910) and exemplified in the work of reformers like Lillian Wald and Vida Scudder, had since the 1880s attempted to rectify some of the worst living and employment problems of the urban poor and to acculturate the poor to middle-class values. Their efforts contributed to the passage of local, state, and federal laws regulating the hours and working conditions of women and children, providing workers' compensation, and improving living, educational, and recreational facilities in urban slums and ghettoes.

Such laws, the first significant body of reform legislation in the nation's history, represented a major, indeed a profound, shift in national attitudes from those that had prevailed earlier, in the heyday of unrestrained industrial growth. Then, the ideology of Social Darwinism, as purveyed by writers like William Graham Sumner, had justified a hands-off approach to economic development, arguing that social, like biological, evolution was governed by natural laws that should not be interfered with. The literature of social protest constituted a strong collective rejoinder to that ideology, and the reform legislation was official recognition of the need for greater governmental involvement and responsibility, for legislative controls, and for social planning, if American society was to fulfill its democratic promise. Essentially the work of middle-class reformers, the progressive movement functioned to repair some of the damage done by an unfettered capitalist system while containing resistance to capitalism, which remained intact despite a briefly successful challenge from socialists, who mounted a series of political campaigns and in 1912 garnered 900,000 votes for Eugene V. Debs as presidential candidate and elected socialist mayors in thirty-three cities.

Some socialist tendencies colored progressive reform thought, including that of the Social Gospel movement that spread inside liberal Protestantism in the 1880s and 1890s. Dedicated to improving society through the application of Christian ethical precepts, emphasizing morality rather than theology, and social rather than individual redemption, the Social Gospel movement included writers like economist Richard T. Ely, whose arguments appeared in *Social Aspects of Christianity* in 1889; ministers like Walter Rauschenbusch, who offered a form of Christian socialism in *Christianity and the Social Crisis* (1907) and *Christianizing the Social Order* (1912); and popularizers like Congregational minister Charles M. Sheldon, who wrote one of the nation's most popular novels, *In His Steps* (1897), in which urban residents reform a city by asking "what would Jesus do" and acting accordingly. Social Gospel thinking also influenced William Dean Howells, who was increasingly concerned in the mid-1880s with issues of poverty and labor unrest. *The Minister's Charge* (1886) is the story of a clergyman who realizes the need for changed clerical attitudes and broader involvement in issues of social justice and reform.

In the Social Gospel movement, religion remained a visible force in American life, and it continued to be a source of spiritual strength and cultural cohesion for blacks. More generally, the influence of religion, specifically the Protestantism on which the nation had been founded and that had provided a common set of values and assumptions for over 250 years, weakened as new denominations continued to appear and as scientifically derived empirical findings challenged biblical revelation. Darwin's *On the Origin of Species* (1859), which undermined belief in the possibility of a separate creation of the human species by God, dealt religion a powerful blow, and indeed the Social Gospel movement can be seen as an effort to regain for ministers some of the status that science was steadily eroding.

The age had a strong secular strain, however, and intellectual authority increasingly passed to scientists, social scientists, and other university-trained and -based scholars and philosophers, as professionalization replaced the genteel amateurism of earlier New England cultural leaders. The very American philosophy of pragmatism, invented and expounded by William James in the final decades of the century and further developed by John Dewey in the twentieth, was an effort to provide the country with a philosophy that responded to new social complexities while retaining the traditional American belief in individualism: recognizing the constrictions of environment and circumstance on human life, pragmatism nonetheless argued for the ameliorative power of human agency to effect constructive change. Other schools of thought, however, which would gain increased currency in the years after World War I, offered less sanguine outlooks. The ideas of Marx and Freud, brewed in the ferment of nineteenth-century Europe, would constitute major intellectual shifts in the twentieth. Both served to accelerate the undermining of traditional ideas regarding the development and organization of society, and individual psychological and moral development as well, and both reinforced the widespread tendency toward a determinist view of individual and social life. As the twentieth century began to take shape in the years before World War I, these and other powerful new intellectual developments would drastically alter the cultural landscape.

VARIETIES OF POSTWAR REALISM: PROSE AND POETRY

So much of the literature of the postwar era aspired to being realistic that we often use the phrase "the rise of realism" to characterize postbellum literature. But what *was* "realism"? In historical terms, it was a movement in literature and the visual arts that succeeded Romanticism and emerged at somewhat different times in England, Western Europe, Russia, and the United States. While realist fiction in French and Russian was read in English translation, realism differed from country to country. In the United States, the concept promoted by cultural arbiter William Dean Howells carried a great deal of weight—although, as we'll see, it should not be taken as the final word. For Howells, realism was "nothing more and nothing less than the truthful treatment of material" (*Criticism and Fiction*, 1891). In reviews, editorial columns, and his book *Criticism and Fiction*, Howells explained what that entailed, taking pains to distinguish realism from Romanticism. Realist writing, he maintained, portrayed real people—individuals, including very ordinary people, not the stock types that romantic fiction featured (he strongly disapproved of the novels of Sir Walter Scott, for instance). Realist plots were plausible, not fantastic, and they turned not only on romantic love but on the broad range of human concerns. Dialogue was not stylized but vernacular, reflecting the great variety that comprised American English. Howells also asserted that realism strove for objectivity. Realist literature did not explain or moralize or seek to manipulate readers' emotions or beliefs, he insisted; it sought to present people and social life as they really were, giving the responsibility of making moral judgments to readers. In structural terms, this meant that narrators should be reticent; unlike the narrator of, say, Stowe's (sentimental) *Uncle Tom's Cabin*, they should not comment or otherwise intrude.

Howells' criteria were grounded in what he saw as the governing principle of realism: its truth to "the motives, the impulses, the principles that shape the life of actual men and women" (*Criticism and Fiction*). That principle was at once aesthetic, ethical, and political; for Howells, realism was democratic—about commonplace people and conveying our common humanity. Until he became discouraged by economic inequity and other undemocratic aspects of U.S. life, Howells also held that realism was therefore uniquely American.

Howells not only wrote prolifically about realism; as the era's most influential editor and critic, he had a strong hand in its success. He championed the writing of Henry James and Mark Twain (both good friends), Hamlin Garland, Charles W. Chesnutt, Mary E. Wilkins Freeman, Sarah Orne Jewett—all included in this volume—and many others. However, his efforts alone could not have made realism the predominant trend in postwar American literature that it was. The phenomenal changes that took place in the decades after national unification were vital to its success. The introduction to Volume C goes into detail about these changes, so mention of a few of the salient ones will suffice here. Geographically, the country was both expanding and changing. Increasingly, Americans were living in cities, and cities were increasing in both size and number. The population too was growing and changing. Heavy industry and mass production were firmly established. Class stratification, and differences and tensions between classes, were becoming more entrenched. Discrete regions and local cultures, along with the diversity of Americans' speech, were coming into sharp focus while a somewhat uniform national culture was also solidifying. All of this, and more, fed Americans' interest in reading about who they were, how they themselves (now) lived, and the lives of other Americans.

While writers, critics, and many readers recognized that these conditions favored realism, other circumstances, less apparent at the time, also contributed to realism's ascendancy. One of the most important was the consolidation of publishing into an industry. Centralized and streamlined, with large houses in New York, Boston, Philadelphia, and Chicago dominating the field (examples include Harpers in New York, Houghton Mifflin in Boston, Lippincott in Philadelphia, Herbert Stone in Chicago), publishers simplified the production process, promoted their products through innovative advertising, and used sophisticated distribution and sales networks. They also more or less determined what would appear in print. Realism *sold*: it met the interests of an increasingly literate public with greater leisure and somewhat more discretionary income than most Americans had had before the Civil War. It also helped finally establish authorship as a remunerative profession. All of this functioned synergistically with the renewed American literary nationalism of the postwar era—the call for "the great American novel" was first made by John William De Forest in *The Nation* magazine in 1868—and Americans' interest in American life to create an ideal environment for the flourishing of realism.

Other factors contributed as well. One was the take-off of photography. Not only were Americans flooded with visual images; photography seemed to promise that objective presentation was possible, whether it was of individuals and groups (which anyone with a Kodak could produce), of major events (as in photographs of Lincoln's funeral procession), or of aspects of contemporary life from which many Americans were normally shielded, such as the photographs of Jacob Reiss's muckraking exposé of poverty, *How The Other Half Lives*. (See the photographs reproduced at the beginning of Volume C.) Enhancing the seeming possibility of objectivity were both the premises and practices of the new field of sociology, which sought to characterize society using empirical approaches, and new journalistic practices. The latter included on-the-scene reporting (the practice of newspapers publishing reports by their army correspondents began during the Civil War; Louisa May Alcott's *Hospital Sketches* of 1863 was based on letters in which she had described her experiences as a nurse in the Union Hospital in Washington, DC) and investigative journalism, of which Ida B. Wells' *The Red Record* and Ambrose Bierce's articles exposing California railroads' involvement in political and economic corruption are exemplary. All of this affirmed realist fiction's confidence in its ability to capture the truth. More specifically, Alcott's short story "My Contraband" draws partly on her nursing experiences, Upton Sinclair's *The Jungle* is novelistic investigative journalism, and Stephen Crane may well have been familiar with Civil War journalism when he wrote his celebrated novel *The Red Badge of Courage*.

In light of this ferment and of Howells's emphasis on the democratic character of realism, one might suppose that "realism" accommodated virtually any writing committed to "telling the truth." It did not. General definitions were necessary to characterize realist writing, as they are for any class of literature. To be sure these were capacious. Alcott's Civil War fiction and her literature for children, Constance Fennimore Woolson's short stories, and some of Harriet Prescott Spoffod's rather gothic fiction more or less qualified. However, Howells sought to establish a *cordon sanitaire* that set realism apart from the sensational, sometimes racy fiction that was also popular, as well as from Romantic fiction. Much harsher were Henry James's efforts to elevate realist authors to the status of artists, for they included ruling out openly emotional writing, sentimental writing in particular. One of James's prime targets was the fiction of women novelists, which had been extremely popular since midcentury. His review of Rebecca Harding Davis's *Waiting for the Verdict* (in the "Literature and Aesthetics" section of this volume) exemplifies his disdain for this writing—a disdain so intense that Stowe biographer Joan Hedrick concludes that James was determined to make authorship a masculine profession.

In actuality, realism far exceeded such efforts to delimit it. For neither Howells nor James was the character of "reality" established once and for all. As Jennifer Emory-Peck shows in her introduction to the James selections, realism as he practiced it shifted markedly over time, and his increasingly intricate prose style kept pace with his deepening concern with psychology and with the twists and turns of consciousness. Realist fiction took paths in other directions as well. Although Charles W. Chesnutt's stories of southern life and of life on the color line in the North found favor with Howells (and were published by Houghton Mifflin), as Chesnutt's work became more directly engaged with racial apartheid and white violence, it became unpalatable to white readers: eventually he was unable to publish. "The Doll," a new inclusion in our Chesnutt section, is an example of his piercing, ironic realism about race and the policing of racial boundaries in late nineteenth-century America.

Moreover, realism was by no means a postbellum phenomenon. Howells himself knew this, but he tended to extend the term to highly esteemed antebellum writers like Hawthorne. In fact, the sentimental literature that James so disdained pioneered realist fiction in the United States. Harding Davis herself published the ground-breaking novella about the lives of Welsh miners in West Virginia, *Life in the Iron Mills* in 1861, while the authors of women's domestic fiction focused on the emotional texture, the relationships, the practices and the economics, the struggles, and the rewards that constituted middle-class white women's lives. (Susan Warner's best-selling novel of 1850, *The Wide, Wide World*, remained popular throughout the nineteenth century.) Slave narratives, too, were pointedly realistic: Douglass's *Life of Frederick Douglass: An American Slave* (1845), William Wells Brown's *Narrative of William Wells Brown, now a fugitive Slave* (1845), Harriet Jacobs' *Incidents in the Life of a Slave Girl* (1861), and many others laid out the realities of slavery—the cruelties, violence, and other horrendous circumstances that comprised the ordinary lives of slaves as well as the strategies for survival practiced by many enslaved people. So compelling were these narratives that Augusta Rohrbach posits that their success spurred the emergence of realist fiction. In addition, the claims to fact and truth of *Uncle*

Tom's Cabin (1850–1851) were so important to its effect that Stowe produced *A Key to Uncle Tom's Cabin* in 1854, the subtitle of which reads *Presenting the Original Facts and Documents Upon Which the Story Is Founded, Together with Corroborative Statements Verifying the Truth of the Work*.

What is more, even though Howells, James, and many publishers and readers identified realist writing almost exclusively with the novel and short story, it took other prose forms. Biographies of the great and the more ordinary, memoirs and other autobiographical writing, journalistic pieces on well-known writers—all appealed to a readership eager to know about other people's lives. (A total of 350,000 copies of Ulysses S. Grant's two-volume *Memoirs* [1885–1886] was purchased shortly after its publication.) While Julia A. Foote's *A Brand Plucked from the Fire* (1879) belongs within the tradition of African American women's spiritual autobiography, it can also be seen in conjunction with other autobiographical pieces included in this volume, including Sui Sin Far's *Leaves from the Mental Portfolio of an Euraisan Woman* and Mary Austin's *Earth Horizon*.

Just as significantly, realism was not limited to prose, for poetry had long had a realist strain. James Russell Lowell's *Biglow Papers* (1848) features Hosea Biglow's Yankee vernacular and Yankee outlook. Whitman's *Leaves of Grass*, the first edition of which appeared in 1855, pioneered a different kind of poetic realism, one that presents Americans of all kinds in straightforward language and gives voice to the bodily, sexual, emotional, and spiritual life of "Walt Whitman, an American, one of the roughs, a kosmos" and other Americans. In words that anticipate Howells (who was at best ambivalent about him), Whitman proclaims in his Preface that "I tell what I tell for precisely what it is.... You [the reader] shall stand by my side and look in the mirror with me."

Whitman continued to develop his poetic realism alongside other modes in the many versions of *Leaves of Grass* he created (the last appeared in 1891–1892), and his poetry was enormously popular. Realism in poetry took other directions as well. Sarah Morgan Bryan Piatt's poetry is realistic in its expression of "a full range of emotions and perspectives" in all its contradiction (Paula Bennett, author of this description and editor of the Piatt section, suggests that stylistically, Piatt's poetry anticipates modernism, an observation that points to how slippery many of the distinctions posited by critics and literary historians are). Dialect poetry, which was fantastically popular towards the end of the century, dovetailed with prose realism, as Howells recognized—he called Lowell "almost the greatest and finest realist who ever wrought in verse" and promoted the dialect poetry of James Whitcomb Riley and Paul Laurence Dunbar. However, Howells did not take note of Dunbar's nondialect poetry, which includes the powerful reflection on the suffering that lay behind African Americans' masks of smiles, "We Wear the Mask," and it is doubtful that he would have been aware of the dialect poetry of Francis E. W. Harper (see the Harper section of this volume).

The literature in this section goes some distance towards showcasing the range of postwar realism. Realist writing, however, in all its variety, is to be found throughout this volume, whether it characterizes a work in full or is one strain among several coexisting ones. It also informs its offspring, naturalist writing, selections of which are in the last section of this volume, "On the Cusp of a New Century." Moreover, owing to its malleability and an enduring interest in—the absence of consensus about—reality, realism throve in a variety of forms and styles throughout the twentieth century. It continues to do so.

Sandra A. Zagarell
Oberlin College

■ JULIA A. J. FOOTE ■
1823–1900

Julia A. J. Foote's autobiography, *A Brand Plucked from the Fire* (1879), is representative of a large number of similar texts published by nineteenth-century black and white women who believed that Christianity had made them the spiritual equals of men and hence equally authorized to lead the church. Her belief in the androgyny of the Christian spirit and her refusal to defer to husband or minister when her own intuitive sense of personal authority was at stake mark Foote's autobiographical work as an important early expression of the American feminist literary tradition.

Foote was born in Schenectady, New York, the daughter of former slaves. Her parents were strongly committed to Methodism and to the education of their children. Because Schenectady's schools were segregated, Foote's parents hired her out as a domestic servant to a white family who used their influence to place her in a country school outside the city. Here, between the ages of ten and twelve, Julia Foote received the only formal education of her life. Despite the fact that her teenage years were devoted to the care of her younger siblings, she read considerably, especially in the Bible, and attended many church meetings. When she was fifteen, she had a profound conversion experience and joined an African Methodist Episcopal church in Albany, New York. Three years later she married George Foote, a sailor, and moved with him to Boston.

Having no children, Foote devoted a great deal of her time to informal evangelistic work in her community, in which she testified to her belief in the doctrine of "sanctification." The controversial idea that a Christian could be sanctified—totally freed from sin and empowered to lead a life of spiritual perfection—had been under debate in Methodist circles for decades. Advocates of sanctification and perfectionism became leaders in the rise of "holiness" movements in evangelical denominations in the United States during the mid- and late-nineteenth century. Foote's belief that she herself had been sanctified by the Holy Spirit contributed to her growing conviction that her destiny was to become a preacher. George Foote was skeptical about his wife's religious beliefs and attempted to curb her public activities; when she resisted his arguments, he drifted out of her life.

Foote knew that a woman who claimed a divine calling to the ministry challenged Christian tradition and American social prejudice. Women were not expected to assume public leadership positions, nor were they allowed to speak, except under restrictions, in most Christian churches. Yet Foote could neither deny her conscience nor shirk the work that she felt had been given her to do. When the minister of her church in Boston refused her access to his pulpit and threatened to expel her from the congregation, she refused to be daunted. She took her case to higher denominational authorities, and when she received no support from them, she set out on an independent preaching career.

In the mid-1840s, she evangelized the upstate New York region, often accompanied or invited by ministers of the A.M.E. church. By 1850 she had crossed the Allegheny Mountains in search of new converts in Ohio and Michigan. She participated in the holiness revivals that swept the Midwest during the 1870s and later became a missionary in the A.M.E. Zion church. During the last decade of her life, she became the first woman to be ordained a deacon and the second woman to hold the office of elder in her denomination. Although her autobiography attacks racism and other social abuses, it is the subordination of women, especially in the spiritual realm, and her desire to inspire faith in her Christian sisters that endow her story with its distinctive voice and intensity.

William L. Andrews
University of North Carolina–Chapel Hill

PRIMARY WORKS

William L. Andrews, ed., *Sisters of the Spirit: Three Black Women's Autobiographies of the Nineteenth Century*, 1986.

from **A Brand Plucked from the Fire**

Chapter XVII. My Call to Preach the Gospel

For months I had been moved upon to exhort and pray with the people, in my visits from house to house; and in meetings my whole soul seemed drawn out for the salvation of souls. The love of Christ in me was not limited. Some of my mistaken friends said I was too forward, but a desire to work for the Master, and to promote the glory of his kingdom in the salvation of souls, was food to my poor soul.

When called of God, on a particular occasion, to a definite work, I said, "No, Lord, not me." Day by day I was more impressed that God would have me work in his vineyard. I thought it could not be that I was called to preach—I, so weak and ignorant. Still, I knew all things were possible with God, even to confounding the wise by the foolish things of this earth. Yet in me there was a shrinking.

I took all my doubts and fears to the Lord in prayer, when, what seemed to be an angel, made his appearance. In his hand was a scroll, on which were these words: "Thee have I chosen to preach my Gospel without delay." The moment my eyes saw it, it appeared to be printed on my heart. The angel was gone in an instant, and I, in agony, cried out, "Lord, I cannot do it!" It was eleven o'clock in the morning, yet everything grew dark as night. The darkness was so great that I feared to stir.

At last "Mam" Riley[1] entered. As she did so, the room grew lighter, and I arose from my knees. My heart was so heavy I scarce could speak. Dear "Mam" Riley saw my distress, and soon left me.

From that day my appetite failed me and sleep fled from my eyes. I seemed as one tormented. I prayed, but felt no better. I belonged to a band of sisters whom I loved dearly, and to them I partially opened my mind. One of them seemed to understand my case at once, and advised me to do as God had bid me, or I would never be happy here or hereafter. But it seemed too hard—I could not give up and obey.

One night as I lay weeping and beseeching the dear Lord to remove this burden from me, there appeared the same angel that came to me before, and on his breast were these words: "You are lost unless you obey God's righteous commands." I saw the writing, and that was enough. I covered my head and awoke my husband, who had returned a few days before. He asked me why I trembled so, but I had not power to answer him. I remained in that condition until morning, when I tried to arise and go about my usual duties, but was too ill. Then my husband called a physician, who prescribed medicine, but it did me no good.

I had always been opposed to the preaching of women, and had spoken against it, though, I acknowledge, without foundation. This rose before me like a mountain, and when I thought of the difficulties they had to encounter, both from professors and non-professors, I shrank back and cried, "Lord, I cannot go!"

The trouble my heavenly Father has had to keep me out of the fire that is never quenched, he alone knoweth. My husband and friends said I would die or go crazy if something favorable did not take place soon. I expected to die and be lost, knowing I had been enlightened and had tasted the heavenly gift. I read again and again the sixth chapter of Hebrews.[2]

Chapter XIX. Public Effort—Excommunication

From this time the opposition to my lifework commenced, instigated by the minister, Mr. Beman.[3] Many in the church were anxious to have me preach in the hall, where our meetings were held at that time, and were not a little astonished at the minister's cool treatment of me. At length two of the trustees got some of the elder sisters to call on the minister and ask him to let me preach. His answer was: "No; she can't preach her holiness stuff here, and I am astonished that you should ask it of me." The sisters said he seemed to be in quite a rage, although he said he was not angry.

---

[1]A close friend and confidante of Foote's in Boston.

[2]In this chapter Paul the Apostle urges his readers to remember God as "a sure and steadfast anchor of the soul" and to shun all forms of apostasy or disobedience to God's commands.

[3]Soon after Foote's experience of having been divinely called to preach, Rev. Jehiel C. Beman, pastor of the African Methodist Episcopal Zion church of Boston, informed her of his doubts about the authenticity of her call.

There being no meeting of the society on Monday evening, a brother in the church opened his house to me, that I might preach, which displeased Mr. Beman very much. He appointed a committee to wait upon the brother and sister who had opened their doors to me, to tell them they must not allow any more meetings of that kind, and that they must abide by the rules of the church, making them believe they would be excommunicated if they disobeyed him. I happened to be present at this interview, and the committee remonstrated with me for the course I had taken. I told them my business was with the Lord, and wherever I found a door opened I intended to go in and work for my Master.

There was another meeting appointed at the same place, which I, of course, attended; after which the meetings were stopped for that time, though I held many more there after these people had withdrawn from Mr. Beman's church.

I then held meetings in my own house; whereat the minister told the members that if they attended them he would deal with them, for they were breaking the rules of the church. When he found that I continued the meetings, and that the Lord was blessing my feeble efforts, he sent a committee of two to ask me if I considered myself a member of his church. I told them I did, and should continue to do so until I had done something worthy of dismemberment.

At this, Mr. Beman sent another committee with a note, asking me to meet him with the committee, which I did. He asked me a number of questions, nearly all of which I have forgotten. One, however, I do remember: he asked if I was willing to comply with the rules of the discipline. To this I answered: "Not if the discipline prohibits me from doing what God has bidden me to do; I fear God more than man." Similar questions were asked and answered in the same manner. The committee said what they wished to say, and then told me I could go home. When I reached the door, I turned and said: "I now shake off the dust of my feet as a witness against you [Mark 6:11; Luke 9:5]. See to it that this meeting does not rise in judgment against you."

The next evening, one of the committee came to me and told me that I was no longer a member of the church, because I had violated the rules of the discipline by preaching.

When this action became known, the people wondered how any one could be excommunicated for trying to do good. I did not say much, and my friends simply said I had done nothing but hold meetings. Others, anxious to know the particulars, asked the minister what the trouble was. He told them he had given me the privilege of speaking or preaching as long as I chose, but that he could not give me the right to use the pulpit, and that I was not satisfied with any other place. Also, that I had appointed meeting on the evening of his meetings, which was a thing no member had a right to do. For these reasons he said he had turned me out of the church.

Now, if the people who repeated this to me told the truth—and I have no doubt but they did—Mr. Beman told an actual falsehood. I had never asked for his pulpit, but had told him and others, repeatedly, that I did not care where I stood—any corner of the hall would do. To which Mr. Beman had answered: "You cannot have any place in the hall." Then I said: "I'll preach in a private house." He answered me: "No, not in this place; I am stationed over all Boston." He was determined I should not preach in the city of Boston. To cover up his deceptive, unrighteous course toward me, he told the above falsehoods.

From his statements, many erroneous stories concerning me gained credence with a large number of people. At that time, I thought it my duty as well as privilege to address a letter to the Conference, which I took to them in person, stating all the facts. At the same time I told them it was not in the power of Mr. Beman, or any one else, to truthfully bring anything against my moral or religious character—that my only offence was in trying to preach the Gospel of Christ—and that I cherished no ill feelings toward Mr. Beman or any one else, but that I desired the Conference to give the case an impartial hearing, and then give me a written statement expressive of their opinion. I also said I considered myself a member of the Conference, and should do so until they said I was not, and gave me their reasons, that I might let the world know what my offence had been.

My letter was slightingly noticed, and then thrown under the table. Why should they notice it? It was only the grievance of a woman, and there was no justice meted out to women in those days. Even ministers of Christ did not feel that women had any rights which they were bound to respect.[4]

Chapter XX. Women in the Gospel

Thirty years ago[5] there could scarcely a person be found, in the churches, to sympathize with any one who talked of Holiness. But, in my simplicity, I did think that a body of Christian ministers would understand my case and judge righteously. I was, however, disappointed.

It is no little thing to feel that every man's hand is against us, and ours against every man, as seemed to be the case with me at this time; yet how precious, if Jesus but be with us. In this severe trial I had constant access to God, and a clear consciousness that he heard me; yet I did not seem to have that plenitude of the Spirit that I had before. I realized most keenly that the closer the communion that may have existed, the keener the suffering of the slightest departure from God. Unbroken communion can only be retained by a constant application of the blood which cleanseth.

Though I did not wish to pain any one, neither could I please any one only as I was led by the Holy Spirit. I saw, as never before, that the best men were liable to err, and that the only safe way was to fall on Christ, even though censure and reproach fell upon me for obeying his voice. Man's

[4]A parody of the language of the Supreme Court's Dred Scott decision of 1857, in which Chief Justice Roger B. Taney stated that black Americans "had no rights which the white man was bound to respect."
[5]1850.

opinion weighed nothing with me, for my commission was from heaven, and my reward was with the Most High.

I could not believe that it was a short-lived impulse or spasmodic influence that impelled me to preach. I read that on the day of Pentecost[6] was the Scripture fulfilled as found in Joel ii. 28, 29; and it certainly will not be denied that women as well as men were at the time filled with the Holy Ghost, because it is expressly stated that women were among those who continued in prayer and supplication, waiting for the fulfillment of the promise. Women and men are classed together, and if the power to preach the Gospel is short-lived and spasmodic in the case of women, it must be equally so in that of men; and if women have lost the gift of prophecy, so have men.

We are sometimes told that if a woman pretends to a Divine call, and thereon grounds the right to plead the cause of a crucified Redeemer in public, she will be believed when she shows credentials from heaven; that is, when she works a miracle. If it be necessary to prove one's right to preach the Gospel, I ask of my brethren to show me their credentials, or I can not believe in the propriety of their ministry.

But the Bible puts an end to this strife when it says: "There is neither male nor female in Christ Jesus" [Gal. 3:28]. Philip had four daughters that prophesied, or preached. Paul called Priscilla, as well as Aquila, his "helper," or, as in the Greek, his "fellow-laborer." Rom. xv. 3; 2 Cor. viii. 23; Phil. ii. 5; 1 Thess. iii. 2. The same word, which, in our common translation, is now rendered a "servant of the church," in speaking of Phebe (Rom. xix. 1.), is rendered "minister" when applied to Tychicus. Eph. vi. 21. When Paul said, "Help those women who labor with me in the Gospel," he certainly meant that they did more than to pour out tea. In the eleventh chapter of First Corinthians Paul gives directions, to men and women, how they should appear when they prophesy or pray in public assemblies; and he defines prophesying to be speaking to edification, exhortation and comfort.

I may further remark that the conduct of holy women is recorded in Scripture as an example to others of their sex. And in the early ages of Christianity many women were happy and glorious in martyrdom. How nobly, how heroically, too, in later ages, have women suffered persecution and death for the name of the Lord Jesus.

In looking over these facts, I could see no miracle wrought for those women more than in myself.

Though opposed, I went forth laboring for God, and he owned and blessed my labors, and has done so wherever I have been until this day. And while I walk obediently, I know he will, though hell may rage and vent its spite.

1879

---

[6]According to Acts 2, on the day of Pentecost (Greek for *fifty*), which took place fifty days after Christ's Resurrection, the Holy Spirit descended on Jesus' disciples in the form of tongues of fire.

■ LOUISA MAY ALCOTT ■
1832–1888

Louisa May Alcott is best known for her children's novel *Little Women* (1868), but there are almost three hundred works in the Alcott canon. In much of this writing, Alcott, who never married, ostensibly proposes that women's true work is found in marriage and family, yet her journals and letters illustrate the dichotomy between her own life and her fictional world. Compared with the lives of many of her heroines and contemporaries, Alcott's life was atypical.

Louisa was born in 1832 to Abigail May (Abba) and Amos Bronson Alcott. Her parents were closely tied to many important philosophical and social issues of the day—Transcendentalism, abolition, women's suffrage, and educational reform. Close family friends, including Emerson, Thoreau, Hawthorne, Margaret Fuller, and William Garrison, composed a virtual *Who's Who* of the time. Although the Alcott girls were exposed to great ideas and surrounded by books, the family was impoverished and moved often, generally to smaller quarters, a consequence of Bronson's inability to provide financial support reliably. Louisa's impractical father was determined to implement his experimental teaching methods, but his efforts met with little success. After the dismal failure of his Utopian experiment in communal living at Fruitlands in 1843–1844, parodied in Louisa's "Transcendental Wild Oats" (1873), the task of supporting the family largely fell to Abba, with help from her relatives and from Emerson. In 1858 the Alcotts purchased Orchard House in Concord, Massachusetts, with the help of Emerson and Abba's relatives, but the family struggled financially until Louisa's success with *Little Women*. At this time Louisa supplanted her father in the "unwomanly" role of family provider. Named "Duty's Faithful Child" by him, Louisa helped to support her family by repeatedly working at jobs she disliked—teacher, seamstress, and maid. These experiences became the raw material for much of her writing.

Alcott published her first work, a poem, in 1851, but not until the 1860s did she find success. Before the publication of *Little Women*, she had over eighty works published in periodicals as diverse as the prestigious *Atlantic Monthly* and the sensational-ist *Frank Leslie's Illustrated Newspaper*. Searching for her literary form while trying to support her family, she wrote poetry, fairy tales, short stories, domestic sketches, melodramatic plays, gothic thrillers, adult novels, and Civil War stories. Beginning in 1863 with the anonymous publication of "Pauline's Passion and Punishment," she wrote secret thrillers for several popular newspapers for five years. She clearly enjoyed writing these stories and told a reporter that her "natural ambition is for the lurid style," but she believed that it was not "natural" for a woman to write plays and stories full of bloodshed and wronged women aggressively seeking revenge.

Alcott also did not want to be identified with the popular "scribbling" ladies of her time; she wanted to be identified with the great writers she had known since childhood. To that end, during the early 1860s, she worked on two adult novels, *Moods* (1864; revised edition 1882) and *Work* (1873), in which she struggled to define for women a role that relieved them of the rigid code of behavior prescribed in nineteenth-century New England. In these novels, she strove for a realistic middle ground between the heroines' vengeful disregard for convention of her thrillers and the adherence to the idea of proper "True Womanhood" proposed in much of the popular literature of the day. In a radical departure for young women in nineteenth-century New England, both novels emphasize the growth their heroines must undergo to become intellectually and emotionally independent. In Alcott's vision of womanhood, only when a woman can stand alone and is not dependent on a man for fulfillment is she capable of finding happiness, whether married or not. Alcott had great difficulty in finding a publisher for *Moods*, and when it was originally published in 1864, it received generally poor reviews. Devastated, she wrote in her journal, "My next book shall have no *ideas* in it, only facts, and the people shall be as ordinary as possible." In 1882, after she had attained wealth and fame—as well as influence with publishers, who begged for her work—she revised and reissued *Moods*. Her perseverance with it testifies to her desire for recognition for work other than her literature for children.

One acceptable outlet for Alcott's need for independence and relief from family duties occurred during the Civil War. An avid abolitionist like her parents, Alcott was determined to join the nursing service, and although single women were not usually allowed to participate, her family and friends used their considerable influence to help her gain a post. In December 1862, she left for the Union Hotel Hospital in Georgetown. The work was grueling, conditions were deplorable, and after only a month Alcott contracted a severe case of typhoid fever and had to be taken home to Concord. Although the treatment she received caused lifelong health problems, her war experience provided ideas for three antislavery stories published in 1863–1864: "M. L.," "My Contraband," and "An Hour." In these stories, published under her own name, Alcott broke with convention by creating heroines who reverse gender roles by acting to save men. She also tacitly supported inter-racial marriage, a sharp break with most abolitionist thinking.

Although Alcott found satisfaction in writing these stories, as she did her secret thrillers, she was still seeking a more reliable genre that would allow her to earn the money her family desperately needed. Again, the Civil War provided material. During her short stint as a nurse, she wrote letters to friends and family, and when her health improved, her family encouraged her to edit them for publication. Although she wasn't enthusiastic about the project, to her delight, *Hospital Sketches* (1863) was warmly received. This volume was significant to her writing career because she discovered a formula for realistic fiction that she would use later in much of her writing for young people, beginning with the loosely autobiographical March family of *Little Women*. She based the characters and some events on the lives of her family and friends but created an idealized family who enjoyed the stability her own early years lacked. In a period when middle-class fathers typically left home each day to work, her father's unconventional example of allowing his wife, daughters, and friends to support him would have been as difficult for readers to understand as it was for Louisa to accept. The universality of the characters and events she created and her emphasis on the importance of family, strong moral values, and shared social responsibilities help to explain why *Little Women* was an instant bestseller in 1868 and remains popular.

Cynthia Butos
Trinity College

PRIMARY WORKS

Hospital Sketches, 1863; *Moods*, 1864 (rev. ed. 1882); *Little Women*, 1868–1869; *Little Men*, 1871; *Work: A Story of Experience*, 1873; *Transcendental Wild Oats*, 1873; *A Modern Mephistopheles*, 1877; *Jo's Boys*, 1886; Joel Myerson, Daniel Shealy, and Madeleine B. Stern, eds., *The Selected Letters*, 1987, *The Journals*, 1989; *Selected Fiction*, 1990.

My Contraband[1]

Doctor Franck came in as I sat sewing up the rents in an old shirt, that Tom might go tidily to his grave. New shirts were needed for the living, and there was no wife or mother to "dress him handsome when he went to meet the Lord," as one woman said, describing the fine funeral she had pinched herself to give her son.

"Miss Dane, I'm in a quandary," began the Doctor, with that expression of countenance which says as plainly as words, "I want to ask a favor, but I wish you'd save me the trouble."

"Can I help you out of it?"

"Faith! I don't like to propose it, but you certainly can, if you please."

"Then name it, I beg."

"You see a Reb[2] has just been brought in crazy with typhoid; a bad case every way; a drunken, rascally little captain somebody took the trouble to capture, but whom nobody wants to take the trouble to cure. The wards are full, the ladies worked to death, and willing to be for our own boys, but rather slow to risk their lives for a Reb. Now, you've had the fever, you like queer patients, your mate will see to your ward for a while, and I will find you a good attendant. The fellow won't last long, I fancy; but he can't die without some sort of care, you know. I've put him in the fourth story of the west wing, away from the rest. It is airy, quiet, and comfortable there. I'm on that ward, and will do my best for you in every way. Now, then, will you go?"

"Of course I will, out of perversity, if not common charity; for some of these people think that because I'm an abolitionist I am also a heathen, and I should rather like to show them that, though I cannot quite love my enemies, I am willing to take care of them."

---

[1]Originally published as "The Brothers" in the *Atlantic Monthly* (November 1863). Reprinted as "My Contraband," Alcott's preferred title, in *Hospital Sketches and Camp and Fireside Stories* (1869). During the Civil War, "contraband" referred to a black slave who escaped to or was brought within Union lines.

[2]During the Civil War, Union supporters referred to Confederate soldiers as "reb" or "rebel."

"Very good; I thought you'd go; and speaking of abolition reminds me that you can have a contraband for servant, if you like. It is that fine mulatto fellow who was found burying his rebel master after the fight, and, being badly cut over the head, our boys brought him along. Will you have him?"

"By all means,—for I'll stand to my guns on that point, as on the other; these black boys are far more faithful and handy than some of the white scamps given me to serve, instead of being served by. But is this man well enough?"

"Yes, for that sort of work, and I think you'll like him. He must have been a handsome fellow before he got his face slashed; not much darker than myself; his master's son, I dare say, and the white blood makes him rather high and haughty about some things. He was in a bad way when he came in, but vowed he'd die in the street rather than turn in with the black fellows below; so I put him up in the west wing, to be out of the way, and he's seen to the captain all the morning. When can you go up?"

"As soon as Tom is laid out, Skinner moved, Haywood washed, Marble dressed, Charley rubbed, Downs taken up, Upham laid down, and the whole forty fed."

We both laughed, though the Doctor was on his way to the dead-house and I held a shroud on my lap. But in a hospital one learns that cheerfulness is one's salvation; for, in an atmosphere of suffering and death, heaviness of heart would soon paralyze usefulness of hand, if the blessed gift of smiles had been denied us.

In an hour I took possession of my new charge, finding a dissipated-looking boy of nineteen or twenty raving in the solitary little room, with no one near him but the contraband in the room adjoining. Feeling decidedly more interest in the black man than in the white, yet remembering the Doctor's hint of his being "high and haughty," I glanced furtively at him as I scattered chloride of lime about the room to purify the air, and settled matters to suit myself. I had seen many contrabands, but never one so attractive as this. All colored men are called "boys," even if their heads are white; this boy was five-and-twenty at least, strong-limbed and manly, and had the look of one who never had been cowed by abuse or worn with oppressive labor. He sat on his bed doing nothing; no book, no pipe, no pen or paper anywhere appeared, yet anything less indolent or listless than his attitude and expression I never saw. Erect he sat, with a hand on either knee, and eyes fixed on the bare wall opposite, so rapt in some absorbing thought as to be unconscious of my presence, though the door stood wide open and my movements were by no means noiseless. His face was half averted, but I instantly approved the Doctor's taste, for the profile which I saw possessed all the attributes of comeliness belonging to his mixed race. He was more quadroon[3] than mulatto, with Saxon features, Spanish complexion darkened by exposure, color in lips and cheek, waving hair, and an eye full of the passionate melancholy which in such men always seems to utter a mute protest

---

[3]A person of one-quarter black ancestry.

against the broken law that doomed them at their birth. What could he be thinking of? The sick boy cursed and raved, I rustled to and fro, steps passed the door, bells rang, and the steady rumble of army-wagons came up from the street, still he never stirred. I had seen colored people in what they call "the black sulks," when, for days, they neither smiled nor spoke, and scarcely ate. But this was something more than that; for the man was not dully brooding over some small grievance; he seemed to see an all-absorbing fact or fancy recorded on the wall, which was a blank to me. I wondered if it were some deep wrong or sorrow, kept alive by memory and impotent regret; if he mourned for the dead master to whom he had been faithful to the end; or if the liberty now his were robbed of half its sweetness by the knowledge that some one near and dear to him still languished in the hell from which he had escaped. My heart quite warmed to him at that idea; I wanted to know and comfort him; and, following the impulse of the moment, I went in and touched him on the shoulder.

In an instant the man vanished and the slave appeared. Freedom was too new a boon to have wrought its blessed changes yet; and as he started up, with his hand at his temple, and an obsequious "Yes, Missis," any romance that had gathered round him fled away, leaving the saddest of all sad facts in living guise before me. Not only did the manhood seem to die out of him, but the comeliness that first attracted me; for, as he turned, I saw the ghastly wound that had laid open cheek and forehead. Being partly healed, it was no longer bandaged, but held together with strips of that transparent plaster which I never see without a shiver, and swift recollections of the scenes with which it is associated in my mind. Part of his black hair had been shorn away, and one eye was nearly closed; pain so distorted, and the cruel sabre-cut so marred that portion of his face, that, when I saw it, I felt as if a fine medal had been suddenly reversed, showing me a far more striking type of human suffering and wrong than Michael Angelo's bronze prisoner.[4] By one of those inexplicable processes that often teach us how little we understand ourselves, my purpose was suddenly changed; and, though I went in to offer comfort as a friend, I merely gave an order as a mistress.

"Will you open these windows? this man needs more air."

He obeyed at once, and, as he slowly urged up the unruly sash, the handsome profile was again turned toward me, and again I was possessed by my first impression so strongly that I involuntarily said,—

"Thank you."

Perhaps it was fancy, but I thought that in the look of mingled surprise and something like reproach which he gave me, there was also a trace of grateful pleasure. But he said, in that tone of spiritless humility these poor souls learn so soon,—

"I isn't a white man, Missis, I'se a contraband."

---

[4]Michelangelo (1475–1564), Italian artist. Alcott seems to be referring to one of the six statues of slaves that he created in marble, not bronze.

"Yes, I know it; but a contraband is a free man, and I heartily congratulate you." He liked that; his face shone, he squared his shoulders, lifted his head, and looked me full in the eye with a brisk,—

"Thank ye, Missis; anything more to do fer yer?"

"Doctor Franck thought you would help me with this man, as there are many patients and few nurses or attendants. Have you had the fever?"

"No, Missis."

"They should have thought of that when they put him here; wounds and fevers should not be together. I'll try to get you moved."

He laughed a sudden laugh: if he had been a white man, I should have called it scornful; as he was a few shades darker than myself, I suppose it must be considered an insolent, or at least an unmannerly one.

"It don't matter, Missis. I'd rather be up here with the fever than down with those niggers; and there isn't no other place fer me."

Poor fellow! that was true. No ward in all the hospital would take him in to lie side by side with the most miserable white wreck there. Like the bat in Æsop's fable, he belonged to neither race; and the pride of one and the helplessness of the other, kept him hovering alone in the twilight a great sin has brought to over-shadow the whole land.

"You shall stay, then; for I would far rather have you than my lazy Jack. But are you well and strong enough?"

"I guess I'll do, Missis."

He spoke with a passive sort of acquiescence,—as if it did not much matter if he were not able, and no one would particularly rejoice if he were.

"Yes, I think you will. By what name shall I call you?"

"Bob, Missis."

Every woman has her pet whim; one of mine was to teach the men self-respect by treating them respectfully. Tom, Dick, and Harry would pass, when lads rejoiced in those familiar abbreviations; but to address men often old enough to be my father in that style did not suit my old-fashioned ideas of propriety. This "Bob" would never die; I should have found it as easy to call the chaplain "Gus" as my tragical-looking contraband by a title so strongly associated with the tail of a kite.

"What is your other name?" I asked. "I like to call my attendants by their last names rather than by their first."

"I'se got no other, Missis; we has our master's names, or do without. Mine's dead, and I won't have anything of his 'bout me."

"Well, I'll call you Robert, then, and you may fill this pitcher for me, if you will be so kind."

He went; but, through all the tame obedience years of servitude had taught him, I could see that the proud spirit his father gave him was not yet subdued, for the look and gesture with which he repudiated his master's name was a more effective declaration of independence than any Fourth-of-July orator could have prepared.

We spent a curious week together. Robert seldom left his room, except upon my errands; and I was a prisoner all day, often all night, by the bedside of the rebel. The fever burned itself rapidly away, for there seemed little vitality to feed it in the feeble frame of this old young man, whose life had been none of the most righteous, judging from the revelations made by his unconscious lips; since more than once Robert authoritatively silenced him, when my gentler hushings were of no avail, and blasphemous wanderings or ribald camp-songs made my cheeks burn and Robert's face assume an aspect of disgust. The captain was a gentleman in the world's eye, but the contraband was the gentleman in mine;—I was a fanatic, and that accounts for such depravity of taste, I hope. I never asked Robert of himself, feeling that somewhere there was a spot still too sore to bear the lightest touch; but, from his language, manner, and intelligence, I inferred that his color had procured for him the few advantages within the reach of a quick-witted, kindly-treated slave. Silent, grave, and thoughtful, but most serviceable, was my contraband; glad of the books I brought him, faithful in the performance of the duties I assigned to him, grateful for the friendliness I could not but feel and show toward him. Often I longed to ask what purpose was so visibly altering his aspect with such daily deepening gloom. But I never dared, and no one else had either time or desire to pry into the past of this specimen of one branch of the chivalrous "F.F.Vs."[5]

On the seventh night, Dr. Franck suggested that it would be well for some one, besides the general watchman of the ward, to be with the captain, as it might be his last. Although the greater part of the two preceding nights had been spent there, of course I offered to remain,—for there is a strange fascination in these scenes, which renders one careless of fatigue and unconscious of fear until the crisis is past.

"Give him water as long as he can drink, and if he drops into a natural sleep, it may save him. I'll look in at midnight, when some change will probably take place. Nothing but sleep or a miracle will keep him now. Good-night."

Away went the Doctor; and, devouring a whole mouthful of grapes, I lowered the lamp, wet the captain's head, and sat down on a hard stool to begin my watch. The captain lay with his hot, haggard face turned toward me, filling the air with his poisonous breath, and feebly muttering, with lips and tongue so parched that the sanest speech would have been difficult to understand. Robert was stretched on his bed in the inner room, the door of which stood ajar, that a fresh draught from his open window might carry the fever-fumes away through mine. I could just see a long, dark figure, with the lighter outline of a face, and, having little else to do just then, I fell to thinking of this curious contraband, who evidently prized his freedom highly, yet seemed in no haste to enjoy it. Dr. Franck had offered to send him on to safer quarters, but he had said, "No, thank yer, sir, not yet," and then had gone away to fall into one of those black moods of his, which began to disturb me, because I had no power to lighten them. As I sat listening to the clocks from the steeples all about us, I amused myself with

[5]First Families of Virginia.

planning Robert's future, as I often did my own, and had dealt out to him a generous hand of trumps wherewith to play this game of life which hitherto had gone so cruelly against him, when a harsh choked voice called,—

"Lucy!"

It was the captain, and some new terror seemed to have gifted him with momentary strength.

"Yes, here's Lucy," I answered, hoping that by following the fancy I might quiet him,—for his face was damp with the clammy moisture, and his frame shaken with the nervous tremor that so often precedes death. His dull eye fixed upon me, dilating with a bewildered look of incredulity and wrath, till he broke out fiercely,—

"That's a lie! she's dead,—and so's Bob, damn him!"

Finding speech a failure, I began to sing the quiet tune that had often soothed delirium like this; but hardly had the line,—

See gentle patience smile on pain,

passed my lips, when he clutched me by the wrist, whispering like one in mortal fear,—

"Hush! she used to sing that way to Bob, but she never would to me. I swore I'd whip the devil out of her, and I did; but you know before she cut her throat she said she'd haunt me, and there she is!"

He pointed behind me with an aspect of such pale dismay, that I involuntarily glanced over my shoulder and started as if I had seen a veritable ghost; for, peering from the gloom of that inner room, I saw a shadowy face, with dark hair all about it, and a glimpse of scarlet at the throat. An instant showed me that it was only Robert leaning from his bed's foot, wrapped in a gray army-blanket, with his red shirt just visible above it, and his long hair disordered by sleep. But what a strange expression was on his face! The unmarred side was toward me, fixed and motionless as when I first observed it,—less absorbed now, but more intent. His eye glittered, his lips were apart like one who listened with every sense, and his whole aspect reminded me of a hound to which some wind had brought the scent of unsuspected prey.

"Do you know him, Robert? Does he mean you?"

"Laws, no, Missis; they all own half-a-dozen Bobs; but hearin' my name woke me, that's all."

He spoke quite naturally, and lay down again, while I returned to my charge, thinking that this paroxysm was probably his last. But by another hour I perceived a hopeful change; for the tremor had subsided, the cold dew was gone, his breathing was more regular, and Sleep, the healer, had descended to save or take him gently away. Doctor Franck looked in at midnight, bade me keep all cool and quiet, and not fail to administer a certain draught as soon as the captain woke. Very much relieved, I laid my head on my arms, uncomfortably folded on the little table, and fancied I was about to perform one of the feats which practice renders possible,—"sleeping with one eye open," as we say: a half-and-half doze, for all senses sleep but that of hearing; the faintest murmur, sigh, or motion will break it, and give one back one's wits much brightened by the brief permission to "stand at ease." On this night the experiment was a failure, for previous vigils, confinement, and much care had rendered naps a dangerous indulgence. Having roused half-a-dozen times in an hour to find all quiet, I dropped my heavy head on my arms, and, drowsily resolving to look up again in fifteen minutes, fell fast asleep.

The striking of a deep-voiced clock awoke me with a start. "That is one," thought I; but, to my dismay, two more strokes followed, and in remorseful haste I sprang up to see what harm my long oblivion had done. A strong hand put me back into my seat, and held me there. It was Robert. The instant my eye met his my heart began to beat, and all along my nerves tingled that electric flash which foretells a danger that we cannot see. He was very pale, his mouth grim, and both eyes full of sombre fire; for even the wounded one was open now, all the more sinister for the deep scar above and below. But his touch was steady, his voice quiet, as he said,—

"Sit still, Missis; I won't hurt yer, nor scare yer, ef I can help it, but yer waked too soon."

"Let me go, Robert,—the captain is stirring,—I must give him something." "No, Missis, yer can't stir an inch. Look here!"

Holding me with one hand, with the other he took up the glass in which I had left the draught, and showed me it was empty.

"Has he taken it?" I asked, more and more bewildered.

"I flung it out o' winder, Missis; he'll have to do without."

"But why, Robert? why did you do it?"

"Kase I hate him!"

Impossible to doubt the truth of that; his whole face showed it, as he spoke through his set teeth, and launched a fiery glance at the unconscious captain. I could only hold my breath and stare blankly at him, wondering what mad act was coming next. I suppose I shook and turned white, as women have a foolish habit of doing when sudden danger daunts them; for Robert released my arm, sat down upon the bedside just in front of me, and said, with the ominous quietude that made me cold to see and hear,—

"Don't yer be frightened, Missis; don't try to run away, fer the door's locked and the key in my pocket; don't yer cry out, fer yer'd have to scream a long while, with my hand on yer mouth, 'efore yer was heard. Be still, an' I'll tell yer what I'm gwine to do."

"Lord help us! he has taken the fever in some sudden, violent way, and is out of his head. I must humor him till some one comes"; in pursuance of which swift determination, I tried to say, quite composedly,—

"I will be still and hear you; but open the window. Why did you shut it?"

"I'm sorry I can't do it, Missis; but yer'd jump out, or call, if I did, an' I'm not ready yet. I shut it to make yer sleep, an' heat would do it quicker'n anything else I could do."

The captain moved, and feebly muttered, "Water!" Instinctively I rose to give it to him, but the heavy hand came down upon my shoulder, and in the same decided tone Robert said,—

"The water went with the physic; let him call."

"Do let me go to him! he'll die without care!"

"I mean he shall;—don't yer meddle, if yer please, Missis."

In spite of his quiet tone and respectful manner, I saw murder in his eyes, and turned faint with fear; yet the fear excited me, and, hardly knowing what I did, I seized the hands that had seized me, crying,—

"No, no; you shall not kill him! It is base to hurt a helpless man. Why do you hate him? He is not your master."

"He's my brother."

I felt that answer from head to foot, and seemed to fathom what was coming, with a prescience vague, but unmistakable. One appeal was left to me, and I made it.

"Robert, tell me what it means? Do not commit a crime and make me accessory to it. There is a better way of righting wrong than by violence;—let me help you find it."

My voice trembled as I spoke, and I heard the frightened flutter of my heart; so did he, and if any little act of mine had ever won affection or respect from him, the memory of it served me then. He looked down, and seemed to put some question to himself; whatever it was, the answer was in my favor, for when his eyes rose again, they were gloomy, but not desperate.

"I will tell yer, Missis; but mind, this makes no difference; the boy is mine. I'll give the Lord a chance to take him fust: if He don't, I shall."

"Oh, no! remember he is your brother."

An unwise speech; I felt it as it passed my lips, for a black frown gathered on Robert's face, and his strong hands closed with an ugly sort of grip. But he did not touch the poor soul gasping there behind him, and seemed content to let the slow suffocation of that stifling room end his frail life.

"I'm not like to forgit dat, Missis, when I've been thinkin' of it all this week. I knew him when they fetched him in, an' would 'a' done it long 'fore this, but I wanted to ask where Lucy was; he knows,—he told tonight,—an' now he's done for."

"Who is Lucy?" I asked hurriedly, intent on keeping his mind busy with any thought but murder.

With one of the swift transitions of a mixed temperament like this, at my question Robert's deep eyes filled, the clenched hands were spread before his face, and all I heard were the broken words,—

"My wife,—he took her—"

In that instant every thought of fear was swallowed up in burning indignation for the wrong, and a perfect passion of pity for the desperate man so tempted to avenge an injury for which there seemed no redress but this. He was no longer slave nor contraband, no drop of black blood marred him in my sight, but an infinite compassion yearned to save, to help, to comfort him. Words seemed so powerless I offered none, only put my hand on his poor head, wounded, homeless, bowed down with grief for which I had no cure, and softly smoothed the long, neglected hair, pitifully wondering the while where was the wife who must have loved this tender-hearted man so well.

The captain moaned again, and faintly whispered, "Air!" but I never stirred. God forgive me! just then I hated him only as a woman thinking of a sister woman's wrong could hate. Robert looked up; his eyes were dry again, his mouth grim. I saw that, said, "Tell me more," and he did; for sympathy is a gift the poorest may give, the proudest stoop to receive.

"Yer see, Missis, his father,—I might say ours, ef I warn't ashamed of both of 'em,—his father died two years ago, an' left us all to Marster Ned,— that's him here, eighteen then. He always hated me, I looked so like old Marster: he don't,—only the light skin an' hair. Old Marster was kind to all of us, me 'specially, an' bought Lucy off the next plantation down there in South Car'lina, when he found I liked her. I married her, all I could; it warn't much, but we was true to one another till Marster Ned come home a year after an' made hell fer both of us. He sent my old mother to be used up in his rice-swamp in Georgy; he found me with my pretty Lucy, an' though young Miss cried, an' I prayed to him on my knees, an' Lucy ran away, he wouldn't have no mercy; he brought her back, an'—took her."

"Oh, what did you do?" I cried, hot with helpless pain and passion.

How the man's outraged heart sent the blood flaming up into his face and deepened the tones of his impetuous voice, as he stretched his arm across the bed, saying, with a terribly expressive gesture,—

"I half murdered him, an' to-night I'll finish."

"Yes, yes,—but go on now; what came next?"

He gave me a look that showed no white man could have felt a deeper degradation in remembering and confessing these last acts of brotherly oppression.

"They whipped me till I couldn't stand, an' they sold me further South. Yer thought I was a white man once,—look here!"

With a sudden wrench he tore the shirt from neck to waist, and on his strong, brown shoulders showed me furrows deeply ploughed, wounds which, though healed, were ghastlier to me than any in that house. I could not speak to him, and, with the pathetic dignity a great grief lends the humblest sufferer, he ended his brief tragedy by simply saying,—

"That's all, Missis. I'se never seen her since, an' now I never shall in this world,—maybe not in t'other."

"But, Robert, why think her dead? The captain was wandering when he said those sad things; perhaps he will retract them when he is sane. Don't despair; don't give up yet."

"No, Missis, I'spect he's right; she was too proud to bear that long. It's like her to kill herself. I told her to, if there was no other way; an' she always minded me, Lucy did. My poor girl! Oh, it warn't right! No, by God, it warn't!"

As the memory of this bitter wrong, this double bereavement, burned in his sore heart, the devil that lurks in every strong man's blood leaped up; he put his hand upon his brother's throat, and, watching the white face before him, muttered low between his teeth,—

"I'm lettin' him go too easy; there's no pain in this; we a'n't even yet. I wish he knew me. Marster Ned! it's Bob; where's Lucy?"

From the captain's lips there came a long faint sigh, and nothing but a flutter of the eyelids showed that he still lived. A strange stillness filled the room as the elder brother held the younger's life suspended in his hand, while wavering between a dim hope and a deadly hate. In the whirl of thoughts that went on in my brain, only one was clear enough to act upon. I must prevent murder, if I could,—but how? What could I do up there alone, locked in with a dying man and a lunatic?—for any mind yielded utterly to any unrighteous impulse is mad while the impulse rules it. Strength I had not, nor much courage, neither time nor wit for strategem, and chance only could bring me help before it was too late. But one weapon I possessed,—a tongue,—often a woman's best defence; and sympathy, stronger than fear, gave me power to use it. What I said Heaven only knows, but surely Heaven helped me; words burned on my lips, tears streamed from my eyes, and some good angel prompted me to use the one name that had power to arrest my hearer's hand and touch his heart. For at that moment I heartily believed that Lucy lived, and this earnest faith roused in him a like belief.

He listened with the lowering look of one in whom brute instinct was sovereign for the time,—a look that makes the noblest countenance base. He was but a man,—a poor, untaught, outcast, outraged man. Life had few joys for him; the world offered him no honors, no success, no home, no love. What future would this crime mar? and why should he deny himself that sweet, yet bitter morsel called revenge? How many white men, with all New England's freedom, culture, Christianity, would not have felt as he felt then? Should I have reproached him for a human anguish, a human longing for redress, all now left him from the ruin of his few poor hopes? Who had taught him that self-control, self-sacrifice, are attributes that make men masters of the earth, and lift them nearer heaven? Should I have urged the beauty of forgiveness, the duty of devout submission? He had no religion, for he was no saintly "Uncle Tom," and Slavery's black shadow seemed to darken all the world to him, and shut out God. Should I have warned him of penalties, of judgments, and the potency of law? What did he know of justice, or the mercy that should temper that stern virtue, when every law, human and divine, had been broken on his hearthstone? Should I have tried to touch him by appeals to filial duty, to brotherly love? How had his appeals been answered? What memories had father and brother stored up in his heart to plead for either now? No,—all those influences, those associations, would have proved worse than useless, had I been calm enough to try them. I was not; but instinct, subtler than reason, showed me the one safe clue by which to lead this troubled soul from the labyrinth in which it groped and nearly fell. When I paused, breathless, Robert turned to me, asking, as if human assurances could strengthen his faith in Divine Omnipotence,—

"Do you believe, if I let Marster Ned live, the Lord will give me back my Lucy?"

"As surely as there is a Lord, you will find her here or in the beautiful hereafter, where there is no black or white, no master and no slave."

He took his hand from his brother's throat, lifted his eyes from my face to the wintry sky beyond, as if searching for that blessed country, happier even than the happy North. Alas, it was the darkest hour before the dawn!—there was no star above, no light below but the pale glimmer of the lamp that showed the brother who had made him desolate. Like a blind man who believes there is a sun, yet cannot see it, he shook his head, let his arms drop nervelessly upon his knees, and sat there dumbly asking that question which many a soul whose faith is firmer fixed than his has asked in hours less dark than this,—"Where is God?" I saw the tide had turned, and strenuously tried to keep this rudderless life-boat from slipping back into the whirlpool wherein it had been so nearly lost.

"I have listened to you, Robert; now hear me, and heed what I say, because my heart is full of pity for you, full of hope for your future, and a desire to help you now. I want you to go away from here, from the temptation of this place, and the sad thoughts that haunt it. You have conquered yourself once, and I honor you for it, because, the harder the battle, the more glorious the victory; but it is safer to put a greater distance between you and this man. I will write you letters, give you money, and send you to good old Massachusetts to begin your new life a freeman,—yes, and a happy man; for when the captain is himself again, I will learn where Lucy is, and move heaven and earth to find and give her back to you. Will you do this, Robert?"

Slowly, very slowly, the answer came; for the purpose of a week, perhaps a year, was hard to relinquish in an hour.

"Yes, Missis, I will."

"Good! Now you are the man I thought you, and I'll work for you with all my heart. You need sleep, my poor fellow; go, and try to forget. The captain is alive, and as yet you are spared that sin. No, don't look there; I'll care for him. Come, Robert, for Lucy's sake."

Thank Heaven for the immortality of love! for when all other means of salvation failed, a spark of this vital fire softened the man's iron will, until a woman's hand could bend it. He let me take from him the key, let me draw him gently away, and lead him to the solitude which now was the most healing balm I could bestow. Once in his little room, he fell down on his bed and lay there, as if spent with the sharpest conflict of his life. I slipped the bolt across his door, and unlocked my own, flung up the window, steadied myself with a breath of air, then rushed to Doctor Franck. He came; and till dawn we worked together, saving one brother's life, and taking earnest thought how best to secure the other's liberty. When the sun came up as blithely as if it shone only upon happy homes, the Doctor went to Robert. For an hour I heard the murmur of their voices; once I caught the sound of heavy sobs, and for a time a reverent hush, as if in the silence that good man were ministering to soul as well as body. When he departed he took Robert with him, pausing to tell me he should get him off as soon as possible, but not before we met again.

Nothing more was seen of them all day; another surgeon came to see the captain, and another attendant came to fill the empty place. I tried to rest, but could not, with the thought of poor Lucy tugging at my heart, and was soon back at my post again, anxiously hoping that my contraband had not been too hastily spirited away. Just as night fell there came a tap, and, opening, I saw Robert literally "clothed, and in his right mind." The Doctor had replaced the ragged suit with tidy garments, and no trace of that tempestuous night remained but deeper lines upon the forehead, and the docile look of a repentant child. He did not cross the threshold, did not offer me his hand,—only took off his cap, saying, with a traitorous falter in his voice,—

"God bless yer, Missis! I'm gwine."

I put out both my hands, and held his fast.

"Good-by, Robert! Keep up good heart, and when I come home to Massachusetts we'll meet in a happier place than this. Are you quite ready, quite comfortable for your journey?"

"Yes, Missis, yes; the Doctor's fixed everything; I'se gwine with a friend of his; my papers are all right, an' I'm as happy as I can be till I find"——

He stopped there; then went on, with a glance into the room,—

"I'm glad I didn't do it, an' I thank yer, Missis, fer hinderin' me,—thank yer hearty; but I'm afraid I hate him jest the same."

Of course he did; and so did I; for these faulty hearts of ours cannot turn perfect in a night, but need frost and fire, wind and rain, to ripen and make them ready for the great harvest-home. Wishing to divert his mind, I put my poor mite into his hand, and, remembering the magic of a certain little book, I gave him mine, on whose dark cover whitely shone the Virgin Mother and the Child, the grand history of whose life the book contained. The money went into Robert's pocket with a grateful murmur, the book into his bosom, with a long look and a tremulous—

"I never saw *my* baby, Missis."

I broke down then; and though my eyes were too dim to see, I felt the touch of lips upon my hands, heard the sound of departing feet, and knew my contraband was gone.

When one feels an intense dislike, the less one says about the subject of it the better; therefore I shall merely record that the captain lived,—in time was exchanged; and that, whoever the other party was, I am convinced the Government got the best of the bargain. But long before this occurred, I had fulfilled my promise to Robert; for as soon as my patient recovered strength of memory enough to make his answer trustworthy, I asked, without any circumlocution,—

"Captain Fairfax, where is Lucy?"

And too feeble to be angry, surprised, or insincere, he straightway answered,—"Dead, Miss Dane."

"And she killed herself when you sold Bob?"

"How the devil did you know that?" he muttered, with an expression half-remorseful, half-amazed; but I was satisfied, and said no more.

Of course this went to Robert, waiting far away there in a lonely home,—waiting, working, hoping for his Lucy. It almost broke my heart to do it; but delay was weak, deceit was wicked; so I sent the heavy tidings, and very soon the answer came,—only three lines; but I felt that the sustaining power of the man's life was gone.

"I tort I'd never see her any more; I'm glad to know she's out of trouble. I thank yer, Missis; an' if they let us, I'll fight fer yer till I'm killed, which I hope will be 'fore long."

Six months later he had his wish, and kept his word.

Every one knows the story of the attack on Fort Wagner;[6] but we should not tire yet of recalling how our Fifty-Fourth, spent with three sleepless nights, a day's fast, and a march under the July sun, stormed the fort as night fell, facing death in many shapes, following their brave leaders through a fiery rain of shot and shell, fighting valiantly for "God and Governor Andrew,"—how the regiment that went into action seven hundred strong, came out having had nearly half its number captured, killed, or wounded, leaving their young commander to be buried, like a chief of earlier times, with his body-guard around him, faithful to the death. Surely, the insult turns to honor, and the wide grave needs no monument but the heroism that consecrates it in our sight; surely, the hearts that held him nearest, see through their tears a noble victory in the seeming sad defeat; and surely, God's benediction was bestowed, when this loyal soul answered, as Death called the roll, "Lord, here am I, with the brothers Thou hast given me!"

The future must show how well that fight was fought; for though Fort Wagner once defied us, public prejudice is down; and through the cannon-smoke of that black night, the manhood of the colored race shines before many eyes that would not see, rings in many ears that would not hear, wins many hearts that would not hitherto believe.

When the news came that we were needed, there was none so glad as I to leave teaching contrabands, the new work I had taken up, and go to nurse "our boys," as my dusky flock so proudly called the wounded of the Fifty-Fourth. Feeling more satisfaction, as I assumed my big apron and turned up my cuffs, than if dressing for the President's levee, I fell to work in Hospital No. 10 at Beaufort. The scene was most familiar, and yet strange; for only dark faces looked up at me from the pallets so thickly laid along the floor, and I missed the sharp accent of my Yankee boys in the slower, softer voices calling cheerily to one another, or answering my questions with a stout, "We'll never give it up, Missis, till the last Reb's dead," or, "If our people's free, we can afford to die."

Passing from bed to bed, intent on making one pair of hands do the work of three, at least, I gradually washed, fed, and bandaged my way down the long line of sable heroes, and coming to the very last, found that he was

---

[6]In July 1863, Union forces assaulted Fort Wagner as part of the siege of Charleston, S.C., a battle the Union eventually won. The 54th Massachusetts Infantry, the first all-black regiment from the North, was created largely due to the efforts of abolitionist John Albion Andrew, governor of Massachusetts from 1860 to 1866.

my contraband. So old, so worn, so deathly weak and wan, I never should have known him but for the deep scar on his cheek. That side lay uppermost, and caught my eye at once; but even then I doubted, such an awful change had come upon him, when, turning to the ticket just above his head, I saw the name, "Robert Dane." That both assured and touched me, for, remembering that he had no name, I knew that he had taken mine. I longed for him to speak to me, to tell how he had fared since I lost sight of him, and let me perform some little service for him in return for many he had done for me; but he seemed asleep; and as I stood re-living that strange night again, a bright lad, who lay next to him softly waving an old fan across both beds, looked up and said,—

"I guess you know him, Missis?"

"You are right. Do you?"

"As much as any one was able to, Missis."

"Why do you say 'was,' as if the man were dead and gone?"

"I s'pose because I know he'll have to go. He's got a bad jab in the breast, an' is bleedin' inside, the Doctor says. He don't suffer any, only gets weaker 'n' weaker every minute. I've been fannin' him this long while, an' he's talked a little; but he don't know me now, so he's most gone, I guess."

There was so much sorrow and affection in the boy's face, that I remembered something, and asked, with redoubled interest,—

"Are you the one that brought him off? I was told about a boy who nearly lost his life in saving that of his mate."

I dare say the young fellow blushed, as any modest lad might have done; I could not see it, but I heard the chuckle of satisfaction that escaped him, as he glanced from his shattered arm and bandaged side to the pale figure opposite.

"Lord, Missis, that's nothin'; we boys always stan' by one another, an' I warn't goin' to leave him to be tormented any more by them cussed Rebs. He's been a slave once, though he don't look half so much like it as me, an' I was born in Boston."

He did not; for the speaker was as black as the ace of spades,—being a sturdy specimen, the knave of clubs would perhaps be a fitter representative,— but the dark freeman looked at the white slave with the pitiful, yet puzzled expression I have so often seen on the faces of our wisest men, when his tangled question of Slavery presented itself, asking to be cut or patiently undone.

"Tell me what you know of this man; for, even if he were awake, he is too weak to talk."

"I never saw him till I joined the regiment, an' no one 'peared to have got much out of him. He was a shut-up sort of feller, an' didn't seem to care for anything but gettin' at the Rebs. Some say he was the fust man of us that enlisted; I know he fretted till we were off, an' when we pitched into old Wagner, he fought like the devil."

"Were you with him when he was wounded? How was it?"

"Yes, Missis. There was somethin' queer about it; for he 'peared to know the chap that killed him, an' the chap knew him. I don't dare to ask, but rather guess one owned the other some time; for, when they clinched, the chap sung out, 'Bob!' an' Dane, 'Marster Ned!'—then they went at it."

I sat down suddenly, for the old anger and compassion struggled in my heart, and I both longed and feared to hear what was to follow.

"You see, when the Colonel,—Lord keep an' send him back to us!—it a'n't certain yet, you know, Missis, though it's two days ago we lost him,— well, when the Colonel shouted, 'Rush on, boys, rush on!' Dane tore away as if he was goin' to take the fort alone; I was next him, an' kept close as we went through the ditch an' up the wall. Hi! warn't that a rusher!" and the boy flung up his well arm with a whoop, as if the mere memory of that stirring moment came over him in a gust of irrepressible excitement.

"Were you afraid?" I said, asking the question women often put, and receiving the answer they seldom fail to get.

"No, Missis!"—emphasis on the "missis"—"I never thought of anything but the damn' Rebs, that scalp, slash, an' cut our ears off, when they git us. I was bound to let daylight into one of 'em at least, an' I did. Hope he liked it!"

"It is evident that you did. Now go on about Robert, for I should be at work."

"He was one of the fust up; I was just behind, an' though the whole thing happened in a minute, I remember how it was, for all I was yellin' an' knockin' round like mad. Just where we were, some sort of an officer was wavin' his sword an' cheerin' on his men; Dane saw him by a big flash that come by; he flung away his gun, give a leap, an' went at that feller as if he was Jeff, Beauregard, an' Lee, all in one. I scrabbled after as quick as I could, but was only up in time to see him git the sword straight through him an' drop into the ditch. You needn't ask what I did next, Missis, for I don't quite know myself; all I'm clear about is, that I managed somehow to pitch that Reb into the fort as dead as Moses, git hold of Dane, an' bring him off. Poor old feller! we said we went in to live or die; he said he went in to die, an' he's done it."

I had been intently watching the excited speaker; but as he regretfully added those last words I turned again, and Robert's eyes met mine,—those melancholy eyes, so full of an intelligence that proved he had heard, remembered, and reflected with that preternatural power which often outlives all other faculties. He knew me, yet gave no greeting; was glad to see a woman's face, yet had no smile wherewith to welcome it; felt that he was dying, yet uttered no farewell. He was too far across the river to return or linger now; departing thought, strength, breath, were spent in one grateful look, one murmur of submission to the last pang he could ever feel. His lips moved, and, bending to them, a whisper chilled my cheek, as it shaped the broken words,—

"I'd 'a' done it,—but it's better so,—I'm satisfied."

Ah! well he might be,—for, as he turned his face from the shadow of the life that was, the sunshine of the life to be touched it with a beautiful content, and in the drawing of a breath my contraband found wife and home, eternal liberty and God.

1863

■ HARRIET PRESCOTT SPOFFORD ■
1835–1921

Like the majority of women writers of her time, Harriet Prescott Spofford turned to authorship out of financial need. When barely in her twenties she began writing to help support her parents and younger siblings. Although some anonymous stories were published in Boston family story-papers, she never acknowledged these earliest money-making ventures. Her literary career officially began with the publication of the short story "In a Cellar" in the February 1859 issue of the *Atlantic Monthly* and continued from her 1865 marriage to Richard S. Spofford, Jr. until her last collection, *The Elder's People*, which appeared in 1920, the year before her death.

During a writing career that spanned more than sixty years in two centuries, Spofford published continuously in periodicals, offering short stories, serialized novels, poetry, and articles—much of it still uncollected—for adults and children. Her first book was a romance called *Sir Rohan's Ghost* (1860), but Spofford's short stories would soon outweigh her other writings in lasting importance. She published *The Amber Gods* (1863), her first short-story collection, and two book-length romances before her marriage. In *The Amber Gods*, "Circumstance," "Knitting Sale-Socks," and "The South Breaker" offered the realistic dialect and the social and economic realities of the rural and small-town New England life that she knew best.

"'Circumstance,'" which first appeared in the *Atlantic Monthly* in May 1860 and was later included in W. D. Howells's collection, *The Great Modern American Stories* (1921), is a fine example of Spofford's realism. Based on a true incident in her family history, "'Circumstance'" is nonetheless startlingly unusual. It impressed Emily Dickinson as "the only thing I ever read in my life that I didn't think I could have imagined myself!" Spofford's gift is to treat the sensational or implicitly "romantic" event realistically: a very real wife and mother draws on the art of her life—the hymns and lullabies and folk tunes she has sung—to placate a wild beast and defend herself against death.

In other stories of women's lives Spofford rebuked the prevalent nineteenth-century stereotypes that divided women into good and bad, angels and whores. The title story of *The Amber Gods* presented one such pair: the passionate Yone and the patient Lu. Each is defined by the jewelry she wears—"pagan" amber beads or "light" and "limpid" aquamarine. (Spofford asserted in her nonfiction *Art Decoration Applied to Furniture* (1878) that styles reflect the people who adopt them, a tactic she frequently used in her own fiction.) Yone and Lu foreshadow pairs of contrasting women in later Spofford stories who remind us that they are but two possible sides of one woman. Frequently also in Spofford's fiction, male characters must learn to appreciate individual differences among women. Men know *woman*, not *women*, Spofford suggests in the story "The Composite Wife" in *A Scarlet Poppy and Other Stories;* when Mr. Chipperley plans to take a fourth wife, he sees her as a composite of the other three.

A *Scarlet Poppy* did not appear until 1894, but the years between 1863 and 1898 were filled with other writings. In her 1935 study of Spofford, Elizabeth K. Halbeisen identifies eight books and at least 374 works published in periodicals during that period. The works collected in *A Scarlet Poppy* are light satire, quite different from the more somber collection *Old Madame and Other Tragedies* (1900). Spofford's days in Washington with her husband provide the basis for the sentimental stories in *Old Washington* (1906), and her final collection, often considered her best, *The Elder's People* (1920), returns to New England. The dry humor, the New England realities, the believable dialect, and the restraint with which she individualizes each character earned Spofford high praise.

Spofford expresses the sisterhood of women in her final collection in a story called "A Village Dressmaker." In this tale of self-sacrifice, the dressmaker Susanna gives the wedding gown she made for herself to Rowena Mayhew, who is marrying the man they both loved. Spofford's women face the realistic necessities of life, live with the limited perceptions of their men, and triumph through the art they create (songs, quilts, and dresses that only a widened perspective recognizes as true art forms) and the choices they willingly make. Spofford always finds the vermilion and azure threads woven into the duns and grays of the New England life and women she knew so well.

Thelma Shinn Richard
Arizona State University

PRIMARY WORKS

The Amber Gods and Other Stories, 1863; *A Scarlet Poppy and Other Stories,* 1894; *Old Madame and Other Tragedies,* 1900; *Old Washington,* 1906; *The Elder's People,* 1920.

Circumstance

She had remained, during all that day, with a sick neighbor,—those eastern wilds of Maine in that epoch frequently making neighbors and miles synonymous,—and so busy had she been with care and sympathy that she did not at first observe the approaching night. But finally the level rays, reddening the snow, threw their gleam upon the wall, and, hastily donning cloak and hood, she bade her friends farewell and sallied forth on her return. Home lay some three miles distant, across a copse, a meadow, and a piece of woods,—the woods being a fringe on the skirts of the great forests that stretch far away into the North. That home was one of a dozen loghouses lying a few furlongs apart from each other, with their half-cleared demesnes separating them at the rear from a wilderness untrodden save by stealthy native or deadly panther tribes.

She was in a nowise exalted frame of spirit,—on the contrary, rather depressed by the pain she had witnessed and the fatigue she had endured; but in certain temperaments such a condition throws open the mental pores, so to speak, and renders one receptive of every influence. Through the little copse she walked slowly, with her cloak folded about her, lingering to imbibe the sense of shelter, the sunset filtered in purple through the mist of woven spray and twig, the companionship of growth not sufficiently dense to band against her, the sweet homefeeling of a young and tender wintry wood. It was therefore just on the edge of the evening that she emerged from the place and began to cross the meadowland. At one hand lay the forest to which her path wound; at the other the evening star hung over a tide of failing orange that slowly slipped down the earth's broad side to sadden other hemispheres with sweet regret. Walking rapidly now, and with her eyes wide-open, she distinctly saw in the air before her what was not there a moment ago, a winding-sheet,—cold, white, and ghastly, waved by the likeness of four wan hands,—that rose with a long inflation, and fell in rigid folds, while a voice, shaping itself from the hollowness above, spectral and melancholy, sighed,—"The Lord have mercy on the people! The Lord have mercy on the people!" Three times the sheet with its corpse-covering outline waved beneath the pale hands, and the voice, awful in its solemn and mysterious depth, sighed, "The Lord have mercy on the people!" Then all was gone, the place was clear again, the gray sky was obstructed by no deathly blot; she looked about her, shook her shoulders decidedly, and, pulling on her hood, went forward once more.

She might have been a little frightened by such an apparition, if she had led a life of less reality than frontier settlers are apt to lead; but dealing with hard fact does not engender a flimsy habit of mind, and this woman was too sincere and earnest in her character, and too happy in her situation, to be thrown by antagonism, merely, upon superstitious fancies and chimeras of the second-sight. She did not even believe herself subject to an hallucination, but smiled simply, a little vexed that her thought could have framed such a glamour from the day's occurrences, and not sorry to lift the bough of the warder of the woods and enter and disappear in their sombre path. If she had been imaginative, she would have hesitated at her first step into a region whose dangers were not visionary; but I suppose that the thought of a little child at home would conquer that propensity in the most habituated. So, biting a bit of spicy birch, she went along. Now and then she came to a gap where the trees had been partially felled, and here she found that the lingering twilight was explained by that peculiar and perhaps electric film which sometimes sheathes the sky in diffused light for many hours before a brilliant aurora. Suddenly, a swift shadow, like the fabulous flying-dragon, writhed through the air before her, and she felt herself instantly seized and borne aloft. It was that wild beast—the most savage and serpentine and subtle and fearless of our latitudes—known by hunters as the Indian Devil, and he held her in his clutches on the broad floor of a swinging fir-bough. His long sharp claws were caught in her clothing, he worried them sagaciously a little, then, finding that ineffectual to free them, he commenced licking her bare arm with his rasping tongue and pouring over her the wide streams of his hot, foetid breath. So quick had this flashing action been that the woman had had no time for alarm; moreover, she was not of the screaming kind: but now, as she felt him endeavoring to disentangle his claws, and the horrid sense of her fate smote her, and she saw instinctively the fierce plunge of those weapons, the long strips of living flesh torn from her bones, the agony, the quivering disgust, itself a worse agony,—while by her side, and holding her in his great lithe embrace, the monster crouched, his white tusks whetting and gnashing, his eyes glaring through all the darkness like balls of red fire,—a shriek, that rang in every forest hollow, that startled every winter-housed thing, that stirred and woke the least needle of the tasselled pines, tore through her lips. A moment afterward, the beast left the arm, once white, now crimson, and looked up alertly.

She did not think at this instant to call upon God. She called upon her husband. It seemed to her that she had but one friend in the world; that was he; and again the cry, loud, clear, prolonged, echoed through the woods. It was not the shriek that disturbed the creature at his relish; he was not born in the woods to be scared of an owl, you know; what then? It must have been the echo, most musical, most resonant, repeated and yet repeated, dying with long sighs of sweet sound, vibrated from rock to river and back again from depth to depth of cave and cliff. Her thought flew after it; she knew, that, even if her husband heard it, he yet could not reach her in time; she saw that while the beast listened he would not gnaw,—and this she *felt* directly, when the rough, sharp, and multiplied stings of his tongue retouched her arm. Again her lips opened by instinct, but the sound that issued thence came by reason. She had heard that music charmed wild beasts,—just this point between life and death intensified every faculty,—and when she opened her lips the third time, it was not for shrieking, but for singing.

A little thread of melody stole out, a rill of tremulous motion; it was the cradle-song with which she rocked her baby;—how could she sing that? And then she remembered the baby sleeping rosily on the long settee before the fire,—the father cleaning his gun, with one foot on the green wooden rundle,—the merry light from the chimney dancing out and through the room, on the rafters of the ceiling with their tassels of onions and herbs, on the log walls painted with lichens and festooned with apples, on the king's-arm slung across the shelf with the old pirate's-cutlass, on the snow-pile of the bed, and on the great brass clock,—dancing, too, and lingering on the baby, with his fringed-gentian eyes, his chubby fists clenched on the pillow, and his fine breezy hair fanning with the motion of his father's foot. All this struck her in one, and made a sob of her breath, and she ceased.

Immediately the long red tongue thrust forth again. Before it touched, a song sprang to her lips, a wild sea-song, such as some sailor might be singing far out on trackless blue water that night, the shrouds whistling with frost and the sheets glued in ice,—a song with the wind in its burden and the spray in its chorus. The monster raised his head and flared the fiery eyeballs upon her, then fretted the imprisoned claws a moment and was quiet; only the breath like the vapor from some hell-pit still swathed her. Her voice, at first faint and fearful, gradually lost its quaver, grew under her control and subject to her modulation; it rose on long swells, it fell in subtile cadences, now and then its tones pealed out like bells from distant belfries on fresh sonorous mornings. She sung the song through, and, wondering lest his name of Indian Devil were not his true name, and if he would not detect her, she repeated it. Once or twice now, indeed, the beast stirred uneasily, turned, and made the bough sway at his movement. As she ended, he snapped his jaws together, and tore away the fettered member, curling it under him with a snarl,—when she burst into the gayest reel that ever answered a fiddle-bow. How many a time she had heard her husband play it on the homely fiddle made by himself from birch and cherrywood! how many a time she had seen it danced on the floor of their one room, to the patter of wooden clogs and the rustle of homespun petticoat! how many a time she had danced it herself!—and did she not remember once, as they joined clasps for eight-hands-round, how it had lent its gay, bright measure to her life? And here she was singing it alone, in the forest, at midnight, to a wild beast! As she sent her voice trilling up and down its quick oscillations between joy and pain, the creature who grasped her uncurled his paw and scratched the bark from the bough; she must vary the spell; and her voice spun leaping along the projecting points of tune of a hornpipe. Still singing, she felt herself twisted about with a low growl and a lifting of the red lip from the glittering teeth; she broke the hornpipe's thread, and commenced unravelling a lighter, livelier thing, an Irish jig. Up and down and round about her voice flew, the beast threw back his head so that the diabolical face fronted hers, and the torrent of his breath prepared her for his feast as the anaconda slimes his prey. Franticly she darted from tune to tune; his restless movements followed her. She tired herself with dancing and vivid national airs, growing feverish and singing spasmodically as she felt her horrid tomb yawning wider. Touching in this manner all the slogan and keen clan cries, the beast moved again, but only to lay the disengaged paw across her with heavy satisfaction. She did not dare to pause; through the clear cold air, the frosty starlight, she sang. If there were yet any tremor in the tone, it was not fear,—she had learned the secret of sound at last; nor could it be chill,—far too high a fever throbbed her pulses; it was nothing but the thought of the log-house and of what might be passing within it. She fancied the baby stirring in his sleep and moving his pretty lips,—her husband rising and opening the door, looking out after her, and wondering at her absence. She fancied the light pouring through the chink and then shut in again with all the safety and comfort and joy, her husband taking down the fiddle and playing lightly with his head inclined, playing while she sang, while she sang for her life to an Indian Devil. Then she knew he was fumbling for and finding some shining fragment and scoring it down the yellowing hair, and unconsciously her voice forsook the wild wartunes and drifted into the half-gay, half-melancholy Rosin the Bow.

Suddenly she woke pierced with a pang, and the daggered tooth penetrating her flesh;—dreaming of safety, she had ceased singing and lost it.
The beast had regained the use of all his limbs, and now, standing and raising his back, bristling and foaming, with sounds that would have been like
hisses but for their deep and fearful sonority, he withdrew step by step toward the trunk of the tree, still with his flaming balls upon her. She was all
at once free, on one end of the bough, twenty feet from the ground. She did
not measure the distance, but rose to drop herself down, careless of any
death, so that it were not this. Instantly, as if he scanned her thoughts, the
creature bounded forward with a yell and caught her again in his dreadful
hold. It might be that he was not greatly famished; for, as she suddenly
flung up her voice again, he settled himself composedly on the bough, still
clasping her with invincible pressure to his rough, ravenous breast, and listening in a fascination to the sad, strange U-la-lu that now moaned forth in
loud, hollow tones above him. He half closed his eyes, and sleepily reopened
and shut them again.

What rending pains were close at hand! Death! and what a death! worse
than any other that is to be named! Water, be it cold or warm, that which
buoys up blue icefields, or which bathes tropical coasts with currents of
balmy bliss, is yet a gentle conqueror, kisses as it kills, and draws you down
gently through darkening fathoms to its heart. Death at the sword is the
festival of trumpet and bugle and banner, with glory ringing out around you
and distant hearts thrilling through yours. No gnawing disease can bring
such hideous end as this; for that is a fiend bred of your own flesh, and
this—is it a fiend, this living lump of appetites? What dread comes with the
thought of perishing in flames! but fire, let it leap and hiss never so hotly, is
something too remote, too alien, to inspire us with such loathly horror as a
wild beast; if it have a life, that life is too utterly beyond our comprehension. Fire is not half ourselves; as it devours, arouses neither hatred nor disgust; is not to be known by the strength of our lower natures let loose; does
not drip our blood into our faces with foaming chaps, nor mouth nor slaver
above us with vitality. Let us be ended by fire, and we are ashes, for the
winds to bear, the leaves to cover; let us be ended by wild beasts, and the
base, cursed thing howls with us forever through the forest. All this she felt
as she charmed him, and what force it lent to her song God knows. If her
voice should fail! If the damp and cold should give her any fatal hoarseness!
If all the silent powers of the forest did not conspire to help her! The dark,
hollow night rose indifferently over her; the wide, cold air breathed rudely
past her, lifted her wet hair and blew it down again; the great boughs swung
with a ponderous strength, now and then clashed their iron lengths together and shook off a sparkle of icy spears or some long-lain weight of
snow from their heavy shadows. The green depths were utterly cold and
silent and stern. These beautiful haunts that all the summer were hers and
rejoiced to share with her their bounty, these heavens that had yielded their
largess, these stems that had thrust their blossoms into her hands, all these
friends of three moons ago forgot her now and knew her no longer.

Feeling her desolation, wild, melancholy, forsaken songs rose thereon from that frightful aerie,—weeping, wailing tunes, that sob among the people from age to age, and overflow with otherwise unexpressed sadness,—all rude, mournful ballads,—old tearful strains, that Shakespeare heard the vagrants sing, and that rise and fall like the wind and tide,—sailor-songs, to be heard only in lone mid-watches beneath the moon and stars,—ghastly rhyming romances, such as that famous one of the Lady Margaret, when

> *"She slipped on her gown of green*
> *A piece below the knee,—*
> *And 't was all a long cold winter's night*
> *A dead corse followed she."*

Still the beast lay with closed eyes, yet never relaxing his grasp. Once a half-whine of enjoyment escaped him,—he fawned his fearful head upon her; once he scored her cheek with his tongue—savage caresses that hurt like wounds. How weary she was! and yet how terribly awake! How fuller and fuller of dismay grew the knowledge that she was only prolonging her anguish and playing with death! How appalling the thought that with her voice ceased her existence! Yet she could not sing forever; her throat was dry and hard; her very breath was a pain; her mouth was hotter than any desert-worn pilgrim's;—if she could but drop upon her burning tongue one atom of the ice that glittered about her!—but both of her arms were pinioned in the giant's vice. She remembered the winding-sheet, and for the first time in her life shivered with spiritual fear. Was it hers? She asked herself, as she sang, what sins she had committed, what life she had led, to find her punishment so soon and in these pangs,—and then she sought eagerly for some reason why her husband was not up and abroad to find her. He failed her,—her one sole hope in life; and without being aware of it, her voice forsook the songs of suffering and sorrow for old Covenanting hymns,—hymns with which her mother had lulled her, which the class-leader pitched in the chimney-corners,—grand and sweet Methodist hymns, brimming with melody and with all fantastic involutions of tune to suit that ecstatic worship,—hymns full of the beauty of holiness, steadfast, relying, sanctified by the salvation they had lent to those in worse extremity than hers,—for they had found themselves in the grasp of hell, while she was but in the jaws of death. Out of this strange music, peculiar to one character of faith, and than which there is none more beautiful in its degree nor owning a more potent sway of sound, her voice soared into the glorified chants of churches. What to her was death by cold or famine or wild beasts? "Though He slay me, yet will I trust in him," she sang. High and clear through the frore[1] fair night, the level moonbeams splintering in the wood, the scarce glints of stars in the shadowy roof of branches, these sacred anthems rose,—rose as a hope from despair, as some snowy spray of flower-bells from blackest mould. Was she not in God's hands? Did not the world swing

---

[1]Frosty, cold.

at his will? If this were in his great plan of providence, was it not best, and should she not accept it?

"He is the Lord our God; his judgments are in all the earth."

Oh, sublime faith of our fathers, where utter self-sacrifice alone was true love, the fragrance of whose unrequired subjection was pleasanter than that of golden censers swung in purple-vapored chancels!

Never ceasing in the rhythm of her thoughts, articulated in music as they thronged, the memory of her first communion flashed over her. Again she was in that distant place on that sweet spring morning. Again the congregation rustled out, and the few remained, and she trembled to find herself among them. How well she remembered the devout, quiet faces, too accustomed to the sacred feast to glow with their inner joy! how well the snowy linen at the altar, the silver vessels slowly and silently shifting! and as the cup approached and passed, how the sense of delicious perfume stole in and heightened the transport of her prayer, and she had seemed, looking up through the windows where the sky soared blue in constant freshness, to feel all heaven's balms dripping from the portals, and to scent the lilies of eternal peace! Perhaps another would not have felt so much ecstasy as satisfaction on that occasion; but it is a true, if a later disciple, who has said, "The Lord bestoweth his blessings there, where he findeth the vessels empty."

"And does it need the walls of a church to renew my communion?" she asked. "Does not every moment stand a temple four-square to God? And in that morning, with its buoyant sunlight, was I any dearer to the Heart of the World than now?—'My beloved is mine, and I am his,'" she sang over and over again, with all varied inflection and profuse tune. How gently all the winter-wrapt things bent toward her then! into what relation with her had they grown! how this common dependence was the spell of their intimacy! how at one with Nature had she become! how all the night and the silence and the forest seemed to hold its breath, and to send its soul up to God in her singing! It was no longer despondency, that singing. It was neither prayer nor petition. She had left imploring, "How long wilt thou forget me, O Lord? Lighten mine eyes, lest I sleep the sleep of death! For in death there is no remembrance of thee,"—with countless other such fragments of supplication. She cried rather, "Yea, though I walk through the valley of the shadow of death, I will fear no evil: for thou art with me; thy rod and thy staff, they comfort me,"—and lingered, and repeated, and sang again, "I shall be satisfied, when I awake, with thy likeness."

Then she thought of the Great Deliverance, when he drew her up out of many waters, and the flashing old psalm pealed forth triumphantly:—

> "The Lord descended from above,
>   and bow'd the heavens hie:
> And underneath his feet he cast
>   the darknesse of the skie.
> On cherubs and on cherubins
>   full royally he road:
> And on the wings of all the winds
>   came flying all abroad."

She forgot how recently, and with what a strange pity for her own shapeless form that was to be, she had quaintly sung,—

"O lovely appearance of death!
What sight upon earth is so fair?
Not all the gay pageants that breathe,
Can with a dead body compare!"

She remembered instead,—"In thy presence is fulness of joy; at thy right hand there are pleasures forevermore. God will redeem my soul from the power of the grave: for he shall receive me. He will swallow up death in victory." Not once now did she say, "Lord, how long wilt thou look on; rescue my soul from their destructions, my darling from the lions,"—for she knew that the young lions roar after their prey and seek their meat from God. "O Lord, thou preservest man and beast!" she said.

She had no comfort or consolation in this season, such as sustained the Christian martyrs in the amphitheatre. She was not dying for her faith; there were no palms in heaven for her to wave; but how many a time had she declared,—"I had rather be a doorkeeper in the house of my God, than to dwell in the tents of wickedness!" And as the broad rays here and there broke through the dense covert of shade and lay in rivers of lustre on crystal sheathing and frozen fretting of trunk and limb and on the great spaces of refraction, they builded up visibly that house, the shining city on the hill, and singing, "Beautiful for situation, the joy of the whole earth, is Mount Zion, on the sides of the North, the city of the Great King," her vision climbed to that higher picture where the angel shows the dazzling thing, the holy Jerusalem descending out of heaven from God, with its splendid battlements and gates of pearls, and its foundations, the eleventh a jacinth, the twelfth an amethyst,—with its great white throne, and the rainbow round about it, in sight like unto an emerald: "And there shall be no night there,— for the Lord God giveth them light," she sang.

What whisper of dawn now rustled through the wilderness? How the night was passing? And still the beast crouched upon the bough, changing only the posture of his head, that again he might command her with those charmed eyes;—half their fire was gone; she could almost have released herself from his custody; yet, had she stirred, no one knows what malevolent instinct might have dominated anew. But of that she did not dream; long ago stripped of any expectation, she was experiencing in her divine rapture how mystically true it is that "he that dwelleth in the secret place of the Most High shall abide under the shadow of the Almighty."

Slow clarion cries now wound from the distance as the cocks caught the intelligence of day and re-echoed it faintly from farm to farm,—sleepy sentinels of night, sounding the foe's invasion, and translating that dim intuition to ringing notes of warning. Still she chanted on. A remote crash of brushwood told of some other beast on his depredations, or some night-belated traveller groping his way through the narrow path. Still she chanted on. The far, faint echoes of the chanticleers died into distance, the crashing of the branches grew nearer. No wild beast that, but a man's step,—a man's form in the moonlight, stalwart and strong,—on one arm slept a little child, in the other hand he held his gun. Still she chanted on.

Perhaps, when her husband last looked forth, he was half ashamed to find what a fear he felt for her. He knew she would never leave the child so long but for some direst need,—and yet he may have laughed at himself, as he lifted and wrapped it with awkward care, and, loading his gun and strapping on his horn, opened the door again and closed it behind him, going out and plunging into the darkness and dangers of the forest. He was more singularly alarmed than he would have been willing to acknowledge; as he had sat with his bow hovering over the strings, he had half believed to hear her voice mingling gayly with the instrument, till he paused and listened if she were not about to lift the latch and enter. As he drew nearer the heart of the forest, that intimation of melody seemed to grow more actual, to take body and breath, to come and go on long swells and ebbs of the night-breeze, to increase with tune and words, till a strange shrill singing grew ever clearer, and, as he stepped into an open space of moonbeams, far up in the branches, rocked by the wind, and singing, "How beautiful upon the mountains are the feet of him that bringeth good tidings, that publisheth peace," he saw his wife,—his wife,—but, great God in heaven! how? Some mad exclamation escaped him, but without diverting her. The child knew the singing voice, though never heard before in that unearthly key, and turned toward it through the veiling dreams. With a celerity almost instantaneous, it lay, in the twinkling of an eye, on the ground at the father's feet, while his gun was raised to his shoulder and levelled at the monster covering his wife with shaggy form and flaming gaze,—his wife so ghastly white, so rigid, so stained with blood, her eyes so fixedly bent above, and her lips, that had indurated into the chiselled pallor of marble, parted only with that flood of solemn song.

I do not know if it were the mother-instinct that for a moment lowered her eyes,—those eyes, so lately riveted on heaven, now suddenly seeing all life-long bliss possible. A thrill of joy pierced and shivered through her like a weapon, her voice trembled in its course, her glance lost its steady strength, fever-flushes chased each other over her face, yet she never once ceased chanting. She was quite aware, that, if her husband shot now, the ball must pierce her body before reaching any vital part of the beast,—and yet better that death, by his hand, than the other. But this her husband also knew, and he remained motionless, just covering the creature with the sight. He dared not fire, lest some wound not mortal should break the spell exercised by her voice, and the beast, enraged with pain, should rend her in atoms; moreover, the light was too uncertain for his aim. So he waited. Now and then he examined his gun to see if the damp were injuring its charge, now and then he wiped the great drops from his forehead. Again the cocks crowed with the passing hour,—the last time they were heard on that night. Cheerful home sound then, how full of safety and all comfort and rest it seemed! what sweet morning incidents of sparkling fire and sunshine, of gay household bustle, shining dresser, and cooing baby, of steaming cattle in the yard, and brimming milk-pails at the door! what pleasant voices! what laughter! what security! and here—

Now, as she sang on in the slow, endless, infinite moments, the fervent vision of God's peace was gone. Just as the grave had lost its sting, she was snatched back again to the arms of earthly hope. In vain she tried to sing, "There remaineth a rest for the people of God,"—her eyes trembled on her husband's, and she could only think of him, and of the child, and of happiness that yet might be, but with what a dreadful gulf of doubt between! She shuddered now in the suspense; all calm forsook her; she was tortured with dissolving heats or frozen with icy blasts; her face contracted, growing small and pinched; her voice was hoarse and sharp,—every tone cut like a knife,—the notes became heavy to lift,—withheld by some hostile pressure,—impossible. One gasp, a convulsive effort, and there was silence,—she had lost her voice.

The beast made a sluggish movement,—stretched and fawned like one awaking,—then, as if he would have yet more of the enchantment, stirred her slightly with his muzzle. As he did so, a sidelong hint of the man standing below with the raised gun smote him; he sprung round furiously, and, seizing his prey, was about to leap into some unknown airy den of the topmost branches now waving to the slow dawn. The late moon had rounded through the sky so that her gleam at last fell full upon the bough with fairy frosting; the wintry morning light did not yet penetrate the gloom. The woman, suspended in mid-air an instant, cast only one agonized glance beneath,—but across and through it, ere the lids could fall, shot a withering sheet of flame,—a rifle-crack, half-heard, was lost in the terrible yell of desperation that bounded after it and filled her ears with savage echoes, and in the wide arc of some eternal descent she was falling;—but the beast fell under her.

I think that the moment following must have been too sacred for us, and perhaps the three have no special interest again till they issue from the shadows of the wilderness upon the white hills that skirt their home. The father carries the child hushed again into slumber, the mother follows with no such feeble step as might be anticipated. It is not time for reaction,—the tension not yet relaxed, the nerves still vibrant, she seems to herself like some one newly made; the night was a dream; the present stamped upon her in deep satisfaction, neither weighed nor compared with the past; if she has the careful tricks of former habit, it is as an automaton; and as they slowly climb the steep under the clear gray vault and the paling morning star, and as she stops to gather a spray of the red-rose berries or a feathery tuft of dead grasses for the chimney-piece of the log-house, or a handful of brown cones for the child's play,—of these quiet, happy folk you would scarcely dream how lately they had stolen from under the banner and encampment of the great King Death. The husband proceeds a step or two in advance; the wife lingers over a singular footprint in the snow, stoops and examines it, then looks up with a hurried word. Her husband stands alone on the hill, his arms folded across the babe, his gun fallen,—stands defined as a silhouette against the pallid sky. What is there in their home, lying below and yellowing in the light, to fix him with such a stare? She springs to his side. There is no home there. The log-house, the barns, the neighboring farms, the fences, are all blotted out and mingled in one smoking ruin. Desolation and death were indeed there, and beneficence and life in the forest. Tomahawk and scalping-knife, descending during that night, had left behind them only this work of their accomplished hatred and one subtle foot-print in the snow.

For the rest,—the world was all before them, where to choose.[2]

1860

■ SAMUEL LANGHORNE CLEMENS (MARK TWAIN) ■
1835–1910

Mark Twain—the historical Samuel Langhorne Clemens—is variously known as a writer of humor, regionalist and historical fiction, travel narratives, and tales, sketches, allegories, and political commentary. His moods range from thumbing his nose at the establishment through lyrical evocations of America's past to angry condemnations of the "damned human race." And his works play the temporal keyboard from the Middle Ages through the nineteenth century to a timeless, nightmare world. Although many of his readers think they know Mark Twain, he is notoriously hard to pin down.

Samuel Clemens was born in rural America—Florida, Missouri—in 1835 and died in the exurbs of New York City—Redding, Connecticut—in 1910. Between his youth and his death, he had visited most parts of the globe and met many of the world's most prominent men and women. Reared in the dialect tradition of American writing, he became its master practitioner. Language— what it is, how it is used, and what it can tell us about the people speaking it— was the central literary preoccupation of his life. He was also fascinated by technologies, such as the telegraph, that suggested the human capability to conquer time and space. As he moved through his century, he responded both to contemporary events as they unfolded and to the specter of his contemporaries' grappling with choice, morality, and law. By the time he died, he no longer believed that human beings were capable of moral action.

Twain's writings reflect both his moods and his movements. Novels such as *Tom Sawyer* (1876) and *The Adventures of Huckleberry Finn* (1885) reflect the landscapes and characters of his antebellum childhood, which was primarily

[2]Concluding lines of John Milton's *Paradise Lost* (1667) describing Adam and Eve's departure from the Garden of Eden.

passed in the Mississippi riverboat town of Hannibal, Missouri. In these, his best-known works, he rides his contemporaries' interest in books about young boys' adventures. Unlike most writers in this genre, however, Twain was less interested in teaching young readers how to conform to social norms than in presenting realistic images of adolescents who are facing serious moral issues, such as, in *The Adventures of Huckleberry Finn*, whether to turn in an escaped slave. As a result, this novel in particular has been read very differently by subsequent generations. For instance, while initial reviews worried that its ragged protagonist presented a bad example for young readers because he smoked, stole watermelons, and spoke in dialect, late twentieth-century readers agonized about its racial politics, with some readers praising its depiction of the relationship between a white boy and a black man and others finding it racist.

In a very different vein, tales such as "The Celebrated Jumping Frog of Calaveras County" (1865), and travel narratives such as *Life on the Mississippi* (1883) and *Roughing It* (1872), reflect Twain's experiences just before and during the Civil War years, when he left Hannibal, first to become a steamboat pilot on the Mississippi River and, later, to head west to the Nevada and California territories, where he became a journalist and started learning his craft. *The Innocents Abroad* (1869), his first long publication, shows him moving in the opposite direction geographically, as a "tourist" visiting Europe and the Holy Land. *The Gilded Age* (1873), his first novel, coauthored with the writer Charles Dudley Warner, took on—and named—the era of excess through which the United States passed just after the Civil War. Both early works demonstrate Twain's capacity for biting satire—directed against both arrogant Europeans and pretentious Americans.

After he had established his reputation as a satirist, regionalist, and writer of travel narratives, and after he had traveled extensively in Europe, Twain turned to European history and geography. The novels *A Connecticut Yankee in King Arthur's Court* (1889) and *Personal Recollections of Joan of Arc* (1895), and the travel narrative *A Tramp Abroad* (1880), show him moving into other times and places as he sought to use Old World materials to comment on contemporary life. In his last two decades, sketches such as "My Platonic Sweetheart" (1898) and novels such as *Puddn'head Wilson* (1894), as well as parts of his *Autobiography* (1906–1907), show him revisiting scenes of his childhood as he pondered questions of racial identity and the possibility that dream life might be as "real" as waking life. *Following the Equator* (1897), his last travel narrative, exhibits his response to non-European peoples and their cultures. In the early twentieth century, political commentaries such as "The Czar's Soliloquy" (1905), "King Leopold's Soliloquy"(1905), and "To the Person Sitting in Darkness" (1901) demonstrate his direct, and angry, response to contemporary events, especially Europeans' and Americans' imperialist interventions into other countries.

Because Mark Twain wrote in so many genres, on so many topics, reading Mark Twain is often a matter of determining which of his many themes is most compelling, and for whom. For instance, in addition to the racial debates about *Huck Finn*, readers of *A Connecticut Yankee in King Arthur's Court*, which transports a nineteenth-century workman into sixth-century England, have long noted that the novel can be read either as a comic time-travel story or as a serious (and contradictory) polemic on American politics and on humans' capacity for moral action. Twain's outspoken sympathy for Chinese immigrants, and his protests against their treatment, is offset by his contemptuous attitudes toward Native Americans. And his extraordinary dexterity with language—words, phrases, syntax, and punctuation—can result not only in some of the most lyrical passages in the American language, but also in some of the most scurrilous. Mark Twain is alternately explosive, lyrical, satirical, and tendentious, but he is always compelling. His love of language, and his engagement with issues that transcend his generation, make him central to the American tradition that calls readers to question their own assumptions.

Susan K. Harris
University of Kansas

PRIMARY WORKS

The Innocents Abroad, 1869; *Roughing It,* 1872; *The Adventures of Tom Sawyer,* 1876; *A Tramp Abroad,* 1880; *The Prince and the Pauper,* 1882; *Life on the Mississippi,* 1883; *Adventures of Huckleberry Finn,* 1885; *A Connecticut Yankee in King Arthur's Court,* 1889; *The Tragedy of Pudd'nhead Wilson and the Comedy of Those Extraordinary Twins,* 1894; *Personal Recollections of Joan of Arc,* 1896; *Following the Equator,* 1897; *Autobiography,* 1924; *Mark Twain in Eruption: Hitherto Unpublished Pages about Men and Events,* 1940; *The Mysterious Stranger Manuscripts,* 1969; *What Is Man? and Other Philosophical Writings,* 1973; *Letters,* 1988–; *The Oxford Mark Twain,* 29 vols., Shelley Fisher Fishkin, gen. ed., 1997.

Jim Smiley and His Jumping Frog[1]

Mr. A. Ward.

Dear Sir:—Well, I called on good-natured, garrulous old Simon Wheeler, and I inquired after your friend Leonidas W. Smiley, as you requested me to do, and I here-unto append the result. If you can get any information out of it you are cordially welcome to it. I have a lurking suspicion that your Leonidas W. Smiley is a myth—that you never knew such a personage, and that you only conjectured that if I asked old Wheeler about him it would remind him of his infamous *Jim* Smiley, and he would go to work and bore me nearly to death with some infernal reminiscence of him as long and tedious as it should be useless to me. If that was your design, Mr. Ward, it will gratify you to know that it succeeded.

* * *

[1]In 1865, while living in California, Mark Twain sent "Jim Smiley and His Jumping Frog" to the comic writer Artemus Ward, who had asked for a sketch for a book he was putting together. But because it arrived too late, it was published elsewhere, in the *New York Saturday Press,* on November 18, 1865. Told by two narrators, Mark Twain and Simon Wheeler, the ironic sketch allows readers to feel superior to Wheeler, but ultimately they find that they have been taken in. The story of the jumping frog made Mark Twain famous because it was copied repeatedly by other publications. Later the author revised the sketch substantially and gave it a new name, "The Celebrated Jumping Frog of Calaveras County," when he included it in his *Sketches, New and Old* (1875). [Notes by Everett Emerson.]

I found Simon Wheeler dozing comfortably by the barroom stove of the little old dilapidated tavern in the ancient mining camp of Boomerang, and I noticed that he was fat and bald-headed, and had an expression of winning gentleness and simplicity upon his tranquil countenance. He roused up and gave me good-day. I told him a friend of mine had commissioned me to make some inquiries about a cherished companion of his boyhood named Leonidas W. Smiley—Rev. Leonidas W. Smiley—a young minister of the gospel, who he had heard was at one time a resident of this village of Boomerang. I added that if Mr. Wheeler could tell me anything about this Rev. Leonidas W. Smiley, I would feel under many obligations to him.

Simon Wheeler backed me into a corner and blockaded me there with his chair—and then sat down and reeled off the monotonous narrative which follows this paragraph. He never smiled, he never frowned, he never changed his voice from the quiet, gently-flowing key to which he turned the initial sentence, he never betrayed the slightest suspicion of enthusiasm—but all through the interminable narrative there ran a vein of impressive earnestness and sincerity, which showed me plainly that so far from his imagining that there was anything ridiculous or funny about his story, he regarded it as a really important matter, and admired its two heroes as men of transcendent genius in finesse. To me, the spectacle of a man drifting serenely along through such a queer yarn without ever smiling was exquisitely absurd. As I said before, I asked him to tell me what he knew of Rev. Leonidas W. Smiley, and he replied as follows. I let him go on in his own way, and never interrupted him once:

There was a feller here once by the name of *Jim* Smiley, in the winter of '49—or maybe it was the spring of '50—I don't recollect exactly, some how, though what makes me think it was one or the other is because I remember the big flume wasn't finished when he first come to the camp; but anyway, he was the curiosest man about always betting on anything that turned up you ever see, if he could get anybody to bet on the other side, and if he couldn't he'd change sides—any way that suited the other man would suit *him*—any way just so's he got a bet, *he* was satisfied. But still, he was lucky—uncommon lucky; he most always come out winner. He was always ready and laying for a chance; there couldn't be no solitry thing mentioned but what that feller'd offer to bet on it—and take any side you please, as I was just telling you: if there was a horse race, you'd find him flush or you find him busted at the end of it; if there was a dog-fight, he'd bet on it; if there was a cat-fight, he'd bet on it; if there was a chicken-fight, he'd bet on it; why if there was two birds setting on a fence, he would bet you which one would fly first—or if there was a camp-meeting he would be there reglar to bet on parson Walker, which he judged to be the best exhorter about here, and so he was, too, and a good man; if he even see a straddle-bug start to go any wheres, he would bet you how long it would take him to get wherever he was going to, and if you took him up he would foller that strad-dle-bug to Mexico but what he would find out where he was bound for and how long he was on the road. Lots of the boys here has seen that Smiley and can tell you about him. Why, it never made no difference to *him*—he would bet on *anything*—the dangdest feller. Parson Walker's wife laid very sick, once, for a good while, and it seemed as if they warn't going to save her; but one morning he come in and Smiley asked him how she was, and he said she was considerable better—thank the Lord for his inf'nit mercy—and coming on so smart that with the blessing of Providence she'd get well yet—and Smiley, before he thought, says, "Well, I'll resk two-and-a-half that she don't, anyway."

Thish-yer Smiley had a mare—the boys called her the fifteen-minute nag, but that was only in fun, you know, because, of course, she was faster than that—and he used to win money on that horse, for all she was so slow and always had the asthma, or the distemper, or the consumption, or some-thing of that kind. They used to give her two or three hundred yards' start, and then pass her under way; but always at the fag-end of the race she'd get excited and desperate-like, and come cavorting and spraddling up, and scat-tering her legs around limber, sometimes in the air, and sometimes out to one side amongst the fences, and kicking up m-o-r-e dust, and raising m-o-r-e racket with her coughing and sneezing and blowing her nose—and always fetch up at the stand just about a neck ahead, as near as you could cipher it down.

And he had a little small bull-pup, that to look at him you'd think he warn't worth a cent, but to set around and look ornery, and lay for a chance to steal something. But as soon as money was up on him he was a different dog—his under-jaw'd begin to stick out like the for'castle of a steamboat, and his teeth would uncover, and shine savage like the furnaces. And a dog might tackle him, and bully-rag him, and bite him, and throw him over his shoulder two or three times, and Andrew Jackson—which was the name of the pup—Andrew Jackson would never let on but what he was satisfied, and hadn't expected nothing else—and the bets being doubled and doubled on the other side all the time, till the money was all up—and then all of a sudden he would grab that other dog just by the joint of his hind legs and freeze to it—not chaw, you understand, but only just grip and hang on till they throwed up the sponge, if it was a year. Smiley always came out winner on that pup till he harnessed a dog once that didn't have no hind legs, because they'd been sawed off in a circular saw, and when the thing had gone along far enough, and the money was all up, and he came to make a snatch for his pet holt, he saw in a minute how he'd been imposed on, and how the other dog had him in the door, so to speak, and he 'peared sur-prised, and then he looked sorter discouraged like, and didn't try no more to win the fight, and so he got shucked out bad. He gave Smiley a look as much as to say his heart was broke, and it was *his* fault, for putting up a dog that hadn't no hind legs for him to take holt of, which was his main depen-dence in a fight, and then he limped off a piece, and laid down and died. It was a good pup, was that Andrew Jackson, and would have made a name for hisself if he'd lived, for the stuff was in him, and he had genius—I know it, because he hadn't had no opportunities to speak of, and it don't stand to reason that a dog could make such a fight as he could under them circumstances, if he hadn't no talent. It always makes me feel sorry when I think of that last fight of his'on, and the way it turned out.

Well, thish-yer Smiley had rat-terriers and chicken cocks, and tom-cats, and all them kind of things, till you couldn't rest, and you couldn't fetch nothing for him to bet on but he'd match you. He ketched a frog one day and took him home and said he cal'lated to educate him; and so he never done nothing for three months but set in his back yard and learn that frog to jump. And you bet you he *did* learn him, too. He'd give him a little hunch behind, and the next minute you'd see that frog whirling in the air like a doughnut—see him turn one summerset, or maybe a couple, if he got a good start, and come down flat-footed and all right, like a cat. He got him up so in the matter of ketching flies, and kept him in practice so constant, that he'd nail a fly every time as far as he could see him. Smiley said all a frog wanted was education, and he could do most anything—and I believe him. Why, I've seen him set Dan'l Webster down here on this floor—Dan'l Webster was the name of the frog—and sing out, "Flies! Dan'l, flies," and quicker'n you could wink, he'd spring straight up, and snake a fly off'n the counter there, and flop down on the floor again as solid as a gob of mud, and fall to scratching the side of his head with his hind foot as indifferent as if he hadn't no idea he'd done any more'n any frog might do. You never see a frog so modest and straightfor'ard as he was, for all he was so gifted. And when it come to fair-and-square jumping on a dead level, he could get over more ground at one straddle than any animal of his breed you ever see. Jumping on a dead level was his strong suit, you understand, and when it come to that, Smiley would ante up money on him as long as he had a red. Smiley was monstrous proud of his frog, and well he might be, for fellers that had travelled and ben everywheres all said he laid over any frog that ever *they* see.

Well, Smiley kept the beast in a little lattice box, and he used to fetch him down town sometimes and lay for a bet. One day a feller—a stranger in the camp, he was—come across him with his box, and says:

"What might it be that you've got in the box?"

And Smiley says, sorter indifferent like, "It might be a parrot, or it might be a canary, maybe, but it ain't—it's only just a frog."

And the feller took it, and looked at it careful, and turned it round this way and that, and says, "H'm—so 'tis. Well, what's *he* good for?"

"Well," Smiley says, easy and careless, "He's good enough for *one* thing I should judge—he can out-jump ary frog in Calaveras county."

The feller took the box again, and took another long, particular look, and give it back to Smiley and says, very deliberate, "Well—I don't see no points about that frog that's any better'n any other frog."

"Maybe you don't," Smiley says. "Maybe you understand frogs, and maybe you don't understand 'em; maybe you've had experience, and maybe you ain't only a amature, as it were. Anyways, I've got *my* opinion, and I'll resk forty dollars that he can outjump ary frog in Calaveras county."

And the feller studied a minute, and then says, kinder sad, like, "Well—I'm only a stranger here, and I ain't got no frog—but if I had a frog I'd bet you."

And then Smiley says, "That's all right—that's all right—if you'll hold my box a minute I'll go and get you a frog;" and so the feller took the box, and put up his forty dollars along with Smiley's, and set down to wait.

So he set there a good while thinking and thinking to hisself, and then he got the frog out and prized his mouth open and took a teaspoon and filled him full of quail-shot—filled him pretty near up to his chin—and set him on the floor. Smiley he went out to the swamp and slopped around in the mud for a long time, and finally he ketched a frog and fetched him in and give him to this feller and says:

"Now if you're ready, set him alongside of Dan'l, with his fore-paws just even with Dan'ls, and I'll give the word." Then he says, "one—two—three—jump!" and him and the feller touched up the frogs from behind, and the new frog hopped off lively, but Dan'l give a heave, and hysted up his shoulders—so—like a Frenchman, but it wasn't no use—he couldn't budge; he was planted as solid as a anvil, and he couldn't no more stir than if he was anchored out. Smiley was a good deal surprised, and he was disgusted too, but he didn't have no idea what the matter was, of course.

The feller took the money and started away, and when he was going out at the door he sorter jerked his thumb over his shoulder—this way—at Dan'l, and says again, very deliberate, "Well—*I* don't see no points about that frog that's any better'n any other frog."

Smiley he stood scratching his head and looking down at Dan'l a long time, and at last he says, "I do wonder what in the nation that frog throwed off for—I wonder if there ain't something the matter with him—he 'pears to look mighty baggy, somehow"—and he ketched Dan'l by the nap of the neck, and lifted him up and says, "Why blame my cats if he don't weigh five pound"—and turned him upside down, and he belched out about a double-handful of shot. And then he see how it was, and he was the maddest man—he set the frog down and took out after that feller, but he never ketched him. And——

[Here Simon Wheeler heard his name called from the front-yard, and got up to go and see what was wanted.] And turning to me as he moved away, he said: "Just sit where you are, stranger, and rest easy—I ain't going to be gone a second."

But by your leave, I did not think that a continuation of the history of the enterprising vagabond Jim Smiley would be likely to afford me much information concerning the Rev. Leonidas W. Smiley, and so I started away.

At the door I met the sociable Wheeler returning, and he buttonholed me and recommenced:

"Well, thish-yer Smiley had a yaller one-eyed cow that didn't have no tail only just a short stump like a bannanner and——"

"O, curse Smiley and his afflicted cow!" I muttered, good-naturedly, and bidding the old gentleman good-day, I departed.

Yours, truly

Mark Twain

1865

from **Roughing It**

Buck Fanshaw's Funeral[1]

Somebody has said that in order to know a community, one must observe the style of its funerals and know what manner of men they bury with most ceremony. I cannot say which class we buried with most eclat in our "flush times," the distinguished public benefactor or the distinguished rough—possibly the two chief grades or grand division of society honored their illustrious dead about equally; and hence, no doubt the philosopher I have quoted from would have needed to see two representative funerals in Virginia before forming his estimate of the people.

There was a grand time over Buck Fanshaw when he died. He was a representative citizen. He had "killed his man"—not in his own quarrel, it is true, but in defence of a stranger unfairly beset by numbers. He had kept a sumptuous saloon. He had been the proprietor of a dashing helpmeet whom he could have discarded without the formality of a divorce. He had held a high position in the fire department and been a very Warwick in politics. When he died there was great lamentation throughout the town, but especially in the vast bottom-stratum of society.

On the inquest it was shown that Buck Fanshaw, in the delirium of a wasting typhoid fever, had taken arsenic, shot himself through the body, cut his throat, and jumped out a four-story window and broken his neck—and after due deliberation, the jury, sad and tearful, but with intelligence unblinded by its sorrow, brought in a verdict of death "by the visitation of God." What could the world do without juries?

Prodigious preparations were made for the funeral. All the vehicles in town were hired, all the saloons put in mourning, all the municipal and fire-company flags hung at half-mast, and all the firemen ordered to muster in uniform and bring their machines duly draped in black. Now—let us remark

---

[1]*Roughing It*, Mark Twain's second travel narrative, recalls his western adventures. In this selection, we see Twain's delight in language play, his ear not only for dialects from particular geographical areas, but also for dialects peculiar to specific classes and professions.

in parenthesis—as all the peoples of the earth had representative adventurers in the Silverland, and as each adventurer had brought the slang of his nation or his locality with him, the combination made the slang of Nevada the richest and the most infinitely varied and copious that had ever existed anywhere in the world, perhaps, except in the mines of California in the "early days." Slang was the language of Nevada. It was hard to preach a sermon without it, and be understood. Such phrases as "You bet!" "Oh, no, I reckon not!" "No Irish need apply," and a hundred others, became so common as to fall from the lips of a speaker unconsciously—and very often when they did not touch the subject under discussion and consequently failed to mean anything.

After Buck Fanshaw's inquest, a meeting of the short-haired brotherhood was held, for nothing can be done on the Pacific coast without a public meeting and an expression of sentiment. Regretful resolutions were passed and various committees appointed; among others, a committee of one was deputed to call on the minister, a fragile, gentle, spirituel new fledgling from an Eastern theological seminary, and as yet unacquainted with the ways of the mines. The committeeman, "Scotty" Briggs, made his visit; and in after days it was worth something to hear the minister tell about it. Scotty was a stalwart rough, whose customary suit, when on weighty official business, like committee work, was a fire helmet, flamming red flannel shirt, patent leather belt with spanner and revolver attached, coat hung over arm, and pants stuffed into boot tops. He formed something of a contrast to the pale theological student. It is fair to say of Scotty, however, in passing, that he had a warm heart, and a strong love for his friends, and never entered into a quarrel when he could reasonably keep out of it. Indeed, it was commonly said that whenever one of Scotty's fights was investigated, it always turned out that it had originally been no affair of his, but that out of native goodheartedness he had dropped in of his own accord to help the man who was getting the worst of it. He and Buck Fanshaw were bosom friends, for years, and had often taken adventurous "pot-luck" together. On one occasion, they had thrown off their coats and taken the weaker side in a fight among strangers, and after gaining a hard-earned victory, turned and found that the men they were helping had deserted early, and not only that, but had stolen their coats and made off with them! But to return to Scotty's visit to the minister. He was on a sorrowful mission, now, and his face was the picture of woe. Being admitted to the presence he sat down before the clergyman, placed his fire-hat on an unfinished manuscript sermon under the minister's nose, took from it a red silk handkerchief, wiped his brow and heaved a sigh of dismal impressiveness, explanatory of his business. He choked, and even shed tears; but with an effort he mastered his voice and said in lugubrious tones:

"Are you the duck that runs the gospel-mill next door?"

"Am I the—pardon me, I believe I do not understand?"

With another sigh and a half-sob, Scotty rejoined:

"Why you see we are in a bit of trouble, and the boys thought maybe you would give us a lift, if we'd tackle you—that is, if I've got the rights of it and you are the head clerk of the doxology-works next door."

"I am the shepherd in charge of the flock whose fold is next door."

"The which?"

"The spiritual adviser of the little company of believers whose sanctuary adjoins these premises."

Scotty scratched his head, reflected a moment, and then said:

"You ruther hold over me, pard. I reckon I can't call that hand. Ante and pass the buck."

"How? I beg pardon. What did I understand you to say?"

"Well, you've ruther got the bulge on me. Or maybe we've both got the bulge, somehow. You don't smoke me and I don't smoke you. You see, one of the boys has passed in his checks and we want to give him a good send-off, and so the thing I'm on now is to roust out somebody to jerk a little chin-music for us and waltz him through handsome."

"My friend, I seem to grow more bewildered. Your observations are wholly incomprehensible to me. Cannot you simplify them in some way? At first I thought perhaps I understood you, but I grope now. Would it not expedite matters if you restricted yourself to categorical statements of fact unencumbered with obstructing accumulations of metaphor and allegory?"

Another pause, and more reflection. Then, said Scotty:

"I'll have to pass, I judge."

"How?"

"You've raised me out, pard."

"I still fail to catch your meaning."

"Why, that last lead of yourn is too many for me—that's the idea. I can't neither trump nor follow suit."

The clergyman sank back in his chair perplexed. Scotty leaned his head on his hand and gave himself up to thought. Presently his face came up, sorrowful but confident.

"I've got it now, so's you can savvy," he said. "What we want is a gospel-sharp. See?"

"A what?"

"Gospel-sharp. Parson."

"Oh! Why did you not say so before? I am a clergyman—a parson."

"Now you talk! You see my blind and straddle it like a man. Put it there!"—extending a brawny paw, which closed over the minister's small hand and gave it a shake indicative of fraternal sympathy and fervent gratification.

"Now we're all right, pard. Let's start fresh. Don't you mind my snuffling a little—becuz we're in the power of trouble. You see, one of the boys has gone up the flume—"

"Gone where?"

"Up the flume—throwed up the sponge, you understand."

"Thrown up the sponge?"

"Yes—kicked the bucket—"

"Ah—has departed to that mysterious country from whose bourne no traveler returns."

"Return! I reckon not. Why pard, he's *dead*!"

"Yes, I understand."

"Oh, you do? Well I thought maybe you might be getting tangled some more. Yes, you see he's dead again—"

"*Again?* Why, has he ever been dead before?"

"Dead before? No! Do you reckon a man has got as many lives as a cat? But you bet you he's awful dead now, poor old boy, and I wish I'd never seen this day. I don't want no better friend than Buck Fanshaw. I knowed him by the back; and when I know a man and like him, I freeze to him—you hear *me*. Take him all round, pard, there never was a bullier man in the mines. No man ever knowed Buck Fanshaw to go back on a friend. But it's all up, you know, it's all up. It ain't no use. They've scooped him."

"Scooped him?"

"Yes—death has. Well, well, well, we've got to give him up. Yes indeed. It's a kind of hard world, after all, *ain't* it! But pard, he was a rustler! You ought to seen him get started once. He was a bully boy with a glass eye! Just spit in his face and give him room according to his strength, and it was just beautiful to see him peel and go in. He was the worst son of a thief that ever drawed breath. Pard, he was *on* it! He was on it bigger than an Injun!"

"On it? On what?"

"On the shoot. On the shoulder. On the fight, you understand. *He* didn't give a continental for *any*body. *Beg* your pardon, friend, for coming so near saying a cuss-word—but you see I'm on an awful strain, in this palaver, on account of having to cramp down and draw everything so mild. But we've got to give him up. There ain't any getting around that, I don't reckon. Now if we can get you to help plant him—"

"Preach the funeral discourse? Assist at the obsequies?"

"Obs'quies is good. Yes. That's it—that's our little game. We are going to get the thing up regardless, you know. He was always nifty himself, and so you bet you his funeral ain't going to be no slouch—solid silver door-plate on his coffin, six plumes on the hearse, and a nigger on the box in a biled shirt and a plug hat—how's that for high? And we'll take care of *you*, pard. We'll fix you all right. There'll be a kerridge for you; and whatever you want, you just 'scape out and we'll 'tend to it. We've got a shebang fixed up for you to stand behind, in No. 1's house, and don't you be afraid. Just go in and toot your horn, if you don't sell a clam. Put Buck through as bully as you can, pard, for anybody that knowed him will tell you that he was one of the whitest men that was ever in the mines. You can't draw it too strong. He never could stand it to see things going wrong. He's done more to make this town quiet and peaceable than any man in it. I've seen him lick four Greasers in eleven minutes, myself. If a thing wanted regulating, *he* warn't a man to go browsing around after somebody to do it, but he would prance in and regulate it himself. He warn't a Catholic. Scasely. He was down on 'em.

His word was, 'No Irish need apply!' But it didn't make no difference about that when it came down to what a man's rights was—and so, when some roughs jumped the Catholic bone-yard and started in to stake out town-lots in it he *went* for 'em! And he *cleaned* 'em, too! I was there, pard, and I seen it myself."

"That was very well indeed—at least the impulse was—whether the act was strictly defensible or not. Had deceased any religious convictions? That is to say, did he feel a dependence upon, or acknowledge allegiance to a higher power?"

More reflection.

"I reckon you've stumped me again, pard. Could you say it over once more, and say it slow?"

"Well, to simplify it somewhat, was he, or rather had he ever been connected with any organization sequestered from secular concerns and devoted to self-sacrifice in the interests of morality?"

"All down but nine—set 'em up on the other alley, pard."

"What did I understand you to say?"

"Why, you're most too many for me, you know. When you get in with your left I hunt grass every time. Every time you draw, you fill; but I don't seem to have any luck. Lets have a new deal."

"How? Begin again?"

"That's it."

"Very well. Was he a good man, and—"

"There—I see that; don't put up another chip till I look at my hand. A good man, says you? Pard, it ain't no name for it. He was the best man that ever—pard, you would have doted on that man. He could lam any galoot of his inches in America. It was him that put down the riot last election before it got a start; and everybody said he was the only man that could have done it. He waltzed in with a spanner in one hand and a trumpet in the other, and sent fourteen men home on a shutter in less than three minutes. He had that riot all broke up and prevented nice before anybody ever got a chance to strike a blow. He was always for peace, and he would *have* peace—he could not stand disturbances. Pard, he was a great loss to this town. It would please the boys if you could chip in something like that and do him justice. Here once when the Micks got to throwing stones through the Methodis' Sunday school windows, Buck Fanshaw, all of his own notion, shut up his saloon and took a couple of six-shooters and mounted guard over the Sunday school. Says he, 'No Irish need apply!' And they didn't. He was the bulliest man in the mountains, pard! He could run faster, jump higher, hit harder, and hold more tangle-foot whisky without spilling it than any man in seventeen counties. Put that in, pard—it'll please the boys more than anything you could say. And you can say, pard, that he never shook his mother."

"Never shook his mother?"

"That's it—any of the boys will tell you so."

"Well, but why *should* he shake her?"

"That's what *I* say—but some people does."

"Not people of any repute?"

"Well, some that averages pretty so-so."

"In my opinion the man that would offer personal violence to his own mother, ought to—"

"Cheese it, pard; you've banked your ball clean outside the string. What I was a drivin' at, was, that he never *throwed off* on his mother—don't you see? No indeedy. He give her a house to live in, and town lots, and plenty of money; and he looked after her and took care of her all the time; and when she was down with the small-pox I'm d—d if he didn't set up nights and nuss her himself! *Beg* your pardon for saying it, but it hopped out too quick for yours truly. You've treated me like a gentleman, pard, and I ain't the man to hurt your feelings intentional. I think you're white. I think you're a square man, pard. I like you, and I'll lick any man that don't. I'll lick him till he can't tell himself from a last year's corpse! Put it *there*!" [Another fraternal handshake—and exit.]

The obsequies were all that "the boys" could desire. Such a marvel of funeral pomp had never been seen in Virginia. The plumed hearse, the dirge-breathing brass bands, the closed marts of business, the flags drooping at half mast, the long, plodding procession of uniformed secret societies, military battalions and fire companies, draped engines, carriages of officials, and citizens in vehicles and on foot, attracted multitudes of spectators to the sidewalks, roofs and windows; and for years afterward, the degree of grandeur attained by any civic display in Virginia was determined by comparison with Buck Fanshaw's funeral.

Scotty Briggs, as a pall-bearer and a mourner, occupied a prominent place at the funeral, and when the sermon was finished and the last sentence of the prayer for the dead man's soul ascended, he responded, in a low voice, but with feeling:

"AMEN. No Irish need apply."

As the bulk of the response was without apparent relevancy, it was probably nothing more than a humble tribute to the memory of the friend that was gone; for, as Scotty had once said, it was "his word."

Scotty Briggs, in after days, achieved the distinction of becoming the only convert to religion that was ever gathered from the Virginia roughs; and it transpired that the man who had it in him to espouse the quarrel of the weak out of inborn nobility of spirit was no mean timber whereof to construct a Christian. The making him one did not warp his generosity or diminish his courage; on the contrary it gave intelligent direction to the one and a broader field to the other. If his Sunday school class progressed faster than the other classes, was it matter for wonder? I think not. He talked to his pioneer small-fry in a language they understood! It was my large privilege, a month before he died, to hear him tell the beautiful story of Joseph and his brethren to his class "without looking at the book." I leave it to the reader to fancy what it was like, as it fell, riddled with slang, from the lips of that grave, earnest teacher, and was listened to by his little learners with a consuming interest that showed that they were as unconscious as he was that any violence was being done to the sacred proprieties!

1865

A True Story[1]

Repeated Word for Word as I Heard It

It was summer-time, and twilight. We were sitting on the porch of the farm-house, on the summit of the hill, and "Aunt Rachel" was sitting respectfully below our level, on the steps—for she was our servant, and colored. She was a mighty frame and stature; she was sixty years old, but her eye was undimmed and her strength unabated. She was a cheerful, hearty soul, and it was no more trouble for her to laugh than it is for a bird to sing. She was under fire now, as usual when the day was done. That is to say, she was being chaffed without mercy, and was enjoying it. She would let off peal after peal of laughter, and then sit with her face in her hands and shake with throes of enjoyment which she could no longer get breath enough to express. At such a moment as this a thought occurred to me, and I said:

"Aunt Rachel, how is it that you've lived sixty years and never had any trouble?"

She stopped quaking. She paused, and there was a moment of silence. She turned her face over her shoulder toward me, and said, without even a smile in her voice:

"Misto C—, is you in 'arnest?"

It surprised me a good deal; and it sobered my manner and my speech, too. I said:

"Why, I thought—that is, I meant—why, you *can't* have had any trouble. I've never heard you sigh, and never seen your eye when there wasn't a laugh in it."

She faced fairly around now, and was full of earnestness.

"Has I had any trouble? Misto C—, I's gwyne to tell you, den I leave it to you. I was bawn down 'mongst de slaves; I knows all 'bout slavery, 'case I ben one of 'em my own se'f. Well, sah, my ole man—dat's my husban'—he was lovin' an kind to me, jist as kind as you is to yo' own wife. An' we had chil'en—seven chil'en—an' we loved dem chil'en just de same as you loves yo' chil'en. Dey was black, but de Lord can't make no chil'en so black but what dey mother loves 'em an' wouldn't give 'em up, no, not for anything dat's in dis whole world.

[1]This was the first piece that Mark Twain published in the *Atlantic Monthly*. It records the painful experiences of the cook at Quarry Farm in Elmira, New York, where the Clemenses summered. According to the author's letter to W. D. Howells, the editor and soon to become his close friend, it was reproduced as he heard it from "Auntie Cord" in the summer of 1874, "not altered, except to begin at the beginning, instead of the middle, as she did—and travelled both ways." [Note by Everett Emerson.]

"Well, sah, I was raised in ole Fo'ginny, but my mother she was raised in Maryland; an' my *souls*! she was turrible when she'd git started! My *lan'*! but she'd make de fur fly! When she'd git into dem tantrums, she always had one word dat she said. She'd straighten herse'f up an' put her fists in her hips an' say, 'I want you to understan' dat I wa'n't bawn in the mash to be fool' by trash! I's one o' de ole Blue Hen's Chickens, I is!' 'ca'se, you see, dat's what folks dat's bawn in Maryland calls deyselves, an' dey's proud of it. Well, dat was her word. I don't ever forgit it, beca'se she said it so much, an' beca'se she said it one day when my little Henry tore his wris' awful, and most busted his head, right up at de top of his forehead, an' de niggers didn't fly aroun' fas' enough to 'tend to him. An' when dey talk' back at her, she up an' she says, 'Look-a-heah!' she says, 'I want you niggers to understan' dat I wa'n't bawn in de mash to be fool' by trash! I's one o' de ole Blue Hen's Chickens, *I* is!' an' den she clar' dat kitchen an' bandage' up de chile herse'f. So I says dat word, too, when I's riled.

"Well, bymeby my ole mistis say she's broke, an' she got to sell all de niggers on de place. An' when I heah dat dey gwyne to sell us all off at oction in Richmon', oh, de good gracious! I know what dat mean!"

Aunt Rachel had gradually risen, while she warmed to her subject, and now she towered above us, black against the stars.

"Dey put chains on us an' put us on a stan' as high as dis po'ch—twenty foot high—an' all de people stood aroun', crowds an' crowds. An' dey'd come up dah an' look at us all roun', an' squeeze our arm, an' make us git up an' walk, an' den say, 'Dis one too ole,' or 'Dis one lame,' or 'Dis one don't 'mount to much.' An' dey sole my ole man, an' took him away, an' dey begin to sell my chil'en an' take *dem* away, an' I begin to cry; an' de man say, 'Shet up yo' damn blubberin',' an' hit me on de mouf wid his han'. An' when de las' one was gone but my little Henry, I grab' *him* clost up to my breas' so, an' I ris up an' says, 'You sha'n't take him away,' I says; 'I'll kill de man dat tetches him!' I says. But my little Henry whisper an' say, 'I gwyne to run away, an' den I work an' buy yo' freedom.' Oh, bless de chile, he always so good! But dey got him—dey got him, de men did; but I took and tear de clo'es mos' off of 'em an' beat 'em over de head wid my chain; an' *dey* give it to *me*, too, but I didn't mine dat.

"Well, dah was my ole man gone, an' all my chil'en, all my seven chi-l'en—an' six of 'em I hain't set eyes on ag'in to this day, an' dat's twenty-two years ago las' Easter. De man dat bought me b'long' in Newbern, an' he took me dah. Well, bymeby de years roll on an' de waw come. My marster he was a Confedrit colonel, an' I was his family's cook. So when de Unions took dat town, dey all run away an' lef' me all by myse'f wid de other niggers in dat mons'us big house. So de big Union officers move in dah, an' dey ask me would I cook for *dem*. 'Lord bless you,' says I, 'dat's what I's *for*.'

"Dey wa'n't no small-fry officers, mine you, dey was de biggest dey *is*; an' de way dey made dem sojers mosey roun'! De Gen'l he tole me to boss dat kitchen; an' he say, 'If anybody come meddlin' wid you, you just make 'em walk chalk; don't you be afeared,' he say; 'you's 'mong frens now.'

"Well, I thinks to myse'f, if my little Henry ever got a chance to run away, he'd make to de Norf, o' course. So one day I comes in dah whar de big officers was, in de parlor, an' I drops a kurtchy, so, an' I up an' tole 'em 'bout my Henry, dey a-listenin' to my troubles jist de same as if I was white folks; an' I says, 'What I come for is beca'se if he got away and got up Norf whar you gemmen comes from, you might 'a' seen him, maybe, an' could tell me so as I could fine him ag'in; he was very little, an' he had a sk-yar on his lef' wris' an' at de top of his forehead.' Den dey look mournful, an' de Gen'l says, 'How long sence you los' him?' an' I say, 'Thirteen year.' Den de Gen'l say, 'He wouldn't be little no mo' now—he's a man!'

"I never thought o' dat befo'! He was only dat little feller to *me* yit. I never thought 'bout him growin' up an' bein' big. But I see it den. None o' de gemmen had run acrost him, so dey couldn't do nothin' for me. But all dat time, do' *I* didn't know it, my Henry *was* run off to de Norf, years an' years, an' he was a barber, too, an' worked for hisse'f. An' bymeby, when de waw come he ups an' he says: 'I's done barberin',' he says, 'I's gwyne to fine my ole mammy, less'n she's dead.' So he sole out an' went to whar dey was recruitin', an' hired hisse'f out to de colonel for his servant; an' den he went all froo de battles everywhah, huntin' for his ole mammy; yes, indeedy, he'd hire to fust one officer an' den another, tell he'd ransacked de whole Souf; but you see *I* didn't know nuffin 'bout *dis*. How was *I* gwyne to know it?

"Well, one night we had a big sojer ball; de sojers dah at Newbern was always havin' balls an' carryin' on. Dey had 'em in my kitchen, heaps o' times, 'ca'se it was so big. Mine you, I was *down* on sich doin's; beca'se my place was wid de officers, an' it rasp me to have dem common sojers cavortin' roun' my kitchen like dat. But I alway' stood aroun' an' kep' things straight, I did; an' sometimes dey'd git my dander up, an' den I'd make 'em clar dat kitchen, mine I *tell* you!

"Well, one night—it was a Friday night—dey comes a whole platoon f'm a *nigger* ridgment dat was on guard at de house—de house was headquarters, you know—an' den I was just a-*bilin*'! Mad? I was just a-*boomin*'! I swelled aroun', an' swelled aroun'; I just was a-itchin' for 'em to do somefin for to start me. An' dey was awaltzin' an' a-dancin'! *my*! but dey was havin' a time! an' I jist a-swellin' an' aswellin' up! Pooty soon, 'long comes *sich* a spruce young nigger a-sailin' down de room wid a yaller wench roun' de wais'; an' roun' an' roun' an' roun' dey went, enough to make a body drunk to look at 'em; an' when dey got abreas' o' me, dey went to kin' o' balancin' aroun' fust on one leg an' den on t'other, an' smilin' at my big red turban, an' makin' fun, an' I ups an' says '*Git* along wid you!—rubbage!' De young man's face kin' o' changed, all of a sudden, for 'bout a second, but den he went to smilin' ag'in, same as he was befo'. Well, 'bout dis time, in comes some niggers dat played music and b'long to de ban', an' dey *never* could git along widout puttin' on airs. An' de very fust air dey put on dat night, I lit into 'em! Dey laughed, an' dat made me wuss. De res' o' de niggers got to laughin', an' den my soul *alive* but I was hot! My eye was just ablazin'! I jist straightened myself up so—jist as I is now, plum to de ceilin' mos'—an' I digs my fists into my hips, an' I says, 'Look-a-heah!' I says, 'I want you niggers to understan' dat I wa'n't bawn in de mash to be fool' by trash! I's one o' de ole Blue Hen's Chickens, *I* is!' an' den I see dat young man stan' a-starin' an' stiff, lookin' kin' o' up at de ceilin' like he fo'got somefin, an' couldn't 'member it no mo'. Well, I jist march' on dem niggers—so lookin' like a gen'l—an' dey jist cave' away befo' me an' out at de do'. An as dis young man was a-goin' out, I heah him say to another nigger, 'Jim,' he says, 'you go 'long an' tell de cap'n I be on han' 'bout eight o'clock in de mawnin'; dey's somefin on my mine,' he says; 'I don't sleep no mo' dis night. You go 'long,' he says, 'an' leave me by my own se'f.'

"Dis was 'bout one o'clock in de mawnin'. Well, 'bout seven, I was up an' on han', gittin' de officers' breakfast. I was a-stoppin' down by de stove—just so, same as if yo' foot was de stove—an' I'd opened de stove do' wid my right han'—so, pushin' it back, just as I pushes yo' foot—an' I'd jist got de pan o' hot biscuits in my han' an' was 'bout to raise up, when I see a black face come aroun' under mine, an' de eyes alookin' up into mine, just as I's a-lookin' up close under yo' face now; an' I just stopped *right dah*, an' never budged! jist gazed an' gazed so; an' de pan begin to tremble, an' all of a sudden I *knowed*! De pan drop' on de flo' an' I grab his lef han' an' shove back his sleeve—jist so, as I's doin' to you—an' den I goes for his forehead an' push de hair back so, an' 'Boy!' I says, 'if you ain't my Henry, what is you doin' wid dis welt on yo' wris' an' dat sk-yar on yo' forehead? De Lord God ob heaven be praise', I got my own ag'in!'

"Oh no, Misto C—, *I* hain't had no trouble. An' no *joy*!"

1874

The Man That Corrupted Hadleyburg[1]

I

It was many years ago. Hadleyburg was the most honest and upright town in all the region round about it. It had kept that reputation unsmirched during three generations, and was prouder of it than of any other of its possessions. It was so proud of it, and so anxious to insure its perpetuation, that it began to teach the principles of honest dealing to its babies in the cradle, and made the like teachings the staple of their culture thenceforward through all the years devoted to their education. Also, throughout the formative years temptations were kept out of the way of the young people, so that their honesty could have every chance to harden and solidify, and became a part of their very bone. The neighboring towns were jealous of this honorable supremacy and affected to sneer at Hadleyburg's pride in it and

[1]"Hadleyburg," written while the Clemens family was living in Austria in 1898, was one of the few short stories that Mark Twain wrote that was not connected to a larger, framing narrative. "Hadleyburg" engages questions of moral agency, determinism, character stereotyping, and plot that Twain had been playing with for much of his professional life.

call it vanity; but all the same they were obliged to acknowledge that Hadleyburg was in reality an incorruptible town; and if pressed they would also acknowledge that the mere fact that a young man hailed from Hadleyburg was all the recommendation he needed when he went forth from his natal town to seek for responsible employment.

But at last, in the drift of time, Hadleyburg had the ill luck to offend a passing stranger—possibly without knowing it, certainly without caring, for Hadleyburg was sufficient unto itself, and cared not a rap for strangers or their opinions. Still, it would have been well to make an exception in this one's case, for he was a bitter man and revengeful. All through his wanderings during a whole year he kept his injury in mind, and gave all his leisure moments to trying to invent a compensating satisfaction for it. He contrived many plans, and all of them were good, but none of them was quite sweeping enough; the poorest of them would hurt a great many individuals, but what he wanted was a plan which would comprehend the entire town, and not let so much as one person escape unhurt. At last he had a fortunate idea, and when it fell into his brain it lit up his whole head with an evil joy. He began to form a plan at once, saying to himself, "That is the thing to do—I will corrupt the town."

Six months later he went to Hadleyburg, and arrived in a buggy at the house of the old cashier of the bank about ten at night. He got a sack out of the buggy, shouldered it, and staggered with it through the cottage yard, and knocked at the door. A woman's voice said "Come in," and he entered, and set his sack behind the stove in the parlor, saying politely to the old lady who sat reading the *Missionary Herald* by the lamp:

"Pray keep your seat, madam, I will not disturb you. There—now it is pretty well concealed; one would hardly know it was there. Can I see your husband a moment, madam?"

No, he was gone to Brixton, and might not return before morning.

"Very well, madam, it is no matter. I merely wanted to leave that sack in his care, to be delivered to the rightful owner when he shall be found. I am a stranger; he does not know me; I am merely passing through the town tonight to discharge a matter which has been long in my mind. My errand is now completed, and I go pleased and a little proud, and you will never see me again. There is a paper attached to the sack which will explain everything. Goodnight, madam."

The old lady was afraid of the mysterious big stranger, and was glad to see him go. But her curiosity was roused, and she went straight to the sack and brought away the paper. It began as follows:

"TO BE PUBLISHED; or, the right man sought out by private inquiry— either will answer. This sack contains gold coin weighing a hundred and sixty pounds four ounces—"

* * *

"Mercy on us, and the door is not locked!"

Mrs. Richards flew to it all in a tremble and locked it, then pulled down the window-shades and stood frightened, worried, and wondering if there was anything else she could do toward making herself and the money more safe. She listened awhile for burglars, then surrendered to curiosity and went back to the lamp and finished reading the paper:

"I am a foreigner, and am presently going back to my own country, to remain there permanently. I am grateful to America for what I have received at her hands during my long stay under her flag; and to one of her citizens—a citizen of Hadleyburg—I am especially grateful for a great kindness done me a year or two ago. Two great kindnesses, in fact. I will explain. I was a gambler. I say I WAS. I was a ruined gambler. I arrived in this village at night, hungry and without a penny. I asked for help—in the dark; I was ashamed to beg in the light. I begged of the right man. He gave me twenty dollars— that is to say, he gave me life, as I considered it. He also gave me fortune; for out of that money I have made myself rich at the gaming-table. And finally, a remark which he made to me has remained with me to this day, and has at last conquered me; and in conquering has saved the remnant of my morals: I shall gamble no more. Now I have no idea who that man was, but I want him found, and I want him to have this money, to give away, throw away, or keep, as he pleases. It is merely my way of testifying my gratitude to him. If I could stay, I would find him myself; but no matter, he will be found. This is an honest town, an incorruptible town, and I know I can trust it without fear. This man can be identified by the remark which he made to me; I feel persuaded that he will remember it.

"And now my plan is this: If you prefer to conduct the inquiry privately, do so. Tell the contents of this present writing to any one who is likely to be the right man. If he shall answer, 'I am the man; the remark I made was so-and-so,' apply the test—to wit: open the sack, and in it you will find a sealed envelope containing that remark. If the remark mentioned by the candidate tallies with it, give him the money, and ask no further questions, for he is certainly the right man.

"But if you shall prefer a public inquiry, then publish this present writing in the local paper—with these instructions added, to wit: Thirty days from now, let the candidate appear at the town-hall at eight in the evening (Friday), and hand his remark, in a sealed envelope, to the Rev. Mr. Burgess (if he will be kind enough to act): and let Mr. Burgess there and then destroy the seals of the sack, open it, and see if the remark is correct; if correct, let the money be delivered, with my sincere gratitude, to my benefactor thus identified."

Mrs. Richards sat down, gently quivering with excitement, and was soon lost in thinkings—after this pattern: "What a strange thing it is! . . . And what a fortune for that kind man who set his bread afloat upon the waters! . . . If it had only been my husband that did it!—for we are so poor, so old and poor! . . ." Then, with a sigh—"But it was not my Edward; no, it was not he that gave a stranger twenty dollars. It is a pity too; I see it now. . . ." Then, with a shudder—"But it is *gambler's* money! the wages of sin; we couldn't take it; we couldn't touch it. I don't like to be near it; it seems a defilement." She moved to a farther chair.... "I wish Edward would come, and take it to the bank; a burglar might come at any moment; it is dreadful to be here all alone with it."

At eleven Mr. Richards arrived, and while his wife was saying, "I am *so* glad you've come!" he was saying, "I'm so tired—tired clear out; it is dreadful to be poor, and have to make these dismal journeys at my time of life. Always at the grind, grind, grind, on a salary—another man's slave, and he sitting at home in his slippers, rich and comfortable."

"I am so sorry for you, Edward, you know that; but be comforted; we have our livelihood; we have our good name—"

"Yes, Mary, and that is everything. Don't mind my talk—it's just a moment's irritation and doesn't mean anything. Kiss me—there, it's all gone now, and I am not complaining any more. What have you been getting? What's in the sack?"

Then his wife told him the great secret. It dazed him for a moment; then he said:

"It weighs a hundred and sixty pounds? Why, Mary, it's for-ty thou-sand dollars—think of it—a whole fortune! Not ten men in this village are worth that much. Give me the paper."

He skimmed through it and said:

"Isn't it an adventure! Why, it's a romance; it's like the impossible things one reads about in books, and never sees in life." He was well stirred up now; cheerful, even gleeful. He tapped his old wife on the cheek, and said, humorously, "Why, we're rich, Mary, rich; all we've got to do is to bury the money and burn the papers. If the gambler ever comes to inquire, we'll merely look coldly upon him and say: 'What is this nonsense you are talking? We have never heard of you and your sack of gold before;' and then he would look foolish, and—"

"And in the mean time, while you are running on with your jokes, the money is still here, and it is fast getting along toward burglar-time."

"True. Very well, what shall we do—make the inquiry private? No, not that; it would spoil the romance. The public method is better. Think what a noise it will make! And it will make all the other towns jealous; for no stranger would trust such a thing to any town but Hadleyburg, and they know it. It's a great card for us. I must get to the printing office now, or I shall be too late."

"But stop—stop—don't leave me here alone with it, Edward!"

But he was gone. For only a little while, however. Not far from his own house he met the editor-proprietor of the paper, and gave him the document, and said, "Here is a good thing for you, Cox—put it in."

"It may be too late, Mr. Richards, but I'll see."

At home again he and his wife sat down to talk the charming mystery over; they were in no condition for sleep. The first question was, Who could the citizen have been who gave the stranger the twenty dollars? It seemed a simple one; both answered it in the same breath—

"Barclay Goodson."

"Yes," said Richards, "he could have done it, and it would have been like him, but there's not another in the town."

"Everybody will grant that, Edward—grant it privately, anyway. For six months, now, the village has been its own proper self once more—honest, narrow, self-righteous, and stingy."

"It is what he always called it, to the day of his death—said it right out publicly, too."

"Yes, and he was hated for it."

"Oh, of course; but he didn't care. I reckon he was the best-hated man among us, except the Reverend Burgess."

"Well, Burgess deserves it—he will never get another congregation here. Mean as the town is, it knows how to estimate *him*. Edward, doesn't it seem odd that the stranger should appoint Burgess to deliver the money?"

"Well, yes—it does. That is—that is—"

"Why so much that-*is*-ing? Would *you* select him?"

"Mary, maybe the stranger knows him better than this village does."

"Much *that* would help Burgess!"

The husband seemed perplexed for an answer; the wife kept a steady eye upon him, and waited. Finally Richards said, with the hesitancy of one who is making a statement which is likely to encounter doubt,

"Mary, Burgess is not a bad man."

His wife was certainly surprised.

"Nonsense!" she exclaimed.

"He is not a bad man. I know. The whole of his unpopularity had its foundation in that one thing—the thing that made so much noise."

"That 'one thing,' indeed! As if that 'one thing' wasn't enough, all by itself."

"Plenty. Plenty. Only he wasn't guilty of it."

"How you talk! Not guilty of it! Everybody knows he *was* guilty."

"Mary, I give you my word—he was innocent."

"I can't believe it, and I don't. How do you know?"

"It is a confession. I am ashamed, but I will make it. I was the only man who knew he was innocent. I could have saved him, and—well, you know how the town was wrought up—I hadn't the pluck to do it. It would have turned everybody against me. I felt mean, ever so mean; but I didn't dare; I hadn't the manliness to face that."

Mary looked troubled, and for a while was silent. Then she said, stammeringly:

"I—I didn't think it would have done for you to—to—One mustn't—er—public opinion—one has to be so careful—so—" It was a difficult road, and she got mired; but after a little she got started again. "It was a great pity, but—Why, we couldn't afford it, Edward—we couldn't indeed. Oh, I wouldn't have had you do it for anything!"

"It would have lost us the good-will of so many people, Mary; and then—and then—"

"What troubles me now is, what *he* thinks of us, Edward."

"He? *He* doesn't suspect that I could have saved him."

"Oh," exclaimed the wife, in a tone of relief, "I am glad of that. As long as he doesn't know that you could have saved him, he—he—well, that makes it a great deal better. Why, I might have known he didn't know, because he is always trying to be friendly with us, as little encouragement as we give him. More than once people have twitted me with it. There's the Wilsons, and the Wilcoxes, and the Harknesses, they take a mean pleasure in saying, '*Your friend* Burgess,' because they know it pesters me. I wish he wouldn't persist in liking us so; I can't think why he keeps it up."

"I can explain it. It's another confession. When the thing was new and hot, and the town made a plan to ride him on a rail, my conscience hurt me so that I couldn't stand it, and I went privately and gave him notice, and he got out of the town and staid out till it was safe to come back."

"Edward! If the town had found it out—"

"*Don't*! It scares me yet, to think of it. I repented of it the minute it was done; and I was even afraid to tell you, lest your face might betray it to somebody. I didn't sleep any that night, for worrying. But after a few days I saw that no one was going to suspect me, and after that I got to feeling glad I did it. And I feel glad yet, Mary—glad through and through."

"So do I, now, for it would have been a dreadful way to treat him. Yes, I'm glad; for really you did owe him that, you know. But Edward, suppose it should come out yet, some day!"

"It won't."

"Why?"

"Because everybody thinks it was Goodson."

"Of course they would!"

"Certainly. And of course *he* didn't care. They persuaded poor old Sawlsberry to go and charge it on him, and he went blustering over there and did it. Goodson looked him over, like as if he was hunting for a place on him that he could despise the most, then he says, 'So you are the Committee of Inquiry, are you?' Sawlsberry said that was about what he was. 'Hm. Do they require particulars, or do you reckon a kind of a *general* answer will do?' 'If they require particulars, I will come back, Mr. Goodson; I will take the general answer first.' 'Very well, then, tell them to go to hell—I reckon that's general enough. And I'll give you some advice, Sawlsberry; when you come back for the particulars, fetch a basket to carry the relics of yourself home in.'"

"Just like Goodson; it's got all the marks. He had only one vanity; he thought he could give advice better than any other person."

"It settled the business, and saved us, Mary. The subject was dropped."

"Bless you, I'm not doubting *that*."

Then they took up the gold-sack mystery again, with strong interest. Soon the conversation began to suffer breaks—interruptions caused by absorbed thinkings. The breaks grew more and more frequent. At last Richards lost himself wholly in thought. He sat long, gazing vacantly at the floor, and by-and-by he began to punctuate his thoughts with little nervous movements of his hands that seemed to indicate vexation. Meantime his wife too had relapsed into a thoughtful silence, and her movements were beginning to show a troubled discomfort. Finally Richards got up and strode aimlessly about the room, ploughing his hands through his hair, much as a somnambulist might do who was having a bad dream. Then he seemed to arrive at a definite purpose; and without a word he put on his hat and passed quickly out of the house. His wife sat brooding, with a drawn face, and did not seem to be aware that she was alone. Now and then she murmured, "Lead us not into t.... but—but—we are so poor, so poor! ... Lead us not into.... Ah, who would be hurt by it?—and no one would ever know.... Lead us...." The voice died out in mumblings. After a little she glanced up and muttered in a half-frightened, half-glad way—

"He is gone! But, oh dear, he may be too late—too late.... Maybe not— maybe there is still time." She rose and stood thinking, nervously clasping and unclasping her hands. A slight shudder shook her frame, and she said, out of a dry throat, "God forgive me—it's awful to think such things—but.... Lord, how we are made—how strangely we are made!"

She turned the light low, and slipped stealthily over and kneeled down by the sack and felt of its ridgy sides with her hands, and fondled them lovingly; and there was a gloating light in her poor old eyes. She fell into fits of absence; and came half out of them at times to mutter, "If we had only waited!—oh, if we had only waited a little, and not been in such a hurry!"

Meantime Cox had gone home from his office and told his wife all about the strange thing that had happened, and they had talked it over eagerly, and guessed that the late Goodson was the only man in the town who could have helped a suffering stranger with so noble a sum as twenty dollars. Then there was a pause, and the two became thoughtful and silent. And by-and-by nervous and fidgety. At last the wife said, as if to herself,

"Nobody knows this secret but the Richardses ... and us ... nobody."

The husband came out of his thinkings with a slight start, and gazed wistfully at his wife, whose face was becoming very pale; then he hesitatingly rose, and glanced furtively at his hat, then at his wife—a sort of mute inquiry. Mrs. Cox swallowed once or twice, with her hand at her throat, then in place of speech she nodded her head. In a moment she was alone, and mumbling to herself.

And now Richards and Cox were hurrying through the deserted streets, from opposite directions. They met, panting, at the foot of the printing-office stairs; by the night-light where they read each other's face. Cox whispered,

"Nobody knows about this but us?"

The whispered answer was,

"Not a soul—on honor, not a soul!"

"If it isn't too late to—"

The men were starting up-stairs; at this moment they were overtaken by a boy, and Cox asked,

"Is that you, Johnny?"

"Yes, sir."

"You needn't ship the early mail—nor *any* mail; wait till I tell you."

"It's already gone, sir."

"*Gone?*" It had the sound of an unspeakable disappointment in it.

"Yes, sir. Time-table for Brixton and all the towns beyond changed to-day, sir—had to get the papers in twenty minutes earlier than common. I had to rush; if I had been two minutes later—"

The men turned and walked slowly away, not waiting to hear the rest. Neither of them spoke during ten minutes; the Cox said, in a vexed tone,

"What possessed you to be in such a hurry, *I* can't make out."

The answer was humble enough:

"I see it now, but somehow I never thought, you know, until it was too late. But the next time—"

"Next time be hanged! It won't come in a thousand years."

Then the friends separated without a good-night, and dragged themselves home with the gait of mortally stricken men. At their homes their wives sprang up with an eager "Well?"—then saw the answer with their eyes and sank down sorrowing, without waiting for it to come in words. In both houses a discussion followed of a heated sort—a new thing; there had been discussions before, but not heated ones, not ungentle ones. The discussions to-night were a sort of seeming plagiarisms of each other. Mrs. Richards said,

"If you had only waited, Edward—if you had only stopped to think; but no, you must run straight to the printing-office and spread it all over the world."

"It *said* publish it."

"That is nothing; it also said do it privately, if you liked. There, now—is that true, or not?"

"Why, yes—yes, it is true; but when I thought what a stir it would make, and what a compliment it was to Hadleyburg that a stranger should trust it so—"

"Oh, certainly, I know all that; but if you had only stopped to think, you would have seen that you *couldn't* find the right man, because he is in his grave, and hasn't left chick nor child nor relation behind him; and as long as the money went to somebody that awfully needed it, and nobody would be hurt by it, and—and—"

She broke down, crying. Her husband tried to think of some comforting thing to say, and presently came out with this:

"But after all, Mary, it must be for the best—it *must* be; we know that. And we must remember that it was so ordered—"

"Ordered! Oh, everything's *ordered*, when a person has to find some way out when he has been stupid. Just the same, it was *ordered* that the money should come to us in this special way, and it was you that must take it on yourself to go meddling with the designs of Providence—and who gave you the right? It was wicked, that is what it was—just blasphemous presumption, and no more becoming to a meek and humble professor of—"

"But, Mary, you know how we have been trained all our lives long, like the whole village, till it is absolutely second nature to us to stop not a single moment to think when there's an honest thing to be done—"

"Oh, I know it, I know it—it's been one everlasting training and training and training in honesty—honesty shielded, from the very cradle, against every possible temptation, and so it's *artificial* honesty, and weak as water when temptation comes, as we have seen this night. God knows I never had shade nor shadow of a doubt of my petrified and indestructible honesty until now—and now, under the very first big and real temptation, I— Edward, it is my belief that this town's honesty is as rotten as mine is; as rotten as yours is. It is a mean town, a hard, stingy town, and hasn't a virtue in the world but this honesty it is so celebrated for and so conceited about; and so help me, I do believe that if ever the day comes that its honesty falls under great temptation, its grand reputation will go to ruin like a house of cards. There, now, I've made confession, and I feel better; I am a humbug, and I've been one all my life, without knowing it. Let no man call me honest again—I will not have it."

"I—well, Mary, I feel a good deal as you do; I certainly do. It seems strange, too, so strange. I never could have believed it—never."

A long silence followed; both were sunk in thought. At last the wife looked up and said,

"I know what you are thinking, Edward."

Richards had the embarrassed look of a person who is caught.

"I am ashamed to confess it, Mary, but—"

"It's no matter, Edward, I was thinking the same question myself."

"I hope so. State it."

"You were thinking, if a body could only guess out *what the remark was* that Goodson made to the stranger."

"It's perfectly true. I feel guilty and ashamed. And you?"

"I'm past it. Let us make a pallet here; we've got to stand watch till the bank vault opens in the morning and admits the sack.... Oh, dear, oh, dear—if we hadn't made the mistake!"

The pallet was made, and Mary said:

"The open sesame—what could it have been? I do wonder what that remark could have been? But come; we will get to bed now."

"And sleep?"

"No; think."

"Yes, think."

By this time the Coxes too had completed their spat and their reconciliation, and were turning in—to think, to think, and toss, and fret, and worry over what the remark could possibly have been which Goodson made to the stranded derelict: that golden remark; that remark worth forty thousand dollars, cash.

The reason that the village telegraph-office was open later than usual that night was this: The foreman of Cox's paper was the local representative of the Associated Press. One might say its honorary representative, for it wasn't four times a year that he could furnish thirty words that would be accepted. But this time it was different. His despatch stating what he had caught got an instant answer:

Send the whole thing—all the details—twelve hundred words.

A colossal order! The foreman filled the bill; and he was the proudest man in the State. By breakfast-time the next morning the name of Hadleyburg the Incorruptible was on every lip in America, from Montreal to the Gulf, from the glaciers of Alaska to the orange-groves of Florida; and millions and millions of people were discussing the stranger and his money-sack, and wondering if the right man would be found, and hoping some more news about the matter would come soon—right away.

II

Hadleyburg village woke up world-celebrated—astonished—happy—vain. Vain beyond imagination. Its nineteen principal citizens and their wives went about shaking hands with each other, and beaming, and smiling, and congratulating, and saying *this* thing adds a new word to the dictionary—*Hadleyburg*, synonym for *incorruptible*—destined to live in dictionaries forever! And the minor and unimportant citizens and their wives went around acting in much the same way. Everybody ran to the bank to see the gold-sack; and before noon grieved and envious crowds began to flock in from Brixton and all neighboring towns; and that afternoon and next day reporters began to arrive from everywhere to verify the sack and its history and write the whole thing up anew, and make dashing free-hand pictures of the sack, and of Richards's house, and the bank, and the Presbyterian church, and the Baptist church, and the public square, and the town-hall where the test would be applied and the money delivered; and damnable portraits of the Richardses, and Pinkerton the banker, and Cox, and the foreman, and Reverend Burgess, and the postmaster—and even of Jack Halliday, who was the loafing, good-natured, no-account, irreverent fisherman, hunter, boys' friend, stray-dogs' friend, typical "Sam Lawson" of the town. The little mean, smirking, oily Pinkerton showed the sack to all comers, and rubbed his sleek palms together pleasantly, and enlarged upon the town's fine old reputation for honesty and upon this wonderful endorsement of it, and hoped and believed that the example would now spread far and wide over the American world, and be epoch-making in the matter of moral regeneration. And so on, and so on.

By the end of a week things had quieted down again; the wild intoxication of pride and joy had sobered to a soft, sweet, silent delight—a sort of deep, nameless, unutterable content. All faces bore a look of peaceful, holy happiness.

Then a change came. It was a gradual change: so gradual that its beginnings were hardly noticed; maybe were not noticed at all, except by Jack Halliday, who always noticed everything; and always made fun of it, too, no matter what it was. He began to throw out chaffing remarks about people not looking quite so happy as they did a day or two ago; and next he claimed that the new aspect was deepening to positive sadness; next, that it was taking on a sick look; and finally he said that everybody was become so moody, thoughtful, and absent-minded that he could rob the meanest man in town of a cent out of the bottom of his breeches pocket and not disturb his revery.

At this stage—or at about this stage—a saying like this was dropped at bedtime—with a sigh, usually—by the head of each of the nineteen principal households:

"Ah, what *could* have been the remark that Goodson made!"

And straightway—with a shudder—came this, from the man's wife:

"Oh, *don't!* What horrible thing are you mulling in your mind? Put it away from you, for God's sake!"

But that question was wrung from those men again the next night—and got the same retort. But weaker.

And the third night the men uttered the question yet again—with anguish, and absently. This time—and the following night—the wives fidgeted feebly, and tried to say something. But didn't.

And the night after that they found their tongues and responded—longingly,

"Oh, if we *could* only guess!"

Halliday's comments grew daily more and more sparklingly disagreeable and disparaging. He went diligently about, laughing at the town, individually and in mass. But his laugh was the only one left in the village: it fell upon a hollow and mournful vacancy and emptiness. Not even a smile was findable anywhere; Halliday carried a cigar-box around on a tripod, playing that it was a camera, and halted all passers and aimed the thing and said, "Ready!—now look pleasant, please," but not even this capital joke could surprise the dreary faces into any softening.

So three weeks passed—one week was left. It was Saturday evening—after supper. Instead of the aforetime Saturday-evening flutter and bustle and shopping and larking, the streets were empty and desolate. Richards and his old wife sat apart in their little parlor—miserable and thinking. This was become their evening habit now: the life-long habit which had preceded it, of reading, knitting, and contented chat, or receiving or paying neighborly calls, was dead and gone and forgotten, ages ago—two or three weeks ago; nobody talked now, nobody read, nobody visited—the whole village sat at home, sighing, worrying, silent. Trying to guess out that remark.

The postman left a letter. Richards glanced listlessly, at the superscription and the post-mark—unfamiliar, both—and tossed the letter on the table and resumed his might-have-beens and his hopeless dull miseries where he had left them off. Two or three hours later his wife got wearily up and was going away to bed without a good-night—custom now—but she stopped near the letter and eyed it awhile with a dead interest, then broke it open, and began to skim it over. Richards, sitting there with his chair tilted back against the wall and his chin between his knees, heard something fall. It was his wife. He sprang to her side, but she cried out:

"Leave me alone, I am too happy. Read the letter—read it!"

He did. He devoured it, his brain reeling. The letter was from a distant State, and it said:

"I am a stranger to you, but no matter: I have something to tell. I have just arrived home from Mexico, and learned about that episode. Of course you do not know who made that remark, but I know, and I am the only person living who does know. It was GOODSON. *I knew him well, many years ago. I passed through your village that very night, and was his guest till the midnight train came along. I overheard him make that remark to the stranger in the dark—it was in Hale Alley. He and I talked of it the rest of the way home, and while smoking in his house. He mentioned many of your villagers in the course of his talk—most of them in a very uncomplimentary way, but two or three favorably: among these latter yourself. I say 'favorably'—nothing stronger. I remember his saying he did not actually* LIKE *any person in the town—not one; but that you—I* THINK *he said you—am almost sure—had done him a very great service once, possibly without knowing the full value of it, and he wished he had a fortune, he would leave it to you when he died, and a curse apiece for the rest of the citizens. Now, then, if it was you that did him that service, you are his legitimate heir, and entitled to the sack of gold. I know that I can trust to your honor and honesty, for in a citizen of Hadleyburg these virtues are an unfailing inheritance, and so I am going to reveal to you the remark, well satisfied that if you are not the right man you will seek and find the right one and see that poor Goodson's debt of gratitude for the service referred to is paid. This is the remark: '*YOU ARE FAR FROM BEING A BAD MAN: GO, AND REFORM.*'*

"Howard L. Stephenson."

"Oh, Edward, the money is ours, and I am so grateful, oh, so grateful—kiss me, dear, it's forever since we kissed—and we needed it so—the money—and now you are free of Pinkerton and his bank, and nobody's slave any more; it seems to me I could fly for joy."

It was a happy half-hour that the couple spent there on the settee caressing each other; it was the old days come again—days that had begun with their courtship and lasted without a break till the stranger brought the deadly money. By-and-by the wife said:

"Oh, Edward, how lucky it was you did him that grand service, poor Goodson! I never liked him, but I love him now. And it was fine and beautiful of you never to mention it or brag about it." Then, with a touch of reproach, "But you ought to have told *me*, Edward, you ought to have told your wife, you know."

"Well, I—er—well, Mary, you see—"

"Now stop hemming and hawing, and tell me about it, Edward. I always loved you, and now I'm proud of you. Everybody believes there was only one good generous soul in this village, and now it turns out that you—Edward, why don't you tell me?"

"Well—er—er—Why, Mary, I can't!"

"You *can't? Why* can't you?"

"You see, he—well, he—he made me promise I wouldn't."

The wife looked him over, and said, very slowly,

"Made—you—promise? Edward, what do you tell me that for?"

"Mary, do you think I would lie?"

She was troubled and silent for a moment, then she laid her hand within his and said:

"No ... no. We have wandered far enough from our bearings—God spare us that! In all your life you have never uttered a lie. But now—now that the foundations of things seem to be crumbling from under us, we— we—" She lost her voice for a moment, then said, brokenly, "Lead us not into temptation ... I think you made the promise, Edward. Let it rest so. Let us keep away from that ground. Now—that is all gone by; let us be happy again; it is no time for clouds."

Edward found it something of an effort to comply, for his mind kept wandering—trying to remember what the service was that he had done Goodson.

The couple lay awake the most of the night, Mary happy and busy, Edward busy, but not so happy. Mary was planning what she would do with the money. Edward was trying to recall that service. At first his conscience was sore on account of the lie he had told Mary—if it was a lie. After much reflection—suppose it *was* a lie? What then? Was it such a great matter? Aren't we always *acting* lies? Then why not *tell* them? Look at Mary—look what she had done. While he was hurrying off on his honest errand, what was she doing? Lamenting because the papers hadn't been destroyed and the money kept! Is theft better than lying?

That point lost its sting—the lie dropped into the background and left comfort behind it. The next point came to the front: *had* he rendered that service? Well, here was Goodson's own evidence as reported in Stephenson's letter; there could be no better evidence than that—it was even *proof* that he had rendered it. Of course. So that point was settled.... No, not quite. He recalled with a wince that this unknown Mr. Stephenson was just a trifle unsure as to whether the performer of it was Richards or some other—and, oh dear, he had put Richards on his honor! He must himself decide whither that money must go—and Mr. Stephenson was not doubting that if he was the wrong man he would go honorably and find the right one. Oh, it was odious to put a man in such a situation—ah, why couldn't Stephenson have left out that doubt! What did he want to intrude that for?

Further reflection. How did it happen that *Richards's* name remained in Stephenson's mind as indicating the right man, and not some other man's name? That looked good. Yes, that looked very good. In fact, it went on looking better and better, straight along—until by-and-by it grew into positive *proof*. And then Richards put the matter at once out of his mind, for he had a private instinct that a proof once established is better left so.

He was feeling reasonably comfortable now, but there was still one other detail that kept pushing itself on his notice: of course he had done that service—that was settled; but what *was* that service? He must recall it—he would not go to sleep till he had recalled it; it would make his peace of mind perfect. And so he thought and thought. He thought of a dozen things—possible services, even probable services—but none of them seemed adequate, none of them seemed large enough, none of them seemed worth the money—worth the fortune Goodson had wished he could leave in his will. And besides, he couldn't remember having done them, anyway. Now, then—now, then—what *kind* of a service would it be that would make a man so inordinately grateful? Ah—the saving of his soul! That must be it. Yes, he could remember, now, how he once set himself the task of converting Goodson, and labored at it as much as—he was going to say three months; but upon closer examination it shrunk to a month, then to a week, then to a day, then to nothing. Yes, he remembered now, and with unwelcome vividness, that Goodson had told him to go to thunder and mind his own business—*he* wasn't hankering to follow Hadleyburg to heaven!

So that solution was a failure—he hadn't saved Goodson's soul. Richards was discouraged. Then after a little came another idea: had he saved Goodson's property? No, that wouldn't do—he hadn't any. His life? That is it! Of course. Why, he might have thought of it before. This time he was on the right track, sure. His imagination-mill was hard at work in a minute, now.

Thereafter during a stretch of two exhausting hours he was busy saving Goodson's life. He saved it in all kinds of difficult and perilous ways. In every case he got it saved satisfactorily up to a certain point; then, just as he was beginning to get well persuaded that it had really happened, a troublesome detail would turn up which made the whole thing impossible. As in the matter of drowning, for instance. In that case he had swum out and tugged Goodson ashore in an unconscious state with a great crowd looking on and applauding, but when he had got it all thought out and was just beginning to remember all about it a whole swarm of disqualifying details arrived on the ground: the town would have known of the circumstance, Mary would have known of it, it would glare like a limelight in his own memory instead of being an inconspicuous service which he had possibly rendered "without knowing its full value." And at this point he remembered that he couldn't swim, anyway.

Ah—*there* was a point which he had been overlooking from the start; it had to be a service which he had rendered "possibly without knowing the full value of it." Why, really, that ought to be an easy hunt—much easier than those others. And sure enough, by-and-by he found it. Goodson, years and years ago, came near marrying a very sweet and pretty girl named Nancy Hewitt, but in some way or other the match had been broken off; the girl died, Goodson remained a bachelor, and by-and-by became a soured one and a frank despiser of the human species. Soon after the girl's death the village found out, or thought it had found out, that she carried a spoonful of negro blood in her veins. Richards worked at these details a good while, and in the end he thought he remembered things concerning them which must have gotten mis-laid in his memory through long neglect. He seemed to dimly remember that it was *he* that found out about the negro blood; that it was he that told the village; that the village told Goodson where they got it; that he thus saved Goodson from marrying the tainted girl; that he had done him this great service "without knowing the full value of it," in fact without knowing that he *was* doing it; but that Goodson knew the value of it, and what a narrow escape he had had, and so went to his grave grateful to his benefactor and wishing he had a fortune to leave him. It was all clear and simple now, and the more he went over it the more luminous and certain it grew; and at last, when he nestled to sleep satisfied and happy, he remembered the whole thing just as if it had been yesterday. In fact, he dimly remembered Goodson's *telling* him his gratitude once. Meantime Mary had spent six thousand dollars on a new house for herself and a pair of slippers for her pastor, and then had fallen peacefully to rest.

That same Saturday evening the postman had delivered a letter to each of the other principal citizens—nineteen letters in all. No two of the envelopes were alike, and no two of the superscriptions were in the same hand, but the letters inside were just like each other in every detail but one. They were exact copies of the letter received by Richards—handwriting and all— and were all signed by Stephenson, but in place of Richards's name each receiver's own name appeared.

All night long eighteen principal citizens did what their caste-brother Richards was doing at the same time—they put in their energies trying to remember what notable service it was that they had unconsciously done Barclay Goodson. In no case was it a holiday job; still they succeeded.

And while they were at this work, which was difficult, their wives put in the night spending the money, which was easy. During that one night the nineteen wives spent an average of seven thousand dollars each out of the forty thousand in the sack—a hundred and thirty-three thousand altogether.

Next day there was a surprise for Jack Halliday. He noticed that the faces of the nineteen chief citizens and their wives bore that expression of peaceful and holy happiness again. He could not understand it, neither was he able to invent any remarks about it that could damage it or disturb it. And so it was his turn to be dissatisfied with life. His private guesses at the reasons for the happiness failed in all instances, upon examination. When he met Mrs. Wilcox and noticed the placid ecstasy in her face, he said to himself, "Her cat has had kittens"—and went and asked the cook; it was not so; the cook had detected the happiness, but did not know the cause. When Halliday found the duplicate ecstasy in the face of "Shadbelly" Billson (village nickname), he was sure some neighbor of Billson's had broken his leg, but inquiry showed that this had not happened. The subdued ecstasy in Gregory Yates's face could mean but one thing—he was a mother-in-law short; it was another mistake. "And Pinkerton—Pinkerton—he has collected ten cents that he thought he was going to lose." And so on, and so on. In some cases the guesses had to remain in doubt, in the others they proved distinct errors. In the end Halliday said to himself, "Anyway it foots up that there's nineteen Hadleyburg families temporarily in heaven: I don't know how it happened; I only know Providence is off duty to-day."

An architect and builder from the next State had lately ventured to set up a small business in this unpromising village, and his sign had now been hanging out a week. Not a customer yet; he was a discouraged man, and sorry he had come. But his weather changed suddenly now. First one and then another chief citizen's wife said to him privately:

"Come to my house Monday week—but say nothing about it for the present. We think of building."

He got eleven invitations that day. That night he wrote his daughter and broke off her match with her student. He said she could marry a mile higher than that.

Pinkerton the banker and two or three other well-to-do men planned country-seats—but waited. That kind don't count their chickens until they are hatched.

The Wilsons devised a grand new thing—a fancy-dress ball. They made no actual promises, but told all their acquaintanceship in confidence that they were thinking the matter over and thought they should give it"—"and if we do, you will be invited, of course." People were surprised, and said, one to another, "Why, they are crazy, those poor Wilsons, they can't afford it." Several among the nineteen said privately to their husbands, "It is a good idea, we will keep still till their cheap thing is over, then *we* will give one that will make it sick."

The days drifted along, and the bill of future squanderings rose higher and higher, wilder and wilder, more and more foolish and reckless. It began to look as if every member of the nineteen would not only spend his whole forty thousand dollars before receiving-day, but be actually in debt by the time he got the money. In some cases light-headed people did not stop with planning to spend, they really spent—on credit. They bought land, mortgages, farms, speculative stocks, fine clothes, horses, and various other things, paid down the bonus, and made themselves liable for the rest—at ten days. Presently the sober second thought came, and Halliday noticed that a ghastly anxiety was beginning to show up in a good many faces. Again he was puzzled, and didn't know what to make of it. "The Wilcox kittens aren't dead, for they weren't born; nobody's broken a leg; there's no shrinkage in mother-in-laws; *nothing* has happened—it is an insolvable mystery."

There was another puzzled man, too—the Rev. Mr. Burgess. For days, wherever he went, people seemed to follow him or to be watching out for him; and if he ever found himself in a retired spot, a member of the nineteen would be sure to appear, thrust an envelope privately into his hand, whisper "To be opened at the town-hall Friday evening," then vanish away like a guilty thing. He was expecting that there might be one claimant for the sack—doubtful, however, Goodson being dead—but it never occurred to him that all this crowd might be claimants. When the great Friday came at last, he found that he had nineteen envelopes.

III

The town-hall had never looked finer. The platform at the end of it was backed by a showy draping of flags; at intervals along the walls were festoons of flags; the gallery fronts were clothed in flags; the supporting columns were swathed in flags; all this was to impress the stranger, for he would be there in considerable force, and in a large degree he would be connected with the press. The house was full. The 412 fixed seats were occupied; also the 68 extra chairs which had been packed into the aisles; the steps of the platform were occupied; some distinguished strangers were given seats on the platform; at the horseshoe of tables which fenced the front and sides of the platform sat a strong force of special correspondents who had come from everywhere. It was the best-dressed house the town had ever produced. There were some tolerably expensive toilets there, and in several cases the ladies who wore them had the look of being unfamiliar with that kind of clothes. At least the town thought they had that look, but the notion could have arisen from the town's knowledge of the fact that these ladies had never inhabited such clothes before.

The gold-sack stood on a little table at the front of the platform where all the house could see it. The bulk of the house gazed at it with a burning interest, a mouth-watering interest, a wistful and pathetic interest; a minority of nineteen couples gazed at it tenderly, lovingly, proprietarily, and the male half of this minority kept saying over to themselves the moving little impromptu speeches of thankfulness for the audience's applause and congratulations which they were presently going to get up and deliver. Every now and then one of these got a piece of paper out of his vest pocket and privately glanced at it to refresh his memory.

Of course there was a buzz of conversation going on—there always is, but at last when the Rev. Mr. Burgess rose and laid his hand on the sack he could hear his microbes gnaw, the place was so still. He related the curious history of the sack, then went on to speak in warm terms of Hadleyburg's old and well-earned reputation for spotless honesty, and of the town's just pride in this reputation. He said that this reputation was a treasure of priceless value; that under Providence its value had now become inestimably enhanced, for the recent episode had spread this fame far and wide, and thus had focussed the eyes of the American world upon this village, and made its name for all time, as he hoped and believed, a synonym for commercial incorruptibility. [*Applause.*] "And who is to be the guardian of this noble treasure—the community as a whole? No! The responsibility is individual, not communal. From this day forth each and every one of you is in his own person its special guardian, and individually responsible that no harm shall come to it. Do you—does each of you—accept this great trust? [*Tumultuous assent.*] Then all is well. Transmit it to your children and to your children's children. To-day your purity is beyond reproach—see to it that it shall remain so. To-day there is not a person in your community who could be beguiled to touch a penny not his own—see to it that you abide in this grace. ["*We will! we will!*"] This is not the place to make comparisons between ourselves and other communities—some of them ungracious toward us; they have their ways, we have ours; let us be content. [*Applause.*] I am done. Under my hand, my friends, rests a stranger's eloquent recognition of what we are: through him the world will always henceforth know what we are. We do not know who he is, but in your name I utter your gratitude, and ask you to raise your voices in indorsement."

The house rose in a body and made the walls quake with the thunders of its thankfulness for the space of a long minute. Then it sat down, and Mr. Burgess took an envelope out of his pocket. The house held its breath while he slit the envelope open and took from it a slip of paper. He read its contents—slowly and impressively—the audience listening with tranced attention to this magic document, each of whose words stood for an ingot of gold:

"'*The remark which I made to the distressed stranger was this: "You are very far from being a bad man: go, and reform."*'" Then he continued:

"We shall know in a moment now whether the remark here quoted corresponds with the one concealed in the sack; and if that shall prove to be so—and it undoubtedly will—this sack of gold belongs to a fellow-citizen who will henceforth stand before the nation as the symbol of the special virtue which has made our town famous throughout the land—Mr. Billson!"

The house had gotten itself all ready to burst into the proper tornado of applause; but instead of doing it, it seemed stricken with a paralysis; there was a deep hush for a moment or two, then a wave of whispered murmurs swept the place—of about this tenor: "*Billson!* oh, come, this is *too* thin! Twenty dollars to a stranger—or *anybody*—Billson! Tell it to the marines!" And now at this point the house caught its breath all of a sudden, in a new access of astonishment, for it discovered that whereas in one part of the hall Deacon Billson was standing up with his head meekly bowed, in another part of it Lawyer Wilson was doing the same. There was a wondering silence now for a while. Everybody was puzzled, and nineteen couples were surprised and indignant.

Billson and Wilson turned and stared at each other. Billson asked, bitingly.

"Why do *you* rise, Mr. Wilson?"

"Because I have a right to. Perhaps you will be good enough to explain to the house why *you* rise?

"With great pleasure. Because I wrote that paper."

"It is an impudent falsity! I wrote it myself."

It was Burgess's turn to be paralyzed. He stood looking vacantly at first one of the men and then the other, and did not seem to know what to do. The house was stupefied. Lawyer Wilson spoke up, now, and said,

"I ask the Chair to read the name signed to that paper."

That brought the Chair to itself, and it read out the name,

"'John Wharton *Billson*.'"

"There!" shouted Billson, "what have you got to say for yourself, now? And what kind of apology are you going to make to me and to this insulted house for the imposture which you have attempted to play here?"

"No apologies are due, sir; and as for the rest of it, I publicly charge you with pilfering my note from Mr. Burgess and substituting a copy of it signed with your own name. There is no other way by which you could have gotten hold of the test-remark; I alone, of living men, possessed the secret of its wording."

There was likely to be a sandalous state of things if this went on; everybody noticed with distress that the short-hand scribes were scribbling like mad; many people were crying "Chair, Chair! Order! order!" Burgess rapped with his gavel, and said:

"Let us not forget the proprieties due. There has evidently been a mistake somewhere, but surely that is all. If Mr. Wilson gave me an envelope—and I remember now that he did—I still have it."

He took one out of his pocket, opened it, glanced at it, looked surprised and worried, and stood silent a few moments. Then he waved his hand in a wandering and mechanical way, and made an effort or two to say something, then gave it up, despondently. Several voices cried out:

"Read it! read it! What is it?"

So he began in a dazed and sleep-walker fashion:

"*The remark which I made to the unhappy stranger was this: "You are far from being a bad man.* [The house gazed at him, marvelling.] *Go, and reform.*'" [*Murmurs:* "Amazing! what can this mean?"] This one," said the Chair, "is signed Thurlow G. Wilson."

"There!" cried Wilson. "I reckon that settles it! I knew perfectly well my note was purloined."

"Purloined!" retorted Billson. "I'll let you know that neither you nor any man of your kidney must venture to—"

The Chair. "Order, gentlemen, order! Take your seats, both of you, please."

They obeyed, shaking their heads and grumbling angrily. The house was profoundly puzzled; it did not know what to do with this curious emergency. Presently Thompson got up. Thompson was the hatter. He would have liked to be a Nineteener; but such was not for him; his stock of hats was not considerable enough for the position. He said:

"Mr. Chairman, if I may be permitted to make a suggestion, can both of these gentlemen be right? I put it to you, sir, can both have happened to say the very same words to the stranger? It seems to me—"

The tanner got up and interrupted him. The tanner was a disgruntled man; he believed himself entitled to be a Nineteener, but he couldn't get recognition. It made him a little unpleasant in his ways and speech. Said he:

"Sho, *that's* not the point! *That* could happen—twice in a hundred years—but not the other thing. *Neither* of them gave the twenty dollars!" [*A ripple of applause.*]

Billson. "*I* did!"

Wilson. "*I* did!"

Then each accused the other of pilfering.

The Chair. "Order! Sit down, if you please—both of you. Neither of the notes has been out of my possession at any moment."

A Voice. "Good—that settles *that!*"

The Tanner. "Mr. Chairman, one thing is now plain: one of these men has been eavesdropping under the other one's bed, and filching family secrets. If it is not un-parliamentary to suggest it, I will remark that both are equal to it. [THE CHAIR: "Order! order!"] I withdraw the remark, sir, and will confine myself to suggesting that *if* one of them has overheard the other reveal the test-remark to his wife, we shall catch him now."

A Voice. "How?"

The Tanner. "Easily. The two have not quoted the remark in exactly the same words. You would have noticed that, if there hadn't been a considerable stretch of time and an exciting quarrel inserted between the two readings."

A Voice. "Name the difference."

The Tanner. "The word *very* is in Billson's note, and not in the other."

Many Voices. "That's so—he's right!"

The Tanner. "And so, if the Chair will examine the test-remark in the sack, we shall know which of these two frauds—[THE CHAIR: "Order!"]—which of these two adventurers—[THE CHAIR: "Order! order!"]—which of these two gentlemen—[*laughter and applause*]—is entitled to wear the belt as being the first dishonest blatherskite ever bred in this town—which he has dishonored, and which will be a sultry place for him from now out!" [*Vigorous applause.*]

Many Voices. "Open it!—open the sack!"

Mr. Burgess made a slit in the sack, slid his hand in and brought out an envelope. In it were a couple of folded notes. He said:

"One of these is marked, 'Not to be examined until all written communications which have been addressed to the Chair—if any—shall have been read.' The other is marked '*The Test.*' Allow me. It is worded—to wit:

"'I do not require that the first half of all the remark which was made to me by my benefactor shall be quoted with exactness, for it was not striking, and could be forgotten; but its closing fifteen words are quite striking, and I think easily rememberable; unless *these* shall be accurately reproduced, let the applicant be regarded as an imposter. My benefactor began by saying he seldom gave advice to any one, but that it always bore the hall-mark of high value when he did give it. Then he said this—and it has never faded from my memory: "*You are far from being a bad man*—"""

Fifty Voices. "That settles it—the money's Wilson's! Wilson! Wilson! Speech! Speech!"

People jumped up and crowded around Wilson, wringing his hand and congratulating fervently—meantime the Chair was hammering with the gavel and shouting:

"Order, gentlemen! Order! Order! Let me finish reading, please." When quiet was restored, the reading was resumed as follows:

""*Go, and reform—or, mark my words—some day, for your sins, you will die and go to hell or Hadleyburg—*TRY AND MAKE IT THE FORMER.""""

A ghastly silence followed. First an angry cloud began to settle darkly upon the faces of the citizenship; after a pause the cloud began to rise, and a tickled expression tried to take its place; tried so hard that it was only kept under with great and painful difficulty; the reporters, the Brixtonites, and other strangers bent their heads down and shielded their faces with their hands, and managed to hold in by main strength and heroic courtesy. At this most inopportune time burst upon the stillness the roar of a solitary voice—Jack Halliday's:

"*That's* got the hall-mark on it!"

Then the house let go, strangers and all. Even Mr. Burgess's gravity broke down presently, then the audience considered itself officially absolved from all restraint, and it made the most of its privilege. It was a good long laugh, and a tempestuously whole-hearted one, but it ceased at last—long enough for Mr. Burgess to try to resume, and for the people to get their eyes partially wiped; then it broke out again; and afterward yet again; then at last Burgess was able to get out these serious words:

"It is useless to try to disguise the fact—we find ourselves in the presence of a matter of grave import. It involves the honor of your town, it strikes at the town's good name. The difference of a single word between the test-remarks offered by Mr. Wilson and Mr. Billson was itself a serious thing, since it indicated that one of the other of these gentlemen had committed a theft—"

The two men were sitting limp, nerveless, crushed; but at these words both were electrified into movement, and started to get up—

"Sit down!" said the Chair, sharply, and they obeyed. "That, as I have said, was a serious thing. And it was—but for only one of them. But the matter has become graver; for the honor of *both* is now in formidable peril. Shall I go even further, and say in inextricable peril? *Both* left out the crucial fifteen words." He paused. During several moments he allowed the pervading stillness to gather and deepen its impressive effects, then added: "There would seem to be but one way whereby this could happen. I ask these gentlemen—Was there *collusion?—agreement?*"

A low murmur sifted through the house; its import was, "He's got them both."

Billson was not used to emergencies; he sat in a helpless collapse. But Wilson was a lawyer. He struggled to his feet, pale and worried, and said:

"I ask the indulgence of the house while I explain this most painful matter. I am sorry to say what I am about to say, since it must inflict irreparable injury upon Mr. Billson, whom I have always esteemed and respected until now, and in whose invulnerability to temptation I entirely believed—as did you all. But for the preservation of my own honor I must speak—and with frankness. I confess with shame—and I now beseech your pardon for it—that I said to the ruined stranger all of the words contained in the test-remark, including the disparaging fifteen. [*Sensation.*] When the late publication was made I recalled them, and I resolved to claim the sack of coin, for by every right I was entitled to it. Now I will ask you to consider this point, and weigh it well: that stranger's gratitude to me that night knew no bounds; he said himself that he could find no words for it that were adequate, and that if he should ever be able he would repay me a thousandfold. Now, then, I ask you this: could I expect—could I believe—could I even remotely imagine—that, feeling as he did, he would do so ungrateful a thing as to add those quite unnecessary fifteen words to his test?—set a trap for me?—expose me as a slanderer of my own town before my own people assembled in a public hall? It was preposterous; it was impossible. His test would contain only the kindly opening clause of my remark. Of that I had no shadow of doubt. You would have thought as I did. You would not have expected a base betrayal from one whom you had befriended and against whom you had committed no offence. And so, with perfect confidence, perfect trust, I wrote on a piece of paper the opening words—ending with 'Go, and reform,'—and signed it. When I was about to put it in an envelope I was called into my back office, and without thinking I left the paper lying open on my desk." He stopped, turned his head slowly toward Billson, waited a moment, then added: "I ask you to note this: when I returned, a little later, Mr. Billson was retiring by my street door." [*Sensation.*]

In a moment Billson was on his feet shouting:

"It's a lie! It's an infamous lie!"

The Chair. "Be seated, sir! Mr. Wilson has the floor."

Billson's friends pulled him into his seat and quieted him, and Wilson went on:

"Those are the simple facts. My note was now lying in a different place on the table from where I had left it. I noticed that, but attached no importance to it, thinking a draught had blown it there. That Mr. Billson would read a private paper was a thing which could not occur to me; he was an honorable man, and he would be above that. If you will allow me to say it, I think his extra word '*very*' stands explained; it is attributable to a defect of memory. I was the only man in the world who could furnish here any detail of the test-mark—by *honorable* means. I have finished."

There is nothing in the world like a persuasive speech to fuddle the mental apparatus and upset the convictions and debauch the emotions of an audience not practised in the tricks and delusions of oratory. Wilson sat down victorious. The house submerged him in tides of approving applause; friends swarmed to him and shook him by the hand and congratulated him, and Billson was shouted down and not allowed to say a word. The Chair hammered and hammered with its gavel, and kept shouting,

"But let us proceed, gentlemen, let us proceed!"

At last there was a measurable degree of quiet, and the hatter said,

"But what is there to proceed with, sir, but to deliver the money?"

Voices. "That's it! That's it! Come forward, Wilson!"

The Hatter. "I move three cheers for Mr. Wilson, Symbol of the special virtue which—"

The cheers burst forth before he could finish; and in the midst of them—and in the midst of the clamor of the gavel also—some enthusiasts mounted Wilson on a big friend's shoulder and were going to fetch him in triumph to the platform. The Chair's voice now rose above the noise—

"Order! To your places! You forget that there is still a document to be read." When quiet had been restored he took up the document, and was going to read it, but laid it down again, saying, "I forgot; this is not to be read until all written communications received by me have first been read." He took an envelope out of his pocket, removed its enclosure, glanced at it—seemed astonished—held it out and gazed at it—stared at it.

Twenty or thirty voices cried out:

"What is it? Read it! read it!"

And he did—slowly, and wondering:

"'The remark which I made to the stranger—[Voices. "Hello! how's this?"]—was this: "You are far from being a bad man. [Voices. "Great Scott!"] Go, and reform."' [Voice. "Oh, saw my leg off!"] Signed by Mr. Pinkerton the banker."

The pandemonium of delight which turned itself loose now was of a sort to make the judicious weep. Those whose withers were unwrung laughed till the tears ran down; the reporters, in throes of laughter, set down disordered pot-hooks which would never in the world be decipherable; and a sleeping dog jumped up, scared out of its wits, and barked itself crazy at the turmoil. All manner of cries were scattered through the din: "We're getting rich—two Symbols of Incorruptibility!—without counting Billson!" "Three!—count Shadbelly in—we can't have too many!" "All right—Billson's elected!" "Alas, poor Wilson—victim of two thieves!"

A Powerful Voice. "Silence! The Chair's fished up something more out of its pocket."

Voices. "Hurrah! Is it something fresh? Read it! read! read!"

The Chair [reading]. "'The remark which I made,' etc. 'You are far from being a bad man. Go,' etc. Signed, 'Gregory Yates.'"

Tornado of Voices. "Four Symbols!" "'Rah for Yates!" "Fish again!"

The house was in a roaring humor now, and ready to get all the fun out of the occasion that might be in it. Several Nineteeners, looking pale and distressed, got up and began to work their way toward the aisles, but a score of shouts went up:

"The doors, the doors—close the doors; no Incorruptible shall leave this place! Sit down, everybody!"

The mandate was obeyed.

"Fish again! Read! read!"

The Chair fished again, and once more the familiar words began to fall from its lips—"'You are far from being a bad man—'"

"Name! name! What's his name?"

"'L. Ingoldsby Sargent.'"

"Five elected! Pile up the Symbols! Go on, go on!"

"'You are far from being a bad—'"

"Name! name!"

"'Nicholas Whitworth.'"

"Hooray! hooray! it's a symbolical day!"

Somebody wailed in, and began to sing this rhyme (leaving out "it's") to the lovely "Mikado" tune of "When a man's afraid of a beautiful maid"; the audience joined in, with joy; then, just in time, somebody contributed another line—

> *"And don't you this forget—"*

The house roared it out. A third line was at once furnished—

> *"Corruptibles far from Hadleyburg are—"*

The house roared that one too. As the last note died, Jack Halliday's voice rose high and clear, freighted with a final line—

> *"But the Symbols are here, you bet!"*

That was sung, with booming enthusiasm. Then the happy house started in at the beginning and sang the four lines through twice, with immense swing and dash, and finished up with a crashing three-times-three and a tiger for "Hadleyburg the Incorruptible and all Symbols of it which we shall find worthy to receive the hall-mark to-night."

Then the shoutings at the Chair began again, all over the place:

"Go on! go on! Read! read some more! Read all you've got!"

"That's it—go on! We are winning eternal celebrity."

A dozen men got up now and began to protest. They said that this farce was the work of some abandoned joker, and was an insult to the whole community. Without a doubt these signatures were all forgeries—

"Sit down! sit down! Shut up! You are confessing. We'll find *your* names in the lot."

"Mr. Chairman, how many of those envelopes have you got?"

The Chair counted.

"Together with those that have been already examined, there are nineteen."

A storm of derisive applause broke out.

"Perhaps they all contain the secret. I move that you open them all and read every signature that is attached to a note of that sort—and read also the first eight words of the note."

"Second that motion!"

It was put and carried—uproariously. Then poor old Richards got up, and his wife rose and stood at his side. Her head was bent down, so that none might see that she was crying. Her husband gave her his arm, and so supporting her, he began to speak in a quavering voice:

"My friends, you have known us two—Mary and me—all our lives, and I think you have liked us and respected us—"

The Chair interrupted him:

"Allow me. It is quite true—that which you are saying, Mr. Richards; this town *does* know you two; it *does* like you; it *does* respect you; more—it honors you and *loves* you—"

Halliday's voice rang out:

"That's the hall-marked truth, too! If the Chair is right, let the house speak up and say it. Rise! Now, then—hip! hip! hip—all together!"

The house rose in mass, faced toward the old couple eagerly, filled the air with a snow-storm of waving handkerchiefs, and delivered the cheers with all its affectionate heart.

The Chair then continued:

"What I was going to say is this: We know your good heart, Mr. Richards, but this is not a time for the exercise of charity toward offenders. [Shouts of "Right right!"] I see your generous purpose in your face, but I cannot allow you to plead for these men—"

"But I was going to—"

"Please take your seat, Mr. Richards. We must examine the rest of these notes—simple fairness to the men who have already been exposed requires this. As soon as that has been done—I give you my word for this—you shall be heard."

Many Voices. "Right!—the Chair is right—no interruption can be permitted at this stage! Go on!—the names! the names!—according to the terms of the motion!"

The old couple sat reluctantly down, and the husband whispered to the wife, "It is pitifully hard to have to wait; the shame will be greater than ever when they find we were only going to plead for *ourselves*."

Straightway the jollity broke loose again with the reading of the names.

"'You are far from being a bad man—' Signature, 'Robert J. Titmarsh.'"

"'You are far from being a bad man—' Signature, 'Eliphalet Weeks.'"

"'You are far from being a bad man—' Signature, 'Oscar B. Wilder.'"

At this point the house lit upon the idea of taking the eight words out of the Chairman's hands. He was not unthankful for that. Thenceforward he held up each note in its turn, and waited. The house droned out the eight words in a massed and measured and musical deep volume of sound (with a daringly close resemblance to a well-known church chant)—"'You are f-a-r from being a b-a-a-a-d man.'" Then the Chair said, "Signature, 'Archibald

Wilcox.'" And so on, and so on, name after name, and everybody had an increasingly and gloriously good time except the wretched Nineteen. Now and then, when a particularly shining name was called, the house made the Chair wait while it chanted the whole of the test-remark from the beginning to the closing words. "And go to hell or Hadleyburg—try and make it the for-or-m-e-r!" and in these special cases they added a grand and agonized and imposing "A-a-a-a-*men!*"

The list dwindled, dwindled, dwindled, poor old Richards keeping tally of the count, wincing when a name resembling his own was pronounced, and waiting in miserable suspense for the time to come when it would be his humiliating privilege to rise with Mary and finish his plea, which he was intending to word thus: ". . . for until now we have never done any wrong thing, but have gone our humble way un-reproached. We are very poor, we are old, and have no chick nor child to help us; we were sorely tempted, and we fell. It was my purpose when I got up before to make confession and beg that my name might not be read out in this public place, for it seemed to us that we could not bear it; but I was prevented. It was just; it was our place to suffer with the rest. It has been hard for us. It is the first time we have ever heard our name fall from any one's lips—sullied. Be merciful—for the sake of the better days; make our shame as light to bear as in your charity you can." At this point in his revery Mary nudged him, perceiving that his mind was absent. The house was chanting, "You are f-a-r," etc.

"Be ready," Mary whispered. "Your name comes now; he has read eighteen."

The chant ended.

"Next! next! next!" came volleying from all over the house.

Burgess put his hand into his pocket. The old couple, trembling, began to rise. Burgess fumbled a moment, then said,

"I find I have read them all."

Faint with joy and surprise, the couple sank into their seats, and Mary whispered.

"Oh, bless God, we are saved!—he has lost ours—I wouldn't give this for a hundred of those sacks!"

The house burst out with its "Mikado" travesty, and sang it three times with ever-increasing enthusiasm, rising to its feet when it reached for the third time the closing line—

"But the Symbols are here, you bet!"

and finishing up with cheers and a tiger for "Hadleyburg purity and our eighteen immortal representatives of it."

Then Wingate, the saddler, got up and proposed cheers "for the cleanest man in town, the one solitary important citizen in it who didn't try to steal that money—Edward Richards."

They were given with great and moving heartiness; then somebody proposed that Richards "be elected sole Guardian and Symbol of the now Sacred Hadleyburg Tradition, with power and right to stand up and look the whole sarcastic world in the face."

Passed, by acclamation; then they sang the "Mikado" again, and ended it with,

"And there's one Symbol left, you bet!"

There was a pause; then—

A Voice. "Now, then, who's to get the sack?"

The Tanner (*with bitter sarcasm*). "That's easy. The money has to be divided among the eighteen Incorruptibles. They gave the suffering stranger twenty dollars apiece—and that remark—each in his turn—it took twenty-two minutes for the procession to move past. Staked the stranger—total contribution, $360. All they want is just the loan back—and interest—forty thousand dollars altogether."

Many Voices [*derisively*]. "That's it Divvy! divvy! Be kind to the poor—don't keep them waiting!"

The Chair. "Order! I now offer the stranger's remaining document. It says: 'If no claimant shall appear [*grand chorus of groans*], I desire that you open the sack and count out the money to the principal citizens of your town, they to take it in trust [*cries of "Oh! Oh! Oh!"*], and use it in such ways as to them shall seem best for the propagation and preservation of your community's noble reputation for incorruptible honesty [*more cries*]—a reputation to which their names and their efforts will add a new and far-reaching lustre.' [*Enthusiastic outburst of sarcastic applause.*] That seems to be all. No—here is a postscript:

"'P.S.—Citizens of Hadleyburg. There *is* no test-remark—nobody made one.

[*Great sensation*] There wasn't any pauper stranger, nor any twenty-dollar contribution, nor any accompanying benediction and compliment—these are all inventions. [*General buzz and hum of astonishment and delight.*] Allow me to tell my story—it will take but a word or two. I passed through your town at a certain time, and received a deep offence which I had not earned. Any other man would have been content to kill one or two of you and call it square, but to me that would have been a trivial revenge, and inadequate; for the dead do not *suffer*. Besides, I could not kill you all—and, anyway, made as I am, even that would not have satisfied me. I wanted to damage every man in the place, and every woman—and not in their bodies or in their estate, but in the vanity—the place where feeble and foolish people are most vulnerable. So I disguised myself and came back and studied you. You were easy game. You had an old and lofty reputation for honesty, and naturally you were proud of it—it was your treasure of treasures, the very apple of your eye. As soon as I found out that you carefully and vigilantly kept yourselves and your children *out of temptation*, I knew how to proceed. Why, you simple creatures, the weakest of all weak thing is a virtue which has not been tested in the fire. I laid a plan, and gathered a list of names. My project was to corrupt Hadleyburg the Incorruptible. My idea was to make liars and thieves of nearly half a hundred smirchless men and women who had never in their lives uttered a lie or stolen a penny. I was afraid of

Goodson. He was neither born nor reared in Hadleyburg. I was afraid that if I started to operate my scheme by getting my letter laid before you, you would say to yourselves, "Goodson is the only man among us who would give away twenty dollars to a poor devil"—and then you might not bite at my bait. But Heaven took Goodson; then I knew I was safe, and I set my trap and baited it. It may be that I shall not catch all the men to whom I mailed the pretended test secret, but I shall catch the most of them, if I know Hadleyburg nature. [*Voices.* "Right—he got every last one of them."] I believe they will even steal ostensible *gamble*-money, rather than miss, poor, tempted, and mistrained fellows. I am hoping to eternally and ever-lastingly squelch your vanity and give Hadleyburg a new renown—one that will *stick*—and spread far. If I have succeeded, open the sack and summon the Committee on Propagation and Preservation of the Hadleyburg Reputation.'"

A Cyclone of Voices. "Open it! Open it! The Eighteen to the front! Committee on Propagation of the Tradition! Forward—the Incorruptibles!"

The chair ripped the sack wide, and gathered up a handful of bright, broad yellow coins, shook them together, then examined them—

"Friends, they are only gilded disks of lead!"

There was a crashing outbreak of delight over this news, and when the noise had subsided, the tanner called out:

"By right of apparent seniority in this business, Mr. Wilson is Chairman of the Committee on Propagation of the Tradition. I suggested that he step forward on behalf of his pals, and receive in trust the money."

A Hundred Voices. "Wilson! Wilson! Wilson! Speech! Speech!"

Wilson. [*in a voice trembling with anger*]. "You will allow me to say, and without apologies for my language, *damn* the money!"

A Voice. "Oh, and him a Baptist!"

A Voice. "Seventeen Symbols left! Step up, gentlemen, and assume your trust!"

There was a pause—no response.

The Saddler. "Mr. Chairman, we've got *one* clean man left, anyway, out of the late aristocracy; and he needs money, and deserves it. I move that you appoint Jack Halliday to get up there and auction off that sack of gilt twenty-dollar pieces, and give the result to the right man—the man whom Hadleyburg delights to honor—Edward Richards."

This was received with great enthusiasm, the dog taking a hand again; the saddler started the bids at a dollar, the Brixton folk and Barnum's representative fought hard for it, the people cheered every jump that the bids made, the excitement climbed moment by moment higher and higher, the bidders got on their mettle and grew steadily more and more daring, more and more determined, the jumps went from a dollar up to five, then to ten, then to twenty, then fifty, then to a hundred, then—

At the beginning of the auction Richards whispered in distress to his wife: "Oh, Mary, can we allow it? It—it—you see, it is an honor-reward, a testimonial to purity of character, and—and—can we allow it? Hadn't I better get up and—Oh, Mary, what ought we to do?—what do you think we—" [*Halliday's voice, "Fifteen I'm bid!—fifteen for the sack!—twenty!—ah, thanks!—thirty—thanks again! Thirty, thirty, thirty—do I hear forty?—forty it is! Keep the ball rolling, gentlemen, keep it rolling!—fifty!—thanks noble Roman!—going at fifty, fifty, fifty!—seventy!—ninety!—splendid!—a hundred!—pile it up, pile it up!—hundred and twenty—forty!—just in time!—hundred and fifty;—TWO hundred!—superb! Do I hear two h—thanks!—two hundred and fifty!—"*]

"It is another temptation, Edward—I'm all in a tremble—but, oh, we've escaped *one* temptation, and that ought to warn us, to—["*Six did I hear?—thanks!—six fifty, six f—*SEVEN *hundred!"*] And yet, Edward, when you think—nobody susp—["*Eight hundred dollars!—hurrah!—make it nine!—Mr. Parsons, did I hear you say—thanks!—nine!—this noble sack of virgin lead going at only nine hundred dollars, gilding and all—come! do I hear—a thousand!—gratefully yours!—did some one say eleven?—a sack which is going to be the most celebrated in the whole Uni—"*] Oh, Edward" (beginning to sob), "we are so poor!—but—but—do as you think best—do as you think best."

Edward fell—that is, he sat still; sat with a conscience which was not satisfied, but which was overpowered by circumstances.

Meantime a stranger, who looked like an amateur detective gotten up as an impossible English earl, had been watching the evening's proceedings with manifest interest, and with a contented expression in his face; and he had been privately commenting to himself. He was now soliloquizing somewhat like this: "None of the Eighteen are bidding; that is not satisfactory; I must change that—the dramatic unities require it; they must buy the sack they tried to steal; they must pay a heavy price, too—some of them are rich. And another thing, when I make a mistake in Hadleyburg nature the man that puts that error upon me is entitled to a high honorarium, and some one must pay it. This poor old Richards has brought my judgment to shame; he is an honest man:—I don't understand it, but I acknowledge it. Yes, he saw my deuces *and* with a straight flush, and by rights the pot is his. And it shall be a jack-pot, too, if I can manage it. He disappointed me, but let that pass."

He was watching the bidding. At a thousand, the market broke; the prices tumbled swiftly. He waited—and still watched. One competitor dropped out; then another, and another. He put in a bid or two, now. When the bids had sunk to ten dollars, he added a five; some one raised him a three; he waited a moment, then flung in a fifty-dollar jump, and the sack was his—at $1282. The house broke out in cheers—then stopped; for he was on his feet, and had lifted his hand. He began to speak.

"I desire to say a word, and ask a favor. I am a speculator in rarities, and I have dealings with persons interested in numismatics all over the world. I can make a profit on this purchase, just as it stands; but there is a way, if I can get your approval, whereby I can make every one of these leaden twenty-dollar pieces worth its face in gold, and perhaps more. Grant me that

approval, and I will give part of my gains to your Mr. Richards, whose invulnerable probity you have so justly and so cordially recognized to-night; his
share will be ten thousand dollars, and I will hand him the money to-morrow. [*Great applause from the house.* But the "invulnerable probity" made the
Richardses blush prettily; however, it went for modesty, and did no harm.]
If you will pass my proposition by a good majority—I would like a two-
thirds vote—I will regard that as the town's consent, and that is all I ask.
Rarities are always helped by any device which will rouse curiosity and compel remark. Now if I may have your permission to stamp upon the faces of
each of these ostensible coins the names of the eighteen gentlemen who—"

Nine-tenths of the audience were on their feet in a moment—dog and
all—and the proposition was carried with a whirlwind of approving applause
and laughter.

They sat down, and all the Symbols except "Dr." Clay Harkness, got up,
violently protesting against the proposed outrage, and threatening to—

"I beg you not to threaten me," said the stranger, calmly. "I know my
legal rights, and am not accustomed to being frightened at bluster."
[*Applause.*] He sat down. "Dr." Harkness saw an opportunity here. He was
one of the two very rich men of the place, and Pinkerton was the other.
Harkness was proprietor of a mint; that is to say, a popular patent medicine. He was running for the Legislature on one ticket, and Pinkerton on
the other. It was a close race and a hot one, and getting hotter every day.
Both had strong appetites for money; each had bought a great tract of
land, with a purpose; there was going to be a new railway, and each wanted
to be in the Legislature and help locate the route to his own advantage; a
single vote might make the decision, and with it two or three fortunes.
The stake was large, and Harkness was a daring speculator. He was sitting
close to the stranger. He leaned over while one or another of the other
Symbols was entertaining the house with protests and appeals, and asked,
in a whisper,

"What is your price for the sack?"

"Forty thousand dollars."

"I'll give you twenty."

"No."

"Twenty-five."

"No."

"Say thirty."

"The price is forty thousand dollars; not a penny less."

"All right, I'll give it. I will come to the hotel at ten in the morning. I
don't want it known; will see you privately."

"Very good." Then the stranger got up and said to the house:

"I find it late. The speeches of these gentlemen are not without merit,
not without interest, not without grace; yet if I may be excused I will take
my leave. I thank you for the great favor which you have shown me
in granting my petition. I ask the Chair to keep the sack for me until

to-morrow, and to hand these three five-hundred-dollar notes to Mr. Richards." They were passed up to the Chair. "At nine I will call for the sack, and at eleven will deliver the rest of the ten thousand to Mr. Richards in person, at his home. Good-night."

Then he slipped out, and left the audience making a vast noise, which was composed of a mixture of cheers, the "Mikado" song, dog-disapproval, and the chant. "You are f-a-r from being a b-a-a-d man—a-a-a-men!"

IV

At home the Richardses had to endure congratulations and compliments until midnight. Then they were left to themselves. They looked a little sad, and they sat silent and thinking. Finally Mary sighed and said,

"Do you think we are to blame, Edward—*much* to blame?" and her eyes wandered to the accusing triplet of big bank-notes lying on the table, where the congratulators had been gloating over them and reverently fingered them. Edward did not answer at once; then he brought out a sigh, and said hesitatingly:

"We—we couldn't help it, Mary. It—well, it was ordered. *All* things are."

Mary glanced up and looked at him steadily; but he didn't return the look. Presently she said:

"I thought congratulations and praises always tasted good. But—it seems to me, now—Edward?"

"Well?"

"Are you going to stay in the bank?"

"N-no."

"Resign?"

"In the morning—by note."

"It does seem best."

Richards bowed his head in his hands and muttered:

"Before, I was not afraid to let oceans of people's money pour through my hands, but—Mary, I am so tired, so tired—"

"We will go to bed."

At nine in the morning the stranger called for the sack and took it to the hotel in a cab. At ten Harkness had a talk with him privately. The stranger asked for and got five checks on a metropolitan bank—drawn to "Bearer,"—four for $1,500 each, and one for $34,000. He put the former in his pocketbook, and the remainder, representing $38,500, he put in an envelope, and with these he added a note, which he wrote after Harkness was gone. At eleven he called at the Richards house and knocked. Mrs. Richards peeped through the shutters, then went and received the envelope, and the stranger disappeared without a word. She came back flushed and a little unsteady on her legs, and gasped out:

"I am sure I recognized him! Last night it seemed to me that maybe I had seen him somewhere before."

"He is the man that brought the sack here?"

"I am almost sure of it."

"Then he is the ostensible Stephenson too, and sold every important citizen in this town with his bogus secret. Now if he has sent checks instead of money, we are sold too, after we thought we had escaped. I was beginning to feel fairly comfortable once more, after my night's rest, but the look of that envelope makes me sick. It isn't fat enough; $8500 in even the largest bank-notes makes more bulk than that."

"Edward, why do you object to checks?"

"Checks signed by Stephenson! I am resigned to take the $8500 if it could come in bank-notes—for it does seem that it was so ordered, Mary—but I have never had much courage, and I have not the pluck to try to market a check signed with that disastrous name. It would be a trap. That man tried to catch me; we escaped somehow or other; and now he is trying a new way. If it is checks—"

"Oh, Edward, it is *too* bad!" and she held up the checks and began to cry.

"Put them in the fire! quick! we mustn't be tempted. It is a trick to make the world laugh at *us*, along with the rest, and—Give them to *me*, since you can't do it!" He snatched them and tried to hold his grip till he could get to the stove; but he was human, he was a cashier, and he stopped a moment to make sure of the signature. Then he came near to fainting.

"Fan me, Mary, fan me! They are the same as gold!"

"Oh, how lovely, Edward! Why?"

"Signed by Harkness. What can the mystery of that be, Mary?"

"Edward, do you think—"

"Look here—look at this! Fifteen—fifteen—fifteen—thirty-four. Thirty-eight thousand five hundred! Mary, the sack isn't worth twelve dollars, and Harkness—apparently—has paid about par for it."

"And does it all come to us, do you think—instead of the ten thousand?"

"Why, it looks like it. And the checks are made to 'Bearer,' too."

"Is that good, Edward? What is it for?"

"A hint to collect them at some distant bank, I reckon. Perhaps Harkness doesn't want the matter known. What is that—a note?"

"Yes. It was with the checks."

It was in the "Stephenson" handwriting, but there was no signature. It said:

> *I am a disappointed man. Your honesty is beyond the reach of temptation. I had a different idea about it, but I wronged you in that, and I beg pardon, and do it sincerely. I honor you—and that is sincere, too. This town is not worthy to kiss the hem of your garment. Dear sir, I made a square bet with myself that there were nineteen debauchable men in your self-righteous community. I have lost. Take the whole pot, you are entitled to it.*

Richards drew a deep sigh, and said:

"It seems written with fire—it burns so. Mary—I am miserable again."

"I, too. Ah, dear, I wish—"

"To think, Mary——he *believes* in me."

"Oh, don't Edward—I can't bear it."

"If those beautiful words were deserved, Mary—and God knows I believed I deserved them once—I think I could give the forty thousand dollars for them. And I would put that paper away, as representing more than gold and jewels, and keep it always. But now—We could not live in the shadow of its accusing presence, Mary."

He put it in the fire.

A messenger arrived and delivered an envelope. Richards took from it a note and read it; it was from Burgess.

> *You saved me, in a difficult time. I saved you last night. It was at cost of a lie, but I made the sacrifice freely, and out of a grateful heart. None in this village knows so well as I know how brave and good and noble you are. At bottom you cannot respect me, knowing as you do of that matter of which I am accused, and by the general voice condemned; but I beg that you will at least believe that I am a grateful man; it will help me to bear my burden.*
>
> [Signed]   "BURGESS."

"Saved, once more. And on such terms!" He put the note in the fire. "I—I wish I were dead, Mary, I wish I were out of it all."

"Oh, these are bitter, bitter days, Edward. The stabs, through their very generosity, are so deep—and they come so fast!"

Three days before the election each of two thousand voters suddenly found himself in possession of a prized momento—one of the renowned bogus double-eagles. Around one of its faces was stamped these words: "THE REMARK I MADE TO THE POOR STRANGER WAS—" Around the other face was stamped these "GO, AND REFORM. [SIGNED] PINKERTON." Thus the entire remaining refuse of the renowned joke was emptied upon a single head, and with calamitous effect. It revived the recent vast laugh and concentrated it upon Pinkerton; and Harkness's election was a walk-over.

Within twenty-four hours after the Richardses had received their checks their consciences were quieting down, discouraged; the old couple were learning to reconcile themselves to the sin which they had committed. But they were to learn, now, that a sin takes on new and real terrors when there seems a chance that it is going to be found out. This gives it a fresh and most substantial and important aspect. At church the morning sermon was of the usual pattern; it was the same old things said in the same old way; they had heard them a thousand times and found them innocuous, next to meaningless, and easy to sleep under; but now it was different: the sermon seemed to bristle with accusations; it seemed aimed straight and specially at people who were concealing deadly sins. After church they got away from the mob of congratulators as soon as they could and hurried homeward, chilled to the bone as they did not know what—vague, shadowy, indefinite fears. And by chance they caught a glimpse of Mr. Burgess as he turned a corner. He paid no attention to their nod of recognition! He hadn't seen it; but they did not know that. What could his conduct mean? It might mean—it might mean—oh, a dozen dreadful things. Was it possible that he knew that Richards could have cleared him of guilt in that bygone time, and had been silently waiting for a chance to even up accounts? At home, in their distress they got to imagining that their servant might have been in the next room listening when Richards revealed the secret to his wife that he knew of Burgess's innocence; next Richards began to imagine that he had heard the swish of a gown in there at that time; next, he was sure he *had* heard it. They would call Sarah in, on a pretext, and watch her face: if she had been betraying them to Mr. Burgess, it would show in her manner. They asked her some questions—questions which were so random and incoherent and seemingly purposeless that the girl felt sure that the old people's minds had been affected by their sudden good fortune; the sharp and watchful gaze which they bent upon her frightened her, and that completed the business. She blushed, she became nervous and confused, and to the old people these were plain signs of guilt—guilt of some fearful sort or other—without doubt she was a spy and a traitor. When they were alone again they began to piece many unrelated things together and get horrible results out of the combination. When things had got about to the worst, Richards was delivered of a sudden gasp, and his wife asked,

"Oh, what is it?—what is it?"

"The note—Burgess's note! Its language was sarcastic, I see it now." He quoted: "'At bottom you cannot respect me, *knowing* as you do, of *that matter* of which I am accused'—oh, it is perfectly plain, now, God help me! He knows that I know! You see the ingenuity of the phrasing. It was a trap—and like a fool, I walked into it. And Mary—?"

"Oh, it is dreadful—I know what you are going to say—he didn't return your transcript of the pretended test-remark."

"No—kept it to destroy us with. Mary, he has exposed us to some already. I know it—I know it well. I saw it in a dozen faces after church. Ah, he wouldn't answer our nod of recognition—*he* knew what he had been doing!"

In the night the doctor was called. The news went around in the morning that the old couple were rather seriously ill—prostrated by the exhausting excitement growing out of their great windfall, the congratulations, and the late hours, the doctor said. The town was sincerely distressed; for these old people were about all it had left to be proud of now.

Two days later the news was worse. The old couple were delirious, and were doing strange things. By witness of the nurses, Richards had exhibited checks—for $8,500? No—for an amazing sum—$38,500! What could be the explanation of this gigantic piece of luck?

The following day the nurses had more news—and wonderful. They had concluded to hide the checks, lest harm come to them; but when they searched they were gone from under the patient's pillow—vanished away. The patient said:

"Let the pillow alone; what do you want?"

"We thought it best that the checks—"

"You will never see them again—they are destroyed. They came from Satan. I saw the hell-brand on them, and I knew they were sent to betray me to sin." Then he fell to gabbling strange and dreadful things which were not clearly understandable, and which the doctor admonished them to keep to themselves.

Richards was right; the checks were never seen again.

A nurse must have talked in her sleep, for within two days the forbidden gabblings were the property of the town; and they were of a surprising sort. They seemed to indicate that Richards had been a claimant for the sack himself, and that Burgess had concealed that fact and then maliciously betrayed it.

Burgess was taxed with this and stoutly denied it. And he said it was not fair to attach weight to the chatter of a sick old man who was out of his mind. Still, suspicion was in the air, and there was much talk.

After a day or two it was reported that Mrs. Richards's delirious deliveries were getting to be duplicates of her husband's. Suspicion flamed up into conviction now, and the town's pride in the purity of its one undiscredited important citizen began to dim down and flicker toward extinction.

Six days passed, then came more news. The old couple were dying. Richards's mind cleared in his latest hour, and he sent for Burgess. Burgess said:

"Let the room be cleared. I think he wishes to say something in privacy."

"No!" said Richards; "I want witnesses. I want you all to hear my confession, so that I may die a man, and not a dog. I was clean—artificially—like the rest; and like the rest I fell when temptation came. I signed a lie, and claimed the miserable sack. Mr. Burgess remembered that I had done him a service, and in gratitude (and ignorance) he suppressed my claim and saved me. You know the thing that was charged against Burgess years ago. My testimony, and mine alone, could have cleared him, and I was a coward, and left him to suffer disgrace—"

"No—no—Mr. Richards, you—"

"My servant betrayed my secret to him—"

"No one has betrayed anything to me—"

—"and then he did a natural and justifiable thing, he repented of the saving kindness which he had done me, and he *exposed* me—as I deserved—"

"Never!—I make oath—"

"Out of my heart I forgive him."

Burgess's impassioned protestations fell upon deaf ears; the dying man passed away without knowing that once more he had done poor Burgess a wrong. The old wife died that night.

The last of the sacred Nineteen had fallen a prey to the fiendish sack; the town was stripped the last rag of its ancient glory. Its mourning was not showy, but it was deep.

By act of the Legislature—upon prayer and petition—Hadleyburg was allowed to change its name to (never mind what—I will not give it away), and leave one word out of the motto that for many generations had graced the town's official seal.

It is an honest town once more, and the man will have to rise early that catches it napping again.

1899, 1900

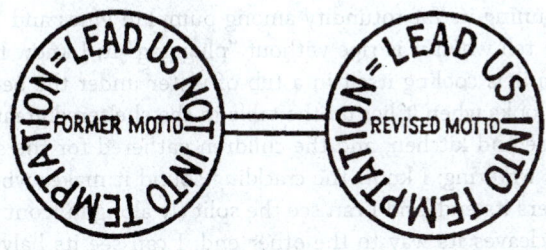

from **The Autobiography of Mark Twain**

Chapter 4[1] ...

As I have said, I spent some part of every year at the farm until I was twelve or thirteen years old. The life which I led there with my cousins was full of charm, and so is the memory of it yet. I can call back the solemn twilight and mystery of the deep woods, the earthy smells, the faint odors of the wild flowers, the sheen of rainwashed foliage, the rattling clatter of drops when the wind shook the trees, the far-off hammering of woodpeckers and the muffled drumming of wood pheasants in the remoteness of the forest, the snapshot glimpses of disturbed wild creatures scurrying through the grass—I can call it all back and make it as real as it ever was, and as blessed. I can call back the prairie, and its loneliness and peace, and a vast hawk hanging motionless in the sky, with his wings spread wide and the blue of the vault showing through the fringe of their end feathers. I can see the woods in their autumn dress, the oaks purple, the hickories washed with gold, the maples and the sumachs luminous with crimson fires, and I can hear the rustle made by the fallen leaves as we plowed through them. I can see the blue clusters of wild grapes hanging among the foliage of the saplings, and I remember the taste of them and the smell. I know how the wild blackberries looked, and how they tasted, and the same with the pawpaws, the hazelnuts, and the persimmons; and I can feel the thumping rain, upon my head, of hickory nuts and walnuts when we were out in the frosty dawn

[1]Mark Twain composed his autobiography as a series of stream-of-consciousness dictations that roamed throughout most phases of his history. This selection records his memories of summer days spent at his Uncle John Quarles's farm, four miles from Sam Clemens's birthplace in Florida, Missouri.

to scramble for them with the pigs, and the gusts of wind loosed them and sent them down. I know the stain of blackberries, and how pretty it is, and I know the stain of walnut hulls, and how little it minds soap and water, also what grudged experience it had of either of them. I know the taste of maple sap, and when to gather it, and how to arrange the troughs and the delivery tubes, and how to boil down the juice, and how to hook the sugar after it is made, also how much better hooked sugar tastes than any that is honestly come by, let bigots say what they will. I know how a prize watermelon looks when it is sunning its fat rotundity among pumpkin vines and "simblins"; I know how to tell when it is ripe without "plugging" it; I know how inviting it looks when it is cooling itself in a tub of water under the bed, waiting; I know how it looks when it lies on the table in the sheltered great floor space between house and kitchen, and the children gathered for the sacrifice and their mouths watering; I know the crackling sound it makes when the carving knife enters its end, and I can see the split fly along in front of the blade as the knife cleaves its way to the other end; I can see its halves fall apart and display the rich red meat and the black seeds, and the heart standing up, a luxury fit for the elect; I know how a boy looks behind a yard-long slice of that melon, and I know how he feels; for I have been there. I know the taste of the watermelon which has been honestly come by, and I know the taste of the watermelon which has been acquired by art. Both taste good, but the experienced know which tastes best. I know the look of green apples and peaches and pears on the trees, and I know how entertaining they are when they are inside of a person. I know how ripe ones look when they are piled in pyramids under the trees, and how pretty they are and how vivid their colors. I know how a frozen apple looks, in a barrel down cellar in the wintertime, and how hard it is to bite, and how the frost makes the teeth ache, and yet how good it is, nowithstanding. I know the disposition of elderly people to select the speckled apples for the children, and I once knew ways to beat the game. I know the look of an apple that is roasting and sizzling on a hearth on a winter's evening, and I know the comfort that comes of eating it hot, along with some sugar and a drench of cream. I know the delicate art and mystery of so cracking hickory nuts and walnuts on a flatiron with a hammer that the kernels will be delivered whole, and I know how the nuts, taken in conjunction with winter apples, cider, and doughnuts, make old people's old tales and old jokes sound fresh and crisp and enchanting, and juggle an evening away before you know what went with the time. I know the look of Uncle Dan'l's kitchen as it was on the privileged nights, when I was a child, and I can see the white and black children grouped on the hearth, with the firelight playing on their faces and the shadows flickering upon the walls, clear back toward the cavernous gloom of the rear, and I can hear Uncle Dan'l telling the immortal tales which Uncle Remus Harris was to gather into his books and charm the world with, by and by; and I can feel again the creepy joy which quivered through me when the time for the ghost story of the "Golden Arm" was reached—and the sense of regret, too, which came over me, for it was always the last story of the evening and there was nothing between it and the unwelcome bed.

I can remember the bare wooden stairway in my uncle's house, and the turn to the left above the landing, and the rafters and the slanting roof over my bed, and the squares of moonlight on the floor, and the white cold world of snow outside, seen through the curtainless window. I can remember the howling of the wind and the quaking of the house on stormy nights, and how snug and cozy one felt, under the blankets, listening; and how the powdery snow used to sift in, around the sashes, and lie in little ridges on the floor and make the place look chilly in the morning and curb the wild desire to get up—in case there was any. I can remember how very dark that room was, in the dark of the moon, and how packed it was with ghostly stillness when one woke up by accident away in the night, and forgotten sins came flocking out of the secret chambers of the memory and wanted a hearing; and how ill chosen the time seemed for this kind of business; and how dismal was the hoohooing of the owl and the wailing of the wolf, sent mourning by on the night wind.

I remember the raging of the rain on that roof, summer nights, and how pleasant it was to lie and listen to it, and enjoy the white splendor of the lightning and the majestic booming and crashing of the thunder. It was a very satisfactory room, and there was a lightning rod which was reachable from the window, and adorable and skittish thing to climb up and down, summer nights, when there were duties on hand of a sort to make privacy desireable.

I remember the 'coon and 'possum hunts, nights, with the negroes, and the long marches through the black gloom of the woods, and the excitement which fired everybody when the distant bay of an experienced dog announced that the game was treed; then the wild scramblings and stumblings through briers and bushes and over roots to get to the spot; then the lighting of a fire and the felling of the tree, the joyful frenzy of the dogs and the negroes, and the weird picture it all made in the red glare—I remember it all well, and the delight that everyone got out of it, except the 'coon.

I remember the pigeon seasons, when the birds would come in millions and cover the trees and by their weight break down the branches. They were clubbed to death with sticks; guns were not necessary and were not used. I remember the squirrel hunts, and prairie-chicken hunts, and wild-turkey hunts, and all that; and how we turned out, mornings, while it was still dark, to go on these expeditions, and how chilly and dismal it was, and how often I regretted that I was well enough to go. A toot on a tin horn brought twice as many dogs as were needed, and in their happiness they raced and scampered about, and knocked small people down, and made no end of unnecessary noise. At the word, they vanished away toward the woods, and we drifted silently after them in the melancholy gloom. But presently the gray dawn stole over the world, the birds piped up, then the sun rose and poured light and comfort all around, everything was fresh and dewy and fragrant, and life was a boon again. After three hours of tramping we arrived back wholesomely tired, overladen with game, very hungry, and just in time for breakfast.

1901

As Regards Patriotism[1]

It is agreed, in this country, that if a man can arrange his religion so that it perfectly satisfies his conscience, it is not incumbent upon him to care whether the arrangement is satisfactory to anyone else or not.

In Austria and some other countries this is not the case. There the State arranges a man's religion for him, he has no voice in it himself.

Patriotism is merely a religion—love of country, worship of country, devotion to the country's flag and honor and welfare.

In absolute monarchies it is furnished from the Throne, cut and dried, to the subject; in England and America it is furnished, cut and dried, to the citizen by the politician and the newspaper.

The newpaper-and-politician-manufactured Patriot often gags in private over his dose; but he takes it, and keeps it on his stomach the best he can. Blessed are the meek.

Sometimes, in the beginning of an insane and shabby political upheaval, he is strongly moved to revolt, but he doesn't do it—he knows better. He knows that his maker would find it out—the maker of his Patriotism, the windy and incoherent six-dollar sub-editor of his village newspaper—and would bray out in print and call him a Traitor. And how dreadful that would be. It makes him tuck his tail between his legs and shiver. We all know—the reader knows it quite well—that two or three years ago nine-tenths of the human tails in England and America performed just that act. Which is to say, nine-tenths of the Patriots in England and America turned Traitor to keep from being called Traitor. Isn't it true? You know it to be true. Isn't it curious?

Yet it was not a thing to be very seriously ashamed of. A man can seldom—very seldom—fight a winning fight against his training; the odds are too heavy. For many a year—perhaps always—the training of the two nations had been dead against independence in political thought, persistently inhospitable toward Patriotism manufactured on a man's own premises, Patriotism reasoned out in the man's own head and fire-assayed and tested and proved in his own conscience. The resulting Patriotism was a shop-worn product procured at second hand. The Patriot did not know just how or when or where he got his opinions, neither did he care, so long as he was with what seemed the majority—which was the main thing, the safe

---

[1]The late Mark Twain responded strongly to world events, especially as they concerned imperialism. He had become a confirmed determinist, convinced that human beings lack moral agency. "As Regards Patriotism" was probably composed in 1901, but it was not published in Twain's lifetime. Here we see Twain struggling to understand how citizens of a republic can substitute "patriotism" for reasoned judgment. From Chapter 5 of his autobiography.

thing, the comfortable thing. Does the reader believe he knows three men who have actual reasons for their pattern of Patriotism—and can furnish them? Let him not examine, unless he wants to be disappointed. He will be likely to find that his men got their Patriotism at the public trough, and had no hand in their preparation themselves.

Training does wonderful things. It moved the people of this country to oppose the Mexican war; then moved them to fall in with what they supposed was the opinion of the majority—majority-Patriotism is the customary Patriotism—and go down there and fight. Before the Civil War it made the North indifferent to slavery and friendly to the slave interest; in that interest it made Massachusetts hostile to the American flag, and she would not allow it to be hoisted on her State House—in her eyes it was the flag of a faction. Then by and by, training swung Massachusetts the other way, and she went raging South to fight under that very flag and against that foretime protected-interest of hers.

Training made us nobly anxious to free Cuba; training made us give her a noble promise; training has enabled us to take it back. Long training made us revolt at the idea of wantonly taking any weak nation's country and liberties away from it, a short training has made us glad to do it, and proud of having done it. Training made us loathe Weyler's cruel concentration camps, training has persuaded us to prefer them to any other device for winning the love of our "wards."

There is nothing that training cannot do. Nothing is above its reach or below it. It can turn bad morals to good, good morals to bad; it can destroy principles, it can re-create them; it can debase angels to men and lift men to angelship. And it can do any one of these miracles in a year—even in six months.

Then men can be trained to manufacture their own Patriotism. They can be trained to labor it out in their own heads and hearts and in the privacy and independence of their own premises. It can train them to stop taking it by command, as the Austrian takes his religion.

1901

The War Prayer[1]

It was a time of great and exalting excitement. The country was up in arms, the war was on, in every breast burned the holy fire of patriotism; the drums were beating, the bands playing, the toy pistols popping, the bunched firecrackers hissing and spluttering; on every hand and far down the receding and fading spread of roofs and balconies a fluttering wilderness of flags flashed in the sun; daily the young volunteers marched down the wide avenue gay and fine in their new uniforms, the proud fathers and mothers and sisters and sweethearts cheering them with voices choked with happy

[1]Also never published in Twain's lifetime, "The War Prayer" asks readers to consider what they really mean when they ask God to help them win a battle.

emotion as they swung by; nightly the packed mass meetings listened, panting, to patriot oratory which stirred the deepest deeps of their hearts, and which they interrupted at briefest intervals with cyclones of applause, the tears running down their cheeks the while; in the churches the pastors preached devotion to flag and country, and invoked the God of Battles, beseeching His aid in our good cause in outpouring of fervid eloquence which moved every listener. It was indeed a glad and gracious time, and the half dozen rash spirits that ventured to disapprove of the war and cast a doubt upon its righteousness straightway got such a stern and angry warning that for their personal safety's sake they quickly shrank out of sight and offended no more in that way.

Sunday morning came—next day the battalions would leave for the front; the church was filled; the volunteers were there, their young faces alight with martial dreams—visions of the stern advance, the gathering momentum, the rushing charge, the flashing sabers, the flight of the foe, the tumult, the enveloping smoke, the fierce pursuit, and surrender!—then home from the war, bronzed heroes, welcomed, adored, submerged in golden seas of glory! With the volunteers sat their dear ones, proud, happy, and envied by the neighbors and friends who had no sons and brothers to send forth to the field of honor, there to win for the flag, or, failing, die the noblest of noble deaths. The service proceeded; a war chapter from the Old Testament was read; the first prayer was said; it was followed by an organ burst that shook the building, and with one impulse the house rose, with glowing eyes and beating hearts, and poured out that tremendous invocation—

"God the all-terrible! Thou who ordainest,
Thunder thy clarion and lightning thy sword!"

Then came the "long" prayer. None could remember the like of it for passionate pleading and moving and beautiful language. The burden of its supplication was, that an ever-merciful and benignant Father of us all would watch over our noble young soldiers, and aid, comfort, and encourage them in their patriotic work; bless them, shield them in the day of battle and the hour of peril, bear them in His mighty hand, make them strong and confident, invincible in the bloody onset; help them to crush the foe, grant to them and to their flag and country imperishable honor and glory—

An aged stranger entered and moved with slow and noiseless step up the main aisle, his eyes fixed upon the minister, his long body clothed in a robe that reached to his feet, his head bare, his white hair descending in a frothy cataract to his shoulders, his seamy face unnaturally pale, pale even to ghastliness. With all eyes following him and wondering, he made his silent way; without pausing, he ascended to the preacher's side and stood there, waiting. With shut lids the preacher, unconscious of his presence, continued his moving prayer, and at last finished it with the words, uttered in fervent appeal, "Bless our arms, grant us the victory, O Lord our God, Father and Protector of our land and flag!"

The stranger touched his arm, motioned him to step aside—which the startled minister did—and took his place. During some moments he surveyed the spellbound audience with solemn eyes, in which burned an uncanny light; then in a deep voice he said:

"I come from the Throne—bearing a message from Almighty God!" The words smote the house with a shock; if the stranger perceived it he gave no attention. "He has heard the prayer of His servant your shepherd, and will grant it if such shall be your desire after I, His messenger, shall have explained to you its import—that is to say, its full import. For it is like unto many of the prayers of men, in that it asks for more than he who utters it is aware of—except he pause and think.

"God's servant and yours has prayed his prayer. Has he paused and taken thought? Is it one prayer? No, it is two—one uttered, the other not. Both have reached the ear of Him Who heareth all supplications, the spoken and the unspoken. Ponder this—keep it in mind. If you would beseech a blessing upon yourself, beware! lest without intent you invoke a curse upon a neighbor at the same time. If you pray for the blessing of rain upon your crop which needs it, by that act you are possibly praying for a curse upon some neighbor's crop which may not need rain and can be injured by it.

"You have heard your servant's prayer—the uttered part of it. I am commissioned of God to put into words the other part of it—that part which the pastor—and also you in your hearts—fervently prayed silently. And ignorantly and unthinkingly? God grant that it was so! You heard these words: 'Grant us the victory, O Lord our God!' That is sufficient. The *whole* of the uttered prayer is compact into those pregnant words. Elaborations were not necessary. When you have prayed for victory you have prayed for many unmentioned results which follow victory—*must* follow it, cannot help but follow it. Upon the listening spirit of God the Father fell also the unspoken part of the prayer. He commandeth me to put it into words. Listen!

"O Lord our Father, our young patriots, idols of our hearts, go forth to battle—be Thou near them! With them—in spirit—we also go forth from the sweet peace of our beloved firesides to smite the foe. O Lord our God, help us to tear their soldiers to bloody shreds with our shells; help us to cover their smiling fields with the pale forms of their patriot dead; help us to drown the thunder of the guns with the shrieks of their wounded, writhing in pain; help us to lay waste their humble homes with a hurricane of fire; help us to wring the hearts of their unoffending widows with unavailing grief; help us to turn them out roofless with their little children to wander unfriended the wastes of their desolated land in rags and hunger and thirst, sports of the sun flames of summer and the icy winds of winter, broken in spirit, worn with travail, imploring Thee for the refuge of the grave and denied it—for our sakes who adore Thee, Lord, blast their hopes, blight their lives, protract their bitter pilgrimage, make heavy their steps, water their way with their tears, stain the white snow with the blood of their wounded feet! We ask it, in the spirit of love, or Him Who is the Source of

Love, and Who is the ever-faithful refuge and friend of all that are sore beset and seek His aid with humble and contrite hearts. Amen."

(After a pause.) "Ye have prayed it; if ye still desire it, speak! The messenger of the Most High waits."

It was believed afterward that the man was a lunatic, because there was no sense in what he said.

1905

■ SARAH MORGAN BRYAN PIATT ■
1836–1919

As a native-born Kentuckian and daughter of slaveholders, Sarah Piatt brought to her poetry a political subjectivity that was formed in the borderland separating North from South. Highly intelligent and honest, she used her poetry to explore the principal social issues of her day—slavery, the Civil War, the myth of the Lost Cause, the displacement of southern blacks, bourgeois corruption in the North, social and economic inequities both here and abroad, changing gender and social values, and the questionable judgments of God. Driven by her personal knowledge of war's waste, Piatt was a political poet for whom issues of social justice (in heaven as well as on earth) were central.

For all the strength of her political commitments, however, Piatt's poetry is of greatest interest for the way that it subsists thematically and structurally in the in-between world of her borderland mentality—a mentality that, like the speaker's in her signature poem, "The Palace-Burner," is never at home in its own contradictions and never able to ignore its complicity in the evil it condemns. Too ironic and too tough-minded to be popular in her own day and yet too accomplished to be ignored, Piatt's poems are striking both for the range and complexity of their concerns and for their stylistic anticipations of modernism, particularly the use of fragmented speakers, rough rhythms, and dialogic structures. In an age given to admiring smoothness and musicality over originality, her voice was unique.

Born on her maternal grandmother's plantation outside Lexington, Kentucky, on August 11, 1836, Sarah Morgan Bryan Piatt came from one of her state's most illustrious founding families, the Bryans, who had migrated west from North Carolina with Daniel Boone in the late 1700s. The Boones and Bryans intermarried over many generations, making the mythic frontiersman Sarah's kinsman through marriage several times over. In 1844 Piatt's mother, Mary Spiers Bryan, died, the first of many deaths that reverberate through her poetry, including those of three children lost in infancy or childhood. As was the custom in the South after a mother's death, Sarah and her younger siblings were sent to various relatives. Sarah and her sister Ellen returned to their grandmother's plantation, and Sarah later lived with her father's sister, Aunt

"Annie" Boone of New Castle, Kentucky. While there, Sarah completed her formal education, graduating from Henry Female College in 1855 with a strong foundation in the sciences and humanities, especially British poetry.

While in New Castle, Sarah began submitting poems to the *Louisville Journal*, whose waspish editor, George D. Prentice, a well-known advocate of women poets, took her under his wing. Prentice introduced her to her future husband, John James Piatt, a young Ohioan, also from an extensive pioneering family. A year older than Sarah, J.J., as he called himself, was a journalist, litterateur, and poet-in-the-making. (In 1860, J.J. published his first volume of verse, *Poems of Two Friends*, coauthored with William Dean Howells.) On June 18, 1861, two months after Union troops surrendered Fort Sumter in Charleston harbor to Confederate forces, J.J. and Sarah married, and the couple moved north to Washington, D.C., where J.J. had a clerkship in the Treasury Department, the first of many patronage positions he would hold—and lose.

Ephemeral as his jobs were (his only successful venture was an eleven-year stint as American consul in Ireland), obtaining them proved disproportionately costly, forcing J.J. to constantly beg for favors in ways that alienated him from virtually everyone that he asked for help, even his oldest friends, Howells and E. C. Stedman. By 1902, Howells reported to John Hay that J.J. was "quite pathetically poor." In the final years of their very long lives together, both he and Sarah depended on the generosity of others to survive. In 1914 J.J. was left incapacitated by a carriage accident. After his death in 1917, increasing ill health forced Sarah to leave the family homestead in North Bend, Ohio. She died at the home of her son, Cecil, in New Jersey in 1919.

In its entirety, Piatt's publishing spanned the years 1854 to 1911. She produced seventeen books, two of which she coauthored with her husband, and hundreds of her poems appeared in leading British, Irish, and American literary periodicals. Although the literary establishment of her day clearly recognized that she was the superior poet of the two spouses (for example, the *Atlantic Monthly* published thirty of her poems and only nine of J.J.'s), after their deaths, only J.J.'s name was preserved, probably because of his close ties to Howells, a master figure in the literature of the day. However, even J.J. recognized his wife's gifts and original talent. "Sallie is writing ... some very good poems.... Nearly everything she writes has a sort of dramatic play in it," J.J. told Stedman in 1869, speaking of the striking evolution that occurred in Sarah's poetry after the war. Two years later, he clarified "Sallie's" new style: "I think you'll like the poems; they seem ... new in measure and individual in ... tone—not following ... any school or favorite. Their subjects are often taken directly from some experience of life, or suggestion of experience."

Piatt's "new" poems were in fact a sharp departure from both the poetry she had written before the war and that written by most of the key literary figures of her day, especially in the centrality of dialogue to them. Lyric poets had never been shy about using dialogue as a rhetorical device, but its use was generally occasional, not constitutive. Not so with Piatt. For this self-divided poet, dialogue with its potential for clashing perspectives became the central building block of her verse. She used direct and indirect dialogue (or what J.J. refers to as "dramatic play") to root her poetry in "life," often taking her cue for a poem from something someone else said. In "The Palace-Burner," for instance, a child's question leads the speaker-mother into an internal dialogue about her own moral complicity in the revolutionary activities she condemns. Other voices that appear in her poems are those of husbands, lovers, friends, acquaintances, critics, wayside strangers, overheard speakers, and, as in the brilliant "We Two," her most Job-like performance, false comforters.

In using dialogue in this way, Piatt stripped from her verse both the excesses of her antebellum newspaper poetry (which reflected her youthful immersion in the narcissistic conventions of antebellum romantic poetry, wherein the speaker's suffering was all) and also the more restrained but no less conventional idealism encouraged by the elite postbellum periodicals and by men like Stedman, editor and poet Richard Gilder, and abolitionist and liberal author Thomas Wentworth Higginson. Instead, she made her poems a vehicle for the expression of a full range of complex emotions and perspectives. With tragic irony ("Giving Back the Flower" and "The Palace-Burner"), bitter intensity and even blasphemy ("We Two" and "Her Blindness in Grief"), tightly controlled wit ("Hearing the Battle," "Shapes of a Soul," and "The Funeral for a Doll"), and playfulness ("The Witch in the Glass," one of few poems that achieved wide-spread popularity in her lifetime), Piatt pushed hard at the limits of Victorian language and the Victorian female persona, staging in her language a multiply fractured persona that was divided not just between North and South but between love and anger, tiger and dove, romanticism and cynicism, piety and apostasy, submissiveness and rebellion.

Without attempting to transcend her own time, Piatt opened her poetry to the divergent voices of her period and culture and to those constituting her own fractured and multiple "self." She was, one graduate student wrote in a response paper, not just a political but "a deeply ethical" writer. After nearly a hundred years of silence and changes in the way we approach literature and particularly poetry, she is receiving the reception her poetic achievements deserve.

Paula Bernat Bennett
Professor Emerita, Southern Illinois University–Carbondale

PRIMARY WORKS

A Woman's Poems, 1871; *That New World and Other Poems*, 1877; *Dramatic Persons and Moods, with Other New Poems*, 1880; *An Enchanted Castle and Other Poems, Pictures, Portraits and People in Ireland*, 1893; *Poems*, 2 vols., 1894; *The Palace-Burner: The Selected Poetry of Sarah Piatt*, ed. Paula Bernat Bennett, 2001.

Hearing the Battle.—July 21, 1861.[1]

One day in the dreamy summer,
　On the Sabbath hills, from afar
We heard the solemn echoes
　Of the first fierce words of war.

[1]*Nests at Washington* (1864).

Ah, tell me, thou veilèd Watcher   5
  Of the storm and the calm to come,
How long by the sun or shadow
  Till these noises again are dumb.

And soon in a hush and glimmer
  We thought of the dark, strange fight,   10
Whose close in a ghastly quiet
  Lay dim in the beautiful night.

Then we talk'd of coldness and pallor,
  And of things with blinded eyes
That stared at the golden stillness   15
  Of the moon in those lighted skies;

And of souls, at morning wrestling
  In the dust with passion and moan,
So far away at evening
  In the silence of worlds unknown.   20

But a delicate wind beside us
  Was rustling the dusky hours,
As it gather'd the dewy odors
  Of the snowy jessamine-flowers.

And I gave you a spray of the blossoms,   25
  And I said: "I shall never know
How the hearts in the land are breaking,
  My dearest, unless you go."

                                           1864

Giving Back the Flower

So, because you chose to follow me into the subtle sadness of night,
  And to stand in the half-set moon with the weird fall-light on your
      glimmering hair,
Till your presence hid all of the earth and all of the sky from my sight,
  And to give me a little scarlet bud, that was dying of frost, to wear,   5

Say, must you taunt me forever, forever? You looked at my hand and
     you knew
That I was the slave of the Ring,[1] while you were as free as the wind
     is free.

---

[1] Her wedding ring.

When I saw your corpse in your coffin, I flung back your flower to   10
    you;
  It was all of yours that I ever had; you may keep it, and—keep from
    me.

Ah? so God is your witness. Has God, then, no world to look after
    but ours?   15
  May He not have been searching for that wild star, with trailing
    plumage, that flew
Far over a part of our darkness while we were there by the freezing
    flowers,
  Or else brightening some planet's luminous rings, instead of   20
    thinking of you?

Or, if He was near us at all, do you think that He would sit listening
    there
  Because you sang "Hear me, Norma,"[2] to a woman in jewels and
    lace,   25
While, so close to us, down in another street, in the wet, unlighted air,
  There were children crying for bread and fire, and mothers who
    questioned His grace?

Or perhaps He had gone to the ghastly field where the fight had been
    that day,   30
  To number the bloody stabs that were there, to look at and judge
    the dead;
Or else to the place full of fever and moans where the wretched
    wounded lay;
  At least I do not believe that He cares to remember a word that you   35
    said.

So take back your flower, I tell you—of its sweetness I now have no
    need;
  Yes, take back your flower down into the stillness and mystery to
    keep;   40
When you wake I will take it, and God, then, perhaps will witness
    indeed,
  But go, now, and tell Death he must watch you, and not let you
    walk in your sleep.

1867

[2]Albeit inexactly, Piatt is quoting from the opera *Norma* (1831) by Vincenzo Bellini. Presumably, like the Druidic heroine of the opera, who carries on a secret liaison with the Roman proconsul of Britain, the speaker has taken a lover from among the enemy. The meeting narrated in the poem appears to occur in Washington, D.C., where Piatt and her husband spent time during the Civil War.

Shapes of a Soul

White with the starlight folded in its wings,
  And nestling timidly against your love,
At this soft time of hushed and glimmering things,
  You call my soul a dove, a snowy dove.

If I shall ask you in some shining hour,   5
  When bees and odors through the clear air pass,
You'll say my soul buds as a small flush'd flower,
  Far off, half hiding, in the old home-grass.

Ah, pretty names for pretty moods; and you,
  Who love me, such sweet shapes as these can see;   10
But, take it from its sphere of bloom and dew,
  And where will then your bird or blossom be?

Could you but see it, by life's torrid light,
  Crouch in its sands and glare with fire-red wrath,
My soul would seem a tiger, fierce and bright   15
  Among the trembling passions in its path.

And, could you sometimes watch it coil and slide,
  And drag its colors through the dust a while,
And hiss its poison under-foot, and hide,
  My soul would seem a snake—ah, do not smile!   20

Yet fiercer forms and viler it can wear;
  No matter, though, when these are of the Past,
If as a lamb in the Good Shepherd's care
  By the still waters it lie down at last.[1]

                                                        1867

The Funeral of a Doll[1']

They used to call her Little Nell,
  In memory of that lovely child
Whose story each had learned to tell.
  She, too, was slight and still and mild,
  Blue-eyed and sweet; she always smiled,   5

---

[1]Piatt's point here is less that after death our sins will be forgiven than that the speaker's interlocutor (presumably her husband) will get what he wants (an "angel-wife") only when she is dead.

[1']*Poems in Company with Children* (1877).

And never troubled any one
Until her pretty life was done.
And so they tolled a tiny bell,
  That made a wailing fine and faint,
As fairies ring, and all was well.   10
  Then she became a waxen saint.

Her funeral it was small and sad.
  Some birds sang bird-hymns in the air.
The humming-bee seemed hardly glad,
  Spite of the honey everywhere.   15
  The very sunshine seemed to wear
Some thought of death, caught in its gold,
That made it waver wan and cold.
Then, with what broken voice he had,
  The Preacher slowly murmured on   20
(With many warnings to the bad)
  The virtues of the Doll now gone.

A paper coffin rosily-lined
  Had Little Nell. There, drest in white,
With buds about her, she reclined,
  A very fair and piteous sight—   25
  Enough to make one sorry, quite.
And, when at last the lid was shut
Under white flowers, I fancied——but
No matter. When I heard the wind   30
  Scatter Spring-rain that night across
The Doll's wee grave, with tears half-blind
  One child's heart felt a grievous loss.

"It was a funeral, mamma. Oh,
  Poor Little Nell is dead, is dead.   35
How dark!—and do you hear it blow?
  She is afraid." And, as she said
  These sobbing words, she laid her head
Between her hands and whispered: "Here
Her bed is made, the precious dear—   40
She cannot sleep in it, I know.
  And there is no one left to wear
Her pretty clothes. *Where did she go?*
——See, this poor ribbon tied her hair!"

                                            1877

The Palace-Burner[1]

A Picture in a Newspaper

She has been burning palaces. "To see
   The sparks look pretty in the wind?" Well, yes—
And something more. But women brave as she
   Leave much for cowards, such as I, to guess.

But this is old, so old that everything   5
   Is ashes here—the woman and the rest.
Two years are—oh! so long. Now you may bring
   Some newer pictures. You like this one best?

You wish that you had lived in Paris then?—
   You would have loved to burn a palace, too?   10
But they had guns in France, and Christian men
   Shot wicked little Communists like you.

You would have burned the palace?—Just because
   You did not live in it yourself! Oh! why
Have I not taught you to respect the laws?   15
   You would have burned the palace—would not *I*?

Would I? Go to your play. Would I, indeed?
   I? Does the boy not know my soul to be
Languid and worldly, with a dainty need
   For light and music? Yet he questions me.   20

Can he have seen my soul more near than I?
   Ah! in the dusk and distance sweet she seems,
With lips to kiss away a baby's cry,
   Hands fit for flowers, and eyes for tears and dreams.

Can he have seen my soul? And could she wear   25
   Such utter life upon a dying face:
Such unappealing, beautiful despair:
   Such garments—soon to be a shroud—with grace?

[1]A striking illustration of the execution of a *Petroleuse*—or "palace-burner," as the female members of the Paris Commune were called—appeared in *Harper's Weekly*, July 8, 1871. The principal speaker in the poem is a bourgeois mother, who is talking with her young son about this illustration.

Has she a charm so calm that it could breathe
  In damp, low places till some frightened hour;   30
Then start, like a fair, subtle snake, and wreathe
  A stinging poison with a shadowy power?

Would *I* burn palaces? The child has seen
  In this fierce creature of the Commune here,
So bright with bitterness and so serene,   35
  A being finer than my soul, I fear.

1872

Her Blindness in Grief[1]

What if my soul is left to me?
Oh! sweeter than my soul was he.
  Its breast broods on a coffin lid;
Its empty eyes stare at the dust.
  Tears follow tears, for treasure hid   5
Forevermore from moth and rust.

The sky a shadow is; how much
I long for something I can touch!
  God is a silence: could I hear
Him whisper once, "Poor child," to me!   10
  God is a dream, a hope, a fear,
A vision—that the seraphs see.

"Woman, why weepest thou?" One said,
To His own mother, from the dead.
  If He should come to mock me now,   15
Here in my utter loneliness,
  And say to me, "Why weepest thou?"
I wonder would I weep the less.

Or, could I, through these endless tears,
Look high into the lovely spheres   20
  And see him there—my little child—
Nursed tenderly at Mary's breast,
  Would not my sorrow be as wild?
Christ help me. Who shall say the rest?

There is no comfort anywhere.   25
My baby's clothes, my baby's hair,

---

[1] *The Independent* (1873).

My baby's grave are all I know.
What could have hurt my baby? Why,
  Why did he come; why did he go?
And shall I have him by and by?   30

Poor grave of mine, so strange, so small,
You cover all, you cover all!
  The flush of every flower, the dew,
The bird's old song, the heart's old trust,
  The star's fair light, the darkness, too,   35
Are hidden in your heavy dust.

Oh! but to kiss his little feet,
And say to them, "So sweet, so sweet,"
  I would give up whatever pain
(What else is there to give, I say?)   40
  This wide world holds. Again, again,
I yearn to follow him away.

My cry is but a human cry.
Who grieves for angels? Do they die?
  Oh! precious hands, as still as snows,   45
How your white fingers hold my heart!
  Yet keep your buried buds of rose,
Though earth and Heaven are far apart.

The grief is bitter. Let me be.
He lies beneath that lonesome tree.   50
  I've heard the fierce rain beating there.
Night covers it with cold moonshine.
  Despair can only be despair.
God has his will. I have not mine.

                                                                   1873

We Two

God's will is—the bud of the rose for your hair,
  The ring for your hand and the pearl for your breast;
God's will is—the mirror that makes you look fair.
  No wonder you whisper: "God's will is the best."

But what if God's will were the famine, the flood?   5
  And were God's will the coffin shut down in your face?
And were God's will the worm in the fold of the bud,
  Instead of the picture, the light, and the lace?

Were God's will the arrow that flieth by night,
  Were God's will the pestilence walking by day,[1]   10
The clod in the valley,[2] the rock on the hight—
  I fancy "God's will" would be harder to say.

God's will is—your own will. What honor have you
  For having your own will, awake or asleep?
Who praises the lily for keeping the dew,   15
  When the dew is so sweet for the lily to keep?

God's will unto me is not music or wine.
  With helpless reproaching, with desolate tears
God's will I resist, for God's will is divine;
  And I—shall be dust to the end of my years.   20

God's will is—not mine. Yet one night I shall lie
  Very still at his feet, where the stars may not shine.
"Lo! I am well pleased"[3] I shall hear from the sky;
  Because—it is God's will I do, and not mine.

                          1874

The Witch in the Glass[1']

"My mother says I must not pass
  Too near that glass;
She is afraid that I will see
A little witch that looks like me,
With a red, red mouth, to whisper low   5
The very thing I should not know!"

Alack for all your mother's care!
  A bird of the air,
A wistful wind, or (I suppose
Sent by some hapless boy) a rose,   10
With breath too sweet, will whisper low,
The very thing you should not know!

                          1880

---

[1] Psalm 91:5-6. "Thou shalt not be afraid for the terror by night, nor for the arrow that flieth by day, nor the pestilence that stalks in the darkness, nor the destruction that wastes at noonday."

[2] Job 21:33. "The clods of the valley are sweet to him," spoken by Job of the wicked who are nevertheless favored by God. The centrality of the Book of Job to this poem cannot be overstressed, despite the fleetingness of this allusion. The "rock" that follows appears to be a more general allusion to the safety and security those in God's favor enjoy.

[3] Matthew 3:17. "This is my beloved son, with whom I am well pleased." Given that these words are spoken by God at the baptism of Christ, Piatt, like Dickinson, appears to be adopting the role of the female Christus, along with that of a female Job.

[1'] The Union of American Poetry and Art (1880), text from Scribner's Monthly (1881).

■ WILLIAM DEAN HOWELLS ■
1837–1920

The most influential American novelist, editor, and critic of his generation, W. D. Howells was at the center of American literary culture for over fifty years. Born and raised in frontier Ohio, Howells was also one of the first important western writers to emigrate to the publishing centers of the East. Largely self-educated, he visited New England in July 1860 and met Nathaniel Hawthorne, Ralph Waldo Emerson, Henry David Thoreau, and other luminaries. As he later reminisced, Hawthorne gave him a note to pass to Emerson: "I find this young man worthy." And while hosting Howells at dinner at the Parker House, James T. Fields said to James Russell Lowell, "this is something like the apostolic succession; this is the laying on of hands." Later in the same year, Howells published a campaign biography of Abraham Lincoln, and after Lincoln's election he was rewarded with an appointment as U.S. consul in Venice. There he wrote the essays collected in his first major book, *Venetian Life* (1866). Settling in Boston the same year, he became the assistant editor of the redoubtable *Atlantic Monthly*, the most important magazine in America, and upon the retirement of Fields in 1871, Howells became its editor, a position he held for the next ten years. In this office he became a dominant critical voice, an arbiter of taste and fashion, and a champion of literary realism or "the truthful treatment of material."

For Howells, realism was a democratic movement in the arts, a focus on the normal and commonplace, distinct from romanticism or "romanticistic" fiction with its emphasis on the more ideal, bizarre, sentimental, or aristocratic. In a word, he promoted such writers as Henry James and Mark Twain and criticized others such as Sir Walter Scott and William Makepeace Thackeray. He urged readers to apply this singular test to any work of the imagination: "Is it true?— true to the motives, the impulses, the principles that shape the life of actual men and women?" He was profoundly moved in the late 1880s by Leo Tolstoy's ideas about nonviolence and economic equality. The Russian realist "has not influenced me in aesthetics only, but in ethics, too," he explained, "so that I can never again see life in the way I saw it before I knew him." Howells summarized his notion of moral complicity in his novel *The Minister's Charge* (1886). No one "sinned or suffered to himself alone," a character remarks. "If a community was corrupt, if an age was immoral, it was not because of the vicious, but the virtuous who fancied themselves indifferent spectators." Faithful to such principles in his life as well as in his art, Howells flirted with socialism and inveighed against imperialism, as in his story "Editha" (1905), a satire of a young woman who challenges her weak-willed lover to win glorious honors in battle.

Nowhere were Howells's democratic ethics more apparent than in his courageous but ill-fated defense of the Haymarket anarchists. On May 4, 1886, after a wave of labor strikes in Chicago in favor of an eight-hour workday, a policeman was killed, and seven others were mortally wounded by a bomb of unknown origin thrown during a rally in Haymarket Square organized by anarchists to protest police brutality. Eight anarchists were arrested, though none was identified as the bomb-thrower, and tried for murder. All were found guilty on August 20 and seven of them sentenced to hang. Howells fairly believed they had been railroaded. After the Supreme Court of Illinois denied their appeal on November 2, he resolved to take a stand on their behalf. On November 4 he sent a letter to the editor of the *New-York Tribune* in which he urged readers to petition the governor of Illinois to commute the anarchists' sentences. The letter appeared in the newspaper on November 6 under the banner "Clemency for the Anarchists/A Letter from W. D. Howells." Howells stood virtually alone on behalf of the doomed men and became the target of public scorn. Even his friends refused to help. As Lowell wrote him, "I thought those Chicago ruffians well hanged," though he "honored your [Howells's] courage in saying what you did about them." After one of the men committed suicide and the sentences of two others were commuted to life in prison, the other four anarchists were executed on August 11. The next day Howells wrote a second letter to the *Tribune* entitled "A Word for the Dead," though it was not published in the paper and probably was never sent. However, Howells expressed similar views in his portrayal of the German socialist Lindau in *A Hazard of New Fortunes* (1890), the novel many critics consider his best. In 1893 the new governor of Illinois pardoned the three surviving anarchists, vindicating Howells's position.

Theodore Dreiser once compared Howells to a sentry "on the watch tower, straining for a first glimpse of approaching genius." As an editor of the *Atlantic* for fifteen years and later as the contributor of the "Editor's Study" and "Editor's Easy Chair" series to *Harper's*, Howells befriended and promoted the careers of such writers as James, Twain, Bret Harte, Sarah Orne Jewett, Mary E. Wilkins (later Freeman), Frank Norris, Charles W. Chesnutt, John W. De Forest, Paul Laurence Dunbar, Hamlin Garland, Edith Wharton, Charlotte Perkins Gilman, Abraham Cahan, and Stephen Crane. Such selections from Howells's late critical writing as his reviews of Wilkins's stories in 1891 and Chesnutt's stories in 1900 and his introduction to Dunbar's *Lyrics of Lowly Life* (1896) illustrate his sponsorship of women writers and writers of color. (Howells also endorsed women's suffrage and was one of the founding members of the NAACP in 1909.)

Known late in life as "the Dean of American letters," Howells was the first president of the American Academy of Arts and Letters and served in that office for thirteen years before his death. Though he became a favorite target of such iconoclasts as H. L. Mencken and Sinclair Lewis, for whom he seemed to epitomize Victorian gentility, he deserves better from his critics. Frank Norris dismissed realism as "the drama of a broken teacup," but as practiced by Howells it both affirmed and subtly questioned bourgeois values. While he once asserted that the "smiling aspects of life" are the "more truly American," Howells was neither snob nor prig but an influential literary theorist, a prolific author, and a courageous spokesman for unpopular, progressive, and occasionally radical causes.

Gary Scharnhorst
University of New Mexico

PRIMARY WORKS

A Foregone Conclusion, 1875; *A Modern Instance*, 1882; *The Rise of Silas Lapham*, 1885; *Indian Summer*, 1886; *The Minister's Charge*, 1886; *A Hazard of New Fortunes*, 1890; *Criticism and Fiction*, 1891; *An Imperative Duty*, 1892; *A Traveler from Altruria*, 1894; *The Landlord at Lion's Head*, 1897; *Literary Friends and Acquaintance*, 1900; *My Mark Twain*, 1910; *A Selected Edition of W. D. Howells*, 1968–; *Selected Letters of W. D. Howells*, 1979–1983.

from **The Editor's Study**

Nevertheless, we are in hopes that the communistic era in taste foreshadowed by Burke[1] is approaching, and that it will occur within the lives of men now overawed by the foolish old superstition that literature and art are anything but the expression of life, and are to be judged by any other test than that of their fidelity to it. The time is coming, we trust, when each new author, each new artist, will be considered, not in his proportion to any other author or artist, but in his relation to the human nature, known to us all, which it is his privilege, his high duty, to interpret. "The true standard of the artist is in every man's power," already as Burke says; Michelangelo's[2] "light of the piazza," the glance of the common eye, is and always was the best light on a statue; Goethe's[3] "boys and blackbirds" have in all ages been the real connoisseurs of berries; but hitherto the mass of common men have been afraid to apply their own simplicity, naturalness, and honesty to the appreciation of the beautiful. They have always cast about for the instruction of some one who professed to know better, and who browbeat wholesome common-sense into the self-distrust that ends in sophistication. They have fallen generally to the worst of this bad species, and have been "amused and misled" (how pretty that quaint old use of *amuse* is!) "by the false lights" of critical vanity and self-righteousness. They have been taught to compare what they see and what they read, not with the things that they have observed and known, but with the things that some other artist or writer has done. Especially if they have themselves the artistic impulse in any direction they are taught to form themselves, not upon life, but upon the masters who became masters only by forming themselves upon life. The seeds of death are planted in them, and they can produce only the stillborn, the academic. They are not told to take their work into the public square and see if it seems true to the chance passer, but to test it by the work of the very men who refused and decried any other test of their own work. The young writer who attempts to report the phrase and carriage of everyday life, who tries to tell just how he has heard men talk and seen them look, is made to feel guilty of something low and unworthy by the stupid

[1] Edmund Burke (1729–1797), British statesman and political essayist.
[2] Michelangelo (1475–1564), Italian artist, one of the greatest figures of the Italian Renaissance.
[3] Johann Wolfgang von Goethe (1749–1832), German poet, novelist, and playwright.

people who would like to have him show how Shakespeare's men talked and looked, or Scott's, or Thackeray's, or Balzac's, or Hawthorne's, or Dickens's;[4] he is instructed to idealize his personages, that is, to take the life-likeness out of them, and put the literary-likeness into them. He is approached in the spirit of the wretched pedantry into which learning, much or little, always decays when it withdraws itself and stands apart from experience in an attitude of imagined superiority, and which would say with the same confidence to the scientist: "I see that you are looking at a grasshopper there which you have found in the grass, and I suppose you intend to describe it. Now don't waste your time and sin against culture in *that* way. I've got a grasshopper here, which has been evolved at considerable pains and expense out of the grasshopper in general; in fact, it's a type. It's made up of wire and card-board, very prettily painted in a conventional tint, and it's perfectly indestructible. It isn't very much like a real grasshopper, but it's a great deal nicer, and it's served to represent the notion of a grasshopper ever since man emerged from barbarism. You may say that it's artificial. Well, it *is* artificial: but then it's ideal too; and what you want to do is to cultivate the ideal. You'll find the books full of my kind of grasshopper, and scarcely a trace of yours in any of them. The thing that you are proposing to do is commonplace; but if you say that it isn't commonplace, for the very reason that it hasn't been done before, you'll have to admit that it's photographic."

As we said, we hope the time is coming when not only the artist, but the common, average man, who always "has the standard of the arts in his power," will have also the courage to apply it, and will reject the ideal grasshopper wherever he finds it, in science, in literature, in art, because it is not "simple, natural, and honest," because it is not like a real grasshopper. But we will own that we think the time is yet far off, and that the people who have been brought up on the ideal grasshopper, the heroic grasshopper, the impassioned grasshopper, the self-devoted, adventureful, good old romantic card-board grasshopper, must die out before the simple, honest, and natural grasshopper can have a fair field.

1887

Letters to the Editor of the *New York Tribune*

4 November 1887, Dansville, New York,
to the Editor of the *New York Tribune*

Sir:[1]

As I have petitioned the Governor of Illinois to commute the death penalty of the Anarchists to imprisonment, and have also personally written him

---

[4]William Shakespeare (1564–1616); Sir Walter Scott (1771–1832); William Makepeace Thackeray (1811–1863); Honoré de Balzac (1799–1850); Nathaniel Hawthorne (1804–1864);

Charles Dickens (1812–1870)—all eminent men of letters.
[1]Whitelaw Reid (1837–1912), editor-in-chief of the *New York Tribune* from 1872 to 1905.

in their behalf, I ask your leave to express here the hope that those who are inclined to do either will not lose faith in themselves because the Supreme Court has denied the condemned a writ of error. That court simply affirmed the legality of the forms under which the Chicago court proceeded; it did not affirm the propriety of trying for murder men fairly indictable for conspiracy alone; and it by no means approved the principle of punishing them because of their frantic opinions, for a crime which they were not shown to have committed. The justice or injustice of their sentence was not before the highest tribunal of our law, and unhappily could not be got there. That question must remain for history, which judges the judgment of courts, to deal with; and I, for one, cannot doubt what the decision of history will be.

But the worst is still for a very few days reparable; the men sentenced to death are still alive, and their lives may be finally saved through the clemency of the Governor, whose prerogative is now the supreme law in their case.[2] I conjure all those who believe that it would be either injustice or impolicy to put them to death, to join in urging him by petition, by letter, through the press, and from the pulpit and the platform, to use his power, in the only direction where power can never be misused, for the mitigation of their punishment.

William Dean Howells
Dansville, N.Y., Nov. 4, 1887

12 November 1887, Dansville, New York,
to the Editor of the New York Tribune

To the Editor of The Tribune:

I have borne with what patience I must, during the past fortnight, to be called by the Tribune, day after day imbecile and bad citizen, with the others who desired mercy for the men killed yesterday at Chicago, in conformity with our still barbarous law. I now ask you to have a little patience with me.

It seems, of course, almost a pity to mix a note of regret with the hymn of thanksgiving for blood going up from thousands of newspapers all over the land this morning; but I reflect that though I write amidst this joyful noise, my letter cannot reach the public before Monday at the earliest, and cannot therefore be regarded as an indecent interruption of the *Te Deum*.

By that time journalism will not have ceased, but history will have at least begun. All over the world where civilized men can think and feel, they are even now asking themselves, For what, really, did those four men die so bravely? Why did one other die so inexorably? Next week the journalistic theory that they died so because they were desperate murderers will have grown even more insufficient than it is now for the minds and hearts of dispassionate inquirers, and history will make the answer to which she must adhere for all time, *They died, in the prime of the freest Republic the world has ever known, for their opinions' sake.*

---

[2]Richard J. Oglesby (1824–1899) commuted to life in prison the sentences of two of the convicted men.

It is useless to deny this truth, to cover it up, to turn our backs upon it, to frown it down, or sneer it down. We have committed an atrocious andir-reparable wrong. We have been undergoing one of those spasms of paroxysmal righteousness to which our Anglo-Saxon race is peculiarly subject, and in which, let us hope, we are not more responsible for our actions than the victim of *petit mal*.[3] Otherwise, we could not forgive ourselves; and I say we, because this deed has apparently been done with the approval of the whole nation. The dead men who now accuse us of the suicidal violence in which they perished, would be alive to-day, if one thousandth part of the means employed to compass their death had been used by the people to inquire into the question of their guilt; for, under the forms of law, their trial has not been a trial by justice, but a trial by passion, by terror, by prejudice, by hate, by newspaper.

To the minority who asked mercy for them because they had made this inquiry (but who were hooted at in your columns as ignorant sentimentalists and cowards) the whole business of their conviction, except for the hideous end attained, might seem a colossal piece of that American humor, so much admired by the English for its grotesque surprises in material and proportion. But perhaps the wildest of our humorists could not have conceived of a joke so monstrous as the conviction of seven men for a murderous conspiracy which they carried into effect while one was at home playing cards with his family, another was addressing a meeting five miles away, another was present with his wife and little children, two others had made pacific speeches, and not one, except on the testimony of a single, notoriously untruthful witness,[4] was proven to have had anything to do with throwing the Haymarket bomb, or to have even remotely instigated the act. It remained for a poetic brain to imagine this, and bring its dream yesterday to homicidal realization.

I mean the brain of Mr. State's Attorney Grinnell,[5] who has shown gifts of imagination that would perhaps fit him better for the functions of a romantic novelist than for the duties of official advocate in a free commonwealth.

It was apparently inconceivable to him that it was the civic duty as well as the sacred privilege of such an officer to seek the truth concerning the accused rather than to seek their destruction. He brought into court the blood-curdling banners of the Anarchists, and unfurled them before the eyes of a jury on which eight or nine men had owned themselves prejudiced against Anarchists before the law delivered the lives of these Anarchists into their hands. He appealed to the already heated passions of the jury; he said the seven were no more guilty than a thousand other men in Chicago, but he told them that if they would hang the seven men before them the other nine hundred and ninety-three equally guilty contrivers of bombs would not

---

[3] A type of epilepsy.

[4] A painter named Harry Gilmer had testified that the anarchist August Spies supplied the match that lit the bomb.

[5] Julius S. Grinnell, the prosecuting attorney.

explode them in the bosom of the impartial jurymen's families and Society would be saved.

If he proved absolutely nothing against the Anarchists worthy of death, it cannot be denied that he at least posed successfully as a Savior of Society—the rôle once filled by the late Emperor of the French, (on the famous 2d December)[6] with great effect against the Socialists of his day. He was, throughout, the expression of the worst passions of the better classes, their fear, their hate, their resentment, which I do not find so much better than the worst passions of the worst classes that I can altogether respect them. He did not show that any of the accused threw the bomb, or had anything to do with throwing it; but he got them convicted of murder all the same. Spies was convicted of murder partly because he conspired against Society with men some of whom he was not on speaking terms with. Among the crimes for which Parsons was convicted of murder was quoting in his paper General Sheridan's belief that a dynamite bomb might kill a regiment of soldiers; and the Supreme Court of Illinois, reviewing the testimony, located him at two points, a block apart, when the bomb was thrown, and found him doubly privy to the act upon this bold topographical conception.

But Mr. Grinnell does not deserve all the honor—if it is an honor—of bringing the Anarchists to their death. He was ably seconded by Judge Gary,[7] whose interpretation of the law against murder, to make it do the work of the law against conspiracy, is a masterpiece of its kind; though perhaps even this is surpassed by his recommendation of Fielden and Schwab to the Governor's mercy because (it is like the logic of a "Bab Ballad")[8] they were pretty-behaved when brought up for sentence. It had indeed been proved, as proof went in that amusingly credulous court, that Fielden was the very man who gave the signal for throwing the bomb; but Judge Gary contributes to the science of jurisprudence the novel principle that if you are pretty-behaved when asked to say why you should not be hung for a crime of which you know your innocence, you ought afterwards to have your sentence commuted. He himself was not always pretty-behaved. When he asked Parsons that comical question, and Parsons entered upon his reasons, he refused to let him pause for a moment's refreshment while delivering his long protest, and thought it good taste and good feeling to sneer at him for reading extracts from the newspapers. Perhaps it was so; or perhaps the judge was tired—the prosecution had been reading whole files of newspapers.

When he said that the seven were no more guilty than a thousand other Anarchists, Mr. Grinnell was counting for Chicago alone; but he could doubtless have figured up ten thousand men equally guilty, upon the same medieval principle, if he took in the whole country. Seven is rather a small percentage, though seven is a mystical number, and he may have thought it had peculiar properties for that reason; but it always struck me as much too

[6]Louis Napoleon Bonaparte (1803–1873) remained president of France by ordering the army to take power on December 2, 1851.

[7]Judge Joseph E. Gary (1821–1906) of the Cooke County Superior Court.
[8]A nonsense song.

few, or wholly too many, according as the men accused did or did not do murder. With his love of poetic justice, (I will call it melodramatic justice if the word poetic seems too strong) I rather wonder that Mr. Grinnell did not at least want the men's families hanged; but since he did not ask this, I do not see why he could not have satisfied himself with having the seven Anarchists hanged in effigy. Possibly if Parsons, believing that he could suffer no wrong in an American court, had not come back and voluntarily given himself up after having made good his escape,[9] Mr. Grinnell would have demanded that sort of expiation for him.

But this is mere conjecture, and I have wished to deal with facts. One of these is that we had a political execution in Chicago yesterday. The sooner we realize this, the better for us. By such a perversion of law as brought the Anarchists to their doom, William Lloyd Garrison who published a paper denouncing the constitution as a compact with hell and a covenant with death, and every week stirred up the blacks and their friends throughout the country to abhor the social system of the South, could have been sent to the gallows if a slave had killed his masters.[10] Emerson, Parker, and Howe, Giddings and Wade, Sumner and Greeley,[11] and all who encouraged the war against slavery in Kansas, and the New England philanthropists[12] who supplied the Free State men with Sharp's rifles could have been held "morally responsible," and made to pay with their persons, when John Brown took seven Missourians out of their beds and shot them. Wendell Phillips, and Thoreau, and the other literary men whose sympathy inflamed Brown to homicidal insurrection at Harper's Ferry, could have been put to death with the same justice that consigned the Anarchists to the gallows in Chicago. The American law yesterday was made to do a deed beside which the treatment of William O'Brien by British law for the like offence, is caressing tenderness.[13]

But the men are dead. They are with God, as the simple, devout old phrase goes; or if the scientific spirit of the age does not consent to this idea, I will say that they are at least not with the newspapers. They are where, as men your words cannot hurt, nor mine help them more. But as memories, they are not beyond the reach of either, and I protest against any farther attempt to defame them. They were no vulgar or selfish murderers. However they came by their craze against society it was not through hate of

---

[9]Parsons escaped to Wisconsin after the bombing, then surrendered to authorities in Chicago six weeks later.

[10]In his abolitionist paper, the *Liberator*, Garrison (1805–1879) had described the U.S. Constitution as a "covenant with hell" because it sanctioned slavery.

[11]Ralph Waldo Emerson (1803–1882), Theodore Parker (1810–1860), Samuel G. Howe (1801–1876), Joshua R. Giddings (1795–1864), Benjamin Franklin Wade (1800–1878), William Sumner (1811–1874), and Horace Greeley (1811–1872) were all outspoken in their opposition to slavery.

[12]The "secret six" New Englanders who supported militant abolitionists such as John Brown were Parker, Howe, Thomas Wentworth Higginson (1823–1911), Gerrit Smith (1799–1874), F. B. Sanborn (1831–1917), and George L. Stearns (1809–1867).

[13]William O'Brien had been convicted in British courts of sedition and sentenced to ninety days in jail for a speech he had delivered in Ireland.

the rich so much as love of the poor. Let both rich and poor remember this, and do them this piece of justice at least.

I dread the Anarchy of the Courts, but I have never been afraid of the prevalence of the dead Anarchists' doctrine, because that must always remain to plain common sense, unthinkable; and I am not afraid of any acts of revenge from their fellow conspirators because I believe they never were part of any conspiracy. I have no doubt that Judge Gary will live long to enjoy the reward upon which he has already entered in his re-election. I have no question either as to the safety of Mr. State's Attorney Grinnell, and I hope he has not suffered too keenly from the failure to realize his poetical ideal in the number of the Anarchists finally hanged. He himself helped to reduce it to four; perhaps he will yet wish that none had died.

W. D. Howells
Dansville, Nov. 12, 1887

Mary E. Wilkins's[1] Short Stories

To turn from this great world of *Gentlemen*, to the small, lowly sphere where Miss Wilkins's humble folk have their being, is a vast change, but there is a kind of consolation in it. Here at least are real interests, passions, ambitions; and yonder there do not seem to be any. The scenes of *A New England Nun and Other Stories* are laid in that land of little village houses which the author of *A Humble Romance* has made her own. The record never strays beyond; there is hardly a person in the dramas who does not work for a living; the tragedies and comedies are those of the simplest and commonest people, who speak a crabbed Yankee through their noses, and whose dress and address would be alike shocking to *Gentlemen*. Still they may be borne with, at least in the hands of an artist such as Miss Wilkins has shown herself to be. We are not sure that there is anything better in this volume than in her first; we note the same powers, the same weaknesses; the never-erring eye, the sometimes mistaken fancy. The figures are drawn with the same exquisitely satisfying veracity; but about half the time we doubt whether they would do what they are shown doing. We have a lurking fear at moments that Miss Wilkins would like to write entirely romantic stories about these honest people of hers; but her own love of truth and her perfect knowledge of such life as theirs forbid her actually to do this. There is apparently a conflict of purposes in her sketches which gives her art an undecided effect, or a divided effect, as in certain of them where we make the acquaintance of her characters in their village of little houses, and lose it in the No Man's Land of exaggerated action and conventional emotion. In the interest of her art, which is so perfectly satisfying in the service of reality, it could almost be wished that she might once write a thoroughly romantic story, and wreak in it all the impulses she has in that

[1]Mary E. Wilkins, later Freeman (1852–1930),
New England regionalist writer.

direction. Then perhaps she might return to the right exercise of a gift which is one of the most precious in fiction. But perhaps this could not happen; perhaps the Study is itself romantic in imagining such a thing. It may be that we shall always have to content ourselves with now a story of the real and unreal mixed, and now one of unmixed reality, such as Miss Wilkins alone can give us. At any rate her future is not in the keeping of criticism, to shape or to direct. Who can forecast the course of such a talent? Not even the talent itself; and what we must be grateful for is what it has already given us in the two volumes of tales, which are as good in their way as anything ever done amongst us; that is, among any people. In form they instinctively approach that of the best work everywhere in the fine detail of the handling; but in spirit they are distinctively ours. The humor is American, and they are almost all humorously imagined, with a sort of direct reference to the facts of the usual rustic American experience. The life of the human heart, its affections, its hopes, its fears, however these mask themselves from low to high, or high to low, is always the same, in every time and land; but in each it has a special physiognomy. What our artist has done is to catch the American look of life, so that if her miniatures remain to other ages they shall know just the expression of that vast average of Americans who do the hard work of the country, and live narrowly on their small earnings and savings. If there is no gayety in that look, it is because the face of hard work is always sober, and because the consciousness of merciless fortuities and inexorable responsibilities comes early and stays late with our people.

1891

from **Criticism and Fiction**

I am not sure that the Americans have not brought the short story nearer perfection in the all-round sense than almost any other people, and for reasons very simple and near at hand. It might be argued from the national hurry and impatience that it was a literary form peculiarly adapted to the American temperament, but I suspect that its extraordinary development among us is owing much more to more tangible facts. The success of American magazines, which is nothing less than prodigious, is only commensurate with their excellence. Their sort of success is not only from the courage to decide what ought to please, but from the knowledge of what does please; and it is probable that, aside from the pictures, it is the short stories which please the readers of our best magazines. The serious novels they must have, of course; but rather more of course they must have short stories, and by operation of the law of supply and demand, the short stories, abundant in quantity and excellent in quality, are forthcoming because they are wanted. By another operation of the same law, which political economists have more recently taken account of, the demand follows the supply, and short stories are sought for because there is a proven ability to furnish them, and people read them willingly because they are usually very good. The art of writing them is now so disciplined and diffused with us that there is no lack either for the magazines or for the newspaper "syndicates" which deal in them almost to the exclusion of the serials. In other countries the feuilleton[1] of the journals is a novel continued from day to day, but with us the papers, whether daily or weekly, now more rarely print novels, whether they get them at first hand from the writers, as a great many do, or through the syndicates, which purvey a vast variety of literary wares, chiefly for the Sunday editions of the city journals. In the country papers the short story takes the place of the chapters of a serial which used to be given.

An interesting fact in regard to the different varieties of the short story among us is that the sketches and studies by the women seem faithfuler and more realistic than those of the men, in proportion to their number. Their tendency is more distinctly in that direction, and there is a solidity, an honest observation, in the work of such women as Mrs. Cooke, Miss Murfree, Miss Wilkins and Miss Jewett,[2] which often leaves little to be desired. I should, upon the whole, be disposed to rank American short stories only below those of such Russian writers as I have read, and I should praise rather than blame their free use of our different local parlances, or "dialects," as people call them. I like this because I hope that our inherited English may be constantly freshened and revived from the native sources which our literary decentralization will help to keep open, and I will own that as I turn over novels coming from Philadelphia, from New Mexico, from Boston, from Tennessee, from rural New England, from New York, every local flavor of diction gives me courage and pleasure.

M. Alphonse Daudet, in a conversation which Mr. H. H. Boyesen has set down in a recently recorded interview with him, said, in speaking of Tourguéneff.[3] "What a luxury it must be to have a great big untrodden barbaric language to wade into! We poor fellows who work in the language of an old civilization, we may sit and chisel our little verbal felicities, only to find in the end that it is a borrowed jewel we are polishing. The crown of jewels of our French tongue have passed through the hands of so many generations of monarchs that it seems like presumption on the part of any late-born pretender to attempt to wear them."

This grief is, of course, a little whimsical, yet it has a certain measure of reason in it, and the same regret has been more seriously expressed by the Italian poet Aleardi:[4]

---

[1] The literary section of a newspaper or magazine.
[2] Rose Terry Cooke (1827–1892); Mary Noailles Murfree (a.k.a. Charles Egbert Craddock) (1850–1922); Mary E. Wilkins Freeman (1852–1930); Sarah Orne Jewett (1849–1909).

[3] M. Alphonse Daudet (1840–1897), French writer; Hjalmar Hjorth Boyesen (1848–1895), a prolific American magazinist; Ivan Tourguéneff or Turgenev (1818–1883), Russian novelist.
[4] Gaetano Aleardi (1812–1878), Italian poet and politician.

> *Muse of an aged people, in the eve*
> *Of fading civilization, I was born.*
> *......... Oh, fortunate,*
> *My sisters, who in the heroic dawn*
> *Of races sung! To them did destiny give*
> *The virgin fire and chaste ingenuousness*
> *Of their land's speech; and, reverenced, their hands*
> *Ran over potent strings.*

It will never do to allow that we are at such a desperate pass in English, but something of this divine despair we may feel too in thinking of "the spacious times of great Elizabeth,"[5] when the poets were trying the stops of the young language, and thrilling with the surprises of their own music. We may comfort ourselves, however, unless we prefer a luxury of grief, by remembering that no language is ever old on the lips of those who speak it, no matter how decrepit it drops from the pen. We have only to leave our studies, editorial and other, and go into the shops and fields to find the "spacious times" again; and from the beginning Realism, before she had put on her capital letter, had divined this near-at-hand truth along with the rest. Mr. Lowell,[6] almost the greatest and finest realist who ever wrought in verse, showed us that Elizabeth was still Queen where he heard Yankee farmers talk. One need not invite slang into the company of its betters, though perhaps slang has been dropping its "s" and becoming language ever since the world began, and is certainly sometimes delightful and forcible beyond the reach of the dictionary. I would not have any one go about for new words, but if one of them came aptly, not to reject its help. For our novelists to try to write Americanly, from any motive, would be a dismal error, but being born Americans, I would have them use "Americanism" whenever these serve their turn; and when their characters speak, I should like to hear them speak true American, with all the varying Tennessean, Philadelphian, Bostonian, and New York accents. If we bother ourselves to write what the critics imagine to be "English," we shall be priggish and artificial, and still more so if we make our Americans talk "English." There is also this serious disadvantage about "English," that if we wrote the best "English" in the world, probably the English themselves would not know it, or, if they did, certainly would not own it. It has always been supposed by grammarians and purists that a language can be kept as they find it; but languages, while they live, are perpetually changing. God apparently meant them for the common people—whom Lincoln believed God liked because he had made so many of them; and the common people will use them freely as they use other gifts of God. On their lips our continental English will differ

---

[5]Alfred Lord Tennyson, "A Dream of Fair Women" (1832): "Dan Chaucer, the first warbler, whose sweet breath/Preluded those melodious bursts that fill/the spacious times of great Elizabeth."

[6]James Russell Lowell (1819–1891), American poet.

more and more from the insular English, and I believe that this is not deplorable, but desirable.

In fine, I would have our American novelists be as American as they unconsciously can. Matthew Arnold[7] complained that he found no "distinction" in our life, and I would gladly persuade all artists intending greatness in any kind among us that the recognition of the fact pointed out by Mr. Arnold ought to be a source of inspiration to them, and not discouragement. We have been now some hundred years building up a state on the affirmation of the essential equality of men in their rights and duties, and whether we have been right or wrong the gods have taken us at our word, and have responded to us with a civilization in which there is no "distinction" perceptible to the eye that loves and values it. Such beauty and such grandeur in which the quality of solidarity so prevails that neither distinguishes itself to the disadvantage of anything else. It seems to me that these conditions invite the artist to the study and the appreciation of the common, and to the portrayal in every art of those finer and higher aspects which unite rather than sever humanity, if he would thrive in our new order of things. The talent that is robust enough to front the everyday world and catch the charm of its work-worn, care-worn, brave, kindly face, need not fear the encounter, though it seems terrible to the sort nurtured in the superstition of the romantic, the bizarre, the heroic, the distinguished, as the things alone worthy of painting or carving or writing. The arts must become democratic, and then we shall have the expression of America in art; and the reproach which Mr. Arnold was half right in making us shall have no justice in it any longer; we shall be "distinguished."

1891

Paul Laurence Dunbar

I think I should scarcely trouble the reader with a special appeal in behalf of this book, if it had not specially appealed to me for reasons apart from the author's race, origin, and condition. The world is too old now, and I find myself too much of its mood, to care for the work of a poet because he is black, because his father and mother were slaves, because he was, before and after he began to write poems, an elevator-boy. These facts would certainly attract me to him as a man, if I knew him to have a literary ambition, but when it came to his literary art, I must judge it irrespective of these facts, and enjoy or endure it for what it was in itself.

It seems to me that this was my experience with the poetry of Paul Laurence Dunbar when I found it in another form, and in justice to him I cannot wish that it should be otherwise with his readers here. Still, it will

---

[7]Matthew Arnold (1822–1888): one of England's most influential poets and cultural critics. One of his criticisms of the United States, which he had visited in 1883–1884 and again in 1886, was that its culture lacked "distinction."

legitimately interest those who like to know the causes, or, if these may not be known, the sources, of things, to learn that the father and mother of the first poet of his race in our language were negroes without admixture of white blood. The father escaped from slavery in Kentucky to freedom in Canada, while there was still no hope of freedom otherwise; but the mother was freed by the events of the civil war, and came North to Ohio, where their son was born at Dayton, and grew up with such chances and mischances for mental training as everywhere befall the children of the poor. He has told me that his father picked up the trade of a plasterer, and when he had taught himself to read, loved chiefly to read history. The boy's mother shared his passion for literature, with a special love of poetry, and after the father died she struggled on in more than the poverty she had shared with him. She could value the faculty which her son showed first in prose sketches and attempts at fiction, and she was proud of the praise and kindness they won him among the people of the town, where he has never been without the warmest and kindest friends.

In fact, from every part of Ohio and from several cities of the adjoining States, there came letters in cordial appreciation of the critical recognition which it was my pleasure no less than my duty to offer Paul Dunbar's work in another place.[1] It seemed to me a happy omen for him that so many people who had known him, or known of him, were glad of a stranger's good word; and it was gratifying to see that at home he was esteemed for the things he had done rather than because as the son of negro slaves he had done them. If a prophet is often without honor in his own country, it surely is nothing against him when he has it. In this case it deprived me of the glory of a discoverer; but that is sometimes a barren joy, and I am always willing to forego it.

What struck me in reading Mr. Dunbar's poetry was what had already struck his friends in Ohio and Indiana, in Kentucky and Illinois. They had felt, as I felt, that however gifted his race had proven itself in music, in oratory, in several of the other arts, here was the first intance of an American negro who had evinced innate distinction in literature. In my criticism of his book I had alleged Dumas in France, and I had forgetfully failed to allege the far greater Pushkin in Russia;[2] but these were both mulattoes, who might have been supposed to derive their qualities from white blood vastly more artistic than ours, and who were the creatures of an environment more favorable to their literary development. So far as I could remember, Paul Dunbar was the only man of pure African blood and of American civilization to feel the negro life æsthetically and express it lyrically. It seemed to me that this had come to its most modern consciousness in him, and that his brilliant and unique achievement was to have studied the American negro objectively, and to have represented him as he found him to be, with humor, with sympathy, and yet with what the reader must instinctively feel

---

[1] Howells had reviewed Dunbar's *Majors and Minors* in *Harper's Weekly* for June 27, 1896.

[2] Alexandre Dumas, or Dumas *père* (the father) (1802–1870), French novelist and playwright; Alexander Pushkin (1799–1837), Russian poet.

to be entire truthfulness. I said that a race which had come to this effect in any member of it, had attained civilization in him, and I permitted myself the imaginative prophecy that the hostilities and the prejudices which had so long constrained his race were destined to vanish in the arts; that these were to be the final proof that God had made of one blood all nations of men. I thought his merits positive and not comparative; and I held that if his black poems had been written by a white man, I should not have found them less admirable. I accepted them as an evidence of the essential unity of the human race, which does not think or feel black in one and white in another, but humanly in all.

Yet it appeared to me then, and it appears to me now, that there is a precious difference of temperament between the races which it would be a great pity ever to lose, and that this is best preserved and most charmingly suggested by Mr. Dunbar in those pieces of his where he studies the moods and traits of his race in its own accent of our English. We call such pieces dialect pieces for want of some closer phrase, but they are really not dialect so much as delightful personal attempts and failures for the written and spoken language. In nothing is his essentially refined and delicate art so well shown as in these pieces, which, as I ventured to say, describe the range between appetite and emotion, with certain lifts far beyond and above it, which is the range of the race. He reveals in these a finely ironical perception of the negro's limitations, with a tenderness for them which I think so very rare as to be almost quite new. I should say, perhaps, that it was this humorous quality which Mr. Dunbar had added to our literature, and it would be this which would most distinguish him, now and hereafter. It is something that one feels in nearly all the dialect pieces; and I hope that in the present collection he has kept all of these in his earlier volume, and added others to them. But the contents of this book are wholly of his own choosing, and I do not know how much or little he may have preferred the poems in literary English. Some of these I thought very good, and even more than very good, but not distinctively his contribution to the body of American poetry. What I mean is that several people might have written them; but I do not know any one else at present who could quite have written the dialect pieces. These are divinations and reports of what passes in the hearts and minds of a lowly people whose poetry had hitherto been inarticulately expressed in music, but now finds, for the first time in our tongue, literary interpretation of a very artistic completeness.

I say the event is interesting, but how important it shall be can be determined only by Mr. Dunbar's future performance. I cannot undertake to prophesy concerning this; but if he should do nothing more than he has done, I should feel that he had made the strongest claim for the negro in English literature that the negro has yet made. He has at least produced something that, however we may critically disagree about it, we cannot well refuse to enjoy; in more than one piece he has produced a work of art.

1896

Mr. Charles W. Chesnutt's Stories

The critical reader of the story called The Wife of his Youth, which appreared in these pages two years ago, must have noticed uncommon traits in what was altogether a remarkable piece of work. The first was the novelty of the material; for the writer dealt not only with people who were not white, but with people who were not black enough to contrast grotesquely with white people,—who in fact were of that near approach to the ordinary American in race and color which leaves, at the last degree, every one but the connoisseur in doubt whether they are Anglo-Saxon or Anglo-African. Quite as striking as this novelty of the material was the author's thorough mastery of it, and his unerring knowledge of the life he had chosen in its peculiar racial characteristics. But above all, the story was notable for the passionless handling of a phase of our common life which is tense with potential tragedy; for the attitude, almost ironical, in which the artist observes the play of contesting emotions in the drama under his eyes; and for his apparently reluctant, apparently helpless consent to let the spectator know his real feeling in the matter. Any one accustomed to study methods in fiction, to distinguish between good and bad art, to feel the joy which the delicate skill possible only from a love of truth can give, must have known a high pleasure in the quiet self-restraint of the performance; and such a reader would probably have decided that the social situation in the piece was studied wholly from the outside, by an observer with special opportunities for knowing it, who was, as it were, surprised into final sympathy.

Now, however, it is known that the author of this story is of negro blood,—diluted, indeed, in such measure that if he did not admit this descent few would imagine it, but still quite of that middle world which lies next, though wholly outside, our own. Since his first story appeared he has contributed several others to these pages, and he now makes a showing palpable to criticism in a volume called The Wife of his Youth, and Other Stories of the Color Line; a volume of Southern sketches called The Conjure Woman; and a short life of Frederick Douglass, in the Beacon Series of biographies. The last is a simple, solid, straight piece of work, not remarkable above many other biographical studies by people entirely white, and yet important as the work of a man not entirely white treating of a great man of his inalienable race. But the volumes of fiction *are* remarkable above many, above most short stories by people entirely white, and would be worthy of unusual notice if they were not the work of a man not entirely white.

It is not from their racial interest that we could first wish to speak of them, though that must have a very great and very just claim upon the critic. It is much more simply and directly, as works of art, that they make their appeal, and we must allow the force of this quite independently of the other interest. Yet it cannot always be allowed. There are times in each of the stories of the first volume when the simplicity lapses, and the effect is as of a weak and uninstructed touch. There are other times when the attitude, severely impartial and studiously aloof, accuses itself of a little pompousness. There are still other times when the literature is a little too ornate for beauty, and the diction is journalistic, reporteristic. But it is right to add that these are the exceptional times, and that for far the greatest part Mr. Chesnutt seems to know quite as well what he wants to do in a given case as Maupassant,[1] or Tour-guénief, or Mr. James, or Miss Jewett, or Miss Wilkins, in other given cases, and has done it with an art of kindred quiet and force. He belongs, in other words, to the good school, the only school, all aberrations from nature being so much truancy and anarchy. He sees his people very clearly, very justly, and he shows them as he sees them, leaving the reader to divine the depth of his feeling for them. He touches all the stops, and with equal delicacy in stories of real tragedy and comedy and pathos, so that it would be hard to say which is the finest in such admirably rendered effects as The Web of Circumstance, The Bouquet, and Uncle Wellington's Wives. In some others the comedy degenerates into satire, with a look in the reader's direction which the author's friend must deplore.

As these stories are of our own time and country, and as there is not a swash-buckler of the seventeenth century, or a sentimentalist of this, or a princess of an imaginary kingdom, in any of them, they will possibly not reach half a million readers in six months, but in twelve months possibly more readers will remember them than if they had reached the half million. They are new and fresh and strong, as life always is, and fable never is; and the stories of The Conjure Woman have a wild, indigenous poetry, the creation of sincere and original imagination, which is imparted with a tender humorousness and a very artistic reticence. As far as his race is concerned, or his sixteenth part of a race, it does not greatly matter whether Mr. Chesnutt invented their motives, or found them, as he feigns, among his distant cousins of the Southern cabins. In either case, the wonder of their beauty is the same; and whatever is primitive and sylvan or campestral in the reader's heart is touched by the spells thrown on the simple black lives in these enchanting tales. Character, the most precious thing in fiction, is as faithfully portrayed against the poetic background as in the setting of the Stories of the Color Line.

Yet these stories, after all, are Mr. Chesnutt's most important work, whether we consider them merely as realistic fiction, apart from their author, or as studies of that middle world of which he is naturally and voluntarily a citizen. We had known the nethermost world of the grotesque and comical negro and the terrible and tragic negro through the white observer on the outside, and black character in its lyrical moods we had known from such an inside witness as Mr. Paul Dunbar; but it had remained for Mr. Chesnutt to acquaint us with those regions where the paler shades dwell as hopelessly, with relation to ourselves, as the blackest negro. He has not shown the dwellers there as very different from ourselves. They have within their own circles the same social ambitions and prejudices; they intrigue and

[1]Guy de Maupassant (1850–1893), French novelist.

truckle and crawl, and are snobs, like ourselves, both of the snobs that snub and the snobs that are snubbed. We may choose to think them droll in their parody of pure white society, but perhaps it would be wiser to recognize that they are like us because they are of our blood by more than a half, or three quarters, or nine tenths. It is not, in such cases, their negro blood that characterizes them; but it is their negro blood that excludes them, and that will imaginably fortify them and exalt them. Bound in that sad solidarity from which there is no hope of entrance into polite white society for them, they may create a civilization of their own, which need not lack the highest quality. They need not be ashamed of the race from which they have sprung, and whose exile they share; for in many of the arts it has already shown, during a single generation of freedom, gifts which slavery apparently only obscured. With Mr. Booker Washington the first American orator of our time,[2] fresh upon the time of Frederick Douglass; with Mr. Dunbar among the truest of our poets; with Mr. Tanner, a black American, among the only three Americans from whom the French government ever bought a picture,[3] Mr. Chesnutt may well be willing to own his color.

But that is his personal affair. Our own more universal interest in him arises from the more than promise he has given in a department of literature where Americans hold the foremost place. In this there is, happily, no color line; and if he has it in him to go forward on the way which he has traced for himself, to be true to life as he has known it, to deny himself the glories of the cheap success which awaits the charlatan in fiction, one of the places at the top is open to him. He has sounded a fresh note, boldly, not blatantly, and he has won the ear of the more intelligent public.

1900

Editha

The air was thick with the war feeling,[1] like the electricity of a storm which has not yet burst. Editha sat looking out into the hot spring afternoon, with her lips parted, and panting with the intensity of the question whether she could let him go. She had decided that she could not let him stay, when she saw him at the end of the still leafless avenue, making slowly up toward the house, with his head down, and his figure relaxed. She ran impatiently out on the veranda, to the edge of the steps, and imperatively demanded greater haste of him with her will before she called aloud to him, "George!"

He had quickened his pace in mystical response to her mystical urgence, before he could have heard her; now he looked up and answered, "Well?"

"Oh, how united we are!" she exulted, and then she swooped down the steps to him. "What is it?" she cried.

---

[2]Booker T. Washington (1856–1915), the principal of Tuskegee Institute in Alabama.
[3]Henry Ossawa Tanner (1859–1937), American painter.

[1]Howells apparently alludes to the then-recent Spanish-American War of 1898, which he opposed.

"It's war," he said, and he pulled her up to him, and kissed her.

She kissed him back intensely, but irrelevantly, as to their passion, and uttered from deep in her throat, "How glorious!"

"It's war," he repeated, without consenting to her sense of it; and she did not know just what to think at first. She never knew what to think of him; that made his mystery, his charm. All through their courtship, which was contemporaneous with the growth of the war feeling, she had been puzzled by his want of seriousness about it. He seemed to despise it even more than he abhorred it. She could have understood his abhorring any sort of bloodshed; that would have been a survival of his old life when he thought he would be a minister, and before he changed and took up the law. But making light of a cause so high and noble seemed to show a want of earnestness at the core of his being. Not but that she felt herself able to cope with a congenital defect of that sort, and make his love for her save him from himself. Now perhaps the miracle was already wrought in him. In the presence of the tremendous fact that he announced, all triviality seemed to have gone out of him; she began to feel that. He sank down on the top step, and wiped his forehead with her handkerchief, while she poured out upon him her question of the origin and authenticity of his news.

All the while, in her duplex emotioning, she was aware that now at the very beginning she must put a guard upon herself against urging him, by any word or act, to take the part that her whole soul willed him to take, for the completion of her ideal of him. He was very nearly perfect as he was, and he must be allowed to perfect himself. But he was peculiar, and he might very well be reasoned out of his peculiarity. Before her reasoning went her emotioning: her nature pulling upon his nature, her womanhood upon his manhood, without her knowing the means she was using to the end she was willing. She had always supposed that the man who won her would have done something to win her; she did not know what, but something. George Gearson had simply asked her for her love, on the way home from a concert, and she gave her love to him, without, as it were, thinking. But now, it flashed upon her, if he could do something worthy to *have* won her—be a hero, *her* hero—it would be even better than if he had done it before asking her; it would be grander. Besides, she had believed in the war from the beginning.

"But don't you see, dearest," she said, "that it wouldn't have come to this, if it hadn't been in the order of Providence? And I call any war glorious that is for the liberation of people who have been struggling for years against the cruelest oppression. Don't you think so too?"

"I suppose so," he returned, languidly. "But war! Is it glorious to break the peace of the world?"

"That ignoble peace! It was no peace at all, with that crime and shame at our very gates." She was conscious of parroting the current phrases of the newspapers, but it was no time to pick and choose her words. She must sacrifice anything to the high ideal she had for him, and after a good deal of rapid argument she ended with the climax: "But now it doesn't matter about the how or why. Since the war has come, all that is gone. There are no two sides, any more. There is nothing now but our country."

He sat with his eyes closed and his head leant back against the veranda, and he said with a vague smile, as if musing aloud, "Our country—right or wrong."

"Yes, right or wrong!" she returned fervidly. "I'll go and get you some lemonade." She rose rustling, and whisked away; when she came back with two tall glasses of clouded liquid, on a tray, and the ice clucking in them, he still sat as she left him, and she said as if there had been no interruption: "But there is no question of wrong in this case. I call it a sacred war. A war for liberty, and humanity, if ever there was one. And I know you will see it just as I do, yet."

He took half the lemonade at a gulp, and he answered as he set the glass down: "I know you always have the highest ideal. When I differ from you, I ought to doubt myself."

A generous sob rose in Editha's throat for the humility of a man, so very nearly perfect, who was willing to put himself below her.

Besides, she felt, more subliminally, that he was never so near slipping through her fingers as when he took that meek way.

"You shall not say that! Only, for once I happen to be right." She seized his hand in her two hands, and poured her soul from her eyes into his. "Don't you think so?" she entreated him.

He released his hand and drank the rest of his lemonade, and she added, "Have mine, too," but he shook his head in answering, "I've no business to think so, unless I act so, too."

Her heart stopped a beat before it pulsed on with leaps that she felt in her neck. She had noticed that strange thing in men; they seemed to feel bound to do what they believed, and not think a thing was finished when they said it, as girls did. She knew what was in his mind, but she pretended not, and she said, "Oh, I am not sure," and then faltered.

He went on as if to himself without apparently heeding her, "There's only one way of proving one's faith in a thing like this."

She could not say that she understood, but she did understand.

He went on again. "If I believed—if I felt as you do about this war—Do you wish me to feel as you do?"

Now she was really not sure; so she said, "George, I don't know what you mean."

He seemed to muse away from her as before. "There is a sort of fascination in it. I suppose that at the bottom of his heart every man would like at times to have his courage tested; to see how he would act."

"How can you talk in that ghastly way!"

"It *is* rather morbid. Still, that's what it comes to, unless you're swept away by ambition, or driven by conviction. I haven't the conviction or the ambition, and the other thing is what it comes to with me. I ought to have been a preacher, after all; then I couldn't have asked it of myself, as I must, now I'm a lawyer. And you believe it's a holy war, Editha?" he suddenly addressed her. "Or, I know you do! But you wish me to believe so, too?"

She hardly knew whether he was mocking or not, in the ironical way he always had with her plainer mind. But the only thing was to be outspoken with him.

"George, I wish you to believe whatever you think is true, at any and every cost. If I've tried to talk you into anything, I take it all back."

"Oh, I know that, Editha. I know how sincere you are, and how—I wish I had your undoubting spirit! I'll think it over; I'd like to believe as you do. But I don't, now; I don't, indeed. It isn't this war alone; though this seems peculiarly wanton and needless; but it's every war—so stupid; it makes me sick. Why shouldn't this thing have been settled reasonably?"

"Because," she said, very throatily again, "God meant it to be war."

"You think it was God? Yes, I suppose that is what people will say."

"Do you suppose it would have been war if God hadn't meant it?"

"I don't know. Sometimes it seems as if God had put this world into men's keeping to work it as they pleased."

"Now, George, that is blasphemy."

"Well, I won't blaspheme. I'll try to believe in your pocket Providence," he said, and then he rose to go.

"Why don't you stay to dinner?" Dinner at Balcom's Works was at one o'clock.

"I'll come back to supper, if you'll let me. Perhaps I shall bring you a convert." "Well, you may come back, on that condition."

"All right. If I don't come, you'll understand."

He went away without kissing her, and she felt it a suspension of their engagement. It all interested her intensely; she was undergoing a tremendous experience, and she was being equal to it. While she stood looking after him, her mother came out through one of the long windows, on to the veranda, with a catlike softness and vagueness.

"Why didn't he stay to dinner?"

"Because—because—war has been declared," Editha pronounced, without turning.

Her mother said, "Oh, my!" and then said nothing more until she had sat down in one of the large Shaker chairs, and rocked herself for some time. Then she closed whatever tacit passage of thought there had been in her mind with the spoken words, "Well, I hope *he* won't go."

"And *I* hope he *will*," the girl said, and confronted her mother with a stormy exaltation that would have frightened any creature less unimpressionable than a cat.

Her mother rocked herself again for an interval of cogitation. What she arrived at in speech was, "Well, I guess you've done a wicked thing, Editha Balcom."

The girl said, as she passed indoors through the same window her mother had come out by, "I haven't done anything—yet."

In her room, she put together all her letters and gifts from Gearson, down to the withered petals of the first flower he had offered, with that timidity of his veiled in that irony of his. In the heart of the packet she enshrined her engagement ring which she had restored to the pretty box he had brought it her in. Then she sat down, if not calmly yet strongly, and wrote:

> "George: I understood—when you left me. But I think we had better empha-
> size your meaning that if we cannot be one in everything we had better be
> one in nothing. So I am sending these things for your keeping till you have
> made up your mind.
>
> "I shall always love you, and therefore I shall never marry any one else.
> But the man I marry must love his country first of all, and be able to say to
> me,
>
>> 'I could not love thee, dear, so much,
>> Loved I not honor more,'[2]
>
> "There is no honor above America with me. In this great hour there is
> no other honor.
>
> "Your heart will make my words clear to you. I had never expected to
> say so much, but it has come upon me that I must say the utmost.
>
> Editha."

She thought she had worded her letter well, worded it in a way that could not be bettered; all had been implied and nothing expressed.

She had it ready to send with the packet she had tied with red, white, and blue ribbon, when it occurred to her that she was not just to him, that she was not giving him a fair chance. He had said he would go and think it over, and she was not waiting. She was pushing, threatening, compelling. That was not a woman's part. She must have him free, free, free. She could not accept for her country or herself a forced sacrifice.

In writing her letter she had satisfied the impulse from which it sprang; she could well afford to wait till he had thought it over. She put the packet and the letter by, and rested serene in the consciousness of having done what was laid upon her by her love itself to do, and yet used patience, mercy, justice.

She had her reward. Gearson did not come to tea, but she had given him till morning, when, late at night there came up from the village the sound of a fife and drum with a tumult of voices, in shouting, singing, and laughing. The noise drew nearer and nearer; it reached the street end of the avenue; there it silenced itself, and one voice, the voice she knew best, rose over the silence. It fell; the air was filled with cheers; the fife and drum struck up, with the shouting, singing, and laughing again, but now retreating; and a single figure came hurrying up the avenue.

She ran down to meet her lover and clung to him. He was very gay, and he put his arm round her with a boisterous laugh. "Well, you must call me Captain, now; or Cap, if you prefer; that's what the boys call me. Yes, we've had a meeting at the town hall, and everybody has volunteered; and they

[2]Editha cites the final lines of "To Lucasta,
Going to the Wars," by Richard Lovelace
(1618– 1658).

selected me for captain, and I'm going to the war, the big war, the glorious war, the holy war ordained by the pocket Providence that blesses butchery. Come along; let's tell the whole family about it. Call them from their downy beds, father, mother, Aunt Hitty, and all the folks!"

But when they mounted the veranda steps he did not wait for a larger audience; he poured the story out upon Editha alone.

"There was a lot of speaking, and then some of the fools set up a shout for me. It was all going one way, and I thought it would be a good joke to sprinkle a little cold water on them. But you can't do that with a crowd that adores you. The first thing I knew I was sprinkling hell-fire on them. 'Cry havoc, and let slip the dogs of war.'[3] That was the style. Now that it had come to the fight, there were no two parties; there was one country, and the thing was to fight the fight to a finish as quick as possible. I suggested volunteering then and there, and I wrote my name first of all on the roster. Then they elected me—that's all. I wish I had some ice-water!"

She left him walking up and down the veranda, while she ran for the ice-pitcher and a goblet, and when she came back he was still walking up and down, shouting the story he had told her to her father and mother, who had come out more sketchily dressed than they commonly were by day. He drank goblet after goblet of the ice-water without noticing who was giving it, and kept on talking, and laughing through his talk wildly. "It's astonishing," he said, "how well the worse reason looks when you try to make it appear the better. Why, I believe I was the first convert to the war in that crowd to-night! I never thought I should like to kill a man; but now, I shouldn't care; and the smokeless powder lets you see the man drop that you kill. It's all for the country! What a thing it is to have a country that *can't* be wrong, but if it is, is right anyway!"

Editha had a great, vital thought, an inspiration. She set down the ice-pitcher on the veranda floor, and ran up-stairs and got the letter she had written him. When at last he noisily bade her father and mother, "Well, good night. I forgot I woke you up; I sha'n't want any sleep myself," she followed him down the avenue to the gate. There, after the whirling words that seemed to fly away from her thoughts and refuse to serve them, she made a last effort to solemnize the moment that seemed so crazy, and pressed the letter she had written upon him.

"What's this?" he said, "Want me to mail it?"

"No, no. It's for you. I wrote it after you went this morning. Keep it— keep it—and read it sometime—" She thought, and then her inspiration came: "Read it if ever you doubt what you've done, or fear that I regret your having done it. Read it after you've started."

They strained each other in embraces that seemed as ineffective as their words, and he kissed her face with quick, hot breaths that were so unlike him, that made her feel as if she had lost her old lover and found a stranger

[3]George quotes Mark Antony in Shakespeare's
Julius Caesar, act 2, scene 1, line 273.

in his place. The stranger said, "What a gorgeous flower you are, with your red hair, and your blue eyes that look black now, and your face with the color painted out by the white moonshine! Let me hold you under my chin, to see whether I love blood, you tiger-lily!" Then he laughed Gearson's laugh, and released her, scared and giddy. Within her willfulness she had been frightened by a sense of subtler force in him, and mystically mastered as she had never been before.

She ran all the way back to the house, and mounted the steps panting. Her mother and father were talking of the great affair. Her mother said: "Wa'n't Mr. Gearson in rather of an excited state of mind? Didn't you think he acted curious?"

"Well, not for a man who'd just been elected captain and had to set 'em up for the whole of Company A," her father chuckled back.

"What in the world do you mean, Mr. Balcom? Oh! There's Editha!" She offered to follow the girl indoors.

"Don't come, mother!" Editha called, vanishing.

Mrs. Balcom remained to reproach her husband. "I don't see much of anything to laugh at."

"Well, it's catching. Caught it from Gearson. I guess it won't be much of a war, and I guess Gearson don't think so, either. The other fellows will back down as soon as they see we mean it. I wouldn't lose any sleep over it. I'm going back to bed, myself."

Gearson came again next afternoon, looking pale, and rather sick, but quite himself, even to his languid irony. "I guess I'd better tell you, Editha, that I consecrated myself to your god of battles last night by pouring too many libations to him down my own throat. But I'm all right, now. One has to carry off the excitement, somehow."

"Promise me," she commanded, "that you'll never touch it again!"

"What! Not let the cannikin clink? Not let the soldier drink? Well, I promise."

"You don't belong to yourself now; you don't even belong to me. You belong to your country, and you have a sacred charge to keep yourself strong and well for your country's sake. I have been thinking, thinking all night and all day long."

"You look as if you had been crying a little, too," he said with his queer smile.

"That's all past. I've been thinking, and worshipping you. Don't you suppose I know all that you've been through, to come to this? I've followed you every step from your old theories and opinions."

"Well, you've had a long row to hoe."

"And I know you've done this from the highest motives—"

"Oh, there won't be much pettifogging to do till this cruel war is—"

"And you haven't simply done it for my sake. I couldn't respect you if you had."

"Well, then we'll say I haven't. A man that hasn't got his own respect intact wants the respect of all the other people he can corner. But we won't go into that. I'm in for the thing now, and we've got to face our future. My idea is that this isn't going to be a very protracted struggle; we shall just scare the enemy to death before it comes to a fight at all. But we must provide for contingencies, Editha. If anything happens to me—"

"Oh, George!" She clung to him sobbing.

"I don't want you to feel foolishly bound to my memory. I should hate that, wherever I happened to be."

"I am yours, for time and eternity—time and eternity." She liked the words; they satisfied her famine for phrases.

"Well, say eternity; that's all right; but time's another thing; and I'm talking about time. But there is something! My mother! If anything happens—"

She winced, and he laughed. "You're not the bold soldier-girl of yesterday!" Then he sobered. "If anything happens, I want you to help my mother out. She won't like my doing this thing. She brought me up to think war a fool thing as well as a bad thing. My father was in the civil war; all through it; lost his arm in it." She thrilled with the sense of the arm round her; what if that should be lost? He laughed as if divining her: "Oh, it doesn't run in the family, as far as a I know!" Then he added, gravely, "He came home with misgivings about war, and they grew on him. I guess he and mother agreed between them that I was to be brought up in his final mind about it; but that was before my time. I only knew him from my mother's report of him and his opinions; I don't know whether they were hers first; but they were hers last. This will be a blow to her. I shall have to write and tell her—"

He stopped, and she asked, "Would you like me to write too, George?"

"I don't believe that would do. No, I'll do the writing. She'll understand a little if I say that I thought the way to minimize it was to make war on the largest possible scale at once—that I felt I must have been helping on the war somehow if I hadn't helped keep it from coming, and I knew I hadn't; when it came, I had no right to stay out of it."

Whether his sophistries satisfied him or not, they satisfied her. She clung to his breast, and whispered, with closed eyes and quivering lips, "Yes, yes, yes!"

"But if anything should happen, you might go to her, and see what you could do for her. You know? It's rather far off; she can't leave her chair—"

"Oh, I'll go, if it's the ends of the earth! But nothing will happen! Nothing *can*! I—"

She felt herself lifted with his rising, and Gearson was saying, with his arm still round her, to her father: "Well, we're off at once, Mr. Balcom. We're to be formally accepted at the capital, and then bunched up with the rest somehow, and sent into camp somewhere, and got to the front as soon as possible. We all want to be in the van, of course; we're the first company to report to the Governor. I came to tell Editha, but I hadn't got round to it."

* * *

She saw him again for a moment at the capital, in the station, just before the train started southward with his regiment. He looked well, in his uniform, and very soldierly, but somehow girlish, too, with his clean-shaven face and slim figure. The manly eyes and the strong voice satisfied her, and his preoccupation with some unexpected details of duty flattered her. Other girls were weeping and bemoaning themselves, but she felt a sort of noble distinction in the abstraction, the almost unconsciousness, with which they parted. Only at the last moment he said, "Don't forget my mother. It mayn't be such a walk-over as I supposed," and he laughed at the notion.

He waved his hand to her, as the train moved off—she knew it among a score of hands that were waved to other girls from the platform of the car, for it held a letter which she knew was hers. Then he went inside the car to read it, doubtless, and she did not see him again. But she felt safe for him through the strength of what she called her love. What she called her God, always speaking the name in a deep voice and with the implication of a mutual understanding, would watch over him and keep him and bring him back to her. If with an empty sleeve, then he should have three arms instead of two, for both of hers should be his for life. She did not see, though, why she should always be thinking of the arm his father had lost.

There were not many letters from him, but they were such as she could have wished, and she put her whole strength into making hers such as she imagined he could have wished, glorifying and supporting him. She wrote to his mother glorifying him as their hero, but the brief answer she got was merely to the effect that Mrs. Gearson was not well enough to write herself, and thanking her for her letter by the hand of some one who called herself "Yrs truly, Mrs. W.J. Andrews."

Editha determined not to be hurt, but to write again quite as if the answer had been all she expected. But before it seemed as if she could have written, there came news of the first skirmish, and in the list of the killed which was telegraphed as a trifling loss on our side, was Gearson's name. There was a frantic time of trying to make out that it might be, must be, some other Gearson; but the name, and the company and the regiment, and the State were too definitely given.

Then there was a lapse into depths out of which it seemed as if she never could rise again; then a lift into clouds far above all grief, black clouds, that blotted out the sun, but where she soared with him, with George, George! She had the fever that she expected of herself, but she did not die in it; she was not even delirious, and it did not last long. When she was well enough to leave her bed, her one thought was of George's mother, of his strangely worded wish that she should go to her and see what she could do for her. In the exaltation of the duty laid upon her—it buoyed her up instead of burdening her—she rapidly recovered.

Her father went with her on the long railroad journey from northern New York to western Iowa; he had business out at Davenport, and he said he could just as well go then as any other time; and he went with her to the little country town where George's mother lived in a little house on the edge of illimitable corn-fields, under trees pushed to a top of the rolling prairie. George's father had settled there after the civil war, as so many other old soldiers had done; but they were Eastern people, and Editha fancied touches of the East in the June rose overhanging the front door, and the garden with early summer flowers stretching from the gate of the paling fence.

It was very low inside the house, and so dim, with the closed blinds, that they could scarcely see one another: Editha tall and black in her crapes which filled the air with the smell of their dyes; her father standing decorously apart with his hat on his forearm, as at funerals; a woman rested in a deep armchair, and the woman who had let the strangers in stood behind the chair.

The seated woman turned her head round and up, and asked the woman behind her chair, "*Who* did you say?"

Editha, if she had done what she expected of herself, would have gone down on her knees at the feet of the seated figure and said, "I am George's Editha," for answer.

But instead of her own voice she heard that other woman's voice, saying, "Well, I don't know as I *did* get the name just right. I guess I'll have to make a little more light in here," and she went and pushed two of the shutters ajar.

Then Editha's father said in his public will-now-address-a-few-remarks tone, "My name is Balcom, ma'am; Junius H. Balcom, of Balcom's Works, New York; my daughter—"

"Oh!" The seated woman broke in, with a powerful voice, the voice that always surprised Editha from Gearson's slender frame. "Let me see you! Stand round where the light can strike on your face," and Editha dumbly obeyed. "So, you're Editha Balcom," she sighed.

"Yes," Editha said, more like a culprit than a comforter.

"What did you come for?" Mrs. Gearson asked.

Editha's face quivered, and her knees shook. "I came—because—because George—" She could go no farther.

"Yes," the mother said, "he told me he had asked you to come if he got killed. You didn't expect that, I suppose, when you sent him."

"I would rather have died myself than done it!" Editha said with more truth in her deep voice than she ordinarily found in it. "I tried to leave him free—"

"Yes, that letter of yours, that came back with his other things, left him free."

Editha saw now where George's irony came from.

"It was not to be read before—unless—until—I told him so," she faltered.

"Of course, he wouldn't read a letter of yours, under the circumstances, till he thought you wanted him to. Been sick?" the woman abruptly demanded.

"Very sick," Editha said, with self-pity.

"Daughter's life," her father interposed, "was almost despaired of, at one time."

Mrs. Gearson gave him no heed. "I suppose you would have been glad to die, such a brave person as you! I don't believe *he* was glad to die. He was always a timid boy, that way; he was afraid of a good many things; but if he was afraid he did what he made up his mind to. I suppose he made up his mind to go, but I knew what it cost him, by what it cost me when I heard of it. I had been through *one* war before. When you sent him you didn't expect he would get killed?"

The voice seemed to compassionate Editha, and it was time. "No," she huskily murmured.

"No, girls don't; women don't, when they give their men up to their country. They think they'll come marching back, somehow, just as gay as they went, or if it's an empty sleeve, or even an empty pantaloon, it's all the more glory, and they're so much the prouder of them, poor things."

The tears began to run down Editha's face; she had not wept till then; but it was now such a relief to be understood that the tears came.

"No, you didn't expect him to get killed," Mrs. Gearson repeated in a voice which was startlingly like Gearson's again. "You just expected him to kill some one else, some of those foreigners, that weren't there because they had any say about it, but because they had to be there, poor wretches— conscripts, or whatever they call 'em. You thought it would be all right for my George, *your* George, to kill the sons of those miserable mothers and the husbands of those girls that you would never see the faces of." The woman lifted her powerful voice in a psalmlike note. "I thank my God he didn't live to do it! I thank my God they killed him first, and that he ain't livin' with their blood on his hands!" She dropped her eyes which she had raised with her voice, and glared at Editha. "What you got that black on for?" She lifted herself by her powerful arms so high that her helpless body seemed to hang limp its full length. "Take it off, take it off, before I tear it from your back!"

The lady who was passing the summer near Balcom's Works was sketching Editha's beauty, which lent itself wonderfully to the effects of a colorist. It had come to that confidence which is rather apt to grow between artist and sitter, and Editha had told her everything.

"To think of your having such a tragedy in your life!" the lady said. She added: "I suppose there are people who feel that way about war. But when you consider the good this war had done—how much it has done for the country! I can't understand such people, for my part. And when you had come all the way out there to console her—got up out of a sick bed! Well!"

"I think," Editha said, magnanimously, "she wasn't quite in her right mind; and so did papa."

"Yes," the lady said, looking at Editha's lips in nature and then at her lips in art, and giving an empirical touch to them in the picture. "But how dreadful of her! How perfectly—excuse me—how *vulgar*!"

A light broke upon Editha in the darkness which she felt had been without a gleam of brightness for weeks and months. The mystery that had bewildered her was solved by the word; and from that moment she rose from grovelling in shame and self-pity, and began to live again in the ideal.

1905

■ CONSTANCE FENIMORE WOOLSON ■
1840–1894

On February 12, 1882, Constance Fenimore Woolson wrote to Henry James, "Death is not terrible to me. . . . To me it is only a release; and if, at any time, you should hear that I had died, always be sure that I was quite willing, and even glad, to go. I do'nt [sic] think this is a morbid feeling, because it is accompanied by a very strong belief, that, while we *are* here, we should do our very best, and be as courageous and work as hard, as we possibly can." A dozen years later, Woolson's body lay on the pavement beneath a window of her Venice apartment. Ill from influenza, or possibly a condition she knew to be more serious, plagued by bouts of depression that she had inherited from her father, isolated from society by increasing deafness, disconnected from the places in the United States that she knew and loved, Woolson jumped from her rented rooms on the second floor of the Casa Semeticolo. She had just completed, but not yet seen through publication, her fourth novel, *Horace Chase*, in which she had imagined a similar death for one of her characters, though she has that character rescued at the last moment from the window ledge he has mounted in the delirium of illness.

Given the drama of her death, it is easy to read Woolson as the poor, suffering artist who, as her friend John Hay put it, "had not as much happiness as a convict." She never knew three of her sisters, who died in a scarlet fever epidemic within a month of her birth. After their deaths her family quickly left the Woolson roots in Claremont, New Hampshire, to settle in Cleveland, Ohio. In Cleveland, she watched her mother grieve over the death of another daughter in infancy and grieved with her when the two older Woolson daughters died shortly after their marriages. When her father died in 1869, Woolson left Cleveland for St. Augustine, Florida, where she, her mother, and her one living sister, who was widowed with a young daughter to raise, could live more cheaply. For the next ten years, they used this oldest city in the United States as a base for travels throughout the Reconstruction South. They maintained contact with the youngest child in the family, the only son, but the letters that mention him are fraught with justifiable worry about this troubled young man who died under mysterious circumstances in California in 1883. When Woolson's mother died in 1879, Woolson moved again, this time to Europe, where she lived, occasionally in England, more often in Florence and Venice, until her death on January 24, 1894.

But to paint Woolson as a suffering artist debilitated by the deaths in her family and by unrequited love—she has been dismissed by biographer Leon

Edel as a spinster in love with Henry James—is to miss the strength reflected in her insistence that "while we *are* here, we should do our very best, and be as courageous and work as hard, as we possibly can." In a nineteenth century that had created an ideal of physical weakness, even invalidism, for many women of her class, including James's sister, Alice, Woolson embraced physical activity, especially rowing and walking. From childhood on, she traveled to remote or distant places: to Mackinac Island, Michigan; to the Blue Ridge Mountains and coastal regions of the South; to Mentone, Egypt, and Corfu. Drawing on powers of close observation developed in an education that included the study of geology and botany, she directed her gaze both to her natural surroundings and to the customs of the people she encountered. She wrote travel sketches, poems, and a children's novel (*The Old Stone House* under the pseudonym Anne March in 1872), as well as a novella, four novels, and more than fifty short stories that appeared in the major literary magazines of the nineteenth century.

Woolson published "'Miss Grief'" in *Lippincott's Magazine* in May 1880. This publication date places it near the middle of her career, and to notice what is missing in the story tells us much about that career and about the careers of many women writers in the nineteenth century. Woolson uses her story to show how publishers, and thus readers, miss the names of women writers who write in a different voice. She raises questions about the pressure to satisfy publishers in order to find an audience and to make money, about the dangers of refusing to revise, about the anxiety of influence in the face of more successful writers, and about the way writing that has not been championed by publishers and readers disappears.

"'Miss Grief,'" more than any other of Woolson's best stories, was missed—perhaps even suppressed—by the very publishers it indicts: they did not collect it in either of her two posthumous volumes of Italian short stories, though its setting in Rome makes it eligible. Ironically, to read it now as reflective of Woolson's relationship with Henry James or as representative of her entire body of work is to miss the depth and range that Woolson showed in a successful twenty-five-year career. The story is only one of many she wrote about artist figures and about Americans living in Europe, and, in some ways, it is atypical even of these artist stories. Alone in her fiction, it omits the centrality of setting, perhaps because Woolson had not been in Europe long enough to observe its landscape and to incorporate that landscape as an essential part of her characters' lives as she does in her stories about the Great Lakes and the Reconstruction South and as she would do later in her European stories. Nor does it contain any of her caustic humor, perhaps again because she had not been in Europe long enough to observe the people from whose language and mannerisms she creates her satire. Although "'Miss Grief'" misses the fullness of Woolson's career, it nevertheless tells us much about the unsaid and the unsayable in the lives of people who lived in the nineteenth century, particularly women artists.

After Woolson's death, Henry James helped her sister sort through her belongings. Scholars believe that he burned many of her letters at this time, and, indeed, precious little remains from which to construct a life of Woolson. An anecdote circulates that James tried to drown Woolson's black silk dresses in a Venice canal, but that, refusing to sink, the dresses rose like black balloons surrounding him in his rented gondola. Happily, like those black dresses, Woolson's name, nearly submerged by the literary canon, has refused to drown.

Sharon L. Dean
Rivier College

PRIMARY WORKS

Castle Nowhere: Lake-Country Sketches, 1875; *Rodman the Keeper: Southern Sketches*, 1880; *Anne*, 1882; *For the Major*, 1883; *East Angels*, 1886; *Jupiter Lights*, 1889; *Horace Chase*, 1894; *The Front Yard and Other Italian Stories*, 1895; *Dorothy and Other Italian Stories*, 1896; Jay B. Hubbell, "Some New Letters of Constance Fenimore Woolson," *New England Quarterly* 14 (1941): 715–35; Alice Hall Petry, ed., "'Always Your Attached Friend': The Unpublished Letters of Constance Fenimore Woolson to John and Clara Hay," *Books at Brown* (1982–83): 11–108.

Miss Grief

"A conceited fool" is a not uncommon expression. Now, I know that I am not a fool, but I also know that I am conceited. But, candidly, can it be helped if one happens to be young, well and strong, passably good-looking, with some money that one has inherited and more that one has earned—in all, enough to make life comfortable—and if upon this foundation rests also the pleasant superstructure of a literary success? The success is deserved, I think: certainly it was not lightly gained. Yet even with this I fully appreciate its rarity. Thus, I find myself very well entertained in life: I have all I wish in the way of society, and a deep, although of course carefully concealed, satisfaction in my own little fame; which fame I foster by a gentle system of non-interference. I know that I am spoken of as "that quiet young fellow who writes those delightful little studies of society, you know;" and I live up to that definition.

A year ago I was in Rome, and enjoying life particularly. There was a large number of my acquaintants there, both American and English, and no day passed without its invitation. Of course I understood it: it is seldom that you find a literary man who is good-tempered, well-dressed, sufficiently provided with money, and amiably obedient to all the rules and requirements of "society." "When found, make a note of it;"[1] and the note was generally an invitation.

One evening, upon returning to my lodgings, my man Simpson informed me that a person had called in the afternoon, and upon learning that I was absent had left not a card, but her name—"Miss Grief." The title lingered—Miss Grief! "Grief has not so far visited me here," I said to myself, dismissing Simpson and seeking my little balcony for a final smoke, "and she shall not now. I shall take care to be 'not at home' to her if she

[1]The line comes from *Dombey and Son* by Charles Dickens (1812–1870). Woolson's reference to this novel is apt because it concerns an industrialist whose son dies, leaving him with a less-valued daughter.

continues to call." And then I fell to thinking of Ethelind[2] Abercrombie, in whose society I had spent that and many evenings: they were golden thoughts.

The next day there was an excursion: it was late when I reached my rooms, and again Simpson informed me that Miss Grief had called.

"Is she coming continuously?" I said, half to myself.

"Yes, sir: she mentioned that she should call again."

"How does she look?"

"Well, sir, a lady, but not so prosperous as she was, I should say," answered Simpson discreetly.

"Young?"

"No, sir."

"Alone?"

"A maid with her, sir."

But once outside in my little high-up balcony with my cigar, I again forgot Miss Grief and whatever she might represent. Who would not forget in that moonlight, with Ethelind Abercrombie's face to remember?

The stranger came a third time, and I was absent: then she let two days pass, and began again. It grew to be a regular dialogue between Simpson and myself when I came in at night: "Grief today?"

"Yes, sir."

"What time?"

"Four, sir."

"Happy the man," I thought, "who can keep her confined to a particular hour!" But I should not have treated my visitor so cavalierly if I had not felt sure that she was eccentric and unconventional—qualities extremely tiresome in a woman no longer young or attractive, and without money to gild them over. If she were not eccentric she would not have persisted in coming to my door day after day in this silent way, without stating her errand, leaving a note or presenting her credentials in any shape. I made up my mind that she had something to sell—a bit of carving or some intaglio[3] supposed to be antique. It was known that I had a fancy for oddities. I said to myself, "She has read or heard of my 'Old Gold' story or else 'The Buried God,' and she thinks me an idealizing ignoramus upon whom she can impose. Her sepulchral name is at least not Italian: probably she is a sharp country-woman of mine, turning by means of aesthetic lies an honest penny when she can."

She had called seven times during a period of two weeks without seeing me, when one day I happened to be at home in the afternoon, owing to a pouring rain and a fit of doubt concerning Miss Abercrombie. For I had constructed a careful theory of that young lady's characteristics in my own mind, and she had lived up to it delightfully until the previous evening,

---

[2]When "'Miss Grief'" appeared in *Stories by American Authors* (1884), the name Ethelind was changed to Isabel. Whether Woolson initiated or approved the change is unclear. Several reprints have incorrectly identified the name Isabel as appearing in the original *Lippincott*'s publication, and most scholars have referred to this character as Isabel rather than as Ethe-lind.

[3]A design engraved in metal or stone.

when with one word she had blown it to atoms and taken flight, leaving me standing, as it were, on a desolate shore, with nothing but a handful of mistaken inductions wherewith to console myself. I do not know a more exasperating frame of mind, at least for a constructor of theories. I could not write, and so I took up a French novel (I model myself a little on Balzac).[4] I had been turning over its pages but a few moments when Simpson knocked, and, entering softly, said, with just a shadow of a smile on his well-trained face, "Miss Grief." I briefly consigned Miss Grief to all the Furies,[5] and then, as he still lingered—perhaps not knowing where they resided—I asked where the visitor was.

"Outside, sir—in the hall. I told her I would see if you were at home."

"She must be unpleasantly wet if she had no carriage."

"No carriage, sir: they always come on foot. I think she *is* a little damp, sir."

"Well, let her in, but I don't want the maid. I may as well see her now, I suppose, and end the affair."

"Yes, sir."

I did not put down my book. My visitor should have a hearing, but not much more: she had sacrificed her womanly claims by her persistent attacks upon my door. Presently Simpson ushered her in. "Miss Grief," he said, and then went out, closing the curtain behind him.

A woman—yes, a lady—but shabby, unattractive and more than middleaged.

I rose, bowed slightly, and then dropped into my chair again, still keeping the book in my hand. "Miss Grief?" I said interrogatively as I indicated a seat with my eyebrows.

"Not Grief," she answered—"Crief: my name is Crief."

She sat down, and I saw that she held a small flat box.

"Not carving, then," I thought—"probably old lace, something that belonged to Tullia[6] or Lucrezia Borgia."[7] But as she did not speak I found myself obliged to begin: "You have been here, I think, once or twice before?"

"Seven times: this is the eighth."

A silence.

"I am often out: indeed, I may say that I am never in," I remarked carelessly.

"Yes: you have many friends."

"Who will perhaps buy old lace," I mentally added. But this time I too remained silent: why should I trouble myself to draw her out? She had sought me: let her advance her idea, whatever it was, now that entrance was gained.

But Miss Grief (I preferred to call her so) did not look as though she could advance anything: her black gown, damp with rain, seemed to retreat

---

[4]Honoré de Balzac (1799–1850) was known for his novels about French society.

[5]In Greek mythology, the Furies were winged women who represented vengeance.

[6]In Roman legend, Tullia murdered her husband and married her brother-in-law. He then murdered her father so that he could be king; she drove over her father's body in her chariot.

[7]Lucrezia Borgia (1480–1519) belonged to a notoriously cruel Italian family.

fearfully to her thin self, while her thin self retreated as far as possible from me, from the chair, from everything. Her eyes were cast down: an old-fashioned lace veil with a heavy border shaded her face. She looked at the floor, and I looked at her.

I grew a little impatient, but I made up my mind that I would continue silent and see how long a time she would consider necessary to give due effect to her little pantomime. Comedy? Or was it tragedy? I suppose full five minutes passed thus in our double silence; and that is a long time when two persons are sitting opposite each other alone in a small still room.

At last my visitor, without raising her eyes, said slowly, "You are very happy, are you not, with youth, health, friends, riches, fame?"

It was a singular beginning. Her voice was clear, low and very sweet as she thus enumerated my advantages one by one in a list. I was attracted by it, but repelled by her words, which seemed to me flattery both dull and bold.

"Thanks," I said, "for your kindness, but I fear it is undeserved. I seldom discuss myself even when with my friends."

"I am your friend," replied Miss Grief. Then, after a moment, she added slowly, "I have read every word you have written."

I curled the edges of my book indifferently: I am not a fop,[8] I hope, but—others have said the same.

"What is more, I know much of it by heart," continued my visitor. "Wait: I will show you;" and then, without pause, she began to repeat something of mine word for word, just as I had written it. On she went, and I—listened. I intended interrupting her after a moment, but I did not, because she was reciting so well, and also because I felt a desire gaining upon me to see what she would make of a certain conversation which I knew was coming—a conversation between two of my characters which was, to say the least, sphinx-like,[9] and somewhat incandescent also. What won me a little, too, was the fact that the scene she was reciting (it was hardly more than that, although called a story) was secretly my favorite among all the sketches from my pen with which a gracious public had been favored. I never said so, but it was; and I had always felt a wondering annoyance that the aforesaid public, while kindly praising beyond their worth other attempts of mine, had never noticed the higher purpose of this little shaft, aimed not at the balconies and lighted windows of society, but straight up toward the distant stars. So she went on, and presently reached the conversation: my two people began to talk. She had raised her eyes now, and was looking at me soberly as she gave the words of the woman, quiet, gentle, cold, and the replies of the man, bitter, hot and scathing. Her very voice changed, and took, although always sweetly, the different tones required, while no point of meaning, however small, no breath of delicate emphasis

[8]A fool.
[9]The Sphinx, part lion and part woman, kept Thebes under her power until Oedipus solved a riddle that asked what goes on four legs in the morning, two in the afternoon, and three in the evening (mankind). Hence, to be sphinxlike is to be enigmatic or mysterious.

which I had meant, but which the dull types could not give, escaped appreciative and full, almost overfull, recognition which startled me. For she had understood me—understood me almost better than I had understood myself. It seemed to me that while I had labored to interpret partially a psychological riddle, she, coming after, had comprehended its bearings better than I had, although confining herself strictly to my own words and emphasis. The scene ended (and it ended rather suddenly), she dropped her eyes, and moved her hand nervously to and fro over the box she held: her gloves were old and shabby, her hands small.

I was secretly much surprised by what I had heard, but my ill-humor was deep-seated that day, and I still felt sure, besides, that the box contained something that I was expected to buy.

"You recite remarkably well," I said carelessly, "and I am much flattered also by your appreciation of my efforts. But it is not, I presume, to that alone that I owe the pleasure of this visit?"

"Yes," she answered, still looking down, "it is, for if you had not written that scene I should not have sought you. Your other sketches are interiors—exquisitely painted and delicately finished, but of small scope. *This* is a sketch in a few bold, masterly lines—work of entirely different spirit and purpose."

I was nettled by her insight. "You have bestowed so much of your kind attention upon me that I feel your debtor," I said, conventionally. "It may be that there is something I can do for you—connected, possibly, with that box?"

It was a little impertinent, but it was true, for she answered, "Yes."

I smiled, but her eyes were cast down and she did not see the smile.

"What I have to show you is a manuscript," she said after a pause which I did not break: "it is a drama. I thought that perhaps you would read it."

"An authoress! This is worse than old lace," I said to myself in dismay.—Then, aloud, "My opinion would be worth nothing, Miss Crief."

"Not in a business way, I know. But it might be—an assistance personally." Her voice had sunk to a whisper: outside, the rain was pouring steadily down. She was a very depressing object to me as she sat there with her box.

"I hardly think I have the time at present—" I began.

She had raised her eyes and was looking at me: then, when I paused, she rose and came suddenly toward my chair. "Yes, you will read it," she said with her hand on my arm—"you will read it. Look at this room; look at yourself; look at all you have. Then look at me, and have pity."

I had risen, for she held my arm and her damp skirt was brushing my knees. Her large dark eyes looked intently into mine as she went on: "I have no shame in asking. Why should I have? It is my last endeavor, but a calm and well-considered one. If you refuse I shall go away, knowing that Fate has willed it so. And I shall be content."

"She is mad," I thought. But she did not look so and she had spoken quietly, even gently.—"Sit down," I said, moving away from her. I felt as if I had been magnetized, but it was only the nearness of her eyes to mine, and their intensity. I drew forward a chair, but she remained standing.

"I cannot," she said in the same sweet, gentle tone, "unless you promise."

"Very well, I promise; only sit down."

As I took her arm to lead her to the chair I perceived that she was trembling, but her face continued unmoved.

"You do not, of course, wish me to look at your manuscript now?" I said, temporizing: "it would be much better to leave it. Give me your address, and I will return it to you with my written opinion; although, I repeat, the latter will be of no use to you. It is the opinion of an editor or publisher that you want."

"It shall be as you please. And I will go in a moment," said Miss Grief, pressing her palms together, as if trying to control the tremor that had seized her slight frame.

She looked so pallid that I thought of offering her a glass of wine: then I remembered that if I did it might be a bait to bring her there again, and this I was desirous to prevent. She rose while the thought was passing through my mind. Her pasteboard box lay on the chair she had first occupied: she took it, wrote an address on the cover, laid it down, and then, bowing with a little air of formality, drew her black shawl around her shoulders and turned toward the door.

I followed, after touching the bell. "You will hear from me by letter," I said.

Simpson opened the door, and I caught a glimpse of the maid, who was waiting in the anteroom. She was an old woman, shorter than her mistress, equally thin, and dressed like her in rusty black. As the door opened she turned toward it a pair of small, dim blue eyes with a look of furtive suspense. Simpson dropped the curtain, shutting me into the inner room: he had no intention of allowing me to accompany my visitor farther. But I had the curiosity to go to a bay-window in an angle from whence I could command the street-door, and presently I saw them issue forth in the rain and walk away side by side, the mistress, being the taller, holding the umbrella: probably there was not much difference in rank between persons so poor and forlorn as these.

It grew dark. I was invited out for the evening, and I knew that if I went I should meet Miss Abercrombie. I said to myself that I would not go. I got out my paper for writing, I made my preparations for a quiet evening at home with myself; but it was of no use. It all ended slavishly in my going. At the last allowable moment I presented myself, and—as a punishment for my vacillation, I suppose—I never passed a more disagreeable evening. I drove homeward in a vixenish temper: it was foggy without, and very foggy within. What Ethelind really was, now that she had broken through my elaborately-built theories, I was not able to decide. There was, to tell the truth, a certain young Englishman—But that is apart from this story.

I reached home, went up to my rooms and had a supper. It was to console myself: I am obliged to console myself scientifically once in a while. I was walking up and down afterward, smoking and feeling somewhat better, when my eye fell upon the pasteboard box. I took it up: on the cover was written an address which showed that my visitor must have walked a long distance in order to see me: "A. Crief."—"A Grief," I thought; "and so she is. I positively believe she has brought all this trouble upon me: she has the evil eye." I took out the manuscript and looked at it. It was in the form of a little volume, and clearly written: on the cover was the word "Armor" in German text,[10] and underneath a pen-and-ink sketch of a helmet, breastplate and shield.

"Grief certainly needs armor," I said to myself, sitting down by the table and turning over the pages. "I may as well look over the thing now: I could not be in a worse mood." And then I began to read.

Early the next morning Simpson took a note from me to the given address, returning with the following reply: "No; I prefer to come to you; at four; A. CRIEF." These words, with their three semicolons, were written in pencil upon a piece of coarse printing-paper, but the handwriting was as clear and delicate as that of the manuscript in ink.

"What sort of a place was it, Simpson?"

"Very poor, sir, but I did not go all the way up. The elder person came down, sir, took the note, and requested me to wait where I was."

"You had no chance, then, to make inquiries?" I said, knowing full well that he had emptied the entire neighborhood of any information it might possess concerning these two lodgers.

"Well, sir, you know how these foreigners will talk, whether one wants to hear or not. But it seems that these two persons have been there but a few weeks: they live alone, and are uncommonly silent and reserved. The people around there call them something that signifies 'the Madames American, thin and dumb.'"

At four the "Madames American" arrived: it was raining again, and they came on foot under their old umbrella. The maid waited in the anteroom, and Miss Grief was ushered into my bachelor's parlor, which was library and dining-room in one. I had thought that I should meet her with great deference, but she looked so forlorn that my deference changed to pity. It was the woman that impressed me then, more than the writer—the fragile, nerveless body more than the inspired mind. For it was inspired: I had sat up half the night over her drama, and had felt thrilled through and through more than once by its earnestness, passion and power.

No one could have been more surprised than I was to find myself thus enthusiastic. I thought I had outgrown that sort of thing. And one would have supposed, too (I myself should have supposed so the day before), that the faults of the drama, which were many and prominent, would have chilled any liking I might have felt, I being a writer myself, and therefore critical; for writers are as apt to make much of the "how," rather than the "what," as painters, who, it is well known, prefer an exquisitely rendered

[10]A gothic-style typeface.

representation of a commonplace theme to an imperfectly executed picture of even the most striking subject. But in this case, on the contrary, the scattered rays of splendor in Miss Grief's drama had made me forget the dark spots, which were numerous and disfiguring; or, rather, the splendor had made me anxious to have the spots removed. And this also was a philanthropic state very unusual for me. Regarding unsuccessful writers my motto had been "Vae victis!"[11]

My visitor took a seat and folded her hands: I could see, in spite of her quiet manner, that she was in breathless suspense. It seemed so pitiful that she should be trembling there before me—a woman so much older than I was, a woman who possessed the divine spark of genius, which I was by no means sure, in spite of my success, had been granted to me—that I felt as if I ought to go down on my knees before her and entreat her to take her proper place of supremacy at once. But there! one does not go down on one's knees combustively, as it were, before a woman over fifty, plain in feature, thin, dejected and ill-dressed. I contented myself with taking her hands (in their miserable old gloves) in mine, while I said cordially "Miss Crief, your drama seems to me full of original power. It has roused my enthusiasm: I sat up half the night reading it."

The hands I held shook, but something (perhaps a shame for having evaded the knees business) made me tighten my hold and bestow upon her also a reassuring smile. She looked at me for a moment, and then, suddenly and noiselessly, tears rose and rolled down her cheeks. I dropped her hands and retreated. I had not thought her tearful: on the contrary, her voice and face had seemed rigidly controlled. But now here she was bending herself over the side of the chair with her head resting on her arms, not sobbing aloud, but her whole frame shaken by the strength of her emotion. I rushed for a glass of wine: I pressed her to take it. I did not quite know what to do, but, putting myself in her place, I decided to praise the drama; and praise it I did. I do not know when I have used so many adjectives. She raised her head and began to wipe her eyes.

"Do take the wine," I said, interrupting myself in my cataract of language.

"I dare not," she answered: then added humbly, "that is, unless you have a biscuit here or a bit of bread."

I found some biscuit: she ate two, and then slowly drank the wine while I resumed my verbal Niagara. Under its influence—and that of the wine too, perhaps—she began to show new life. It was not that she looked radiant—she could not—but simply that she looked warm. I now perceived what had been the principal discomfort of her appearance heretofore: it was that she had looked all the time as if suffering from cold.

At last I could think of nothing more to say, and stopped. I really admired the drama, but I thought I had exerted myself sufficiently as an anti-hysteric, and that adjectives enough, for the present at least, had been

---

[11]Woe to the vanquished.

administered. She had put down her empty wine-glass, and was resting her hands on the broad cushioned arms of her chair with a sort of expanded content.

"You must pardon my tears," she said, smiling: "it was the revulsion of feeling. My life was at a low ebb: if your sentence had been against me it would have been my end."

"Your end?"

"Yes, the end of my life: I should have destroyed myself."

"Then you would have been a weak as well as wicked woman," I said in a tone of disgust: I do hate sensationalism.

"Oh no, you know nothing about it. I should have destroyed only this poor worn tenement of clay. But I can well understand how *you* would look upon it. Regarding the desirableness of life the prince and the beggar may have different opinions.—We will say no more of it, but talk of the drama instead." As she spoke the word "drama" a triumphant brightness came into her eyes.

I took the manuscript from a drawer and sat down beside her. "I suppose you know that there are faults," I said, expecting ready acquiescence.

"I was not aware that there were any," was her gentle reply.

Here was a beginning! After all my interest in her—and, I may say under the circumstances, my kindness—she received me in this way! However, my belief in her genius was too sincere to be altered by her whimsies; so I persevered. "Let us go over it together," I said. "Shall I read it to you, or will you read it to me?"

"I will not read it, but recite it."

"That will never do: you will recite it so well that we shall see only the good points, and what we have to concern ourselves with now is the bad ones."

"I will recite it," she repeated.

"Look here, Miss Crief," I said bluntly, "for what purpose did you come to me? Certainly not merely to recite: I am no stage-manager. In plain English, was it not your idea that I might help you in obtaining a publisher?"

"Yes, yes," she answered, looking at me apprehensively, all her old manner returning.

I followed up my advantage, opened the little paper volume and began. I first took the drama line by line, and spoke of the faults of expression and structure: then I turned back and touched upon two or three glaring impossibilities in the plot. "Your absorbed interest in the motive of the whole no doubt made you forget these blemishes," I said apologetically.

But, to my surprise, I found that she did not see the blemishes—that she appreciated nothing I had said, comprehended nothing. Such unaccountable obtuseness puzzled me. I began again, going over the whole with even greater minuteness and care. I worked hard: the perspiration stood in beads upon my forehead as I struggled with her—what shall I call it—obstinacy? But it was not exactly obstinacy. She simply could not see the faults of her own work, any more than a blind man can see the smoke that dims a patch of blue sky. When I had finished my task the second time she still remained as gently impassive as before. I leaned back in my chair exhausted and looked at her.

Even then she did not seem to comprehend (whether she agreed with it or not) what I must be thinking. "It is such a heaven to me that you like it!" she murmured dreamily, breaking the silence. Then, with more animation, "And *now* you will let me recite it?"

I was too weary to oppose her: she threw aside her shawl and bonnet, and, standing in the centre of the room, began.

And she carried me along with her: all the strong passages were doubly strong when spoken, and the faults, which seemed nothing to her, were made by her earnestness to seem nothing to me, at least for that moment. When it was ended she stood looking at me with a triumphant smile.

"Yes," I said, "I like it, and you see that I do. But I like it because my taste is peculiar. To me originality and force are everything—perhaps because I have them not to any marked degree myself—but the world at large will not overlook as I do your absolutely barbarous shortcomings on account of them. Will you trust me to go over the drama and correct it at my pleasure?" This was a vast deal for me to offer: I was surprised at myself.

"No," she answered softly, still smiling. "There shall not be so much as a comma altered." Then she sat down and fell into a reverie as though she were alone.

"Have you written anything else?" I said after a while, when I had become tired of the silence.

"Yes."

"Can I see it? Or is it *them*?"

"It is *them*. Yes, you can see all."

"I will call upon you for the purpose."

"No, you must not," she said, coming back to the present nervously: "I prefer to come to you."

At this moment Simpson entered to light the room, and busied himself rather longer than was necessary over the task. When he finally went out I saw that my visitor's manner had sunk into its former depression: the presence of the servant seemed to have chilled her.

"When did you say I might come?" I repeated, ignoring her refusal.

"I did not say it. It would be impossible."

"Well, then, when will you come here?" There was, I fear, a trace of fatigue in my tone.

"At your good pleasure, sir," she answered humbly.

My chivalry was touched by this: after all, she was a woman. "Come tomorrow," I said. "By the way, come and dine with me then: why not?" I was curious to see what she would reply.

"Why not, indeed? Yes, I will come. I am forty-three: I might have been your mother."

This was not quite true, as I am over thirty; but I look young, while she—Well, I had thought her over fifty. "I can hardly call you 'mother,' but then we might compromise upon 'aunt,'" I said, laughing. "Aunt what?"

"My name is Aaronna,"[12] she gravely answered. "My father was much disappointed that I was not a boy, and gave me as nearly as possible the name he had prepared—Aaron."

"Then come and dine with me to-morrow, and bring with you the other manuscripts, Aaronna," I said, amused at the quaint sound of the name. On the whole, I did not like "aunt."

"I will come," she answered.

It was twilight and still raining, but she refused all offers of escort or carriage, departing with her maid, as she had come, under the brown umbrella.

The next day we had the dinner. Simpson was astonished—and more than astonished, grieved—when I told him that he was to dine with the maid; but he could not complain in words, since my own guest, the mistress, was hardly more attractive. When our preparations were complete I could not help laughing: the two prim little tables, one in the parlor and one in the anteroom, and Simpson disapprovingly going back and forth between them, were irresistible.

I greeted my guest hilariously when she arrived, and, fortunately, her manner was not quite so depressed as usual: I could never have accorded myself with a tearful mood. I had thought that perhaps she would make, for the occasion, some change in her attire: I have never known a woman who had not some scrap of finery, however small, in reserve for that unexpected occasion of which she is ever dreaming. But no: Miss Grief wore the same black gown, unadored and unaltered. I was glad that there was no rain that day, so that the skirt did not at least look so damp and rheumatic.

She ate quietly, almost furtively, yet with a good appetite, and she did not refuse the wine. Then, when the meal was over and Simpson had removed the dishes, I asked for the new manuscripts. She gave me an old green copybook filled with short poems, and a prose sketch by itself: I lit a cigar and sat down at my desk to look them over.

"Perhaps you will try a cigarette?" I suggested, more for amusement than anything else, for there was not a shade of Bohemianism about her: her whole appearance was puritanical.

"I have not yet succeeded in learning to smoke." "You have tried?" I said, turning around.

"Yes: Serena[13] and I tried, but we did not succeed."

---

[12]Cheryl Torsney reads the name Aaronna as a feminization of the biblical Aaron. The first of Israel's high priests and the brother of Moses, Aaron wore armorlike clothing and served as an intermediary with God. In Torsney's interpretation, Woolson uses the meagerly clothed Aaronna to predict a time when female artists will overturn patriarchal traditions and assert their own powerful voices. See Exodus 28–29.

[13]Woolson changes this name to Martha at the end of the story. Cheryl Torsney equates Martha with the biblical Martha (Luke 10:39–42; John 11:21–27), the sister of Lazarus, who works at household tasks while her sister Mary listens to the words of Jesus. Torsney reads the narrator as a Jesus figure who does not deserve to be heard and who does not perform an act of resurrection as the biblical Jesus does with Lazarus.

"Serena is your maid?"

"She lives with me."

I was seized with inward laughter, and began hastily to look over her manuscripts with my back toward her, so that she might not see it. A vision had risen before me of those two forlorn women, alone in their room with locked doors, patiently trying to acquire the smoker's art.

But my attention was soon absorbed by the papers before me. Such a fantastic collection of words, lines and epithets I had never before seen, or even in dreams imagined. In truth, they were like the work of dreams: they were *Kubla Khan*,[14] only more so. Here and there was radiance like the flash of a diamond, but each poem, almost each verse and line, was marred by some fault or lack which seemed wilful perversity, like the work of an evil sprite. It was like a case of jeweller's wares set before you, with each ring unfinished, each bracelet too large or too small for its purpose, each breast-pin without its fastening, each necklace purposely broken. I turned the pages, marvelling. When about half an hour had passed, and I was leaning back for a moment to light another cigar, I glanced toward my visitor. She was behind me, in an easy-chair before my small fire, and she was—fast asleep! In the relaxation of her unconsciousness I was struck anew by the poverty her appearance expressed: her feet were visible, and I saw the miserable worn old shoes which hitherto she had kept concealed.

After looking at her for a moment I returned to my task and took up the prose story: in prose she must be more reasonable. She was less fantastic perhaps, but hardly more reasonable. The story was that of a profligate and commonplace man forced by two of his friends, in order not to break the heart of a dying girl who loves him, to live up to a high imaginary ideal of himself which her pure but mistaken mind has formed. He has a handsome face and sweet voice, and repeats what they tell him. Her long, slow decline and happy death, and his own inward ennui and profound weariness of the rôle he has to play, made the vivid points of the story. So far, well enough, but here was the trouble: through the whole narrative moved another character, a physician of tender heart and exquisite mercy, who practised murder as a fine art, and was regarded (by the author) as a second Messiah! This was monstrous. I read it through twice, and threw it down: then, fatigued, I turned round and leaned back, waiting for her to wake. I could see her profile against the dark hue of the easy-chair.

Presently she seemed to feel my gaze, for she stirred, then opened her eyes. "I have been asleep," she said, rising hurriedly.

"No harm in that, Aaronna."

But she was deeply embarrassed and troubled, much more so than the occasion required; so much so, indeed, that I turned the conversation back upon the manuscripts as a diversion. "I cannot stand that doctor of yours," I said, indicating the prose story: "no one would. You must cut him out."

---

[14]A poem by Samuel Taylor Coleridge (1772–1834) that he claimed came from a dream vision.

Her self-possession returned as if by magic. "Certainly not," she answered haughtily.

"Oh, if you do not care—I had labored under the impression that you were anxious these things should find a purchaser."

"I am, I am," she said, her manner changing to deep humility with wonderful rapidity. With such alternations of feeling as this sweeping over her like great waves, no wonder she was old before her time.

"Then you must take out that doctor."

"I am willing, but do not know how," she answered, pressing her hands together helplessly. "In my mind he belongs to the story so closely that he cannot be separated from it."

Here Simpson entered, bringing a note for me: it was a line from Mrs. Abercrombie inviting me for that evening—an unexpected gathering, and therefore likely to be all the more agreeable. My heart bounded in spite of me: I forgot Miss Grief and her manuscripts for the moment as completely as though they had never existed. But, bodily, being still in the same room with her, her speech brought me back to the present.

"You have had good news?" she said.

"Oh no, nothing especial—merely an invitation."

"But good news also," she repeated. "And now, as for me, I must go."

Not supposing that she would stay much later in any case, I had that morning ordered a carriage to come for her at about that hour. I told her this. She made no reply beyond putting on her bonnet and shawl.

"You will hear from me soon," I said: "I shall do all I can for you."

She had reached the door, but before opening it she stopped, turned and extended her hand. "You are good," she said: "I give you thanks. Do not think me ungrateful or envious. It is only that you are young, and I am so—so old." Then she opened the door and passed through the anteroom without pause, her maid accompanying her and Simpson with gladness lighting the way. They were gone. I dressed hastily and went out—to continue my studies in psychology.

Time passed: I was busy, amused and perhaps a little excited (sometimes psychology is delightful). But, although much occupied with my own affairs, I did not altogether neglect my self-imposed task regarding Miss Grief. I began by sending her prose story to a friend, the editor of a monthly magazine, with a letter making a strong plea for its admittance. It should have a chance first on its own merits. Then I forwarded the drama to a publisher, also an acquaintance, a man with a taste for phantasms and a soul above mere common popularity, as his own coffers knew to their cost. This done, I waited with conscience clear.

Four weeks passed. During this waiting period I heard nothing from Miss Grief. At last one morning came a letter from my editor. "The story has force, but I cannot stand that doctor," he wrote. "Let her cut him out, and I might print it." Just what I myself had said. The package lay there on my table, travelworn and grimed: a returned manuscript is, I think, the most melancholy object on earth. I decided to wait, before writing to Aaronna, until the second letter was received. A week later it came. "Armor" was declined. The publisher had been "impressed" by the power displayed in certain passages, but the "impossibilities of the plot" rendered it "unavailable for publication"—in fact, would "bury it in ridicule" if brought before the public, a public "lamentably" fond of amusement, "seeking it, undaunted, even in the cannon's mouth." I doubt if he knew himself what he meant. But one thing, at any rate, was clear: "Armor" was declined.

Now, I am, as I have remarked before, a little obstinate. I was determined that Miss Grief's work should be received. I would alter and improve it myself, without letting her know: the end justified the means. Surely the sieve of my own good taste, whose mesh had been pronounced so fine and delicate, would serve for two. I began, and utterly failed.

I set to work first upon "Armor." I amended, altered, left out, put in, pieced, condensed, lengthened: I did my best, and all to no avail. I could not succeed in completing anything that satisfied me, or that approached, in truth, Miss Grief's own work just as it stood. I suppose I went over that manuscript twenty times: I covered sheets of paper with my copies. But the obstinate drama refused to be corrected: as it was it must stand or fall.

Wearied and annoyed, I threw it aside and took up the prose story: that would be easier. But, to my surprise, I found that that apparently gentle "doctor" would not out: he was so closely interwoven with every part of the tale that to take him out was like taking out one especial figure in a carpet: that is impossible unless you unravel the whole. At last I did unravel the whole, and then the story was no longer good, or Aaronna's: it was weak, and mine. All this took time, for of course I had much to do in connection with my own life and tasks. But, although slowly and at my leisure, I really did try my best as regarded Miss Grief, and without success. I was forced at last to make up my mind that either my own powers were not equal to the task, or else that her perversities were as essential a part of her work as her inspirations, and not to be separated from it. Once during this period I showed two of the short poems to Ethelind, withholding of course the writer's name. "They were written by a woman," I explained.

"Her mind must have been disordered, poor thing!" Ethelind said in her gentle way when she returned them—"at least, judging by these. They are hopelessly mixed and vague."

Now, they were not vague so much as vast. But I knew that I could not make Ethelind comprehend it, and (so complex a creature is man) I do not know that I wanted her to comprehend it. These were the only ones in the whole collection that I would have shown her, and I was rather glad that she did not like even these. Not that poor Aaronna's poems were evil: they were simply unrestrained, large, vast, like the skies or the wind. Ethelind was bounded on all sides, like a violet in a garden-bed. And I liked her so.

One afternoon, about the time when I was beginning to see that I could not "improve" Miss Grief, I came upon the maid. I was driving, and she had stopped on the crossing to let the carriage pass. I recognized her at a glance (by her general forlornness), and called to the driver to stop. "How is Miss Crief?" I said. "I have been intending to write to her for some time."

"And your note, when it comes," answered the old woman on the cross-walk fiercely, "she shall not see."

"What?"

"I say she shall not see it. Your patronizing face shows that you have no good news, and you shall not rack and stab her any more on *this* earth, please God, while I have authority."

"Who has racked or stabbed her, Serena?"

"Serena, indeed! Rubbish! I'm no Serena: I'm her aunt. And as to who has racked and stabbed her, I say you, *you*—YOU literary men!" She had put her old head inside my carriage, and flung out these words at me in a shrill, menacing tone. "But she shall die in peace in spite of you," she continued. "Vampires! you take her ideas and fatten on them, and leave her to starve. You know you do—*you* who have had her poor manuscripts these months and months!"

"Is she ill?" I asked in real concern, gathering that much at least from the incoherent tirade.

"She is dying," answered the desolate old creature, her voice softening and her dim eyes filling with tears.

"Oh, I trust not. Perhaps something can be done. Can I help you in any way?" "In all ways if you would," she said, breaking down and beginning to sob weakly, with her head resting on the sill of the carriage-window. "Oh, what have we not been through together, we two! Piece by piece I have sold all."

I am good-hearted enough, but I do not like to have old women weeping across my carriage-door. I suggested, therefore, that she should come inside and let me take her home. Her shabby old skirt was soon beside me, and, following her directions, the driver turned toward one of the most wretched quarters of the city, the abode of poverty, crowded and unclean. Here, in a large bare chamber up many flights of stairs, I found Miss Grief.

As I entered I was startled: I thought she was dead. There seemed no life present until she opened her eyes, and even then they rested upon us vaguely, as though she did not know who we were. But as I approached a sudden light came into them: she recognized me, and this sudden animation, this return of the soul to the windows of the almost deserted body, was the most wonderful thing I ever saw. "You have good news of the drama?" she whispered as I bent over her: "tell me. I *know* you have good news."

What was I to answer? Pray, what would you have answered, puritan?

"Yes, I have good news, Aaronna," I said. "The drama will appear." (And who knows? Perhaps it will in some other world.)

She smiled, and her now brilliant eyes did not leave my face.

"He knows I'm your aunt: I told him," said the old woman, coming to the bedside.

"Did you?" whispered Miss Grief, still gazing at me with a smile. "Then please, dear Aunt Martha, give me something to eat."

Aunt Martha hurried across the room, and I followed her. "It's the first time she's asked for food in weeks," she said in a husky tone.

She opened a cupboard-door vaguely, but I could see nothing within. "What have you for her?" I asked with some impatience, although in a low voice.

"Please God, nothing!" answered the poor old woman, hiding her reply and her tears behind the broad cupboard-door. "I was going out to get a little something when I met you."

"Good Heavens! is it money you need? Here, take this and send; or go yourself in the carriage waiting below."

She hurried out breathless, and I went back to the bedside, much disturbed by what I had seen and heard. But Miss Grief's eyes were full of life, and as I sat down beside her she whispered earnestly, "Tell me."

And I did tell her—a romance invented for the occasion. I venture to say that none of my published sketches could compare with it. As for the lie involved, it will stand among my few good deeds, I know, at the judgment-bar.

And she was satisfied. "I have never known what it was," she whispered, "to be fully happy until now." She closed her eyes, and when the lids fell I again thought that she had passed away. But no, there was still pulsation in her small, thin wrist. As she perceived my touch she smiled. "Yes, I am happy," she said again, although without audible sound.

The old aunt returned: food was prepared, and she took some. I myself went out after wine that should be rich and pure. She rallied a little, but I did not leave her: her eyes dwelt upon me and compelled me to stay, or rather my conscience compelled me. It was a damp night, and I had a little fire made. The wine, fruit, flowers and candles I had ordered made the bare place for the time being bright and fragrant. Aunt Martha dozed in her chair from sheer fatigue—she had watched many nights—but Miss Grief was awake, and I sat beside her.

"I make you my executor," she murmured, "as to the drama. But my other manuscripts place, when I am gone, under my head, and let them be buried with me. They are not many—those you have and these. See!"

I followed her gesture, and saw under her pillows the edges of two more copy-books like the one I had. "Do not look at them—my poor dead children!" she said tenderly. "Let them depart with me—unread, as I have been."

Later she whispered, "Did you wonder why I came to you? It was the contrast. You were young—strong—rich—praised—loved—successful: all that I was not. I wanted to look at you—and imagine how it would feel. You had success—but I had the greater power. Tell me: did I not have it?"

"Yes, Aaronna."

"It is all in the past now. But I am satisfied."

After another pause she said with a faint smile, "Do you remember when I fell asleep in your parlor? It was the good and rich food. It was so long since I had had food like that!"

I took her hand and held it, conscience-stricken, but now she hardly seemed to perceive my touch. "And the smoking?" she whispered. "Do you remember how you laughed? I saw it. But I had heard that smoking soothed—that one was no longer tired and hungry—with a cigar."

In little whispers of this sort, separated by long rests and pauses, the night passed. Once she asked if her aunt was asleep, and when I answered in the affirmative she said, "Help her to return home—to America: the drama will pay for it. I ought never to have brought her away."

I promised, and she resumed her bright-eyed silence.

I think she did not speak again. Toward morning the change came, and soon after sunrise, with her old aunt kneeling by her side, she passed away.

All was arranged as she had wished. Her manuscripts, covered with violets, formed her pillow. No one followed her to the grave save her aunt and myself: I thought she would prefer it so. Her name was not "Crief," after all, but "Moncrief:" I saw it written out by Aunt Martha for the coffinplate, as follows: "Aaronna Moncrief, aged forty-three years two months and eight days."

I never knew more of her history than is written here. If there was more that I might have learned, it remained unlearned, for I did not ask.

And the drama? I keep it here in this locked case. I could have had it published at my own expense, but I think that now she knows its faults herself, and would not like it.

I keep it, and once in a while I read it over—not as a *memento mori*[15] exactly, but rather as a memento of my own good-fortune, for which I should continually give thanks. The want of one grain made all her work void, and that one grain was given to me. She, with the greater power, failed—I, with the less, succeeded. But no praise is due to me for that. When I die "Armor" is to be destroyed unread: not even Ethelind is to see it. For women will misunderstand each other; and, dear and precious to me as my sweet wife is, I could not bear that she or any one should cast so much as a thought of scorn upon the memory of the writer, upon my poor dead, "unavailable," unaccepted "Miss Grief."

1880

HENRY JAMES
1843–1916

Henry James has a unique position on the borderline between many intersecting national, cultural, and aesthetic frontiers. His life spanned the U.S. Civil War and World War I, and his national allegiance and residence shifted between America and England. His prolific literary output bridges the gap between the nineteenth and twentieth centuries and between the literary periods of Realism and Modernism. Thus, Henry James—dubbed "The Master"—often finds

---

[15]A reminder of death.

himself on a vast array of college syllabi and has inspired an enormous variety of critical conversations for more than a century. Indeed, a quick scan of the table of contents of the immensely useful recent resource *Henry James in Context* (Cambridge 2010)—which comprises an incredibly diverse 41 entries—speaks to how richly James's work rewards a multiplicity of critical perspectives and possibilities. I cite this text as a useful resource for further reading about Henry James and also to emphasize his central importance to a wide range of scholarly pursuits and his usefulness for an enormous variety of interests in the undergraduate classroom.

Born in 1843 in New York City, Henry James was born into a wealthy and idiosyncratic family of thinkers and writers. His father, Henry James Sr., inherited wealth and property, which enabled his self-published writing about spirituality, self-questioning, and individualism inspired partly by his beliefs in the Swedish mystic Swedenborg. Henry James's elder brother, William James, became an influential thinker in the fields of psychology and philosophy. His sister Alice James wrote a diary that was published posthumously and has received critical attention for its compelling account of her experience. As a boy Henry James traveled throughout Europe and he spent his early career as a journalist reporting back from the "Old World" to his American brethren. He settled in England in 1876 and maintained a career-long interest in the cultural differences between Americans and Europeans. Indeed, shortly after his relocation to Europe, James wrote novels entitled *The American* (1877), in which the protagonist experiences the culture shock of Paris, and *The Europeans* (1878), in which two siblings from the Old World arrive in Boston to experience the "New World" order of America. James was deeply interested in relationships brokered across cultural differences and in the effects of transplantation into an alien society; he took up these problems from various vantage points throughout his career. James's novels have been taken as critiques of both American and European societies. The novels often feature innocent young wealthy American girls "going abroad" only to be damaged by the sinister seductions of the Old World, as is the fate of Isabel Archer (the "lady" in *Portrait of a Lady*, 1880–1881) and Daisy Miller (of "Daisy Miller," 1878). Yet in other texts, the ultimate coming-into-power of such young women—Milly Theale (of *The Wings of the Dove*, 1902, and Maggie Verver (of *The Golden Bowl*, 1904)—suggests a criticism of the voracious and morally dubious power of purchase enabled by American capitalism. James rarely depicts anything in black and white, and his many explorations of these conflicts of national character and experiences in foreign environments are ubiquitously cast in a morally murky grayscale.

James's writing resists the absolute and instead revels in ambiguity—embracing shifts in narrative perspective and multiplying possibilities. Appropriately then, his travel writing registers a similar inversion and flipping of perspective: while he started his literary career as a traveling journalist reporting back on Europe to American periodicals near the end of his career, he turned the tables and wrote the controversial, *The American Scene* (1907), reflecting—often harshly—upon his return visit to the United States in 1904–1905. In his fiction, he also takes up protagonists who grapple with understanding their identities through national contexts. Spencer Brydon (the protagonist of "The Jolly Corner," 1908) negotiates a complex return back to the States after years spent abroad in Europe; he is overwhelmed by the disorienting changes to the American scene and is haunted by the spectral vision of what his own identity might have been if he had never left. Other Jamesian protagonists are often disoriented by foreign environments and attempt to understand their Americanness from their distanced position in Europe; these include Christopher Newman, the titular hero of *The American* (1876–1877), and Lambert Strether, the protagonist of *The Ambassadors* (1903). Throughout his career, James was fascinated by the shifting constructions of national and personal identities and rendered the disorienting experiences of these problems through complex narratives filled with stylistic doubling and shaded ambiguity.

James's interest in representing the nuances of the often confused consciousnesses of his characters stylistically marks his development of what many have termed a "psychological realism" and what others have taken as modernism or at least proto-modernism. In one of his most famous works, the 1898 novella *The Turn of the Screw*, he plays with an unreliable narrator, the unnamed governess who has recorded the story of strange happenings at a country estate. The governess's shifty style of narration—her use of ambiguous pronouns, dizzying syntactical chains, and frequent interruptive dashes—maintains the story's irresolvable ambiguity about whether the cause of the unfortunate events arises from a supernatural haunting or rather from her own gothic imagination turned to madness. Indeed, James's style in his later works is the element that most fosters his persistent ambiguity; he often ends his texts with doubling language and syntax that resist clear resolution, generating lively debates among his readers about the fates of his characters and the meanings of the final pages and paragraphs of his texts.

Henry James is an author who has long been associated with "Realism" as a literary movement and style, and yet his views on how to represent the "real thing" shifted dramatically throughout his career. In his early work, realism appeared as a relatively direct manner of presentation and an interest in representing both internal and external responses to events. In his review of *Waiting for the Verdict* (1867; elsewhere in this volume), James accuses novelist Rebecca Harding Davis of failing to achieve realism because of her overly sentimentalized style. For James here, "Realism" was bound up with a particular style. However, in "The Art of Fiction" (1884), James expresses the difficulties of pinning down the novel to any set of rules and instead prescribes that "the good health of an art which undertakes so immediately to reproduce life must demand that it be perfectly free." Later in the essay, James explains the difficulties of defining "reality" and the impossibility of teaching a precise recipe to achieve those effects: he asserts that "you will not write a good novel unless you possess the sense of reality; but it will be difficult to give you a recipe for calling that sense into being. Humanity is immense, and reality has myriad forms." In the middle of his career, James questioned how to best represent the "real" and challenged whether "the real thing" was even possible to represent; in the short story aptly titled "The Real Thing" (1892), he explores these questions of representation and "realness" through the story of an illustrator who finds that he prefers the "represented thing" over the "real thing"—leading to his rejection of potential models who are so "real" that they cannot be transformed in his artistic creations. In his later novels, considered by many to be the least "real" by virtue of their incredibly nuanced, complex, and challenging style of expression, James seemed most satisfied that he has successfully executed his intentions to show "as much of [his characters] as a coherent literary form permits."

Contemporary critics were divided about James's achievement of realism in these later novels, some challenging the plausibility of his plots, his characters, and his language and others extolling his unique aesthetic capturing of the experience of the "real." One early review of *The Golden Bowl* criticizes James for his almost supernatural unreality: "Mr. James appears more than ever to detach himself from earth, and to write of human beings as if he were observing them from some faraway and inaccessible planet." In contrast, another contemporary review praises James for striving to represent experience through characters' perspectives: "We learn [about events] always through the refracting medium of some person's mind—and that often is rather not his notion of the event in itself, but his suspicion of somebody else's notion of it. Now this is in reality the only way in which events, either personal or historical, exist for any of us." These critical responses—and James's dynamic career—suggest that the demands of realism changed as the experience and understanding of the human mind and its interaction with a changing world also developed and shifted. The second reviewer, writing in 1904, suggests that James's innovation in "psychological realism" was the most effective means of narrating "in reality" the way that things "exist"—at least from that particular reviewer's vantage point.

Critics have often divided James's long career and massive textual output into stages, phases, or periods. While strict divisions are dubious, 1897 did mark a major shift in how Henry James composed his fiction. He began a distinctly different method of composition—moving from writing his manuscripts out by hand to dictating to a typist who would then transcribe his oral speech acts.[1] This shift to a mediated form of textual composition made James especially aware of the material production of literary texts and of the unique expressive opportunities afforded by different media and by different forms of circulation. James's novella *In the Cage* (1898)—written just after this shift to dictation— takes up the perspective of an unnamed telegraphist whose job requires her mediation within communication as she processes and transmits the telegrams of her affluent clientele. In this story, James plays with the partitions between operators and customers, between different classes and genders, and between readers and authors as he explores the mediated transmissions of telegraphy and experiments with mediation in his own narrative technologies.

James articulates his complex relationship to his own work in a series of prefaces written as part of the reissuing of his career-long work in the twenty-six volumes of Scribner's New York Edition (1907–1917) as "the act of revision, the act of seeing it again." Through the New York Edition prefaces, James emerges as an author immensely concerned with his own legacy, with finding an audience, and, more than anything, with being understood. In "The Figure in the Carpet" (1896), James constructs a tale of several obsessive readers (including the narrator) who devote themselves entirely to discovering the elusive

---

[1]For further insight about James's compositional practices and idiosyncrasies, read Theodora Bosanquet's intriguing tales of her time as his amanuensis (the typist to whom he dictated) in *Henry James at Work* (1924).

thread hidden in the fictional author Hugh Vereker's work, which is described by the baffled narrator as a "complex figure in a Persian carpet." James articulates his own fantasies of inspiring such an intense readerly desire in the preface to *The Golden Bowl* (1909), as he imagines the New York Edition project as "an earnest invitation to the reader to dream again in my company and in the interest of his own larger absorption of my sense." In other words, he hoped that this dedicated reader would go back through all twenty-six volumes and follow in James's "footsteps" to "dream" it all again through his framing prefaces and his revisions. Indeed, James imagines his relationship with his readers as a joint quest for meaning and pleasure in clearer understanding or "larger absorption": "It all comes back to that, to my and your 'fun'—if we but allow the term its full extension, to the production of which no humblest question involved, even to that of the shade of a cadence or the position of a comma, is not richly pertinent." In characteristically elaborate phrasing, James exemplifies his point—we need to investigate such "shades" and "commas" to get at the full richness of James's meaning and to "see" everything that he was after. Hopefully after reading these selections, you will see that such readerly attentiveness and labor can also be "fun."

Jennifer Emory-Peck
Oberlin College

PRIMARY WORKS

The Novels and Tales of Henry James (New York Edition), 26 Vols., 1907–1917; Leon Edel and Lyall H. Powers, eds. *The Complete Notebooks of Henry James,* 1987; Leon Edel and Mark Wilson, eds., *Henry James: Literary Criticism: Essays on Literature, American Writers & English Writers* (1984) and *Henry James: Literary Criticism: French Writers, Other European Writers, The Prefaces to the New York Edition* (Library of America) (1984); *Complete Stories* (5 volumes of stories from 1864–1910 by Library of America, 1996–1999); Richard Howard, ed. *Henry James: Collected Travel Writings: Great Britain and America* (Library of America) (1993).

Daisy Miller: A Study

I

At the little town of Vevey, in Switzerland, there is a particularly comfortable hotel. There are, indeed, many hotels; for the entertainment of tourists is the business of the place, which, as many travellers will remember, is seated upon the edge of a remarkably blue lake—a lake that it behoves every tourist to visit. The shore of the lake presents an unbroken array of establishments of this order, of every category, from the "grand hotel" of the newest fashion, with a chalk-white front, a hundred balconies, and a dozen flags flying from its roof, to the little Swiss *pension*[1] of an elder day, with its name inscribed in German-looking lettering upon a pink or yellow wall, and

---

[1]European boarding house (notes by Alfred Habegger).

an awkward summer-house in the angle of the garden. One of the hotels at Vevey, however, is famous, even classical, being distinguished from many of its upstart neighbours by an air both of luxury and of maturity. In this region, in the month of June, American travellers are extremely numerous; it may be said, indeed, that Vevey assumes at this period some of the characteristics of an American watering-place. There are sights and sounds which evoke a vision, an echo, of Newport and Saratoga.[2] There is a flitting hither and thither of "stylish" young girls, a rustling of muslin flounces, a rattle of dance-music in the morning hours, a sound of high-pitched voices at all times. You receive an impression of these things at the excellent inn of the "Trois Couronnes,"[3] and are transported in fancy to the Ocean House or to Congress Hall.[4] But at the "Trois Couronnes," it must be added, there are other features that are much at variance with these suggestions: neat German waiters, who look like secretaries of legation; Russian princesses sitting in the garden; little Polish boys walking about, held by the hand, with their governors; a view of the snowy crest of the Dent du Midi[5] and the picturesque towers of the Castle of Chillon.

I hardly know whether it was the analogies or the differences that were uppermost in the mind of a young American, who, two or three years ago, sat in the garden of the "Trois Couronnes," looking about him, rather idly, at some of the graceful objects I have mentioned. It was a beautiful summer morning, and in whatever fashion the young American looked at things, they must have seemed to him charming. He had come from Geneva the day before, by the little steamer, to see his aunt, who was staying at the hotel—Geneva having been for a long time his place of residence. But his aunt had a headache—his aunt had almost always a headache—and now she was shut up in her room, smelling camphor, so that he was at liberty to wander about. He was some seven-and-twenty years of age; when his friends spoke of him, they usually said that he was at Geneva, "studying." When his enemies spoke of him they said—but, after all, he had no enemies; he was an extremely amiable fellow, and universally liked. What I should say is, simply, that when certain persons spoke of him they affirmed that the reason of his spending so much time at Geneva was that he was extremely devoted to a lady who lived there—a foreign lady—a person older than himself. Very few Americans—indeed I think none—had ever seen this lady, about whom there were some singular stories. But Winterbourne had an old attachment for the little metropolis of Calvinism; he had been put to school there as a boy, and he had afterwards gone to college there—circumstances which had led to his forming a great many youthful friendships. Many of these he had kept, and they were a source of great satisfaction to him.

After knocking at his aunt's door and learning that she was indisposed, he had taken a walk about the town, and then he had come in to his

---

[2]Upper-class resort towns in Rhode Island and New York, respectively.
[3]French: "Three Crowns."
[4]Hotels in Newport and Saratoga.
[5]Swiss mountain peak visible from Vevey.

breakfast. He had now finished his breakfast; but he was drinking a small cup of coffee, which had been served to him on a little table in the garden by one of the waiters who looked like an *attaché*.[6] At last he finished his coffee and lit a cigarette. Presently a small boy came walking along the path—an urchin of nine or ten. The child, who was diminutive for his years, had an aged expression of countenance, a pale complexion, and sharp little features. He was dressed in knickerbockers, with red stockings, which displayed his poor little spindleshanks; he also wore a brilliant red cravat. He carried in his hand a long alpenstock, the sharp point of which he thrust into everything that he approached—the flower-beds, the garden-benches, the trains of the ladies' dresses. In front of Winterbourne he paused, looking at him with a pair of bright, penetrating little eyes.

"Will you give me a lump of sugar?" he asked, in a sharp, hard little voice—a voice immature, and yet, somehow, not young.

Winterbourne glanced at the small table near him, on which his coffee-service rested, and saw that several morsels of sugar remained. "Yes, you may take one," he answered; "but I don't think sugar is good for little boys."

This little boy stepped forward and carefully selected three of the coveted fragments, two of which he buried in the pocket of his knickerbockers, depositing the other as promptly in another place. He poked his alpenstock, lance-fashion, into Winterbourne's bench, and tried to crack the lump of sugar with his teeth.

"Oh, blazes; it's har-r-d!" he exclaimed, pronouncing the adjective in a peculiar manner.

Winterbourne had immediately perceived that he might have the honour of claiming him as a fellow-countryman. "Take care you don't hurt your teeth," he said, paternally.

"I haven't got any teeth to hurt. They have all come out. I have only got seven teeth. My mother counted them last night, and one came out right afterwards. She said she'd slap me if any more came out. I can't help it. It's this old Europe. It's the climate that makes them come out. In America they didn't come out. It's these hotels."

Winterbourne was much amused. "If you eat three lumps of sugar, your mother will certainly slap you," he said.

"She's got to give me some candy, then," rejoined his young interlocutor. "I can't get any candy here—any American candy. American candy's the best candy."

"And are American little boys the best little boys?" asked Winterbourne.

"I don't know. I'm an American boy," said the child.

"I see you are one of the best!" laughed Winterbourne.

"Are you an American man?" pursued this vivacious infant. And then, on Winterbourne's affirmative reply—"American men are the best," he declared.

His companion thanked him for the compliment; and the child, who had now got astride of his alpenstock, stood looking about him, while he

[6]Member of a diplomatic staff.

attacked a second lump of sugar. Winterbourne wondered if he himself had been like this in his infancy, for he had been brought to Europe at about this age.

"Here comes my sister!" cried the child, in a moment. "She's an American girl."

Winterbourne looked along the path and saw a beautiful young lady advancing. "American girls are the best girls," he said, cheerfully, to his young companion.

"My sister ain't the best!" the child declared. "She's always blowing at me."

"I imagine that is your fault, not hers," said Winterbourne. The young lady meanwhile had drawn near. She was dressed in white muslin, with a hundred frills and flounces, and knots of pale-coloured ribbon. She was bare-headed; but she balanced in her hand a large parasol, with a deep border of embroidery; and she was strikingly, admirably pretty. "How pretty they are!" thought Winterbourne, straightening himself in his seat, as if he were prepared to rise.

The young lady paused in front of his bench, near the parapet of the garden, which overlooked the lake. The little boy had now converted his alpenstock into a vaulting-pole, by the aid of which he was springing about in the gravel, and kicking it up not a little.

"Randolph," said the young lady, "what *are* you doing?"

"I'm going up the Alps," replied Randolph. "This is the way!" And he gave another little jump, scattering the pebbles about Winterbourne's ears.

"That's the way they come down," said Winterbourne.

"He's an American man!" cried Randolph, in his little hard voice.

The young lady gave no heed to this announcement, but looked straight at her brother. "Well, I guess you had better be quiet," she simply observed.

It seemed to Winterbourne that he had been in a manner presented. He got up and stepped slowly towards the young girl, throwing away his cigarette. "This little boy and I have made acquaintance," he said, with great civility. In Geneva, as he had been perfectly aware, a young man was not at liberty to speak to a young unmarried lady except under certain rarely-occurring conditions; but here at Vevey, what conditions could be better than these?—a pretty American girl coming and standing in front of you in a garden. This pretty American girl, however, on hearing Winterbourne's observation, simply glanced at him; she then turned her head and looked over the parapet, at the lake and the opposite mountains. He wondered whether he had gone too far; but he decided that he must advance farther, rather than retreat. While he was thinking of something else to say, the young lady turned to the little boy again.

"I should like to know where you got that pole," she said.

"I bought it!" responded Randolph.

"You don't mean to say you're going to take it to Italy."

"Yes, I am going to take it to Italy!" the child declared.

The young girl glanced over the front of her dress, and smoothed out a knot or two of ribbon. Then she rested her eyes upon the prospect again. "Well, I guess you had better leave it somewhere," she said, after a moment.

"Are you going to Italy?" Winterbourne inquired, in a tone of great respect. The young lady glanced at him again. "Yes, sir," she replied. And she said nothing more.

"Are you—a—going over the Simplon?"[7] Winterbourne pursued, a little embarrassed.

"I don't know," she said. "I suppose it's some mountain. Randolph, what mountain are we going over?"

"Going where?" the child demanded.

"To Italy," Winterbourne explained.

"I don't know," said Randolph. "I don't want to go to Italy. I want to go to America."

"Oh, Italy is a beautiful place!" rejoined the young man.

"Can you get candy there?" Randolph loudly inquired.

"I hope not," said his sister. "I guess you have had enough candy, and mother thinks so too."

"I haven't had any for ever so long—for a hundred weeks!" cried the boy, still jumping about.

The young lady inspected her flounces and smoothed her ribbons again; and Winterbourne presently risked an observation upon the beauty of the view. He was ceasing to be embarrassed, for he had begun to perceive that she was not in the least embarrassed herself. There had not been the slightest alteration in her charming complexion; she was evidently neither offended nor fluttered. If she looked another way when he spoke to her, and seemed not particularly to hear him, this was simply her habit, her manner. Yet, as he talked a little more, and pointed out some of the objects of interest in the view, with which she appeared quite unacquainted, she gradually gave him more of the benefit of her glance; and then he saw that this glance was perfectly direct and unshrinking. It was not, however, what would have been called an immodest glance, for the young girl's eyes were singularly honest and fresh. They were wonderfully pretty eyes; and, indeed, Winterbourne had not seen for a long time anything prettier than his fair countrywoman's various features—her complexion, her nose, her ears, her teeth. He had a great relish for feminine beauty; he was addicted to observing and analysing it; and as regards this young lady's face he made several observations. It was not at all insipid, but it was not exactly expressive; and though it was eminently delicate Winterbourne mentally accused it—very forgivingly—of a want of finish. He thought it very possible that Master Randolph's sister was a coquette; he was sure she had a spirit of her own; but in her bright, sweet, superficial little visage there was no mockery, no irony. Before long it became obvious that she was much disposed towards

[7]Mountain pass between Switzerland and Italy.

conversation. She told him that they were going to Rome for the winter—she and her mother and Randolph. She asked him if he was a "real American;" she wouldn't have taken him for one; he seemed more like a German—this was said after a little hesitation, especially when he spoke. Winterbourne, laughing, answered that he had met Germans who spoke like Americans; but that he had not, so far as he remembered, met an American who spoke like a German. Then he asked her if she would not be more comfortable in sitting upon the bench which he had just quitted. She answered that she liked standing up and walking about; but she presently sat down. She told him she was from New York State—"if you know where that is." Winterbourne learned more about her by catching hold of her small, slippery brother and making him stand a few minutes by his side.

"Tell me your name, my boy," he said.

"Randolph C. Miller," said the boy, sharply. "And I'll tell you her name;" and he levelled his alpenstock at his sister.

"You had better wait till you are asked!" said this young lady, calmly.

"I should like very much to know your name," said Winterbourne.

"Her name is Daisy Miller!" cried the child. "But that isn't her real name; that isn't her name on her cards."

"It's a pity you haven't got one of my cards!" said Miss Miller.

"Her real name is Annie P. Miller," the boy went on.

"Ask him *his* name," said his sister, indicating Winterbourne.

But on this point Randolph seemed perfectly indifferent; he continued to supply information with regard to his own family. "My father's name is Ezra B. Miller," he announced. "My father ain't in Europe; my father's in a better place than Europe."

Winterbourne imagined for a moment that this was the manner in which the child had been taught to intimate that Mr. Miller had been removed to the sphere of celestial rewards. But Randolph immediately added, "My father's in Schenectady. He's got a big business. My father's rich, you bet."

"Well!" ejaculated Miss Miller, lowering her parasol and looking at the embroidered border. Winterbourne presently released the child, who departed, dragging his alpenstock along the path. "He doesn't like Europe," said the young girl. "He wants to go back."

"To Schenectady, you mean?"

"Yes; he wants to go right home. He hasn't got any boys here. There is one boy here, but he always goes round with a teacher; they won't let him play."

"And your brother hasn't any teacher?" Winterbourne inquired.

"Mother thought of getting him one, to travel round with us. There was a lady told her of a very good teacher; an American lady—perhaps you know her—Mrs. Sanders. I think she came from Boston. She told her of this teacher, and we thought of getting him to travel round with us. But Randolph said he didn't want a teacher travelling round with us. He said he wouldn't have lessons when he was in the cars. And we *are* in the cars about half the time. There was an English lady we met in the cars[8]—I think her name was Miss Featherstone; perhaps you know her. She wanted to know why I didn't give Randolph lessons—give him "instruction," she called it. I guess he could give me more instruction than I could give him. He's very smart."

"Yes," said Winterbourne; "he seems very smart."

"Mother's going to get a teacher for him as soon as we get to Italy. Can you get good teachers in Italy?"

"Very good, I should think," said Winterbourne.

"Or else she's going to find some school. He ought to learn some more. He's only nine. He's going to college." And in this way Miss Miller continued to converse upon the affairs of her family, and upon other topics. She sat there with her extremely pretty hands, ornamented with very brilliant rings, folded in her lap, and with her pretty eyes now resting upon those of Winterbourne, now wandering over the garden, the people who passed by, and the beautiful view. She talked to Winterbourne as if she had known him a long time. He found it very pleasant. It was many years since he had heard a young girl talk so much. It might have been said of this unknown young lady, who had come and sat down beside him upon a bench, that she chattered. She was very quiet, she sat in a charming tranquil attitude; but her lips and her eyes were constantly moving. She had a soft, slender, agreeable voice, and her tone was decidedly sociable. She gave Winterbourne a history of her movements and intentions, and those of her mother and brother, in Europe, and enumerated, in particular, the various hotels at which they had stopped. "That English lady in the cars," she said—"Miss Featherstone—asked me if we didn't all live in hotels in America. I told her I had never been in so many hotels in my life as since I came to Europe. I have never seen so many—it's nothing but hotels." But Miss Miller did not make this remark with a querulous accent; she appeared to be in the best humour with everything. She declared that the hotels were very good, when once you got used to their ways, and that Europe was perfectly sweet. She was not disappointed—not a bit. Perhaps it was because she had heard so much about it before. She had ever so many intimate friends that had been there ever so many times. And then she had had ever so many dresses and things from Paris. Whenever she put on a Paris dress she felt as if she were in Europe.

"It was a kind of a wishing-cap," said Winterbourne.

"Yes," said Miss Miller, without examining this analogy; "it always made me wish I was here. But I needn't have done that for dresses. I am sure they send all the pretty ones to America; you see the most frightful things here. The only thing I don't like," she proceeded, "is the society. There isn't any society; or, if there is, I don't know where it keeps itself. Do you? I suppose there is some society somewhere, but I haven't seen anything of it. I'm very fond of society, and I have always had a great deal of it. I don't mean only

[8]I.e., by rail.

in Schenectady, but in New York. I used to go to New York every winter. In New York I had lots of society. Last winter I had seventeen dinners given me; and three of them were by gentlemen," added Daisy Miller. "I have more friends in New York than in Schenectady—more gentlemen friends; and more young lady friends too," she resumed in a moment. She paused again for an instant; she was looking at Winterbourne with all her prettiness in her lively eyes and in her light, slightly monotonous smile. "I have always had," she said, "a great deal of gentlemen's society."

Poor Winterbourne was amused, perplexed, and decidedly charmed. He had never yet heard a young girl express herself in just this fashion; never, at least, save in cases where to say such things seemed a kind of demonstrative evidence of a certain laxity of deportment. And yet was he to accuse Miss Daisy Miller of actual or potential *inconduite*,[9] as they said at Geneva? He felt that he had lived at Geneva so long that he had lost a good deal; he had become dishabituated to the American tone. Never, indeed, since he had grown old enough to appreciate things, had he encountered a young American girl of so pronounced a type as this. Certainly she was very charming; but how deucedly sociable! Was she simply a pretty girl from New York State—were they all like that, the pretty girls who had a good deal of gentlemen's society? Or was she also a designing, an audacious, an unscrupulous young person? Winterbourne had lost his instinct in this matter, and his reason could not help him. Miss Daisy Miller looked extremely innocent. Some people had told him that, after all, American girls were exceedingly innocent; and others had told him that, after all, they were not. He was inclined to think Miss Daisy Miller was a flirt—a pretty American flirt. He had never, as yet, had any relations with young ladies of this category. He had known, here in Europe, two or three women—persons older than Miss Daisy Miller, and provided, for respectability's sake, with husbands—who were great coquettes—dangerous, terrible women, with whom one's relations were liable to take a serious turn. But this young girl was not a coquette in that sense; she was very unsophisticated; she was only a pretty American flirt. Winterbourne was almost grateful for having found the formula that applied to Miss Daisy Miller. He leaned back in his seat; he remarked to himself that she had the most charming nose he had ever seen; he wondered what were the regular conditions and limitations of one's intercourse with a pretty American flirt. It presently became apparent that he was on the way to learn.

"Have you been to that old castle?" asked the young girl, pointing with her parasol to the far-gleaming walls of the Château de Chillon.

"Yes, formerly, more than once," said Winterbourne. "You too, I suppose, have seen it?"

"No; we haven't been there. I want to go there dreadfully. Of course I mean to go there. I wouldn't go away from here without having seen that old castle."

[9]French: misconduct.

"It's a very pretty excursion," said Winterbourne, "and very easy to make. You can drive, you know, or you can go by the little steamer."

"You can go in the cars," said Miss Miller.

"Yes; you can go in the cars," Winterbourne assented.

"Our courier says they take you right up to the castle," the young girl continued. "We were going last week; but my mother gave out. She suffers dreadfully from dyspepsia. She said she couldn't go. Randolph wouldn't go either; he says he doesn't think much of old castles. But I guess we'll go this week, if we can get Randolph."

"Your brother is not interested in ancient monuments?" Winterbourne inquired, smiling.

"He says he don't care much about old castles. He's only nine. He wants to stay at the hotel. Mother's afraid to leave him alone, and the courier won't stay with him; so we haven't been to many places. But it will be too bad if we don't go up there." And Miss Miller pointed again at the Château de Chillon.

"I should think it might be arranged," said Winterbourne. "Couldn't you get some one to stay—for the afternoon—with Randolph?"

Miss Miller looked at him a moment; and then, very placidly—"I wish *you* would stay with him!" she said.

Winterbourne hesitated a moment. "I would much rather go to Chillon with you."

"With me?" asked the young girl, with the same placidity.

She didn't rise, blushing, as a young girl at Geneva would have done; and yet Winterbourne, conscious that he had been very bold, thought it possible she was offended. "With your mother," he answered very respectfully.

But it seemed that both his audacity and his respect were lost upon Miss Daisy Miller. "I guess my mother won't go, after all," she said. "She don't like to ride round in the afternoon. But did you really mean what you said just now; that you would like to go up there?"

"Most earnestly," Winterbourne declared.

"Then we may arrange it. If mother will stay with Randolph, I guess Eugenio will."

"Eugenio?" the young man inquired.

"Eugenio's our courier. He doesn't like to stay with Randolph; he's the most fastidious man I ever saw. But he's a splendid courier. I guess he'll stay at home with Randolph if mother does, and then we can go to the castle."

Winterbourne reflected for an instant as lucidly as possible—"we" could only mean Miss Daisy Miller and himself. This programme seemed almost too agreeable for credence; he felt as if he ought to kiss the young lady's hand. Possibly he would have done so—and quite spoiled the project; but at this moment another person—presumably Eugenio—appeared. A tall, handsome man, with superb whiskers, wearing a velvet morning-coat and a brilliant watch-chain, approached Miss Miller, looking sharply at her companion. "Oh, Eugenio!" said Miss Miller, with the friendliest accent.

Eugenio had looked at Winterbourne from head to foot; he now bowed gravely to the young lady. "I have the honour to inform mademoiselle that luncheon is upon the table."

Miss Miller slowly rose. "See here, Eugenio," she said. "I'm going to that old castle, any way."

"To the Château de Chillon, mademoiselle?" the courier inquired. "Mademoiselle has made arrangements?" he added, in a tone which struck Winterbourne as very impertinent.

Eugenio's tone apparently threw, even to Miss Miller's own apprehension, a slightly ironical light upon the young girl's situation. She turned to Winterbourne, blushing a little—a very little. "You won't back out?" she said.

"I shall not be happy till we go!" he protested.

"And you are staying in this hotel?" she went on. "And you are really an American?"

The courier stood looking at Winterbourne, offensively. The young man, at least, thought his manner of looking an offence to Miss Miller; it conveyed an imputation that she "picked up" acquaintances. "I shall have the honour of presenting to you a person who will tell you all about me," he said smiling, and referring to his aunt.

"Oh, well, we'll go some day," said Miss Miller. And she gave him a smile and turned away. She put up her parasol and walked back to the inn beside Eugenio. Winterbourne stood looking after her; and as she moved away, drawing her muslin furbelows over the gravel, said to himself that she had the *tournure*[10] of a princess.

II

He had, however, engaged to do more than proved feasible, in promising to present his aunt, Mrs. Costello, to Miss Daisy Miller. As soon as the former lady had got better of her headache he waited upon her in her apartment; and, after the proper inquiries in regard to her health, he asked her if she had observed, in the hotel, an American family—a mamma, a daughter, and a little boy.

"And a courier?" said Mrs. Costello. "Oh, yes, I have observed them. Seen them—heard them—and kept out of their way." Mrs. Costello was a widow with a fortune; a person of much distinction, who frequently intimated that, if she were not so dreadfully liable to sick-headaches, she would probably have left a deeper impress upon her time. She had a long pale face, a high nose, and a great deal of very striking white hair, which she wore in large puffs and *rouleaux*[11] over the top of her head. She had two sons married in New York, and another who was now in Europe. This young man was amusing himself at Homburg,[12] and, though he was on his travels, was rarely perceived to visit any particular city at the moment selected by his

---

[10]French: figure, bearing.
[11]French: rolls.

[12]German resort famed for its curative waters and (before 1872) its casino.

mother for her own appearance there. Her nephew, who had come up to Vevey expressly to see her, was therefore more attentive than those who, as she said, were nearer to her. He had imbibed at Geneva the idea that one must always be attentive to one's aunt. Mrs. Costello had not seen him for many years, and she was greatly pleased with him, manifesting her approbation by initiating him into many of the secrets of that social sway which, as she gave him to understand, she exerted in the American capital. She admitted that she was very exclusive; but, if he were acquainted with New York, he would see that one had to be. And her picture of the minutely hierarchical constitution of the society of that city, which she presented to him in many different lights, was, to Winterbourne's imagination, almost oppressively striking.

He immediately perceived, from her tone, that Miss Daisy Miller's place in the social scale was low. "I am afraid you don't approve of them," he said.

"They are very common," Mrs. Costello declared. "They are the sort of Americans that one does one's duty by not—not accepting."

"Ah, you don't accept them?" said the young man.

"I can't, my dear Frederick. I would if I could, but I can't."

"The young girl is very pretty," said Winterbourne, in a moment.

"Of course she's pretty. But she is very common."

"I see what you mean, of course," said Winterbourne, after another pause.

"She has that charming look that they all have," his aunt resumed. "I can't think where they pick it up; and she dresses in perfection—no, you don't know how well she dresses. I can't think where they get their taste."

"But, my dear aunt, she is not, after all, a Comanche savage."

"She is a young lady," said Mrs. Costello, "who has an intimacy with her mamma's courier?"

"An intimacy with the courier?" the young man demanded.

"Oh, the mother is just as bad! They treat the courier like a familiar friend—like a gentleman. I shouldn't wonder if he dines with them. Very likely they have never seen a man with such good manners, such fine clothes, so like a gentleman. He probably corresponds to the young lady's idea of a Count. He sits with them in the garden, in the evening. I think he smokes."

Winterbourne listened with interest to these disclosures; they helped him to make up his mind about Miss Daisy. Evidently she was rather wild. "Well," he said, "I am not a courier, and yet she was very charming to me."

"You had better have said at first," said Mrs. Costello with dignity, "that you had made her acquaintance."

"We simply met in the garden, and we talked a bit."

"*Tout bonnement!*[13] And pray what did you say?"

"I said I should take the liberty of introducing her to my admirable aunt."

[13]French: As simply as that!

"I am much obliged to you."

"It was to guarantee my respectability," said Winterbourne.

"And pray who is to guarantee hers?"

"Ah, you are cruel!" said the young man. "She's a very nice girl."

"You don't say that as if you believed it," Mrs. Costello observed.

"She is completely uncultivated," Winterbourne went on. "But she is wonderfully pretty, and, in short, she is very nice. To prove that I believe it, I am going to take her to the Château de Chillon."

"You two are going off there together? I should say it proved just the contrary. How long had you known her, may I ask, when this interesting project was formed? You haven't been twenty-four hours in the house."

"I had known her half-an-hour!" said Winterbourne, smiling.

"Dear me!" cried Mrs. Costello. "What a dreadful girl!"

Her nephew was silent for some moments. "You really think, then," he began, earnestly, and with a desire for trustworthy information—"you really think that— —" But he paused again.

"Think what, sir?" said his aunt.

"That she is the sort of young lady who expects a man—sooner or later—to carry her off?"

"I haven't the least idea what such young ladies expect a man to do. But I really think that you had better not meddle with little American girls that are uncultivated, as you call them. You have lived too long out of the country. You will be sure to make some great mistake. You are too innocent."

"My dear aunt, I am not so innocent," said Winterbourne, smiling and curling his moustache.

"You are too guilty, then!"

Winterbourne continued to curl his moustache, meditatively. "You won't let the poor girl know you then?" he asked at last.

"Is it literally true that she is going to the Château de Chillon with you?"

"I think that she fully intends it."

"Then, my dear Frederick," said Mrs. Costello, "I must decline the honour of her acquaintance. I am an old woman, but I am not too old—thank Heaven—to be shocked!"

"But don't they all do these things—the young girls in America?" Winterbourne inquired.

Mrs. Costello stared a moment. "I should like to see my granddaughters do them!" she declared, grimly.

This seemed to throw some light upon the matter, for Winterbourne remembered to have heard that his pretty cousins in New York were "tremendous flirts." If, therefore, Miss Daisy Miller exceeded the liberal license allowed to these young ladies, it was probable that anything might be expected of her. Winterbourne was impatient to see her again, and he was vexed with himself that, by instinct, he should not appreciate her justly.

Though he was impatient to see her, he hardly knew what he should say to her about his aunt's refusal to become acquainted with her; but he discovered, promptly enough, that with Miss Daisy Miller there was no great need of walking on tiptoe. He found her that evening in the garden, wandering about in the warm starlight, like an indolent sylph, and swinging to and fro the largest fan he had ever beheld. It was ten o'clock. He had dined with his aunt, had been sitting with her since dinner, and had just taken leave of her till the morrow. Miss Daisy Miller seemed very glad to see him; she declared it was the longest evening she had ever passed.

"Have you been all alone?" he asked.

"I have been walking round with mother. But mother gets tired walking round," she answered.

"Has she gone to bed?"

"No; she doesn't like to go to bed," said the young girl. "She doesn't sleep—not three hours. She says she doesn't know how she lives. She's dreadfully nervous. I guess she sleeps more than she thinks. She's gone somewhere after Randolph; she wants to try to get him to go to bed. He doesn't like to go to bed."

"Let us hope she will persuade him," observed Winterbourne.

"She will talk to him all she can; but he doesn't like her to talk to him," said Miss Daisy, opening her fan. "She's going to try to get Eugenio to talk to him. But he isn't afraid of Eugenio. Eugenio's a splendid courier, but he can't make much impression on Randolph! I don't believe he'll go to bed before eleven." It appeared that Randolph's vigil was in fact triumphantly prolonged, for Winterbourne strolled about with the young girl for some time without meeting her mother. "I have been looking round for that lady you want to introduce me to," his companion resumed. "She's your aunt." Then, on Winterbourne's admitting the fact, and expressing some curiosity as to how she had learned it, she said she had heard all about Mrs. Costello from the chambermaid. She was very quiet and very *comme il faut;*[14] she wore white puffs; she spoke to no one, and she never dined at the *table d'hôte.*[15] Every two days she had a headache. "I think that's a lovely description, headache and all!" said Miss Daisy, chattering along in her thin, gay voice. "I want to know her ever so much. I know just what *your* aunt would be; I know I should like her. She would be very exclusive. I like a lady to be exclusive; I'm dying to be exclusive myself. Well, we *are* exclusive, mother and I. We don't speak to every one—or they don't speak to us. I suppose it's about the same thing. Any way, I shall be ever so glad to know your aunt."

Winterbourne was embarrassed. "She would be most happy," he said; "but I am afraid those headaches will interfere."

The young girl looked at him through the dusk. "But I suppose she doesn't have a headache every day," she said, sympathetically.

Winterbourne was silent a moment. "She tells me she does," he answered at last—not knowing what to say.

Miss Daisy Miller stopped and stood looking at him. Her prettiness was still visible in the darkness; she was opening and closing her enormous fan.

---

[14]French: correct, proper.   [15]French: common table for hotel guests.

"She doesn't want to know me!" she said, suddenly. "Why don't you say so? You needn't be afraid. I'm not afraid!" And she gave a little laugh.

Winterbourne fancied there was a tremor in her voice; he was touched, shocked, mortified by it. "My dear young lady," he protested, "she knows no one. It's her wretched health."

The young girl walked on a few steps, laughing still. "You needn't be afraid," she repeated. "Why should she want to know me?" Then she paused again; she was close to the parapet of the garden, and in front of her was the starlit lake. There was a vague sheen upon its surface, and in the distance were dimly-seen mountain forms. Daisy Miller looked out upon the mysterious prospect, and then she gave another little laugh. "Gracious! she *is* exclusive!" she said. Winterbourne wondered whether she was seriously wounded, and for a moment almost wished that her sense of injury might be such as to make it becoming in him to attempt to reassure and comfort her. He had a pleasant sense that she would be very approachable for consolatory purposes. He felt then, for the instant, quite ready to sacrifice his aunt, conversationally; to admit that she was a proud, rude woman, and to declare that they needn't mind her. But before he had time to commit himself to this perilous mixture of gallantry and impiety, the young lady, resuming her walk, gave an exclamation in quite another tone. "Well; here's mother! I guess she hasn't got Randolph to go to bed." The figure of a lady appeared, at a distance, very indistinct in the darkness, and advancing with a slow and wavering movement. Suddenly it seemed to pause.

"Are you sure it is your mother? Can you distinguish her in this thick dusk?" Winterbourne asked.

"Well!" cried Miss Daisy Miller, with a laugh, "I guess I know my own mother. And when she has got on my shawl, too! She is always wearing my things."

The lady in question, ceasing to advance, hovered vaguely about the spot at which she had checked her steps.

"I am afraid your mother doesn't see you," said Winterbourne. "Or perhaps," he added—thinking, with Miss Miller, the joke permissible—"perhaps she feels guilty about your shawl."

"Oh, it's a fearful old thing!" the young girl replied, serenely. "I told her she could wear it. She won't come here, because she sees you."

"Ah, then," said Winterbourne, "I had better leave you."

"Oh no; come on!" urged Miss Daisy Miller.

"I'm afraid your mother doesn't approve of my walking with you."

Miss Miller gave him a serious glance. "It isn't for me; it's for you—that is, it's for *her*. Well; I don't know who it's for! But mother doesn't like any of my gentlemen friends. She's right down timid. She always makes a fuss if I introduce a gentleman. But I *do* introduce them—almost always. If I didn't introduce my gentlemen friends to mother," the young girl added, in her little soft, flat monotone, "I shouldn't think I was natural."

"To introduce me," said Winterbourne, "you must know my name." And he proceeded to pronounce it.

"Oh, dear; I can't say all that!" said his companion, with a laugh. But by this time they had come up to Mrs. Miller, who, as they drew near, walked to the parapet of the garden and leaned upon it, looking intently at the lake and turning her back upon them. "Mother!" said the young girl, in a tone of decision. Upon this the elder lady turned round. "Mr. Winterbourne," said Miss Daisy Miller, introducing the young man very frankly and prettily. "Common," she was, as Mrs. Costello had pronounced her; yet it was a wonder to Winterbourne that, with her commonness, she had a singularly delicate grace.

Her mother was a small, spare, light person, with a wandering eye, a very exiguous nose, and a large forehead, decorated with a certain amount of thin, much-frizzled hair. Like her daughter, Mrs. Miller was dressed with extreme elegance; she had enormous diamonds in her ears. So far as Winterbourne could observe, she gave him no greeting—she certainly was not looking at him. Daisy was near her, pulling her shawl straight. "What are you doing, poking round here?" this young lady inquired; but by no means with that harshness of accent which her choice of words may imply.

"I don't know," said her mother, turning towards the lake again.

"I shouldn't think you'd want that shawl!" Daisy exclaimed.

"Well—I do!" her mother answered, with a little laugh.

"Did you get Randolph to go to bed?" asked the young girl.

"No; I couldn't induce him," said Mrs. Miller, very gently. "He wants to talk to the waiter. He likes to talk to that waiter."

"I was telling Mr. Winterbourne," the young girl went on; and to the young man's ear her tone might have indicated that she had been uttering his name all her life.

"Oh, yes!" said Winterbourne; "I have the pleasure of knowing your son."

Randolph's mamma was silent; she turned her attention to the lake. But at last she spoke. "Well, I don't see how he lives!"

"Anyhow, it isn't so bad as it was at Dover,"[16] said Daisy Miller.

"And what occurred at Dover?" Winterbourne asked.

"He wouldn't go to bed at all. I guess he sat up all night—in the public parlour. He wasn't in bed at twelve o'clock: I know that."

"It was half-past twelve," declared Mrs. Miller, with mild emphasis.

"Does he sleep much during the day?" Winterbourne demanded.

"I guess he doesn't sleep much," Daisy rejoined.

"I wish he would!" said her mother. "It seems as if he couldn't."

"I think he's real tiresome," Daisy pursued.

Then, for some moments, there was silence. "Well, Daisy Miller," said the elder lady, presently, "I shouldn't think you'd want to talk against your own brother!"

"Well, he *is* tiresome, mother," said Daisy, quite without the asperity of a retort. "He's only nine," urged Mrs. Miller.

[16]English coastal town, point of departure for France.

"Well, he wouldn't go to that castle," said the young girl. "I'm going there with Mr. Winterbourne."

To this announcement, very placidly made, Daisy's mamma offered no response. Winterbourne took for granted that she deeply disapproved of the projected excursion; but he said to himself that she was a simple, easily-managed person, and that a few deferential protestations would take the edge from her displeasure. "Yes," he began; "your daughter has kindly allowed me the honour of being her guide."

Mrs. Miller's wandering eyes attached themselves, with a sort of appealing air, to Daisy, who, however, strolled a few steps farther, gently humming to herself. "I presume you will go in the cars," said her mother.

"Yes; or in the boat," said Winterbourne.

"Well, of course, I don't know," Mrs. Miller rejoined. "I have never been to that castle."

"It is a pity you shouldn't go," said Winterbourne, beginning to feel reassured as to her opposition. And yet he was quite prepared to find that, as a matter of course, she meant to accompany her daughter.

"We've been thinking ever so much about going," she pursued; "but it seems as if we couldn't. Of course Daisy—she wants to go round. But there's a lady here—I don't know her name—she says she shouldn't think we'd want to go to see castles *here*; she should think we'd want to wait till we got to Italy. It seems as if there would be so many there," continued Mrs. Miller, with an air of increasing confidence. "Of course, we only want to see the principal ones. We visited several in England," she presently added.

"Ah, yes! in England there are beautiful castles," said Winterbourne. "But Chillon, here, is very well worth seeing."

"Well, if Daisy feels up to it— —," said Mrs. Miller, in a tone impregnated with a sense of the magnitude of the enterprise. "It seems as if there was nothing she wouldn't undertake."

"Oh, I think she'll enjoy it!" Winterbourne declared. And he desired more and more to make it a certainty that he was to have the privilege of a *tête-à-tête* with the young lady, who was still strolling along in front of them, softly vocalising. "You are not disposed, madam," he inquired, "to undertake it yourself?"

Daisy's mother looked at him, an instant, askance, and then walked forward in silence. Then—"I guess she had better go alone," she said, simply.

Winterbourne observed to himself that this was a very different type of maternity from that of the vigilant matrons who massed themselves in the forefront of social intercourse in the dark old city at the other end of the lake. But his meditations were interrupted by hearing his name very distinctly pronounced by Mrs. Miller's unprotected daughter.

"Mr. Winterbourne!" murmured Daisy.

"Mademoiselle!" said the young man.

"Don't you want to take me out in a boat?"

"At present?" he asked.

"Of course!" said Daisy.

"Well, Annie Miller!" exclaimed her mother.

"I beg you, madam, to let her go," said Winterbourne, ardently; for he had never yet enjoyed the sensation of guiding through the summer starlight a skiff freighted with a fresh and beautiful young girl.

"I shouldn't think she'd want to," said her mother. "I should think she'd rather go indoors."

"I'm sure Mr. Winterbourne wants to take me," Daisy declared. "He's so awfully devoted!"

"I will row you over to Chillon, in the starlight."

"I don't believe it!" said Daisy.

"Well!" ejaculated the elder lady again.

"You haven't spoken to me for half-an-hour," her daughter went on.

"I have been having some very pleasant conversation with your mother," said Winterbourne.

"Well; I want you to take me out in a boat!" Daisy repeated. They had all stopped, and she had turned round and was looking at Winterbourne. Her face wore a charming smile, her pretty eyes were gleaming, she was swinging her great fan about. No; it's impossible to be prettier than that, thought Winterbourne.

"There are half-a-dozen boats moored at that landing-place," he said, pointing to certain steps which descended from the garden to the lake. "If you will do me the honour to accept my arm, we will go and select one of them."

Daisy stood there smiling; she threw back her head and gave a little light laugh. "I like a gentleman to be formal!" she declared.

"I assure you it's a formal offer."

"I was bound I would make you say something," Daisy went on.

"You see it's not very difficult," said Winterbourne. "But I am afraid you are chaffing me."

"I think not, sir," remarked Mrs. Miller, very gently.

"Do, then, let me give you a row," he said to the young girl.

"It's quite lovely, the way you say that!" cried Daisy.

"It will be still more lovely to do it."

"Yes, it would be lovely!" said Daisy. But she made no movement to accompany him; she only stood there laughing.

"I should think you had better find out what time it is," interposed her mother.

"It is eleven o'clock, madam," said a voice, with a foreign accent, out of the neighbouring darkness; and Winterbourne, turning, perceived the florid personage who was in attendance upon the two ladies. He had apparently just approached.

"Oh, Eugenio," said Daisy, "I am going out in a boat!"

Eugenio bowed. "At eleven o'clock, mademoiselle?"

"I am going with Mr. Winterbourne. This very minute."

"Do tell her she can't," said Mrs. Miller to the courier.

"I think you had better not go out in a boat, mademoiselle," Eugenio declared.

Winterbourne wished to Heaven this pretty girl were not so familiar with her courier; but he said nothing.

"I suppose you don't think it's proper!" Daisy exclaimed. "Eugenio doesn't think anything's proper."

"I am at your service," said Winterbourne.

"Does mademoiselle propose to go alone?" asked Eugenio of Mrs. Miller.

"Oh, no; with this gentleman!" answered Daisy's mamma.

The courier looked for a moment at Winterbourne—the latter thought he was smiling—and then, solemnly, with a bow, "As mademoiselle pleases!" he said.

"Oh, I hoped you would make a fuss!" said Daisy. "I don't care to go now."

"I myself shall make a fuss if you don't go," said Winterbourne.

"That's all I want—a little fuss!" And the young girl began to laugh again.

"Mr. Randolph has gone to bed!" the courier announced, frigidly.

"Oh, Daisy; now we can go!" said Mrs. Miller.

Daisy turned away from Winterbourne, looking at him, smiling and fanning herself. "Good night," she said; "I hope you are disappointed, or disgusted, or something!"

He looked at her, taking the hand she offered him. "I am puzzled," he answered.

"Well; I hope it won't keep you awake!" she said, very smartly; and, under the escort of the privileged Eugenio, the two ladies passed towards the house.

Winterbourne stood looking after them; he was indeed puzzled. He lingered beside the lake for a quarter of an hour, turning over the mystery of the young girl's sudden familiarities and caprices. But the only very definite conclusion he came to was that he should enjoy deucedly "going off" with her somewhere.

Two days afterwards he went off with her to the Castle of Chillon. He waited for her in the large hall of the hotel, where the couriers, the servants, the foreign tourists were lounging about and staring. It was not the place he would have chosen, but she had appointed it. She came tripping downstairs, buttoning her long gloves, squeezing her folded parasol against her pretty figure, dressed in the perfection of a soberly elegant travelling-costume. Winterbourne was a man of imagination and, as our ancestors used to say, of sensibility; as he looked at her dress and, on the great staircase, her little rapid, confiding step, he felt as if there were something romantic going forward. He could have believed he was going to elope with her. He passed out with her among all the idle people that were assembled there; they were all looking at her very hard; she had begun to chatter as soon as she joined him. Winterbourne's preference had been that they should be conveyed to Chillon in a carriage; but she expressed a lively wish to go in the little steamer; she declared that she had a passion for steamboats. There was always such a lovely breeze upon the water, and you saw such lots of people. The sail was not long, but Winterbourne's companion found time to say a great many things. To the young man himself their little excursion was so much of an escapade—an adventure—that, even allowing for her habitual sense of freedom, he had some expectation of seeing her regard it in the same way. But it must be confessed that, in this particular, he was disappointed. Daisy Miller was extremely animated, she was in charming spirits; but she was apparently not at all excited; she was not fluttered; she avoided neither his eyes nor those of any one else; she blushed neither when she looked at him nor when she saw that people were looking at her. People continued to look at her a great deal, and Winterbourne took much satisfaction in his pretty companion's distinguished air. He had been a little afraid that she would talk loud, laugh overmuch, and even, perhaps, desire to move about the boat a good deal. But he quite forgot his fears; he sat smiling, with his eyes upon her face, while, without moving from her place, she delivered herself of a great number of original reflections. It was the most charming garrulity he had ever heard. He had assented to the idea that she was "common;" but was she so, after all, or was he simply getting used to her commonness? Her conversation was chiefly of what metaphysicians term the objective cast; but every now and then it took a subjective turn.

"What on *earth* are you so grave about?" she suddenly demanded, fixing her agreeable eyes upon Winterbourne's.

"Am I grave?" he asked. "I had an idea I was grinning from ear to ear."

"You look as if you were taking me to a funeral. If that's a grin, your ears are very near together."

"Should you like me to dance a hornpipe on the deck?"

"Pray do, and I'll carry round your hat. It will pay the expenses of our journey."

"I never was better pleased in my life," murmured Winterbourne.

She looked at him a moment, and then burst into a little laugh. "I like to make you say those things! You're a queer mixture!"

In the castle, after they had landed, the subjective element decidedly prevailed. Daisy tripped about the vaulted chambers, rustled her skirts in the corkscrew staircases, flirted back with a pretty little cry and a shudder from the edge of the *oubliettes*,[17] and turned a singularly well-shaped ear to everything that Winterbourne told her about the place. But he saw that she cared very little for feudal antiquities, and that the dusky traditions of Chillon made but a slight impression upon her. They had the good fortune to have been able to walk about without other companionship than that of the custodian; and Winterbourne arranged with this functionary that they should not be hurried—that they should linger and pause wherever they chose. The custodian interpreted the bargain generously—Winterbourne, on his side, had been generous—and ended by leaving them quite to themselves. Miss Miller's observations were not remarkable for logical consistency; for anything she wanted to say she was sure to find a pretext. She found a great many pretexts in the rugged embrasures of Chillon for asking

---

[17]French: dungeons opening beneath the floor.

Winterbourne sudden questions about himself—his family, his previous history, his tastes, his habits, his intentions—and for supplying information upon corresponding points in her own personality. Of her own tastes, habits and intentions Miss Miller was prepared to give the most definite, and indeed the most favourable, account.

"Well; I hope you know enough!" she said to her companion, after he had told her the history of the unhappy Bonivard.[18] "I never saw a man that knew so much!" The history of Bonivard had evidently, as they say, gone into one ear and out of the other. But Daisy went on to say that she wished Winterbourne would travel with them and "go round" with them; they might know something, in that case. "Don't you want to come and teach Randolph?" she asked. Winterbourne said that nothing could possibly please him so much; but that he had unfortunately other occupations. "Other occupations? I don't believe it!" said Miss Daisy. "What do you mean? You are not in business." The young man admitted that he was not in business; but he had engagements which, even within a day or two, would force him to go back to Geneva. "Oh, bother!" she said, "I don't believe it!" and she began to talk about something else. But a few moments later, when he was pointing out to her the pretty design of an antique fireplace, she broke out irrelevantly, "You don't mean to say you are going back to Geneva?"

"It is a melancholy fact that I shall have to return to Geneva to-morrow."

"Well, Mr. Winterbourne," said Daisy; "I think you're horrid!"

"Oh, don't say such dreadful things!" said Winterbourne—"just at the last."

"The last!" cried the young girl; "I call it the first. I have half a mind to leave you here and go straight back to the hotel alone." And for the next ten minutes she did nothing but call him horrid. Poor Winterbourne was fairly bewildered; no young lady had as yet done him the honour to be so agitated by the announcement of his movements. His companion, after this, ceased to pay any attention to the curiosities of Chillon or the beauties of the lake; she opened fire upon the mysterious charmer in Geneva, whom she appeared to have instantly taken it for granted that he was hurrying back to see. How did Miss Daisy Miller know that there was a charmer in Geneva? Winterbourne, who denied the existence of such a person, was quite unable to discover; and he was divided between amazement at the rapidity of her induction and amusement at the frankness of her *persiflage*.[19] She seemed to him, in all this, an extraordinary mixture of innocence and crudity. "Does she never allow you more than three days at a time?" asked Daisy, ironically. "Doesn't she give you a vacation in summer? There's no one so hard worked but they can get leave to go off somewhere at this season. I suppose, if you stay another day, she'll come after you in the boat. Do wait over till Friday, and I will go down to the landing to see her arrive!" Winterbourne began to think he had been wrong to feel disappointed in the temper in which the

[18]A leader of the Genevan resistance against foreign domination, imprisoned in the Castle of Chillon, 1532–1536. Byron's famous poem, "The Prisoner of Chillon" (1816), gave nineteenth-century readers a romantic image of Bonivard's sufferings.
[19]Raillery, banter.

young lady had embarked. If he had missed the personal accent, the personal accent was now making its appearance. It sounded very distinctly, at last, in her telling him she would stop "teasing" him if he would promise her solemnly to come down to Rome in the winter.

"That's not a difficult promise to make," said Winterbourne. "My aunt has taken an apartment in Rome for the winter, and has already asked me to come and see her."

"I don't want you to come for your aunt," said Daisy; "I want you to come for me." And this was the only allusion that the young man was ever to hear her make to his invidious kinswoman. He declared that, at any rate, he would certainly come. After this Daisy stopped teasing. Winterbourne took a carriage, and they drove back to Vevey in the dusk; the young girl was very quiet.

In the evening Winterbourne mentioned to Mrs. Costello that he had spent the afternoon at Chillon, with Miss Daisy Miller.

"The Americans—of the courier?" asked this lady.

"Ah, happily," said Winterbourne, "the courier stayed at home."

"She went with you all alone?"

"All alone."

Mrs. Costello sniffed a little at her smelling-bottle. "And that," she exclaimed, "is the young person you wanted me to know!"

III

Winterbourne, who had returned to Geneva the day after his excursion to Chillon, went to Rome towards the end of January. His aunt had been established there for several weeks, and he had received a couple of letters from her. "Those people you were so devoted to last summer at Vevey have turned up here, courier and all," she wrote. "They seem to have made several acquaintances, but the courier continues to be the most *intime*.[20] The young lady, however, is also very intimate with some third-rate Italians, with whom she rackets about in a way that makes much talk. Bring me that pretty novel of Cherbuliez's—'Paule Méré'[21]—and don't come later than the 23rd."

In the natural course of events, Winterbourne, on arriving in Rome, would presently have ascertained Mrs. Miller's address at the American banker's and have gone to pay his compliments to Miss Daisy. "After what happened at Vevey I certainly think I may call upon them," he said to Mrs. Costello.

"If, after what happens—at Vevey and everywhere—you desire to keep up the acquaintance, you are very welcome. Of course a man may know every one. Men are welcome to the privilege!"

"Pray what is it that happens—here, for instance?" Winterbourne demanded.

[20]French: familiar, confidential, intimate.
[21]This 1864 novel by a popular Swiss-French novelist told of a spontaneous young woman who runs afoul of the rigid social code of Geneva.

"The girl goes about alone with her foreigners. As to what happens farther, you must apply elsewhere for information. She has picked up half-a-dozen of the regular Roman fortune-hunters, and she takes them about to people's houses. When she comes to a party she brings with her a gentleman with a good deal of manner and a wonderful moustache."

"And where is the mother?"

"I haven't the least idea. They are very dreadful people."

Winterbourne meditated a moment. "They are very ignorant—very innocent only. Depend upon it they are not bad."

"They are hopelessly vulgar," said Mrs. Costello. "Whether or not being hopelessly vulgar is being 'bad' is a question for the metaphysicians. They are bad enough to dislike, at any rate; and for this short life that is quite enough."

The news that Daisy Miller was surrounded by half-a-dozen wonderful moustaches checked Winterbourne's impulse to go straightway to see her. He had perhaps not definitely flattered himself that he had made an ineffaceable impression upon her heart, but he was annoyed at hearing of a state of affairs so little in harmony with an image that had lately flitted in and out of his own meditations; the image of a very pretty girl looking out of an old Roman window and asking herself urgently when Mr. Winterbourne would arrive. If, however, he determined to wait a little before reminding Miss Miller of his claims to her consideration, he went very soon to call upon two or three other friends. One of these friends was an American lady who had spent several winters at Geneva, where she had placed her children at school. She was a very accomplished woman and she lived in the Via Gregoriana.[22] Winterbourne found her in a little crimson drawing-room, on a third-floor; the room was filled with southern sunshine. He had not been there ten minutes when the servant came in, announcing "Madame Mila!" This announcement was presently followed by the entrance of little Randolph Miller, who stopped in the middle of the room and stood staring at Winterbourne. An instant later his pretty sister crossed the threshold; and then, after a considerable interval, Mrs. Miller slowly advanced.

"I know you!" said Randolph.

"I'm sure you know a great many things," exclaimed Winterbourne, taking him by the hand. "How is your education coming on?"

Daisy was exchanging greetings very prettily with her hostess; but when she heard Winterbourne's voice she quickly turned her head. "Well, I declare!" she said.

"I told you I should come, you know," Winterbourne rejoined, smiling.

"Well—I didn't believe it," said Miss Daisy.

"I am much obliged to you," laughed the young man.

"You might have come to see me!" said Daisy.

"I arrived only yesterday."

---

[22]A fashionable street near the Spanish Steps, the center of Rome's English quarter.

"I don't believe that!" the young girl declared.

Winterbourne turned with a protesting smile to her mother; but this lady evaded his glance, and seating herself, fixed her eyes upon her son. "We've got a bigger place than this," said Randolph. "It's all gold on the walls."

Mrs. Miller turned uneasily in her chair. "I told you if I were to bring you, you would say something!" she murmured.

"I told *you!*" Randolph exclaimed. "I tell *you,* sir!" he added jocosely, giving Winterbourne a thump on the knee. "It *is* bigger, too!"

Daisy had entered upon a lively conversation with her hostess; Winterbourne judged it becoming to address a few words to her mother. "I hope you have been well since we parted at Vevey," he said.

Mrs. Miller now certainly looked at him—at his chin. "Not very well, sir," she answered.

"She's got the dyspepsia," said Randolph. "I've got it too. Father's got it. I've got it worst!"

This announcement, instead of embarrassing Mrs. Miller, seemed to relieve her. "I suffer from the liver," she said. "I think it's this climate; it's less bracing than Schenectady, especially in the winter season. I don't know whether you know we reside at Schenectady. I was saying to Daisy that I certainly hadn't found any one like Dr. Davis, and I didn't believe I should. Oh, at Schenectady, he stands first; they think everything of him. He has so much to do, and yet there was nothing he wouldn't do for me. He said he never saw anything like my dyspepsia, but he was bound to cure it. I'm sure there was nothing he wouldn't try. He was just going to try something new when we came off. Mr. Miller wanted Daisy to see Europe for herself. But I wrote to Mr. Miller that it seems as if I couldn't get on without Dr. Davis. At Schenectady he stands at the very top; and there's a great deal of sickness there, too. It affects my sleep."

Winterbourne had a good deal of pathological gossip with Dr. Davis's patient, during which Daisy chattered unremittingly to her own companion. The young man asked Mrs. Miller how she was pleased with Rome. "Well, I must say I am disappointed," she answered. "We had heard so much about it; I suppose we had heard too much. But we couldn't help that. We had been led to expect something different."

"Ah, wait a little, and you will become very fond of it," said Winterbourne. "I hate it worse and worse every day!" cried Randolph.

"You are like the infant Hannibal,"[23] said Winterbourne.

"No, I ain't!" Randolph declared, at a venture.

"You are not much like an infant," said his mother. "But we have seen places," she resumed, "that I should put a long way before Rome." And in reply to Winterbourne's interrogation, "There's Zurich," she observed; "I think Zurich is lovely; and we hadn't heard half so much about it."

---

[23]Carthaginian general, 247–183 B.C., trained from early childhood to seek vengeance against Rome.

"The best place we've seen is the City of Richmond!" said Randolph.

"He means the ship," his mother explained. "We crossed in that ship. Randolph had a good time on the City of Richmond."

"It's the best place I've seen," the child repeated. "Only it was turned the wrong way."

"Well, we've got to turn the right way some time," said Mrs. Miller, with a little laugh. Winterbourne expressed the hope that her daughter at least found some gratification in Rome, and she declared that Daisy was quite carried away. "It's on account of the society—the society's splendid. She goes round everywhere; she has made a great number of acquaintances. Of course she goes round more than I do. I must say they have been very sociable; they have taken her right in. And then she knows a great many gentlemen. Oh, she thinks there's nothing like Rome. Of course, it's a great deal pleasanter for a young lady if she knows plenty of gentlemen."

By this time Daisy had turned her attention again to Winterbourne. "I've been telling Mrs. Walker how mean you were!" the young girl announced.

"And what is the evidence you have offered?" asked Winterbourne, rather annoyed at Miss Miller's want of appreciation of the zeal of an admirer who on his way down to Rome had stopped neither at Bologna nor at Florence, simply because of a certain sentimental impatience. He remembered that a cynical compatriot had once told him that American women—the pretty ones, and this gave a largeness to the axiom—were at once the most exacting in the world and the least endowed with a sense of indebtedness.

"Why, you were awfully mean at Vevey," said Daisy. "You wouldn't do anything. You wouldn't stay there when I asked you."

"My dearest young lady," cried Winterbourne, with eloquence, "have I come all the way to Rome to encounter your reproaches?"

"Just hear him say that!" said Daisy to her hostess, giving a twist to a bow on this lady's dress. "Did you ever hear anything so quaint?"

"So quaint, my dear?" murmured Mrs. Walker, in the tone of a partisan of Winterbourne.

"Well, I don't know," said Daisy, fingering Mrs. Walker's ribbons. "Mrs. Walker, I want to tell you something."

"Motherr," interposed Randolph, with his rough ends to his words, "I tell you you've got to go. Eugenio'll raise something!"[24]

"I'm not afraid of Eugenio," said Daisy, with a toss of her head. "Look here, Mrs. Walker," she went on, "you know I'm coming to your party."

"I am delighted to hear it."

"I've got a lovely dress."

"I am very sure of that."

"But I want to ask a favour—permission to bring a friend."

"I shall be happy to see any of your friends," said Mrs. Walker, turning with a smile to Mrs. Miller.

[24]*I.e.*, raise hell.

"Oh, they are not my friends," answered Daisy's mamma, smiling shyly, in her own fashion. "I never spoke to them!"

"It's an intimate friend of mine—Mr. Giovanelli," said Daisy, without a tremor in her clear little voice or a shadow on her brilliant little face.

Mrs. Walker was silent a moment, she gave a rapid glance at Winterbourne. "I shall be glad to see Mr. Giovanelli," she then said.

"He's an Italian," Daisy pursued, with the prettiest serenity. "He's a great friend of mine—he's the handsomest man in the world—except Mr. Winterbourne! He knows plenty of Italians, but he wants to know some Americans. He thinks ever so much of Americans. He's tremendously clever. He's perfectly lovely!"

It was settled that this brilliant personage should be brought to Mrs. Walker's party, and then Mrs. Miller prepared to take her leave. "I guess we'll go back to the hotel," she said.

"You may go back to the hotel, mother, but I'm going to take a walk," said Daisy.

"She's going to walk with Mr. Giovanelli," Randolph proclaimed.

"I am going to the Pincio,"[25] said Daisy, smiling.

"Alone, my dear—at this hour?" Mrs. Walker asked. The afternoon was drawing to a close—it was the hour for the throng of carriages and of contemplative pedestrians. "I don't think it's safe, my dear," said Mrs. Walker.

"Neither do I," subjoined Mrs. Miller. "You'll get the fever as sure as you live. Remember what Dr. Davis told you!"[26]

"Give her some medicine before she goes," said Randolph.

The company had risen to its feet; Daisy, still showing her pretty teeth, bent over and kissed her hostess. "Mrs. Walker, you are too perfect," she said. "I'm not going alone; I am going to meet a friend."

"Your friend won't keep you from getting the fever," Mrs. Miller observed. "Is it Mr. Giovanelli?" asked the hostess.

Winterbourne was watching the young girl; at this question his attention quickened. She stood there smiling and smoothing her bonnet-ribbons; she glanced at Winterbourne. Then, while she glanced and smiled, she answered without a shade of hesitation, "Mr. Giovanelli—the beautiful Giovanelli."

"My dear young friend," said Mrs. Walker, taking her hand, pleadingly, "don't walk off to the Pincio at this hour to meet a beautiful Italian."

"Well, he speaks English," said Mrs. Miller.

"Gracious me!" Daisy exclaimed, "I don't want to do anything improper. There's an easy way to settle it." She continued to glance at Winterbourne. "The Pincio is only a hundred yards distant, and if Mr. Winterbourne were as polite as he pretends he would offer to walk with me!"

---

[25]An elevated terrace laid out in gardens, walks, and driveways, much frequented for the afternoon promenade.

[26]Roman fever, malaria.

Winterbourne's politeness hastened to affirm itself, and the young girl gave him gracious leave to accompany her. They passed down-stairs before her mother, and at the door Winterbourne perceived Mrs. Miller's carriage drawn up, with the ornamental courier whose acquaintance he had made at Vevey seated within. "Good-bye, Eugenio!" cried Daisy, "I'm going to take a walk." The distance from the Via Gregoriana to the beautiful garden at the other end of the Pincian Hill is, in fact, rapidly traversed. As the day was splendid, however, and the concourse of vehicles, walkers, and loungers numerous, the young Americans found their progress much delayed. This fact was highly agreeable to Winterbourne, in spite of his consciousness of his singular situation. The slow-moving, idly-gazing Roman crowd bestowed much attention upon the extremely pretty young foreign lady who was passing through it upon his arm; and he wondered what on earth had been in Daisy's mind when she proposed to expose herself, unattended, to its appreciation. His own mission, to her sense, apparently, was to consign her to the hands of Mr. Giovanelli; but Winterbourne, at once annoyed and gratified, resolved that he would do no such thing.

"Why haven't you been to see me?" asked Daisy. "You can't get out of that."

"I have had the honour of telling you that I have only just stepped out of the train."

"You must have stayed in the train a good while after it stopped!" cried the young girl, with her little laugh. "I suppose you were asleep. You have had time to go to see Mrs. Walker."

"I knew Mrs. Walker—" Winterbourne began to explain.

"I knew where you knew her. You knew her at Geneva. She told me so. Well, you knew me at Vevey. That's just as good. So you ought to have come." She asked him no other question than this; she began to prattle about her own affairs. "We've got splendid rooms at the hotel; Eugenio says they're the best rooms in Rome. We are going to stay all winter—if we don't die of the fever; and I guess we'll stay then. It's a great deal nicer than I thought; I thought it would be fearfully quiet; I was sure it would be awfully poky. I was sure we should be going round all the time with one of those dreadful old men that explain about the pictures and things. But we only had about a week of that, and now I'm enjoying myself. I know ever so many people, and they are all so charming. The society's extremely select. There are all kinds—English, and Germans, and Italians. I think I like the English best. I like their style of conversation. But there are some lovely Americans. I never saw anything so hospitable. There's something or other every day. There's not much dancing; but I must say I never thought dancing was everything. I was always fond of conversation. I guess I shall have plenty at Mrs. Walker's—her rooms are so small." When they had passed the gate of the Pincian Gardens, Miss Miller began to wonder where Mr. Giovanelli might be. "We had better go straight to that place in front," she said, "where you look at the view."

"I certainly shall not help you to find him," Winterbourne declared.

"Then I shall find him without you," said Miss Daisy.

"You certainly won't leave me!" cried Winterbourne.

She burst into her little laugh. "Are you afraid you'll get lost—or run over? But there's Giovanelli, leaning against that tree. He's staring at the women in the carriages: did you ever see anything so cool?"

Winterbourne perceived at some distance a little man standing with folded arms, nursing his cane. He had a handsome face, an artfully poised hat, a glass in one eye and a nosegay in his button-hole. Winterbourne looked at him a moment and then said, "Do you mean to speak to that man?"

"Do I mean to speak to him? Why, you don't suppose I mean to communicate by signs?"

"Pray understand, then," said Winterbourne, "that I intend to remain with you."

Daisy stopped and looked at him, without a sign of troubled consciousness in her face; with nothing but the presence of her charming eyes and her happy dimples. "Well, she's a cool one!" thought the young man.

"I don't like the way you say that," said Daisy. "It's too imperious."

"I beg your pardon if I say it wrong. The main point is to give you an idea of my meaning."

The young girl looked at him more gravely, but with eyes that were prettier than ever. "I have never allowed a gentleman to dictate to me, or to interfere with anything I do."

"I think you have made a mistake," said Winterbourne. "You should sometimes listen to a gentleman—the right one?"

Daisy began to laugh again. "I do nothing but listen to gentlemen!" she exclaimed. "Tell me if Mr. Giovanelli is the right one?"

The gentleman with the nosegay in his bosom had now perceived our two friends, and was approaching the young girl with obsequious rapidity. He bowed to Winterbourne as well as to the latter's companion; he had a brilliant smile, an intelligent eye; Winterbourne thought him not a bad-looking fellow. But he nevertheless said to Daisy—"No, he's not the right one."

Daisy evidently had a natural talent for performing introductions; she mentioned the name of each of her companions to the other. She strolled along with one of them on each side of her; Mr. Giovanelli, who spoke English very cleverly—Winterbourne afterwards learned that he had practised the idiom upon a great many American heiresses—addressed her a great deal of very polite nonsense; he was extremely urbane, and the young American, who said nothing, reflected upon that profundity of Italian cleverness which enables people to appear more gracious in proportion as they are more acutely disappointed. Giovanelli, of course, had counted upon something more intimate; he had not bargained for a party of three. But he kept his temper in a manner which suggested far-stretching intentions. Winterbourne flattered himself that he had taken his measure. "He is not a gentleman," said the young American; "he is only a clever imitation of one. He is a music-master, or a penny-a-liner, or a third-rate artist. Damn his good looks!" Mr. Giovanelli had certainly a very pretty face; but Winterbourne felt

a superior indignation at his own lovely fellow-country-woman's not knowing the difference between a spurious gentleman and a real one. Giovanelli
chattered and jested and made himself wonderfully agreeable. It was true
that if he was an imitation the imitation was very skilful. "Nevertheless,"
Winterbourne said to himself, "a nice girl ought to know!" And then he
came back to the question whether this was in fact a nice girl. Would a nice
girl—even allowing for her being a little American flirt—make a rendezvous
with a presumably low-lived foreigner? The rendezvous in this case, indeed,
had been in broad daylight, and in the most crowded corner of Rome; but
was it not impossible to regard the choice of these circumstances as a proof
of extreme cynicism? Singular though it may seem, Winterbourne was vexed
that the young girl, in joining her *amoroso*,[27] should not appear more impatient of his own company, and he was vexed because of his inclination. It
was impossible to regard her as a perfectly well-conducted young lady; she
was wanting in a certain indispensable delicacy. It would therefore simplify
matters greatly to be able to treat her as the object of one of those sentiments which are called by romancers "lawless passions." That she should
seem to wish to get rid of him would help him to think more lightly of her,
and to be able to think more lightly of her would make her much less perplexing. But Daisy, on this occasion, continued to present herself as an inscrutable combination of audacity and innocence.

She had been walking some quarter of an hour, attended by her two cav-
aliers, and responding in a tone of very childish gaiety, as it seemed to Winterbourne, to the pretty speeches of Mr. Giovanelli, when a carriage that
had detached itself from the revolving train drew up beside the path. At the
same moment Winterbourne perceived that his friend Mrs. Walker—the
lady whose house he had lately left—was seated in the vehicle and was beckoning to him. Leaving Miss Miller's side, he hastened to obey her summons.
Mrs. Walker was flushed; she wore an excited air. "It is really too dreadful,"
she said. "That girl must not do this sort of thing. She must not walk here
with you two men. Fifty people have noticed her."

Winterbourne raised his eyebrows. "I think it's a pity to make too much
fuss about it."

"It's a pity to let the girl ruin herself!"

"She is very innocent," said Winterbourne.

"She's very crazy!" cried Mrs. Walker. "Did you ever see anything so
imbecile as her mother? After you had all left me, just now, I could not sit
still for thinking of it. It seemed too pitiful, not even to attempt to save her.
I ordered the carriage and put on my bonnet, and came here as quickly as
possible. Thank heaven I have found you!"

"What do you propose to do with us?" asked Winterbourne, smiling.

"To ask her to get in, to drive her about here for half-an-hour, so that
the world may see she is not running absolutely wild, and then to take her
safely home."

---

[27]Italian: admirer, suitor.

"I don't think it's a very happy thought," said Winterbourne; "but you can try." Mrs. Walker tried. The young man went in pursuit of Miss Miller, who had simply nodded and smiled at his interlocutrix in the carriage and had gone her way with her own companion. Daisy, on learning that Mrs. Walker wished to speak to her, retraced her steps with a perfect good grace and with Mr. Giovanelli at her side. She declared that she was delighted to have a chance to present this gentleman to Mrs. Walker. She immediately achieved the introduction, and declared that she had never in her life seen anything so lovely as Mrs. Walker's carriage-rug.

"I am glad you admire it," said this lady, smiling sweetly. "Will you get in and let me put it over you?"

"Oh, no, thank you," said Daisy. "I shall admire it much more as I see you driving round with it."

"Do get in and drive with me," said Mrs. Walker.

"That would be charming, but it's so enchanting just as I am!" and Daisy gave a brilliant glance at the gentlemen on either side of her.

"It may be enchanting, dear child, but it is not the custom here," urged Mrs. Walker, leaning forward in her victoria[28] with her hands devoutly clasped.

"Well, it ought to be, then!" said Daisy. "If I didn't walk I should expire."

"You should walk with your mother, dear," cried the lady from Geneva, losing patience.

"With my mother dear!" exclaimed the young girl.

Winterbourne saw that she scented interference. "My mother never walked ten steps in her life. And then, you know," she added with a laugh, "I am more than five years old."

"You are old enough to be more reasonable. You are old enough, dear Miss Miller, to be talked about."

Daisy looked at Mrs. Walker, smiling intensely. "Talked about? What do you mean?"

"Come into my carriage and I will tell you."

Daisy turned her quickened glance again from one of the gentlemen beside her to the other. Mr. Giovanelli was bowing to and fro, rubbing down his gloves and laughing very agreeably; Winterbourne thought it a most unpleasant scene. "I don't think I want to know what you mean," said Daisy presently. "I don't think I should like it."

Winterbourne wished that Mrs. Walker would tuck in her carriage-rug and drive away; but this lady did not enjoy being defied, as she afterwards told him. "Should you prefer being thought a very reckless girl?" she demanded.

"Gracious me!" exclaimed Daisy. She looked again at Mr. Giovanelli, then she turned to Winterbourne. There was a little pink flush in her cheek; she was tremendously pretty. "Does Mr. Winterbourne think," she asked

---

[28]Four-wheeled pleasure carriage for two.

slowly, smiling, throwing back her head and glancing at him from head to foot, "that—to save my reputation—I ought to get into the carriage?"

Winterbourne coloured; for an instant he hesitated greatly. It seemed so strange to hear her speak that way of her "reputation." But he himself, in fact, must speak in accordance with gallantry. The finest gallantry, here, was simply to tell her the truth; and the truth, for Winterbourne, as the few indications I have been able to give have made him known to the reader, was that Daisy Miller should take Mrs. Walker's advice. He looked at her exquisite prettiness; and then he said very gently, "I think you should get into the carriage."

Daisy gave a violent laugh. "I never heard anything so stiff! If this is improper, Mrs. Walker," she pursued, "then I am all improper, and you must give me up. Good-bye; I hope you'll have a lovely ride!" and, with Mr. Giovanelli, who made a triumphantly obsequious salute, she turned away.

Mrs. Walker sat looking after her, and there were tears in Mrs. Walker's eyes. "Get in here, sir," she said to Winterbourne, indicating the place beside her. The young man answered that he felt bound to accompany Miss Miller; whereupon Mrs. Walker declared that if he refused her this favour she would never speak to him again. She was evidently in earnest. Winterbourne overtook Daisy and her companion and, offering the young girl his hand, told her that Mrs. Walker had made an imperious claim upon his society. He expected that in answer she would say something rather free, something to commit herself still farther to that "recklessness" from which Mrs. Walker had so charitably endeavoured to dissuade her. But she only shook his hand, hardly looking at him, while Mr. Giovanelli bade him farewell with a too emphatic flourish of the hat.

Winterbourne was not in the best possible humour as he took his seat in Mrs. Walker's victoria. "That was not clever of you," he said candidly, while the vehicle mingled again with the throng of carriages.

"In such a case," his companion answered, "I don't wish to be clever, I wish to be *earnest!*"

"Well, your earnestness has only offended her and put her off."

"It has happened very well," said Mrs. Walker. "If she is so perfectly determined to compromise herself, the sooner one knows it the better; one can act accordingly."

"I suspect she meant no harm," Winterbourne rejoined.

"So I thought a month ago. But she has been going too far."

"What has she been doing?"

"Everything that is not done here. Flirting with any man she could pick up; sitting in corners with mysterious Italians; dancing all the evening with the same partners; receiving visits at eleven o'clock at night. Her mother goes away when visitors come."

"But her brother," said Winterbourne, laughing, "sits up till midnight."

"He must be edified by what he sees. I'm told that at their hotel every one is talking about her, and that a smile goes round among the servants when a gentleman comes and asks for Miss Miller."

"The servants be hanged!" said Winterbourne angrily. "The poor girl's only fault," he presently added, "is that she is very uncultivated."

"She is naturally indelicate," Mrs. Walker declared. "Take that example this morning. How long had you known her at Vevey?"

"A couple of days."

"Fancy, then, her making it a personal matter that you should have left the place!"

Winterbourne was silent for some moments; then he said, "I suspect, Mrs. Walker, that you and I have lived too long at Geneva!" And he added a request that she should inform him with what particular design she had made him enter her carriage.

"I wished to beg you to cease your relations with Miss Miller—not to flirt with her—to give her no farther opportunity to expose herself—to let her alone, in short."

"I'm afraid I can't do that," said Winterbourne. "I like her extremely."

"All the more reason that you shouldn't help her to make a scandal."

"There shall be nothing scandalous in my attentions to her."

"There certainly will be in the way she takes them. But I have said what I had on my conscience," Mrs. Walker pursued. "If you wish to rejoin the young lady I will put you down. Here, by-the-way, you have a chance."

The carriage was traversing that part of the Pincian Garden which overhangs the wall of Rome and overlooks the beautiful Villa Borghese.[29] It is bordered by a large parapet, near which there are several seats. One of the seats, at a distance, was occupied by a gentleman and a lady, towards whom Mrs. Walker gave a toss of her head. At the same moment these persons rose and walked towards the parapet. Winterbourne had asked the coachman to stop; he now descended from the carriage. His companion looked at him a moment in silence; then, while he raised his hat, she drove majestically away. Winterbourne stood there; he had turned his eyes towards Daisy and her cavalier. They evidently saw no one; they were too deeply occupied with each other. When they reached the low garden-wall they stood a moment looking off at the great flat-topped pine-clusters of the Villa Borghese; then Giovanelli seated himself familiarly upon the broad ledge of the wall. The western sun in the opposite sky sent out a brilliant shaft through a couple of cloud-bars; whereupon Daisy's companion took her parasol out of her hands and opened it. She came a little nearer and he held the parasol over her; then, still holding it, he let it rest upon her shoulder, so that both of their heads were hidden from Winterbourne. This young man lingered a moment, then he began to walk. But he walked—not towards the couple with the parasol; towards the residence of his aunt, Mrs. Costello.

[29]The Borghese mansion/museum and its large
  wooded park.

IV

He flattered himself on the following day that there was no smiling among the servants when he, at least, asked for Mrs. Miller at her hotel. This lady and her daughter, however, were not at home; and on the next day after, repeating his visit, Winterbourne again had the misfortune not to find them. Mrs. Walker's party took place on the evening of the third day, and in spite of the frigidity of his last interview with the hostess Winterbourne was among the guests. Mrs. Walker was one of those American ladies who, while residing abroad, make a point, in their own phrase, of studying European society; and she had on this occasion collected several specimens of her diversely-born fellow-mortals to serve, as it were, as text-books. When Winterbourne arrived Daisy Miller was not there; but in a few moments he saw her mother come in alone, very shyly and ruefully. Mrs. Miller's hair, above her exposed-looking temples, was more frizzled than ever. As she approached Mrs. Walker, Winterbourne also drew near.

"You see I've come all alone," said poor Mrs. Miller. "I'm so frightened; I don't know what to do; it's the first time I've ever been to a party alone—especially in this country. I wanted to bring Randolph or Eugenio, or some one, but Daisy just pushed me off by myself. I ain't used to going round alone."

"And does not your daughter intend to favour us with her society?" demanded Mrs. Walker, impressively.

"Well, Daisy's all dressed," said Mrs. Miller, with that accent of the dispassionate, if not of the philosophic, historian with which she always recorded the current incidents of her daughter's career. "She got dressed on purpose before dinner. But she's got a friend of hers there; that gentleman—the Italian—that she wanted to bring. They've got going at the piano; it seems as if they couldn't leave off. Mr. Giovanelli sings splendidly. But I guess they'll come before very long," concluded Mrs. Miller hopefully.

"I'm sorry she should come—in that way," said Mrs. Walker.

"Well, I told her that there was no use in her getting dressed before dinner if she was going to wait three hours," responded Daisy's mamma. "I didn't see the use of her putting on such a dress as that to sit round with Mr. Giovanelli."

"This is most horrible!" said Mrs. Walker, turning away and addressing herself to Winterbourne. "*Elle s'affiche*.[30] It's her revenge for my having ventured to remonstrate with her. When she comes I shall not speak to her."

Daisy came after eleven o'clock, but she was not, on such an occasion, a young lady to wait to be spoken to. She rustled forward in radiant loveliness, smiling and chattering, carrying a large bouquet and attended by Mr. Giovanelli. Every one stopped talking, and turned and looked at her. She came straight to Mrs. Walker. "I'm afraid you thought I never was coming, so I sent mother off to tell you. I wanted to make Mr. Giovanelli practise

[30]French: She is making a spectacle of herself.

some things before he came; you know he sings beautifully, and I want you to ask him to sing. This is Mr. Giovanelli; you know I introduced him to you; he's got the most lovely voice and he knows the most charming set of songs. I made him go over them this evening, on purpose; we had the greatest time at the hotel." Of all this Daisy delivered herself with the sweetest, brightest audibleness, looking now at her hostess and now round the room, while she gave a series of little pats, round her shoulders, to the edges of her dress. "Is there any one I know?" she asked.

"I think every one knows you!" said Mrs. Walker pregnantly, and she gave a very cursory greeting to Mr. Giovanelli. This gentleman bore himself gallantly. He smiled and bowed and showed his white teeth, he curled his moustaches and rolled his eyes, and performed all the proper functions of a handsome Italian at an evening party. He sang, very prettily, half-a-dozen songs, though Mrs. Walker afterwards declared that she had been quite unable to find out who asked him. It was apparently not Daisy who had given him his orders. Daisy sat at a distance from the piano, and though she had publicly, as it were, professed a high admiration for his singing, talked, not inaudibly, while it was going on.

"It's a pity these rooms are so small; we can't dance," she said to Winterbourne, as if she had seen him five minutes before.

"I am not sorry we can't dance," Winterbourne answered; "I don't dance."

"Of course you don't dance; you're too stiff," said Miss Daisy. "I hope you enjoyed your drive with Mrs. Walker."

"No, I didn't enjoy it; I preferred walking with you."

"We paired off, that was much better," said Daisy. "But did you ever hear anything so cool as Mrs. Walker's wanting me to get into her carriage and drop poor Mr. Giovanelli; and under the pretext that it was proper? People have different ideas! It would have been most unkind; he had been talking about that walk for ten days."

"He should not have talked about it at all," said Winterbourne; "he would never have proposed to a young lady of this country to walk about the streets with him."

"About the streets?" cried Daisy, with her pretty stare. "Where then would he have proposed to her to walk? The Pincio is not the streets, either; and I, thank goodness, am not a young lady of this country. The young ladies of this country have a dreadfully poky time of it, so far as I can learn; I don't see why I should change my habits for *them*."

"I am afraid your habits are those of a flirt," said Winterbourne gravely.

"Of course they are," she cried, giving him her little smiling stare again. "I'm a fearful, frightful flirt! Did you ever hear of a nice girl that was not? But I suppose you will tell me now that I am not a nice girl."

"You're a very nice girl, but I wish you would flirt with me, and me only," said Winterbourne.

"Ah! thank you, thank you very much; you are the last man I should think of flirting with. As I have had the pleasure of informing you, you are too stiff."

"You say that too often," said Winterbourne.

Daisy gave a delighted laugh. "If I could have the sweet hope of making you angry, I would say it again."

"Don't do that; when I am angry I'm stiffer than ever. But if you won't flirt with me, do cease at least to flirt with your friend at the piano; they don't understand that sort of thing here."

"I thought they understood nothing else!" exclaimed Daisy.

"Not in young unmarried women."

"It seems to me much more proper in young unmarried women than in old married ones," Daisy declared.

"Well," said Winterbourne, "when you deal with natives you must go by the custom of the place. Flirting is a purely American custom; it doesn't exist here. So when you show yourself in public with Mr. Giovanelli and without your mother— —"

"Gracious! poor mother!" interposed Daisy.

"Though you may be flirting, Mr. Giovanelli is not; he means something else." "He isn't preaching, at any rate," said Daisy with vivacity. "And if you want very much to know, we are neither of us flirting; we are too good friends for that; we are very intimate friends."

"Ah!" rejoined Winterbourne, "if you are in love with each other it is another affair."

She had allowed him up to this point to talk so frankly that he had no expectation of shocking her by this ejaculation; but she immediately got up, blushing visibly, and leaving him to exclaim mentally that little American flirts were the queerest creatures in the world. "Mr. Giovanelli, at least," she said, giving her interlocutor a single glance, "never says such very disagreeable things to me."

Winterbourne was bewildered; he stood staring. Mr. Giovanelli had finished singing; he left the piano and came over to Daisy. "Won't you come into the other room and have some tea?" he asked, bending before her with his decorative smile.

Daisy turned to Winterbourne, beginning to smile again. He was still more perplexed, for this inconsequent smile made nothing clear, though it seemed to prove, indeed, that she had a sweetness and softness that reverted instinctively to the pardon of offences. "It has never occurred to Mr. Winterbourne to offer me any tea," she said, with her little tormenting manner.

"I have offered you advice," Winterbourne rejoined.

"I prefer weak tea!" cried Daisy, and she went off with the brilliant Giovanelli. She sat with him in the adjoining room, in the embrasure of the window, for the rest of the evening. There was an interesting performance at the piano, but neither of these young people gave heed to it. When Daisy came to take leave of Mrs. Walker, this lady conscientiously repaired the weakness of which she had been guilty at the moment of the young girl's arrival. She turned her back straight upon Miss Miller and left her to depart with what grace she might. Winterbourne was standing near the door; he saw it all. Daisy turned very pale and looked at her mother, but Mrs. Miller was humbly unconscious of any violation of the usual social forms. She appeared, indeed, to have felt an incongruous impulse to draw attention to her own striking observance of them. "Good night, Mrs. Walker," she said; "we've had a beautiful evening. You see if I let Daisy come to parties without me, I don't want her to go away without me." Daisy turned away, looking with a pale, grave face at the circle near the door; Winterbourne saw that, for the first moment, she was too much shocked and puzzled even for indignation. He on his side was greatly touched.

"That was very cruel," he said to Mrs. Walker.

"She never enters my drawing-room again," replied his hostess.

Since Winterbourne was not to meet her in Mrs. Walker's drawing-room, he went as often as possible to Mrs. Miller's hotel. The ladies were rarely at home, but when he found them the devoted Giovanelli was always present. Very often the polished little Roman was in the drawing-room with Daisy alone, Mrs. Miller being apparently constantly of the opinion that discretion is the better part of surveillance.[31] Winterbourne noted, at first with surprise, that Daisy on these occasions was never embarrassed or annoyed by his own entrance; but he very presently began to feel that she had no more surprises for him; the unexpected in her behaviour was the only thing to expect. She showed no displeasure at her *tête-à-tête* with Giovanelli being interrupted; she could chatter as freshly and freely with two gentlemen as with one; there was always in her conversation, the same odd mixture of audacity and puerility. Winterbourne remarked to himself that if she was seriously interested in Giovanelli it was very singular that she should not take more trouble to preserve the sanctity of their interviews, and he liked her the more for her innocent-looking indifference and her apparently inexhaustible good humour. He could hardly have said why, but she seemed to him a girl who would never be jealous. At the risk of exciting a somewhat derisive smile on the reader's part, I may affirm that with regard to the women who had hitherto interested him it very often seemed to Winterbourne among the possibilities that, given certain contingencies, he should be afraid—literally afraid—of these ladies. He had a pleasant sense that he should never be afraid of Daisy Miller. It must be added that this sentiment was not altogether flattering to Daisy; it was part of his conviction, or rather of his apprehension, that she would prove a very light young person.

But she was evidently very much interested in Giovanelli. She looked at him whenever he spoke; she was perpetually telling him to do this and to do that; she was constantly "chaffing" and abusing him. She appeared completely to have forgotten that Winterbourne had said anything to displease her at Mrs. Walker's little party. One Sunday afternoon, having gone to St. Peter's[32] with his aunt, Winterbourne perceived Daisy strolling about the great church in company with the inevitable Giovanelli. Presently he pointed

---

[31]A variation on Falstaff's statement in *Henry IV*, Part I, that "the better part of valour is discretion."

[32]The Papal church, the largest and most imposing in Christendom.

out the young girl and her cavalier to Mrs. Costello. This lady looked at them a moment through her eyeglass, and then she said:

"That's what makes you so pensive in these days, eh?"

"I had not the least idea I was pensive," said the young man.

"You are very much pre-occupied, you are thinking of something."

"And what is it," he asked, "that you accuse me of thinking of?"

"Of that young lady's—Miss Baker's, Miss Chandler's—what's her name?—Miss Miller's intrigue with that little barber's block."

"Do you call it an intrigue," Winterbourne asked—"an affair that goes on with such peculiar publicity?"

"That's their folly," said Mrs. Costello, "it's not their merit."

"No," rejoined Winterbourne, with something of that pensiveness to which his aunt had alluded. "I don't believe that there is anything to be called an intrigue."

"I have heard a dozen people speak of it; they say she is quite carried away by him."

"They are certainly very intimate," said Winterbourne.

Mrs. Costello inspected the young couple again with her optical instrument. "He is very handsome. One easily sees how it is. She thinks him the most elegant man in the world, the finest gentleman. She has never seen anything like him; he is better even than the courier. It was the courier probably who introduced him, and if he succeeds in marrying the young lady, the courier will come in for a magnificent commission."

"I don't believe she thinks of marrying him," said Winterbourne, "and I don't believe he hopes to marry her."

"You may be very sure she thinks of nothing. She goes on from day to day, from hour to hour, as they did in the Golden Age. I can imagine nothing more vulgar. And at the same time," added Mrs. Costello, "depend upon it that she may tell you any moment that she is 'engaged.'"

"I think that is more than Giovanelli expects," said Winterbourne.

"Who is Giovanelli?"

"The little Italian. I have asked questions about him and learned something. He is apparently a perfectly respectable little man. I believe he is in a small way a *cavaliere avvocato*.[33] But he doesn't move in what are called the first circles. I think it is really not absolutely impossible that the courier introduced him. He is evidently immensely charmed with Miss Miller. If she thinks him the finest gentleman in the world, he, on his side, has never found himself in personal contact with such splendour, such opulence, such expensiveness, as this young lady's. And then she must seem to him wonderfully pretty and interesting. I rather doubt whether he dreams of marrying her. That must appear to him too impossible a piece of luck. He has nothing but his handsome face to offer, and there is a substantial Mr. Miller

[33]A lawyer given an honorary knighthood (the lowest noble ranking) by the Italian government.

in that mysterious land of dollars. Giovanelli knows that he hasn't a title to offer. If he were only a count or a *marchese*![34] He must wonder at his luck at the way they have taken him up."

"He accounts for it by his handsome face, and thinks Miss Miller a young lady *qui se passe ses fantaisies*!"[35] said Mrs. Costello.

"It is very true," Winterbourne pursued, "that Daisy and her mamma have not yet risen to that stage of—what shall I call it?—of culture, at which the idea of catching a count or a *marchese* begins. I believe that they are intellectually incapable of that conception."

"Ah! but the *cavaliere* can't believe it," said Mrs. Costello.

Of the observation excited by Daisy's "intrigue," Winterbourne gathered that day at St. Peter's sufficient evidence. A dozen of the American colonists in Rome came to talk with Mrs. Costello, who sat on a little portable stool at the base of one of the great pilasters. The vesper-service was going forward in splendid chants and organ-tones in the adjacent choir, and meanwhile, between Mrs. Costello and her friends, there was a great deal said about poor little Miss Miller's going really "too far." Winterbourne was not pleased with what he heard; but when, coming out upon the great steps of the church, he saw Daisy, who had emerged before him, get into an open cab with her accomplice and roll away through the cynical streets of Rome, he could not deny to himself that she was going very far indeed. He felt very sorry for her—not exactly that he believed that she had completely lost her head, but because it was painful to hear so much that was pretty and undefended and natural assigned to a vulgar place among the categories of disorder. He made an attempt after this to give a hint to Mrs. Miller. He met one day in the Corso[36] a friend—a tourist like himself—who had just come out of the Doria Palace,[37] where he had been walking through the beautiful gallery. His friend talked for a moment about the superb portrait of Innocent X. by Velasquez, which hangs in one of the cabinets of the palace, and then said, "And in the same cabinet, by-the-way, I had the pleasure of contemplating a picture of a different kind—that pretty American girl whom you pointed out to me last week." In answer to Winterbourne's inquiries, his friend narrated that the pretty American girl—prettier than ever—was seated with a companion in the secluded nook in which the great papal portrait is enshrined.

"Who was her companion?" asked Winterbourne.

"A little Italian with a bouquet in his button-hole. The girl is delightfully pretty, but I thought I understood from you the other day that she was a young lady *du meilleur monde*."[38]

---

[34]Italian: marquis.

[35]French: who indulges her whims.

[36]"The finest street in Rome," according to Hare's *Walks in Rome*.

[37]Famed for its picture gallery. The painting of Pope Innocent X by the seventeenth-century Spanish painter Velasquez is still exhibited in a small room.

[38]French: of good society.

"So she is!" answered Winterbourne; and having assured himself that his informant had seen Daisy and her companion but five minutes before, he jumped into a cab and went to call on Mrs. Miller. She was at home; but she apologised to him for receiving him in Daisy's absence.

"She's gone out somewhere with Mr. Giovanelli," said Mrs. Miller. "She's always going round with Mr. Giovanelli."

"I have noticed that they are very intimate," Winterbourne observed.

"Oh! it seems as if they couldn't live without each other!" said Mrs. Miller. "Well, he's a real gentleman, anyhow. I keep telling Daisy she's engaged!"

"And what does Daisy say?"

"Oh, she says she isn't engaged. But she might as well be!" this impartial parent resumed. "She goes on as if she was. But I've made Mr. Giovanelli promise to tell me, if *she* doesn't. I should want to write to Mr. Miller about it—shouldn't you?"

Winterbourne replied that he certainly should; and the state of mind of Daisy's mamma struck him as so unprecedented in the annals of parental vigilance that he gave up as utterly irrelevant the attempt to place her upon her guard.

After this Daisy was never at home, and Winterbourne ceased to meet her at the houses of their common acquaintance, because, as he perceived, these shrewd people had quite made up their minds that she was going too far. They ceased to invite her, and they intimated that they desired to express to observant Europeans the great truth that, though Miss Daisy Miller was a young American lady, her behaviour was not representative— was regarded by her compatriots as abnormal. Winterbourne wondered how she felt about all the cold shoulders that were turned towards her, and sometimes it annoyed him to suspect that she did not feel at all. He said to himself that she was too light and childish, too uncultivated and unreasoning, too provincial, to have reflected upon her ostracism or even to have perceived it. Then at other moments he believed that she carried about in her elegant and irresponsible little organism a defiant, passionate, perfectly observant consciousness of the impression she produced. He asked himself whether Daisy's defiance came from the consciousness of innocence or from her being, essentially, a young person of the reckless class. It must be admitted that holding oneself to a belief in Daisy's "innocence" came to seem to Winterbourne more and more a matter of fine-spun gallantry. As I have already had occasion to relate, he was angry at finding himself reduced to chopping logic about this young lady; he was vexed at his want of instinctive certitude as to how far her eccentricities were generic, national, and how far they were personal. From either view of them he had somehow missed her, and now it was too late. She was "carried away" by Mr. Giovanelli.

A few days after his brief interview with her mother, he encountered her in that beautiful abode of flowering desolation known as the Palace of the Caesars. The early Roman spring had filled the air with bloom and perfume, and the rugged surface of the Palatine[39] was muffled with tender verdure. Daisy was strolling along the top of one of those great mounds of ruin that are embanked with mossy marble and paved with monumental inscriptions. It seemed to him that Rome had never been so lovely as just then. He stood looking off at the enchanting harmony of line and colour that remotely encircles the city, inhaling the softly humid odours and feeling the freshness of the year and the antiquity of the place reaffirm themselves in mysterious interfusion. It seemed to him also that Daisy had never looked so pretty; but this had been an observation of his whenever he met her. Giovanelli was at her side, and Giovanelli, too, wore an aspect of even unwonted brilliancy.

"Well," said Daisy, "I should think you would be lonesome!"

"Lonesome?" asked Winterbourne.

"You are always going round by yourself. Can't you get any one to walk with you?"

"I am not so fortunate," said Winterbourne, "as your companion."

Giovanelli, from the first, had treated Winterbourne with distinguished politeness; he listened with a deferential air to his remarks; he laughed, punctiliously, at his pleasantries; he seemed disposed to testify to his belief that Winterbourne was a superior young man. He carried himself in no degree like a jealous wooer; he had obviously a great deal of tact; he had no objection to your expecting a little humility of him. It even seemed to Winterbourne at times that Giovanelli would find a certain mental relief in being able to have a private understanding with him—to say to him, as an intelligent man, that, bless you, *he* knew how extraordinary was this young lady, and didn't flatter himself with delusive—or at least *too* delusive—hopes of matrimony and dollars. On this occasion he strolled away from his companion to pluck a sprig of almond blossom, which he carefully arranged in his button-hole.

"I know why you say that," said Daisy, watching Giovanelli. "Because you think I go round too much with *him*!" And she nodded at her attendant.

"Every one thinks so—if you care to know," said Winterbourne.

"Of course I care to know!" Daisy exclaimed seriously. "But I don't believe it. They are only pretending to be shocked. They don't really care a straw what I do. Besides, I don't go round so much."

"I think you will find they do care. They will show it—disagreeably."

Daisy looked at him a moment. "How—disagreeably?"

"Haven't you noticed anything?" Winterbourne asked.

"I have noticed you. But I noticed you were as stiff as an umbrella the first time I saw you."

"You will find I am not so stiff as several others," said Winterbourne, smiling. "How shall I find it?"

"By going to see the others."

---

[39]Numerous Roman emperors had their official residences on this hill.

"What will they do to me?"

"They will give you the cold shoulder. Do you know what that means?"

Daisy was looking at him intently; she began to colour. "Do you mean as Mrs. Walker did the other night?"

"Exactly!" said Winterbourne.

She looked away at Giovanelli, who was decorating himself with his almond-blossom. Then looking back at Winterbourne—"I shouldn't think you would let people be so unkind!" she said.

"How can I help it?" he asked.

"I should think you would say something."

"I do say something;" and he paused a moment. "I say that your mother tells me that she believes you are engaged."

"Well, she does," said Daisy very simply.

Winterbourne began to laugh. "And does Randolph believe it?" he asked.

"I guess Randolph doesn't believe anything," said Daisy. Randolph's scepticism excited Winterbourne to farther hilarity, and he observed that Giovanelli was coming back to them. Daisy, observing it too, addressed herself again to her countryman. "Since you have mentioned it," she said, "I *am* engaged." ... Winterbourne looked at her; he had stopped laughing. "You don't believe it!" she added.

He was silent a moment; and then, "Yes, I believe it!" he said.

"Oh, no, you don't," she answered. "Well, then—I am not!"

The young girl and her cicerone were on their way to the gate of the enclosure, so that Winterbourne, who had but lately entered, presently took leave of them. A week afterwards he went to dine at a beautiful villa on the Cælian Hill,[40] and, on arriving, dismissed his hired vehicle. The evening was charming, and he promised himself the satisfaction of walking home beneath the Arch of Constantine[41] and past the vaguely-lighted monuments of the Forum.[42] There was a waning moon in the sky, and her radiance was not brilliant, but she was veiled in a thin cloud-curtain which seemed to diffuse and equalise it. When, on his return from the villa (it was eleven o'clock), Winterbourne approached the dusky circle of the Colosseum,[43] it occurred to him, as a lover of the picturesque, that the interior, in the pale moonshine, would be well worth a glance. He turned aside and walked to one of the empty arches, near which, as he observed, an open carriage—one of the little Roman street-cabs—was stationed. Then he passed in among the cavernous shadows of the great structure, and emerged upon the clear and silent arena. The place had never seemed to him more impressive. One-half of the gigantic circus was in deep shade; the other was sleeping in the

---

[40]The Coelian Hill, sparsely inhabited in the 1870s, was known for its views and quiet walks.

[41]Erected in the fourth century to celebrate a military victory by the first Christian emperor.

[42]The heart of ancient Rome, site of the senate and various temples and memorials.

[43]The great amphitheater where gladiators fought and Christians were martyred. James pictures it as it was before 1872, when the large cross was removed and the arena excavated.

luminous dusk. As he stood there he began to murmur Byron's famous lines, out of "Manfred;"[44] but before he had finished his quotation he remembered that if nocturnal meditations in the Colosseum are recommended by the poets, they are deprecated by the doctors. The historic atmosphere was there, certainly; but the historic atmosphere, scientifically considered, was no better than a villainous miasma. Winterbourne walked to the middle of the arena, to take a more general glance, intending thereafter to make a hasty retreat. The great cross in the centre was covered with shadow; it was only as he drew near it that he made it out distinctly. Then he saw that two persons were stationed upon the low steps which formed its base. One of these was a woman, seated; her companion was standing in front of her.

Presently the sound of the woman's voice came to him distinctly in the warm night-air. "Well, he looks at us as one of the old lions or tigers may have looked at the Christian martyrs!" These were the words he heard, in the familiar accent of Miss Daisy Miller.

"Let us hope he is not very hungry," responded the ingenious Giovanelli. "He will have to take me first; you will serve for dessert!"

Winterbourne stopped, with a sort of horror; and, it must be added, with a sort of relief. It was as if a sudden illumination had been flashed upon the ambiguity of Daisy's behaviour and the riddle had become easy to read. She was a young lady whom a gentleman need no longer be at pains to respect. He stood there looking at her—looking at her companion, and not reflecting that though he saw them vaguely, he himself must have been more brightly visible. He felt angry with himself that he had bothered so much about the right way of regarding Miss Daisy Miller. Then, as he was going to advance again, he checked himself; not from the fear that he was doing her injustice, but from a sense of the danger of appearing unbecomingly exhilarated by this sudden revulsion from cautious criticism. He turned away towards the entrance of the place; but as he did so he heard Daisy speak again.

"Why, it was Mr. Winterbourne! He saw me—and he cuts me!"

What a clever little reprobate she was, and how smartly she played an injured innocence! But he wouldn't cut her. Winterbourne came forward again, and went towards the great cross. Daisy had got up; Giovanelli lifted his hat. Winterbourne had now begun to think simply of the craziness, from a sanitary point of view, of a delicate young girl lounging away the evening in this nest of malaria. What if she *were* a clever little reprobate? that was no reason for her dying of the *perniciosa*.[45] "How long have you been here?" he asked, almost brutally.

Daisy, lovely in the flattering moonlight, looked at him a moment. Then—"All the evening," she answered gently.... "I never saw anything so pretty."

[44]"... upon such a night I stood within the Coliseum's wall, Midst the chief relics of almighty Rome." *Manfred*, III, iv, 9–11

[45]*I.e.*, malaria.

"I am afraid," said Winterbourne, "that you will not think Roman fever very pretty. This is the way people catch it. I wonder," he added, turning to Giovanelli, "that you, a native Roman, should countenance such a terrible indiscretion."

"Ah," said the handsome native, "for myself, I am not afraid."

"Neither am I—for you! I am speaking for this young lady."

Giovanelli lifted his well-shaped eyebrows and showed his brilliant teeth. But he took Winterbourne's rebuke with docility. "I told the Signorina[46] it was a grave indiscretion; but when was the Signorina ever prudent?"

"I never was sick, and I don't mean to be!" the Signorina declared. "I don't look like much, but I'm healthy! I was bound to see the Colosseum by moonlight; I shouldn't have wanted to go home without that; and we have had the most beautiful time, haven't we, Mr. Giovanelli? If there has been any danger, Eugenio can give me some pills. He has got some splendid pills."

"I should advise you," said Winterbourne, "to drive home as fast as possible and take one!"

"What you say is very wise," Giovanelli rejoined. "I will go and make sure the carriage is at hand." And he went forward rapidly.

Daisy followed with Winterbourne. He kept looking at her; she seemed not in the least embarrassed. Winterbourne said nothing; Daisy chattered about the beauty of the place. "Well, I *have* seen the Colosseum by moonlight!" she exclaimed. "That's one good thing." Then, noticing Winterbourne's silence, she asked him why he didn't speak. He made no answer; he only began to laugh. They passed under one of the dark archways; Giovanelli was in front with the carriage. Here Daisy stopped a moment, looking at the young American. "*Did* you believe I was engaged the other day?" she asked.

"It doesn't matter what I believed the other day," said Winterbourne, still laughing.

"Well, what do you believe now?"

"I believe that it makes very little difference whether you are engaged or not!"

He felt the young girl's pretty eyes fixed upon him through the thick gloom of the archway; she was apparently going to answer. But Giovanelli hurried her forward. "Quick, quick," he said; "if we get in by midnight we are quite safe."

Daisy took her seat in the carriage, and the fortunate Italian placed himself beside her. "Don't forget Eugenio's pills!" said Winterbourne, as he lifted his hat.

"I don't care," said Daisy, in a little strange tone, "whether I have Roman fever or not!" Upon this the cab-driver cracked his whip, and they rolled away over the desultory patches of the antique pavement.

Winterbourne—to do him justice, as it were—mentioned to no one that he had encountered Miss Miller, at midnight, in the Colosseum with a gentleman; but nevertheless, a couple of days later, the fact of her having been

[46]The Miss, the young lady.

there under these circumstances was known to every member of the little American circle, and commented accordingly. Winterbourne reflected that they had of course known it at the hotel, and that, after Daisy's return, there had been an exchange of jokes between the porter and the cab-driver. But the young man was conscious at the same moment that it had ceased to be a matter of serious regret to him that the little American flirt should be "talked about" by low-minded menials. These people, a day or two later, had serious information to give: the little American flirt was alarmingly ill. Winterbourne, when the rumour came to him, immediately went to the hotel for more news. He found that two or three charitable friends had preceded him, and that they were being entertained in Mrs. Miller's salon by Randolph.

"It's going round at night," said Randolph—"that's what made her sick. She's always going round at night. I shouldn't think she'd want to—it's so plaguey dark. You can't see anything here at night, except when there's a moon. In America there's always a moon!" Mrs. Miller was invisible; she was now, at least, giving her daughter the advantage of her society. It was evident that Daisy was dangerously ill.

Winterbourne went often to ask for news of her, and once he saw Mrs. Miller, who, though deeply alarmed, was—rather to his surprise—perfectly composed, and, as it appeared, a most efficient and judicious nurse. She talked a good deal about Dr. Davis, but Winterbourne paid her the compliment of saying to himself that she was not, after all, such a monstrous goose. "Daisy spoke of you the other day," she said to him. "Half the time she doesn't know what she's saying, but that time I think she did. She gave me a message; she told me to tell you. She told me to tell you that she never was engaged to that handsome Italian. I am sure I am very glad; Mr. Giovanelli hasn't been near us since she was taken ill. I thought he was so much of a gentleman; but I don't call that very polite! A lady told me that he was afraid I was angry with him for taking Daisy round at night. Well, so I am; but I suppose he knows I'm a lady. I would scorn to scold him. Any way, she says she's not engaged. I don't know why she wanted you to know; but she said to me three times—'Mind you tell Mr. Winterbourne.' And then she told me to ask if you remembered the time you went to that castle, in Switzerland. But I said I wouldn't give any such messages as that. Only, if she is not engaged, I'm sure I'm glad to know it."

But, as Winterbourne had said, it mattered very little. A week after this the poor girl died; it had been a terrible case of the fever. Daisy's grave was in the little Protestant cemetery, in an angle of the wall of imperial Rome, beneath the cypresses and the thick spring-flowers. Winterbourne stood there beside it, with a number of other mourners; a number larger than the scandal excited by the young lady's career would have led you to expect. Near him stood Giovanelli, who came nearer still before Winterbourne turned away. Giovanelli was very pale; on this occasion he had no flower in his button-hole; he seemed to wish to say something. At last he said, "She was the most beautiful young lady I ever saw, and the most amiable." And then he added in a moment, "And she was the most innocent."

Winterbourne looked at him, and presently repeated his words, "And the most innocent?"

"The most innocent!"

Winterbourne felt sore and angry. "Why the devil," he asked, "did you take her to that fatal place?"

Mr. Giovanelli's urbanity was apparently imperturbable. He looked on the ground a moment, and then he said, "For myself, I had no fear; and she wanted to go."

"That was no reason!" Winterbourne declared.

The subtle Roman again dropped his eyes. "If she had lived, I should have got nothing. She would never have married me, I am sure."

"She would never have married you?"

"For a moment I hoped so. But no. I am sure."

Winterbourne listened to him; he stood staring at the raw protuberance among the April daisies. When he turned away again Mr. Giovanelli, with his light slow step, had retired.

Winterbourne almost immediately left Rome; but the following summer he again met his aunt, Mrs. Costello, at Vevey. Mrs. Costello was fond of Vevey. In the interval Winterbourne had often thought of Daisy Miller and her mystifying manners. One day he spoke of her to his aunt—said it was on his conscience that he had done her injustice.

"I am sure I don't know," said Mrs. Costello. "How did your injustice affect her?"

"She sent me a message before her death which I didn't understand at the time. But I have understood it since. She would have appreciated one's esteem."

"Is that a modest way," asked Mrs. Costello, "of saying that she would have reciprocated one's affection?"

Winterbourne offered no answer to this question; but he presently said, "You were right in that remark that you made last summer. I was booked to make a mistake. I have lived too long in foreign parts."

Nevertheless, he went back to live at Geneva, whence there continue to come the most contradictory accounts of his motives of sojourn: a report that he is "studying" hard—an intimation that he is much interested in a very clever foreign lady.

1878

The Art of Fiction

I should not have affixed so comprehensive a title to these few remarks, necessarily wanting in any completeness upon a subject the full consideration of which would carry us far, did I not seem to discover a pretext for my temerity in the interesting pamphlet lately published under this name by Mr. Walter Besant.[1] Mr Besant's lecture at the Royal Institution—the original form of his pamphlet—appears to indicate that many persons are

[1]Sir Walter Besant (1836–1901), English novelist known for his romantic style and his concern for social causes. (Notes by Alfred Habegger.)

interested in the art of fiction, and are not indifferent to such remarks, as those who practise it may attempt to make about it. I am therefore anxious not to lose the benefit of this favourable association, and to edge in a few words under cover of the attention which Mr. Besant is sure to have excited. There is something very encouraging in his having put into form certain of his ideas on the mystery of story-telling.

It is a proof of life and curiosity—curiosity on the part of the brother-hood of novelists as well as on the part of their readers. Only a short time ago it might have been supposed that the English novel was not what the French call *discutable*.[2] It had no air of having a theory, a conviction, a con-sciousness of itself behind it—of being the expression of an artistic faith, the result of choice and comparison. I do not say it was necessarily the worse for that: it would take much more courage than I possess to intimate that the form of the novel as Dickens[3] and Thackeray[4] (for instance) saw it had any taint of incompleteness. It was, however, *naïf* (if I may help myself out with another French word); and evidently if it be destined to suffer in any way for having lost its *naïveté* it has now an idea of making sure of the corresponding advantages. During the period I have alluded to there was a comfortable, good-humoured feeling abroad that a novel is a novel, as a pud-ding is a pudding, and that our only business with it could be to swallow it. But within a year or two, for some reason or other, there have been signs of returning animation—the era of discussion would appear to have been to a certain extent opened. Art lives upon discussion, upon experiment, upon cu-riosity, upon variety of attempt, upon the exchange of views and the com-parison of standpoints; and there is a presumption that those times when no one has anything particular to say about it, and has no reason to give for practice or preference, though they may be times of honour, are not times of development—are times, possibly even, a little of dulness. The successful application of any art is a delightful spectacle, but the theory too is interest-ing; and though there is a great deal of the latter without the former I sus-pect there has never been a genuine success that has not had a latent core of conviction. Discussion, suggestion, formulation, these things are fertilis-ing when they are frank and sincere. Mr. Besant has set an excellent exam-ple in saying what he thinks, for his part, about the way in which fiction should be written, as well as about the way in which it should be published; for his view of the "art," carried on into an appendix, covers that too. Other labourers in the same field will doubtless take up the argument, they will give it the light of their experience, and the effect will surely be to make our interest in the novel a little more what it had for some time threatened to fail to be—a serious, active, inquiring interest, under protection of which

[2]French: questionable.
[3]Charles Dickens (1812–1870), the most pop-ular English novelist of the nineteenth cen-tury, wrote prolifically about all levels of British society employing a variety of literary modes from the sensational and the dra-matic to the sentimental.
[4]William Makepeace Thackeray (1811–1863), satiric Victorian novelist.

this delightful study may, in moments of confidence, venture to say a little more what it thinks of itself.

It must take itself seriously for the public to take it so. The old superstition about fiction being "wicked" has doubtless died out in England; but the spirit of it lingers in a certain oblique regard directed toward any story which does not more or less admit that it is only a joke. Even the most jocular novel feels in some degree the weight of the proscription that was formerly directed against literary levity: the jocularity does not always succeed in passing for orthodoxy. It is still expected, though perhaps people are ashamed to say it, that a production which is after all only a "make-believe" (for what else is a "story"?) shall be in some degree apologetic—shall renounce the pretension of attempting really to represent life. This, of course, any sensible, wide-awake story declines to do, for it quickly perceives that the tolerance granted to it on such a condition is only an attempt to stifle it disguised in the form of generosity. The old evangelical hostility to the novel, which was as explicit as it was narrow, and which regarded it as little less favourable to our immortal part than a stage-play, was in reality far less insulting. The only reason for the existence of a novel is that it does attempt to represent life. When it relinquishes this attempt, the same attempt that we see on the canvas of the painter, it will have arrived at a very strange pass. It is not expected of the picture that it will make itself humble in order to be forgiven; and the analogy between the art of the painter and the art of the novelist is, so far as I am able to see, complete. Their inspiration is the same, their process (allowing for the different quality of the vehicle), is the same, their success is the same. They may learn from each other, they may explain and sustain each other. Their cause is the same, and the honour of one is the honour of another. The Mahometans[5] think a picture an unholy thing, but it is a long time since any Christian did, and it is therefore the more odd that in the Christian mind the traces (dissimulated though they may be) of a suspicion of the sister art should linger to this day. The only effectual way to lay it to rest is to emphasise the analogy to which I just alluded—to insist on the fact that as the picture is reality, so the novel is history. That is the only general description (which does it justice) that we may give of the novel. But history also is allowed to represent life; it is not, any more than painting, expected to apologise. The subject-matter of fiction is stored up likewise in documents and records, and if it will not give itself away, as they say in California, it must speak with assurance, with the tone of the historian. Certain accomplished novelists have a habit of giving themselves away which must often bring tears to the eyes of people who take their fiction seriously. I was lately struck, in reading over many pages of Anthony Trollope,[6] with his want of discretion in this particular. In a digression, a parenthesis or an aside, he concedes to the

---

[5]Muslims.
[6]English novelist noted for the verisimilitude of his Victorian fiction (1815–1882).

reader that he and this trusting friend are only "making believe." He admits that the events he narrates have not really happened, and that he can give his narrative any turn the reader may like best. Such a betrayal of a sacred office seems to me, I confess, a terrible crime; it is what I mean by the attitude of apology, and it shocks me every whit as much in Trollope as it would have shocked me in Gibbon[7] or Macaulay.[8] It implies that the novelist is less occupied in looking for the truth (the truth, of course I mean, that he assumes, the premises that we must grant him, whatever they may be), than the historian, and in doing so it deprives him at a stroke of all his standing-room. To represent and illustrate the past, the actions of men, is the task of either writer, and the only difference that I can see is, in proportion as he succeeds, to the honour of the novelist, consisting as it does in his having more difficulty in collecting his evidence, which is so far from being purely literary. It seems to me to give him a great character, the fact that he has at once so much in common with the philosopher and the painter; this double analogy is a magnificent heritage.

It is of all this evidently that Mr. Besant is full when he insists upon the fact that fiction is one of the *fine* arts, deserving in its turn of all the honours and emoluments that have hitherto been reserved for the successful profession of music, poetry, painting, architecture. It is impossible to insist too much on so important a truth, and the place that Mr. Besant demands for the work of the novelist may be represented, a trifle less abstractly, by saying that he demands not only that it shall be reputed artistic, but that it shall be reputed very artistic indeed. It is excellent that he should have struck this note, for his doing so indicates that there was need of it, that his proposition may be to many people a novelty. One rubs one's eyes at the thought; but the rest of Mr. Besant's essay confirms the revelation. I suspect in truth that it would be possible to confirm it still further, and that one would not be far wrong in saying that in addition to the people to whom it has never occurred that a novel ought to be artistic, there are a great many others who, if this principle were urged upon them, would be filled with an indefinable mistrust. They would find it difficult to explain their repugnance, but it would operate strongly to put them on their guard. "Art," in our Protestant communities, where so many things have got so strangely twisted about, is supposed in certain circles to have some vaguely injurious effect upon those who make it an important consideration, who let it weigh in the balance. It is assumed to be opposed in some mysterious manner to morality, to amusement, to instruction. When it is embodied in the work of the painter (the sculptor is another affair!) you know what it is: it stands there before you, in the honesty of pink and green and a gilt frame; you can see the worst of it at a glance, and you can be on your guard. But when it is introduced into literature it becomes more insidious—there is danger of its

[7]Edward Gibbon (1737–1794), English historian.
[8]Thomas Babbington Macaulay (1800–1859), English historian, author, and politician.

hurting you before you know it. Literature should be either instructive or amusing, and there is in many minds an impression that these artistic pre-occupations, the search for form, contribute to neither end, interfere indeed with both. They are too frivolous to be edifying, and too serious to be diverting; and they are moreover priggish and paradoxical and superfluous. That, I think, represents the manner in which the latent thought of many people who read novels as an exercise in skipping would explain itself if it were to become articulate. They would argue, of course, that a novel ought to be "good," but they would interpret this term in a fashion of their own, which indeed would vary considerably from one critic to another. One would say that being good means representing virtuous and aspiring characters, placed in prominent positions; another would say that it depends on a "happy ending," on a distribution at the last of prizes, pensions, husbands, wives, babies, millions, appended paragraphs, and cheerful remarks. Another still would say that it means being full of incident and movement, so that we shall wish to jump ahead, to see who was the mysterious stranger, and if the stolen will was ever found, and shall not be distracted from this pleasure by any tiresome analysis or "description." But they would all agree that the "artistic" idea would spoil some of their fun. One would hold it accountable for all the description, another would see it revealed in the absence of sym-pathy. Its hostility to a happy ending would be evident, and it might even in some cases render any ending at all impossible. The "ending" of a novel is, for many persons, like that of a good dinner, a course of dessert and ices, and the artist in fiction is regarded as a sort of meddlesome doctor who for-bids agreeable aftertastes. It is therefore true that this conception of Mr. Besant's of the novel as a superior form encounters not only a negative but a positive indifference. It matters little that as a work of art it should really be as little or as much of its essence to supply happy endings, sympathetic characters, and an objective tone, as if it were a work of mechanics: the association of ideas, however incongruous, might easily be too much for it if an eloquent voice were not sometimes raised to call attention to the fact that it is at once as free and as serious a branch of literature as any other.

Certainly this might sometimes be doubted in presence of the enormous number of works of fiction that appeal to the credulity of our generation, for it might easily seem that there could be no great character in a commod-ity so quickly and easily produced. It must be admitted that good novels are much compromised by bad ones, and that the field at large suffers discredit from overcrowding. I think, however, that this injury is only superficial, and that the superabundance of written fiction proves nothing against the prin-ciple itself. It has been vulgarised, like all other kinds of literature, like everything else to-day, and it has proved more than some kinds accessible to vulgarisation. But there is as much difference as there ever was between a good novel and a bad one: the bad is swept with all the daubed canvases and spoiled marble into some unvisited limbo, or infinite rubbish-yard beneath the back-windows of the world, and the good subsists and emits its light and stimulates our desire for perfection. As I shall take the liberty of making but a single criticism of Mr. Besant, whose tone is so full of the love of his art, I may as well have done with it at once. He seems to me to mistake in attempting to say so definitely beforehand what sort of an affair the good novel will be. To indicate the danger of such an error as that has been the purpose of these few pages; to suggest that certain traditions on the subject, applied *a priori*, have already had much to answer for, and that the good health of an art which undertakes so immediately to reproduce life must demand that it be perfectly free. It lives upon exercise, and the very meaning of exercise is freedom. The only obligation to which in advance we may hold a novel, without incurring the accusation of being arbitrary, is that it be interesting. That general responsibility rests upon it, but it is the only one I can think of. The ways in which it is at liberty to accomplish this result (of interesting us) strike me as innumerable, and such as can only suffer from being marked out or fenced in by prescription. They are as various as the temperament of man, and they are successful in proportion as they reveal a particular mind, different from others. A novel is in its broadest definition a personal, a direct impression of life; that, to begin with, constitutes its value, which is greater or less according to the intensity of the impression. But there will be no intensity at all, and therefore no value, unless there is freedom to feel and say. The tracing of a line to be followed, of a tone to be taken, of a form to be filled out, is a limitation of that freedom and a suppression of the very thing that we are most curious about. The form, it seems to me, is to be appreciated after the fact: then the author's choice has been made, his standard has been indicated; then we can follow lines and directions and compare tones and resemblances. Then in a word we can enjoy one of the most charming of pleasures, we can estimate quality, we can apply the test of execution. The execution belongs to the author alone; it is what is most personal to him, and we measure him by that. The advantage, the luxury, as well as the torment and responsibility of the novelist, is that there is no limit to what he may attempt as an executant—no limit to his possible experiments, efforts, discoveries, successes. Here it is especially that he works, step by step, like his brother of the brush, of whom we may always say that he has painted his picture in a manner best known to himself. His manner is his secret, not necessarily a jealous one. He cannot disclose it as a general thing if he would; he would be at a loss to teach it to others. I say this with a due recollection of having insisted on the community of method of the artist who paints a picture and the artist who writes a novel. The painter *is* able to teach the rudiments of his practice, and it is possible, from the study of good work (granted the aptitude), both to learn how to paint and to learn how to write. Yet it remains true, without injury to the *rapprochement*,[9] that the literary artist would be obliged to say to his pupil much more than the other, "Ah, well, you must do it as you can!" It is a question of degree, a matter of delicacy. If there are

---

[9]French: accord.

exact sciences, there are also exact arts, and the grammar of painting is so much more definite that it makes the difference.

I ought to add, however, that if Mr. Besant says at the beginning of his essay that the "laws of fiction may be laid down and taught with as much precision and exactness as the laws of harmony, perspective, and proportion," he mitigates what might appear to be an extravagance by applying his remark to "general" laws, and by expressing most of these rules in a manner with which it would certainly be unaccommodating to disagree. That the novelist must write from his experience, that his "characters must be real and such as might be met with in actual life;" that "a young lady brought up in a quiet country village should avoid descriptions of garrison life," and "a writer whose friends and personal experiences belong to the lower middleclass should carefully avoid introducing his characters into society," that one should enter one's notes in a common-place book;[10] that one's figures should be clear in outline; that making them clear by some trick of speech or of carriage is a bad method, and "describing them at length" is a worse one; that English Fiction should have a "conscious moral purpose;" that "it is almost impossible to estimate too highly the value of careful workmanship— that is, of style;" that "the most important point of all is the story," that "the story is everything": these are principles with most of which it is surely impossible not to sympathise. That remark about the lower middle-class writer and his knowing his place is perhaps rather chilling; but for the rest I should find it difficult to dissent from any one of these recommendations. At the same time, I should find it difficult positively to assent to them, with the exception, perhaps, of the injunction as to entering one's notes in a common-place book. They scarcely seem to me to have the quality that Mr. Besant attributes to the rules of the novelist—the "precision and exactness" of "the laws of harmony, perspective, and proportion." They are suggestive, they are even inspiring, but they are not exact, though they are doubtless as much so as the case admits of: which is a proof of that liberty of interpretation for which I just contended. For the value of these different injunctions—so beautiful and so vague—is wholly in the meaning one attaches to them. The characters, the situation, which strike one as real will be those that touch and interest one most, but the measure of reality is very difficult to fix. The reality of Don Quixote[11] or of Mr. Micawber[12] is a very delicate shade; it is a reality so coloured by the author's vision that, vivid as it may be, one would hesitate to propose it as a model: one would expose one's self to some very embarrassing questions on the part of a pupil. It goes without saying that you will not write a good novel unless you possess the sense of reality; but it will be difficult to give you a recipe for calling that sense into being. Humanity is

---

[10]A book in which quotations, poems, extracts, comments, and so on are recorded for future use.

[11]Protagonist of Miguel de Cervantes's romance *Don Quixote de la Mancha* (1605), who lived according to chivalrous but impractical ideals.

[12]Wilkins Micawber, a character in Charles Dickens's *David Copperfield*, known for his good heart and erratic temperament.

immense, and reality has a myriad forms; the most one can affirm is that some of the flowers of fiction have the odour of it, and others have not; as for telling you in advance how your nosegay should be composed, that is another affair. It is equally excellent and inconclusive to say that one must write from experience; to our supposititious aspirant such a declaration might savour of mockery. What kind of experience is intended, and where does it begin and end? Experience is never limited, and it is never complete; it is an immense sensibility, a kind of huge spider-web of the finest silken threads suspended in the chamber of consciousness, and catching every air-borne particle in its tissue. It is the very atmosphere of the mind; and when the mind is imaginative—much more when it happens to be that of a man of genius—it takes to itself the faintest hints of life, it converts the very pulses of the air into revelations. The young lady living in a village has only to be a damsel upon whom nothing is lost to make it quite unfair (as it seems to me) to declare to her that she shall have nothing to say about the military. Greater miracles have been seen than that, imagination assisting, she should speak the truth about some of these gentlemen. I remember an English novelist, a woman of genius, telling me that she was much commended for the impression she had managed to give in one of her tales of the nature and way of life of the French Protestant youth. She had been asked where she learned so much about this recondite being, she had been congratulated on her peculiar opportunities. These opportunities consisted in her having once, in Paris, as she ascended a staircase, passed an open door where, in the household of a *pasteur*,[13] some of the young Protestants were seated at table round a finished meal. The glimpse made a picture; it lasted only a moment, but that moment was experience. She had got her direct personal impression, and she turned out her type. She knew what youth was, and what Protestantism; she also had the advantage of having seen what it was to be French, so that she converted these ideas into a concrete image and produced a reality. Above all, however, she was blessed with the faculty which when you give it an inch takes an ell, and which for the artist is a much greater source of strength than any accident of residence or of place in the social scale. The power to guess the unseen from the seen, to trace the implication of things, to judge the whole piece by the pattern, the condition of feeling life in general so completely that you are well on your way to knowing any particular corner of it—this cluster of gifts may almost be said to constitute experience, and they occur in country and in town, and in the most differing stages of education. If experience consists of impressions, it may be said that impressions *are* experience, just as (have we not seen it?) they are the very air we breathe. Therefore, if I should certainly say to a novice, "Write from experience and experience only," I should feel that this was rather a tantalising monition if I were not careful immediately to add, "Try to be one of the people on whom nothing is lost!"

I am far from intending by this to minimise the importance of exactness—of truth of detail. One can speak best from one's own taste, and I may

[13]French: minister, priest.

therefore venture to say that the air of reality (solidity of specification) seems to me to be the supreme virtue of a novel—the merit on which all its other merits (including that conscious moral purpose of which Mr. Besant speaks) helplessly and submissively depend. If it be not there they are all as nothing, and if these be there, they owe their effect to the success with which the author has produced the illusions of life. The cultivation of this success, the study of this exquisite process, form, to my taste, the beginning and the end of the art of the novelist. They are his inspiration, his despair, his reward, his torment, his delight. It is here in very truth that he competes with life; it is here that he competes with his brother the painter in *his* attempt to render the look of things, the look that conveys their meaning, to catch the colour, the relief, the expression, the surface, the substance of the human spectacle. It is in regard to this that Mr. Besant is well inspired when he bids him take notes. He cannot possibly take too many, he cannot possibly take enough. All life solicits him, and to "render" the simplest surface, to produce the most momentary illusion, is a very complicated business. His case would be easier, and the rule would be more exact, if Mr. Besant had been able to tell him what notes to take. But this, I fear, he can never learn in any manual; it is the business of his life. He has to take a great many in order to select a few, he has to work them up as he can, and even the guides and philosophers who might have most to say to him must leave him alone when it comes to the application of precepts, as we leave the painter in communion with his palette. That his characters "must be clear in outline," as Mr. Besant says—he feels that down to his boots; but how he shall make them so is a secret between his good angel and himself. It would be absurdly simple if he could be taught that a great deal of "description" would make them so, or that on the contrary the absence of description and the cultivation of dialogue, or the absence of dialogue and the multiplication of "incident," would rescue him from his difficulties. Nothing, for instance, is more possible than that he be of a turn of mind for which this odd, literal opposition of description and dialogue, incident and description, has little meaning and light. People often talk of these things as if they had a kind of internecine[14] distinctness, instead of melting into each other at every breath, and being intimately associated parts of one general effort of expression. I cannot imagine composition existing in a series of blocks, nor conceive, in any novel worth discussing at all, of a passage of dialogue that is not in its intention descriptive, a touch of truth of any sort that does not partake of the nature of incident, or an incident that derives its interest from any other source than the general and only source of the success of a work of art—that of being illustrative. A novel is a living thing, all one and continuous, like any other organism, and in proportion as it lives will it be found, I think, that in each of the parts there is something of each of the other parts. The critic who over the close texture of a finished work shall pretend to trace a geography of items will mark some frontiers as

---

[14]Mutually destructive.

artificial, I fear, as any that have been known to history. There is an old-fashioned distinction between the novel of character and the novel of incident which must have cost many a smile to the intending fabulist who was keen about his work. It appears to me as little to the point as the equally celebrated distinction between the novel and the romance—to answer as little to any reality. There are bad novels and good novels, as there are bad pictures and good pictures; but that is the only distinction in which I see any meaning, and I can as little imagine speaking of a novel of character as I can imagine speaking of a picture of character. When one says picture one says of character, when one says novel one says of incident, and the terms may be transposed at will. What is character but the determination of incident? What is incident but the illustration of character? What is either a picture or a novel that is *not* of character? What else do we seek in it and find in it? It is an incident for a woman to stand up with her hand resting on a table and look out at you in a certain way; or if it be not an incident I think it will be hard to say what it is. At the same time it is an expression of character. If you say you don't see it (character in *that*—*allons donc!*),[15] this is exactly what the artist who has reasons of his own for thinking he *does* see it undertakes to show you. When a young man makes up his mind that he has not faith enough after all to enter the church as he intended, that is an incident, though you may not hurry to the end of the chapter to see whether perhaps he doesn't change once more. I do not say that these are extraordinary or startling incidents. I do not pretend to estimate the degree of interest proceeding from them, for this will depend upon the skill of the painter. It sounds almost puerile to say that some incidents are intrinsically much more important than others, and I need not take this precaution after having professed my sympathy for the major ones in remarking that the only classification of the novel that I can understand is into that which has life and that which has it not.

The novel and the romance, the novel of incident and that of character—these clumsy separations appear to me to have been made by critics and readers for their own convenience, and to help them out of some of their occasional queer predicaments, but to have little reality or interest for the producer, from whose point of view it is of course that we are attempting to consider the art of fiction. The case is the same with another shadowy category which Mr. Besant apparently is disposed to set up—that of the "modern English novel"; unless indeed it be that in this matter he has fallen into an accidental confusion of standpoints. It is not quite clear whether he intends the remarks in which he alludes to it to be didactic or historical. It is as difficult to suppose a person intending to write a modern English as to suppose him writing an ancient English novel: that is a label which begs the question. One writes the novel, one paints the picture, of one's language and of one's time, and calling it modern English will not, alas! make the difficult task any easier. No more, unfortunately, will calling this or that work of one's fellow-artist a romance—unless it be, of course,

[15]French: come on!

simply for the pleasantness of the thing, as for instance when Hawthorne[16] gave this heading to his story of *Blithedale*. The French, who have brought the theory of fiction to remarkable completeness, have but one name for the novel, and have not attempted smaller things in it, that I can see, for that. I can think of no obligation to which the "romancer" would not be held equally with the novelist; the standard of execution is equally high for each. Of course it is of execution that we are talking—that being the only point of a novel that is open to contention. This is perhaps too often lost sight of, only to produce interminable confusions and cross-purposes. We must grant the artist his subject, his idea, his *donnée*:[17] our criticism is applied only to what he makes of it. Naturally I do not mean that we are bound to like it or find it interesting: in case we do not our course is perfectly simple—to let it alone. We may believe that of a certain idea even the most sincere novelist can make nothing at all, and the event may perfectly justify our belief; but the failure will have been a failure to execute, and it is in the execution that the fatal weakness is recorded. If we pretend to respect the artist at all, we must allow him his freedom of choice, in the face, in particular cases, of innumerable presumptions that the choice will not fructify. Art derives a considerable part of its beneficial exercise from flying in the face of presumptions, and some of the most interesting experiments of which it is capable are hidden in the bosom of common things. Gustave Flaubert[18] has written a story about the devotion of a servant-girl to a parrot, and the production, highly finished as it is, cannot on the whole be called a success. We are perfectly free to find it flat, but I think it might have been interesting; and I, for my part, am extremely glad he should have written it; it is a contribution to our knowledge of what can be done—or what cannot. Ivan Turgénieff[19] has written a tale about a deaf and dumb serf and a lap-dog, and the thing is touching, loving, a little masterpiece. He struck the note of life where Gustave Flaubert missed it—he flew in the face of a presumption and achieved a victory.

Nothing, of course, will ever take the place of the good old fashion of "liking" a work of art or not liking it: the most improved criticism will not abolish that primitive, that ultimate test. I mention this to guard myself from the accusation of intimating that the idea, the subject, of a novel or a picture, does not matter. It matters, to my sense, in the highest degree, and if I might put up a prayer it would be that artists should select none but the richest. Some, as I have already hastened to admit, are much more remunerative than others, and it would be a world happily arranged in which persons intending to treat them should be exempt from confusions and mistakes. This fortunate condition will arrive only, I fear, on the same day

---

[16]Nathaniel Hawthorne (1804–1864), antebellum American writer known for romance fiction set mainly in New England.

[17]French: literally, "given"; refers to the autonomy of a writer's material and standpoint.

[18]French novelist noted for his realist fiction and artistry (1821–1880).

[19]Ivan Sergeevich Turgenieff (Turgenev) (1818–1883), Russian realist novelist recognized for his engagement with social and political issues.

that critics become purged from error. Meanwhile, I repeat, we do not judge the artist with fairness unless we say to him, "Oh, I grant you your starting-point, because if I did not I should seem to prescribe to you, and heaven forbid I should take that responsibility. If I pretend to tell you what you must not take, you will call upon me to tell you then what you must take; in which case I shall be prettily caught. Moreover, it isn't till I have accepted your data that I can begin to measure you. I have the standard, the pitch; I have no right to tamper with your flute and then criticise your music. Of course I may not care for your idea at all; I may think it silly, or stale, or unclean; in which case I wash my hands of you altogether. I may content myself with believing that you will not have succeeded in being interesting, but I shall, of course, not attempt to demonstrate it, and you will be as indifferent to me as I am to you. I needn't remind you that there are all sorts of tastes: who can know it better? Some people, for excellent reasons, don't like to read about carpenters; others, for reasons even better, don't like to read about courtesans. Many object to Americans. Others (I believe they are mainly editors and publishers) won't look at Italians. Some readers don't like quiet subjects; others don't like bustling ones. Some enjoy a complete illusion, others the consciousness of large concessions. They choose their novels accordingly, and if they don't care about your idea they won't, *a fortiori*,[20] care about your treatment."

So that it comes back very quickly, as I have said, to the liking: in spite of M. Zola,[21] who reasons less powerfully than he represents, and who will not reconcile himself to this absoluteness of taste, thinking that there are certain things that people ought to like, and that they can be made to like. I am quite at a loss to imagine anything (at any rate in this matter of fiction) that people *ought* to like or to dislike. Selection will be sure to take care of itself, for it has a constant motive behind it. That motive is simply experience. As people feel life, so they will feel the art that is most closely related to it. This closeness of relation is what we should never forget in talking of the effort of the novel. Many people speak of it as a factitious, artificial form, a product of ingenuity, the business of which is to alter and arrange the things that surround us, to translate them into conventional, traditional moulds. This, however, is a view of the matter which carries us but a very short way, condemns the art to an eternal repetition of a few familiar *clichés*, cuts short its development, and leads us straight up to a dead wall. Catching the very note and trick, the strange irregular rhythm of life, that is the attempt whose strenuous force keeps Fiction upon her feet. In proportion as in what she offers us we see life *without* rearrangement do we feel that we are touching the truth; in proportion as we see it *with* rearrangement do we feel that we are being put off with a substitute, a compromise and convention. It is not uncommon to hear an extraordinary assurance of

[20]Latin: all the more so.
[21]Émile Zola (1840–1902), French novelist noted for his naturalistic novels.

remark in regard to this matter of rearranging, which is often spoken of as if it were the last word of art. Mr. Besant seems to me in danger of falling into the great error with his rather unguarded talk about "selection." Art is essentially selection, but it is a selection whose main care is to be typical, to be inclusive. For many people art means rose-coloured window-panes and selection means picking a bouquet for Mrs. Grundy.[22] They will tell you glibly that artistic considerations have nothing to do with the disagreeable, with the ugly; they will rattle off shallow commonplaces about the province of art and the limits of art till you are moved to some wonder in return as to the province and the limits of ignorance. It appears to me that no one can ever have made a seriously artistic attempt without becoming conscious of an immense increase—a kind of revelation—of freedom. One perceives in that case—by the light of a heavenly ray—that the province of art is all life, all feeling, all observation, all vision. As Mr. Besant so justly intimates, it is all experience. That is a sufficient answer to those who maintain that it must not touch the sad things of life, who stick into its divine unconscious bosom little prohibitory inscriptions on the end of sticks, such as we see in public gardens—"It is forbidden to walk on the grass; it is forbidden to touch the flowers; it is not allowed to introduce dogs or to remain after dark; it is requested to keep to the right." The young aspirant in the line of fiction whom we continue to imagine will do nothing without taste, for in that case his freedom would be of little use to him; but the first advantage of his taste will be to reveal to him the absurdity of the little sticks and tickets. If he have taste, I must add, of course he will have ingenuity, and my disrespectful reference to that quality just now was not meant to imply that it is useless in fiction. But it is only a secondary aid; the first is a capacity for receiving straight impressions.

Mr. Besant has some remarks on the question of "the story" which I shall not attempt to criticise, though they seem to me to contain a singular ambiguity, because I do not think I understand them. I cannot see what is meant by talking as if there were a part of a novel which is the story and part of it which for mystical reasons is not—unless indeed the distinction be made in a sense in which it is difficult to suppose that any one should attempt to convey anything. "The story," if it represents anything, represents the subject, the idea, the *donnée* of the novel; and there is surely no "school"—Mr. Besant speaks of a school—which urges that a novel should be all treatment and no subject. There must assuredly be something to treat; every school is intimately conscious of that. This sense of the story being the idea, the starting-point, of the novel, is the only one that I see in which it can be spoken of as something different from its organic whole; and since in proportion as the work is successful the idea permeates and penetrates it, informs and animates it, so that every word and every punctuation-point contribute directly to the expression, in that proportion do we lose our

---

[22]A narrow-minded or priggish person (after a character by the same name featured in *Speed the Plough* [1798], a play by Thomas Morton).

sense of the story being a blade which may be drawn more or less out of its sheath. The story and the novel, the idea and the form, are the needle and thread, and I never heard of a guild of tailors who recommended the use of the thread without the needle, or the needle without the thread. Mr. Besant is not the only critic who may be observed to have spoken as if there were certain things in life which constitute stories, and certain others which do not. I find the same odd implication in an entertaining article in the *Pall Mall Gazette*[23] devoted, as it happens, to Mr. Besant's lecture. "The story is the thing!" says this graceful writer, as if with a tone of opposition to some other idea. I should think it was, as every painter who, as the time for "sending in" his picture looms in the distance, finds himself still in quest of a subject—as every belated artist not fixed about his theme will heartily agree. There are some subjects which speak to us and others which do not, but he would be a clever man who should undertake to give a rule—an index expurgatorius—by which the story and the no-story should be known apart. It is impossible (to me at least) to imagine any such rule which shall not be altogether arbitrary. The writer in the *Pall Mall* opposes the delightful (as I suppose) novel of *Margot la Balafrée* to certain tales in which "Bostonian nymphs" appear to have "rejected English dukes for psychological reasons." I am not acquainted with the romance just designated, and can scarcely forgive the *Pall Mall* critic for not mentioning the name of the author, but the title appears to refer to a lady who may have received a scar in some heroic adventure. I am inconsolable at not being acquainted with this episode, but am utterly at a loss to see why it is a story when the rejection (or acceptance) of a duke is not, and why a reason, psychological or other, is not a subject when a cicatrix is. They are all particles of the multitudinous life with which the novel deals, and surely no dogma which pretends to make it lawful to touch the one and unlawful to touch the other will stand for a moment on its feet. It is the special picture that must stand or fall, according as it seem to possess truth or to lack it. Mr. Besant does not, to my sense, light up the subject by intimating that a story must, under penalty of not being a story, consist of "adventures." Why of adventures more than of green spectacles? He mentions a category of impossible things, and among them he places "fiction without adventure." Why without adventure, more than without matrimony, or celibacy, or parturition, or cholera, or hydropathy, or Jansenism?[24] This seems to me to bring the novel back to the hapless little *rôle* of being an artificial, ingenious thing—bring it down from its large, free character of an immense and exquisite correspondence with life. And what *is* adventure, when it comes to that, and by what sign is the listening pupil to recognize it? It is an adventure—an immense one— for me to write this little article; and for a Bostonian nymph to reject an

---

[23]A liberal London "penny paper."
[24]"Hydropathy": a kind of medical treatment, originated in 1825 by Vincenz Preissnitz at Gräfenberg in Germany, consisting of the external and internal application of water;

the water-cure. Jansenism: A religious doctrine based upon the predestinarian teachings of Cornelis Jansen (1585– 1638), a Dutch Roman Catholic theologian.

English duke is an adventure only less stirring, I should say, than for an English duke to be rejected by a Bostonian nymph. I see dramas within dramas in that, and innumerable points of view. A psychological reason is, to my imagination, an object adorably pictorial; to catch the tint of its complexion—I feel as if that idea might inspire one to Titianesque[25] efforts. There are few things more exciting to me, in short, than a psychological reason, and yet, I protest, the novel seems to me the most magnificent form of art. I have just been reading, at the same time, the delightful story of *Treasure Island*, by Mr. Robert Louis Stevenson[26] and, in a manner less consecutive, the last tale from M. Edmond de Goncourt,[27] which is entitled *Chérie*. One of these works treats of murders, mysteries, islands of dreadful renown, hairbreadth escapes, miraculous coincidences and buried doubloons. The other treats of a little French girl who lived in a fine house in Paris, and died of wounded sensibility because no one would marry her. I call *Treasure Island* delightful, because it appears to me to have succeeded wonderfully in what it attempts; and I venture to bestow no epithet upon *Chérie*, which strikes me as having failed deplorably in what it attempts— that is in tracing the development of the moral consciousness of a child. But one of these productions strikes me as exactly as much of a novel as the other, and as having a "story" quite as much. The moral consciousness of a child is as much a part of life as the islands of the Spanish Main, and the one sort of geography seems to me to have those "surprises" of which Mr. Besant speaks quite as much as the other. For myself (since it comes back in the last resort, as I say, to the preference of the individual), the picture of the child's experience has the advantage that I can at successive steps (an immense luxury, near to the "sensual pleasure" of which Mr. Besant's critic in the *Pall Mall* speaks) say Yes or No, as it may be, to what the artist puts before me. I have been a child in fact, but I have been on a quest for a buried treasure only in supposition, and it is a simple accident that with M. de Goncourt I should have for the most part to say No. With George Eliot,[28] when she painted that country with a far other intelligence, I always said Yes.

The most interesting part of Mr. Besant's lecture is unfortunately the briefest passage—his very cursory allusion to the "conscious moral purpose" of the novel. Here again it is not very clear whether he be recording a fact or laying down a principle; it is a great pity that in the latter case he should not have developed his idea. This branch of the subject is of immense importance, and Mr. Besant's few words point to considerations of the widest reach, not to be lightly disposed of. He will have treated the art of fiction but superficially who is not prepared to go every inch of the way that these considerations will carry him. It is for this reason that at the beginning of

---

[25]After Titian (Italian name Tiziano Vecellio), the Venetian painter (1490–1576).

[26]Scottish novelist, essayist, and poet known for his adventure tales and thrillers (1850–1894).

[27]French art critic, novelist, and historian (1822–1896).

[28]George Eliot (pseudonym of Mary Ann Evans, 1819–1880), English novelist noted for the great depth and intellectual range of her realist novels.

these remarks I was careful to notify the reader that my reflections on so large a theme have no pretension to be exhaustive. Like Mr. Besant, I have left the question of the morality of the novel till the last, and at the last I find I have used up my space. It is a question surrounded with difficulties, as witness the very first that meets us, in the form of a definite question, on the threshold. Vagueness, in such a discussion, is fatal, and what is the meaning of your morality and your conscious moral purpose? Will you not define your terms and explain how (a novel being a picture) a picture can be either moral or immoral? You wish to paint a moral picture or carve a moral statue: will you not tell us how you would set about it? We are discussing the Art of Fiction; questions of art are questions (in the widest sense) of execution; questions of morality are quite another affair, and will you not let us see how it is that you find it so easy to mix them up? These things are so clear to Mr. Besant that he has deduced from them a law which he sees embodied in English Fiction, and which is "a truly admirable thing and a great cause for congratulation." It is a great cause for congratulation indeed when such thorny problems become as smooth as silk. I may add that in so far as Mr. Besant perceives that in point of fact English Fiction has addressed itself preponderantly to these delicate questions he will appear to many people to have made a vain discovery. They will have been positively struck, on the contrary, with the moral timidity of the usual English novelist; with his (or with her) aversion to face the difficulties with which on every side the treatment of reality bristles. He is apt to be extremely shy (whereas the picture that Mr. Besant draws is a picture of boldness), and the sign of his work, for the most part, is a cautious silence on certain subjects. In the English novel (by which of course I mean the American as well), more than in any other, there is a traditional difference between that which people know and that which they agree to admit that they know, that which they see and that which they speak of, that which they feel to be a part of life and that which they allow to enter into literature. There is the great difference, in short, between what they talk of in conversation and what they talk of in print. The essence of moral energy is to survey the whole field, and I should directly reverse Mr. Besant's remark and say not that the English novel has a purpose, but that it has a diffidence. To what degree a purpose in a work of art is a source of corruption I shall not attempt to inquire; the one that seems to me least dangerous is the purpose of making a perfect work. As for our novel, I may say lastly on this score that as we find it in England today it strikes me as addressed in a large degree to "young people," and that this in itself constitutes a presumption that it will be rather shy. There are certain things which it is generally agreed not to discuss, not even to mention, before young people. That is very well, but the absence of discussion is not a symptom of the moral passion. The purpose of the English novel—"a truly admirable thing, and a great cause for congratulation"—strikes me therefore as rather negative.

There is one point at which the moral sense and the artistic sense lie very near together; that is in the light of the very obvious truth that the deepest quality of a work of art will always be the quality of the mind of the producer. In proportion as that intelligence is fine will the novel, the picture, the statue partake of the substance of beauty and truth. To be constituted of such elements is, to my vision, to have purpose enough. No good novel will ever proceed from a superficial mind; that seems to me an axiom which, for the artist in fiction, will cover all needful moral ground: if the youthful aspirant take it to heart it will illuminate for him many of the mysteries of "purpose." There are many other useful things that might be said to him, but I have come to the end of my article, and can only touch them as I pass. The critic in the *Pall Mall Gazette*, whom I have already quoted, draws attention to the danger, in speaking of the art of fiction, of generalising. The danger that he has in mind is rather, I imagine, that of particularising, for there are some comprehensive remarks which, in addition to those embodied in Mr. Besant's suggestive lecture, might without fear of misleading him be addressed to the ingenuous student. I should remind him first of the magnificence of the form that is open to him, which offers to sight so few restrictions and such innumerable opportunities. The other arts, in comparison, appear confined and hampered; the various conditions under which they are exercised are so rigid and definite. But the only condition that I can think of attaching to the composition of the novel is, as I have already said, that it be sincere. This freedom is a splendid privilege, and the first lesson of the young novelist is to learn to be worthy of it. "Enjoy it as it deserves," I should say to him; "take possession of it, explore it to its utmost extent, publish it, rejoice in it. All life belongs to you, and do not listen either to those who would shut you up into corners of it and tell you that it is only here and there that art inhabits, or to those who would persuade you that this heavenly messenger wings her way outside of life altogether, breathing a superfine air, and turning away her head from the truth of things. There is no impression of life, no manner of seeing it and feeling it, to which the plan of the novelist may not offer a place; you have only to remember that talents so dissimilar as those of Alexandre Dumas[29] and Jane Austen,[30] Charles Dickens and Gustave Flaubert have worked in this field with equal glory. Do not think too much about optimism and pessimism; try and catch the colour of life itself. In France to-day we see a prodigious effort (that of Emile Zola, to whose solid and serious work no explorer of the capacity of the novel can allude without respect), we see an extraordinary effort vitiated by a spirit of pessimism on a narrow basis. M. Zola is magnificent, but he strikes an English reader as ignorant; he has an air of working in the dark; if he had as much light as energy, his results would be of the highest value. As for the aberrations of a shallow optimism, the ground (of English fiction especially) is strewn with their brittle particles as with broken glass. If you must indulge in conclusions, let them have the

---

[29]Either Alexandre Dumas, the father (1802–1870), or Alexandre Dumas, the son (1824–1895), both French novelists and playwrights.

[30]English novelist recognized for her witty novels of middle-class mores and manners (1775–1817).

taste of a wide knowledge. Remember that your first duty is to be as complete as possible—to make as perfect a work. Be generous and delicate and pursue the prize."

1884

The Figure in the Carpet[1]

I

I had done a few things and earned a few pence—I had perhaps even had time to begin to think *I* was finer than was perceived by the patronising; but when I take the little measure of my course (a fidgety habit, for it's none of the longest yet) I count my real start from the evening George Corvick, breathless and worried, came in to ask me a service. He had done more things than I, and earned more pence, though there were chances for cleverness I thought he sometimes missed. I could only however that evening declare to him that he never missed one for kindness. There was almost rapture in hearing it proposed to me to prepare for *The Middle*, the organ of our lucubrations,[2] so called from the position in the week of its day of appearance, an article for which he had made himself responsible and of which, tied up with a stout string, he laid on my table the subject. I pounced upon my opportunity—that is on the first volume of it—and paid scant attention to my friend's explanation of his appeal. What explanation could be more to the point than my obvious fitness for the task? I had written on Hugh Vereker, but never a word in *The Middle*, where my dealings were mainly with the ladies and the minor poets. This was his new novel, an advance copy, and whatever much or little it should do for his reputation I was clear on the spot as to what it should do for mine. Moreover if I always read him as soon as I could get hold of him I had a particular reason for wishing to read him now: I had accepted an invitation to Bridges for the following Sunday, and it had been mentioned in Lady Jane's note that Mr. Vereker was to be there. I was young enough for a flutter at meeting a man of his renown, and innocent enough to believe the occasion would demand the display of an acquaintance with his "last."

Corvick, who had promised a review of it, had not even had time to read it; he had gone to pieces in consequence of news requiring—as on precipitate reflexion he judged—that he should catch the night-mail[3] to Paris. He had had a telegram from Gwendolen Erme in answer to his letter offering to fly to her aid. I knew already about Gwendolen Erme; I had never seen her,

[1]"The Figure in the Carpet" first appeared in *Cosmopolis*, January–February 1896, and was first published in book form in *Embarrassments* (1896). The text here is taken from the revised version from the New York Edition *Volume XV: The Lesson of the Master, The Death of the Lion, The Next Time and Other Tales*, pp 217–279. (Notes by Jennifer Emory-Peck.)

[2]The product of nocturnal study and meditation; hence, a literary work showing signs of careful elaboration.

[3]A train that carries mail across the country by night (*i.e.*, the overnight train to Paris).

but I had my ideas, which were mainly to the effect that Corvick would marry her if her mother would only die. That lady seemed now in a fair way to oblige him; after some dreadful mistake about a climate or a "cure" she had suddenly collapsed on the return from abroad. Her daughter, unsupported and alarmed, desiring to make a rush for home but hesitating at the risk, had accepted our friend's assistance, and it was my secret belief that at sight of him Mrs. Erme would pull round. His own belief was scarcely to be called secret; it discernibly at any rate differed from mine. He had showed me Gwendolen's photograph with the remark that she wasn't pretty but was awfully interesting; she had published at the age of nineteen a novel in three volumes, "Deep Down," about which, in *The Middle*, he had been really splendid. He appreciated my present eagerness and undertook that the periodical in question should do no less; then at the last, with his hand on the door, he said to me: "Of course you'll be all right, you know." Seeing I was a trifle vague he added: "I mean you won't be silly."

"Silly—about Vereker! Why what do I ever find him but awfully clever?"

"Well, what's that but silly? What on earth does 'awfully clever' mean? For God's sake try to get at him. Don't let him suffer by our arrangement. Speak of him, you know, if you can, as *I* should have spoken of him."

I wondered an instant. "You mean as far and away the biggest of the lot—that sort of thing?"

Corvick almost groaned. "Oh you know, I don't put them back to back that way; it's the infancy of art! But he gives me a pleasure so rare; the sense of"—he mused a little—"something or other."

I wondered again. "The sense, pray, of what?"

"My dear man, that's just what I want you to say!"

Even before he had banged the door I had begun, book in hand, to prepare myself to say it. I sat up with Vereker half the night; Corvick couldn't have done more than that. He was awfully clever—I stuck to that, but he wasn't a bit the biggest of the lot. I didn't allude to the lot, however; I flattered myself that I emerged on this occasion from the infancy of art. "It's all right," they declared vividly at the office; and when the number appeared I felt there was a basis on which I could meet the great man. It gave me confidence for a day or two—then that confidence dropped. I had fancied him reading it with relish, but if Corvick wasn't satisfied how could Vereker himself be? I reflected indeed that the heat of the admirer was sometimes grosser even than the appetite of the scribe. Corvick at all events wrote me from Paris a little ill-humouredly. Mrs. Erme was pulling round, and I hadn't at all said what Vereker gave him the sense of.

II

The effect of my visit to Bridges was to turn me out for more profundity. Hugh Vereker, as I saw him there, was of a contact so void of angles that I blushed for the poverty of imagination involved in my small precautions. If he was in spirits it wasn't because he had read my review; in fact on the

Sunday morning I felt sure he hadn't read it, though *The Middle* had been out three days and bloomed, I assured myself, in the stiff garden of periodicals which gave one of the ormolu[4] tables the air of a stand at a station. The impression he made on me personally was such that I wished him to read it, and I corrected to this end with a surreptitious[5] hand what might be wanting in the careless conspicuity[6] of the sheet. I'm afraid I even watched the result of my manoeuvre, but up to luncheon I watched in vain.

When afterwards, in the course of our gregarious[7] walk, I found myself for half an hour, not perhaps without another manoeuvre, at the great man's side, the result of his affability[8] was a still livelier desire that he shouldn't remain in ignorance of the peculiar justice I had done him. It wasn't that he seemed to thirst for justice; on the contrary I hadn't yet caught in his talk the faintest grunt of a grudge—a note for which my young experience had already given me an ear. Of late he had had more recognition, and it was pleasant, as we used to say in *The Middle*, to see how it drew him out. He wasn't of course popular, but I judged one of the sources of his good humour to be precisely that his success was independent of that. He had none the less become in a manner the fashion; the critics at least had put on a spurt and caught up with him. We had found out at last how clever he was, and he had had to make the best of the loss of his mystery. I was strongly tempted, as I walked beside him, to let him know how much of that unveiling was my act; and there was a moment when I probably should have done so had not one of the ladies of our party, snatching a place at his other elbow, just then appealed to him in a spirit comparatively selfish. It was very discouraging: I almost felt the liberty had been taken with myself.

I had had on my tongue's end, for my own part, a phrase or two about the right word at the right time; but later on I was glad not to have spoken, for when on our return we clustered at tea I perceived Lady Jane, who had not been out with us, brandishing *The Middle* with her longest arm. She had taken it up at her leisure; she was delighted with what she had found, and I saw that, as a mistake in a man may often be a felicity in a woman, she would practically do for me what I hadn't been able to do for myself. "Some sweet little truths that needed to be spoken," I heard her declare, thrusting the paper at rather a bewildered couple by the fireplace. She grabbed it away from them again on the reappearance of Hugh Vereker, who after our walk had been upstairs to change something. "I know you don't in general look at this kind of thing, but it's an occasion really for doing so. You *haven't* seen it? Then you must. The man has actually got at you, at what *I* always feel, you know." Lady Jane threw into her eyes a look evidently intended to give an idea of what she always felt; but she added that she couldn't have expressed it. The man in the paper expressed it in a striking manner. "Just see there, and there, where I've dashed it, how he brings it out." She had

---

[4]Gilded bronze or a gold-coloured alloy of copper, zinc, and tin used to decorate furniture.
[5]Done by stealth or secretly.

[6]Clearly visible, easy to be seen, obvious or striking to the eye.
[7]Inclined to associate with others, sociable.
[8]Civility, courteousness, openness of manner.

literally marked for him the brightest patches of my prose, and if I was a little amused Vereker himself may well have been. He showed how much he was when before us all Lady Jane wanted to read something aloud. I liked at any rate the way he defeated her purpose by jerking the paper affectionately out of her clutch. He'd take it upstairs with him and look at it on going to dress. He did this half an hour later—I saw it in his hand when he repaired to his room. That was the moment at which, thinking to give her pleasure, I mentioned to Lady Jane that I was the author of the review. I did give her pleasure, I judged, but perhaps, not quite so much as I had expected. If the author was "only me" the thing didn't seem quite so remarkable. Hadn't I had the effect rather of diminishing the lustre of the article than of adding to my own? Her ladyship was subject to the most extraordinary drops. It didn't matter; the only effect I cared about was the one it would have on Vereker up there by his bedroom fire.

At dinner I watched for the signs of this impression, tried to fancy some happier light in his eyes; but to my disappointment Lady Jane gave me no chance to make sure. I had hoped she'd call triumphantly down the table, publicly demand if she hadn't been right. The party was large—there were people from outside as well, but I had never seen a table long enough to deprive Lady Jane of a triumph. I was just reflecting in truth that this interminable board would deprive me of one when the guest next me, dear woman—she was Miss Poyle, the vicar's sister, a robust unmodulated person—had the happy inspiration and the unusual courage to address herself across it to Vereker, who was opposite, but not directly, so that when he replied they were both leaning forward. She enquired, artless body, what he thought of Lady Jane's "panegyric,"[9] which she had read—not connecting it however with her right-hand neighbour; and while I strained my ear for his reply I heard him, to my stupefaction, call back gaily, his mouth full of bread: "Oh it's all right—the usual twaddle!"

I had caught Vereker's glance as he spoke, but Miss Poyle's surprise was a fortunate cover for my own.

"You mean he doesn't do you justice?" said the excellent woman.

Vereker laughed out, and I was happy to be able to do the same. "It's a charming article," he tossed us.

Miss Poyle thrust her chin half across the cloth. "Oh you're so deep!" she drove home.

"As deep as the ocean! All I pretend is that the author doesn't see—" But a dish was at this point passed over his shoulder, and we had to wait while he helped himself.

"Doesn't see what?" my neighbour continued.

"Doesn't see anything."

"Dear me—how very stupid!"

[9]A public speech or published text in praise of a person or thing; a laudatory discourse; a eulogy, an encomium.

"Not a bit," Vereker laughed again. "Nobody does."

The lady on his further side appealed to him and Miss Poyle sank back to myself. "Nobody sees anything!" she cheerfully announced; to which I replied that I had often thought so too, but had somehow taken the thought for a proof on my own part of a tremendous eye. I didn't tell her the article was mine; and I observed that Lady Jane, occupied at the end of the table, had not caught Vereker's words.

I rather avoided him after dinner, for I confess he struck me as cruelly conceited, and the revelation was a pain. "The usual twaddle"—my acute little study! That one's admiration should have had a reserve or two could gall him to that point? I had thought him placid, and he was placid enough; such a surface was the hard polished glass that encased the bauble of his vanity. I was really ruffled, and the only comfort was that if nobody saw anything George Corvick was quite as much out of it as I. This comfort however was not sufficient, after the ladies had dispersed, to carry me in the proper manner—I mean in a spotted jacket and humming an air—into the smoking-room. I took my way in some dejection to bed; but in the passage I encountered Mr. Vereker, who had been up once more to change, coming out of his room. *He* was humming an air and had on a spotted jacket, and as soon as he saw me his gaiety gave a start.

"My dear young man," he exclaimed, "I'm so glad to lay hands on you! I'm afraid I most un-wittingly wounded you by those words of mine at dinner to Miss Poyle. I learned but half an hour ago from Lady Jane that you're the author of the little notice in *The Middle*."

I protested that no bones were broken; but he moved with me to my own door, his hand, on my shoulder, kindly feeling for a fracture; and on hearing that I had come up to bed he asked leave to cross my threshold and just tell me in three words what his qualification of my remarks had represented. It was plain he really feared I was hurt, and the sense of his solicitude[10] suddenly made all the difference to me. My cheap review fluttered off into space, and the best things I had said in it became flat enough beside the brilliancy of his being there. I can see him there still, on my rug, in the firelight and his spotted jacket, his fine clear face all bright with the desire to be tender to my youth. I don't know what he had at first meant to say, but I think the sight of my relief touched him, excited him, brought up words to his lips from far within. It was so these words presently conveyed to me something that, as I afterwards knew, he had never uttered to any one. I've always done justice to the generous impulse that made him speak; it was simply compunction[11] for a snub unconsciously administered to a man of letters in a position inferior to his own, a man of letters moreover in the very act of praising him. To make the thing right he talked to me exactly as an equal and on the ground of what we both loved best. The hour, the place, the unexpectedness deepened the impression: he couldn't have done anything more intensely effective.

---

[10]Care, concern, anxiety.   [11]Remorse, contrition.

III

"I don't quite know how to explain it to you," he said, "but it was the very fact that your notice of my book had a spice of intelligence, it was just your exceptional sharpness, that produced the feeling—a very old story with me, I beg you to believe—under the momentary influence of which I used in speaking to that good lady the words you so naturally resent. I don't read the things in the newspapers unless they're thrust upon me as that one was—it's always one's best friend who does it! But I used to read them sometimes—ten years ago. I dare say they were in general rather stupider then; at any rate it always struck me they missed my little point with a perfection exactly as admirable when they patted me on the back as when they kicked me in the shins. Whenever since I've happened to have a glimpse of them they were still blazing away—still missing it, I mean, deliciously. You miss it, my dear fellow, with inimitable[12] assurance; the fact of your being awfully clever and your article's being awfully nice doesn't make a hair's breadth of difference. It's quite with you rising young men," Vereker laughed, "that I feel most what a failure I am!"

I listened with keen interest; it grew keener as he talked. "You a failure—heavens! What then may your 'little point' happen to be?"

"Have I got to *tell* you, after all these years and labours?" There was something in the friendly reproach of this—jocosely[13] exaggerated—that made me, as an ardent young seeker for truth, blush to the roots of my hair. I'm as much in the dark as ever, though I've grown used in a sense to my obtuseness; at that moment, however, Vereker's happy accent made me appear to myself, and probably to him, a rare dunce. I was on the point of exclaiming "Ah yes, don't tell me: for my honour, for that of the craft, don't!" when he went on in a manner that showed he had read my thought and had his own idea of the probability of our some day redeeming ourselves. "By my little point I mean—what shall I call it?—the particular thing I've written my books most *for*. Isn't there for every writer a particular thing of that sort, the thing that most makes him apply himself, the thing without the effort to achieve which he wouldn't write at all, the very passion of his passion, the part of the business in which, for him, the flame of art burns most intensely? Well, it's *that*!"

I considered a moment—that is I followed at a respectful distance, rather gasping. I was fascinated—easily, you'll say; but I wasn't going after all to be put off my guard. "Your description's certainly beautiful, but it doesn't make what you describe very distinct."

"I promise you it would be distinct if it should dawn on you at all." I saw that the charm of our topic overflowed for my companion into an emotion as lively as my own. "At any rate," he went on, "I can speak for myself: there's an idea in my work without which I wouldn't have given a straw for the whole job. It's the finest fullest intention of the lot, and the application

---

[12]Incapable of being imitated, peerless.   [13]Jokingly.

of it has been, I think, a triumph of patience, of ingenuity. I ought to leave that to somebody else to say; but that nobody does say it is precisely what we're talking about. It stretches, this little trick of mine, from book to book, and everything else, comparatively, plays over the surface of it. The order, the form, the texture of my books will perhaps some day constitute for the initiated a complete representation of it. So it's naturally the thing for the critic to look for. It strikes me," my visitor added, smiling, "even as the thing for the critic to find."

This seemed a responsibility indeed. "You call it a little trick?"

"That's only my little modesty. It's really an exquisite scheme."

"And you hold that you've carried the scheme out?"

"The way I've carried it out is the thing in life I think a bit well of myself for."

I had a pause. "Don't you think you ought—just a trifle—to assist the critic?"

"Assist him? What else have I done with every stroke of my pen? I've shouted my intention in his great blank face!" At this, laughing out again, Vereker laid his hand on my shoulder to show the allusion wasn't to my personal appearance.

"But you talk about the initiated. There must therefore, you see, *be* initiation."

"What else in heaven's name is criticism supposed to be?" I'm afraid I coloured at this too; but I took refuge in repeating that his account of his silver lining was poor in something or other that a plain man knows things by. "That's only because you've never had a glimpse of it," he returned. "If you had had one the element in question would soon have become practically all you'd see. To me it's exactly as palpable as the marble of this chimney. Besides, the critic just isn't a plain man: if he were, pray, what would he be doing in his neighbour's garden? You're anything but a plain man yourself, and the very *raison d'etre* of you all is that you 're little demons of subtlety. If my great affair's a secret, that's only because it's a secret in spite of itself—the amazing event has made it one. I not only never took the smallest precaution to keep it so, but never dreamed of any such accident. If I had I shouldn't in advance have had the heart to go on. As it was, I only became aware little by little, and meanwhile I had done my work."

"And now you quite like it?" I risked.

"My work?"

"Your secret. It's the same thing."

"Your guessing that," Vereker replied, "is a proof that you're as clever as I say!" I was encouraged by this to remark that he would clearly be pained to part with it, and he confessed that it was indeed with him now the great amusement of life. "I live almost to see if it will ever be detected." He looked at me for a jesting challenge; something far within his eyes seemed to peep out. "But I needn't worry—it won't!"

"You fire me as I've never been fired," I declared; "you make me determined to do or die." Then I asked: "Is it a kind of esoteric message?"

His countenance fell at this—he put out his hand as if to bid me good-night. "Ah my dear fellow, it can't be described in cheap journalese!"

I knew of course he'd be awfully fastidious, but our talk had made me feel how much his nerves were exposed. I was unsatisfied—I kept hold of his hand. "I won't make use of the expression then," I said, "in the article in which I shall eventually announce my discovery, though I dare say I shall have hard work to do without it. But meanwhile, just to hasten that difficult birth, can't you give a fellow a clue?" I felt much more at my ease.

"My whole lucid effort gives him the clue—every page and line and letter. The thing's as concrete there as a bird in a cage, a bait on a hook, a piece of cheese in a mouse-trap. It's stuck into every volume as your foot is stuck into your shoe. It governs every line, it chooses every word, it dots every i, it places every comma."

I scratched my head. "Is it something in the style or something in the thought? An element of form or an element of feeling?"

He indulgently shook my hand again, and I felt my questions to be crude and my distinctions pitiful. "Good-night, my dear boy—don't bother about it. After all, you do like a fellow."

"And a little intelligence might spoil it?" I still detained him.

He hesitated. "Well, you've got a heart in your body. Is that an element of form or an element of feeling? What I contend that nobody has ever mentioned in my work is the organ of life."

"I see—it's some idea about life, some sort of philosophy. Unless it be," I added with the eagerness of a thought perhaps still happier, "some kind of game you're up to with your style, something you're after in the language. Perhaps it's a preference for the letter P!" I ventured profanely to break out. "Papa, potatoes, prunes—that sort of thing?" He was suitably indulgent: he only said I hadn't got the right letter. But his amusement was over; I could see he was bored. There was nevertheless something else I had absolutely to learn. "Should you be able, pen in hand, to state it clearly yourself—to name it, phrase it, formulate it?"

"Oh," he almost passionately sighed, "if I were only, pen in hand, one of *you* chaps!"

"That would be a great chance for you of course. But why should you despise us chaps for not doing what you can't do yourself?"

"Can't do?" He opened his eyes. "Haven't I done it in twenty volumes? I do it in my way," he continued. "Go *you* and don't do it in yours."

"Ours is so devilish difficult," I weakly observed.

"So's mine! We each choose our own. There's no compulsion. You won't come down and smoke?"

"No. I want to think this thing out."

"You'll tell me then in the morning that you've laid me bare?"

"I'll see what I can do; I'll sleep on it. But just one word more," I added. We had left the room—I walked again with him a few steps along the passage. "This extraordinary 'general intention,' as you call it—for that's the most vivid description I can induce you to make of it—is then, generally, a sort of buried treasure?"

His face lighted. "Yes, call it that, though it's perhaps not for me to do so."

"Nonsense!" I laughed. "You know you're hugely proud of it."

"Well, I didn't propose to tell you so; but it *is* the joy of my soul!"

"You mean it's a beauty so rare, so great?"

He waited a little again. "The loveliest thing in the world!" We had stopped, and on these words he left me; but at the end of the corridor, while I looked after him rather yearningly, he turned and caught sight of my puzzled face. It made him earnestly, indeed I thought quite anxiously, shake his head and—wave his finger. "Give it up—give it up!"

This wasn't a challenge—it was fatherly advice. If I had had one of his books at hand I'd have repeated my recent act of faith—I'd have spent half the night with him. At three o'clock in the morning, not sleeping, remembering moreover how indispensable he was to Lady Jane, I stole down to the library with a candle. There wasn't, so far as I could discover, a line of his writing in the house.

IV

Returning to town I feverishly collected them all; I picked out each in its order and held it up to the light. This gave me a maddening month, in the course of which several things took place. One of these, the last, I may as well immediately mention, was that I acted on Vereker's advice: I renounced my ridiculous attempt. I could really make nothing of the business; it proved a dead loss. After all I had always, as he had himself noted, liked him; and what now occurred was simply that my new intelligence and vain preoccupation damaged my liking. I not only failed to run a general intention to earth, I found myself missing the subordinate intentions I had formerly enjoyed. His books didn't even remain the charming things they had been for me; the exasperation of my search put me out of conceit of them. Instead of being a pleasure the more they became a resource the less; for from the moment I was unable to follow up the author's hint I of course felt it a point of honour not to make use professionally of my knowledge of them. I *had* no knowledge—nobody had any. It was humiliating, but I could bear it—they only annoyed me now. At last they even bored me, and I accounted for my confusion—perversely, I allow—by the idea that Vereker had made a fool I of me. The buried treasure was a bad joke, the general intention a monstrous *pose*.

The great point of it all is, however, that I told George Corvick what had befallen me and that my information had an immense effect on him. He had at last come back, but so, unfortunately, had Mrs. Erme, and there was as yet, I could see, no question of his nuptials. He was immensely stirred up by the anecdote I had brought from Bridges; it fell in so completely with the sense he had had from the first that there was more in Vereker than met the eye. When I remarked that the eye seemed what the printed page had been expressly invented to meet he immediately accused me of being spiteful because I had been foiled. Our commerce had always that pleasant latitude. The thing Vereker had mentioned to me was exactly the thing he, Corvick, had wanted me to speak of in my review. On my suggesting at last that with the assistance I had now given him he would doubtless be prepared to speak of it himself he admitted freely that before doing this there was more he must understand. What he would have said, had he reviewed the new book, was that there was evidently in the writer's inmost art something to *be* understood. I hadn't so much as hinted at that: no wonder the writer hadn't been flattered! I asked Corvick what he really considered he meant by his own supersubtlety, and, unmistakeably kindled, he replied: "It isn't for the vulgar—it isn't for the vulgar!" He had hold of the tail of something: he would pull hard, pull it right out. He pumped me dry on Vereker's strange confidence and, pronouncing me the luckiest of mortals, mentioned half a dozen questions he wished to goodness I had had the gumption to put. Yet on the other hand he didn't want to be told too much—it would spoil the fun of seeing what would come. The failure of *my* fun was at the moment of our meeting not complete, but I saw it ahead, and Corvick saw that I saw it. I, on my side, saw likewise that one of the first things he would do would be to rush off with my story to Gwendolen.

On the very day after my talk with him I was surprised by the receipt of a note from Hugh Vereker, to whom our encounter at Bridges had been recalled, as he mentioned, by his falling, in a magazine, on some article to which my signature was attached. "I read it with great pleasure," he wrote, "and remembered under its influence our lively conversation by your bedroom fire. The consequence of this has been that I begin to measure the temerity of my having saddled you with a knowledge that you may I find something of a burden. Now that the fit's over I can't imagine how I came to be moved so much beyond my wont. I had never before mentioned, no matter in what state of expansion, the fact of my little secret, and I shall never speak of that mystery again. I was accidentally so much more explicit with you than it had ever entered into my game to be, that I find this game—I mean the pleasure of playing it—suffers considerably. In short, if you can understand it, I've rather spoiled my sport. I really don't want to give anybody what I believe you clever young men call the tip. That's of course a selfish solicitude, and I name it to you for what it may be worth to you. If you're disposed to humour me don't repeat my revelation. Think me demented—it's your right; but don't tell anybody why."

The sequel to this communication was that as early on the morrow as I dared I drove straight to Mr. Vereker's door. He occupied in those years one of the honest old houses in Kensington Square.[14] He received me immediately, and as soon as I came in I saw I hadn't lost my power to minister to

---

[14]A garden square neighborhood in Kensington, a fashionable area of London.

his mirth. He laughed out at sight of my face, which doubtless expressed my perturbation.[15] I had been indiscreet—my compunction was great. "I have told somebody," I panted, "and I'm sure that person will by this time have told somebody else! It's a woman, into the bargain."

"The person you've told?"

"No, the other person. I'm quite sure he must have told her."

"For all the good it will do her—or do *me*! A woman will never find out."

"No, but she'll talk all over the place: she'll do just what you don't want."

Vereker thought a moment, but wasn't so disconcerted as I had feared: he felt that if the harm was done it only served him right. "It doesn't matter—don't worry."

"I'll do my best, I promise you, that your talk with me shall go no further."

"Very good; do what you can."

"In the meantime," I pursued, "George Corvick's possession of the tip may, on his part, really lead to something."

"That will be a brave day."

I told him about Corvick's cleverness, his admiration, the intensity of his interest in my anecdote; and without making too much of the divergence of our respective estimates mentioned that my friend was already of opinion that he saw much further into a certain affair than most people. He was quite as fired as I had been at Bridges. He was moreover in love with the young lady: perhaps the two together would puzzle something out.

Vereker seemed struck with this. "Do you mean they're to be married?"

"I dare say that's what it will come to."

"That may help them," he conceded, "but we must give them time!"

I spoke of my own renewed assault and confessed my difficulties; whereupon he repeated his former advice: "Give it up, give it up!" He evidently didn't think me intellectually equipped for the adventure. I stayed half an hour, and he was most good-natured, but I couldn't help pronouncing him a man of unstable moods. He had been free with me in a mood, he had repented in a mood, and now in a mood he had turned indifferent. This general levity helped me to believe that, so far as the subject of the tip went, there wasn't much in it. I contrived however to make him answer a few more questions about it, though he did so with visible impatience. For himself, beyond doubt, the thing we were all so blank about was vividly there. It was something, I guessed, in the primal plan; something like a complex figure in a Persian carpet. He highly approved of this image when I used it, and he used another himself.

"It's the very string," he said, "that my pearls are strung on!" The reason of his note to me had been that he really didn't want to give us a grain of succour[16]—our density was a thing too perfect in its way to touch. He had

---

[15]Mental or spiritual agitation or disturbance.   [16]Aid, help, assistance.

formed the habit of depending on it, and if the spell was to break it must break by some force of its own. He comes back to me from that last occasion—for I was never to speak to him again—as a man with some safe preserve for sport. I wondered as I walked away where he had got *his* tip.

V

When I spoke to George Corvick of the caution I had received he made me feel that any doubt of his delicacy would be almost an insult. He had instantly told Gwendolen, but Gwendolen's ardent response was in itself a pledge of discretion. The question would now absorb them and would offer them a pastime too precious to be shared with the crowd. They appeared to have caught instinctively at Vereker's high idea of enjoyment. Their intellectual pride, however, was not such as to make them indifferent to any further light I might throw on the affair they had in hand. They were indeed of the "artistic temperament," and I was freshly struck with my colleague's power to excite himself over a question of art. He'd call it letters, he'd call it life, but it was all one thing. In what he said I now seemed to understand that he spoke equally for Gwendolen, to whom, as soon as Mrs. Erme was sufficiently better to allow her a little leisure, he made a point of introducing me. I remember our going together one Sunday in August to a huddled house in Chelsea,[17] and my renewed envy of Corvick's possession of a friend who had some light to mingle with his own. He could say things to her that I could never say to him. She had indeed no sense of humour and, with her pretty way of holding her head on one side, was one of those persons whom you want, as the phrase is, to shake, but who have learnt Hungarian by themselves. She conversed perhaps in Hungarian with Corvick; she had remarkably little English for his friend. Corvick afterwards told me that I had chilled her by my apparent indisposition to oblige them with the detail of what Vereker had said to me. I allowed that I felt I had given thought enough to that indication: hadn't I even made up my mind that it was vain and would lead nowhere? The importance they attached to it was irritating and quite envenomed my doubts.

That statement looks unamiable, and what probably happened was that I felt humiliated at seeing other persons deeply beguiled by an experiment that had brought me only chagrin.[18] I was out in the cold while, by the evening fire, under the lamp, they followed the chase for which I myself had sounded the horn. They did as I had done, only more deliberately and sociably—they went over their author from the beginning. There was no hurry, Corvick said—the future was before them and the fascination could only grow; they would take him page by page, as they would take one of the classics, inhale him in slow draughts and let him sink all the way in. They would scarce have got so wound up, I think, if they hadn't been in love: poor

[17]Residential neighborhood in west London.
[18]Acute vexation, annoyance, or mortification, arising from disappointment, thwarting, or failure.

Vereker's inner meaning gave them endless occasion to put and to keep their young heads together. None the less it represented the kind of problem for which Corvick had a special aptitude, drew out the particular pointed patience of which, had he lived, he would have given more striking and, it is to be hoped, more fruitful examples. He at least was, in Vereker's words, a little demon of subtlety. We had begun by disputing, but I soon saw that without my stirring a finger his infatuation would have its bad hours. He would bound off on false scents as I had done—he would clap his hands over new lights and see them blown out by the wind of the turned page. He was like nothing, I told him, but the maniacs who embrace some bedlamitical[19] theory of the cryptic character of Shakespeare. To this he replied that if we had had Shakespeare's own word for his being cryptic he would at once have accepted it. The case there was altogether different—we had nothing but the word of Mr. Snooks.[20] I returned that I was stupefied to see him attach such importance even to the word of Mr. Vereker. He wanted thereupon to know if I treated Mr. Vereker's word as a lie. I wasn't perhaps prepared, in my unhappy rebound, to go so far as that, but I insisted that till the contrary was proved I should view it as too fond an imagination. I didn't, I confess, say—I didn't at that time quite know—all I felt. Deep down, as Miss Erme would have said, I was uneasy, I was expectant. At the core of my disconcerted state—for my wonted curiosity lived in its ashes—was the sharpness of a sense that Corvick would at last probably come out somewhere. He made, in defence of his credulity, a great point of the fact that from of old, in his study of this genius, he had caught whiffs and hints of he didn't know what, faint wandering notes of a hidden music. That was just the rarity, that was the charm: it fitted so perfectly into what I reported.

If I returned on several occasions to the little house in Chelsea I dare say it was as much for news of Vereker as for news of Miss Erme's ailing parent. The hours spent there by Corvick were present to my fancy as those of a chessplayer bent with a silent scowl, all the lamplit winter, over his board and his moves. As my imagination filled it out the picture held me fast. On the other side of the table was a ghostlier form, the faint figure of an antagonist good-humouredly but a little wearily secure—an antagonist who leaned back in his chair with his hands in his pockets and a smile on his fine clear face. Close to Corvick, behind him, was a girl who had begun to strike me as pale and wasted and even, on more familiar view, as rather handsome, and who rested on his shoulder and hung on his moves. He would take up a chessman and hold it poised a while over one of the little squares, and then would put it back in its place with a long sigh of disappointment. The young lady, at this, would slightly but uneasily shift her

---

[19]Bedlamitical means "lunatic" or "mad," and the longer phrase suggests theories that Shakespeare's works were written by someone else whose identity might be cryptically hidden inside the texts.

[20]Most likely James invented name for one of these critics.

position and look across, very hard, very long, very strangely, at their dim participant. I had asked them at an early stage of the business if it mightn't contribute to their success to have some closer communication with him. The special circumstances would surely be held to have given me a right to introduce them. Corvick immediately replied that he had no wish to approach the altar before he had prepared the sacrifice. He quite agreed with our friend both as to the delight and as to the honour of the chase— he would bring down the animal with his own rifle. When I asked him if Miss Erme were as keen a shot he said after thinking: "No, I'm ashamed to say she wants to set a trap. She'd give anything to see him; she says she requires another tip. She's really quite morbid about it. But she must play fair—she *shan't* see him!" he emphatically added. I wondered if they hadn't even quarrelled a little on the subject—a suspicion not corrected by the way he more than once exclaimed to me: "She's quite incredibly literary, you know—quite fantastically!" I remember his saying of her that she felt in italics and thought in capitals. "Oh when I've run him to earth," he also said, "then, you know, I shall knock at his door. Rather—I beg you to believe. I'll have it from his own lips: 'Right you are, my boy; you've done it this time!' He shall crown me victor—with the critical laurel."[21]

Meanwhile he really avoided the chances London life might have given him of meeting the distinguished novelist; a danger, however, that disappeared with Vereker's leaving England for an indefinite absence, as the newspapers announced—going to the south for motives connected with the health of his wife, which had long kept her in retirement. A year—more than a year—had elapsed since the incident at Bridges, but I had had no further sight of him. I think I was at bottom rather ashamed—I hated to remind him that, though I had irremediably missed his point, a reputation for acuteness was rapidly overtaking me. This scruple led me a dance; kept me out of Lady Jane's house, made me even decline, when in spite of my bad manners she was a second time so good as to make me a sign, an invitation to her beautiful seat. I once became aware of her under Vereker's escort at a concert, and was sure I was seen by them, but I slipped out without being caught. I felt, as on that occasion I splashed along in the rain, that I couldn't have done anything else; and yet I remember saying to myself that it was hard, was even cruel. Not only had I lost the books, but I had lost the man himself: they and their author had been alike spoiled for me. I knew too which was the loss I most regretted. I had taken to the man still more than I had ever taken to the books.

VI

Six months after our friend had left England George Corvick, who made his living by his pen, contracted for a piece of work which imposed on him an absence of some length and a journey of some difficulty, and his

[21]As in the laurel wreaths awarded in ancient Greece to victors in athletics and poetry; here the crowned victory would be in criticism.

undertaking of which was much of a surprise to me. His brother-in-law had become editor of a great provincial paper, and the great provincial paper, in a fine flight of fancy, had conceived the idea of sending a "special commissioner" to India. Special commissioners had begun, in the "metropolitan press," to be the fashion, and the journal in question must have felt it had passed too long for a mere country cousin. Corvick had no hand, I knew, for the big brush of the correspondent, but that was his brother-in-law's affair, and the fact that a particular task was not in his line was apt to be with himself exactly a reason for accepting it. He was prepared to out-Herod[22] the metropolitan press; he took solemn precautions against priggishness, he exquisitely outraged taste. Nobody ever knew it—that offended principle was all his own. In addition to his expenses he was to be conveniently paid, and I found myself able to help him, for the usual fat book, to a plausible arrangement with the usual fat publisher. I naturally inferred that his obvious desire to make a little money was not unconnected with the prospect of a union with Gwendolen Erme. I was aware that her mother's opposition was largely addressed to his want of means and of lucrative abilities, but it so happened that, on my saying the last time I saw him something that bore on the question of his separation from our young lady, he brought out with an emphasis that startled me: "Ah I'm not a bit engaged to her, you know!"

"Not overtly," I answered, "because her mother doesn't like you. But I've always taken for granted a private understanding."

"Well, there *was* one. But there isn't now." That was all he said save something about Mrs. Erme's having got on her feet again in the most extraordinary way—a remark pointing, as I supposed, the moral that private understandings were of little use when the doctor didn't share them. What I took the liberty of more closely inferring was that the girl might in some way have estranged him. Well, if he had taken the turn of jealousy for instance it could scarcely be jealousy of me. In that case—over and above the absurdity of it—he wouldn't have gone away just to leave us together. For some time before his going we had indulged in no allusion to the buried treasure, and from his silence, which my reserve simply emulated, I had drawn a sharp conclusion. His courage had dropped, his ardour had gone the way of mine—this appearance at least he left me to scan. More than that he couldn't do; he couldn't face the triumph with which I might have greeted an explicit admission. He needn't have been afraid, poor dear, for I had by this time lost all need to triumph. In fact I considered I showed magnanimity in not reproaching him with his collapse, for the sense of his having thrown up the game made me feel more than ever how much I at last depended on him. If Corvick had broken down I should never know; no one would be of any use if he wasn't. It wasn't a bit true I had ceased to care for knowledge; little by little my curiosity not only had begun to ache again, but

---

[22]A term meaning to out-do or be more extreme or outrageous than someone else; often alluding to Shakespeare's usage in *Hamlet* (III ii 14).

had become the familiar torment of my days and my nights. There are doubtless people to whom torments of such an order appear hardly more natural than the contortions of disease; but I don't after all know why I should in this connexion so much as mention them. For the few persons, at any rate, abnormal or not, with whom my anecdote is concerned, literature was a game of skill, and skill meant courage, and courage meant honour, and honour meant passion, meant life. The stake on the table was of a special substance and our roulette the revolving mind, but we sat round the green board as intently as the grim gamblers at Monte Carlo.[23] Gwendolen Erme, for that matter, with her white face and her fixed eyes, was of the very type of the lean ladies one had met in the temples of chance. I recognised in Corvick's absence that she made this analogy vivid. It was extravagant, I admit, the way she lived for the art of the pen. Her passion visibly preyed on her, and in her presence I felt almost tepid. I got hold of "Deep Down" again: it was a desert in which she had lost herself, but in which too she had dug a wonderful hole in the sand—a cavity out of which Corvick had still more remarkably pulled her.

Early in March I had a telegram from her, in consequence of which I repaired immediately to Chelsea, where the first thing she said to me was: "He has got it, he has got it!"

She was moved, as I could see, to such depths that she must mean the great thing. "Vereker's idea?"

"His general intention. George has cabled from Bombay."

She had the missive open there; it was emphatic though concise. "Eureka. Immense." That was all—he had saved the cost of the signature. I shared her emotion, but I was disappointed. "He doesn't say what it is."

"How could he—in a telegram? He'll write it."

"But how does he know?"

"Know it's the real thing? Oh I'm sure that when you see it you do know. *Vera incessu patuit dea!*"[24]

"It's you, Miss Erme, who are a 'dear' for bringing me such news!"—I went all lengths in my high spirits. "But fancy finding our goddess in the temple of Vishnu![25] How strange of George to have been able to go into the thing again in the midst of such different and such powerful solicitations!"

"He hasn't gone into it, I know; it's the thing itself, let severely alone for six months, that has simply sprung out at him like a tigress out of the jungle. He didn't take a book with him—on purpose; indeed he wouldn't have needed to—he knows every page, as I do, by heart. They all worked in him together, and some day somewhere, when he wasn't thinking, they fell, in all their superb intricacy, into the one right combination. The figure in the carpet came out. That's the way he knew it would come and the real reason—you didn't in the least understand, but I suppose I may tell you

---

[23]European gambling resort containing many "temples of chance."

[24]Latin: By her gait she was revealed as a true goddess (Virgil's *Aeniad*, I.405).

[25]One of the principle Hindu gods.

now—why he went and why I consented to his going. We knew the change would do it—that the difference of thought, of scene, would give the needed touch, the magic shake. We had perfectly, we had admirably calculated. The elements were all in his mind, and in the *secousse*[26] of a new and intense experience they just struck light." She positively struck light herself—she was literally, facially luminous. I stammered something about unconscious cerebration, and she continued: "He'll come right home—this will bring him."

"To see Vereker, you mean?"

"To see Vereker—and to see *me*. Think what he 'll have to tell me!"

I hesitated. "About India?"

"About fiddlesticks! About Vereker—about the figure in the carpet."

"But, as you say, we shall surely have that in a letter."

She thought like one inspired, and I remembered how Corvick had told me long before that her face was interesting. "Perhaps it can't be got into a letter if it's 'immense.'"

"Perhaps not if it's immense bosh.[27] If he has hold of something that can't be got into a letter he hasn't hold of *the* thing. Vereker's own statement to me was exactly that the 'figure' *would* fit into a letter."

"Well, I cabled to George an hour ago—two words," said Gwendolen.

"Is it indiscreet of me to ask what they were?"

She hung fire,[28] but at last brought them out. "'Angel, write.'"

"Good!" I cried. "I'll make it sure—I'll send him the same."

VII

My words however were not absolutely the same—I put something instead of "angel"; and in the sequel my epithet seemed the more apt, for when eventually we heard from our traveller it was merely, it was thoroughly to be tantalised. He was magnificent in his triumph, he described his discovery as stupendous; but his ecstasy only obscured it—there were to be no particulars till he should have submitted his conception to the supreme authority. He had thrown up his commission, he had thrown up his book, he had thrown up everything but the instant need to hurry to Rapallo, on the Genoese shore,[29] where Vereker was making a stay. I wrote him a letter which was to await him at Aden[30]—I besought him to relieve my suspense. That he had found my letter was indicated by a telegram which, reaching me after weary days and in the absence of any answer to my laconic dispatch to him at Bombay, evidently intended as a reply to both communications. Those few words were in familiar French, the French of the day, which Corvick often made use of to show he wasn't a prig. It had for some persons the opposite effect, but his message may fairly be paraphrased.

[26]French: a jolt, shake, or shock.

[27]Contemptible nonsense, foolish talk.

[28]One of James's favorite phrases for a pregnant pause, a deliberate hesitation before speech or action.

[29]A municipality in the province of Genoa in the north of Italy.

[30]A major port in Yemen that served as a way-station for sea travel between India and Europe.

"Have patience; I want to see, as it breaks on you, the face you'll make!" "Tellement en vie de voir ta tête!"[31]—that was what I had to sit down with. I can certainly not be said to have sat down, for I seem to remember myself at this time as rattling constantly between the little house in Chelsea and my own. Our impatience, Gwendolen's and mine, was equal, but I kept hoping her light would be greater. We all spent during this episode, for people of our means, a great deal of money in telegrams and cabs, and I counted on the receipt of news from Rapallo immediately after the junction of the discoverer with the discovered. The interval seemed an age, but late one day I heard a hansom[32] precipitated to my door with the crash engendered by a hint of liberality. I lived with my heart in my mouth and accordingly bounded to the window—a movement which gave me a view of a young lady erect on the footboard of the vehicle and eagerly looking up at my house. At sight of me she flourished a paper with a movement that brought me straight down, the movement with which, in melodramas, handkerchiefs and reprieves are flourished at the foot of the scaffold.

"Just seen Vereker—not a note wrong. Pressed me to bosom—keeps me a month." So much I read on her paper while the cabby dropped a grin from his perch. In my excitement I paid him profusely and in hers she suffered it; then as he drove away we started to walk about and talk. We had talked, heaven knows, enough before, but this was a wondrous lift. We pictured the whole scene at Rapallo, where he would have written, mentioning my name, for permission to call; that is *I* pictured it, having more material than my companion, whom I felt hang on my lips as we stopped on purpose before shop-windows we didn't look into. About one thing we were clear: if he was staying on for fuller communication we should at least have a letter from him that would help us through the dregs of delay. We understood his staying on, and yet each of us saw, I think, that the other hated it. The letter we were clear about arrived; it was for Gwendolen, and I called on her in time to save her the trouble of bringing it to me. She didn't read it out, as was natural enough; but she repeated to me what it chiefly embodied. This consisted of the remarkable statement that he'd tell her after they were married exactly what she wanted to know.

"Only *then*, when I'm his wife—not before," she explained. "It's tantamount to saying—isn't it?—that I must marry him straight off!" She smiled at me while I flushed with disappointment, a vision of fresh delay that made me at first unconscious of my surprise. It seemed more than a hint that on me as well he would impose some tiresome condition. Suddenly, while she reported several more things from his letter, I remembered what he had told me before going away. He had found Mr. Vereker deliriously interesting and his own possession of the secret a real intoxication. The buried treasure was all gold and gems. Now that it was there it seemed to grow and grow before

---

[31]French: I long to see your face.
[32]A hansom cab or a low-hung two-wheeled carriage holding two persons inside, with the driver being mounted on an elevated seat behind and the reins going over the roof.

him; it would have been, through all time and taking all tongues, one of the most wonderful flowers of literary art. Nothing, in especial, once you were face to face with it, could show for more consummately *done*. When once it came out it came out, was there with a splendour that made you ashamed; and there hadn't been, save in the bottomless vulgarity of the age, with every one tasteless and tainted, every sense stopped, the smallest reason why it should have been overlooked. It was great, yet so simple, was simple, yet so great, and the final knowledge of it was an experience quite apart. He intimated that the charm of such an experience, the desire to drain it, in its freshness, to the last drop, was what kept him there close to the source. Gwendolen, frankly radiant as she tossed me these fragments, showed the elation of a prospect more assured than my own. That brought me back to the question of her marriage, prompted me to ask if what she meant by what she had just surprised me with was that she was under an engagement.

"Of course I am!" she answered. "Didn't you know it?" She seemed astonished, but I was still more so, for Corvick had told me the exact contrary. I didn't mention this, however; I only reminded her how little I had been on that score in her confidence, or even in Corvick's, and that moreover I wasn't in ignorance of her mother's interdict.[33] At bottom I was troubled by the disparity of the two accounts; but after a little I felt Corvick's to be the one I least doubted. This simply reduced me to asking myself if the girl had on the spot improvised an engagement—vamped up an old one or dashed off a new—in order to arrive at the satisfaction she desired. She must have had resources of which I was destitute, but she made her case slightly more intelligible by returning presently: "What the state of things has been is that we felt of course bound to do nothing in mamma's lifetime."

"But now you think you'll just dispense with mamma's consent?"

"Ah it mayn't come to that!" I wondered what it might come to, and she went on: "Poor dear, she may swallow the dose. In fact, you know," she added with a laugh, "she really *must*!"—a proposition of which, on behalf of every one concerned, I fully acknowledged the force.

VIII

Nothing more vexatious[34] had ever happened to me than to become aware before Corvick's arrival in England that I shouldn't be there to put him through. I found myself abruptly called to Germany by the alarming illness of my younger brother, who, against my advice, had gone to Munich to study, at the feet indeed of a great master, the art of portraiture in oils. The near relative who made him an allowance had threatened to withdraw it if he should, under specious pretexts, turn for superior truth to Paris—Paris being somehow, for a Cheltenham aunt,[35] the school of evil, the abyss. I

---

[33]An authoritative prohibition, an act of forbidding.

[34]Annoying and troubling.

[35]Cheltenham is a spa town in Gloucester in southwest England, and the aunt's views of Paris suggest her moral conservatism.

deplored this prejudice at the time, and the deep injury of it was now visible—first in the fact that it hadn't saved the poor boy, who was clever frail and foolish, from congestion of the lungs, and second in the greater break with London to which the event condemned me. I'm afraid that what was uppermost in my mind during several anxious weeks was the sense that if we had only been in Paris I might have run over to see Corvick. This was actually out of the question from every point of view: my brother, whose recovery gave us both plenty to do, was ill for three months, during which I never left him and at the end of which we had to face the absolute prohibition of a return to England. The consideration of climate imposed itself, and he was in no state to meet it alone. I took him to Meran[36] and there spent the summer with him, trying to show him by example how to get back to work and nursing a rage of another sort that I tried *not* to show him.

The whole business proved the first of a series of phenomena so strangely interlaced that, taken all together—which was how I had to take them—they form as good an illustration as I can recall of the manner in which, for the good of his soul doubtless, fate sometimes deals with a man's avidity.[37] These incidents certainly had larger bearings than the comparatively meagre consequence we are here concerned with—though I feel that consequence also a thing to speak of with some respect. It's mainly in such a light, I confess, at any rate, that the ugly fruit of my exile is at this hour present to me. Even at first indeed the spirit in which my avidity, as I have called it, made me regard that term owed no element of ease to the fact that before coming back from Rapallo George Corvick addressed me in a way I objected to. His letter had none of the sedative action I must today profess myself sure he had wished to give it, and the march of occurrences was not so ordered as to make up for what it lacked. He had begun on the spot, for one of the quarterlies, a great last word on Vereker's writings, and this exhaustive study, the only one that would have counted, have existed, was to turn on the new light, to utter—oh so quietly!—the unimagined truth. It was in other words to trace the figure in the carpet through every convolution, to reproduce it in every tint. The result, according to my friend, would be the greatest literary portrait ever painted, and what he asked of me was just to be so good as not to trouble him with questions till he should hang up his masterpiece before me. He did me the honour to declare that, putting aside the great sitter himself, all aloft in his indifference, I was individually the connoisseur he was most working for. I was therefore to be a good boy and not try to peep under the curtain before the show was ready: I should enjoy it all the more if I sat very still.

I did my best to sit very still, but I couldn't help giving a jump on seeing in *The Times*, after I had been a week or two in Munich and before, as I knew, Corvick had reached London, the announcement of the sudden death of poor Mrs. Erme. I instantly, by letter, appealed to Gwendolen for

---

[36]Also known as Merano, a town in northern Italy with many spas.

[37]Extreme eagerness or greediness.

particulars, and she wrote me that her mother had yielded to long-threatened failure of the heart. She didn't say, but I took the liberty of reading into her words, that from the point of view of her marriage and also of her eagerness, which was quite a match for mine, this was a solution more prompt than could have been expected and more radical than waiting for the old lady to swallow the dose. I candidly admit indeed that at the time—for I heard from her repeatedly—I read some singular things into Gwendolen's words and some still more extraordinary ones into her silences. Pen in hand, this way, I live the time over, and it brings back the oddest sense of my having been, both for months and in spite of myself, a kind of coerced spectator. All my life had taken refuge in my eyes, which the procession of events appeared to have committed itself to keep astare.[38] There were days when I thought of writing to Hugh Vereker and simply throwing myself on his charity. But I felt more deeply that I hadn't fallen quite so low—besides which, quite properly, he would send me about my business. Mrs. Erme's death brought Corvick straight home, and within the month he was united "very quietly"—as quietly, I seemed to make out, as he meant in his article to bring out his *trouvaille*[39]—to the young lady he had loved and quitted. I use this last term, I may parenthetically say, because I subsequently grew sure that at the time he went to India, at the time of his great news from Bombay, there had been no positive pledge between them whatever. There had been none at the moment she was affirming to me the very opposite. On the other hand he had certainly become engaged the day he returned. The happy pair went down to Torquay[40] for their honeymoon, and there, in a reckless hour, it occurred to poor Corvick to take his young bride a drive. He had no command of that business: this had been brought home to me of old in a little tour we had once made together in a dog-cart.[41] In a dog-cart he perched his companion for a rattle over Devonshire hills, on one of the likeliest of which he brought his horse, who, it was true, had bolted, down with such violence that the occupants of the cart were hurled forward and that he fell horribly on his head. He was killed on the spot; Gwendolen escaped unhurt.

I pass rapidly over the question of this unmitigated tragedy, of what the loss of my best friend meant for me, and I complete my little history of my patience and my pain by the frank statement of my having, in a postscript to my very first letter to her after the receipt of the hideous news, asked Mrs. Corvick whether her husband mightn't at least have finished the great article on Vereker. Her answer was as prompt as my question: the article, which had been barely begun, was a mere heartbreaking scrap. She explained that our friend, abroad, had just settled down to it when interrupted by her mother's death, and that then, on his return, he had been kept from work

---

[38]Referring to his eyes as staring and wide open.

[39]French: a lucky find, a windfall.

[40]Fashionable seaside resort in Devon, England.

[41]An open carriage with two transverse seats back to back, the rear seat originally converting into a box for dogs.

by the engrossments into which that calamity[42] was to plunge them. The opening pages were all that existed; they were striking, they were promising, but they didn't unveil the idol. That great intellectual feat was obviously to have formed his climax. She said nothing more, nothing to enlighten me as to the state of her own knowledge—the knowledge for the acquisition of which I had fancied her prodigiously acting. This was above all what I wanted to know: had *she* seen the idol unveiled? Had there been a private ceremony for a palpitating audience of one? For what else but that ceremony had the nuptials taken place? I didn't like as yet to press her, though when I thought of what had passed between us on the subject in Corvick's absence her reticence surprised me. It was therefore not till much later, from Meran, that I risked another appeal, risked it in some trepidation, for she continued to tell me nothing. "Did you hear in those few days of your blighted bliss," I wrote, "what we desired so to hear?" I said "we" as a little hint; and she showed me she could take a little hint. "I heard everything," she replied, "and I mean to keep it to myself!"

IX

It was impossible not to be moved with the strongest sympathy for her, and on my return to England I showed her every kindness in my power. Her mother's death had made her means sufficient, and she had gone to live in a more convenient quarter. But her loss had been great and her visitation cruel; it never would have occurred to me moreover to suppose she could come to feel the possession of a technical tip, of a piece of literary experience, a counterpoise to her grief. Strange to say, none the less, I couldn't help believing after I had seen her a few times that I caught a glimpse of some such oddity. I hasten to add that there had been other things I couldn't help believing, or at least imagining; and as I never felt I was really clear about these, so, as to the point I here touch on, I give her memory the benefit of the doubt. Stricken and solitary, highly accomplished and now, in her deep mourning, her maturer grace and her uncomplaining sorrow, incontestably handsome, she presented herself as leading a life of singular dignity and beauty. I had at first found a way to persuade myself that I should soon get the better of the reserve formulated, the week after the catastrophe, in her reply to an appeal as to which I was not unconscious that it might strike her as mistimed. Certainly that reserve was something of a shock to me—certainly it puzzled me the more I thought of it and even though I tried to explain it (with moments of success) by an imputation[43] of exalted sentiments, of superstitious scruples, of a refinement of loyalty. Certainly it added at the same time hugely to the price of Vereker's secret, precious as this mystery already appeared. I may as well confess abjectly that Mrs. Corvick's unexpected attitude was the final tap on the nail that was to

---

[42]Deep distress, struggle, or misery.   [43]Accusation or charge.

fix fast my luckless idea, convert it into the obsession of which I'm for ever conscious.

But this only helped me the more to be artful, to be adroit,[44] to allow time to elapse before renewing my suit. There were plenty of speculations for the interval, and one of them was deeply absorbing. Corvick had kept his information from his young friend till after the removal of the last barrier to their intimacy—then only had he let the cat out of the bag. Was it Gwendolen's idea, taking a hint from him, to liberate this animal only on the basis of the renewal of such a relation? Was the figure in the carpet traceable or describable only for husbands and wives—for lovers supremely united? It came back to me in a mystifying manner that in Kensington Square, when I mentioned that Corvick would have told the girl he loved, some word had dropped from Vereker that gave colour to this possibility. There might be little in it, but there was enough to make me wonder if I should have to marry Mrs. Corvick to get what I wanted. Was I prepared to offer her this price for the blessing of her knowledge? Ah that way madness lay![45]—so I at least said to myself in bewildered hours. I could see meanwhile the torch she refused to pass on flame away in her chamber of memory—pour through her eyes a light that shone in her lonely house. At the end of six months I was fully sure of what this warm presence made up to her for. We had talked again and again of the man who had brought us together—of his talent, his character, his personal charm, his certain career, his dreadful doom, and even of his clear purpose in that great study which was to have been a supreme literary portrait, a kind of critical Vandyke or Velasquez.[46] She had conveyed to me in abundance that she was tongue-tied by her perversity, by her piety, that she would never break the silence it had not been given to the "right person," as she said, to break. The hour however finally arrived. One evening when I had been sitting with her longer than usual I laid my hand firmly on her arm. "Now at last what *is* it?"

She had been expecting me and was ready. She gave a long slow soundless headshake, merciful only in being inarticulate. This mercy didn't prevent its hurling at me the largest finest coldest "Never!" I had yet, in the course of a life that had known denials, had to take full in the face. I took it and was aware that with the hard blow the tears had come into my eyes. So for a while we sat and looked at each other; after which I slowly rose. I was wondering if some day she would accept me; but this was not what I brought out. I said as I smoothed down my hat: "I know what to think then. It's nothing!"

---

[44]Dexterous, clever.

[45]An adapted allusion to "O, that way madness lies," spoken by King Lear III.iv.91.

[46]"Vandyke" or Sir Anthony Van Dyk (1599–1641) was a Flemish-born painter who became a leading painter of portraits of the English court, including King Charles I. Diego Rodríguez de Silva y Velázquez (1599–1660) was a Spanish painter also famous for his work in portraits in the court of King Philip IV.

A remote disdainful pity for me gathered in her dim smile; then she spoke in a voice that I hear at this hour. "It's my *life*!" As I stood at the door she added: "You've insulted him!"

"Do you mean Vereker?"

"I mean the Dead!"

I recognised when I reached the street the justice of her charge. Yes, it was her life—recognised that too; but her life none the less made room with the lapse of time for another interest. A year and a half after Corvick's death she published in a single volume her second novel, "Overmastered," which I pounced on in the hope of finding in it some tell-tale echo or some peeping face. All I found was a much better book than her younger performance, showing I thought the better company she had kept. As a tissue tolerably intricate it was a carpet with a figure of its own; but the figure was not the figure I was looking for. On sending a review of it to *The Middle* I was surprised to learn from the office that a notice was already in type. When the paper came out I had no hesitation in attributing this article, which I thought rather vulgarly overdone, to Drayton Deane, who in the old days had been something of a friend of Corvick's, yet had only within a few weeks made the acquaintance of his widow. I had had an early copy of the book, but Deane had evidently had an earlier. He lacked all the same the light hand with which Corvick had gilded the gingerbread—he laid on the tinsel in splotches.

X

Six months later appeared "The Right of Way," the last chance, though we didn't know it, that we were to have to redeem ourselves. Written wholly during Vereker's sojourn abroad, the book had been heralded, in a hundred paragraphs, by the usual ineptitudes. I carried it, as early a copy as any, I this time flattered myself, straightway to Mrs. Corvick. This was the only use I had for it; I left the inevitable tribute of *The Middle* to some more ingenious mind and some less irritated temper. "But I already have it," Gwendolen said. "Drayton Deane was so good as to bring it to me yesterday, and I've just finished it."

"Yesterday? How did he get it so soon?"

"He gets everything so soon! He's to review it in *The Middle*."

"He—Drayton Deane—review Vereker?" I couldn't believe my ears.

"Why not? One fine ignorance is as good as another."

I winced but I presently said: "You ought to review him yourself!"

"I don't review,'" she laughed. "I'm reviewed!"

Just then the door was thrown open. "Ah yes, here's your reviewer!" Drayton Deane was there with his long legs and his tall forehead: he had come to see what she thought of "The Right of Way," and to bring news that was singularly relevant. The evening papers were just out with a telegram on the author of that work, who, in Rome, had been ill for some days with an attack of malarial fever. It had at first not been thought grave, but had taken, in consequence of complications, a turn that might give rise to anxiety. Anxiety had indeed at the latest hour begun to be felt.

I was struck in the presence of these tidings with the fundamental detachment that Mrs. Corvick's overt concern quite failed to hide: it gave me the measure of her consummate independence. That independence rested on her knowledge, the knowledge which nothing now could destroy and which nothing could make different. The figure in the carpet might take on another twist or two, but the sentence had virtually been written. The writer might go down to his grave: she was the person in the world to whom—as if she had been his favoured heir—his continued existence was least of a need. This reminded me how I had observed at a particular moment—after Corvick's death—the drop of her desire to see him face to face. She had got what she wanted without that. I had been sure that if she hadn't got it she wouldn't have been restrained from the endeavour to sound him personally by those superior reflexions, more conceivable on a man's part than on a woman's, which in my case had served as a deterrent. It wasn't however, I hasten to add, that my case, in spite of this invidious comparison, wasn't ambiguous enough. At the thought that Vereker was perhaps at that moment dying there rolled over me a wave of anguish—a poignant sense of how inconsistently I still depended on him. A delicacy that it was my one compensation to suffer to rule me had left the Alps and the Apennines between us, but the sense of the waning occasion suggested that I might in my despair at last have gone to him. Of course I should really have done nothing of the sort. I remained five minutes, while my companions talked of the new book, and when Drayton Deane appealed to me for my opinion of it I made answer, getting up, that I detested Hugh Vereker and simply couldn't read him. I departed with the moral certainty that as the door closed behind me Deane would brand me for awfully superficial. His hostess wouldn't contradict *that* at least.

I continue to trace with a briefer touch our intensely odd successions. Three weeks after this came Vereker's death, and before the year was out the death of his wife. That poor lady I had never seen, but I had had a futile theory that, should she survive him long enough to be decorously accessible, I might approach her with the feeble flicker of my plea. Did she know and if she knew would she speak? It was much to be presumed that for more reasons than one she would have nothing to say; but when she passed out of all reach I felt renunciation indeed my appointed lot. I was shut up in my obsession for ever—my gaolers[47] had gone off with the key. I find myself quite as vague as a captive in a dungeon about the time that further elapsed before Mrs. Corvick became the wife of Drayton Deane. I had foreseen, through my bars, this end of the business, though there was no indecent haste and our friendship had rather fallen off. They were both so "awfully intellectual" that it struck people as a suitable match, but I had measured better than any one the wealth of understanding the bride would contribute

[47]Jailers.

to the union. Never, for a marriage in literary circles—so the newspapers described the alliance—had a lady been so bravely dowered. I began with due promptness to look for the fruit of the affair—that fruit, I mean, of which the premonitory[48] symptoms would be peculiarly visible in the husband. Taking for granted the splendour of the other party's nuptial gift, I expected to see him make a show commensurate with his increase of means. I knew what his means had been—his article on "The Right of Way" had distinctly given one the figure. As he was now exactly in the position in which still more exactly I was not I watched from month to month, in the likely periodicals, for the heavy message poor Corvick had been unable to deliver and the responsibility of which would have fallen on his successor. The widow and wife would have broken by the rekindled hearth the silence that only a widow and wife might break, and Deane would be as aflame with the knowledge as Corvick in his own hour, as Gwendolen in hers, had been. Well, he was aflame doubtless, but the fire was apparently not to become a public blaze. I scanned the periodicals in vain: Drayton Deane filled them with exuberant pages, but he withheld the page I most feverishly sought. He wrote on a thousand subjects, but never on the subject of Vereker. His special line was to tell truths that other people either "funked," as he said, or overlooked, but he never told the only truth that seemed to me in these days to signify. I met the couple in those literary circles referred to in the papers: I have sufficiently intimated that it was only in such circles we were all constructed to revolve. Gwendolen was more than ever committed to them by the publication of her third novel, and I myself definitely classed by holding the opinion that this work was inferior to its immediate predecessor. Was it worse because she had been keeping worse company? If her secret was, as she had told me, her life—a fact discernible in her increasing bloom, an air of conscious privilege that, cleverly corrected by pretty charities, gave distinction to her appearance—it had yet not a direct influence on her work. That only made one—everything only made one—yearn the more for it; only rounded it off with a mystery finer and subtler.

XI

It was therefore from her husband I could never remove my eyes: I beset him in a manner that might have made him uneasy. I went even so far as to engage him in conversation. Didn't he know, hadn't he come into it as a matter of course?—that question hummed in my brain. Of course he knew; otherwise he wouldn't return my stare so queerly. His wife had told him what I wanted and he was amiably amused at my impotence. He didn't laugh—he wasn't a laugher: his system was to present to my irritation, so that I should crudely expose myself, a conversational blank as vast as his big bare brow. It always happened that I turned away with a settled conviction from these unpeopled expanses, which seemed to complete each other

[48]Serving to warn or notify beforehand.

geographically and to symbolise together Drayton Deane's want of voice, want of form. He simply hadn't the art to use what he knew; he literally was incompetent to take up the duty where Corvick had left it. I went still further—it was the only glimpse of happiness I had. I made up my mind that the duty didn't appeal to him. He wasn't interested, he didn't care. Yes, it quite comforted me to believe him too stupid to have joy of the thing I lacked. He was as stupid after as he had been before, and that deepened for me the golden glory in which the mystery was wrapped. I had of course none the less to recollect that his wife might have imposed her conditions and exactions. I had above all to remind myself that with Vereker's death the major incentive dropped. He was still there to be honoured by what might be done—he was no longer there to give it his sanction. Who alas but he had the authority?

Two children were born to the pair, but the second cost the mother her life. After this stroke I seemed to see another ghost of a chance. I jumped at it in thought, but I waited a certain time for manners, and at last my opportunity arrived in a remunerative way. His wife had been dead a year when I met Drayton Deane in the smoking-room of a small club of which we both were members, but where for months—perhaps because I rarely entered it—I hadn't seen him. The room was empty and the occasion propitious.[49] I deliberately offered him, to have done with the matter for ever, that advantage for which I felt he had long been looking.

"As an older acquaintance of your late wife's than even you were," I began, "you must let me say to you something I have on my mind. I shall be glad to make any terms with you that you see fit to name for the information she must have had from George Corvick—the information, you know, that had come to *him*, poor chap, in one of the happiest hours of his life, straight from Hugh Vereker."

He looked at me like a dim phrenological bust.[50] "The information—?"

"Vereker's secret, my dear man—the general intention of his books: the string the pearls were strung on, the buried treasure, the figure in the carpet."

He began to flush—the numbers on his bumps[51] to come out. "Vereker's books had a general intention?"

I stared in my turn. "You don't mean to say you don't know it?" I thought for a moment he was playing with me. "Mrs. Deane knew it; she had it, as I say, straight from Corvick, who had, after infinite search and to Vereker's own delight, found the very mouth of the cave. Where *is* the mouth? He told after their marriage—and told alone—the person who, when the circumstances were reproduced, must have told *you*. Have I been wrong in taking for granted that she admitted you, as one of the highest privileges of the relation in which you stood to her, to the knowledge of

---

[49]Boding well, promising.
[50]A bust used for phrenology or the study of the cranium for determination of mental faculties.

[51]Another reference to phrenological bust, on which the different areas of the brain were numbered.

which she was after Corvick's death the sole depositary? All *I* know is that that knowledge is infinitely precious, and what I want you to understand is that if you'll in your turn admit me to it you 'll do me a kindness for which I shall be lastingly grateful."

He had turned at last very red; I dare say he had begun by thinking I had lost my wits. Little by little he followed me; on my own side I stared with a livelier surprise. Then he spoke. "I don't know what you 're talking about."

He wasn't acting—it was the absurd truth. "She *didn't* tell you—?"

"Nothing about Hugh Vereker."

I was stupefied; the room went round. It had been too good even for that! "Upon your honour?"

"Upon my honour. What the devil's the matter with you?" he growled.

"I'm astounded—I'm disappointed. I wanted to get it out of you."

"It isn't *in* me!" he awkwardly laughed. "And even if it were—"

"If it were you'd let me have it—oh yes, in common humanity. But I believe you. I see—I see!" I went on, conscious, with the full turn of the wheel, of my great delusion, my false view of the poor man's attitude. What I saw, though I couldn't say it, was that his wife hadn't thought him worth enlightening. This struck me as strange for a woman who had thought him worth marrying. At last I explained it by the reflexion that she couldn't possibly have married him for his understanding. She had married him for something else.

He was to some extent enlightened now, but he was even more astonished, more disconcerted: he took a moment to compare my story with his quickened memories. The result of his meditation was his presently saying with a good deal of rather feeble form: "This is the first I hear of what you allude to. I think you must be mistaken as to Mrs. Drayton Deane's having had any unmentioned, and still less any unmentionable, knowledge of Hugh Vereker.

She'd certainly have wished it—should it have borne on his literary character—to be used."

"It *was* used. She used it herself. She told me with her own lips that she 'lived' on it." I had no sooner spoken than I repented of my words; he grew so pale that I felt as if I had struck him. "Ah 'lived'—!" he murmured, turning short away from me.

My compunction was real; I laid my hand on his shoulder. "I beg you to forgive me—I've made a mistake. You don't know what I thought you knew. You could, if I had been right, have rendered me a service; and I had my reasons for assuming that you'd be in a position to meet me."

"Your reasons?" he echoed. "What were your reasons?"

I looked at him well; I hesitated; I considered. "Come and sit down with me here and I'll tell you." I drew him to a sofa, I lighted another cigar and, beginning with the anecdote of Vereker's one descent from the clouds, I recited to him the extraordinary chain of accidents that had, in spite of the original gleam, kept me till that hour in the dark. I told him in a word just what I've written out here. He listened with deepening attention, and I became aware, to my surprise, by his ejaculations, by his questions, that he would have been after all not unworthy to be trusted by his wife. So abrupt an experience of her want of trust had now a disturbing effect on him; but I saw the immediate shock throb away little by little and then gather again into waves of wonder and curiosity—waves that promised, I could perfectly judge, to break in the end with the fury of my own highest tides. I may say that to-day as victims of unappeased desire there isn't a pin to choose between us. The poor man's state is almost my consolation; there are really moments when I feel it to be quite my revenge.

1908

NATION WITHIN A NATION: LAKOTAS/ DAKOTAS/NAKOTAS

Sioux. It is a word that, for people unfamiliar with Native America, conjures up the Hollywood image of an "Indian;" a stern man in a long warbonnet, his face painted, his horse painted. He lives on the Great Plains, where he hunts bison or fights the cavalry. If we do not see him doing these things, we see him all alone, on a tired horse, disappearing into the sunset. This is an unchanging, monolithic notion of what Native America was, in the long ago.

In fact, "Sioux" describes an association of many Native nations, nations that existed before European horses replaced the dogs that once aided the people in transport and hunting. "Sioux" describes nations that continue to exist today, nations that continue to define themselves as other than, and sovereign from, the settler colonial nation of the United States.

The Dakota, Nakota, and Lakota, each also divided into smaller bands, form the three main branches of the Sioux. The term "Sioux" should conjure up an image of diverse communities of men and women in constant movement, constant negotiation with changing circumstances. It should conjure up an image of an affiliation of nations, linked to one another by story, tradition, and culture, but also different from one another, not always in agreement, and not always responding to change in the same way.

The Siouxan peoples were originally from around the headwaters of the Mississippi. They had horses by the early eighteenth century and moved west onto the Great Plains by the late eighteenth century, in response to the pressures of other Native nations being pushed further west by white settlement. When Lewis and Clark met them in the early nineteenth century, they met people who could curse in both French and English, wore wool, had guns, and were perfectly aware of and in adaptive relation to white cultural presence. By the middle of the nineteenth century, these nations stretched from Minnesota to the Dakotas and Wyoming. Dakotas lived in the upper Mississippi and western Minnesota. Nakotas lived between the Mississippi and the Missouri. Lakotas lived west of the Missouri.

The Great Plains, figured often as a desert landscape by white writers, became, across the nineteenth century, an arena of intense competition for hunting territory and resources among Native people. With the pressure for territory always increasing, warfare became a constant of High Plains life. Prestige as a warrior was essential for masculine power in the community. Warrior societies were the basis of government, but acts of bravery, witnessed by others and recounted at home, were the most important feature of war. Raids that brought back many horses, or striking an enemy harmlessly—"counting coup"—were more honored than killing.

Women's work changed, too. Bison had once been hunted on foot and with dogs. Few animals were killed. However, horses and guns made the killing of bison easier, and with increased demand for bison robes in the east, bison hunting became essential for trade with whites and other Native nations. Women's place in the community consequently became tied to the laborious preparation of the skins for trade.

Pressure continued to grow among competing Native nations, however. The railroad came, and the vast bison herds were systematically brought to the brink of extinction under the aegis of the U.S. government. Genocide became the goal of U.S. military encounters with High Plains people. The reservation system crushed Native mobility, gender roles, and cultural and political sovereignty. Children were taken away to boarding school, and they returned—if they returned—forever different. The people had to change again.

The decades covered by this volume encompassed for the Dakota, Lakota, and Nakota a period of enormous change and enormous loss. The Civil War, which was as much about the future of the west as it was about the north and south, enabled increased white expansion. The "Indian Wars" that spread across the plains during and after the Civil War are more honestly described as "wars of extermination"—a term that was in use at the time. These violent encounters between whites and Native people ranged from massacres of whole villages to skirmishes between small groups of militia and Native hunters to fully fledged battles between soldiers and warriors.

Palaneapope's 1865 explanation of "How the Indians are Victimized by Government Agents and Soldiers" gives a portrait of the everyday irritation, often erupting into outright violence, of colonial presence immediately following the Civil War. In 1868, the Treaty of Fort Laramie formed the Great Sioux Reservation. This treaty guaranteed the Black Hills as well as hunting rights in South Dakota, Wyoming, and Montana. In 1874, however, General George Armstrong Custer's Black Hills Expedition discovered gold in the Black Hills, and prospectors began invading. Full-scale war broke out.

The Black Hills War is most famous among non-Native people for the Battle of Greasy Grass Creek, or The Battle of Little Big Horn, in which Custer and all of the 7th Cavalry were killed by a combined force of Lakota, Northern Cheyenne, and Arapaho warriors. Two Moons' description of the battle is surprising, if one expects to see Native jubilation over a great "victory." He says that after the battle the warriors were sad. Honor in traditional warfare came not from killing but from acts of bravery. The outcome—all the enemy dead—was not, in fact, commensurate with traditional notions of victory. In his description, Two Moons is careful to point out which white soldier was the bravest; he is more interested in honoring that man than in identifying Custer. He also explains that "war-women" had mutilated some soldiers. Women were present at the battle and in fact were responsible for humiliating the enemy, which was as much a part of the traditional structures of honor as the men's roles.

In spite of Greasy Grass Creek, the war ended in defeat. The reservation was made smaller, and a portion of the Black Hills was lost. Horses and guns were taken away. Religion was suppressed. Children began to be taken away to be "educated" in eastern boarding schools. This so-called "education" was in fact part of a plan of assimilation hailed by Richard Henry Pratt, the mastermind of Indian boarding school education, as a means to "kill the Indian . . . and save the man." Children arrived at school as young as five years old. Their hair was cut—for them, this was a sign of cowardice and mourning. They were punished if they spoke their language. They were forced to conform to white gender norms, and they weren't allowed to go home for years on end. Meanwhile, at home on the reservation, sickness, starvation, and suicide were rampant. In the selections by Zitkala-Sa, we have a portrayal of both reservation life and school life. Born in 1876, the year of the Battle of Greasy Grass Creek, Zitkala-Sa was enticed away to boarding school at the age of eight. She eventually taught at Carlisle Indian School, but the experience disgusted her and she published her memoir in 1900 in an attempt to reveal to white America the cultural genocide perpetrated by the boarding school system.

In John Grass, Sitting Bull, and Red Cloud, we see three leaders of three different groups responding differently to the imperative to change as the Lakota, Dakota, and Nakota were confined on the reservation—forced to give up their religion, horses, and guns—and not allowed to move with the seasons. John Grass, a leader of the Blackfoot Lakota, rose to importance in 1876 and the years following because of his willingness to contemplate some aspects of assimilation, namely Christianity, farming, and white educational goals. However, he had little faith in the government. The piece included here shows his understanding of government trickery, and we see him demanding that his people be given good tools and strong animals and that their children be educated in a way that made them able to return and be useful to their own people. He asks that mixed and white people who understand themselves as Blackfoot also be understood by the United States government as belonging to the Blackfoot nation. This rejection of "race" as the signifier of Indianness is important. Indianness, Grass is arguing, is defined not by blood, but by participation in the culture.

In contrast to John Grass, Sitting Bull, a leader and holy man of the Hunkpapa Lakota, remained anti-assimilationist his whole life; after the Battle of Greasy Grass Creek, he took his band north to Canada rather than settle on the reservation. He and his people returned to the reservation in 1881, but, as we can see from his speech, he utterly rejected white definitions of virtue.

Red Cloud was a war-leader and a chief of the Oglala Lakota. He led the Oglala from 1868 to 1909; in other words, he led his nation both in the wars against the United States, in which he proved to be a brilliant strategist, and across his nation's transition to the reservation. In the selection here he explains why the Ghost Dance religion was so compelling to Native people. We include several of the Ghost Dance Songs in this section of the volume; the headnote to the Ghost Dance Songs discusses the context in which they arose. Red Cloud blames white depredations for the extreme suffering of High Plains people. It isn't the Ghost Dance that causes unrest, he explains. It is starvation and continually blasted hope.

In 1887 reservation life changed again. The Dawes Act (see this volume pp. 552–554) authorized the surveying of Indian land for the purpose of dividing it into allotments. The Great Sioux Reservation was broken up, and vast acreage was lost. Families were reorganized and gender roles redefined. In the wake of allotment, the Ghost Dance religion sparked anxiety in white America;

would it erupt in violence and prompt a return to the Indian wars? Newspapers called on the army to put a stop to the singing and dancing. Sitting Bull, who was sympathetic to the Ghost Dancers, was seen as a threat. It was feared that he would join them, and lend his strength to the movement. Reservation police were sent to arrest him on December 14, 1870; instead, they killed him. A group of his followers fled and met up with another band under the leadership of Big Foot. On the evening of December 28, at Wounded Knee creek, they were surrounded by the 7th Cavalry and surrendered. In the morning, during a search for weapons, shooting began, and the army proceeded to indiscriminately kill men, women, and children. Turning Hawk, Captain Sword, Spotted Horse, and American Horse give an account of the massacre in the pages that follow.

The massacre at Wounded Knee marks the end of nineteenth century armed resistance to white colonialism. New kinds of resistance and adaptation had to be found. Charles Eastman and Zitkala-Sa (Gertrude Bonnin) are each the child of a white and a Native parent, and they each represent the struggles of their generation to account for the transition from traditional to reservation life. Eastman, whose mother was a white woman, was educated in white schools and became a physician. He returned to the reservation, where he witnessed both the Ghost Dance religion and the aftermath of the Wounded Knee massacre, both of which are described by him here. Zitkala-Sa's "Why I Am a Pagan" shows that Native religious sovereignty survived Wounded Knee; this hopeful piece insists upon the "survivance" of Native America, in the land and in the people.

Across the decades covered by this volume, the Lakota, Dakota, and Nakota people were faced with reinterpreting and rebuilding their cultures under terrible conditions. The losses were huge and the violence unremitting. However, the Lakota, Nakota, and Dakota came and continue to come through. "Survivance" is a neologism coined by Anishinaanbe scholar Gerald Vizenor. It is a word that aims to move us past an understanding of Native cultures as always in a state of disappearance, crushed by genocidal machineries of colonialism. Instead, seeing Native cultures as always engaging in a practice of "survivance" is to see Native cultures in dynamic, creative, and enduring modes of generation. Devastation, loss, and grief must not be minimized, but survivance—which combines an understanding of survival, resistance, and active futurity—repudiates disappearance. Loss is certainly threaded through, but it is neither the beginning, the middle, nor the end of the story.

Bethany Ridgway Schneider
Bryn Mawr College

PALANEAPOPE (YANKTON SIOUX)
UNKNOWN DATES

from "How the Indians are Victimized by Government Agents and Soldiers"[1]

My friend, we are now done with the agent, and we will now commence with the soldiers. The first year they came up in this country, I think my grandfather must have told them to commence on me, and that is the reason I commence thus with them. I would like to know if my grandfather told them to commence against me first; I should think so, the way they treated us. The first time they came up our young men had nothing to eat, and had gone over the Missouri river to hunt, and the soldiers killed seven of them. The Two-Kettle band and the Low Yanktonais were friendly, and were then on my reservation at the time, and some of them went out with my young men to hunt, and were among, the seven that were killed; they were all friendly to the whites. When General Sully returned from his expedition, and was crossing my reserve, there were some of the Indian women married to half-breeds, and they had houses, and the soldiers went in and drove all the persons in them out, and robbed the houses of all there was in them. I would like to know if my grandfather told them to do so. I do not think he did. (All the chiefs present assent to this.) One of my chiefs, Little Swan, now here, had a house, and the soldiers broke in and destroyed all his goods, furniture, utensils and tools, and all the property of his band, the same being stored there. I would like to know if my grandfather told the soldiers when they returned from the expedition with their horses worn out, lost or stolen, to take horses from the Yanktons, in place of those they had lost or had worn out and broken down; I don't believe he did, but that is the way the soldiers did. I think the way the white men treated us is worse than the wolves do. We have a way in the winter of putting our dead up on scaffolds up from the ground, but the soldiers cut down the scaffolds and cut off the hair of the dead, and if they had good teeth they pulled them out, and some of them cut off the heads of the dead and carried them away. One time one of my young men and two squaws went over the river to Fort Randall, and a soldier wanted one of the squaws to do something with; he wanted to sleep with her, and she refused to sleep with him; one of the Indians asked the other squaw if she would sleep with the soldier, and she said she would; but the soldier would not have her, but wanted the other squaw, and claimed that the Indian was trying to prevent him from sleeping with his (the Indian's) squaw, his wife, and the Indian, fearing trouble, started

[1]From Senate Report No. 156, U.S. Congress (1867). "Grandfather" is a respectful way of referring to the U.S. president.

for the ferry, and the soldier shot the Indian, though the Indian got over it. Another time when General Sully came up he passed through the middle of our field, turned all his cattle and stock into our corn and destroyed the whole of it. The ears of some were then a foot long; the corn was opposite Fort Randall, and they not only destroyed the corn but burnt up the fence. I think no other white man would do so; I do not think my grandfather told them to do so. The soldiers set fire to the prairie and burnt up four of our lodges and all there was in them, and three horses. When my corn is good to eat they cross the river from Fort Randall and eat it, and when it is not good they throw it in the river. I think my reserve is very small; the soldiers cut all my wood and grass, and I think this is bad treatment. The above in regard to the soldiers applies to my three chiefs on the reserve opposite Fort Randall, and I will now speak of things at my agency when the soldiers came down from the expedition last fall. At that time myself and others were out on a hunt, and had put our goods under the floors; but when the expedition came down the soldiers broke open the houses, destroyed our pans and kettles, and fired into the stoves and kettles. The soldiers are very drunken and come to our place—they have arms and guns; they run after our women and fire into our houses and lodges; one soldier came along and wanted one of our young men to drink, but he would not, and turned to go away, and the soldier shot at him. Before the soldiers came along we had good health; but once the soldiers come along they go to my squaws and want to sleep with them, and the squaws being hungry will sleep with them in order to get something to eat, and will get a bad disease, and then the squaws turn to their husbands and give them the bad disease.

I would like to know if my grandfather tells the soldiers to get all my hay. Every year great contracts are made for cutting hay for Fort Randall, and they cut the hay all off our land, and I would like to know if my grandfather gave them permission to cut all the hay and take the money. I never see any of the money myself. They take all my mowing machines, bought with my money, to cut hay to sell to the soldiers, and I cannot get the mowing machines to cut anything for ourselves, and I have no use of them. I think the agents are in partnership with these men cutting hay to sell to the soldiers. The reason I think the agent had a hand in cutting hay for the soldiers is, because one year Burleigh gave all of us chiefs fifty dollars each for the hay cut upon the contract. Last spring I asked him for the money for the hay he cut last year, and he told me he could not give it to me, because he had spent it last winter to get us something to eat; but I do not know whether he did or not. I hope you will report these things to my grandfather, and have him stop those men from cutting the hay right off. I think if they would return me my mowing machine I could cut part of the hay on the contract, and I must have some for my ponies; I wish you would attend to it. When I started to come down here they were getting ready to cut hay on another contract for the soldiers at Fort Randall. If they would return our mowing machines we could take the contract ourselves; we have some white men and half-breeds who could assist us, but they want it all themselves. The reason I talk thus is, I think all is wrong. I know the young man who has the contract; I think he has had it two years before. When he breaks any part of the mowing machine he goes to my blacksmith shop and carpenter shop to repair it; it is all paid for out of my annuity fund. It is Hedges who has the contract. Thompson, our blacksmith, has had charge of cutting the hay on the contracts for the past two years, and is getting ready to cut it this year....

Since I made the treaty I am an American. My new agent told me the other day that the old Commissioner of Indian Affairs had been stealing part of the annuities, and that a better man had been put in his place. At this I felt good, and I put on my hat, I felt so good, my heart so big. My new agent is an entirely different man; he shows me the invoices, and I think he is a good man for us. He hired a blacksmith right off. My friend, what I am going to tell you is the truth. We only get five dollars apiece; we have only had one trader; he often makes us feel bad; he sells us goods so high it makes us cry; I think there ought to be two traders; I want two traders. I think if you come up to our agency you will laugh in the first place, and then be mad to see our storehouse in the same building with the trader's store. I want the store moved away a mile, so that it won't be so handy to our goods; I want you to have this changed. I hope my grandfather will see that the store is moved away from my warehouse, because the trader's store is under the floor where my goods are stored. I sometimes have bad dreams; I feel that there may be cracks that my goods may fall through.

I am done. Again I say, my friend, I am glad you have come to see us, and I hope will report all I have said to the Great Father, and that you will do us good. The Great Spirit knows that I have Spoken the truth.

1867

■ ## TWO MOONS (CHEYENNE) ■
UNKNOWN DATES

The Battle of the Little Bighorn, Narrated by an Indian Who Fought in It, June 25, 1876[1]

[The Black Hills region of the Dakotas was recognized as inviolable Indian land by the federal government. But the onset of a gold rush there in 1874–75 led the administration of President Ulysses S. Grant to decide that it would be easier to contrive a war against the Indians and seize the land than it would be to oust the white intruders. The campaign of 1876 was

[1]From *McClure's Magazine*, September, 1898.

commanded by Generals George Crook and Alfred Terry. General George A.
Custer and his 7th Cavalry arrived at the huge Sioux encampment in
eastern Montana, and there he hoped to achieve fame and advancement by
defeating the Indians.]

That spring [1876] I was camped on Powder River with fifty lodges of my
people—Cheyennes. The place is near what is now Fort Mc-Kenney. One
morning soldiers charged my camp. They were in command of Three Fingers
[Colonel McKenzie]. We were surprised and scattered, leaving our ponies. The
soldiers ran all our horses off. That night the soldiers slept, leaving the horses
one side; so we crept up and stole them back again, and then we went away.

We traveled far, and one day we met a big camp of Sioux at Charcoal
Butte. We camped with the Sioux, and had a good time, plenty grass, plenty
game, good water. Crazy Horse was head chief of the camp. Sitting Bull was
camped a little ways below, on the Little Missouri River.

Crazy Horse said to me, "I'm glad you are come. We are going to fight
the white man again."

The camp was already full of wounded men, women, and children.

I said to Crazy Horse, "All right. I am ready to fight. I have fought already. My people have been killed, my horses stolen; I am satisfied to fight."

[Here the old man paused a moment, and his face took on a lofty and
somber expression.]

I believed at that time the Great Spirits had made Sioux, put them there
[he drew a circle to the right], and white men and Cheyennes here [indicat-
ing two places to the left], expecting them to fight. The Great Spirits I
thought liked to see the fight; it was to them all the same like playing. So I
thought then about fighting. [As he said this, he made me feel for one
moment the power of a sardonic god whose drama was the wars of men.]

About May, when the grass was tall and the horses strong, we broke
camp and started across the country to the mouth of the Tongue River.
Then Sitting Bull and Crazy Horse and all went up the Rosebud. There we
had a big fight with General Crook, and whipped him. Many soldiers were
killed—few Indians. It was a great fight, much smoke and dust.

From there we all went over the divide, and camped in the valley of Little Horn. Everybody thought, "Now we are out of the white man's country.
He can live there, we will live here." After a few days, one morning when I
was in camp north of Sitting Bull, a Sioux messenger rode up and said, "Let
everybody paint up, cook, and get ready for a big dance."

Cheyennes then went to work to cook, cut up tobacco, and get ready.
We all thought to dance all day. We were very glad to think we were far
away from the white man.

I went to water my horses at the creek, and washed them off with cool
water, then took a swim myself. I came back to the camp afoot. When I got
near my lodge, I looked up the Little Horn towards Sitting Bull's camp. I
saw a great dust rising. It looked like a whirlwind. Soon Sioux horseman
came rushing into camp shouting: "Soldiers come! Plenty white soldiers."

I ran into my lodge, and said to my brother-in-law, "Get your horses; the white man is coming. Everybody run for horses."

Outside, far up the valley, I heard a battle cry, *Hay-ay, hay-ay!* I heard shooting, too, this way [clapping his hands very fast]. I couldn't see any Indians. Everybody was getting horses and saddles. After I had caught my horse, a Sioux warrior came again and said, "Many soldiers are coming."

Then he said to the women, "Get out of the way, we are going to have hard fight."

I said, "All right, I am ready."

I got on my horse, and rode out into my camp. I called out to the people all running about: "I am Two Moon, your chief. Don't run away. Stay here and fight. You must stay and fight the white soldiers. I shall stay even if I am to be killed."

I rode swiftly toward Siting Bull's camp. There I saw the white soldiers fighting in a line [Reno's men]. Indians covered the flat. They began to drive the soldiers all mixed up—Sioux, then soldiers, then more Sioux, and all shooting. The air was full of smoke and dust. I saw the soldiers fall back and drop into the river-bed like buffalo fleeing. They had no time to look for a crossing. The Sioux chased them up the hill, where they met more soldiers in wagons, and then messengers came saying more soldiers were going to kill the women, and the Sioux turned back. Chief Gall was there fighting, Crazy Horse also.

I then rode toward my camp, and stopped squaws from carrying off lodges. While I was sitting on my horse I saw flags come up over the hill to the east like that [he raised his finger-tips]. Then the soldiers rose all at once, all on horses, like this [he put his fingers behind each other to indicate that Custer appeared marching in columns of fours]. They formed into three bunches [squadrons] with a little ways between. Then a bugle sounded, and they all got off horses, and some soldiers led the horses back over the hill.

Then the Sioux rode up the ridge on all sides, riding very fast. The Cheyennes went up the left way. Then the shooting was quick, quick, Pop—pop—pop very fast. Some of the soldiers were down on their knees, some standing. Officers all in front. The smoke was like a great cloud, and everywhere the Sioux went the dust rose like smoke. We circled all round him—swirling like water round a stone. We shoot, we ride fast, we shoot again. Soldiers drop, and horses fall on them. Soldiers in line drop, but one man rides up and down the line—all the time shouting. He rode a sorrel horse with white face and white fore-legs. I don't know who he was. He was a brave man.

Indians keep swirling round and round, and the soldiers killed only a few. Many soldiers fell. At last all horses killed but five. Once in a while some man would break out and run toward the river, but he would fall. At last about a hundred men and five horsemen stood on the hill all bunched together. All along the bugler kept blowing his commands. He was very brave too. Then a chief was killed. I hear it was Long Hair [Custer], I don't know; and then the five horsemen and the bunch of men, may be so forty, started toward the river. The man on the sorrel horse led, them, shouting all the time. He wore a buckskin shirt, and had long black hair and mustache. He fought hard with a big knife. His men were all covered with white dust. I couldn't tell whether they were officers or not. One man all alone ran far down toward the river, then round up over the hill. I thought he was going to escape, but a Sioux fired and hit him in the head. He was the last man. He wore braid on his arms [sergeant].

All the soldiers were now killed, and the bodies were stripped. After that no one could tell which were officers. The bodies were left where they fell. We had no dance that night. We were sorrowful.

Next day four Sioux chiefs and two Cheyennes and I, Two Moon, went upon the battlefield to count the dead. One man carried a little bundle of sticks. When we came to dead men, we took a little stick and gave it to another man, so we counted the dead. There were 388. There were thirty-nine. Sioux and seven Cheyennes killed, and about a hundred wounded.

Some white soldiers were cut with knives, to make sure they were dead; and the war women had mangled some. Most of them were left just where they fell. We came to the man with the big mustache; he lay down the hills towards the river. The Indians did not take his buckskin shirt. The Sioux said, "That is a big chief. That is Long Hair," I don't know. I had never seen him. The man on the white-faced horse was the bravest man.

That day as the sun was getting low our young men came up the Little Horn riding hard. Many white soldiers were coming in a big boat, and when we looked we could see the smoke rising. I called my people together, and we hurried up the Little Horn, into Rotten Grass Valley. We camped there three days, and then rode swiftly back over our old trail to the east. Sitting Bull went back into the Rosebud and down the Yellowstone, and away to the north. I did not see him again.

1876

▪ JOHN GRASS (BLACKFOOT SIOUX) ▪
1837–1918

Indian Conditions for Treaty Renewal, October 11, 1876[1]

My friends, this day I behold you, and I behold you with a glad heart. We are going this day to renew a treaty; that is why my heart is glad. You saw me and you pray to the Great Spirit, which pleases me very much. The

[1] From Senate Executive Document No. 9, 44th Congress, 2nd Session, pp. 47–48.

Great Spirit made this earth for me and He raised me on it; you brought this to my mind and I am thankful. Our Great Father selected this commission from just and kind-hearted men. Look well at me with both eyes and listen to me with both ears. What I am looking forward to in the future I want you to remember always. The white people look for a country that pleases them; they find one, make a selection, locate themselves there, and consider that as an inheritance for their children; the Indians do the same, The different countries that the Great Spirit has made, the people inhabiting these countries, are bargaining with each other for land. You come here from the Great Father to inquire of me about my land. I will never find another land better than the one I have. I cannot look upon my land as cheap and valueless. You speak to us about a strange country. We want you to strike that out. My father had the white people for friends. Our grandfathers, our fathers, and all of our kindred were raised on the Missouri River. I told my grandchildren that I would never leave the land on the Missouri River. Red Cloud and Spotted Tail's people are not pleased to live on the Missouri River, hence you take them off to look at other countries, but we are not displeased with this country; we are pleased with the country on the Missouri River, and consequently we wish to remain here. You have come to us with the words from her other agencies. If the majority of Indians desire to remain on the Missouri River I wish the commission would decide that Red Cloud and Spotted Tail should also be brought to the Missouri River. I am going to say something that will not please you before I sign the agreement: I desire to know whether the commissioners are willing to erase that part of the propositions where you ask the Indians to go to a strange country?...

My friends, I have considered the words you have brought me, and I am ready to answer you. The chiefs you see here have all come to the same conclusion. You have brought words to the chiefs here that will bring life to their children; that will make their children live; they answer *how* [signifying their approval] to that. And now since they have ceded their country to you, they want to tell you of certain things that they shall want for their families, and people, and children in the future. What we shall need for our children to succeed in life, to instruct our children so that they will become self-supporting—the things you have spoken to us about. The affairs at this agency are allotted to a society of Christians. They are to think for our people, and to instruct our people in the way they should live. I want them to live in this country with us and instruct our children. We want wagons that are good wagons, and will last for ten years; and we want some light wagons so that can ride over the country rapidly. We want cows and bulls for breeding purposes. We want some sheep and hogs. We want mares and stallions for breeding purposes. We want mowing-machines, and large plows; we also want small plows, and cultivators, and harrows. We want yokes of heavy cattle for plowing. I want a house with at least three rooms in it. I want furniture for the house—stoves, tables and other house furniture. We have not seen the Great Father and discussed this matter with him. I wish that I could see him and talk these matters over with him. If I could see him, I think he would have a reply for me in regard to these things that I am asking for. I wish when the Great Father buys anything for my people—provisions, annuity, goods, etc.—that he would send |jrne a list of the articles purchased. I want this list to be sent to me every year, for all goods purchased. I also want a copy of this agreement left with me. Is the present President the one that has been buying goods and annuities for the Indians? Are the men that have been our agents here, from time to time, still living? The Great Father has not been respected nor obeyed; I have not been respected, I have been abused together with the Great Father. The Great Father thinks that I have received all that has been purchased for me, but that which I have received is the smallest part of what has been provided for us. Notwithstanding that I did not receive them, they are mine still; they were all for me, and are still mine, and I expect to get them, and shall look for them. I want the Great Father to look these things up, and make the men that have made away with them pay for them. These things have been made away with, and I am an Indian, and am not able to tell the Great Father. I meet these just men, and hope you will tell a straight story to the Great Father. The things that would enable me to become self-supporting on this river, this day you remind me of them, but they are all gone. This day I want to learn something, to learn a lesson, to learn how to do something. You have talked to me well, spoken to me well, and I am going to state in what way I can learn something to-day. You are writing here [referring to the stenographer], and you have a paper underneath the one upon which you are writing that is not written on. In times past we used to know such things as that; we have seen business done the same way in past times—a blank paper underneath the? one we sign. I wish the Great Father would select a physician, a man who is capable of treating sick Indians, and who can cure them, and send him to us. I want a sawyer, a blacksmith, and a man that can work in tin to make pans, kettles, cups, etc., I also wants an expert carpenter. I want a trader that will trade with us at the same prices that he trades with the whites, one that will not charges an Indian more than he does a white man. I have a trader here, but he treats me badly. He has a bad way of trading. Tell the Greats Father to take him away and send a man in his place who is acquainted with Indians and with Indian ways, a man who can live with the Indians and be their friend. I wish they would send me three or four traders. We want you to consider our half-breeds and the white men who are married to our women as a part of our people.

1876

■ SITTING BULL (HUNKPAPA SIOUX) ■
1831–1890

Keeping Treaties[1]

What treaty that the whites have kept has the red man broken? Not one.
What treaty that the whites ever made with us red men have they kept?
Not one. When I was a boy the Sioux owned the world. The sun rose and set
in their lands. They sent 10,000 horsemen to battle. Where are the warriors
to-day? Who slew them? Where are our lands? Who owns them? What white
man can say I ever stole his lands or a penny of his money? Yet they say I
am a thief. What white woman, however lonely, was ever when a captive
insulted by me? Yet they say I am a bad Indian. What white man has ever
seen me drunk? Who has ever come to me hungry and gone unfed? Who
has ever seen me beat my wives or abuse my children? What law have I broken? Is it wrong for me to love my own? Is it wicked in me because my skin
is red; because I am a Sioux; because I was born where my fathers lived;
because I would die for my people and my country?

1891

■ RED CLOUD (OGALA SIOUX) ■
1822–1908

Reasons for the Trouble between the Indians and the
Government During the Excitement of the Ghost Dance
Excitement of 1890[1']

Everybody seems to think that the belief in the coming of the Messiah has
caused all the trouble. This is a mistake. I will tell you the cause.

When we first made treaties with the Government, this was our position: Our old life and our old customs were about to end; the game upon
which we lived was disappearing; the whites were closing around us, and
nothing remained for us but to adopt their ways and have the same rights
with them if we wished to save ourselves. The Government promised us all

---

[1]From W. Fletcher Johnson, *Life of Sitting Bull*
(1891), p. 201.

[1']From W. Fletcher Jones, *Life of Sitting Bull*
(1891). For background on the Ghost Dance
religion and the massacre at Wounded Knee,
see the introduction to the "Ghost Dance
Songs" and Charles Eastman, "The Ghost
Dance War," both in this section.

the means necessary make our living out of our land, and to instruct us how to do it, and abundant food to support us until we could take care of ourselves. We looked forward with hope to the time when we could be as independent as the whites, and have a voice in the Government.

The officers of the army could have helped us better than any others, but we were not left to them. An Indian Department was made, with a large number of agents and other officials drawing large salaries, and these men were supposed to teach us the ways of the whites. Then came the beginning of trouble. These men took care of themselves but not of us. It was made very hard for us to deal with the Government except through them. It seems to me that they thought they could make more by keeping us back than by helping us forward. We did not get the means to work our land. The few things given were given in such a way as to do us little or no good. Our rations began to be reduced. Some said that we were lazy and wanted to live on rations and not to work. That is false. How does any man of sense suppose that so great a number of people could get to work at once, unless they were at once supplied with means to work, and instructors enough to teach them how to use them?

Remember that even our little ponies were taken away under the promise that they would be replaced by oxen and large horses and that it was long before we saw any, and then we got very few. We tried, even with the means we had, but on one pretext or another we were shifted from place to place or were told that such a transfer was coming. Great efforts were made to break up our customs, but nothing was done to introduce the customs of the whites. Everything was done to break the power of the real chiefs who really wished their people to improve, and little men, so-called chiefs, were made to act as disturbers and agitators. Spotted Tail wanted the ways of the whites, and a cowardly assassin was found to remove him. This was charged upon the Indians, because an Indian did it, but who set on the Indian?

I was abused and slandered, to weaken my influence for good and make me seem like one who did not want to advance. This was done by the men paid by the Government to teach us the ways of the whites. I have visited many other tribes, and find that the same things were done among them. All was done to discourage and nothing to encourage. I saw the men paid by the Government to help us all very busy making money for themselves, but doing nothing for us.

Now, don't you suppose we saw all this? Of course we did, but what could we do? We were prisoners, not in the hands of the army, but in the hands of robbers. Where was the army? Set by the Government to watch us, but having no voice in setting thing right, so that they would not need to watch us. They could not speak for us, though we wished it very much. Those who held us pretended to be very anxious about our welfare, and said our condition was a great mystery. We tried to speak and clear up this mystery, but were laughed at and treated as children. So things went on from year to year. Other treaties were made, and it was all the same. Rations were further reduced, and we were starving, sufficient food not given us, and no means to get food from the land were provided. Rations were still further reduced. A family got for two weeks what was not enough for one week.

What did we eat when that was gone? The people were desperate from starvation—they had no hope. They did not think of fighting. What good would it do? They might die like men, but what would the women and children do? Some say they saw the son of God. All did not see Him. I did not see Him. If He had come He would do some great thing as He did before. We doubted it, because we saw neither Him nor His works. Then Gen. Crook came. His words sounded well; but how could we know that a new treaty would be kept any better than the old one? For that reason we did not care to sign. He promised to see that his promises would be kept. He, at least, had never lied to us. His words gave the people hope. They signed. They hoped. He died. Their hope died with him. Despair came again. The people were counted, and wrongly counted. Our rations were again reduced. The white men seized on the land we sold them through Gen. Crook, but our pay was as distant as ever. The man who counted us told all over that we were feasting and wasting food. Where did he see this?

How can we eat or waste what we have not? We felt that we were mocked in our misery. We had no newspapers, and no one to speak for us. We had no redress. Our rations were again reduced. You who eat three times each day, and see your children well and happy around you, can't understand what starving Indians feel. We were faint with hunger and maddened by despair. We held our dying children, and felt their little bodies tremble as their souls went out and left only a dead weight in our hands. They were not very heavy, but we ourselves were very faint, and the dead weighed us down. There was no hope on earth, and God seemed to have forgotten us. Some one had again been talking of the Son of God, and said He had come. The people did not know; they did not care. They snatched at the hope. They screamed like crazy men to Him for mercy. They caught at the promises they heard He had made.

The white men were frightened, and called for soldiers. We had begged for life, and the white men thought we wanted theirs. We heard that soldiers were coming. We did not fear. We hoped that he could tell them our troubles and get help. A white man said the Soldiers meant to kill us. We did not believe it, but some were frightened and ran away to the Bad Lands. The soldiers came. They said: "Don't be afraid; we come to make peace, and not war." It was true. They brought us food, and did not threaten us. If the Messiah has really come, it must be in this way. The people prayed for life, and the army brought it. The Black Robe, Father Jule, went to the Bad Lands and brought in some Indians to talk to Gen. Brooke. The General was very kind to them, and quieted their fears, and was a real friend. He sent out Indians to call in the other Indians from the Bad Lands. I sent all my horses and all my young men to help Gen. Brooke save the Indians. Am I not right when I say that he will know how to settle this trouble? He has settled it.

The Indian Department called for soldiers to shoot down the Indians whom it had starved into despair. Gen. Brooke said, "No, what have they done? They are dying. They must live." He brought us food. He gave us hope. I trust to him now to see that we will be well treated. I hope that the despair that he has driven away will never return again. If the army had been with us from the first there never would have been any trouble. The army will, I hope, keep us safe and help us to become as independent as the whites.

[What do you think of the killing of Sitting Bull?]

Sitting Bull was nothing but what the white men made him. He was a conceited man who never did anything great, but wanted to get into notice, and white men who had something to make by it, encouraged him and used him. When they had made him as great as they could they killed him to get a name by it. The fight at his arrest would have been made for any one arrested in the same way. If he was a little man, he was a man, and should not have been murdered uselessly. What is worse, many good men were killed also. The soldiers came in time to prevent more murders, but too late to save all. If the army had wanted to arrest him they knew how to do it, and never would have done it in that way. You see how they are doing here. The agent does not interfere with the army, and the army saves lives and does not do anything foolish. No Indian wants to fight; they want to eat, and work, and live; and as the soldiers are peace-makers there will be no trouble here.

The Indian Department has almost destroyed us. Save us from it. Let the army take charge of us. We know it can help us. Let it manage our affairs in its own way. If this can be done I will think that all this late trouble has been only a storm that broke the clouds. Let the sun shine on us again.

1891

■ TURNING HAWK, CAPTAIN SWORD, SPOTTED ■ HORSE, AND AMERICAN HORSE (SIOUX)
UNKNOWN DATES

The Massacre at Wounded Knee, South Dakota, on December 29, 1890[1]

TURNING HAWK, Pine Ridge (Mr Cook, interpreter). Mr Commissioner, my purpose to-day is to tell you what I know of the condition of affairs at the agency where I live. A certain falsehood came to our agency from the west which had the effect of a fire upon the Indians, and when this certain fire came upon our people those who had farsightedness and could see into the

[1]From *Fourteenth Annual Report of the Bureau of American Ethnology* (1896), Part 2, pp. 884–886.

matter made up their minds to stand up against it and fight it. The reason we took this hostile attitude to this fire was because we believed that you yourself would not be in favor of this particular mischief-making thing; but just as we expected, the people in authority did not like this thing and we were quietly told that we must give up or have nothing to do with this certain movement. Though this is the advice from our good friends in the east, there were, of course, many silly young men who were longing to become identified with the movement, although they knew that there was nothing absolutely bad, nor did they know there was anything absolutely good, in connection with the movement.

In the course of time we heard that the soldiers were moving toward the scene of trouble. After awhile some of the soldiers finally reached our place and we heard that a number of them also reached our friends at Rosebud. Of course, when a large body of soldiers is moving toward a certain direction they inspire a more or less amount of awe, and it is natural that the women and children who see this large moving mass are made afraid of it and be put in a condition to make them run away. At first we thought that Pine Ridge and Rosebud were the only two agencies where soldiers were sent, but finally we heard that the other agencies fared likewise. We heard and saw that about half our friends at Rosebud agency, from fear at seeing the soldiers, began the move of running away from their agency toward ours (Pine Ridge), and when they had gotten inside of our reservation they there learned that right ahead of them at our agency was another large crowd of soldiers, and while the soldiers were there, there was constantly a great deal of false rumor flying back and forth. The special rumor I have in mind is the threat that the soldiers had come there to disarm the Indians entirely and to take away all their horses from them. That was the oft-repeated story.

So constantly repeated was this story that our friends from Rosebud, instead of going to Pine Ridge, the place of their destination, veered off and went to some other direction toward the "Bad Lands." We did not know definitely how many, but understood there were 300 lodges of them, about 1,700 people. Eagle Pipe, Turning Bear, High Hawk, Short Bull, Lance, No Flesh, Pine Bird, Crow Dog, Two Strike, and White Horse were the leaders.

Well, the people after veering off in this way, many of them who believe in peace and order at our agency, were very anxious that some influence should be brought upon these people. In addition to our love of peace we remembered that many of these people were related to us by blood. So we sent out peace commissioners to the people who were thus running away from their agency.

I understood at the time that they were simply going away from fear because of so many soldiers. So constant was the word of these good men from Pine Ridge agency that finally they succeeded in getting away half of the party from Rosebud, from the place where they took refuge, and finally were brought to the agency at Pine Ridge. Young-Man-Afraid-of-his-Horses, Little Wound, Fast Thunder, Louis Shangreau, John Grass, Jack Red Cloud, and myself were some of these peacemakers.

The remnant of the party from Rosebud not taken to the agency finally reached the wilds of the Bad Lands. Seeing that we had succeeded so well, once more we sent to the same party in the Bad Lands and succeeded in bringing these very Indians out of the depths of the Bad Lands and were being brought toward the agency. When we were about a day's journey from our agency we heard that a certain party of Indians (Big Foot's band) from the Cheyenne River agency was coming toward Pine Ridge in flight.

CAPTAIN SWORD. Those who actually went off of the Cheyenne River agency probably number 303, and there were a few from the Standing Rock reserve with them, but as to their number I do not know. There were a number of Ogalallas, old men and several school boys, coming back with that very same party, and one of the very seriously wounded boys was a member of the Ogalalla boarding school at Pine Ridge agency. He was not on the warpath, but was simply returning home to his agency and to his school after a summer visit to relatives on the Cheyenne river.

TURNING HAWK. When we heard that these people were coming toward our agency we also heard this. These people were coming toward Pine Ridge agency, and when they were almost on the agency they were met by the soldiers and surrounded and finally taken to the Wounded Knee creek, and there at a given time their guns were demanded. When they had delivered them up, the men were separated from their families, from their tipis, and taken to a certain spot. When the guns were thus taken and the men thus separated, there was a crazy man, a young man of very bad influence and in fact a nobody, among that bunch of Indians fired his gun, and of course the firing of a gun must have been the breaking of a military rule of some sort, because immediately the soldiers returned fire and indiscriminate killing followed.

SPOTTED HORSE. This man shot an officer in the army; the first shot killed this officer. I was a voluntary scout at that encounter and I saw exactly what was done, and that was what I noticed; that the first shot killed an officer. As soon as this shot was fired the Indians immediately began drawing their knives, and they were exhorted from all sides to desist, but this was not obeyed. Consequently the firing began immediately on the part of the soldiers.

TURNING HAWK. All the men who were in a bunch were killed right there, and those who escaped that first fire got into the ravine, and as they went along up the ravine for a long distance they were pursued on both sides by the soldiers and shot down, as the dead bodies showed afterwards. The women were standing off at a different place from where the men were stationed, and when the firing began, those of the men who escaped the first onslaught went in one direction up the ravine, and then the women, who were bunched together at another place, went entirely in a different direction through an open field, and the women fared the same fate as the men who went up the deep ravine.

AMERICAN HORSE. The men were separated, as has already been said, from the women, and they were surrounded by the soldiers. Then came next the village of the Indians and that was entirely surrounded by the soldiers also. When the firing began, of course the people who were standing immediately around the young man who fired the first shot were killed right together, and then they turned their guns, Hotchkiss guns, etc., upon the women who were in the lodges standing there under a flag of truce, and of course as soon as they were fired upon they fled, the men fleeing in one direction and the women running in two different directions. So that there were three general directions in which they took flight. There was a women with an infant in her arms who was killed as she almost touched the flag of truce, and the women and children of course were strewn all along the circular village until they were dispatched. Right near the flag of truce a mother was shot down with her infant; the child not knowing that its mother was dead was still nursing, and that especially was a very sad sight. The women as they were fleeing with their babes were killed together, shot right through, and the women who were very heavy with child were also killed. All the Indians fled in these three directions, and after most all of them had been killed a cry was made that all those who were not killed or wounded should come forth and they would be safe. Little boys who were not wounded came out of their places of refuge, and as soon as they came in sight a number of soldiers surrounded them and butchered them there.

Of course we all feel very sad about this affair. I stood very loyal to the government all through those troublesome days, and believing so much in the government and being so loyal to it, my disappointment was very strong, and I have come to Washington with a very great blame on my heart. Of course it would have been all right if only the men were killed; we would feel almost grateful for it. But the fact of the killing of the women, and more especially the killing of the young boys and girls who are to go to make up the future strength of the Indian people, is the saddest part of the whole affair and we feel it very sorely.

I was not there at the time before the burial of the bodies, but I did go there with some of the police and the Indian doctor and a great many of the people, men from the agency, and we went through the battlefield and saw where the bodies were from the track of the blood.

TURNING HAWK. I had just reached the point where I said that the women were killed. We heard, besides the killing of the men, of the onslaught also made upon the women and children, and they were treated as roughly and indiscriminately as the men and boys were.

Of course this affair brought a great deal of distress upon all the people, but especially upon the minds of those who stood loyal to the government and who did all that they were able to do in the matter of bringing about peace. They especially have suffered much distress and are very much hurt at heart. These peacemakers continued on in their good work, but there were a great many fickle young men who were ready to be moved by the change in the events there, and consequently, in spite of the great fire that was brought upon all, they were ready to assume any hostile attitude. These young men got themselves in readiness and went in the direction of the scene of battle so they might be of service there. They got there and finally exchanged shots with the soldiers. This party of young men was made up from Rosebud, Ogalalla (Pine

Ridge), and members of any other agencies that happened to be there at the time. While this was going on in the neighborhood of Wounded Knee—the Indians and soldiers exchanging shots—the agency, our home, was also fired into by the Indians. Matters went on in this strain until the evening came on, and then the Indians went off down by White Clay creek. When the agency was fired upon by the Indians from the hillside, of course the shots were returned by the Indian police who were guarding the agency buildings.

Although fighting seemed to have been in the air, yet those who believed in peace were still constant at their work. Young-Man-Afraid-of-his-Horses, who had been on a visit to some other agency in the north or northwest, returned, and immediately went out to the people living about White Clay creek, on the border of; the Bad Lands, and brought his people out. He succeeded in obtaining the consent of the people to come out of their place of refuge and return to the agency. Thus the remaining portion of the Indians who started from Rosebud were brought back into the agency. Mr. Commissioner, during the days of the great whirlwind out there, those good men tried to hold up a counteracting power, land that was "Peace," We have now come to realize that peace has prevailed and won the day. While we were engaged in bringing about peace our property was left behind, of course, and most of us have lost everything, even down to the matter of guns with which to kill ducks, rabbits, etc, shotguns, and guns of that order. When Young-Man-Afraid brought the people in and their guns were asked for, both men who were called hostile and men who stood loyal to the government delivered up their guns.

1896

GHOST DANCE SONGS

In 1871 Congress terminated the U.S. policy of making treaties with Native peoples as sovereign nations, thus making the tribes subject to the will of Congress and the administrative rulings of the president. The pace of Anglo-American expansion and expropriation of Native lands quickened, culminating within a decade in the destruction of the vast buffalo herds and the forcible confinement of many tribes to unproductive reservation land, where starvation threatened their lives and acculturation threatened their traditional cultures with extinction. The response of many Native people to threats to their way of life was a powerful apocalyptic dream of a future time when enemies would be overthrown and the world returned to the divine order established in the beginning.

The Ghost Dance, the most dramatic and widespread manifestation of this phenomenon, began when the Paiute prophet Wovoka experienced such a vision. He prophesied that the crow would bring whirlwinds and earthquakes to cleanse the earth and destroy the white invaders, and that the Native dead (the "ghosts") and the slaughtered buffalo would return to reclaim the land. The vision and the trance-inducing round dance and songs accompanying it spread like wildfire among reservation communities from California to the Dakotas.

Among the Sioux, facing a desperate struggle for both physical and cultural survival, the Ghost Dance became especially powerful, catching up men like Sitting Bull in its fervor and persuading others of their invulnerability to the white man's bullets. Fear swept over whites living on and near the Pine Ridge Reservation in South Dakota, provoking confrontations. In 1890, when Sitting Bull was killed while being arrested, others like Big Foot and his band saw no future and left the reservation. They made it into the Dakota Badlands as far as a place called Wounded Knee, where members of the U.S. cavalry armed with machine guns surrounded and searched them for weapons. A few shots were heard, then many from the machine guns. When silence settled, around 200 Native American men, women, and children were dead, and so was the hope awakened by Wovoka's dream. The Ghost Dance songs that follow should be read with the account of Charles Eastman, a Dakota trained in medicine, who returned to the Pine Ridge Reservation in time to witness the calamity at Wounded Knee.

Andrew O. Wiget
New Mexico State University

PRIMARY SOURCES

James Mooney, *The Ghost Dance Religion and Sioux Outbreak of 1890.* Fourteenth Annual Report of the Bureau of American Ethnology, Pt. 2. Washington: GPO, 1893.

Ghost Dance Songs

I

My children,[1] when at first I liked the whites,
My children, when at first I liked the whites,
I gave them fruits,
I gave them fruits.

II

Father, have pity on me,   5
Father, have pity on me;
I am crying for thirst,
I am crying for thirst;
All is gone—I have nothing to eat.
All is gone—I have nothing to eat.   10

---

[1]The songs are sung as a dialogue, with the Sun ("Our Father") addressing the Indians ("my children").

III

My son, let me grasp your hand,
My son, let me grasp your hand,
Says the father,
Says the father.
You shall live,   15
You shall live,
Says the father,
Says the father.
I bring you a pipe,[2]
I bring you a pipe,   20
Says the father,
Says the father.
By means of it you shall live,
By means of it you shall live,
Says the father,   25
Says the father.

IV

My children, my children,
I take pity on those who have been taught,
I take pity on those who have been taught,
Because they push on hard,   30
Because they push on hard.
Says our father,
Says our father.

V

The whole world is coming,
A nation is coming, a nation is coming,   35
The Eagle has brought the message to the tribe.
The father says so, the father says so.
Over the whole earth they are coming.
The buffalo are coming, the buffalo are coming.
The Crow has brought the message to his tribe,   40
The father says so, the father says so.

---

[2]*I.e.,* "a vision." The pipe was smoked to put one in prayerful contact with the sacred. Here "a pipe" functions as symbol for the vision that smoking the pipe would induce.

VI

The spirit host is advancing, they say,
The spirit host is advancing, they say,
They are coming with the buffalo, they say,
They are coming with the buffalo, they say.   45
They are coming with the new earth, they say,
They are coming with the new earth, they say.

VII

He' yoho' ho! He' yoho' ho![3]
The yellow-hide, the white skin
I have now put him aside—   50
I have now put him aside—
I have no more sympathy with him,
I have no more sympathy with him,
He' yoho' ho! he' yoho' ho!

VIII

I' yehe! my children—*Uhi 'yeye 'heye!*   55
I' yehe! my children—*Uhi 'yeye 'heye!*
I' yehe! we have rendered them desolate—*Eye' ae 'yuhe' yu!*
I' yehe! we have rendered them desolate—*Eye' ae 'yuhe' yu!*
The whites are crazy—*Ahe 'yuhe' yu!*

                                                      1893

■ ## CHARLES ALEXANDER EASTMAN (SIOUX) ■
1858–1939

What's in a name? In the case of Charles Eastman, a complicated story of cross
cultural relations. Born in 1858, he was given the name Hakadah ("Pitiful Last"),
because his mother soon died. Raised in the culture of the Santee Sioux, at the
age of four he was given a new name, Ohiyesa ("The Winner"), after his village
won a game of lacrosse. Eastman was in more ways than one a champion, but
he would also face more than his share of losses.

---

[3]The words are vocables, with no referential
significance.

Tensions between encroaching whites and Native people in Minnesota were mounting, and the failure of the U.S. government to adhere to its treaty obligations created a desperate situation. In 1862 some Sioux rebelled, killing a number of settlers. When the U.S. Army put down the insurrection, some three hundred Sioux were imprisoned and sentenced to die—including Eastman's father, Many Lightnings. His uncle and grandmother escaped with other Santee into the "deep woods" of Canada. His uncle gave Ohiyesa a warrior's education, preparing him to take revenge.

In 1873, however, Ohiyesa's father reappeared, as if back from the dead. Abraham Lincoln had commuted his sentence to a term in prison, where he had converted to Christianity. The elder Eastman now read the Bible and took up the plow, following a model that reformers had advocated for hunting-and-gathering Natives. To symbolize the change, he adopted the last name of his deceased wife Mary Eastman, whose father was a white soldier. He expected his son to follow in his footsteps along this new path, and thus Ohiyesa journeyed with him to his farm in South Dakota and was there christened Charles Eastman.

Eastman began his cultural reeducation by going to a nearby missionary-run school, where he soon excelled. Reversing the westward route of manifest destiny, he then traveled ever eastward from school to school—Beloit in Wisconsin, Knox in Illinois, Dartmouth in New Hampshire, and finally Boston University, where he earned a medical degree in 1890. He was then ready to go back to the West to serve his people at the Pine Ridge Agency in South Dakota, where he became known as the "white doctor who is an Indian."

In 1890 the Ghost Dance religion was spreading among the Sioux. Following the vision of the prophet Wovoka, some Sioux believed that if the Ghost Dance was performed, whites would vanish, the buffalo would return, and Native land, life, and culture would be restored. Attempting to quell this millenarian movement, the army ended up massacring approximately 200 men, women, and children at Wounded Knee. Although Eastman had adopted much of what the white world offered, the sight of so many brutalized bodies shattered the idea that white society represented only light and progress.

Many reformers of his day clung to this idea and tried to convince both Native people and whites that Native cultures were inferior and backward. They espoused a "Kill the Indian and save the man" philosophy, believing that the only way Natives could survive in modern America was to wash their hands of the old ways and completely assimilate. Reformers often held up educated Native people like Eastman as confirmation of their views. While Eastman's life proved that Native people could succeed on the white man's terms, he himself insisted that Native cultures were valuable in their own right and, further, that they had much to offer modern America. While the missionaries believed that Christianity would civilize the "savage," Eastman held that Native people could educate white Americans on how to become truly civilized and spiritual. His motto could have been "Save the Indian and save the American."

Interestingly, he found a receptive audience among white Americans. As the country stepped up the pace of industrialization, many people became unsettled in the increasingly urbanized landscape. Seeking a kind of therapy for the anxieties of the machine age, many turned to Native peoples to try to reconnect with nature and recover a soul seemingly being exhausted by smoke-stack America.

Much of what Eastman wrote responded to this desire. His wife, Elaine Goodale, a poet and writer whom he had met at Pine Ridge in 1890 when she was serving as a supervisor of Native education, encouraged his literary efforts. In 1902, in *Indian Boyhood*, he told the story of the years before his introduction to white education. With the editorial help of his wife he wrote several other popular works, becoming a leading light in the Boy Scout movement and lecturing widely. In books such as *The Soul of an Indian* (1911) and his autobiographical *From Deep Woods to Civilization* (1916), Eastman acted as a spokesperson, explaining Native cultures to white America. In the process of explaining, though, he was also creating, for, as he well knew, there was no single Native culture. Eastman was helping forge a pan-Native identity that could both command the respect of whites and offer a vantage point from which to criticize the materialism and other drawbacks of mainstream American culture. The traditional ways and wisdom he celebrated were thus reinvented for a new audience, a new time, and a new purpose.

Eastman's legacy is perhaps best illustrated by the work he did between 1903 and 1909 to standardize the family names of the Sioux. This project involved more than simple translation from Lakota into English, because the Sioux followed a different cultural logic in their naming than did the dominant society. Eastman had to negotiate between two cultures in order to create a synthesis that was somehow true to both sides. This was the sort of challenge Eastman faced his whole life, and because he met this particular one, his people gave him a new and most appropriate appellation: Name Giver. Through his writing and other work, Eastman made a name both for himself and for Native peoples at a time when they otherwise might have been deleted from the rolls of the nation.

Douglas C. Sackman
University of Puget Sound

PRIMARY WORKS

Indian Boyhood, 1902; *Red Hunters and the Animal People*, 1904; *Old Indian Days*, 1907; *Wigwam Evenings* (with Elaine Goodale Eastman), 1909; *The Soul of the Indian*, 1911; *Indian Child Life*, 1913; *Indian Scout Talks*, 1914; *The Indian To-Day*, 1915; *From the Deep Woods to Civilization*, 1916; *Indian Heroes and Great Chieftains*, 1918.

from **The Soul of the Indian**

I. The Great Mystery[1]

The original attitude of the American Indian toward the Eternal, the "Great Mystery" that surrounds and embraces us, was as simple as it was exalted.

---

[1]In subsequent chapters, Eastman describes the family's role in religious training, the social reinforcement of religious views through ritual and ceremony, the nurturing of morality in Indian society, the role of oral tradition in religion, and Indian concepts regarding the spirit world. [All footnotes by Daniel F. Littlefield, Jr.]

To him it was the supreme conception, bringing with it the fullest measure of joy and satisfaction possible in this life.

The worship of the "Great Mystery" was silent, solitary, free from all self-seeking. It was silent, because all speech is of necessity feeble and imperfect; therefore the souls of my ancestors ascended to God in wordless adoration. It was solitary, because they believed that He is nearer to us in solitude, and there were no priests authorized to come between a man and his Maker. None might exhort or confess or in any way meddle with the religious experience of another. Among us all men were created sons of God and stood erect, as conscious of their divinity. Our faith might not be formulated in creeds, nor forced upon any who were unwilling to receive it; hence there was no preaching, proselyting, nor persecution, neither were there any scoffers or atheists.

There were no temples or shrines among us save those of nature. Being a natural man, the Indian was intensely poetical. He would deem it sacrilege to build a house for Him who may be met face to face in the mysterious, shadowy aisles of the primeval forest, or on the sunlit bosom of virgin prairies, upon dizzy spires and pinnacles of naked rock, and yonder in the jeweled vault of the night sky! He who en-robes Himself in filmy veils of cloud, there on the rim of the visible world where our Great-Grandfather Sun kindles his evening camp-fire, He who rides upon the rigorous wind of the north, or breathes forth His spirit upon aromatic southern airs, whose war-canoe is launched upon majestic rivers and inland seas—He needs no lesser cathedral!

That solitary communion with the Unseen which was the highest expression of our religious life is partly described in the word *hambeday*, literally "mysterious feeling," which has been variously translated "fasting" and "dreaming." It may better be interpreted as "consciousness of the divine."

The first *hambeday*, or religious retreat, marked an epoch in the life of the youth, which may be compared to that of confirmation or conversion in Christian experience. Having first prepared himself by means of the purifying vapor-bath, and cast off as far as possible all human or fleshly influences, the young man sought out the noblest height, the most commanding summit in all the surrounding region. Knowing that God sets no value upon material things, he took with him no offerings or sacrifices other than symbolic objects, such as paints and tobacco. Wishing to appear before Him in all humility, he wore no clothing save his moccasins and breech-clout. At the solemn hour of sunrise or sunset he took up his position, overlooking the glories of earth and facing the "Great Mystery," and there he remained, naked, erect, silent, and motionless, exposed to the elements and forces of His arming, for a night and a day to two days and nights, but rarely longer. Sometimes he would chant a hymn without words, or offer the ceremonial "filled pipe." In this holy trance or ecstasy the Indian mystic found his highest happiness and the motive power of his existence.

When he returned to the camp, he must remain at a distance until he had again entered the vapor-bath and prepared himself for intercourse with his fellows. Of the vision or sign vouchsafed to him he did not speak, unless it had included some commission which must be publicly fulfilled. Sometimes an old man, standing upon the brink of eternity, might reveal to a chosen few the oracle of his long-past youth.

The native American has been generally despised by his white conquerors for his poverty and simplicity. They forget, perhaps, that his religion forbade the accumulation of wealth and the enjoyment of luxury. To him, as to other single-minded men in every age and race, from Diogenes to the brothers of Saint Francis, from the Montanists to the Shakers,[2] the love of possessions has appeared a snare, and the burdens of a complex society a source of needless peril and temptation. Furthermore, it was the rule of his life to share the fruits of his skill and success with his less fortunate brothers. Thus he kept his spirit free from the clog of pride, cupidity, or envy, and carried out, as he believed, the divine decree—a matter profoundly important to him.

It was not, then, wholly from ignorance or improvidence that he failed to establish permanent towns and to develop a material civilization. To the untutored sage, the concentration of population was the prolific mother of all evils, moral no less than physical. He argued that food is good, while surfeit kills; that love is good, but lust destroys; and not less dreaded than the pestilence following upon crowded and unsanitary dwellings was the loss of spiritual power inseparable from too close contact with one's fellow-men. All who have lived much out of doors know that there is a magnetic and nervous force that accumulates in solitude and that is quickly dissipated by life in a crowd; and even his enemies have recognized the fact that for a certain innate power and self-poise, wholly independent of circumstances, the American Indian is unsurpassed among men.

The red man divided mind into two parts,—the spiritual mind and the physical mind. The first is pure spirit, concerned only with the essence of things, and it was this he sought to strengthen by spiritual prayer, during which the body is subdued by fasting and hardship. In this type of prayer there was no beseeching of favor or help. All matters of personal or selfish concern, as success in hunting or warfare, relief from sickness, or the sparing of a beloved life, were definitely relegated to the plane of the lower or material mind, and all ceremonies, charms, or incantations designed to

---

[2]Diogenes of Sinope (c. 400–c. 325 B.C.), as an exile in Athens, lived in poverty and believed that happiness resulted from satisfaction of one's natural needs as easily and cheaply as possible and that any natural act was decent and honorable. The doctrine of poverty espoused by St. Francis of Assisi was practiced by the Franciscan friars he founded in 1209. Montanism, based on the apocalyptic teachings of Montanus of Phrygia (who lived sometime in the second century), was characterized by asceticism, zeal, and anti-institutionalism in the Church. Shakers grew out of the Quaker revival in England in 1747. In America, after 1774, they formed communal societies in which property was held in common.

secure a benefit or to avert a danger, were recognized as emanating from the physical self.

The rites of this physical worship, again, were wholly symbolic, and the Indian no more worshiped the Sun than the Christian adores the Cross. The Sun and the Earth, by an obvious parable, holding scarcely more of poetic metaphor than of scientific truth, were in his view the parents of all organic life. From the Sun, as the universal father, proceeds the quickening principle in nature, and in the patient and fruitful womb of our mother, the Earth, are hidden embryos of plants and men. Therefore our reverence and love for them was really an imaginative extension of our love for our immediate parents, and with this sentiment of filial piety was joined a willingness to appeal to them, as to a father, for such good gifts as we may desire. This is the material or physical prayer.

The elements and majestic forces in nature, Lightning, Wind, Water, Fire, and Frost, were regarded with awe as spiritual powers, but always secondary and intermediate in character. We believed that the spirit pervades all creation and that every creature possesses a soul in some degree, though not necessarily a soul conscious of itself. The tree, the waterfall, the grizzly bear, each is an embodied Force, and as such an object of reverence.

The Indian loved to come into sympathy and spiritual communion with his brothers of the animal kingdom, whose inarticulate souls had for him something of the sinless purity that we attribute to the innocent and irresponsible child. He had faith in their instincts, as in a mysterious wisdom given from above; and while he humbly accepted the supposedly voluntary sacrifice of their bodies to preserve his own, he paid homage to their spirits in prescribed prayers and offerings.

In every religion there is an element of the supernatural, varying with the influence of pure reason over its devotees. The Indian was a logical and clear thinker upon matters within the scope of his understanding, but he had not yet charted the vast field of nature or expressed her wonders in terms of science. With his limited knowledge of cause and effect, he saw miracles on every hand,—the miracle of life in seed and egg, the miracle of death in lightning flash and in the swelling deep! Nothing of the marvelous could astonish him; as that a beast should speak, or the sun stand still. The virgin birth would appear scarcely more miraculous than is the birth of every child that comes into the world, or the miracle of the loaves and fishes excite more wonder than the harvest that springs from a single ear of corn.

Who may condemn his superstition? Surely not the devout Catholic, or even Protestant missionary, who teaches Bible miracles as literal fact! The logical man must either deny all miracles or none, and our American Indian myths and hero stories are perhaps, in themselves, quite as credible as those of the Hebrews of old. If we are of the modern type of mind, that sees in natural law a majesty and grandeur far more impressive than any solitary infraction of it could possibly be, let us not forget that, after all, science has not explained everything. We have still to face the ultimate miracle,—the origin and principle of life! Here is the supreme mystery that is the essence of worship, without which there can be no religion, and in the presence of this mystery our attitude cannot be very unlike that of the natural philosopher, who beholds with awe the Divine in all creation.

It is simple truth that the Indian did not, so long as his native philosophy held sway over his mind, either envy or desire to imitate the splendid achievements of the white man. In his own thought he rose superior to them! He scorned them, even as a lofty spirit absorbed in its stern task rejects the soft beds, the luxurious food, the pleasure-worshiping dalliance of a rich neighbor. It was clear to him that virtue and happiness are independent of these things, if not incompatible with them.

There was undoubtedly much in primitive Christianity to appeal to this man, and Jesus' hard sayings to the rich and about the rich would have been entirely comprehensible to him. Yet the religion that is preached in our churches and practiced by our congregations, with its element of display and self-aggrandizement, its active proselytism, and its open contempt of all religions but its own, was for a long time extremely repellent. To his simple mind, the professionalism of the pulpit, the paid exhorter, the moneyed church, was an unspiritual and unedifying thing, and it was not until his spirit was broken and his moral and physical constitution undermined by trade, conquest, and strong drink, that Christian missionaries obtained any real hold upon him. Strange as it may seem, it is true that the proud pagan in his secret soul despised the good men who came to convert and to enlighten him!

Nor were its publicity and its Phariseeism the only elements in the alien religion that offended the red man. To him, it appeared shocking and almost incredible that there were among this people who claimed superiority many irreligious, who did not even pretend to profess the national faith. Not only did they not profess it, but they stooped so low as to insult their God with profane and sacrilegious speech! In our own tongue His name was not spoken aloud, even with utmost reverence, much less lightly or irreverently.

More than this, even in those white men who professed religion we found much inconsistency of conduct. They spoke much of spiritual things, while seeking only the material. They bought and sold everything: time, labor, personal independence, the love of woman, and even the ministrations of their holy faith! The lust for money, power, and conquest so characteristic of the Anglo-Saxon race did not escape moral condemnation at the hands of his untutored judge, nor did he fail to contrast this conspicuous trait of the dominant race with the spirit of the meek and lowly Jesus.

He might in time come to recognize that the drunkards and licentious among white men, with whom he too frequently came in contact, were condemned by the white man's religion as well, and must not be held to discredit it. But it was not so easy to overlook or to excuse national bad faith. When distinguished emissaries from the Father at Washington, some of them ministers of the gospel and even bishops, came to the Indian nations, and pledged to them in solemn treaty the national honor, with prayer and mention of their God; and when such treaties, so made, were promptly and shamelessly broken, is it strange that the action should arouse not only anger, but contempt? The historians of the white race admit that the Indian was never the first to repudiate his oath.

It is my personal belief, after thirty-five years' experience of it, that there is no such thing as "Christian civilization." I believe that Christianity and modern civilization are opposed and irreconcilable, and that the spirit of Christianity and of our ancient religion is essentially the same.

1911

from **From the Deep Woods to Civilization**

VII. The Ghost Dance War[1]

A religious craze such as that of 1890–91 was a thing foreign to the Indian philosophy.[2] I recalled that a hundred years before, on the overthrow of the Algonquin nations, a somewhat similar faith was evolved by the astute Delaware prophet, brother to Tecumseh.[3] It meant that the last hope of race entity had departed, and my people were groping blindly after spiritual relief in their bewilderment and misery. I believe that the first prophets of the "Red Christ" were innocent enough and that the people generally were sincere, but there were doubtless some who went into it for self-advertisement, and who introduced new and fantastic features to attract the crowd.[4]

The ghost dancers had gradually concentrated on the Medicine Root creek and the edge of the "Bad Lands,"[5] and they were still further isolated by a new order from the agent, calling in all those who had not adhered to the new religion.[6] Several thousand of these "friendlies" were soon encamped on the White Clay creek, close by the agency.[7] It was near the

---

[1] In earlier chapters, Eastman describes his life as a student at Santee Normal Training School, Dartmouth College, and Boston University Medical School. Subsequent chapters relate his career as a government physician, as a lecturer and writer, and as a leader in the Indian Y.M.C.A. His final chapter contains his estimation of how well Indians have fared in the assimilation process.

[2] The Ghost Dance and the messianic religion with which it was associated. See headnote to *Ghost Dance Songs*.

[3] Tenskwatawa rose to prominence in 1805 when, in a vision, the Master of Life announced to him a new mode of action, which his people must take in order to regain divine favor. They must reject witchcraft and the white man's whiskey, dress, and technology, and Indian women must no longer marry whites. Only when they returned to their former life ways would they find the happiness that they had known in aboriginal days. Tenskwatawa's teachings, like Wovoka's,

were a response to the cultural discontinuity that came with white contact. Tenskwatawa and Tecumseh were Shawnees, not Delawares as Eastman says.

[4] Eastman may refer here to the trances common among dancers and their belief that bullets could not penetrate the Ghost Dance shirts they wore.

[5] An area of rough, broken land just off the reservation, about fifty miles northwest of the Pine Ridge agency, South Dakota.

[6] Agency officials, Washington bureaucrats, and military officers considered the Ghost Dance movement a serious threat to their authority and control over the Indians. As Eastman indicates below, the excitement at the time of the so-called Ghost Dance War was heightened by political differences among the Indians, personal ambitions, and real grievances against the federal government.

[7] The agency was located near the Nebraska border, southwest of the Wounded Knee massacre site.

middle of December, with weather unusually mild for that season. The dancers held that there would be no snow so long as their rites continued.

An Indian called Little[8] had been guilty of some minor offense on the reservation and had hitherto evaded arrest. Suddenly he appeared at the agency on an issue day, for the express purpose, as it seemed, of defying the authorities. The assembly room of the Indian police, used also as a council room, opened out of my dispensary[9] and on this particular morning a council was in progress. I heard some loud talking, but was too busy to pay particular attention, though my assistant had gone in to listen to the speeches. Suddenly the place was in an uproar, and George[10] burst into the inner office, crying excitedly "Look out for yourself, friend! They are going to fight!"

I went around to see what was going on. A crowd had gathered just outside the council room, and the police were surrounded by wild Indians with guns and drawn knives in their hands. "Hurry up with them!" one shouted, while another held his stone war-club over a policeman's head. The attempt to arrest Little had met with a stubborn resistance.

At this critical moment, a fine-looking Indian in citizen's clothes faced the excited throng, and spoke in a clear, steady, almost sarcastic voice.

"Stop! Think! What are you going to do? Kill these men of our own race? Then what? Kill all these helpless white men, women and children? And what then? What will these brave words, brave deeds lead to in the end? How long can you hold out? Your country is surrounded with a network of railroads; thousands of white soldiers will be here within three days. What ammunition have you? what provisions? What will become of your families? Think, think, my brothers! this is a child's madness."

It was the "friendly" chief, American Horse,[11] and it seems to me as I recall the incident that this man's voice had almost magic power. It is likely that he saved us all from massacre, for the murder of the police, who represented the authority of the Government, would surely have been followed by a general massacre. It is a fact that those Indians who upheld the agent were in quite as much danger from their wilder brethren as were the whites, indeed it was said that the feeling against them was even stronger. Jack Red Cloud, son of the chief,[12] thrust the muzzle of a cocked revolver almost into the face of American Horse. "It is you and your kind," he shouted, "who

[8]Little had been arrested and brought to the agency, but had been rescued by his friends a few weeks earlier.

[9]Eastman had been appointed government physician at Pine Ridge only weeks earlier, after graduation from medical school at Boston University.

[10]Perhaps George Sword, captain of the agency's Indian police squad.

[11]American Horse, an Oglala, had signed a treaty in 1887 by which the Sioux reservation was reduced by one half. Objections to the treaty added to the discontent of the

Ghost Dance adherents and led them to their so-called "hostile" state in 1890. American Horse worked to resolve differences and to convince the "hostiles" to relent.

[12]Red Cloud (1822–1909), an Oglala, had been one of the most famous and powerful chiefs and since 1867 had been on peaceful terms with the United States. Old and partially blind, he took no part in the events of 1890. Jack Red Cloud was one of the Ghost Dancers who had earlier been induced to leave the Bad Lands and come to the agency.

have brought us to this pass!" That brave man never flinched. Ignoring his rash accuser, he quietly reentered the office; the door closed behind him; the mob dispersed, and for the moment the danger seemed over.

I scarcely knew at the time, but gradually learned afterward, that the Sioux had many grievances and causes for profound discontent, which lay back of and were more or less closely related to the ghost dance craze and the prevailing restlessness and excitement. Rations had been cut from time to time; the people were insufficiently fed, and their protests and appeals were disregarded. Never was more ruthless fraud and graft practiced upon a defenseless people than upon these poor natives by the politicians! Never were there more worthless "scraps of paper" anywhere in the world than many of the Indian treaties and Government documents! Sickness was prevalent and the death rate alarming, especially among the children. Trouble from all these causes had for some time been developing, but might have been checked by humane and conciliatory measures. The "Messiah craze" in itself was scarcely a source of danger, and one might almost as well call upon the army to suppress Billy Sunday[13] and his hysterical followers. Other tribes than the Sioux who adopted the new religion were let alone, and the craze died a natural death in the course of a few months.

Among the leaders of the malcontents at this time were Jack Red Cloud, No Water, He Dog, Four Bears, Yellow Bear, and Kicking Bear.[14] Friendly leaders included American Horse, Young Man Afraid of His Horses, Bad Wound, Three Stars.[15] There was still another set whose attitude was not clearly defined, and among these men was Red Cloud, the greatest of them all. He who had led his people so brilliantly and with such remarkable results, both in battle and diplomacy, was now an old man of over seventy years, living in a frame house which had been built for him within a half mile of the agency. He would come to council, but said little or nothing. No one knew exactly where he stood, but it seemed that he was broken in spirit as in body and convinced of the hopelessness of his people's cause.

It was Red Cloud who asked the historic question, at a great council held in the Black Hills region with a Government commission, and after good Bishop Whipple[16] had finished the invocation, "Which God is our brother praying to now? Is it the same God whom they have twice deceived, when they made treaties with us which they afterward broke?"

Early in the morning after the attempted arrest of Little, George rushed into my quarters and awakened me. "Come quick!" he shouted, "the soldiers

[13]William Ashley Sunday (1862–1935), a well-known American evangelist.
[14]No Water's camp on the White River near Pine Ridge was the site of much Ghost Dance activity. In 1891, He Dog served as one of the Sioux delegates to Washington, sent to try to resolve tribal differences. Kicking Bear, from the Cheyenne River reservation, was a Ghost Dance priest who had organized the first dance at Sitting Bull's camp on the Standing Rock reservation. Four Bears and Yellow Bear have not been identified.
[15]Young Man Afraid of His Horses, an Oglala, had made his reputation in the wars of the 1860s but, like Red Cloud, had lived peaceably since 1867 and counseled peace during the crisis. Bad Wound and Three Stars have not been identified.
[16]Episcopal Bishop Henry Benjamin Whipple.

are here!" I looked along the White Clay creek toward the little railroad town of Rushville, Nebraska, twenty-five miles away, and just as the sun rose above the knife-edged ridges black with stunted pine, I perceived a moving cloud of dust that marked the trail of the Ninth Cavalry. There was instant commotion among the camps of friendly Indians. Many women and children were coming in to the agency for refuge, evidently fearing that the dreaded soldiers might attack their villages by mistake. Some who had not heard of their impending arrival hurried to the offices to ask what it meant. I assured those who appealed to me that the troops were here only to preserve order, but their suspicions were not easily allayed.

As the cavalry came nearer, we saw that they were colored troopers, wearing buffalo overcoats and muskrat caps; the Indians with their quick wit called them "buffalo soldiers." They halted, and established their temporary camp in the open space before the agency enclosure. The news had already gone out through the length and breadth of the reservation, and the wildest rumors were in circulation. Indian scouts might be seen upon every hill top, closely watching the military encampment.

At this juncture came the startling news from Fort Yates, some two hundred and fifty miles to the north of us, that Sitting Bull had been killed by Indian police while resisting arrest, and a number of his men with him, as well as several of the police. We next heard that the remnant of his band had fled in our direction, and soon afterward, that they had been joined by Big Foot's band from the western part of Cheyenne River agency, which lay directly in their road.[17] United States troops continued to gather at strategic points, and of course the press seized upon the opportunity to enlarge upon the strained situation and predict an "Indian uprising." The reporters were among us, and managed to secure much "news" that no one else ever heard of. Border towns were fortified and cowboys and militia gathered in readiness to protect them against the "red devils." Certain classes of the frontier population industriously fomented the excitement for what there was in it for them, since much money is apt to be spent at such times. As for the poor Indians, they were quite as badly scared as the whites and perhaps with more reason.

General Brooke[18] undertook negotiations with the ghost dancers, and finally induced them to come within reach. They camped on a flat about a mile north of us and in full view, while the more tractable bands were still gathered on the south and west. The large boarding school had locked its doors and succeeded in holding its hundreds of Indian children, partly for their own sakes, and partly as hostages for the good behavior of their fathers. At the agency were now gathered all the government employees and their families, except such as had taken flight, together with traders,

[17]After Sitting Bull's death, the Hunkpapa Ghost Dancers fled from the Standing Rock reservation. The group Eastman refers to fled to the camp of Big Foot, a Minneconjou. Big Foot, gravely ill, yet considered dangerous by the authorities, started with his people toward the Pine Ridge reservation, where he hoped to find refuge.

[18]General J. R. Brooke, commander of the troops sent to Pine Ridge.

missionaries, and ranchmen, army officers, and newspaper men. It was a conglomerate population.

During this time of grave anxiety and nervous tension, the cooler heads among us went about our business, and still refused to believe in the tragic possibility of an Indian war. It may be imagined that I was more than busy, though I had not such long distances to cover, for since many Indians accustomed to comfortable log houses were compelled to pass the winter in tents, there was even more sickness than usual. I had access and welcome to the camps of all the various groups and factions, a privilege shared by my good friend Father Jutz,[19] the Catholic missionary, who was completely trusted by his people.

Three days later, we learned that Big Foot's band of ghost dancers from the Cheyenne river reservation north of us was approaching the agency, and that Major Whiteside[20] was in command of troops with orders to intercept them.

Late that afternoon, the Seventh Cavalry under Colonel Forsythe[21] was called to the saddle and rode off toward Wounded Knee creek, eighteen miles away. Father Craft,[22] a Catholic priest with some Indian blood, who knew Sitting Bull and his people, followed an hour or so later, and I was much inclined to go too, but my fiancée[23] pointed out that my duty lay rather at home with our Indians, and I stayed.

The morning of December 29th was sunny and pleasant. We were all straining our ears toward Wounded Knee, and about the middle of the forenoon we distinctly heard the reports of the Hotchkiss guns. Two hours later, a rider was seen approaching at full speed, and in a few minutes he had dismounted from his exhausted horse and handed his message to General Brooke's orderly. The Indians were watching their own messenger, who ran on foot along the northern ridges and carried the news to the so-called "hostile" camp. It was said that he delivered his message at almost the same time as the mounted officer.

The resulting confusion and excitement was unmistakable. The white teepees disappeared as if by magic and soon the caravans were in motion, going toward the natural fortress of the "Bad Lands." In the "friendly" camp there was almost as much turmoil, and crowds of frightened women and children poured into the agency. Big Foot's band had been wiped out by the troops, and reprisals were naturally looked for. The enclosure was not barricaded in any way and we had but a small detachment of troops for our

[19]Father John Jutz.

[20]Major Samuel Whiteside, with a detachment of the Seventh Cavalry, intercepted Big Foot on December 28 and convinced him to encamp for the night at Wounded Knee.

[21]Colonel James W. Forsyth, commander of the Seventh Cavalry, joined Whiteside at Wounded Knee on the night of December 28.

[22]Father Craft was at the massacre and was wounded.

[23]Elaine Goodale, who had taught for a number of years on the Great Sioux Reservation, was then superintendent for Indian education in the Dakotas. She and Eastman married in 1891. In later years, an author in her own right, she encouraged Eastman to write and lecture and collaborated with him on many works. The extent of her influence on his writing may never be known, but it was certainly great.

protection. Sentinels were placed, and machine guns trained on the various approaches.

A few hot-headed young braves fired on the sentinels and wounded two of them. The Indian police began to answer by shooting at several braves who were apparently about to set fire to some of the outlying buildings. Every married employee was seeking a place of safety for his family, the interpreter among them. Just then General Brooke ran out into the open, shouting at the top of his voice to the police: "Stop, stop! Doctor, tell them they must not fire until ordered!" I did so, as the bullets whistled by us, and the General's coolness perhaps saved all our lives, for we were in no position to repel a large attacking force. Since we did not reply, the scattered shots soon ceased, but the situation remained critical for several days and nights.

My office was full of refugees. I called one of my good friends aside and asked him to saddle my two horses and stay by them. "When general fighting begins, take them to Miss Goodale and see her to the railroad if you can," I told him. Then I went over to the rectory. Mrs. Cook refused to go without her husband,[24] and Miss Goodale would not leave while there was a chance of being of service. The house was crowded with terrified people, most of them Christian Indians, whom our friends were doing their best to pacify.

At dusk, the Seventh Cavalry returned with their twenty-five dead and I believe thirty-four wounded, most of them by their own comrades, who had encircled the Indians, while few of the latter had guns.[25] A majority of the thirty or more Indian wounded were women and children, including babies in arms. As there were not tents enough for all, Mr. Cook offered us the mission chapel, in which the Christmas tree still stood, for a temporary hospital. We tore out the pews and covered the floor with hay and quilts. There we laid the poor creatures side by side in rows, and the night was devoted to caring for them as best we could. Many were frightfully torn by pieces of shells, and the suffering was terrible. General Brooke placed me in charge and I had to do nearly all the work, for although the army surgeons were more than ready to help as soon as their own men had been cared for, the tortured Indians would scarcely allow a man in uniform to touch them. Mrs. Cook, Miss Goodale, and several of Mr. Cook's Indian helpers acted as volunteer nurses. In spite of all our efforts, we lost the greater part of them, but a few recovered, including several children who had lost all their relatives and who were adopted into kind Christian families.

On the day following the Wounded Knee massacre there was a blizzard, in the midst of which I was ordered out with several Indian police, to look for a policeman who was reported to have been wounded and left some two

[24]The Reverend Charles Smith Cook, an Oglala, was an 1881 graduate of Trinity College and had studied theology at Seabury Divinity School. He was ordained and served as a teacher and minister on the Pine Ridge reservation. Cook died in 1892.

[25]The few Indians who had weapons had been disarmed, except one, when the firing commenced.

miles from the agency. We did not find him. This was the only time during the whole affair that I carried a weapon; a friend lent me a revolver which I put in my overcoat pocket, and it was lost on the ride. On the third day it cleared, and the ground was covered with an inch or two of fresh snow. We had feared that some of the Indian wounded might have been left on the field, and a number of us volunteered to go and see. I was placed in charge of the expedition of about a hundred civilians, ten or fifteen of whom were white men. We were supplied with wagons in which to convey any of whom we might find still alive. Of course a photographer and several reporters were of the party.

Fully three miles from the scene of the massacre we found the body of a woman completely covered with a blanket of snow, and from this point on we found them scattered along as they had been relentlessly hunted down and slaughtered while fleeing for their lives. Some of our people discovered relatives or friends among the dead, and there was much wailing and mourning. When we reached the spot where the Indian camp had stood, among the fragments of burned tents and other belongings we saw the frozen bodies lying close together or piled one upon another. I counted eighty bodies of men who had been in the council and who were almost as helpless as the women and babes when the deadly fire began, for nearly all their guns had been taken from them. A reckless and desperate young Indian fired the first shot when the search for weapons was well under way,[26] and immediately the troops opened fire from all sides, killing not only unarmed men, women, and children, but their own comrades who stood opposite them, for the camp was entirely surrounded.

It took all of my nerve to keep my composure in the face of this spectacle, and of the excitement and grief of my Indian companions, nearly every one of whom was crying aloud or singing his death song. The white men became very nervous, but I set them to examining and uncovering every body to see if one were living. Although they had been lying untended in the snow and cold for two days and nights, a number had survived. Among them I found a baby of about a year old warmly wrapped and entirely unhurt. I brought her in, and she was afterward adopted and educated by an army officer. One man who was severely wounded begged me to fill his pipe. When we brought him into the chapel he was welcomed by his wife and daughters with cries of joy, but he died a day or two later.

Under a wagon I discovered an old woman, totally blind and entirely helpless. A few had managed to crawl away to some place of shelter, and we found in a log store near by several who were badly hurt and others who had died after reaching there. After we had dispatched several wagon loads to the agency, we observed groups of warriors watching us from adjacent buttes; probably friends of the victims who had come there for the same purpose as ourselves. A majority of our party, fearing an attack, insisted

[26]The young man who fired the first shot was Black Coyote, alleged to have been deaf.

that some one ride back to the agency for an escort of soldiers, and as mine was the best horse, it fell to me to go. I covered the eighteen miles in quick time and was not interfered with in any way, although if the Indians had meant mischief they could easily have picked me off from any of the ravines and gulches.

All this was a severe ordeal for one who had so lately put all his faith in the Christian love and lofty ideals of the white man. Yet I passed no hasty judgment, and was thankful that I might be of some service and relieve even a small part of the suffering. An appeal published in a Boston paper brought us liberal supplies of much needed clothing, and linen for dressings. We worked on. Bishop Hare of South Dakota[27] visited us, and was overcome by faintness when he entered his mission chapel, thus transformed into a rude hospital.

After some days of extreme tension, and weeks of anxiety, the "hostiles," so called, were at last induced to come in and submit to a general disarmament. Father Jutz, the Catholic missionary, had gone bravely among them and used all his influence toward a peaceful settlement. The troops were all recalled and took part in a grand review before General Miles,[28] no doubt intended to impress the Indians with their superior force.

1916

■ GERTRUDE BONNIN (ZITKALA-SA) (SIOUX) ■
1876–1938

In her writings as well as her work as an Indian rights activist, Gertrude Simmons Bonnin, or Zitkala-Sa (Red Bird), is a vital link between the oral culture of tribal America in conflict with its colonizers and the literate culture of contemporary American Indians. A Yankton, born on the Pine Ridge Reservation in South Dakota, she was the third child of Ellen Tate 'Iyohiwin Simmons, a full-blood Sioux. Little is known of her father, a white man. Her mother brought up the children in traditional ways. At the age of eight, Zitkala-Sa left the reservation to attend a Quaker missionary school in Wabash, Indiana. She returned to the reservation but was culturally unhinged, "neither a wild Indian nor a tame one," as she described herself later in "The Schooldays of an Indian Girl." After four unhappy years she returned to her school, graduated, and at age nineteen enrolled—against her mother's wish—at Earlham College in Richmond, Indiana.

---

[27]Bishop W. D. Hare, long-time Episcopal missionary bishop among the Sioux.

[28]General Nelson A. Miles, commander of the Army Department of the Missouri, who had ordered the arrest of Sitting Bull.

She later taught at Carlisle Indian School for about two years. Having become an accomplished violinist, she also studied at the Boston Conservatory of Music.

Meanwhile, the estrangement from her mother and the old ways of the reservation had grown, as had her indignation over the treatment of American Indians by the state, church, and population at large. Around 1900 she began to express her feelings publicly in writing. In articles in the *Atlantic Monthly* and other journals, she struggled with the issues of cultural dislocation and injustice that brought suffering to her people. Her authorial voice was not merely critical, however. She was earnestly committed to being a bridge builder between cultures, for example, by writing *Old Indian Legends*, published in 1901. "I have tried," she says in the introduction to that work, "to transplant the native spirit of these tales—root and all—into the English language, since America in the last few centuries has acquired a second tongue."

In the following decades, Zitkala-Sa's writing efforts were increasingly part of, and finally supplanted by, her work as an Indian rights activist. She had accepted a clerkship at the Standing Rock Reservation, where she met and married Raymond T. Bonnin, another Sioux employee of the Indian service. The Bonnins then transferred to a reservation in Utah where they became affiliated with the Society of American Indians. Zitkala-Sa was elected secretary of the Society in 1916, and the Bonnins moved to Washington, D.C., where she worked with the Society and edited the *American Indian Magazine*. In 1926 she founded the National Council of American Indians and continued to pursue reforms through public speaking and lobbying efforts. She was instrumental in the passage of the Indian Citizenship Bill and secured powerful outside interests in Indian reform. Zitkala-Sa died in Washington, D.C., in 1938 and was buried in Arlington Cemetery.

Although her output was limited, her artistic accomplishment is noteworthy. In addition to her earlier works, in 1913 she collaborated with William P. Hanson in producing an Indian opera, "Sundance." In 1921 her collection of *American Indian Stories* was published, combining her previously printed work with some new essays and merging autobiography and fiction in a unique way. In her writings, Zitkala-Sa anticipated some aspects of the work of present-day American Indian fiction writers like N. Scott Momaday and Leslie Silko and advocates of the Indian cause like Vine Deloria, Jr. As her collection of *Old Indian Legends* proves, she realized that political rights would be fruitless unless they were rooted in a recovery of cultural identity through a revitalization of the oral tradition.

Zitkala-Sa's autobiographical work makes her perhaps the first American Indian woman to write her own story without the aid of an editor, interpreter, or ethnographer. Her essay, "Why I am a Pagan," merits special attention because at the time it was published it was popular for American Indians to describe their conversions to Christianity.

Kristin Herzog
University of North Carolina–Chapel Hill

PRIMARY WORKS

Old Indian Legends, 1901, 1985; *American Indian Stories,* 1921, 1985.

from **Impressions of an Indian Childhood**[1]

I. My Mother

A wigwam of weather-stained canvas stood at the base of some irregularly ascending hills. A footpath wound its way gently down the sloping land till it reached the broad river bottom; creeping through the long swamp grasses that bent over it on either side, it came out on the edge of the Missouri.

Here, morning, noon, and evening, my mother came to draw water from the muddy stream for our household use. Always, when my mother started for the river, I stopped my play to run along with her. She was only of medium height. Often she was sad and silent, at which times her full arched lips were compressed into hard and bitter lines, and shadows fell under her black eyes. Then I clung to her hand and begged to know what made the tears fall.

"Hush; my little daughter must never talk about my tears;" and smiling through them, she patted my head and said, "Now let me see how fast you can run to-day." Whereupon I tore away at my highest possible speed, with my long black hair blowing in the breeze.

I was a wild little girl of seven. Loosely clad in a slip of brown buckskin, and light-footed with a pair of soft moccasins on my feet, I was as free as the wind that blew my hair, and no less spirited than a bounding deer. These were my mother's pride, – my wild freedom and overflowing spirits. She taught me no fear save that of intruding myself upon others.

Having gone many paces ahead I stopped, panting for breath, and laughing with glee as my mother watched my every movement. I was not wholly conscious of myself, but was more keenly alive to the fire within. It was as if I were the activity, and my hands and feet were only experiments for my spirit to work upon.

Returning from the river, I tugged beside my mother, with my hand upon the bucket I believed I was carrying. One time, on such a return, I remember a bit of conversation we had. My grown-up cousin, Warca-Ziwin (Sunflower), who was then seventeen, always went to the river alone for water for her mother. Their wigwam was not far from ours; and I saw her daily going to and from the river. I admired my cousin greatly. So I said: "Mother, when I am tall as my cousin Warca-Ziwin, you shall not have to come for water. I will do it for you."

With a strange tremor in her voice which I could not understand, she answered, "If the paleface does not take away from us the river we drink."

"Mother, who is this bad paleface?" I asked.

"My little daughter, he is a sham, – a sickly sham! The bronzed Dakota is the only real man."

---

[1]"Impressions of an Indian Childhood" initially appeared in *Atlantic Monthly* 85 (1900), pp. 37–47. It was reprinted in Zitkala-Sa's *American Indian Stories* (1921).

I looked up into my mother's face while she spoke; and seeing her bite her lips, I knew she was unhappy. This aroused revenge in my small soul. Stamping my foot on the earth, I cried aloud, "I hate the paleface that makes my mother cry!"

Setting the pail of water on the ground, my mother stooped, and stretching her left hand out on the level with my eyes, she placed her other arm about me; she pointed to the hill where my uncle and my only sister lay buried.

"There is what the paleface has done! Since then your father too has been buried in a hill nearer the rising sun. We were once very happy. But the paleface has stolen our lands and driven us hither. Having defrauded us of our land, the paleface forced us away.

"Well, it happened on the day we moved camp that your sister and uncle were both very sick. Many others were ailing, but there seemed to be no help. We traveled many days and nights; not in the grand happy way that we moved camp when I was a little girl, but we were driven, my child, driven like a herd of buffalo. With every step, your sister, who was not as large as you are now, shrieked with the painful jar until she was hoarse with crying. She grew more and more feverish. Her little hands and cheeks were burning hot. Her little lips were parched and dry, but she would not drink the water I gave her. Then I discovered that her throat was swollen and red. My poor child, how I cried with her because the Great Spirit had forgotten us!

"At last, when we reached this western country, on the first weary night your sister died. And soon your uncle died also, leaving a widow and an orphan daughter, your cousin Warca-Ziwin. Both your sister and uncle might have been happy with us to-day, had it not been for the heartless paleface."

My mother was silent the rest of the way to our wigwam. Though I saw no tears in her eyes, I knew that was because I was with her. She seldom wept before me.

1900

The School Days of an Indian Girl[1]

I. The Land of Red Apples

There were eight in our party of bronzed children who were going East with the missionaries. Among us were three young braves, two tall girls, and we three little ones, Judéwin, Thowin, and I.

We had been very impatient to start on our journey to the Red Apple Country,[2] which, we were told, lay a little beyond the great circular horizon

---

[1]"The School Days of an Indian Girl" appeared in *Atlantic*, 85 (February, 1900), 185–194. It was reprinted in Zitkala-Sa's *American Indian Stories* (1921).

[2]I.e., Indiana.

of the Western prairie. Under a sky of rosy apples we dreamt of roaming as freely and happily as we had chased the cloud shadows on the Dakota plains. We had anticipated much pleasure from a ride on the iron horse, but the throngs of staring palefaces disturbed and troubled us.

On the train, fair women, with tottering babies on each arm, stopped their haste and scrutinized the children of absent mothers. Large men, with heavy bundles in their hands, halted near by, and riveted their glassy blue eyes upon us.

I sank deep into the corner of my seat, for I resented being watched. Directly in front of me, children who were no larger than I hung themselves upon the backs of their seats, with their bold white faces toward me. Sometimes they took their forefingers out of their mouths and pointed at my moccasined feet. Their mothers, instead of reproving such rude curiosity, looked closely at me, and attracted their children's further notice to my blanket. This embarrassed me, and kept me constantly on the verge of tears.

I sat perfectly still, with my eyes downcast, daring only now and then to shoot long glances around me. Chancing to turn to the window at my side, I was quite breathless upon seeing one familiar object. It was the telegraph pole which strode by at short paces. Very near my mother's dwelling, along the edge of a road thickly bordered with wild sunflowers, some poles like these had been planted by white men. Often I had stopped, on my way down the road, to hold my ear against the pole, and, hearing its low moaning, I used to wonder what the paleface had done to hurt it. Now I sat watching for each pole that glided by to be the last one.

In this way I had forgotten my uncomfortable surroundings, when I heard one of my comrades call out my name. I saw the missionary standing very near, tossing candies and gums into our midst. This amused us all, and we tried to see who could catch the most of the sweet-meats. The missionary's generous distribution of candies was impressed upon my memory by a disastrous result which followed. I had caught more than my share of candies and gums, and soon after our arrival at the school I had a chance to disgrace myself, which, I am ashamed to say, I did.

Though we rode several days inside of the iron horse, I do not recall a single thing about our luncheons.

It was night when we reached the school grounds. The lights from the windows of the large buildings fell upon some of the icicled trees that stood beneath them. We were led toward an open door, where the brightness of the lights within flooded out over the heads of the excited palefaces who blocked the way. My body trembled more from fear than from the snow I trod upon.

Entering the house, I stood close against the wall. The strong glaring light in the large whitewashed room dazzled my eyes. The noisy hurrying of hard shoes upon a bare wooden floor increased the whirring in my ears. My only safety seemed to be in keeping next to the wall. As I was wondering in which direction to escape from all this confusion, two warm hands grasped me firmly, and in the same moment I was tossed high in midair. A rosy-cheeked paleface woman caught me in her arms. I was both frightened and insulted by such trifling. I stared into her eyes, wishing her to let me stand on my own feet, but she jumped me up and down with increasing enthusiasm. My mother had never made a plaything of her wee daughter. Remembering this I began to cry aloud.

They misunderstood the cause of my tears, and placed me at a white table loaded with food. There our party were united again. As I did not hush my crying, one of the older ones whispered to me, "Wait until you are alone in the night."

It was very little I could swallow besides my sobs, that evening.

"Oh, I want my mother and my brother Dawée! I want to go to my aunt!" I pleaded; but the ears of the palefaces could not hear me.

From the table we were taken along an upward incline of wooden boxes, which I learned afterward to call a stairway. At the top was a quiet hall, dimly lighted. Many narrow beds were in one straight line down the entire length of the wall. In them lay sleeping brown faces, which peeped just out of the coverings. I was tucked into bed with one of the tall girls, because she talked to me in my mother tongue and seemed to soothe me.

I had arrived in the wonderful land of rosy skies, but I was not happy, as I had thought I should be. My long travel and the bewildering sights had exhausted me. I fell asleep, heaving deep, tired sobs. My tears were left to dry themselves in streaks, because neither my aunt nor my mother was near to wipe them away.

II. The Cutting of My Long Hair

The first day in the land of apples was a bitter-cold one; for the snow still covered the ground, and the trees were bare. A large bell rang for breakfast, its loud metallic voice crashing through the belfry overhead and into our sensitive ears. The annoying clatter of shoes on bare floors gave us no peace. The constant clash of harsh noises, with an undercurrent of many voices murmuring an unknown tongue, made a bedlam within which I was securely tied. And though my spirit tore itself in struggling for its lost freedom, all was useless.

A paleface woman, with white hair, came up after us. We were placed in a line of girls who were marching into the dining room. These were Indian girls, in stiff shoes and closely clinging dresses. The small girls wore sleeved aprons and shingled hair. As I walked noiselessly in my soft moccasins, I felt like sinking to the floor, for my blanket had been stripped from my shoulders. I looked hard at the Indian girls, who seemed not to care that they were even more immodestly dressed than I, in their tightly fitting clothes. While we marched in, the boys entered at an opposite door. I watched for the three young braves who came in our party. I spied them in the rear ranks, looking as uncomfortable as I felt.

A small bell was tapped, and each of the pupils drew a chair from under the table. Supposing this act meant they were to be seated, I pulled out mine and at once slipped into it from one side. But when I turned my head, I saw that I was the only one seated, and all the rest at our table remained standing. Just as I began to rise, looking shyly around to see how chairs were to be used, a second bell was sounded. All were seated at last, and I had to crawl back into my chair again. I heard a man's voice at one end of the hall, and I looked around to see him. But all the others hung their heads over their plates. As I glanced at the long chain of tables, I caught the eyes of a paleface woman upon me. Immediately I dropped my eyes, wondering why I was so keenly watched by the strange woman. The man ceased his mutterings, and then a third bell was tapped. Every one picked up his knife and fork and began eating. I began crying instead, for by this time I was afraid to venture anything more.

But this eating by formula was not the hardest trial in that first day. Late in the morning, my friend Judéwin gave me a terrible warning. Judéwin knew a few words of English; and she had overheard the paleface woman talk about cutting our long, heavy hair. Our mothers had taught us that only unskilled warriors who were captured had their hair shingled by the enemy. Among our people, short hair was worn by mourners, and shingled hair by cowards!

We discussed our fate some moments, and when Judéwin said, "We have to submit, because they are strong," I rebelled.

"No, I will not submit! I will struggle first!" I answered.

I watched my chance, and when no one noticed I disappeared. I crept up the stairs as quietly as I could in my squeaking shoes,—my moccasins had been exchanged for shoes. Along the hall I passed, without knowing whither I was going. Turning aside to an open door, I found a large room with three white beds in it. The windows were covered with dark green curtains, which made the room very dim. Thankful that no one was there, I directed my steps toward the corner farthest from the door. On my hands and knees I crawled under the bed, and cuddled myself in the dark corner.

From my hiding place I peered out, shuddering with fear whenever I heard footsteps near by. Though in the hall loud voices were calling my name, and I knew that even Judéwin was searching for me, I did not open my mouth to answer. Then the steps were quickened and the voices became excited. The sounds came nearer and nearer. Women and girls entered the room. I held my breath, and watched them open closet doors and peep behind large trunks. Some one threw up the curtains, and the room was filled with sudden light. What caused them to stoop and look under the bed I do not know. I remember being dragged out, though I resisted by kicking and scratching wildly. In spite of myself, I was carried downstairs and tied fast in a chair.

I cried aloud, shaking my head all the while until I felt the cold blades of the scissors against my neck, and heard them gnaw off one of my thick braids. Then I lost my spirit. Since the day I was taken from my mother I had suffered extreme indignities. People had stared at me. I had been tossed about in the air like a wooden puppet. And now my long hair was shingled like a coward's! In my anguish I moaned for my mother, but no one came to comfort me. Not a soul reasoned quietly with me, as my own mother used to do: for now I was only one of many little animals driven by a herder.

III. The Snow Episode

A short time after our arrival we three Dakotas were playing in the snow-drifts. We were all still deaf to the English language, excepting Judéwin, who always heard such puzzling things. One morning we learned through her ears that we were forbidden to fall lengthwise in the snow, as we had been doing, to see our own impressions. However, before many hours we had forgotten the order, and were having great sport in the snow, when a shrill voice called us. Looking up, we saw an imperative hand beckoning us into the house. We shook the snow off ourselves, and started toward the woman as slowly as we dared.

Judéwin said: "Now the paleface is angry with us. She is going to punish us for falling into the snow. If she looks straight into your eyes and talks loudly, you must wait until she stops. Then, after a tiny pause, say, 'No.'" The rest of the way we practiced upon the little word "no."

As it happened, Thowin was summoned to judgment first. The door shut behind her with a click.

Judéwin and I stood silently listening at the keyhole. The paleface woman talked in very severe tones. Her words fell from her lips like crackling embers, and her inflection ran up like the small end of a switch. I understood her voice better than the things she was saying. I was certain we had made her very impatient with us. Judéwin heard enough of the words to realize all too late that she had taught us the wrong reply.

"Oh, poor Thowin!" she gasped, as she put both hands over her ears.

Just then I heard Thowin's tremulous answer, "No."

With an angry exclamation, the woman gave her a hard spanking. Then she stopped to say something. Judéwin said it was this: "Are you going to obey my word the next time?"

Thowin answered again with the only word at her command, "No."

This time the woman meant her blows to smart, for the poor frightened girl shrieked at the top of her voice. In the midst of the whipping the blows ceased abruptly, and the woman asked another question: "Are you going to fall in the snow again?"

Thowin gave her bad password another trial. We heard her say feebly, "No! No!"

With this the woman hid away her half-worn slipper, and led the child out, stroking her black shorn head. Perhaps it occurred to her that brute force is not the solution for such a problem. She did nothing to Judéwin nor to me. She only returned to us our unhappy comrade, and left us alone in the room.

During the first two or three seasons misunderstandings as ridiculous as this one of the snow episode frequently took place, bringing unjustifiable frights and punishments into our little lives.

Within a year I was able to express myself somewhat in broken English. As soon as I comprehended a part of what was said and done, a mischievous spirit of revenge possessed me. One day I was called in from my play for some misconduct. I had disregarded a rule which seemed to me very needlessly binding. I was sent into the kitchen to mash the turnips for dinner. It was noon, and steaming dishes were hastily carried into the dining room. I hated turnips, and their odor which came from the brown jar was offensive to me. With fire in my heart, I took the wooden tool that the paleface woman held out to me. I stood upon a step, and, grasping the handle with both hands, I bent in hot rage over the turnips. I worked my vengeance upon them. All were so busily occupied that no one noticed me. I saw that the turnips were in a pulp, and that further beating could not improve them; but the order was, "Mash these turnips," and mash them I would! I renewed my energy; and as I sent the masher into the bottom of the jar, I felt a satisfying sensation that the weight of my body had gone into it.

Just here a paleface woman came up to my table. As she looked into the jar, she shoved my hands roughly aside. I stood fearless and angry. She placed her red hands upon the rim of the jar. Then she gave one lift and a stride away from the table. But lo! the pulpy contents fell through the crumbled bottom to the floor! She spared me no scolding phrases that I had earned. I did not heed them. I felt triumphant in my revenge, though deep within me I was a wee bit sorry to have broken the jar.

As I sat eating my dinner, and saw that no turnips were served, I whooped in my heart for having once asserted the rebellion within me.

IV. The Devil

Among the legends the old warriors used to tell me were many stories of evil spirits. But I was taught to fear them no more than those who stalked about in material guise. I never knew there was an insolent chieftain among the bad spirits, who dared to array his forces against the Great Spirit, until I heard this white man's legend from a paleface woman.

Out of a large book she showed me a picture of the white man's devil. I looked in horror upon the strong claws that grew out of his fur-covered fingers. His feet were like his hands. Trailing at his heels was a scaly tail tipped with a serpent's open jaws. His face was a patchwork: he had bearded cheeks, like some I had seen palefaces wear; his nose was an eagle's bill, and his sharp-pointed ears were pricked up like those of a sly fox. Above them a pair of cow's horns curved upward. I trembled with awe, and my heart throbbed in my throat, as I looked at the king of evil spirits. Then I heard the paleface woman say that this terrible creature roamed loose in the world, and that little girls who disobeyed school regulations were to be tortured by him.

That night I dreamt about this evil divinity. Once again I seemed to be in my mother's cottage. An Indian woman had come to visit my mother. On opposite sides of the kitchen stove, which stood in the centre of the small house, my mother and her guest were seated in straight-backed chairs. I played with a train of empty spools hitched together on a string. It was night, and the wick burned feebly. Suddenly I heard some one turn our door-knob from without.

My mother and the woman hushed their talk, and both looked toward the door. It opened gradually. I waited behind the stove. The hinges squeaked as the door was slowly, very slowly pushed inward.

Then in rushed the devil! He was tall! He looked exactly like the picture I had seen of him in the white man's papers. He did not speak to my mother, because he did not know the Indian language, but his glittering yellow eyes were fastened upon me. He took long strides around the stove, passing behind the woman's chair. I threw down my spools, and ran to my mother. He did not fear her, but followed closely after me. Then I ran round and round the stove, crying aloud for help. But my mother and the woman seemed not to know my danger. They sat still, looking quietly upon the devil's chase after me. At last I grew dizzy. My head revolved as on a hidden pivot. My knees became numb, and doubled under my weight like a pair of knife blades without a spring. Beside my mother's chair I fell in a heap. Just as the devil stooped over me with outstretched claws my mother awoke from her quiet indifference, and lifted me on her lap. Whereupon the devil vanished, and I was awake.

On the following morning I took my revenge upon the devil. Stealing into the room where a wall of shelves was filled with books, I drew forth *The Stories of the Bible*. With a broken slate pencil I carried in my apron pocket, I began by scratching out his wicked eyes. A few moments later, when I was ready to leave the room, there was a ragged hole in the page where the picture of the devil had once been.

V. Iron Routine

A loud-clamoring bell awakened us at half past six in the cold winter mornings. From happy dreams of Western rolling lands and unlassoed freedom we tumbled out upon chilly bare floors back again into a paleface day. We had short time to jump into our shoes and clothes, and wet our eyes with icy water, before a small hand bell was vigorously rung for roll call.

There were too many drowsy children and too numerous orders for the day to waste a moment in any apology to nature for giving her children such a shock in the early morning. We rushed downstairs, bounding over two high steps at a time, to land in the assembly room.

A paleface woman, with a yellow-covered roll book open on her arm and a gnawed pencil in her hand, appeared at the door. Her small, tired face was coldly lighted with a pair of large gray eyes.

She stood still in a halo of authority, while over the rim of her spectacles her eyes pried nervously about the room. Having glanced at her long list of names and called out the first one, she tossed up her chin and peered through the crystals of her spectacles to make sure of the answer "Here."

Relentlessly her pencil black-marked our daily records if we were not present to respond to our names, and no chum of ours had done it successfully for us. No matter if a dull headache or the painful cough of slow consumption had delayed the absentee, there was only time enough to mark the tardiness. It was next to impossible to leave the iron routine after the civilizing machine had once begun its day's buzzing; and as it was inbred in me to suffer in silence rather than to appeal to the ears of one whose open eyes could not see my pain, I have many times trudged in the day's harness heavy-footed, like a dumb sick brute.

Once I lost a dear classmate. I remember well how she used to mope along at my side, until one morning she could not raise her head from her pillow. At her deathbed I stood weeping, as the paleface woman sat near her moistening the dry lips. Among the folds of the bedclothes I saw the open pages of the white man's Bible. The dying Indian girl talked disconnectedly of Jesus the Christ and the paleface who was cooling her swollen hands and feet.

I grew bitter, and censured the woman for cruel neglect of our physical ills. I despised the pencils that moved automatically, and the one teaspoon which dealt out, from a large bottle, healing to a row of variously ailing Indian children. I blamed the hard-working, well-meaning, ignorant woman who was inculcating in our hearts her superstitious ideas. Though I was sullen in all my little troubles, as soon as I felt better I was ready again to smile upon the cruel woman. Within a week I was again actively testing the chains which tightly bound my individuality like a mummy for burial.

The melancholy of those black days has left so long a shadow that it darkens the path of years that have since gone by. These sad memories rise above those of smoothly grinding school days. Perhaps my Indian nature is the moaning wind which stirs them now for their present record. But, however tempestuous this is within me, it comes out as the low voice of a curiously colored sea-shell, which is only for those ears that are bent with compassion to hear it.

VI. Four Strange Summers

After my first three years of school, I roamed again in the Western country through four strange summers.

During this time I seemed to hang in the heart of chaos, beyond the touch or voice of human aid. My brother, being almost ten years my senior, did not quite understand my feelings. My mother had never gone inside of a schoolhouse, and so she was not capable of comforting her daughter who could read and write. Even nature seemed to have no place for me. I was neither a wee girl nor a tall one; neither a wild Indian nor a tame one. This deplorable situation was the effect of my brief course in the East, and the unsatisfactory "teenth" in a girl's years.

It was under these trying conditions that, one bright afternoon, as I sat restless and unhappy in my mother's cabin, I caught the sound of the spirited step of my brother's pony on the road which passed by our dwelling. Soon I heard the wheels of a light buckboard, and Dawée's familiar "Ho!" to his pony. He alighted upon the bare ground in front of our house. Tying his pony to one of the projecting corner logs of the low-roofed cottage, he stepped upon the wooden doorstep.

I met him there with a hurried greeting, and, as I passed by, he looked a quiet "What?" into my eyes.

When he began talking with my mother, I slipped the rope from the pony's bridle. Seizing the reins and bracing my feet against the dashboard, I wheeled around in an instant. The pony was ever ready to try his speed. Looking backward, I saw Dawée waving his hand to me. I turned with the curve in the road and disappeared. I followed the winding road which crawled upward between the bases of little hillocks. Deep water-worn ditches ran parallel on either side. A strong wind blew against my cheeks and fluttered my sleeves. The pony reached the top of the highest hill, and began an even race on the level lands. There was nothing moving within that great circular horizon of the Dakota prairies save the tall grasses, over which the wind blew and rolled off in long, shadowy waves.

Within this vast wigwam of blue and green I rode reckless and insignificant. It satisfied my small consciousness to see the white foam fly from the pony's mouth.

Suddenly, out of the earth a coyote came forth at a swinging trot that was taking the cunning thief toward the hills and the village beyond. Upon the moment's impulse, I gave him a long chase and a wholesome fright. As I turned away to go back to the village, the wolf sank down upon his haunches for rest, for it was a hot summer day; and as I drove slowly homeward, I saw his sharp nose still pointed at me, until I vanished below the margin of the hilltops.

In a little while I came in sight of my mother's house. Dawée stood in the yard, laughing at an old warrior who was pointing his forefinger, and again waving his whole hand, toward the hills. With his blanket drawn over one shoulder, he talked and motioned excitedly. Dawée turned the old man by the shoulder and pointed me out to him.

"Oh, han!" (Oh, yes) the warrior muttered, and went his way. He had climbed the top of his favorite barren hill to survey the surrounding prairies, when he spied my chase after the coyote. His keen eyes recognized the pony and driver. At once uneasy for my safety, he had come running to my mother's cabin to give her warning. I did not appreciate his kindly interest, for there was an unrest gnawing at my heart.

As soon as he went away, I asked Dawée about something else.

"No, my baby sister. I cannot take you with me to the party to-night," he replied. Though I was not far from fifteen, and I felt that before long I should enjoy all the privileges of my tall cousin, Dawée persisted in calling me his baby sister.

That moonlight night, I cried in my mother's presence when I heard the jolly young people pass by our cottage. They were no more young braves in blankets and eagle plumes, nor Indian maids with prettily painted cheeks.

They had gone three years to school in the East, and had become civilized. The young men wore the white man's coat and trousers, with bright neckties. The girls wore tight muslin dresses, with ribbons at neck and waist. At these gatherings they talked English. I could speak English almost as well as my brother, but I was not properly dressed to be taken along. I had no hat, no ribbons, and no close-fitting gown. Since my return from school I had thrown away my shoes, and wore again the soft moccasins.

While Dawée was busily preparing to go I controlled my tears. But when I heard him bounding away on his pony, I buried my face in my arms and cried hot tears.

My mother was troubled by my unhappiness. Coming to my side, she offered me the only printed matter we had in our home. It was an Indian Bible,[3] given her some years ago by a missionary. She tried to console me. "Here, my child, are the white man's papers. Read a little from them," she said most piously.

I took it from her hand, for her sake; but my enraged spirit felt more like burning the book, which afforded me no help, and was a perfect delusion to my mother. I did not read it, but laid it unopened on the floor, where I sat on my feet. The dim yellow light of the braided muslin burning in a small vessel of oil flickered and sizzled in the awful silent storm which followed my rejection of the Bible.

Now my wrath against the fates consumed my tears before they reached my eyes. I sat stony, with a bowed head. My mother threw a shawl over her head and shoulders, and stepped out into the night.

After an uncertain solitude, I was suddenly aroused by a loud cry piercing the night. It was my mother's voice wailing among the barren hills which held the bones of buried warriors. She called aloud for her brothers' spirits to support her in her helpless misery. My fingers grew icy cold, as I realized that my unrestrained tears had betrayed my suffering to her, and she was grieving for me.

Before she returned, though I knew she was on her way, for she had ceased her weeping, I extinguished the light, and leaned my head on the window sill.

Many schemes of running away from my surroundings hovered about in my mind. A few more moons of such a turmoil drove me away to the Eastern school. I rode on the white man's iron steed, thinking it would bring me back to my mother in a few winters, when I should be grown tall, and there would be congenial friends awaiting me.

VII. Incurring My Mother's Displeasure

In the second journey to the East I had not come without some precautions. I had a secret interview with one of our best medicine men, and when I left

---

[3]Selections from the Bible had been published in Dakota as early as 1839. The reference is probably to *Dakota Wowapi Wakan*, translated by Thomas S. Williamson and Stephen R. Riggs and published in 1879.

his wigwam I carried securely in my sleeve a tiny bunch of magic roots. This possession assured me of friends wherever I should go. So absolutely did I believe in its charms that I wore it through all the school routine for more than a year. Then, before I lost my faith in the dead roots, I lost the little buckskin bag containing all my good luck.

At the close of this second term of three years I was the proud owner of my first diploma. The following autumn I ventured upon a college career against my mother's will.

I had written for her approval, but in her reply I found no encouragement. She called my notice to her neighbors' children, who had completed their education in three years. They had returned to their homes, and were then talking English with the frontier settlers. Her few words hinted that I had better give up my slow attempt to learn the white man's ways, and be content to roam over the prairies and find my living upon wild roots. I silenced her by deliberate disobedience.

Thus, homeless and heavy-hearted, I began anew my life among strangers.

As I hid myself in my little room in the college dormitory, away from the scornful and yet curious eyes of the students, I pined for sympathy. Often I wept in secret, wishing I had gone West, to be nourished by my mother's love, instead of remaining among a cold race whose hearts were frozen hard with prejudice.

During the fall and winter seasons I scarcely had a real friend, though by that time several of my classmates were courteous to me at a safe distance.

My mother had not yet forgiven my rudeness to her, and I had no moment for letterwriting. By daylight and lamplight, I spun with reeds and thistles, until my hands were tired from their weaving, the magic design which promised me the white man's respect.

At length, in the spring term, I entered an oratorical contest among the various classes. As the day of competition approached, it did not seem possible that the event was so near at hand, but it came. In the chapel the classes assembled together, with their invited guests. The high platform was carpeted, and gayly festooned with college colors. A bright white light illumined the room, and outlined clearly the great polished beams that arched the domed ceiling. The assembled crowds filled the air with pulsating murmurs. When the hour for speaking arrived all were hushed. But on the wall the old clock which pointed out the trying moment ticked calmly on.

One after another I saw and heard the orators. Still, I could not realize that they longed for the favorable decision of the judges as much as I did. Each contestant received a loud burst of applause, and some were cheered heartily. Too soon my turn came, and I paused a moment behind the curtains for a deep breath. After my concluding words, I heard the same applause that the others had called out.

Upon my retreating steps, I was astounded to receive from my fellow-students a large bouquet of roses tied with flowing ribbons. With the lovely flowers I fled from the stage. This friendly token was a rebuke to me for the hard feelings I had borne them.

Later, the decision of the judges awarded me the first place. Then there was a mad uproar in the hall, where my classmates sang and shouted my name at the top of their lungs; and the disappointed students howled and brayed in fearfully dissonant tin trumpets. In this excitement, happy students rushed forward to offer their congratulations. And I could not conceal a smile when they wished to escort me in a procession to the students' parlor, where all were going to calm themselves. Thanking them for the kind spirit which prompted them to make such a proposition, I walked alone with the night to my own little room.

A few weeks afterward, I appeared as the college representative in another contest. This time the competition was among orators from different colleges in our State. It was held at the State capital, in one of the largest opera houses.

Here again was a strong prejudice against my people. In the evening, as the great audience filled the house, the student bodies began warring among themselves. Fortunately, I was spared witnessing any of the noisy wrangling before the contest began. The slurs against the Indian that stained the lips of our opponents were already burning like a dry fever within my breast.

But after the orations were delivered a deeper burn awaited me. There, before that vast ocean of eyes, some college rowdies threw out a large white flag, with a drawing of a most forlorn Indian girl on it. Under this they had printed in bold black letters words that ridiculed the college which was represented by a "squaw." Such worse than barbarian rudeness embittered me. While we waited for the verdict of the judges, I gleamed fiercely upon the throngs of palefaces. My teeth were hard set, as I saw the white flag still floating insolently in the air.

Then anxiously we watched the man carry toward the stage the envelope containing the final decision.

There were two prizes given, that night, and one of them was mine!

The evil spirit laughed within me when the white flag dropped out of sight, and the hands which hurled it hung limp in defeat.

Leaving the crowd as quickly as possible, I was soon in my room. The rest of the night I sat in an armchair and gazed into the crackling fire. I laughed no more in triumph when thus alone. The little taste of victory did not satisfy a hunger in my heart. In my mind I saw my mother far away on the Western plains, and she was holding a charge against me.

1900

Why I Am a Pagan[1]

When the spirit swells my breast I love to roam leisurely among the green hills; or sometimes, sitting on the brink of the murmuring Missouri, I marvel at the great blue overhead. With half closed eyes I watch the huge cloud

[1]This essay appeared in *Atlantic,* 90 (December, 1902), 801–803.

shadows in their noiseless play upon the high bluffs opposite me, while into my ear ripple the sweet, soft cadences of the river's song. Folded hands lie in my lap, for the time forgot. My heart and I lie small upon the earth like a grain of throbbing sand. Drifting clouds and tinkling waters, together with the warmth of a genial summer day, bespeak with eloquence the loving Mystery round about us. During the idle while I sat upon the sunny river brink, I grew somewhat, though my response be not so clearly manifest as in the green grass fringing the edge of the high bluff back of me.

At length retracing the uncertain footpath scaling the precipitous embankment, I seek the level lands where grow the wild prairie flowers. And they, the lovely little folk, soothe my soul with their perfumed breath.

Their quaint round faces of varied hue convince the heart which leaps with glad surprise that they, too, are living symbols of omnipotent thought. With a child's eager eye I drink in the myriad star shapes wrought in luxuriant color upon the green. Beautiful is the spiritual essence they embody.

I leave them nodding in the breeze, but take along with me their impress upon my heart. I pause to rest me upon a rock embedded on the side of a foothill facing the low river bottom. Here the Stone-Boy,[2] of whom the American aborigine tells, frolics about, shooting his baby arrows and shouting aloud with glee at the tiny shafts of lightning that flash from the flying arrow-beaks. What an ideal warrior he became, baffling the siege of the pests of all the land till he triumphed over their united attack. And here he lay,—Inyan our great-great-grandfather, older than the hill he rested on, older than the race of men who love to tell of his wonderful career.

Interwoven with the thread of this Indian legend of the rock, I fain would trace a subtle knowledge of the native folk which enabled them to recognize a kinship to any and all parts of this vast universe. By the leading of an ancient trail I move toward the Indian village.

With the strong, happy sense that both great and small are so surely enfolded in His magnitude that, without a miss, each has his allotted individual ground of opportunities, I am buoyant with good nature.

Yellow Breast, swaying upon the slender stem of a wild sunflower, warbles a sweet assurance of this as I pass near by. Breaking off the clear crystal song, he turns his wee head from side to side eyeing me wisely as slowly I plod with moccasined feet. Then again he yields himself to his song of joy. Flit, flit hither and yon, he fills the summer sky with his swift, sweet melody. And truly does it seem his vigorous freedom lies more in his little spirit than in his wing.

With these thoughts I reach the log cabin whither I am strongly drawn by the tie of a child to an aged mother. Out bounds my four-footed friend to meet me, frisking about my path with unmistakable delight. Chän is a black shaggy dog, "a thorough bred little mongrel" of whom I am very fond. Chän seems to understand many words in Sioux, and will go to her mat

[2]Stone Boy, or Inyanhoksila, possessed of supernatural powers, was a popular figure in Dakota lore.

even when I whisper the word, though generally I think she is guided by the tone of the voice. Often she tries to imitate the sliding inflection and long drawn out voice to the amusement of our guests, but her articulation is quite beyond my ear. In both my hands I hold her shaggy head and gaze into her large brown eyes. At once the dilated pupils contract into tiny black dots, as if the roguish spirit within would evade my questioning.

Finally resuming the chair at my desk I feel in keen sympathy with my fellow creatures, for I seem to see clearly again that all are akin.

The racial lines, which once were bitterly real, now serve nothing more than marking out a living mosaic of human beings. And even here men of the same color are like the ivory keys of one instrument where each resembles all the rest, yet varies from them in pitch and quality of voice. And those creatures who are for a time mere echoes of another's note are not unlike the fable of the thin sick man whose distorted shadow, dressed like a real creature, came to the old master to make him follow as a shadow. Thus with a compassion for all echoes in human guise, I greet the solemn-faced "native preacher" whom I find awaiting me. I listen with respect for God's creature, though he mouth most strangely the jangling phrases of a bigoted creed.

As our tribe is one large family, where every person is related to all the others, he addressed me:—

"Cousin, I came from the morning church service to talk with you."

"Yes?" I said interrogatively, as he paused for some word from me.

Shifting uneasily about in the straight-backed chair he sat upon, he began: "Every holy day (Sunday) I look about our little God's house, and not seeing you there, I am disappointed. This is why I come to-day. Cousin, as I watch you from afar, I see no unbecoming behavior and hear only good reports of you, which all the more burns me with the wish that you were a church member. Cousin, I was taught long years ago by kind missionaries to read the holy book. These godly men taught me also the folly of our old beliefs.

"There is one God who gives reward or punishment to the race of dead men. In the upper region the Christian dead are gathered in unceasing song and prayer. In the deep pit below, the sinful ones dance in torturing flames.

"Think upon these things, my cousin, and choose now to avoid the after-doom of hell fire!" Then followed a long silence in which he clasped tighter and unclasped again his interlocked fingers.

Like instantaneous lightning flashes came pictures of my own mother's making, for she, too, is now a follower of the new superstition.

"Knocking out the chinking of our log cabin, some evil hand thrust in a burning taper of braided dry grass, but failed of his intent, for the fire died out and the half burned brand fell inward to the floor. Directly above it, on a shelf, lay the holy book. This is what we found after our return from a several days' visit. Surely some great power is hid in the sacred book!"

Brushing away from my eyes many like pictures, I offered midday meal to the converted Indian sitting wordless and with downcast face. No sooner had he risen from the table with "Cousin, I have relished it," than the church bell rang.

Thither he hurried forth with his afternoon sermon. I watched him as he hastened along, his eyes bent fast upon the dusty road till he disappeared at the end of a quarter of a mile.

The little incident recalled to mind the copy of a missionary paper brought to my notice a few days ago, in which a "Christian" pugilist commented upon a recent article of mine, grossly perverting the spirit of my pen. Still I would not forget that the pale-faced missionary and the hoodooed aborigine are both God's creatures, though small indeed their own conceptions of Infinite Love. A wee child toddling in a wonder world, I prefer to their dogma my excursions into the natural gardens where the voice of the Great Spirit is heard in the twittering of birds, the rippling of mighty waters, and the sweet breathing of flowers. If this is Paganism, then at present, at least, I am a Pagan.

1902

WRITING AND PLACE

*P*lace seems like a perfectly simple concept. A place is "here" or "there" or "over there." Still, what makes a place "here" or "there" can be complicated and has been on this continent since the early days of exploration, colonization, and settlement. The Native peoples who were often slaughtered and almost always displaced by Europeans mourned for the places from which they had been forced; for decades, they regarded the places to which they were removed as resettlements. The generations of Africans and Europeans who came to this continent, whatever the conditions under which they came, tended to view places "here" in light of those they had left. And the Euro Americans who founded settlements in what was euphemistically seen as "virgin land" sometimes designed those new places to resemble the ones from which they came (many New Englanders who moved west reproduced the layout of New England villages) and often compared those settlements, for good and ill, to the places they had left.

Further complicating the picture, different places within the United States have different histories and to some extent distinctive characters. Before European settlement, Natchez, Taensea, and other Native peoples lived in what would become Louisiana, and the area was French for almost 100 years, then Spanish, then French again, before it became part of the United States. Massachusetts was inhabited mainly by Algonquin-speaking Native peoples and settled by English Protestants in the seventeenth century. Michigan was part of the country's western frontier in the 1820s, 1830s, and 1840s. The Mormons who settled in Utah in 1847 did so before the territory became part of the United States in 1848, and Mormon practices, especially polygamy, created a vexed relationship between Utah Territory and the United States for decades.

By the Reconstruction era, distinctions among different places within the United States seemed so well established that the nation was thought to comprise specific regions: the South, New England, the Midwest, the Southwest, the West. However, the character of regions was also complicated. Distinctive as each region may have been geographically and historically, and distinctive as each may have seemed demographically, culturally, and economically, each was also embedded in—and partly shaped or reshaped by—the nationwide forces that accelerated in the same period, from ever-expanding networks of transportation, industry, and commerce to intensified class stratification to a deepening conviction that the United States was rightly a nation-as-empire.

The example of the railroad offers a valuable window on how places were enmeshed within large-scale networks *and* appeared to be local and particular in the late nineteenth century. Railroads played a major role in that dynamic. Most obvious was their contribution to the consolidation of a national economy and culture. During the decades after the Civil War, railroads increasingly crisscrossed and linked various parts of the country; in 1873 they connected the east and west coasts. They thus underwrote the expansion of industry and commerce; not only were railroads themselves a business and an industry, but they also facilitated the transportation of agricultural products, raw materials, and goods. They also spurred the extension of the telegraph, which accompanied the laying of track, and contributed to the establishment of rural federal delivery of the mails, which became national policy in 1896. Because of them, local life was enhanced—some of the same canned goods, clothing, furniture, magazines, and books that were available in large cities (Chicago, Cleveland, New York) were also to be had in small towns in Wisconsin or Nebraska or Texas. Yet this also brought significant standardization, as literature and other reading material, clothing, and food became more uniform throughout the country.

Railroads also had what we might call a localizing effect. In the Midwest and especially the Great Plains, they were instrumental in *creating* localities. They sold land lots and underwrote the transportation of timber and crops that sustained local life, and they played a role, sometimes a central one, in forming the character of many places. In some places they were instrumental in limiting peoples' possibilities and intensifying their hardships. Hamlin Garland's "Up the Coulée" dwells on the bleak lives of Wisconsin farmers weighed down by mortgages from banks whose reach paralleled that of the railroads. Garland shows that the railroad did provide opportunity for a select few—the story's protagonist travels by train to high school in a nearby city, then leaves rural Wisconsin and becomes a successful actor—but, as "Up the Coulée" emphasizes, the departure of the fortunate could contribute to the desolation of local life by loosening family ties. The railroad was also vital in the emergence of certain places as industrial centers. Chicago's role as a major railroad hub coordinated with its status as the home of the meat-packing industry, a circumstance that itself went hand in hand with the creation of a large pool of industrial workers, many of them immigrants, and the proliferation of the slums in which most workers lived. Upton Sinclair's *The Jungle* (1906) dramatically exposed the conditions of immigrant workers' lives in Chicago.

More subtly, the railroad also contributed to the perceived divide between "modern" cities like New York, Chicago, Cleveland, and San Francisco and places that seemed either to be left behind, like Garland's "little town," or, like many rural New England villages, to be preserves of a traditional way of life. As they linked various parts of the United States, moreover, railroads helped make some places seem remote or nonmodern in ways that were themselves very modern. The appeal that the image of Garland's backwater town had for his urban readers rested partly on those readers' prior view that midwestern farm towns were desolate backwaters. Along different lines, villages on the coast of Maine, such as Ogunquit, Wells, and York, became thriving summer resorts for city dwellers when they were redesigned to mimic contemporary ideas of what New England villages untouched by modern life should look like. Railroad-sponsored photographs of the landscape and Native peoples of the Southwest, complemented by ethnographic writing by Mary Austin, Charles Loomis, and others, produced images of the area as sublime and starkly beautiful, and populated by authentically traditional Native peoples—an area ripe for the tourism that itself was made possible by the railroads.

If many Americans were aware that places that seemed straightforwardly local were not actually so at all, writing played a significant part in that awareness. A good deal of writing in the late nineteenth century focused intently on life in a specific place. Much of it participated in the regionalist movement in literature, the visual arts, and music that was devoted to representing the nation's regions. Regionalist writing usually presented local life as multiply situated: grounded in the environment, history, population, and practices of a place and also enmeshed in the nation's culture and its demographic trends, its history, and economy. Indeed, the richest regionalist writing was by authors who could assume both an insider's and an outsider's perspective: they had firsthand knowledge of the places and people they depicted as well as a distance that cast extra-local elements with which the local was intertwined in high relief. Sarah Orne Jewett and Mary E. Wilkins Freeman portray villages in Maine, New Hampshire, and elsewhere in New England that are traditionally or quirkily Yankee—and that means they are affected by immigration, outmigration, industrialism, commodity capitalism, and tourism, as well as by the region's earlier history and culture. The population and dialects in Rowland E. Robinson's fictional rural Vermont town of Danvis include French Canadians who speak accented English and Anglo-Protestants who speak in a Yankee vernacular. On the West coast, the lower California that Maria Ruiz de Burton depicts in *The Squatter and the Don* is a cauldron of conflicting local interests and racial tension that embroil *Californios* (Spanish-descended large landowners who were once members of the Mexican aristocracy but lost their status when *Alta California* was ceded to the United States by the Treaty of Guadaloupe-Hidalgo), white settlers (the squatters of the title), and Indian farm workers; these conflicts are themselves outgrowths of the Spanish colonization of *Alta California*, war between the United States and Mexico, and the spread of white settlement. While Frank Norris's ironically titled *"Fantasie Printanière"* (A Spring Fantasy") characterizes discord as a permanent feature of life among Irish immigrants in the tenements of San Francisco, his scope too was generally much broader. His planned *Epic of Wheat* trilogy probed the interconnections among the railroads, other corporate interests, and finance as they affected California wheat ranchers. The two novels he completed before his death, *The Octopus* and *The Pit*, spotlight the relentless expansion of the new large-scale forces of industrial and finance capitalism, which did not preclude the use of violence.

Regional writing's representation of place is still more complicated than this, for most regionalist literature was put out by major publishing houses in New York, Chicago, and Boston and was often influenced by the decisions and taste of editors and publishers. Much of it was also more openly pitched to readers who did not live in the places it represented than to those who did. For example, the frames of reference of the narrators of many works of regionalist fiction, including Jewett's brilliant *The Country of the Pointed Firs* (1896), are more cosmopolitan than are the people they portray. This makes local people and places seem provincial, even as in other ways the same works emphasize intersections of the local and the large scale.

During this period some work also concentrated on a particular place, emerged from within it, was created for the people it featured, and situated the local within the larger in ways that spoke eloquently to its intended audience. Alexander Posey's *Fus Fixico's* letters, for example, were satiric columns in Creek dialect that Posey wrote for his newspaper, the *Eufaula* (Okla.) *Indian Journal*.

Addressing matters of concern to the Creek Nation, of which Posey was a member, the letters connect such aspects of local life as the influx of commodities with the larger U.S. economy and culture and suggest that Creeks themselves should determine the extent to which commodities should be adopted; the letters also consistently air debates about whether Creek Territory, and Indian Territory more generally, should enter the Union as a state—and abandon tribal rule in consequence. Somewhat similarly, *corridos*—Spanish-language ballads that originated in Mexico and flourished along the Mexican–United States border—feature the arduousness of Latinos' labor, the complexities of their family lives, their resistance and resilience in the face of the violence to which U.S. law officers and the Texas rangers subjected them, and the heroism of figures like Gregorio Cortez.

The selections in this section of Volume C suggest that the writing of place kept pace with the many places that comprised the United States and that, almost always, rather than reproducing a preestablished script, it explored the relationships between a given place, with its own particularities, and the large-scale institutions and forces of which it was inevitably a part. It should be noted that writing about the South was so deeply invested in defining that region to itself and to the nation, particularly in redefining "black" and "white" once slavery had officially ended, that we devote a separate section to that writing. Yet even if we consider the South on its own, we should recognize that the writing of place does not comprise a body of work that, when taken together, yields a composite picture of the United States. Rather, it offers many perspectives on the complex relationships that made and remade places during a time of extraordinary change. We gain the most when we read it in that spirit.

Sandra A. Zagarell
Oberlin College

■ SARAH ORNE JEWETT ■
1849–1909

Sarah Orne Jewett was born in South Berwick, Maine, part of an extended family with deep roots in the Piscataqua River region. Her stories are intimately connected with that place. But she grew up to be a citizen of the world as well (by the standards of her day), through reading, a network of friendships, and travel. Jewett once wrote in a letter that she was "made of Berwick dust," and she also posted quotations from the French realist Gustave Flaubert above her writing desk. Both the local and the cosmopolitan are integral to her life and her fiction.

Jewett began publishing at a very early age. When she was just fourteen, some verses and a story appeared locally. At eighteen she placed a story in a popular Boston newspaper and began sending her work to the premier literary journal in America, *The Atlantic Monthly*. William Dean Howells, then assistant editor, accepted her third submission, and she was twenty when the first of many stories she would publish in the *Atlantic* appeared.

Jewett was not a professional writer, in the sense of depending on what she earned for her living. Her family, with merchants and sea captains in its past, was well off; her maternal grandfather and father were doctors. She herself considered becoming a physician, deciding against it because her health was not strong—although she was active and loved to be outdoors, all her life Jewett suffered from attacks of what we would now call rheumatoid arthritis. (She later wrote a novel about a woman becoming *A Country Doctor* [1884].) By the 1870s, however, when she was doing extensive revisions on a group of sketches about two girls spending the summer in an old village by the sea to produce her first book, *Deephaven* (1877), she could not possibly have worked harder at her writing—in fact, she exhausted herself and became ill. For the rest of her life, Jewett felt a commitment to literature and—amid her family responsibilities, social life, and travel—worked as much as she could and was a prolific author. It mattered a great deal, both for her sense of self and for her situation, that her publications eventually made Jewett financially independent.

Jewett may be better served in an anthology than many other writers, because she worked so much and so well in short narratives. Readers today may find it an obstacle, however, that she often experimented with forms that do not follow predictable linear patterns. For example, the sketch, a genre developed primarily though not exclusively by women during the nineteenth century, provided a short, flexible structure that encourages realistic depiction of specific environments, moods, relationships, customs, and characters without requiring pronounced conflicts and closure. Her maxims from Flaubert were "*Écrire la vie ordinaire comme on écrit l'histoire*"—write about daily life as you would write history—and "*Ce n'est pas de faire rire, ni de faire pleurer, ni de vous mettre à fureur, mais d'agir à la façon de la nature, c'est à dire de faire rêver*"—it is not to provoke tears, laughter, or rage, but to act as nature does, that is, to provoke dreaming. Her focus is often less on what happens than on the profound significance of the ordinary, on what is said and implied and imagined.

Central to Jewett's sense of vocation was her belief that she could do good through her writing. Her religious doubts and affinities—ranging from the seventeenth-century French Catholic François Fénelon to Theophilus Parsons, an American exponent of the eccentric visionary Swedenborg, and culminating in her shift from her family's Congregationalism to confirmation in the Episcopal Church—are well documented. In the early years of her career she often wrote for children, especially girls, and those stories are explicitly moral. All her work is informed by Christian faith—more implicitly decade by decade, as the tide of literary opinion turned against didacticism, and as her own views mellowed. It is not necessary to read her work through the lens of religion, but she represents a world that is fundamentally ordered and benevolent. Compassion and gratitude are not just sensations—they are cognitive principles. Jewett writes within the conventions of an increasingly secular realism, but she writes with the conviction that, as she put it in a letter, "Love isn't blind—it's only love that sees."

Jewett focused throughout her career on loving relationships among women. She grounded her own personal life in close friendships with women, the most important of which was her long relationship with Annie Fields, a woman prominent and powerful in her own right in the Boston literary and publishing world. The two women's commitment to each other began in the early 1880s, shortly after the death of Annie's husband, the publisher James Fields, and became the strongest bond in the author's adult life. Fields and Jewett traveled widely in Europe and the eastern United States and lived a large part of every year together, dividing their time between Boston and the New England shore (the remainder of the year Jewett lived in her family home in South Berwick). Their household on Charles Street in the Back Bay in Boston served as an important literary center where well-known figures in the publishing world, from Howells in the 1880s to Cather in the early 1900s, visited and gathered.

Jewett connected two generations of women writers. She counted among her influences Harriet Beecher Stowe, whose New England fiction she greatly admired, and she figured prominently in the tradition of women realists and regionalists active in the second half of the nineteenth century: Rose Terry Cooke, Celia Thaxter, Mary E. Wilkins Freeman, Alice Brown, Elizabeth Stuart Phelps. At the turn of the century, writers as different as Kate Chopin and Willa Cather looked to Jewett as a model. (Edith Wharton did as well, though she chose to call attention to her independence from Jewett rather than her affinity with her.) Cather acknowledged a strong debt to Jewett, dedicated *O Pioneers!* (1913)—her first novel centered on a woman—to Jewett, and said in 1925 that *The Country of the Pointed Firs* ranked with *The Scarlet Letter* and *Huckleberry Finn* as an American classic.

Toward the end of her career, Jewett brilliantly fused her interests in rural community, female friendship, the making of art, and the structure of narrative in *The Country of the Pointed Firs*. These concerns also shape "A White Heron" (1881), probably Jewett's best-known individual story; "Martha's Lady"; and "The Foreigner" (1900), which is set in the world of Dunnet Landing created in *The Country of the Pointed Firs*.

"A White Heron" may be seen as dramatizing the clash of competing sets of values in late-nineteenth-century industrial America: urban/rural, scientific/empathic, masculine/feminine. However, it was much less the collection of specimens by ornithologists, than their harvesting for plumes to decorate women's hats, that had endangered the Snowy Egret. A story of female initiation—or perhaps anti-initiation—it offers a highly critical perspective on heterosexual romantic attraction in modern Western culture and presciently poses problems now being addressed by ecocriticism and environmental history.

"Martha's Lady" appears to set aside those tensions in its focus on the life-changing, lifelong devotion that a provincial servant feels for a privileged woman whom she meets only twice. Its moving exploration of transfiguring friendship depends on the sense that the past is alive in the present, that the quietest and most obscure life matters—but also on the asymmetries of social class. Indeed, Jewett's work consistently assumes the benevolence of hierarchies we may question today. They are underpinned by a racialized vision of civilization that takes for granted the local, national, and global dominance of particular ethnic groups, and the West in general. Jewett's Dunnet Landing story "The Queen's Twin," which appeared in the same volume of stories as "Martha's Lady," places women's almost-occult bonds into the framework of empire and even implies a link to the emerging power of celebrity in a world of mass communications.

"The Foreigner" takes Jewett's lifelong fascination with the mysteries of connectedness a step further. She wrote in *The Country of the Pointed Firs* that "Tact is a form of mind-reading," and she is willing to speculate that communication across the boundary between life and death may be possible. Jewett's work invites us into, and asks us to value, a quite particular regional world. At the same time, it implies the possibility—perhaps the promise—of other realities. Her stories project an alternative, female-centered world of bonds between mothers and daughters, and sisterly friends; they imagine a "golden chain of love and dependence" (to quote *The Country of the Pointed Firs*) linking individuals into an enduring, virtually utopian community quite different from the "Gilded Ages" of her turn of the century or our own. "A White Heron" suggests a mysterious connection between species, and "The Foreigner" shows the supernatural surfacing in an everyday setting. For Jewett, just as South Berwick is not separate from but part of the Atlantic world, the ordinary and the extraordinary are one.

June Howard
University of Michigan

Elizabeth Ammons
Tufts University

PRIMARY WORKS

Deephaven, 1877; *A Country Doctor*, 1884; *A White Heron and Other Stories*, 1886; *Strangers and Wayfarers*, 1890; *The Country of the Pointed Firs*, 1896; *The Queen's Twin and Other Tales*, 1899; *The Tory Lover*, 1901; *The Irish Stories of Sarah Orne Jewett*, ed. Jack Morgan and Louis A. Renza, 1996.

A White Heron

I

The woods were already filled with shadows one June evening, just before eight o'-clock, though a bright sunset still glimmered faintly among the trunks of the trees. A little girl was driving home her cow, a plodding, dilatory, provoking creature in her behavior, but a valued companion for all that. They were going away from whatever light there was, and striking deep into the woods, but their feet were familiar with the path, and it was no matter whether their eyes could see it or not.

There was hardly a night the summer through when the old cow could be found waiting at the pasture bars; on the contrary, it was her greatest pleasure to hide herself away among the huckleberry bushes, and though she wore a loud bell she had made the discovery that if one stood perfectly still it would not ring. So Sylvia had to hunt for her until she found her, and call Co'! Co'! with never an answering Moo, until her childish patience was quite spent. If the creature had not given good milk and plenty of it, the case would have seemed very different to her owners. Besides, Sylvia had all the time there was, and very little use to make of it. Sometimes in pleasant weather it was a consolation to look upon the cow's pranks as an intelligent attempt to play hide and seek, and as the child had no playmates she lent herself to this amusement with a good deal of zest. Though this chase had been so long that the wary animal herself had given an unusual signal of her whereabouts, Sylvia had only laughed when she came upon Mistress Moolly at the swampside, and urged her affectionately homeward with a twig of birch leaves. The old cow was not inclined to wander farther, she even turned in the right direction for once as they left the pasture, and stepped along the road at a good pace. She was quite ready to be milked now, and seldom stopped to browse. Sylvia wondered what her grandmother would say because they were so late. It was a great while since she had left home at half-past five o'clock, but everybody knew the difficulty of making this errand a short one. Mrs. Tilley had chased the hornéd torment too many summer evenings herself to blame any one else for lingering, and was only thankful as she waited that she had Sylvia, nowadays, to give such valuable assistance. The good woman suspected that Sylvia loitered occasionally on her own account; there never was such a child for straying about out-of-doors since the world was made! Everybody said that it was a good change for a little maid who had tried to grow for eight years in a crowded manu-facturing town, but, as for Sylvia herself, it seemed as if she never had been alive at all before she came to live at the farm. She thought often with wist-ful compassion of a wretched geranium that belonged to a town neighbor.

"'Afraid of folks,'" old Mrs. Tilley said to herself, with a smile, after she had made the unlikely choice of Sylvia from her daughter's houseful of chil-dren, and was returning to the farm. "'Afraid of folks,' they said! I guess she won't be troubled no great with 'em up to the old place!" When they reached the door of the lonely house and stopped to unlock it, and the cat came to purr loudly, and rub against them, a deserted pussy, indeed, but fat with young robins, Sylvia whispered that this was a beautiful place to live in, and she never should wish to go home.

The companions followed the shady woodroad, the cow taking slow steps and the child very fast ones. The cow stopped long at the brook to drink, as if the pasture were not half a swamp, and Sylvia stood still and waited, letting her bare feet cool themselves in the shoal water, while the great twilight moths struck softly against her. She waded on through the brook as the cow moved away, and listened to the thrushes with a heart that beat fast with pleasure. There was a stirring in the great boughs overhead. They were full of little birds and beasts that seemed to be wide awake, and going about their world, or else saying good-night to each other in sleepy twitters. Sylvia herself felt sleepy as she walked along. However, it was not much farther to the house, and the air was soft and sweet. She was not of-ten in the woods so late as this, and it made her feel as if she were a part of the gray shadows and the moving leaves. She was just thinking how long it seemed since she first came to the farm a year ago, and wondering if every-thing went on in the noisy town just the same as when she was there; the thought of the great red-faced boy who used to chase and frighten her made her hurry along the path to escape from the shadow of the trees.

Suddenly this little woods-girl is horror-stricken to hear a clear whistle not very far away. Not a bird's-whistle, which would have a sort of friendli-ness, but a boy's whistle, determined, and somewhat aggressive. Sylvia left the cow to whatever sad fate might await her, and stepped discreetly aside into the bushes, but she was just too late. The enemy had discovered her, and called out in a very cheerful and persuasive tone, "Halloa, little girl, how far is it to the road?" and trembling Sylvia answered almost inaudibly, "A good ways."

She did not dare to look boldly at the tall young man, who carried a gun over his shoulder, but she came out of her bush and again followed the cow, while he walked alongside.

"I have been hunting for some birds," the stranger said kindly, "and I have lost my way, and need a friend very much. Don't be afraid," he added gallantly. "Speak up and tell me what your name is, and whether you think I can spend the night at your house, and go out gunning early in the morning."

Sylvia was more alarmed than before. Would not her grandmother con-sider her much to blame? But who could have foreseen such an accident as this? It did not seem to be her fault, and she hung her head as if the stem of it were broken, but managed to answer "Sylvy," with much effort when her companion again asked her name.

Mrs. Tilley was standing in the doorway when the trio came into view. The cow gave a loud moo by way of explanation.

"Yes, you'd better speak up for yourself, you old trial! Where'd she tucked herself away this time, Sylvy?" But Sylvia kept an awed silence; she knew by instinct that her grandmother did not comprehend the gravity of the situation. She must be mistaking the stranger for one of the farmer-lads of the region.

The young man stood his gun beside the door, and dropped a lumpy game-bag beside it; then he bade Mrs. Tilley good-evening, and repeated his wayfarer's story, and asked if he could have a night's lodging.

"Put me anywhere you like," he said. "I must be off early in the morning, before day; but I am very hungry, indeed. You can give me some milk at any rate, that's plain."

"Dear sakes, yes," responded the hostess, whose long slumbering hospi-tality seemed to be easily awakened. "You might fare better if you went out to the main road a mile or so, but you're welcome to what we've got. I'll milk right off, and you make yourself at home. You can sleep on husks or feath-ers," she proffered graciously. "I raised them all myself. There's good pastur-ing for geese just below here towards the ma'sh. Now step round and set a plate for the gentleman, Sylvy!" And Sylvia promptly stepped. She was glad to have something to do, and she was hungry herself.

It was a surprise to find so clean and comfortable a little dwelling in this New England wilderness. The young man had known the horrors of its most primitive housekeeping, and the dreary squalor of that level of society which does not rebel at the companionship of hens. This was the best thrift of an old-fashioned farmstead, though on such a small scale that it seemed like a hermitage. He listened eagerly to the old woman's quaint talk, he watched Sylvia's pale face and shining gray eyes with ever growing enthusiasm, and insisted that this was the best supper he had eaten for a month, and afterward the new-made friends sat down in the door-way together while the moon came up.

Soon it would be berry-time, and Sylvia was a great help at picking. The cow was a good milker, though a plaguy thing to keep track of, the hostess gossiped frankly, adding presently that she had buried four children, so Sylvia's mother, and a son (who might be dead) in California were all the children she had left. "Dan, my boy, was a great hand to go gunning," she explained sadly. "I never wanted for pa'tridges or gray squer'ls while he was to home. He's been a great wand'rer, I expect, and he's no hand to write letters. There, I don't blame him, I'd ha' seen the world myself if it had been so I could."

"Sylvy takes after him," the grandmother continued affectionately, after a minute's pause. "There ain't a foot o' ground she don't know her way over, and the wild creatures counts her one o' themselves. Squer'ls she'll tame to come an' feed right out o' her hands, and all sorts o' birds. Last winter she got the jaybirds to bangeing[1] here, and I believe she'd 'a' scanted herself of her own meals to have plenty to throw out amongst 'em, if I had n't kep' watch. Anything but crows, I tell her, I'm willin' to help support—though Dan he had a tamed one o' them that did seem to have reason same as folks. It was round here a good spell after he went away. Dan an' his father they did n't hitch,—but he never held up his head ag'in after Dan had dared him an' gone off."

The guest did not notice this hint of family sorrows in his eager interest in something else.

"So Sylvy knows all about birds, does she?" he exclaimed, as he looked round at the little girl who sat, very demure but increasingly sleepy, in the moonlight. "I am making a collection of birds myself. I have been at it ever since I was a boy." (Mrs. Tilley smiled.) "There are two or three very rare ones I have been hunting for these five years. I mean to get them on my own ground if they can be found."

"Do you cage 'em up?" asked Mrs. Tilley doubtfully, in response to this enthusiastic announcement.

"Oh no, they're stuffed and preserved, dozens and dozens of them," said the ornithologist, "and I have shot or snared every one myself. I caught a glimpse of a white heron a few miles from here on Saturday, and I have followed it in this direction. They have never been found in this district at all.

[1] A New England term for loafing or lounging about.

The little white heron, it is," and he turned again to look at Sylvia with the hope of discovering that the rare bird was one of her acquaintances.

But Sylvia was watching a hop-toad in the narrow footpath.

"You would know the heron if you saw it," the stranger continued eagerly. "A queer tall white bird with soft feathers and long thin legs. And it would have a nest perhaps in the top of a high tree, made of sticks, something like a hawk's nest."

Sylvia's heart gave a wild beat; she knew that strange white bird, and had once stolen softly near where it stood in some bright green swamp grass, away over at the other side of the woods. There was an open place where the sunshine always seemed strangely yellow and hot, where tall, nodding rushes grew, and her grandmother had warned her that she might sink in the soft black mud underneath and never be heard of more. Not far beyond were the salt marshes just this side the sea itself, which Sylvia wondered and dreamed much about, but never had seen, whose great voice could sometimes be heard above the noise of the woods on stormy nights.

"I can't think of anything I should like so much as to find that heron's nest," the handsome stranger was saying. "I would give ten dollars to anybody who could show it to me," he added desperately, "and I mean to spend my whole vacation hunting for it if need be. Perhaps it was only migrating, or had been chased out of its own region by some bird of prey."

Mrs. Tilley gave amazed attention to all this, but Sylvia still watched the toad, not divining, as she might have done at some calmer time, that the creature wished to get to its hole under the door-step, and was much hindered by the unusual spectators at that hour of the evening. No amount of thought, that night, could decide how many wished-for treasures the ten dollars, so lightly spoken of, would buy.

The next day the young sportsman hovered about the woods, and Sylvia kept him company, having lost her first fear of the friendly lad, who proved to be most kind and sympathetic. He told her many things about the birds and what they knew and where they lived and what they did with themselves. And he gave her a jackknife, which she thought as great a treasure as if she were a desert-islander. All day long he did not once make her troubled or afraid except when he brought down some unsuspecting singing creature from its bough. Sylvia would have liked him vastly better without his gun; she could not understand why he killed the very birds he seemed to like so much. But as the day waned, Sylvia still watched the young man with loving admiration. She had never seen anybody so charming and delightful; the woman's heart, asleep in the child, was vaguely thrilled by a dream of love. Some premonition of that great power stirred and swayed these young creatures who traversed the solemn woodlands with soft-footed silent care. They stopped to listen to a bird's song; they pressed forward again eagerly, parting the branches—speaking to each other rarely and in whispers; the young man going first and Sylvia following, fascinated, a few steps behind, with her gray eyes dark with excitement.

She grieved because the longed-for white heron was elusive, but she did not lead the guest, she only followed, and there was no such thing as speaking first. The sound of her own unquestioned voice would have terrified her—it was hard enough to answer yes or no when there was need of that. At last evening began to fall, and they drove the cow home together, and Sylvia smiled with pleasure when they came to the place where she heard the whistle and was afraid only the night before.

II

Half a mile from home, at the farther edge of the woods, where the land was highest, a great pine-tree stood, the last of its generation. Whether it was left for a boundary mark, or for what reason, no one could say; the wood-choppers who had felled its mates were dead and gone long ago, and a whole forest of sturdy trees, pines and oaks and maples, had grown again. But the stately head of this old pine towered above them all and made a landmark for sea and shore miles and miles away. Sylvia knew it well. She had always believed that whoever climbed to the top of it could see the ocean; and the little girl had often laid her hand on the great rough trunk and looked up wistfully at those dark boughs that the wind always stirred, no matter how hot and still the air might be below. Now she thought of the tree with a new excitement, for why, if one climbed it at break of day could not one see all the world, and easily discover from whence the white heron flew, and mark the place, and find the hidden nest?

What a spirit of adventure, what wild ambition! What fancied triumph and delight and glory for the later morning when she could make known the secret! It was almost too real and too great for the childish heart to bear.

All night the door of the little house stood open and the whippoorwills came and sang upon the very step. The young sportsman and his old hostess were sound asleep, but Sylvia's great design kept her broad awake and watching. She forgot to think of sleep. The short summer night seemed as long as the winter darkness, and at last when the whippoorwills ceased, and she was afraid the morning would after all come too soon, she stole out of the house and followed the pasture path through the woods, hastening toward the open ground beyond, listening with a sense of comfort and companionship to the drowsy twitter of a half-awakened bird, whose perch she had jarred in passing. Alas, if the great wave of human interest which flooded for the first time this dull little life should sweep away the satisfactions of an existence heart to heart with nature and the dumb life of the forest!

There was the huge tree asleep yet in the paling moonlight, and small and silly Sylvia began with utmost bravery to mount to the top of it, with tingling, eager blood coursing the channels of her whole frame, with her bare feet and fingers, that pinched and held like bird's claws to the monstrous ladder reaching up, up, almost to the sky itself. First she must mount the white oak tree that grew alongside, where she was almost lost among

the dark branches and the green leaves heavy and wet with dew; a bird fluttered off its nest, and a red squirrel ran to and fro and scolded pettishly at
the harmless housebreaker. Sylvia felt her way easily. She had often climbed
there, and knew that higher still one of the oak's upper branches chafed
against the pine trunk, just where its lower boughs were set close together.
There, when she made the dangerous pass from one tree to the other, the
great enterprise would really begin.

She crept out along the swaying oak limb at last, and took the daring
step across into the old pine-tree. The way was harder than she thought;
she must reach far and hold fast, the sharp dry twigs caught and held her
and scratched her like angry talons, the pitch made her thin little fingers
clumsy and stiff as she went round and round the tree's great stem, higher
and higher upward. The sparrows and robins in the woods below were beginning to wake and twitter to the dawn, yet it seemed much lighter there
aloft in the pine-tree, and the child knew she must hurry if her project were
to be of any use.

The tree seemed to lengthen itself out as she went up, and to reach farther and farther upward. It was like a great main-mast to the voyaging
earth; it must truly have been amazed that morning through all its ponderous frame as it felt this determined spark of human spirit wending its way
from higher branch to branch. Who knows how steadily the least twigs held
themselves to advantage this light, weak creature on her way! The old pine
must have loved his new dependent. More than all the hawks, and bats, and
moths, and even the sweet voiced thrushes, was the brave, beating heart of
the solitary gray-eyed child. And the tree stood still and frowned away the
winds that June morning while the dawn grew bright in the east.

Sylvia's face was like a pale star, if one had seen it from the ground,
when the last thorny bough was past, and she stood trembling and tired but
wholly triumphant, high in the treetop. Yes, there was the sea with the
dawning sun making a golden dazzle over it, and toward that glorious east
flew two hawks with slow-moving pinions. How low they looked in the air
from that height when one had only seen them before far up, and dark
against the blue sky. Their gray feathers were as soft as moths; they seemed
only a little way from the tree, and Sylvia felt as if she too could go flying
away among the clouds. Westward, the woodlands and farms reached miles
and miles into the distance; here and there were church steeples, and white
villages, truly it was a vast and awesome world!

The birds sang louder and louder. At last the sun came up bewilder-
ingly bright. Sylvia could see the white sails of ships out at sea, and the
clouds that were purple and rose-colored and yellow at first began to fade
away. Where was the white heron's nest in the sea of green branches, and
was this wonderful sight and pageant of the world the only reward for
having climbed to such a giddy height? Now look down again, Sylvia,
where the green marsh is set among the shining birches and dark hem-
locks; there where you saw the white heron once you will see him again;
look, look! a white spot of him like a single floating feather comes up from

the dead hemlock and grows larger, and rises, and comes close at last, and goes by the landmark pine with steady sweep of wing and outstretched slender neck and crested head. And wait! wait! do not move a foot or a finger, little girl, do not send an arrow of light and consciousness from your two eager eyes, for the heron has perched on a pine bough not far beyond yours, and cries back to his mate on the nest and plumes his feathers for the new day!

The child gives a long sigh a minute later when a company of shouting cat-birds comes also to the tree, and vexed by their fluttering and lawlessness the solemn heron goes away. She knows his secret now, the wild, light, slender bird that floats and wavers, and goes back like an arrow presently to his home in the green world beneath. Then Sylvia, well satisfied, makes her perilous way down again, not daring to look far below the branch she stands on, ready to cry sometimes because her fingers ache and her lamed feet slip. Wondering over and over again what the stranger would say to her, and what he would think when she told him how to find his way straight to the heron's nest.

"Sylvy, Sylvy!" called the busy old grandmother again and again, but nobody answered, and the small husk bed was empty and Sylvia had disappeared.

The guest waked from a dream, and remembering his day's pleasure hurried to dress himself that might it sooner begin. He was sure from the way the shy little girl looked once or twice yesterday that she had at least seen the white heron, and now she must really be made to tell. Here she comes now, paler than ever, and her worn old frock is torn and tattered, and smeared with pine pitch. The grandmother and the sportsman stand in the door together and question her, and the splendid moment has come to speak of the dead hemlock-tree by the green marsh.

But Sylvia does not speak after all, though the old grandmother fretfully rebukes her, and the young man's kind, appealing eyes are looking straight in her own. He can make them rich with money; he has promised it, and they are poor now. He is so well worth making happy, and he waits to hear the story she can tell.

No, she must keep silence! What is it that suddenly forbids her and makes her dumb? Has she been nine years growing and now, when the great world for the first time puts out a hand to her, must she thrust it aside for a bird's sake? The murmur of the pine's green branches is in her ears, she remembers how the white heron came flying through the golden air and how they watched the sea and the morning together, and Sylvia cannot speak; she cannot tell the heron's secret and give its life away.

Dear loyalty, that suffered a sharp pang as the guest went away disappointed later in the day, that could have served and followed him and loved him as a dog loves! Many a night Sylvia heard the echo of his whistle haunting the pasture path as she came home with the loitering cow. She forgot even her sorrow at the sharp report of his gun and the sight of thrushes and sparrows dropping silent to the ground, their songs hushed and their pretty feathers stained and wet with blood. Were the birds better friends than their hunter might have been,—who can tell? Whatever treasures were lost to her, woodlands and summer-time, remember! Bring your gifts and graces and tell your secrets to this lonely country child!

1886

The Foreigner

1

One evening, at the end of August, in Dunnet Landing, I heard Mrs. Todd's firm footstep crossing the small front entry outside my door, and her conventional cough which served as a herald's trumpet, or a plain New England knock, in the harmony of out fellowship.

"Oh, please come in!" I cried, for it had been so still in the house that I supposed my friend and hostess had gone to see one of her neighbors. The first cold north-easterly storm of the season was blowing hard outside. Now and then there was a dash of great raindrops and a flick of wet lilac leaves against the window, but I could hear that the sea was already stirred to its dark depths, and the great rollers were coming in heavily against the shore. One might well believe that Summer was coming to a sad end that night, in the darkness and rain and sudden access of autumnal cold. It seemed as if there must be danger offshore among the outer islands.

"Oh, there!" exclaimed Mrs. Todd, as she entered. "I know nothing ain't ever happened out to Green Island since the world began, but I always do worry about mother in these great gales. You know those tidal waves occur sometimes down to the West Indies, and I get dwellin' on 'em so I can't set still in my chair, nor knit a common row to a stocking. William might get mooning, out in his small bo't, and not observe how the sea was making, an' meet with some accident. Yes, I thought I'd come in and set with you if you wa'n't busy. No, I never feel any concern about 'em in winter 'cause then they're prepared, and all ashore and everything snug. William ought to keep help, as I tell him; yes, he ought to keep help."

I hastened to reassure my anxious guest by saying that Elijah Tilley had told me in the afternoon, when I came along the shore past the fish houses, that Johnny Bowden and the Captain were out at Green Island; he had seen them beating up the bay, and thought they must have put into Burnt Island cove, but one of the lobstermen brought word later that he saw them hauling out at Green Island as he came by, and Captain Bowden pointed ashore and shook his head to say that he did not mean to try to get in. "The old Miranda just managed it, but she will have to stay at home a day or two and put new patches in her sail," I ended, not without pride in so much circumstantial evidence.

Mrs. Todd was alert in a moment. "Then they'll all have a very pleasant evening," she assured me, apparently dismissing all fears of tidal waves and other sea-going disasters. "I was urging Alick Bowden to go ashore some day and see mother before cold weather. He's her own nephew; she sets a great deal by him. And Johnny's a great chum o' William's; don't you know the first day we had Johnny out 'long of us, he took an' give William his money to keep for him that he'd been a savin', and William showed it to me an' was so affected I thought he was goin' to shed tears? 'T was a dollar an' eighty cents; yes, they'll have a beautiful evenin' all together, and like's not the sea'll be flat as a doorstep come morning."

I had drawn a large wooden rocking-chair before the fire, and Mrs. Todd was sitting there jogging herself a little, knitting fast, and wonderfully placid of countenance. There came a fresh gust of wind and rain, and we could feel the small wooden house rock and hear it creak as if it were a ship at sea.

"Lord, hear the great breakers!" exclaimed Mrs. Todd. "How they pound!—there, there! I always run of an idea that the sea knows anger these nights and gets full o' fight. I can hear the rote o' them old black ledges way down the thoroughfare. Calls up all those stormy verses in the Book o' Psalms; David he knew how old seagoin' folks have to quake at the heart."

I thought as I had never thought before of such anxieties. The families of sailors and coastwise adventurers by sea must always be worrying about somebody, this side of the world or the other. There was hardly one of Mrs. Todd's elder acquaintances, men or women, who had not at some time or other made a sea voyage, and there was often no news until the voyagers themselves came back to bring it.

"There's a roaring high overhead, and a roaring in the deep sea," said Mrs. Todd solemnly, "and they battle together nights like this. No, I could n't sleep; some women folks always goes right to bed an' to sleep, so's to forget, but 't aint my way. Well, it's a blessin' we don't all feel alike; there's hardly any of our folks at sea to worry about, nowadays, but I can't help my feelin's, an' I got thinking of mother all alone, if William had happened to be out lobsterin' and could n't make the cove gettin' back."

"They will have a pleasant evening," I repeated. "Captain Bowden is the best of good company."

"Mother'll make him some pancakes for his supper, like's not," said Mrs. Todd, clicking her knitting needles and giving a pull at her yarn. Just then the old cat pushed open the unlatched door and came straight toward her mistress's lap. She was regarded severely as she stepped about and turned on the broad expanse, and then made herself into a round cushion of fur, but was not openly admonished. There was another great blast of wind overhead, and a puff of smoke came down the chimney.

"This makes me think o' the night Mis' Cap'n Tolland died," said Mrs. Todd, half to herself. "Folks used to say these gales only blew when somebody's a-dyin', or the devil was a-comin' for his own, but the worst man I ever knew died a real pretty mornin' in June."

"You have never told me any ghost stories," said I; and such was the gloomy weather and the influence of the night that I was instantly filled with reluctance to have this suggestion followed. I had not chosen the best of moments; just before I spoke we had begun to feel as cheerful as possible. Mrs. Todd glanced doubtfully at the cat and then at me, with a strange absent look, and I was really afraid that she was going to tell me something that would haunt my thoughts on every dark stormy night as long as I lived.

"Never mind now; tell me to-morrow by daylight, Mrs. Todd," I hastened to say, but she still looked at me full of doubt and deliberation.

"Ghost stories!" she answered. "Yes, I don't know but I've heard a plenty of 'em first an' last. I was just sayin' to myself that this is like the night Mis' Cap'n Tolland died. 'T was the great line storm in September all of thirty, or maybe forty, year ago. I ain't one that keeps much account o' time."

"Tolland? That's a name I have never heard in Dunnet," I said.

"Then you have n't looked well about the old part o' the buryin' ground, no'th-east corner," replied Mrs. Todd. "All their women folks lies there; the sea's got most o' the men. They were a known family o' shipmasters in early times. Mother had a mate, Ellen Tolland, that she mourns to this day; died right in her bloom with quick consumption, but the rest o' that family was all boys but one, and older than she, an' they lived hard seafarin' lives an' all died hard. They were called very smart seamen. I've heard that when the youngest went into one o' the old shippin' houses in Boston, the head o' the firm called out to him: 'Did you say Tolland from Dunnet? That's recommendation enough for any vessel!' There was some o' them old shipmasters as tough as iron, an' they had the name o' usin' their crews very severe, but there wa'n't a man that would n't rather sign with 'em an' take his chances, than with the slack ones that did n't know how to meet accidents."

II

There was so long a pause, and Mrs. Todd still looked so absent-minded, that I was afraid she and the cat were growing drowsy together before the fire, and I should have no reminiscences at all. The wind struck the house again, so that we both started in our chairs and Mrs. Todd gave a curious, startled look at me. The cat lifted her head and listened too, in the silence that followed, while after the wind sank we were more conscious than ever of the awful roar of the sea. The house jarred now and then, in a strange, disturbing way.

"Yes, they'll have a beautiful evening out to the island," said Mrs. Todd again; but she did not say it gayly. I had not seen her before in her weaker moments.

"Who was Mrs. Captain Tolland?" I asked eagerly, to change the current of our thoughts.

"I never knew her maiden name; if I ever heard it, I've gone an' forgot; 't would mean nothing to me," answered Mrs. Todd.

"She was a foreigner, an' he met with her out in the Island o' Jamaica. They said she'd been left a widow with property. Land knows what become of it; she was French born, an' her first husband was a Portugee, or somethin'."

I kept silence now, a poor and insufficient question being worse than none.

"Cap'n John Tolland was the least smartest of any of 'em, but he was full smart enough, an' commanded a good brig at the time, in the sugar trade; he'd taken out a cargo o' pine lumber to the islands from somewheres up the river, an' had been loadin' for home in the port o' Kingston, an' had gone ashore that afternoon for his papers, an' remained afterwards 'long of three friends o' his, all shipmasters. They was havin' their suppers together in a tavern; 't was late in the evenin' an' they was more lively than usual, an' felt boyish; and ever opposite was another house full o' company, real bright and pleasant lookin', with a lot o' lights, an' they heard somebody singin' very pretty to a guitar, They wa'n't in no go-to-meetin' condition, an' one of 'em, he slapped the table an' said, 'Le' 's go over an' hear that lady sing!' an' over they all went, good honest sailors, but three sheets in the wind, and stepped in as if they was invited, an' made their bows inside the door, an' asked if they could hear the music; they were all respectable well-dressed men. They saw the woman that had the guitar, an' there was a company a-listenin', regular highbinders[1] all of 'em; an' there was a long table all spread out with big candlesticks like little trees o' light, and a sight o' glass an' silver ware; an' part o' the men was young officers in uniform, an' the colored folks was steppin' round servin' 'em, an' they had the lady singin'. 'T was a wasteful scene, an' a loud talkin' company, an' though they was three sheets in the wind themselves there wa'n't one o' them cap'ns but had sense to perceive it. The others had pushed back their chairs, an' their decanters an' glasses was standin' thick about, an' they was teasin' the one that was singin' as if they'd just got her in to amuse 'em. But they quieted down; one o' the young officers had beautiful manners, an' invited the four cap'ns to join 'em, very polite; 't was a kind of public house, and after they 'd all heard another song, he come to consult with 'em whether they would n't git up and dance a hornpipe or somethin' to the lady's music.

"They was all elderly men an' shipmasters, and owned property; two of 'em was church members in good standin'," continued Mrs. Todd loftily, "an' they would n't lend theirselves to no such kick-shows as that, an' spite o' bein' three sheets in the wind, as I have once observed; they waved aside the tumblers of wine the young officer was pourin' out for 'em so free-handed, and said they should rather be excused. An' when they all rose, still very dignified, as I've been well informed, and made their partin' bows and was goin' out, them young sports got round 'em, an' tried to prevent 'em, and they had to push an' strive considerable, but out they come. There was this Cap'n Tolland and two Cap'n Bowdens, and the fourth was my own father." (Mrs. Todd spoke slowly, as if to impress the value of her authority.) "Two of them was very religious, upright men, but they would have

---

[1]The Highbinders were a gang of vagabonds in New York City in the early 1800s; the term came to refer to any ruffian or swindler.

their night off sometimes, all o' them old-fashioned cap'ns, when they was free of business and ready to leave port.

"An' they went back to their tavern an' got their bills paid, an' set down kind o' mad with everybody by the front windows, mistrusting some o' their tavern charges, like's not, by that time, an' when they got tempered down, they watched the house over across, where the party was.

"There was a kind of a grove o' trees between the house an' the road, an' they heard the guitar a-goin' an' a-stoppin' short by turns, and pretty soon somebody began to screech, an' they saw a white dress come runnin' out through the bushes, an' tumbled over each other in their haste to offer help; an' out she come, with the guitar, cryin' into the street, and they just walked off four square with her amongst 'em, down toward the wharves where they felt more to home. They could n't make out at first what 't was she spoke,— Cap'n Lorenzo Bowden was well acquainted in Havre an' Bordeaux, an' spoke a poor quality o' French, an' she knew a little mite o' English, but not much; and they come somehow or other to discern that she was in real distress. Her husband and her children had died o' yellow fever; they 'd all come up to Kingston from one o' the far Wind'ard Islands to get passage on a steamer to France, an' a negro had stole their money off her husband while he lay sick o' the fever, an' she had been befriended some, but the folks that knew about her had died too; it had been a dreadful run o' the fever that season, an' she fell at last to playin' an' singin' for hire, and for what money they'd throw to her round them harbor houses.

"'T was a real hard case, an' when them cap'ns made out about it, there wa'n't one that meant to take leave without helpin' of her. They was pretty mellow, an' whatever they might lack o' prudence they more 'n made up with charity: they did n't want to see nobody abused, an' she was sort of a pretty woman, an' they stopped in the street then an' there an' drew lots who should take her aboard, bein' all bound home. An' the lot fell to Cap'n Jonathan Bowden who did act discouraged; his vessel had but small accommodations, though he could stow a big freight, an' she was a dreadful slow sailer through bein' square as a box, an' his first wife, that was livin' then, was a dreadful jealous woman. He threw himself right onto the mercy o' Cap'n Tolland."

Mrs. Todd indulged herself for a short time in a season of calm reflection.

"I always thought they 'd have done better, and more reasonable, to give her some money to pay her passage home to France, or wherever she may have wanted to go," she continued.

I nodded and looked for the rest of the story.

"Father told mother," said Mrs. Todd confidentially, "that Cap'n Jonathan Bowden an' Cap'n John Tolland had both taken a little more than usual; I would n't have you think, either, that they both was n't the best o' men, an' they was solemn as owls, and argued the matter between 'em, an' waved aside the other two when they tried to put their oars in. An' spite o' Cap'n Tolland's bein' a settled old bachelor they fixed it that he was to take the prize on his brig; she was a fast sailer, and there was a good spare cabin or two where he'd sometimes carried passengers, but he'd filled 'em with bags o' sugar on his own account an' was loaded very heavy beside. He said he'd shift the sugar an' get along somehow, an' the last the other three cap'ns saw of the party was Cap'n John handing the lady into his bo't, guitar and all, an' off they all set tow'ds their ships with their men rowin' 'em in the bright moonlight down to Port Royal where the anchorage was, an' where they all lay, goin' out with the tide an' mornin' wind at break o' day. An' the others thought they heard music of the guitar, two o' the bo'ts kept well together, but it may have come from another source."

"Well; and then?" I asked eagerly after a pause. Mrs. Todd was almost laughing aloud over her knitting and nodding emphatically. We had forgotten all about the noise of the wind and sea.

"Lord bless you! he come sailing into Portland with his sugar, all in good time, an' they stepped right afore a justice o' the peace, and Cap'n John Tolland come paradin' home to Dunnet Landin' a married man. He owned one o' them thin, narrow-lookin' houses with one room each side o' the front door, and two slim black spruces spindlin' up against the front windows to make it gloomy inside. There was no horse nor cattle of course, though he owned pasture land, an' you could see rifts o' light right through the barn as you drove by. And there was a good excellent kitchen, but his sister reigned over that; she had a right to two rooms, and took the kitchen an' a bedroom that led out of it; an' bein' given no rights in the kitchen had angered the cap'n so they were n't on no kind o' speakin' terms. He preferred his old brig for comfort, but now and then, between voyages, he'd come home for a few days, just to show he was master over his part o' the house, and show Eliza she could n't commit no trespass.

"They stayed a little while; 't was pretty spring weather, an' I used to see Cap'n John rollin' by with his arms full o' bundles from the store, lookin' as pleased and important as a boy; an' then they went right off to sea again, an' was gone a good many months. Next time he left her to live there alone, after they'd stopped at home together some weeks, an' they said she suffered from bein' at sea, but some said that the owners would n't have a woman aboard. 'T was before father was lost on that last voyage of his, an' he and mother went up once or twice to see them. Father said there wa'n't a mite o' harm in her, but somehow or other a sight o' prejudice arose; it may have been caused by the remarks of Eliza an' her feelin's tow'ds her brother. Even my mother had no regard for Eliza Tolland. But mother asked the cap'n's wife to come with her one evenin' to a social circle that was down to the meetin'-house vestry, so she'd get acquainted a little, an' she appeared very pretty until they started to have some singin' to the melodeon. Mari' Harris an' one o' the younger Caplin girls undertook to sing a duet, an' they sort o' flatted, an' she put her hands right up to her ears, and give a little squeal, an' went quick as could be an' give 'em the right notes, for she could read the music like plain print, an' made 'em try it over again. She was real willin' an' pleasant, but that did n't suit, an' she made faces when they got it wrong. An' then there fell a dead calm, an' we was all settin' round prim as dishes, an' my mother, that never expects ill feelin', asked her if she would n't sing somethin', an' up she got,—poor creatur', it all seems so different to me now,—an' sung a lovely little song standin' in the floor; it seemed to have something gay about it that kept a-repeatin', an' nobody could help keepin' time, an' all of a sudden she looked round at the tables and caught up a tin plate that somebody 'd fetched a Washin'ton pie in, an' she begun to drum on it with her fingers like one o' them tambourines, an' went right on singin' faster an' faster, and next minute she begun to dance a little pretty dance between the verses, just as light and pleasant as a child. You could n't help seein' how pretty 't was; we all got to trottin' a foot, an' some o' the men clapped their hands quite loud, a-keepin' time, 't was so catchin', an' seemed so natural to her. There wa'n't one of 'em but enjoyed it; she just tried to do her part, an' some urged her on, till she stopped with a little twirl of her skirts an' went to her place again by mother. And I can see mother now, reachin' over an' smilin' an' pattin' her hand.

"But next day there was an awful scandal goin' in the parish, an' Mari' Harris reproached my mother to her face, an' I never wanted to see her since, but I've had to a good many times. I said Mis' Tolland did n't intend no impropriety,—I reminded her of David's dancin' before the Lord; but she said such a man as David never would have thought o' dancin' right there in the Orthodox vestry, and she felt I spoke with irreverence.

"And next Sunday Mis' Tolland come walkin' into our meeting, but I must say she acted like a cat in a strange garret, and went right out down the aisle with her head in air, from the pew Deacon Caplin had showed her into. 'T was just in the beginning of the long prayer. I wish she'd stayed through, whatever her reasons were. Whether she'd expected somethin' different, or misunderstood some o' the pastor's remarks, or what 't was, I don't really feel able to explain, but she kind o' declared war, at least folks thought so, an' war 't was from that time. I see she was cryin', or had been, as she passed by me; perhaps bein' in meetin' was what had power to make her feel homesick and strange.

"Cap'n John Tolland was away fittin' out; that next week he come home to see her and say farewell. He was lost with his ship in the Straits of Malacca, and she lived there alone in the old house a few months longer till she died. He left her well off; 't was said he hid his money about the house and she knew where 't was. Oh, I expect you've heard that story told over an' over twenty times, since you've been here at the Landin'?"

"Never one word," I insisted.

"It was a good while ago," explained Mrs. Todd, with reassurance. "Yes, it all happened a great while ago."

III

At this moment, with a sudden flaw of the wind, some wet twigs outside blew against the window panes and made a noise like a distressed creature trying to get in. I started with sudden fear, and so did the cat, but Mrs. Todd knitted away and did not even look over her shoulder.

"She was a good-looking woman; yes, I always thought Mis' Tolland was good-looking, though she had, as was reasonable, a sort of foreign cast, and she spoke very broken English, no better than a child. She was always at work about her house, or settin' at a front window with her sewing; she was a beautiful hand to embroider. Sometimes, summer evenings, when the windows was open, she'd set an' drum on her guitar, but I don't know as I ever heard her sing but once after the cap'n went away. She appeared very happy about havin' him, and took on dreadful at partin' when he was down here on the wharf, going back to Portland by boat to take ship for that last v'y'ge. He acted kind of ashamed, Cap'n John did; folks about here ain't so much accustomed to show their feelings. The whistle had blown an' they was waitin' for him to get aboard, an' he was put to it to know what to do and treated her very affectionate in spite of all impatience; but mother happened to be there and she went an' spoke, and I remember what a comfort she seemed to be. Mis' Tolland clung to her then, and she would n't give a glance after the boat when it had started, though the captain was very eager a-wavin' to her. She wanted mother to come home with her an' would n't let go her hand, and mother had just come in to stop all night with me an' had plenty o' time ashore, which did n't always happen, so they walked off together, an' 't was some considerable time before she got back.

"'I want you to neighbor with that poor lonesome creatur',' says mother to me, lookin' reproachful. 'She's a stranger in a strange land,' says mother. 'I want you to make her have a sense that somebody feels kind to her.'

"'Why, since that time she flaunted out o' meetin', folks have felt she liked other ways better 'n our'n,' says I. I was provoked, because I'd had a nice supper ready, an' mother 'd let it wait so long 't was spoiled. 'I hope you'll like your supper!' I told her. I was dreadful ashamed afterward of speakin' so to mother.

"'What consequence is my supper?' says she to me; mother can be very stern,—'or your comfort or mine, beside letting a foreign person an' a stranger feel so desolate; she's done the best a woman could do in her lonesome place, and she asks nothing of anybody except a little common kindness. Think if 't was you in a foreign land!'

"And mother set down to drink her tea, an' I set down humbled enough over by the wall to wait till she finished. An' I did think it all over, an' next day I never said nothin', but I put on my bonnet, and went to see Mis' Cap'n Tolland, if 't was only for mother's sake. 'T was about three quarters of a mile up the road here, beyond the schoolhouse. I forgot to tell you that the cap'n had bought out his sister's right at three or four times what 't was worth, to save trouble, so they'd got clear o' her, an' I went round into the side yard sort o' friendly an' sociable, rather than stop an' deal with the knocker an' the front door. It looked so pleasant an' pretty I was glad I come; she had set a little table for supper, though 't was still early, with a white cloth on it, right out under an old apple tree close by the house. I noticed 't was same as with me at home, there was only one plate. She was just coming out with a dish; you could n't see the door nor the table from the road.

"In the few weeks she'd been there she 'd got some bloomin' pinks an' other flowers next the doorstep. Somehow it looked as if she'd known how to make it homelike for the cap'n. She asked me to set down; she was very polite, but she looked very mournful, and I spoke of mother, an' she put down her dish and caught holt o' me with both hands an' said my mother was an angel. When I see the tears in her eyes 't was all right between us, and we were always friendly after that, and mother had us come out and make a little visit that summer; but she come a foreigner and she went a foreigner, and never was anything but a stranger among our folks. She taught me a sight o' things about herbs I never knew before nor since; she was well acquainted with the virtues o' plants. She'd act awful secret about some things too, an' used to work charms for herself sometimes, an' some o' the neighbors told to an' fro after she died that they knew enough not to provoke her, but 't was all nonsense; 't is the believin' in such things that causes 'em to be any harm, an' so I told 'em," confided Mrs. Todd contemptuously. "That first night I stopped to tea with her she'd cooked some eggs with some herb or other sprinkled all through, and 't was she that first led me to discern mushrooms; an' she went right down on her knees in my garden here when she saw I had my different officious herbs. Yes, 't was she that learned me the proper use o' parsley too; she was a beautiful cook."

Mrs. Todd stopped talking, and rose, putting the cat gently in the chair, while she went away to get another stick of apple-tree wood. It was not an evening when one wished to let the fire go down, and we had a splendid bank of bright coals. I had always wondered where Mrs. Todd had got such an unusual knowledge of cookery, of the varieties of mushrooms, and the use of sorrel as a vegetable, and other blessings of that sort. I had long ago learned that she could vary her omelettes like a child of France, which was indeed a surprise in Dunnet Landing.

IV

All these revelations were of the deepest interest, and I was ready with a question as soon as Mrs. Todd came in and had well settled the fire and herself and the cat again.

"I wonder why she never went back to France, after she was left alone?"

"She come here from the French islands," explained Mrs. Todd. "I asked her once about her folks, an' she said they were all dead; 't was the fever took 'em. She made this her home, lonesome as 't was; she told me she had n't been in France since she was 'so small,' and measured me off a child o' six. She'd lived right out in the country before, so that part wa'n't unusual to her. Oh yes, there was something very strange about her, and she had n't been brought up in high circles not nothing o' that kind. I think she'd been really pleased to have the cap'n marry her an' give her a good home, after all she'd passed through, and leave her free with his money an' all that. An' she got over bein' so strange-looking to me after a while, but 't was a very singular expression: she wore a fixed smile that wa'n't a smile; there wa'n't no light behind it, same 's a lamp can't shine if it ain't lit. I don't know just how to express it, 't was a sort of made countenance."

One could not help thinking of Sir Philip Sidney's phrase, "A made countenance, between simpering and smiling."

"She took it hard, havin' the captain go off on that last voyage," Mrs. Todd went on. "She said somethin' told her when they was partin' that he would never come back. He was lucky to speak a home-bound ship this side o' the Cape o' Good Hope, an' got a chance to send her a letter, an' that cheered her up. You often felt as if you was dealin' with a child's mind, for all she had so much information that other folks had n't. I was a sight younger than I be now, and she made me imagine new things, and I got interested watchin' her an' findin' out what she had to say, but you could n't get to no affectionateness with her. I used to blame me sometimes; we used to be real good comrades goin' off for an afternoon, but I never give her a kiss till the day she laid in her coffin and it come to my heart there wa'n't no one else to do it."

"And Captain Tolland died," I suggested after a while.

"Yes, the cap'n was lost," said Mrs. Todd, "and of course word did n't come for a good while after it happened. The letter come from the owners to my uncle, Cap'n Lorenzo Bowden, who was in charge of Cap'n Tolland's affairs at home, and he come right up for me an' said I must go with him to the house. I had known what it was to be a widow, myself, for near a year, an' there was plenty o' widow women along this coast that the sea had made desolate, but I never saw a heart break as I did then.

"'T was this way: we walked together along the road, me an' uncle Lorenzo. You know how it leads straight from just above the schoolhouse to the brook bridge, and their house was just this side o' the brook bridge on the left hand; the cellar's there now, and a couple or three good-sized gray birches growin' in it. And when we come near enough I saw that the best room, this way, where she most never set, was all lighted up, and the curtains up so that the light shone bright down the road, and as we walked, those lights would dazzle and dazzle in my eyes, and I could hear the guitar a-goin', an' she was singin'. She heard our steps with her quick ears and come running to the door with her eyes a-shinin', an' all that set look gone out of her face, an' begun to talk French, gay as a bird, an' shook hands and behaved very pretty an' girlish, sayin' 't was her fête day.[2] I did n't know what she meant then. And she had gone an' put a wreath o' flowers on her hair an' wore a handsome gold chain that the cap'n had given her; an' there she was, poor creatur', makin' believe have a party all alone in her best room; 't was prim enough to discourage a person, with too many

---

[2]In France, one's fête day is the day which the Roman Catholic Church has assigned as the festival of the saint who bears one's first name. This day is often celebrated in preference to one's birthday.

chairs set close to the walls, just as the cap'n's mother had left it, but she had put sort o' long garlands on the walls, droopin' very graceful, and a sight of green boughs in the corners, till it looked lovely, and all lit up with a lot o' candles."

"Oh dear!" I sighed. "Oh, Mrs. Todd, what did you do?"

"She beheld our countenances," answered Mrs. Todd solemnly. "I expect they was telling everything plain enough, but Cap'n Lorenzo spoke the sad words to her as if he had been her father; and she wavered a minute and then over she went on the floor before we could catch hold of her, and then we tried to bring her to herself and failed, and at last we carried her upstairs, an' I told uncle to run down and put out the lights, and then go fast as he could for Mrs. Begg, being very experienced in sickness, an' he so did. I got off her clothes and her poor wreath, and I cried as I done it. We both stayed there that night, and the doctor said 't was a shock when he come in the morning; he'd been over to Black Island an' had to stay all night with a very sick child."

"You said that she lived alone some time after the news came," I reminded Mrs. Todd then.

"Oh yes, dear," answered my friend sadly, "but it wa'n't what you'd call livin'; no, it was only dyin', though at a snail's pace. She never went out again those few months, but for a while she could manage to get about the house a little, and do what was needed, an' I never let two days go by without seein' her or hearin' from her. She never took much notice as I came an' went except to answer if I asked her anything. Mother was the one who gave her the only comfort."

"What was that?" I asked softly.

"She said that anybody in such trouble ought to see their minister, mother did, and one day she spoke to Mis' Tolland, and found that the poor soul had been believin' all the time that there were n't any priests here. We'd come to know she was a Catholic by her beads and all, and that had set some narrow minds against her. And mother explained it just as she would to a child; and uncle Lorenzo sent word right off somewheres up river by a packet that was bound up the bay, and the first o' the week a priest come by the boat, an' uncle Lorenzo was on the wharf 'tendin' to some business; so they just come up for me, and I walked with him to show him the house. He was a kind-hearted old man; he looked so benevolent an' fatherly I could ha' stopped an' told him my own troubles; yes, I was satisfied when I first saw his face, an' when poor Mis' Tolland beheld him enter the room, she went right down on her knees and clasped her hands together to him as if he'd come to save her life, and he lifted her up and blessed her, an' I left 'em together, and slipped out into the open field and walked there in sight so if they needed to call me, and I had my own thoughts. At last I saw him at the door; he had to catch the return boat. I meant to walk back with him and offer him some supper, but he said no, and said he was comin' again if needed, and signed me to go into the house to her, and shook his head in a way that meant he understood everything. I can see him now; he walked with a cane, rather tired and feeble; I wished somebody would come along, so's to carry him down to the shore.

"Mis' Tolland looked up at me with a new look when I went in, an' she even took hold o' my hand and kept it. He had put some oil on her forehead, but nothing anybody could do would keep her alive very long; 't was his medicine for the soul rather 'n the body. I helped her to bed, and next morning she could n't get up to dress her, and that was Monday, and she began to fail, and 't was Friday night she died." (Mrs. Todd spoke with unusual haste and lack of detail.) "Mrs. Begg and I watched with her, and made everything nice and proper, and after all the ill will there was a good number gathered to the funeral. 'T was in Reverend Mr. Bascom's day, and he done very well in his prayer, considering he could n't fill in with mentioning all the near connections by name as was his habit. He spoke very feeling about her being a stranger and twice widowed, and all he said about her being reared among the heathen was to observe that there might be roads leadin' up to the New Jerusalem from various points. I says to myself that I guessed quite a number must ha' reached there that wa'n't able to set out from Dunnet Landin'!"

Mrs. Todd gave an odd little laugh as she bent toward the firelight to pick up a dropped stitch in her knitting, and then I heard a heartfelt sigh.

"'T was most forty years ago," she said; "most everybody's gone a'ready that was there that day."

V

Suddenly Mrs. Todd gave an energetic shrug of her shoulders, and a quick look at me, and I saw that the sails of her narrative were filled with a fresh breeze.

"Uncle Lorenzo, Cap'n Bowden that I have referred to"—

"Certainly!" I agreed with eager expectation.

"He was the one that had been left in charge of Cap'n John Tolland's affairs, and had now come to be of unforeseen importance.

"Mrs. Begg an' I had stayed in the house both before an' after Mis' Tolland's decease, and she was now in haste to be gone, having affairs to call her home; but uncle come to me as the exercises was beginning, and said he thought I'd better remain at the house while they went to the buryin' ground. I could n't understand his reasons, an' I felt disappointed, bein' as near to her as most anybody; 't was rough weather, so mother could n't get in, and did n't even hear Mis' Tolland was gone till next day. I just nodded to satisfy him, 't wa'n't no time to discuss anything. Uncle seemed flustered; he'd gone out deep-sea fishin' the day she died, and the storm I told you of rose very sudden, so they got blown off way down the coast beyond Monhegan, and he'd just got back in time to dress himself and come.

"I set there in the house after I'd watched her away down the straight road far 's I could see from the door; 't was a little short walkin' funeral an' a cloudy sky, so everything looked dull an' gray, an' it crawled along all in one piece, same 's walking funerals do, an' I wondered how it ever come to the Lord's mind to let her begin down among them gay islands all heat and sun, and end up here among the rocks with a north wind blowin'. 'T was a gale that begun the afternoon before she died, and had kept blowin' off an' on ever since. I'd thought more than once how glad I should be to get home an' out o' sound o' them black spruces a-beatin' an' scratchin' at the front windows.

"I set to work pretty soon to put the chairs back, an' set outdoors some that was borrowed, an' I went out in the kitchen, an' I made up a good fire in case somebody come an' wanted a cup o' tea; but I did n't expect any one to travel way back to the house unless 't was uncle Lorenzo. 'T was growin' so chilly that I fetched some kindlin' wood and made fires in both the fore rooms. Then I set down an' begun to feel as usual, and I got my knittin' out of a drawer. You can't be sorry for a poor creatur' that's come to the end o' all her troubles; my only discomfort was I thought I'd ought to feel worse at losin' her than I did; I was younger then than I be now. And as I set there, I begun to hear some long notes o' dronin' music from upstairs that chilled me to the bone."

Mrs. Todd gave a hasty glance at me.

"Quick 's I could gather me, I went right upstairs to see what 't was," she added eagerly, "an' 't was just what I might ha' known. She'd always kept her guitar hangin' right against the wall in her room; 't was tied by a blue ribbon, and there was a window left wide open; the wind was veerin' a good deal, an' it slanted in and searched the room. The strings was jarrin' yet.

"'T was growin' pretty late in the afternoon, an' I begun to feel lonesome as I should n't now, and I was disappointed at having to stay there, the more I thought it over, but after a while I saw Cap'n Lorenzo polin' back up the road all alone, and when he come nearer I could see he had a bundle under his arm and had shifted his best black clothes for his every-day ones. I run out and put some tea into the teapot and set it back on the stove to draw, an' when he come in I reached down a little jug o' spirits,—Cap'n Toll-and had left his house well provisioned as if his wife was goin' to put to sea same's himself, an' there she'd gone an' left it. There was some cake that Mis' Begg an' I had made the day before. I thought that uncle an' me had a good right to the funeral supper, even if there wa'n't any one to join us. I was lookin' forward to my cup o' tea; 't was beautiful tea out of a green lacquered chest that I 've got now."

"You must have felt very tired," said I, eagerly listening.

"I was 'most beat out, with watchin' an' tendin' and all," answered Mrs. Todd, with as much sympathy in her voice as if she were speaking of another person. "But I called out to uncle as he came in, 'Well, I expect it's all over now, an' we 've all done what we could. I thought we'd better have some tea or somethin' before we go home. Come right out in the kitchen, sit,' says I, never thinking but we only had to let the fires out and lock up everything safe an' eat our refreshment, an' go home.

"'I want both of us to stop here tonight,' says uncle, looking at me very important.

"'Oh, what for?' says I, kind o' fretful.

"'I've got my proper reasons,' says uncle. 'I'll see you well satisfied, Almira. Your tongue ain't so easy-goin' as some o' the women folks, an' there's property here to take charge of that you don't know nothin' at all about.'

"'What do you mean?' says I.

"'Cap'n Tolland acquainted me with his affairs; he had n't no sort o' confidence in nobody but me an' his wife, after he was tricked into signin' that Portland note, an' lost money. An' she did n't know nothin' about business; but what he didn't take to sea to be sunk with him he's hid somewhere in this house. I expect Mis' Tolland may have told you where she kept things?' said uncle.

"I see he was dependin' a good deal on my answer," said Mrs. Todd, "but I had to disappoint him; no, she had never said nothin' to me.

"'Well, then, we 've got to make a search,' says he, with considerable relish; but he was all tired and worked up, and we set down to the table, an' he had somethin', an' I took my desired cup o' tea, and then I begun to feel more interested.

"'Where you goin' to look first?' says I, but he give me a short look an' made no answer, and begun to mix me a very small portion out of the jug, in another glass. I took it to please him; he said I looked tired, speakin' real fatherly, and I did feel better for it, and we set talkin' a few minutes, an' then he started for the cellar, carrying an old ship's lantern he fetched out o' the stairway an' lit.

"'What are you lookin' for, some kind of a chist?' I inquired, and he said yes. All of a sudden it come to me to ask who was the heirs; Eliza Tolland, Cap'n John's own sister, had never demeaned herself to come near the funeral, and uncle Lorenzo faced right about and begun to laugh, sort o' pleased. I thought queer of it; 't wa'n't what he'd taken, which would be nothin' to an old weathered sailor like him.

"'Who's the heir?' says I the second time.

"'Why, it's *you*, Almiry,' says he; and I was so took aback I set right down on the turn o' the cellar stairs.

"'Yes 't is,' said uncle Lorenzo. 'I'm glad of it too. Some thought she did n't have no sense but foreign sense, an' a poor stock o' that, but she said you was friendly to her, an' one day after she got news of Tolland's death, an' I had fetched up his will that left everything to her, she said she was goin' to make a writin', so's you could have things after she was gone, an' she give five hundred to me for bein' executor. Square Pease fixed up the paper, an' she signed it; it's all accordin' to law.' There, I begun to cry," said Mrs. Todd; "I could n't help it. I wished I had her back again to do somethin' for, an' to make her know I felt sisterly to her more 'n I'd ever showed, an' it come over me 't was all too late, an' I cried the more, till uncle showed impatience, an' I got up an' stumbled along down cellar with my apern to my eyes the greater part of the time.

"'I'm goin' to have a clean search,' says he; 'you hold the light.' An' I held it, and he rummaged in the arches an' under the stairs, an' over in some old closet where he reached out bottles an' stone jugs an' canted some kags an' one or two casks, an' chuckled well when he heard there was somethin' inside,—but there wa'n't nothin' to find but things usual in a cellar, an' then the old lantern was givin' out an' we come away.

"'He spoke to me of a chist, Cap'n Tolland did,' says uncle in a whisper. 'He said a good sound chist was as safe a bank as there was, an' I beat him out of such nonsense, 'count o' fire an' other risks,' 'There's no chist in the rooms above,' says I; 'no, uncle, there ain't no sea-chist, for I've been here long enough to see what there was to be seen.' Yet he would n't feel contented till he'd mounted up into the toploft; 't was one o' them single, hip-roofed houses that don't give proper accommodation for a real garret, like Cap'n Littlepage's down here at the Landin'. There was broken furniture and rubbish, an' he let down a terrible sight o' dust into the front entry, but sure enough there was n't no chist. I had it all to sweep up next day.

"'He must have took it away to sea,' says I to the cap'n, an' even then he did n't want to agree, but we was both beat out. I told him where I'd always seen Mis' Tol-land get her money from, and we found much as a hundred dollars there in an old red morocco wallet. Cap'n John had been gone a good while a'ready, and she had spent what she needed. 'T was in an old desk o' his in the settin' room that we found the wallet."

"At the last minute he may have taken his money to sea," I suggested.

"Oh yes," agreed Mrs. Todd. "He did take considerable to make his venture to bring home, as was customary, an' that was drowned with him as uncle agreed; but he had other property in shipping, and a thousand dollars invested in Portland in a cordage shop, but 't was about the time shipping begun to decay, and the cordage shop faded, and in the end I wa'n't so rich as I thought I was goin' to be for those few minutes on the cellar stairs. There was an auction that accumulated something. Old Mis' Tolland, the cap'n's mother, had heired some good furniture from a sister: there was above thirty chairs in all, and they 're apt to sell well. I got over a thousand dollars when we come to settle up, and I made uncle take his five hundred; he was getting along in years and had met with losses in navigation, and he left it back to me when he died, so I had a real good lift. It all lays in the bank over to Rockland, and I draw my interest fall an' spring, with the little Mr. Todd was to leave me; but that's kind o' sacred money; 't was earnt and saved with the hope o' youth, an' I'm very particular what I spend it for. Oh yes, what with ownin' my house, I've been enabled to get along very well, with prudence!" said Mrs. Todd contentedly.

"But there was the house and land," I asked,—"what became of that part of the property?"

Mrs. Todd looked into the fire, and a shadow of disapproval flitted over her face.

"Poor old uncle!" she said, "he got childish about the matter. I was hoping to sell at first, and I had an offer, but he always run of an idea that there was more money hid away, and kept wanting me to delay; an' be used to go up there all alone and search, and dig in the cellar, empty an' bleak as 't was in winter weather or any time. An' he'd come and tell me he'd dreamed he found gold behind a stone in the cellar wall, or somethin'. And one night we all see the light o' fire up that way, an' the whole Landin' took the road, and run to look, and the Tolland property was all in a light blaze. I expect the old gentleman had dropped fire about; he said he'd been up there to see if everything was safe in the afternoon. As for the land, 't was so poor that everybody used to have a joke that the Tolland boys preferred to farm the sea instead. It's 'most all grown up to bushes now, where it ain't poor water grass in the low places. There's some upland that has a pretty view, after you cross the brook bridge. Years an' years after she died, there was some o' her flowers used to come up an' bloom in the door garden. I brought two or three that was unusual down here; they always come up and remind me of her, constant as the spring. But I never did want to fetch home that guitar, some way or 'nother; I would n't let it go at the auction, either. It was hangin' right there in the house when the fire took place. I've got some o' her other little things scattered about the house: that picture on the mantel-piece belonged to her."

I had often wondered where such a picture had come from, and why Mrs. Todd had chosen it; it was a French print of the statue of the Empress Josephine[3] in the Savane at old Fort Royal, in Martiniqu.

VI

Mrs. Todd drew her chair closer to mine; she held the cat and her knitting with one hand as she moved, but the cat was so warm and so sound asleep that she only stretched a lazy paw in spite of what must have felt like a slight earthquake. Mrs. Todd began to speak almost in a whisper.

"I ain't told you all," she continued; "no, I have n't spoken of all to but very few. The way it came was this," she said solemnly, and then stopped to listen to the wind, and sat for a moment in deferential silence, as if she waited for the wind to speak first. The cat suddenly lifted her head with quick excitement and gleaming eyes, and her mistress was leaning forward toward the fire with an arm laid on either knee, as if they were consulting the glowing coals for some augury. Mrs. Todd looked like an old prophetess as she sat there with the firelight shining on her strong face; she was posed for some great painter. The woman with the cat was as unconscious and as mysterious as any sibyl of the Sistine Chapel.[4]

"There, that's the last struggle o' the gale," said Mrs. Todd, nodding her head with impressive certainty and still looking into the bright embers of

---

[3]The Empress Josephine (1763–1814) was the wife of Napoleon Bonaparte and Empress of France. She was often considered the epitome of foreign elegance and extravagance.

[4]The ceiling of the Sistine Chapel in Rome, painted by Michelangelo, is ringed by sibyls, prophetesses of the pagan religion of Greece and Rome.

the fire. "You'll see!" She gave me another quick glance, and spoke in a low tone as if we might be overheard.

"'T was such a gale as this the night Mis' Tolland died. She appeared more comfortable first o' the evenin'; and Mrs. Begg was more spent than I, bein' older, and a beautiful nurse that was the first to see and think of everything, but perfectly quiet an' never asked a useless question. You remember her funeral when you first come to the Landing? And she consented to goin' an' havin' a good sleep while she could, and left me one o' those good little pewter lamps that burnt whale oil an' made plenty o' light in the room, but not too bright to be disturbin'.

"Poor Mis' Tolland had been distressed the night before, an' all that day, but as night come on she grew more and more easy, an' was layin' there asleep; 't was like settin' by any sleepin' person, and I had none but usual thoughts. When the wind lulled and the rain, I could hear the seas, though more distant than this, and I don' know's I observed any other sound than what the weather made; 't was a very solemn feelin' night. I set close by the bed; there was times she looked to find somebody when she was awake. The light was on her face, so I could see her plain; there was always time when she wore a look that made her seem a stranger you'd never set eyes on before. I did think what a world it was that her an' me should have come together so, and she have nobody but Dunnet Landin' folks about her in her extremity. 'You're one o' the stray ones, poor creatur',' I said. I remember those very words passin' through my mind, but I saw reason to be glad she had some comforts, and did n't lack friends at the last, though she'd seen misery an' pain. I was glad she was quiet; all day she'd been restless, and we could n't understand what she wanted from her French speech. We had the window open to give her air, an' now an' then a gust would strike that guitar that was on the wall and set it swinging by the blue ribbon, and soundin' as if somebody begun to play it. I come near takin' it down, but you never know what'll fret a sick person an' put 'em on the rack, an' that guitar was one o' the few things she'd brought with her."

I nodded assent, and Mrs. Todd spoke still lower.

"I set there close by the bed; I'd been through a good deal for some days back, and I thought I might's well be droppin' asleep too, bein' a quick person to wake. She looked to me as if she might last a day longer, certain, now she'd got more comfortable, but I was real tired, an' sort o' cramped as watchers will get, an' a fretful feeling begun to creep over me such as they often do have. If you give way, there ain't no support for the sick person; they can't count on no composure o' their own. Mis' Tolland moved then, a little restless, an' I forgot me quick enough, an' begun to hum out a little part of a hymn tune just to make her feel everything was as usual an' not wake up into a poor uncertainty. All of a sudden she set right up in bed with her eyes wide open, an' I stood an' put my arm behind her; she had n't moved like that for days. And she reached out both her arms toward the door, an' I looked the way she was lookin', an' I see some one was standin' there against the dark. No, 't wa'n't Mis' Begg; 't was somebody a good deal shorter than Mis' Begg. The lamplight struck across the room between us. I could n't tell the shape, but 't was a woman's dark face lookin' right at us; 't wa'n't but an instant I could see. I felt dreadful cold, and my head begun to swim; I thought the light went out; 't wa'n't but an instant, as I say, an' when my sight come back I could n't see nothing there. I was one that did n't know what it was to faint away, no matter what happened; time was I felt above it in others, but 't was somethin' that made poor human natur' quail. I saw very plain while I could see; 't was a pleasant enough face, shaped somethin' like Mis' Tolland's, and a kind of expectin' look.

"No, I don't expect I was asleep," Mrs. Todd assured me quietly, after a moment's pause, though I had not spoken. She gave a heavy sigh before she went on. I could see that the recollection moved her in the deepest way.

"I suppose if I had n't been so spent an' quavery with long watchin', I might have kept my head an' observed much better," she added humbly; "but I see all I could bear. I did try to act calm, an' I laid Mis' Tolland down on her pillow, an' I was ashakin' as I done it. All she did was to look up to me so satisfied and sort o' questioning, an' I looked back to her.

"'You saw her, did n't you?' she says to me, speakin' perfectly reasonable. ''T is my mother,' she says again, very feeble, but lookin' straight up at me, kind of surprised with the pleasure, and smiling as if she saw I was overcome, an' would have said more if she could, but we had hold of hands. I see then her change was comin', but I did n't call Mis' Begg, nor make no uproar. I felt calm then, an' lifted to some-thin' different as I never was since. She opened her eyes just as she was goin'—

"'You saw her, did n't you?' she said the second time, an' I says, '*Yes, dear I did; you ain't never goin' to feel strange an' lonesome no more.*' An' then in a few quiet minutes 't was all over. I felt they'd gone away together. No, I wa'n't alarmed afterward; 't was just that one moment I could n't live under, but I never called it beyond reason I should see the other watcher. I saw plain enough there was somebody there with me in the room.

VII

"'T was just such a night as this Mis' Tolland died," repeated Mrs. Todd, returning to her usual tone and leaning back comfortably in her chair as she took up her knitting. " 'T was just such a night as this. I've told the circumstances to but very few; but I don't call it beyond reason. When folks is goin' 't is all natural, and only common things can jar upon the mind. You know plain enough there's somethin' beyond this world; the doors stand wide open. 'There's somethin' of us that must still live on, we've got to join both worlds together an' live in one but for the other. The doctor said that to me one day, an' I never could forget it; he said 't was in one o' his old doctor's books.'

We sat together in silence in the warm little room; the rain dropped heavily from the eaves, and the sea still roared, but the high wind had done blowing. We heard the far complaining fog horn of a steamer up the Bay.

"There goes the Boston boat out, pretty near on time," said Mrs. Todd with satisfaction. "Sometimes these late August storms 'll sound a good deal worse than they really be. I do hate to hear the poor steamers callin' when they're bewildered in thick nights in winter, comin' on the coast. Yes, there goes the boat; they 'll find it rough at sea, but the storm 's all over."

1900

Martha's Lady[1]

I

One day, many years ago, the old Judge Pyne house wore an unwonted look of gayety and youthfulness. The high-fenced green garden was bright with June flowers. Under the elms in the large shady front yard you might see some chairs placed near together, as they often used to be when the family were all at home and life was going on gayly with eager talk and pleasure-making; when the elder judge, the grandfather, used to quote that great author, Dr. Johnson, and say to his girls, "Be brisk, be splendid, and be public."[2]

One of the chairs had a crimson silk shawl thrown carelessly over its straight back, and a passer-by, who looked in through the latticed gate between the tall gate-posts with their white urns, might think that this piece of shining East Indian color was a huge red lily that had suddenly bloomed against the syringa bush. There were certain windows thrown wide open that were usually shut, and their curtains were blowing free in the light wind of a summer afternoon; it looked as if a large household had returned to the old house to fill the prim best rooms and find them full of cheer.

It was evident to every one in town that Miss Harriet Pyne, to use the village phrase, had company. She was the last of her family, and was by no means old; but being the last, and wonted to live with people much older than herself, she had formed all the habits of a serious elderly person. Ladies of her age, something past thirty, often wore discreet caps in those days, especially if they were married, but being single, Miss Harriet clung to youth in this respect, making the one concession of keeping her waving chestnut hair as smooth and stiffly arranged as possible. She had been the dutiful companion of her father and mother in their latest years, all her elder brothers and sisters having married and gone, or died and gone, out of the house. Now that she was left alone it seemed quite the best thing frankly to accept the fact of age, and to turn more resolutely than ever to the companionship of duty and serious books. She was more serious and given to routine than her elders themselves, as sometimes happened when the daughters of New England gentlefolks were brought up wholly in the society of their elders. At thirty-five she had more reluctance than her mother

---

[1]Originally published in the *Atlantic Monthly* in October 1897, "Martha's Lady" was collected in *The Queen's Twin* in 1899.   [2]Dr. Johnson: Samuel Johnson (1709–1784).

to face an unforeseen occasion, certainly more than her grandmother, who had preserved some cheerful inheritance of gayety and worldliness from colonial times.

There was something about the look of the crimson silk shawl in the front yard to make one suspect that the sober customs of the best house in a quiet New England village were all being set at defiance, and once when the mistress of the house came to stand in her own doorway, she wore the pleased but somewhat apprehensive look of a guest. In these days in New England life held the necessity of much dignity and discretion of behavior; there was the truest hospitality and good cheer in all occasional festivities, but it was sometimes a self-conscious hospitality, followed by an inexorable return to asceticism both of diet and behavior. Miss Harriet Pyne belonged to the very dullest days of New England, those which perhaps held the most priggishness for the learned professions, the most limited interpretation of the word "evangelical," and the prettiest indifference to large things. The outbreak of a desire for larger religious freedom caused at first a most determined reaction toward formalism, especially in small and quiet villages like Ashford, intently busy with their own concerns. It was high time for a little leaven to begin its work, in this moment when the great impulses of the war for liberty had died away and those of the coming war for patriotism and a new freedom had hardly yet begun.

The dull interior, the changed life of the old house, whose former activities seemed to have fallen sound asleep, really typified these larger conditions, and a little leaven had made its easily recognized appearance in the shape of a light-hearted girl. She was Miss Harriet's young Boston cousin, Helena Vernon, who, half-amused and half-impatient at the unnecessary sober-mindedness of her hostess and of Ashford in general, had set herself to the difficult task of gayety. Cousin Harriet looked on at a succession of ingenious and, on the whole, innocent attempts at pleasure, as she might have looked on at the frolics of a kitten who easily substitutes a ball of yarn for the uncertainties of a bird or a wind-blown leaf, and who may at any moment ravel the fringe of a sacred curtain-tassel in preference to either.

Helena, with her mischievous appealing eyes, with her enchanting old songs and her guitar, seemed the more delightful and even reasonable because she was so kind to everybody, and because she was a beauty. She had the gift of most charming manners. There was all the unconscious lovely ease and grace that had come with the good breeding of her city home, where many pleasant people came and went; she had no fear, one had almost said no respect, of the individual, and she did not need to think of herself. Cousin Harriet turned cold with apprehension when she saw the minister coming in at the front gate, and wondered in agony if Martha were properly attired to go to the door, and would by any chance hear the knocker; it was Helena who, delighted to have anything happen, ran to the door to welcome the Reverend Mr. Crofton as if he were a congenial friend of her own age. She could behave with more or less propriety during the stately first visit, and even contrive to lighten it with modest mirth, and to extort the confession that the guest had a tenor voice, though sadly out of practice; but when the minister departed a little flattered, and hoping that he had not expressed himself too strongly for a pastor upon the poems of Emerson, and feeling the unusual stir of gallantry in his proper heart, it was Helena who caught the honored hat of the late Judge Pyne from its last resting-place in the hall, and holding it securely in both hands, mimicked the minister's self-conscious entrance. She copied his pompous and anxious expression in the dim parlor in such delicious fashion that Miss Harriet, who could not always extinguish a ready spark of the original sin of humor, laughed aloud.

"My dear!" she exclaimed severely the next moment, "I am ashamed of your being so disrespectful!" and then laughed again, and took the affecting old hat and carried it back to its place.

"I would not have had any one else see you for the world," she said sorrowfully as she returned, feeling quite self-possessed again, to the parlor doorway; but Helena still sat in the minister's chair, with her small feet placed as his stiff boots had been, and a copy of his solemn expression before they came to speaking of Emerson and of the guitar. "I wish I had asked him if he would be so kind as to climb the cherry-tree," said Helena, unbending a little at the discovery that her cousin would consent to laugh no more. "There are all those ripe cherries on the top branches. I can climb as high as he, but I can't reach far enough from the last branch that will bear me. The minister is so long and thin"—

"I don't know what Mr. Crofton would have thought of you; he is a very serious young man," said cousin Harriet, still ashamed of her laughter. "Martha will get the cherries for you, or one of the men. I should not like to have Mr. Crofton think you were frivolous, a young lady of your opportunities"— but Helena had escaped through the hall and out at the garden door at the mention of Martha's name. Miss Harriet Pyne sighed anxiously, and then smiled, in spite of her deep convictions, as she shut the blinds and tried to make the house look solemn again.

The front door might be shut, but the garden door at the other end of the broad hall was wide open upon the large sunshiny garden, where the last of the red and white peonies and the golden lilies, and the first of the tall blue larkspurs lent their colors in generous fashion. The straight box borders were all in fresh and shining green of their new leaves, and there was a fragrance of the old garden's inmost life and soul blowing from the honeysuckle blossoms on a long trellis. It was now late in the afternoon, and the sun was low behind great apple-trees at the garden's end, which threw their shadows over the short turf of the bleaching-green. The cherry-trees stood at one side in full sunshine, and Miss Harriet, who presently came to the garden steps to watch like a hen at the water's edge, saw her cousin's pretty figure in its white dress of India muslin hurrying across the grass. She was accompanied by the tall, ungainly shape of Martha the new maid, who, dull and indifferent to every one else, showed a surprising willingness and allegiance to the young guest.

"Martha ought to be in the dining-room, already, slow as she is; it wants but half an hour of tea-time," said Miss Harriet, as she turned and went into the shaded house. It was Martha's duty to wait at table, and there had been many trying scenes and defeated efforts toward her education. Martha was certainly very clumsy, and she seemed the clumsier because she had replaced her aunt, a most skillful person, who had but lately married a thriving farm and its prosperous owner. It must be confessed that Miss Harriet was a most bewildering instructor, and that her pupil's brain was easily confused and prone to blunders. The coming of Helena had been somewhat dreaded by reason of this incompetent service, but the guest took no notice of frowns or futile gestures at the first tea-table, except to establish friendly relations with Martha on her own account by a reassuring smile. They were about the same age, and next morning, before cousin Harriet came down, Helena showed by a word and a quick touch the right way to do something that had gone wrong and been impossible to understand the night before. A moment later the anxious mistress came in without suspicion, but Martha's eyes were as affectionate as a dog's, and there was a new look of hopefulness on her face; this dreaded guest was a friend after all, and not a foe come from proud Boston to confound her ignorance and patient efforts.

The two young creatures, mistress and maid, were hurrying across the bleaching-green.

"I can't reach the ripest cherries," explained Helena politely, "and I think that Miss Pyne ought to send some to the minister. He has just made a call. Why Martha, you haven't been crying again!"

"Yes'm," said Martha sadly. "Miss Pyne always loves to send something to the minister," she acknowledged with interest, as if she did not wish to be asked to explain these latest tears.

"We'll arrange some of the best cherries in a pretty dish. I'll show you how, and you shall carry them over to the parsonage after tea," said Helena cheerfully, and Martha accepted the embassy with pleasure. Life was beginning to hold moments of something like delight in the last few days.

"You'll spoil your pretty dress, Miss Helena," Martha gave shy warning, and Miss Helena stood back and held up her skirts with unusual care while the country girl, in her heavy blue checked gingham, began to climb the cherry-tree like a boy.

Down came the scarlet fruit like bright rain into the green grass.

"Break some nice twigs with the cherries and leaves together; oh, you're a duck, Martha!" and Martha, flushed with delight, and looking far more like a thin and solemn blue heron, came rustling down to earth again, and gathered the spoils into her clean apron.

That night at tea, during her handmaiden's temporary absence, Miss Harriet announced, as if by way of apology, that she thought Martha was beginning to understand something about her work. "Her aunt was a treasure, she never had to be told anything twice; but Martha has been as clumsy as a calf," said the precise mistress of the house. "I have been afraid sometimes that I never could teach her anything. I was quite ashamed to have you come just now, and find me so unprepared to entertain a visitor."

"Oh, Martha will learn fast enough because she cares so much," said the visitor eagerly. "I think she is a dear good girl. I do hope that she will never go away. I think she does things better every day, cousin Harriet," added Helena pleadingly, with all her kind young heart. The china-closet door was open a little way, and Martha heard every word. From that moment, she not only knew what love was like, but she knew love's dear ambitions. To have come from a stony hill-farm and a bare small wooden house, was like a cave-dweller's coming to make a permanent home in an art museum, such had seemed the elaborateness and elegance of Miss Pyne's fashion of life; and Martha's simple brain was slow enough in its processes and recognitions. But with this sympathetic ally and defender, this exquisite Miss Helena who believed in her, all difficulties appeared to vanish.

Later that evening, no longer homesick or hopeless, Martha returned from her polite errand to the minister, and stood with a sort of triumph before the two ladies, who were sitting in front of the doorway, as if they were waiting for visitors, Helena still in her white muslin and red ribbons, and Miss Harriet in a thin black silk. Being happily self-forgetful in the greatness of the moment, Martha's manners were perfect, and she looked for once almost pretty and quite as young as she was.

"The minister came to the door himself, and returned his thanks. He said that cherries were always his favorite fruit, and he was much obliged to both Miss Pyne and Miss Vernon. He kept me waiting a few minutes, while he got this book ready to send to you, Miss Helena."

"What are you saying, Martha? I have sent him nothing!" exclaimed Miss Pyne, much astonished. "What does she mean, Helena?"

"Only a few cherries," explained Helena. "I thought Mr. Crofton would like them after his afternoon of parish calls. Martha and I arranged them before tea, and I sent them with our compliments."

"Oh, I am very glad you did," said Miss Harriet, wondering, but much relieved. "I was afraid"—

"No, it was none of my mischief," answered Helena daringly. "I did not think that Martha would be ready to go so soon. I should have shown you how pretty they looked among their green leaves. We put them in one of your best white dishes with the openwork edge. Martha shall show you tomorrow; mamma always likes to have them so." Helena's fingers were busy with the hard knot of a parcel.

"See this, cousin Harriet!" she announced proudly, as Martha disappeared round the corner of the house, beaming with the pleasures of adventure and success. "Look! the minister has sent me a book: Sermons on what? Sermons—it is so dark that I can't quite see."

"It must be his 'Sermons on the Seriousness of Life;' they are the only ones he has printed, I believe," said Miss Harriet, with much pleasure. "They are considered very fine discourses. He pays you a great compliment, my dear. I feared that he noticed your girlish levity."

"I behaved beautifully while he stayed," insisted Helena. "Ministers are only men," but she blushed with pleasure. It was certainly something to receive a book from its author, and such a tribute made her of more value to the whole reverent household. The minister was not only a man, but a bachelor, and Helena was at the age that best loves conquest; it was at any rate comfortable to be reinstated in cousin Harriet's good graces.

"Do ask the kind gentleman to tea! He needs a little cheering up," begged the siren in India muslin, as she laid the shiny black volume of sermons on the stone doorstep with an air of approval, but as if they had quite finished their mission.

"Perhaps I shall, if Martha improves as much as she has within the last day or two," Miss Harriet promised hopefully. "It is something I always dread a little when I am all alone, but I think Mr. Crofton likes to come. He converses so elegantly."

II

These were the days of long visits, before affectionate friends thought it quite worth while to take a hundred miles' journey merely to dine or to pass a night in one another's houses. Helena lingered through the pleasant weeks of early summer, and departed unwillingly at last to join her family at the White Hills,[3] where they had gone, like other households of high social station, to pass the month of August out of town. The happy-hearted young guest left many lamenting friends behind her, and promised each that she would come back again next year. She left the minister a rejected lover, as well as the preceptor of the academy, but with their pride unwounded, and it may have been with wider outlooks upon the world and a less narrow sympathy both for their own work in life and for their neighbors' work and hindrances. Even Miss Harriet Pyne herself had lost some of the unnecessary provincialism and prejudice which had begun to harden a naturally good and open mind and affectionate heart. She was conscious of feeling younger and more free, and not so lonely. Nobody had ever been so gay, so fascinating, or so kind as Helena, so full of social resource, so simple and undemanding in her friendliness. The light of her young life cast no shadow on either young or old companions, her pretty clothes never seemed to make other girls look dull or out of fashion. When she went away up the street in Miss Harriet's carriage to take the slow train toward Boston and the gayeties of the new Profile House,[4] where her mother waited impatiently with a group of Southern friends, it seemed as if there would never be any more picnics or parties in Ashford, and as if society had nothing left to do but to grow old and get ready for winter.

Martha came into Miss Helena's bedroom that last morning, and it was easy to see that she had been crying; she looked just as she did in the first sad week of homesickness and despair. All for love's sake she had been

---

[3]The White Mountains (northern New Hampshire). [4]A resort hotel in the White Mountains.

learning to do many things, and to do them exactly right; her eyes had grown quick to see the smallest chance for personal service. Nobody could be more humble and devoted; she looked years older than Helena, and wore already a touching air of caretaking.

"You spoil me, you dear Martha!" said Helena from the bed. "I don't know what they will say at home, I am so spoiled."

Martha went on opening the blinds to let in the brightness of the summer morning, but she did not speak.

"You are getting on splendidly, aren't you?" continued the little mistress. "You have tried so hard that you make me ashamed of myself. At first you crammed all the flowers together, and now you make them look beautiful. Last night cousin Harriet was so pleased when the table was so charming, and I told her that you did everything yourself, every bit. Won't you keep the flowers fresh and pretty in the house until I come back? It's so much pleasanter for Miss Pyne, and you'll feed my little sparrows, won't you? They're growing so tame."

"Oh, yes, Miss Helena!" and Martha looked almost angry for a moment, then she burst into tears and covered her face with her apron. "I couldn't understand a single thing when I first came. I never had been anywhere to see anything, and Miss Pyne frightened me when she talked. It was you made me think I could ever learn. I wanted to keep the place, 'count of mother and the little boys; we're dreadful hard pushed. Hepsy has been good in the kitchen; she said she ought to have patience with me, for she was awkward herself when she first came."

Helena laughed; she looked so pretty under the tasseled white curtains.

"I dare say Hepsy tells the truth," she said. "I wish you had told me about your mother. When I come again, some day we'll drive up country, as you call it, to see her. Martha! I wish you would think of me sometimes after I go away. Won't you promise?" and the bright young face suddenly grew grave. "I have hard times myself; I don't always learn things that I ought to learn, I don't always put things straight. I wish you wouldn't forget me ever, and would just believe in me. I think it does help more than anything."

"I won't forget," said Martha slowly. "I shall think of you every day." She spoke almost with indifference, as she had been asked to dust a room, but she turned aside quickly and pulled the little mat under the hot water jug quite out of its former straightness; then she hastened away down the long white entry, weeping as she went.

III

To lose out of sight the friend whom one has loved and lived to please is to lose joy out of life. But if love is true, there comes presently a higher joy of pleasing the ideal, that is to say, the perfect friend. The same old happiness is lifted to a higher level. As for Martha, the girl who stayed behind in Ashford, nobody's life could seem duller to those who could not understand; she was slow of step, and her eyes were almost always downcast as if intent upon incessant toil; but they startled you when she looked up, with their shining light. She as capable of the happiness of holding fast to a great sentiment, the ineffable satisfaction of trying to please one whom she truly loved. She never thought of trying to make other people pleased with herself; all she lived for was to do the best she could for others, and to conform to an ideal, which grew at last to be like a saint's vision, a heavenly figure painted upon the sky.

On Sunday afternoons in summer, Martha sat by the window of her chamber, a low-storied little room, which looked into the side yard and the great branches of an elm tree. She never sat in the old wooden rocking-chair except on Sundays like this; it belonged to the day of rest and to happy meditation. She wore her plain black dress and a clean white apron, and held in her lap a little wooden box, with a brass ring on top for a handle. She was past sixty years of age and looked even older, but there was the same look on her face that it had sometimes worn in girlhood. She was the same Martha; her hands were old-looking and work-worn, but her face still shone. It seemed like yesterday that Helena Vernon had gone away, and it was more than forty years.

War and peace had brought their changes and great anxieties, the face of the earth was furrowed by floods and fire, the faces of mistress and maid were furrowed by smiles and tears, and in the sky the stars shone on as if nothing had happened. The village of Ashford added a few pages to its unexciting history, the minister preached, the people listened; now and then a funeral crept along the street, and now and then the bright face of a little child rose above the horizon of a family pew. Miss Harriet Pyne lived on in the large white house, which gained more and more distinction because it suffered no changes, save successive repaintings and a new railing about its stately roof. Miss Harriet herself had moved far beyond the uncertainties of an anxious youth. She had long ago made all her decisions, and settled all necessary questions; her scheme of life was as faultless as the miniature landscape of a Japanese garden, and as easily kept in order. The only important change she would ever be capable of making was the final change to another and a better world; and for that nature itself would gently provide, and her own innocent life.

Hardly any great social event had ruffled the easy current of life since Helena Vernon's marriage. To this Miss Pyne had gone, stately in appearance and carrying gifts of some old family silver which bore the Vernon crest, but not without some protest in her heart against the uncertainties of married life. Helena was so equal to a happy independence and even to the assistance of other lives grown strangely dependent upon her quick sympathies and instinctive decisions, that it was hard to let her sink her personality in the affairs of another. Yet a brilliant English match was not without its attractions to an old-fashioned gentlewoman like Miss Pyne, and Helena herself was amazingly happy; one day there had come a letter to Ashford, in which her very heart seemed to beat with love and self-forgetfulness, to tell cousin Harriet of such new happiness and high hope. "Tell Martha all that I say about my dear Jack," wrote the eager girl; "please show my letter to Martha, and tell her that I shall come home next summer and bring the handsomest and best man in the world to Ashford. I have told him all about the dear house and the dear garden; there never was such a lad to reach for cherries with his six-foot-two." Miss Pyne, wondering a little, gave the letter to Martha, who took it deliberately and as if she wondered too, and went away to read it slowly by herself. Martha cried over it, and felt a strange sense of loss and pain; it hurt her heart a little to read about the cherry-picking. Her idol seemed to be less her own since she had become the idol of a stranger. She never had taken such a letter in her hands before, but love at last prevailed, since Miss Helena was happy, and she kissed the last page where her name was written, feeling overbold, and laid the envelope on Miss Pyne's secretary without a word.

The most generous love cannot but long for reassurance, and Martha had the joy of being remembered. She was not forgotten when the day of the wedding drew near, but she never knew that Miss Helena had asked if cousin Harriet would not bring Martha to town; she should like to have Martha there to see her married. "She would help about the flowers," wrote the happy girl; "I know she will like to come, and I'll ask mamma to plan to have some one take her all about Boston and make her have a pleasant time after the hurry of the great day is over."

Cousin Harriet thought it was very kind and exactly like Helena, but Martha would be out of her element; it was most imprudent and girlish to have thought of such a thing. Helena's mother would be far from wishing for any unnecessary guest just then, in the busiest part of her household, and it was best not to speak of the invitation. Some day Martha should go to Boston if she did well, but not now. Helena did not forget to ask if Martha had come, and was astonished by the indifference of the answer. It was the first thing which reminded her that she was not a fairy princess having everything her own way in that last day before the wedding. She knew that Martha would have loved to be near, for she could not help understanding in that moment of her own happiness the love that was hidden in another heart. Next day this happy young princess, the bride, cut a piece of a great cake and put it into a pretty box that had held one of her wedding presents. With eager voices calling her, and all her friends about her, and her mother's face growing more and more wistful at the thought of parting, she still lingered and ran to take one or two trifles from her dressing-table, a little mirror and some tiny scissors that Martha would remember, and one of the pretty handkerchiefs marked with her maiden name. These she put in the box too; it was half a girlish freak and fancy, but she could not help trying to share her happiness, and Martha's life was so plain and dull. She whispered a message, and put the little package into cousin Harriet's hand for Martha as she said good-by. She was very fond of cousin Harriet. She smiled with a gleam of her old fun; Martha's puzzled look and tall awkward figure seemed to stand suddenly before her eyes, as she promised to come again to

Ashford. Impatient voices called to Helena, her lover was at the door, and she hurried away, leaving her old home and her girlhood gladly. If she had only known it, as she kissed cousin Harriet good-by, they were never going to see each other again until they were old women. The first step that she took out of her father's house that day, married, and full of hope and joy, was a step that led her away from the green elms of Boston Common and away from her own country and those she loved best, to a brilliant, much-varied foreign life, and to nearly all the sorrows and nearly all the joys that the heart of one woman could hold or know.

On Sunday afternoons Martha used to sit by the window in Ashford and hold the wooden box which a favorite young brother, who afterward died at sea, had made for her, and she used to take out of it the pretty little box with a gilded cover that had held the piece of wedding-cake, and the small scissors, and the blurred bit of a mirror in its silver case; as for the handkerchief with the narrow lace edge, once in two or three years she sprinkled it as if it were a flower, and spread it out in the sun on the old bleaching-green, and sat near by in the shrubbery to watch lest some bold robin and cherry-bird should seize it and fly away.

IV

Miss Harriet Pyne was often congratulated upon the good fortune of having such a helper and friend as Martha. As time went on this tall, gaunt woman, always thin, always slow, gained a dignity of behavior and simple affectionateness of look which suited the charm and dignity of the ancient house. She was unconsciously beautiful like a saint, like the picturesqueness of a lonely tree which lives to shelter unnumbered lives and to stand quietly in its place. There was such rustic homeliness and constancy belonging to her, such beautiful powers of apprehension, such reticence, such gentleness for those who were troubled or sick; all these gifts and graces Martha hid in her heart. She never joined the church because she thought she was not good enough, but life was such a passion and happiness of service that it was impossible not to be devout, and she was always in her humble place on Sundays, in the back pew next to the door. She had been educated by a remembrance; Helena's young eyes forever looked at her reassuringly from a gay girlish face. Helena's sweet patience in teaching her own awkwardness could never be forgotten.

"I owe everything to Miss Helena," said Martha, half aloud, as she sat alone by the window; she had said it to herself a thousand times. When she looked in the little keepsake mirror she always hoped to see some faint reflection of Helena Vernon, but there was only her own brown old New England face to look back at her wonderingly.

Miss Pyne went less and less often to pay visits to her friends in Boston; there were very few friends left to come to Ashford and make long visits in the summer, and life grew more and more monotonous. Now and then there came news from across the sea and messages of remembrance, letters that were closely written on thin sheets of paper, and that spoke of lords and ladies, of great journeys, of the death of little children and the proud successes of boys at school, of the wedding of Helena Dysart's only daughter; but even that had happened years ago. These things seemed far away and vague, as if they belonged to a story and not to life itself; the true links with the past were quite different. There was the unvarying flock of ground-sparrows that Helena had begun to feed; every morning Martha scattered crumbs for them from the side doorsteps while Miss Pyne watched from the dining-room window, and they were counted and cherished year by year.

Miss Pyne herself had many fixed habits, but little ideality or imagination, and so at last it was Martha who took thought for her mistress, and gave freedom to her own good taste. After a while, without any one's observing the change, the every-day ways of doing things in the house came to be the stately ways that had once belonged only to the entertainment of guests. Happily both mistress and maid seized all possible chances for hospitality, yet Miss Harriet nearly always sat alone at her exquisitely served table with its fresh flowers, and the beautiful old china which Martha handled so lovingly that there was not good excuse for keeping it hidden on closet shelves. Every year when the old cherry-trees were in fruit, Martha carried the round white old English dish with a fretwork edge, full of pointed green leaves and scarlet cherries, to the minister, and his wife never quiet understood why every year he blushed and looked so conscious of the pleasure, and thanked Martha as if he had received a very particular attention. There was no pretty suggestion toward the pursuit of the fine art of housekeeping in Martha's limited acquaintance with newspapers that she did not adopt; there was no refined old custom of the Pyne housekeeping that she consented to let go. And every day, as she had promised, she thought of Miss Helena,—oh, many times in every day: whether this thing would please her, or that be likely to fall in with her fancy or ideas of fitness. As far as was possible the rare news that reached Ashford through an occasional letter or the talk of guests was made part of Martha's own life, the history of her own heart. A worn old geography often stood open at the map of Europe on the lightstand in her room, and a little old-fashioned gilt button, set with a bit of glass like a ruby, that had broken and fallen from the trimming of one of Helena's dresses, was used to mark the city of her dwelling-place. In the changes of a diplomatic life Martha followed her lady all about the map. Sometimes the button was at Paris, and sometimes at Madrid; once, to her great anxiety, it remained long at St. Petersburg. For such a slow scholar Martha was not unlearned at last, since everything about life in these foreign towns was of interest to her faithful heart. She satisfied her own mind as she threw crumbs to the tame sparrows; it was all part of the same thing and for the same affectionate reasons.

V

One Sunday afternoon in early summer Miss Harriet Pyne came hurrying along the entry that led to Martha's room and called two or three times before its inhabitant could reach the door. Miss Harriet looked unusually cheerful and excited, and she held something in her hand. "Where are you, Martha?" she called again. "Come quick, I have something to tell you!"

"Here I am, Miss Pyne," said Martha, who had only stopped to put her precious box in the drawer, and to shut the geography.

"Who do you think is coming this very night at half-past six? We must have everything as nice as we can; I must see Hannah at once. Do you remember my cousin Helena who has lived abroad so long? Miss Helena Vernon,—the Honorable Mrs. Dysart, she is now."

"Yes, I remember her," answered Martha, turning a little pale.

"I knew that she was in this country, and I had written to ask her to come for a long visit," continued Miss Harriet, who did not often explain things, even to Martha, though she was always conscientious about the kind messages that were sent by grateful guests. "She telegraphs that she means to anticipate her visit by a few days and come to me at once. The heat is beginning in town, I suppose. I daresay, having been a foreigner so long, she does not mind traveling on Sunday. Do you think Hannah will be prepared? We must have tea a little later."

"Yes, Miss Harriet," said Martha. She wondered that she could speak as usual, there was such a ringing in her ears. "I shall have time to pick some fresh strawberries; Miss Helena is so fond of our strawberries."

"Why, I had forgotten," said Miss Pyne, a little puzzled by something quite unusual in Martha's face. "We must expect to find Mrs. Dysart a good deal changed, Martha; it is a great many years since she was here; I have not seen her since her wedding, and she has had a great deal of trouble, poor girl. You had better open the parlor chamber, and make it ready before you go down."

"It is all ready," said Martha. "I can carry some of those little sweet-brier roses upstairs before she comes."

"Yes, you are always thoughtful," said Miss Pyne, with unwonted feeling.

Martha did not answer. She glanced at the telegram wistfully. She had never really suspected before that Miss Pyne knew nothing of the love that had been in her heart all these years; it was half a pain and half a golden joy to keep such a secret; she could hardly bear this moment of surprise.

Presently the news gave wings to her willing feet. When Hannah, the cook, who never had known Miss Helena, went to the parlor an hour later on some errand to her old mistress, she discovered that this stranger guest must be a very important person. She had never seen the tea-table look exactly as it did that night, and in the parlor itself there were fresh blossoming boughs in the old East India jars, and lilies in the paneled hall, and flowers everywhere, as if there were some high festivity.

Miss Pyne sat by the window watching, in her best dress, looking stately and calm; she seldom went out now, and it was almost time for the carriage. Martha was just coming in from the garden with the strawberries, and with more flowers in her apron. It was a bright cool evening in June, the golden robins sang in the elm, and the sun was going down behind the apple-trees at the foot of the garden. The beautiful old house stood wide open to the long-expected guest.

"I think that I shall go down to the gate," said Miss Pyne, looking at Martha for approval, and Martha nodded and they went together slowly down the broad front walk.

There was a sound of horses and wheels on the roadside turf: Martha could not see at first; she stood back inside the gate behind the white lilac-bushes as the carriage came. Miss Pyne was there; she was holding out both arms and taking a tired, bent little figure in black to her heart. "Oh, my Miss Helena is an old woman like me!" and Martha gave a pitiful sob; she had never dreamed it would be like this; this was the one thing she could not bear.

"Where are you, Martha?" called Miss Pyne. "Martha will bring these in; you have not forgotten my good Martha, Helena?" Then Mrs. Dysart looked up and smiled just as she used to smile in the old days. The young eyes were there still in the changed face, and Miss Helena had come.

That night Martha waited in her lady's room just as she used, humble and silent, and went through with the old unforgotten loving services. The long years seemed like days. At last she lingered a moment trying to think of something else that might be done, then she was going silently away, but Helena called her back. She suddenly knew the whole story and could hardly speak.

"Oh, my dear Martha!" she cried, "won't you kiss me good-night? Oh, Martha, have you remembered like this, all these long years!"

1897

MARY E. WILKINS FREEMAN
1852–1930

Mary E. Wilkins Freeman is best known for the short stories she began to publish in 1883 in *Harper's Bazaar*, some of the finest of which were collected in *A New England Nun and Other Stories*. In a letter to Sarah Orne Jewett, the regionalist writer whose work she most admired, dated December 10, 1889, Freeman wrote: "I suppose it seems to you as it does to me that everything you have heard, seen, or done, since you opened your eyes on the world, is coming back to you sooner or later, to go into stories." Drawing from what she had heard, seen, or done in Randolph, Massachusetts, her birthplace, and in Brattleboro, Vermont, Freeman developed strategies to step beyond her editors' expectations for genteel and conventional women's stories, often by adding a sentimental ending or beginning while also exploring the connection between feminine identity and place or subverting the domestic realm as an arena for female rebellion.

Early literary historians frequently categorized Freeman as a "local colorist" whose primary interest was to depict the peculiarities of her region. Since the rise of feminist criticism in the 1970s, however, critics have recognized that Freeman's work resists the representation of region in terms that merely preserve traditional images of New England rural culture. Marjorie Pryse, Judith Fetterly, Sandra Zagarell, Elizabeth Ammons, and many others point to the ways in which Freeman defied the standard definitions of region; she set traditions in new contexts that exposed limitations and defied expectations and boundaries, writing "out of place" rather than merely "of place," as Judith Fetterly and Marjorie Pryse explain in *Writing Out of Place: Regionalism, Women, and American Literary Culture*. Sandra Zagarell, in her introduction to the Penguin collection of Freeman's fiction, suggests that Freeman's best work "not only creatively reworks the literary formulas it sometimes uses, but also even actively disputes or complicates standard regionalist images of rural life as the 'sanctuary' of a 'traditional' America, untouched by industrial or commodity culture." Like Henry James, Freeman was interested in inner as well as outer landscape, as is evinced in her depth of characterization, and like Mark Twain, she experimented with dialect and humor while probing the larger questions of the complexities of public and private life. However, Freeman also shifted her readers' attention to alternative ways of reading domesticity within the seemingly "separate sphere" to which women of her time were assigned, exploring the psychology of women's lives and focusing on large battles fought on humble turf.

Much of Freeman's life reflects the complexities of growing up female and in economic hardship in nineteenth-century New England. Mary Ella Wilkins was born in Randolph, Massachusetts, a small rural town near Boston (she later changed her middle name to Eleanor in memory of her mother); as the daughter of orthodox Congregationalists, Warren and Eleanor Wilkins, she was nurtured in the context of repression and with the expectation of conformity to traditional standards of female passivity. Further, because she was a delicate child whose health was unpredictable, she grew up under close watch. Her childhood was shadowed by profound loss. A first child had died in infancy prior to her birth, and in 1858 her brother died. Her father, a builder, moved the family to Brattleboro, Vermont, in the hope of improving their financial circumstances when she was fifteen. Instead, Warren's goal to build a new home for his family had to be cast aside as his business failed, and in 1877 the family moved in with an established local family, the Tylers, for whom Eleanor Wilkins had to work as housekeeper. After graduating from Brattleboro High School, Mary attended Mount Holyoke Female Seminary, but like Emily Dickinson, she attended for only a year. Her brief effort to contribute to family finances as a teacher soon shifted to a determination to have a successful writing career. In 1875 she wrote to an editor, Edward Everett Hale, thanking him for his critique of her work, which she described as "cold water to a thirsty soul." All along, she resisted the pressure to marry, which was her father's hope for her financial security. After her first check for a major story, twenty-five dollars, for "Two Old Lovers" (1882), writing became her source of income and the center of her life. As she described it in an undated, untitled manuscript given to Edward Foster by Mrs. A. B. Mann, "I felt my wings spring from my shoulders capable of flight, and I flew home." Home shifted as well. This was a pivotal period in her professional and personal life, for she had lost her sister Anna in 1876 and her mother, with whom she was very close, in 1880. Just after the publication of "Two Old Lovers," her father died. In 1883 Freeman returned to Randolph, Massachusetts, to live with her childhood friend Mary John Wales on the farm she had come to love as a child. Here she spent the twenty most productive years of her literary career, writing in a room reserved for her on the second floor of the homestead and thriving in her relationship with Mary John Wales, who was her primary reader and source of emotional support. She also expanded her connections with editors such as Louisa Maria Booth and frequently traveled to Boston on trips related to her publications.

Freeman married Charles Freeman in 1902, after nine years of seeming hesitation according to the elaborate newspaper coverage, speculation, and surprise over the length of time it took for her to say yes (this public commentary was yet another reflection of her time). At forty-nine, she was comfortably past the childbearing years, yet the marriage still required some sacrifices, most importantly that she part with what she called "the old me," and leave Randolph, the locale for so much of her work, for Metuchen, New Jersey, where she found "I have not a blessed thing to write about." The marriage to Charles dissolved in 1921, largely due to Charles's decline into severe alcoholism and drug addiction. One of the most interesting things she wrote after marrying Charles Freeman was "Old Maid Aunt," the chapter she contributed to the collaborative novel *The Whole Family*. Here she redefines conventional views of spinsterhood, creating a lively, sexy, self-possessed (though also ambivalent) woman, the envy of all married women. Freeman wrote that the objections of some of her male cowriters, such as William Dean Howells, reflected a time when "women of thirty put on caps, and renounced the world." Her heroine, Lily Talbert, shakes up the novel and changes its direction in its second chapter.

Mary E. Wilkins Freeman died of a heart attack at seventy-eight, having received in her lifetime considerable recognition for her work, the scope of which includes fourteen novels, two hundred fifty short stories, fifteen short story collections, and several plays, children's works, and essays. She was honored with the Howells Medal for fiction from the American Academy of Arts and Letters; the bronze doors of the Academy still carry the inscription "Dedicated to the Memory of Mary E. Wilkins Freeman and the Women Writers of America." For further detail on Freeman's life in relation to her work, see Glasser, *In a Closet Hidden: The Life and Work of Mary E. Wilkins Freeman*.

Freeman was among the first American women writers to write openly about women's sexuality, the role of work in women's lives, the experience of poverty and aging, the stigma of nineteenth-century spinsterhood, the relationships that women formed outside of marriage and motherhood, and the role of place in relation to the quest for autonomy. "A New England Nun," "The Revolt of 'Mother,'" and "Old Woman Magoun" serve as examples of Freeman's powerful prose. David Hirsch, one of the pioneer critics to bring Freeman's fiction back into literary consciousness, summed up the effect Freeman's language still has on readers, as she invests "the minutest and most ordinary details with deeper psychic significance." Her brand of regionalism, too, is subtle. It is what Sandra Zagarell terms "critical regionalism"; she "often conveys her take on rural New England and its relationship with 'modern' America obliquely," using the conventions of regionalism in "off-center ways that unsettle the presumption that rural life is fully separate from modern life." Her characterizations and their depth transform traditional stereotypes of rural New Englanders.

In "A New England Nun," "The Revolt of 'Mother,'" and "Old Woman Magoun," Freeman reconstructs spinsterhood, wifehood, motherhood, girlhood, and grand-motherhood through a lens that captures their complexities in profoundly evocative dramas set within the context of place. "A New England Nun" was once generally read as a story that emphasizes the repression of its main character, Louisa, who rejects her fiancé after fifteen years of waiting for his return, and chooses to continue her life as an "uncloistered nun." Over the years, perception of this story shifted to an understanding of Louisa's choice in the context of her effort to sustain independence, despite the possible cost of such autonomy. The story interestingly positioned Louisa and her plain apron, donned for self-service rather than the service of others, in deliberate contrast to the dominant images of acceptable women in fashionable attire throughout *Harper's Bazaar*. Freeman's most frequently anthologized story, "The Revolt of 'Mother,'" proved to be so relevant to future generations that it was adapted for television in 1986. Here Freeman demonstrates her ability to address critical issues within the domestic realm and to reframe the meaning of the word "battle" and "home" in women's terms. Freeman's regionalism also makes use of region to critique gender and class, as one of her darkest stories, "Old Woman Magoun," demonstrates. The hamlet of Barry's Ford and the bridge a grandmother and child must cross become the stage for a drama that, like all of Freeman's finest fiction, transcends time and place.

Leah B. Glasser
Mt. Holyoke College

PRIMARY WORKS

A Humble Romance and Other Stories, 1887; *A New England Nun and Other Stories*, 1891; *Pembroke*, 1894; *By the Light of the Soul*, 1906; "The Girl Who Wants to Write: Things to Do and Avoid," *Harper's Bazaar* (June 1913), 272; *The Infant Sphinx: Collected Letters of Mary E. Wilkins Freeman*, ed. Brent L. Kendrick, 1985; *The Uncollected Stories of Mary Wilkins Freeman*, ed. Mary Reichardt, 1992; *Mary E. Wilkins Freeman Reader*, ed. Mary Reichardt, 1997; *A New England Nun and Other Stories*, ed. Sandra A. Zagarell, 2000.

A New England Nun

It was late in the afternoon, and the light was waning. There was a difference in the look of the tree shadows out in the yard. Somewhere in the distance cows were lowing and a little bell was tinkling; now and then a farm-wagon tilted by, and the dust flew; some blue-shirted laborers with shovels over their shoulders plodded past; little swarms of flies were dancing up and down before the peoples' faces in the soft air. There seemed to be a gentle stir arising over everything for the mere sake of subsidence—a very premonition of rest and hush and night.

This soft diurnal commotion was over Louisa Ellis also. She had been peacefully sewing at her sitting-room window all the afternoon. Now she quilted her needle carefully into her work, which she folded precisely, and laid in a basket with her thimble and thread and scissors. Louisa Ellis could not remember that ever in her life she had mislaid one of these little feminine appurtenances, which had become, from long use and constant association, a very part of her personality.

Louisa tied a green apron round her waist, and got out a flat straw hat with a green ribbon. Then she went into the garden with a little blue crockery bowl, to pick some currants for her tea. After the currants were picked she sat on the back doorstep and stemmed them, collecting the stems carefully in her apron, and afterwards throwing them into the hen-coop. She looked sharply at the grass beside the step to see if any had fallen there.

Louisa was slow and still in her movements; it took her a long time to prepare her tea; but when ready it was set forth with as much grace as if she had been a veritable guest to her own self. The little square table stood exactly in the centre of the kitchen, and was covered with a starched linen cloth whose border pattern of flowers glistened. Louisa had a damask napkin on her tea-tray, where were arranged a cut-glass tumbler full of teaspoons, a silver cream-pitcher, a china sugar-bowl, and one pink china cup and saucer. Louisa used china every day—something which none of her neighbors did. They whispered about it among themselves. Their daily tables were laid with common crockery, their sets of best china stayed in the parlor closet, and Louisa Ellis was no richer nor better bred than they. Still she would use the china. She had for her supper a glass dish full of sugared currants, a plate of little cakes, and one of light white biscuits. Also a leaf or two of lettuce, which she cut up daintily. Louisa was very fond of lettuce, which she raised to perfection in her little garden. She ate quite heartily, though in a delicate, pecking way; it seemed almost surprising that any considerable bulk of the food should vanish.

After tea she filled a plate with nicely baked thin corn-cakes, and carried them out into the back-yard.

"Caesar!" she called. "Caesar! Caesar!"

There was a little rush, and the clank of a chain, and a large yellow-and-white dog appeared at the door of his tiny hut, which was half hidden among the tall grasses and flowers. Louisa patted him and gave him the corn-cakes. Then she returned to the house and washed the tea-things, polishing the china carefully. The twilight had deepened; the chorus of the frogs floated in at the open window wonderfully loud and shrill, and once in a while a long sharp drone from a tree-toad pierced it. Louisa took off her green gingham apron, disclosing a shorter one of pink and white print. She lighted her lamp, and sat down again with her sewing.

In about half an hour Joe Dagget came. She heard his heavy step on the walk, and rose and took off her pink-and-white apron. Under that was still another—white linen with a little cambric edging on the bottom; that was Louisa's company apron. She never wore it without her calico sewing apron over it unless she had a guest. She had barely folded the pink and white one with methodical haste and laid it in a table drawer when the door opened and Joe Dagget entered.

He seemed to fill up the whole room. A little yellow canary that had been asleep in his green cage at the south window woke up and fluttered wildly, beating his little yellow wings against the wires. He always did so when Joe Dagget came into the room.

"Good-evening," said Louisa. She extended her hand with a kind of solemn cordiality.

"Good-evening, Louisa," returned the man, in a loud voice.

She placed a chair for him, and they sat facing each other, with the table between them. He sat bolt-upright, toeing out his heavy feet squarely, glancing with a good-humored uneasiness around the room. She sat gently erect, folding her slender hands in her white-linen lap.

"Been a pleasant day," remarked Dagget.

"Real pleasant," Louisa assented, softly. "Have you been haying?" she asked, after a little while.

"Yes, I've been haying all day, down in the ten-acre lot. Pretty hot work."

"It must be."

"Yes, it's pretty hot work in the sun."

"Is your mother well to-day?"

"Yes, mother's pretty well."

"I suppose Lily Dyer's with her now?"

Dagget colored. "Yes, she's with her," he answered, slowly.

He was not very young, but there was a boyish look about his large face. Louisa was not quite as old as he, her face was fairer and smoother, but she gave people the impression of being older.

"I suppose she's a good deal of help to your mother," she said, further.

"I guess she is; I don't know how mother'd get along without her," said Dagget, with a sort of embarrassed warmth.

"She looks like a real capable girl. She's pretty-looking too," remarked Louisa.

"Yes, she is pretty fair looking."

Presently Dagget began fingering the books on the table. There was a square red autograph album, and a Young Lady's Gift-Book[1] which had belonged to Louisa's mother. He took them up one after the other and opened them; then laid them down again, the album on the Gift-Book.

Louisa kept eyeing them with mild uneasiness. Finally she rose and changed the position of the books, putting the album underneath. That was the way they had been arranged in the first place.

Dagget gave an awkward little laugh. "Now what difference did it make which book was on top?" said he.

Louisa looked at him with a deprecating smile. "I always keep them that way," murmured she.

"You do beat everything," said Dagget, trying to laugh again. His large face was flushed.

[1]*Young Lady's Gift-Book: A Common-Place Book of Prose and Poetry* (Providence, R.I., 1836) or a similar anthology of writing intended for young women.

He remained about an hour longer, then rose to take leave. Going out, he stumbled over a rug, and trying to recover himself, hit Louisa's work-basket on the table and knocked it on the floor.

He looked at Louisa, then at the rolling spools; he ducked himself awkwardly toward them, but she stopped him. "Never mind," said she; "I'll pick them up after you're gone."

She spoke with a mild stiffness. Either she was a little disturbed, or his nervousness affected her, and made her seem constrained in her effort to reassure him.

When Joe Dagget was outside he drew in the sweet evening air with a sigh, and felt much as an innocent and perfectly well-intentioned bear might after his exit from a china shop.

Louisa, on her part, felt much as the kind-hearted, long-suffering owner of the china shop might have done after the exit of the bear.

She tied on the pink, then the green apron, picked up all the scattered treasures and replaced them in her work-basket, and straightened the rug. Then she set the lamp on the floor, and began sharply examining the carpet. She even rubbed her fingers over it, and looked at them.

"He's tracked in a good deal of dust," she murmured. "I thought he must have."

Louisa got a dust-pan and brush, and swept Joe Dagget's track carefully.

If he could have known it, it would have increased his perplexity and uneasiness, although it would not have disturbed his loyalty in the least. He came twice a week to see Louisa Ellis, and every time, sitting there in her delicately sweet room, he felt as if surrounded by a hedge of lace. He was afraid to stir lest he should put a clumsy foot or hand through the fairy web, and he had always the consciousness that Louisa was watching fearfully lest he should.

Still the lace and Louisa commanded perforce his perfect respect and patience and loyalty. They were to be married in a month, after a singular courtship which had lasted for a matter of fifteen years. For fourteen out of the fifteen years the two had not once seen each other, and they had seldom exchanged letters. Joe had been all those years in Australia, where he had gone to make his fortune, and where he had stayed until he made it. He would have stayed fifty years if it had taken so long, and come home feeble and tottering, or never come home at all, to marry Louisa.

But the fortune had been made in the fourteen years, and he had come home now to marry the woman who had been patiently and unquestioningly waiting for him all that time.

Shortly after they were engaged he had announced to Louisa his determination to strike out into new fields, and secure a competency before they should be married. She had listened and assented with the sweet serenity which never failed her, not even when her lover set forth on that long and uncertain journey. Joe, buoyed up as he was by his sturdy determination, broke down a little at the last, but Louisa kissed him with a mild blush, and said good-by.

"It won't be for long," poor Joe had said, huskily; but it was for fourteen years.

In that length of time much had happened. Louisa's mother and brother had died, and she was all alone in the world. But greatest happening of all—a subtle happening which both were too simple to understand—Louisa's feet had turned into a path, smooth maybe under a calm, serene sky, but so straight and unswerving that it could only meet a check at her grave, and so narrow that there was no room for any one at her side.

Louisa's first emotion when Joe Dagget came home (he had not apprised her of his coming) was consternation, although she would not admit it to herself, and he never dreamed of it. Fifteen years ago she had been in love with him—at least she considered herself to be. Just at that time, gently acquiescing with and falling into the natural drift of girlhood, she had seen marriage ahead as a reasonable feature and a probable desirability of life. She had listened with calm docility to her mother's views upon the subject. Her mother was remarkable for her cool sense and sweet, even temperament. She talked wisely to her daughter when Joe Dagget presented himself, and Louisa accepted him with no hesitation. He was the first lover she had ever had.

She had been faithful to him all these years. She had never dreamed of the possibility of marrying any one else. Her life, especially for the last seven years, had been full of a pleasant peace, she had never felt discontented nor impatient over her lover's absence; still she had always looked forward to his return and their marriage as the inevitable conclusion of things. However, she had fallen into a way of placing it so far in the future that it was almost equal to placing it over the boundaries of another life.

When Joe came she had been expecting him, and expecting to be married for fourteen years, but she was as much surprised and taken aback as if she had never thought of it.

Joe's consternation came later. He eyed Louisa with an instant confirmation of his old admiration. She had changed but little. She still kept her pretty manner and soft grace, and was, he considered, every whit as attractive as ever. As for himself, his stent was done; he had turned his face away from fortune-seeking, and the old winds of romance whistled as loud and sweet as ever through his ears. All the song which he had been wont to hear in them was Louisa; he had for a long time a loyal belief that he heard it still, but finally it seemed to him that although the winds sang always that one song, it had another name. But for Louisa the wind had never more than murmured; now it had gone down, and everything was still. She listened for a little while with half-wistful attention; then she turned quietly away and went to work on her wedding clothes.

Joe had made some extensive and quite magnificent alterations to his house. It was the old homestead; the newly-married couple would live there, for Joe could not desert his mother, who refused to leave her old home. So Louisa must leave hers. Every morning, rising and going about among her neat maidenly possessions, she felt as one looking her last upon the faces of dear friends. It was true that in a measure she could take them with her, but, robbed of their old environments, they would appear in such new guises that they would almost cease to be themselves. Then there were some peculiar features of her happy solitary life which she would probably be obliged to relinquish altogether. Sterner tasks than these graceful but half-needless ones would probably devolve upon her. There would be a large house to care for; there would be company to entertain; there would be Joe's rigorous and feeble old mother to wait upon; and it would be contrary to all thrifty village traditions for her to keep more than one servant. Louisa had a little still, and she used to occupy herself pleasantly in summer weather with distilling the sweet and aromatic essences from roses and peppermint and spearmint. By-and-by her still must be laid away. Her store of essences was already considerable, and there would be no time for her to distil for the mere pleasure of it. Then Joe's mother would think it foolishness; she had already hinted her opinion in the matter. Louisa dearly loved to sew a linen seam, not always for use, but for the simple, mild pleasure which she took in it. She would have been loath to confess how more than once she had ripped a seam for the mere delight of sewing it together again. Sitting at her window during long sweet afternoons, drawing her needle gently through the dainty fabric, she was peace itself. But there was small chance of such foolish comfort in the future. Joe's mother, domineering, shrewd old matron that she was even in her old age, and very likely even Joe himself, with his honest masculine rudeness, would laugh and frown down all these pretty but senseless old maiden ways.

Louisa had almost the enthusiasm of an artist over the mere order and cleanliness of her solitary home. She had throbs of genuine triumph at the sight of the window-panes which she had polished until they shone like jewels. She gloated gently over her orderly bureau-drawers, with their exquisitely folded contents redolent with lavender and sweet clover and very purity. Could she be sure of the endurance of even this? She had visions, so startling that she half repudiated them as indelicate, of coarse masculine belongings strewn about in endless litter; of dust and disorder arising necessarily from a coarse masculine presence in the midst of all this delicate harmony.

Among her forebodings of disturbance, not the least was with regard to Caesar. Caesar was a veritable hermit of a dog. For the greater part of his life he had dwelt in his secluded hut, shut out from the society of his kind and all innocent canine joys. Never had Caesar since his early youth watched at a woodchuck's hole; never had he known the delights of a stray bone at a neighbor's kitchen door. And it was all on account of a sin committed when hardly out of his puppyhood. No one knew the possible depth of remorse of which this mild-visaged, altogether innocent-looking old dog might be capable; but whether or not he had encountered remorse, he had encountered a full measure of righteous retribution. Old Caesar seldom lifted up his voice in a growl or a bark; he was fat and sleepy; there were yellow rings which looked like spectacles around his dim old eyes; but there was a neighbor who bore on his hand the imprint of several of Caesar's sharp white youthful teeth, and for that he had lived at the end of a chain, all alone in a little hut, for fourteen years. The neighbor, who was choleric and smarting with the pain of his wound, had demanded either Caesar's death or complete ostracism. So Louisa's brother, to whom the dog had belonged, had built him his little kennel and tied him up. It was now fourteen years since, in a flood of youthful spirits, he had inflicted that memorable bite, and with the exception of short excursions, always at the end of the chain, under the strict guardianship of his master or Louisa, the old dog had remained a close prisoner. It is doubtful if, with his limited ambition, he took much pride in the fact, but it is certain that he was possessed of considerable cheap fame. He was regarded by all the children in the village and by many adults as a very monster of ferocity. St. George's dragon[2] could hardly have surpassed in evil repute Louisa Ellis's old yellow dog. Mothers charged their children with solemn emphasis not to go too near to him, and the children listened and believed greedily, with a fascinated appetite for terror, and ran by Louisa's house stealthily, with many sidelong and backward glances at the terrible dog. If perchance he sounded a hoarse bark, there was a panic. Wayfarers chancing into Louisa's yard eyed him with respect, and inquired if the chain were stout. Caesar at large might have seemed a very ordinary dog, and excited no comment whatever; chained, his reputation overshadowed him, so that he lost his own proper outlines and looked darkly vague and enormous. Joe Dagget, however, with his good-humored sense and shrewdness, saw him as he was. He strode valiantly up to him and patted him on the head, in spite of Louisa's soft clamor of warning, and even attempted to set him loose. Louisa grew so alarmed that he desisted, but kept announcing his opinion in the matter quite forcibly at intervals. "There ain't a better-natured dog in town," he would say, "and it's downright cruel to keep him tied up there. Some day I'm going to take him out."

Louisa had very little hope he would not, one of these days, when their interests and possessions should be more completely fused in one. She pictured to herself Caesar on the rampage through the quiet and unguarded village. She saw innocent children bleeding in his path. She was herself very fond of the old dog, because he had belonged to her dead brother, and he was always very gentle with her; still she had great faith in his ferocity. She always warned people not to go too near him. She fed him on ascetic fare of corn-mush and cakes, and never fired his dangerous temper with heating and sanguinary diet of flesh and bones. Louisa looked at the old dog munching his simple fare, and thought of her approaching marriage and trembled. Still no anticipation of disorder and confusion in lieu of sweet peace and harmony, no forebodings of Caesar on the rampage, no wild fluttering of her little yellow canary, were sufficient to turn her a hair's-breadth. Joe Dagget had been fond of her and working for her all these years. It was not

[2]Dragon slain by St. George, patron saint of England.

for her, whatever came to pass, to prove untrue and break his heart. She put the exquisite little stitches into her wedding-garments, and time went on until it was only a week before her wedding-day. It was a Tuesday evening, and the wedding was to be a week from Wednesday.

There was a full moon that night. About nine o'clock Louisa strolled down the road a little way. There were harvest-fields on either hand, bordered by low stone walls. Luxuriant clumps of bushes grew beside the wall, and trees—wild cherry and old apple-trees—at intervals. Presently Louisa sat down on the wall and looked about her with mildly sorrowful reflectiveness. Tall shrubs of blueberry and meadow-sweet, all woven together and tangled with blackberry vines and horsebriers, shut her in on either side. She had a little clear space between them. Opposite her, on the other side of the road, was a spreading tree; the moon shone between its boughs, and the leaves twinkled like silver. The road was bespread with a beautiful shifting dapple of silver and shadow; the air was full of a mysterious sweetness. "I wonder if it's wild grapes?" murmured Louisa. She sat there some time. She was just thinking of rising, when she heard footsteps and low voices, and remained quiet. It was a lonely place, and she felt a little timid. She thought she would keep still in the shadow and let the persons, whoever they might be, pass her.

But just before they reached her the voices ceased, and the footsteps. She understood that their owners had also found seats upon the stone wall. She was wondering if she could not steal away unobserved, when the voice broke the stillness. It was Joe Dagget's. She sat still and listened.

The voice was announced by a loud sigh, which was as familiar as itself. "Well," said Dagget, "you've made up your mind, then, I suppose?"

"Yes," returned another voice; "I'm going day after to-morrow."

"That's Lily Dyer," thought Louisa to herself. The voice embodied itself in her mind. She saw a girl tall and full-figured, with a firm, fair face, looking fairer and firmer in the moonlight, her strong yellow hair braided in a close knot. A girl full of a calm, rustic strength and bloom, with a masterful way which might have beseemed a princess. Lily Dyer was a favorite with the village folk; she had just the qualities to arouse the admiration. She was good and handsome and smart. Louisa had often heard her praises sounded.

"Well," said Joe Dagget. "I ain't got a word to say."

"I don't know what you could say," returned Lily Dyer.

"Not a word to say," repeated Joe, drawing out the words heavily. Then there was a silence. "I ain't sorry," he began at last, "that that happened yesterday—that we kind of let on how we felt to each other. I guess it's just as well we knew. Of course I can't do anything different. I'm going right on an' get married next week. I ain't going back on a woman that's waited for me fourteen years, an' break her heart."

"If you should jilt her to-morrow, I wouldn't have you," spoke up the girl, with sudden vehemence.

"Well, I ain't going to give you the chance," said he; "but I don't believe you would, either."

"You'd see I wouldn't. Honor's honor, an' right's right. An' I'd never think anything of any man that went against 'em for me or any other girl; you'd find that out, Joe Dagget."

"Well, you'll find out fast enough that I ain't going against 'em for you or any other girl," returned he. Their voices sounded almost as if they were angry with each other. Louisa was listening eagerly.

"I'm sorry you feel as if you must go away," said Joe, "but I don't know but it's best."

"Of course it's best. I hope you and I have got common-sense."

"Well, I suppose you're right." Suddenly Joe's voice got an undertone of tenderness. "Say, Lily," said he, "I'll get along well enough myself, but I can't bear to think—You don't suppose you're going to fret much over it?"

"I guess you'll find out I sha'n't fret much over a married man."

"Well, I hope you won't—I hope you won't, Lily. God knows I do. And— I hope—one of these days—you'll—come across somebody else—"

"I don't see any reason why I shouldn't." Suddenly her tone changed. She spoke in a sweet, clear voice, so loud that she could have been heard across the street. "No, Joe Dagget," said she, "I'll never marry any other man as long as I live. I've got good sense, an' I ain't going to break my heart nor make a fool of myself; but I'm never going to be married, you can be sure of that. I ain't that sort of a girl to feel this way twice."

Louisa heard an exclamation and a soft commotion behind the bushes; then Lily spoke again,—the voice sounded as if she had risen. "This must be put a stop to," said she. "We've stayed here long enough. I'm going home."

Louisa sat there in a daze, listening to their retreating steps. After a while she got up and slunk softly home herself. The next day she did her housework methodically; that was as much a matter of course as breathing; but she did not sew on her wedding-clothes. She sat at her window and meditated. In the evening Joe came. Louisa Ellis had never known that she had any diplomacy in her, but when she came to look for it that night she found it, although meek of its kind, among her little feminine weapons. Even now she could hardly believe that she had heard aright, and that she would not do Joe a terrible injury should she break her troth-plight. She wanted to sound him without betraying too soon her own inclinations in the matter. She did it successfully, and they finally came to an understanding; but it was a difficult thing, for he was as afraid of betraying himself as she.

She never mentioned Lily Dyer. She simply said that while she had no cause of complaint against him, she had lived so long in one way that she shrank from making a change.

"Well, I never shrank, Louisa," said Dagget. "I'm going to be honest enough to say that I think maybe it's better this way; but if you'd wanted to keep on, I'd have stuck to you till my dying day. I hope you know that."

"Yes, I do," said she.

That night she and Joe parted more tenderly than they had done for a long time. Standing in the door, holding each other's hands, a last great wave of regretful memory swept over them.

"Well, this ain't the way we've thought it was all going to end, is it, Louisa?" said Joe.

She shook her head. There was a little quiver on her placid face.

"You let me know if there's ever anything I can do for you," said he. "I ain't ever going to forget you, Louisa." Then he kissed her, and went down the path.

Louisa, all alone by herself that night, wept a little, she hardly knew why; but the next morning, on waking, she felt like a queen who, after fearing lest her domain be wrested away from her, sees it firmly insured in her possession.

Now the tall weeds and grasses might cluster around Caesar's little hermit hut, the snow might fall on its roof year in and year out, but he never would go on a rampage through the unguarded village. Now the little canary might turn itself into a peaceful yellow ball night after night, and have no need to wake and flutter with wild terror against its bars. Louisa could sew linen seams, and distil roses, and dust and polish and fold away in lavender, as long as she listed. That afternoon she sat with her needle-work at the window, and felt fairly steeped in peace. Lily Dyer, tall and erect and blooming, went past; but she felt no qualm. If Louisa Ellis had sold her birthright she did not know it, the taste of the pottage was so delicious, and had been her sole satisfaction for so long. Serenity and placid narrowness had become to her as the birthright itself. She gazed ahead through a long reach of future days strung together like pearls in a rosary, every one like the others, and all smooth and flawless and innocent, and her heart went up in thankfulness. Outside was the fervid summer afternoon; the air was filled with the sounds of the busy harvest of men and birds and bees; there were halloos, metallic clatterings, sweet calls, and long hummings. Louisa sat, prayerfully numbering her days, like an uncloistered nun.

1887

The Revolt of "Mother"

"Father!"

"What is it?"

"What are them men diggin' over there in the field for?"

There was a sudden dropping and enlarging of the lower part of the old man's face, as if some heavy weight had settled therein; he shut his mouth tight, and went on harnessing the great bay mare. He hustled the collar on to her neck with a jerk.

"Father!"

The old man slapped the saddle upon the mare's back.

"Look here, father, I want to know what them men are diggin' over in the field for, an' I'm goin' to know."

"I wish you'd go into the house, mother, an' 'tend to your own affairs," the old man said then. He ran his words together, and his speech was almost as inarticulate as a growl.

But the woman understood; it was her most native tongue. "I ain't goin' into the house till you tell me what them men are doin' over there in the field," said she.

Then she stood waiting. She was a small woman, short and straight-waisted like a child in her brown cotton gown. Her forehead was mild and benevolent between the smooth curves of gray hair; there were meek downward lines about her nose and mouth; but her eyes, fixed upon the old man, looked as if the meekness had been the result of her own will, never of the will of another.

They were in the barn, standing before the wide open doors. The spring air, full of the smell of growing grass and unseen blossoms, came in their faces. The deep yard in front was littered with farm wagons and piles of wood; on the edges, close to the fence and the house, the grass was a vivid green, and there were some dandelions.

The old man glanced doggedly at his wife as he tightened the last buckles on the harness. She looked as immovable to him as one of the rocks in his pasture-land, bound to the earth with generations of blackberry vines. He slapped the reins over the horse, and started forth from the barn.

"*Father!*" said she.

The old man pulled up. "What is it?"

"I want to know what them men are diggin' over there in that field for."

"They're diggin' a cellar, I s'pose, if you've got to know."

"A cellar for what?"

"A barn."

"A barn? You ain't goin' to build a barn over there where we was goin' to have a house, father?"

The old man said not another word. He hurried the horse into the farm wagon, and clattered out of the yard, jouncing as sturdily on his seat as a boy.

The woman stood a moment looking after him, then she went out of the barn across a corner of the yard to the house. The house, standing at right angles with the great barn and a long reach of sheds and out-buildings, was infinitesimal compared with them. It was scarcely as commodious for people as the little boxes under the barn eaves were for doves.

A pretty girl's face, pink and delicate as a flower, was looking out of one of the house windows. She was watching three men who were digging over in the field which bounded the yard near the road line. She turned quietly when the woman entered.

"What are they digging for, mother?" said she. "Did he tell you?"

"They're diggin' for—a cellar for a new barn."

"Oh, mother, he ain't going to build another barn?"

"That's what he says."

A boy stood before the kitchen glass combing his hair. He combed slowly and painstakingly, arranging his brown hair in a smooth hillock over his forehead. He did not seem to pay any attention to the conversation.

"Sammy, did you know father was going to build a new barn?" asked the girl.

The boy combed assiduously.

"Sammy!"

He turned, and showed a face like his father's under his smooth crest of hair. "Yes, I s'pose I did," he said, reluctantly.

"How long have you known it?" asked his mother.

"'Bout three months, I guess."

"Why didn't you tell of it?"

"Didn't think 'twould do no good."

"I don't see what father wants another barn for," said the girl, in her sweet, slow voice. She turned again to the window, and stared out at the digging men in the field. Her tender, sweet face was full of a gentle distress. Her forehead was as bald and innocent as a baby's, with the light hair strained back from it in a row of curl-papers. She was quite large, but her soft curves did not look as if they covered muscles.

Her mother looked sternly at the boy. "Is he goin' to buy more cows?" said she.

The boy did not reply; he was tying his shoes.

"Sammy, I want you to tell me if he's goin' to buy more cows."

"I s'pose he is."

"How many?"

"Four, I guess."

His mother said nothing more. She went into the pantry, and there was a clatter of dishes. The boy got his cap from a nail behind the door, took an old arithmetic from the shelf, and started for school. He was lightly built, but clumsy. He went out of the yard with a curious spring in the hips, that made his loose homemade jacket tilt up in the rear.

The girl went to the sink, and began to wash the dishes that were piled up there. Her mother came promptly out of the pantry, and shoved her aside. "You wipe 'em," said she; "I'll wash. There's a good many this mornin'."

The mother plunged her hands vigorously into the water, the girl wiped the plates slowly and dreamily. "Mother," said she, "don't you think it's too bad father's going to build that new barn, much as we need a decent house to live in?"

Her mother scrubbed a dish fiercely. "You ain't found out yet we're women-folks, Nanny Penn," said she. "You ain't seen enough of men-folks yet to. One of these days you'll find it out, an' then you'll know that we know only what men-folks think we do, so far as any use of it goes, an' how we'd ought to reckon men-folks in with Providence, an' not complain of what they do any more than we do of the weather."

"I don't care; I don't believe George is anything like that, anyhow," said Nanny. Her delicate face flushed pink, her lips pouted softly, as if she were going to cry.

"You wait an' see. I guess George Eastman ain't no better than other men. You hadn't ought to judge father, though. He can't help it, 'cause he don't look at things jest the way we do. An' we've been pretty comfortable here, after all. The roof don't leak—ain't never but once—that's one thing. Father's kept it shingled right up."

"I do wish we had a parlor."

"I guess it won't hurt George Eastman any to come to see you in a nice clean kitchen. I guess a good many girls don't have as good a place as this. Nobody's ever heard me complain."

"I ain't complained either, mother."

"Well, I don't think you'd better, a good father an' a good home as you've got. S'pose your father made you go out an' work for your livin'? Lots of girls have to that ain't no stronger an' better able to than you be."

Sarah Penn washed the frying-pan with a conclusive air. She scrubbed the outside of it as faithfully as the inside. She was a masterly keeper of her box of a house. Her one living-room never seemed to have in it any of the dust which the friction of life with inanimate matter produces. She swept, and there seemed to be no dirt to go before the broom; she cleaned, and one could see no difference. She was like an artist so perfect that he has apparently no art. To-day she got out a mixing bowl and a board, and rolled some pies, and there was no more flour upon her than upon her daughter who was doing finer work. Nanny was to be married in the fall, and she was sewing on some white cambric and embroidery. She sewed industriously while her mother cooked, her soft milk-white hands and wrists showed whiter than her delicate work.

"We must have the stove moved out in the shed before long," said Mrs. Penn. "Talk about not havin' things, it's been a real blessin' to be able to put a stove up in that shed in hot weather. Father did one good thing when he fixed that stove-pipe out there."

Sarah Penn's face as she rolled her pies had that expression of meek vigor which might have characterized one of the New Testament saints. She was making mince-pies. Her husband, Adoniram Penn, liked them better than any other kind. She baked twice a week. Adoniram often liked a piece of pie between meals. She hurried this morning. It had been later than usual when she began, and she wanted to have a pie baked for dinner. However deep a resentment she might be forced to hold against her husband, she would never fail in sedulous attention to his wants.

Nobility of character manifests itself at loop-holes when it is not provided with large doors. Sarah Penn's showed itself to-day in flaky dishes of pastry. So she made the pies faithfully, while across the table she could see, when she glanced up from her work, the sight that rankled in her patient and steadfast soul—the digging of the cellar of the new barn in the place where Adoniram forty years ago had promised her their new house should stand.

The pies were done for dinner. Adoniram and Sammy were home a few minutes after twelve o'clock. The dinner was eaten with serious haste. There was never much conversation at the table in the Penn family. Adoniram asked a blessing, and they ate promptly, then rose up and went about their work.

Sammy went back to school, taking soft sly lopes out of the yard like a rabbit. He wanted a game of marbles before school, and feared his father would give him some chores to do. Adoniram hastened to the door and called after him, but he was out of sight.

"I don't see what you let him go for, mother," said he. "I wanted him to help me unload that wood."

Adoniram went to work out in the yard unloading wood from the wagon. Sarah put away the dinner dishes, while Nanny took down her curl-papers and changed her dress. She was going down to the store to buy some more embroidery and thread.

When Nanny was gone, Mrs. Penn went to the door. "Father!" she called.

"Well, what is it!"

"I want to see you jest a minute, father."

"I can't leave this wood nohow. I've got to git it unloaded an' go for a load of gravel afore two o'clock. Sammy had ought to helped me. You hadn't ought to let him go to school so early."

"I want to see you jest a minute."

"I tell ye I can't, nohow, mother."

"Father, you come here." Sarah Penn stood in the door like a queen; she held her head as if it bore a crown; there was the patience which makes authority royal in her voice. Adoniram went.

Mrs. Penn led the way into the kitchen, and pointed to a chair. "Sit down, father," said she; "I've got somethin' I want to say to you."

He sat down heavily; his face was quite stolid, but he looked at her with restive eyes. "Well, what is it, mother?"

"I want to know what you're buildin' that new barn for, father?"

"I ain't got nothin' to say about it."

"It can't be you think you need another barn?"

"I tell ye I ain't got nothin' to say about it, mother; an' I ain't goin' to say nothin'."

"Be you goin' to buy more cows?"

Adoniram did not reply; he shut his mouth tight.

"I know you be, as well as I want to. Now, father, look here"—Sarah Penn had not sat down; she stood before her husband in the humble fashion of a Scripture woman—"I'm goin' to talk real plain to you; I never have sence I married you, but I'm goin' to now. I ain't never complained, an' I ain't goin' to complain now, but I'm goin' to talk plain. You see this room here, father; you look at it well. You see there ain't no carpet on the floor, an' you see the paper is all dirty, an' droppin' off the walls. We ain't had no new paper on it for ten year, an' then I put it on myself, an' it didn't cost but ninepence a roll. You see this room, father; it's all the one I've had to work in an' eat in an' sit in sence we was married. There ain't another woman in the whole town whose husband ain't got half the means you have but what's got better. It's all the room Nanny's got to have her company in; an' there ain't one of her mates but what's got better, an' their fathers not so able as hers is. It's all the room she'll have to be married in. What would you have thought, father, if we had had our weddin' in a room no better than this? I was married in my mother's parlor, with a carpet on the floor, an' stuffed furniture, an' a mahogany card-table. An' this is all the room my daughter will have to be married in. Look here, father!"

Sarah Penn went across the room as though it were a tragic stage. She flung open a door and disclosed a tiny bedroom, only large enough for a bed and bureau, with a path between. "There, father," said she—"there's all the room I've had to sleep in forty year. All my children were born there—the two that died, an' the two that's livin'. I was sick with a fever there."

She stepped to another door and opened it. It led into the small, ill-lighted pantry. "Here," said she, "is all the buttery I've got—every place I've got for my dishes, to set away my victuals in, an' to keep my milk-pans in. Father, I've been takin' care of the milk of six cows in this place, an' now you're goin' to build a new barn, an' keep more cows, an' give me more to do in it."

She threw open another door. A narrow crooked flight of stairs wound upward from it. "There, father," said she, "I want you to look at the stairs that go up to them two unfinished chambers that are all the places our son an' daughter have had to sleep in all their lives. There ain't a prettier girl in town nor a more ladylike one than Nanny, an' that's the place she has to sleep in. It ain't so good as your horse's stall; it ain't so warm an' tight."

Sarah Penn went back and stood before her husband. "Now, father," said she, "I want to know if you think you're doin' right an' accordin' to what you profess. Here, when we was married, forty year ago, you promised me faithful that we should have a new house built in that lot over in the field before the year was out. You said you had money enough, an' you wouldn't ask me to live in no such place as this. It is forty year now, an' you've been makin' more money, an' I've been savin' of it for you ever since, an' you ain't built no house yet. You've built sheds an' cow-houses an' one new barn, an' now you're goin' to build another. Father, I want to know if you think it's right. You're lodgin' your dumb beasts better than you are your own flesh an' blood. I want to know if you think it's right."

"I ain't got nothin' to say."

"You can't say nothin' without ownin' it ain't right, father. An' there's another thing—I ain't complained; I've got along forty year, an' I s'pose I should forty more, if it wa'n't for that—if we don't have another house. Nanny she can't live with us after she's married. She'll have to go somewheres else to live away from us, an' it don't seem as if I could have it so, noways, father. She wa'n't ever strong. She's got considerable color, but there wa'n't ever any backbone to her. I've always took the heft of everything off her, an' she ain't fit to keep house an' do everything herself. She'll be all worn out inside of a year. Think of her doin' all the washin' an' ironin' an' bakin' with them soft white hands an' arms, an' sweepin'! I can't have it so, noways, father."

Mrs. Penn's face was burning; her mild eyes gleamed. She had pleaded her little cause like a Webster;[1] she had ranged from severity to pathos; but

[1]Daniel Webster, congressman and famous nineteenth-century orator.

her opponent employed that obstinate silence which makes eloquence futile with mocking echoes. Adoniram arose clumsily.

"Father, ain't you got nothin' to say?" said Mrs. Penn.

"I've got to go off after that load of gravel. I can't stan' here talkin' all day."

"Father, won't you think it over, an' have a house built there instead of a barn?"

"I ain't got nothin' to say."

Adoniram shuffled out. Mrs. Penn went into her bedroom. When she came out, her eyes were red. She had a roll of unbleached cotton cloth. She spread it out on the kitchen table, and began cutting out some shirts for her husband. The men over in the field had a team to help them this afternoon; she could hear their halloos. She had a scanty pattern for the shirts; she had to plan and piece the sleeves.

Nanny came home with her embroidery, and sat down with her needle-work. She had taken down her curl-papers, and there was a soft roll of fair hair like an aureole over her forehead; her face was as delicately fine and clear as porcelain. Suddenly she looked up, and the tender red flamed all over her face and neck. "Mother," said she.

"What say?"

"I've been thinking—I don't see how we're goin' to have any—wedding in this room. I'd be ashamed to have his folks come if we didn't have any-body else."

"Mebbe we can have some new paper before then; I can put it on. I guess you won't have no call to be ashamed of your belongin's."

"We might have the wedding in the new barn," said Nanny, with gentle pettishness. "Why, mother, what makes you look so?"

Mrs. Penn had started, and was staring at her with a curious expression. She turned again to her work, and spread out a pattern carefully on the cloth. "Nothin'," said she.

Presently Adoniram clattered out of the yard in his two-wheeled dump cart, standing as proudly upright as a Roman charioteer. Mrs. Penn opened the door and stood there a minute looking out; the halloos of the men sounded louder.

It seemed to her all through the spring months that she heard nothing but the halloos and the noises of saws and hammers. The new barn grew fast. It was a fine edifice for this little village. Men came on pleasant Sun-days, in their meeting suits and clean shirt bosoms, and stood around it admiringly. Mrs. Penn did not speak of it, and Adoniram did not mention it to her, although sometimes, upon a return from inspecting it, he bore him-self with injured dignity.

"It's a strange thing how your mother feels about the new barn," he said, confidentially, to Sammy one day.

Sammy only grunted after an odd fashion for a boy; he had learned it from his father.

The barn was all completed ready for use by the third week in July. Ado-niram had planned to move his stock in on Wednesday; on Tuesday he received a letter which changed his plans. He came in with it early in the morning. "Sammy's been to the post-office," said he, "an' I've got a letter from Hiram." Hiram was Mrs. Penn's brother, who lived in Vermont.

"Well," said Mrs. Penn, "what does he say about the folks?"

"I guess they're all right. He says he thinks if I come up country right off there's a chance to buy jest the kind of a horse I want." He stared reflectively out of the window at the new barn.

Mrs. Penn was making pies. She went on clapping the rolling-pin into the crust, although she was very pale, and her heart beat loudly.

"I dun' know but what I'd better go," said Adoniram. "I hate to go off jest now, right in the midst of hayin', but the ten-acre lot's cut, an' I guess Rufus an' the others can git along without me three or four days. I can't get a horse round here to suit me, nohow, an' I've got to have another for all that wood-haulin' in the fall. I told Hiram to watch out, an' if he got wind of a good horse to let me know. I guess I'd better go."

"I'll get out your clean shirt an' collar," said Mrs. Penn calmly.

She laid out Adoniram's Sunday suit and his clean clothes on the bed in the little bedroom. She got his shaving-water and razor ready. At last she buttoned on his collar and fastened his black cravat.

Adoniram never wore his collar and cravat except on extra occasions. He held his head high, with a rasped dignity. When he was all ready, with his coat and hat brushed, and a lunch of pie and cheese in a paper bag, he hesitated on the threshold of the door. He looked at his wife, and his manner was defiantly apologetic. "*If* them cows come to-day, Sammy can drive 'em into the new barn," said he; "an' when they bring the hay up, they can pitch it in there."

"Well," replied Mrs. Penn.

Adoniram set his shaven face ahead and started. When he had cleared the doorstep, he turned and looked back with a kind of nervous solemnity. "I shall be back by Saturday if nothin' happens," said he.

"Do be careful, father," returned his wife.

She stood in the door with Nanny at her elbow and watched him out of sight. Her eyes had a strange, doubtful expression in them; her peaceful forehead was contracted. She went in, and about her baking again. Nanny sat sewing. Her wedding-day was drawing nearer, and she was getting pale and thin with her steady sewing. Her mother kept glancing at her.

"Have you got that pain in your side this mornin'?" she asked.

"A little."

Mrs. Penn's face, as she worked, changed, her perplexed forehead smoothed, her eyes were steady, her lips firmly set. She formed a maxim for herself, although incoherently with her unlettered thoughts. "Unsolicited opportunities are the guide-posts of the Lord to the new roads of life," she repeated in effect, and she made up her mind to her course of action.

"S'posin' I *had* wrote to Hiram," she muttered once, when she was in the pantry—"s'posin' I had wrote, an' asked him if he knew of any horse? But I didn't, an' father's goin' wa'n't none of my doin'. It looks like a providence." Her voice rang out quite loud at the last.

"What you talkin' about, mother?" called Nanny.

"Nothin'."

Mrs. Penn hurried her baking; at eleven o'clock it was all done. The load of hay from the west field came slowly down the cart track, and drew up at the new barn. Mrs. Penn ran out. "Stop!" she screamed—"stop!"

The men stopped and looked; Sammy upreared from the top of the load, and stared at his mother.

"Stop!" she cried out again. "Don't you put the hay in that barn; put it in the old one."

"Why, he said to put it in here," returned one of the hay-makers, wonderingly. He was a young man, a neighbor's son, whom Adoniram hired by the year to help on the farm.

"Don't you put the hay in the new barn; there's room enough in the old one, ain't there?" said Mrs. Penn.

"Room enough," returned the hired man, in his thick, rustic tones. "Didn't need the new barn, nohow, far as room's concerned. Well, I s'pose he changed his mind." He took hold of the horses' bridles.

Mrs. Penn went back to the house. Soon the kitchen windows were darkened, and a fragrance like warm honey came into the room.

Nanny laid down her work. "I thought father wanted them to put the hay into the new barn?" she said, wonderingly.

"It's all right," replied her mother.

Sammy slid down from the load of hay, and came in to see if dinner was ready.

"I ain't goin' to get a regular dinner to-day, as long as father's gone," said his mother. "I've let the fire go out. You can have some bread an' milk an' pie. I thought we could get along." She set out some bowls of milk, some bread and a pie on the kitchen table. "You'd better eat your dinner now," said she. "You might jest as well get through with it. I want you to help me afterward."

Nanny and Sammy stared at each other. There was something strange in their mother's manner. Mrs. Penn did not eat anything herself. She went into the pantry, and they heard her moving dishes while they ate. Presently she came out with a pile of plates. She got the clothes-basket out of the shed, and packed them in it. Nanny and Sammy watched. She brought out cups and saucers, and put them in with the plates.

"What you goin' to do, mother?" inquired Nanny, in a timid voice. A sense of something unusual made her tremble, as if it were a ghost. Sammy rolled his eyes over his pie.

"You'll see what I'm goin' to do," replied Mrs. Penn. "If you're through, Nanny, I want you to go up-stairs an' pack up your things; an' I want you, Sammy, to help me take down the bed in the bedroom."

"Oh, mother, what for?" gasped Nanny.

"You'll see."

During the next few hours a feat was performed by this simple, pious New England mother which was equal in its way to Wolfe's storming of the

Heights of Abraham.[2] It took no more genius and audacity of bravery for Wolfe to cheer his wondering soldiers up those steep precipices, under the sleeping eyes of the enemy, than for Sarah Penn, at the head of her children, to move all their little household goods into the new barn while her husband was away.

Nanny and Sammy followed their mother's instructions without a murmur; indeed, they were overawed. There is a certain uncanny and superhuman quality about all such purely original undertakings as their mother's was to them. Nanny went back and forth with her light loads, and Sammy tugged with sober energy.

At five o'clock in the afternoon the little house in which the Penns had lived for forty years had emptied itself into the new barn.

Every builder builds somewhat for unknown purposes, and is in a measure a prophet. The architect of Adoniram Penn's barn, while he designed it for the comfort of four-footed animals, had planned better than he knew for the comfort of humans. Sarah Penn saw at a glance its possibilities. These great box-stalls, with quilts hung before them, would make better bedrooms than the one she had occupied for forty years, and there was a tight carriage-room. The harness-room, with its chimney and shelves, would make a kitchen of her dreams. The great middle space would make a parlor, by-and-by, fit for a palace. Up-stairs there was as much room as down. With partitions and windows, what a house would there be! Sarah looked at the row of stanchions before the allotted space for cows, and reflected that she would have her front entry there.

At six o'clock the stove was up in the harness-room, the kettle was boiling, and the table set for tea. It looked almost as home-like as the abandoned house across the yard had ever done. The young hired man milked, and Sarah directed him calmly to bring the milk to the new barn. He came gaping, dropping little blots of foam from the brimming pails on the grass. Before the next morning he had spread the story of Adoniram Penn's wife moving into the new barn all over the little village. Men assembled in the store and talked it over, women with shawls over their heads scuttled into each other's houses before their work was done. Any deviation from the ordinary course of life in this quiet town was enough to stop all progress in it. Everybody paused to look at the staid, independent figure on the side track. There was a difference of opinion with regard to her. Some held her to be insane; some, of a lawless and rebellious spirit.

Friday the minister went to see her. It was in the forenoon, and she was at the barn door shelling pease for dinner. She looked up and returned his salutation with dignity, then she went on with her work. She did not invite him in. The saintly expression of her face remained fixed, but there was an angry flush over it.

[2]James Wolfe, a British general, scored a decisive victory against Quebec in the Seven Years War (1756–1763). Since the bluffs were considered unscalable, his was a very daring and heroic exploit.

The minister stood awkwardly before her, and talked. She handled the pease as if they were bullets. At last she looked up, and her eyes showed the spirit that her meek front had covered for a lifetime.

"There ain't no use talkin', Mr. Hersey," said she. "I've thought it all over an' over, an' I believe I'm doin' what's right. I've made it the subject of prayer, an' it's betwixt me an' the Lord an' Adoniram. There ain't no call for nobody else to worry about it."

"Well, of course, if you have brought it to the Lord in prayer, and feel satisfied that you are doing right, Mrs. Penn," said the minister, helplessly. His thin gray-bearded face was pathetic. He was a sickly man; his youthful confidence had cooled; he had to scourge himself up to some of his pastoral duties as relentlessly as a Catholic ascetic, and then he was prostrated by the smart.

"I think it's right jest as much as I think it was right for our forefathers to come over from the old country 'cause they didn't have what belonged to 'em," said Mrs. Penn. She arose. The barn threshold might have been Plymouth Rock from her bearing. "I don't doubt you mean well, Mr. Hersey," said she, "but there are things people hadn't ought to interfere with. I've been a member of the church for over forty year. I've got my own mind an' my own feet, an' I'm goin' to think my own thoughts an' go my own ways, an' nobody but the Lord is goin' to dictate to me unless I've a mind to have him. Won't you come in an' set down? How is Mis' Hersey?"

"She is well, I thank you," replied the minister. He added some more perplexed apologetic remarks; then he retreated.

He could expound the intricacies of every character study in the Scriptures, he was competent to grasp the Pilgrim Fathers and all historical innovators, but Sarah Penn was beyond him. He could deal with primal cases, but parallel ones worsted him. But, after all, although it was aside from his province, he wondered more how Adoniram Penn would deal with his wife than how the Lord would. Everybody shared the wonder. When Adoniram's four new cows arrived, Sarah ordered three to be put in the old barn, the other in the house shed where the cooking-stove had stood. That added to the excitement. It was whispered that all four cows were domiciled in the house.

Towards sunset on Saturday, when Adoniram was expected home, there was a knot of men in the road near the new barn. The hired man had milked, but he still hung around the premises. Sarah Penn had supper all ready. There were brown-bread and baked beans and a custard pie; it was the supper Adoniram loved on a Saturday night. She had a clean calico, and she bore herself imperturbably. Nanny and Sammy kept close at her heels. Their eyes were large, and Nanny was full of nervous tremors. Still there was to them more pleasant excitement than anything else. An in-born confidence in their mother over their father asserted itself.

Sammy looked out of the harness-room window. "There he is," he announced, in an awed whisper. He and Nanny peeped around the casing. Mrs. Penn kept on about her work. The children watched Adoniram leave the new horse standing in the drive while he went to the house door. It was fastened. Then he went around to the shed. That door was seldom locked, even when the family was away. The thought how her father would be confronted by the cow flashed upon Nanny. There was a hysterical sob in her throat. Adoniram emerged from the shed and stood looking about in a dazed fashion. His lips moved; he was saying something, but they could not hear what it was. The hired man was peeping around a corner of the old barn, but nobody saw him.

Adoniram took the new horse by the bridle and led him across the yard to the new barn. Nanny and Sammy slunk close to their mother. The barn doors rolled back, and there stood Adoniram, with the long mild face of the great Canadian farm horse looking over his shoulder.

Nanny kept behind her mother, but Sammy stepped suddenly forward, and stood in front of her.

Adoniram stared at the group. "What on airth you all down here for?" said he. "What's the matter over to the house?"

"We've come here to live, father," said Sammy. His shrill voice quavered out bravely.

"What"—Adoniram sniffed—"what is it smells like cookin'?" said he. He stepped forward and looked in the open door of the harness-room. Then he turned to his wife. His old bristling face was pale and frightened. "What on airth does this mean, mother?" he gasped.

"You come in here, father," said Sarah. She led the way into the harness-room and shut the door. "Now, father," said she, "you needn't be scared. I ain't crazy. There ain't nothin' to be upset over. But we've come here to live, an' we're goin' to live here. We've got jest as good a right here as new horses an' cows. The house wa'n't fit for us to live in any longer, an' I made up my mind I wa'n't goin' to stay there. I've done my duty by you forty year, an' I'm goin' to do it now; but I'm goin' to live here. You've got to put in some windows and partitions; an' you'll have to buy some furniture."

"Why, mother!" the old man gasped.

"You'd better take your coat off an' get washed—there's the wash-basin—an' then we'll have supper."

"Why, mother!"

Sammy went past the window, leading the new horse to the old barn. The old man saw him, and shook his head speechlessly. He tried to take off his coat, but his arms seemed to lack the power. His wife helped him. She poured some water into the tin basin, and put in a piece of soap. She got the comb and brush, and smoothed his thin gray hair after he had washed. Then she put the beans, hot bread, and tea on the table. Sammy came in, and the family drew up. Adoniram sat looking dazedly at his plate, and they waited.

"Ain't you goin' to ask a blessin', father?" said Sarah.

And the old man bent his head and mumbled.

All through the meal he stopped eating at intervals, and stared furtively at his wife; but he ate well. The home food tasted good to him, and his old frame was too sturdily healthy to be affected by his mind. But after supper he went out, and sat down on the step of the smaller door at the right of the barn, through which he had meant his Jerseys to pass in stately file, but which Sarah designed for her front house door, and he leaned his head on his hands.

After the supper dishes were cleared away and the milk-pans washed, Sarah went out to him. The twilight was deepening. There was a clear green glow in the sky. Before them stretched the smooth level of field; in the distance was a cluster of haystacks like the huts of a village; the air was very cool and calm and sweet. The landscape might have been an ideal one of peace.

Sarah bent over and touched her husband on one of his thin, sinewy shoulders. "Father!"

The old man's shoulders heaved: he was weeping.

"Why, don't do so, father," said Sarah.

"I'll—put up the—partitions, an'—everything you—want, mother."

Sarah put her apron up to her face; she was overcome by her own triumph.

Adoniram was like a fortress whose walls had no active resistance, and went down the instant the right besieging tools were used. "Why, mother," he said, hoarsely, "I hadn't no idee you was so set on't as all this comes to."

1891

Old Woman Magoun

The hamlet of Barry's Ford is situated in a sort of high valley among the mountains. Below it the hills lie in moveless curves like a petrified ocean; above it they rise in green-cresting waves which never break. It is *Barry's* Ford because at one time the Barry family was the most important in the place; and *Ford* because just at the beginning of the hamlet the little turbulent Barry River is fordable. There is, however, now a rude bridge across the river.

Old Woman Magoun was largely instrumental in bringing the bridge to pass. She haunted the miserable little grocery, wherein whiskey and hands of tobacco were the most salient features of the stock in trade, and she talked much. She would elbow herself into the midst of a knot of idlers and talk.

"That bridge ought to be built this very summer," said Old Woman Magoun. She spread her strong arms like wings, and sent the loafers, half laughing, half angry, flying in every direction. "If I were a *man*," said she, "I'd go out this very minute and lay the fust log. If I were a passel of lazy men layin' round, I'd start up for once in my life, I would." The men cowered visibly—all except Nelson Barry; he swore under his breath and strode over to the counter.

Old Woman Magoun looked after him majestically. "You can cuss all you want to, Nelson Barry," said she; "I ain't afraid of you. I don't expect you to lay ary log of the bridge, but I'm goin' to have it built this very summer."

She did. The weakness of the masculine element in Barry's Ford was laid low before such strenuous feminine assertion.

Old Woman Magoun and some other women planned a treat—two sucking pigs, and pies, and sweet cake—for a reward after the bridge should be finished. They even viewed leniently the increased consumption of ardent spirits.

"It seems queer to me," Old Woman Magoun said to Sally Jinks, "that men can't do nothin' without havin' to drink and chew to keep their sperits up. Lord! I've worked all my life and never done nuther."

"Men is different," said Sally Jinks.

"Yes, they be," assented Old Woman Magoun, with open contempt.

The two women sat on a bench in front of Old Woman Magoun's house, and little Lily Barry, her granddaughter, sat holding her doll on a small mossy stone near by. From where they sat they could see the men at work on the new bridge. It was the last day of the work.

Lily clasped her doll—a poor old rag thing—close to her childish bosom, like a little mother, and her face, round which curled her long yellow hair, was fixed upon the men at work. Little Lily had never been allowed to run with the other children of Barry's Ford. Her grandmother had taught her everything she knew—which was not much, but tending at least to a certain measure of spiritual growth—for she, as it were, poured the goodness of her own soul into this little receptive vase of another. Lily was firmly grounded in her knowledge that it was wrong to lie or steal or disobey her grandmother. She had also learned that one should be very industrious. It was seldom that Lily sat idly holding her doll-baby, but this was a holiday because of the bridge. She looked only a child, although she was nearly fourteen; her mother had been married at sixteen. That is, Old Woman Magoun said that her daughter, Lily's mother, had married at sixteen; there had been rumors, but no one had dared openly gainsay the old woman. She said that her daughter had married Nelson Barry, and he had deserted her. She had lived in her mother's house, and Lily had been born there, and she had died when the baby was only a week old. Lily's father, Nelson Barry, was the fairly dangerous degenerate of a good old family. Nelson's father before him had been bad. He was now the last of the family, with the exception of a sister of feeble intellect, with whom he lived in the old Barry house. He was a middle-aged man, still handsome. The shiftless population of Barry's Ford looked up to him as to an evil deity. They wondered how Old Woman Magoun dared brave him as she did. But Old Woman Magoun had within her a mighty sense of reliance upon herself as being on the right track in the midst of a maze of evil, which gave her courage. Nelson Barry had manifested no interest whatever in his daughter. Lily seldom saw her father. She did not often go to the store which was his favorite haunt. Her grandmother took care that she should not do so.

However, that afternoon she departed from her usual custom and sent Lily to the store.

She came in from the kitchen, whither she had been to baste the roasting pig. "There's no use talkin'," said she, "I've got to have some more salt.

I've jest used the very last I had to dredge over that pig. I've got to go to the store."

Sally Jinks looked at Lily. "Why don't you send her?" she asked.

Old Woman Magoun gazed irresolutely at the girl. She was herself very tired. It did not seem to her that she could drag herself up the dusty hill to the store. She glanced with covert resentment at Sally Jinks. She thought that she might offer to go. But Sally Jinks said again, "Why don't you let her go?" and looked with a languid eye at Lily holding her doll on the stone.

Lily was watching the men at work on the bridge, with her childish delight in a spectacle of any kind, when her grandmother addressed her.

"Guess I'll let you go down to the store an' git some salt, Lily," said she.

The girl turned uncomprehending eyes upon her grandmother at the sound of her voice. She had been filled with one of the innocent reveries of childhood. Lily had in her the making of an artist or a poet. Her prolonged childhood went to prove it, and also her retrospective eyes, as clear and blue as blue light itself, which seemed to see past all that she looked upon. She had not come of the old Barry family for nothing. The best of the strain was in her, along with the splendid stanchness in humble lines which she had acquired from her grandmother.

"Put on your hat," said Old Woman Magoun; "the sun is hot, and you might git a headache." She called the girl to her, and put back the shower of fair curls under the rubber band which confined the hat. She gave Lily some money, and watched her knot it into a corner of her little cotton handkerchief. "Be careful you don't lose it," said she, "and don't stop to talk to anybody, for I am in a hurry for that salt. Of course, if anybody speaks to you answer them polite, and then come right along."

Lily started, her pocket-handkerchief weighted with the small silver dangling from one hand, and her rag doll carried over her shoulder like a baby. The absurd travesty of a face peeped forth from Lily's yellow curls. Sally Jinks looked after her with a sniff.

"She ain't goin' to carry that rag doll to the store?" said she.

"She likes to," replied Old Woman Magoun, in a half-shamed yet defiantly extenuating voice.

"Some girls at her age is thinkin' about beaux instead of rag dolls," said Sally Jinks.

The grandmother bristled, "Lily ain't big nor old for her age," said she. "I ain't in any hurry to have her git married. She ain't none too strong."

"She's got a good color," said Sally Jinks. She was crocheting white cotton lace, making her thick fingers fly. She really knew how to do scarcely anything except to crochet that coarse lace; somehow her heavy brain or her fingers had mastered that.

"I know she's got a beautiful color," replied Old Woman Magoun, with an odd mixture of pride and anxiety, "but it comes an' goes."

"I've heard that was a bad sign," remarked Sally Jinks, loosening some thread from her spool.

"Yes, it is," said the grandmother. "She's nothin' but a baby, though she's quicker than most to learn."

Lily Barry went on her way to the store. She was clad in a scanty short frock of blue cotton; her hat was tipped back, forming an oval frame for her innocent face. She was very small, and walked like a child, with the clap-clap of little feet of babyhood. She might have been considered, from her looks, under ten.

Presently she heard footsteps behind her; she turned around a little timidly to see who was coming. When she saw a handsome, well-dressed man, she felt reassured. The man came alongside and glanced down carelessly at first, then his look deepened. He smiled, and Lily saw he was very handsome indeed, and that his smile was not only reassuring but wonderfully sweet and compelling.

"Well, little one," said the man, "where are you bound, you and your dolly?"

"I am going to the store to buy some salt for grandma," replied Lily, in her sweet treble. She looked up in the man's face, and he fairly started at the revelation of its innocent beauty. He regulated his pace by hers, and the two went on together. The man did not speak again at once. Lily kept glancing timidly up at him, and every time that she did so the man smiled and her confidence increased. Presently when the man's hand grasped her little childish one hanging by her side, she felt a complete trust in him. Then she smiled up at him. She felt glad that this nice man had come along, for just here the road was lonely.

After a while the man spoke. "What is your name, little one?" he asked, caressingly.

"Lily Barry."

The man started. "What is your father's name?"

"Nelson Barry," replied Lily.

The man whistled. "Is your mother dead?"

"Yes, sir."

"How old are you, my dear?"

"Fourteen," replied Lily.

The man looked at her with surprise. "As old as that?"

Lily suddenly shrank from the man. She could not have told why. She pulled her little hand from his, and he let it go with no remonstrance. She clasped both her arms around her rag doll, in order that her hand should not be free for him to grasp again.

She walked a little farther away from the man, and he looked amused.

"You still play with your doll?" he said, in a soft voice.

"Yes, sir," replied Lily. She quickened her pace and reached the store.

When Lily entered the store, Hiram Gates, the owner, was behind the counter. The only man besides in the store was Nelson Barry. He sat tipping his chair back against the wall; he was half asleep, and his handsome face was bristling with a beard of several days' growth and darkly flushed. He opened his eyes when Lily entered, the strange man following. He brought his chair down on all fours, and he looked at the man—not noticing Lily at all—with a look compounded of defiance and uneasiness.

"Hullo, Jim!" he said.

"Hullo, old man!" returned the stranger.

Lily went over to the counter and asked for the salt, in her pretty little voice. When she had paid for it and was crossing the store, Nelson Barry was on his feet.

"Well, how are you, Lily? It is Lily, isn't it?" he said.

"Yes, sir," replied Lily, faintly.

Her father bent down and, for the first time in her life, kissed her, and the whiskey odor of his breath came into her face.

Lily involuntarily started, and shrank away from him. Then she rubbed her mouth violently with her little cotton handkerchief, which she held gathered up with the rag doll.

"Damn it all! I believe she is afraid of me," said Nelson Barry, in a thick voice.

"Looks a little like it," said the other man, laughing.

"It's that damned old woman," said Nelson Barry. Then he smiled again at Lily. "I didn't know what a pretty little daughter I was blessed with," said he, and he softly stroked Lily's pink cheek under her hat.

Now Lily did not shrink from him. Hereditary instincts and nature itself were asserting themselves in the child's innocent, receptive breast.

Nelson Barry looked curiously at Lily. "How old are you, anyway, child?" he asked.

"I'll be fourteen in September," replied Lily.

"But you still play with your doll?" said Barry, laughing kindly down at her.

Lily hugged her doll more tightly, in spite of her father's kind voice. "Yes, sir," she replied.

Nelson glanced across at some glass jars filled with sticks of candy. "See here, little Lily, do you like candy?" said he.

"Yes, sir."

"Wait a minute."

Lily waited while her father went over to the counter. Soon he returned with a package of the candy.

"I don't see how you are going to carry so much," he said, smiling. "Suppose you throw away your doll?"

Lily gazed at her father and hugged the doll tightly, and there was all at once in the child's expression something mature. It became the reproach of a woman. Nelson's face sobered.

"Oh, it's all right, Lily," he said; "keep your doll. Here, I guess you can carry this candy under your arm."

Lily could not resist the candy. She obeyed Nelson's instructions for carrying it, and left the store laden. The two men also left, and walked in the opposite direction, talking busily.

When Lily reached home, her grandmother, who was watching for her, spied at once the package of candy.

"What's that?" she asked, sharply.

"My father gave it to me," answered Lily, in a faltering voice. Sally regarded her with something like alertness.

"Your father?"

"Yes, ma'am."

"Where did you see him?"

"In the store."

"He gave you this candy?"

"Yes, ma'am."

"What did he say?"

"He asked me how old I was, and—"

"And what?"

"I don't know," replied Lily; and it really seemed to her that she did not know, she was so frightened and bewildered by it all, and, more than anything else, by her grandmother's face as she questioned her.

Old Woman Magoun's face was that of one upon whom a long-anticipated blow had fallen. Sally Jinks gazed at her with a sort of stupid alarm.

Old Woman Magoun continued to gaze at her grandchild with that look of terrible solicitude, as if she saw the girl in the clutch of a tiger. "You can't remember what else he said?" she asked, fiercely, and the child began to whimper softly.

"No, ma'am," she sobbed. "I—don't know, and—"

"And what? Answer me."

"There was another man there. A real handsome man."

"Did he speak to you?" asked Old Woman Magoun.

"Yes ma'am; he walked along with me a piece," confessed Lily, with a sob of terror and bewilderment.

"What did *he* say to you?" asked Old Woman Magoun, with a sort of despair.

Lily told, in her little, faltering, frightened voice, all of the conversation which she could recall. It sounded harmless enough, but the look of the realization of a long-expected blow never left her grandmother's face.

The sun was getting low, and the bridge was nearing completion. Soon the workmen would be crowding into the cabin for their promised supper. There became visible in the distance, far up the road, the heavily plodding figure of another woman who had agreed to come and help. Old Woman Magoun turned again to Lily.

"You go right up-stairs to your own chamber now," said she.

"Good land! ain't you goin' to let that poor child stay up and see the fun?" said Sally Jinks.

"You jest mind your own business," said Old Woman Magoun, forcibly, and Sally Jinks shrank. "You go right up there now, Lily," said the grandmother, in a softer tone, "and grandma will bring you up a nice plate of supper."

"When be you goin' to let that girl grow up?" asked Sally Jinks, when Lily had disappeared.

"She'll grow up in the Lord's good time," replied Old Woman Magoun, and there was in her voice something both sad and threatening. Sally Jinks again shrank a little.

Soon the workmen came flocking noisily into the house. Old Woman Magoun and her two helpers served the bountiful supper. Most of the men had drunk as much as, and more than, was good for them, and Old Woman Magoun had stipulated that there was to be no drinking of anything except coffee during supper.

"I'll git you as good a meal as I know how," she said, "but if I see ary one of you drinkin' a drop, I'll run you all out. If you want anything to drink, you can go up to the store afterward. That's the place for you to go to, if you've got to make hogs of yourselves. I ain't goin' to have no hogs in my house."

Old Woman Magoun was implicitly obeyed. She had a curious authority over most people when she chose to exercise it. When the supper was in full swing, she quietly stole up-stairs and carried some food to Lily. She found the girl, with the rag doll in her arms, crouching by the window in her little rocking-chair—a relic of her infancy, which she still used.

"What a noise they are makin', grandma!" she said, in a terrified whisper, as her grandmother placed the plate before her on a chair.

"They've 'most all of 'em been drinkin'. They air a passel of hogs," replied the old woman.

"Is the man that was with—with my father down there?" asked Lily, in a timid fashion. Then she fairly cowered before the look in her grandmother's eyes.

"No, he ain't; and what's more, he never will be down there if I can help it," said Old Woman Magoun, in a fierce whisper. "I know who he is. They can't cheat me. He's one of them Willises—that family the Barrys married into. They're worse than the Barrys, ef they *have* got money. Eat your supper, and put him out of your mind, child."

It was after Lily was asleep, when Old Woman Magoun was alone, clearing away her supper dishes, that Lily's father came. The door was closed, and he knocked, and the old woman knew at once who was there. The sound of that knock meant as much to her as the whir of a bomb to the defender of a fortress. She opened the door, and Nelson Barry stood there.

"Good-evening, Mrs. Magoun," he said.

Old Woman Magoun stood before him, filling up the doorway with her firm bulk.

"Good-evening, Mrs. Magoun," said Nelson Barry again.

"I ain't got no time to waste," replied the old woman, harshly. "I've got my supper dishes to clean up after them men."

She stood there and looked at him as she might have looked at a rebellious animal which she was trying to tame. The man laughed.

"It's no use," said he. "You know me of old. No human being can turn me from my way when I am once started in it. You may as well let me come in."

Old Woman Magoun entered the house, and Barry followed her.

Barry began without any preface. "Where is the child?" asked he.

"Up-stairs. She has gone to bed."

"She goes to bed early."

"Children ought to," returned the old woman, polishing a plate.

Barry laughed. "You are keeping her a child a long while," he remarked, in a soft voice which had a sting in it.

"She *is* a child," returned the old woman, defiantly.

"Her mother was only three years older when Lily was born."

The old woman made a sudden motion toward the man which seemed fairly menacing. Then she turned again to her dish-washing.

"I want her," said Barry.

"You can't have her," replied the old woman, in a still stern voice.

"I don't see how you can help yourself. You have always acknowledged that she was my child."

The old woman continued her task, but her strong back heaved. Barry regarded her with an entirely pitiless expression.

"I am going to have the girl, that is the long and short of it," he said, "and it is for her best good, too. You are a fool, or you would see it."

"Her best good?" muttered the old woman.

"Yes, her best good. What are you going to do with her, anyway? The girl is a beauty, and almost a woman grown, although you try to make out that she is a baby. You can't live forever."

"The Lord will take care of her," replied the old woman, and again she turned and faced him, and her expression was that of a prophetess.

"Very well, let Him," said Barry, easily. "All the same I'm going to have her, and I tell you it is for her best good. Jim Willis saw her this afternoon, and—"

Old Woman Magoun looked at him. "Jim Willis!" she fairly shrieked.

"Well, what of it?"

"One of them Willises!" repeated the old woman, and this time her voice was thick. It seemed almost as if she were stricken with paralysis. She did not enunciate clearly.

The man shrank a little. "Now what is the need of your making such a fuss?" he said. "I will take her, and Isabel will look out for her."

"Your half-witted sister?" said Old Woman Magoun.

"Yes, my half-witted sister. She knows more than you think."

"More wickedness."

"Perhaps. Well, a knowledge of evil is a useful thing. How are you going to avoid evil if you don't know what it is like? My sister and I will take care of my daughter."

The old woman continued to look at the man, but his eyes never fell. Suddenly her gaze grew inconceivably keen. It was as if she saw through all externals.

"I know what it is!" she cried. "You have been playing cards and you lost, and this is the way you will pay him."

Then the man's face reddened, and he swore under his breath.

"Oh, my God!" said the old woman; and she really spoke with her eyes aloft as if addressing something outside of them both. Then she turned again to her dishwashing.

The man cast a dogged look at her back. "Well, there is no use talking. I have made up my mind," said he, "and you know me and what that means. I am going to have the girl."

"When?" said the old woman, without turning around.

"Well, I am willing to give you a week. Put her clothes in good order before she comes."

The old woman made no reply. She continued washing dishes. She even handled them so carefully that they did not rattle.

"You understand," said Barry. "Have her ready a week from to-day."

"Yes," said Old Woman Magoun, "I understand."

Nelson Barry, going up the mountain road, reflected that Old Woman Magoun had a strong character, that she understood much better than her sex in general the futility of withstanding the inevitable.

"Well," he said to Jim Willis when he reached home, "the old woman did not make such a fuss as I expected."

"Are you going to have the girl?"

"Yes; a week from to-day. Look here, Jim; you've got to stick to your promise."

"All right," said Willis. "Go you one better."

The two were playing at cards in the old parlor, once magnificent, now squalid, of the Barry house. Isabel, the half-witted sister, entered, bringing some glasses on a tray. She had learned with her feeble intellect some tricks, like a dog. One of them was the mixing of sundry drinks. She set the tray on a little stand near the two men, and watched them with her silly simper.

"Clear out now and go to bed," her brother said to her, and she obeyed.

Early the next morning Old Woman Magoun went up to Lily's little sleeping-chamber, and watched her a second as she lay asleep, with her yellow locks spread over the pillow. Then she spoke. "Lily," said she—"Lily, wake up. I am going to Greenham across the new bridge, and you can go with me."

Lily immediately sat up in bed and smiled at her grandmother. Her eyes were still misty, but the light of awakening was in them.

"Get right up," said the old woman. "You can wear your new dress if you want to."

Lily gurgled with pleasure like a baby. "And my new hat?" asked she.

"I don't care."

Old Woman Magoun and Lily started for Greenham before Barry Ford, which kept late hours, was fairly awake. It was three miles to Greenham. The old woman said that, since the horse was a little lame, they would walk. It was a beautiful morning, with a diamond radiance of dew over everything. Her grandmother had curled Lily's hair more punctiliously than usual. The little face peeped like a rose out of two rows of golden spirals. Lily wore her new muslin dress with a pink sash, and her best hat of a fine white straw trimmed with a wreath of rosebuds; also the neatest black open-work stockings and pretty shoes. She even had white cotton gloves. When they set out, the old, heavily stepping woman, in her black gown and cape and bonnet, looked down at the little pink fluttering figure. Her face was full of the tenderest love and admiration, and yet there was something terrible about it. They crossed the new bridge—a primitive structure built of logs in a slovenly fashion. Old Woman Magoun pointed to a gap.

"Jest see that," said she. "That's the way men work."

"Men ain't very nice, be they?" said Lily, in her sweet little voice.

"No, they ain't, take them all together," replied her grandmother.

"That man that walked to the store with me was nicer than some, I guess," Lily said, in a wishful fashion. Her grandmother reached down and took the child's hand in its small cotton glove. "You hurt me, holding my hand so tight," Lily said presently, in a deprecatory little voice.

The old woman loosened her grasp. "Grandma didn't know how tight she was holding your hand," said she. "She wouldn't hurt you for nothin', except it was to save your life, or somethin' like that." She spoke with an undertone of tremendous meaning which the girl was too childish to grasp. They walked along the country road. Just before they reached Greenham they passed a stone wall overgrown with blackberry-vines, and, an unusual thing in that vicinity, a lusty spread of deadly nightshade full of berries.

"Those berries look good to eat, grandma," Lily said.

At that instant the old woman's face became something terrible to see. "You can't have any now," she said, and hurried Lily along.

"They look real nice," said Lily.

When they reached Greenham, Old Woman Magoun took her way straight to the most pretentious house there, the residence of the lawyer, whose name was Mason. Old Woman Magoun bade Lily wait in the yard for a few moments, and Lily ventured to seat herself on a bench beneath an oak-tree; then she watched with some wonder her grandmother enter die lawyer's office door at the right of the house. Presently the lawyer's wife came out and spoke to Lily under the tree. She had in her hand a little tray containing a plate of cake, a glass of milk, and an early apple. She spoke very kindly to Lily; she even kissed her, and offered her the tray of refreshments, which Lily accepted gratefully. She sat eating, with Mrs. Mason watching her, when Old Woman Magoun came out of the lawyer's office with a ghastly face.

"What are you eatin'?" she asked Lily, sharply. "Is that a sour apple?"

"I thought she might be hungry," said the lawyer's wife, with loving, melancholy eyes upon the girl.

Lily had almost finished the apple. "It's real sour, but I like it; it's real nice, grandma," she said.

"You ain't been drinkin' milk with a sour apple?"

"It was real nice milk, grandma."

"You ought never to have drunk milk and eat a sour apple," said her grandmother. "Your stomach was all out of order this mornin', an' sour apples and milk is always apt to hurt anybody."

"I don't know but they are," Mrs. Mason said, apologetically, as she stood on the green lawn with her lavender muslin sweeping around her. "I am real sorry, Mrs. Magoun. I ought to have thought. Let me get some soda for her."

"Soda never agrees with her," replied the old woman, in a harsh voice. "Come," she said to Lily, "it's time we were goin' home."

After Lily and her grandmother had disappeared down the road, Lawyer Mason came out of his office and joined his wife, who had seated herself on the bench beneath the tree. She was idle, and her face wore the expression of those who review joys forever past. She had lost a little girl, her only child, years ago, and her husband always knew when she was thinking about her. Lawyer Mason looked older than his wife; he had a dry, shrewd, slightly one-sided face.

"What do you think, Maria?" he said. "That old woman came to me with the most pressing entreaty to adopt that little girl."

"She is a beautiful little girl," said Mrs. Mason, in a slightly husky voice.

"Yes, she is a pretty child," assented the lawyer, looking pityingly at his wife; "but it is out of the question, my dear. Adopting a child is a serious measure, and in this case a child who comes from Barry's Ford."

"But the grandmother seems a very good woman," said Mrs. Mason.

"I rather think she is. I never heard a word against her. But the father! No, Maria, we cannot take a child with Barry blood in her veins. The stock has run out; it is vitiated physically and morally. It won't do, my dear."

"Her grandmother had her dressed up as pretty as a little girl could be," said Mrs. Mason, and this time the tears welled into her faithful, wistful eyes.

"Well, we can't help that," said the lawyer, as he went back to his office.

Old Woman Magoun and Lily returned, going slowly along the road to Barry's Ford. When they came to the stone wall where the blackberry-vines and the deadly nightshade grew, Lily said she was tired, and asked if she could not sit down for a few minutes. The strange look on her grandmother's face had deepened. Now and then Lily glanced at her and had a feeling as if she were looking at a stranger.

"Yes, you can set down if you want to," said Old Woman Magoun, deeply and harshly.

Lily started and looked at her, as if to make sure that is was her grandmother who spoke. Then she sat down on a stone which was comparatively free of the vines.

"Ain't you goin' to set down, grandma? "Lily asked, timidly.

"No; I don't want to get into that mess," replied her grandmother. "I ain't tired. I'll stand here."

Lily sat still; her delicate little face was flushed with heat. She extended her tiny feet in her best shoes and gazed at them. "My shoes are all over dust," said she.

"It will brush off," said her grandmother, still in that strange voice.

Lily looked around. An elm-tree in the field behind her cast a spray of branches over her head; a little cool puff of wind came on her face. She gazed at the low mountains on the horizon, in the midst of which she lived, and she sighed, for no reason that she knew. She began idly picking at the blackberry-vines; there were no berries on them; then she put her little fingers on the berries of the deadly nightshade: "These look like nice berries," she said.

Old Woman Magoun, standing stiff and straight in the road, said nothing.

"They look good to eat," said Lily.

Old Woman Magoun still said nothing, but she looked up into the ineffable blue of the sky, over which spread at intervals great white clouds shaped like wings.

Lily picked some of the deadly nightshade berries and ate them. "Why, they are real sweet," said she. "They are nice." She picked some more and ate them.

Presently her grandmother spoke. "Come," she said, "it is time we were going. I guess you have set long enough."

Lily was still eating the berries when she slipped down from the wall and followed her grandmother obediently up the road.

Before they reached home, Lily complained of being very thirsty. She stopped and made a little cup of a leaf and drank long at a mountain brook. "I am dreadful dry, but it hurts me to swallow," she said to her grandmother when she stopped drinking and joined the old woman waiting for her in the road. Her grandmother's face seemed strangely dim to her. She took hold of Lily's hand as they went on. "My stomach burns," said Lily, presently. "I want some more water."

"There is another brook a little farther on," said Old Woman Magoun, in a dull voice.

When they reached that brook, Lily stopped and drank again, but she whimpered a little over her difficulty in swallowing. "My stomach burns, too," she said, walking on, "and my throat is so dry, grandma." Old Woman Magoun held Lily's hand more tightly. "You hurt me holding my hand so tight, grandma," said Lily, looking up at her grandmother, whose face she seemed to see through a mist, and the old woman loosened her grasp.

When at last they reached home, Lily was very ill. Old Woman Magoun put her on her own bed in the little bedroom out of the kitchen. Lily lay there and moaned, and Sally Jinks came in.

"Why, what ails her?" she asked. "She looks feverish."

Lily unexpectedly answered for herself. "I ate some sour apples and drank some milk," she moaned.

"Sour apples and milk are dreadful apt to hurt anybody," said Sally Jinks. She told several people on her way home that Old Woman Magoun was dreadful careless to let Lily eat such things.

Meanwhile Lily grew worse. She suffered cruelly from the burning in her stomach, the vertigo, and the deadly nausea. "I am so sick, I am so sick, grandma," she kept moaning. She could no longer see her grandmother as she bent over her, but she could hear her talk.

Old Woman Magoun talked as Lily had never heard her talk before, as nobody had ever heard her talk before. She spoke from the depths of her soul; her voice was as tender as the coo of a dove, and it was grand and exalted. "You'll feel better very soon, little Lily," said she.

"I am so sick, grandma."

"You will feel better very soon, and then—"

"I am sick."

"You shall go to a beautiful place."

Lily moaned.

"You shall go to a beautiful place," the old woman went on.

"Where?" asked Lily, groping feebly with her cold little hands. Then she moaned again.

"A beautiful place, where the flowers grow tall."

"What color? Oh, grandma, I am so sick."

"A blue color," replied the old woman. Blue was Lily's favorite color. "A beautiful blue color, and as tall as your knees, and the flowers always stay there, and they never fade."

"Not if you pick them, grandma? Oh!"

"No, not if you pick them; they never fade, and they are so sweet you can smell them a mile off; and there are birds that sing, and all the roads have gold stones in them, and the stone walls are made of gold."

"Like the ring grandpa gave you? I am so sick, grandma."

"Yes, gold like that. And all the houses are built of silver and gold, and the people all have wings, so when they get tired walking they can fly, and—"

"I am so sick, grandma."

"And all the dolls are alive," said Old Woman Magoun. "Dolls like yours can run, and talk, and love you back again."

Lily had her poor old rag doll in bed with her, clasped close to her agonized little heart. She tried very hard with her eyes, whose pupils were so dilated they looked black, to see her grandmother's face when she said that, but she could not. "It is dark," she moaned, feebly.

"There where you are going it is always light," said the grandmother, "and the commonest things shine like that breastpin Mrs. Lawyer Mason had on to-day."

Lily moaned pitifully, and said something incoherent. Delirium was commencing. Presently she sat straight up in bed and raved; but even then her grandmother's wonderful compelling voice had an influence over her.

"You will come to a gate with all the colors of the rainbow," said her grandmother; "and it will open, and you will go right in and walk up the gold street, and cross the field where the blue flowers come up to your knees, until you find your mother, and she will take you home where you are going to live. She has a little white room all ready for you, white curtains at the windows, and a little white looking-glass, and when you look in it you will see—"

"What will I see? I am so sick, grandma."

"You will see a face like yours, only it's an angel's; and there will be a little white bed, and you can lay down an' rest."

"Won't I be sick, grandma?" asked Lily. Then she moaned and babbled wildly, although she seemed to understand through it all what her grandmother said.

"No, you will never be sick anymore. Talkin' about sickness won't mean anything to you."

It continued. Lily talked on wildly and her grandmother's great voice of soothing never ceased, until the child fell into a deep sleep, or what resembled sleep; but she lay stiffly in that sleep, and a candle flashed before her eyes made no impression on them.

Then it was that Nelson Barry came. Jim Willis waited outside the door. When Nelson entered he found Old Woman Magoun on her knees beside the bed, weeping with dry eyes and a might of agony which fairly shook Nelson Barry, the degenerate of a fine old race.

"Is she sick?" he asked, in a hushed voice.

Old Woman Magoun gave another terrible sob, which sounded like the gasp of one dying.

"Sally Jinks said that Lily was sick from eating milk and sour apples," said Barry, in a tremulous voice. "I remember that her mother was very sick once from eating them."

Lily lay still, and her grandmother on her knees shook with her terrible sobs.

Suddenly Nelson Barry started. "I guess I had better go to Greenham for a doctor if she's as bad as that," he said. He went close to the bed and looked at the sick child. He gave a great start. Then he felt of her hands and reached down under the bedclothes for her little feet. "Her hands and feet are like ice," he cried out. "Good God! why didn't you send for some one—for me—before? Why, she's dying; she's almost gone!"

Barry rushed out and spoke to Jim Willis, who turned pale and came in and stood by the bedside.

"She's almost gone," he said, in a hushed whisper.

"There's no use going for the doctor, she'd be dead before he got here," said Nelson, and he stood regarding the passing child with a strange, sad face—unutterably sad, because of his incapability of the truest sadness.

"Poor little thing, she's past suffering, anyhow," said the other man, and his own face also was sad with a puzzled, mystified sadness.

Lily died that night. There was quite a commotion in Barry's Ford until after the funeral, it was all so sudden, and then everything went on as usual. Old Woman Magoun continued to live as she had done before. She supported herself by the produce of her tiny farm; she was very industrious, but people said that she was a trifle touched, since every time she went over the log bridge with her eggs or her garden vegetables to sell in Greenham, she carried with her, as one might have carried an infant, Lily's old rag doll.

1909

■   ROWLAND E. ROBINSON   ■
1833–1900

Rowland E. Robinson was born in 1833 at Rokeby, his parents' homestead, in Ferrisburgh, Vermont, and died there in 1900. Except for learning to engrave when he lived in New York City during his teens and living there again in his late thirties, Robinson spent his life in the forests of the green mountains, the broad Champlain Valley, and on Lake Champlain.

Robinson worked some as an engraver and a painter, and his daughter Rachel Robinson Elme became an especially fine artist, her skills far surpassing her father's. He also wrote outdoor articles about hunting, fishing, and trapping for *Forest and Stream*—precursor to *Field and Stream*. Houghton Mifflin became the regular publisher for his fiction in book form. This writing, the Danvis stories, features the activities and people in the fictitious town of Danvis, located somewhere on the western slopes of the Green Mountains. From there, residents traverse the broad Champlain Valley to Lake Champlain to hunt, fish, trap, and camp.

Although Robinson wrote articles about hunting, fishing, and trapping for nationally distributed magazines such as *Forest and Stream*, and his stories of the people of Danvis were published in *Scribner's*, the *Atlantic Monthly*, and other magazines with national circulations, his reputation and readership were for the most part local. He was the most-read and best-loved of all nineteenth-century Vermont authors. School children and adults alike read his books; in an age before radio, ordinary people read the stories aloud in the evening as entertainment.

Several key factors influenced Robinson's writing. First, his parents and grandparents were committed Quakers and Abolitionists. The Robinson household was a station on the Underground Railroad, and the young Rowland encountered numerous escaped slaves sheltered at Rokeby. As "A Side Track of the U.G.R.R." suggests, Robinson probably did not share completely his parents' commitment to either Quakerism or the Abolitionist movement. This may have been simply a form of rebellion against his parents. In any case, Sam Lovell, the main character in the Danvis stories, does not like Quakerism one bit. He can't stand the moaning and groaning he hears coming from the Quaker church as he passes by on a Sunday morning. And he is ambivalent about Abolitionists and refers to African Americans as "niggers." Yet he also risks his neck to get an escaping slave, Bob, safely onto an apple boat bound for Montreal. Robinson's willingness to convey his characters' ambivalences contributes to their realism; they have what Julia Alvarez calls the "dignity of complexity."

Important as the Underground Railroad movement and runaway slaves are to the progress of the Danvis stories, nothing is more important than Rowland's passionate commitment to telling realistic stories about the people of Danvis and of the wild. His visual sense—his ability to make the written word paint vivid pictures of his fictional world—is uncanny. That he was an illustrator and painter must have had something to do with his ability to paint pictures with words. This is especially striking because almost all of the Danvis stories were written *after* Robinson became totally blind. I believe Robinson's ability to describe the natural world comes from his desperate urgency to "see" the world again through words.

His method for writing the stories after he was blind combined orality with writing, which is especially notable in light of his captivating and brilliant use of dialect. He used a piece of heavy cardboard with grooves running horizontally from top to bottom; these were manufactured specifically for the blind. He placed a piece of paper over the grooves, then, following the grooves from left to right, wrote in straight lines across the page. After he drafted a story, his wife read it back to him; he made oral revisions which she inserted. Finally, she rewrote the story in her own hand.

Central to Robinson's work is his commitment to capturing the dialects used in the mid-nineteenth-century Champlain Valley in western Vermont. His representation of the French-Canadian dialect reflects his own ambivalence about French Canadians. He not only tried to get down on paper the way Antoine Bassette, Sam Lovell's best camping, fishing, and hunting pal, actually spoke, but he also ridiculed French Canadians for "butchering" the English language. In late-nineteenth-century New England, such prejudice against French Canadians—and against the Irish—was commonplace. In a Vermont dominated by white, Anglo-Saxon Protestants, Roman Catholics were an anathema. In addition, the French and Irish were foreigners and often poor. Moreover, the French were non-English speakers. Constituting a large proportion of Vermont's population, they were perceived as a threat by many white Protestant Vermonters. Yet Antoine is resourceful as well as irascible and hilarious—testimony to Robinson's use of dialect in creating multifaceted characters who cannot be reduced to stereotypes.

Among the few who still know Robinson, he has a reputation as a folksy, funny, down-home, merely popular writer. Although all of those adjectives are superficially apt, there is far more to him. For example, at a time when there were no set fishing and hunting seasons or other game laws, he campaigned for game laws in essays and fiction. Indeed, along with his contemporary, John Muir, he was one of America's first ecologists. His fiction is substantive *and* entertaining. Certainly some twenty-first-century readers will initially find his prose off-putting. Unlike the writing we are used to, it blends dialogue and dialect with an almost Elizabethan syntax. Reading it aloud, however, can make the rhythms and language come alive, and once you get into Robinson's "groove," his writing can be as captivating now as it was for his contemporaries.

David Budbill
Poet and Playwright, Wolcott, Vermont

PRIMARY SOURCES

Uncle Lisha's Camp, 1884; *Sam Lovel's Camps*, 1889; *Danvis Folks*, 1894; *Uncle Lisha's Outing*, 1897; *Sam Lovel's Boy*, 1901; *Danvis Tales: Selected Stories*, ed. David Budbill, introduction, Hayden Carruth, 1996.

A Rainy Day[1]

It was a May day with April weather. The rain had poured down in intermittent showers during the night. In the morning the rising sun transmuted the gray mist to floating gold, and turned the tremulous strings of sundrops on every bending twig to resplendent jewels.

The sheep began to scatter over the pastures, mumbling out calls to their lambs as they cropped the wet grass.

But the robins sang vociferously for more rain; the sun veiled itself with a drifting cloud, bordering it with gold, and shooting from behind it broad, divergent, watery bolts; a film of shower was trailed along the mountainside; the blotches of sunlight narrowed and faded into the universal somber gray, and, after a brief pattering prelude, the rain poured down again, and swept across the blurred landscape in majestic columns, that fled along the earth while they upheld the narrow sky.

Then it stopped as suddenly as it began, the sun shone out and revived the drowned splendor of the earth, the bedraggled robins sang again, and the murmur of the swollen brooks rose and fell more distinctly with the puffs and lulls of the inconstant wind. Then the sky would darken and blot out the patches of blue and the half-built arch of a rainbow, and the new showers chase away the straggling sunbeams, and the pour of the downfall overbear all other sounds.

Thus it was pouring, when Uncle Lisha came into the shop from the house and put on his apron, stooping low as he tied the strings to look out through the blurred panes upon the narrow landscape. He saw the innumerable jets of the puddles leaping up to meet the rain, the pelted, dodging leaves of the plum and cherry trees bending over their fallen blossoms, that like untimely snow, lay beneath them, where a group of fowls stood, bedraggled and forlorn, with shortened necks and slanted tails.

Beyond, all objects became flattened and more indistinct till, in the gray background, mountain and sky met and dissolved in each other.

An umbrella was coming up the road, dodging from side to side as the bearer avoided puddles and sprang across rivulets. The misty fabric materialized into blue cotton, and presently entered the shop, closed, with its depressed point streaming like a conduit, followed by Pelatiah, who set it to dribble in a corner as he said, "Haow de do," and then "Gosh," as a sufficient comment on the weather.

"I'm tumble glad you 've come, Peltier," said Uncle Lisha, searching among his tools for his pipe, "fer it's a lunsome kinder day, an' I wa'n't expectin' nob'dy. It 's kinder chilly, an' I don't b'lieve but what you 'd better whittle up some kindlin' an' start a fire in the stove."

Nothing loath, Pelatiah got some wood from the box, and, kneeling before the stove, whittled some kindling, laid and lighted it, and, still kneeling, intently watched the slow progress of the flame.

"Wal," said the old man, looking at him with kindly anxiety, "haow be ye gittin' 'long? Feelin' any comf'tabler in yer mind?"

[1] From *Danvis Folks* (1894).

"It aches contin'al," Pelatiah answered.

"You don't go tu Hamner's no more?"

Pelatiah shook his head as he got on all fours to blow the reluctant fire, and answered, "Not sence you gin me a talkin' tu 'n under the bridge."

"You done almighty well, boy, an' you jest stick to 't. When you hain't tu work, you go a-fishin' as often 's ye can, an' when it gits so 't there hain't no fishin', go a-huntin', an' 'twixt 'em they 'll fetch ye aout."

The two doors opened almost at the same moment, and Sam entered from the kitchen leading his now toddling boy, followed by his father, bringing in an ox-bow to whittle and scrape where litter offered no offence, while Solon and Antoine came in from the rainy outer world.

"Hoddy do, all de company?" Antoine saluted. "What you 'll said 'bout fishin's? Ah s'pose prob'ly you an Peltiet tink you felt pooty plump for ketch so many feesh, ant it?" He got beside the stove, steaming in the growing warmth, and preparing also to smoke. "Wal, seh, One' Lasha, dat ant not'- ing, not'ing for wat Ah 'll do wen Ah leeve in Canada."

"Naow lie, dum ye," Uncle Lisha growled.

"Haow many tam," Antoine demanded with grieved impressiveness, "Ah 'll gat for tol' you Ah ant never lie? M'sieu Mumpson, he 'll read me 'baout George Washin's son chawp a happle-tree wid hees new saw, an' tol' hees fader he 'll do it 'cause he 'll can'lie. Ah 'll chawp more as forty happle, prob'ly feefty tree 'fore Ah 'll lie, me. Yas, sah. But Ah 'll goin' tol' you. Great many tam, but one teekly tam Ah 'll go feeshins an' Ah 'll trow mah hook wid nice waum on it an' de traout was so hongry in hees belly an' so crazy in hees head dey 'll go after it so fas', de fus one git it, de nex' one touch hol' hees mouf of dat one's tail an' de nex' de sem way till dey was twenty prob'ly 'f dey ant fif- teen all in string, an' Ah 'll pull it mos' so hard Ah 'll can't, an' seh, Ah 'll gat all of it honly de middlin' one was kan o' slimber, an' broke off, so Ah 'll loss de hine en' of de row. Hol' on," as Uncle. Lisha began to open his mouth, "Ah 'll ant fineesh. W'en de traout in de water see where Ah 'll sot mah deesh of waum on de bank, he 'll beegin jomp on de bank for gat it, an' tumble top of herself for gat it. Den, seh, Onc' Lasha, Ah'll peek up mah deesh an' shook it, an' holly 'caday, caday' an' dat traouts folla me home so fas' Ah 'll had to run an' shut de door for keep it from feel up de haouse."

"Ann Twine," said Uncle Lisha, heaving a sigh of relief and sinking back into his seat till the leathern bottom creaked, "I Was raly afeared you was a-goin' tu tell one o' your lies."

1894

A Side Track of the U.G.R.R.[1]

The shadows of the trees that skirted the west shore stretched far across the marsh and channel as Sam drove the canoe up the creek with quick,

[1]From *Uncle Lisha's Outing* (1897).

strong strokes quite regardless of the throngs of incoming waterfowl that swept past him or those already arrived that arose from the marsh on either hand and the open water before him, for he had left the temptation of the gun behind him. When he entered the East Slang all lesser shadows were dissolved in the overwhelming shadow of the Adirondacks, and when he stepped on shore at the old camp landing the twilight was thickening into gloom in the woods, through which he took the now dimly defined path and hastened toward the log house of the negro.

When he came in sight of it, it was a dark blotch in the clearing against the faint light of the afterglow, with one spot of light in it, where a candle shone from its single front window. As he approached he heard the voices and frequent laughter of his acquaintances of the morning, with the softer voice of a woman sometimes breaking in. He knocked at the door and the voices were suddenly hushed, and in the stillness he heard the puff that blew out the candle, followed by excited whispers and cautious steps across the floor. He knocked again, and the woman's voice demanded:

"Who 's there?"

"It's me! Sam Lovel! the man 'at was here this mornin'. I want tu speak tu the man they call James."

There was more whispering before Jim asked, jerking out the words with the characteristic nervous twitches of the head that Sam could almost see in spite of the intervening door:—

"What d' you want? Be you alone? Can't you talk through the door?"

"I don't want tu holler," said Sam in a low voice, answering the last question first. "It 's suthin' 'baout the man 'at you call your brother er cousin. He wants tu be makin' himself sca'ce raoun' here. I 'm all alone, an' you need n't be afeared tu open the door."

After more whispering inside, the door was unfastened and cautiously opened far enough for Jim to thrust his head outside and assure himself of Sam's identity and that he was alone. Then the door was held wide open and the visitor invited to enter by a jerk of the head and motion of the hand. The door was closed so quickly behind Sam that it nearly caught the skirts of his coat. By the glimmer of light from the stove he saw the lilting, dancing negro of the morning transformed into a stern, threatening giant confronting him with an axe uplifted above his shoulder. The figure of a woman shrank behind the stove, with a child, wide-eyed with fright and wonder, clinging to her gown.

"You need n't be afeared tu light your light an' see who I be," said Sam. "The' hain't nob'dy else."

While Jim relighted the candle with a splinter the others looked intently at Sam, as his features grew distinct in the increasing glow, when, being assured that his honest face masked no evil purpose, the tall negro lowered his axe, and the woman, a handsome mulatto, sat down and took the child upon her knee.

Sam told them of his suspicion that the visitors at camp were in search of Jim's guest. "And naow," he said in conclusion, "the chances is they 'll be here arter you to-morrow. I 've laid in with a feller tu take ye tu Canerdy on his boat, but he won't go afore to-morrow night or nex' day, an' you 'll haf-ter lay low either in the woods or up tu Mr. Bartlett's. I cal'late his haouse is the best place, an' I come tu take ye up there an' tell him abaout gittin' on ye off, an' if that suits ye we 'll be a-moggin' soon as you c'n git ready."

"I 'se ready," said Bob, snatching his hat and coat from a peg on the log wall and moving toward the door.

"It don't take Bob long tu pack his trunk, no sir," Jim said with a nerv-ous laugh. "Lord, haow you did scare me when you knocked. Twice in one day is 'baout often 'nough to scare a man in one day, yes, sir! But naow you 're putty nigh scarin' of me ag'in. You s'pose them fellers r'ally was huntin' arter Bob?"

"I 'se ready," Bob repeated as he drew a small pistol from his coat pocket, and turning stooped to the candle light to examine the cap. Replac-ing it in his pocket, he turned to Sam and said:—

"I s'pec 's you 're gwine ter sot me 'cross de run, Marse Lovel?"

"The run? Oh, the Slang; yes, I was cal'latin' tu, an' tu go up tu Mr. Bar-tlett's with ye. I want tu see him. My canew 's up there tu the landin'."

"What! you did n't never come clean raound to the Slang to-night? You might ha' come right acrost the crik no time."

"I did n't know who might be a-watchin'," Sam answered. "The longest way raoun' 's the surest. Come, le' 's be a-moggin'."

"I 'se done b'en ready," said Bob. "Goo'-by, Nancy; goo'-by, little Jimmy. De good Lawd bress ye an' ta' keer on ye."

He shook hands with the woman and laid his huge hand on the child's curly head, and then stretched it out to Jim.

"Goo'-by, Jeems, er is you gwine 'long?"

"You stay along wi' me, Jim," said the woman anxiously.

"I guess mebby you 'd better," said Sam.

The two negroes looked at him suspiciously, and exchanged questioning glances.

"I guess I'll go a piece," Jim said with an emphatic jerk of the head.

"All right, suit yourself. I only cal'lated it 'ould look better if anybody come. S'posin' yu put the light aout ag'in, so the' can't nob'dy see us goin' aout."

Jim blew out the candle and the three went out into the night, now lighted only by the stars and the flicker of the northern lights.

They took their way across the clearing at a brisk pace, Jim taking the lead as being most familiar with the path, Sam next, and the runaway in the rear. The latter cast frequent glances behind and started nervously when an alarmed bird fluttered suddenly from a bush, or some night prowler scurried among the fallen leaves and dry twigs, while Sam and Jim held steadily on, quite regardless of such harmless sounds. Feeling their way more slowly along the unseen wood path, they came to where they saw the stars again, then saw them repeated in the still water of the channel, and then were at the landing. There was a soft splash in the channel like the cautious dip of an oar.

"Fo' de Lawd," Bob gasped, starting back and thrusting his hand in his pocket, "dern fellers out dar layin' fo' me. My Gawd, Marse Lovel, you ain't de man to fool a pore niggah what 's bein' hunted to de eends of de airth!" and he tried to scan Sam's face in the dim starlight, but holding aloof in a half-crouching attitude that might be a preparation for either a fight or a run.

"I guess it hain't nothin' but a mushrat or a duck," Sam whispered, looking intently in the direction of the sound, "but mebby Jim hed better shove aout there in his canew an' see."

Jim pushed his dugout to the edge of the channel and presently jerked back a loud disjointed whisper.

"Everything 's all right. Jist as clear 's a Christian's eye. Yes, sir, jist eg-zackly."

With this assurance Bob took his place in the canoe where Sam had already kneeled, with his paddle in his hand, and he now pushed out and laid his craft alongside of Jim's.

"I do' know jest where I 'm a-goin' tu land," he said with a questioning inflection.

"You go up 'baout fifty rod an' you 'll come tu the John Clark place, where ol' John Clark allus used tu fish. You can run right up to the hard bank there. Mr. Bartlett's is the furdest north in that string o' lights. You put right straight for it an' you 'll strike a big holler where a brook runs, which you cross it an' follow up the north bank an' you 'll hit the secont road right by his haouse. I guess I won't go no furder an' I 'll bid you good-by, Bob, an' good luck to ye."

"Goo'-by, Jeems; ta' keer yo'se'f, boy."

They shook hands across the gunwales and the bark canoe slid silently up the channel, breaking the smooth surface with wake and paddle strokes that set the mirrored stars a-dancing and startled the sleeping ducks to sudden, noisy flight. Without greater incident the brief voyage was made, and the two men set forth across the fields, guided by the house light and the deep-cut watercourse to which they presently came. They approached the first road with scarcely a precaution of secrecy, for there was not a house upon it nearer than the tavern at the corner, where the bar-room lights shone out with hospitable gleam.

They were beginning to climb the fence when they heard the sound of a wagon and voices in low but earnest conversation close at hand and drawing nearer. Then they saw the intermittent glow of a pipe, and as they sank back and crouched in a weed-grown fence corner they caught a whiff of its odor.

"Fo' de Lawd," Bob whispered, sniffing it eagerly, "I hain't felt de smell o' no terbacca lak dat sence I done lef' Ol' Firginny."

Sam laid a cautionary hand on his arm. "What be they talkin' 'baout?"

The wagon stopped almost in front of them, and as its clatter and the footfalls of the horse ceased, the guarded voices of the occupants were distinctly heard.

"I tell you the rwud cross lots is consid'able furder on," said one. "The' hain't no gap ner barway here, fer I c'n see stakes an' caps tu ev'ry corner."

Sam held his breath while he knew that two pairs of eyes were closely scanning the fence and the very corner where he crouched beside his companion, whose hand he could hear stealthily creeping to the pocket that held the pistol.

"I reckon yo' ah right," the other occupant of the wagon said at last, and Sam recognized the smooth voice of the quiet visitor at camp; "but 'pears like we 'd come fah enough."

"No, sir," the other rejoined emphatically, "the 's a reg'lar rwud when we come tu it, an' it runs through a paster. This 'ere 's a medder; I can see a stack a-loomin' up."

"All right," the other conceded, "go ahade and hurry up yo' cakes, foh I'll be bound Baker and his man s thah with the boat foh now."

The driver spoke sharply to his horse, and the wagon went rattling down the road at a rapid pace.

"Wal," said Sam, rising and letting out his long-held breath, "I cal'late you stayed to Jim's 'baout as long as was healthy for ye."

"Sho 's yo' bawn, Marse Lovel! Dat 'ar man saoun' des lak Cap'n Clahk," Bob whispered excitedly. "De shaapes' man faw huntin' niggahs dey is in all dem pahts. Lawd, if I did n't t'ink he was lookin' right squaar' at me."

"Wal, he hain't a-huntin' on his own groun', an' that makes lots o' odds. My sakes, won't they hev fun a-hoofin on't raound the head o' the Slang in the dark! It would be tew all-killin' bad if they should break the' necks a-tumblin' through the woods."

When the two came to the broad stage road, no one was astir in the quiet neighborhood, and leaving Bob hidden in an adjacent fence corner, Sam went to Friend Bartlett's kitchen door and knocked, and presently a handsome young woman came forth. Her plain dress wore some un-Quakerly adornments, but her face was so kindly that Sam felt sure she must be in full sympathy with her parents in all benevolent work.

"Good evenin', Miss Bartlett; I fetched up a couple o' ducks tu your father, an' I wanted tu speak tu him abaout a little business."

"Yes," she said, with a questioning affirmative, as she took the proffered ducks. "Thee may leave any message for father with me. Why, these ducks are very nice, and I 'm sure he 'll be very much obliged to thee. Won't thee come in?"

Sam declined and she stepped out, closing the door behind her. "You tell your father," Sam hastened to say in a low voice, "'at the' 's som'b'dy arter that nigger an' they 've faound aout where he was hid, so I fetched him up here."

"The colored man at James's? Where is he?" Margaret Bartlett asked anxiously.

"I did n't cal'late tu hev nob'dy see him but your father, an' hid him in the fence aout here. But he can't stay there all night, an' what be I goin' tu du with him?"

"Thee must put him in the barn, in the bay on the west side of the barn floor. No one will go there, and 'll tell Father when he comes."

"All right, an' you tell your father 'at I 've laid in wi' a Canuck 'at's a-buyin' apples tu take the nigger tu Canerdy in a day or two. Your father 'll want tu take daown a lwud to-morrer an' find aout when, an' we 'll git the nigger there tu rights."

"I wish thee would n't call colored people niggers," said Margaret.

"Why," said Sam, "That's what he calls himself, an' I rather guess from his looks he is one. Good night. I'll mow him away all right."

Groping his way into the unknown interior of the barn, guided only by feeling and a knowledge of the common internal arrangement of barns in general, Sam led his charge to this safe retreat, and bidding him good-by departed on his devious, dark, and solitary way back to camp.

As he silently passed the landing where Jim's dugout lay he saw the light of a lantern glimmering unsteadily along the wood path and heard the hunters returning in bad humor from their unsuccessful quest, stumbling and grumbling over the rough trail.

"Wal," said Sam to himself, as he listened to their floundering progress up the wooded bank of the Slang, "you faound the holler tree, but the coon was n't in it. By the gre't horn spoon! I 'd ha gi'n a fo'pence tu ha' be'n there an' seen 'em an' seen Jim shake that head o' his 'n."

When he reached the mouth of the Slang he heard the regular sound of oars and saw another light steadily advancing up the channel of the creek, shining far along the quiet water before it, while glittering reflections flickered out like floating sparks where the wake stirred the rushes.

Sam ran his canoe into the weeds till the other boat had passed. The lantern shining on the face of the man in the stern revealed the features of Baker, the other visitor at the camp.

"You planned it fust rate," Sam soliloquized again, "but it's a dre'f'l poor night for huntin' niggers. Oh, you cussed slinks! I don't lay it up so much ag'in that other feller, for that's the way he was brought up; but you—V'monters—huntin' niggers! Damn ye! I 'd lufter sink ye in the mud!"

So, by turns boiling with wrath and chuckling over the discomfiture of the slave-hunters, Sam pursued his way to where the candle was burning low in the socket of the tin lantern which was hung out to beacon him to the upper landing.

The northern horizon was glowing with the pulsating flame of the aurora, and the dark forest of the eastern shore echoed at intervals with the solemn challenges of the horned owls, remotely answered by their brethren who held sway over the somber realm of the Porterboro woods that stretched their dark expanse along the west bank of the South Slang and beyond the sluggish rivulets of its source.

"'Cordin' tu the signs we 're a-goin' tu git some sort o' fallin' weather," Uncle Lisha remarked as he gave an eye and ear to these prognostics of a storm.

"The north'n lights is shinin' tol'able bright," said Joseph, peeping through the trees at the celestial display.

Antoine rolled himself off his seat on to all fours, and in that position intently regarded such glimpses of the flickering arch as could be seen between the tree trunks that stood in black relief against it, then turning his searching gaze to the creek, descried a light moving about in the black shadows of the farther shore.

"Look, see dar!" he said in a suppressed tone of alarm, as he pointed to the moving light.

The Canadian watched the light till it vanished in fitful gleams among the woods, and then he turned and stooped to the campfire to rekindle his neglected pipe.

Before seating himself at the fire he looked again in the direction where the light had disappeared. If he had been given the vision of an owl he might have seen a boat with two figures in it stealthily landing at the farther shore; but the faint light of the aurora, that barely defined in dimmed silver the course of the channel, revealed nothing to him.

The owls had quit their dismal calling, and not a sound was to be heard from the woods or waters save the occasional splash of a fish or a waterfowl or a muskrat busy with its nightly labors.

"What ye s'pose has become o' that 'ere tormented boy?" Uncle Lisha demanded sharply, after some inward fuming at the apparent apathy of his companions, "or don' ye car' whether he 's draownded or lost in the ma'sh? Why don't ye say suthin?"

"Wal, Ah guess Sam gat hol' 'nough for took care heese'f of it, prob'ly," Antoine answered with some sharpness. "He 'll ant leetly boy, ant it?"

Uncle Lisha deigned no reply to the Canadian. Then after a moment of intent listening, "I 'm a dumbed good min' to holler. I c'n make him hear if he 's alive within a mild o' here."

As he drew in his breath for a mighty shout they heard disturbed waterfowl, one after another, nearer and nearer, taking sudden flight, the flutter of uprising and cries of alarm continually drawing nearer, till at last the thump of a paddle was heard at the landing, and then the lantern began to sway and undulate, now hidden behind a tree or knoll, now shining brighter till its sprinkled light disclosed Sam's illuminated legs quite close at hand.

"Wal, folks, here I be," he announced as he let the full light of the candle upon his face through the open door and then extinguished it with a puff.

"An' high time 'at you was," and Uncle Lisha spent his hoarded breath in a growl. "What ye be'n shoolin' raound these 'ere ma'shes for, a-ketchin' the fever 'n' aig an' freezin' tu death? I'm a tarnal good min' ter shake ye, so I be. Sed daown there by the fire an' warm ye whilst I put on some more wood. An' say, Ann Twine, hain't ye got a col' duck for him an' a hunk o' bread? I know he's hungry."

"I ain't a mite hungry, ner cold nuther," Sam declared, seating himself by the fire and preparing for a restful smoke. "On'y a leetle mite tired. I stayed tu Mr. Bartlett's longer'n what I meant tu an' it's kinder slow poky work a-keepin' the channel in the dark, 'spesherly in the Slang. I 'm sorry you got worried."

"Sho, I wan't worryin' none, but I was a leetle riled," said the old man as he ran his hand down Sam's long shank. "Why, your laigs is kinder damp. You want tu dry 'em good 'fore you go tu bed!"

"Say, Sam," Antoine whispered cautiously, "Where you was, hein?"

Sam cast a scrutinizing glance upon him as he answered, "Why, up to Mr. Bartlett's. Where d' ye s'pose. Le' 's go tu bed."

1897

▪ PAULINE ELIZABETH HOPKINS ▪
1859–1930

Pauline Elizabeth Hopkins was one of several pioneering post-Reconstruction black writers whose fiction sharpened awareness of political and racial issues central to African Americans at the turn of the twentieth century. Born in Portland, Maine, Hopkins moved to Boston with her parents, William and Sarah Allen Hopkins, during her childhood. Always possessing a strong desire to write, she won her first award at fifteen for an essay in a contest sponsored by the escaped slave, abolitionist, and novelist William Wells Brown (*Clotelle*, 1853). After graduating from Girls High School in Boston, she began to pursue a dual career in writing and theater; at the age of twenty, she composed and produced a musical drama entitled *Slaves' Escape; or, the Underground Railroad*. Hopkins played a central character in this production, and subsequent theatrical performances led to her fame as "Boston's Favorite Soprano." Eventually, she left the stage to become a stenographer and public lecturer so that she might better support herself as a writer.

In her lifetime Hopkins produced four novels, a novella, a play, several short stories, and numerous works of nonfiction. *Contending Forces: A Romance Illustrative of Negro Life North and South*, published by the Colored Co-operative Publishing Company in 1900 and her most famous novel, is an ambitious story about several generations of a black family from their pre–Civil War Caribbean and North Carolina origins to their later life in the North. The narrative dramatizes essential American historical realities: slavery, Klan violence and lynching, hidden inter-racial blood lines, post-Reconstruction voting disenfranchisement, and job discrimination against blacks. What sets Hopkins apart from her male contemporaries is her outrage at black women's victimization, their sexual exploitation by white men.

The heroine of *Contending Forces*, Sappho, functions in behavior and appearance to overturn the Jezebel stereotype historically applied to African American women. Rather than embodying seductiveness, Sappho stonily rebuffs male advances as a way of erasing her personal history of rape and victimization. In creating Sappho as a counterimage to the Jezebel stereotype, Hopkins also contended with the color prejudice in American society that exalted an ideal of beauty based on Anglo-Saxon features, skin, and hair. Sappho, of mixed parentage, has "hair of a golden cast" and an "aquiline nose," features that exemplify the culture contradictions in which post–Civil War African American writers were also caught in their effort, as Hopkins describes in her preface, "to raise the stigma of degradation from the race." In Chapter 14, Hopkins introduces Luke Sawyer, a gifted speaker at the American Colored League meeting, and his "very black" complexion emphasizes Luke's intellectual and moral capability, despite racist attitudes toward him. In much of her work, then, Hopkins uses skin color as a device to develop her characters' strengths and vulnerabilites.

A large part of the interest and significance of Hopkins's work lies in her use of popular fictional techniques to convey her political perspectives. She uses both the romance form and the conventions of domestic realism, juxtaposing imperiled heroines, concupiscent villains, and tragic misunderstandings with serene domestic scenes celebrating the pleasures of homemaking, marriage, love, and motherhood. At the same time, rhetorical devices with serious political implications permeate the melodrama. Sappho may possess the predictable beauty of a romance heroine, but Hopkins uses her atractiveness to expose the victimization that has accompanied beauty for African American women in a racist society. Her villians perpetrate racial crimes—the sexual coercion of women and the ritualized murder of men. And Hopkins infuses the cult of domesticity with polical messages, so that ordinary gatherings of women, such as sewing circles or tea parties, become the occasions for polical expression. Specifically, Hopkins proclaims the vibrancy of the black women's club movement, which was developed by the 1890s, as a powerful collective force that fought against lynching and black female sexual abuse. Coincidence, a device that earmarks romance, is a central fixture in Hopkins's fiction, underscoring her efforts to point out the remarkable events—in her words "all the fire and romance"—in African American history. Hopkins's choice of the romance form places her in the tradition of African American writers initiated by Harriet Wilson's *Our Nig* in 1859 and continued by Hopkins's contemporaries Frances Ellen Watkins Harper and Amelia Johnson. Her feminist insistence on women's instrumentality in history and her desire to empower her characters to regard themselves as actors rather than victims anticipates recent African American novelists such as Toni Morrison and Alice Walker.

Most of Hopkins's work, including three of her novels, was published in the *Colored American Magazine*. Established in 1900 as a forum for African American literary talent and the only monthly magazine of its sort at the time, the *Colored American Magazine* was a forerunner of present-day magazines addressed to black audiences. Hopkins was a founding staff member and one of its powerful editorial forces, working not only to showcase African American creative efforts but to strengthen racial solidarity. Both in her writings and in her editorial work, she pursued the goals to which other post–Civil War black writers were also committed: furthering pride in African American history and creating respect for the intelligence and dignity of the race.

Jane Campbell
Purdue University, Calumet

PRIMARY WORKS

Contending Forces: A Romance Illustrative of Negro Life North and South, 1900, reprint 1988; *The Magazine Novels: Hagar's Daughter, A Story of Southern Caste Prejudice,*

1902; *Winona: A Tale of Negro Life in the South and Southwest*, 1902; *Of One Blood, or, the Hidden Self*, 1903, reprint 1988; *Short Fiction by Black Women: 1900–1920* [reprints of most stories], 1991; "Pauline Elizabeth Hopkins," in *The Roots of African-American Drama: A Collection of Early Plays, 1858–1938*, ed. Leo Hamalian and Robert Latham, 1991.

from **Contending Forces: A Romance Illustrative of Negro Life North and South**

Chapter VIII. The Sewing Circle

[This chapter serves as a thematic focal point of *Contending Forces*, for "The Sewing Circle" clearly demonstrates Hopkin's belief that women can change the course of history by transforming a traditional womanly activity, such as sewing garments for a church fair, into a political forum. Miss Willis represents the leaders of the black women's club movement, a network of organizations which, during post-Reconstruction, crusaded against Jim Crow laws, lynching, and segregation. Moreover, the club movement urged African American women to celebrate their innate morality in the face of historical sexual trespass and concubinage. Although Mrs. Willis enunciates this celebration and adumbrates Hopkin's theme that solidarity among women can effect historical change, she also appears to Sappho as somewhat insincere, perhaps reflecting Hopkin's ambivalence toward some of the movement leaders.]

> *Where village statesmen talked with looks profound, . . .*
> *Imagination fondly stoops to trace*
> *The parlor splendors of that festive place.*
>
> .   .   .
>
> *Yes! let the rich deride, the proud disdain,*
> *These simple blessings of the lowly train;*
> *To me more dear, . . .*
> *One native charm than all the gloss of art.*
>
> —GOLDSMITH[1]

Ma Smith was a member of the church referred to in the last chapter, the most prominent one of color in New England. It was situated in the heart of the West End, and was a very valuable piece of property. Every winter this church gave many entertainments to aid in paying off the mortgage, which at this time amounted to about eight thousand dollars. Mrs. Smith, as the chairman of the board of stewardesses, was inaugurating a fair—one that should eclipse anything of a similar nature ever attempted by the colored people, and numerous sewing-circles were being held among the members all over the city. Parlor entertainments where an admission fee of ten cents was collected from every patron, were also greatly in vogue, and the money thus obtained was put into a fund to defray the expense of purchasing

[1]From "The Deserted Village" (1770), by Oliver Goldsmith.

eatables and decorations, and paying for the printing of tickets, circulars, etc., for the fair. The strongest forces of the colored people in the vicinity were to combine and lend their aid in making a supreme effort to clear this magnificent property.

Boston contains a number of well-to-do families of color whose tax-bills show a most comfortable return each year to the city treasury. Strange as it may seem, these well-to-do people, in goodly numbers, distribute themselves and their children among the various Episcopal churches with which the city abounds, the government of which holds out the welcome hand to the brother in black, who is drawn to unite his fortunes with the members of this particular denomination. It may be true that the beautiful ritual of the church is responsible in some measure for this. Colored people are nothing if not beauty-lovers, and for such a people the grandeur of the service has great attractions. But in justice to this church one must acknowledge that it has been instrumental in doing much toward helping this race to help itself, along the lines of brotherly interest.

These people were well represented within the precincts of Mrs. Smith's pretty parlor one afternoon, all desirous of lending their aid to help along the great project.

As we have said, Mrs. Smith occupied the back parlor of the house as her chamber, and within this room the matrons had assembled to take charge of the cutting out of different garments; and here, too, the sewing machine was placed ready to use. In the parlor proper all the young ladies were seated ready to perform any service which might be required of them in the way of putting garments together.

By two o'clock all the members of the sewing-circle were in their places. The parlor was crowded. Mrs. Willis, the brilliant widow of a bright Negro politician had charge of the girls, and after the sewing had been given out the first business of the meeting was to go over events of interest to the Negro race which had transpired during the week throughout the country. These facts had been previously tabulated upon a blackboard which was placed upon an easel, and occupied a conspicuous position in the room. Each one was supposed to contribute anything of interest that she had read or heard in that time for the benefit of all. After these points had been gone over, Mrs. Willis gave a talk upon some topic of interest. At six o'clock tea was to be served in the kitchen, the company taking refreshment in squads of five. At eight o'clock all unfinished work would be folded and packed away in the convenient little Boston bag, to be finished at home, and the male friends of the various ladies were expected to put in an appearance. Music and recitations were to be enjoyed for two hours, ice cream and cake being sold for the benefit of the cause.

Mrs. Willis was a good example of a class of women of color that came into existence at the close of the Civil War. She was not a *rara avis*, but one of many possibilities which the future will develop from among the colored women of New England. Every city or town from Maine to New York has its Mrs. Willis. Keen in her analysis of human nature, most people realized, after a short acquaintance, in which they ran the gamut of emotions from strong attraction to repulsion, that she had sifted them thoroughly, while they had gained nothing in return. Shrewd in business matters, many a subtle business man had been worsted by her apparent womanly weakness and charming simplicity. With little money, she yet contrived to live in quiet elegance, even including the little journeys from place to place, so adroitly managed as to increase her influence at home and her fame abroad. Well-read and thoroughly conversant will all current topics, she impressed one as having been liberally educated and polished by travel, whereas a high-school course more than covered all her opportunities.

Even today it is erroneously believed that all racial development among colored people has taken place since emancipation. It is impossible of belief for some, that little circles of educated men and women of color have existed since the Revolutionary War. Some of these people were born free, some have lost the memory of servitude in the dim past; a greater number by far were recruited from the energetic slaves of the South, who toiled when they should have slept, for the money that purchased their freedom, or else they boldly took the rights which man denied. Mrs. Willis was one from among these classes. The history of her descent could not be traced, but somewhere, somehow, a strain of white blood had filtered through the African stream. At sixty odd she was vigorous, well-preserved, broad and comfortable in appearance, with an aureole of white hair crowning a pleasant face.

She had loved her husband with a love ambitious for his advancement. His foot on the stairs mounting to the two-room tenement which constituted their home in the early years of married life, had sent a thrill to her very heart as she sat sewing baby clothes for the always expected addition to the family. But twenty years make a difference in all our lives. It brought many changes to the colored people of New England—social and business changes. Politics had become the open sesame for the ambitious Negro. A seat in the Legislature then was not a dream to this man, urged by the loving woman behind him. Other offices of trust were quickly offered him when his worth became known. He grasped his opportunity; grew richer, more polished, less social, and the family broadened out and overflowed from old familiar "West End" environments across the River Charles into the aristocratic suburbs of Cambridge. Death comes to us all.

Money, the sinews of living and social standing, she did not possess upon her husband's death. Therefore she was forced to begin a weary pilgrimage—a hunt for the means to help her breast the social tide. The best opening, she decided after looking carefully about her, was in the great cause of the evolution of true womanhood in the work of the "Woman Question" as embodied in marriage and suffrage. She could talk dashingly on many themes, for which she had received much applause in by-gone days, when in private life she had held forth in the drawing-room of some Back Bay philanthropist who sought to use her talents as an attraction for a worthy charitable object, the discovery of a rare species of versatility in the

Negro character being a sure drawing-card. It was her boast that she had made the fortunes of her family and settled her children well in life. The advancement of the colored woman should be the new problem in the woman question that should float her upon its tide into the prosperity she desired. And she succeeded well in her plans: conceived in selfishness, they yet bore glorious fruit in the formation of clubs of colored women banded together for charity, for study, for every reason under God's glorious heavens that can better the condition of mankind.

Trivialities are not to be despised. Inborn love implanted in a woman's heart for a luxurious, esthetic home life, running on well-oiled wheels amid flowers, sunshine, books and priceless pamphlets, easy chairs and French gowns, may be the means of developing a Paderewski[2] or freeing a race from servitude. It was amusing to watch the way in which she governed societies and held her position. In her hands committees were as wax, and loud murmuring against the tyranny of her rule died down to judicious whispers. If a vote went contrary to her desires, it was in her absence. Thus she became the pivot about which all the social and intellectual life of the colored people of her section revolved. No one had yet been found with the temerity to contest her position, which, like a title of nobility, bade fair to descend to her children. It was thought that she might be eclipsed by the younger and more brilliant women students on the strength of their alma mater, but she still held her own by sheer force of will-power and indomitable pluck.

The subject of the talk at this meeting was: "The place which the virtuous woman occupies in upbuilding a race." After a few explanatory remarks, Mrs. Willis said:

"I am particularly anxious that you should think upon this matter seriously, because of its intrinsic value to all of us as race women. I am not less anxious because you represent the coming factors of our race. Shortly, you must fill the positions now occupied by your mothers, and it will rest with you and your children to refute the charges brought against us as to our moral irresponsibility, and the low moral standard maintained by us in comparison with other races."

"Did I understand you to say that the Negro woman in her native state is truly a virtuous woman?" asked Sappho, who had been very silent during the bustle attending the opening of the meeting.

"Travelers tell us that the native African woman is impregnable in her virtue," replied Mrs. Willis.

"So we have sacrificed that attribute in order to acquire civilization," chimed in Dora.

"No, not 'sacrificed' but pushed one side by the force of circumstances. Let us thank God that it *is* an essential attribute peculiar to us—a racial

---

[2]Ignace Jan Paderewski (1860–1941), Polish pianist, composer, and statesman, who wrote his first musical piece at the age of six. One of the most acclaimed masters of the piano, Paderewski also played a significant role in obtaining Poland's status as an independent nation by the Treaty of Versailles and gave his vast fortune to the cause of his country.

characteristic which is slumbering but not lost," replied Mrs. Willis. "But let us not forget the definition of virtue—'Strength to do the right thing under all temptations.' Our ideas of virtue are too narrow. We confine them to that conduct which is ruled by our animal passions alone. It goes deeper than that—general excellence in every duty of life is what we may call virtue."

"Do you think, then, that Negro women will be held responsible for all the lack of virtue that is being laid to their charge today? I mean, do you think that God will hold us responsible for the *illegitimacy* with which our race has been obliged, as it were, to flood the world?" asked Sappho.

"I believe that we shall not be held responsible for wrongs which we have unconsciously committed, or which we have committed under compulsion. We are virtuous or non-virtuous only when we have a choice under temptation. We cannot by any means apply the word to a little child who has never been exposed to the African brought to these shores against his will—the state of morality which implies willpower on his part does not exist, therefore he is not a responsible being. The sin and its punishment lies with the person consciously false to his knowledge of right. From this we deduce the truism that 'the civility of no race is perfect whilst another race is degraded.'"

"I shall never forget my feelings," chimed in Anna Stevens, a school teacher of a very studious temperament, "at certain remarks made by the Rev. John Thomas at one of his noonday lectures in the Temple. He was speaking on 'Different Races,' and had in his vigorous style been sweeping his audience with him at a high elevation of thought which was dazzling to the faculties, and almost impossible to follow in some points. Suddenly he touched upon the Negro, and with impressive gesture and lowered voice thanked God that the mulatto race was dying out, because it was a mongrel mixture which combined the worst elements of two races. Lo, the poor mulatto! despised by the blacks of his own race, scorned by the whites! Let him go out and hang himself!" In her indignation Anna forgot the scissors, and bit her thread off viciously with her little white teeth.

Mrs. Willis smiled as she said calmly: "My dear Anna, I would not worry about the fate of the mulatto, for the fate of the mulatto will be the fate of the entire race. Did you never think that today the black race on this continent has developed into a race of mulattoes?"

"Why, Mrs. Willis!" came in a chorus of voices.

"Yes," continued Mrs. Willis, still smiling. "It is an incontrovertible truth that there is no such thing as an unmixed black on the American continent. Just bear in mind that we cannot tell by a person's complexion whether he be dark or light in blood, for by the working of the natural laws the white father and black mother produce the mulatto offspring; the black father and white mother the mulatto offspring also; while the black father and quadroon mother produce the black child, which to the eye alone is a child of unmixed black blood. I will venture to say that out of a hundred apparently pure black men not one will be able to trace an unmixed flow of African blood since landing upon these shores! What an unhappy example of the frailty of the human intellects, when such a man and scholar as Doctor Thomas could so far allow his prejudices to dominate his better judgment as to add one straw to the burden which is popularly supposed to rest upon the unhappy mulattoes of a despised race," finished the lady, with a dangerous flash of her large dark eyes.

"Mrs. Willis," said Dora, with a scornful little laugh, "I am not unhappy, and I am a mulatto. I just enjoy my life, and I don't want to die before my time comes, either. There are lots of good things left on earth to be enjoyed even by mulattoes, and I want my share."

"Yes, my dear; and I hope you may all live and take comfort in the proper joys of your lives. While we are all content to accept life, and enjoy it along the lines which God has laid down for us as individuals as well as a race, we shall be happy and get the best out of life. Now, let me close this talk by asking you to remember one maxim written of your race by a good man: 'Happiness and social position are not to be gained by pushing.' Let the world, by its need of us along certain lines, and our intrinsic fitness for these lines, push us into the niche which God has prepared for us. So shall our lives be beautiful and our race raised in the civilization of the future as we grow away from all these prejudices which have been the instruments of our advancement according to the intention of an All-seeing Omnipotence, from the beginning. Never mind our poverty, ignorance, and the slights and injuries which we bear at the hands of a higher race. With the thought ever before us of what the Master suffered to raise all humanity to its present degree of prosperity and intelligence, let us cultivate, while we go about our daily tasks, no matter how inferior they may seem to us, beauty of the soul and mind, which being transmitted to our children by the law of heredity, shall improve the race by eliminating *immorality* from our midst and raising *morality* and virtue to their true place. Thirty-five years of liberty have made us a new people. The marks of servitude and oppression are dropping slowly from us; let us hasten the transformation of the body by the nobility of the soul."

> For of the soul of the body form doth take,
> For soul is form and doth the body make,

quoted Dora.

"Yes," said Mrs. Willis with a smile, "that is the idea exactly, and well expressed. Now I hope that through the coming week you will think of what we have talked about this afternoon, for it is of the very first importance to all people, but particularly so to young folks."

Sappho, who had been thoughtfully embroidering pansies on white linen, now leaned back in her chair for a moment and said: "Mrs. Willis, there is one thing which puzzles me—how are we to overcome the nature which is given us? I mean how can we eliminate passion from our lives, and emerge into the purity which marked the life of Christ? So many of us desire purity and think to have found it, but in a moment of passion, or under the pressure of circumstances which we cannot control, we commit some horrid sin, and the taint of it sticks and will not leave us, and we grow to loathe ourselves."

"Passion, my dear Miss Clark, is a state in which the will lies dormant, and all other desires become subservient to one. Enthusiasm for any one object or duty may become a passion. I believe that in some degree passion may be beneficial, but we must guard ourselves against a sinful growth of any appetite. All work of whatever character, as I look at it, needs a certain amount of absorbing interest to become successful, and it is here that the Christian life gains its greatest glory in teaching us how to keep ourselves from abusing any of our human attributes. We are not held responsible for compulsory sin, only for the sin that is pleasant to our thoughts and palatable to our appetites. All desires and hopes with which we are endowed are good in the sight of God, only it is left for us to discover their right uses. Do I cover your ground?"

"Yes and no," replied Sappho; "but perhaps at some future time you will be good enough to talk with me personally upon this subject."

"Dear child, sit here by me. It is a blessing to look at you. Beauty like yours is inspiring. You seem to be troubled; what is it? If I can comfort or strengthen, it is all I ask." She pressed the girl's hand in hers and drew her into a secluded corner. For a moment the flood-gates of suppressed feeling flew open in the girl's heart, and she longed to lean her head on that motherly breast and unburden her sorrows there.

"Mrs. Willis, I am troubled greatly," she said at length.

"I am *so* sorry; tell me, my love, what it is all about."

Just as the barriers of Sappho's reserve seemed about to be swept away, there followed, almost instantly, a wave of repulsion toward this woman and her effusiveness, so forced and insincere. Sappho was very impressionable, and yielded readily to the influence which fell like a cold shadow between them. She drew back as from an abyss suddenly beheld stretching before her.

"On second thoughts, I think I ought to correct my remarks. It is not really *trouble*, but more a desire to confirm me in my own ideas."

"Well, if you feel you are right, dear girl, stand for the uplifting of the race and womanhood. Do not shrink from duty."

"I was simply a thought raised by your remarks on morality. I once knew a woman who had sinned. No one in the community in which she lived knew it but herself. She married a man who would have despised her had he known her story; but as it is, she is looked upon as a pattern of virtue for all women."

"And then what?" asked Mrs. Willis, with a searching glance at the fair face beside her.

"Ought she not to have told her husband before marriage? Was it not her duty to have thrown herself upon his clemency?"

"I think not," replied Mrs. Willis dryly. "See here, my dear, I am a practical woman of the world, and I think your young woman builded wiser than she knew. I am of the opinion that most men are like the lower animals in many things—they don't always know what is for their best good. If the husband had been left to himself, he probably would not have married the one woman in the world best fitted to be his wife. I think in her case she did her duty."

"Ah, that word 'duty,' What is our duty" queried the girl, with a sad droop to the sensitive mouth. "It is so hard to know our duty. We are told that all hidden things shall be revealed. Must repented and atoned-for sin rise at last to be our curse?"

"Here is a point, dear girl. God does not look upon the constitution of sin as we do. His judgment is not ours; ours is finite, his infinite. *Your* duty is not to be morbid, thinking these thoughts that have puzzled older heads than yours. *Your* duty is, also, to be happy and bright for the good of those about you. Just blossom like the flowers, have faith and *trust*." At this point the entrance of the men made an interruption, and Mrs. Willis disappeared in a crowd of other matrons. Sappho was impressed in spite of herself, by the woman's words. She sat buried in deep thought.

There was evidently more in this woman than appeared upon the surface. With all the centuries of civilization and culture that have come to this grand old world, no man has yet been found able to trace the windings of God's inscrutable ways. There are men and women whose seeming uselessness fit perfectly into the warp and woof of Destiny's web. All things work together for good.

Supper being over, the elderly people began to leave. It was understood that after nine o'clock the night belonged to the young people. A committee had been formed from among them to plan for their enjoyment, and they consulted with Ma Smith, in the kitchen, as to the best plan of procedure.

"The case is this," said the chairman, who was also the church chorister: "Ma Smith has brought four gallons of ice cream, to be sold for the benefit of this fair. It's *got* to go, and it rests with us to devise ways and means of getting rid of it."

"Get up a dance," suggested Sam Washington, a young fellow who was the life of all social functions.

"Dance!" exclaimed Ma Smith, "not in this house."

The choir-master surreptitiously kicked Sam on the shins, as he said soothingly: "Under the circumstances I see no other way, as we've *got* to sell the cream, and there's not harm in dancing, anyway."

"You ain't going to object to our dancing, are you Ma? It's all old fogyism about dancing being a sin," chimed in Sam.

"Oh, but my son, I've been a church member over thirty years, a consistent Christian, and I never was up before the board for behavior unbecoming a professor. Think of the disgrace on me if the church took it up," she expostulated tearfully.

"Look here, Ma, the deacons and ministers are all fooling you. It's the style for church members to go to the theatre and the circus, to balls and everything you can mention. Why, I've seen our own pastor up to see the *Black Crook*,[3] and laughing like all possessed at the sights. Fact!"

"Why, Samuel!" said Ma Smith, "how can you stand there and tell me such awful stories?"

"Not a bit of a story," declared the brazen-faced Sam, "it's as true as gospel. I'll find out what seat the minister gets next June when the circus comes into town, and I'll get a set for you right behind him. If you've never been to the circus, Ma, and to see the seven-headed lady and the dancing mokes, you ought to go as soon as possible. Think of the fun your missing."

"Oh!" groaned the good woman in holy horror, "how you do go on."

"But that ain't nothing to the ice cream," continued Sam, "and them girls in there have got to be warmed up, or the cream will be left, and there won't be a thing doing when the committee calls for the money."

"That's so," replied Ma Smith, beginning to weaken in her opposition.

"Well, mother," said Will, who had been an amused listener to the dialogue, "we'll have the dance, and it shall be *my* dance for *my* company. No one shall trouble you; you will have nothing to do with it."

"Well, if you say so, Willie, it's all right," replied his mother with a fond smile; "you are master in this house."

In the meantime the furniture in the parlors had been moved out by other members of the committee, and in one corner a set of whist-players were enjoying themselves at ten cents a head for a thirty-minute game, which ended at the stroke of a small silver bell, their places being taken by others.

Already it was getting very warm in the crowded rooms. The doors leading into the entry had been thrown open, and couples were finding seats in convenient nooks waiting for dancing to begin. The girls were thinking of ice cream. Rev. Tommy James gravitated toward Mrs. Davis's corner. She had not gone out with the other matrons.

"I enjoy a real good time as much as anybody, children," she said; "and when it comes to dancing, you can't lose your Aunt Hannah."

The Reverend Tommy was always at his ease with Mrs. Davis. She led him along paths which caused him no embarrassment. He knew that she looked up to him because of his education and his clerical dignity. On his side, he admired her rugged common-sense, which put him at his ease, and banished the last atom of his "ladylike" bashfulness. Early in the winter he had been brought to realize the nature of his feeling for Mrs. Davis, by seeing Brother Silas Hamm, recently left a widower, and having ten children, making a decided stampede in the widow's direction. Revered Tommy was grieved. To be sure, she was old enough to be his mother, but she had many good points to be considered. She was a good worker, experienced in married life and ways of making a man comfortable. Then her savings must be considered. When Tommy reached this last point he always felt sure that

---

[3]A musical extravaganza first performed in 1866. Considered risqué in its day, *The Black Crook* is also known as America's first musical comedy.

she was the most desirable woman in the world for a young minister. He felt hopeful tonight, because he had seen Brother Hamm and his bride in church the Sunday before. Mrs. Davis opened the conversation by speaking of the bride and groom.

"Hamm and his bride looked mighty comfut'ble in church Sunday, didn't they?"

"*He* did. I'm glad he's settled again. It is not good for man to be alone."

"'Deed I'm glad, too."

"*You*—well, well, I'm really glad to hear *you* say it."

"What for?" asked the widow coyly, looking down and playing with her fan.

"I—I didn't know how you and Brother Hamm stood."

"Stood! Well I never."

"I thought Brother Hamm had been trying to get you," whispered Tommy, sitting closer and putting his arm across the back of her chair.

"Law suz, Mr. Jeems, how nervous you does make me. Do take yer arm away, everybody'll be a-lookin' at yer, honey. I'm 'sprised at yer thinkin' I'd look at Hamm an' all them chillun. Massy knows what the 'ooman he's got's gwine to do with 'em." But she looked so mild and smiling that Tommy went into the seventh heaven of delight, and so lost his head that when he heard the call "Another couple wanted here!" he took Mrs. Davis on his arm and stood up on the floor, forgetful of the fact that he was within a few months of his ordination. A good-natured matron not connected with the church had volunteered to supply the lace of an orchestra. Waltzing was soon in full blast, and the demand on the ice-cream cans was filling Ma Smith's heart with joy, tempered with inward stings of conscience and fear of the Steward's Board. Dora was dancing assiduously and eating ice cream at John's expense, he meantime saying that if she kept on she would turn into a frozen dainty, to say nothing of a frost in his pocketbook. Dora declared that it was for the good of the cause, and he'd "just got to stand it." She was wildly happy because of the tender familiarity between her brother and her friend. A long-stemmed rose that Will wore in his button-hole had been transferred to Sappho's corsage. Dora smiled as she caught the half puzzled, half-wondering expression on her mother's face.

It was approaching twelve o'clock when it was proposed to wind up the festivities with the good old "Virginy" reel. Sam Washington was the caller, and did his work with the fancy touch peculiar to a poetic Southern temperament. He was shrewd and good-natured, and a bit of a wag. He knew all the secret sighings of the ladies and their attendant swains. A lively girl whom everyone called "Jinny," remarked to Same, referring to the fact that Sam was on probation: "Your class-leader won't recommend you to the Board for membership after tonight."

"Now, Jinny," replied Sam, stopping his business of arranging couples, "don't make yourself obnoxious bringing up unpleasant subjects. I'll take my medicine like a man when the time comes; but I'd bust, sho, if I didn't get loose tonight. I'm in good company, too," he grinned, nodding toward

Reverend Tommy and Mrs. Davis, who were just taking their places on the floor. "If this is good for Tommy, it is good enough for me."

All reserve was broken down the instant the familiar strains of the Virginia reel were heard. The dance was soon in full swing—an up-and-down, dead-in-earnest seeking for a good time, and a determination to have it was to be got. It was a vehement rhythmic thump, thump, thumpity thump, with a great stamping of the feet and cutting of the pigeon wing. Sam had provided himself with the lively Jinny for a partner, and was cutting grotesque juba figures[4] in the pauses of the music, to the delight of the company. His partner, in wild vivacity, fairly vied with him in his efforts at doing the hoe-down and the heel-and-toe. Not to be outdone, the Rev. Tommy James and Mrs. Davis scored great hits in cutting pigeon wings and in reviving forgotten beauties of the "walk-'round." Tommy "allowed" he hadn't enjoyed himself so much since he came up North.

"Yes," said Sam, "this beats the cake-walk all holler. Now then, one more turn and we're done. Forward on the head; balance yer partner; swing the next gent; swing that lady. Now swing yer rose, yer pretty rose, yer yaller rose of Texas. All promenade."

Everybody declared it had been a wonderful evening. "Thank the Lord it's over," said Ma Smith to Mrs. Sarah Ann White, who was helping her in the kitchen.

"Well," said the latter, pausing in her work with her arms akimbo, "sech sights as I've seen tonight I never would have believed. 'Phelia Davis, what ought ter be a mother in Jerusalem, kickin' up her heels in your parlor like a colt in a corn-field; and that Tommy Jeems, no more fittin' fer a minister than a suckin' babe, a-traipsin' after her like a bald-headed rooster."

1900

Chapter XIV. Luke Sawyer Speaks to the League.

[This chapter contains two key passages from *Contending Forces*, both narrated by Luke Sawyer at a meeting of the American Colored League, a fictional group representing organizatons that have addressed political issues in the African American community. Described as having a "very black" complexion, Sawyer reflects Hopkins's insistence that an African American can possess the intellect and character of "a Cromwell, a Robespierre, a Lincoln," notwithstanding the various "contending forces" with which he must wrestle. The chapter puts a face on the horrible practice of lynching, which reached record numbers during the late nineteenth and early twentieth centuries. These years became known by African Americans as the "Decades of Disapppointment" because for most black citizens, the American dream was completely unattainable. Mob violence, along with other forms of repression, almost succeeded in destroying hope. In Mabelle

---

[4] "Juba" is the name of a joyful dance originating in Africa.

Beaubean's story, Luke reminds readers that America's liberty and equality were not experienced by all citizens: interracial marriage was illegal, and black women were regarded as sexual chattel.]

> My ear is pained,
> My soul is sick with every day's report
> Of wrong and outrage with which the earth is filled.
> There is no flesh in man's obdurate heart;
> It does not feel for man: the natural bond
> Of brotherhood is severed as the flax
> That falls asunder at the touch of fire.
> He finds his fellow guilty of a skin
> *Not colored like his own;* and, having power
> To enforce the wrong *for such a worthy cause,*
> Dooms and devotes him as a lawful prey.
>
> —COWPER

Scarcely had the speaker taken his seat amid suppressed murmurs of discontent, when a tall, gaunt man of very black complexion arose in his seat among the delegates, and in a sonorous bass voice uttered the solemn protest of Patrick Henry, so famous in history: "Gentlemen may cry 'Peace! peace!' but there is no peace!"

In an instant confusion reigned. Women fluttered their handkerchiefs, and above waves of applause and cheers could be heard cries of "Hear, hear!" "Platform! platform!" The chairman rapped for order, and when he could make himself heard, asked the delegate to come to the platform; another speaker was waiting, but the audience would be glad to hear anything he might have to say. As he passed up the aisle and mounted the steps of the rostrum, the people saw a man of majestic frame, rugged physique and immense muscular development. His face was kindly, but withal bore the marks of superior intelligence, shrewdness and great strength of character. He might have been a Cromwell, a Robespierre, a Lincoln. Men of his physiological development—when white—mould humanity, and leave their own characteristics engraved upon the pages of the history of their times.

"Friends," said he, when he stood before them, "I come from Williamstown, in the western part of this state, to be a delegate at this meeting. Here are my credentials to show that I am in good standing in the League where I belong. (He handed his papers to the chairman.) I want to impress that fact upon the minds of this assembly, because I am going to tell you some awful facts before I get through." He paused, and with his handkerchief wiped the tears and perspiration from his face. "Friends, I am thirty years old and look fifty. I want to tell you why this is so. I want to tell you what brought me *here.* I want to tell the gentlemen who have spoken here tonight that conservatism, lack of brotherly affiliation, lack of energy for the right and the power of the almighty dollar which deadens men's hearts to the sufferings of their brothers, and makes them feel that if only *they* can rise to the top of the ladder may God help the hindmost man, are the forces which are ruining the Negro in this country. It is killing him off by thousands, destroying his self-respect, and degrading him to the level of the brute. *These are the contending forces that are dooming this race to despair!*

"My name is Lycurgus Sawyer; Luke they call me for short. When I was about ten years old my father kept a large store in a little town in the state of Louisany. I had two brothers and a sister. My mother was a fine woman, somewhat better educated than my father. Through her influence he went into this business of trading, and soon had the largest business and as much money as any man in the county. Father didn't care to meddle with politics, for, with the natural shrewdness of many of us, he saw that that might be made an excuse for his destruction. When I was about ten years old, then, a white man in the village, seeing the headway my father was making in accumulating property, opened a store on the same street. Father said nothing, but his customers still continued to trade with him, and it seemed that the other man would be compelled to give up. About this time father received threatening letters ordering him to move, and saying that in case he did not do as ordered he would lose his life. Mother was frightened, and advised father to get out of the place, but he, anxious to save some part of his hard earnings, waited to sell his stock and houses before seeking a home elsewhere. One night a posse of men came to our house and began smoking us out. You don't know anything about that up here, do you? Well, you'll get there if things keep on as they're going. My father had arms. He raised the window of his sleeping-room and fired into the mob of cowardly hounds. Thoroughly enraged, they broke open the doors back and front, seized my father and hung him to the nearest tree, whipped my mother and sister, and otherwise abused them so that they died the next day. My brothers were twins, still so small that there were but babes. The mob took them by the heels and dashed their brains out against the walls of the house! Then they burned the house. I saw all this, and frenzied with horror, half-dead with fright, crept into the woods to die. I was found there by a colored planter named Beaubean, who lived in the next township. He pitied me and took me home. *That*, gentlemen, was my *first* experience of lynching. Do you think it is possible to preach 'peace' to a man like me?"

The house was filled with the cries and groans of the audience. Sobs shook the women, while the men drank in the words of the speaker with darkening brows and hands which involuntarily clinched themselves in sympathy with his words.

"But that is not the only story I can tell. Here's another. I will tell it to you, and you can digest it at your leisure.

"Monsieur Beaubean was an educated man, descended from a very wealthy family. His father had been his owner. When the father died he left to his son, born of a black mother, an equal share of the estate along with his legitimate heirs. They made no objections, so he got it.

"Monsieur Beaubean had married a quadroon woman of great beauty— Louisany abounds in handsome women of color; they had two children, a boy and a girl. She was three years old when I went to live with them. I remained in the family twelve years. I learned many things there; along with the trade of blacksmithing I learned to esteem myself as a man.

"I cannot describe to you the beauty and loveliness of that child. As a boy I worshipped her, and as a man I loved her; not with the hope of ever having a return of the feeling she had aroused in me, but as a faithful dog that would lay down his life for those who shelter and care for him, so I felt to Beaubean's family, and especially that child. When Mabelle, as we called her, was old enough, she was sent to the Colored Sisters' School in the city of New Orleans. It was my pleasant duty to drive her into the city each day and go for her at night.

"Monsieur Beaubean had a half-brother—a white man—who was very wealthy and stood very high in politics. In fact, he was in the State Senate. He was very warm in his expressions of friendship for the family, and especially so in his assumption of relationship. I noticed that he seemed extremely fond of Mabelle. One day, after she had passed her fourteenth birthday, she had a holiday from school, and went with some schoolfel-lows to visit a companion who lived in the city. They returned at night without her, saying that she went into a store with Monsieur Beaubean's brother, and they had not seen her since.

"Can you imagine what a night was passed by that family? No, you cannot, unless you have been through the same experience. The father went in one direction and I in another. All night long we searched the city streets; nothing could be heard of her. Finally we went to police headquarters and secured the services of a detective. After *three weeks* of incessant searching we found her a prisoner in a house of the vilest character in the lowest portion of the city of New Orleans—a poor, ruined, half-crazed creature in whom it was almost impossible to trace a resemblance to the beautiful pet of our household. These arms bore her forth from that vile den and restored her to a broken-hearted parent. I think that I must have gone mad. If I had had the man there that committed the crime (he raised one gaunt arm above his head, and standing in that attitude seemed the embodiment of vengeance) I would have taken him by the throat and shaken him (he hissed the words through clinched teeth), shaken him as a dog would a rat until he was *dead!* DEAD! DEAD! We took her home, but I believe that her father was a madman from the time he placed his eyes upon her until he was murdered. And who do you think had done this foul crime? Why, the father's *half-brother, uncle* of the victim!

"Crazed with grief, Monsieur Beaubean faced his brother and accused him of this crime. 'Well,' said he, 'whatever damage I have done I am willing to pay for. But your child is no better than her mother or her grandmother. What does a woman of mixed blood, or any Negress, for that matter, know of virtue? It is my belief that they were a direct creation by God to be the pleasant companions of men of my race. Now, I am willing to give you a thousand dollars and call it square.' He handed Monsieur Beaubean a roll of bills as he spoke. Beaubean seized them and hurled them into the villain's face with these words: 'I leave you to carry my case into the Federal courts and appeal for justice.' Unhappy man! That night his house was mobbed. The crowd surrounded the building after firing it, and as an inmate would show his head at a window in the struggle to escape from the burning building, someone would pick him off. So it went all night. I seized Mabelle and wrapped her in a blanket. Watching my chance I stole her from the house after the fire was well under way, and miraculously reached a place of safety. I took Mabelle to the colored convent at New Orleans, and left her there in the care of the sisters. *There she died when her child was born!*"

As the speaker stood silently contemplating his weeping, grief-convulsed audience, a woman was borne from the auditorium in a fainting condition. John Langley from his seat on the platform leaned over and asked an usher who the lady was. "Miss Sappho Clark," was his reply.

Amid universal silence, the silence which comes from feeling too deep for outward expression, the speaker concluded: "A tax too heavy placed on tea and things like that, made the American Colonies go to war with Great Britain to get their liberty. I ask you what you think the American Colonies would have done if they had suffered as we have suffered and are still suffering?

"Mr. Chairman, gentlemen call for peace, and I reply: 'Peace if possible; justice at any rate.' Where is there peace for men like me? When the grave has closed over me and my memories, I shall have peace.

"Under such conditions as I have described, contentment, amity—call it by what name you will—is impossible; justice alone remains to us."

Talma Gordon[1]

The Canterbury Club of Boston was holding its regular monthly meeting at the palatial Beacon-street residence of Dr. William Thornton, expert medical practitioner and specialist.[2] All the members were present, because some rare opinions were to be aired by men of profound thought on a question of vital importance to the life of the Republic, and because the club celebrated its anniversary in a home usually closed to society. The Doctor's winters, since his marriage, were passed at his summer home near his celebrated sanatorium. This winter found him in town with his wife and two boys. We had heard much of the beauty of the former, who was entirely unknown to social life, and about whose life and marriage we felt sure a romantic interest attached. The Doctor himself was too bright a luminary of the professional world to remain long hidden without creating comment. We had accepted the invitation to dine with alacrity, knowing that we should be welcomed to a banquet that would feast both eye and palate; but we had not been favored by even a glimpse of the hostess. The subject for discussion was: "Expansion; Its Effect upon the Future Development of the Anglo-Saxon throughout the World."

Dinner was over, but we still sat about the social board discussing the question of the hour. The Hon. Herbert Clapp, eminent jurist and politician,

[1] *Colored American Magazine* 1 (Oct. 1900): 271–90.
[2] The Canterbury Club was an Episcopalian social club. Beacon Street was, and remains, a wealthy and historic area of Boston.

had painted in glowing colors the advantages to be gained by the increase of wealth and the exalted position which expansion would give the United States in the councils of the great governments of the world. In smoothly flowing sentences marshalled in rhetorical order, with compact ideas, and incisive argument, he drew an effective picture with all the persuasive eloquence of the trained orator.

Joseph Whitman, the theologian of world-wide fame, accepted the arguments of Mr. Clapp, but subordinated all to the great opportunity which expansion would give to the religious enthusiast. None could doubt the sincerity of this man, who looked once into the idealized face on which heaven had set the seal of consecration.

Various opinions were advanced by the twenty-five men present, but the host said nothing; he glanced from one to another with a look of amusement in his shrewd gray-blue eyes. "Wonderful eyes," said his patients who came under their magic spell. "A wonderful man and a wonderful mind," agreed his contemporaries, as they heard in amazement of some great cure of chronic or malignant disease which approached the supernatural.

"What do you think of this question, Doctor?" finally asked the president, turning to the silent host.

"Your arguments are good; they would convince almost anyone."

"But not Doctor Thornton," laughed the theologian.

"I acquiesce which ever way the result turns. Still, I like to view both sides of a question. We have considered but one tonight. Did you ever think that in spite of our prejudices against amalgamation, some of our descendants, indeed many of them, will inevitably intermarry among those far-off tribes of dark-skinned peoples, if they become a part of this great Union?"

"Among the lower classes that may occur, but not to any great extent," remarked a college president.

"My experience teaches me that it will occur among all classes, and to an appalling extent," replied the Doctor.

"You don't believe in intermarriage with other races?"

"Yes, most emphatically, when they possess decent moral development and physical perfection, for then we develop a superior being in the progeny born of the intermarriage. But if we are not ready to receive and assimilate the new material which will be brought to mingle with our pure Anglo-Saxon stream, we should call a halt in our expansion policy."

"I must confess, Doctor, that in the idea of amalgamation you present a new thought to my mind. Will you not favor us with a few of your main points?" asked the president of the club, breaking the silence which followed the Doctor's remarks.

"Yes, Doctor, give us your theories on the subject. We may not agree with you, but we are all open to conviction."

The Doctor removed the half-consumed cigar from his lips, drank what remained in his glass of the choice Burgundy, and leaning back in his chair contemplated the earnest faces before him.

We may make laws, but laws are but straws in the hands of Omnipotence.

"There's a divinity that shapes our ends,
Rough-hew them how we will."[3]

And no man may combat fate. Given a man, propinquity, opportunity, fascinating femininity, and there you are. Black, white, green, yellow—nothing will prevent intermarriage. Position, wealth, family, friends—all sink into insignificance before the God-implanted instinct that made Adam, awakening from a deep sleep and finding the woman beside him, accept Eve as bone of his bone; he cared not nor questioned whence she came. So it is with the sons of Adam ever since, through the law of heredity which makes us all one common family. And so it will be with us in our reformation of this old Republic. Perhaps I can make my meaning clearer by illustration, and with your permission I will tell you a story which came under my observation as a practitioner.

Doubtless all of you heard of the terrible tragedy which occurred at Gordonville, Mass., some years ago, when Capt. Jonathan Gordon, his wife and little son were murdered. I suppose that I am the only man on this side the Atlantic, outside of the police, who can tell you the true story of that crime.

I knew Captain Gordon well; it was through his persuasions that I bought a place in Gordonville and settled down to spending my summers in that charming rural neighborhood. I had rendered the Captain what he was pleased to call valuable medical help, and I became his family physician. Captain Gordon was a retired sea captain, formerly engaged in the East India trade. All his ancestors had been such; but when the bottom fell out of that business he established the Gordonville Mills with his first wife's money, and settled down as a money-making manufacturer of cotton cloth. The Gordons were old New England Puritans who had come over in the "Mayflower"; they had owned Gordon Hall for more than a hundred years. It was a baronial-like pile of granite with towers, standing on a hill which commanded a superb view of Massachusetts Bay and the surrounding country. I imagine the Gordon star was under a cloud about the time Captain Jonathan married his first wife, Miss Isabel Franklin of Boston, who brought to him the money which mended the broken fortunes of the Gordon house, and restored this old Puritan stock to its rightful position. In the person of Captain Gordon the austerity of manner and indomitable will-power that he had inherited were combined with a temper that brooked no contradiction.

The first wife died at the birth of her third child, leaving him two daughters, Jeannette and Talma. Very soon after her death the Captain married again. I have heard it rumored that the Gordon girls did not get on very well with their stepmother. She was a woman with no fortune of her own, and envied the large portion left by the first Mrs. Gordon to her daughters.

Jeannette was tall, dark, and stern like her father; Talma was like her dead mother, and possessed of great talent, so great that her father sent her

---

[3]William Shakespeare, *Hamlet*, 5.2, ll. 10–11.

to the American Academy at Rome, to develop the gift. It was the hottest of July days when her friends were bidden to an afternoon party on the lawn and a dance in the evening, to welcome Talma Gordon among them again. I watched her as she moved about among her guests, a fairylike blonde in floating white draperies, her face a study in delicate changing tints, like the heart of a flower, sparkling in smiles about the mouth to end in merry laughter in the clear blue eyes. There were all the subtle allurements of birth, wealth and culture about the exquisite creature:

> "Smiling, frowning evermore,
> Thou art perfect in love-lore,
> Ever varying Madeline,"[4]

quoted a celebrated writer as he stood apart with me, gazing upon the scene before us. He sighed as he looked at the girl.

"Doctor, there is genius and passion in her face. Sometime our little friend will do wonderful things. But is it desirable to be singled out for special blessings by the gods? Genius always carries with it intense capacity for suffering: 'Whom the gods love die young.'"

"Ah," I replied, "do not name death and Talma Gordon together. Cease your dismal croakings; such talk is rank heresy."

The dazzling daylight dropped slowly into summer twilight. The merriment continued; more guests arrived; the great dancing pagoda built for the occasion was lighted by myriads of Japanese lanterns. The strains from the band grew sweeter and sweeter, and "all went merry as a marriage bell." It was a rare treat to have this party at Gordon Hall, for Captain Jonathan was not given to hospitality. We broke up shortly before midnight, with expressions of delight from all the guests.

I was a bachelor then, without ties. Captain Gordon insisted upon my havng a bed at the Hall. I did not fall asleep readily; there seemed to be something in the air that forbade it. I was still awake when a distant clock struck the second hour of the morning. Suddenly the heavens were lighted by a sheet of ghastly light; a terrific midsummer thunderstorm was breaking over the sleeping town. A lurid flash lit up all the landscape, painting the trees in grotesque shapes against the murky sky, and defining clearly the sullen blackness of the waters of the bay breaking in grandeur against the rocky coast. I had arisen and put back the draperies from the windows, to have an unobstructed view of the grand scene. A low muttering coming nearer and nearer, a terrific roar, and then a tremendous downpour. The storm had burst.

Now the uncanny howling of a dog mingled with the rattling volleys of thunder. I heard the opening and closing of doors; the servants were about looking after things. It was impossible to sleep. The lightning was more vivid. There was a blinding flash of a greenish-white tinge mingled with the crash of falling timbers. Then before my startled gaze arose columns of red

---

[4]Alfred Lord Tennyson, "Madeline," ll. 8–10.

flames reflected against the sky. "Heaven help us!" I cried; "it is the left tower; it has been struck and is on fire!"

I hurried on my clothes and stepped into the corridor; the girls were there before me. Jeannette came up to me instantly with anxious face. "Oh, Doctor Thornton, what shall we do? Papa and mamma and little Johnny are in the old left tower. It is on fire. I have knocked and knocked, but get no answer."

"Don't be alarmed," said I soothingly. "Jenkins, ring the alarm bell," I continued, turning to the butler who was standing near; "the rest follow me. We will force the entrance to the Captain's room."

Instantly, it seemed to me, the bell boomed out upon the now silent air, for the storm had died down as quickly as it arose; and as our little procession paused before the entrance to the old left tower, we could distinguish the sound of the fire engines already on their way from the village.

The door resisted all our efforts; there seemed to be a barrier against it which nothing could move. The flames were gaining headway. Still the same deadly silence within the rooms.

"Oh, will they never get here?" cried Talma, ringing her hands in terror. Jeannette said nothing, but her face was ashen. The servants were huddled together in a panic-stricken group. I can never tell you what a relief it was when we heard the first sound of the firemen's voices, saw their quick movements, and heard the ringing of the axes with which they cut away every obstacle to our entrance to the rooms. The neighbors who had just enjoyed the hospitality of the house were now gathered around offering all the assistance in their power. In less than fifteen minutes the fire was out, and the men began to bear the unconscious inmates from the ruins. They carried them to the pagoda so lately the scene of mirth and pleasure, and I took up my station there, ready to assume my professional duties. The Captain was nearest me; and as I stooped to make the necessary examination I reeled away from the ghastly sight which confronted me—*gentlemen, across the Captain's throat was a deep gash that severed the jugular vein!*

The Doctor paused, and the hand with which he refilled his glass trembled violently.

"What is it, Doctor?" cried the men, gathering about me.

"Take the women away; this is murder!"

"Murder!" cried Jeannette, as she fell against the side of the pagoda.

"Murder!" screamed Talma, staring at me as if unable to grasp my meaning.

I continued my examination of the bodies, and found that the same thing had happened to Mrs. Gordon and to little Johnny.

The police were notified; and when the sun rose over the dripping town he found them in charge of Gordan Hall, the servants standing in excited knots talking over the crime, the friends of the family confounded, and the two girls trying to comfort each other and realize the terrible misfortune that had overtaken them.

Nothing in the rooms of the left tower seemed to have been disturbed. The door of communication between the rooms of the husband and wife was open, as they had arranged it for the night. Little Johnny's crib was placed beside his mother's bed. In it he was found as though never awakened by the storm. It was quite evident that the assassin was no common ruffian. The chief gave strict orders for a watch to be kept on all strangers or suspicious characters who were seen in the neighborhood. He made inquiries among the servants, seeing each one separately, but there was nothing gained from them. No one had heard anything suspicious; all had been awakened by the storm. The chief was puzzled. Here was a triple crime for which no motive could be assigned.

"What do you think of it?" I asked him, as we stood together on the lawn.

"It is my opinion that the deed was committed by one of the higher classes, which makes the mystery more difficult to solve. I tell you, Doctor, there are mysteries that never come to light, and this, I think, is one of them."

While we were talking Jenkins, the butler, an old and trusted servant, came up to the chief and saluted respectfully. "Want to speak with me, Jenkins?" he asked. The man nodded, and they walked away together.

The story of the inquest was short, but appalling. It was shown that Talma had been allowed to go abroad to study because she and Mrs. Gordon did not get on well together. From the testimony of Jenkins it seemed that Talma and her father had quarrelled bitterly about her lover, a young artist whom she had met at Rome, who was unknown to fame, and very poor. There had been terrible things said by each, and threats even had passed, all of which now rose up in judgment against the unhappy girl. The examination of the family solicitor revealed the fact that Captain Gordon intended to leave his daughers only a small annuity, the bulk of the fortune going to his son Jonathan, junior. This was a monstrous injustice, as everyone felt. In vain Talma protested her innocence. Someone must have done it. No one would be benefited so much by these deaths as she and her sister. Moreover, the will, together with other papers, was nowhere to be found. Not the slightest clue bearing upon the disturbing elements in this family, if any there were, was to be found. As the only surviving relatives, Jeannette and Talma became joint heirs to an immense fortune, which only for the bloody tragedy just enacted would, in all probability, have passed them by. Here was the motive. The case was very black against Talma. The foreman stood up. The silence was intense: We "find that Capt. Jonathan Gordon, Mary E. Gordon and Jonathan Gordon, junior, all deceased, came to their deaths by means of a knife or other sharp instrument in the hands of Talma Gordon." The girl was like one stricken with death. The flower-like mouth was drawn and pinched; the great sapphire-blue eyes were black with passionate anguish, terror and despair. She was placed in jail to await her trial at the fall session of the criminal court. The excitement in the hitherto quiet town rose to fever heat. Many points in the evidence seemed incomplete to thinking men. The weapon could not be found, nor could it be divined what had become of it. No reason could be given for the murder except the quarrel between Talma and her father and the ill will which existed between the girl and her stepmother.

When the trial was called Jeannette sat beside Talma in the prisoner's dock; both were arrayed in deepest mourning. Talma was pale and careworn, but seemed uplifted, spiritualized, as it were. Upon Jeannette the full realization of her sister's peril seemed to weigh heavily. She had changed much too: hollow cheeks, tottering steps, eyes blazing with fever, all suggestive of rapid and premature decay. From far-off Italy Edward Turner, growing famous in the art world, came to stand beside his girl-love in this hour of anguish.

The trial was a memorable one. No additional evidence had been collected to strengthen the prosecution; when the attorney-general rose to open the case against Talma he knew, as everyone else did, that he could not convict solely on the evidence adduced. What was given did not always bear upon the case, and brought out strange stories of Captain Jonathan's methods. Tales were told of sailors who had sworn to take his life, in revenge for injuries inflicted upon them by his hand. One or two clues were followed, but without avail. The judge summed up the evidence impartially, giving the prisoner the benefit of the doubt. The points in hand furnished valuable collateral evidence, but were not direct proof. Although the moral presumption was against the prisoner, legal evidence was lacking to actually convict. The jury found the prisoner "Not Guilty," owing to the fact that the evidence was entirely circumstantial. The verdict was received in painful silence; then a murmur of discontent ran through the great crowd.

"She must have done it," said one; "who else has been benefited by the horrible deed?"

"A poor woman would not have fared so well at the hands of the jury, nor a homely one either, for that matter," said another.

The great Gordon trial was ended; innocent or guilty, Talma Gordon could not be tried again. She was free; but her liberty, with blasted prospects and fair fame gone forever, was valueless to her. She seemed to have but one object in her mind: to find the murderer or murderers of her parents and half-brother. By her direction the shrewdest of detectives were employed and money flowed like water, but to no purpose; the Gordon tragedy remained a mystery. I had consented to act as one of the trustees of the immense Gordon estates and business interests, and by my advice the Misses Gordon went abroad. A year later I received a letter from Edward Turner, saying that Jeannette Gordon had died suddenly at Rome, and that Talma, after refusing all his entreaties for an early marriage, had disappeared, leaving no clue as to her whereabouts. I could give the poor fellow no comfort, although I had been duly notified of the death of Jeannette by Talma, in a letter telling me where to forward her remittances, and at the same time requesting me to keep her present residence secret, especially from Edward.

I had established a sanitarium for the cure of chronic diseases at Gordonville, and absorbed in the cares of my profession I gave little thought to the Gordons. I seemed fated to be involved in mysteries.

A man claiming to be an Englishman, and fresh from the California gold fields, engaged board and professional service at my retreat. I found him suffering in the grasp of the tubercle-fiend—the last stages. He called himself Simon Cameron. Seldom have I seen so fascinating and wicked a face. The lines of the mouth were cruel, the eyes cold and sharp, the smile mocking and evil. He had money in plenty but seemed to have no friends, for he had received no letters and had had no visitors in the time he had been with us. He was an enigma to me; and his nationality puzzled me, for of course I did not believe his story of being English. The peaceful influence of the house seemed to soothe him in a measure, and make his last steps to the mysterious valley as easy as possible. For a time he improved, and would sit or walk about the grounds and sing sweet songs for the pleasure of the other inmates. Strange to say, his malady only affected his voice at times. He sang quaint songs in a silvery tenor of great purity and sweetness that was delicious to the listening ear:

> "A wet sheet and a flowing sea,
> A wind that follows fast,
> And fills the white and rustling sail
> And bends the gallant mast;
> And bends the gallant mast, my boys;
> While like the eagle free,
> Away the good ship flies, and leaves
> Old England on the lea."

There are few singers on the lyric stage who could surpass Simon Cameron.

One night, a few weeks after Cameron's arrival, I sat in my office making up my accounts when the door opened and closed; I glanced up, expecting to see a servant. A lady advanced toward me. She threw back her veil, and then I saw that Talma Gordon, or her ghost, stood before me. After the first excitement of our meeting was over, she told me she had come direct from Paris, to place herself in my care. I had studied her attentively during the first moments of our meeting, and I felt that she was right; unless something unforeseen happened to arouse her from the stupor into which she seemed to have fallen, the last Gordon was doomed to an early death. The next day I told her I had cabled Edward Turner to come to her.

"It will do no good; I cannot marry him," was her only comment.

"Have you no feeling of pity for that faithful fellow?" I asked her sternly, provoked by her seeming indifference. I shall never forget the varied emotions depicted on her speaking face. Fully revealed to my gaze was the sight of a human soul tortured beyond the point of endurance; suffering all things, enduring all things, in the silent agony of despair.

In a few days Edward arrived, and Talma consented to see him and explain her refusal to keep her promise to him. "You must be present, Doctor; it is due your long, tried friendship to know that I have not been fickle, but have acted from the best and strongest motives."

I shall never forget that day. It was directly after lunch that we met in the library. I was greatly excited, expecting I knew not what. Edward was agitated, too. Talma was the only calm one. She handed me what seemed to be a letter, with the request that I would read it. Even now I think I can repeat every word of the document, so indelibly are the words engraved upon my mind:

My Darling Sister Talma:

When you read these lines I shall be no more, for I shall not live to see your life blasted by the same knowledge that has blighted mine.

One evening, about a year before your expected return from Rome, I climbed into a hammock in one corner of the veranda outside the breakfast-room windows, intending to spend the twilight hours in lazy comfort, for it was very hot, enervating August weather. I fell asleep. I was awakened by voices. Because of the heat the rooms had been left in semi-darkness. As I lay there, lazily enjoying the beauty of the perfect summer night, my wandering thoughts were arrested by words spoken by our father to Mrs. Gordon, for they were the occupants of the breakfast-room.

"Never fear, Mary; Johnny shall have it all—money, houses, land and business."

"But if you do go first, Jonathan, what will happen if the girls contest the will? People will think that they ought to have the money as it appears to be theirs by law. I never could survive the terrible disgrace of the story."

"Don't borrow trouble; all you would need to do would be to show them papers I have drawn up, and they would be glad to take their annuity and say nothing. After all, I do not think it is so bad. Jeannette can teach; Talma can paint; six hundred dollars a year is quite enough for them."

I had been somewhat mystified by the conversation until now. This last remark solved the riddle. What could he mean? teach, paint, six hundred a year! With my usual impetuosity I sprang from my resting-place, and in a moment stood in the room confronting my father, and asking what he meant. I could see plainly that both were disconcerted by my unexpected appearance.

"Ah, wretched girl! you have been listening. But what could I expect of your mother's daughter?"

At these words I felt the indignant blood rush to my head in a torrent. So it had been all my life. Before you could remember, Talma, I had felt my little heart swell with anger at the disparaging hints and slurs concerning our mother. Now was my time. I determined that tonight I would know why she was looked upon as an outcast, and her children subjected to every humiliation. So I replied to my father in bitter anger:

"I was not listening; I fell asleep in the hammock. What do you mean by a paltry six hundred a year each to Talma and to me? 'My mother's daughter' demands an explanation from you, sir, of the meaning of the monstrous injustice that you have always practised toward my sister and me."

"Speak more respectfully to your father, Jeannette," broke in Mrs. Gordon.

"How is it, madam, that you look for respect from one whom you have delighted to torment ever since you came into this most unhappy family?"

"Hush, both of you," said Captain Gordon, who seemed to have recovered from the dismay into which my sudden appearance and passionate words had plunged him. "I think I may as well tell you as to wait. Since you know so much, you may as well know the whole miserable story." He motioned me to a seat. I could see that he was deeply agitated. I seated myself in a chair he pointed out, in wonder and expectation,—expectation of I knew not what. I trembled. This was a supreme moment in my life; I felt it. The air was heavy with the intense stillness that had settled over us as the common sounds of day gave place to the early quiet of the rural evening. I could see Mrs. Gordon's face as she sat within the radius of the lighted hallway. There was a smile of triumph upon it. I clinched my hands and bit my lips until the blood came, in the effort to keep from screaming. What was I about to hear? At last he spoke:

"I was disappointed at your birth, and also at the birth of Talma. I wanted a male heir. When I knew that I should again be a father I was torn by hope and fear, but I comforted myself with the thought that luck would be with me in the birth of the third child. When the doctor brought me word that a son was born to the house of Gordon, I was wild with delight, and did not notice his disturbed countenance. In the midst of my joy he said to me:

"Captain Gordon, there is something strange about this birth. I want you to see this child."

Quelling my exultation I followed him to the nursery, and there, lying in the cradle, I saw a child dark as a mulatto, with the characteristic features of the Negro! I was stunned. Gradually it dawned upon me that there was something radically wrong. I turned to the doctor for an explanation.

"There is but one explanation, Captain Gordon; there is Negro blood in this child."

"There is no Negro blood in my veins," I said proudly. Then I paused—the mother!—I glanced at the doctor. He was watching me intently. The same thought was in his mind. I must have lived a thousand years in that cursed five seconds that I stood there confronting the physician and trying to think. "Come," said I to him, "let us end this suspense." Without thinking of consequences, I hurried away to your mother and accused her of infidelity to her marriage vows. I raved like a madman. Your mother fell into convulsions; her life was despaired of. I sent for Mr. and Mrs. Franklin, and then I learned the truth. They were childless. One year while on a Southern tour, they befriended an octoroon girl who had been abandoned by her white lover. Her child was a beautiful girl baby. They, being Northern born, thought little of caste distinction because the child showed no trace of Negro blood. They determined to adopt it. They went abroad, secretly sending back word to their friends at a proper time, of the birth of a little daughter. No one doubted the truth of the statement. They made Isabel their heiress, and all went well until the birth of your brother. Your mother and the unfortunate babe died. This is the story which, if known, would bring dire disgrace upon the Gordon family.

> *To appease my righteous wrath, Mr. Franklin left a codicil to his will by which all the property is left at my disposal save a small annuity to you and your sister."*
>
> *I sat there after he had finished his story, stunned by what I had heard. I understood, now, Mrs. Gordon's half contemptuous toleration and lack of consideration for us both. As I rose from my seat to leave the room I said to Captain Gordon:*
>
> *"Still, in spite of all, sir, I am a Gordon, legally born. I will not tamely give up my birthright."*
>
> *I left that room a broken-hearted girl, filled with a desire for revenge upon this man, my father, who by his manner disowned us without a regret. Not once in that remarkable interview did he speak of our mother as his wife; he quietly repudiated her and us with all the cold cruelty of relentless caste prejudice. I heard the treatment of your lover's proposal: I knew why Captain Gordon's consent to your marriage was withheld.*
>
> *The night of the reception and dance was the chance for which I had waited, planned and watched. I crept from my window into the ivy-vines, and so down, down, until I stood upon the window-sill of Captain Gordon's room in the old left tower. How did I do it, you ask? I do not know. The house was silent after the revel; the darkness of the gathering storm favored me, too. The lawyer was there that day. The will was signed and put safely away among my father's papers. I was determined to have the will and the other documents bearing upon the case, and I would have revenge, too, for the cruelties we had suffered. With the old East Indian dagger firmly grasped I entered the room and found—that my revenge had been forestalled! The horror of the discovery I made that night restored me to reason and a realization of the crime I meditated. Scarce knowing what I did, I sought and found the papers, and crept back to my room as I had come. Do you wonder that my disease is past medical aid?*

I looked at Edward as I finished. He sat, his face covered with his hands. Finally he looked up with a glance of haggard despair: "God! Doctor, but this is too much. I could stand the stigma of murder, but add to that the pollution of Negro blood! No man is brave enough to face such a situation."

"It is as I thought it would be," said Talma sadly, while the tears poured over her white face. "I do not blame you, Edward."

He rose from his chair, wrung my hand in a convulsive clasp, turned to Talma and bowed profoundly, with his eyes fixed upon the floor, hesitated, turned, paused, bowed again and abruptly left the room. So those two who had been lovers, parted. I turned to Talma, expecting her to give way. She smiled a pitiful smile, and said: "You see, Doctor, I knew best."

From that on she failed rapidly. I was restless. If only I could rouse her to an interest in life, she might live to old age. So rich, so young, so beautiful, so talented, so pure; I grew savage thinking of the injustice of the world. I had not reckoned on the power that never sleeps. Something was about to happen.

On visiting Cameron next morning I found him approaching the end. He had been sinking for a week very rapidly. As I sat by the bedside holding his emaciated hand, he fixed his bright, wicked eyes on me, and asked: "How long have I got to live?"

"Candidly, but a few hours."

"Thank you; well, I want death; I am not afraid to die. Doctor, Cameron is not my name."

"I never supposed it was."

"No? You are sharper than I thought. I heard all your talk yesterday with Talma Gordon. Curse the whole race!"

He clasped his bony fingers around my arm and gasped: "*I murdered the Gordons!*"

Had I the pen of a Dumas I could not paint Cameron as he told his story. It is a question with me whether this wheeling planet, home of the suffering, doubting, dying, may not hold worse agonies on its smiling surface than those of the conventional hell. I sent for Talma and a lawyer. We gave him stimulants, and then with broken intervals of coughing and prostration we got the story of the Gordon murder. I give it to you in a few words:

"I am an East Indian, but my name does not matter, Cameron is as good as any. There is many a soul crying in heaven and hell for vengeance on Jonathan Gordon. Gold was his idol; and many a good man walked the plank, and many a gallant ship was stripped of her treasure, to satisfy his lust for gold. His blackest crime was the murder of my father, who was his friend, and had sailed with him for many a year as mate. One night these two went ashore together to bury their treasure. My father never returned from that expedition. His body was afterward found with a bullet through the heart on the shore where the vessel stopped that night. It was the custom then among pirates for the captain to kill the men who helped bury their treasure. Captain Gordon was no better than a pirate. An East Indian never forgets, and I swore by my mother's deathbed to hunt Captain Gordon down until I had avenged my father's murder. I had the plans of the Gordon estate, and fixed on the night of the reception in honor of Talma as the time for my vengeance. There is a secret entrance from the shore to the chambers where Captain Gordon slept; no one knew of it save the Captain and trusted members of his crew. My mother gave me the plans, and entrance and escape were easy."

"So the great mystery was solved. In a few hours Cameron was no more. We placed the confession in the hands of the police, and there the matter ended."

"But what became of Talma Gordon?" questioned the president. "Did she die?"

"Gentlemen," said the doctor, rising to his feet and sweeping the faces of the company with his eagle gaze, "gentlemen, if you will follow me to the drawing-room, I shall have much pleasure in introducing you to my wife— *nee* Talma Gordon."

1900

JAMES WHITCOMB RILEY
1849–1916

James Whitcomb Riley was born in Greenfield, Indiana, in 1849. Riley's family initially prospered on this frontier, and idealized memories of an idyllic childhood in rural Indiana would shape many of his most popular poems. However, his family's fortunes declined after the Civil War, and he took to the road, earning money as a sign painter and patent medicine salesman. He began writing poems in the 1870s in association with his advertising work and became known locally as the "Painter Poet" (during this time he also took on heavy debts and developed a drinking problem; he struggled with both for much of his life). His poems of the 1870s and 1880s appeared in local newspapers and addressed an Indiana audience, but as he became a more confident writer, he sought national attention. A supportive letter from Longfellow in 1876 encouraged Riley to submit poems to the country's most influential magazines, although it would take another decade for him to succeed outside the state.

By the end of the 1870s, Riley had achieved local renown as a poet. He modeled himself on humorists like Samuel Clemens ("Mark Twain") and Henry Wheeler Shaw ("Josh Billings"), whose performances combined lecture, recitation, and stand-up comedy in the regionally specific voice of a small-town philosopher or wag. Riley wrote therefore with public performance in mind: he was as much actor as author, and the performative nature of his work led him to publish under carefully crafted fictional personae, such as "Benjamin F. Johnson of Boone," whose volume *The Old Swimmin'-Hole and 'Leven Other Poems* (1883) was Riley's first book and his first nationwide success.

With that success, Riley was in even greater demand as a performer, across the Midwest and eventually the East Coast. His lecture tours were profitable but exhausting and stressful, and his partnerships often ended acrimoniously. He first performed in the Northeast in 1882, but his breakthrough came at a publicity event for the International Copyright League in 1887 in New York City. His hugely successful reading there—in the homespun voice of an Indiana Hoosier—earned him national renown. For the next thirty years he was the most popular poet in America, while his books, which were usually published around Christmas (and became little more than compilations of older material) sold hundreds of thousands of copies.

But what did readers find in his work? In the nineteenth-century geographic imagination, Indiana was "the West" and "Hoosier" Indiana was a distinctive regional identity. Novels like Edward Eggleston's *The Hoosier Schoolmaster* (1871) had portrayed Indiana as a barbarous region with only the barest sheen of civilization. Riley sought to counter such negative portrayals of the state with humorous portraits of Hoosier characters, often cast in a tone of sentimental nostalgia.

"The Old Swimmin' Hole" is a characteristic example of Riley's power to evoke a rural childhood realm now lost amid the modern world. The scene of barefoot summers beside "a baby-river that was laying half asleep" gives way at the poem's end to a view of "the bridge of the railroad," which now "crosses the spot/Whare the old divin'-log lays sunk and fergot." However, Riley's poetry often juxtaposes this lost setting with situations relevant to the 1880s and 1890s. His glancing references to contemporary events always blend hard facts with humor: the allusion to mob violence at the end of "Down on Wriggle Crick" is passed off with the wry claim that "Circumstances alters cases/Down on Wriggle Crick!" while the light-hearted tone of "A Hobo Voluntary" eases but does not erase the grim circumstances of vagrancy.

Although he wrote many poems in Standard English, Riley was known best for poems in Hoosier dialect. His work fits into the explosion of regionalist writing popular after the American Civil War, and his literary persona resembles that of dialect poets like Will Carleton or Paul Laurence Dunbar, patterned on the model of Robert Burns ("To Robert Burns" expresses Riley's admiration while also displaying his facility with Burns's Ayrshire Scots). Like Burns, Dunbar, and other dialect authors, Riley was read as though he had captured a picturesque world that was rapidly disappearing behind the advance of postbellum modernity. Even though he was one of the wealthiest writers at the time of his death, readers felt Riley to be a folk poet who translated into aesthetic forms the vernacular speech and philosophy of a bygone mode of life.

Michael C. Cohen
University of California at Los Angeles

PRIMARY WORKS

The Old Swimmin'-Hole and 'Leven Other Poems, 1883; *The Boss Girl, A Christmas Story and Other Sketches*, 1885; *Afterwhiles*, 1887; *Pipes o' Pan at Zekesbury*, 1889; *Rhymes of Childhood*, 1890; *Neghborly Poems*, 1891; *Armazindy*, 1894; *A Child-World*, 1896; *The Rubaiyat of Doc Sifers*, 1897.

Scraps

There's a habit I have nurtured,
    From the sentimental time
When my life was like a story,
    And my heart a happy rhyme,—
Of clipping from the paper,   5
    Or magazine, perhaps,
The idle songs of dreamers,
    Which I treasure as my scraps.

They hide among my letters,
    And they find a cozy nest   10
In the bosom of my wrapper,
    And the pockets of my vest;
They clamber in my fingers
    Till my dreams of wealth relapse
In fairer dreams than Fortune's   15
    Though I find them only scraps.

Sometimes I find, in tatters
    Like a beggar, form as fair
As ever gave to Heaven
    The treasure of a prayer;   20
And words all dim and faded,
    And obliterate in part,
Grow into fadeless meanings
    That are printed on the heart.

Sometimes a childish jingle   25
    Flings an echo, sweet and clear,
And thrills me as I listen
    To the laughs I used to hear;
And I catch the gleam of faces,
    And the glimmer of glad eyes   30
That peep at me expectant
    O'er the walls of Paradise.

O syllables of measure!
    Though you wheel yourselves in line,
And await the further order   35
    Of this eager voice of mine;
You are powerless to follow
    O'er the field my fancy maps,
So I lead you back to silence
    Feeling you are only scraps.   40

1876

Down on Wriggle Crick

Best time to kill a hog's when he's fat

—OLD SAW.

Mostly, folks is law-abidin'
    Down on Wriggle Crick,—
Seein' they's no Squire residin'
    In our bailywick;
No grand juries, no suppeenies,   5
    Ner no vested rights to pick
Out yer man, jerk up and jail ef
    He's outragin' Wriggle Crick!

Wriggle Crick hain't got no lawin',
    Ner no suits to beat;   10
Ner no court-house gee-and-hawin'

Like a County-seat;
Hain't no waitin' round fer verdicks,
    Ner non-gittin' witness-fees;
Ner no thiefs 'at gits "new hearin's,"   15
    By some lawyer slick as grease!

Wriggle Crick's leadin' spirit
    Is old Johnts Culwell,—
Keeps post-office, and right near it
    Owns what's called "The Grand   20
        Hotel"—
(Warehouse now)—buys wheat and ships it;
    Gits out ties, and trades in stock,
And knows all the high-toned drummers
    'Twixt South Bend and Mishawauk   25

Last year comes along a feller—
    Sharper 'an a lance—
Stovepipe-hat and silk umbreller,
    And a boughten all-wool pants,—
Tinkerin' of clocks and watches;   30
    Says a trial's all he wants—
And rents out the tavern-office
    Next to Uncle Johnts.

Well.—He tacked up his k'dentials,
    And got down to biz.—   35
Captured Johnts by cuttin' stenchils
    Fer them old wheat-sacks o' his.—
Fixed his clock, in the post-office—
    Painted fer him, clean and slick,
'Crost his safe, in gold-leaf letters,   40
    "J. Culwells's, Wriggle Crick."

Any kind o' job you keered to
    Resk him with, and bring,
He'd fix fer you—jes' appeared to
    Turn his hand to anything!—   45
Rings, er earbobs, er umbrellers—
    Glue a cheer er chany doll,—
W'y, of all the beatin' fellers,
    He jes' beat 'em all!

Made his friends, but wouldn't stop   50
        there,—

One mistake he learnt,
That was, sleepin' in his shop there.—
    And one Sund'y night it burnt!
Come in one o' jes' a-sweepin'   55
    All the whole town high and dry—
And that feller, when they waked him,
    Suffocatin', mighty nigh!

Johnts he drug him from the buildin',
    He'pless—'peared to be,—   60
And the women and the childern
    Drenchin' him with sympathy!
But I noticed Johnts helt on him
    With a' extry lovin' grip,
And the men-folks gathered round him   65
    In most warmest pardnership!

That's the whole mess, grease-and-dopin'!
    Johnts's safe was saved,—
But the lock was found sprung open,
    And the inside caved.   70
Was no trial—ner no jury—
    Ner no jedge ner court-house-click.—
Circumstances alters cases
    Down on Wriggle Crick!

                        1885

To Robert Burns

Sweet Singer that I loe the maist
    O' ony, sin' wi' eager haste
I smacket bairn-lips ower the taste
    O' hinnied sang,
I hail thee, though a blessed ghaist   5
    In Heaven lang!

For, weel I ken, nae cantie phrase,
Nor courtly airs, nor lairdly ways,
Could gar me freer blame, or praise,
    Or proffer hand,   10
Where "Rantin' Robbie" and his lays
    Thegither stand.

And sae these hamely lines I send,
Wi' jinglin' words at ilka end,

In echo o' the sangs that wend   15
    Frae thee to me
Like simmer-brooks, wi' mony a bend
    O' wimplin' glee.

In fancy, as, wi' dewy een,
    I part the clouds aboon the scene   20
Where thou wast born, and peer
        atween,
    I see nae spot
In a' the Hielands half sae green
    And unforgot!   25

I see nae storied castle-hall,
Wi' banners flauntin' ower the wall
And serf and page in ready call,
    Sae grand to me
As ane puir cotter's hut, wi' all   30
    Its poverty.

There where the simple daisy grew
Sae bonnie sweet, and modest, too,
Thy liltin' filled its wee head fu'
    O' sic a grace,   35
It aye is weepin' tears o' dew
    Wi' droopit face.

Frae where the heather bluebells fling
Their sangs o' fragrance to the Spring,
To where the lavrock soars to sing,   40
    Still lives thy strain,
For a' the birds are twittering
    Sangs like thine ain.

And aye, by light, o' sun or moon,
By banks o' Ayr, or Bonnie Doon,   45
The waters lilt nae tender tune
    But sweeter seems
Because they poured their limpid rune
    Through a' thy dreams.

Wi' brimmin' lip, and laughin' ee,   50
    Thou shookest even Grief wi' glee,
Yet had nae niggart sympathy
    Where Sorrow bowed,

But gavest a' thy tears as free
 As a' thy gowd.   55

And sae it is we loe thy name
To see bleeze up wi' sic a flame,
That a' pretentious stars o' fame
 Maun blink asklent,
To see how simple worth may shame   60
 Their brightest glent.

               1880

The Old Swimmin'-Hole

Oh! the old swimmin'-hole! whare the crick so still and deep
Looked like a baby-river that was laying half asleep,
And the gurgle of the worter round the drift jest below
Sounded like the laugh of something we onc't ust to know
Before we could remember anything but the eyes   5
Of the angels lookin' out as we left Paradise;
But the merry days of youth is beyond our controle,
And it's hard to part ferever with the old swimmin'-hole.

Oh! the old swimmin'-hole! In the happy days of yore,
When I ust to lean above it on the old sickamore,   10
Oh! it showed me a face in its warm sunny tide
That gazed back at me so gay and glorified,
It made me love myself, as I leaped to caress
My shadder smilin' up at me with sich tenderness.
But them days is past and gone, and old Time's tuck his toll 15
From the old man come back to the old swimmin'-hole.

Oh! the old swimmin'-hole! In the long, lazy days
When the humdrum of school made so many run-a-ways,
How plesant was the jurney down the old dusty lane,
Whare the tracks of our bare feet was all printed so plane 20
You could tell by the dent of the heel and the sole
They was lots o' fun on hands at the old swimmin'-hole.
But the lost joys is past! Let your tears in sorrow roll
Like the rain that ust to dapple up the old swimmin'-hole.

Thare the bullrushes growed, and the cattails so tall,   25
Arid the sunshine and shadder fell over it all;
And it mottled the worter with amber and gold
Tel the glad lilies rocked in the ripples that rolled;
And the snake-feeder's four gauzy wings fluttered by

Like the ghost of a daisy dropped out of the sky,   30
Or a wownded apple-blossom in the breeze's controle
As it cut acrost some orchurd to'rds the old swimmin'-hole.

Oh! the old swimmin'-hole! When I last saw the place,
The scenes was all changed, like the change in my face;
The bridge of the railroad now crosses the spot   35
Whare the old divin'-log lays sunk and fergot.
And I stray down the banks whare the trees ust to be—
But never again will theyr shade shelter me!
And I wish in my sorrow I could strip to the soul,
And dive off in my grave like the old swimmin'-hole.   40

                                                                                    1882

A Hobo Voluntary

Oh, the hobo's life is a roving life;
*   It robs pretty maids of their heart's delight—*
It causes them to weep and it causes
*   them to mourn*
For the life of a hobo, never to return.   5

The hobo's heart it is light and free,
Though it's Sweethearts all, farewell to thee!—
Farewell to thee, for it's far away
The homeless hobo's footsteps stray.

In the morning bright, or the dusk so dim,   10
It's any path is the one for him!
He'll take his chances, long or short,
For to meet his fate with a valiant heart.

Oh, it's beauty mops out the side-tracked-car,
And it's beauty-beaut' at the pigs-feet bar;   15
But when his drinks and his eats is made
Then the hobo shunts off down the grade.
He camps near town, on the old crick bank,
And he cuts his name on the water tank—
He cuts his name and the hobo sign,—   20
"Bound for the land of corn and wine!"

He's lonesome-like, so he gits run in,
To git the hang o' the world again;
But the laundry circles he moves in there
Makes him sigh for the country air,—   25

So it's Good-by gals! and he takes his chance
And wads hisself through the work house-fence:
He sheds the town and the railroad, too,
And strikes mud roads for a change of view.

The jay drives by on his way to town,   30
And looks on the hobo in high score
And so likewise does the farmhands stare—
But what the haids does the hobo care!
He hits the pike, in the summer's heat
Or the winter's cold, with its snow and sleet—   35
With a boot on one foot, and one shoe—
Or he goes barefoot, if he chooses to.
But he likes the best when the day is warm,
With his bum prince-albert on his arm—
He likes to size up a farmhouse where   40
They haint no man nor bulldog there.

Oh, he gits his meals wherever he can,
So natchurly he's a handy man—
He's a handy man both day and night,
And he's always blest with an appetite!   45

(Oh, it's I like friends that he'ps me through,
And the friends also that he'ps you, too,—
Oh, I like all friends, 'most every kind
But I don't like friends that don't like mine.)

There's friends of mine when they gits the hunch   50
Comes a swarmin' in, the blasted bunch,—
"Clog-step Jonny" and "Flat-wheel Bill"
Aad "Brockey Ike" from Circleville.
With "Cooney Ward" and "Sikes the Kid"
And old "Pop Lawson"—the best we had—   55
The rankest mug and the worst for lush
And the dandiest of the whole blame push.
Oh, them's the times I remembers best
When I took my chance with all the rest,
And hogged fried chicken and roastin' ears, too,   60
And sucked cheroots when the feed was through.

Oh, the hobo's way is the railroad line,
And it's little he cares for schedule time;
Whatever town he's a-striken for
Will wait for him till he gits there.   65

And whatever burg that he lands in
There's beauties there just thick for him—
There's beauty at "The Queen's Taste Lunchstand," sure,
Or "The Last Chance Boardin' House" back door.

A tin o' black coffee, and a rhubarb pie—   70
Be they old and cold as charity—
They're hot-stuff enough for the pore hobo,
And it's "Thanks, kind lady, for to treat me so!"

Then he fills his pipe with a stub cigar
And swipes a coal from the kitchen-fire,   75
And the hired girl says, in a smilin' tone,—
"It's good-by John, if you call that goin'!"
Oh, the hobo's life is a roving life,
It robs pretty maids of their heart's delight—
It causes them to weep and it causes them to mourn   80
For the life of a hobo, never to return.

                                                             1915

■ # UPTON SINCLAIR ■
1878–1968

A savage indictment of wage slavery and of the unsanitary and harrowing conditions in the Chicago meatpacking industry, as well as a call for socialism as the
only means by which to end the exploitation of the working class in an industrial society, Upton Sinclair's *The Jungle* has been one of the most widely read of
American novels. In its own day it was responsible for federal legislation to correct some of the worst abuses in the meatpacking industry, and since then,
widely translated, it has offered an image of America that other cultures have
found profoundly significant.

Sinclair was born in Baltimore and raised in New York City, where he
attended City College of New York and Columbia University. Before he was
twenty he had begun supporting himself by selling juvenile fiction to various
magazines and newspapers, and by 1900 he had given up his academic study to
become a full-time writer. His first four novels were sentimental and immature,
but in 1904 he published *Manassas*, a neo-abolitionist novel about the Civil War
that marked an important step in Sinclair's development as a writer—his shift
to the historical novel. In the summer of 1904, Sinclair became an official member of the Socialist Party of America, then in the decade of its greatest success.
Later that same year Fred D. Warren, the editor of *Appeal to Reason*, a weekly

socialist journal published in Kansas, challenged Sinclair to write a novel dealing with contemporary wage slavery as opposed to the antebellum slavery he had written about in *Manassas*. Sinclair accepted the challenge, and a $500 offer for the serial rights to his new novel, then traveled to the stockyards of Chicago, where he lived for seven weeks in November and December of 1904 while he investigated the conditions of the men and women who lived and worked in Packingtown. When *The Jungle* was released in book form on January 25, 1906, its impact was immediate. Meat sales sharply declined, and President Theodore Roosevelt, after inviting Sinclair to the White House, ordered an investigation of the meatpacking industry that in turn led Congress to pass the Beef Inspection Act and the nation's first Pure Food and Drug Act. Ironically, readers of the novel tended to focus on the vivid, often gruesome descriptions of the meatpacking industry rather than on the plea for socialism that Sinclair included in his final chapters. "I aimed at the public's heart, and by accident hit it in the stomach," Sinclair observed. This, despite the fact that Sinclair cut the original version of the novel, which had appeared in serial form in a socialist journal in 1905, by one-third in order to make it more palatable to a mass audience.

The Jungle follows the shifting fortunes of Jurgis Rudkus and his family, Lithuanian peasants who immigrate to Chicago and find employment in Packingtown. The novel describes the horrifying working conditions in the industries in Packingtown and the family's gradual disintegration, including Jurgis's imprisonment for attacking a man who seduces his wife, the family's loss of their house, the deaths of Jurgis's wife and son, and his own impoverished and hopeless drifting from city to city. In the novel's final chapters, however, Sinclair introduces Jurgis to socialism, and through his involvement with the socialist movement Jurgis becomes a "new man," who finds himself at long last "delivered from the thralldom of despair." The famous last line of *The Jungle*—"CHICAGO WILL BE OURS!"—refers to the widespread socialist gains in the 1904 elections.

The Jungle's flaws are obvious; it is openly didactic; its plot is melodramatic; its characters often lack psychological complexity; and its style is heavy and redundant with detail. However, as a muck-raking novel that documented and exposed working conditions in the Chicago stockyards, and as a political novel that illustrated the industrial exploitation of immigrants like the Rudkus family, *The Jungle* possesses a raw emotional power that is undiminished in the ninety years since its publication. Sinclair's other major novels, all written in the form he referred to as the "contemporary historical novel," possess the same strengths and weaknesses as *The Jungle*. *King Coal* (1917) concerns the Colorado mine wars of 1913–1914, *Oil* (1927) the Teapot Dome Scandal, and *Boston* (1928) the Sacco and Vanzetti executions. His "Lanny Budd" series, 1940–1949, for one volume of which he won the Pulitzer Prize in 1946, was his personal interpretation of the two World Wars. The historical fictions of later American writers, especially John Steinbeck and John Dos Passos, show the influence of Sinclair.

Throughout his long career, Sinclair remained a passionate critic of the social and political inequities of modern capitalism. His political efforts often extended outside the realm of literature, as, for instance, when in 1906 he founded Helicon Hall, an experiment in cooperative living, and when in 1934 he ran as the Democratic candidate for governor of California on his EPIC ("End Poverty in California") platform. By the time Sinclair died in 1968 at the age of ninety, he had published over fifty novels and twenty books of nonfiction.

James C. Wilson
University of Cincinnati

PRIMARY WORKS

The Jungle, 1906; *King Coal,* 1917; *The Profits of Religion,* 1918; *The Brass Check: A Study of American Journalism,* 1919; *Oil,* 1927; *Boston,* 1928.

from **The Jungle**

from Chapter II

Jurgis[1] talked lightly about work, because he was young. They told him stories about the breaking down of men, there in the stockyards of Chicago,[2] and of what had happened to them afterwards—stories to make your flesh creep, but Jurgis would only laugh. He had only been there four months, and he was young, and a giant besides. There was too much health in him. He could not even imagine how it would feel to be beaten. "That is well enough for men like you," he would say, "*silpnas,* puny fellows—but my back is broad."

Jurgis was like a boy, a boy from the country. He was the sort of man the bosses like to get hold of, the sort they make it a grievance they cannot get hold of. When he was told to go to a certain place, he would go there on the run. When he had nothing to do for the moment, he would stand round fidgeting, dancing, with the overflow of energy that was in him. If he were working in a line of men, the line always moved too slowly for him, and you could pick him out by his impatience and restlessness. That was why he had been picked out on one important occasion; for Jurgis had stood outside of Brown and Company's "Central Time Station" not more than half an hour, the second day of his arrival in Chicago, before he had been beckoned by one of the bosses. Of this he was very proud, and it made him more disposed than ever to laugh at the pessimists. In vain would they all tell him that there were men in that crowd from which he had been chosen who had stood there a month—yes, many months—and not been chosen yet. "Yes," he would say, "but what sort of men? Broken-down tramps and good-for-nothings, fellows who have spent all their money drinking, and want to get more for it. Do you want me to believe that with these arms"—and he

---

[1]Jurgis Rudkus and his wife, Ona Lukoszaite, are young Lithuanian immigrants who have moved with their families to Chicago. Jurgis (pronounced *Yoorghis*), the central character in *The Jungle,* has found work in the stockyards of Chicago.

[2]Located on the south side of Chicago, the stockyards (founded 1865) include some of the largest slaughterhouses and meat-processing facilities in the world.

would clench his fists and hold them up in the air, so that you might see the rolling muscles—"that with these arms people will ever let me starve?"

"It is plain," they would answer to this, "that you have come from the country, and from very far in the country." And this was the fact, for Jurgis had never seen a city, and scarcely even a fair-sized town, until he had set out to make his fortune in the world and earn his right to Ona. His father, and his father's father before him, and as many ancestors back as legend could go, had lived in that part of Lithuania known as *Brelovicz*, the Imperial Forest.[3] This is a great tract of a hundred thousand acres, which from time immemorial has been a hunting preserve of the nobility. There are a very few peasants settled in it, holding title from ancient times; and one of these was Antanas Rudkus, who had been reared himself, and had reared his children in turn, upon half a dozen acres of cleared land in the midst of a wilderness. There had been one son besides Jurgis, and one sister. The former had been drafted into the army; that had been over ten years ago, but since that day nothing had ever been heard of him. The sister was married, and her husband had bought the place when old Antanas had decided to go with his son.

It was nearly a year and a half ago that Jurgis had met Ona, at a horse-fair a hundred miles from home. Jurgis had never expected to get married—he had laughed at it as a foolish trap for a man to walk into; but here, without ever having spoken a word to her, with no more than the exchange of half a dozen smiles, he found himself, purple in the face with embarrassment and terror, asking her parents to sell her to him for his wife—and offering his father's two horses he had been sent to the fair to sell. But Ona's father proved as a rock—the girl was yet a child, and he was a rich man, and his daughter was not to be had in that way. So Jurgis went home with a heavy heart, and that spring and summer toiled and tried hard to forget. In the fall, after the harvest was over, he saw that it would not do, and tramped the full fortnight's journey that lay between him and Ona.

He found an unexpected state of affairs—for the girl's father had died, and his estate was tied up with creditors; Jurgis's heart leaped as he realized that now the prize was within his reach. There was Elzbieta Lukoszaite, Teta, or Aunt, as they called her, Ona's stepmother, and there were her six children, of all ages. There was also her brother Jonas, a dried-up little man who had worked upon the farm. They were people of great consequence, as it seemed to Jurgis, fresh out of the woods; Ona knew how to read, and knew many other things that he did not know; and now the farm had been sold, and the whole family was adrift—all they owned in the world being about seven hundred roubles, which is half as many dollars. They would have had three times that, but it had gone to court, and the judge had

---

[3]Apparently in the southeastern, heavily forested part of Lithuania. Located on the Baltic Sea just north of Poland, Lithuania was one of the component republics of the U.S.S.R. from 1940 to 1990. Lithuania has been an independent nation since March 1990.

decided against them, and it had cost the balance to get him to change his decision.

Ona might have married and left them, but she would not, for she loved Teta Elzbieta. It was Jonas who suggested that they all go to America, where a friend of his had gotten rich. He would work, for his part, and the women would work, and some of the children, doubtless—they would live somehow. Jurgis, too, had heard of America. That was a country where, they said, a man might earn three roubles a day; and Jurgis figured what three roubles a day would mean, with prices as they were where he lived, and decided forthwith that he would go to America and marry, and be a rich man in the bargain. In that country, rich or poor, a man was free, it was said; he did not have to go into the army, he did not have to pay out his money to rascally officials,—he might do as he pleased, and count himself as good as any other man. So America was a place of which lovers and young people dreamed. If one could only manage to get the price of a passage, he could count his troubles at an end.

It was arranged that they should leave the following spring, and meantime Jurgis sold himself to a contractor for a certain time, and tramped nearly four hundred miles from home with a gang of men to work upon a railroad in Smolensk.[4] This was a fearful experience, with filth and bad food and cruelty and overwork; but Jurgis stood it and came out in fine trim, and with eighty roubles sewed up in his coat. He did not drink or fight, because he was thinking all the time of Ona; and for the rest, he was a quiet, steady man, who did what he was told to, did not lose this temper often, and when he did lose it made the offender anxious that he should not lose it again. When they paid him off he dodged the company gamblers and dramshops, and so they tried to kill him; but he escaped, and tramped it home, working at odd jobs, and sleeping always with one eye open.

So in the summer time they had all set out for America. At the last moment there joined them Marija Berczynskas, who was a cousin of Ona's. Marija was an orphan, and had worked since childhood for a rich farmer of Vilna, who beat her regularly. It was only at the age of twenty that it had occurred to Marija to try her strength, when she had risen up and nearly murdered the man, and then come away.

There were twelve in all in the party, five adults and six children—and Ona, who was a little of both. They had a hard time on the passage; there was an agent who helped them, but he proved a scoundrel, and got them into a trap with some officials, and cost them a good deal of their precious money, which they clung to with such horrible fear. This happened to them again in New York—for, of course, they knew nothing about the country, and had no one to tell them, and it was easy for a man in a blue uniform to lead them away, and to take them to a hotel and keep them there, and make them pay

[4]A city about 220 miles southwest of Moscow. One of Russia's oldest cities, Smolensk is a port on the Dnieper River and an important railroad junction and distribution point for the region's agricultural products.

enormous charges to get away. The law says that the rate-card shall be on the door of a hotel, but it does not say that it shall be in Lithuanian.

It was in the stockyards that Jonas's friend had gotten rich, and so to Chicago the party was bound. They knew that one word, Chicago,—and that was all they needed to know, at least, until they reached the city. Then, tumbled out of the cars without ceremony, they were no better off than before; they stood staring down the vista of Dearborn Street, with its big black buildings towering in the distance, unable to realize that they had arrived, and why, when they said "Chicago," people no longer pointed in some direction, but instead looked perplexed, or laughed, or went on without paying any attention. They were pitiable in their helplessness; above all things they stood in deadly terror of any sort of person in official uniform, and so whenever they saw a policeman they would cross the street and hurry by. For the whole of the first day they wandered about in the midst of deafening confusion, utterly lost; and it was only at night that, cowering in the doorway of a house, they were finally discovered and taken by a policeman to the station. In the morning an interpreter was found, and they were taken and put upon a car, and taught a new word—"stockyards." Their delight at discovering that they were to get out of this adventure without losing another share of their possessions, it would not be possible to describe.

They sat and stared out of the window. They were on a street which seemed to run on forever, mile after mile—thirty-four of them, if they had known it—and each side of it one uninterrupted row of wretched little two-story frame buildings. Down every side street they could see, it was the same,—never a hill and never a hollow, but always the same endless vista of ugly and dirty little wooden buildings. Here and there would be a bridge crossing a filthy creek, with hard-baked mud shores and dingy sheds and docks along it; here and there would be a railroad crossing, with a tangle of switches, and locomotives puffing, and rattling freight-cars filing by; here and there would be a great factory, a dingy building with innumerable windows in it, and immense volumes of smoke pouring from the chimneys, darkening the air above and making filthy the earth beneath. But after each of these interruptions, the desolate procession would begin again—the procession of dreary little buildings.

A full hour before the party reached the city they had begun to note the perplexing changes in the atmosphere. It grew darker all the time, and upon the earth the grass seemed to grow less green. Every minute, as the train sped on, the colors of things became dingier; the fields were grown parched and yellow, the landscape hideous and bare. And along with the thickening smoke they began to notice another circumstance, a strange, pungent odor. They were not sure that it was unpleasant, this odor; some might have called it sickening, but their taste in odors was not developed, and they were only sure that it was curious. Now, sitting in the trolley car, they realized that they were on their way to the home of it—that they had travelled all the way from Lithuania to it. It was now no longer something far-off and faint, that you caught in whiffs; you could literally taste it, as well as smell it—you could take hold of it, almost, and examine it at your leisure. They were divided in their opinions about it. It was an elemental odor, raw and crude; it was rich, almost rancid, sensual, and strong. There were some who drank it in as if it were an intoxicant; there were others who put their handkerchiefs to their faces. The new emigrants were still tasting it, lost in wonder, when suddenly the car came to a halt, and the door was flung open, and a voice shouted—"Stockyards!"

They were left standing upon the corner, staring; down a side street there were two rows of brick houses, and between them a vista: half a dozen chimneys, tall as the tallest of buildings, touching the very sky—and leaping from them half a dozen columns of smoke, thick, oily, and black as night. It might have come from the centre of the world, this smoke, where the fires of the ages still smoulder. It came as if self-impelled, driving all before it, a perpetual explosion. It was inexhaustible; one stared, waiting to see it stop, but still the great streams rolled out. They spread in vast clouds overhead, writhing, curling; then, uniting in one giant river, they streamed away down the sky, stretching a black pall as far as the eye could reach.

Then the party became aware of another strange thing. This, too, like the odor, was a thing elemental; it was a sound, a sound made up of ten thousand little sounds. You scarcely noticed it at first—it sunk into your consciousness, a vague disturbance, a trouble. It was like the murmuring of the bees in the spring, the whisperings of the forest; it suggested endless activity, the rumblings of a world in motion. It was only by an effort that one could realize that it was made by animals, that it was the distant lowing of ten thousand cattle, the distant grunting of ten thousand swine.

They would have liked to follow it up, but, alas, they had no time for adventures just then. The policeman on the corner was beginning to watch them; and so, as usual, they started up the street. Scarcely had they gone a block, however, before Jonas was heard to give a cry, and began pointing excitedly across the street. Before they could gather the meaning of his breathless ejaculations he had bounded away, and they saw him enter a shop, over which was a sign: "J. Szedvilas, Delicatessen." When he came out again it was in company with a very stout gentleman in shirt sleeves and an apron, clasping Jonas by both hands and laughing hilariously. Then Teta Elzbieta recollected suddenly that Szedvilas had been the name of the mythical friend who had made his fortune in America. To find that he had been making it in the delicatessen business was an extraordinary piece of good fortune at this juncture; though it was well on in the morning, they had not breakfasted, and the children were beginning to whimper.

Thus was the happy ending of a woeful voyage. The two families literally fell upon each other's necks—for it had been years since Jokubas Szedvilas had met a man from his part of Lithuania. Before half the day they were lifelong friends. Jokubas understood all the pitfalls of this new world, and could explain all of its mysteries; he could tell them the things they ought to have done in the different emergencies—and what was still more to the point, he could tell them what to do now. He would take them to poni Aniele, who kept a boarding-house the other side of the yards; old Mrs. Jukniene, he explained, had not what one would call choice accommodations, but they might do for the moment. To this Teta Elzbieta hastened to respond that nothing could be too cheap to suit them just then; for they were quite terrified over the sums they had had to expend. A very few days of practical experience in this land of high wages had been sufficient to make clear to them the cruel fact that it was also a land of high prices, and that in it the poor man was almost as poor as in any other corner of the earth; and so there vanished in a night all the wonderful dreams of wealth that had been haunting Jurgis. What had made the discovery all the more painful was that they were spending, at American prices, money which they had earned at home rates of wages—and so were really being cheated by the world! The last two days they had all but starved themselves—it made them quite sick to pay prices that the railroad people asked them for food.

Yet, when they saw the home of the Widow Jukniene they could not but recoil, even so. In all their journey they had seen nothing so bad as this. Poni Aniele had a four-room flat in one of that wilderness of two-story frame tenements that lie "back of the yards." There were four such flats in each building, and each of the four was a "boarding-house" for the occupancy of foreigners—Lithuanians, Poles, Slovaks, or Bohemians. Some of these places were kept by private persons, some were coöperative. There would be an average of half a dozen boarders to each room—sometimes there were thirteen or fourteen to one room, fifty or sixty to a flat. Each one of the occupants furnished his own accommodations—that is, a mattress and some bedding. The mattresses would be spread upon the floor in rows—and there would be nothing else in the place except a stove. It was by no means unusual for two men to own the same mattress in common, one working by day and using it by night, and the other at night and using it in the daytime. Very frequently a lodging-house keeper would rent the same beds to double shifts of men.

Mrs. Jukniene was a wizened-up little woman, with a wrinkled face. Her home was unthinkably filthy; you could not enter by the front door at all, owing to the mattresses, and when you tried to go up the backstairs you found that she had walled up most of the porch with old boards to make a place to keep her chickens. It was a standing jest of the boarders that Aniele cleaned house by letting the chickens loose in the rooms. Undoubtedly this did keep down the vermin, but it seemed probable, in view of all the circumstances, that the old lady regarded it rather as feeding the chickens than as cleaning the rooms. The truth was that she had definitely given up the idea of cleaning anything, under pressure of an attack of rheumatism, which had kept her doubled up in one corner of her room for over a week; during which time eleven of her boarders, heavily in her debt, had concluded to try their chances of employment in Kansas City. This was July, and the fields were green. One never saw the fields, nor any green thing whatever, in Packingtown;[5] but one could go out on the road and "hobo it," as the men phrased it, and see the country, and have a long rest, and an easy time riding on the freight cars....

from **Chapter IX**

... Jurgis heard of these things little by little, in the gossip of those who were obliged to perpetrate them. It seemed as if every time you met a person from a new department, you heard of new swindles and new crimes. There was, for instance, a Lithuanian who was a cattle-butcher for the plant where Marija had worked, which killed meat for canning only; and to hear this man describe the animals which came to his place would have been worth while for a Dante[6] or a Zola.[7] It seemed that they must have agencies all over the country, to hunt out old and crippled and diseased cattle to be canned. There were cattle which had been fed on "whiskey malt," the refuse of the breweries, and had become what the men called "steerly"—which means covered with boils. It was a nasty job killing these, for when you plunged your knife into them they would burst and splash foul-smelling stuff into your face; and when a man's sleeves were smeared with blood, and his hands steeped in it, how was he ever to wipe his face, or to clear his eyes so that he could see? It was stuff such as this that made the "embalmed beef" that had killed several times as many United States soldiers as all the bullets of the Spaniards;[8] only the army beef, besides, was not fresh canned, it was old stuff that had been lying for years in the cellars.

Then one Sunday evening, Jurgis sat puffing his pipe by the kitchen stove, and talking with an old fellow whom Jonas had introduced, and who worked in the canning-rooms at Durham's; and so Jurgis learned a few things about the great and only Durham canned goods, which had become a national institution. They were regular alchemists at Durham's; they advertised a mushroom-catsup, and the men who made it did not know what a mushroom looked like. They advertised "potted chicken,"—and it was like the boarding-house soup of the comic papers, through which a chicken had walked with rubbers on. Perhaps they had a secret process for making chickens chemically—who knows? said Jurgis's friend; the things that went into the mixture were tripe, and the fat of pork, and beef suet, and hearts of beef, and finally the waste ends of veal, when they had any. They put these up in several grades, and sold them at several prices; but the contents of the

---

[5]The area surrounding the stockyards on the south side of Chicago.

[6]Dante Alighieri, Italian poet, 1265–1321. Author of the *Divine Comedy*. The reference here is to the *Inferno*, the first of three parts of the *Divine Comedy*, in which the poet is conducted by the spirit of the poet Virgil through the twenty-four great circles of Hell on the first stage of his journey toward God.

[7]Emile Zola, French novelist, 1840–1902. With such novels as *Nana* (1880) and *Germinal* (1885), Zola became the leading exponent of French Naturalism. Zola was famous for his journalistic, ostensibly scientific rendering of social milieu, based on minute and often sordid details. Like Sinclair, Zola was an ardent social reformer.

[8]The Spanish-American War, 1898.

cans all came out of the same hopper. And then there was "potted game" and "potted grouse," "potted ham," and "devilled ham"—de-vyled, as the men called it. "De-vyled" ham was made out of the waste ends of smoked beef that were too small to be sliced by the machines; and also tripe, dyed with chemicals so that it would not show white; and trimmings of hams and corned beef; and potatoes, skins and all; and finally the hard cartilaginous gullets of beef, after the tongues had been cut out. All this ingenious mixture was ground up and flavored with spices to make it taste like something. Anybody who could invent a new imitation had been sure of a fortune from old Durham, said Jurgis's informant; but it was hard to think of anything new in a place where so many sharp wits had been at work for so long; where men welcomed tuberculosis in the cattle they were feeding, because it made them fatten more quickly; and where they bought up all the old rancid butter left over in the grocery-stores of a continent, and "oxidized" it by a forced-air process, to take away the odor, rechurned it with skim-milk, and sold it in bricks in the cities! Up to a year or two ago it had been the custom to kill horses in the yards—ostensibly for fertilizer; but after long agitation the newspapers had been able to make the public realize that the horses were being canned. Now it was against the law to kill horses in Packingtown, and the law was really complied with—for the present, at any rate. Any day, however, one might see sharp-horned and shaggy-haired creatures running with the sheep—and yet what a job you would have to get the public to believe that a good part of what it buys for lamb and mutton is really goat's flesh!

There was another interesting set of statistics that a person might have gathered in Packingtown—those of the various afflictions of the workers. When Jurgis had first inspected the packing-plants with Szedvilas, he had marvelled while he listened to the tale of all the things that were made out of the carcasses of animals, and of all the lesser industries that were maintained there; now he found that each one of these lesser industries was a separate little inferno, in its way as horrible as the killing-beds, the source and fountain of them all. The workers in each of them had their own peculiar diseases. And the wandering visitor might be sceptical about all the swindles, but he could not be sceptical about these, for the worker bore the evidence of them about on his own person—generally he had only to hold out his hand.

There were the men in the pickle-rooms, for instance, where old Antanas had gotten his death; scarce a one of these that had not some spot of horror on his person. Let a man so much as scrape his finger pushing a truck in the pickle-rooms, and he might have a sore that would put him out of the world; all the joints in his fingers might be eaten by the acid, one by one. Of the butchers and floorsmen, the beef-boners and trimmers, and all those who used knives, you could scarcely find a person who had the use of his thumb; time and time again the base of it had been slashed, till it was a mere lump of flesh against which the man pressed the knife to hold it. The hands of these men would be criss-crossed with cuts, until you could no longer pretend to count them or to trace them. They would have no nails,—they had worn them off pulling hides; their knuckles were swollen so that their fingers spread out like a fan. There were men who worked in the cooking-rooms, in the midst of steam and sickening odors, by artificial light; in these rooms the germs of tuberculosis might live for two years, but the supply was renewed every hour. There were the beef-luggers, who carried two-hundred-pound quarters into the refrigerator-cars; a fearful kind of work, that began at four o'clock in the morning, and that wore out the most powerful men in a few years. There were those who worked in the chilling-rooms, and whose special disease was rheumatism; the time-limit that a man could work in the chilling-rooms was said to be five years. There were the wool-pluckers, whose hands went to pieces even sooner than the hands of the pickle-men; for the pelts of the sheep had to be painted with acid to loosen the wool, and then the pluckers had to pull out this wool with their bare hands, till the acid had eaten their fingers off. There were those who made the tins for the canned-meat; and their hands, too, were a maze of cuts, and each cut represented a chance for blood-poisoning. Some worked at the stamping-machines, and it was seldom that one could work long there at the pace that was set, and not give out and forget himself, and have a part of his hand chopped off. There were the "hoisters," as they were called, whose task it was to press the lever which lifted the dead cattle off the floor. They ran along upon a rafter, peering down through the damp and the steam; and as old Durham's architects had not built the killing-room for the convenience of the hoisters, at every few feet they would have to stoop under a beam, say four feet above the one they ran on; which got them into the habit of stooping, so that in a few years they would be walking like chimpanzees. Worst of any, however, were the fertilizer-men, and those served in the cooking-rooms. These people could not be shown to the visitor,—for the odor of a fertilizer-man would scare any ordinary visitor at a hundred yards, and as for the other men, who worked in tank-rooms full of steam, and in some of which there were open vats near the level of the floor, their peculiar trouble was that they fell into the vats; and when they were fished out, there was never enough of them left to be worth exhibiting,—sometimes they would be overlooked for days, till all but the bones of them had gone out to the world as Durham's Pure Leaf Lard! ...

from Chapter XI

... A time of peril on the killing-beds when a steer broke loose. Sometimes, in the haste of speeding-up, they would dump one of the animals out on the floor before it was fully stunned, and it would get upon its feet and run amuck. Then there would be a yell of warning—the men would drop everything and dash for the nearest pillar, slipping here and there on the floor, and tumbling over each other. This was bad enough in the summer, when a man could see; in winter-time it was enough to make your hair stand up, for the room would be so full of steam that you could not make anything out five feet in front of you. To be sure, the steer was generally blind and frantic, and not especially bent on hurting any one; but think of the chances of running upon a knife, while nearly every man had one in his hand! And then, to cap the climax, the floor-boss would come rushing up with a rifle and begin blazing away!

It was in one of these mêlées that Jurgis fell into his trap. That is the only word to describe it; it was so cruel, and so utterly not to be foreseen. At first he hardly noticed it, it was such a slight accident—simply that in leaping out of the way he turned his ankle. There was a twinge of pain, but Jurgis was used to pain, and did not coddle himself. When he came to walk home, however, he realized that it was hurting him a great deal; and in the morning his ankle was swollen out nearly double its size, and he could not get his foot into his shoe. Still, even then, he did nothing more than swear a little, and wrapped his foot in old rags, and hobbled out to take the car. It chanced to be a rush day at Durham's, and all the long morning he limped about with his aching foot; by noon-time the pain was so great that it made him faint, and after a couple of hours in the afternoon he was fairly beaten, and had to tell the boss. They sent for the company doctor, and he examined the foot and told Jurgis to go home to bed, adding that he had probably laid himself up for months by his folly. The injury was not one that Durham and Company could be held responsible for, and so that was all there was to it, so far as the doctor was concerned.

Jurgis got home somehow, scarcely able to see for the pain, and with an awful terror in his soul. Elzbieta helped him into bed and bandaged his injured foot with cold water, and tried hard not to let him see her dismay; when the rest came home at night she met them outside and told them, and they, too, put on a cheerful face, saying it would only be for a week or two, and that they would pull him through.

When they had gotten him to sleep, however, they sat by the kitchen fire and talked it over in frightened whispers. They were in for a siege, that was plainly to be seen. Jurgis had only about sixty dollars in the bank, and the slack season was upon them. Both Jonas and Marija might soon be earning no more than enough to pay their board, and besides that there were only the wages of Ona and the pittance of the little boy. There was the rent to pay, and still some on the furniture; there was the insurance just due, and every month there was sack after sack of coal. It was January, midwinter, an awful time to have to face privation. Deep snows would come again, and who would carry Ona to her work now? She might lose her place— she was almost certain to lose it. And then little Stanislovas[9] began to whimper—who would take care of him?

It was dreadful that an accident of this sort, that no man can help, should have meant such suffering. The bitterness of it was the daily food and drink of Jurgis. It was of no use for them to try to deceive him; he knew as much about the situation as they did, and he knew that the family might

---

[9]Son of Teta Elzbieta, Ona's stepmother.

literally starve to death. The worry of fairly ate him up—he began to look haggard the first two or three days of it. In truth, it was almost maddening for a strong man like him, a fighter, to have to lie there helpless on his back. It was for all the world the old story of Prometheus[10] bound. As Jurgis lay on his bed, hour after hour, there came to him emotions that he had never known before. Before this he had met life with a welcome—it had its trials, but none that a man could not face. But now, in the night-time, when he lay tossing about, there would come stalking into his chamber a grisly phantom, the sight of which made his flesh curl and his hair to bristle up. It was like seeing the world fall away from underneath his feet; like plunging down into a bottomless abyss, into yawning caverns of despair. It might be true, then, after all, what others had told him about life, that the best powers of a man might not be equal to it! It might be true that, strive as he would, toil as he would, he might fail, and go down and be destroyed! The thought of this was like an icy hand at his heart; the thought that here, in this ghastly home of all horror, he and all those who were dear to him might lie and perish of starvation and cold, and there would be no ear to hear their cry, no hand to help them! It was true, it was true,—that here in this huge city, with its stores of heaped-up wealth, human creatures might be hunted down and destroyed by the wild-beast powers of nature, just as truly as ever they were in the days of the cave men! ...

from Chapter XII

... The latter part of April Jurgis went to see the doctor, and was given a bandage to lace about his ankle, and told that he might go back to work. It needed more than the permission of the doctor, however, for when he showed up on the killing-floor of Brown's, he was told by the foreman that it had not been possible to keep his job for him. Jurgis knew that this meant simply that the foreman had found some one else to do the work as well and did not want to bother to make a change. He stood in the doorway, looking mournfully on, seeing his friends and companions at work, and feeling like an outcast. Then he went out and took his place with the mob of the unemployed.

This time, however, Jurgis did not have the same fine confidence, nor the same reason for it. He was no longer the finest-looking man in the throng, and the bosses no longer made for him; he was thin and haggard, and his clothes were seedy, and he looked miserable. And there were hundreds who looked and felt just like him, and who had been wandering about Packingtown for months begging for work. This was a critical time in Jurgis's life, and if he had been a weaker man he would have gone the way the rest did. Those out-of-work wretches would stand about the packing-houses every morning till the police drove them away, and then they would

[10]Greek Titan, the son of Iapetus and Clymene, who stole fire from heaven, for which crime Zeus ordered him chained to a rock on Mount Caucasus where a vulture fed daily on his liver.

scatter among the saloons. Very few of them had the nerve to face the rebuffs that they would encounter by trying to get into the buildings to interview the bosses; if they did not get a chance in the morning, there would be nothing to do but hang about the saloons the rest of the day and night. Jurgis was saved from all this—partly, to be sure, because it was pleasant weather, and there was no need to be indoors; but mainly because he carried with him always the pitiful little face of his wife. He must get work, he told himself, fighting the battle with despair every hour of the day. He must get work! He must have a place again and some money saved up, before the next winter came.

But there was no work for him. He sought out all the members of his union—Jurgis had stuck to the union through all this—and begged them to speak a word for him. He went to every one he knew, asking for a chance, there or anywhere. He wandered all day through the buildings; and in a week or two, when he had been all over the yards, and into every room to which he had access, and learned that there was not a job anywhere, he persuaded himself that there might have been a change in the places he had first visited, and began the round all over; till finally the watchmen and the "spotters" of the companies came to know him by sight and to order him out with threats. Then there was nothing more for him to do but go with the crowd in the morning, and keep in the front row and look eager, and when he failed, go back home, and play with little Kotrina[11] and the baby.[12]

The peculiar bitterness of all this was that Jurgis saw so plainly the meaning of it. In the beginning he had been fresh and strong, and he had gotten a job the first day; but now he was second-hand, a damaged article, so to speak, and they did not want him. They had got the best out of him,—they had worn him out, with their speeding-up and their carelessness, and now they had thrown him away! And Jurgis would make the acquaintance of others of these unemployed men and find that they had all had the same experience. There were some, of course, who had wandered in from other places, who had been ground up in other mills; there were others who were out from their own fault—some, for instance, who had not been able to stand the awful grind without drink. The vast majority, however, were simply the worn-out parts of the great merciless packing-machine; they had toiled there, and kept up with the pace, some of them for ten or twenty years, until finally the time had come when they could not keep up with it any more. Some had been frankly told that they were too old, that a sprier man was needed; others had given occasion, by some act of carelessness or incompetence; with most, however, the occasion had been the same as with Jurgis. They had been overworked and underfed so long, and finally some disease had laid them on their backs; or they had cut themselves, and had blood-poisoning, or met with some other accident. When a man came back after that, he would get his place back only by the courtesy of the boss. To

---

[11]Daughter of Teta Elzbieta, Ona's stepmother.   [12]Jurgis and Ona's infant son.

this there was no exception, save when the accident was one for which the firm was liable; in that case they would send a slippery lawyer to see him, first to try to get him to sign away his claims, but if he was too smart for that, to promise him that he and his should always be provided with work. This promise they would keep, strictly and to the letter—for two years. Two years was the "statute of limitations," and after that the victim could not sue.

What happened to a man after any of these things, all depended upon the circumstances. If he were of the highly skilled workers, he would probably have enough saved up to tide him over. The best-paid men, the "splitters," made fifty cents an hour, which would be five or six dollars a day in the rush seasons, and one or two in the dullest. A man could live and save on that; but then there were only half a dozen splitters in each place, and one of them that Jurgis knew had a family of twenty-two children, all hoping to grow up to be splitters like their father. For an unskilled man, who made ten dollars a week in the rush seasons and five in the dull, it all depended upon his age and the number he had dependent upon him. An unmarried man could save, if he did not drink, and if he was absolutely selfish—that is, if he paid no heed to the demands of his old parents, or of his little brothers and sisters, or of any other relatives he might have, as well as of the members of his union, and his chums, and the people who might be starving to death next door....

from Chapter XIV

With one member trimming beef in a cannery, and another working in a sausage factory, the family had a first-hand knowledge of the great majority of Packingtown swindles. For it was the custom, as they found, whenever meat was so spoiled that it could not be used for anything else, either to can it or else to chop it up into sausage. With what had been told them by Jonas, who had worked in the pickle-rooms, they could now study the whole of the spoiled-meat industry on the inside, and read a new and grim meaning into that old Packingtown jest,—that they use everything of the pig except the squeal.

Jonas had told them how the meat that was taken out of pickle would often be found sour, and how they would rub it up with soda to take away the smell, and sell it to be eaten on free-lunch counters; also of all the miracles of chemistry which they performed, giving to any sort of meat, fresh or salted, whole or chopped, any color and any flavor and any odor they chose. In the pickling of hams they had an ingenious apparatus, by which they saved time and increased the capacity of the plant—a machine consisting of a hollow needle attached to a pump; by plunging this needle into the meat and working with his foot, a man could fill a ham with pickle in a few seconds. And yet, in spite of this, there would be hams found spoiled, some of them with an odor so bad that a man could hardly bear to be in the room with them. To pump into these the packers had a second and much stronger pickle which destroyed the odor—a process known to the workers as "giving them thirty per cent." Also, after the hams had been smoked, there would be found some that had gone to the bad. Formerly these had been sold as "Number Three Grade," but later on some ingenious person had hit upon a new device, and now they would extract the bone, about which the bad part generally lay, and insert in the hole a white-hot iron. After this invention there was no longer Number One, Two and Three Grade—there was only Number One Grade. The packers were always originating such schemes—they had what they called "boneless hams," which were all the odds and ends of pork stuffed into casings; and "California hams," which were the shoulders, with big knuckle-joints, and nearly all the meat cut out; and fancy "skinned hams," which were made of the oldest hogs, whose skins were so heavy and coarse that no one would buy them—that is, until they had been cooked and chopped fine and labelled "head cheese"!

It was only when the whole ham was spoiled that it came into the department of Elzbieta. Cut up by the two-thousand-revolutions-a-minute flyers, and mixed with half a ton of other meat, no odor that ever was in a ham could make any difference. There was never the least attention paid to what was cut up for sausage; there would come all the way back from Europe old sausage that had been rejected, and that was mouldy and white—it would be dosed with borax and glycerine, and dumped into the hoppers, and made over again for home consumption. There would be meat that had tumbled out on the floor, in the dirt and sawdust, where the workers had tramped and spit uncounted billions of consumption germs. There would be meat stored in great piles in rooms; and the water from leaky roofs would drip over it, and thousands of rats would race about on it. It was too dark in these storage places to see well, but a man could run his hand over these piles of meat and sweep off handfuls of the dried dung of rats. These rats were nuisances, and the packers would put poisoned bread out for them; they would die, and then rats, bread, and meat would go into the hoppers together. This is no fairy story and no joke; the meat would be shovelled into carts, and the man who did the shovelling would not trouble to lift out a rat even when he saw one— there were things that went into the sausage in comparison with which a poisoned rat was a tidbit. There was no place for the men to wash their hands before they ate dinner, and so they made a practice of washing them in the water that was to be ladled into the sausage. There were the butt-ends of smoked meat, and the scraps of corned beef, and all the odds and ends of the waste of the plants, that would be dumped into old barrels in the cellar and left there. Under the system of rigid economy which the packers enforced, there were some jobs that it only paid to do once in a long time, and among these was the cleaning out of the waste-barrels. Every spring they did it; and in the barrels would be dirt and rust and old nails and stale water—and cart load after cart load of it would be taken up and dumped into the hoppers with fresh meat, and sent out to the public's breakfast. Some of it they would make into "smoked" sausage—but as the smoking took time, and was therefore expensive, they would call upon their chemistry department, and preserve it with borax and color it with gelatine to make it brown. All of their sausage came out of the same bowl, but when they came to wrap it they would stamp some of it "special," and for this they would charge two cents more a pound.

Such were the new surroundings in which Elzbieta was placed, and such was the work she was compelled to do. It was stupefying, brutalizing work; it left her no time to think, no strength for anything. She was part of the machine she tended, and every faculty that was not needed for the machine was doomed to be crushed out of existence. There was only one mercy about the cruel grind—that it gave her the gift of insensibility. Little by little she sank into a torpor—she fell silent. She would meet Jurgis and Ona in the evening, and the three would walk home together, often without saying a word. Ona, too, was falling into a habit of silence—Ona, who had once gone about singing like a bird. She was sick and miserable, and often she would barely have strength enough to drag herself home. And there they would eat what they had to eat, and afterwards, because there was only their misery to talk of, they would crawl into bed and fall into a stupor and never stir until it was time to get up again, and dress by candlelight, and go back to the machines. They were so numbed that they did not even suffer from hunger, now; only the children continued to fret when the food ran short.

Yet the soul of Ona was not dead—the souls of none of them were dead, but only sleeping; and now and then they would waken, and these were cruel times. The gates of memory would roll open—old joys would stretch out their arms to them, old hopes and dreams would call to them, and they would stir beneath the burden that lay upon them, and feel its forever immeasurable weight. They could not even cry out beneath it; but anguish would seize them, more dreadful than the agony of death. It was a thing scarcely to be spoken—a thing never spoken by all the world, that will not know its own defeat.

They were beaten; they had lost the game, they were swept aside. It was not less tragic because it was so sordid, because that it had to do with wages and grocery bills and rents. They had dreamed of freedom; of a chance to look about them and learn something; to be decent and clean, to see their child grow up to be strong. And now it was all gone—it would never be! They had played the game and they had lost. Six years more of toil they had to face before they could expect the least respite, the cessation of the payments upon the house; and how cruelly certain it was that they could never stand six years of such a life as they were living! They were lost, they were going down—and there was no deliverance for them, no hope; for all the help it gave them the vast city in which they lived might have been an ocean waste, a wilderness, a desert, a tomb. So often this mood would come to Ona, in the night-time, when something wakened her; she would lie, afraid of the beating of her own heart, fronting the blood-red eyes of the old primeval terror of life. Once she cried aloud, and woke Jurgis, who was tired and cross. After that she learned to weep silently—their moods so seldom came together now! It was as if their hopes were buried in separate graves. . . .

1906

■ HAMLIN GARLAND ■
1860–1940

Hannibal Hamlin Garland's childhood and youth epitomize the late-nineteenth-century American westering movement he would represent in fiction and auto-biography. Born on a farm in Wisconsin, Garland moved with his family to successive farming locations in Minnesota and Iowa, a movement spurred by his father's restless drive for new land and a fresh start. Garland's lifelong sensitivity to the situation of women appears to have stemmed from his view of his mother's suffering and hardship in attempting to establish a home on these farms on the raw prairie. In 1876 the family was settled in Osage, Iowa, where Garland enrolled in the Cedar Valley Seminary. Following his graduation in 1881 and a trip east with his brother, Garland returned to the West to stake a claim in the Dakota Territory, where his family was now settled.

Garland's growing dissatisfaction with what he took to be the bleakness of upper-midwestern farm life together with his fresh, favorable impressions of the more settled and established East crystallized in 1884 with a decision to move to Boston to pursue further education and to attempt to establish a career. Working on his own at the Boston Public Library, Garland studied widely, from the poetry of Walt Whitman to the evolutionary philosophy of Charles Darwin and Herbert Spencer. His reading of Henry George's economic theories convinced Garland that radical reform of the tax system was needed to bring justice to working farmers in relation to the land owners, an idea that informed much of his subsequent fiction.

Gradually establishing himself, Garland obtained a teaching position at the Boston School of Oratory, gave lectures on literature, and started to write about the prairie life that was engraved upon his memory. Visits to his parents in 1887 and 1888 renewed those memories and stimulated a series of stories that were collected with the title *Main-Travelled Roads* (1891). These stories, including "Up the Coulé," "The Return of a Private," and "Under the Lion's Paw," are unsparing in their depiction of harsh realities of midwestern farm life and are especially noteworthy for their knowledgeable portrayal of the lives of farm women and of the need for economic reform. William Dean Howells, a central figure in American letters, hailed *Main-Travelled Roads* as a strong contribution to the movement toward realism in literature. *Prairie Folks* (1893) collects more of Garland's early stories of farm life and, with *Main-Travelled Roads*, represents the best of Garland's short fiction. In 1892 Garland followed up his successful short stories with the publication of three novels of strongly polemical bent: *Jason Edwards: Average Man*, which expounds the tax theories of Henry George;

A Spoil of Office, an exposé of political corruption and exploration of possibilities of reform along Populist Party lines; and *A Member of the Third House*, a depiction of the influence of the railroad monopoly on a state legislature. Garland's career as novelist climaxed in 1895 with the publication of *Rose of Dutcher's Coolly*, which presents, in a sense, a female alter ego to Garland. Like Garland, Rose, born on a farm, wearies of the monotony of farm life and dreams of escape through establishing herself as an author. When Rose leaves the farm, her guilt toward her father, left behind, recalls themes of guilt felt by the departing young in relation to farm families that we see in "Up the Coulé" and elsewhere in Garland's fiction and autobiography. With marriage, Rose and her husband pledge to live as equals, a relationship Garland explicitly sought with the artist Zulime Taft, whom he married in 1899.

In essays collected in *Crumbling Idols* (1894), Garland gave his theory of the literary realism, or "Veritism" as he called it, that he championed in the earlier part of his career. In the mid-1890s, with an eye to attracting a larger readership, Garland turned to the production of romantic adventure stories. One of the better of these later novels, *The Captain of the Gray-Horse Troop* (1902), deals with the abuse of American Indians by cattlemen. Garland's knowledgeable interest in American Indians, based on his travels to Indian reservations, is also strongly apparent in stories collected in his late *Book of the American Indian* (1923).

Garland's literary career yielded a final, rich harvest with the publication of his autobiographies. *A Son of the Middle Border* (1917), a recognized classic American personal narrative, was followed by the sequel *A Daughter of the Middle Border* (1921), which was awarded the Pulitzer Prize. Subsequent autobiographical works (some semi-fictionalized), including *Trail-Makers of the Middle Border* (1926) and *Back-Trailers from the Middle Border* (1928), though perhaps lacking the power of the first two, remain a lasting and rich resource for students of American life and literary history.

James Robert Payne
New Mexico State University

PRIMARY WORKS

Main-Travelled Roads, 1891; *Jason Edwards*, 1892; *Crumbling Idols*, 1894; *Rose of Dutcher's Coolly*, 1895, ed. Donald Pizer, 1969; *A Son of the Middle Border*, 1917; *The Book of the American Indian*, 1923; *Hamlin Garland's Diary*, ed. Donald Pizer, 1968.

Up the Coulé[1]

A Story of Wisconsin

"Keep the main-travelled road up the Coolly—it's the second house after crossin' the crick."

___

[1] A valley or ravine often with a stream at the bottom. Among Garland's various spellings are *coule*, *coulé*, and *coolly*.

The ride from Milwaukee to the Mississippi is a fine ride at any time, superb in summer. To lean back in a reclining-chair and whirl away in a breezy July day, past lakes, groves of oak, past fields of barley being reaped, past hay-fields, where the heavy grass is toppling before the swift sickle, is a panorama of delight, a road full of delicious surprises, where down a sudden vista lakes open, or a distant wooded hill looms darkly blue, or swift streams, foaming deep down the solid rock, send whiffs of cool breezes in at the window.

It has majesty, breadth. The farming has nothing apparently petty about it. All seems vigorous, youthful, and prosperous. Mr. Howard McLane in his chair let his newspaper fall on his lap, and gazed out upon it with dreaming eyes. It had a certain mysterious glamour to him; the lakes were cooler and brighter to his eye, the greens fresher, and the grain more golden than to any one else, for he was coming back to it all after an absence of ten years. It was, besides, *his* West. He still took pride in being a Western man.

His mind all day flew ahead of the train to the little town far on toward the Mississippi, where he had spent his boyhood and youth. As the train passed the Wisconsin River, with its curiously carved cliffs, its cold, dark, swift-swirling water eating slowly under cedar-clothed banks, Howard began to feel curious little movements of the heart, like a lover as he nears his sweetheart.

The hills changed in character, growing more intimately recognizable. They rose higher as the train left the ridge and passed down into the Black River valley, and specifically into the La Crosse valley.[2] They ceased to have any hint of upheavals of rock, and became simply parts of the ancient level left standing after the water had practically given up its post-glacial, scooping action.

It was about six o'clock as he caught sight of the dear broken line of hills on which his baby eyes had looked thirty-five years ago. A few minutes later and the train drew up at the grimy little station set in at the hillside, and, giving him just time to leap off, plunged on again toward the West. Howard felt a ridiculous weakness in his legs as he stepped out upon the broiling hot splintery planks of the station and faced the few idlers lounging about. He simply stood and gazed with the same intensity and absorption one of the idlers might show standing before the Brooklyn Bridge.

The town caught and held his eyes first. How poor and dull and sleepy and squalid it seemed! The one main street ended at the hillside at his left, and stretched away to the north, between two rows of the usual village stores, unrelieved by a tree or a touch of beauty. An unpaved street, drab-colored, miserable, rotting wooden buildings, with the inevitable battlements—the same, only worse, was the town.

The same, only more beautiful still, was the majestic amphitheatre of green wooded hills that circled the horizon, and toward which he lifted his eyes. He thrilled at the sight.

"Glorious!" he cried involuntarily.

---

[2]In western Wisconsin.

Accustomed to the White Mountains, to the Alleghanies,[3] he had wondered if these hills would retain their old-time charm. They did. He took off
his hat to them as he stood there. Richly wooded, with gently-sloping green
sides, rising to massive square or rounded tops with dim vistas, they glowed
down upon the squalid town, gracious, lofty in their greeting, immortal in
their vivid and delicate beauty.

He was a goodly figure of a man as he stood there beside his valise.
Portly, erect, handsomely dressed, and with something unusually winning in
his brown mustache and blue eyes, something scholarly suggested by the
pinch-nose glasses, something strong in the repose of the head. He smiled
as he saw how unchanged was the grouping of the old loafers on the salt-
barrels and nail-kegs. He recognized most of them—a little dirtier, a little
more bent, and a little grayer.

They sat in the same attitudes, spat tobacco with the same calm delight,
and joked each other, breaking into short and sudden fits of laughter, and
pounded each other on the back, just as when he was a student at the La
Crosse Seminary, and going to and fro daily on the train.

They ruminated on him as he passed, speculating in a perfectly audible
way upon his business.

"Looks like a drummer."

"No, he ain't no drummer. See them Boston glasses?"

"That's so. Guess he's a teacher."

"Looks like a moneyed cuss."

"Bos'n, I *guess*."

He knew the one who spoke last—Freeme Cole, a man who was the fighting wonder of Howard's boyhood, now degenerated into a stoop-shouldered,
faded, garrulous, and quarrelsome old man. Yet there was something epic in
the old man's stories, something enthralling in the dramatic power of recital.

Over by the blacksmith shop the usual game of "quaits"[4] was in progress, and the drug-clerk on the corner was chasing a crony with the squirt-
pump, with which he was about to wash the windows. A few teams stood
ankle-deep in the mud, tied to the fantastically-gnawed pine pillars of the
wooden awnings. A man on a load of hay was "jawing" with the attendant
of the platform scales, who stood below, pad and pencil in hand.

"Hit 'im! hit 'im! Jump off and knock 'im!" suggested a bystander, jovially.

Howard knew the voice.

"Talk's cheap. Takes money t' buy whiskey," he said, when the man on
the load repeated his threat of getting off and whipping the scales-man.

"You're William McTurg," Howard said, coming up to him.

"I am, sir," replied the soft-voiced giant, turning and looking down on
the stranger, with an amused twinkle in his deep brown eyes. He stood as
erect as an Indian, though his hair and beard were white.

---

[3]Both the White Mountains, in northern New
Hampshire and southwestern Maine, and the
Alleghenies, extending from northern Pennsylvania to southwestern Virginia, are parts
of the Appalachian system. [4]A ring toss game.

"I'm Howard McLane."

"Ye begin t' look it," said McTurg, removing his right hand from his pocket. "How are yeh?"

"I'm first-rate. How's mother and Grant?"

"Saw 'im ploughing corn as I came down. Guess he's all right. Want a boost?"

"Well, yes. Are you down with a team?"

"Yep. 'Bout goin' home. Climb right in. That's my rig, right there," nodding at a sleek bay colt hitched in a covered buggy. "Heave y'r grip under the seat."

They climbed into the seat after William had lowered the buggy-top and unhitched the horse from the post. The loafers were mildly curious. Guessed Bill had got hooked onto by a lightnin'-rod peddler, or somethin' o' that kind.

"Want to go by river, or 'round by the hills?"

"Hills, I guess."

The whole matter began to seem trivial, as if he had only been away for a month or two.

William McTurg was a man little given to talk. Even the coming back of a nephew did not cause any flow of questions or reminiscences. They rode in silence. He sat a little bent forward, the lines held carelessly in his hands, his great leonine head swaying to and fro with the movement of the buggy.

As they passed familiar spots, the younger man broke the silence with a question.

"That's old man McElvaine's place, ain't it?"

"Yep."

"Old man living?"

"I *guess* he is. Husk more corn 'n any man he c'n hire."

In the edge of the village they passed an open lot on the left, marked with circus-rings of different eras.

"There's the old ball-ground. Do they have circuses on it just the same as ever?"

"Just the same."

"What fun that field calls up! The games of ball we used to have! Do you play yet?"

"Sometimes. Can't stoop so well as I used to." He smiled a little. "Too much fat."

It all swept back upon Howard in a flood of names and faces and sights and sounds; something sweet and stirring somehow, though it had little of aesthetic charm at the time. They were passing along lanes now, between superb fields of corn, wherein ploughmen were at work. Kingbirds flew from post to post ahead of them; the insects called from the grass. The valley slowly outspread below them. The workmen in the fields were "turning out" for the night. They all had a word of chaff with McTurg.

Over the western wall of the circling amphitheatre the sun was setting. A few scattering clouds were drifting on the west wing, their shadows sliding down the green and purpled slopes. The dazzling sunlight flamed along the luscious velvety grass, and shot amid the rounded, distant purple peaks, and streamed in bars of gold and crimson across the blue mist of the narrower upper Coulés.

The heart of the young man swelled with pleasure almost like pain, and the eyes of the silent older man took on a far-off, dreaming look, as he gazed at the scene which had repeated itself a thousand times in his life, but of whose beauty he never spoke.

Far down to the left was the break in the wall, through which the river ran, on its way to join the Mississippi. As they climbed slowly among the hills, the valley they had left grew still more beautiful, as the squalor of the little town was hid by the dusk of distance. Both men were silent for a long time. Howard knew the peculiarities of his companion too well to make any remarks or ask any questions, and besides it was a genuine pleasure to ride with one who could feel that silence was the only speech amid such splendors.

Once they passed a little brook singing in a mournfully sweet way its eternal song over its pebbles. It called back to Howard the days when he and Grant, his younger brother, had fished in this little brook for trout, with trousers rolled above the knee and wrecks of hats upon their heads.

"Any trout left?" he asked.

"Not many. Little fellers." Finding the silence broken, William asked the first question since he met Howard. "Less see: you're a show feller now? B'long to a troupe?"

"Yes, yes; I'm an actor."

"Pay much?"

"Pretty well."

That seemed to end William's curiosity about the matter.

"Ah, there's our old house, ain't it?" Howard broke out, pointing to one of the houses farther up the Coulé. It'll be a surprise to them, won't it?"

"Yep; only they don't live there."

"What! They don't!"

"No."

"Who does?"

"Dutchman."

Howard was silent for some moments. "Who lives on the Dunlap place?"

"'Nother Dutchman."

"Where's Grant living, anyhow?"

"Farther up the Coolly."

"Well, then I'd better get out here, hadn't I?"

"Oh, I'll drive yeh up."

"No, I'd rather walk."

The sun had set, and the Coulé was getting dusk when Howard got out of Mc-Turg's carriage, and set off up the winding lane toward his brother's house. He walked slowly to absorb the coolness and fragrance and color of the hour. The katydids sang a rhythmic song of welcome to him. Fireflies were in the grass. A whippoorwill in the deep of the wood was calling weirdly, and an occasional nighthawk, flying high gave his grating shriek, or hollow boom, suggestive and resounding.

He had been wonderfully successful, and yet had carried into his success as a dramatic author as well as actor a certain puritanism that made him a paradox to his fellows. He was one of those actors who are always in luck, and the best of it was he kept and made use of his luck. Jovial as he appeared, he was inflexible as granite against drink and tobacco. He retained through it all a certain freshness of enjoyment that made him one of the best companions in the profession; and now as he walked on, the hour and the place appealed to him with great power. It seemed to sweep away the life that came between.

How close it all was to him, after all! In his restless life, surrounded by the glare of electric lights, painted canvas, hot colors, creak of machinery, mock trees, stones, and brooks, he had not lost but gained appreciation for the coolness, quiet and low tones, the shyness of the wood and field.

In the farm-house ahead of him a light was shining as he peered ahead, and his heart gave another painful movement. His brother was awaiting him there, and his mother, whom he had not seen for ten years and who had grown unable to write. And when Grant wrote, which had been more and more seldom of late, his letters had been cold and curt.

He began to feel that in the pleasure and excitement of his life he had grown away from his mother and brother. Each summer he had said, "Well, now I'll go home *this* year sure." But a new play to be produced, or a yachting trip, or a tour of Europe, had put the home-coming off; and now it was with a distinct consciousness of neglect of duty that he walked up to the fence and looked into the yard, where William had told him his brother lived.

It was humble enough—a small white house, story-and-a-half structure, with a wing, set in the midst of a few locust-trees; a small drab-colored barn, with a sagging ridge-pole; a barnyard full of mud, in which a few cows were standing, fighting the flies and waiting to be milked. An old man was pumping water at the well; the pigs were squealing from a pen near by; a child was crying.

Instantly the beautiful, peaceful valley was forgotten. A sickening chill struck into Howard's soul as he looked at it all. In the dim light he could see a figure milking a cow. Leaving his valise at the gate, he entered, and walked up to the old man, who had finished pumping and was about to go to feed the hogs.

"Good-evening," Howard began. "Does Mr. Grant McLane live here?"

"Yes, sir, he does. He's right over there milkin'."

"I'll go over there an—"

"Don't b'lieve I would. It's darn muddy over there. It's been turrible rainy. He'll be done in a minute, anyway."

"Very well; I'll wait."

As he waited, he could hear a woman's fretful voice, and the impatient jerk and jar of kitchen things, indicative of ill-temper or worry. The longer he stood absorbing this farm-scene, with all its sordidness, dulness, triviality, and its endless drudgeries, the lower his heart sank. All the joy of the home-coming was gone, when the figure arose from the cow and approached the gate, and put the pail of milk down on the platform by the pump.

"Good-evening," said Howard, out of the dusk.

Grant stared a moment. "Good-evening."

Howard knew the voice, though it was older and deeper and more sullen. "Don't you know me, Grant? I am Howard."

The man approached him, gazing intently at his face. "You are?" after a pause. "Well, I'm glad to see yeh, but I can't shake hands. That damned cow had laid down in the mud."

They stood and looked at each other. Howard's cuffs, collar, and shirt, alien in their elegance, showed through the dusk, and a glint of light shot out from the jewel of his necktie, as the light from the house caught it at the right angle. As they gazed in silence at each other, Howard divined something of the hard, bitter feeling which came into Grant's heart, as he stood there, ragged, ankle-deep in muck, his sleeves rolled up, a shapeless old straw hat on his head.

The gleam of Howard's white hands angered him. When he spoke, it was in a hard, gruff tone, full of rebellion.

"Well, go in the house and set down. I'll be in soon's I strain the milk and wash the dirt off my hands."

"But mother—"

"She's 'round somewhere. Just knock on the door under the porch round there."

Howard went slowly around the corner of the house, past a vilely smelling rain-barrel, toward the west. A gray-haired woman was sitting in a rocking-chair on the porch, her hands in her lap, her eyes fixed on the faintly yellow sky, against which the hills stood dim purple silhouettes, and the locust-trees were etched as fine as lace. There was sorrow, resignation, and a sort of dumb despair in her attitude.

Howard stood, his throat swelling till it seemed as if he would suffocate. This was his mother—the woman who bore him, the being who had taken her life in her hand for him; and he, in his excited and pleasurable life, had neglected her!

He stepped into the faint light before her. She turned and looked at him without fear. "Mother!" he said. She uttered one little, breathing, gasping cry, called his name, rose, and stood still. He bounded up the steps and took her in his arms.

"Mother! Dear old mother!"

In the silence, almost painful, which followed, an angry woman's voice could be heard inside: "I don't care. I ain't goin' to wear myself out fer him. He c'n eat out here with us, or else—"

Mrs. McLane began speaking. "Oh, I've longed to see yeh, Howard. I was afraid you wouldn't come till—too late."

"What do you mean, mother? Ain't you well?"

"I don't seem to be able to do much now 'cept sit around and knit a little. I tried to pick some berries the other day, and I got so dizzy I had to give it up."

"You mustn't work. You *needn't* work. Why didn't you write to me how you were?" Howard asked in an agony of remorse.

"Well, we felt as if you probably had all you could do to take care of yourself."

"Are you married, Howard?"

"No, mother; and there ain't any excuse for me—not a bit," he said, dropping back into her colloquialisms. "I'm ashamed when I think of how long it's been since I saw you. I could have come."

"It don't matter now," she interrupted gently. "It's the way things go. Our boys grow up and leave us."

"Well, come in to supper," said Grant's ungracious voice from the doorway. "Come, mother."

Mrs. McLane moved with difficulty. Howard sprang to her aid, and leaning on his arm she went through the little sitting-room, which was unlighted, out into the kitchen, where the supper-table stood near the cook-stove.

"How, this is my wife," said Grant, in a cold, peculiar tone.

Howard bowed toward a remarkably handsome young woman, on whose forehead was a scowl, which did not change as she looked at him and the old lady.

"Set down, anywhere," was the young woman's cordial invitation.

Howard sat down next his mother, and facing the wife, who had a small, fretful child in her arms. At Howard's left was the old man, Lewis. The supper was spread upon a gay-colored oilcloth, and consisted of a pan of milk, set in the midst, with bowls at each plate. Beside the pan was a dipper and a large plate of bread, and at one end of the table was a dish of fine honey.

A boy of about fourteen leaned upon the table, his bent shoulders making him look like an old man. His hickory shirt, like that of Grant, was still wet with sweat, and discolored here and there with grease, or green from grass. His hair, freshly wet and combed, was smoothed away from his face, and shone in the light of the kerosene lamp. As he ate, he stared at Howard, as if he would make an inventory of each thread of the visitor's clothing.

"Did I look like that at his age?" thought Howard.

"You see we live jest about the same's ever," said Grant, as they began eating, speaking with a grim, almost challenging inflection.

The two brothers studied each other curiously, as they talked of neighborhood scenes. Howard seemed incredibly elegant and handsome to them all, with his rich, soft clothing, his spotless linen, and his exquisite enunciation and ease of speech. He had always been "smooth-spoken," and he had become "elegantly persuasive," as his friends said of him, and it was a large factor in his success.

Every detail of the kitchen, the heat, the flies buzzing aloft, the poor furniture, the dress of the people—all smote him like the lash of a wire whip. His brother was a man of great character. He could see that now. His deep-set, gray eyes and rugged face showed at thirty a man of great natural ability. He had more of the Scotch in his face than Howard, and he looked much older.

He was dressed, like the old man and the boy, in a checked shirt without vest. His suspenders, once gay-colored, had given most of their color to his shirt, and had marked irregular broad bands of pink and brown and green over his shoulders. His hair was uncombed, merely pushed away from his face. He wore a mustache only, though his face was covered with a week's growth of beard. His face was rather gaunt, and was brown as leather.

Howard could not eat much. He was disturbed by his mother's strange silence and oppression, and sickened by the long-drawn gasps with which the old man ate his bread and milk, and by the way the boy ate. He had his knife gripped tightly in his fist, knuckles up, and was scooping honey upon his bread.

The baby, having ceased to be afraid, was curious, gazing silently at the stranger.

"Hello, little one! Come and see your uncle. Eh? Course 'e will," cooed Howard in the attempt to escape the depressing atmosphere. The little one listened to his inflections as a kitten does, and at last lifted its arms in sign of surrender.

The mother's face cleared up a little. "I declare, she wants to go to you."

"Course she does. Dogs and kittens always come to me when I call 'em. Why shouldn't my own niece come?"

He took the little one and began walking up and down the kitchen with her, while she pulled at his beard and nose. "I ought to have you, my lady, in my new comedy. You'd bring down the house."

"You don't mean to say you put babies on the stage, Howard," said his mother in surprise.

"Oh, yes. Domestic comedy must have a baby these days."

"Well, that's another way of makin' a livin', sure," said Grant. The baby had cleared the atmosphere a little. "I s'pose you fellers make a pile of money."

"Sometimes we make a thousand a week; oftener we don't."

"A thousand dollars!" They all stared.

"A thousand dollars sometimes, and then lose it all the next week in another town. The dramatic business is a good deal like gambling—you take your chances."

"I wish you weren't in it, Howard. I don't like to have my son—"

"I wish I was in somethin' that paid better'n farmin'. Anything under God's heavens is better'n farmin'," said Grant.

"No, I ain't laid up much," Howard went on, as if explaining why he hadn't helped them. "Costs me a good deal to live, and I need about ten thousand dollars leeway to work on. I've made a good living, but I—I ain't made any money."

Grant looked at him, darkly meditative.

Howard went on:

"How'd ye come to sell the old farm? I was in hopes—"

"How'd we come to sell it?" said Grant with terrible bitterness. "We had something on it that didn't leave anything to sell. You probably don't remember anything about it, but there was a mortgage on it that eat us up in just four years by the almanac. 'Most killed mother to leave it. We wrote to you for money, but I don't s'pose you remember *that*."

"No, you didn't."

"Yes, I did."

"When was it? I don't—why, it's—I never received it. It must have been that summer I went with Rob Manning to Europe." Howard put the baby down and faced his brother. "Why, Grant, you didn't think I refused to help?"

"Well, it looked that way. We never heard a word from yeh all summer, and when y' did write, it was all about yerself'n plays 'n things we didn't know anything about. I swore to God I'd never write to you again, and I won't."

"But, good heavens! I never got it."

"Suppose you didn't. You might of known we were poor as Job's off-ox.[5] Everybody is that earns a living. We fellers on the farm have to earn a livin' for ourselves and you fellers that don't work. I don't blame yeh. I'd do it if I could."

"Grant, don't talk so! Howard didn't realize—"

"I tell yeh I don't blame 'im. Only I don't want him to come the brotherly business over me, after livin' as he has—that's all." There was a bitter accusation in the man's voice.

Howard leaped to his feet, his face twitching. "By God, I'll go back tomorrow morning!" he threatened.

"Go, an' be damned! I don't care what yeh do," Grant growled, rising and going out.

"Boys," called the mother, piteously, "it's terrible to see you quarrel."

"But I'm not to blame, mother," cried Howard in a sickness that made him white as chalk. "The man is a savage. I came home to help you all, not to quarrel."

"Grant's got one o' his fits on," said the young wife, speaking for the first time. "Don't pay any attention to him. He'll be all right in the morning."

"If it wasn't for you, mother, I'd leave now, and never see that savage again."

---

[5]The Old Testament figure Job traditionally possesses qualities of poverty and patience. With reference to a team of oxen, the *off-ox* would be the one on the far side, the one of less use.

He lashed himself up and down in the room, in horrible disgust and hate of his brother and of this home in his heart. He remembered his tender anticipations of the home-coming with a kind of self-pity and disgust. This was his greeting!

He went to bed, to toss about on the hard, straw-filled mattress in the stuffy little best room. Tossing, writhing under the bludgeoning of his brother's accusing inflections, a dozen times he said, with a half-articulate snarl:

"He can go to hell! I'll not try to do anything more for him. I don't care if he *is* my brother; he has no right to jump on me like that. On the night of my return, too. My God! he is a brute, a savage!"

He thought of the presents in his trunk and valise which he couldn't show to him that night, after what had been said. He had intended to have such a happy evening of it, such a tender reunion! It was to be so bright and cheery!

In the midst of his cursings, his hot indignation, would come visions of himself in his own modest rooms. He seemed to be yawning and stretching in his beautiful bed, the sun shining in, his books, foils, pictures around him, to say good-morning and tempt him to rise, while the squat little clock on the mantel struck eleven warningly.

He could see the olive walls, the unique copper-and-crimson arabesque frieze (his own selection), and the delicate draperies; an open grate full of glowing coals, to temper the sea-winds; and in the midst of it, between a landscape by Enneking and an Indian in a canoe in a cañon, by Brush, he saw a sombre landscape by a master greater than Millet,[6] a melancholy subject, treated with pitiless fidelity.

A farm in the valley! Over the mountains swept jagged, gray, angry, sprawling clouds, sending a freezing, thin drizzle of rain, as they passed, upon a man following a plough. The horses had a sullen and weary look, and their manes and tails streamed sidewise in the blast. The ploughman clad in a ragged gray coat, with uncouth, muddy boots upon his feet, walked with his head inclined towards the sleet, to shield his face from the cold and sting of it. The soil rolled away, black and sticky and with a dull sheen upon it. Near by, a boy with tears on his cheeks was watching cattle, a dog seated near, his back to the gale.

As he looked at this picture, his heart softened. He looked down at the sleeve of his soft and fleecy night-shirt, at his white, rounded arm, muscular yet fine as a woman's, and when he looked for the picture it was gone. Then came again the assertive odor of stagnant air, laden with camphor; he felt the springless bed under him, and caught dimly a few soap-advertising lithographs on the walls. He thought of his brother, in his still more inhospitable bedroom, disturbed by the child, condemned to rise at five o'clock and begin

[6]John Joseph Enneking (1841–1916), American painter noted for landscapes; George de Forest Brush (1855–1941), American painter of American Indian subjects; Jean François Millet (1814–1875), French painter known for realistic portrayal of peasant life.

another day's pitiless labor. His heart shrank and quivered, and the tears started to his eyes.

"I forgive him, poor fellow! He's not to blame."

II

He woke, however, with a dull, languid pulse, and an oppressive melancholy on his heart. He looked around the little room, clean enough, but oh, how poor! how barren! Cold plaster walls, a cheap wash-stand, a wash-set of three pieces, with a blue band around each; the windows, rectangular, and fitted with fantastic green shades.

Outside he could hear the bees humming. Chickens were merrily moving about. Cow-bells far up the road were sounding irregularly. A jay came by and yelled an insolent reveille, and Howard sat up. He could hear nothing in the house but the rattle of pans on the back side of the kitchen. He looked at his watch and saw it was half-past seven. His brother was in the field by this time, after milking, currying the horses, and eating breakfast—had been at work two hours and a half.

He dressed himself hurriedly in a négligé shirt with a windsor scarf, light-colored, serviceable trousers with a belt, russet shoes and a tennis hat—a knock-about costume, he considered. His mother, good soul, thought it a special suit put on for her benefit, and admired it through her glasses.

He kissed her with a bright smile, nodded at Laura the young wife, and tossed the baby, all in a breath, and with the manner as he himself saw, of the returned captain in the war-dramas of the day.

"Been to breakfast?" He frowned reproachfully. "Why didn't you call me? I wanted to get up, just as I used to, at sunrise."

"We thought you was tired, and so we didn't—"

"Tired! Just wait till you see me help Grant pitch hay or something. Hasn't finished his haying, has he?"

"No, I guess not. He will to-day if it don't rain again."

"Well, breakfast is all ready—Howard," said Laura, hesitating a little on his name.

"Good! I am ready for it. Bacon and eggs, as I'm a jay![7] Just what I was wanting. I was saying to myself: 'Now if they'll only get bacon and eggs and hot biscuits and honey—' Oh, say, mother, I heard the bees humming this morning; same noise they used to make when I was a boy, exactly. Must be the same bees.—Hey, you young rascal! come here and have some breakfast with your uncle."

"I never saw her take to any one so quick," Laura smiled. Howard noticed her in particular for the first time. She had on a clean calico dress and a gingham apron, and she looked strong and fresh and handsome. Her head was intellectual, her eyes full of power. She seemed anxious to remove the impression of her unpleasant looks and words the night before. Indeed it would have been hard to resist Howard's sunny good-nature.

[7]A country person.

The baby laughed and crowed. The old mother could not take her dim eyes off the face of her son, but sat smiling at him as he ate and rattled on. When he rose from the table at last, after eating heartily and praising it all, he said, with a smile:

"Well, now I'll just telephone down to the express and have my trunk brought up. I've got a few little things in there you'll enjoy seeing. But this fellow," indicating the baby, "I didn't take into account. But never mind; Uncle How'll make that all right."

"You ain't goin' to lay it up agin Grant, be you, my son?" Mrs. McLane faltered, as they went out into the best room.

"Of course not! He didn't mean it. Now can't you send word down and have my trunk brought up? Or shall I have to walk down?"

"I guess I'll see somebody goin' down," said Laura.

"All right. Now for the hay-field," he smiled, and went out into the glorious morning.

The circling hills the same, yet not the same as at night. A cooler, tenderer, more subdued cloak of color upon them. Far down the valley a cool, deep, impalpable, blue mist lay, under which one divined the river ran, under its elms and basswoods and wild grapevines. On the shaven slopes of the hills cattle and sheep were feeding, their cries and bells coming to the ear with a sweet suggestiveness. There was something immemorial in the sunny slopes dotted with red and brown and gray cattle.

Walking toward the haymakers, Howard felt a twinge of pain and distrust. Would he ignore it all and smile—

He stopped short. He had not seen Grant smile in so long—he couldn't quite see him smiling. He had been cold and bitter for years. When he came up to them, Grant was pitching on; the old man was loading, and the boy was raking after.

"Good-morning," Howard cried cheerily. The old man nodded, the boy stared. Grant growled something, without looking up. These "finical" things of saying good-morning and good-night are not much practised in such homes as Grant McLane's.

"Need some help? I'm ready to take a hand. Got on my regimentals this morning."

Grant looked at him a moment.

"You look like it."

"Gimme a hold on that fork, and I'll show you. I'm not so soft as I look, now you bet."

He laid hold upon the fork in Grant's hands, who released it sullenly and stood back sneering. Howard stuck the fork into the pile in the old way, threw his left hand to the end of the polished handle, brought it down into the hollow of his thigh, and laid out his strength till the handle bent like a bow. "Oop she rises!" he called laughingly, as the whole pile began slowly to rise, and finally rolled upon the high load.

"Oh, I ain't forgot how to do it," he laughed, as he looked around at the boy, who was studying the jacket and hat with a devouring gaze.

Grant was studying him too, but not in admiration.

"I shouldn't say you had," said the old man, tugging at the forkful.

"Mighty funny to come out here and do a little of this. But if you had to come here and do it all the while, you wouldn't look so white and soft in the hands," Grant said, as they moved on to another pile. "Give me that fork. You'll be spoiling your fine clothes."

"Oh, these don't matter. They're made for this kind of thing."

"Oh, are they? I guess I'll dress in that kind of a rig. What did that shirt cost? I need one."

"Six dollars a pair; but then it's old."

"And them pants," he pursued; "they cost six dollars too, didn't they?"

Howard's face darkened. He saw his brother's purpose. He resented it. "They cost fifteen dollars, if you want to know, and the shoes cost six-fifty. This ring on my cravat cost sixty dollars and the suit I had on last night cost eighty-five. My suits are made by Breckstein, on Fifth Avenue and Twentieth Street, if you want to patronize him," he ended brutally, spurred on by the sneer in his brother's eyes. "I'll introduce you."

"Good idea," said Grant, with a forced, mocking smile. "I need just such a getup for haying and corn-ploughing. Singular I never thought of it. Now my pants cost eighty-five cents, s'penders fifteen, hat twenty, shoes one-fifty; stockin's I don't bother about."

He had his brother at a disadvantage, and he grew fluent and caustic as he went on, almost changing places with Howard, who took the rake out of the boy's hands and followed, raking up the scatterings.

"Singular we fellers here are discontented and mulish, ain't it? Singular we don't believe your letters when you write, sayin', 'I just about make a live of it'? Singular we think the country's goin' to hell, we fellers, in a two-dollar suit, wadin' around in the mud or sweatin' around in the hay-field, while you fellers lay around New York and smoke and wear good clothes and toady to millionaires?"

Howard threw down the rake and folded his arms. "My God! you're enough to make a man forget the same mother bore us!"

"I guess it wouldn't take much to make you forget that. You ain't put much thought on me nor her for ten years."

The old man cackled, the boy grinned, and Howard, sick and weak with anger and sorrow, turned away and walked down toward the brook. He had tried once more to get near his brother, and had failed. Oh, God! how miserably, pitiably! The hot blood gushed all over him as he thought of the shame and disgrace of it.

He, a man associating with poets, artists, sought after by brilliant women, accustomed to deference even from such people, to be sneered at, outfaced, shamed, shoved aside, by a man in a stained hickory shirt and patched overalls, and that man his brother! He lay down on the bright grass, with the sheep all around him, and writhed and groaned with the agony and despair of it.

And worst of all, underneath it was a consciousness that Grant was right in distrusting him. He *had* neglected him; he *had* said, "I guess they're getting along all right." He had put them behind him when the invitation to spend summer on the Mediterranean or in the Adirondacks,[8] came.

"What can I do? What can I do?" he groaned.

The sheep nibbled the grass near him, the jays called pertly, "Shame, shame," a quail piped somewhere on the hillside, and the brook sung a soft, soothing melody that took away at last the sharp edge of his pain, and he sat up and gazed down the valley, bright with the sun and apparently filled with happy and prosperous people.

Suddenly a thought seized him. He stood up so suddenly the sheep fled in affright. He leaped the brook, crossed the flat, and began searching in the bushes on the hillside. "Hurrah!" he said, with a smile.

He had found an old road which he used to travel when a boy—a road that skirted the edge of the valley, now grown up to brush, but still passable for footmen. As he ran lightly along down the beautiful path, under oaks and hickories, past masses of poison-ivy, under hanging grapevines, through clumps of splendid hazel-nut bushes loaded with great sticky, rough, green burs, his heart threw off part of its load.

How it all came back to him! How many days, when the autumn sun burned the frost off the bushes, had he gathered hazel-nuts here with his boy and girl friends—Hugh and Shelley McTurg, Rome Sawyer, Orrin McIlvaine, and the rest! What had become of them all? How he had forgotten them!

This thought stopped him again, and he fell into a deep muse, leaning against an oak-tree and gazing into the vast fleckless space above. The thrilling, inscrutable mystery of life fell upon him like a blinding light. Why was he living in the crush and thunder and mental unrest of a great city, while his companions, seemingly his equals, in powers, were milking cows, making butter, and growing corn and wheat in the silence and drear monotony of the farm?

His boyish sweethearts! their names came back to his ear now, with a dull, sweet sound as of faint bells. He saw their faces, their pink sunbonnets tipped back upon their necks, their brown ankles flying with the swift action of the scurrying partridge. His eyes softened; he took off his hat. The sound of the wind and the leaves moved him almost to tears.

A woodpecker gave a shrill, high-keyed, sustained cry. "Ki, ki, ki!" and he started from his revery, the dapples of sun and shade falling upon his lithe figure as he hurried on down the path.

He came at last to a field of corn that ran to the very wall of a large weather-beaten house, the sight of which made his breathing quicker. It was the place where he was born. The mystery of his life began there. In the branches of those poplar and hickory trees he had swung and sung in the rushing breeze, fearless as a squirrel. Here was the brook where, like a larger

---

[8]Mountains in northeastern New York.

Kildee, he with Grant had waded after craw-fish, or had stolen upon some wary trout, rough-cut pole in hand.

Seeing someone in the garden, he went down along the corn-row through the rustling ranks of green leaves. An old woman was picking berries, a squat and shapeless figure.

"Good-morning," he called cheerily.

"Morgen,"[9] she said, looking up at him with a startled and very red face. She was German in every line of her body.

"Ich bin Herr McLane,"[10] he said, after a pause.

"So?"[11] she replied, with a questioning inflection.

"Yah; ich bin Herr Grant's Bruder."[12]

"Ach, so!"[13] she said, with a downward inflection. "Ich no spick Inglish. No spick Inglis."

"Ich bin durstig,"[14] he said. Leaving her pans, she went with him to the house, which was what he wanted to see.

"Ich bin hier geboren."[15]

"Ach, so!" She recognized the little bit of sentiment, and said some sentences in German whose general meaning was sympathy. She took him to the cool cellar where the spring had been trained to run into a tank containing pans of cream and milk, she gave him a cool draught from a large tin cup, and then at his request they went upstairs. The house was the same, but somehow seemed cold and empty. It was clean and sweet, but it had so little evidence of being lived in. The old part, which was built of logs, was used as best room, and modelled after the best rooms of the neighboring Yankee homes, only it was emptier, without the cabinet organ and the rag-carpet and the chromos.[16]

The old fireplace was bricked up and plastered—the fireplace beside which in the far-off days he had lain on winter nights, to hear his uncles tell tales of hunting, or to hear them play the violin, great dreaming giants that they were.

The old woman went out and left him sitting there, the centre of a swarm of memories coming and going like so many ghostly birds and butterflies.

A curious heartache and listlessness, a nerveless mood came on him. What was it worth, anyhow—success? Struggle, strife, trampling on some one else. His play crowding out some other poor fellow's hope. The hawk eats the partridge, the partridge eats the flies and bugs, the bugs eat each other and the hawk, when he in his turn is shot by man. So, in the world of business, the life of one man seemed to him to be drawn from the life of another man, each success to spring from other failures.

---

[9]German: "Morning."
[10]German: "I am Mr. McLane."
[11]German: "Indeed?"
[12]Howard's German: "Yes; I am Mr. Grant's brother."
[13]German: "Oh, I see!"

[14]German: "I am thirsty."
[15]Howard's German: "I was born here."
[16]Short form of *chromolithographs*, pictures printed in colors from lithographic stones or plates.

He was like a man from whom all motives had been withdrawn. He was sick, sick to the heart. Oh, to be a boy again! An ignorant baby, pleased with a block and string, with no knowledge and no care of the great unknown! To lay his head again on his mother's bosom and rest! To watch the flames on the hearth!—

Why not? Was not that the very thing to do? To buy back the old farm? It would cripple him a little for the next season, but he could do it. Think of it! To see his mother back in the old home, with the fireplace restored, the old furniture in the sitting-room around her, and fine new things in the parlor!

His spirits rose again. Grant couldn't stand out when he brought to him a deed of the farm. Surely his debt would be cancelled when he had seen them all back in the wide old kitchen. He began to plan and to dream. He went to the windows, and looked out on the yard to see how much it had changed.

He'd build a new barn, and buy them a new carriage. His heart glowed again, and his lips softened into their usual feminine grace—lips a little full and falling easily into curves.

The old German woman came in at length, bringing some cakes and a bowl of milk, smiling broadly and hospitably as she waddled forward.

"Ach! Goot!" he said, smacking his lips over the pleasant draught.

"Wo ist ihre goot mann?"[17] he inquired, ready for business.

III

When Grant came in at noon Mrs. McLane met him at the door, with a tender smile on her face.

"Where's Howard, Grant?"

"I don't know," he replied in a tone that implied "I don't care."

The dim eyes clouded with quick tears.

"Ain't you seen him?"

"Not since nine o'clock."

"Where d'you think he is?"

"I tell yeh I don't know. He'll take care of himself; don't worry."

He flung off his hat and plunged into the washbasin. His shirt was wet with sweat and covered with dust of the hay and fragments of leaves. He splashed his burning face with the water, paying no further attention to his mother. She spoke again, very gently, in reproof:

"Grant, why do you stand out against Howard so?"

"I don't stand out against him," he replied harshly, pausing with the towel in his hands. His eyes were hard and piercing. "But if he expects me to gush over his coming back, he's fooled, that's all. He's left us to paddle our own canoe all this while, and, so far as *I'm* concerned, he can leave us alone hereafter. He looked out for his precious hide mighty well, and now

[17]Howard's German: "Where is your good husband?"

he comes back here to play big-gun and pat us on the head. I don't propose to let him come that over me."

Mrs. McLane knew too well the temper of her son to say any more, but she inquired about Howard of the old hired man.

"He went off down the valley. He 'n' Grant had s'm *words*, and he pulled out down toward the old farm. That's the last I see of 'im."

Laura took Howard's part at the table. "Pity you can't be decent," she said, brutally direct as usual. "You treat Howard as if he was a—a—I do' know what."

"Will you let me alone?"

"No, I won't. If you think I'm going to set by an' agree to your bullyrag-gin[18] him, you're mistaken. It's a shame! You're mad 'cause he's succeeded and you ain't. He ain't to blame for his brains. If you and I'd had any, we'd 'a 'succeeded too. It ain't our fault and it ain't his; so what's the use?"

There was a look came into Grant's face that the wife knew. It meant bitter and terrible silence. He ate his dinner without another word.

It was beginning to cloud up. A thin, whitish, all-pervasive vapor which meant rain was dimming the sky, and he forced his hands to their utmost during the afternoon in order to get most of the down hay in before the rain came. He was pitching hay up into the barn when Howard came by just before one o'clock.

It was windless there. The sun fell through the white mist with undiminished fury, and the fragrant hay sent up a breath that was hot as an oven-draught. Grant was a powerful man, and there was something majestic in his action as he rolled the huge flakes of hay through the door. The sweat poured from his face like rain, and he was forced to draw his dripping sleeve across his face to clear away the blinding sweat that poured into his eyes.

Howard stood and looked at him in silence, remembering how often he had worked there in that furnace-heat, his muscles quivering, cold chills running over his flesh, red shadows dancing before his eyes.

His mother met him at the door, anxiously, but smiled as she saw his pleasant face and cheerful eyes.

"You're a little late, m' son."

Howard spent most of the afternoon sitting with his mother on the porch, or under the trees, lying sprawled out like a boy, resting at times with sweet forgetfulness of the whole world, but feeling a dull pain whenever he remembered the stern, silent man pitching hay in the hot sun on the torrid side of the barn.

His mother did not say anything about the quarrel; she feared to reopen it. She talked mainly of old times in a gentle monotone of reminiscence, while he listened, looking up into her patient face.

The heat slowly lessened as the sun sank down toward the dun clouds rising like a more distant and majestic line of mountains beyond the western hills. The sound of cow-bells came irregularly to the ear, and the voices

---

[18]Bullying.

and sounds of the haying-fields had a jocund, thrilling effect on the ear of the city-dweller.

He was very tender. Everything conspired to make him simple, direct, and honest.

"Mother, if you'll only forgive me for staying away so long, I'll surely come to see you every summer."

She had nothing to forgive. She was so glad to have him there at her feet—her great, handsome, successful boy! She could only love him and enjoy him every moment of the precious days. If Grant would only reconcile himself to Howard! That was the great thorn in her flesh.

Howard told her how he had succeeded.

"It was luck, mother. First I met Cooke, and he introduced me to Jake Saulsman of Chicago. Jake asked me to go to New York with him, and—I don't know why—took a fancy to me some way. He introduced me to a lot of the fellows in New York, and they all helped me along. I did nothing to merit it. Everybody helps me. Anybody can succeed in that way."

The doting mother thought it not at all strange that they all helped him.

At the supper-table Grant was gloomily silent, ignoring Howard completely. Mrs. McLane sat and grieved silently, not daring to say a word in protest. Laura and the baby tried to amuse Howard, and under cover of their talk the meal was eaten.

The boy fascinated Howard. He "sawed wood"[19] with a rapidity and uninterruptedness which gave alarm. He had the air of coaling up for a long voyage.

"At that age," Howard thought, "I must have gripped my knife in my right hand so, and poured my tea into my saucer so. I must have buttered and bit into a huge slice of bread just so, and chewed at it with a smacking sound in just that way. I must have gone to the length of scooping up honey with my knife-blade."

It was magically, mystically beautiful over all this squalor and toil and bitterness, from five till seven—a moving hour. Again the falling sun streamed in broad banners across the valleys; again the blue mist lay far down the Coulé over the river; the cattle called from the hills in the moistening, sonorous air; the bells came in a pleasant tangle of sound; the air pulsed with the deepening chorus of katydids and other nocturnal singers.

Sweet and deep as the very springs of his life was all this to the soul of the elder brother; but in the midst of it, the younger man, in ill-smelling clothes and great boots that chafed his feet, went out to milk the cows—on whose legs the flies and mosquitoes swarmed, bloated with blood,—to sit by the hot side of the cow and be lashed with her tail as she tried frantically to keep the savage insects from eating her raw.

"The poet who writes of milking the cows does it from the hammock, looking on," Howard soliloquized, as he watched the old man Lewis racing around the filthy yard after one of the young heifers that had kicked over

---

[19]To focus on one's own business; here, of course, on the business of eating.

the pail in her agony with the flies and was unwilling to stand still and be eaten alive.

"So, *so!* you beast!" roared the old man, as he finally cornered the shrinking, nearly frantic creature.

"Don't you want to look at the garden?" asked Mrs. McLane of Howard; and they went out among the vegetables and berries.

The bees were coming home heavily laden and crawling slowly into the hives. The level, red light streamed through the trees, blazed along the grass, and lighted a few old-fashioned flowers into red and gold flame. It was beautiful, and Howard looked at it through his half-shut eyes as the painters do, and turned away with a sigh at the sound of blows where the wet and grimy men were assailing the frantic cows.

"There's Wesley with your trunk," Mrs. McLane said, recalling him to himself.

Wesley helped him carry the trunk in, and waved off thanks.

"Oh, that's all right," he said; and Howard knew the Western man too well to press the matter of pay.

As he went in an hour later and stood by the trunk, the dull ache came back into his heart. How he had failed! It seemed like a bitter mockery now to show his gifts.

Grant had come in from his work, and with his feet released from his chafing boots, in his wet shirt and milk-splashed overalls, sat at the kitchen table reading a newspaper which he held close to a small kerosene lamp. He paid no attention to any one. His attitude, curiously like his father's, was perfectly definite to Howard. It meant that from that time forward there were to be no words of any sort between them. It meant that they were no longer brothers, not even acquaintances. "How inexorable that face!" thought Howard.

He turned sick with disgust and despair, and would have closed his trunk without showing any of the presents, only for the childish expectancy of his mother and Laura.

"Here's something for you, mother," he said, assuming a cheerful voice, as he took a fold of fine silk from the trunk and held it up. "All the way from Paris."

He laid it on his mother's lap and stooped and kissed her, and then turned hastily away to hide the tears that came to his own eyes as he saw her keen pleasure.

"And here's a parasol for Laura. I don't know how I came to have that in here. And here's General Grant's[20] autobiography for his namesake," he said, with an effort at carelessness, and waited to hear Grant rise.

"Grant, won't you come in?" asked his mother, quaveringly.

Grant did not reply nor move. Laura took the handsome volumes out and laid them beside him on the table. He simply pushed them one side and went on with his reading.

[20]General Ulysses S. Grant (1822–1885), commander-in-chief of the U.S. Army in the Civil War, became the 18th U.S. President (1869–1877).

Again that horrible anger swept hot as flame over Howard. He could have cursed him. His hands shook as he handed out other presents to his mother and Laura and the baby. He tried to joke.

"I didn't know how old the baby was, so she'll have to grow to some of these things."

But the pleasure was all gone for him and for the rest. His heart swelled almost to a feeling of pain as he looked at his mother. There she sat with the presents in her lap. The shining silk came too late for her. It threw into appalling relief her age, her poverty, her work-weary frame. "My God!" he almost cried aloud, "how little it would have taken to lighten her life!"

Upon this moment, when it seemed as if he could endure no more, came the smooth voice of William McTurg:

"Hello, folkses!"

"Hello, Uncle Bill! Come in."

"That's what we came for," laughed a woman's voice.

"Is that you, Rose?" asked Laura.

"It's me—Rose," replied the laughing girl, as she bounced into the room and greeted everybody in a breathless sort of way.

"You don't mean little Rosy?"

"Big Rosy now," said William.

Howard looked at the handsome girl and smiled, saying in a nasal sort of tone, "Wal, wal! Rosy, how you've growed since I saw yeh!"

"Oh, look at all this purple and fine linen! Am I left out?"

Rose was a large girl of twenty-five or there-abouts, and was called an old maid. She radiated good-nature from every line of her buxom self. Her black eyes were full of drollery, and she was on the best of terms with Howard at once. She had been a teacher, but that did not prevent her from assuming a peculiar directness of speech. Of course they talked about old friends.

"Where's Rachel?" Howard inquired. Her smile faded away.

"Shellie married Orrin McIlvaine. They're way out in Dakota. Shellie's havin' a hard row of stumps."

There was a little silence.

"And Tommy?"

"Gone West. Most all the boys have gone West. That's the reason there's so many old maids."

"You don't mean to say—"

"I don't *need* to say—I'm an old maid. Lots of the girls are."

"It don't pay to marry these days."

"Are you married?"

"Not *yet*." His eyes lighted up again in a humorous way.

"Not yet! That's good! That's the way old maids all talk."

"You don't mean to tell me that no young fellow comes prowling around—"

"Oh, a young Dutchman or Norwegian once in a while. Nobody that counts. Fact is, we're getting like Boston—four women to one man; and when you consider that we're getting more particular each year, the outlook is—well, it's dreadful!"

"It certainly is."

"Marriage is a failure these days for most of us. We can't live on the farm, and can't get a living in the city, and there we are." She laid her hand on his arm. "I declare, Howard, you're the same boy you used to be. I ain't a bit afraid of you, for all your success."

"And you're the same girl? No, I can't say that. It seems to me you've grown more than I have—I don't mean physically, I mean mentally," he explained, as he saw her smile in the defensive way a fleshy girl has, alert to ward off a joke.

They were in the midst of talk. Howard telling one of his funny stories, when a wagon clattered up to the door, and merry voices called loudly:

"Whoa, there, Sampson!"

"Hullo, the house!"

Rose looked at her father with a smile in her black eyes exactly like his. They went to the door.

"Hullo! What's wanted?"

"Grant McLane live here?"

"Yup. Right here."

A moment later there came a laughing, chatting squad of women to the door. Mrs. McLane and Laura stared at each other in amazement. Grant went out-doors.

Rose stood at the door as if she were hostess.

"Come in, Nettie. Glad to see yeh—glad to see yeh! Mrs. McIlvaine, come right in! Take a seat. Make yerself to home, *do!* And Mrs. Peavey! Wal, I never! This must be a surprise-party. Well, I swan! How many more o' ye air they?"

All was confusion, merriment, hand-shakings as Rose introduced them in her roguish way.

"Folks, this is Mr. Howard McLane of New York. He's an actor, but it hain't spoiled him a bit as *I* can see. How, this is Nettie McIlvaine—Wilson that was."

Howard shook hands with Nettie, a tall, plain girl with prominent teeth.

"This is Ma McIlvaine."

"She looks just the same," said Howard, shaking her hand and feeling how hard and work-worn it was.

And so amid bustle, chatter, and invitations "to lay off y'r things an' stay awhile," the women got disposed about the room at last. Those that had rocking-chairs rocked vigorously to and fro to hide their embarrassment. They all talked in loud voices.

Howard felt nervous under this furtive scrutiny. He wished his clothes didn't look so confoundedly dressy. Why didn't he have sense enough to go and buy a fifteen-dollar suit of diagonals for every-day wear.

Rose was the life of the party. Her tongue rattled on in the most delightful way.

"It's all Rose an' Bill's doin's," Mrs. McIlvaine explained. "They told us to come over an' pick up anybody we see on the road. So we did."

Howard winced a little at her familiarity of tone. He couldn't help it for the life of him.

"Well, I wanted to come to-night because I'm going away next week, and I wanted to see how he'd act at a surprise-party again," Rose explained.

"Married, I s'pose," said Mrs. McIlvaine, abruptly.

"No, not yet."

"Good land! Why, y' mus' be thirty-five, How. Must 'a' dis'p'inted y'r mam not to have a young 'un to call 'er granny."

The men came clumping in, talking about haying and horses. Some of the older ones Howard knew and greeted, but the younger ones were mainly too much changed. They were all very ill at ease. Most of them were in compromise dress—something lying between working "rig" and Sunday dress. Most of them had on clean shirts and paper collars, and wore their Sunday coats (thick woollen garments) over rough trousers. All of them crossed their legs at once, and most of them sought the wall and leaned back perilously upon the hind legs of their chairs, eyeing Howard slowly.

For the first few minutes the presents were the subjects of conversation. The women especially spent a good deal of talk upon them.

Howard found himself forced to taking the initiative, so he inquired about the crops and about the farms.

"I see you don't plough the hills as we used to. And reap! *What* a job it ust to be. It makes the hills more beautiful to have them covered with smooth grass and cattle."

There was only dead silence to this touching upon the idea of beauty.

"I s'pose it pays reasonably."

"Not enough to kill," said one of the younger men. "You c'n see that by the houses we live in—that is, most of us. A few that came in early an' got land cheap, like McIlvaine, here—he got a lift that the rest of us can't get."

"I'm a free-trader,[21] myself," said one young fellow, blushing and looking away as Howard turned and said cheerily:

"So 'm I."

The rest seemed to feel that this was a tabooed subject—a subject to be talked out of doors, where one could prance about and yell and do justice to it.

Grant sat silently in the kitchen doorway, not saying a word, not looking at his brother.

"Well, I don't never use hot vinegar for mine," Mrs. McIlvaine was heard to say. "I jest use hot water, an' I rinse 'em out good, and set 'em bottom-side up in the sun. I do' know but what hot vinegar *would* be more cleansin'."

[21]Many western farmers at the time of the story were advocates of free trade, or limitations on tariffs, which they believed artificially increased the prices of many items they required.

Rose had the younger folks in a giggle with a droll telling of a joke on herself.

"How'd y' stop 'em from laffin'?"

"I let 'em laugh. Oh, my school is a disgrace—so one director says. But I like to see children laugh. It broadens their cheeks."

"Yes, that's all hand-work." Laura was showing the baby's Sunday clothes.

"Goodness Peter! How do you find time to do so much?"

"I take time."

Howard, being the lion of the evening, tried his best to be agreeable. He kept near his mother, because it afforded her so much pride and satisfaction, and because he was obliged to keep away from Grant, who had begun to talk to the men. Howard talked mainly about their affairs, but still was forced more and more into talking of life in the city. As he told of the theatre and the concerts, a sudden change fell upon them; they grew sober, and he felt deep down in the hearts of these people a melancholy which was expressed only elusively with little tones or sighs. Their gayety was fitful.

They were hungry for the world, for art—these young people. Discontented and yet hardly daring to acknowledge it; indeed, few of them could have made definite statement of their dissatisfaction. The older people felt it less. They practically said, with a sigh of pathetic resignation:

"Well, I don't expect ever to see these things *now*."

A casual observer would have said, "What a pleasant bucolic—this little surprise-party of welcome!" But Howard with his native ear and eye had no such pleasing illusion. He knew too well these suggestions of despair and bitterness. He knew that, like the smile of the slave, this cheerfulness was self-defence; deep down was another self.

Seeing Grant talking with a group of men over by the kitchen door, he crossed over slowly and stood listening. Wesley Cosgrove—a tall, raw-boned young fellow with a grave, almost tragic face—was saying:

"Of course I ain't. Who is? A man that's satisfied to live as we do is a fool."

"The worst of it is," said Grant, without seeing Howard, "a man can't get out of it during his lifetime, and *I* don't know that he'll have any chance in the next—the speculator'll be there ahead of us."

The rest laughed, but Grant went on grimly:

"Ten years ago Wess, here, could have got land in Dakota pretty easy, but now it's about all a feller's life's worth to try it. I tell you things seem shuttin' down on us fellers."

"Plenty o' land to rent?" suggested some one.

"Yes, in terms that skin a man alive. More than that, farmin' ain't so free a life as it used to be. This cattle-raisin' and butter-makin' makes a nigger of a man. Binds him right down to the grindstone, and he gets nothin' out of it—that's what rubs it in. He simply wallers around in the manure for somebody else. I'd like to know what a man's life is worth who lives as we do? How much higher is it than the lives the niggers used to live?"

These brutally bald words made Howard thrill with emotion like some great tragic poem. A silence fell on the group.

"That's the God's truth, Grant," said young Cosgrove, after a pause.

"A man like me is helpless," Grant was saying. "Just like a fly in a pan of molasses. There ain't any escape for him. The more he tears around the more liable he is to rip his legs off."

"What can he do?"

"Nothin'."

The men listened in silence.

"Oh come, don't talk politics all night!" cried Rose, breaking in. "Come, let's have a dance. Where's that fiddle?"

"Fiddle!" cried Howard, glad of a chance to laugh. "Well, now! Bring out that fiddle. Is it William's?"

"Yes, pap's old fiddle."

"O Gosh! he don't want to hear me play," protested William. "He's heard s' many fiddlers."

"Fiddlers! I've heard a thousand violinists, but not fiddlers. Come, give us 'Honest John.'"

William took the fiddle in his work-calloused and crooked hands and began tuning it. The group at the kitchen door turned to listen, their faces lighting up a little. Rose tried to get a set on the floor.

"Oh, good land!" said some. "We're all tuckered out. What makes you so anxious?"

"She wants a chance to dance with the New Yorker."

"That's it exactly," Rose admitted.

"Wal, if you'd churned and mopped and cooked for hayin' hands as I have today, you wouldn't be so full o' nonsense."

"Oh, bother! Life's short. Come quick, get Bettie out. Come, Wess, never mind your hobby-horse."

By incredible exertion she got a set on the floor, and William got the fiddle in tune. Howard looked across at Wesley, and thought the change in him splendidly dramatic. His face had lighted up into a kind of deprecating, boyish smile. Rose could do anything with him.

William played some of the old tunes that had a thousand associated memories in Howard's brain, memories of harvest-moons, of melon-feasts, and of clear, cold winter nights. As he danced, his eyes filled with a tender, luminous light. He came closer to them all than he had been able to do before. Grant had gone out into the kitchen.

After two or three sets had been danced, the company took seats and could not be stirred again. So Laura and Rose disappeared for a few moments, and returning, served strawberries and cream, which Laura said she "just happened to have in the house."

And then William played again. His fingers, now grown more supple, brought out clearer, firmer tones. As he played, silence fell on these people. The magic of music sobered every face; the women looked older and more care-worn, the men slouched sullenly in their chairs, or leaned back against the wall.

It seemed to Howard as if the spirit of tragedy had entered this house. Music had always been William's unconscious expression of his unsatisfied desires. He was never melancholy except when he played. Then his eyes grew sombre, his drooping face full of shadows.

He played on slowly, softly, wailing Scotch tunes and mournful Irish songs. He seemed to find in the songs of these people, and especially in a wild, sweet, low-keyed negro song, some expression for his indefinable inner melancholy.

He played on, forgetful of everybody, his long beard sweeping the violin, his toil-worn hands marvellously obedient to his will.

At last he stopped, looked up with a faint, deprecating smile, and said with a sigh:

"Well, folkses, time to go home."

The going was quiet. Not much laughing. Howard stood at the door and said good-night to them all, his heart very tender.

"Come and see us," they said.

"I will," he replied cordially. "I'll try and get around to see everybody, and talk over old times, before I go back."

After the wagons had driven out of the yard, Howard turned and put his arm about his mother's neck.

"Tired?"

"A little."

"Well, now good-night. I'm going for a little stroll."

His brain was too active to sleep. He kissed his mother good-night, and went out into the road, his hat in his hand, the cool, moist wind on his hair.

It was very dark, the stars being partly hidden by a thin vapor. On each side the hills rose, every line familiar as the face of an old friend. A whip-poorwill called occasionally from the hillside, and the spasmodic jangle of a bell now and then told of some cow's battle with the mosquitoes.

As he walked, he pondered upon the tragedy he had re-discovered in these people's lives. Out here under the inexorable spaces of the sky, a deep distaste of his own life took possession of him. He felt like giving it all up. He thought of the infinite tragedy of these lives which the world loves to call "peaceful and pastoral." His mind went out in the aim to help them. What could he do to make life better worth living? Nothing. They must live and die practically as he saw them to-night.

And yet he knew this was a mood, and that in a few hours the love and the habit of life would come back upon him and upon them; that he would go back to the city in a few days; that these people would live on and make the best of it.

"I'll make the best of it," he said at last, and his thought came back to his mother and Grant.

IV

The next day was a rainy day; not a shower, but a steady rain—an unusual thing in mid-summer in the West. A cold, dismal day in the fireless, color-less farm-houses. It came to Howard in that peculiar reaction which surely comes during a visit of this character, when thought is a weariness, when the visitor longs for his own familiar walls and pictures and books, and longs to meet his friends, feeling at the same time the tragedy of life which makes friends nearer and more congenial than blood-relations.

Howard ate his breakfast alone, save Baby and Laura, its mother, going about the room. Baby and mother alike insisted on feeding him to death. Already dyspeptic pangs were setting in.

"Now ain't there something more I can—"

"Good heavens! No!" he cried in dismay. "I'm likely to die of dyspepsia now. This honey and milk, and these delicious hot biscuits—"

"I'm afraid it ain't much like the breakfasts you have in the city."

"Well, no, it ain't," he confessed. "But this is the kind a man needs when he lives in the open air."

She sat down opposite him, with her elbows on the table, her chin in her palm, her eyes full of shadows.

"I'd like to go to a city once. I never saw a town bigger'n Lumberville. I've never seen a play, but I've read of 'em in the magazines. It must be won-derful; they say they have wharves and real ships coming up to the wharf, and people getting off and on. How do they do it?"

"Oh, that's too long a story to tell. It's a lot of machinery and paint and canvas. If I told you how it was done, you wouldn't enjoy it so well when you come on and see it."

"Do you ever expect to see *me* in New York?"

"Why, yes. Why not? I expect Grant to come on and bring you all some day, especially Tonikins here. Tonikins, you hear, sir? I expect you to come on you' forf birfday, sure." He tried thus to stop the woman's gloomy confi-dence.

"I hate farm-life," she went on with a bitter inflection. "It's nothing but fret, fret and work the whole time, never going any place, never seeing any-body but a lot of neighbors just as big fools as you are. I spend my time fighting flies and washing dishes and churning. I'm sick of it all."

Howard was silent. What could he say to such an indictment? The ceil-ing swarmed with flies which the cold rain had driven to seek the warmth of the kitchen. The gray rain was falling with a dreary sound outside, and down the kitchen stove-pipe an occasional drop fell on the stove with a hissing, angry sound.

The young wife went on with a deeper note:

"I lived in Lumberville two years, going to school, and I know a little something of what city life is. If I was a man, I bet I wouldn't wear my life out on a farm, as Grant does. I'd get away and I'd do something. I wouldn't care what, but I'd get away."

There was a certain volcanic energy back of all the woman said, that made Howard feel she'd make the attempt. She didn't know that the struggle for a place to stand on this planet was eating the heart and soul out of men and women in the city, just as in the country. But he could say nothing. If he had said in conventional phrase, sitting there in his soft clothing, "We must make the best of it all," the woman could justly have thrown the dish-cloth in his face. He could say nothing.

"I was a fool for ever marrying," she went on, while the baby pushed a chair across the room. "I made a decent living teaching, I was free to come and go, my money was my own. Now I'm tied right down to a churn or a dish-pan, I never have a cent of my own. *He's* growlin' round half the time, and there's no chance of his ever being different."

She stopped with a bitter sob in her throat. She forgot she was talking to her husband's brother. She was conscious only of his sympathy.

As if a great black cloud had settled down upon him, Howard felt it all—the horror, hopelessness, immanent tragedy of it all. The glory of nature, the bounty and splendor of the sky, only made it the more benumbing. He thought of a sentence Millet once wrote:

"I see very well the aureole of the dandelions, and the sun also, far down there behind the hills, flinging his glory upon the clouds. But not alone that—I see in the plains the smoke of the tired horses at the plough, or, on a stony-hearted spot of ground, a back-broken man trying to raise himself upright for a moment to breathe. The tragedy is surrounded by glories—that is no invention of mine."[22]

Howard arose abruptly and went back to his little bedroom, where he walked up and down the floor till he was calm enough to write, and then he sat down and poured it all out to "Dearest Margaret," and his first sentence was this:

"If it were not for you (just to let you know the mood I'm in)—if it were not *for* you, and I had the world in my hands, I'd crush it like a puffball; evil so predominates, suffering is so universal and persistent, happiness so fleeting and so infrequent."

He wrote on for two hours, and by the time he had sealed and directed several letters he felt calmer, but still terribly depressed. The rain was still falling, sweeping down from the half-seen hills, wreathing the wooded peaks with a gray garment of mist, and filling the valley with a whitish cloud.

It fell around the house drearily. It ran down into the tubs placed to catch it, dripped from the mossy pump, and drummed on the upturned milk-pails, and upon the brown and yellow beehives under the maple-trees. The chickens seemed depressed, but the irrepressible bluejay screamed amid it all, with the same insolent spirit, his plumage untarnished by the wet. The barnyard showed a horrible mixture of mud and mire, through which

[22]The quotation is adapted from a letter from Millet to the art historian Alfred Sensier. A somewhat different, fuller version of Millet's letter appears in Alfred Sensier, *Jean-François Millet: Peasant and Painter*, trans. Helena de Kay, 1880, 157–8.

Howard caught glimpses of the men, slumping to and fro without more additional protection than a ragged coat and a shapeless felt hat.

In the sitting-room where his mother sat sewing there was not an ornament, save the etching he had brought. The clock stood on a small shelf, its dial so much defaced that one could not tell the time of day; and when it struck, it was with noticeably disproportionate deliberation, as if it wished to correct any mistake into which the family might have fallen by reason of its illegible dial.

The paper on the walls showed the first concession of the Puritans to the Spirit of Beauty, and was made up of a heterogeneous mixture of flowers of unheard-of shapes and colors, arranged in four different ways along the wall. There were no books, no music, and only a few newspapers in sight—a bare, blank, cold, drab-colored shelter from the rain, not a home. Nothing cosey, nothing heart-warming; a grim and horrible shed.

"What are they doing? It can't be they're at work such a day as this," Howard said, standing at the window.

"They find plenty to do, even on rainy days," answered his mother. "Grant always has some job to set the men at. It's the only way to live."

"I'll go out and see them." He turned suddenly. "Mother, why should Grant treat me so? Have I deserved it?"

Mrs. McLane sighed in pathetic hopelessness. "I don't know, Howard. I'm worried about Grant. He gets more an' more down-hearted an' gloomy every day. Seems if he'd go crazy. He don't care how he looks any more, won't dress up on Sunday. Days an' days he'll go aroun' not sayin' a word. I was in hopes you could help him, Howard."

"My coming seems to have had an opposite effect. He hasn't spoken a word to me, except when he had to, since I came. Mother, what do you say to going home with me to New York?"

"Oh, I couldn't do that!" she cried in terror. "I couldn't live in a big city—never!"

"There speaks the truly rural mind," smiled Howard at his mother, who was looking up at him through her glasses with a pathetic forlornness which sobered him again. "Why, mother, you could live in Orange, New Jersey, or out in Connecticut, and be just as lonesome as you are here. You wouldn't need to live in the city. I could see you then every day or two."

"Well, I couldn't leave Grant an' the baby, anyway," she replied, not realizing how one could live in New Jersey and do business daily in New York.

"Well, then, how would you like to go back into the old house?" he said, facing her.

The patient hands fell to the lap, the dim eyes fixed in searching glance on his face. There was a wistful cry in the voice.

"Oh, Howard! Do you mean—"

He came and sat down by her, and put his arm about her and hugged her hard. "I mean, you dear, good, patient, work-weary old mother, I'm going to buy back the old farm and put you in it."

There was no refuge for her now except in tears, and she put up her thin, trembling old hands about his neck, and cried in that easy, placid, restful way age has.

Howard could not speak. His throat ached with remorse and pity. He saw his forgetfulness of them all once more without relief,—the black thing it was!

"There, there mother, don't cry!" he said, torn with anguish by her tears. Measured by man's tearlessness, her weeping seemed terrible to him. "I didn't realize how things were going here. It was all my fault—or, at least, most of it. Grant's letter didn't reach me. I thought you were still on the old farm. But no matter; it's all over now. Come, don't cry any more, mother dear. I'm going to take care of you now."

It had been years since the poor, lonely woman had felt such warmth of love. Her sons had been like her husband, chary of expressing their affection; and like most Puritan families, there was little of caressing among them. Sitting there with the rain on the roof and driving through the trees, they planned getting back into the old house. Howard's plan seemed to her full of splendor and audacity. She began to understand his power and wealth now, as he put it into concrete form before her.

"I wish I could eat Thanksgiving dinner there with you," he said at last, "but it can't be thought of. However, I'll have you all in there before I go home. I'm going out now and tell Grant. Now don't worry any more; I'm going to fix it all up with him, sure." He gave her a parting hug.

Laura advised him not to attempt to get to the barn; but as he persisted in going, she hunted up an old rubber coat for him. "You'll mire down and spoil your shoes," she said, glancing at his neat calf gaiters.

"Darn the difference!" he laughed in his old way. "Besides, I've got rubbers."

"Better go round by the fence," she advised, as he stepped out into the pouring rain.

How wretchedly familiar it all was! The miry cow-yard, with the hollow trampled out around the horse-trough, the disconsolate hens standing under the wagons and sheds, a pig wallowing across its sty, and for atmosphere the desolate, falling rain. It was so familiar he felt a pang of the old rebellious despair which seized him on such days in his boyhood.

Catching up courage, he stepped out on the grass, opened the gate and entered the barnyard. A narrow ribbon of turf ran around the fence, on which he could walk by clinging with one hand to the rough boards. In this way he slowly made his way around the periphery, and came at last to the open barn-door without much harm.

It was a desolate interior. In the open floorway Grant, seated upon a half-bushel, was mending a harness. The old man was holding the trace in his brown hard hands; the boy was lying on a wisp of hay. It was a small barn, and poor at that. There was a bad smell, as of dead rats, about it, and the rain fell through the shingles here and there. To the right, and below, the horses stood, looking up with their calm and beautiful eyes, in which the whole scene was idealized.

Grant looked up an instant and then went on with his work.

"Did yeh wade through?" grinned Lewis, exposing his broken teeth.

"No, I kinder circumambiated the pond." He sat down on the little tool-box near Grant. "Your barn is a good deal like that in 'The Arkansas Travel-ler.' Needs a new roof, Grant." His voice had a pleasant sound, full of the tenderness of the scene through which he had just been. "In fact, you need a new barn."

"I need a good many things more'n I'll ever get," Grant replied shortly.

"How long did you say you'd been on this farm?"

"Three years this fall."

"I don't s'pose you've been able to think of buying—Now hold on, Grant," he cried, as Grant threw his head back. "for God's sake, don't get mad again! Wait till you see what I'm driving at."

"I don't see what you're drivin' at, and I don't care. All I want you to do is to let us alone. That ought to be easy enough for you."

"I tell you, I didn't get your letter. I didn't know you'd lost the old farm." Howard was determined not to quarrel. "I didn't suppose—"

"You might 'a' come to see."

"Well, I'll admit that. All I can say in excuse is that since I got to manag-ing plays I've kept looking ahead to making a big hit and getting a barrel of money—just as the old miners used to hope and watch. Besides, you don't understand how much pressure there is on me. A hundred different people pulling and hauling to have me go here or go there, or do this or do that. When it isn't yachting, it's canoeing, or—"

He stopped. His heart gave a painful throb, and a shiver ran through him. Again he saw his life, so rich, so bright, so free, set over against the routine life in the little low kitchen, the barren sitting-room, and this still more horrible barn. Why should his brother sit there in wet and grimy clothing mending a broken trace, while he enjoyed all the light and civiliza-tion of the age?

He looked at Grant's fine figure, his great strong face; recalled his deep, stern, masterful voice. "Am I so much superior to him? Have not circum-stances made me and destroyed him?"

"Grant, for God's sake, don't sit there like that! I'll admit I've been negli-gent and careless. I can't understand it all myself. But let me do something for you now. I've sent to New York for five thousand dollars. I've got terms on the old farm. Let me see you all back there once more before I return."

"I don't want any of your charity."

"It ain't charity. It's only justice to you." He rose. "Come now, let's get at an understanding, Grant. I can't go on this way. I can't go back to New York and leave you here like this."

Grant rose too. "I tell you, I don't ask your help. You can't fix this thing up with money. If you've got more brains 'n I have, why it's all right. I ain't got any right to take anything that I don't earn."

"But you don't get what you do earn. It ain't your fault. I begin to see it now. Being the oldest, I had the best chance. I was going to town to school while you were ploughing and husking corn. Of course I thought you'd be going soon, yourself. I had three years the start of you. If you'd been in my place, *you* might have met a man like Cooke, *you* might have gone to New York and have been where I am."

"Well, it can't be helped now. So drop it."

"But it must be!" Howard said, pacing about, his hands in his coat-pockets. Grant had stopped work, and was gloomily looking out of the door at a pig nosing in the mud for stray grains of wheat at the granary door:

"Good God! I see it all now," Howard burst out in an impassioned tone. "I went ahead with *my* education, got *my* start in life, then father died, and you took up his burdens. Circumstances made me and crushed you. That's all there is about that. Luck made me and cheated you. It ain't right."

His voice faltered. Both men were now oblivious of their companions and of the scene. Both were thinking of the days when they both planned great things in the way of an education, two ambitious, dreamful boys.

"I used to think of you, Grant, when I pulled out Monday morning in my best suit—cost fifteen dollars in those days." He smiled a little at the recollection. "While you in overalls and an old 'wammus'[23] was going out into the field to plough, or husk corn in the mud. It made me feel uneasy, but, as I said, I kept saying to myself, 'His turn'll come in a year or two.' But it didn't."

His voice choked. He walked to the door, stood a moment, came back. His eyes were full of tears.

"I tell you, old man, many a time in my boarding-house down to the city, when I thought of the jolly times I was having, my heart hurt me. But I said: 'It's no use to cry. Better go on and do the best you can, and then help them afterwards. There'll only be one more miserable member of the family if you stay at home.' Besides, it seemed right to me to have first chance. But I never thought you'd be shut off, Grant. If I had, I never would have gone on. Come, old man, I want you to believe that." His voice was very tender now and almost humble.

"I don't know as I blame yeh for that, How," said Grant, slowly. It was the first time he had called Howard by his boyish nickname. His voice was softer, too, and higher in key. But he looked steadily away.

"I went to New York. People liked my work. I was very successful, Grant; more successful than you realize. I could have helped you at any time. There's no use lying about it. And I ought to have done it; but some way—it's no excuse, I don't mean it for an excuse, only an explanation—some way I got in with the boys. I don't mean I was a drinker and all that. But I bought pictures and kept a horse and a yacht, and of course I had to pay my share of all expeditions, and—oh, what's the use!"

---

[23]Loose-fitting work jacket.

He broke off, turned, and threw his open palms out toward his brother, as if throwing aside the last attempt at an excuse.

"I *did* neglect you, and it's a damned shame! and I ask your forgiveness. Come, old man!"

He held out his hand, and Grant slowly approached and took it. There was a little silence. Then Howard went on, his voice trembling, the tears on his face.

"I want you to let me help you, old man. That's the way to forgive me. Will you?"

"Yes, if you can help me."

Howard squeezed his hand. "That's right, old man. Now you make me a boy again. Course I can help you. I've got ten—"

"I don't mean that, How." Grant's voice was very grave. "Money can't give me a chance now."

"What do you mean?"

"I mean life ain't worth very much to me. I'm too old to take a new start. I'm a dead failure. I've come to the conclusion that life's a failure for ninety-nine per cent of us. You can't help me now. It's too late."

The two men stood there, face to face, hands clasped, the one fair-skinned, full-lipped, handsome in his neat suit; the other tragic, sombre in his softened mood, his large, long, rugged Scotch face bronzed with sun and scarred with wrinkles that had histories, like sabre-cuts on a veteran, the record of his battles.

1891

■ STANDING BEAR (MACHUNAZHA; PONCA) ■
1829–1908

The heritage of eloquence in Native American oral tradition reflects the notion that selected individuals possess the gifts of thought, language, and moral courage to lead us to recognize the underlying meaning of human existence. Thus, life experience, historical circumstance, personal character, and oral rhetorical skill combine to allow speakers to share with their audience a moment of authentic understanding, the momentary recognition of the confluence of real events and their verbal interpretation.

The Ponca people of north-central Nebraska and south-central South Dakota, centered on the Niobrara River of Nebraska, established a record of peaceful relations with their non-Indian neighbors and with the U.S. government. Having entered into four previous treaties with the United States, the Poncas nevertheless were callously deprived of their homeland in a treaty in which they were not even a participant. In the Fort Laramie Treaty of 1868 with the bands of the Lakota (Western Sioux), the U.S. government inexplicably and carelessly granted the ancestral Ponca homelands to the Lakota as part of the Great Sioux Reservation. Then, fearing warfare between the two tribal nations, government representatives unilaterally determined that the Poncas should be removed to Indian Territory, present-day Oklahoma.

In May 1877, the Poncas were forcibly removed to Baxter Springs in eastern Oklahoma and then to Ponca City in north-central Oklahoma. In the Ponca version of the Trail of Tears, eight chiefs were selected to visit Indian Territory to select a new homeland. Upon seeing their choices, the chiefs expressed their dissatisfaction and requested to be allowed to return to their northern home. Although denied permission, they defiantly made the 500-mile trip back to their homeland. In spite of all their appeals, E. C. Kemble, U.S. Indian inspector, ordered the Ponca removal, which concluded on July 29, 1878. As a result of climatic difficulties, exposure, and poor nutrition, only 681 Poncas arrived in Indian Territory, having lost one-third of their number along the way.

The tribulations of the Poncas crested as the death of Chief Standing Bear's son was linked with the son's request to be buried in the Niobrara homeland. In the winter of 1879, Chief Standing Bear and sixty-six Poncas set out from Indian Territory for Nebraska. Taken into custody by General George Crook, Standing Bear and his people were able to attract public attention with the assistance of *Omaha Daily Herald* assistant editor Thomas Henry Tibbles, who was committed to the principle of "equality of all men before the law." With help from two prominent attorneys, Tibbles was able to assist Standing Bear in obtaining a writ of habeas corpus in the court of federal judge Elmer S. Dundy, who ruled in *Standing Bear et al. v. Crook* in favor of Standing Bear, in effect declaring that "an Indian is a person within the meaning of the laws of the United States." By thus invoking the protection of the Fourteenth Amendment of the United States Constitution, Standing Bear's small band was able to prevent its return to Indian Territory. As a result of this decision, Standing Bear and the members of his party were released, and their legal possession of their reservation was subsequently affirmed by Judge Dundy.

Among the notables taking up the cause of the injustices imposed upon the Poncas was Helen Hunt Jackson, who attacked Secretary of the Interior Carl Schurz and his policies regarding Indian nations. In 1881 she published *A Century of Dishonor*, which condemned federal policy toward Native American people. In response to public pressure, a U.S. Senate commission in its report to President Rutherford B. Hayes in 1881 determined that the Poncas should be allowed to remain on their lands in Nebraska with every member who so desired receiving an allotment on the "old Dakota Reservation." Poncas who chose to remain in the north became known as Northern Ponca; so-called Southern Ponca remained in Indian Territory. Because of the allotment policy of 1887, most northern Ponca land was lost to non-Indian ownership in the decades that followed.

In another period of detrimental federal policy after the 1950s, in April 1962, Senator Frank Church of Idaho introduced a bill terminating the Northern Ponca band's federal trust relationship. On September 5, 1962, Congress passed Public Law 870-629, in effect terminating the Ponca Tribe of Nebraska. Today, the Northern Poncas are engaged in an effort to restore their federal recognition as a tribe. In May 1989, the Northern Ponca Restoration Committee initiated an ongoing effort to restore federal recognition to the Northern Poncas.

In his statement to the presidential commission in January 1881, Standing Bear intended to move his audience through the organization of his thoughts and the power of his language (in translation) to share the Poncas' view of their treatment by the U.S. government. Although Standing Bear's words were translated by David Le Clair, a Ponca, in the presence of James Owen Dorsey, a well-known non-Indian ethnographer and linguist, the quality of the translation, as of other Native American texts, continues to be of some concern. Nevertheless, Standing Bear's abilities as a public speaker are evident. He begins by establishing his goodwill toward the audience—a common practice of Native American orators—and then his credibility in relation to God. Using another common device of tribal spokesmen, he traces the pertinent history of his people in the body of his statement, making appropriate references to previous speakers, speaking directly and humbly from a personal point of view with repeated rhetorical questions. His conclusion presents the issues at hand and appeals for justice and fair treatment for his people.

Standing Bear and his band were allowed to move back to their old lands and received allotments there in 1890. He often went to visit his Southern Ponca relatives in Indian Territory. He died in 1908.

R. D. Theisz
Black Hills State University

PRIMARY WORK

Speech to the Ponca Commission, 1881.

What I Am Going to Tell You Here Will Take Me until Dark[1]

I do not think we have made this day, but I think that God has caused it, and my heart is glad to see you all here. Why should I tell you a different word? I have told to God my troubles, and why should I deceive Him?[2] I have told my troubles to Him. Whatever God does is good, I think; even if a thing happens which may not suit us or which may be unfortunate, still God causes it, I think. If a man gets by accident or puts himself into a bad place, or gets frightened, he remembers God and asks Him to help him. You have seen that land, my friends. God made us there,[3] my friends, and He

---

[1]Standing Bear's talk appeared in *Senate Executive Document 30* of the third session of the Forty-sixth Congress (p. 31). The occasion was a January 1881 session of a presidential commission sent to Nebraska to take testimony concerning the Ponca removal. Standing Bear's speech was translated by David Le Clair, a Ponca. [All footnotes by Daniel F. Littlefield, Jr.]

[2]General George Crook had asked Standing Bear for his account of the removal but asked him to be brief, saying rather impatiently that he had heard the story before. Standing Bear's question is the chief's way of politely asserting the truth of his statement.
[3]I.e., to the east.

made you, too, but I have been very weak. You have driven me from the East to this place, and I have been here two thousand years or more.[4]

I don't know how it came about that I encountered misfortunes. My friends, they spoke of carrying me away. I was unwilling. My friends, if you took me away from this land it would be very hard for me. I wish to die in this land. I wish to be an old man here. As I was unwilling, they fastened me and made a prisoner of me and carried me to the fort.[5] When I came back, the soldiers came with their guns and bayonets; they aimed their guns at us, and our people and our children were crying. This was a very different thing that was done to me; I had hoped the Great Father had not done this thing to me—forcing me to leave this land. They took me and carried me without stopping; they traveled all day until night came, and they carried me down to Baxter Springs——.[6]

——I reached that place,[7] and that while I was there fully 150 of my people died. The land was truly bad, and so I came back again. One of the employees of the President—a commissioner—came to see me, and I said to him: "I am going back to my own land. I have never given it to you—I have never sold it to you. You have not paid me for it. I am going back to my own land. The lawyers, ministers, and those who are with them—those who control the land, and God Himself, if He desire it—all will help me." I came back, and there was some talk about this affair; they took pity on me, just as you here take pity on me, and there was a suit brought about it in the courts, and the affair was settled, and I came back successful.[8] Some of my people have gone to my Great Father in Washington. Are they there now?——[9]

——My friends, I haven't got much brain, but you whites have a great deal of brain. The Indians do not know much, but the Great Father has caused you to come to look into our affairs. I refer to this land, not knowing about it. The Indians are ignorant about it. When they went from Indian Territory to sell their lands they didn't know all about it, and the Great Father should have told them correctly. Which of the Great Fathers was it? He should have released me—let me alone. Was it the Secretary of the Interior? What I am going to tell you here will take me until dark. Since I got from the Territory up to this time I have not wished to give even a part of it to the Great Father. Though he were to give me a million dollars I would not give him the land. Even if the Great Father should wish to buy a part of the

---

[4]Such use of the first person is common in Indian oratory. It indicates that the speaker does not distinguish himself from his people, past or present.

[5]Fort Randall, South Dakota.

[6]In southeastern Kansas. The removal plan called for settling the Poncas on Quapaw lands just south of Baxter Springs in Indian Territory because the Quapaws were a cognate tribe with the Omaha, Ponca, Osage, and Kansa, having similar language, tribal organization, and religion.

[7]I.e., Indian Territory.

[8]Standing Bear refers to the famous case of *Standing Bear et al. v. Crook*, which said that an Indian is a person under the laws of the United States.

[9]Standing Bear refers to a delegation of the Indian Territory Poncas that had gone to Washington to air their concerns. General Crook's response to Standing Bear's question was that the delegation had returned to the Indian Territory.

land from me the Indians up the river would hear of it and would be unwilling. My friends, I have been in your lands—to Omaha, Chicago, New York, Boston, Philadelphia, Washington, all these cities, and I've been to the Dakotas, and they've given me my land back——[10]

——I wish to take back my own people from the Indian Territory. I wish them to live. I hadn't heard what you've done with regard to them. If the Secretary is sick or foolish, I hope you'll act as physicians and heal him—I mean the one who speaks German.[11] If one man cheats another, tries to make sport of him, or to kill him, and the other party finds out his danger, he don't have anything more to do with him—he lets him go to one side. I refer to the land. When they went to the Great Father to sell the land, which land did they mean? They live in Indian Territory. Did they want to sell that land or to sell this where I live, and which is mine? One thing I forgot. The land in which you dwell, my friends, is your own. Who would come from another quarter to take it away from you? Your land is your own, and so are your things, and you wouldn't like anybody to come and try to take them away from you. If men want to trade, they say, How much do you want for that piece of property? What price do you put upon it? But nothing of that kind was said; they came and took me away without saying a word.

1881

■ SARAH WINNEMUCCA (THOCMETONY; PAIUTE) ■
c. 1844–1891

Born about 1844 near Humboldt Lake in what is now northwestern Nevada, the daughter of a respected Paiute leader, Sarah Winnemucca (Thocmetony, or Shell Flower) would become one of the principal voices for Indian rights in the late nineteenth century. Although she spent part of her youth in the company of whites as well as Indians, Winnemucca was largely self-educated, fluent in three Indian languages as well as English and Spanish. In a period of extreme upheaval during white incursions on traditional Northern Paiute lands in present-day western Nevada, northern California, and southeastern Oregon, she consistently

---

[10]In the previous summer the Dakotas had attended a grand council of the Sioux, at which Spotted Trail told his people that they must return the disputed land to the Poncas. As one of the major reasons for removing the Poncas, the United States officials had argued that war between the Poncas and the Sioux was inevitable.

[11]Secretary of the Interior Carl Schurz had publicly defended the government's removal policy and had charged that Standing Bear and his entourage were simply troublemakers during their speaking tour of the east in 1879 and 1880.

sought to advance the well-being of her people in the face of daunting personal hardship.

Her major publication, *Life Among the Piutes: Their Wrongs and Claims*, encompasses the first encounters of Paiutes with whites, described in the selection below; the Bannock Indian War of 1878; and the accomplishment of her father's dream, the establishment of a reservation on some of the Paiutes' ancestral lands, in 1889. Winnemucca's remarkable story is complex in both content and form, combining elements of history, autobiography, myth, sentimental appeal, humor, adventure, political tract, and oratory. Reflecting her experiences as a translator for the U.S. Army, an advocate for the Paiutes in Washington, a popular stage performer, and an innovative teacher and school reformer, the volume also seeks to educate white readers about her people. Winnemucca depicts a civilized tribe that deserves whites' sympathy and support. Willing to risk her livelihood and even her life, she gives outspoken testimony against the wrongs committed by reservation agents, whose corruption outraged not only Sarah but many sympathetic observers. She also reveals the efforts of governmental representatives and elected officials to prevent her from lecturing and garnering support for her cause.

One surprise to many contemporary readers may be her praise of the U.S. Army, whose commanding officers often proved to be much more honest and compassionate than government-appointed reservation agents, who were sometimes only nominal Christians. Winnemucca reserves some of her most intense attacks for the latter, who not only profited from government supplies meant for the Indians but regularly permitted their charges to freeze and starve to death. Her fiery stance inspired her to tell one agent to his face that "hell is full of just such Christians as you are."

Negotiating between two worlds was never easy, and Sarah was often placed in a precarious position with her own people by the false promises of white officials as well as by her own goal of assimilation. Her difficulties were also intensified by gender. A favorite claim of detractors—and one leveled at many women reformers of the time—was that she was promiscuous. This charge is ironic in view of the sexual abuse of Indian women by white men that Winnemucca describes in the selection below, abuse so prevalent and unrelenting that she affirms, "the mothers are afraid to have more children, for fear they shall have daughters, who are not safe even in their mother's presence." At least two of the wars that Sarah describes in her book were initiated by such abuse.

After suffering many frustrations and bitter disappointments at the hands of the government and its agents, Winnemucca finally decided that she could best serve her people by opening an Indian-run school. With the financial and emotional support of formidable Boston reformer Elizabeth Palmer Peabody and her sister Mary Mann (also the editor of *Life Among the Piutes*), Sarah founded, managed, and taught at the Peabody Indian School for nearly four years. In contrast to government-run schools, her school not only practiced bilingualism, it also affirmed Paiute values and traditions. During these last few years before her early death, Winnemucca suffered from ill health brought on by long-term physical hardship, as well as from the emotional stresses due to her last marriage to the improvident Lewis Hopkins, who frequently gambled away her hard-won earnings. Winnemucca amply deserves the renewed recognition she is beginning to receive, and we can place her securely in Native American literary and activist traditions begun by William Apess and continued in the late nineteenth and early twentieth centuries by Zitkala-Sa, Alice Callahan, and Mourning Dove.

Karen Kilcup
University of North Carolina–Greensboro

PRIMARY WORKS

Life Among the Piutes: Their Wrongs and Claims, 1883.

from **Life among the Piutes**

Chapter I.
First Meeting of Piutes and Whites

I was born somewhere near 1844, but am not sure of the precise time. I was a very small child when the first white people came into our country. They came like a lion, yes, like a roaring lion, and have continued so ever since, and I have never forgotten their first coming. My people were scattered at that time over nearly all the territory now known as Nevada. My grandfather was chief of the entire Piute nation, and was camped near Humboldt Lake, with a small portion of his tribe, when a party travelling eastward from California was seen coming. When the news was brought to my grandfather, he asked what they looked like? When told that they had hair on their faces, and were white, he jumped up and clasped his hands together, and cried aloud,—

"My white brothers,—my long-looked for white brothers have come at last!"

He immediately gathered some of his leading men, and went to the place where the party had gone into camp. Arriving near them, he was commanded to halt in a manner that was readily understood without an interpreter. Grandpa at once made signs of friendship by throwing down his robe and throwing up his arms to show them he had no weapons; but in vain,—they kept him at a distance. He knew not what to do. He had expected so much pleasure in welcoming his white brothers to the best in the land, that after looking at them sorrowfully for a little while, he came away quite unhappy. But he would not give them up so easily. He took some of his most trustworthy men and followed them day after day, camping near them at night, and travelling in sight of them by day, hoping in this way to gain their confidence. But he was disappointed, poor dear old soul!

I can imagine his feelings, for I have drank deeply from the same cup. When I think of my past life, and the bitter trials I have endured, I can scarcely believe I live, and yet I do; and, with the help of Him who notes the sparrow's fall, I mean to fight for my down-trodden race while life lasts.

Seeing they would not trust him, my grandfather left them, saying, "Perhaps they will come again next year." Then he summoned his whole people, and told them this tradition:—

"In the beginning of the world there were only four, two girls and two boys. Our forefather and mother were only two, and we are their children. You all know that a great while ago there was a happy family in this world. One girl and one boy were dark and the others were white. For a time they got along together without quarrelling, but soon they disagreed, and there was trouble. They were cross to one another and fought, and our parents were very much grieved. They prayed that their children might learn better, but it did not do any good; and afterwards the whole household was made so unhappy that the father and mother saw that they must separate their children; and then our father took the dark boy and girl, and the white boy and girl, and asked them, 'Why are you so cruel to each other?' They hung down their heads, and would not speak. They were ashamed. He said to them, 'Have I not been kind to you all, and given you everything your hearts wished for? You do not have to hunt and kill your own game to live upon. You see, my dear children, I have power to call whatsoever kind of game we want to eat; and I also have the power to separate my dear children, if they are not good to each other.' So he separated his children by a word. He said, 'Depart from each other, you cruel children;—go across the mighty ocean and do not seek each other's lives.'

"So the light girl and boy disappeared by that one word, and their parents saw them no more, and they were grieved, although they knew their children were happy. And by-and-by the dark children grew into a large nation; and we believe it is the one we belong to, and that the nation that sprung from the white children will some time send some one to meet us and heal all the old trouble. Now, the white people we saw a few days ago must certainly be our white brothers, and I want to welcome them. I want to love them as I love all of you. But they would not let me; they were afraid. But they will come again, and I want you one and all to promise that, should I not live to welcome them myself, you will not hurt a hair on their heads, but welcome them as I tried to do."[1]

How good of him to try and heal the wound, and how vain were his efforts! My people had never seen a white man, and yet they existed, and were a strong race. The people promised as he wished, and they all went back to their work.

The next year came a great emigration,[2] and camped near Humboldt Lake. The name of the man in charge of the trains was Captain Johnson, and they stayed three days to rest their horses, as they had a long journey before them without water. During their stay my grandfather and some of his people called upon them, and they all shook hands, and when our white brothers were going away they gave my grandfather a white tin plate. Oh,

---

[1] This story represents a selective retelling of a popular Paiute tradition, the quarreling children. Captain Truckee chooses to emphasize the last section of the story and thus positive relations among whites and Indians; he deemphasizes the opening section that would identify the whites as cannibals. The latter is implied later in Winnemucca's narrative when the mothers bury their children alive.

[2] Of white settlers.

what a time they had over that beautiful gift,—it was so bright! They say that after they left, my grandfather called for all his people to come together, and he then showed them the beautiful gift which he had received from his white brothers. Everybody was so pleased; nothing like it was ever seen in our country before. My grandfather thought so much of it that he bored holes in it and fastened it on his head, and wore it as a hat. He held it in as much admiration as my white sisters hold their diamond rings or a sealskin jacket. So that winter they talked of nothing but their white brothers. The following spring there came great news down the Humboldt River, saying that there were some more of the white brothers coming, and there was something among them that was burning all in a blaze. My grandfather asked them what it was like. They told him it looked like a man; it had legs and hands and a head, but the head had quit burning, and it was left quite black. There was the greatest excitement among my people everywhere about the men in a blazing fire. They were excited because they did not know there were any people in the world but the two,—that is, the Indians and the whites; they thought that was all of us in the beginning of the world, and, of course, we did not know where the others had come from, and we don't know yet. Ha! ha! oh, what a laughable thing that was! It was two negroes wearing red shirts!

The third year more emigrants came, and that summer Captain Fremont, who is now General Fremont.

My grandfather met him, and they were soon friends. They met just where the railroad crosses Truckee River, now called Wadsworth, Nevada. Captain Fremont gave my grandfather the name of Captain Truckee, and he also called the river after him. Truckee is an Indian word, it means *all right*, or *very well*. A party of twelve of my people went to California with Captain Fremont. I do not know just how long they were gone.

During the time my grandfather was away in California, where he staid till after the Mexican war, there was a girl-baby born in our family. I can just remember it. It must have been in spring, because everything was green. I was away playing with some other children when my mother called me to come to her. So I ran to her. She then asked me to sit down, which I did. She then handed me some beautiful beads, and asked me if I would like to buy something with them. I said:—

"Yes, mother,—some pine nuts."

My mother said:—

"Would you like something else you can love and play with? Would you like to have a little sister?" I said,—

"Yes, dear mother, a little, little sister; not like my sister Mary, for she won't let me play with her. She leaves me and goes with big girls to play;" and then my mother wanted to know if I would give my pretty beads for the little sister.

Just then the baby let out such a cry it frightened me; and I jumped up and cried so that my mother took me in her arms, and said it was a little sister for me, and not to be afraid. This is all I can remember about it.

When my grandfather went to California he helped Captain Fremont fight the Mexicans. When he came back he told the people what a beautiful country California was. Only eleven returned home, one having died on the way back.

They spoke to their people in the English language, which was very strange to them all.

Captain Truckee, my grandfather, was very proud of it, indeed. They all brought guns with them. My grandfather would sit down with us for hours, and would say over and over again, "Goodee gun, goodee, goodee gun, heap shoot." They also brought some of the soldiers' clothes with all their brass buttons, and my people were very much astonished to see the clothes, and all that time they were peaceable toward their white brothers. They had learned to love them, and they hoped more of them would come. Then my people were less barbarous than they are nowadays.

That same fall, after my grandfather came home, he told my father to take charge of his people and hold the tribe, as he was going back to California with as many of his people as he could get to go with him. So my father took his place as Chief of the Piutes, and had it as long as he lived. Then my grandfather started back to California again with about thirty families. That same fall, very late, the emigrants kept coming. It was this time that our white brothers first came amongst us. They could not get over the mountains, so they had to live with us. It was on Carson River, where the great Carson City stands now. You call my people bloodseeking. My people did not seek to kill them, nor did they steal their horses,—no, no, far from it. During the winter my people helped them. They gave them such as they had to eat. They did not hold out their hands and say:—

"You can't have anything to eat unless you pay me." No,—no such word was used by us savages at that time; and the persons I am speaking of are living yet; they could speak for us if they choose to do so.

The following spring, before my grandfather returned home, there was a great excitement among my people on account of fearful news coming from different tribes, that the people whom they called their white brothers were killing everybody that came in their way, and all the Indian tribes had gone into the mountains to save their lives. So my father told all his people to go into the mountains and hunt and lay up food for the coming winter. Then we all went into the mountains. There was a fearful story they told us children. Our mothers told us that the whites were killing everybody and eating them. So we were all afraid of them. Every dust that we could see blowing in the valleys we would say it was the white people. In the late fall my father told his people to go to the rivers and fish, and we all went to Humboldt River, and the women went to work gathering wild seed, which they grind between the rocks. The stones are round, big enough to hold in the hands. The women did this when they got back, and when they had gathered all they could they put it in one place and covered it with grass, and then over the grass mud. After it is covered it looks like an Indian wigwam.

Oh, what a fright we all got one morning to hear some white people were coming. Every one ran as best they could. My poor mother was left with my little sister and me. Oh, I never can forget it. My poor mother was carrying my little sister on her back, and trying to make me run; but I was so frightened I could not move my feet, and while my poor mother was trying to get me along my aunt overtook us, and she said to my mother: "Let us bury our girls, or we shall be killed and eaten up." So they went to work and buried us, and told us if we heard any noise not to cry out, for if we did they would surely kill us and eat us. So our mothers buried me and my cousin, planted sage bushes over our faces to keep the sun from burning them, and there we were left all day.

Oh, can any one imagine my feelings *buried alive*, thinking every minute that I was to be unburied and eaten up by the people that my grandfather loved so much? With my heart throbbing, and not daring to breathe, we lay there all day. It seemed that the night would never come. Thanks be to God! the night came at last. Oh, how I cried and said: "Oh, father, have you forgotten me? Are you never coming for me?" I cried so I thought my very heartstrings would break.

At last we heard some whispering. We did not dare to whisper to each other, so we lay still. I could hear their footsteps coming nearer and nearer. I thought my heart was coming right out of my mouth. Then I heard my mother say, "'T is right here!" Oh, can any one in this world ever imagine what were my feelings when I was dug up by my poor mother and father? My cousin and I were once more happy in our mothers' and fathers' care, and we were taken to where all the rest were.

I was once buried alive; but my second burial shall be for ever, where no father or mother will come and dig me up. It shall not be with throbbing heart that I shall listen for coming footsteps. I shall be in the sweet rest of peace,—I, the chieftain's weary daughter.

Well, while we were in the mountains hiding, the people that my grandfather called our white brothers came along to where our winter supplies were. They set everything we had left on fire. It was a fearful sight. It was all we had for the winter, and it was all burnt during that night. My father took some of his men during the night to try and save some of it, but they could not; it had burnt down before they got there.

These were the last white men that came along that fall. My people talked fearfully that winter about those they called our white brothers. My people said they had something like awful thunder and lightning, and with that they killed everything that came in their way.

This whole band of white people perished in the mountains, for it was too late to cross them. We could have saved them, only my people were afraid of them. We never knew who they were, or where they came from. So, poor things, they must have suffered fearfully, for they all starved there. The snow was too deep.

[Soon after these events, Sarah's father has a powerful and prophetic dream about the impending violence of white settlers, and members of the tribe are deeply troubled. Captain Truckee, on the other hand, maintains a vision of peaceful coexistence and white benevolence, even following the murder of one of Sarah's uncles. Shortly afterward, Sarah's grandfather persuades part of his band of Paiutes to go to California, and he insists that his daughter (Tuboitonie, Sarah's mother), Sarah, and her sisters accompany him. In spite of Tuboitonie's pleas, Sarah's father is left behind as the leader of another band. The journey is perilous because of potential white and Mexican hostility, although Captain Truckee manages to negotiate successfully with the former and to gain assistance along the way. Sarah is particularly afraid of the white settlers, who, with their beards and light eyes, seem like the owls in a frightening Paiute myth. She loses this fear when a kind and gentle white woman nurses her through a painful illness that youthful Sarah attributes to "poisoned sugar-bread" (cake), but that is actually a severe case of poison oak. Soon after this episode, they arrive at the ranch of Hiram Scott and Jacob Bonsal, where the men of Captain Truckee's group have been hired to work.]

One of my grandpa's friends was named Scott, and the other Bonsal. After we got there, his friend killed beef for him and his people. We stayed there some time. Then grandpa told us that he had taken charge of Mr. Scott's cattle and horses, and he was going to take them all up the mountains to take care of them for his brothers. He wanted my uncles and their families and my mother and her two sons and three daughters to stay where they were; that is, he told his dear daughter that he wanted her two sons to take care of a few horses and cows that would be left. My mother began to cry, and said,—

"Oh, father, don't leave us here! My children might get sick, and there would be no one to speak for us; or something else might happen." He again said, "I don't think my brothers will do anything that is wrong to you and your children." Then my mother asked my grandfather if he would take my sister with him. My poor mother felt that her daughter was unsafe, for she was young and very good-looking.

"I would like to take her along," he said, "but I want her to learn how to work and cook. Scott and Bonsal say they will take the very best care of you and the children. It is not as if I was going to leave you here really alone; your brothers will be with you." So we staid. Two men owned the ferry, and they had a great deal of money. So my brothers took care of their horses and cows all winter, and they paid them well for their work. But, oh, what trouble we had for a while! The men whom my grandpa called his brothers would come into our camp and ask my mother to give our sister to them. They would come in at night, and we would all scream and cry; but that would not stop them. My sister, and mother, and my uncles all cried and said, "Oh, why did we come? Oh, we shall surely all be killed some night." My uncles and brothers would not dare to say a word, for fear they would be shot down. So we used to go away every night after dark and hide, and come back to our camp every morning. One night we were getting ready to go, and there came five men. The fire was out; we could see two men come into the tent and shut off the postles outside. My uncles and my brothers made such a noise! I don't know what happened; when I woke I asked my mother if they had killed my sister. She said, "We are all safe here. Don't cry."

"Where are we, mother?"

"We are in a boarding-house."

"Are my uncles killed?"

"No, dear, they are all near here too.

I said, "Sister, where are you? I want to come to you."

She said, "Come on."

I laid down, but I could not sleep. I could hear my poor sister's heart beat. Early the next morning we got up and went down stairs, for it was upstairs where we slept. There were a great many in the room. When we came down, my mother said, "We will go outside."

My sister said, "There is no outlet to the house. We can't get out."

Mother looked round and said, "No, we cannot get out." I as usual began to cry. My poor sister! I ran to her, I saw tears in her eyes. I heard some one speak close to my mother. I looked round and saw Mr. Scott holding the door open. Mother said, "Children, come."

He went out with us and pointed to our camp, and shook his head, and motioned to mother to go into a little house where they were cooking. He took my hand in his, and said the same words that I had learned, "Poor little girl." I could see by his looks that he pitied me, so I was not afraid of him. We went in and sat down on the floor. Oh, what pretty things met my eyes. I was looking all round the room, and I saw beautiful white cups, and every beautiful thing on something high and long, and around it some things that were red.

I said to my sister, "Do you know what those are?" for she had been to the house before with my brothers. She said, "That high thing is what they use when eating, and the white cups are what they drink hot water from, and the red things you see is what they sit upon when they are eating." There was one now near us, and I thought if I could sit upon it I should be so happy! I said to my mother, "Can I sit on that one?" She said, "No, they would whip you." I did not say any more, but sat looking at the beautiful red chair. By-and-by the white woman went out, and I wished in my heart I could go and sit upon it while she was gone. Then she came in with her little child in her arms. As she came in she went right to the very chair I wanted to sit in so badly, and set her child in it. I looked up to my mother, and said, "Will she get a whipping?"

"No, dear, it belongs to her father."

So I said no more. Pretty soon a man came in. She said something to him, and he went out, and in a little while they all came in and sat round that high thing, as I called it. That was the table. It was all very strange to me, and they were drinking the hot water as they ate. I thought it was indeed hot water. After they got through, they all went out again, but Mr. Scott staid and talked to the woman and the man a long time. Then the woman fixed five places and the men went out and brought in my brothers, and kept talking to them. My brother said, "Come and sit here, and you, sister, sit there." But as soon as I sat down in the beautiful chair I began to look at the pretty picture on the back of the chair. "Dear, sit nice and eat, or the white woman will whip you," my mother said. I was quiet, but did not eat much. I tasted the black hot water; I did not like it. It was coffee that we called hot water. After we had done, brother said, "Mother, come outside; I want to talk to you." So we all went out. Brother said, "Mother, Mr. Scott wants us all to stay here. He says you and sister are to wash dishes, and learn all kinds of work. We are to stay here all the time and sleep upstairs, and the white woman is going to teach my sister how to sew. I think, dear mother, we had better stay, because grandpa said so, and our father Scott will take good care of us. He is going up into the mountains to see how grandpa is getting along, and he says he will take my uncles with him." All the time brother was talking, my mother and sister were crying. I did not cry, for I wanted to stay so that I could sit in the beautiful red chairs. Mother said,—

"Dear son, you know if we stay here sister will be taken from us by the bad white man. I would rather see her die than see her heart full of fear every night."

"Yes, dear mother, we love our dear sister, and if you say so we will go to papa."

"Yes, dear son, let us go and tell him what his white brothers are doing to us."

"Then I will go and tell Mr. Scott we want to go to our papa." He was gone some time, and at last came back.

"Mother," he says, "we can't go,—that is, brother and I must stay;—but you and sister can go if you wish to."

"Oh no, my dear children, how can I go and leave you here? Oh, how can that bad man keep you from going? You are not his children. How dare he say you cannot go with your mother? He is not your father; he is nothing but a bad white man, and he dares to say you cannot go. Your own father did not say you should not come with me. Oh, had my dear husband said those words I would not have been here today, and see my dear children suffer from day to day. Oh, if your father only knew how his children were suffering, I know he would kill that white man who tried to take your sister. I cannot see for my life why my father calls them his white brothers. They are not people; they have no thought, no mind, no love. They are beasts, or they would know I, a lone woman, am here with them. They tried to take my girl from me and abuse her before my eyes and yours too, and oh, you must go too."

"Oh, mother, here he comes!"

My mother got up. She held out her two hands to him, and cried out,—

"Oh, good father, don't keep my children from me. If you have a heart in you, give them back to me. Let me take them to their good father, where they can be cared for."

We all cried to see our poor mother pleading for us. Mother held on to him until he gave some signs of letting her sons go with her; then he nodded his head,—they might go. My poor mother's crying was turned into joy, and we were all glad. The wagon was got ready,—we were to ride in it. Oh, how I jumped about because I was going to ride in it! I ran up to sister, and said,—

"Ain't you glad we are going to ride in that beautiful red house?" I called it house. My sister said,—

"Not I, dear sister, for I hate everything that belongs to the white dogs. I would rather walk all the way; oh, I hate them so badly!"

When everything was got ready, we got into the red house, as we called the wagon. I soon got tired of riding in the red house and went to sleep. Nothing happened during the day, and after awhile mother told us not to say a word about why we left, for grandpa might get mad with us. So we got to our people, and grandpa ran out to meet us. We were all glad to see him. The white man staid all night, and went home the next day. After he left us my grandpa called my brothers to him.

"Now, my dear little boys, I have something to tell you that will make you happy. Our good father (he did not say my white brother, but he said our good father) has left something with me to give you, and he also told me that he had given you some money for your work. He says you are all good boys, and he likes you very much; and he told me to give you three horses apiece, which makes six in all, and he wants you and your brother to go back and to go on with the same work, and he will pay you well for it. He is to come back in three days; then if you want to go with him you can."

Brother said, "Will mother and sisters go too?"

"No, they will stay with me." My brothers were so happy over their horses.

Now, my dear reader, there is no word so endearing as the word father, and that is why we call all good people father or mother; no matter who it is,—negro, white man, or Indian, and the same with the women. Grandpa talked to my mother a long time, but I did not hear what he said to her, as I went off to play with the other children. But the first thing I knew the white man came and staid four days. Then all the horses were got up, and he saw them all, and the cattle also. I could see my poor mother and sister crying now and then, but I did not know what for. So one morning the man was going away, and I saw mother getting my brothers' horses ready too. I ran to my mother, and said, "Mother, what makes you cry so?" Grandpa was talking to her. He said, "They will not be hurt; they will have quite a number of horses by the time we are ready to go back to our home again."

I knew then that my brothers were going back with this man. Oh, then I began to cry, and said everything that was bad to them. I threw myself down upon the ground.

"Oh, brothers, I will never see them any more. They will kill them, I know. Oh, you naughty, naughty grandpa, you want my poor brothers to be killed by the bad men. You don't know what they do to us. Oh, mother, run,—bring them back again!"

Oh, how we missed our brothers for a long time. We did not see them for a long time, but the men came now and then. They never brought my brothers with them. After they went away, grandpa would come in with his rag friend[3] in hand and say to mother, "My friend here says my boys are all right, not sick."

My mother said, "Father, why can you not have them come and see us sometimes?"

"Dear daughter, we will get ready to go home. It is time now that the snow is off the mountains. In ten days more we will go, and we will get the children as we go by."

Oh, how happy everybody was! Everybody was singing here and there, getting beautiful dresses made, and before we started we had a thanksgiving dance. The day we were to start we partook of the first gathering of food for that summer. So that morning everybody prayed, and sang songs, and danced, and ate before starting. It was all so nice, and everybody was so happy because they were going to see their dear country and the dear ones at home. Grandpa took all the horses belonging to the white men. After we got home the horses were put into the corral for all night, and the two white men counted their horses the next morning. They gave my grandpa eight horses for his work, and two or three horses each to some of the people. To my two brothers they gave sixteen horses and some money, and after we all got our horses, grandpa said to his people,—

"Now, my children, you see that what I have told you about my white brothers is true. You see we have not worked very much, and they have given us all horses. Don't you see they are good people?"

All that time, neither my uncles nor my mother had told what the white men did while we were left all alone.

So the day was set for starting. It was to be in five days. We had been there three days when we saw the very men who were so bad to us. Yes, they were talking to grandpa. Mother said to sister,—

"They are talking about us. You see they are looking this way."

Sister said, "Oh, mother, I hope grandpa will not do such a wicked thing as to give me to those bad men."

Oh, how my heart beat! I saw grandpa shake his head, and he looked mad with them. He came away and left them standing there. From that day my grandma took my sister under her care, and we got along nicely.

Then we started for our home, and after traveling some time we arrived at the head of Carson River. There we met some of our people, and they told us some very bad news, indeed, which made us all cry. They said almost all the tribe had died off, and if one of a family got sick it was a sure thing that

---

[3]A written introduction and testimonial given to Captain Truckee by Captain Fremont for his help in the war against Mexico. Captain Truckee regards the letter as a pledge of friendship between whites and Paiutes.

the whole family would die. He said the white men had poisoned the Humboldt River, and our people had drank the water and died off.[4] Grandpa said,—

"Is my son dead?"

"No, he has been in the mountains all the time, and all who have been there are all right."

The men said a great many of our relations had died off.

We staid there all night, and the next day our hair was all cut off.[5] My sister and my mother had such beautiful hair!

So grandpa said to the man,—

"Go and tell our people we are coming. Send them to each other, and tell my son to come to meet us."

So we went on our journey, and after travelling three days more we came to a place called Genoa, on the west side of Carson River, at the very place where I had first seen a white man. A saw-mill and a grist-mill were there, and five more houses. We camped in the very same place where we did before. We staid there a long time waiting for my father to come to meet us. At last my cousin rode into our camp one evening, and said my father was coming with many of his people. We heard them as they came nearer and nearer; they were all crying, and then we cried too, and as they got off their horses they fell into each other's arms, like so many little children, and cried as if their hearts would break, and told what they had suffered since we went away, and how our people had died off. As soon as one would get sick he would drink water and die right off. Every one of them was in mourning also, and they talked over the sad things which had happened to them during the time we were away. One and all said that the river must have been poisoned by the white people, because that they had prayed, and our spirit-doctors had tried to cure the sick; they too died while they were trying to cure them. After they had told grandpa all, he got angry and said,—

"My dear children, I am heartily sorry to hear your sad story; but I cannot and will not believe my white brothers would do such a thing. Oh, my dear children, do not think so badly of our white fathers, for if they had poisoned the river, why, my dear children, they too would have died when they drank of the water. It is this, my dear children, it must be some fearful disease or sickness unknown to us, and therefore, my dear children, don't blame our brothers. The whole tribe have called me their father, and I have loved you all as my dear children, and those who have died are happy in the Spirit-land, though we mourn their loss here on earth. I know my grandchildren and daughters and brothers are in that happy bright Spirit-land, and I shall soon see them there. Some of you may live a long time yet, and don't let your hearts work against your white fathers; if you do, you will not get along. You see they are already here in our land; here they are all along the river, and we must let our brothers live with us. We cannot tell them to go away. I know your good hearts. I know you won't say *kill them*. Surely you

---

[4]From typhus.

[5]Hair was cut off as a sign of mourning.

all know that they are human. Their lives are just as dear to them as ours to us. It is a very sad thing indeed to have to lose so many of our dear ones; but maybe it was to be. We can do nothing but mourn for their loss." He went on to say,—

"My dear children, you all know the tradition says: 'Weep not for your dead; but sing and be joyful, for the soul is happy in the Spirit-land.' But it is natural for man or woman to weep, because it relieves our hearts to weep together, and we all feel better afterwards."

Every one hung their heads while grandpa talked on. Now and then one could hear some of them cry out, just as the Methodists cry out at their meetings; and grandpa said a great many beautiful things to his people. He talked so long, I for one wished he would stop, so I could go and throw myself into my father's arms, and tell him what the white people were. At last he stopped, and we all ran to our father and threw our arms around his neck, and cried for joy; and then mother came with little sister. Papa took her in his arms, and mother put her hand in his bosom, and we all wept together, because mother had lost two sisters, and their husbands, and all their children but one girl; and thus passed away the day. Grandpa had gone off during our meeting with father, and prayer was offered, and every one washed their face, and were waiting for something else. Pretty soon grandpa came, and said: "This is my friend," holding up his paper in his hand. "Does it look as if it could talk and ask for anything? Yet it does. It can ask for something to eat for me and my people. Yet, it is nothing but a rag. Oh, wonderful things my white brothers can do. I have taken it down to them, and it has asked for sacks of flour for us to eat. Come, we will go and get them," So the men went down and got the flour. Grandpa took his son down to see the white men, and by-and-by we saw them coming back. They had given my father a red blanket and a red shirt.

1883

■ ## CORRIDOS ■

The *corrido* is perhaps the most important expressive form for the Mexican Americans of the Southwest during the period from 1865 to 1915. The *corrido* (from *correr*, the Spanish verb meaning "to run") is a fast-paced narrative ballad whose roots may be traced to the romances of medieval Spain. In colonizing what is now the American Southwest, the Spaniards carried their musical traditions with them and these flourished, simultaneously preserving old songs and themes and adapting to the particular circumstances of life in the New World. Of the various Spanish musical traditions that prospered in the Southwest— the *copla*, the *danza*, and the *décima*, for example—the *corrido* stands out, in terms of quantity, persistence, and historical and cultural interest. Countless *corridos* emerged in the Southwest, generally composed anonymously and transmitted by word of mouth to commemorate events and experiences of sometimes epic proportions. As the distinguished folklorist Américo Paredes has shown, the *corrido* thrived particularly in circumstances of cultural conflict; in the Southwest this often meant between Mexican American and Anglo-American.

As a distinct ballad form, the *corrido* first appeared in Mexico in the mid-nineteenth century and began to emerge in the American Southwest soon thereafter, most conspicuously in the border regions of south Texas where Mexican and Mexican American cultures were virtually indistinguishable.

"Kiansis," the oldest of the *corridos* presented here, dates from the 1860s (a more precise date of origin is impossible for such an anonymous song) when cattle drives from Texas to Kansas were conducted regularly, more often than not with Mexican American as well as Anglo cowboys. "Kiansis," like virtually all *corridos* including the others printed here, was composed in Spanish and is presented in translation without any attempt to preserve its original rhythm or other poetic qualities. Notice that "Kiansis" depicts the sometimes fierce rivalry between Mexican American and Anglo-American cowboys. In their songs, Mexican Americans liked to point out that ranching in the Southwest was essentially a Mexican institution that Anglos had later claimed as their own.

"Gregorio Cortez" and "Jacinto Trevino" are probably the best known of Mexican American *corridos*, again dealing with episodes of conflict between a Mexican American and Anglos, in this case Texas Rangers. These two ballads date from the early 1900s and feature violent conflict. Gregorio Cortez, an ordinary rancher and farmer, shoots the "major sheriff" in defense of his brother and then flees for the Mexican border, knowing he'll not receive justice in a Texas court. He skillfully eludes his hundreds of pursuers but finally surrenders when he realizes that other Mexican Americans are being punished in retribution. "Jacinto Trevino" presents a similar scenario: a fight breaks out in a south Texas saloon, the Texas Rangers come to arrest Trevino and he backs them down, finally making his way to safety. Both *corridos* present admittedly biased versions of Mexican American/Anglo conflict but also provide a necessary counterbalance to the conventional and better-known accounts of Texas Ranger heroics in American folklore and popular culture.

Like the *corridos* noted above, "El Hijo Desobediente" (The Disobedient Son) is from Texas but this time focuses not on a broad cultural issue but a family matter. Considered one of the greatest of all ballads from along the south Texas border, "El Hijo Desobediente" poignantly relates the tragedy of a young man trapped in his excessive masculinity.

The final two *corridos* are of rather recent origin, demonstrating that the *corrido* tradition is still active. "Recordando al Presidente" ("Remembering the President") was composed by Willie López of McAllen, Texas, to commemorate John F. Kennedy, the first Catholic president, who was widely admired in the Mexican American community. The "*Corrido* de César Chávez" is notable for several reasons. It focuses on the work of one of the great contemporary Mexican American heroes, César Chávez, who dedicated his career to fighting for decent working and living conditions for farm workers. Secondly, this ballad was composed and recorded by Lalo Guerrero, one of the most gifted and influential of contemporary Mexican American musicians. Both of the contemporary *corridos* are of known authorship and have been sold commercially, indicating the adaptability of this musical form to contemporary circumstances.

Raymund Paredes
Commissioner of Higher Education, State of Texas

PRIMARY WORKS

Américo Paredes, comp. *A Texas-Mexican Cancionero: Folksongs of the Lower Border*, 1976.

Kiansis I

["Kiansis I" is sung in a slow, reflective tempo, most often by one singer alone and frequently without guitar accompaniment. The rhythm is not the usual *one*-two-three strum used for the *corrido*. It is more of a three-*one*-two-three-*one* rhythm similar to the *colombiana* or *yucateca* strums. "Kiansis II" has a straight *corrido* rhythm. It is more often sung by two voices, with guitar accompaniment. It is a *canción de grito*, the type you would expect to hear at cantinas as well as at ranchos.]

Cuando salimos pa' Kiansis
con una grande partida,
¡ah, qué camino tan largo!
no contaba con mi vida.

Nos decía el caporal,   5
como queriendo llorar:
—Allá va la novillada,
no me la dejen pasar.—

¡Ah, qué caballo tan bueno!
todo se le iba en correr,   10
¡y, ah, qué fuerte aguacerazo!
no contabe yo en volver.

Unos pedían cigarro,
otros pedían que comer,
y el caporal nos decía: 15
—Sea por Dios, qué hemos de hacer.—

En el charco de Palomas
se cortó un novillo bragado,
y el caporal lo lazó
en su caballo melado.   20

Avísenle al caporal
que un vaquero se mató,
en las trancas del corral
nomás la cuera dejó.

Llegamos al Río Salado   25
y nos tiramos a nado,
decía un americano:
—Esos hombres ya se ahogaron.—

Pues qué pensaría ese hombre
que venimos a esp'rimentar,   30
si somos del Río Grande,
de los buenos pa'nadar.

Y le dimos vista a Kiansis,
y nos dice el caporal:
—Ora sí somos de vida,   35
ya vamos a hacer corral.—

Y de vuelta en San Antonio
compramos buenos sombreros,
y aquí se acaban cantando
versos de los aventureros.   40

Kansas I

When we left for Kansas with a great herd of cattle,
ah, what a long trail it was! I was not sure I would survive.

The *caporal* would tell us, as if he was going to cry,
"Watch out for that bunch of steers; don't let them get past
    you."

Ah, what a good horse I had! He did nothing but gallop.   5
And, ah, what a violent cloudburst! I was not sure I would come
    back.
Some of us asked for cigarettes, others wanted something
    to eat;
and the *caporal* would tell us, "So be it, it can't be helped."

By the pond at Palomas a vicious steer left the herd.   10
and the *caporal* lassoed it on his honey-colored horse.

Go tell the *caporal* that a vaquero has been killed;

all he left was his leather jacket hanging on the rails of the
    corral.

We got to the Salado River, and we swam our horses across;
an American was saying, "Those men are as good as drowned."   15

I wonder what the man thought, that we came to learn, perhaps;
why, we're from the Rio Grande, where the good swimmers are
    from.

And then Kansas came in sight, and the *caporal* tells us,
"We have finally made it, we'll soon have them in the corral."   20

Back again in San Antonio, we all bought ourselves good hats,
and this is the end of the singing of the stanzas about the trail
    drivers.

    1976

Gregorio Cortez

["Gregorio Cortez" is sung a bit more slowly than the average *corrido*, with
the basses on the guitar strongly accented.]

    En el condado de El Carmen
miren lo que ha sucedido,
murió el Cherife Mayor,
quedando Román herido.

    En el condado de El Carmen   5
tal desgracia sucedió,
murió el Cherife Mayor,
no saben quién lo mató.

    Se anduvieron informando
como media hora después,   10
supieron que el malhechor
era Gregorio Cortez.

    Ya insortaron a Cortez
por toditito el estado,
que vivo o muerto se aprehenda   15
porque a varios ha matado.

    Decía Gregorio Cortez
con su pistola en la mano:

—No siento haberlo matado,
lo que siento es a mi hermano.—   20

Decía Gregorio Cortez
con su alma muy encendida:
—No siento haberlo matado,
la defensa es permitida.—

Venían los americanos   25
más blancos que una amapola,
de miedo que le tenían
a Cortez con su pistola.

Decían los americanos,
decían con timidez: 30
—Vamos a seguir la huella
que el malhechor es Cortez.—

Soltaron los perros jaunes
pa' que siguieran la huella,
pero alcanzar a Cortez   35
era seguir a una estrella.

Tiró con rumbo a Gonzales
sin ninguna timidez:
—Síganme, rinches cobardes,
yo soy Gregorio Cortez.—   40

Se fue de Belmont al rancho,
lo alcanzaron a rodear,
poquitos más de trescientos,
y allí les brincó el corral.

Cuando les brincó el corral,   45
según lo que aquí se dice,
se agarraron a balazos
y les mató otro cherife.

Decía Gregorio Cortez
con su pistola en la mano: 50
—No corran, rinches cobardes,
con un solo mexicano.—

Salió Gregorio Cortez,
salió con rumbo a Laredo,
no lo quisieron seguir   55

porque le tuvieron miedo.

Decía Gregorio Cortez:
—¿Pa' qué se valen de planes?
No me pueden agarrar
ni con esos perros jaunes.—   60

Decían los americanos:
—Si lo alcanzamos ¿qué hacemos?
Si le entramos por derecho
muy poquitos volveremos.—

Allá por El Encinal,   65
según lo que aquí se dice,
le formaron un corral
y les mató otro cherife.

Decía Gregorio Cortez
echando muchos balazos: 70
—Me he escapado de aguaceros,
contimás de nublinazos.—

Ya se encontró a un mexicano,
le dice con altivez:
—Platícame qué hay de nuevo,   75
yo soy Gregorio Cortez.

—Dicen que por culpa mía
han matado mucha gente,
pues ya me voy a entregar
porque eso no es conveniente.—   80

Cortez le dice a Jesús:
—Ora sí lo vas a ver,
anda diles a los rinches
que me vengan a aprehender.—

Venían todos los rinches,   85
venían que hasta volaban,
porque se iban a ganar
diez mil pesos que les daban.

Cuando rodearon la casa
Cortez se les presentó: 90
—Por la buena sí me llevan
porque de otro modo no.—

Decía el Cherife Mayor
como queriendo llorar:
—Cortez, entrega tus armas,   95
mo te vamos a matar.—

Decía Gregorio Cortez,
les gritaba en alta voz:
—Mis armas no las entrego
hasta estar en calaboz'.—   100

Decía Gregorio Cortez,
decía en su voz divina:
—Mis armas no las entrego
hasta estar en bartolina.—

Ya agarraron a Cortez,   105
ya terminó la cuestión,
la pobre de su familia
lo lleva en el corazón.

Ya con ésta me despido
a la sombra de un ciprés,   110
aquí se acaba el corridor
de don Gregorio Cortez.

Gregorio Cortez

In the county of El Carmen, look what has happened;
the Major Sheriff is dead, leaving Román badly wounded.

In the county of El Carmen such a tragedy took place:
the Major Sheriff is dead; no one knows who killed him.

They went around asking questions about half an hour afterward;   5
they found out that the wrongdoer had been Gregorio Cortez.

Now they have outlawed Cortez throughout the whole of the state;
let him be taken, dead or alive, for he has killed several men.

Then said Gregorio Cortez, with his pistol in his hand,
"I don't regret having killed him; what I regret is my brother's   10
    death."

Then said Gregorio Cortez, with his soul aflame,
"I don't regret having killed him; self-defense is permitted."

The Americans were coming; they were whiter than a poppy
from the fear that they had of Cortez and his pistol.   15

Then the Americans said, and they said it fearfully,
"Come, let us follow the trail, for the wrongdoer is Cortez."

They let loose the bloodhounds so they could follow the trail,
but trying to overtake Cortez was like following a star.

He struck out for Gonzales, without showing any fear: 20
"Follow me, cowardly *rinches*; I am Gregorio Cortez."

From Belmont he went to the ranch, where they succeeded in
    surrounding him,
quite a few more than three hundred, but he jumped out of their
    corral.   25

When he jumped out of their corral, according to what is said
    here,
they got into a gunfight, and he killed them another sheriff.

Then said Gregorio Cortez, with his pistol in his hand,
"Don't run, you cowardly *rinches*, from a single Mexican."   30

Gregorio Cortez went out, he went out toward Laredo;
they would not follow him because they were afraid of him.

Then said Gregorio Cortez, "What is the use of your scheming?
You cannot catch me, even with those bloodhounds."

Then said the Americans, "If we catch up with him, what shall we   35
    do?
If we fight him man to man, very few of us will return."

Way over near El Encinal, according to what is said here,
they made him a corral, and he killed them another sheriff.

Then said Gregorio Cortez, shooting out a lot of bullets,   40
"I have weathered thunderstorms; this little mist doesn't bother me."

Now he has met a Mexican; he says to him haughtily,
"Tell me the news; I am Gregorio Cortez.

"They say that because of me many people have been killed;   45
so now I will surrender, because such things are not right."

Cortez says to Jesús, "At last you are going to see it;
go and tell the *rinches* that they can come and arrest me."

All the *rinches* were coming, so fast that they almost flew,
because they were going to get the ten thousand dollars that were   50
 offered.

When they surrounded the house, Cortez appeared before them:
"You will take me if I'm willing but not any other way."

Then said the Major Sheriff, as if he was going to cry,
"Cortez, hand over your weapons; we do not want to kill you."   55

Then said Gregorio Cortez, shouting to them in a loud voice,
"I won't surrender my weapons until I am in a cell."

Then said Gregorio Cortez, speaking in his godlike voice,
"I won't surrender my weapons until I'm inside a jail."

Now they have taken Cortez, and now the matter is ended;   60
his poor family are keeping him in their hearts.

Now with this I say farewell in the shade of a cypress;
this is the end of the ballad of Don Gregorio Cortez.

1976

Jacinto Treviño

Ya con ésta van tres veces
que se ha visto lo bonito,
la primera fue en Macalen,
en Brónsvil y en San Benito.

Y en la cantina de Bekar   5
se agarraron a balazos,
por dondequiera saltaban
botellas hechas pedazos.

Esa cantina de Bekar
al momento quedó sola,   10
nomás Jacinto Treviño
de carabina y pistola.

—Entrenle, rinches cobardes,
que el pleito no es con un niño,

querían concocer su padre,   15
¡yo soy Jacinto Treviño!

—Entrenle, rinches cobardes,
validos de la ocasión,
no van a comer pan blanco
con tajadas de jamón.—   20

Decía el Rinche Mayor,
como era un americano:
—¡Ah, qué Jacinto tan hombre,
no niega el ser mexicano!—

Decía Jacinto Treviño   25
que se moría de la risa:
—A mí me hacen los ojales,
los puños de la camisa.—

Decía Jacinto Treviño,
abrochándose un zapato: 30
—Aquí traigo más cartuchos
pa' divertirnos un rato.—

Decía Jacinto Treviño,
con su pistola en la mano:
No corran, rinches cobardes,   35
con un solo mexicano.—

Decía Jacinto Treviño:
—Yo ya me vo' a retirar,
me voy para Río Grande
y allá los voy a esperar.—   40

Decía Jacinto Treviño,
al bajar una bajada:
—¡Ay, qué rinches tan cobardes,
que no me haigan hecho nada!—

Decía Jacinto Treviño,   45
andando en Nuevo Laredo:
—Yo soy Jacinto Treviño,
nacido en Montemorelos.—

Ya con ésta me despido
aquí a presencia de todos,   50
yo soy Jacinto Treviño,
vecino de Matamoros.

Jacinto Treviño

With this it will be three times that remarkable things have
    happened;
the first time was in McAllen, then in Brownsville and San
    Benito.

They had a shoot-out at Baker's saloon;
broken bottles were popping all over the place.   5

Baker's saloon was immediately deserted;
only Jacinto Treviño remained, with his rifle and his pistol.

"Come on, you cowardly *rinches*, you're not playing games with a
    child.
You wanted to meet your father? I am Jacinto Treviño!   10

"Come on, you cowardly *rinches*, you always like to take the
    advantage;
this is not like eating white bread with slices of ham."

The chief of the *rinches* said, even though he was an American,
"Ah, what a brave man is Jacinto; you can see he is a Mexican!"   15

Then said Jacinto Treviño, who was dying of laughter,
"All you're good for is to make the buttonholes and the cuffs on
    my shirt."

Then said Jacinto Treviño, as he was tying his shoe,
"I have more cartridges here, so we can amuse ourselves a while."   20

Then said Jacinto Treviño, with his pistol in his hand,
"Don't run, you cowardly *rinches*, from a single Mexican."

Then said Jacinto Treviño, "I am going to retire.
I'm going to Rio Grande City, and I will wait for you there."

Then said Jacinto Treviño, as he came down an incline,   25
"Ah, what a cowardly bunch of *rinches*; they didn't do anything to
    me!"

Then said Jacinto Treviño, when he was in Nuevo Laredo,
"I am Jacinto Treviño, born in Montemorelos."

Now with this I say farewell, here in everybody's presence;   30
I am Jacinto Treviño, a citizen of Matamoros.

1976

El Hijo Desobediente

Un domingo estando herrando
se encontraron dos mancebos,
echando mano a los fieros
como queriendo pelear;
cuando se estaban peleando   5
pues llegó su padre de uno:
—Hijo de mi corazón,
ya no pelees con ninguno.—

—Quítese de aquí mi padre
que estoy más bravo que   10
un león no vaya a sacar la espada
y la parta el corazón.—
—Hijo de mi corazón,
por lo que acabas de hablar
antes de que raye el sol   15
la vida te han de quitar.—

—Lo que le pido a mi padre
que no me entierre en sagrado,
que me entierre en tierra bruta
donde me trille el ganado,   20
con una mano de fuera
y un papel sobre-dorado,
con un letrero que diga,
"Felipe fue desdichado."

—La vaquilla colorada,   25
hace un año que nació.
ahi se la dejo a mi padre
por la crianza que me dió;
los tres caballos que tengo,
ahi se los dejo a los pobres   30
para que digan en vida,
"Felipe, Dios te perdone."—

Bajaron el toro prieto,
que nunca lo habían bajado,
pero ora si ya bajó   35
revuelto con el ganado;
ya con ésta me despido
por la estrella del oriente,
y aquí se acaba el corrido
de El Hijo Desobediente.   40

The Disobedient Son

On a Sunday during branding
Two young cowboys did meet,
Each going for his steel
Each looking to fight;
As they were fighting   5
The father of one arrived:
—My beloved son
Do not fight with anyone.—

—Get away from here, my father
I feel more fierce than a lion,   10
For I may draw my knife
To split your heart in two.—
—My beloved son,
Because of what you have said
Before the next sunrise   15
Your life will be taken away.—

—I only ask of my father
Do not bury me in sacred ground,
Bury me in brute earth
Where the stock may trample me   20
With one hand out of the grave
And a gilded paper,
With an epitaph that reads
"Felipe was an ill-fated man."

The red yearling   25
Born a year ago,
I leave to my father
My upbringing to him I owe;
My three stallions
I leave to the poor   30
So that they may say
"May God forgive you, Felipe."

They brought the black bull down,
Never before brought down,
But now the bull has come down   35
With the rest of the stock;
Now with this I say farewell
Guided by the eastern star
This ends the ballad
Of the disobedient son.   40

Recordando al Presidente

by Willie López

Los latinoaméricanos de esta tierra
recordamos con tristeza al Presidente:
en los tiempos de la paz y de la guerra
estuviste defendiendo al continente.

En la guerra fuiste siempre buen soldado,   5
en la paz fuiste un honrado presidente,
un gran hombre de todos appreciado,
un demócrata sincero y muy valiente.

John F. [efe] Kennedy tu recuerdo vivirá,
que Dios te tenga con el allí en la gloria,   10
te lloramos los de aquí, te sintieron los de allá,
ya tu nombre escrito está en el mundo y en la historia.

Teniendo Cuba muchas armas peligrosas,
a los rusos les hablaste muy en serio,
desafiando los peligros y otras cosas   15
y salvando de la muerte al hemisferio.

Mexicanos, de acá somos residentes,
y por pochos nos distinguen los demas,
te quisimos como a pocos presidentes,
pues pensamos como tú,¡viva la paz!   20

John F. [efe] Kennedy tu recuerdo vivirá,
que Dios te tenga con el allí en la gloria,
te lloramos los de aquí, te sintieron los de allá,
ya tu nombre escrito está en el mundo y en la historia.

Remembering the President

by Willie López

We Latin Americans of this country,
With sadness we remember the President,
In times of war and peace
You were defending the continent.

In the war you were always a good soldier,   5
In peace you were an honorable president,
A great man esteemed by all,
A sincere and brave democrat.

John F. Kennedy your memory will live,
May God have you with him in his glory,   10
We weep for you here and others grieve for you
      elsewhere,
Now your name is inscribed in the world and in history.

When Cuba had many dangerous arms,
You spoke very seriously to the Russians,   15
Facing dangers and other things
And saving the hemisphere from death.

Mexicans here [in Texas] we are citizens,
And others [Mexicans] call us *pochos*,[1]
We loved you as we have loved few presidents,   20
And we believed as you, long live peace!

John F. Kennedy your memory will live,
May God have you with him in his glory,
We weep for you here and others grieve for you
      elsewhere,   25
Now your name is inscribed in the world and in history.

Corrido de César Chávez

Detente mi corazón,
En el pecho no me cabe
El regocijo y orgullo
Al cantarle a César Chávez.

Inspiración de mi gente,   5
Protector del campesino
El es un gran mexicano
Ese sería su destino.

De muy humildes principios
Organizaste a la gente;   10
Y a los hacendados ricos
Te paraste frente a frente.

[1]Slang term for an Americanized Mexican.

Injustamente te acusan
Que intentaste usar violencia
Ayunaste veinticinco días　　　　　　　　　　　　15
Pa' probar tu inocencia.

En el estandarte que lleva
Mi Virgen de Guadalupe,
En tu incesante labor
De bendiciones te tuve.　　　　　　　　　　　　20

A los venticinco días
El ayuno terminó
En el parque de Delano
Una misa celebró.

Junto con ocho mil almas　　　　　　　　　　　　25
Bobby Kennedy asistió;
Admiración y cariño
Nuestra gente le brindó.

Vuela de aquí de me seno,
Paloma, vete a Delano;　　　　　　　　　　　　30
Y por si acaso no sabes
Allí vive César Chávez.

Ballad of César Chávez[1]

Stop, my heart,
In my breast there is no room
For the joy and pride
Of singing of César Chávez.

Inspiration of my people,　　　　　　　　　　　　5
Protector of the farm worker,
He is a great Mexican;
This would be his destiny.

From very humble beginnings
You organized your people;　　　　　　　　　　　　10
And against the rich ranchers
You stood face to face.

---

[1] Head of the United Farm Workers, 1965–1993.

Unjustly they accuse you
Of intending to use violence.
You fasted for twenty-five days   15
In order to prove your innocence.

On the standard that carries
My Virgin of Guadalupe,
In whose presence you came to worship,
I esteemed you with my praise.   20

After twenty-five days
The fast ended;
In the park in Delano
A mass was celebrated.

Together with eight thousand souls   25
Bobby Kennedy attended;
Admiration and affection
Our people offered him a toast.

Fly from my breast,
Dove, go to Delano;   30
And if perhaps you don't know,
There lives César Chávez.

The Dawes Act

I N 1887, PARTLY IN RESPONSE TO DEMANDS FOR REFORM OF U.S. TREATMENT OF Native Americans, Congress passed the General Allotment Act, also known as the Dawes Act. The Act divided tribal lands into plots to be allotted to individual Indian owners and decreed that only Indians agreeing to private property ownership (and rejection of communal ownership) would be granted U.S. citizenship. Whatever the intentions of the reformers who backed it, the Act's chief result was the further devastation of tribes and tribal cultures and the further reduction of land remaining in Native American hands, with unallotted land opened up to white settlers. As Mark Rifkin has argued, the Dawes Act also forced American Indians into family and gender structures that resembled the patriarchal model idealized in American law and culture; the insistence on private property devastated Native cultural models under which gender roles and family structures looked radically different.

John Milton Oskison's short story "The Problem of Old Harjo" highlights the impasse between American and Native cultures by focusing on the family. Portraying a loving Indian family that comprises two wives and one husband, and a Christian missionary torn between U.S. law and custom and respect for this family, Oskison's story brilliantly unsettles the status of "the American" family as a viable model for all Americans, or for the nation. Written for Native people in the Indian Territory that the Dawes Act carved out, Alexander Posey's Fus Fixico letters reflect on aspects of life there and examine the question of whether or not the Territory should become a state (it did—the state of Oklahoma—in 1907). While the Dawes Act does not have direct bearing on other Native selections in Volume C, they situate the Act and its effects within the larger context of the genocide waged against Native peoples and cultures and the resilience as well as the losses that Natives peoples' lives entailed.

U.S. CONGRESS

from **The Dawes Act (1887)**

An Act to provide for the allotment of lands in severalty to Indians on the various reservations, and to extend the protection of the laws of the United States and the Territories over the Indians, and for other purposes.

Be it enacted by the Senate and House of Representatives of the United States of America in Congress assembled, That in all cases where any tribe or band of Indians has been, or shall hereafter be, located upon any reservation created for their use, either by treaty stipulation or by virtue of an act of Congress or executive order setting apart the same for their use, the President of the United States be, and he hereby is, authorized, whenever in his opinion any reservation or any part thereof of such Indians is advantageous for agricultural and grazing purposes, to cause said reservation, or any part thereof, to be surveyed, or resurveyed if necessary, and to allot the lands in said reservation in severalty to any Indian located thereon in quantities as follows:

To each head of a family, one-quarter of a section;
To each single person over eighteen years of age, one-eighth of a section;
To each orphan child under eighteen years of age, one-eighth of a section; and
To each other single person under eighteen years now living, or who may be born prior to the date of the order of the President directing an allotment of the lands embraced in any reservation, one-sixteenth of a section....

[A]t any time after lands have been allotted to all the Indians of any tribe as herein provided, or sooner if in the opinion of the President it shall be for the best interests of said tribe, it shall be lawful for the Secretary of the Interior to negotiate with such Indian tribe for the purchase and release by said tribe of such portions of its reservation not allotted ... *Provided however*, That all lands adapted to agriculture, with or without irrigation so sold or released to the United States by any Indian tribe shall be held by the United States for the sale purpose of securing homes to actual settlers and shall be disposed of by the United States to actual and bona fide settlers only tracts not exceeding one hundred and sixty acres to any one person, on such terms as Congress shall prescribe, subject to grants which Congress may make in aid of education; *And provided further*, That no patents shall issue therefor except to the person so taking the same as and for a homestead, or his heirs, and after the exploration of five years of occupancy of said lands so taken as a homestead, or any contract touching the same, or lien, thereon, created prior to the date of such patent, shall be null and void.... And if any religious society or other organization is now occupying any of the public lands to which this act is applicable, for religious or educational work among the Indians, the Secretary of the Interior is hereby authorized to confirm such occupation to such society or organization, in quantity not exceeding one hundred and sixty acres in any one tract.... That upon the completion of said allotments and the patenting of the lands to said allottees, each and every member of the respective bands or tribes of Indians to whom allotments have been made shall have the benefit of and be subject to the laws, both civil and criminal, of the State or Territory in which they may reside; and no Territory shall pass or enforce any law denying any such Indian within its jurisdiction the equal protection of law.

And every Indian born within the territorial limits of the United States to whom allotments shall have been made under provision of this act, or under law or treaty, and every Indian born within the territorial limits of the United States who has voluntarily taken up.... his residence separate and apart from any tribe of Indians therein, and has adopted the habits of civilized life, is hereby declared to be a citizen of the United State.... And hereafter in the employment of Indian police, or any other employees in the public service among any of the Indian tribes or bands affected by this act, and where Indians can perform the duties required, those Indians who have availed themselves of the provisions of this act and become citizens of the United States shall be preferred.

...[N]othing in this act contained shall be so construed to affect the right and power of Congress to grant the right of way through any lands granted to an Indian, or a tribe of Indians, for railroads or other highways, or telegraph lines, for the public use, or condemn such lands to public uses, upon making just compensation.

[N]othing in this act shall be so construed as to prevent the removal of the Southern Ute Indians from their present reservation in Southwestern Colorado to a new reservation by and with consent of a majority of the adult male members of said tribe.

Approved, February 8, 1887.
United States Congress

■ ALEXANDER LAWRENCE POSEY (CREEK) ■
1873–1908

Alexander Posey's life was cut short on May 27, 1908. At the age of thirty-five, the Creek writer drowned while crossing the flooded Oktahutche River. It was barely a year since Indian Territory and the tribal governments within it had been dissolved. Born in the Creek Nation, Posey died in the brand-new state of Oklahoma. The end of tribal governments and the advent of statehood were long, bitterly contested transitions. As a poet, politician, and political satirist, Posey had a strong and complicated voice in the deliberations.

Often called a "progressivist" because he believed that Native peoples needed at least partially to assimilate to white culture in order to survive, Posey criticized "traditionalists," calling them "pull back" Indians who couldn't possibly survive in the imminent future. Nevertheless, he respected older Creeks who remembered another way of life. Posey has been somewhat reviled among Creeks for his participation in the bureaucracy surrounding the dissolution of tribal government and for his subsequent activities as a real estate speculator in formerly tribal land. However, he is recognized as having penned some of the most cogent and far-sighted critiques of both that bureaucracy and the greed for Indian land. Posey lived during a complicated period of change for the Creek Nation, and his motivations were never simple. They are still difficult to decipher, perhaps because they are so often couched in humor.

Posey's mother was half Creek and half Chickasaw. Because she was from the tribal town of Tuskegee and Creek clan membership follows matrilineal lines, Posey himself was a Wind Clan member of Tuskegee. Although Posey's father was born to white parents, he called himself Creek. He was raised in the Creek Nation from the time he was orphaned, he spoke Creek fluently, and he was a member of the Broken Arrow tribal town. Young Alexander spoke only Creek; when he was fourteen, his father insisted that he speak English and punished him if he spoke in his native language. From that time, Posey received a formal education, including three years at Bacone Indian University in Muskogee. His mixed-blood status, his estrangement from the Creek language, and his education fostered his ambivalence toward Creek traditionalism; this ambivalence separated him from his own culture but gave him a powerful critical voice within it.

Posey began writing while a student at Bacone. Influenced by the conventional English forms he studied in school, Posey's poetry pays homage to Whittier, Longfellow, Kipling, and Tennyson. Naturalists who wrote in English, like Thoreau and John Burroughs, also influenced the aspiring Creek poet. A lover of nature, Posey was passionately attached to the Tulledega Hills, where he spent his childhood. Not satisfied with the English language's abilities to translate Creek experience, Posey tried to replicate in his English poetry the rhythms and cadences of the musical Creek language. His poetry achieved moderate success, regularly appearing in Indian Territory publications. In 1900 and 1901, a few poems appeared in publications in the East and Midwest.

Soon after leaving school, Posey became involved in Creek politics. His leadership skills, intelligence, and personal charm proved highly useful to the struggling Creek Nation. Elected to the Creek National Council at age twenty-two, he would continue his political involvement until his death. By the turn of the century his interest in poetry had waned, and in 1902 he started a career as a journalist, setting the stage for his most effective writing. As owner and editor of the *Eufaula (Okla.) Indian Journal*, Posey achieved national prominence in the United States for establishing the first Indian-published daily newspaper. More important, he was recognized for comic letters written by his fictional persona, Fus Fixico (Heartless Bird), which he printed in the *Indian Journal* as substitutes for editorials. A full-blooded Creek, Fus Fixico wrote to the paper about his everyday life or sent in transcriptions of speeches that he had heard the Creek medicine man Hotgun deliver to an audience of other old men—Kono Harjo, Tookpafka Micco, and Wolf Warrior. The monologues are in dialect and achieve a wickedly satirical perspective on Creek culture and politics.

Sometimes read as expressions of nostalgia for a vanishing way of life, the Fus Fixico letters are also cogent political commentary aimed at influencing Indian Territory, Oklahoma, and United States politics. Across the years when Posey wrote and published the Fus Fixico letters, politics in Indian Territory was a veritable Gordian knot. The Curtis Act of 1898, which decreed that Indian land held in common by tribal governments be broken up and allotted in small portions to individual tribal members, was being implemented, and debates about statehood were raging. Not only were Native peoples ambivalent about statehood, there was a very real possibility that Oklahoma would be admitted as two states—one white, one Indian. Posey was a strong advocate of the two-state proposal and was secretary of the 1905 convention to organize Sequoyah, the proposed Indian state. The Fus Fixico letters satirized every aspect of the debate. Posey was frequently approached by U.S. newspaper syndicates that wanted to publish his Fus Fixico letters nationally. He refused permission. His political satires were intended for Indian Territory readers, and he knew that their dialect and humor would suffer in translation for a national audience that knew little of the intricacies of Indian Territory politics.

Dialect literature was hugely popular at the turn of the twentieth century. Posey's father liked to tell stories in black dialect, and Alexander Posey's favorite poet was Robert Burns, famous for his Scottish dialect poems. Posey read the dialect literatures of poet James Whitcomb Riley and Paul Laurence Dunbar and dialect humorists such as Josh Billings and Max Adler. He was doing far more than simply catering to U.S. national taste, however. He switched from poetry to dialect writing as he became more politically active, and his dialect writings represent Creek life more effectively than does his poetry. Though his characters speak Creek English, the dialect writings are representations of Creek oral culture. Posey had no patience for writers who wrote dialect simply because it was fashionable: "Those cigar store Indian dialect stories ... will fool no one who has lived 'six months in the precinct.' Like the wooden aborigine, they are the product of a white man's factory, and bear no resemblance to the real article."

Posey was mourned throughout the Indian Territory after his premature death. He remains a complicated figure in Creek culture, remembered with mingled respect and suspicion. Two years after his death, his wife collected and published much of his poetry, but his Fus Fixico letters remained uncollected until the 1990s.

Bethany Ridgway Schneider
Bryn Mawr College

PRIMARY WORKS

Edward Everett Dale, ed., The Journal of Alexander Lawrence Posey, January 1 to September 4, 1897, *Chronicles of Oklahoma* 45 (Winter 1967–1968); Minnie Posey, ed., *The Poems of Alexander Lawrence Posey*, 1910; Daniel F. Littlefield, Jr. and Carol A. Petter Hunter, eds., *The Fus Fixico Letters*, 1993.

Ode to Sequoyah[1]

The names of Waitie and Boudinot—[2]
   The valiant warrior and gifted sage—
And other Cherokees, may be forgot,
   But thy name shall descend to every age;
The mysteries enshrouding Cadmus' name[3]   5
Cannot obscure thy claim to fame.

The people's language cannot perish—nay,
   When from the face of this great continent
   Inevitable doom hath swept away
The last memorial—the last fragment   10
   Of tribes,—some scholar learned shall pore
Upon thy letters, seeking ancient lore.

Some bard shall lift a voice in praise of thee,
   In moving numbers tell the world how men
Scoffed thee, hissed thee, charged with lunacy!   15
   And who could not give 'nough honor when
At length, in spite of jeers, of want and need,
Thy genius shaped a dream into a deed.

By cloud-capped summits in the boudless west,
   Or mighty river rolling to the sea   20

---

[1]Sequoyah (George Guess) invented the 86-symbol Cherokee syllabary.

[2]Brothers and leaders of the Cherokee Treaty Party, they supported voluntary Cherokee removal from Georgia to what would become Indian Territory in the West, leading voluntary emigration in 1837. Stand Watie (1806–1871) became a Confederate general. Elias Boudinot, who changed his name from Chuck Watie, edited the *Cherokee Phoenix*. Born in 1802, he was assassinated in 1838 by the Anti-Treaty Party headed by tribal chief John Ross. Volume B contains his "Address to the Whites."

[3]Mythological figure to whom origination of the Greek alphabet was attributed.

Where'er they footsteps led thee on that quest,
    Unknown, rest thee, illustrious Cherokee![4]

1899

Hotgun on the Death of Yadeka Harjo[1]

"Well so," Hotgun he say,
    "My ol'-time frien', Yadeka Harjo, he
Was died the other day,
    An' they was no ol'-timer left but me.

"Hotulk Emathla he   5
    Was go to be good Injin long time 'go,
An' Woxie Harjoche
    Been dead ten years or twenty, maybe so.

All had to die at las';
    I live long time, but now my days was few;   10
'Fore long poke-weeds an' grass
    Be growin' all aroun' my grave-house, too."

Wolf Warrior he listen close,
    An' Kono Harjo pay close 'tention, too;
Tookpafka Micco he almos'   15
    Let his pipe go out a time or two.

1908

Fus Fixico's Letter 44, April 29, 1904

Eufaula [Creek Nation] Tribune

[Hotgun and his friends are discussing the sale of Creeks' and other tribes' land in Indian Territory after the General Allotment Act (1887) and the Curtis Act (1898) effected this sale as well as the end of tribal government. Posey's four fictional "traditional" Indians, all elderly, are disturbed both by dishonest white land brokers and by Indians' enthusiasm for whites' commodities.]

"Well, so," Hotgun he say, "the Injin he sell land and sell land, and the white man he give whiskey and give whiskey and put his arm around the Injin's neck and they was good friends like two Elks out for a time."

---

[4]Sequoyah disappeared while looking for Cherokees who had gone to Mexico rather than "remove" to the West.

[1]Posey's tribute to the much-respected Yadeka Hajro, who had died at an advanced age, is spoken by the fictional central character of his Fus Fuxico Letters, Hotgun; several other figures cited in the poem also appear in the Letters (see next selection). Posey published this poem in the Eufaula (Oklahoma) Indian Journal of January 24, 1908.

"Well, maybe so," Tookpafka Micco he say, "the white man was cut it out when the Injun was all in."

Then Hotgun he make the smoke b'il out a his pipe good and answer Tookpafka Micco, "Well, so the Injin was had to go up against it to learn and, maybe so, after while he catch on, same like the white man and go to Mexico and bunco the greaser."[1]

Then Hotgun he take another puff and go on and say, "Well, so like I start to say history was repeat itself. The Injin he sell his land in the old country (Alabama) and he sell his land in Injin Territory and was had a good time out here like back there in olden times. But back in old country he was live different, 'cause he was sit on a long chair like a fence rail—but he was no mugwump.[2] Now the Injin was sit on a chair that was had fore legs and hind legs too, like a oxen, and also a cushion soft like moss. He was got civilized and called the old chair a bench. He wear a white shirt now and black clothes and shoes that was look like a ripe musk melon. Then he was buy bon bons for his papoose and drop-stitch stockings for his squaw and part his name in the middle, J. Little Bear.

"Then the white man he tell the Injin, 'Well so your wagon was out of date and you better buy you a fine buggy; or, maybe so, a fine surrey.' The Injin he grunt and say, 'Well, so let's see um.' Then the white man he say, 'Well, so I sell it cheap like stealing it—sell it to Injun the fine buggy and harness and all for hundred and fifty dollars. That was cheap, 'cause Injun he was sell land and got it lots a money and was out of date riding on two horse wagon.' Then the Injin he look at fine buggy a long time and make good judgment and buy um. His little pony mare team look mighty weak and woolly and got colt, but they was pulled the fine buggy home all right. Then when the Injin was got home he was put the fine buggy under a tree to look at like fine painting."

(Tookpafka Micco and Wolf Warrior and Kono Harjo they was look in the fire and spit in the ashes and pay close attention like they was interested.)

Then Hotgun he go on and say, "Well, maybe so about three years from now the starch was go out a the Injin's white shirt and make it limber like a dish rag, and his black suit was fade like the last rose a summer and his breeches was get slack like a gunny sack, and his big toe was stick through his tan shoes like a snag in Deep Fork,[3] and his fine buggy was tied together with bailing wire and his old fillies was made good crow bait pulling the fine buggy to stomp dances." Then, Hotgun he go on and say, "Maybe so the Injin was awakened up to his sense a duty and earn his bread by the sweat a his brow like a good republican or maybe so a democrat."

And Tookpafka Micco he say, "Well, maybe so he be a middle of a the roader."

---

[1] The reference is to the Creeks' 1832 agreement to give up their land in the Southeast and move west.

[2] Postbellum Republican Party reformers, whom Hotgun casts as compromisers, or "fence-sitters."

[3] The Deep Fork River served as the southeastern boundary separating the Creek and Choctaw nations. A snag: a tree stump or other item protruding from the river's surface.

Then Hotgun he say, "Well, so they was only two sides to a clapboard and it's the same way in politics. The Injin couldn't cut any ice or raise any sofky sitting on top a the rail looking at the crabgrass."[4]

(Then Tookpafka Micco and Wolf Warrior and Kono Harjo they was grunt and spit in the ashes again and say, "Well, so we vote it straight.")

1904

Fus Fixico's Letter 45, May 7, 1904

"Well, so," Hotgun he say, "It was time to go barefooted and quote poetry and spark some widow woman that was had a good family history on the Loyal Creek roll,[1] 'cause every evening after sun down the frogs was give a concert, like the Muskogee Merchants Band, and the old plow filly was picking up on the green grass and scattering lots a dead hair where she wallows."

(Tookpafka Micco and Wolf Warrior and Kono Harjo they was grunt and look way off towards the creek like they want to go fishing.)

Then Hotgun he smoke slow and look at red ants on the ground, go on and say, "Well, so I don't know what the newspapers was had to fill up on, 'cause Crazy Snake was made a assignment and gone out of business and retired to cabin to fix up the fence around his sofky patch and clean out his old spring and start over again."

"Well, so," Tookpafka Micco he say, "the newspapers could finds lots a stuff to fill up on, like the removal a the restrictions so the niggers could squander they land for a blue suit of clothes and rubber-tired buggy and make room for progress, while the Injin he look on and learn a good object lesson."[2]

Then Wolf Warrior he join in and say, "Well, so the newspapers was had lots other news 'sides that to fill up on, like when Chief Porter go to St. Louis and get married and Secretary Its Cocked was approved the matrimony, or maybe so, when Muskogee was had the state capital and all the railroads and street car lines, and all the senators and congressmen and members a the legislature and judges and road overseers and coroners, notary publics and things like that."[3]

Hotgun he look at the red ants and smoke a long time and say, "Well, so all that kind a thing was looked good in print, but it was not made spicy

---

[4]Hotgun is saying that the middle-of-the-road position that Tookpafka Micco suggests is the equivalent of the Mugwamps' fence-sitting.

[1]Hotgun is proposing that he court a widow whose family is on the list of Creeks loyal to the Union during the Civil War. At the time of this writing, it appeared as if the loyal Creeks might receive a cash settlement in payment for Civil War damages. The fictive

widow would then be in line for a small amount of money.

[2]Many freedmen who had received allotments after the Civil War lost their land when restrictions on sale were lifted.

[3]Wolf Warrior is referring to the possibility that Muskogee would become the state capital if Indian Territory were to become its own state.

reading like bad news from Hickory Ground, where the Snakes was uprising and throwing tomahawks at the pale face prisoner for practice."[4]

"But," Hotgun he go on and say, "like I start to say, Crazy Snake he was called his people together and made a motion to give it up.

"He says, 'Well, so I was want to advise you they was no hope—and no provisions neither. So we better give up and be reconciled, like the Chinese.[5] The United States was break treaty and break treaty, and the white man he has come from Arkansas and come from Arkansas and stay and write back to kinfolks and say this was the garden spot a the earth and you better come out here before it's all gone. So that way the country was settled up and settled up, and they was no game left but swamp rabbits. We couldn't had any fish fry and stomp dance like in olden time. The white man he was make town and make town and build railroad and build railroad and appoint federal judge and appoint federal judge to say it was all right and we couldn't help it. So if we was had a council to talk it over, the marshal and soldiers was arrest us for trying to kill the president and put us in jail to catch consumption and maybe so lice. So I was make a motion to give it up and see what become of us anyhow.' Everybody was give a big grunt and the motion was carried."

(Tookpafka Micco and Wolf Warrior and Kono Harjo they was look mighty sorry.)

"Well, so," Hotgun he go on and say, "that was made me think about the old chief that was want to die long time ago, because he knew too much. The old chief he think he learn everything and maybe so he better lay down and die. So he was called his warriors around his buffalo hide and made 'em long talk about how to run the government when he die. Then he called for his pipe so he could die in peace, and was ask a little boy to get him a coal of fire. The little boy he go to the fire and bring the coal on some ashes in his hand instead of a chip or maybe so bark. The old chief he was watch him do it and jumped up and say, 'Well, so I was a damn fool and was had lots of sense to learn, maybe so from a little boy.'"

1904

Fus Fixico's Letter 46, May 13, 1904

Well, so Hotgun and Tookpafka Micco they was talked politics and Wolf Warrior and Kono Harjo they was paid close attention and grunt.

"Well, so," Hotgun he say, "they was lots a good political timber decaying 'cause we didn't had statehood, and maybe so some of it was rotten enough to make fox fire and lead Bony Parts a long chase for nothing."[1]

[4]Hotgun is distinguishing between news that looks good and news that is interesting; "progress" is boring, whereas insurrection is thrilling. Hotgun is suggesting that the possibility of resistance is over, though, in fact, the Snakes and Chitto Harjo were not acquiescent.
[5]China was divided into "spheres of influence" by European nations.

[1]Fox fire is the dim light cast by decaying wood. The implication is that Charles J. Bonaparte, who was sent to Indian Territory to investigate allegations of fraud by federal agents, was not able to discover the truth.

(Tookpafka Micco and Wolf Warrior and Kono Harjo they was grunt soft and study about it, while Hotgun was filled his pipe so he could warm up to the occasion.)

"But, maybe so," Hotgun he go on and say, "we could afford to let the timber go to waste, 'cause they was plenty more where that was come from 'sides the improved variety that was shipped down here from the states on fifty years trial."

And Tookpafka Micco he say, "Well so who was the most prominent before the people anyhow and was stirred up the most feeling?"

And Hotgun he say, "Well, so I think they was most prominent among themselves and the people didn't had nothing to do with it and was innocent. It was like this way: These politicians was get together like wolves when they was get hungry and want to forage—and the wolf in front was Plenty So Far.[2] He was sit 'round on the knolls a Cooweescoowee prairie looking for signs till he was had big callouses on his hips. When congress was get in session and was busy with statehood bills and didn't had no time to look after the Injun, then Plenty So Far he was sit down on top of a knoll and look 'way off and howl lonesome. Pretty soon Judge My Fee hear him 'way down on Kendall Heights and howl back and pretty soon come to him with lots a black wolves from Cane Creek. Then maybe so the constable 'way down about Eufaula come and join with lots a cayotes [sic]. Then maybe so directly the postmaster down to Okmulgee come trotting up with a big following. So that way they was come to him from Wildcat and Twine till Plenty So Far could look back over his shoulder and see a big pack behind so hungry they couldn't hardly stay together."[3]

(Tookpafka Micco and Wolf Warrior and Kono Harjo they was listen so close they pipes was go out and they didn't know it.)

Then Hotgun he go on and say, "Well, so it was the same way among the Democrats too and it was about a stand off. They was two, three down to Choctaw nation and Chickasaw nation howling with they packs. But I think maybe so Old Hailey was prowling 'round in the hills close to South McAlester with the biggest pack, while Bob Willing was sneaking 'round on the Blue with a few cayotes and Mayor Dick was sent up a lonesome howl from down about Ardmore.[4] So these was the Democrat wolves, but the trouble with them is they was too hungry to stay together and much disturbance among the sheep. The Republican wolves was better organized and had better hunting ground."

---

[2]Pliny Soper was the U.S. attorney for the Northern District of Indian Territory and was heavily involved in the systematic practices of defrauding Native Americans of their land.

[3]Hotgun is painting a portrait of the social geography of Indian Territory. He is saying that the African American populations in areas like Cane Creek, Wildcat, and Pine, who mostly voted Republican, are all rallying behind Soper.

[4]Hotgun is describing prominent Democrats, many of whom went on to benefit from statehood. Robert Lee Williams went on to become governor from 1915 to 1919.

(Then Tookpafka Micco he was passed 'round the "homemade," and Hotgun and Wolf Warrior and Kono Harjo they was pinched off some for a fresh smoke.)

Then Tookpafka Micco he ask Hotgun, "Well, so who all want to be large delegates and little delegates to the big convention in the states to nominate a new president?"

And Hotgun he say, "Well, so the Republicans was already picked out Plenty So Far from the Seminole nation and Cherokee nation and Quapaw agency to lead the delegates from the rest a the Territory. He was had a Choctaw Injun in the bunch that was not old enough to vote and was had to had a white man go with him to show him how to cast his ballot and make excuse for him."[5]

"Then," Hotgun he go on and say, "The Democrats was had lots aspirants to be large delegates and little delegates to trot out nominee for president. The most prominent ones was Cliff Jack's son and Jim's Living and Lick's Broke and Sam Rather Ford and C. B. Stew It."

"But," Hotgun he go on and say, "like I first start to say, the people was busy putting in more land and building shacks and say nothing. Maybe so when the time was ripe they was take a hand in politics and make these spoil hunters look like an order on the store for merchandise during the Loyal Creek payment."

1904

■ JOHN MILTON OSKISON (CHEROKEE) ■
1874–1947

John Oskison was born at Vinita in the Cherokee Nation, to a Cherokee mother and a white father. He began his college career at Willie Halsell College in his home town; one of his classmates was the future movie-star cowboy Will Rogers, who became his lifelong friend. Leaving Indian Territory, Oskison embarked upon an exclusive education, finishing his B.A. at Stanford in 1898, then going to Harvard to study literature. He had already written for Cherokee Nation publications and for the Stanford magazine *Sequoia*, but Oskison's career as a writer took off while he was at Harvard. In 1899 he submitted his short story "Only the Master Shall Praise," which borrowed its title from Rudyard Kipling, to the *Century* magazine competition for college graduates. Oskison won the coveted prize, which brought him to national attention, and he embarked upon a long, flourishing career as a writer.

---

[5]Hotgun is pointing out that the Republican delegation from Indian Territory to the national presidential nominating convention is almost entirely white.

As an adult, Oskison was removed from Cherokee and other Native American populations by both geography and education. He drew upon his childhood in the Cherokee Nation for his material; his regionalist stories are set in Indian Territory and reproduce the cultural idiosyncracies and dialects of the many people who struggled to make the Territory their own. Published in the early years of the twentieth century, his short stories brought to national attention the particular culture and the peculiar conflicts that characterized Indian Territory in the last days before native governments were dissolved and the state of Oklahoma was created in their place. Oskison had a keen eye for the painful ironies that often surface in cultural conflict; his stories are populated with a miscellany of full and mixed-blood Cherokees as well as white cowboys, outlaws, ministers, and missionaries. His tales of Indian Territory, such as "The Problem of Old Harjo," "The Fall of King Chris," and "When the Grass Grew Long," were widely published in national magazines such as *Century*, *North American Review*, and *McClure's*. In spite of his success, Oskison didn't continue writing short stories. Beginning in 1903, he devoted his time to journalism, which he pursued until 1912. Across those years he edited a daily newspaper, wrote for the *Saturday Evening Post*, and climbed the editorial ladder at *Colliers*, ending up as financial editor. His writings on finance were syndicated in several publications, and he was often called upon to write about Indian affairs.

The First World War interrupted Oskison's peaceful professional progression. He served with the American Expeditionary Force in Europe, and upon his return to the United States he began a third writing career, this time as a novelist. Again, he turned to the now long-gone Indian Territory for inspiration. *Wild Harvest* and *Black Jack Davy*, the two novels he published in the 1920s, concern white heroes. They evoke the desperate and ruthless mood that pervaded the final years of Native government in Indian Territory; Oskison condemns the greed of both whites and mixed-bloods who took advantage of the chaos to line their own pockets. In 1929—an ironic year in which to publish the biography of a rich man—Oskison produced *A Texas Titan*, which told the story of Sam Houston. During the Great Depression, Oskison turned his eyes again to Native subject-matter, publishing *Brothers Three*, a novel that traces the tragedy of mixed-blood siblings who give up a traditional relationship to the land in order to pursue the American dream of individual wealth. Although Oskison's novels are not as appreciated as his shorter, earlier works, they round out a lifework concerned with the problems of mixed-race people struggling to make sense of a homeland and politics that were changing more quickly than their own abilities to adapt. In 1938 Oskison published *Tecumseh and His Times*, a biography of the Shawnee leader who led a confederacy of Native American nations to resist white encroachments on land and sovereignty. That biography was Oskison's last completed work. When he died in 1947, he was at work on an autobiography.

Bethany Ridgway Schneider
Bryn Mawr College

PRIMARY WORKS

Wild Harvest; A Novel of Transition Days in Oklahoma, 1925; *Black Jack Davy,* 1926; *A Texas Titan: The Story of Sam Houston,* 1929; *Brothers Three,* 1935; *Tecumseh and His Times: The Story of a Great Indian,* 1938.

The Problem of Old Harjo[1]

The Spirit of the Lord had descended upon old Harjo. From the new missionary, just out from New York, he had learned that he was a sinner. The fire in the new missionary's eyes and her gracious appeal had convinced old Harjo that this was the time to repent and be saved. He was very much in earnest, and he assured Miss Evans that he wanted to be baptized and received into the church at once. Miss Evans was enthusiastic and went to Mrs. Rowell with the news. It was Mrs. Rowell who had said that it was no use to try to convert the older Indians, and she, after fifteen years of work in Indian Territory missions, should have known. Miss Evans was pardonably proud of her conquest.

"Old Harjo converted!" exclaimed Mrs. Rowell. "Dear Miss Evans, do you know that old Harjo has two wives?" To the older woman it was as if some one had said to her "Madame, the Sultan of Turkey wishes to teach one of your mission Sabbath school classes."

"But," protested the younger woman, "he is really sincere, and—"

"Then ask him," Mrs. Rowell interrupted a bit sternly, "if he will put away one of his wives. Ask him, before he comes into the presence of the Lord, if he is willing to conform to the laws of the country in which he lives, the country that guarantees his idle existence. Miss Evans, your work is not even begun." No one who knew Mrs. Rowell would say that she lacked sincerity and patriotism. Her own cousin was an earnest crusader against Mormonism, and had gathered a goodly share of that wagonload of protests that the Senate had been asked to read when it was considering whether a certain statesman of Utah should be allowed to represent his state at Washington.[2]

In her practical, tactful way, Mrs. Rowell had kept clear of such embarrassments. At first, she had written letters of indignant protest to the Indian Office against the toleration of bigamy amongst the tribes. A wise inspector had been sent to the mission, and this man had pointed out that it was better to ignore certain things, "deplorable, to be sure," than to attempt to make over the habits of the old men. Of course, the young Indians would not be permitted to take more than one wife each.

So Mrs. Rowell had discreetly limited her missionary efforts to the young, and had exercised toward the old and bigamous only that strict charity which even a hopeless sinner might claim.

[1]*Southern Workman* 36 (April 1907), 235–41.
[2]Oskison suggests parallels between U.S. anti-Mormonism-based objections to polygamy and U.S. government and Christian missionaries' rejection of the Creek custom of plural marriage. The reference to Utah also raises questions about U.S. government denial of citizenship and political representation: Utah had been denied statehood because of polygamy, and even after it did achieve statehood, Congress excluded, or attempted to exclude, some of its elected representatives on the same ground.

Miss Evans, it was to be regretted, had only the vaguest notions about "expediency;" so weak on matters of doctrine was she that the news that Harjo was living with two wives didn't startle her. She was young and possessed of but one enthusiasm—that for saving souls.

"I suppose," she ventured, "that old Harjo *must* put away one wife before he can join the church?"

"There can be no question about it, Miss Evans."

"Then I shall have to ask him to do it." Miss Evans regretted the necessity for forcing this sacrifice, but had no doubt that the Indian would make it in order to accept the gift of salvation which she was commissioned to bear to him.

Harjo lived in a "double" log cabin three miles from the mission. His ten acres of corn had been gathered into its fence-rail crib; four hogs that were to furnish his winter's bacon had been brought in from the woods and penned conveniently near to the crib; out in a corner of the garden, a fat mound of dirt rose where the crop of turnips and potatoes had been buried against the corrupting frost; and in the hayloft of his log stable were stored many pumpkins, dried corn, onions (suspended in bunches from the rafters) and the varied forage that Mrs. Harjo number one and Mrs. Harjo number two had thriftily provided. Three cows, three young heifers, two colts, and two patient, capable mares bore the Harjo brand, a fantastic "**H-I**" that the old man had designed. Materially, Harjo was solvent; and if the Government had ever come to his aid he could not recall the date.

This attempt to rehabilitate old Harjo morally, Miss Evans felt, was not one to be made at the mission; it should be undertaken in the Creek's own home where the evidences of his sin should confront him as she explained.

When Miss Evans rode up to the block in front of Harjo's cabin, the old Indian came out, slowly and with a broadening smile of welcome on his face. A clean gray flannel shirt had taken the place of the white collarless garment, with crackling stiff bosom, that he had worn to the mission meetings. Comfortable, well-patched moccasins had been substituted for creaking boots, and brown corduroys, belted in at the waist, for tight black trousers. His abundant gray hair fell down on his shoulders. In his eyes, clear and large and black, glowed the light of true hospitality. Miss Evans thought of the patriarchs as she saw him lead her horse out to the stable; thus Abraham might have looked and lived.

"Harjo," began Miss Evans before following the old man to the covered passageway between the disconnected cabins, "is it true that you have two wives?" Her tone was neither stern nor accusatory. The Creek had heard that question before, from scandalized missionaries and perplexed registry clerks when he went to Muscogee to enroll himself and his family in one of the many "final" records ordered to be made by the Government preparatory to dividing the Creek lands among the individual citizens.[3]

---

[3]Much official business was performed by the Indian agency in the town of Muscogee, in what had been Indian Territory and is now the state of Oklahoma.

For answer, Harjo called, first into the cabin that was used as a kitchen and then, in a loud, clear voice, toward the small field, where Miss Evans saw a flock of half-grown turkeys running about in the corn stubble. From the kitchen emerged a tall, thin Indian woman of fifty-five, with a red hand-kerchief bound severely over her head. She spoke to Miss Evans and sat down in the passageway. Presently, a clear, sweet voice was heard in the field; a stout, handsome woman, about the same age as the other, climbed the rail fence and came up to the house. She, also, greeted Miss Evans briefly. Then she carried a tin basin to the well near by, where she filled it to the brim. Setting it down on the horse block, she rolled back her sleeves, tucked in the collar of her gray blouse, and plunged her face in the water. In a minute she came out of the kitchen freshened and smiling. 'Liza Harjo had been pulling dried bean stalks at one end of the field, and it was dirty work. At last old Harjo turned to Miss Evans and said, "These two my wife—this one 'Liza, this one Jennie."

It was done with simple dignity. Miss Evans bowed and stammered. Three pairs of eyes were turned upon her in patient, courteous inquiry.

It was hard to state the case. The old man was so evidently proud of his women, and so flattered by Miss Evans' interest in them, that he would find it hard to understand. Still, it had to be done, and Miss Evans took the plunge.

"Harjo, you want to come into our church?" The old man's face lighted.

"Oh, yes, I would come to Jesus, please, my friend."

"Do you know, Harjo, that the Lord commanded that one man should mate with but one woman? The question was stated again in simpler terms, and the Indian replied, "Me know that now, my friend. Long time ago"—Harjo plainly meant the whole period previous to his conversion—"me did not know. The Lord Jesus did not speak to me in that time and so I was blind. I do what blind man do."

"Harjo, you must have only one wife when you come into our church. Can't you give up one of these women?" Miss Evans glanced at the two, sit-ting by with smiles of polite interest on their faces, understanding nothing. They had not shared Harjo's enthusiasm either for the white man's God or his language.

"Give up my wife?" A sly smile stole over his face. He leaned closer to Miss Evans. "You tell me, my friend, which one I give up." He glanced from 'Liza to Jennie as if to weigh their attractions, and the two rewarded him with their pleasantest smiles. "You tell me which one," he urged.

"Why, Harjo, how can I tell you!" Miss Evans had little sense of humor; she had taken the old man seriously.

"Then," Harjo sighed, continuing the comedy, for surely the missionary was jesting with him, "'Liza and Jennie must say." He talked to the Indian women for a time, and they laughed heartily. 'Liza, pointing to the other, shook her head. At length Harjo explained, "My friend, they cannot say. Jennie, she would run a race to see which one stay, but 'Liza, she say no, she is fat and cannot run."

Miss Evans comprehended at last. She flushed angrily, and protested, "Harjo, you are making a mock of a sacred subject; I cannot allow you to talk like this."

"But did you not speak in fun, my friend?" Harjo queried, sobering. "Surely you have just said what your friend, the white woman at the mission (he meant Mrs. Rowell) would say, and you do not mean what you say."

"Yes, Harjo, I mean it. It is true that Mrs. Rowell raised the point first, but I agree with her. The church cannot be defiled by receiving a bigamist into its membership." Harjo saw that the young woman was serious, distressingly serious. He was silent for a long time, but at last he raised his head and spoke quietly, "It is not good to talk like that if it is not in fun."

He rose and went to the stable. As he led Miss Evans' horse up to the block it was champing a mouthful of corn, the last of a generous portion that Harjo had put before it. The Indian held the bridle and waited for Miss Evans to mount. She was embarrassed, humiliated, angry. It was absurd to be dismissed in this way by—"by an ignorant old bigamist!" Then the humor of it burst upon her, and its human aspect. In her anxiety concerning the spiritual welfare of the sinner Harjo, she had insulted the man Harjo. She began to understand why Mrs. Rowell had said that the old Indians were hopeless.

"Harjo," she begged, coming out of the passageway, "please forgive me. I do not want you to give up one of your wives. Just tell me why you took them."

"I will tell you that, my friend." The old Creek looped the reins over his arm and sat down on the block. "For thirty years Jennie has lived with me as my wife. She is of the Bear people, and she came to me when I was thirty-five and she was twenty-five. She could not come before, for her mother was old, very old, and Jennie, she stay with her and feed her.

"So, when I was thirty years old I took 'Liza for my woman. She is of the Crow people.[4] She help me make this little farm here when there was no farm for many miles around.

"Well, five years 'Liza and me, we live here and work hard. But there was no child. Then the old mother of Jennie she died, and Jennie got no family left in this part of the country. So 'Liza say to me, 'Why don't you take Jennie in here?' I say, 'You don't care?' and she say, 'No, maybe we have children here then.' But we have no children—never have children. We do not like that, but God He would not let it be. So, we have lived here thirty years very happy. Only just now you make me sad."

"Harjo," cried Miss Evans, "forget what I said. Forget that you wanted to join the church." For a young mission worker with a single purpose always before her, Miss Evans was saying a strange thing. Yet she couldn't help saying it; all of her zeal seemed to have been dissipated by a simple statement of the old man.

[4]The Crow and Bear clans were two of the many Creek clans.

"I cannot forget to love Jesus, and I want to be saved." Old Harjo spoke with solemn earnestness. The situation was distracting. On one side stood a convert eager for the protection of the church, asking only that he be allowed to fulfill the obligations of humanity and on the other stood the church, represented by Mrs. Rowell, that set an impossible condition on receiving old Harjo to itself. Miss Evans wanted to cry; prayer, she felt, would be entirely inadequate as a means of expression.

"Oh! Harjo," she cried out, "I don't know what to do. I must think it over and talk with Mrs. Rowell again."

But Mrs. Rowell could suggest no way out; Miss Evans' talk with her only gave the older woman another opportunity to preach the folly of wasting time on the old and "unreasonable" Indians. Certainly the church could not listen even to a hint of a compromise in this case. If Harjo wanted to be saved there was one way and only one—unless—

"Is either of the two women old? I mean, so old that she is—an—"

"Not at all," answered Miss Evans. "They're both strong and—yes, happy. I think they will outlive Harjo."

"Can't you appeal to one of the women to go away? I dare say we could provide for her." Miss Evans, incongruously, remembered Jennie's jesting proposal to race for the right to stay with Harjo. What could the mission provide as a substitute for the little home that 'Liza had helped to create there in the edge of the woods? What other home would satisfy Jennie?

"Mrs. Rowell, are you sure that we ought to try to take one of Harjo's women from him? I'm not sure that it would in the least advance morality amongst the tribe, but I'm certain that it would make three gentle people unhappy for the rest of their lives."

"You may be right, Miss Evans." Mrs. Rowell was not seeking to create unhappiness, for enough of it inevitably came to be pictured in the little mission building. "You may be right," she repeated, "but it is a grevious misfortune that old Harjo should wish to unite with the church."

No one was more regular in his attendance at the mission meetings than old Harjo. Sitting well forward, he was always in plain view of Miss Evans at the organ. Before the service began, and after it was over, the old man greeted the young woman. There was never a spoken question, but in the Creek's eyes was always a mute inquiry.

Once Miss Evans ventured to write to her old pastor in New York, and explain her trouble. This was what he wrote in reply: "I am surprised that you are troubled, for I should have expected you to rejoice, as I do, over this new and wonderful evidence of the Lord's reforming power. Though the church cannot receive the old man so long as he is confessedly a bigamist and violator of his country's just laws, you should be greatly strengthened in your work through bringing him to desire salvation."

"Oh! it's easy to talk when you're free from responsibility!" cried out Miss Evans. "But I woke him up to a desire for this water of salvation that he cannot take. I have seen Harjo's home, and I know how cruel and useless it would be to urge him to give up what he loves—for he does love those two women who have spent half their lives and more with him. What, what can be done!"

Month after month, as old Harjo continued to occupy his seat in the mission meetings, with that mute appeal in his eyes and a persistent light of hope on his face, Miss Evans repeated the question, "What can be done?" If she was sometimes tempted to say to the old man, "Stop worrying about your soul; you'll get to Heaven as surely as any of us," there was always Mrs. Rowell to remind her that she was not a Mormon missionary. She could not run away from her perplexity. If she should secure a transfer to another station, she felt that Harjo would give up coming to the meetings, and in his despair become a positive influence for evil amongst his people. Mrs. Rowell would not waste her energy on an obstinate old man. No, Harjo was her creation, her impossible convert, and throughout the years, until death—the great solvent which is not always a solvent—came to one of them, would continue to haunt her.

And meanwhile, what?

1907

■ MARÍA AMPARO RUIZ DE BURTON ■
1832–1895

The life and writings of María Amparo Ruiz de Burton—the first known Mexican American to write two novels in English—demonstrate the historical contradictions of Mexican American identity. Born in 1832 to an elite, land-holding family in Loreto, Baja California, Mexico, she died destitute in Chicago in 1895. She witnessed the 1846 U.S. invasion of La Paz, Baja California, at the start of the Mexican War and three years later married the captain of the invading army, Henry S. Burton, a West Point graduate from Connecticut. She attended the 1861 inauguration of President Lincoln, but after the Civil War she had private talks with Varina Davis, wife of the Confederacy's ex-president, in which the two women denounced the Yankees. Fluent in English and Spanish, María penned copious letters, wrote a play based on the Spanish classic *Don Quixote*, and wrote two novels that openly critiqued northeastern materialism and portrayed California's land-holding Mexicans as a genteel, white population wrongfully displaced in the United States by racism and corrupt politics. No wonder it took over one hundred years for her life and novels to emerge from obscurity— they challenge traditional American and Mexican American literary histories.

When the Treaty of Guadalupe Hidalgo (1848) ended the Mexican War, the United States gained upper California, along with extensive southwestern territory, but left lower (Baja) California to Mexico. Captain Burton arranged to have over four hundred friendly Mexicans transported north to Monterey, California, granting them full rights of U.S. citizenship as guaranteed by the treaty. María was one of those who made the trip. By most accounts, she and the captain were in love. She was Catholic and he Protestant, and their marriage seemed to signal a happy union between California's Mexican land-holding gentry, known as *californios*, and the upstart Yankee invaders. In 1852 the Burtons moved to San Diego. Henry took command of the army post there and purchased property on Rancho Jamul, a large Mexican land grant that would figure heavily in María's later misfortunes. While she raised their daughter Nellie and two years later gave birth to son Henry Halleck, she and her husband enjoyed an aristocratic way of life.

The Civil War brought an end to the Burtons' California romance. The family moved east in 1859, living in Rhode Island, New York, Washington, D.C., and Virginia. While Burton's war heroics were winning him a promotion to the rank of brigadier general, she was taking in Yankee culture with a skeptical eye. "And it is also necessary that you come for a visit, to stay a winter in Washington and see what a great humbug is this Yankie [sic] nation," she wrote to her friend and fellow *californio*, Mariano G. Vallejo; "A humbug so methodical and well supported that they even almost believe it." Her stay in the East lasted a decade; in 1869 she returned to California a widowed mother of two after General Burton died of malarial fever. The "Maid of Monterey," as she was once remembered in a romantic California ballad, spent the rest of her life fighting the realities of economic hardship, unscrupulous land litigation, and the social dislocation that had already devastated many *californios*.

She returned to find parts of her Rancho Jamul property sold off to pay her husband's debts; she also found fifteen American squatters, each claiming a 160-acre homestead on the Jamul property. In 1851 Congress had passed the California Land Act, which, contrary to the 1848 treaty, considered all Mexican land grants public domain and available for resettlement until a federal Land Commission could verify the legitimacy of land titles. Verification required long legal battles that forced Ruiz de Burton and other *californios* to mortgage their land to lawyers and judges to pay legal fees as they sought to confirm their titles. At one point, Ruiz de Burton wrote her own legal briefs because she could not afford a lawyer. Rival claimants to Jamul kept the title tied up in court long after Ruiz de Burton's death. She never regained the Jamul property and even discovered she never had rights to a tract in Ensenada that she had inherited from her grandfather.

Her personal experiences, legal frustrations, and financial straits led her to a literary career. In 1872, she published *Who Would Have Thought It?*, a biting satire of northeastern culture based in part on her ten-year stay on the east coast. Set during the Civil War and Reconstruction but including significant events in the Southwest during the Mexican War, the novel—published in Philadelphia—exposes Yankee hypocrisy and the shortcomings of liberal democracy. While Lola Medina, a wealthy Mexican American born in Indian captivity, faces the overt racism of her adopted New England family, the novel's narrator provides a critique of unprincipled Yankee politics. Yet *Who Would Have Thought It?* challenges the Northeast's anglocentrism, not by disputing it but by insisting that upper-class Mexicans should be recognized as white. "[I]t happens that this child has no more Indian or Negro blood than you or I have," Lola's adoptive father explains to his family.

Ruiz de Burton's second novel, *The Squatter and the Don* (1885), turns on the same challenge. In the selection reprinted here, the aristocratic Don Mariano proposes a plan that rests on cheap Indian labor to benefit himself and the Anglo squatters who have settled on his ranch. The scene exhibits the novel's reliance on racial and ethnic caricature. It features genteel white Mexicans; vulgar and myopic Anglo squatters; sympathetic, business-minded Yankees; a younger generation of settlers whose attraction to the Don's daughters provides the novel's hope for social reconciliation; and nameless Indian laborers whose presence reminds us that a colonial hierarchy existed in California long before the arrival of American squatters. Although the novel reflects Ruiz de Burton's legal troubles with squatters on Rancho Jamul, its strongest critique is directed at the corruption of the U.S. government, which it traces to the confluence of capitalism and democracy. Squatters and *californios* alike fall victim to railroad barons who bribe state legislators for control of California property. Even the romance between Mercedes Alamar, the Don's daughter, and Clarence Darrell, a squatter's son, cannot prevent both families from being displaced from their homesteads. Their marriage signals a happy ending for the lovers but does not stop the railroad magnates—Stanford, Huntington, Crocker, and Hopkins—from profiting from California land at the expense of both Anglos and *californios*.

Ruiz de Burton works within many established literary traditions. She follows the historical romance tradition set by contemporary British, French, Spanish, and Mexican writers but also incorporates American modes of realism and naturalism later made popular by writers such as Theodore Dreiser and Frank Norris. As a Mexican American female novelist, however, her identity remained marginal. She published her first novel as "Mrs. Henry S. Burton" and her second one anonymously as "C. Loyal," an abbreviated form of *Ciudadano Leal*, "Loyal Citizen," a conventional method of closing official letters in nineteenth-century Mexico that Ruiz de Burton uses ironically to demonstrate her Mexican loyalties and signal her criticism of the corruption of American political ideals. She covers themes central to Mexican American history—Anglo-Mexican cultural clashes, disputes over land, and problems of racial identity—but values aristocratic *californios*, who have more in common with their Anglo counterparts than with working-class Mexican Americans. Her novels level scathing critiques of U.S. colonialism not because it excludes *californios*, but because it does not view them as white and extend class mobility to them.

Jesse Alemán
University of New Mexico

PRIMARY WORKS

Who Would Have Thought It?, ed. Rosaura Sánchez and Beatrice Pita (1872; Houston: Arte Público, 1995); *The Squatter and the Don*, ed. Rosaura Sánchez and Beatrice Pita, 2nd ed. (1885; Houston: Arte Público, 1997); *Don Quixote de la Mancha* (San Francisco: J. H. Carmany, 1876). María Amparo Ruiz de Burton's letters and documents can be found in the Bancroft Collection at the Berkeley Library of the University of California at Berkeley; Mission Santa Barbara in Santa Barbara, California; the Huntington Library in San Marino, California; and the San Diego Historical Society in San Diego, California.

from **The Squatter and the Don**

Chapter V. The Don in His Broad Acres

"The one great principle of English law"—Charles Dickens says, "is to make business for itself. There is no other principle distinctly, certainly and consistently maintained through all its narrow turnings. Viewed by this light, it becomes a coherent scheme ... and not the monstrous maze the laity are apt to think it. Let them but once clearly perceive that its grand principle is to make business for itself at their expense, and surely they will cease to grumble."[1]

The one great principle of American law is very much the same; our law-givers keep giving us laws and then enacting others to explain them. The lawyers find plenty of occupation, but what becomes of the laity?

"No. 189. *An Act to ascertain and settle the private land claims in the State of California,*" says the book.[2]

And by a sad subversion of purposes, all the private land titles became *unsettled*. It ought to have been said, "An Act to *unsettle* land titles, and to upset the rights of the Spanish population of the State of California."

It thus became not only necessary for the Spanish people to present their titles for revision, and litigate to maintain them (in case of anyone contesting their validity, should the least irregularity be discovered, and others covet their possession), but to maintain them against the government before several tribunals; for the government, besides making its own laws, *appeals to itself* as against the landowners, after their titles might have been *approved*. But this benign Act says (in "Sec. II"), "That the Commissioners, the District and Supreme Courts, in deciding on the validity of any claim, shall be governed by the treaty of Guadalupe Hidalgo; the law of nations; the laws, usages, and customs of the government *from which the claim is derived*; the principles of equity, and the decisions of the Supreme Court of the United States, etc., etc."

[1]The quotation is from *Bleak House* (1852–1853). Based on an actual case, Dickens's novel recounts the property dispute between Jarndyce and Jarndyce. While the case is tied up in the legal fog of the Chancery court, characters stake their lives on the pending decision, but when the court finally names the heirs to the Jarndyce fortune, all of it has been eaten up by court costs. The novel's third-person narrator provides a satirical criticism of the legal quagmire while a romance between two characters offers a sense of hope but no resolution to England's social and political ills.

[2]The 1851 Land Law. Three years after the Treaty of Guadalupe Hidalgo granted citizenship rights to Mexicans remaining in the United States, Congress passed the California Land Act, which established a lengthy process for confirming Spanish and Mexican land titles. Claimants had to prove to the Board of Land Commissions that their title was legitimate; if the title could not be verified, the land became public domain and open for resettlement. Even if the title was verified, attorneys or settlers could appeal the case to the U.S. Supreme Court, and squatters were permitted to remain on the disputed land while the Mexican claimant paid the property taxes and compensated the squatters for property improvements. Because it took an average of seventeen years to confirm a land title in California, many land-owning Mexicans had to mortgage their property to American businessmen and lawyers to pay legal fees.

Thus the government washes its hands clean, liberally providing plenty of tribunals, plenty of crooked turnings through which to scourge the wretched landowners.

Don Mariano had been for some years under the lash of the maternal government, whom he had found a cruel stepmother, indeed.

As it was arranged with Clarence, the meeting would take place that day on the broad piazza of John Gasbang's house, this being the most central point in the rancho.

The heads of families all came—the male heads, be it understood—as the squatters did not make any pretense to regard female opinion with any more respect than other men.

All the benches and chairs that the house contained, with the exception of Mrs. Gasbang's sewing rocker, had been brought to the porch, which was quite roomy and airy.

At ten minutes before two, all the settlers were there, that is to say, all the old men, with their elder sons.

Clarence, Romeo, Tom and Jack sat together in a corner, conversing in low tones, while Gasbang was entertaining his guests with some broad anecdotes, which brought forth peals of laughter.

At five minutes to two, Señor Alamar, accompanied by Mr. Mechlin, arrived in a buggy; his two sons followed on horseback.

Clarence had time to look at them leisurely while they dismounted and tied their horses to a hitching post.

"They are gentlemen, no doubt," observed Clarence.

"You bet they are," Romeo coincided. Evidently he admired and liked them.

"How much the boys look like the old man," Tom said.

"They look like Englishmen," was Clarence's next observation.

"Yes, particularly Victoriano; he is so light he looks more like a German, I think," said Romeo.

"I think Gabriel is very handsome," Tom said, "only of late he seems always so sad or thoughtful."

"That won't do for a man who is to marry soon," said Romeo. "I think he has always been rather reserved. He has only a cold salutation to give, while Victoriano will be laughing and talking to everybody. But, perhaps, you are right, and he is changed. I think he is less reconciled than others, to have us settlers helping outselves to what they consider their land. He certainly was far more talkative four or five years ago. I used to work with them in ploughing and harvesting time, and both boys and the Don were always very kind to me, and I can't help liking them."

"The ladies, though, ain't so affable. They are very proud," said Tom; "they walk like queens."

"They didn't seem proud to me, but I never spoke to them," said Romeo.

Gasbang went forward to meet his guests, and all came into the porch.

"Good afternoon, gentlemen," said Don Mariano to the settlers, lifting his hat and bowing. His sons and Mr. Mechlin did the same. Clarence arose, and so did the other young men with him, returning their salutation. The elder Darrell, Pittikin and Hughes followed this example; the other settlers nodded only, and remained sitting with their hats on, looking with affected indifference at the trees beyond.

"I thank you for your courtesy in complying with my request to have this meeting," he said. Some nodded, others grinned and winked, others smiled silently.

"Take this chair, Señor, and you, Mr. Mechlin, take this one. They are the best in my establishment," said Gasbang. "The young gentlemen will find seats somewhere on the benches."

Clarence came forward and offered three chairs. Mr. Mechlin took his arm and presented him to the Alamars.

"I take pleasure in making your acquaintance, and I hope to have the opportunity to thank you for your kind cooperation more appropriately afterward," said Don Mariano. His sons shook hands with Clarence cordially and accepted the proffered chairs.

Don Mariano excused himself for not speaking English more fluently.

"If you don't understand me I will repeat my words until I make my meaning clear, but I hope you will ask me to repeat them; or perhaps, some one of these young gentlemen will do me the kindness to be my interpreter," said he.

"Romeo talks Spanish; he can interpret for you," said Victoriano.

"You talk English better," Romeo proudly replied, thinking he could tell his wife that the Don had asked him to be his interpreter.

"Perhaps Mr. Clarence Darrell would do me the favor," said Don Mariano.

"You speak very good English, Señor. We understand you perfectly. You do not require an interpreter," Clarence said.

"That is so; you speak very well," said Mr. Mechlin.

Gasbang and Pittikin added: "Certainly, we understand him very well."

"You are very kind," said the Don, smiling, "and I will try to be brief, and not detain you long."

"We have all the afternoon," said Hughes.

"That's so; we ain't in a hurry," said several.

"Only let us out in time to bring the milch cows home, before night comes on," said old Miller dryly.

"Exactly, we want to look after our cows, too," said the Don laughing.

All saw the fine irony of the rejoinder and laughed heartily. Miller scratched his ear as if he had felt the retort there, knowing well that, with the exception of Mathews and Gasbang, he had killed and "*corralled*" more of the Don's cattle than any other settler.

"Speaking about cows brings us at once to the object of this meeting"— Don Mariano, still smiling, went on saying: "You know that I have lost many, and that it is natural I should wish to save those I have left. To do this, and yet not ask that you give up your claims, I have one or two propositions to make you. The reason why you have taken up land here is because you want homes. You want to make money. Isn't that the reason? Money! money!"

"That's it, exactly," said many voices, and all laughed.

"Well, I can show you how you may keep your home and make more money than you can by your present methods, while at the same time I also save my cattle. That little point, you know, I must keep in view."

All laughed again.

"To fence your fields, you have said, is too expensive, particularly as the rainy seasons are too uncertain to base upon them any calculations for getting crops to pay for fencing. I believe this is what most of you say; is it not?"

"We could have raised better crops if your cattle hadn't damaged them," said Mathews.[3]

"I beg to differ; but supposing that you are right, do you think you could be sure of good crops if you killed all my stock, or if I took them all away to the mountains? No, most assuredly. The rainy season would still be irregular and unreliable, I think. Yes, I may say, I feel sure, it is a mistake to try to make San Diego County a grain-producing county. It is not so, and I feel certain it never will be, to any great extent. This county is, and has been and will be always, a good grazing county—one of the best counties for cattle-raising on this coast, and the very best for fruit-raising on the face of the earth. God intended it should be. Why, then, not devote your time, your labor and your money to raising vineyards, fruits and cattle, instead of trusting to the uncertain rains to give you grain crops?"

"It takes a long time to get fruit trees to bearing. What are we to do for a living in the meantime?" asked Miller.

"Begin raising cattle—that will support you," the Don replied.

"Where is the capital to buy cattle with?" Gasbang asked.

"You don't require any more capital than you already have. I can let each of you have a number of cows to begin with, and give you four or five years' time to pay me. So you see, it will be with the increase of these cattle you will pay, for I shall charge you no interest."

"What do you expect us to do in return? To give back to you our homesteads?" asked Hughes.

"No, sir; I have said, and repeat again, you will retain your homesteads."

"And will you stop contesting our claims?" asked Mathews.

"I will, and will give each one a quit-claim deed."

"You will not fight our claims, but you don't want us to plant grain on our land," said Gasbang.

---

[3]The point of contention here is the "No Fence Law," a state constitutional amendment that exempted several counties, including San Diego, from California's otherwise strict fencing statutes. Residents of San Diego County were not required to build lawful fences as defined by the state, but the county did enforce state laws on animal trespassing. If an animal trespassed onto private property, the landowner could corral the animal and hold its owner liable for twice the amount of property damage done by the wayward animal. Neither state nor local laws permitted property owners to kill trespassing animals.

"You can plant grain, if you like, but to do so you must fence your land; so, as you all say, that fencing is expensive, I suggest your fencing orchards and vineyards only, but no grain fields—I mean large fields."

"Pshaw! I knew there was to be something behind all that display of generosity," muttered Mathews.

Don Mariano reddened with a thrill of annoyance, but quietly answered:

"You are too good business men to suppose that I should not reserve some slight advantage for myself, when I am willing you should have many more yourselves. All I want to do is to save the few cattle I have left. I am willing to quit-claim to you the land you have taken, and give you cattle to begin the stock business, and all I ask you in return is to put a fence around whatever land you wish to cultivate, so that my cattle cannot go in there. So I say, plant vineyards, plant olives, figs, oranges; make wines and oil and raisins; export olives and dried and canned fruits. I had some very fine California canned fruit sent to me from San Francisco. Why could we not can fruits as well, or better? Our olives are splendid—the same our figs, oranges, apricots, and truly all semitropical fruits are of a superior quality. When this fact becomes generally known, I feel very sure that San Diego Couny will be selected for fruit and grape-growing. In two years grape vines begin to bear; the same with figs, peaches and other fruits. At three years old they bear quite well, and all without irrigation. So you would not have to wait so very long to begin getting a return from your labor and capital. Moreover, an orchard of forty acres or vineyard of twenty will pay better after three years' growth than one hundred and sixty acres of wheat or barley in good seasons, and more than three hundred acres of any grain in moderately good seasons, one thousand acres in bad seasons. You can easily fence twenty or forty or sixty acres for a vineyard or orchard, but not so easily fence a field of one hundred and sixty, and the grain crop would be uncertain, depending on the rains, but not so the trees, for you can irrigate them, and after the trees are rooted that is not required."[4]

"Where is the water to irrigate?" asked Miller.

"The water is in the sea now, for there we let it go every year; but if we were sensible, judicious men, we would not let it go to waste—we would save it. This rancho has many deep ravines which bring water from hills and sierras. These ravines all open into the valleys and run like so many little rivers in the rainy season. By converting these ravines into reservoirs we could have more water than would be needed for irrigating the fruit trees on the foothills. In the low valleys no irrigation would be needed. If we all join forces to put up dams across the most convenient of the ravines, we will have splendid reservoirs.[5] I will defray half the expense if you will get

[4]The Don's plan indicates his eagerness to profit from the changes in California, and it demonstrates Ruiz de Burton's exceptional foresight. Southern California's agricultural industry eventually followed the development the Don outlines here.

[5]The Don seems to be describing Ruiz de Burton's own 1873 plans to establish a waterworks on Rancho Jamul and create a reservoir for San Diego. She enlisted the aid of George Davidson, a friend and professor at Berkeley, who deemed Rancho Jamul an ideal location for a reservoir that would provide water for nearly 100,000 people. However, lack of capital and investors thwarted her plans.

together and stand the other half. Believe me, it will be a great godsend to have a thriving, fruit-growing business in our county. To have the cultivated land well fenced, and the remainder left out for grazing. Then there would not be so many thousands upon thousands of useless acres as now have to be. For every ten acres of cultivated land (not fenced) there are ten thousand, yes, twenty thousand, entirely idle, useless. Why? Because those ten acres of growing grain must be protected, and the cattle which don't know the 'no fence law,' follow their inclination to go and eat the green grass. Then they are "*corralled*" or killed. Is it not a pity to kill the poor dumb brutes, because we can't make them understand the law, and see the wisdom of our Sacramento legislators who enacted it? And is it not a pity to impoverish our county by making the bulk of its land useless? The foolishness of letting all of the rainfall go to waste is an old time folly with us. Still, in old times, we had at least the good excuse that we raised all the fruits we needed for our use, and there was no market for any more. But we were not then, as now, guilty of the folly of making the land useless. We raised cattle and sold hides and tallow every year, and made money. When gold was discovered, we drove our stock north, got a good price for it, and made money. But now no money will be made by anybody out of cattle, if they are to be destroyed, and no money made out of land, for the grazing will be useless when there will be no stock left to eat it. Thus, the county will have no cattle, and the crops be always uncertain. Believe me, in years to come, you will see that the county was impoverished by the 'no fence law,' unless we try to save our county, in spite of foolish legislation. If our wise legislators could enact a law obliging rain to come, so that we could have better chances to raise grain, then there would be some show of excuse for the 'no fence law,' perhaps. I say PERHAPS, because, in my humble opinion, we ought to prefer cattle raising and fruit growing for our county. We should make these our speciality."

"I think it would be much more foolish to trust a few cows to make out a living while trees grow," said Miller, "than to the seasons to give us grain crops."

"No, sir; because cattle are sure to increase, if they are not killed, and you could make cheese and butter, and sell your steers every year, while trees grow. You have been seven years a settler on this rancho. In these seven years you have raised two good crops; three poor, or only middling, and two, no crops at all."

"Yes, because your cattle destroyed them," said Mathews.

"No, sir; my cattle were not all over California; but the bad seasons were, and only in few places, moderately good crops were harvested; in the southern counties none at all. We had rains enough to get sufficiently good grazing, but not to raise grain."

"I think you are right about the uncertainty of our seasons, and I think a good dairy always pays well, also a good orchard and vineyard," said Darrell. "But the question is, whether we can adopt some feasible plan to put your idea into practice."

"Yes, how many cows will you let us have?" asked Hager.

"I will divide with you. Next week I shall have my *rodeo*. We can see then the number of cattle I have left. We shall count them. I shall take half, the other half you divide pro rata, each head of a family taking a proportionate number of cattle."

"That is fair," Darrell said.

"I don't want any cattle. I ain't no *vaquero* to go *busquering* around and *lassoing* cattle.[6] I'll *lasso* myself; what do I know about whirling a *lariat*?" said Mathews.

"Then don't take cattle. You can raise fruit trees and vineyards," said Darrell.

"Yes, and starve meantime," Mathews replied.

"You will not have to be a *vaquero*. I don't go *busquering* around *lassoing*, unless I wish to do so," said the Don. "You can hire an Indian boy to do that part. They know how to handle *la reata* and *echar el lazo*[7] to perfection. You will not starve, either, for if you wish, you can make butter and cheese enough to help to pay expenses. I think this State ought to make and export as good cheese as it now imports, and some day people will see it, and do it, too. Thus, with the produce of your dairies at first, and afterward with your fruits, you will do far better than with grain crops, and not work as hard. Let the northern counties raise grain, while we raise fruits and make wine, butter and cheese. You must not forget, either, that every year you can sell a number of cattle, besides keeping as many milch cows as you need."

"Where can we sell our cattle?" asked Hancock.

"Cattle-buyers will come to buy from you. But if you prefer it, you can drive your stock north yourselves, and make a good profit. Since 1850, I have sent nine times droves of cattle to the northern counties, and made a handsome profit every time. The first time we took stock north was in '50; I took nearly six thousand head—three thousand were mine—and the others belonged to my brothers. We lost very few, and sold at a good price—all the way from eighteen dollars to twenty five dollars per head. About five hundred of mine I sold as high as thirty dollars per head. I made sixty thousand dollars by this operation. Then out of the next lot I made twenty seven thousand dollars. Then I made twenty two thousand, and so on, until my tame cows began to disappear, as you all know. In four years after my cows began to get shot, my cattle decreased more than half. Now I don't think I have many more than three thousand head. So you cannot blame me for wishing to save these few. But believe me, the plan I propose will be as beneficial to you as to me, and also to the entire county, for as soon as it is shown that we can make a success of the industries I propose, others will follow our example."

---

[6]*Vaquero* is Spanish for "cowboy"; *busquering* is an Anglicization of the Spanish verb *buscar*, "to look for." Throughout this section, Ruiz de Burton uses language to mark the difference in cultural and social status between the squatters and the Don. The squatters speak a vernacular English; the Don's English is impeccable, despite his initial statement that he speaks it poorly.
[7]Spanish: "the rope" and "to lasso."

"If you have only three thousand head, you can't spare many to us, and it will hardly be worth while to stop planting crops to get a few cows," said Gasbang.

"I think I will be able to spare five hundred or six hundred cows. I don't know how many I have left."

"We will buy from somebody else, if we want more," said Darrell. "We won't want many to begin with; it will be something of an experiment for some of us."

"For all of us here. Perhaps you understand *vaquering*;[8] we don't," said Hancock; all laughed.

"Then fence your claim and plant grain," Darrell retorted.

"I am not so big a fool as to spend money in fences. The 'no fence law' is better than all the best fences," Mathews said.

"But what if you make more money by following other laws that are more just, more rational?" said the Don.

"The 'no fence law' is rational enough for me," said Miller.

"And so say I," said Mathews.

"And I," said Gasbang.

Hughes nodded approvingly, but he was too much of a hypocrite to commit himself in words.

"We did not come to discuss the 'no fence law,' but only to propose something that will put more money in your pockets than killing dumb beasts," said Mr. Mechlin.

"Then propose something practicable," said Mathews.

"I think what has been proposed is practicable enough," Darrell said.

"Certainly it is," Mr. Mechlin added.

"I don't see it," said Mathews.

"Nor I, either," added Gasbang.

"Nor I, neither," said Hughes.

"Well, gentlemen," said Don Mariano, rising, "I shall leave you now; you know my views, and you perhaps prefer to discuss them, and discuss your own among yourselves, and not in my presence. Take your time, and when you come to a final decision let me know. Perhaps I can advance the money to those of you who do not have it ready to purchase fencing lumber, I shall charge no interest, and give you plenty of time to pay."

"I will do that, Señor Alamar," Clarence said; "if the settlers agree to fence their lands, I will advance the money to them to put up their fences."

"Yes, and if our crops fail, we will be in debt to the ears, with a chain around our necks," Mathews growled.

"I thought you said that if it were not for my cattle, your crops would not have failed," said Don Mariano, smiling.

---

[8]Hancock combines the Spanish word for "cowboy" with an English verb ending to create *cowboying*, "to perform the work of cowboys." The bilingual exchanges between the squatters and the Don undermine an enduring myth about the American West. Cowboy culture is not an American tradition but a Mexican one, with help from hired Indian laborers.

"I said so, and it is so. But you see, that was before we had the 'no fence law,'" answered he, grinning.

Don Mariano shook hands with Clarence, whom he invited to call at his house—this invitation Clarence accepted with warm thanks—and, followed by his sons and his friend Mr. Mechlin, Don Mariano took his leave, bowing to the settlers, who nodded and grinned in return.

"I suppose you, too, think the 'no fence law' iniquitous, as you appear to favor the aristocracy," said Gasbang to Clarence.

"It is worse than that; it is stupid. Now it kills the cattle, afterwards it will kill the county," Clarence answered.

"Shall we plant no wheat, because the Spaniards want to raise cattle?" Mathews asked.

"Plant wheat, if you can do so without killing cattle. But do not destroy the larger industry with the smaller. If, as the Don very properly says, this is a grazing county, no legislation can change it. So it would be wiser to make laws to suit the county, and not expect that the county will change its character to suit absurd laws," Clarence replied.

1885

MARY AUSTIN
1868–1934

The second child of George and Susannah Hunter, Mary Hunter Austin was born in Carlinville, Illinois, and graduated from Blackburn College in 1888, with interests in both science and art. In 1888 her family moved to Southern California, hoping to homestead in the lower San Joaquin Valley. By this time her father and older sister had died, relations between Austin and her mother were strained, and Austin had accustomed herself to a solitary life, in which her most vibrant, meaningful experiences came from a mystical connection to nature. Already predisposed to value the natural world, Austin explored, fell in love with, and began to write about the arid landscapes of the Southwest.

She married Stafford Wallace Austin in 1891, moving with him to the Owens Valley, where both taught in several Southern California small towns, settling finally in Lone Pine. In 1892 her only child, Ruth, was born mentally retarded; eventually Ruth was placed by her mother in a mental institution, where she died in 1918. Austin's marriage to Stafford Austin was in shambles by the time her first, and most famous book, *The Land of Little Rain*, appeared in 1903. They lived separate lives for ten years, finally divorcing in 1914. Austin never remarried, devoting herself instead to intellectual and emotional engagement with the most important writers of her time and to a life of public activism in various causes, including environmental conservation and regional advocacy. An important figure in the artists' colonies of both Carmel, California, and Santa Fe, New Mexico, she also fought for water rights in the Southwest, first in the Owens Valley and later as a delegate to the Boulder Dam Conference in 1927, where she argued against the diversion of the Colorado River to supply water to Los Angeles.

As her autobiography, *Earth Horizon*, makes clear, early in her life Austin felt herself "marked" by a specialness that was evidenced in her drive to influence social customs and political policies through her writings. Author of twenty-seven books and more than two hundred and fifty articles, she saw her mission as essentially twofold: to shift the center of culture from the Euro-American tra-ditions of the East coast to the American Indian and Hispanic traditions of the Southwest and to change her generation's attitudes toward women and women's rights. She was a regionalist who used her considerable energy, influence, and talent in collecting, preserving, and encouraging the continuation of Hispanic and American Indian folk arts. Her involvement with American Indian and His-panic arts in the Southwest poses, however, complex interpretative issues. On the one hand, Austin and her colleagues helped engender national markets for art forms that had been ignored and even suppressed; on the other, they did so by applying Euro-American esthetic standards to indigenous arts, attempting to direct the local artists into patterns not necessarily in keeping with the crafts or their own cultural values.

Austin also used her writings to argue for suffrage and birth control. Her most successful fictional effort, *A Woman of Genius*, ranks alongside Willa Cath-er's *Song of the Lark* as a study in the trials facing a creative woman of the Pro-gressive Era. Austin's remarkable legacy of writings coheres around her intense focus on the conflicts experienced by women of her time. *Earth Horizon* most clearly delineates those tensions in Austin's inventive use of first, second, and third person voices in referring to herself. Realizing that women often operated in two spheres of consciousness—one that was their inner, true self and one that evidenced a husband's or father's projections of ideal womanhood (she, you, or simply, Mary)—Austin wrote movingly about her personal anguish in order to exemplify the changes she hoped to see accomplished. Her struggle was not only with beliefs about women's roles but with the physical spaces they were allowed to occupy. Whether she was writing about desert-induced mirages, or small-town life in Carlinville, Illinois, or the urban canyons of New York City, she described in detail the physical environment and its potential as a place of free movement for women. In this way, Austin's writing offers a broad-ranging critique of the environments—both perceptual and actual—in which women live their lives. Her counsel to herself in *Earth Horizon* remains valuable today as women continue the struggle to establish their own space: "There was some-thing you could do about unsatisfactory conditions besides being heroic or mar-tyr to them, something more satisfactory than enduring or complaining, and that was getting out to hunt for the remedy."

Vera Norwood
University of New Mexico

PRIMARY WORKS

The Land of Little Rain, 1903; *Lost Borders*, 1909; *A Woman of Genius*, 1912; *The Land of Journey's Ending*, 1924; *Starry Adventure*, 1931; *Earth Horizon*, 1932; *Literary America*, 1903–1934; *The Mary Austin Letters*, 1979; *Stories from the Country of Lost Borders*, ed. Marjorie Pryse, 1987; *The Ford*, 1997; *The Basket Woman: A Book of Indian Tales*, 1999.

from **Earth Horizon**

III

After the summer of '82, or thereabouts, events began to present themselves again in an orderly course. We were living on Johnson Street then, in a house my mother built out of the sale of the farm. The pension she had applied for had been allowed, with officer's back pay; other matters had straightened themselves out, so that, though she continued to go out occasionally as general emergency aid, it was chiefly to the houses of her friends, who coveted her warm, consoling interest in their plight. The house was well built, of six rooms arranged in two rows, three bedrooms, parlor, sitting-room, and kitchen; no bath, of course; an outside toilet, and drinking water from the pump, as was the case with all the houses in town except for the very wealthy. There was no central heating such as was beginning to be the fashion for more commodious homes, but there were two fireplaces for burning coal, with imitation black marble mantels, and between the parlor and livingroom there were folding doors. The one extravagance my mother had allowed herself was to have the woodwork of the two 'front' rooms 'grained'; which means that it was treated so as to present the natural aspect of an expensive hardwood finish, like no wood on earth, I am sure. Susie[1] was extremely pleased with it, and the work must have been good of its kind, for when I visited the house forty years later, it was still shining and intact.

Outside, ours was such a house as might have been discovered by the score in any Middlewestern town, clapboarded, white-painted with green blinds, its original Colonial lines corrupted by what in the course of the next decade or two broke out irruptively into what is now known as the 'bungalow' type. We lived there about seven years, and Mary was never at home in it at all. At that time nobody ever thought of inquiring what Mary thought of anything, so nobody found out. Several years after our removing to California, when Mother, who was desperately homesick there, was reproaching her for never having shown any trace of such sickness, said Mary unthoughtfully, 'Homesick for what?' and saw that she would have to turn it quickly; 'Isn't it the family that makes the home?'—and Susie managed to be doubtfully content with that. The place was dear to her; she had built it,

[1]Susie is Mary Austin's mother, Susannah Hunter.

584 ▪ Late Nineteenth Century: 1865–1910

and except that she would have furnished it more handsomely if she could, it satisfied her expectation. But Mary recalls very well her first going there after the workmen had left and the furniture was partly in place, and being struck with a cold blast of what she was to recognize long after as the wind before the dawn of the dreary discontent with the American scene, which has since been made familiar to us all by the present generation of writers in the Middlewest. But Mary's case was rendered more desolate by her not being able to refuse the conviction that was pressed upon her from every side, that any dissatisfaction she might have felt was inherently of herself, that she was queer and ungrateful and insensitive to the finer aspects of existence. To the extent that she wasn't able to shut it out of consciousness by fixing her attention on something else, Mary was always, in that house, a little below herself, without the relief of despising it, which a kindly dispensation granted to the generation next after her.

To begin with, there wasn't a nook or corner of the house which could be differentiated from any other corner, could be made to take the impress of the resident's spirit, or afford even a momentary relief from the general tone and tempo of the family life. It was all neat and hard and squared up with a purely objective domesticity within which it was not possible even to imagine any other sort of life. There wasn't the alteration of pulse such as might be secured by the coming and going of the head of the house, the relief of readjusting details to the drama of affection; a perpetually widowed house.

My mother was in most respects an efficient housekeeper; everything was invariably clean and tidy; she got through her work with a celerity that was the marvel of the neighborhood. She had an extraordinary knack of stretching money to the utmost, of cleaning and turning and pressing her clothes, so that she always looked trim and well-turned-out. She put all of us, and her house, through the same process, without anybody ever suspecting that it might not be the best process imaginable for everybody.

Outside, things were not much better. Johnson Street was north of the town, between the town and the college; it had been chosen partly because of that, so that the children as they grew up might have that advantage, or that Susie might eke out her income, as it proved desirable, with boarders. This last plan never came to anything. In that small house the intrusion of a 'boarder' proved unbearable, even to the brothers, and Susie discovered that a boarder is a poor substitute for the one thing that binds a woman willingly to the unbroken routine of meals and hours.

The neighborhood itself was new; only a few houses had gone up there, newly married couples and the better-paid sort of work-people. All that part of town was originally prairie, stretching north and north unbrokenly, shorn and treeless, to flat horizons. Up and down the street young maples had been planted, but except for a few trees about the Miller place, which had once been a farmhouse, there was nothing to rest the eye upon. Going to school one went past vacant weed-grown lots, past the foundry, which had once been the woolen mills, and was at the moment, I believe, a tool and hoe works, and so to Grandpa's house on First North, and across the square to school. That was the way you took when hurried, but coming back you spared yourself the time as often as possible to come the longest way around, along East Main, up College Avenue, so as to bring yourself past the more attractive gardens.

I am not, after all these years, going to be blamed, as I was blamed by everybody who knew about it, for my preferences in matters of this kind. Mary was more than ordinarily sensitive to form and proportion. Never so much so as during those years of adolescence when the submerged faculty, that is appeased with the mere appearance of things, came so close to the surface that it was chiefly the want of any possible practical way of accomplishing a painting career that decided her between paint and print as a medium of expression.

I felt the outward scene in those days as other people feel music, its structure, its progressions; felt emotion as color and color as tone. All the family except Mary were to some degree musical, but it scarcely occurred to anybody in those days that not having 'an ear for music' was merely an error in the instrumentation, that all the sensitivities that went with a musical gift were merely transferred to another sensory tract and were active there, capable of ecstasy and pain in a similar, even in a more intensive fashion. To this day Mary can be made sick by living in a room of bad color or wrong proportions, even though, in the stress of other preoccupations, often the first notice she has of inharmony in the objective environment, is physical dis-ease. Susie herself was so sensitive to tone that she never hesitated to say when the piano was badly out of tune that it 'gave her the shivers.'

One of the family jokes was that Mary had a notion that the tool and hoe works was pretty, although what Mary had actually said was not 'pretty' but beautiful, as she had seen it once of a winter twilight, rust-red against a dark blue sky faintly streaked with ruddy cloud, and below the long lines of the brick walls in harmony with the horizon, the pond where youngsters went to skate in winter, blue with the deep-sea blue of thick ice lit with reflected fire of the sky. Well, it *was* beautiful. The mistake was in saying so. And that was why Mary said as little as possible about the house in Johnson Street, which only just escaped being unendurable.

The parlor was the worst. The furniture, except for the piano new and ugly, of a popular type of decoration of cut-in designs picked out in black and gilt. People were then beginning to get rid of their good old pieces and stressing a modern note. The blinds at the undraped windows were dark chocolate, the carpet and upholstery chosen of reds and greens which 'set each other off.' Except for a few family photographs, the walls were bare. Later a lithograph of the martyred Garfield[2] adorned one wall and a cheap papier-maché 'placque' of Lily Langtry[3] another. I do not know what else we would have put on them. There were a few houses in Carlinville where you could see good old

---

[2]James Garfield, twentieth president of the United States, who was assassinated in 1881.

[3]Lily Langtry was an English actress of the time.

engravings, Currier and Ives prints, and a few dark portraits in oil. There were other houses in which you might find bright prints of a slightly later date in black and gilt frames; none of them so bad as they became a decade later; sentimental subjects; Fast Asleep and Wide Awake were the names of the two at Grandpa's, and a black and white Landseer Stag at Bay—some such matter. But there were none of these at our house, perhaps because Susie had never cared to own them. There was not even a Whatnot.

Some day someone will write the history of the Whatnot, with its odd, and for the most part attractive, collection of sociohistorical fetishes; the tropic shell carved minutely with the Lord's Prayer; Indian arrow-heads; the glass paper-weight with glass flowers inside, or a picture of the Centennial; the stuffed bird; the wax flowers; the polished buffalo horn; the 'mineral specimens' from California; all those curious keys which unlocked for the ancestors aesthetic emotion and intellectual curiosity. I am sure if I had a proper Whatnot at hand, I could lead you by it through the whole aesthetic history of the Middlewest. I could touch the hidden life, the obscure, the unconfessed root of the art impulse from which I am indubitably sprung. But we had no Whatnot in our house, not even a home-made one of wire-threaded spools and walnut stain.

Looking back, I can realize now that the child with staring eyes and the great mane of tawny curls, who used to creep slowly along the rail that divided the 'art department' of the county fair from the milling crowd, taking in with avid, slow absorption the now obsolete tufted and cut-out and cross-stitched counterpanes, the infinitely fine crocheted antimacassars, the picture frames of shells and acorn cups and prickly seeds, seeing them grow with time more curious and tasteless, and valued for their singularity, was seeing much more than that. She was seeing the passing of that initial impulse toward aestheticism so hardily kept alive for three generations on the contents of Whatnots, and on little else....

It wasn't until the family had settled well into the house on Johnson Street that Mary began to feel herself harassed by family criticism of her individual divergences on no better ground than that they were divergences. That year Mary had finally overcome the two years' difference in their school grades that divided her from Jim,[4] and, though not yet sharing all his classes, they sat under the same teacher, and Mary began to be the subject of that acute sensitivity of brothers to lapses, on the part of their young sisters, from severest propriety. Well, of course, brothers always did tell on you. It seemed to be part of their official prerogative as arbiters of what could or could not be said to or in front of sisters and the obligation to lick other boys who violated these restrictions. But it seemed to Mary that there was too much relish sometimes in the telling, and, besides, Mary had her own notions of the proprieties.

---

[4]Austin's older brother. She was advanced to his grade level because she was an excellent reader, much beyond her age level.

It was in the business of a spirited self-justification that she first explicitly noticed something of which she had been, ever since that summer in Boston, dimly aware, the extent to which her mother was reshaping the family and her own affectional life around her eldest son, shaping him to that part it was so widely agreed was suitable to be played, and 'sweet' to observe him playing, as the widow's son.

One tries to present a situation, usual enough then, not so usual now, as it occurred, as an incident in the education of Mary. What my mother was proceeding toward, with the sanction of the most treasured of American traditions, was constituting my brother, at fifteen or thereabouts, the Head of the family. According to the tradition, she had a right to expect Mary to contribute a certain acquiescence in a situation which kept the shape if not the content of the best my mother's generation knew of the ritual of sex. It was a way to maintain what the high-minded women of her generation esteemed the crown of a woman's life, the privilege of being the utterly giving and devoted wife of one man who could make it still seem a privilege, although it violated all the other natural motions of the woman's being. Susie was justified, in a compulsion of advice and remonstrance, to persuade Mary into the traditional attitudes. What she missed realizing was that a general social change in those attitudes was imminent, and that both her children were probably unconsciously responding to it according to their natures. Hers was not the only household in which struggles between brothers and sisters were going on, prophetic of the somewhat later conflict between traditionalism and realism which was so to alter the whole status of American marriage. Mary wasn't by any means the only girl of that period insisting on going her own way against the traditions, and refusing to come to a bad end on account of it.

Years after, when the feminist fight, marshaled in the direction of Woman Suffrage, became the occasion of conferences of women from all parts of the world, in the relaxing hour between committee meetings and campaign planning, there would be confidences. 'Well, it was seeing what my mother had to go through that started me'; or, 'It was being sacrificed to the boys in the family that set me going'; or, 'My father was one of the old-fashioned kind . . .' I remember three English sisters who all together and at once took to window-smashing and hunger fasts because they simply could not endure for another minute the tyranny of having their father spend their dress money every year in a single bolt of cloth of his own choosing, from which they were expected to make up what they wore. Women of high intelligence and education went white and sick telling how, in their own families, the mere whim of the dominant male member, even in fields which should have been exempt from his interference, had been allowed to assume the whole weight of moral significance.

It was a four-minute egg that set Mary going.

I have already related how, scrambling out of sleep rendered uneasy by too early responsibility and not always untouched by the consciousness of her father's recurrent anguish, Mary had acquired a prejudice against the very soft-boiled egg, so that her never very stable appetite revolted at seeing one broken even unsuspectingly before her. I don't know just when her quite justifiable request to have her egg put in the kettle a minute or two before the others began to break down the general disposition to create, out of her brother's status as the Head of the family, a criterion of how eggs should be served. It was only one of many unimportant oddments in which the necessity arose of considering Mary as a separate item in the family ritual which Susie was happily reconstituting around her eldest son. It was to be for Jim as nearly as possible as it had been when the whole affectional and practical interest of the family had centered on Father having what he wanted and being pleased by it. To remember Mary's egg became a constantly annoying snag in the perfect family gesture of subservience to the Head, which all her woman's life had gone to create. And perhaps there was latent in Susie's mind, in spite of her avowed liberality toward the woman movement, something of the deep-seated conviction, on the part of the house-mother, that drove many girls of Mary's generation from the domestic life, that a different sort of boiled egg was more than a female had a right to claim on her own behalf. I can, at any rate, recall very well the completely justified manner with which she would say, on those increasing occasions when it turned out that Mary's egg had not been remembered, 'Well, my dear, if you can't learn to take your food like the *rest* of the family ...' But even more it proved a distraction and an annoyance when Mary was left to prepare her own egg. 'Oh, Mary, why do you always have to have something different from the *rest* of the family ...' And finally when Jim, consistently playing his part as the complaisant favorite of the house, delivered judgment, 'Somehow you never seem to have any feeling for what a HOME should be'; not in the least realizing that there was growing up in the minds of thousands of young American women at that moment, the notion that it, at least, *shouldn't* be the place of the apotheosis of its male members. In so far as the difficulty about the extra minute and a half proved annoying to Mary, she settled it by deciding that she didn't care for eggs for breakfast. And yet, slight as the incident seems, it served to fix the pattern of family reaction to Mary's divergences....

By the time the Hunters had settled in at Tejon,[5] Mary suffered something like a complete collapse. There had been, in addition to the emotional stress of breaking up home, the two years of exhausting college work, in which so much of the other two years had to be made up by extra hours, after which had come the relaxing California climate, and the problem of food. I suppose few people who pioneered on the Pacific Coast between the Gold Rush in '49 and the Real Estate Rush in the eighties ever realized the natural food poverty of that opulent land. By that time the Spanish with the art

[5]Austin's family moved to an area of homestead land south of Bakersfield, California, in 1888.

of irrigation, and the Chinese, wise in food-growing, had mitigated the handicaps of an almost total want of native roots and fruits and nuts on which the Middlewest pioneers had managed mainly to subsist. It was only the few like the Tejon homesteaders, cast away on a waterless strip in a dry year, who realized that it had been the wiping away of the slowly accumulated Indian knowledge of native foods under the Franciscans, and the replacement of the wild herds with privately owned sheep and cattle, that made the tragedy of the forced abandonment of the Missions. For the settlers on the Tejon there was not so much as a mess of greens to be raised or gathered. It had all to be fetched from the town two days away, at prices that forced a cautious balancing between that and the still expensive and not very satisfactory canned fruits and vegetables. Strange now to recall that my mother never did become skillful in the utilization of canned foods, and that there persisted among housewives out of the self-sustaining rural households of the Middlewest an irreducible remainder of prejudice to their use.

During the first six months of homesteading, Mary suffered the genuine distress of malnutrition. There was no butter, and if anyone remembers what canned milk was like at that time, diluted with stale water from a dry-season waterhole—but I hope nobody does! For meat, we had game, plentiful if monotonous; rabbits, quail, and occasionally bear meat and venison bought from the 'mountain men,' grizzled derelicts of an earlier period, hidden away in tiny valleys, subsisting chiefly on the killing of venison and the robbing of bee trees. Mary, however, did not like game, especially rabbits, though she might have done better about it if she had not had to kill them. Mary was a fair shot, and with George to pick them up after they were killed, contrived to keep the family table reasonably supplied. Every little while the men of the neighborhood would go on a community hunt, especially in the winter months when there were ducks by thousands on the sloughs, and so we managed to live. My brothers, in fact, throve; George, who up till then had shown signs of being under-sized and pudgy, began to shoot up and ended by being the tallest of the family. But Mary grew thinner and thinner, stooping under her weight of hair, and fell into a kind of torpor, of which undernourishment was probably the chief factor, a condition to which nobody paid any attention. Appetite, or the loss of it, was a purely personal matter. People guessed you would eat if you wanted it. What finally worried her mother was that Mary was unable to sleep. She would lie in her bunk with fixed, wide-open eyes, hearing the cu-owls on the roof, the nearly noiseless tread of coyotes going by in the dark, the strange ventriloquist noises they kept up with their cousins miles away beyond Rose Station, hearing the slow shuffling tread of the starved cattle, momentarily stopped by the faint smell of the settlers' water-barrels, but too feeble to turn out of their own tracks to come at them.

Nights when she and her mother slept at Susie's cabin, which was in a sandy wash, Mary would sit out among the dunes in the moonlight—Susie would never sleep there at any other times than full moon—watching the frisking forms of field mouse and kangaroo rat, the noiseless passage of the red fox and the flitting of the elf owls at their mating. By day she would follow a bobcat to its lair in the bank of the Wash, and, lying down before its den, the two would contemplate each other wordlessly for long times, in which Mary remained wholly unaware of what might happen to her should the wildcat at any moment make up its mind to resent her presence. There was a band of antelope on the Tejon range, fully protected by law, roving far down the hollow between the hills, passing between the wires of the fence as cleanly as winged things. There was a lone buck—the one who figures in the story of 'The Last Antelope'—who tolerated her—it was not in his lifetime that the antelope had been accustomed to pursuit from men. Once in a storm of wind and rain they took shelter together in a half-ruined settler's shack. That was how Mary spent the first three months on the Tejon, all the time growing apparently more apathetic, until Susie was genuinely worried. 'I can't help but think,' she would say, 'if you'd rouse yourself to take some interest in things ...'

But the fact is Mary was consumed with interest as with enchantment. Her trouble was that the country failed to explain itself. If it had a history, nobody could recount it. Its creatures had no known life except such as she could discover by unremitting vigilance of observation; its plants no names that her Middlewestern botany could supply. She did not know yet what were its weather signs, nor what the procession of its days might bring forth. Until these things elucidated themselves factually, Mary was spellbound in an effort not to miss any animal behavior, any bird-marking, any weather signal, any signature of tree or flower. Animals are like that, thrust into strange captivity, caught up into fearful question, refusing food and sleep until they die. But in Mary's case there was no fear but that she might miss the significance of the question, to which as yet she had no answer, the magic words which would unlock as much at least as anybody knew of the meaning of what she saw. For Mary is one of those people plagued with an anxiety to know. Other people, satisfied by the mere delight of seeing, think they pay her a compliment when they speak of her 'intuition' about things of the wild, or that they let her down a deserved notch or two by referring to her fortunate guesses.

The deadlock was broken by the discovery, after the leaves were off, of wild grapes in one of the Tejon canyons, and after a week or two of almost exclusive grape diet, Mary began to pick up amazingly. It was so *like* Mary, her family remarked, to almost starve to death on a proper Christian diet and go and get well on something grubbed out of the woods. But there was more to the incident than that; there was the beginning of a notion in Mary's mind of a poor appetite of any sort being cured by its proper food; that there was something you could do about unsatisfactory conditions besides being heroic or a martyr to them, something more satisfactory than enduring or complaining, and that was getting out to hunt for the remedy. This, for young ladies in the eighteen-eighties, was a revolutionary discovery to have made. So that it

appeared in the nature of a happy accident that General Edward Fitzgerald
Beale, the owner of Tejon Ranch, came back to it along in January, 1889, and
released Mary from the black spell of her wanting to know.

1932

■ FRANK NORRIS ■
1870–1902

In late 1899, book reviewers were astounded to find that newcomer Frank Norris
had published yet another novel, his third in twelve months. Even more startling
was the variety of his work. The sensational adventure-romance *Moran of the Lady
Letty* (1898) was followed by his masterpiece, *McTeague* (1899), a graphic and still
gruesome study of sex, greed, violence, and degeneracy in the style of the French
literary Naturalists. *Blix* appeared seven months later, and this pleasant love-idyll
suggested the influence of neither Robert Louis Stevenson nor Emile Zola. Rather,
free from a focus on abnormal behavior and deviant sexuality, it was designed not
to shock but to depict in high relief the optimism about American life that was once
William Dean Howells's. Indeed, its characters would most likely have delighted
Louisa May Alcott. "What would Norris try next?" was the question posed.

Though Norris is now known principally as a Naturalistic novelist and literary theorist, he was known for his versatility then. His growing, eclectic canon
documented American literature and thought at a transitional stage when Norris and his progressive contemporaries were experimentally moving from the
Victorian to the Modern sensibility.

Norris's own life reflected the restlessness of American culture in the 1890s.
Born to a well-to-do family in Chicago in 1870, he moved to San Francisco in
1884. From 1887 to 1889, he studied art at the Académie Julian in Paris. He
returned to California with a determination to pursue another artistic career, in
literature. He spent four years at the University of California, dabbling in higher
education and adjusting to his father's third marriage. From 1894 to 1895, he
studied French literature and creative writing at Harvard University. In addition, his short stories had appeared since 1891 in such prestigious periodicals as
Argonaut and *Overland Monthly*. Like his first book, the narrative poem *Yvernelle:
A Legend of Feudal France* (1892), these early works showed the clear influence
of Romantic writers such as Sir Walter Scott. Starting in 1894 to 1895, however,
Norris updated his repertoire. The new focus in his prose was on the contemporary scene, and his tone was that of ironic and witty observers of life in high society like Richard Harding Davis and Anthony Hope—a tone which was later
carried over to "*Fantaisie Printanière*" (1897). By 1895, he showed the influence
of his reading in French literature and was beginning to play the *enfant terrible*;
he had fallen under the spell of Emile Zola and in his creative writing course he

produced sketches for his two Zolaesque novels of degeneration, *McTeague* and *Vandover and the Brute* (the latter was posthumously published in 1914).

Norris, the peripatetic aspirant to a literary career, soon departed on a journalistic jaunt to South Africa for the *San Francisco Chronicle*. Deported because of his involvement in an English attempt to topple the Boer government, he began in April 1896 a twenty-two-month stint as a writer for the San Francisco weekly, *The Wave*, during which he was frequently on the road in northern California, producing local color sketches. Over one hundred and fifty articles and short stories later, Norris had gained experience in a wide variety of styles. The subjects he chose and would continue to write about were those at the center of the intellectual and social ferment of the 1890s: the New Woman; technological progress and urbanization; evolution and the determinisms of heredity and environment and what he termed "the mystery of sex." Indeed, Norris became one of the most sexually explicit writers of his generation. Further, he did not stop at sex, but deliberately sought out other taboos of genteel culture to violate, as will be seen in the still unsettling, "black humor" treatment of wife-beating featured in "*Fantaisie Printanière*." Like Ambrose Bierce and Stephen Crane, Norris specialized in chilling affronts to not only middle-class mores, but also to all kinds of traditional western values and cherished conceptions. The same year "*Fantaisie Printanière*" was published, "*Miracle Joyeux*" depicts Jesus employing his psychological insight in a peculiar manner, responding to human baseness by blinding two misers. "The Associated Un-Charities" puzzles the reader in much the same way that "*Fantaisie Printanière*" does: in 1897 or now, how should one respond to a comic sketch which turns upon a cruel joke played upon three blind men? On several occasions, then, Norris anticipates the disquieting effects produced in the twentieth century by Erskine Caldwell, Nathanael West, and Flannery O'Connor.

When not engaged in bizarre flirtations with "tasteless" subject matter, Norris soberly analyzed the schools of Realism, Romanticism, and Naturalism—defining his own position in regard to the character that modern art should have. Truthful representation was Norris's passion; and the ideal means to that end, he concluded, was a Naturalism that synthesized the best aspects of the older literacy traditions of Realism and Romanticism: Realism's devotion to empirical fact in modern conditions and Romanticism's probatory dedication to the revelation of truth.

Such a blending of techniques in varying proportions can be seen in the minor novels—*Moran, Blix, A Man's Woman* (1900)—as Norris engaged in revisionist definitions of masculinity and femininity, emphasizing in the first two novels the inadequacies of the Victorian concepts of both. Norris stresses the fact that the "human animal"—males and females—is naturally subject to drives and appetites that a post-Darwinian generation would frankly acknowledge. What Victorians termed the "beast within" also looms large in *McTeague* and *Vandover*: in both cases the "brute" of sexuality naturally emerges in the heroes and heroines, who struggle with the guilt they have been morally conditioned to feel.

Other kinds of determinisms shape the lives of the characters in Norris's *The Octopus* (1901) and *The Pit* (1903). The former is an early muck-raking novel exposing the chicanery of a railroad trust in California. The desire to dominate in the arena of a *laissez-faire* capitalist economy, fueled by the keen acquisitive instincts displayed by both the representatives of the railroad and the wheat growers in the San Joaquin Valley, overtakes all of the principal characters, and the Social Darwinists on the railroad's side prevail as those "fit to survive," crushing the wheat growers. The megalomaniacal hero of *The Pit* is similarly carried along by his passion to prevail in a dog-eat-dog economic order, while his neurotic wife—a victim of Romantic cultural influences rather than economic forces—tries to realize impossibly high expectations of love and life in the manner of the heroines in Gustave Flaubert's *Madame Bovary* and Kate Chopin's *The Awakening*.

Norris's rejection of Victorian proprieties and his many violations of the limits imposed upon literature by the genteel guardians of public morality were both sardonically comical in tone (as in *"Fantaisie Printanière"*) and mordantly serious (as in *Vandover and the Brute*). At the turn of the century, his experiments in making a NEW sense of things encouraged younger writers like Jack London to take risks in revealing the truth of the human condition. Admired and imitated by later authors such as F. Scott Fitzgerald and John Steinbeck, Norris's view of the complex nature of human experience was perpetuated in the modern tradition of American literature.

Joseph R. McElrath, Jr.
Florida State University

PRIMARY WORKS

Yvernelle, 1892; *Moran of the Lady Letty*, 1898; *McTeague*, 1899; *Blix*, 1899; *A Man's Woman*, 1900; *The Octopus*, 1901; *The Pit*, 1903; *A Deal in Wheat*, 1903; *The Responsibilities of the Novelist*, 1903; *The Joyous Miracle*, 1906; Will Irwin, ed., *The Third Circle*, 1909; *Vandover and the Brute*, 1914; Oscar Lewis, ed., *Frank Norris of "The Wave,"* 1931; Donald Pizer, ed., *The Literary Criticism of Frank Norris*, 1964; James D. Hart, ed., *A Novelist in the Making*, 1970; Jesse S. Crisler, ed., *Frank Norris: Collected Letters*, 1986.

SECONDARY WORKS

Franklin Walker, *Frank Norris: A Biography*, 1932; Ernest Marchand, *Frank Norris: A Study*, 1942; Warren French, *Frank Norris*, 1962; Donald Pizer, *The Novels of Frank Norris*, 1966; William B. Dillingham, *Frank Norris: Instinct and Art*; Jesse S. Crisler and Joseph R. McElrath, Jr., *Frank Norris: A Reference Guide*, 1974; Don Graham, *The Fiction of Frank Norris*, 1978; Barbara Hochman, *The Art of Frank Norris, Storyteller*, 1988; Joseph R. McElrath, Jr., *Frank Norris Revisited*, 1992; idem, *Frank Norris: A Descriptive Bibliography*, 1992.

Fantaisie Printanière[1]

The McTeagues and the Ryers lived at the disreputable end of Polk street, away down in the squalid neighborhood by the huge red drum of the gas

---

[1]Springtime fantasy.

works. The drum leaked, of course, and the nasty brassy foulness of the leak mingled with the odors of cooking from the ill-kept kitchens, and the reek of garbage in the vacant lots did not improve the locality.

McTeague had once been a dentist, and had had "parlors" up at the respectable end of the street. But after a while the license office discovered that he had no diploma; in fact, had never attended a college of any sort, and had forbidden him to practice. So McTeague had taken to drink.

Ryer, some years back, had been a sort of small stock-dealer on the outskirts of Butchertown,[2] and had done fairly well until the Health Board reported him to the Supervisors because he had fattened his hogs on poultices obtained from the City and County Hospital. The result was a lamentable scandal, which finally drove him out of business. So Ryer had taken to drink.

The Ryers home (or let us say, the house in which the Ryers ate and slept), adjoined the house in which the McTeagues ate and slept. You would have thought that this propinquity, joined with the coincidence of their common misfortunes—both victims of governmental persecution—would have insured a certain degree of friendship between the two men. But this was not so at all, a state of feud existed between Montague Ryer and Capulet McTeague.[3] The feud had originated some year or so previous to the time of this tale, in the back room of Gerstle's "Wein Stube"[4] on the corner opposite the drum. A discussion had arisen between the two men, both far gone in whiskey, as to the lines of longitude on the surface of the globe. Capulet claimed they were parallel throughout their whole extent—Montague maintained they converged at the poles. They discussed this question at length—first with heady words and vociferation, next with hurled pony glasses and uplifted chairs, and finally, after their ejection from the "Stube," with fists clenched till the knuckles whitened, crooked elbows, and the soles of heavy-shod boots. They arrived at no definite conclusion. Twice since then had they fought. Their original difference of opinion had been speedily forgotten. They fought now, they knew not why—merely for the sake of fighting. The quarrel between them came to be recognized by the "block" as part of the existing order of things, like the reek from the drum and the monthly visit of the rent-collector.

Ryer had something the worst of it in these fights. He was a small, lean, pinkish creature, like a split carrot, his mouth a mere long slit beneath his nose. When he was angry his narrow eyes glistened like streaks of bitumen.

McTeague was a huge blonde giant, carrying his enormous fell of yellow hair, six feet and more above his ponderous, slow-moving feet. His hands, hard as wooden mallets, dangled from arms that suggested twisted cables. His jaw was that of the carnivoral.

---

[2]All of the locations cited are in the environs of San Francisco.

[3]Allusion to the feuding families, Montague and Capulet, in Shakespeare's *Romeo and Juliet*.

[4]Wine pub or saloon.

Both men thrashed their wives, McTeague on the days when he was drunk, which were many, Ryer on the days when he was sober, which were few. They went about it, each in his own peculiar fashion. Ryer found amusement in whipping Missis Ryer with a piece of rubber hose filled with gravel, or (his nature demanded variety of sensation), with a long, thin rawhide, which he kept hidden between the mattress. He never used fists or boots; such methods revolted him. "What! am I a drayman, am I a hod-carrier!" exclaimed Mister Ryer. When McTeague did not use the fist or the foot, he used the club. Refinement, such as characterized Ryer, was foreign to the ex-dentist. He struck out blindly, savagely, and with a colossal, clumsy force that often spent itself upon the air. The difference between the men could be seen in the different modes of punishment they affected. Ryer preferred the lash of the whip, McTeague the butt. Ryer was cruel, McTeague only brutal.

While common grievance had not made friends of the two men, mutual maltreatment had drawn their wives together, until no two women on the "block" were more intimate than Trina McTeague and Ryer's wife. They made long visits to each other in the morning in their wrappers and curl papers, talking for hours over a cuppa tea, served upon the ledge of the sink or a corner of the laundry table. During these visits they avoided speaking of their husbands, because, although the whole "block" knew of the occasional strained relations of their families, the two women feigned to keep the secret from each other. And this in the face of the fact that Missis Ryer would sometimes come over to see Trina with a thin welt across her neck, or Trina return the visit with a blackened eye or a split lip.

Once, however, only once, they broke in upon their reticence. Many things came of the infringement. Among others this *fantaisie*.

During that particular night three dandelions had bloomed in the vacant lot behind the gas works, the unwonted warmth of the last few days had brought back the familiar odor of the garbage heaps, an open car had appeared on the cross town cable line and Bock beer[5] was on draught at the "Wein Stube," and Polk street knew that Spring was at hand.

About nine o'clock Trina McTeague appeared on the back steps of her house rolling her washtub before her, preparing to do her monthly washing in the open air on that fine morning. She and Ryer's wife usually observed this hated rite at the same time, calling shrilly to one another as their backs bent and straightened over the scrubbing-boards. But that morning Trina looked long for Missis Ryer and at last fell a-wondering.

The fact of the matter was that the night before Ryer had come home sober and had found occasion to coerce Missis Ryer with a trunk-strap. By a curious coincidence McTeague had come home drunk the same evening, and for two hours Trina had been hard put to it to dodge his enormous fists and his hurled boots. (Nor had she been invariably successful.)

[5]Beer available in the spring.

At that moment the ex-dentist was sleeping himself sober under the stairs in the front hall, and the whilom stock-dealer was drinking himself drunk in the "Wein Stube" across the street.

When eleven o'clock had struck and Missis Ryer had not appeared, Trina dried her smoking arms on her skirt, and, going through the hole in the backyard fence, entered the kitchen of the Ryers house and called. Missis Ryer came into the kitchen in a blue cotton wrapper and carpet slippers. Her hair was hanging down her back (it was not golden).[6] Evidently she had just arisen.

"Ain't you goin' to wash this mornin', Missis Ryer?" asked Trina McTeague.

"Good Mornin', Trina," said the other, adding doggedly, as she sat down hard in a broken chair: "I'm *sick* and *tired* a-washin' an' workin' for Ryer."

She drew up instinctively to the cold stove, and propped her chin upon her knuckles. The loose sleeve of the wrapper fell away from her forearm, and Trina saw the fresh marks of the trunk-strap. Evidently Ryer had not held that strap by the buckle-end.

This was the first time Missis Ryer had ever mentioned her husband to Trina.

"Hoh!" ejaculated Trina, speaking before she thought, "it ain't alwus such fun workin' for Mac, either."

There was a brief silence. Both the women remained for a moment looking vaguely out of the kitchen door, absorbed in thought, very curious, each wondering what next the other would say. The conversation, almost without their wishing it, had suddenly begun upon untried and interesting ground. Missis Ryer said:

"I'll make a cuppa tea."

She made the tea, slovening languidly about the dirty kitchen, her slippers clap-clapping under her bare heels. Then the two drew up to the washboard of the sink, drinking the tea from the saucers, wiping their lips slowly from time to time with the side of their hands. Each was waiting for the other to speak. Suddenly Missis Ryer broke out.

"It's best not to fight him, or try to git away—hump your back and it's soonest over."

"You couldn't do that with Mac," answered Trina, shaking her head with decision, "if I didunt dodge, if I let um have his own way he'd sure kill me. Mac's that strong he could break me in two."

"Oh, *Ryer's* strong all-right-all-right," returned Missis Ryer, "an' then he's sober when he fights an' knows what he's about, an' that makes it worse. Look there what he did last night." She rolled up her sleeve and Trina glanced at the arm with the critical glance of a connoisseur.

---

[6]Allusion to popular song praising a woman's supreme beauty; "Her golden hair was hanging down her back."

"Hoh," she said scornfully, "that ain't a circumstance. I had a row with Mac last night meself, and this is what he did with his fist. Just his fist, mind you, and it only grazed me as it was." She slipped a discolored shoulder out of her calico gown. The two critically compared bruises. Missis Ryer was forced to admit that Trina's bruise was the worse. She was vexed and disappointed but rallied with:

"Yes that's pirty bad, but I'll show you somethin' that'll open your eyes," and she thrust the blue wrapper down from the nape of the neck. "See that scar there," she said "that's the kind of work Ryer can do when he puts his mind to it; got that nearly four months ago and it's sore yet."

"Ah, yes," said Trina loftily, "little scars, little flesh wounds like that! You never had any bones brokun. Just look at that thumb," she went on proudly, "Mac did that with just a singul grip of his fist. I can't nevur bend it again."

Then the interminable discussion began.

"Look at that, just look at *that*, will you?"

"Ah, that ain't nothun. How about *that?* there's a lick for you."

"Why, Mac's the strongest man you ever *saw*."

"Ah-h, you make me tired, it ain't a strong man, always, that can hurt the most. It's the fellah that knows how and where to hit. It's a whip that hurts the most."

"But it's a club that does the most damage."

"Huh! wait till you git hit with a rubber hose filled with gravel."

"Why, Mac can knock me the length of the house with his left fist. He's done plenty a'times."

Then they came to reminiscences.[7]

"Why, one time when Mac came home from a picnic at Schuetzen Park,[8] he picked me right up offun the ground with one hand and held me right up in the air like that, and let me have it with a kitchun chair. Huh! talk to *me* about Ryer's little whips, Ryer ain't a patch on my man. *You* don't know what a good thrashun is."

"I *don't*, hey? you can just listen to what I tell you, Trina McTeague, when I say that Ryer can lay all over your man. You jest ought a been here one night when I sassed Ryer back, I tell you I'll never do *that* again. Why the worst lickin' Mister McTeague ever gave you was just little love taps to what I got. Besides I don' *believe* your man ever held you up with one hand and banged you like that with a chair, you wouldn't a' lived if he had."

"Oh, I ain't *lyun* to you," cried Trina, with shrill defiance getting to her feet. Missis Ryer rose likewise and clapped her arms akimbo.

"Why," she cried, "you just said as much yourself, that if you didn't dodge and get away he'd kill you."

---

[7]A condensed version of this conversation later appeared in *McTeague*, chapter 16.

[8]In Oakland, a city located across the bay from San Francisco.

"An' I'll say it again. I ain't gowun to eat my words for the best woman that ever wore shoes, an' you can chew on that, Missus Ryer. I tell you Mac's the hardest hittun husband a woman ever had."

"I just like to have you live here with Ryer a week or so, you'd soon find out who was the best man, an'—" here Missis Ryer came close to Trina and shouted the word in her face. "An' don't you sass me either, an' talk about eatin' words, or I'll show; you right here the kind a' whalin' Ryer's taught me."

"I guess Ryer, himself, knows who's the best man of the two, he or Mac," exclaimed Trina, loftily. "How about that last scrap o' theirs? If Mac got hold a you once and gave you one lick, like the kind I get twenty of every week, you wouldunt be as well off as your man was when Mac got through with um the time they fought last Washington's burthday, behind the brick kiln. Why Mac could do for the whole three of us, you an' Ryer an' I, yes he could, with one hand."

"Ah, talk sense, will you?" shouted Missis Ryer, as she moved the previous question. "Ain't Mister McTeague drunk when he dresses you down, and don't it stand to reason that he *can't* give it to you as hard as Ryer gives it to me when he's *sober?*"

"Do you know anything about it anyways?" said Trina, excitedly, "I tell you he's a deal worse to me than Ryer ever *thought* of be-un to you. Ain't he twysut, *three* times as strong?"

"That's a lie," retorted Ryer's wife, vindicating her absent husband with astonishing vehemence.

"Don't you tell me I lie again," shouted Trina, her cheeks flaming, her chin thrust out.

"I guess I'll say what I please in my own kitchin, you dirty little drab," screamed the other. Their faces were by this time close together, neither would draw back an inch.

"No you won't, no you won't," panted Trina, "an' don't you dare call me a drab. Drab yourself; best go back to the pigs your man used to fatten on old poultices, go back to your sty, I guess it won't be any dirtier than this here kitchun."

"Git out of it then."

"Not till I get ready."

"An' I'll call you drab till I'm black in the face, drab, *drab*, damn nasty, dirty little drab. Git out uv my kitchin."

"Ah-h, let me see you put me out."

"Ah dirty little drab."

"Ah, slattern, ah, pig-feeder."

Suddenly they tore at each other like infuriated cats. A handful of black and gray hair came away from Missis Ryer's head. Fingernail marks, long red lines appeared on the curve of Trina's cheeks, very like McTeague's conception of the parallels upon a globe. Missis Ryer, hustling Trina toward the door, pushed her into the arms of McTeague himself. At the same time Ryer, warned of this war of wives, entered the kitchen from the front of the house. He had come over hastily from the "Wein Stube" and was half drunk. McTeague had partially slept off his intoxication and was about half sober.

"Here, here, here," cried the ex-dentist over his wife's shoulder, "you two women fightin', quit it; what the bloody Hell!"

"Scrappin'" shouted Ryer from the doorway, "choke off, ol' woman, if there's any scrappin' to be done, I'll do it meself."

"She called me a drab," gasped Trina, glaring at her enemy from under the protection of her gigantic husband.

"An' she said my kitchin wasn't a place for pigs to live in," retorted Missis Ryer, without taking her eyes from Trina.

The men had not yet looked at each other. They were unwilling to fight this morning, because each one of them was half drunk or half sober (either way you chose to put it), and because Ryer preferred to fight when he had all his wits about him while McTeague was never combative until he had lost *his* wits entirely.

"What started the row, whatcha been fightin' about?" demanded the ex-dentist.

"Yes, sure," put in Ryer, "whatcha been scrappin' about, what started the row?"

The women looked at each other, unable to answer. Then Trina began awkwardly:

"Well I—well—well—a—well she told me—she said—well, she run you down Mac, an' I didunt figure on puttun up with it."

"She tried to make small of you, Ryer," said his wife, "an' I called her down an'—that's all, she tried to make small of you."

"Hey? What'd she say?" demanded McTeague, "out with it."

"Well, *this* is what she said," exclaimed Trina suddenly. "She said Ryer could give her a worse dressing down than you ever gave me, an' I wouldn't stand it."

"Well," declared Missis Ryer, turning to her husband. "I ain't goin' to let every dirty little drab that comes along say—say—throw mud at my man, am I? I guess," added Missis Ryer, defiantly, facing Trina and the ex-dentist. "I guess Ryer can do what he likes in his own house. I ain't goin' to let any woman tell me that her man's better'n mine, in any way."

"An' that's what you two fought over," exclaimed the husbands in the same breath.

"Well, suppose we did?" said Trina with defiance.

"I guess I can quarrel about what I like," observed Missis Ryer, sullenly.

For the first time since they had entered the room the eyes of the two men met and for fully half a dozen seconds they looked squarely at each other. Then the corners of the slit under Ryer's nose began to twitch, and McTeague's huge jaws to widen to a grin in nut-cracker fashion. Suddenly a roar of laughter shook him; he sank into a chair, rocking back and forth, smiting his knee with his palm. Ryer cackled shrilly crying out between peals of laughter: "Well, if this ain't the greatest jolly I've struck yet."

"Fightin' over our fightin' *them*," bellowed McTeague.

"I've seen queer bugs in my time," gasped Ryer, "but the biggest curios yet are women, oh Lord, but this does beat the Dutch."

"Say, ain't this great, Ryer?"

"Mac, this does beat the carpet, sure."

"Look here old man, about them parallel lines, *I* say let's call it off. I ain't got no quarrel against *you*."

"That's a go, Mac, you're a good fellah, sure, put it there."

They shook hands upon their reconciliation, their breasts swelling with magnanimity. They felt that they liked one another hugely, and they slapped each other tremendous blows on the back, exclaiming at intervals *"put* it there," and gripping hands with a cordiality that was effusive beyond words. All at once Ryer had an inspiration.

"Say, Mac, come over to the Stube and have a drink on it."

"Well, I just guess I will," vociferated the ex-dentist.

Bewildered and raging at the unexpected reconciliation of their husbands, the two women had disappeared, Trina slamming the door of the kitchen with a parting cry of "pig feeder," which Missis Ryer immediately answered by thrusting her head out of a second story window and screaming at the top of her voice to the neighborhood in general, "dirty little drab."

Meanwhile the two men strode out of the house and across the street, their arms affectionately locked; the swing doors of the "Stube" flapped after them like a pair of silent wings.

That day settled the matter. Heretofore it had been the men who were enemies and their wives who were friends. Now the two men are fast friends, while the two women maintain perpetual feud. The "block" has come to recognize their quarrel as part of the existing order of things, like the leak from the gas-works and the collector's visits. Occasionally the women fight, and Missis Ryer, who is the larger and heavier, has something the best of it.

However, one particular custom common to both households remains unchanged—both men continue to thrash their wives in the old ratio—McTeague on the days when he is drunk (which are many), Ryer on the days when he is sober (which are few).

1897

REDEFINING THE SOUTH

IN FOCUS

Black and White after Slavery

ALTHOUGH THE CIVIL WAR ENDED IN 1865, TENSIONS CONTINUED TO RUN HIGH as the South—and the entire nation for that matter—sought to come to terms with the unprecedented cultural upheaval triggered by the freeing of the slaves. Indeed, one can argue that the abolition of chattel slavery in the United States entailed a fundamental reconsideration of not just the construction of race but also the very definitions of "freedom" and "citizenship." In the years immediately following the War, it became clear that most Southern whites remained highly resistant to the idea of black freedom, not to mention black political empowerment, and Congress finally decided after much heated debate to impose what was essentially military law on the Southern states in order to safeguard the rights of the former slaves. This controversial exercise in social engineering was known as the "Radical Reconstruction."

For many in the white South, the Reconstruction was the federal government's pouring salt in still-gaping wounds opened by a humiliating defeat in the Civil War. Accordingly, the Compromise of 1877 that led to the withdrawal of U.S. troops from the South was seen by most whites in the region as a key part in the process dubbed the "Redemption." Meanwhile, more extreme elements had been resorting to violence in an attempt to maintain white supremacy in the wake of the Civil War and the end of slavery, with the Ku Klux Klan being the most notorious example. Such groups were but the tip of the iceberg in the burgeoning racial violence that became commonplace throughout the South and that was most horrifically enacted in the sadistic practice of lynching blacks, a form of ritualized brutality that, like most terrorist acts, was designed to intimidate and render insecure an entire population, not simply to attack specific individuals.

Through the 1880s and 1890s, the reconsolidation of white supremacy in the South moved ahead quickly via both *de facto* (informal) and *de jure* (legislative) means. By the end of the century, most blacks in the region were rendered politically powerless after having only just begun to gain a foothold at the local and national governmental levels during Reconstruction. A key mechanism in the repression of blacks at the time was the so-called "Jim Crow" segregation that severely restricted African American mobility and access to public services.

An especially discouraging factor here was the extent to which the federal government's commitment to black security, much less to black enfranchisement and economic progress, had largely dissipated. Perhaps the most sobering indication of this shift in national policy was the 1896 *Plessy v. Ferguson* decision in which the Supreme Court established the legality of "separate but equal" facilities despite the fact that the bulk of such racially segregated facilities were certainly "separate" but almost never "equal." The impact of this ruling cannot be understated, for with the imprimatur of the Supreme Court, Southern states established a thoroughgoing form of racial apartheid that persisted through the middle of the twentieth century. It is understandable why the African American historian Rayford Logan termed the late nineteenth century the "nadir" of the black experience in the United States after slavery.

For many Southern whites, the end of Reconstruction and the withdrawal of the federal government from an active role in managing race relations in the region could not have come a moment too soon. In his famous 1886 speech titled "The New South," the influential editor Henry Grady articulated a vision of the postwar South as primed to take its place as a key contributor in the country's push toward the front rank of Western nations and its drive toward what was widely celebrated as "progress." Such advance depended, Grady and others contended, on an ending of sectional hostility and antagonism. Furthermore, the desired reconciliation between the North and the South would, they felt, be most potently keyed by the recognition that the United States was and would need to remain a *white* nation. Accordingly, the racial bond joining Northern and Southern whites was, it was argued, far too fundamental to be disrupted for long by any bitter debate over the morality of slavery and the subsequent status of the former slave.

A number of white moderate voices attempted to speak out against the rising tide of racist extremism. In this section of the anthology, examples include Albion Tourgée and George Washington Cable. A well-known novelist and the lawyer who argued on behalf of the plaintiff in the *Plessy v. Ferguson* case, Tourgée observed quite astutely in 1888, "Not only is the epoch of the war the favorite field of American fiction to-day, but the Confederate soldier is the popular hero. Our literature has become not only Southern in type, but distinctly Confederate in sympathy" ("The South as a Field for Fiction"). Tourgée's comments acknowledge the remarkable extent to which the white South overwhelmingly won what might today be termed the "culture war" in the last half of the nineteenth century. Built on the myths of the Confederacy as a "Noble Cause" and of slavery as a benign institution benefiting both master and slave, what came to be called the "Plantation Tradition" movement proved powerfully seductive throughout the United States. Accordingly, we see countless plays, novels, songs, stories, poems, advertisements, and paintings that offer up stereotypically conceptualized views of the South. The earliest literary manifestations of the Plantation Tradition predate the Civil War. However, it reaches its apotheosis in the late nineteenth century, with Thomas Nelson Page's "Mars Chan" (1884) embodying the formulaic mixture of humor, nostalgia, sentimentality, superficial racial type, patriarchy, and elitism upon which subsequent authors, South and North, drew with considerable success for years.

Also important to note here is the extent to which the Plantation Tradition participated in a broader turn to dialect, vernacular speech, and folkways that we find throughout American literature of the time. Easily the best-known white Southern writer in this tradition was the Georgia journalist Joel Chandler Harris, whose black fictive creation Uncle Remus served as the mouthpiece for scores of folktales to which Harris exposed most white Americans for the first time. Although many of his tales are, in fact, based on African American oral folk materials and thus valuable from an anthropological perspective, he consistently presents these texts outside an African American social setting in his work. Furthermore, in some of his sketches, Harris has Uncle Remus quite explicitly express cynicism regarding attempts to provide former slaves with a formal education and political rights. Also worth brief mention here is the more extremist and inflammatory antiblack fiction at the time. Perhaps the foremost example of this repugnant strain of popular literature was Thomas Dixon's fiercely provocative and bestselling novel *The Clansman* (1905), which served as the basis for D. W. Griffith's celebrated film *The Birth of a Nation* (1915). Both the novel and the film depict most blacks as corrupt, gullible, incompetent, sexually voracious, dangerous creatures whose freedom from white supervision with the end of slavery constitutes a grave and terrifying threat to the Southern order and to the so-called "white" civilization of the entire nation. Predictably, the exceedingly few positively represented blacks in such texts are favored primarily for their steadfast and selfless loyalty to their white employers, usually their former owners.

In the postbellum period, we see a growing rate of written literacy among African Americans, a development abetted by the new educational opportunities provided by black colleges established primarily in the South during and immediately following Reconstruction. It should thus come as no surprise that a significant number of African Americans sought to use literary expression to counter the racist stereotypes that dominated the mainstream representation of blacks at the time. Even when African American authors did not explicitly treat what was called the "Negro Problem," they almost always depicted their black characters as complex human beings, a choice that constituted a fundamentally resistant act. Building on her earlier career as an activist antislavery writer, Frances Harper continued to produce verse and fiction about the African American community, particularly in the South, and that community's drive toward security and self-determination. Along with other African American female writers such as Anna Julia Cooper, Harper also became involved in the women's rights struggle that was coalescing in the United States toward the end of the century.

Frances Harper is notable as well for her experiments with black Southern vernacular speech in her post–Civil War poetry. Like the celebrated African American writer Paul Laurence Dunbar, she sought to undermine the ways in which what was known as black "dialect" verse had all too often been written and consumed as broad comedy or pathos that did little to offer fully formed representations of blacks. Harper contested such limitations by addressing explicitly political issues in her verse through the down-to-earth voices of her black folk speakers. Another black author who found creative ways to incorporate black vernacular speech into her work is Alice Dunbar-Nelson. In her quite striking sketch "The Praline Woman," Dunbar-Nelson reveals the rich humanity of a Creole woman who speaks a hybridized French-English patois as she sells candies to passersby on a New Orleans street. The Louisiana locale of Dunbar-Nelson's work exemplifies the extent to which that region has long stood out as something of an aberration on the American cultural landscape. Demographically constituted of a mélange of Spanish, African, American Indian, French, and Anglo-American peoples and, before the Civil War, marked by complex interactions among the free, the slave, and the semi-free, Louisiana in the late nineteenth century proved to be a fertile setting for creative considerations of race, class, gender, and nationality. This section of the anthology includes several authors besides Dunbar-Nelson whose work makes use of the rich and diverse cultures of the Louisiana locale—Kate Chopin, George Washington Cable, and Grace King.

Embodying many of the aforementioned literary strategies and concerns was the black author Charles Chesnutt. Although nowhere near as commercially successful as his contemporary Paul Laurence Dunbar, Chesnutt, like Dunbar, was extraordinarily skilled at rendering Southern black vernacular speech and deeply committed to portraying blacks as psychologically complex human beings. Engaging such themes as the ongoing economic exploitation of blacks, the impact of the legacy of slavery on both blacks and whites in the South, color and class tensions in the African American community, the role of violence in race relations in the United States, and the instability of racial categories, Chesnutt was masterful in his ability to subvert popular racial stereotypes even as he could superficially appear to apply them uncritically. The conceptual ambition, finely honed prose, and subtle irony of Chesnutt's work have a great deal to do with the growing critical recognition of his accomplishments in our time. However, one can argue that these very characteristics as well as the literary tide against which he was swimming ensured that he would be misread, underappreciated, or ignored in his own.

Finally, as part of the nationwide explosion of investigative (or "muckraking") journalism in the late nineteenth century, writers like Ida B. Wells exemplified the commitment of a growing number of blacks to using their pens in the struggle against the rampant brutalizing and marginalization of African American citizens, especially in the South. Wells and others sought, often at no small risk to themselves, to contest directly mainstream derogatory narratives regarding blacks. Another compelling example of such literary activism is Kelly Miller, whose open letter to the white novelist Thomas Dixon appears in this section of the anthology. Dixon's popular novel *The Leopard's Spots* (1902) struck Miller as a downright libel on African American character. Miller's angry and yet restrained comments indicate just how clearly African American observers recognized the extraordinary power of popular media representations of blacks in general and of black–white race relations in the South in particular. Their attempts to respond to this challenge through literature manifest both their ideological investments and their ultimate faith in the power of the communicative act of writing.

Richard Yarborough
University of California, Los Angeles

HENRY W. GRADY
1851–1889

from **The New South: Speech Given to the New England Society of New York City in December 1886**[1]

In speaking to the toast with which you have honored me, I accept the term, "The New South," as in no sense disparaging to the Old. Dear to me, sir, is the home of my childhood and the traditions of my people. I would not, if I could, dim the glory they won in peace and war, or by word or deed take aught from the splendor and grace of their civilization—never equaled and, perhaps, never to be equaled in its chivalric strength and grace. There is a New South, not through protest against the Old, but because of new conditions, new adjustments and, if you please, new ideas and aspirations....

[He evokes the spectacle of the defeated Confederate soldiers returned to a South that war has devastated.]

What does he do—this hero in gray with a heart of gold? Does he sit down in sullenness and despair? Not for a day. Surely God, who had stripped him of his prosperity, inspired him in his adversity. As ruin was never before so overwhelming, never was restoration swifter. The soldier stepped from the trenches into the furrow; horses that had charged Federal guns march before the plow, and fields that ran red with human blood in April were green with the harvest in June; women reared in luxury cut up their dresses and made breeches for their husbands, and, with a patience and heroism that fit women always as a garment, gave their hands to work. There was little bitterness in all this. Cheerfulness and frankness prevailed....
[W]e have caught the sunshine in the bricks and mortar of our homes, and have builded therein not one ignoble prejudice or memory. But in all this what have we accomplished? What is the sum of our work? We have found out that in the general summary the free Negro counts more than he did as a slave. We have planted the schoolhouse on the hilltop and made it free to white and black. We have sowed towns and cities in the place of theories and put business above politics. We have challenged your spinners in Massachusetts and your iron-makers in Pennsylvania. We have learned that the $400,000,000 annually received from our cotton crop will make us rich, when the supplies that make it are home-raised. We have reduced the commercial rate of interest from twenty-four to six per cent, and are floating four per cent bonds. We have learned that one Northern immigrant is worth

[1]Edwin DuBois Shurter, ed., *The Complete Orations and Speeches of Henry W. Grady* (Norwood, MA: Norwood Press, 1910). Henry Woodfin Grady (1851–1889) was editor of the *Atlanta Constitution* from 1880 to 1889. He was a spokesman for the New South and a renowned orator.

fifty foreigners, and have smoothed the path to southward, wiped out the place where Mason and Dixon's line used to be, and hung our latch-string out to you and yours. We have reached the point that marks perfect harmony in every household, when the husband confesses that the pies which his wife cooks are as good as those his mother used to bake; and we admit that the sun shines as brightly and the moon as softly as it did "before the war." We have established thrift in city and country. We have fallen in love with work. We have restored comfort to homes from which culture and elegance never departed. We have let economy take root and spread among us as rank as the crabgrass which sprang from Sherman's cavalry camps, until we are ready to lay odds on the Georgia Yankee, as he manufactures relics of the battlefield in a one-story shanty and squeezes pure olive oil out of his cotton-seed, against any downeaster that ever swapped wooden nutmegs for flannel sausages in the valleys of Vermont. Above all, we know that we have achieved in these "piping times of peace" a fuller independence for the South than that which our fathers sought to win in the forum by their eloquence or compel on the field by their swords. . . .

But what of the Negro? Have we solved the problem he presents or progressed in honor and equity towards the solution? Let the record speak to the point. No section shows a more prosperous laboring population than the Negroes of the South; none in fuller sympathy with the employing and land-owning class. He shares our school fund, has the fullest protection of our laws and the friendship of our people. Self-interest, as well as honor, demand that he should have this. Our future, our very existence depend upon our working out this problem in full and exact justice. We understand that when Lincoln signed the Emancipation Proclamation, your victory was assured; for he then committed you to the cause of human liberty, against which the arms of man cannot prevail . . . ; while those of our statesmen who trusted to make slavery the cornerstone of the Confederacy doomed us to defeat as far as they could, committing us to a cause that reason could not defend or the sword maintain in the sight of advancing civilization. . . . [W]henever slavery became entangled in war it must perish, and . . . the chattel in human flesh ended forever in New England when your fathers— not to be blamed for parting with what didn't pay—sold their slaves to our fathers—not to be praised for knowing a paying thing when they saw it. The relations of the Southern people with the Negro are close and cordial. We remember with what fidelity for four years he guarded our defenceless women and children, whose husbands and fathers were fighting against his freedom. To his eternal credit be it said that whenever he struck a blow for his own liberty he fought in open battle, and when at last he raised his black and humble hands that the shackles might be struck off, those hands were innocent of wrong against his helpless charges, and worthy to be taken in loving grasp by every man who honors loyalty and devotion. Ruffians have maltreated him, rascals have misled him, philanthropists established a bank for him, but the South, with the North, protects against injustice to this simple and sincere people. To liberty and enfranchisement is as far as law can carry the Negro. The rest must be left to conscience and common sense. It should be left to those among whom his lot is cast, with whom he is indissolubly connected and whose prosperity depends upon their possessing his intelligent sympathy and confidence. Faith has been kept with him in spite of calumnious assertions to the contrary by those who assume to speak for us or by frank opponents. Faith will be kept with him in the future, if the South holds her reason and integrity....

The Old South rested everything on slavery and agriculture, unconscious that these could neither give nor maintain healthy growth. The New South presents a perfect democracy, the oligarchs leading in the popular movements' social system compact and closely knitted, less splendid on the surface but stronger at the core—a hundred farms for every plantation, fifty homes for every palace, and a diversified industry that meets the complex needs of this complex age.

1886

■ ALBION W. TOURGÉE ■
1838–1905

from **The South as a Field for Fiction**[1]

More than twenty years ago the writer ventured the prediction that the short but eventful lifetime of the Southern Confederacy, the downfall of slavery, and the resulting conditions of Southern life would furnish to the future American novelist his richest and most striking material. At that time he was entirely unknown as a writer of fiction, and it is probable that he is now generally supposed to have turned his attention in this direction more from political bias than from any literary or artistic attraction which it offered. The exact converse was in fact true; the romantic possibility of the situation appealed to him even more vividly than its political difficulty, though, as is always the case in great national crises, the one was unavoidably colored by the other. Slavery as a condition of society has not yet become separable, in the minds of our people, North or South, from slavery as a political idea, a factor of partisan strife. They do not realize that two centuries of bondage left an ineradicable impress on master and slave alike, or that the line of separation between the races, being marked by the fact of color, is as impassable since emancipation as it was before, and perhaps even more portentous. They esteem slavery as simply a dead, unpleasant fact of

[1]*Forum*, December 1888.

which they wish to hear nothing more, and regard any disparaging allusion to its results as an attempt to revive a defunct political sentiment....

[The author] is almost startled ... to find himself averring, in the very glare of expiring conflict, that "within thirty years after the close of the war of rebellion popular sympathy will be with those who upheld the Confederate cause rather than with those by whom it was overthrown; our popular heroes will be Confederate leaders; our fiction will be Southern in its prevailing types and distinctively Southern in its character." There are yet seven years to elapse before the prescribed limit is reached, but the prediction is already almost literally fulfilled. Not only is the epoch of the war the favorite field of American fiction to-day, but the Confederate soldier is the popular hero. Our literature has become not only Southern in type, but distinctly Confederate in sympathy. The federal or Union soldier is not exactly depreciated, but subordinated; the Northern type is not decried, but the Southern is preferred. This is not because of any essential superiority of the one or lack of heroic attributes in the other, but because sentiment does not always follow the lead of conviction, and romantic sympathy is scarcely at all dependent upon merit. The writer makes no pretension to having foreseen the events that have occurred in the interval that has elapsed. Even the results he but imperfectly comprehended, having no clear anticipation of the peculiar forms which Southern fiction would assume. The one thing he did perceive, and the causes of which he clearly outlined, was the almost unparalleled richness of Southern life of that period as a field for fictitious narrative.

But whatever the cause may be, it cannot be denied that American fiction of to-day, whatever may be its origin, is predominantly Southern in type and character....

A foreigner studying our current literature, without knowledge of our history, and judging our civilization by our fiction, would undoubtedly conclude that the South was the seat of intellectual empire in America, and the African the chief romantic element of our population. As an evidence of this, it may be noted that a few months ago every one of our great popular monthlies presented a "Southern story" as one of its most prominent features; and during the past year nearly two-thirds of the stories and sketches furnished to newspapers by various syndicates have been of this character....

But the Negro has of late developed a capacity as a stock character of fiction which no one ever dreamed that he possessed in the good old days when he was a merchantable commodity. It must be admitted, too, that the Southern writers are "working him for all he is worth," as a foil to the aristocratic types of the land of heroic possibilities. The Northern man, no matter what his prejudices, is apt to think of the Negro as having an individuality of his own. To the Southern mind, he is only a shadow—an incident of another's life. As such he is invariably assigned one of two roles. In one he figures as the devoted slave who serves and sacrifices for his master and mistress, and is content to live or die, do good or evil, for those to whom he feels himself under infinite obligation for the privilege of living and serving. There were such miracles no doubt, but they were so rare as never to have lost the miraculous character. The other favorite aspect of the Negro character from the point of view of the Southern fictionist, is that of the poor "nigger" to whom liberty has brought only misfortune, and who is relieved by the disinterested friendship of some white man whose property he once was. There are such cases, too, but they are not so numerous as to destroy the charm of novelty. About the Negro as a man, with hopes, fears, and aspirations like other men, our literature is very nearly silent. Much has been written of the slave and something of the freedman, but thus far no one has been found able to weld the new life to the old.

This indeed is the great difficulty to be overcome. As soon as the American Negro seeks to rise above the level of the former time, he finds himself confronted with the past of his race and the woes of his kindred. It is to him not only a record of subjection but of injustice and oppression. The "twice-told tales" of *his* childhood are animate with rankling memories of wrongs. Slavery colored not only the lives but the traditions of his race. With the father's and the mother's blood is transmitted the story, not merely of their individual wrongs but of a race's woe, which the impenetrable oblivion of the past makes even more terrible and which the sense of color will not permit him to forgot. The white man traces his ancestry back for generations, knows whence they came, where they lived, and guesses what they did. To the American Negro the past is only darkness replete with unimaginable horrors. Ancestors he has none. Until within a quarter of a century he had no record of his kindred. he was simply one number of an infinite "no name series." He had no father, no mother; only a sire and dam. Being bred for market, he had no name, only a distinguishing appellative, like that of a horse or a dog. Even in comparison with these animals he was at a disadvantage; there was no "herdbook" of slaves. A well-bred horse may be traced back in his descent for a thousand years, and may show a hundred strains of noble blood; but even this poor consolation is denied the eight millions of slave-descended men and women in our country.

The remembrance of this condition is not pleasant and can never become so. It is exasperating, galling, degrading. Every freedman's life is colored by this shadow. The farther he gets away from slavery, the more bitter and terrible will be his memory of it. The wrong that was done to his forebears is a continuing and self-magnifying evil. This is the inevitable consequence of the conditions of the past; no kindness can undo it; no success can blot it out. It is the sole inheritance the bondman left his issue, and it must grow heavier rather than lighter until the very suggestion of inequality has disappeared—if indeed such a time shall ever come.

The life of the Negro as a slave, freedman, and racial outcast offers undoubtedly the richest mine of romantic material that has opened to the English-speaking novelist since the Wizard of the North discovered and depicted the common life of Scotland. The Negro as a man has an immense advantage over the Negro as a servant, being an altogether new character in fiction. The slave's devotion to the master was trite in the remote antiquity of letters; but the slave as a man, with his hopes, his fears, his faith, has been touched, and only touched, by the pen of the novelist. The traditions of the freedman's fireside are richer and far more tragic than the folk-lore which genius has recently put into his quaint vernacular. The freedman as a man—not as a "brother in black," with the curse of Cain yet upon him, but a man with hopes and aspirations, quick to suffer, patient to endure, full of hot passion, fervid imagination, desirous of being equal to the best—is sure to be a character of enduring interest. . . .

1888

IDA B. WELLS-BARNETT
1862–1931

from A Red Record[1]

The student of American sociology will find the year 1894 marked by a pronounced awakening of the public conscience to a system of anarchy and outlawry which had grown during a series of ten years to be so common, that scenes of unusual brutality failed to have any visible effect upon the humane sentiments of the people of our land.

Beginning with the emancipation of the Negro, the inevitable result of unbridled power exercised for two and a half centuries, by the white man over the Negro, began to show itself in acts of conscienceless outlawry. During the slave regime, the Southern white man owned the Negro body and soul. It was to his interest to dwarf the soul and preserve the body. . . .

But Emancipation came and the vested interests of the white man in the Negro's body were lost. The white man had no right to scourge the emancipated Negro, still less has he a right to kill him. But the Southern white people had been educated so long in that school of practice, in which might makes right, that they disdained to draw strict lines of action in dealing with the Negro. In slave times the Negro was kept subservient and submissive by the frequency and severity of the scourging, but, with freedom, a new system of intimidation came into vogue; the Negro was not only whipped and scourged; he was killed.

Not all nor nearly all of the murders done by white men, during the past thirty years in the South, have come to light, but the statistics as gathered and preserved by white men, and which have not been questioned, show that during these years more than ten thousand Negroes have been killed in

[1]Chicago, 1895.

cold blood, without the formality of judicial trial and legal execution. And yet, as evidence of the absolute impunity with which the white man dares to kill a Negro, the same record shows that during all these years, and for all these murders only three white men have been tried, convicted, and executed. As no white man has been lynched for the murder of colored people, these three executions are the only instances of the death penalty being visited upon white men for murdering Negroes.

Naturally enough the commission of these crimes began to tell upon the public conscience, and the Southern white man, as a tribute to the nineteenth century civilization, was in a manner compelled to give excuses for his barbarism. His excuses have adapted themselves to the emergency, and are aptly outlined by that greatest of all Negroes, Frederick Douglass, in an article of recent date, in which he shows that there have been three distinct eras of Southern barbarism, to account for which three distinct excuses have been made.

The first excuse given to the civilized world for the murder of unoffending Negroes was the necessity of the white man to repress and stamp out alleged "race riots." For years immediately succeeding the war there was an appalling slaughter of colored people, and the wires usually conveyed to northern people and the world the intelligence, first, that an insurrection was being planned by Negroes, which, a few hours later, would prove to have been vigorously resisted by white men, and controlled with a resulting loss of several killed and wounded. It was always a remarkable feature in these insurrections and riots that only Negroes were killed during the rioting, and that all white men escaped unharmed. . . .

No insurrection ever materialized; no Negro rioter was ever apprehended and proven guilty, and no dynamite ever recorded the black man's protest against oppression and wrong. . . .

Then came the second excuse, which had its birth during the turbulent times of reconstruction. By an amendment to the Constitution the Negro was given the right of franchise, and, theoretically at least, his ballot became his invaluable emblem of citizenship. In a government "of the people, for the people, and by the people," the Negro's vote became an important factor in all matters of state and national politics. But this did not last long. The southern white man would not consider that the Negro had any right which a white man was bound to respect, and the idea of a republican form of government in the southern states grew into general contempt. It was maintained that 'This is a white man's government," and regardless of numbers the white man should rule. "No Negro domination" became the new legend on the sanguinary banner of the sunny South, and under it rode the Ku Klux Klan, the Regulators, and the lawless mobs, which for any cause chose to murder one man or a dozen as suited their purpose best. It was a long, gory campaign; the blood chills and the heart almost loses faith in Christianity when one thinks of Yazoo, Hamburg, Edgefield, Copiah, and the countless massacres of defenseless Negroes, whose only crime was the attempt to exercise their right to vote.

But it was a bootless strife for colored people. The government which had made the Negro a citizen found itself unable to protect him. It gave him the right to vote, but denied him the protection which should have maintained that right. Scourged from his home; hunted through the swamps; hung by midnight raiders, and openly murdered in the light of day, the Negro clung to his right of franchise with a heroism which would have wrung admiration from the hearts of savages. He believed that in that small white ballot there was a subtle something which stood for manhood as well as citizenship, and thousands of brave black men went to their graves, exemplifying the one by dying for the other.

The white man's victory soon became complete by fraud, violence, intimidation and murder. The franchise vouchsafed to the Negro grew to be a "barren ideality," and regardless of numbers, the colored people found themselves voiceless in the councils of those whose duty it was to rule. With no longer the fear of "Negro Domination" before their eyes, the white man's second excuse became valueless. With the Southern governments all subverted and the Negro actually eliminated from all participation in state and national elections, there could be no longer an excuse for killing Negroes to prevent "Negro Domination."

Brutality still continued; Negroes were whipped, scourged, exiled, shot and hung whenever and wherever it pleased the white man so to treat them, and as the civilized world with increasing persistency held the white people of the South to account for its outlawry, the murderers invented the third excuse—that Negroes had to be killed to avenge their assaults upon women. There could be framed no possible excuse more harmful to the Negro and more unanswerable if true in its sufficiency for the white man.

Humanity abhors the assailant of womanhood, and this charge upon the Negro at once placed him beyond the pale of human sympathy. With such unanimity, earnestness and apparent candor was this charge made and reiterated that the world has accepted the story that the Negro is a monster which the Southern white man has painted him. And to-day, the Christian world feels, that while lynching is a crime, and lawlessness and anarchy the certain precursors of a nation's fall, it can not by word or deed, extend sympathy or help to a race of outlaws, who might mistake their plea for justice and deem it an excuse for their continued wrongs.

The Negro has suffered much and is willing to suffer more. He recognizes that the wrongs of two centuries can not be righted in a day, and he tries to bear his burden with patience for to-day and be hopeful for to-morrow. But there comes a time when the veriest worm will turn, and the Negro feels to-day that after all the work he has done, all the sacrifices he has made, and all the suffering he has endured, if he did not, now, defend his name and manhood from this vile accusation, he would be unworthy even of the contempt of mankind. It is to this charge he now feels he must make answer.

If the Southern people in defense of their lawlessness, would tell the truth and admit that colored men and women are lynched for almost any offense, from murder to a misdemeanor, there would not now be the necessity for this defense. But when they intentionally, maliciously and constantly belie the record and bolster up these falsehoods by the words of legislators, preachers, governors and bishops, then the Negro must give to the world his side of the awful story.

A word as to the charge itself. In considering the third reason assigned by the Southern white people for the butchery of blacks, the question must be asked, what the white man means when he charges the black man with rape. Does he mean the crime which the statutes of the civilized states describe as such? Not by any means. With the Southern white man, any mesalliance existing between a white woman and a colored man is a sufficient foundation for the charge of rape. The Southern white man says that it is impossible for a voluntary alliance to exist between a white woman and a colored man, and therefore, the fact of an alliance is a proof of force ...

During all the years of slavery, no such charge was ever made, not even during the dark days of the rebellion, when the white man, following the fortunes of war went to do battle for the maintenance of slavery. While the master was away fighting to forge the fetters upon the slave, he left his wife and children with no protectors save the Negroes themselves. And yet during those years of trust and peril, no Negro proved recreant to his trust and no white man returned to a home that had been dispoiled.

Likewise during the period of alleged "insurrection," and alarming "race riots," it never occurred to the white man, that his wife and children were in danger of assault. Nor in the Reconstruction era, when the hue and cry was against "Negro Domination," was there ever a thought that the domination would ever contaminate a fireside or strike to death the virtue of womanhood. It must appear strange indeed, to every thoughtful and candid man, that more than a quarter of a century elapsed before the Negro began to show signs of such infamous degeneration.

In his remarkable apology for lynching, Bishop Haygood, of Georgia, says: "No race, not the most savage, tolerates the rape of woman, but it may be said without reflection upon any other people that the Southern people are now and always have been most sensitive concerning the honor of their women—their mothers, wives, sisters and daughters." It is not the purpose of this defense to say one word against the white women of the South. Such need not be said, but it is their misfortune that the chivalrous white men of that section, in order to escape the deserved execration of the civilized world, should shield themselves by their cowardly and infamously false excuse, and call into question that very honor about which their distinguished priestly apologist claims they are most sensitive. To justify their own barbarism they assume a chivalry which they do not possess. True chivalry respects all womanhood, and no one who reads the record, as it is written in the faces of the million mulattoes in the South, will for a minute conceive that the southern white man had a very chivalrous regard for the honor due the women of his own race or respect for the womanhood which circumstances placed in his power. That chivalry which is "most sensitive concerning the honor of women" can hope for but little respect from the civilized world, when it confines itself entirely to the women who happen to be white. Virtue knows no color line, and the chivalry which depends upon complexion of skin and texture of hair can command no honest respect.

When emancipation came to the Negroes, there arose in the northern part of the United States an almost divine sentiment among the noblest, purest and best white women of the North, who felt called to a mission to educate and Christianize the millions of southern ex-slaves. From every nook and corner of the North, brave young white women answered that call and left their cultured homes, their happy associations and their lives of ease, and with heroic determination went to the South to carry light and truth to the benighted blacks. It was a heroism no less than that which calls for volunteers for India, Africa and the Isles of the sea. To educate their unfortunate charges; to teach them the Christian virtues and to inspire in them the moral sentiments manifest in their own lives, these young women braved dangers whose record reads more like fiction than fact. They became social outlaws in the South. The peculiar sensitiveness of the southern white men for women, never shed its protecting influence about them. No friendly word from their own race cheered them in their work; no hospital doors gave them the companionship like that from which they had come. No chivalrous white man doffed his hat in honor or respect. They were "Nigger teachers"—unpardonable offenders in the social ethics of the South, and were insulted, persecuted and ostracised, not by Negroes, but by the white manhood which boasts of its chivalry toward women.

And yet these northern women worked on, year after year, unselfishly, with a heroism which amounted almost to martyrdom. Threading their way through dense forests, working in schoolhouse, in the cabin and in the church, thrown at all times and in all places among the unfortunate and lowly Negroes, whom they had come to find and to serve, these northern women, thousands of them, have spent more than a quarter of a century in giving to the colored people their splendid lessons for home and heart and soul. Without protection, save that which innocence gives to every good woman, they went about their work, fearing no assault and suffering none. . . .

It is [the Negro's] regret, that, in his own defense, he must disclose to the world that degree of dehumanizing brutality which fixes upon America the blot of a national crime. Whatever faults and failings other nations may have in their dealings with their own subjects of with other people, no other civilized nation stands condemned before the world with a series of crimes so peculiarly national. It becomes a painful duty of the Negro to reproduce a record which shows that a large portion of the American people avow anarchy, condone murder and defy the contempt of civilization.

These pages are written in no spirit of vindictiveness, for all who give the subject consideration must concede that far too serious is the condition of that civilized government in which the spirit of unrestrained outlawry constantly increases in violence, and casts its blight over a continually growing area of territory.

1895

■ UNITED STATES SUPREME COURT ■

from **Plessy v. Ferguson**[1]

Supreme Court of the United States, May 18, 1896....

Mr. Justice BROWN ... delivered the opinion of the court.

This case turns upon the constitutionality of an act of the general assembly of the state of Louisiana, passed in 1890, providing for separate railway carriages for the white and colored races....

A statute which implies merely a legal distinction between the white and colored races—a distinction which is founded in the color of the two races, and which must always exist so long as white men are distinguished from the other race by color— has no tendency to destroy the legal equality of the two races, or re-establish a state of involuntary servitude....

By the fourteenth amendment, all persons born or naturalized in the United States, and subject to the jurisdiction thereof, are made citizens of the United States and of the state wherein they reside; and the states are forbidden from making or enforcing any law which shall abridge the privileges or immunities of citizens of the United States, or shall deprive any person of life, liberty, or property without due process of law, or deny to any person within their jurisdiction the equal protection of the laws....

The object of the amendment was undoubtedly to enforce the absolute equality of the two races before the law, but, in the nature of things, it could not have been intended to abolish distinctions based upon color, or to enforce social, as distinguished from political, equality, or a commingling of the two races upon terms unsatisfactory to either. Laws permitting, and even requiring, their separation, in places where they are liable to be brought into contact, do not necessarily imply the inferiority of either race to the other, and have been generally, if not universally, recognized as within the competency of the state legislatures in the exercise of their police power. The most common instance of this is connected with the establishment of separate schools for white and colored children, which have been held to be a valid exercise of the legislative power even by courts of states where the political rights of the colored race have been longest and most earnestly enforced....

Laws forbidding the intermarriage of the two races may be said in a technical sense to interfere with the freedom of contract, and yet have been universally recognized as within the police power of the state. *State v. Gibson*, 36 Ind. 389....

So far, ... as a conflict with the fourteenth amendment is concerned, the case reduces itself to the question whether the statute of Louisiana is a reasonable regulation, and with respect to this there must necessarily be a large discretion on the part of the legislature. In determining the question of reasonableness, it is at liberty to act with reference to the established

[1]*Plessy v. Ferguson*, 267 U.S. 163 (1896).

usages, customs, and traditions of the people, and with a view to the promotion of their comfort, and the preservation of the public peace and good order. Gauged by this standard, we cannot say that a law which authorizes or even requires the separation of the two races in public conveyances ... is unreasonable, or more obnoxious to the fourteenth amendment than the acts of congress requiring separate schools for colored children in the District of Columbia, the constitutionality of which does not seem to have been questioned, or the corresponding acts of state legislatures.

We consider the underlying fallacy of the plaintiff's argument to consist in the assumption that the enforced separation of the two races stamps the colored race with a badge of inferiority. If this be so, it is not by reason of anything found in the act, but solely because the colored race chooses to put that construction upon it. The argument necessarily assumes that if, as has been more than once the case, and is not unlikely to be so again, the colored race should become the dominant power in the state legislature, and should enact a law in precisely similar terms, it would thereby relegate the white race to an inferior position. We imagine that the white race, at least, would not acquiesce in this assumption. The argument also assumes that social prejudices may be overcome by legislation, and that equal rights cannot be secured to the negro except by an enforced commingling of the two races. We cannot accept this proposition. If the two races are to meet upon terms of social equality, it must be the result of natural affinities, a mutual appreciation of each other's merits, and a voluntary consent of individuals. As was said by the court of appeals of New York in *People v. Gallagher*, 93 N.Y. 438, 448: 'This end can neither be accomplished nor promoted by laws which conflict with the general sentiment of the community upon whom they are designed to operate. When the government, therefore, has secured to each of its citizens equal rights before the law, and equal opportunities for improvement and progress, it has accomplished the end for which it was organized, and performed all of the functions respecting social advantages with which it is endowed.' Legislation is powerless to eradicate racial instincts, or to abolish distinctions based upon physical differences, and the attempt to do so can only result in accentuating the difficulties of the present situation. If the civil and political rights of both races be equal, one cannot be inferior to the other civilly [163 U.S. 537, 552] or politically. If one race be inferior to the other socially, the constitution of the United States cannot put them upon the same plane....

Mr. Justice HARLAN dissenting....

In respect of civil rights, common to all citizens, the constitution of the United States does not, I think, permit any public authority to know the race of those entitled to be protected in the enjoyment of such rights. Every true man has pride of race, and under appropriate circumstances, when the rights of others, his equals before the law, are not to be affected, it is his privilege to express such pride and to take such action based upon it as to him seems proper. But I deny that any legislative body or judicial tribunal may have regard to the ... race of citizens when the civil rights of those citizens are involved.

Indeed, such legislation as that here in question is inconsistent not only with that equality of rights which pertains to citizenship, national and state, but with the personal liberty enjoyed by every one within the United States.

The thirteenth amendment does not permit the withholding or the deprivation of any right necessarily inhering in freedom. It not only struck down the institution of slavery as previously existing in the United States, but it prevents the imposition of any burdens or disabilities that constitute badges of slavery or servitude. It decreed universal civil freedom in this country. This court has so adjudged. But, that amendment having been found inadequate to the protection of the rights of those who had been in slavery, it was followed by the fourteenth amendment, which added greatly to the dignity and glory of American citizenship, and to the security of personal liberty, by declaring that 'all persons born or naturalized in the United States, and subject to the jurisdiction thereof, are citizens of the United States and of the state wherein they reside,' and that 'no state shall make or enforce any law which shall abridge the privileges or immunities of citizens of the United States; nor shall any state deprive any person of life, liberty or property without due process of law, nor deny to any person within its jurisdiction the equal protection of the laws.' These two amendments, if enforced according to their true intent and meaning, will protect all the civil rights that pertain to freedom and citizenship. Finally, and to the end that no citizen should be denied, on account of his race, the privilege of participating in the political control of his country, it was declared by the fifteenth amendment that 'the right of citizens of the United States to vote shall not be denied or abridged by the United States or by any state on account of race, color or previous condition of servitude."

These notable additions to the fundamental law were welcomed by the friends of liberty throughout the world. They removed the race line from our governmental system....

It was said in argument that the statute of Louisiana does not discriminate against either race, but prescribes a rule applicable alike to white and colored citizens. But this argument does not meet the difficulty. Every one knows that the statute in question had its origin in the purpose, not so much to exclude white persons from railroad cars occupied by blacks, as to exclude colored people from coaches occupied by or assigned to white persons. Railroad corporations of Louisiana did not make discrimination among whites in the matter of commodation for travelers. The thing to accomplish was, under the guise of giving equal accommodation for whites and blacks, to compel the latter to keep to themselves while traveling in railroad passenger coaches. No one would be so wanting in candor as to assert the contrary. The fundamental objection, therefore, to the statute, is that it interferes with the personal freedom of citizens. "Personal liberty," it has been well said, "consists in the power of locomotion, of changing situation, or removing one's person to whatsoever places one's own inclination may direct, without imprisonment or restraint, unless by due course of law." 1 Bl. Comm. *134. If a white man and a black man choose to occupy the same public conveyance on a public highway, it is their right to do so; and no government, proceeding alone on grounds of race, can prevent it without infringing the personal liberty of each....

The white race deems itself to be the dominant race in this country. And so it is, in prestige, in achievements, in education, in wealth, and in power. So, I doubt not, it will continue to be for all time, if it remains true to its great heritage, and holds fast to the principles of constitutional liberty. But in view of the constitution, in the eye of the law, there is in this country no superior, dominant, ruling class of citizens. There is no caste here. Our constitution is color-blind, and neither knows nor tolerates classes among citizens. In respect of civil rights, all citizens are equal before the law. The humblest is the peer of the most powerful. The law regards man as man, and takes no account of his surroundings or of his color when his civil rights as guarantied by the supreme law of the land are involved....

In my opinion, the judgment this day rendered will, in time, prove to be quite as pernicious as the decision made by this tribunal in the *Dred Scott Case.* ... [I]t seems that we have yet, in some of the states, a dominant race,— a superior class of citizens,— which assumes to regulate the enjoyment of civil rights, common to all citizens, upon the basis of race. The present decision, it may well be apprehended, will not only stimulate aggressions, more or less brutal and irritating, upon the admitted rights of colored citizens, but will encourage the belief that it is possible, by means of state enactments, to defeat the beneficent purposes which the people of the United States had in view when they adopted the recent amendments of the constitution, by one of which the blacks of this country were made citizens of the United States and of the states in which they respectively reside, and whose privileges and immunities, as citizens, the states are forbidden to abridge. Sixty millions of whites are in no danger from the presence here of eight millions of blacks. The destinies of the two races, in this country, are indissolubly linked together, and the interests of both require that the common government of all shall not permit the seeds of race hate to be planted under the sanction of law. What can more certainly arouse race hate, what more certainly create and perpetuate a feeling of distrust between these races, than state enactments which, in fact, proceed on the ground that colored citizens are so inferior and degraded that they cannot be allowed to sit in public coaches occupied by white citizens? That, as all will admit, is the real meaning of such legislation as was enacted in Louisiana.

The sure guaranty of the peace and security of each race is the clear, distinct, unconditional recognition by our governments, national and state, of every right that inheres in civil freedom, and of the equality before the law of all citizens of the United States, without regard to race. State enactments regulating the enjoyment of civil rights upon the basis of race, and cunningly devised to defeat legitimate results of the ... war, under the pretense of recognizing equality of rights, can have no other result than to render permanent peace impossible, and to keep alive a conflict of races, the continuance of which must do harm to all concerned. ...

There is a race so different from our own that we do not permit those belonging to it to become citizens of the United States. Persons belonging to it are, with few exceptions, absolutely excluded from our country. I allude to the Chinese race. But, by the statute in question, a Chinaman can ride in the same passenger coach with white citizens of the United States, while citizens of the black race in Louisiana, many of whom, perhaps, risked their lives for the preservation of the Union, who are entitled, by law, to participate in the political control of the state and nation, who are not excluded, by law or by reason of their race, from public stations of any kind, and who have all the legal rights that belong to white citizens, are yet declared to be criminals, liable to imprisonment, if they ride in a public coach occupied by citizens of the white race. It is scarcely just to say that a colored citizen should not object to occupying a public coach assigned to his own race. He does not object, nor, perhaps, would he object to separate coaches for his race if his rights under the law were recognized. But he does object, and he ought never to cease objecting, that citizens of the white and black races can be adjudged criminals because they sit, or claim the right to sit, in the same public coach on a public highway.... The arbitrary separation of citizens, on the basis of race, while they are on a public highway, is a badge of servitude wholly inconsistent with the civil freedom and the equality before the law established by the constitution. It cannot be justified upon any legal grounds.

If evils will result from the commingling of the two races upon public highways established for the benefit of all, they will be infinitely less than those that will surely come from state legislation regulating the enjoyment of civil rights upon the basis of race. We boast of the freedom enjoyed by our people above all other peoples. But it is difficult to reconcile that boast with a state of the law which, practically, puts the brand of servitude and degradation upon a large class of our fellow citizens,—our equals before the law. The thin disguise of 'equal' accommodations for passengers in railroad coaches will not mislead any one, nor atone for the wrong this day done....

1896

■ KELLY MILLER ■
1863–1939

from **As to "The Leopard's Spots"**[1]

An Open Letter to Thomas Dixon, Jr.

As to the Leopard's Spots—"I regard it as the ablest, soundest, and most important document that has appeared on this subject in many years.

—"GEO. W. CABLE."

September, 1905.

[1]From *Race Adjustments: Essays on the Negro in America* (Neale, 1908).

Mr. Thomas Dixon, Jr.

Dear Sir: I am writing you this letter to express the attitude and feeling of ten million of your fellow-citizens toward the evil propagandism of race animosity to which you have lent your great literary powers. Through the widespread influence of your writings you have become the chief priest of those who worship at the shrine of race hatred and wrath. This one spirit runs through all your books and published utterances, like the recurrent theme of an opera. As the general trend of your doctrine is clearly epitomized and put forth in your contribution to the *Saturday Evening Post* of August 19, I beg to consider chiefly the issues therein raised. You are a white man born in the midst of the Civil War; I am a Negro born during the same stirring epoch. You were born with a silver spoon in your mouth; I was born with an iron hoe in my hand. Your race has afflicted accumulated injury and wrong upon mine; mine has borne yours only service and good will. You express your views with the most scathing frankness; I am sure you will welcome an equally candid expression from me....

Your fundamental thesis is that " no amount of education of any kind, industrious, classical or religious, can make a Negro a white man or bridge the chasm of the centuries which separates him from the white man in the evolution of human history." This doctrine is as old as human oppression. Calhoun made it the arch-stone in the defense of Negro slavery—and lost.

This is but a recrudescence of the doctrine which was exploited and exploded during the anti-slavery struggle. Do you recall the school of pro-slavery scientists who demonstrated beyond doubt that the Negro's skull was too thick to comprehend the substance of Aryan knowledge? Have you not read in the now discredited scientific books of that period with what triumphant acclaim it was shown that the shape and size of the Negro's skull, facial angle, and cephalic configuration rendered him forever impervious to the white man's civilization? But all enlightened minds are now as ashamed of that doctrine as they are of the one-time dogma that the Negro had no soul. We become aware of mind through its manifestations. Within forty years of only partial opportunity, while playing, as it were, in the back yard of civilization, the American Negro has cut down his illiteracy by over fifty per cent.; has produced a professional class, some fifty thousand strong, including ministers, teachers, doctors, editors, authors, architects, engineers, and is found in all higher lines of listed pursuits in which white men are engaged; some three thousand Negroes have taken collegiate degrees, over three hundred being from the best institutions in the North and West established for the most favored white youth; there is scarcely a first-class institution in America, excepting some three or four in the South, that is without colored students, who pursue their studies generally with success, and sometimes with distinction; Negro inventors have taken out four hundred patents as a contribution to the mechanical genius of America; there are scores of Negroes who, for conceded ability and achievements, take respectable rank in the company of distinguished Americans....

It devolves upon you, Mr. Dixon, to point out some standard, either of intelligence, character, or conduct, to which the Negro cannot conform. Will you please tell a waiting world just what is the psychological difference between the races? No reputable authority, either of the old or of the new school of psychology, has yet pointed out any sharp psychic discriminant. There is not a single intellectual, moral, or spiritual excellence attained by the white race to which the Negro does not yield an appreciative response. If you could show that the Negro is incapable of mastering the intricacies of Aryan speech; that he could not comprehend the intellectual basis of European culture, or apply the apparatus of practical knowledge; that he could not be made amenable to the white man's ethical code or appreciate his spiritual motive—then your case would be proved. But in default of such demonstration we must relegate your eloquent pronouncement to the realm of generalization and prophecy, an easy and agreeable exercise of the mind in which the romancer is ever prone to indulge....

Our own country has not escaped the odium of intellectual inferiority. The generation has scarcely passed away in whose ears used to ring the standing sneer, "Who reads an American book?" It was in the day of Thomas Jefferson that a learned European declared: "America has not produced one good poet, one able mathematician, one man of genius in a single art or science." In response to this charge Jefferson enters an eloquent special plea. He says: "When we shall have existed as a people as long as the Greeks did before they produced a Homer, the Romans, a Virgil, the French, a Racine, the English, a Shakespeare and Milton, should this reproach be still true, we will inquire from what unfriendly cause it has proceeded." How analogous to this is the reproach which you and Mr. Watson, treading the track of Thomas Nelson Page, and those of his school of thought, now hurl against the Negro race? The response of Jefferson defending the American colonies from the reproach of innate inferiority will apply with augmented emphasis to ward off similar charges against the despised and rejected Negro....

You quote me as being in favor of the amalgamation of the races. A more careful reading of the article referred to would have convinced you that I was arguing against amalgamation as a probable solution of the race problem. I merely stated the intellectual conviction that two races cannot live indefinitely side by side, under the same general regime, without ultimately fusing. This was merely the expression of a belief, and not the utterance of a preference nor the formulation of a policy. I know of no colored man who advocates amalgamation as a feasible policy of solution. You are mistaken. The Negro does not " hope and dream of amalgamation." This would be self-stultification with a vengeance. If such a policy were allowed to dominate the imagination of the colored race its women would give themselves over to the unrestrained passion of white men, in quest of tawny offspring, which would give rise to a state of indescribable moral debauchery. At the same time, you would hardly expect the Negro, in derogation of his common human qualities, to proclaim that he is so diverse from

God's other human creatures as to make the blending of the races contrary to the law of nature. The Negro refuses to become excited or share in your frenzy on this subject. The amalgamation of the races is an ultimate possibility, though not an immediate probability. But what have you and I to do with ultimate questions anyway? Our concern is with duty, not destiny....

But do you know, Mr. Dixon, that you are probably the foremost promoter of amalgamation between the two oceans? Wherever you narrow the scope of the Negro by preaching the doctrine of hate you drive thousands of persons of lighter hue over to the white race, carrying more or less Negro blood in their train. The blending of the races is less likely to take place if the self-respect and manly opportunity of the Negro are respected and encouraged than if he is to be forever crushed beneath the level of his faculties for dread of the fancied result. Hundreds of the composite progeny are daily crossing the color line and carrying as much of the despised blood as an albicant skin can conceal without betrayal. I believe that it was Congressman Tillman, brother of the more famous Senator of that name, who stated on the floor of the Constitutional Convention of South Carolina that he knew of four hundred white families in that State who had a taint of Negro blood in their veins. I personally know, or know of, fifty cases of transition in the city of Washington. It is a momentous thing for one to change one's caste. The man or woman who affects to deny, ignore, or scorn the class with whom he previously associated is usually deemed deficient in the nobler qualities of human nature. It is not conceivable that persons of this class would undergo the self-degradation and humiliation of soul necessary to cross the great "social divide" unless it be to escape for themselves and their descendants an odious and despised status. Your oft expressed and passionately avowed belief that the progressive development of the Negro would hasten amalgamation is not borne out by the facts of observation....

You openly urge your fellow-citizens to override all law, human and divine. Are you aware of the force and effect of these words? "Could fatuity reach a sublimer height than the idea that the white man will stand idly by and see the performance? What will he do when put to the test? He will do exactly what his white neighbor in the North does when the Negro threatens his bread—kill him!" These words breathe out hatred and slaughter and suggest the murder of innocent men whose only crime is quest for the God-given right to work. You poison the mind and pollute the imagination through the subtle influence of literature. Are you aware of the force and effect of evil suggestion when the passions of men are in a state of unstable equilibrium? A heterogeneous population, where the elements are, on any account, easily distinguishable, is an easy prey for the promoter of wrath. The fuse is already prepared for the Spark. The soul of the mob is stirred by suggestion of hatred and slaughter, as a famished beast at the smell of blood. Hatred is the ever-handy dynamic of the demagogue. The rabble responds much more readily to an appeal to passion than to reason. To stir wantonly the fires of race antipathy is as execrable a deed as flaunting a red rag in the face of a bull at a summer's picnic, or raising a false cry of "fire" in a crowded house. Human society could not exist one hour except on the basis of law which holds the baser passions of men in restraint....

You preside at every crossroad lynching of a helpless victim; whenever the midnight murderer rides with rope and torch in quest of the blood of his black brother, you ride by his side; wherever the cries of the crucified victim go up to God from the crackling flame, behold, you are there; when women and children, drunk with ghoulish glee, dance around the funeral pyre and mock the death groans of their fellow-man and fight for ghastly souvenirs, you have your part in the inspiration of it all. When guilefully guided workmen in mine and shop and factory, goaded by a real or imaginary sense of wrong, begin the plunder and pillage of property and murder of rival men, your suggestion is justifier of the dastardly doings. Lawlessness is gnawing at the very vitals of our institutions. It is the supreme duty of every enlightened mind to allay rather than spur on this spirit. You are hastening the time when there is to be a positive and emphatic show of hands—not of white hands against black hands, God forbid! not of Northern hands against Southern hands, heaven forfend! but a determined show of those who believe in law and God and constituted order, against those who would undermine and destroy the organic basis of society, involving all in a common ruin....

But do not think, Mr. Dixon, that when you evoke the evil spirit you can exorcise him at will. The Negro in the end will be the least of his victims. Those who become inoculated with the virus of race hatred are more unfortunate than the victims of it. Voltaire tells us that it is more difficult and more meritorious to wean men of their prejudices than it is to civilize the barbarian. Race hatred is the most malignant poison that can afflict the mind. It freezes up the font of inspiration and chills the higher faculties of the soul. You are a greater enemy to your own race than you are to mine.

1905

AMBROSE BIERCE
1842–1914(?)

Perhaps the most striking aspect of Ambrose Bierce's life is the mystery of his death. In 1913, when he was over seventy years of age, Bierce decided to tour Mexico in order to meet the revolutionary Pancho Villa and understand firsthand the civil war in progress there. He realized he would probably never return from that war-torn country. His last letter was dated December 26, 1913. After that, his whereabouts are simply unknown, although the contemporary Mexican writer Carlos Fuentes insists that one still hears stories about "an old gringo" wandering the Mexican countryside. In spirit, Bierce certainly haunts the South American literary landscape: major writers such as Jorge Luis Borges, Julio Cortázar, and Fuentes have all been influenced and intrigued by his work and his life.

Bierce was tenth of the thirteen children of Laura Sherwood and Marcus Aurelius Bierce, poor farmers in southeastern Ohio who believed in the western dream of expansion. The family moved in 1846 to a farm outside of Warsaw, Indiana, but did not achieve prosperity there either. Bierce early evinced a keen literary imagination and a nonconformist temperament. While still in school, he worked on *The Northern Indianan*, an antislavery newspaper.

In 1861, at the age of eighteen, he enlisted in the Ninth Indiana Infantry. Bierce performed a number of notable acts of bravery during his war years, including carrying a wounded comrade off a battlefield. The soldier died, and Bierce had his first taste of ambivalent heroism. Similarly, occupying the staff position of topographical engineer, Bierce surveyed some of the most famous—and bloodiest—battles of the Civil War, including those at Shiloh, Chickamauga, Lookout Mountain, and Missionary Ridge.

After the war, Bierce traveled for nearly seven years, trying his hand at different careers, and only in 1871 did he publish his first short story, "The Haunted Valley." On Christmas Day of the same year, he married Mollie Day. The couple lived first in San Rafael, California, and then, the following year, moved to London, where Bierce wrote satirical pieces for *Fun* and *Figaro*.

Bierce returned to America in 1875. He settled in San Francisco with his wife and their three children and forged a career as a short story writer and one of the best-known journalists of his age. Unwilling to compromise his principles or tone down his scathing criticisms of those he thought to be unscrupulous or merely pompous, he was known as "bitter Bierce" and "the wickedest man in San Francisco" and seemed to enjoy both titles.

Although his personal life was not happy—he separated from his wife and experienced the tragic deaths of both of his sons—Bierce enjoyed the respect of a number of his contemporaries. He pioneered a number of important literary techniques, including a fluid, sometimes surrealistic prose style, the use of stream of consciousness, and the exploration of the subjectivity of time. In his stories he is particularly preoccupied with the human capacity for self-deception. Whether writing ghost stories or war tales, he often portrays characters who destroy themselves by their unwillingness to examine their own assumptions.

"Chickamauga" is one of the most graphic antiwar stories in American literature. A fictional experimentalist, Ambrose Bierce nonetheless remained a moral writer who believed that the reader might learn from the lessons that his characters typically learn too late.

Cathy N. Davidson
Duke University

PRIMARY WORKS

Tales of Soldiers and Civilians, 1892; *Black Beetles in Amber*, 1892; *Can Such Things Be?*, 1893; *Fantastic Fables*, 1899; *The Cynic's Word Book*, 1906; *The Collected Works of Ambrose Bierce*, 12 vols., 1909–1912.

Chickamauga[1]

One sunny autumn afternoon a child strayed away from its rude home in a small field and entered a forest unobserved. It was happy in a new sense of freedom from control, happy in the opportunity of exploration and adventure; for this child's spirit, in bodies of its ancestors, had for thousands of years been trained to memorable feats of discovery and conquest—victories in battles whose critical moments were centuries, whose victors' camps were cities of hewn stone. From the cradle of its race it had conquered its way through two continents and passing a great sea had penetrated a third, there to be born to war and dominion as a heritage.

The child was a boy aged about six years, the son of a poor planter. In his younger manhood the father had been a soldier, had fought against naked savages and followed the flag of his country into the capital of a civilized race to the far South. In the peaceful life of a planter the warrior-fire survived; once kindled, it is never extinguished. The man loved military books and pictures and the boy had understood enough to make himself a wooden sword, though even the eye of his father would hardly have known it for what it was. This weapon he now bore bravely, as became the son of an heroic race, and pausing now and again in the sunny spaces of the forest assumed, with some exaggeration, the postures of aggression and defense that he had been taught by the engraver's art. Made reckless by the ease with which he overcame invisible foes attempting to stay his advance, he committed the common enough military error of pushing the pursuit to a dangerous extreme, until he found himself upon the margin of a wide but shallow brook, whose rapid waters barred his direct advance against the flying foe that had crossed with illogical ease. But the intrepid victor was not to be baffled; the spirit of the race which had passed the great sea burned unconquerable in that small breast and would not be denied. Finding a place where some bowlders in the bed of the stream lay but a step or a leap apart,

---

[1]The Battle of Chickamauga Creek took place in Georgia on September 19–20, 1863. Casualties in the first four hours of battle ran to over fifty percent on both sides. There were nearly 40,000 casualties in all, making it one of the most confusing and deadly battles of the Civil War.

he made his way across and fell again upon the rear-guard of his imaginary foe, putting all to the sword.

Now that the battle had been won, prudence required that he withdraw to his base of operations. Alas; like many a mightier conquerer, and like one, the mightiest, he could not

> curb the lust for war,
> Nor learn that tempted Fate will leave the loftiest star.[2]

Advancing from the bank of the creek he suddenly found himself confronted with a new and more formidable enemy: in the path that he was following, sat, bolt upright, with ears erect and paws suspended before it, a rabbit. With a startled cry the child turned and fled, he knew not in what direction, calling with inarticulate cries for his mother, weeping, stumbling, his tender skin cruelly torn by brambles, his little heart beating hard with terror—breathless, blind with tears—lost in the forest! Then, for more than an hour, he wandered with erring feet through the tangled undergrowth, till at last, overcome by fatigue, he lay down in a narrow space between two rocks, within a few yards of the stream and still grasping his toy sword, no longer a weapon but a companion, sobbed himself to sleep. The wood birds sang merrily above his head; the squirrels, whisking their bravery of tail, ran barking from tree to tree, unconscious of the pity of it, and somewhere far away was a strange, muffled thunder, as if the partridges were drumming in celebration of nature's victory over the son of her immemorial enslavers. And back at the little plantation, where white men and black were hastily searching the fields and hedges in alarm, a mother's heart was breaking for her missing child.

Hours passed, and then the little sleeper rose to his feet. The chill of the evening was in his limbs, the fear of the gloom in his heart. But he had rested, and he no longer wept. With some blind instinct which impelled to action he struggled through the undergrowth about him and came to a more open ground—on his right the brook, to the left a gentle acclivity studded with infrequent trees; over all, the gathering gloom of twilight. A thin, ghostly mist rose along the water. It frightened and repelled him; instead of recrossing, in the direction whence he had come, he turned his back upon it, and went forward toward the dark inclosing wood. Suddenly he saw before him a strange moving object which he took to be some large animal—a dog, a pig—he could not name it; perhaps it was a bear. He had seen pictures of bears, but knew of nothing to their discredit and had vaguely wished to meet one. But something in form or movement of this object—something in the awkwardness of its approach—told him that it was not a bear, and curiosity was stayed by fear. He stood still and as it came slowly on gained courage every moment, for he saw that at least it had not the long, menacing ears of the rabbit. Possibly his impressionable mind was half conscious

---

[2]From *Childe Harold's Pilgrimage* by Lord Byron.
Byron's "conquerer" is Napoleon.

of something familiar in its shambling, awkward gait. Before it had approached near enough to resolve his doubts he saw that it was followed by another and another. To right and to left were many more; the whole open space about him was alive with them—all moving toward the brook.

They were men. They crept upon their hands and knees. They used their hands only, dragging their legs. They used their knees only, their arms hanging idle at their sides. They strove to rise to their feet, but fell prone in the attempt. They did nothing naturally, and nothing alike, save only to advance foot by foot in the same direction. Singly, in pairs and in little groups, they came on through the gloom, some halting now and again while others crept slowly past them, then resuming their movement. They came by dozens and by hundreds; as far on either hand as one could see in the deepening gloom they extended, and the black wood behind them appeared to be inexhaustible. The very ground seemed in motion toward the creek. Occasionally one who had paused did not again go on, but lay motionless. He was dead. Some, pausing, made strange gestures with their hands, erected their arms and lowered them again, clasped their heads; spread their palms upward, as men are sometimes seen to do in public prayer.

Not all of this did the child note; it is what would have been noted by an elder observer; he saw little but that these were men, yet crept like babes. Being men, they were not terrible, though unfamiliarly clad. He moved among them freely, going from one to another and peering into their faces with childish curiosity. All their faces were singularly white and many were streaked and gouted with red. Something in this—something too, perhaps, in their grotesque attitudes and movements—reminded him of the painted clown whom he had seen last summer in the circus, and he laughed as he watched them. But on and ever on they crept, these maimed and bleeding men, as heedless as he of the dramatic contrast between his laughter and their own ghastly gravity. To him it was a merry spectacle. He had seen his father's negroes creep upon their hands and knees for his amusement—had ridden them so, "making believe" they were his horses. He now approached one of these crawling figures from behind and with an agile movement mounted it astride. The man sank upon his breast, recovered, flung the small boy fiercely to the ground as an unbroken colt might have done, then turned upon him a face that lacked a lower jaw—from the upper teeth to the throat was a great red gap fringed with hanging shreds of flesh and splinters of bone. The unnatural prominence of nose, the absence of chin, the fierce eyes, gave this man the appearance of a great bird of prey crimsoned in throat and breast by the blood of its quarry. The man rose to his knees, the child to his feet. The man shook his fist at the child; the child, terrified at last, ran to a tree near by, got upon the farther side of it and took a more serious view of the situation. And so the clumsy multitude dragged itself slowly and painfully along in hideous pantomime—moved forward down the slope like a swarm of great black beetles, with never a sound of going—in silence profound, absolute.

Instead of darkening, the haunted landscape began to brighten. Through the belt of trees beyond the brook shone a strange red light, the trunks and branches of the trees making a black lacework against it. It struck the creeping figures and gave them monstrous shadows, which caricatured their movements on the lit grass. It fell upon their faces, touching their whiteness with a ruddy tinge, accentuating the stains with which so many of them were freaked and maculated. It sparkled on buttons and bits of metal in their clothing. Instinctively the child turned toward the growing splendor and moved down the slope with his horrible companions; in a few moments had passed the foremost of the throng—not much of a feat, considering his advantages. He placed himself in the lead, his wooden sword still in hand, and solemnly directed the march, conforming his pace to theirs and occasionally turning as if to see that his forces did not straggle. Surely such a leader never before had such a following.

Scattered about upon the ground now slowly narrowing by the encroachment of this awful march to water, were certain articles to which, in the leader's mind, were coupled no significant associations: an occasional blanket, tightly rolled lengthwise, doubled and the ends bound together with a string; a heavy knapsack here, and there a broken rifle—such things, in short, as are found in the rear of retreating troops, the "spoor" of men flying from their hunters. Everywhere near the creek, which here had a margin of lowland, the earth was trodden into mud by the feet of men and horses. An observer of better experience in the use of his eyes would have noticed that these footprints pointed in both directions; the ground had been twice passed over—in advance and in retreat. A few hours before, these desperate, stricken men, with their more fortunate and now distant comrades, had penetrated the forest in thousands. Their successive battalions, breaking into swarms and reforming in lines, had passed the child on every side—had almost trodden on him as he slept. The rustle and murmur of their march had not awakened him. Almost within a stone's throw of where he lay they had fought a battle; but all unheard by him were the roar of the musketry, the shock of the cannon, "the thunder of the captains and the shouting."[3] He had slept through it all, grasping his little wooden sword with perhaps a tighter clutch in unconscious sympathy with his martial environment, but as heedless of the grandeur of the struggle as the dead who had died to make the glory.

The fire beyond the belt of woods on the farther side of the creek, reflected to earth from the canopy of its own smoke, was now suffusing the whole landscape. It transformed the sinuous line of mist to the vapor of gold. The water gleamed with dashes of red, and red, too, were many of the stones protruding above the surface. But that was blood; the less desperately wounded had stained them in crossing. On them, too, the child now crossed with eager steps; he was going to the fire. As he stood upon the farther bank he turned about to look at the companions of his march. The

---

[3]Job 39:25. "He saith among the trumpets, Ha, ha! and he smelleth the battle afar off, the thunder of the captains, and the shouting."

advance was arriving at the creek. The stronger had already drawn themselves to the brink and plunged their faces into the flood. Three or four who lay without motion appeared to have no heads. At this the child's eyes expanded with wonder; even his hospitable understanding could not accept a phenomenon implying such vitality as that. After slaking their thirst these men had not the strength to back away from the water, nor to keep their heads above it. They were drowned. In rear of these, the open spaces of the forest showed the leader as many formless figures of his grim command as at first; but not nearly so many were in motion. He waved his cap for their encouragement and smilingly pointed with his weapon in the direction of the guiding light—a pillar of fire to this strange exodus.[4]

Confident of the fidelity of his forces, he now entered the belt of woods, passed through it easily in the red illumination, climbed a fence, ran across a field, turning now and again to coquet with his responsive shadow, and so approached the blazing ruin of a dwelling. Desolation everywhere! In all the wide glare not a living thing was visible. He cared nothing for that; the spectacle pleased, and he danced with glee in imitation of the wavering flames. He ran about, collecting fuel, but every object that he found was too heavy for him to cast in from the distance to which the heat limited his approach. In despair he flung in his sword—a surrender to the superior forces of nature. His military career was at an end.

Shifting his position, his eyes fell upon some outbuildings which had an oddly familiar appearance, as if he had dreamed of them. He stood considering them with wonder, when suddenly the entire plantation, with its inclosing forest, seemed to turn as if upon a pivot. His little world swung half around; the points of the compass were reversed. He recognized the blazing building as his own home!

For a moment he stood stupefied by the power of the revelation, then ran with stumbling feet, making a half-circuit of the ruin. There, conspicuous in the light of the conflagration, lay the dead body of a woman—the white face turned upward, the hands thrown out and clutched full of grass, the clothing deranged, the long dark hair in tangles and full of clotted blood. The greater part of the forehead was torn away, and from the jagged hole the brain protruded, overflowing the temple, a frothy mass of gray, crowned with clusters of crimson bubbles—the work of a shell.

The child moved his little hands, making wild, uncertain gestures. He uttered a series of inarticulate and indescribable cries—something between the chattering of an ape and the gobbling of a turkey—a startling, soulless, unholy sound, the language of a devil. The child was a deaf mute.

Then he stood motionless, with quivering lips, looking down upon the wreck.

1889

---

[4]Exodus 13:21. During the flight from Egypt, God led the Israelites with a pillar of fire lighting the night.

GEORGE WASHINGTON CABLE
1844–1925

In his early novels and stories, George Washington Cable gave us perhaps our most memorable view of the drama of multicultural Louisiana in the nineteenth century, especially of New Orleans Creole life. Born in New Orleans in 1844, Cable was of New England Puritan background on his mother's side and of a Virginia slaveholding family of German descent on his father's side. Upon the death of his father, Cable had to leave school at age fourteen to take a job at the New Orleans customhouse. At nineteen, during the Civil War, Cable enlisted in the Fourth Mississippi Cavalry, little knowing that he was providing himself with an experience that would form the basis of one of his most popular novels. After the war Cable obtained a position as a surveyor of the Atchafalaya River levees, contracted malaria, and was incapacitated for two years. Taking advantage of the enforced "leisure," he began writing and started to contribute a column to the New Orleans *Picayune*. In 1869 Cable married Louise Bartlett, with whom he was to have five children. As he established a home in New Orleans, he worked as bookkeeper for a cotton firm after a brief stint as a newspaper reporter.

Although he had had to forgo formal education, Cable enjoyed private study, often rising early for reading and writing before work. He mastered French and loved to peruse the old New Orleans city records in that language, thereby developing a store of knowledge and lore that he soon began to transmute into fictional narratives. Cable achieved national attention with the publication of his story "'Sieur George" in *Scribner's Monthly* in 1873. Within the next three years *Scribner's Monthly* would publish "Belles Demoiselles Plantation," "'Tite Poulette," "Madame Délicieuse," "Jean-ah Poquelin," and other stories, which were collected in *Old Creole Days* (1879). On the basis of these stories, Cable gained a national reputation as an important local color realist, adept at suggesting language and character of the varied groups of his region.

Following serial publication in *Scribner's*, Cable's novel *The Grandissimes* appeared as a book in 1880. A short novel, *Madame Delphine*, was published in the following year. Both novels vividly depict dramatic aspects of Creole life in pre–Civil War New Orleans, including black–white relations and problems stemming from the exploitation of African Americans. In spite of complaints of Creole readers that his representation of their community amounted to caricature, Cable's first three books brought him enough success that he could give up his clerical position and devote himself full time to writing.

At the high point of his career, Cable turned his attention to polemical themes. *Dr. Sevier*, a novel dealing with the need for prison reform, was published in 1884, the year that Cable's exposé "The Convict Lease System in the Southern States" appeared in *Century Magazine*. With Creole New Orleans resentful of its portrayal by Cable and with white Southerners in general angered by his writings about injustice toward blacks, Cable found the Northeast, which he enjoyed on several trips, more and more congenial. In 1885 he moved his family to Northampton, Massachusetts, where he would be closer to publishers and to friends like Mark Twain, with whom he had recently conducted a successful reading tour.

Noteworthy among Cable's publications after he moved north is *The Silent South* (1885), a collection of his essays exposing the oppression of African Americans and persistence of racism in the postbellum South; our selection "Freed– Not Free" is from that volume. He also continued to write fiction. His novel *John March, Southerner* (1894) represents an aristocratic Southerner's attempt to transcend limitations of family and regional background. *The Cavalier* (1901), a popularly successful novel for which he drew on his Civil War experience, marks Cable's turn toward a more romantic type of fiction in the latter part of his career. His work at this stage has been criticized for sometimes being excessively tailored to demands of genteel editors and readers. Yet all in all, it can be said that with his unflinching representation of moral dimensions of interethnic relations, his imaginative understanding of the impact of the past on the present, and his aesthetic sensitivity to exotic aspects of his region, Cable helped prepare the ground for William Faulkner, Eudora Welty, Flannery O'Connor, and other modern Southern writers.

James Robert Payne
New Mexico State University

PRIMARY WORKS

Old Creole Days, 1879; *The Grandissimes*, 1880, rev. 1883; *Madame Delphine*, 1881; *Dr. Sevier*, 1884; *The Silent South, together with The Freeman's Case in Equity and The Convict Lease System*, 1885; *John March, Southerner*, 1894; *The Negro Question*, ed. Arlin Turner, 1958.

'Tite Poulette[1]

Kristian Koppig[2] was a rosy-faced, beardless young Dutchman. He was one of that army of gentlemen who, after the purchase of Louisiana, swarmed from all parts of the commercial world, over the mountains of Franco-Spanish exclusiveness, like the Goths over the Pyrenees,[3] and settled down in New Orleans to pick up their fortunes, with the diligence of hungry pigeons. He may have been a German; the distinction was too fine for Creole haste and disrelish.

He made his home in a room with one dormer window looking out, and somewhat down, upon a building opposite, which still stands, flush with the street, a century old. Its big, round-arched windows in a long, second-story row, are walled up, and two or three from time to time have had smaller windows let into them again, with odd little latticed peep-holes in their

[1]French: "little chick."
[2]Dutch: "headstrong, stubborn."
[3]In the fifth century A.D., the Visigoths, a Germanic tribe, crossed the mountain range of the Pyrenees to invade the land that is now Spain. The Visigoths ruled Spain until the Moors conquered them in the eighth century.

batten shutters. This had already been done when Kristian Koppig first began to look at them from his solitary, dormer window.

All the features of the building lead me to guess that it is a remnant of the old Spanish Barracks,[4] whose extensive structure fell by government sale into private hands a long time ago. At the end toward the swamp a great, oriental-looking passage is left, with an arched entrance, and a pair of ponderous wooden doors. You look at it, and almost see Count O'Reilly's[5] artillery come bumping and trundling out, and dash around into the ancient Plaza to bang away at King St. Charles's birthday.[6]

I do not know who lives there now. You might stand about on the opposite *banquette*[7] for weeks and never find out. I suppose it is a residence, for it does not look like one. That is the rule in that region.

In the good old times of duels, and bagatelle-clubs,[8] and theatre-balls,[9] and Cayetano's circus,[10] Kristian Koppig rooming as described, there lived in the portion of this house, partly overhanging the archway, a palish handsome woman, by the name—or going by the name—of Madame John. You would hardly have thought of her being "colored." Though fading, she was still of very attractive countenance, fine, rather severe features, nearly straight hair carefully kept, and that vivid black eye so peculiar to her kind. Her smile, which came and went with her talk, was sweet and exceedingly intelligent; and something told you, as you looked at her, that she was one who had had to learn a great deal in this troublesome life.

"But!"—the Creole lads in the street would say—"her daughter!" and there would be lifting of arms, wringing of fingers, rolling of eyes, rounding of mouths, gaspings and clasping of hands. "So beautiful, beautiful, beautiful! White?—white like a water lily! White—like a magnolia!"

Applause would follow, and invocation of all the saints to witness.

And she could sing.

"Sing?" (disdainfully)—"if a mocking-bird can *sing*! Ha!"

They could not tell just how old she was; they "would give her about seventeen."

---

[4]Residence of the Spanish army. Colonized by France in 1682, Louisiana was ceded to Spain and England in 1763, when New Orleans became the capital of Spanish Louisiana. The French and Creole residents' frequently violent rebellion against Spanish rule required the constant presence of Spanish troops in the city.
[5]Irish-born Alexander O'Reilly (1722–1794), nicknamed "Bloody O'Reilly," the Spanish army officer who defeated the Creole revolt against the first Spanish governor of Louisiana. O'Reilly became governor in 1769 and was made a count in 1771.
[6]November 4 or 5, feast day of St. Charles Borromeo, Catholic saint who cared for the sick and is invoked against the plague.

[7]Brick sidewalk.
[8]*Bagatelle* was a table game similar to pool or billards, popular in Europe at the turn of the nineteenth century.
[9]In 1805, the St. Philip Street Theatre became the first home of New Orlean's so-called quadroon balls or octoroon balls, famous dancing parties limited to white men and free women of mixed race. (See note 11.)
[10]The Cuban Cayetano Mariotini directed one of the first multi-act touring circuses in North America. He established a base in New Orleans in the early 1800s. Cayetano went bankrupt in 1816 when the theater he built failed; he had to sign over his performing horses and his slave William to creditors.

Mother and daughter were very fond. The neighbors could hear them call each other pet names, and see them sitting together, sewing, talking happily to each other in the unceasing French way, and see them go out and come in together on their little tasks and errands. "'Tite Poulette," the daughter was called; she never went out alone.

And who was this Madame John?

"Why, you know!—she was"—said the wig-maker at the corner to Kristian Koppig—"I'll tell you. You know?—she was"—and the rest atomized off in a rasping whisper. She was the best yellow-fever nurse in a thousand yards round; but that is not what the wig-maker said.

A block nearer the river stands a house altogether different from the remnant of old barracks. It is of frame, with a deep front gallery over which the roof extends. It has become a den of Italians, who sell fuel by daylight, and by night are up to no telling what extent of deviltry. This was once the home of a gay gentleman, whose first name happened to be John. He was a member of the Good Children Social Club. As his parents lived with him, his wife would, according to custom, have been called Madame John, but he had no wife. His father died, then his mother; last of all, himself. As he is about to be off, in comes Madame John, with 'Tite Poulette, then an infant, on her arm.

"Zalli," said he, "I am going."

She bowed her head, and wept.

"You have been very faithful to me, Zalli."

She wept on.

"Nobody to take care of you now, Zalli."

Zalli only went on weeping.

"I want to give you this house, Zalli; it is for you and the little one."

An hour after, amid the sobs of Madame John, she and the "little one" inherited the house, such as it was. With the fatal caution which characterizes ignorance, she sold the property and placed the proceeds in a bank, which made haste to fail. She put on widow's weeds, and wore them still when 'Tite Poulette "had seventeen," as the frantic lads would say.

How they did chatter over her. Quiet Kristian Koppig had never seen the like. He wrote to his mother, and told her so. A pretty fellow at the corner would suddenly double himself up with beckoning to a knot of chums; these would hasten up; recruits would come in from two or three other directions; as they reached the corner their countenances would quickly assume a genteel severity, and presently, with her mother, 'Tite Poulette would pass—tall, straight, lithe, her great black eyes made tender by their sweeping lashes, the faintest tint of color in her Southern cheek, her form all grace, her carriage a wonder of simple dignity.

The instant she was gone every tongue was let slip on the marvel of her beauty; but, though theirs were only the loose New Orleans morals of over fifty years ago, their unleashed tongues never had attempted any greater liberty than to take up the pet name, 'Tite Poulette. And yet the mother was soon to be, as we shall discover, a paid dancer at the *Salle de Condé*.

To Zalli, of course, as to all "quadroon[11] ladies," the festivities of the Conde-street ball-room were familiar of old. There, in the happy days when dear Monsieur John was young, and the eighteenth century old, she had often repaired under guard of her mother—dead now, alas!—and Monsieur John would slip away from the dull play and dry society of Théâtre d'Orléans,[12] and come around with his crowd of elegant friends; and through the long sweet hours of the ball she had danced, and laughed, and coquetted under her satin mask, even to the baffling and tormenting of that prince of gentlemen, dear Monsieur John himself. No man of questionable blood dare set his foot within the door. Many noble gentlemen were pleased to dance with her. Colonel De ——— and General La ———: city councilmen and officers from the Government House. There were no paid dancers then. Every thing was decorously conducted indeed! Every girl's mother was there, and the more discreet always left before there was too much drinking. Yes, it was gay, gay!—but sometimes dangerous. Ha! More times than a few had Monsieur John knocked down some long-haired and long-knifed rowdy, and kicked the breath out of him for looking saucily at her; but that was like him, he was so brave and kind;—and he is gone!

There was no room for widow's weeds there. So when she put these on, her glittering eyes never again looked through her pink and white mask, and she was glad of it; for never, never in her life had they so looked for anybody but her dear Monsieur John, and now he was in heaven—so the priest said—and she was a sick-nurse.

Living was hard work; and, as Madame John had been brought up tenderly, and had done what she could to rear her daughter in the same mistaken way, with, of course, no more education than the ladies in society got, they knew nothing beyond a little music and embroidery. They struggled as they could, faintly; now giving a few private dancing lessons, now dressing hair, but ever beat back by the steady detestation of their imperious patronesses; and, by and by, for want of that priceless worldly grace known among the flippant as "money-sense," these two poor children, born of misfortune and the complacent badness of the times, began to be in want.

Kristian Koppig noticed from his dormer window one day a man standing at the big archway opposite, and clanking the brass knocker on the wicket that was in one of the doors. He was a smooth man, with his hair parted in the middle, and his cigarette poised on a tiny gold holder. He waited a moment, politely cursed the dust, knocked again, threw his slender sword-cane under his arm, and wiped the inside of his hat with his handkerchief.

Madame John held a parley with him at the wicket. 'Tite Poulette was nowhere seen. He stood at the gate while Madame John went up-stairs. Kristian Koppig knew him. He knew him as one knows a snake. He was the

---

[11]Legal term for a person with one-fourth black ancestry. *Octoroon* (see note 9) means that the person's ancestry is one-eighth black.

[12]Opera house patronized by elite white Creole society.

manager of the *Salle de Condé*. Presently Madame John returned with a little bundle, and they hurried off together.

And now what did this mean? Why, by any one of ordinary acuteness the matter was easily understood, but, to tell the truth, Kristian Koppig was a trifle dull, and got the idea at once that some damage was being planned against 'Tite Poulette. It made the gentle Dutchman miserable not to be minding his own business, and yet—

"But the woman certainly will not attempt"—said he to himself—"no, no! she cannot." Not being able to guess what he meant, I cannot say whether she could or not. I know that next day Kristian Koppig, glancing eagerly over the *"Ami des Lois,"*[13] read an advertisement which he had always before skipped with a frown. It was headed, *"Salle de Condé,"* and, being interpreted, signified that a new dance was to be introduced, the *Danse de Chinois*,[14] and that *a young lady* would follow it with the famous *"Danse du Shawl."*[15]

It was the Sabbath. The young man watched the opposite window steadily and painfully from early in the afternoon until the moon shone bright; and from the time the moon shone bright until Madame John!—joy!—Madame John! And not 'Tite Poulette, stepped through the wicket, much dressed and well muffled and hurried off toward the *Rue Condé*. Madame John was the "young lady;" and the young man's mind, glad to return to its own unimpassioned affairs, relapsed into quietude.

Madame John danced beautifully. It had to be done. It brought some pay, and pay was bread; and every Sunday evening, with a touch here and there of paint and powder, the mother danced the dance of the shawl, the daughter remaining at home alone.

Kirstian Koppig, simple, slow-thinking young Dutchman, never noticing that he staid at home with his window darkened for the very purpose, would see her come to her window and look out with a little wild, alarmed look in her magnificent eyes, and go and come again, and again, until the mother, like a storm-driven bird, came panting home.

Two or three months went by.

One night, on the mother's return, Kristian Koppig coming to his room nearly at the same moment, there was much earnest conversation, which he could see, but not hear.

"'Tite Poulette," said Madame John, "you are seventeen."

"True, Maman."

"Ah! My child, I see not how you are to meet the future." The voice trembled plaintively.

"But how, Maman?"

---

[13]French: "Friend of the Laws," a New Orleans evening newspaper published from 1809 to 1834.
[14]French: "Chinese Dance."
[15]French: "Dance of the Shawl," an erotic dance in which a woman removes some or all of her clothing but remains hidden behind artfully maneuvered shawls or veils. The dance of the shawl was popular in the late nineteenth century when Cable was writing, not during the earlier period in which the story is set.

"Ah! you are not like others; no fortune, no pleasure, no friend."

"Maman!"

"No, no;—I thank God for it; I am glad you are not; but you will be lonely, lonely, all your poor life long. There is no place in this world for us poor women. I wish that we were either white or black!"—and the tears, two "shining ones," stood in the poor quadroon's eyes.

The daughter stoop up, her eyes flashing.

"God made us, Maman," she said with a gentle, but stately smile.

"Ha!" said the mother, her keen glance darting through her tears, "Sin made *me*, yes."

"No," said 'Tite Poulette, "God made us. He made us just as we are; not more white, not more black."

"He made you, truly!" said Zalli. "You are so beautiful; I believe it well." She reached and drew the fair form to a kneeling posture. "My sweet, white daughter!"

Now the tears were in the girl's eyes. "And could I be whiter than I am?" she asked.

"Oh, no, no! 'Tite Poulette," cried the other; "but if we were only *real white!*— both of us; so that some gentleman might come to see me and say 'Madame John, I want your pretty little chick. She is so beautiful. I want to take her home. She is so good—I want her to be my wife.' Oh, my child, my child, to see that I would give my life—I would give my soul! Only you should take me along to be your servant. I walked behind two young men to-night; they were coming home from their office; presently they began to talk about you."

'Tite Poulette's eyes flashed fire.

"No, my child, they spoke only the best things. One laughed a little at times and kept saying 'Beware!' but the other—I prayed the Virgin to bless him, he spoke such kind and noble words. Such gentle pity; such a holy heart! 'May God defend her,' he said, *cherie;*[16] he said, 'May God defend her, for I see no help for her.' The other one laughed and left him. He stopped in the door right across the street. Ah, my child, do you blush? Is that something to bring the rose to your cheek? Many fine gentlemen at the ball ask me often, 'How is your daughter, Madame John?'"

The daughter's face was thrown into the mother's lap, not so well satisfied, now, with God's handiwork. Ah, how she wept! Sob, sob, sob; gasps and sighs and stifled ejaculations, her small right hand clinched and beating on her mother's knee; and the mother weeping over her.

Kristian Koppig shut his window. Nothing but a generous heart and a Dutchman's phlegm could have done so at that moment. And even thou, Kristian Koppig!———for the window closed very slowly.

He wrote to his mother, thus:

"In this wicked city, I see none so fair as the poor girl who lives opposite me, and who, alas! though so fair, is one of those whom the taint of caste has cursed. She lives a lonely, innocent life in the midst of corruption, like

---

[16]French: "sweetheart."

the lilies I find here in the marshes, and I have great pity for her. 'God defend her,' I said to-night to a fellow clerk, 'I see no help for her.' I know there is a natural, and I think proper, horror of mixed blood (excuse the mention, sweet mother), and I feel it, too; and yet if she were in Holland to-day, not one of a hundred suitors would detect the hidden blemish."

In such strain this young man wrote on trying to demonstrate the utter impossibility of his ever loving the loveable unfortunate, until the midnight tolling of the cathedral clock sent him to bed.

About the same hour Zalli and 'Tite Poulette were kissing good-night.

"'Tite Poulette, I want you to promise me one thing."

"Well, Maman?"

"If any gentleman should ever love you and ask you to marry,—not knowing, you know,—promise me you will not tell him you are not white."

"It can never be," said 'Tite Poulette.

"But if it should," said Madame John pleadingly.

"And break the law?"[17] asked 'Tite Poulette, impatiently.

"But the law is unjust," said the mother.

"But it is the law!"

"But you will not, dearie, will you?"

"I would surely tell him!" said the daughter.

When Zalli, for some cause, went next morning to the window, she started.

"'Tite Poulette!"—she called softly without moving. The daughter came. The young man, whose idea of propriety had actuated him to this display, was sitting in the dormer window, reading. Mother and daughter bent a steady gaze at each other. It meant in French, "If he saw us last night!"—

"Ah! dear," said the mother, her face beaming with fun— "What can it be, Maman?"

"He speaks—oh! ha, ha!—he speaks—such miserable French!"

It came to pass one morning at early dawn that Zalli and 'Tite Poulette, going to mass, passed a café, just as—who should be coming out but Monsieur, the manager of the *Salle de Condé*. He had not yet gone to bed. Monsieur was astonished. He had a Frenchman's eye for the beautiful, and certainly there the beautiful was. He had heard of Madame John's daughter, and had hoped once to see her, but did not; but could this be she?

They disappeared within the cathedral. A sudden pang of piety moved him; he followed. 'Tite Poulette was already kneeling in the aisle. Zalli, still in the vestibule, was just taking her hand from the font of holy-water.

"Madame John," whispered the manager.

She courtesied.

---

[17]In 1724, Louis XV of France applied to Louisiana the Code Noir, or Black Code, a series of laws forbidding intermarriage and concubinage between whites and people of color. Although the Code Noir remained in effect throughout Spanish and American possessions, white Louisianans ignored strictures against concubinage, often maintaining separate households for their black mistresses and mixed-race children.

"Madame John, that young lady—is she your daughter?"

"She—she—is my daughter," said Zalli, with somewhat of alarm in her face, which the manager misinterpreted.

"I think not, Madame John." He shook his head, smiling as one too wise to be fooled.

"Yes, Monsieur, she is my daughter."

"O no, Madame John, it is only make-believe, I think." "I swear she is, Monsieur de la Rue."[18]

"Is that possible?" pretending to waver, but convinced in his heart of hearts, by Zalli's alarm, that she was lying. "But how? Why does she not come to our ball-room with you?"

Zalli, trying to get away from him, shrugged and smiled. "Each to his taste, Monsieur; it pleases her not."

She was escaping, but he followed one step more. "I shall come to see you, Madame John."

She whirled and attacked him with her eyes. "Monsieur must not give himself the trouble!" she said, the eyes at the same time adding, "Dare to come!" She turned again, and knelt to her devotions. The manager dipped in the font, crossed himself, and departed.

Several weeks went by, and M. de la Rue had not accepted the fierce challenge of Madame John's eyes. One or two Sunday nights she had succeeded in avoiding him, though fulfilling her engagement in the *Salle*; but by and by pay-day,—a Saturday,—came round, and though the pay was ready, she was loath to go up to Monsieur's little office.

It was an afternoon in May. Madame John came to her own room, and, with a sigh, sank into a chair. Her eyes were wet.

"Did you go to his office, dear mother?" asked 'Tite Poulette.

"I could not," she answered, dropping her face in her hands.

"Maman, he has seen me at the window!"

"While I was gone?" cried the mother.

"He passed on the other side of the street. He looked up purposely, and saw me." The speaker's cheeks were burning red.

Zalli wrung her hands.

"It is nothing, mother; do not go near him."

"But the pay, my child."

"The pay matters not."

"But he will bring it here; he wants the chance."

That was the trouble, sure enough.

About this time Kristian Koppig lost his position in the German importing house where, he had fondly told his mother, he was indispensable.

"Summer was coming on," the senior said, "and you see our young men are almost idle. Yes, our engagement *was* for a year, but ah—we could not foresee"—etc., etc., "besides" (attempting a parting flattery), "your father is

[18]French: "man of the street."

a rich gentleman, and you can afford to take the summer easy. If we can ever be of any service to you," etc., etc.

So the young Dutchman spent the afternoons at his dormer window reading and glancing down at the little casement opposite, where a small, rude shelf had lately been put out, holding a row of cigar-boxes with wretched little botanical specimens in them trying to die. 'Tite Poulette was their gardener; and it was odd to see,—dry weather or wet—how many waterings per day those plants could take. She never looked up from her task; but I know she performed it with that unacknowledged pleasure which all girls love and deny, that of being looked upon by noble eyes.

On this peculiar Saturday afternoon in May, Kristian Koppig had been witness of the distressful scene over the way. It occurred to 'Tite Poulette that such might be the case, and she stepped to the casement to shut it. As she did so, the marvellous delicacy of Kristian Koppig moved him to draw in one of his shutters. Both young heads came out at one moment, while at the same instant—

"Rap, rap, rap, rap, rap!" clanked the knocker on the wicket. The black eyes of the maiden and the blue over the way, from looking into each other for the first time in life, glanced down to the arched doorway upon Monsieur the manager. Then the black eyes disappeared within, and Kristian Koppig thought again, and re-opening his shutter, stood up at the window prepared to become a bold spectator of what might follow.

But for a moment nothing followed.

"Trouble over there," thought the rosy Dutchman, and waited. The manager waited too, rubbing his hat and brushing his clothes with the tips of his kidded fingers.

"They do not wish to see him," slowly concluded the spectator.

"Rap, rap, rap, rap, rap!" quoth the knocker, and M. de la Rue looked up around at the windows opposite and noticed the handsome young Dutchman looking at him.

"Dutch!" said the manager softly, between his teeth.

"He is staring at me," said Kristian Koppig to himself;—"but then I am staring at him, which accounts for it."

A long pause, and then another long rapping.

"They want him to go away," thought Koppig.

"Knock hard!" suggested a street youngster, standing by.

"Rap, rap"—The manager had no sooner recommenced than several neighbors looked out of doors and windows.

"Very bad," thought our Dutchman; "somebody should make him go off. I wonder what they will do."

The manager stepped into the street, looked up at the closed window, returned to the knocker, and stood with it in his hand.

"They are all gone out, Monsieur," said the street youngster.

"You lie!" said the cynosure of neighboring eyes.

"Ah!" thought Kristian Koppig; "I will go down and ask him"—Here his thoughts lost outline; he was only convinced that he had somewhat to say to him, and turned to go down stairs. In going he became a little vexed with himself because he could not help hurrying. He noticed, too, that his arm holding the stair-rail trembled in a silly way, whereas he was perfectly calm. Precisely as he reached the street-door the manager raised the knocker; but the latch clicked and the wicket was drawn slightly ajar.

Inside could just be descried Madame John. The manager bowed, smiled, talked, talked on, held money in his hand, bowed, smiled, talked on, flourished the money, smiled, bowed, talked on and plainly persisted in some intention to which Madame John was steadfastly opposed.

The window above, too,—it was Kristian Koppig who noticed that,— opened a wee bit, like the shell of a terrapin.[19] Presently the manager lifted his foot and put forward an arm, as though he would enter the gate by pushing, but as quick as gunpowder it clapped—in his face!

You could hear the fleeing feet of Zalli pounding up the staircase.

As the panting mother re-entered her room, "See, Maman," said 'Tite Poulette, peeping at the window, "the young gentleman from over the way has crossed!"

"Holy Mary bless him!" said the mother.

"I will go over," thought Kristian Koppig, "and ask him kindly if he is not making a mistake."

"What are they doing, dear?" asked the mother, with clasped hands.

"They are talking; the young man is tranquil, but 'Sieur de la Rue is very angry," whispered the daughter; and just then—pang! came a sharp, keen sound rattling up the walls on either side of the narrow way, and "Aha!" and laughter and clapping of female hands from two or three windows.

"Oh! what a slap!" cried the girl, half in fright, half in glee, jerking herself back from the casement simultaneously with the report. But the "ahas" and laughter, and clapping of feminine hands, which still continued, came from another cause. 'Tite Poulette's rapid action had struck the slender cord that held up an end of her hanging garden, and the whole rank of cigar-boxes slid from their place, turned gracefully over as they shot through the air, and emptied themselves plump upon the head of the slapped manager. Breathless, dirty, pale as whitewash, he gasped a threat to be heard from again, and, getting round the corner as quick as he could walk, left Kristian Koppig, standing motionless, the most astonished man in that street.

"Kristian Koppig, Kristian Koppig," said Greatheart to himself, slowly dragging up-stairs, "what a mischief you have done. One poor woman certainly to be robbed of her bitter wages, and another—so lovely!—put to the burning shame of being the subject of a street brawl! What will this silly neighborhood say? 'Has the gentleman a heart as well as a hand?' 'Is it jealousy?'" There he paused, afraid himself to answer the supposed query; and then—"Oh! Kristian Koppig, you have been such a dunce!" "And I cannot apologize to them. Who in this street would carry my note, and not wink and grin over it with low surmises? I cannot even make restitution. Money?

[19]A kind of turtle.

They would not dare receive it. Oh! Kristian Koppig, why *did* you not mind your own business? Is she any thing to you? Do you love her? *Of course not!* Oh!— such a dunce!"

The reader will eagerly admit that however faulty this young man's course of reasoning, his conclusion was correct. For mark what he did.

He went to his room, which was already growing dark, shut his window, lighted his big Dutch lamp, and sat down to write. "Something *must* be done," said he aloud, taking up his pen; "I will be calm and cool; I will be distant and brief; but—I shall have to be kind or I may offend. Ah! I shall have to write in French; I forgot that; I write it so poorly, dunce that I am, when all my brothers and sisters speak it so well." He got out his French dictionary. Two hours slipped by. He made a new pen, washed and refilled his inkstand, mended his "abominable!" chair, and after two hours more made another attempt, and another failure. "My head aches," said he, and lay down on his couch, the better to frame his phrases.

He was awakened by the Sabbath sunlight. The bells of the Cathedral and the Ursulines' chapel[20] were ringing for high mass, and mocking-bird, perching on a chimney-top above Madame John's rooms, was carolling, whistling, mewing, chirping, screaming, and trilling with the ecstasy of a whole May in his throat. "Oh! sleepy Kristian Koppig," was the young man's first thought, "—such a dance!"

Madame John and daughter did not go to mass. The morning wore away, and their casement remained closed. "They are offended," said Kristian Koppig, leaving the house, and wandering up to the little Protestant affair known as Christ Church.

"No, possibly they are not," he said, returning and finding the shutters thrown back.

By a sad accident, which mortified him extremely, he happened to see, late in the afternoon,—hardly conscious that he was looking across the street,—that Madame John was—dressing. Could it be that she was going to the *Salle de Condé?* He rushed to his table, and began to write.

He had guessed aright. The wages were too precious to be lost. The manager had written her a note. He begged to assure her that he was a gentleman of the clearest cut. If he had made a mistake the previous afternoon, he was glad no unfortunate result had followed except his having been assaulted by a ruffian; that the *Danse du Shawl* was promised in his advertisement, and he hoped Madame John (whose wages were in hand waiting for her) would not fail to assist as usual. Lastly, and delicately put, he expressed his conviction that Mademoiselle was wise and discreet in declining to entertain gentlemen at her home.

So, against much beseeching on the part of 'Tite Poulette, Madame John was going to the ball-room. "Maybe I can discover what 'Sieur de la Rue is planning against Monsieur over the way," she said, knowing certainly the

---

[20]The French Quarter convent of the Ursuline nuns, a Roman Catholic order housed in the oldest building in Louisiana and devoted to educating young women.

slap would not be forgiven; and the daughter, though tremblingly, at once withdrew her objections.

The heavy young Dutchman, now thoroughly electrified, was writing like mad. He wrote and tore up, wrote and tore up, lighted his lamp, started again, and at last signed his name. A letter by a Dutchman in French!—what can be made of it in English? We will see:

Madame and Mademoiselle:

> *A stranger, seeking not to be acquainted, but seeing and admiring all days the goodness and high honor, begs to be pardoned of them for the mistakes, alas! of yesterday, and to make reparation and satisfaction in destroying the ornaments of the window, as well as the loss of compensation from Monsieur the manager, with the enclosed bill of the* Banque de la Louisiane[21] *for fifty dollars ($50). And, hoping they will seeing what he is meaning, remains, respectfully,*
>
> Kristian Koppig

P.S.—Madame must not go to the ball.

He must bear the missive himself. He must speak in French. What should the words be? A moment of study—he has it, and is off down the long three-story stair-way. At the same moment Madame John stepped from the wicket, and glided off to the *Salle de Condé*, a trifle late.

"I shall see Madame John, of course," thought the young man, crushing a hope, and rattled the knocker. 'Tite Poulette sprang up from praying for her mother's safety. "What has she forgotten?" she asked herself, and hastened down. The wicket opened. The two innocents were stunned.

"Aw—aw"—said the pretty Dutchman, "aw,"—blurted out something in virgin Dutch, . . . handed her the letter, and hurried down street.

"Alas! what have I done?" said the poor girl, bending over her candle, and bursting into tears that fell on the unopened letter. "And what shall I do? It may be wrong to open it—and worse not to." Like her sex, she took the benefit of the doubt, and intensified her perplexity and misery by reading and misconstruing the all but unintelligible contents. What then? Not only sobs and sighs, but moaning and beating of little fists together, and outcries of soul-felt agony stifled against the bedside, and temples pressed into knitted palms, because of one who "sought *not to be* acquainted," but offered money— money!—in pity to a poor—shame on her for saying that!—a poor *nigresse*.[22]

And now our self-confessed dolt turned back from a half-hour's walk, concluding there might be an answer to his note. "Surely Madame John will appear this time." He knocked. The shutter stirred above, and something white came fluttering wildly down like a shot dove. It was his own letter containing the fifty-dollar bill. He bounded to the wicket, and softly but eagerly knocked again.

---

[21]A New Orleans bank, the first American bank founded in the Louisiana Territory after the Louisiana Purchase (1803).

[22]French: "negress," a black woman.

"Go away," said a trembling voice from above.

"Madame John?" said he; but the window closed, and he heard a step, the same step on the stair. Step, step, every step one step deeper into his heart. 'Tite Poulette came to the closed door.

"What will you?" said the voice within.

"I—I—don't wish to see you. I wish to see Madame John."

"I must pray Monsieur to go away. My mother is at the *Salle de Condé*."

"At the ball!" Kristian Koppig strayed off, repeating the words for want of definite thought. All at once it occurred to him that at the ball he could make Madame John's acquaintance with impunity. "Was it courting sin to go?" By no means; he should, most likely, save a woman from trouble, and help the poor in their distress.

Behold Kristian Koppig standing on the floor of the *Salle de Condé*. A large hall, a blaze of lamps, a bewildering flutter of fans and floating robes, strains of music, columns of gay promenaders, a long row of turbaned mothers lining either wall, gentlemen of the portlier sort filling the recesses of the windows, whirling waltzers gliding here and there—smiles and grace, smiles and grace; all fair, orderly, elegant, bewitching. A young Creole's laugh mayhap a little loud, and—truly there were many sword-canes.[23] But neither grace nor foulness satisfied the eye of the zealous young Dutchman.

Suddenly a muffled woman passed him, leaning on a gentleman's arm. It looked like—it must be, Madame John. Speak quick, Kristian Koppig; do not stop to notice the man!

"Madame John"—bowing—"I am your neighbor, Kristian Koppig."

Madame John bows low, and smiles—a ball-room smile, but is frightened, and her escort,—the manager,—drops her hand and slips away.

"Ah! Monsieur," she whispers excitedly, "you will be killed if you stay here a moment. Are you armed? No. Take this." She tried to slip a dirk into his hands, but he would not have it.

"Oh, my dear young man, go! Go quickly!" she pleaded, glancing furtively down the hall.

"I wish you not to dance," said the young man.

"I have danced already; I am going home. Come; be quick! we will go together." She thrust her arm through his, and they hastened into the street. When a square had been passed there came a sound of men running behind them.

"Run, Monsieur, run!" she cried, trying to drag him; but Monsieur Dutchman would not.

"*Run*, Monsieur! Oh, my God! it is 'Sieur"—

"*That* for yesterday!" cried the manager, striking fiercely with his cane. Kristian Koppig's fist rolled him in the dirt.

"*That* for 'Tite Poulette!" cried another man dealing the Dutchman a terrible blow from behind.

---

[23]Blades concealed in sheaths designed to resemble walking canes, so that the carrier appears unarmed.

"And *that* for me!" hissed a third, thrusting at him with something bright.

"*That* for yesterday!" screamed the manager, bounding like a tiger; "That!" "THAT!" "Ha!"

Then Kristian Koppig knew that he was stabbed.

"That!" and "That!" and "That!" and the poor Dutchman struck wildly here and there, grasped the air, shut his eyes, staggered, reeled, fell, rose half up, fell again for good, and they were kicking him and jumping on him. All at once they scampered. Zalli had found the night-watch.

"Buz-z-z-z!" went a rattle. "Buz-z-z-z!" went another.

"Pick him up."

"Is he alive?"

"Can't tell; hold him steady; lead the way, misses."

"He's bleeding all over my breeches."

"This way—here—around this corner."

"This way now—only two squares more."

"Here we are."

"Rap-rap-rap!" on the old brass knocker. Curses on the narrow wicket, more on the dark archway, more still on the twisting stairs.

Up at last and into the room.

"Easy, easy, push this under his head! never mind his boots!"

So he lies—on 'Tite Poulette's own bed.

The watch are gone. They pause under the corner lamp to count profits;—a single bill—*Banque de la Louisiane*, fifty dollars. Providence is kind—tolerably so. Break it at the "Guillaume Tell."[24] "But did you ever hear any one scream like that girl did?"

And there lies the young Dutch neighbor. His money will not flutter back to him this time; nor will any voice behind a gate "beg Monsieur to go away." O, Woman!— that knows no enemy so terrible as man! Come nigh, poor Woman, you have nothing to fear. Lay your strange, electric touch upon the chilly flesh; it strikes no eager mischief along the fainting veins. Look your sweet looks upon the grimy face, and tenderly lay back the locks from the congested brows; no wicked misinterpretation lurks to bite your kindness. Be motherly, be sisterly, fear nought. Go, watch him by night; you may sleep at his feet and he will not stir. Yet his lives, and shall live—may live to forget you, who knows? But for all that, be gentle and watchful; be woman-like, we ask no more; and God reward you!

Even while it was taking all the two women's strength to hold the door against Death, the sick man himself laid a grief upon them.

"Mother," he said to Madame John, quite a master of French in his delirium, "dear mother, fear not; trust your boy; fear nothing. I will not marry 'Tite Poulette; I cannot. She is fair, dear mother, but ah! she is not—don't

---

[24]A French ship that, presumably, required no proof of identity upon changing large sums of money.

you know, mother? don't you know? The race! the race! Don't you know that she is jet black. Isn't it?"

The poor nurse nodded "Yes," and gave a sleeping draught; but before the patient quite slept he started once and stared.

"Take her away,"—waving his hand—"take your beauty away. She is jet white. Who could take a jet white wife? O, no, no, no, no!"

Next morning his brain was right.

"Madame," he weakly whispered, "I was delirious last night?"

Zalli shrugged. "Only a very, very, wee, wee trifle of a bit."

"And did I say something wrong or—foolish?"

"O, no, no," she replied; "you only clasped your hands, so, and prayed, prayed all the time to the dear Virgin."

"To the virgin?" asked the Dutchman, smiling incredulously.

"And St. Joseph—yes, indeed," she insisted; "you may strike me dead."

And so, for politeness' sake, he tried to credit the invention, but grew suspicious instead.

Hard was the battle against death. Nurses are sometimes amazons, and such were these. Through the long, enervating summer, the contest lasted; but when at last the cool airs of October came stealing in at the bedside like long-banished little children, Kristian Koppig rose upon his elbow and smiled them a welcome.

The physician, blessed man, was kind beyond measure; but said some inexplicable things, which Zalli tried in vain to make him speak in an undertone. "If I knew Monsieur John?" he said, "certainly! Why, we were chums at school. And he left you so much as that, Madame John? Ah! my old friend John, always noble! And you had it all in that naughty bank? Ah, well, Madame John, it matters little. No, I shall not tell 'Tite Poulette. Adieu."

And another time:—"If I will let you tell me something? With pleasure, Madame John. No, and not tell anybody, Madame John. No, Madame, not even 'Tite Poulette. What?"—a long whistle—"is that pos-si-ble?—and Monsieur John knew it?—encouraged it?—eh, well, eh, well!—But—can I believe you, Madame John? Oh! you have Monsieur John's sworn statement. Ah! very good, truly, but—you *say* you have it; but where is it? Ah! to-mor-row!" a sceptical shrug. "Pardon me, Madame John, I think perhaps, *perhaps* you are telling the truth.

"If I think you did right? Certainly! What nature keeps back, accident sometimes gives, Madame John; either is God's will. Don't cry. 'Stealing from the dead?' No! It was giving, yes! They are thanking you in heaven, Madame John."

Kristian Koppig, lying awake, but motionless and with closed eyes, hears in part, and, fancying he understands, rejoices with silent intensity. When the doctor is gone he calls Zalli.

"I give you a great deal of trouble, eh, Madame John?"

"No, no; you are no trouble at all. Had you the yellow fever—ah! then!"

She rolled her eyes to signify the superlative character of the tribulations attending yellow fever.

"I had a lady and gentleman once—a Spanish lady and gentleman, just off the ship; both sick at once with the fever—delirious—could not tell their names. Nobody to help me but sometimes Monsieur John! I never had such a time,—never before, never since—as that time. Four days and nights this head touched not a pillow."

"And they died!" said Kristian Koppig.

"The third night the gentleman went. Poor Señor! 'Sieur John,—he did not know the harm,—gave him some coffee and toast! The fourth night it rained and turned cool, and just before day the poor lady"—

"Died!" said Koppig.

Zalli dropped her arms listlessly into her lap and her eyes ran brimful.

"And left an infant!" said the Dutchman, ready to shout with exultation.

"Ah! no, Monsieur," said Zalli.

The invalid's heart sank like a stone.

"Madame John,"—his voice was all in a tremor,—"tell me the truth. Is 'Tite Poulette your own child?"

"Ah-h-h, ha! ha! What foolishness! Of course she is my child!" And Madame gave vent to a true Frenchwoman's laugh.

It was too much for the sick man. In the pitiful weakness of his shattered nerves he turned his face into his pillow and wept like a child. Zalli passed into the next room to hide her emotion.

"Maman, dear Maman," said 'Tite Poulette, who had overheard nothing, but only saw the tears.

"Ah! my child, my child, my task—my task is too great—too great for me. Let me go now—another time. Go and watch at his bedside."

"But, Maman,"—for 'Tite Poulette was frightened,—"he needs no care now."

"Nay, but go, my child; I wish to be alone."

The maiden stole in with averted eyes and tiptoed to the window—*that window*. The patient, already a man again, gazed at her till she could feel the gaze. He turned his eyes from her a moment to gather resolution. And now, stout heart, farewell; a word or two of friendly parting—nothing more.

"'Tite Poulette."

The slender figure at the window turned and came to the bedside.

"I believe I owe my life to you," he said.

She looked down meekly, the color rising in her cheek.

"I must arrange to be moved across the street tomorrow, on a litter."

She did not stir or speak.

"And I must now thank you, sweet nurse, for your care. Sweet nurse! Sweet nurse!"

She shook her head in protestation.

"Heaven bless you, 'Tite Poulette!"

Her face sank lower.

"God has made you very beautiful, 'Tite Poulette!"

She stirred not. He reached, and gently took her little hand, and as he drew her one step nearer, a tear fell from her long lashes. From the next room, Zalli, with a face of agonized suspense, gazed upon the pair, undiscovered. The young man lifted the hand to lay it upon his lips, when, with a mild, firm force, it was drawn away, yet still rested in his own upon the bedside, like some weak thing snared, that could only not get free.

"Thou wilt not have my love, 'Tite Poulette?"

No answer.

"Thou wilt not, beautiful?"

"Cannot!" was all that she could utter, and upon their clasped hands the tears ran down.

"Thou wrong'st me, 'Tite Poulette. Thou dost not trust me; thou fearest the kiss may loosen the hands. But I tell thee nay. I have struggled hard, even to this hour, against Love, but I yield me now; I yield; I am his unconditioned prisoner forever. God forbid that I ask aught but that you will be my wife."

Still the maiden moved not, looked not up, only rained down tears.

"Shall it not be, 'Tite Poulette?" He tried in vain to draw her.

"'Tite Poulette?" So tenderly he called? And then she spoke.

"It is against the law."

"It is not!" cried Zalli, seizing her round the waist and dragging her forward. "Take her! she is thine. I have robbed God long enough. Here are the sworn papers—here! Take her; she is as white as snow—so! Take her, kiss her; Mary be praised! I never had a child—she is the Spaniard's daughter!"

1874, 1879

from The Freedman's Case in Equity

V. Freed—Not Free

To be a free man is his still distant goal. Twice he has been a freedman. In the days of compulsory reconstruction he was freed in the presence of his master by that master's victorious foe. In these days of voluntary reconstruction he is virtually freed by the consent of his master, but the master retaining the exclusive right to define the bounds of his freedom. Many everywhere have taken up the idea that this state of affairs is the end to be desired and the end actually sought in reconstruction as handed over to the States. I do not charge such folly to the best intelligence of any American community; but I cannot ignore my own knowledge that the average thought of some regions rises to no better idea of the issue. The belief is all too common that the nation, having aimed at a wrong result and missed, has left us of the Southern States to get now such other result as we think best. I say this belief is not universal. There are those among us who see that America has no room for a state of society which makes its lower classes harmless by abridging their liberties, or, as one of the favored class lately said to me, has "got 'em so they don't give no trouble." There is a growing number who see that the one thing we cannot afford to tolerate at large is a class of people less than citizens; and that every interest in the land demands that the freedman be free to become in all things, as far as his own personal gifts will lift and sustain him, the same sort of American citizen he would be if, with the same intellectual and moral calibre, he were white.

Thus we reach the ultimate question of fact. Are the freedman's liberties suffering any real abridgment? The answer is easy. The letter of the laws, with a few exceptions, recognizes him as entitled to every right of an American citizen; and to some it may seem unimportant that there is scarcely one public relation of life in the South where he is not arbitrarily and unlawfully compelled to hold toward the white man the attitude of an alien, a menial, and a probable reprobate, by reason of his race and color. One of the marvels of future history will be that it was counted a small matter, by a majority of our nation, for six millions of people within it, made by its own decree a component part of it, to be subjected to a system of oppression so rank that nothing could make it seem small except the fact that they had already been ground under it for a century and a half.

Examine it. It proffers to the freedman a certain security of life and property, and then holds the respect of the community, that dearest of earthly boons, beyond his attainment. It gives him certain guarantees against thieves and robbers, and then holds him under the unearned contumely of the mass of good men and women. It acknowledges in constitutions and statutes his title to an American's freedom and aspirations, and then in daily practice heaps upon him in every public place the most odious distinctions, without giving ear to the humblest plea concerning mental or moral character. It spurns his ambition, tramples upon his languishing self-respect, and indignantly refuses to let him either buy with money, or earn by any excellence of inner life or outward behavior, the most momentary immunity from these public indignities even for his wife and daughters. Need we cram these pages with facts in evidence, as if these were charges denied and requiring to be proven? They are simply the present avowed and defended state of affairs peeled of its exteriors.

Nothing but the habit, generations old, of enduring it could make it endurable by men not in actual slavery. Were we whites of the South to remain every way as we are, and our six million blacks to give place to any sort of whites exactly their equals, man for man, in mind, morals, and wealth, provided only that they had tasted two years of American freedom, and were this same system of tyrannies attempted upon them, there would be as bloody an uprising as this continent has ever seen. We can say this quietly. There is not a scruple's weight of present danger. These six million freedmen are dominated by nine million whites immeasurably stronger than they, backed by the virtual consent of thirty odd millions more. Indeed, nothing but the habit of oppression could make such oppression possible to a people of the intelligence and virtue of our Southern whites, and the invitation to practice it on millions of any other than the children of their former slaves would be spurned with a noble indignation.

Suppose, for a moment, the tables turned. Suppose the courts of our Southern States, while changing no laws requiring the impaneling of jurymen without distinction as to race, etc., should suddenly begin to draw their thousands of jurymen all black, and well-nigh every one of them counting not only himself, but all his race, better than any white man. Assuming that their average of intelligence and morals should be not below that of jurymen as now drawn, would a white man, for all that, choose to be tried in one of those courts? Would he suspect nothing? Could one persuade him that his chances of even justice were all they should be, or all they would be were the court not evading the law in order to sustain an outrageous distinction against him because of the accidents of his birth? Yet only read white man for black man, and black man for white man, and that—I speak as an eye-witness—has been the practice for years, and is still so today; an actual emasculation, in the case of six million people both as plaintiff and defendant, of the right of trial by jury.

In this and other practices the outrage falls upon the freedman. Does it stop there? Far from it. It is the first premise of American principles that whatever elevates the lower stratum of the people lifts all the rest, and whatever holds it down holds all down. For twenty years, therefore, the nation has been working to elevate the freedman. It counts this one of the great necessities of the hour. It has poured out its wealth publicly and privately for this purpose. It is confidently hoped that it will soon bestow a royal gift of millions for the reduction of the illiteracy so largely shared by the blacks. Our Southern States are, and for twenty years have been, taxing themselves for the same end. The private charities alone of the other States have given twenty millions in the same good cause. Their colored seminaries, colleges, and normal schools dot our whole Southern country, and furnish our public colored schools with a large part of their teachers. All this and much more has been or is being done in order that, for the good of himself and everybody else in the land, the colored man may be elevated as quickly as possible from all the debasements of slavery and semi-slavery to the full stature and integrity of citizenship. And it is in the face of all this that the adherent of the old régime stands in the way to every public privilege and place—steamer landing, railway platform, theatre, concert-hall, art display, public library, public school, courthouse, church, everything—flourishing the hot branding-iron of ignominious distinctions. He forbids the freedman to go into the water until *he* is satisfied that he knows how to swim, and for fear he should learn hangs mill-stones about his neck. This is what we are told is a small matter that will settle itself. Yes, like a roosting curse, until the outraged intelligence of the South lifts its indignant protest against this stupid firing into our own ranks.

VI. Its Daily Workings

I say the outraged intelligence of the South; for there are thousands of Southern-born white men and women, in the minority in all these places— in churches, courts, schools, libraries, theatres, concert-halls, and on steamers and railway carriages,—who see the wrong and folly of these things, silently blush for them, and withhold their open protests only because their belief is unfortunately stronger in the futility of their counsel than in the power of a just cause. I do not justify their silence; but I affirm their sincerity and their goodly numbers. Of late years, when condemning these evils from the platform in Southern towns, I have repeatedly found that those who I had earlier been told were the men and women in whom the community placed most confidence and pride—they were the ones who, when I had spoken, came forward with warmest hand-grasps and expressions of thanks, and pointedly and cordially justified my every utterance. And were they the young South? Not by half. The gray-beards of the old times have always been among them, saying in effect, not by any means as converts, but as fellow-discoverers, "Whereas we were blind, now we see."

Another sort among our good Southern people make a similar but feeble admission, but with the time-worn proviso that expediency makes a more imperative demand than law, justice, or logic, and demands the preservation of the old order. Somebody must be outraged, it seems; and if not the freedman, then it must be a highly refined and enlightened race of people constantly offended and grossly discommoded, if not imposed upon, by a horde of tatterdemalions, male and female, crowding into a participation in their reserved privileges. Now, look at this plea. It is simply saying in another way that though the Southern whites far outnumber the blacks, and though we hold every element of power in greater degree than the blacks, and though the larger part of us claim to be sealed by nature as an exclusive upper class, and though we have the courts completely in our own hands, with the police on our right and the prisons on our left, and though we justly claim to be an intrepid people, and though we have a superb military experience, with ninety-nine hundredths of all the military equipment and no scarcity of all the accessories, yet with all these facts behind us we cannot make and enforce that intelligent and approximately just assortment of persons in public places and conveyances on the merits of exterior decency that is made in all other enlightened lands. On such a plea are made a distinction and separation that not only are crude, invidious, humiliating, and tyrannous, but which do not reach their ostensible end or come near it; and all that saves such a plea from being a confession of driveling imbecility is its utter speciousness. It is advanced sincerely; and yet nothing is easier to show than that these distinctions on the line of color are really made not from any necessity, but simply for their own sake—to preserve the old arbitrary supremacy of the master class over the menial without regard to the decency or indecency of appearance or manners in either the white individual or the colored.

See its every-day working. Any colored man gains unquestioned admission into innumerable places the moment he appears as the menial attendant of some white person, where he could not cross the threshold in his own right as a well-dressed and well-behaved master of himself. The contrast is even greater in the case of colored women. There could not be a system which when put into practice would more offensively condemn itself. It does more: it actually creates the confusion it pretends to prevent. It blunts the sensibilities of the ruling class themselves. It waives all strict demand for painstaking in either manners or dress of either master or menial, and, for one result, makes the average Southern railway coach more uncomfortable than the average of railway coaches elsewhere. It prompts the average Southern white passenger to find less offense in the presence of a profane, boisterous, or unclean white person than in that of a quiet, well-behaved colored man or woman attempting to travel on an equal footing with him without a white master or mistress. The holders of the old sentiments hold the opposite choice in scorn. It is only when we go on to say that there are regions where the riotous expulsion of a decent and peaceable colored person is preferred to his inoffensive company, that it may seem necessary to bring in evidence. And yet here again it is *prima facie* evidence; for the following extract was printed in the Selma (Alabama) "Times" not six months ago,[1] and not as a complaint, but as a boast:

"A few days since, a negro minister, of this city, boarded the east-bound passenger train on the E. T., V. & G. Railway and took a seat in the coach occupied by white passengers. Some of the passengers complained to the conductor and brakemen, and expressed considerable dissatisfaction that they were forced to ride alongside of a negro. The railroad officials informed the complainants that they were not authorized to force the colored passenger into the coach set apart for the negroes, and they would lay themselves liable should they do so. The white passengers then took the matter in their own hands and ordered the ebony-hued minister to take a seat in the next coach. He positively refused to obey orders, whereupon the white men gave him a sound flogging and forced him to a seat among his own color and equals. We learned yesterday that the vanquished preacher was unable to fill his pulpit on account of the severe chastisement inflicted upon him. Now [says the delighted editor] the query that puzzles is, 'Who did the flogging?'"

And as good an answer as we can give is that likely enough they were some of the men for whom the whole South has come to a halt to let them get over the "feelings engendered by the war." Must such men, such acts, such sentiments, stand alone to represent us of the South before an enlightened world? No. I say, as a citizen of an extreme Southern State, a native of Louisiana, an ex-Confederate soldier, and a lover of my home, my city, and my State, as well as of my country, that this is not the best sentiment in the South, nor the sentiment of her best intelligence; and that it would not ride up and down that beautiful land dominating and domineering were it not for its tremendous power as the *traditional* sentiment of a conservative people. But is not silent endurance criminal? I cannot but repeat my own words, spoken near the scene and about the time of this event. Speech may be silvern and silence golden; but if a lump of gold is only big enough, it can drag us to the bottom of the sea and hold us there while all the world sails over us.

[1] In the summer of 1884. [Author's note.]

The laws passed in the days of compulsory reconstruction requiring "equal accommodations," etc., for colored and white persons were freedmen's follies. On their face they defeated their ends; for even in theory they at once reduced to half all opportunity for those more reasonable and mutually agreeable self-assortments which public assemblages and groups of passengers find it best to make in all other enlightened countries, making them on the score of conduct, dress, and price. They also led the whites to overlook what they would have seen instantly had these invidious distinctions been made against themselves: that their offense does not vanish at the guarantee against the loss of physical comforts. But we made, and are still making, a mistake beyond even this. For years many of us have carelessly taken for granted that these laws were being carried out in some shape that removed all just ground of complaint. It is common to say, "We allow the man of color to go and come at will, only let him sit apart in a place marked off for him." But marked off how? So as to mark him instantly as a menial. Not by railings and partitions merely, which, raised against any other class in the United States with the same invidious intent, would be kicked down as fast as put up, but by giving him besides, in every instance and without recourse, the most uncomfortable, uncleanest, and unsafest place; and the unsafety, uncleanness, and discomfort of most of these places are a shame to any community pretending to practice public justice. If any one can think the freedman does not feel the indignities thus heaped upon him, let him take up any paper printed for colored men's patronage, or ask any colored man of known courageous utterance. Hear them:

> "We ask not Congress, nor the Legislature, nor any other power, to remedy these evils, but we ask the people among whom we live. Those who can remedy them if they will. Those who have a high sense of honor and a deep moral feeling. Those who have one vestige of human sympathy left.... Those are the ones we ask to protect us in our weakness and ill-treatments.... As soon as the colored man is treated by the white man as a man, that harmony and pleasant feeling which should characterize all races which dwell together, shall be the bond of peace between them."

Surely their evidence is good enough to prove their own feelings. We need not lean upon it here for anything else. I shall not bring forward a single statement of fact from them or any of their white friends who, as teachers and missionaries, share many of their humiliations, though my desk is covered with them. But I beg to make the same citation from my own experience that I made last June[2] in the far South. It was this: One hot night in September of last year[3] I was traveling by rail in the State of Alabama. At rather late bed-time there came aboard the train a young mother and her little daughter of three or four years. They were neatly and tastefully dressed in cool, fresh muslins, and as the train went on its way they sat together very still and quiet. At the next station there came aboard a most

---

[2]1884. [Author's note.]

[3]1883. [Author's note.]

melancholy and revolting company. In filthy rags, with vile odors and the clanking of shackles and chains, nine penitentiary convicts chained to one chain, and ten more chained to another, dragged laboriously into the compartment of the car where in one corner sat this mother and child, and packed it full, and the train moved on. The keeper of the convicts told me he should take them in that car two hundred miles that night. They were going to the mines. My seat was not in that car, and I staid in it but a moment. It stank insufferably. I returned to my own place in the coach behind, where there was, and had all the time been, plenty of room. But the mother and child sat on in silence in that foul hole, the conductor having distinctly refused them admission elsewhere because they were of African blood, and not because the mother was, but because she was *not*, engaged at the moment in menial service. Had the child been white, and the mother not its natural but its hired guardian, she could have sat anywhere in the train, and no one would have ventured to object, even had she been as black as the mouth of the coal-pit to which her loathsome fellow-passengers were being carried in chains.

Such is the incident as I saw it. But the illustration would be incomplete here were I not allowed to add the comments I made upon it when in June last I recounted it, and to state the two opposite tempers in which my words were received. I said: "These are the facts. And yet you know and I know we belong to communities that after years of hoping for, are at last taking comfort in the assurance of the nation's highest courts that no law can reach and stop this shameful foul play until we choose to enact a law to that end ourselves. And now the east and north and west of our great and prosperous and happy country, and the rest of the civilized world, as far as it knows our case, are standing and waiting to see what we will write upon the white page of to-day's and to-morrow's history, now that we are simply on our honor and on the mettle of our far and peculiarly famed Southern instinct. How long, then, shall we stand off from such ringing moral questions as these on the flimsy plea that they have a political value, and, scrutinizing the Constitution, keep saying, 'Is it so nominated in the bond? I cannot find it; 'tis not in the bond.'"

With the temper that promptly resented these words through many newspapers of the neighboring regions there can be no propriety in wrangling. When regions so estranged from the world's thought carry their resentment no further than a little harmless invective, it is but fair to welcome it as a sign of progress. If communities nearer the great centers of thought grow impatient with *them*, how shall we resent the impatience of these remoter ones when their oldest traditions are, as it seems to them, ruthlessly assailed? There is but one right thing to do: it is to pour in upon them our reiterations of the truth without malice and without stint.

But I have a much better word to say. It is for those who, not voiced by the newspapers around them, showed both then and constantly afterward in public and private during my two days' subsequent travel and sojourn in the region, by their cordial, frequent, specific approval of my words, that a better intelligence is longing to see the evils of the old régime supplanted by a wiser and more humane public sentiment and practice. And I must repeat my conviction that if the unconscious habit of oppression were not already there, a scheme so gross, irrational, unjust, and inefficient as our present caste distinctions could not find place among a people so generally intelligent and high-minded. I ask attention to their bad influence in a direction not often noticed.

1885

■ ALICE DUNBAR-NELSON ■
1875–1935

Alice Ruth Moore, born in New Orleans on July 19, 1875, aspired to bridge the color line in American letters. She was the daughter of a freed slave woman; her mother may have been the cast-off common-law wife of a white man. Little is known about her father, but a letter suggests shame about her parentage. Yet Dunbar-Nelson's upbringing testifies to what a female-headed family of an ex-slave could achieve. She attended public school and graduated from the private Straight University, now Dillard University, in 1892 as a teacher. Founded after the Civil War to educate freed slaves, the university had become an elite school that Creoles of color whose ancestors had never been slaves also attended. There, despite being the daughter of an ex-slave, the beautiful, gifted young woman excelled. During her senior year, Straight University alumnus Louis Martinet led the "Comité des Citoyens" in urgent appeals throughout the city to help fund the legal challenge to segregated streetcars that ended in the Supreme Court ruling segregation lawful in *Plessy v. Ferguson* in 1896. That decision would darken her generation's prospects.

Nevertheless, Alice Moore acquired the ambition and the education to become a writer in her native cosmopolitan city. She started her career by writing for the black press, and as she turned twenty, she published her first book, *Violets and Other Tales* (1895). In 1896 she left the Jim Crow–ridden South for Boston, where she continued to write. Seeing her picture in a black publication, Paul Laurence Dunbar, already a rising literary star, began courting her. They conducted their romance mainly through letters, finally met in 1897 in New York, and married in 1898. However, their marriage was troubled: although he encouraged her literary aspirations and his publisher brought out her second book, *The Goodness of St. Rocques and Other Tales* (1899), he was addicted to alcohol and sometimes abusive. Complicating their relationship was his poor health from tuberculosis. They separated but never divorced, and despite their private pain, she kept his name and promoted his work after his death in 1906.

The black press proved essential to Dunbar-Nelson's survival as a writer. After 1899 she was unable to publish much in the white mainstream; one prominent editor explicitly rejected her fiction for being race-conscious. However, her columns, "From a Woman's Point of View" (later "Une Femme Dit") and "As in a Looking Glass," were widely syndicated in the Associated Negro Press, and her work appeared in leading black journals, including *Crisis* and *Opportunity*. She coedited and published a black newspaper with Robert J. Nelson, whom she married in 1916. Although she was all but forgotten until Gloria T. Hull unearthed her body of work—including poems, short stories, novels, and the diary she kept sporadically from 1921–1931—her importance is now being recognized. She is seen as a literary trailblazer in the black short story, and, in her antilynching play titled "Mine Eyes Have Seen" (1918), a pioneer of black drama. She is celebrated as one of the women poets of the Harlem Renaissance as well. Her role as an active proponent of black literature has also re-emerged: she published two anthologies, *Masterpieces of Negro Eloquence* (1914) and *The Dunbar Speaker and Entertainer* (1920).

Although Alice Dunbar-Nelson was light enough to pass for white, her lifelong political activism attests to her self-identification as a "colored" American committed to bettering the condition of African Americans. Always active in the National Federation of Colored Women Clubs, she helped found and later taught at the Industrial School for Colored Girls in Delaware. She also taught high school in Wilmington, Delaware, for almost twenty years, and was fired for going to Ohio as part of a women's delegation urging presidential candidate Warren G. Harding to advocate social justice. She had long campaigned for women's suffrage, and in 1921 she was one of three women in a group of thirty black leaders who went to the White House to ask President Harding to pardon black soldiers jailed for rioting. In 1922 she led a statewide antilynching campaign in Delaware. In addition to her political organizing, she was Executive Secretary of the American Friends Inter-Racial Peace Committee from 1928 to 1931.

While modern critics recognize how accomplished Dunbar-Nelson's Creole stories are, there is some disagreement about their racial politics. Some see them as "aracial," or hiding behind a "white veil"; others see her fiction as subtly interrogating racial and cultural difference. In "People of Color in Louisiana" (*Journal of Negro History*, 1916–1917), Dunbar-Nelson challenges dominant interpretations of "race," noting that Louisiana was, from the outset, molded by diverse peoples, including Native Americans, the Spanish, the French, the English, Americans, African slaves, and immigrants of all colors from the Caribbean. Officially, those of Creole ancestry were claimed for the "white" side of the color-line, but she knew that the reality was far more complex. Aware that whites would adamantly object to including people of color as "Creole," she cannily asserts that "a Creole is a native of Louisiana, in whose blood runs mixed strains of everything un-American, with the African strain slightly apparent."

Just as Dunbar-Nelson's fiction takes great care to represent the cultural specificity of Catholic Creoles, her stories, individually and taken together, make it clear that New Orleans is not culturally "white," but "Creole" in the broadest sense—a blend of cultures that defies easy racial categorization but unquestionably includes the "African strain." In "The Praline Woman" (1899), a slice of New Orleans street life, a scrappy Creole woman sells her candies and tells her story; fusing French with nonstandard English influenced by Southern black speech patterns, her dialect offers clues but does not resolve the issue of her racial classification. "Sister Josepha" (1899) explores the few choices open to a young woman whose identity is not fixed by a family name or membership in a racial group. "Mr. Baptiste" (1899) shows the dangers of crossing the color line: for cheering on black strike breakers, an old Creole man is struck down by an Irish mob who rejects working alongside blacks. Dunbar-Nelson refuses to write as if "race" determines "identity," for individuals cannot be reduced to social categories, though they often suffer because of them.

Caroline Gebhard
Tuskegee University

PRIMARY WORKS

Violets and Other Tales, 1895; *The Goodness of St. Rocque and Other Stories,* 1899, in *The Works of Alice Dunbar-Nelson,* 3 vols., ed. Gloria T. Hull, 1988; "People of Color in Louisiana, Part I and II," *Journal of Negro History* 1 (1916): 361–76, and 2 (1917): 51–78; *The Diary of Alice Dunbar-Nelson,* ed. Gloria T. Hull, 1984.

Sister Josepha

Sister Josepha told her beads mechanically, her fingers numb with the accustomed exercise. The little organ creaked a dismal "O Salutaris,"[1] and she still knelt on the floor, her white-bonneted head nodding suspiciously. The Mother Superior gave a sharp glance at the tired figure; then, as a sudden lurch forward brought the little sister back to consciousness, Mother's eyes relaxed into a genuine smile.

The bell tolled the end of vespers, and the sombre-robed nuns filed out of the chapel to go about their evening duties. Little Sister Josepha's work was to attend to the household lamps, but there must have been as much oil spilled upon the table tonight as was put in the vessels. The small brown hands trembled so that most of the wicks were trimmed with points at one corner which caused them to smoke that night.

"Oh, cher Seigneur,"[2] she sighed, giving an impatient polish to a refractory chimney, "it is wicked and sinful, I know, but I am so tired. I can't be happy and sing any more. It doesn't seem right for le bon Dieu[3] to have me all cooped up here with nothing to see but stray visitors, and always the same old work, teaching those mean little girls to sew, and washing and filling the same old lamps. Pah!" And she polished the chimney with a sudden vigorous jerk which threatened destruction.

They were rebellious prayers that the red mouth murmured that night, and a restless figure that tossed on the hard dormitory bed. Sister Dominica called from her couch to know if Sister Josepha were ill.

"No," was the somewhat short reponse; then a muttered, "Why can't they let me alone for a minute? That pale-eyed Sister Dominica never sleeps; that's why she is so ugly."

[1]Opening words of "O Salutaris Hostia," "Oh, Saving Host," the hymn to the Blessed Sacrament consecrated outside of Mass.

[2]French: "dear Lord."

[3]French: "the good Lord/God."

About fifteen years before this night some one had brought to the orphan asylum connected with this convent, du Sacre Coeur, a round, dimpled bit of three-year-old humanity, who regarded the world from a pair of gravely twinkling black eyes, and only took a chubby thumb out of a rosy mouth long enough to answer in monosyllabic French. It was a child without an identity; there was but one name that any one seemed to know, and that, too, was vague,—Camille.

She grew up with the rest of the waifs; scraps of French and American civilization thrown together to develop a seemingly inconsistent miniature world. Mademoiselle Camille was a queen among them, a pretty little tyrant who ruled the children and dominated the more timid sisters in charge.

One day an awakening came. When she was fifteen, and almost fully ripened into a glorious tropical beauty of the type that matures early, some visitors to the convent were fascinated by her and asked the Mother Superior to give the girl into their keeping.

Camille fled like a frightened fawn into the yard, and was only unearthed with some difficulty from behind a group of palms. Sulky and pouting, she was led into the parlour, picking at her blue pinafore like a spoiled infant.

"The lady and gentleman wish you to go home with them, Camille," said the Mother Superior, in the language of the convent. Her voice was kind and gentle apparently; but the child, accustomed to its various inflections, detected a steely ring behind its softness, like the proverbial iron hand in the velvet glove.

"You must understand, madame," continued Mother, in stilted English, "that we never force children from us. We are ever glad to place them in comfortable—how you say that?—quarters—maisons—homes—bien! But we will not make them go if they do not wish."

Camille stole a glance at her would-be guardians, and decided instantly, impulsively, finally. The woman suited her; but the man! It was doubtless intuition of the quick, vivacious sort which belonged to her blood that served her. Untutored in worldly knowledge, she could not divine the meaning of the pronounced leers and admiration of her physical charms which gleamed in the man's face, but she knew it made her feel creepy, and stoutly refused to go.

Next day Camille was summoned from a task to the Mother Superior's parlour. The other girls gazed with envy upon her as she dashed down the courtyard with impetuous movement. Camille, they decided crossly, received too much notice. It was Camille this, Camille that; she was pretty, it was to be expected. Even Father Ray lingered longer in his blessing when his hands pressed her silky black hair.

As she entered the parlour, a strange chill swept over the girl. The room was not an unaccustomed one, for she had swept it many times, but to-day the stiff black chairs, the dismal crucifixes, the gleaming whiteness of the walls, even the cheap lithograph of the Madonna which Camille had always regarded as a perfect specimen of art, seemed cold and mean.

"Camille, ma chere,"[4] said Mother, "I am extremely displeased with you. Why did you not wish to go with Monsieur and Madame Lafaye yesterday?"

The girl uncrossed her hands from her bosom, and spread them out in a deprecating gesture.

"Mais, ma mere,[5] I was afraid."

Mother's face grew stern. "No foolishness now," she exclaimed.

"It is not foolishness, ma mere; I could not help it, but that man looked at me so funny, I felt all cold chills down my back. Oh, dear Mother, I love the convent and the sisters so, I just want to stay and be a sister too, may I?"

And thus it was that Camille took the white veil at sixteen years. Now that the period of novitiate was over, it was just beginning to dawn upon her that she had made a mistake.

"Maybe it would have been better had I gone with the funny-looking lady and gentleman," she mused bitterly one night. "Oh, Seigneur, I'm so tired and impatient; it's so dull here, and, dear God, I'm so young."

There was no help for it. One must arise in the morning, and help in the refectory with the stupid Sister Francesca, and go about one's duties with a prayerful mien, and not even let a sigh escape when one's head ached with the eternal telling of beads.

A great fete day was coming, and an atmosphere of preparation and mild excitement pervaded the brown walls of the convent like a delicate aroma. The old Cathedral around the corner had stood a hundred years, and all the city was rising to do honour to its age and time-softened beauty. There would be a service, oh, but such a one! with two Cardinals, and Archbishops and Bishops, and all the accompanying glitter of soldiers and orchestras. The little sisters of the Convent du Sacre Coeur clasped their hands in anticipation of the holy joy. Sister Josepha curled her lip, she was so tired of churchly pleasures.

The day came, a gold and blue spring day, when the air hung heavy with the scent of roses and magnolias, and the sunbeams fairly laughed as they kissed the houses. The old Cathedral stood gray and solemn, and the flowers in Jackson Square smiled cheery birthday greetings across the way. The crowd around the door surged and pressed and pushed in its eagerness to get within. Ribbons stretched across the banquette were of no avail to repress it, and important ushers with cardinal colours could do little more.

The Sacred Heart sisters filed slowly in at the side door, creating a momentary flutter as they paced reverently to their seats, guarding the blue-bonnetted orphans. Sister Josepha, determined to see as much of the world as she could, kept her big black eyes opened wide, as the church rapidly filled with the fashionably dressed, perfumed, rustling, and self-conscious throng.

---

[4]French: "my dear."   [5]French: "But, mother."

Her heart beat quickly. The rebellious thoughts that will arise in the most philosophical of us surged in her small heavily gowned bosom. For her were the gray things, the neutral tinted skies, the ugly garb, the coarse meats; for them the rainbow, the ethereal airiness of earthly joys, the bonbons and glacés of the world. Sister Josepha did not know that the rainbow is elusive, and its colours but the illumination of tears; she had never been told that earthly ethereality is necessarily ephemeral, nor that bonbons and glaces, whether of the palate or of the soul, nauseate and pall upon the taste. Dear God, forgive her, for she bent with contrite tears over her worn rosary, and glanced no more at the worldly glitter of femininity.

The sunbeams streamed through the high windows in purple and crimson lights upon a veritable fugue of colour. Within the seats, crush upon crush of spring millinery; within the aisles erect lines of gold-braided, gold-buttoned military. Upon the altar, broad sweeps of golden robes, great dashes of crimson skirts, mitres and gleaming crosses, the soft neutral hue of rich lace vestments; the tender heads of childhood in picturesque attire; the proud, golden magnificence of the domed altar with its weighting mass of lilies and wide-eyed roses, and the long candles that sparkled their yellow star points above the reverent throng within the altar rails.

The soft baritone of the Cardinal intoned a single phrase in the suspended silence. The censer took up the note in its delicate clink clink, as it swung to and fro in the hands of a fair-haired child. Then the organ, pausing an instant in a deep, mellow, long-drawn note, burst suddenly into a magnificent strain, and the choir sang forth, "Kyrie Eleison, Christe Eleison."[6] One voice, flute-like, piercing, sweet, rang high over the rest. Sister Josepha heard and trembled, as she buried her face in her hands, and let her tears fall, like other beads, through her rosary.

It was when the final word of the service had been intoned, the last peal of the exit march had died away, that she looked up meekly, to encounter a pair of youthful brown eyes gazing pityingly upon her. That was all she remembered for a moment, that the eyes were youthful and handsome and tender. Later, she saw that they were placed in a rather beautiful boyish face, surmounted by waves of brown hair, curling and soft, and that the head was set on a pair of shoulders decked in military uniform. Then the brown eyes marched away with the rest of the rear guard, and the white-bonneted sisters filed out the side door, through the narrow court, back into the brown convent.

That night Sister Josepha tossed more than usual on her hard bed, and clasped her fingers often in prayer to quell the wickedness in her heart. Turn where she would, pray as she might, there was ever a pair of tender,

[6]"Lord, have mercy, Christ, have mercy," penitential prayer used at the beginning of the liturgy.

pitying brown eyes, haunting her persistently. The squeaky organ at vespers intoned the clank of military accoutrements to her ears, the white bonnets of the sisters about her faded into mists of curling brown hair. Briefly, Sister Josepha was in love.

The days went on pretty much as before, save for the one little heart that beat rebelliously now and then, though it tried so hard to be submissive. There was the morning work in the refectory, the stupid little girls to teach sewing, and the insatiable lamps that were so greedy for oil. And always the tender, boyish brown eyes, that looked so sorrowfully at the fragile, beautiful little sister, haunting, following, pleading.

Perchance, had Sister Josepha been in the world, the eyes would have been an incident. But in this home of self-repression and retrospection, it was a life-story. The eyes had gone their way, doubtless forgetting the little sister they pitied; but the little sister?

The days glided into weeks, the weeks into months. Thoughts of escape had come to Sister Josepha, to flee into the world, to merge in the great city where recognition was impossible, and, working her way like the rest of humanity, perchance encounter the eyes again.

It was all planned and ready. She would wait until some morning when the little band of black-robed sisters wended their way to mass at the Cathedral. When it was time to file out the side-door into the courtway, she would linger at prayers, then slip out another door, and unseen glide up Chartres Street to Canal, and once there, mingle in the throng that filled the wide thoroughfare. Beyond this first plan she could think no further. Penniless, garbed, and shaven though she would be, other difficulties never presented themselves to her. She would rely on the mercies of the world to help her escape from this torturing life of inertia. It seemed easy now that the first step of decision had been taken.

The Saturday night before the final day had come, and she lay feverishly nervous in her narrow little bed, wondering with wide-eyed fear at the morrow. Pale-eyed Sister Dominica and Sister Francesca were whispering together in the dark silence, and Sister Josepha's ears pricked up as she heard her name.

"She is not well, poor child," said Francesca. "I fear the life is too confining."

"It is best for her," was the reply. "You know, sister, how hard it would be for her in the world, with no name but Camille, no friends, and her beauty; and then—"

Sister Josepha heard no more, for her heart beating tumultously in her bosom drowned the rest. Like the rush of the bitter salt tide over a drowning man clinging to a spar, came the complete submerging of her hopes of another life. No name but Camille, that was true; no nationality, for she could never tell from whom or whence she came; no friends, and a beauty that not even an ungainly bonnet and shaven head could hide. In a flash she realised the deception of the life she would lead, and the cruel self-torture of wonder at her own identity. Already, as if in anticipation of the world's questionings, she was asking herself, "Who am I? What am I?"

The next morning the sisters du Sacre Coeur filed into the Cathedral at High Mass, and bent devout knees at the general confession. "Confiteor Deo omnipotenti,"[7] murmured the priest; and tremblingly one little sister followed the words, "Je confesse a Dieu, tout puissant—que j'ai beaucoup peche par pensees—c'est ma faute—c'est ma faute—c'est ma tres grande faute."

The organ pealed forth as mass ended, the throng slowly filed out, and the sisters paced through the courtway back into the brown convent walls. One paused at the entrance, and gazed with swift longing eyes in the direction of narrow, squalid Chartres Street, then, with a gulping sob, followed the rest, and vanished behind the heavy door.

1899

The Praline Woman

The praline woman sits by the side of the Archbishop's quaint little old chapel on Royal Street, and slowly waves her latanier fan over the pink and brown wares.

"Pralines, pralines.[1] Ah, ma'amzelle, you buy? S'il vous plait,[2] ma'amzelle, ces pralines, dey be fine, ver' fresh.

"Mais non, maman, you are not sure?

"Sho', chile, ma bébé, ma petite, she put dese up hissef. He's hans' so small, ma'amzelle, lak you's, mais brune.[3] She put dese up dis morn'. You tak' none? No husban' fo' you den!

"Ah, ma petite, you tak'? Cinq sous,[4] bébé, may le bon Dieu keep you good![5]

"Mais oui, madame, I know you étrangér.[6] You don' look lak dese New Orleans peop'. You lak' dose Yankee dat come down 'fo' de war."

Ding-dong, ding-dong, ding-dong, chimes the Cathedral bell across Jackson Square, and the praline woman crosses herself.

"Hail, Mary, full of grace—

"Pralines, madame? You buy lak' dat? Dix sous,[7] madame, an' one lil' piece fo' lagniappe fo' madame's lil' bébé.[8] Ah, c'est bon!

---

[7] "I confess to God Almighty." The priest begins, in Latin, the formulaic prayer traditionally used to initiate confession. It is taken up in French which translates: "I confess to God Almighty—that I have gravely sinned in my thoughts—it is my fault—it is my most grievous fault."

[1] Originated in antebellum New Orleans, praline candy confections were often sold by African American women on street corners of the French Quarter.

[2] French: if you please, or, please.

[3] French: but dark skinned; or, but black; or, but with a dark complexion.

[4] French: five cents.

[5] French: the good God.

[6] French: stranger.

[7] French: ten cents.

[8] *Langniappe* is a Creole American term for the New Orleans custom of grocers' giving favors of sugar, spice, or candy to customers for each purchase.

"Pralines, pralines, so fresh, so fine! M'sieu would lak' some fo' he's lil' gal' at home? Mais non, what's dat you say? She 's daid! Ah, m'sieu, 't is my lil' gal what died long year ago. Misère, misère![9]

"Here come dat lazy Indien squaw. What she good fo', anyhow? She jes' sit lak dat in de French Market an' sell her filé,[10] an' sleep, sleep, sleep, lak' so in he's blanket. Hey, dere, you, Tonita, how goes you' beezness?

"Pralines, pralines! Holy Father, you give me dat blessin' sho'? Tak' one, I know you lak dat w'ite one. It tas' good, I know, bien.

"Pralines, madame? I lak' you' face. What fo' you wear black? You' lil' boy daid? You tak' one, jes' see how it tas'. I had one lil' boy once, he jes' grow 'twell he 's big lak' dis, den one day he tak' sick an' die. Oh, madame, it mos' brek my po' heart. I burn candle in St. Rocque,[11] I say my beads, I sprinkle holy water roun' he's bed; he jes' lay so, he's eyes turn up, he say 'Maman, maman,' den he die! Madame, you tak' one. Non, non, no l'argent,[12] you tak' one fo' my lil' boy's sake.

"Pralines, pralines, m'sieu? Who mak' dese? My lil' gal, Didele, of co'se. Non, non, I don't mak' no mo'. Po' Tante Marie get too ol'.[13] Didele? She's one lil' gal I 'dopt. I see her one day in de strit. He walk so; hit col' she shiver, an' I say, 'Where you gone, lil' gal?' and he can' tell. He jes' crip close to me, an' cry so! Den I tak' her home wid me, and she say he's name Didele. You see dey wa'nt nobody dere. My lil' gal, she 's daid of de yellow fever; my lil' boy, he 's daid, po' Tante Marie all alone. Didele, she grow fine, she keep house an' mek' pralines. Den, when night come, she sit wid he's guitar an' sing,

> "'Tu l'aime ces trois jours,
> Tu l'aime ces trois jours,
>   Ma cœur à toi,
>   Ma cœur à toi,
> Tu l'aime ces trois jours!'[14]

"Ah, he's fine gal, is Didele!

"Pralines, pralines! Dat lil' cloud, h'it look lak' rain, I hope no.

"Here come dat lazy I'ishman down de strit. I don't lak' I'ishman, me, non, dey so funny. One day one I'ishman, he say to me, 'Auntie, what fo' you talk so?' and I jes' say back, 'What fo' you say "Faith an' be jabers"?'[15] Non, I don' lak' I'ishman, me!

"Here come de rain! Now I got fo' to go. Didele, she be wait fo' me. Down h'it come! H'it fall in de Meesseesip, an' fill up—up—so, clean to de

---

[9]French: misery; an equivalent English expression might be "Oh, woe is me."
[10]Powdered sassafras used in Louisiana cuisine.
[11]A small chapel in New Orleans associated with mixed Catholic and voodoo practices.
[12]French: money.
[13]French: Aunt Marie.

[14]French: You love him these three days / You love him these three days / My heart is yours / My heart is yours / You love him these three days!
[15]A disparaging reference to the Irish expression "Faith an' be jabbers."

levee, den we have big crivasse, an' po' Tante Marie float away. Bon jour, madame, you come again? Pra-lines! Pralines!"

1899

Mr. Baptiste

He might have had another name; we never knew. Some one had christened him Mr. Baptiste long ago in the dim past, and it sufficed. No one had ever been known who had the temerity to ask him for another cognomen, for though he was a mild-mannered little man, he had an uncomfortable way of shutting up oyster-wise and looking disagreeable when approached concerning his personal history.

He was small: most Creole men are small when they are old. It is strange, but a fact. It must be that age withers them sooner and more effectually than those of un-Latinised extraction. Mr. Baptiste was, furthermore, very much wrinkled and lame. Like the Son of Man, he had nowhere to lay his head, save when some kindly family made room for him in a garret or a barn. He subsisted by doing odd jobs, whitewashing, cleaning yards, doing errands, and the like.

The little old man was a frequenter of the levee. Never a day passed that his quaint little figure was not seen moving up and down about the ships. Chiefly did he haunt the Texas and Pacific warehouses and the landing-place of the Morgan-line steamships.[1] This seemed like madness, for these spots are almost the busiest on the levee, and the rough seamen and 'longshoremen have least time to be bothered with small weak folks. Still there was method in the madness of Mr. Baptiste. The Morgan steamships, as every one knows, ply between New Orleans and Central and South American ports, doing the major part of the fruit trade; and many were the baskets of forgotten fruit that Mr. Baptiste took away with him unmolested. Sometimes, you know, bananas and mangoes and oranges and citrons will half spoil, particularly if it has been a bad voyage over the stormy Gulf, and the officers of the ships will give away stacks of fruit, too good to go into the river, too bad to sell to the fruit-dealers.

You could see Mr. Baptiste trudging up the street with his quaint one-sided walk, bearing his dilapidated basket on one shoulder, a nondescript head-cover pulled over his eyes, whistling cheerily. Then he would slip in at the back door of one of his clients with a brisk,—

"Ah, bonjour, madame. Now here ees jus' a lil' bit fruit, some bananas. Perhaps madame would cook some for Mr. Baptiste?"

And madame, who understood and knew his ways, would fry him some of the bananas, and set it before him, a tempting dish, with a bit of

---

[1]The Texas and Pacific Railway, established by federal charter in 1871, ran from Marshall, Texas, to Sierra Blanca, Texas, also extending eastward into New Orleans. The Morgan Line steamships, controlled by Charles Morgan (1795–1882), exemplify the importance of steam navigation through the middle part of the nineteenth century.

madame's bread and meat and coffee thrown in for lagniappe[2]; and Mr. Baptiste would depart, filled and contented, leaving the load of fruit behind as madame's pay. Thus did he eat, and his clients were many, and never too tired or too cross to cook his meals and get their pay in baskets of fruit.

One day he slipped in at Madamae Garcia's kitchen door with such a woebegone air, and slid a small sack of nearly ripe plantains on the table with such a misery-laden sigh, that madame, who was fat and excitable, threw up both hands and cried out:

"Mon Dieu, Mistare Baptiste, fo' w'y you look lak dat? What ees de mattare?"

For answer, Mr. Baptiste shook his head gloomily and sighed again. Madame Garcia moved heavily about the kitchen, putting the plantains in a cool spot and punctuating her footsteps with sundry "Mon Dieux" and "Misères."[3]

"Dose cotton!" ejaculated Mr. Baptiste, at last.

"Ah, mon Dieu!" groaned Madame Garcia, rolling her eyes heavenwards.

"Hit will drive de fruit away!" he continued.

"Misère!" said Madame Garcia.

"Hit will."

"Oui, oui," said Madame Garcia. She had carefully inspected the plantains, and seeing that they were good and wholesome, was inclined to agree with anything Mr. Baptiste said.

He grew excited. "Yaas, dose cotton-yardmans, dose 'longsho'mans, dey go out on one strik'. Dey t'row down dey tool an' say dey work no mo' wid niggers. Les veseaux,[4] dey lay in de river, no work, no cargo, yaas. Den de fruit ship, dey can' mak' lan', de mans, dey t'reaten an' say t'ings. Dey mak' big fight, yaas. Dere no mo' work on de levee, lak dat. Ever'body jus' walk roun' an' say cuss word, yaas!"

"Oh, mon Dieu, mon Dieu!" groaned Madame Garcia, rocking her guinea-blue-clad self to and fro.

Mr. Baptiste picked up his non-descript head-cover and walked out through the brick-reddened alley, talking excitedly to himself. Madame Garcia called after him to know if he did not want his luncheon, but he shook his head and passed on.

Down on the levee it was even as Mr. Baptiste had said. The 'long-shore-men, the cotton-yardmen, and the stevedores had gone out on a strike. The levee lay hot and unsheltered under the glare of a noonday sun. The turgid Mississippi scarce seemed to flow, but gave forth a brazen gleam from its yellow bosom. Great vessels lay against the wharf, silent and unpopulated. Excited groups of men clustered here and there among bales of uncompressed cotton, lying about in disorderly profusion. Cargoes of molasses and sugar

---

[2]*Langniappe* is a Creole American term for the New Orleans custom of grocers' giving favors of sugar, spice, or candy to customers for each purchase.

[3]French: miseries; an equivalent English expression might be "Oh, woe is me."
[4]French: the ships (*vaisseaux*).

gave out a sticky sweet smell, and now and then the fierce rays of the sun would kindle tiny blazes in the cotton and splinter-mixed dust underfoot.

Mr. Baptiste wandered in and out among the groups of men, exchanging a friendly salutation here and there. He looked the picture of woe-begone misery.

"Hello, Mr. Baptiste," cried a big, brawny Irishman, "sure an' you look, as if you was about to be hanged."

"Ah, mon Dieu," said Mr. Baptiste, "dose fruit ship be ruined fo' dees strik'."

"Damn the fruit!" cheerily replied the Irishman, artistically disposing of a mouthful of tobacco juice. "It ain't the fruit we care about, it's the cotton."

"Hear! hear!" cried a dozen lusty comrades.

Mr. Baptiste shook his head and moved sorrowfully away.

"Hey, by howly St. Patrick, here's that little fruit-eater!" called the centre of another group of strikers perched on cotton-bales.

"Hello! Where—" began a second; but the leader suddenly held up his hand for silence, and the men listened eagerly.

It might not have been a sound, for the levee lay quiet and the mules on the cotton-drays dozed languidly, their ears pitched at varying acute angles. But the practised ears of the men heard a familiar sound stealing up over the heated stillness.

"Oh—ho—ho—humph—humph—humph—ho—ho—ho—oh—oh—humph!"

Then the faint rattle of chains, and the steady thump of a machine pounding.

If ever you go on the levee you'll know that sound, the rhythmic song of the stevedores heaving cotton-bales, and the steady thump, thump, of the machine compressing them within the hold of the ship.

Finnegan, the leader, who had held up his hand for silence, uttered an oath.

"Scabs! Men, come on!"

There was no need for a further invitation. The men rose in sullen wrath and went down the levee, the crowd gathering in numbers as it passed along. Mr. Baptiste followed in its wake, now and then sighing a mournful protest which was lost in the roar of the men.

"Scabs!" Finnegan had said; and the word was passed along, until it seemed that the half of the second District knew and had risen to investigate.

"Oh—ho—ho—humph—humph—humph—oh—ho—ho—oh—o—o—humph!"

The rhythmic chorus sounded nearer, and the cause manifested itself when the curve of the levee above the French Market was passed. There rose a White Star steamer, insolently settling itself to the water as each consignment of cotton bales was compressed into her hold.

"Niggers!" roared Finnegan wrathily.

"Niggers! niggers! Kill'em, scabs! chorused the crowd.

With muscles standing out like cables through their blue cotton shirts, and sweat rolling from glossy black skins, the Negro stevedores were at work steadily labouring at the cotton, with the rhythmic song swinging its cadence in the hot air. The roar of the crowd caused the men to look up with momentary apprehension, but at the overseer's reassuring word they bent back to work.

Finnegan was a Titan. With livid face and bursting veins he ran into the street facing the French Market, and uprooted a huge block of paving stone. Staggering under its weight, he rushed back to the ship, and with one mighty effort hurled it into the hold.

The delicate poles of the costly machine tottered in the air, then fell forward with a crash as the whole iron framework in the hold collapsed.

"Damn ye," shouted Finnegan, "now yez can pack yer cotton!"

The crowd's cheers at this changed to howls, as the Negroes, infuriated at their loss, for those costly machines belong to the labourers and not to the ship-owners, turned upon the mob and began to throw brickbats, pieces of iron, chunks of wood, anything that came to hand. It was pandemonium turned loose over a turgid stream, with a malarial sun to heat the passions to fever point.

Mr. Baptiste had taken refuge behind a bread-stall on the outside of the market. He had taken off his cap, and was weakly cheering the Negroes on.

"Bravo!" cheered Mr. Baptiste.

"Will yez look at that damned fruit-eatin' Frinchman!" howled McMahon. "Cheerin' the niggers, are you?" and he let fly a brickbat in the direction of the bread-stall.

"Oh, mon Dieu, mon Dieu!" wailed the bread-woman.

Mr. Baptiste lay very still, with a great ugly gash in his wrinkled brown temple. Fishmen and vegetable marchands gathered around him in a quick, sympathetic mass. The individual, the concrete bit of helpless humanity, had more interest for them than the vast, vague fighting mob beyond.

The noon-hour pealed from the brazen throats of many bells, and the numerous hoarse whistles of the steamboats called the unheeded luncheon-time to the levee workers. The war waged furiously, and groans of the wounded mingled with curses and roars from the combatants.

"Killed instantly," said the surgeon, carefully lifting Mr. Baptiste into the ambulance.

Tramp, tramp, tramp, sounded the milita steadily marching down Decatur Street.

"Whist! do yez hear!" shouted Finnegan; and the conflict had ceased ere the yellow river could reflect the sun from the polished bayonets.

You remember, of course, how long the strike lasted, and how many battles were fought and lives lost before the final adjustment of affairs. It was a fearsome war, and many forgot afterwards whose was the first life lost in the struggle,—poor little Mr. Baptiste's, whose body lay at the Morgue unclaimed for days before it was finally dropped unnamed into Potter's Field.

1899

GRACE KING
1852–1932

Grace King called herself a "southern woman of letters." Persistent assumptions about southern women might suggest that she was a living oxymoron. However, King's life and work have offered recent critics the opportunity to tease out some of the enormous complexities of privilege and oppression in the American South.

Robert Bush's anthology (1973) and biography (1983) have brought recognition to Grace King after decades of oblivion. Bush identifies King's as "the patrician voice" of the post–Civil War South, a voice that spoke for southern tradition against Reconstruction's devastation. Yet her work is polyvocal. She wrote, most crucially, as a woman in a patriarchal literary establishment, a fact that contradicted the very conventions of race, class, and language that she otherwise represented. As a woman whose most honest relationships were with other women, she both manipulated and criticized men's power. As a woman writer, she refused to "just rip the story open and insert a love story!" as advised by Thomas Nelson Page. As a white woman, she wrote about blacks from conflicting positions of racism and identification. She experienced poverty after the Civil War when her family moved to a working-class neighborhood in New Orleans, yet she never identified herself as other than patrician. She defended the South yet befriended writers and feminists in the North. And as a bilingual Protestant writer, equally fluent in French and English, she wrote from a position of "other" about the Roman Catholic Creoles. Thus, though frequently indirectly and perhaps unwittingly, she challenged the very tradition for which she spoke. What difference, if any, such indirect challenges make to a dominant ideology is one of the questions raised by her work.

Grace King was born in New Orleans in 1852. She spent most of her life in New Orleans. After the war, her father slowly rebuilt his law practice; it was a great victory for the King children when, in middle age, they were able in 1904 to own a house that fit the family image. King never married; she lived with her (also unmarried) sisters and traveled widely and independently after gaining fame as a writer.

In 1885 King wrote her first story, "Monsieur Motte," which appeared in the *New Princeton Review*. She wrote it in a state of pique at the popularity of George Washington Cable's representations of New Orleans, particularly his sympathetic portrayals of the oppression of blacks. When Richard Watson Gilder, editor of *Century*, asked her, "Why do not some of you write better?" she sat down to write a story about a black woman's devotion to her young white mistress, suggesting the traditional southern view of "good darkies." Yet she also wrote about the agony of Marcelite's internalized racism. The popularity of "Monsieur Motte" led her to complete three more sections and make it into a novel. The social connections King made in New Orleans with visiting members of the northern literary establishment such as Julia Ward Howe, Richard Watson Gilder, and Charles Dudley Warner gave her a professional entrée. Visiting the enclave of writers in Hartford, Connecticut, she became Olivia Clemens's confidante and befriended the feminist Isabella Hooker. In Paris she befriended Madame Blanc (who published as "Th. Bentzon"), a pupil of George Sand. Her work as well as her person circulated nationally and internationally.

Early in her career King focused on short fiction, of which one story is included here. "The Little Convent Girl" appeared in *Balcony Stories*, a collection that took its title from the habit of New Orleans women to sit on their balconies and tell tales. "The Little Convent Girl" is a good example of the ways in which questions of gender and race become entwined in the South with issues of identity. After publishing another collection of stories, *Tales of a Time and Place*, King moved next to writing histories, appropriating a traditionally public, "masculine" genre for *New Orleans: The Place and the People* and *Stories from Louisiana History*. During the teens, she returned to fiction; she spent years composing what some consider her masterpiece, *The Pleasant Ways of St. Medard*. A "novel" set during Reconstruction, it is arguably an early modernist text in its experimental structure. King's last novel, *La Dame de Sainte Hermine*, appeared in 1924; her autobiography, *Memories of a Southern Woman of Letters*, appeared in the year of her death, 1932.

Anne Jones
University of Florida

PRIMARY WORKS

Monsieur Motte, 1888; *Tales of a Time and Place*, 1892; *Balcony Stories*, 1893; *New Orleans: The Place and the People*, 1895; *Stories from Louisiana History*, 1905; *The Pleasant Ways of St. Medard*, 1916; *La Dame de Sainte Hermine*, 1924; *Memories of a Southern Woman of Letters*, 1932; *Grace King of New Orleans: A Selection of Her Writings*, ed. Robert Bush, 1973.

The Little Convent Girl

She was coming down on the boat from Cincinnati, the little convent girl. Two sisters had brought her aboard. They gave her in charge of the captain, got her a state-room, saw that the new little trunk was put in it, hung the new little satchel up on the wall, showed her how to bolt the door at night, shook hands with her for good-by (good-bys have really no significance for sisters), and left her there. After a while the bells all rang, and the boat, in the awkward elephantine fashion of boats, got into midstream. The chambermaid found her sitting on the chair in the state-room where the sisters had left her, and showed her how to sit on a chair in the saloon. And there she sat until the captain came and hunted her up for supper. She could not do anything of herself; she had to be initiated into everything by some one else.

She was known on the boat only as "the little convent girl." Her name, of course, was registered in the clerk's office, but on a steamboat no one thinks of consulting the clerk's ledger. It is always the little widow, the fat madam, the tall colonel, the parson, etc. The captain, who pronounced by the letter, always called her the little con-*vent* girl. She was the beau-ideal of the little convent girl. She never raised her eyes except when spoken to. Of course she never spoke first, even to the chambermaid, and when she did speak it was in the wee, shy, furtive voice one might imagine a just-budding violet to have; and she walked with such soft, easy, carefully calculated steps that one naturally felt the penalties that must have secured them—penalties dictated by a black code of deportment.

She was dressed in deep mourning. Her black straw hat was trimmed with stiff new crape, and her stiff new bombazine dress had crape collar and cuffs. She wore her hair in two long plaits fastened around her head tight and fast. Her hair had a strong inclination to curl, but that had been taken out of it as austerely as the noise out of her footfalls. Her hair was as black as her dress; her eyes, when one saw them, seemed blacker than either, on account of the bluishness of the white surrounding the pupil. Her eyelashes were almost as thick as the black veil which the sisters had fastened around her hat with an extra pin the very last thing before leaving. She had a round little face, and a tiny pointed chin; her mouth was slightly protuberant from the teeth, over which she tried to keep her lips well shut, the effort giving them a pathetic little forced expression. Her complexion was sallow, a pale sallow, the complexion of a brunette bleached in darkened rooms. The only color about her was a blue taffeta ribbon from which a large silver medal of the Virgin hung over the place where a breastpin should have been. She was so little, so little, although she was eighteen, as the sisters told the captain; otherwise they would not have permitted her to travel all the way to New Orleans alone.

Unless the captain or the clerk remembered to fetch her out in front, she would sit all day in the cabin, in the same place, crocheting lace, her spool of thread and box of patterns in her lap, on the handkerchief spread to save her new dress. Never leaning back—oh, no! always straight and stiff, as if the conventual back board were there within call. She would eat only convent fare at first, notwithstanding the importunities of the waiters, and the jocularities of the captain, and particularly of the clerk. Every one knows the fund of humor possessed by a steamboat clerk, and what a field for display the table at meal-times affords. On Friday she fasted rigidly, and she never began to eat, nor finished, without a little Latin movement of the lips and a sign of the cross. And always at six o'clock of the evening she remembered the angelus, although there was no church bell to remind her of it.

She was in mourning for her father, the sisters told the captain, and she was going to New Orleans to her mother. She had not seen her mother since she was an infant, on account of some disagreement between the parents, in consequence of which the father had brought her to Cincinnati and placed her in the convent. There she had been for twelve years, only going to her father for vacations and holidays. So long as the father lived he would never let the child have any communication with her mother. Now that he was dead all that was changed, and the first thing the girl herself wanted to do was to go to her mother.

The mother superior had arranged it all with the mother of the girl, who was to come personally to the boat in New Orleans, and receive her child from the captain, presenting a letter from the mother superior, a fac-simile of which the sisters gave the captain.

It is a long voyage from Cincinnati to New Orleans, the rivers doing their best to make it interminable, embroidering themselves *ad libitum* all over the country. Every five miles, and sometimes oftener, the boat would stop to put off or take on freight, if not both. The little convent girl, sitting in the cabin, had her terrible frights at first from the hideous noises attend-ant on these landings—the whistles, the ringings of the bells, the running to and fro, the shouting. Every time she thought it was shipwreck, death, judgment, purgatory; and her sins! her sins! She would drop her crochet, and clutch her prayer-beads from her pocket, and relax the constraint over her lips, which would go to rattling off prayers with the velocity of a relaxed windlass. That was at first, before the captain took to fetching her out in front to see the boat make a landing. Then she got to liking it so much that she would stay all day just where the captain put her, going inside only for her meals. She forgot herself at times so much that she would draw her chair a little closer to the railing, and put up her veil, actually, to see better. No one ever usurped her place, quite in front, or intruded upon her either with word or look; for every one learned to know her shyness, and began to feel a personal interest in her, and all wanted the little convent girl to see everything that she possibly could.

And it was worth seeing—the balancing and *chasséeing* and waltzing of the cumbersome old boat to make a landing. It seemed to be always attended with the difficulty and the improbability of a new enterprise; and the relief when it did sidle up anywhere within rope's-throw of the spot aimed at! And the roustabout throwing the rope from the perilous end of the dangling gang-plank! And the dangling roustabouts hanging like drops of water from it—dropping sometimes twenty feet to the land, and not infrequently into the river itself. And then what a rolling of barrels, and shouldering of sacks, and singing of Jim Crow songs, and pacing of Jim Crow steps; and black skins glistening through torn shirts, and white teeth gleaming through red lips, and laughing, and talking and—bewildering! entrancing! Surely the little convent girl in her convent walls never dreamed of so much unpunished noise and movement in the world!

The first time she heard the mate—it must have been like the first time woman ever heard man—curse and swear, she turned pale, and ran quickly, quickly into the saloon, and—came out again? No, indeed! not with all the soul she had to save, and all the other sins on her conscience. She shook her head resolutely, and was not seen in her chair on deck again until the cap-tain not only reassured her, but guaranteed his reassurance. And after that, whenever the boat was about to make a landing, the mate would first glance up to the guards, and if the little convent girl were sitting there he would change his invective to sarcasm, and politely request the colored gentlemen not to hurry themselves—on no account whatever; to take their time about shoving out the plank; to send the rope ashore by post office—write him when it got there; begging them not to strain their backs; calling them mister, colonel, major, general, prince, and your royal highness, which was vastly amusing. At night, however, or when the little convent girl was not there, language flowed in its natural curve, the mate swearing like a pagan to make up for lost time.

The captain forgot himself one day: it was when the boat ran aground in the most unexpected manner and place, and he went to work to express his opinion, as only steamboat captains can, of the pilot, mate, engineer, crew, boat, river, country, and the world in general, ringing the bell, first to back, then to head, shouting himself hoarser than his own whistle—when he chanced to see the little black figure hurrying through the chaos on the deck; and the captain stuck as fast aground in midstream as the boat had done.

In the evening the little convent girl would be taken on the upper deck, and there was such confusion, going up, in keeping the black skirts down over the stiff white petticoats; and, coming down, such blushing when suspicion would cross the un-prepared face that a rim of white stocking might be visible; and the thin feet, laced so tightly in the glossy new leather boots, would cling to each successive round as if they could never, never make another venture; and then one boot would (there is but that word) hesitate out, and feel and feel around, and have such a pause of helpless agony as if indeed the next step must have been wilfully removed, or was nowhere to be found on the wide, wide earth.

It was a miracle that the pilot ever got her up into the pilot-house; but pilots have a lonely time, and do not hesitate even at miracles when there is a chance for company. He would place a box for her to climb to the tall bench behind the wheel, and he would arrange the cushions, and open a window here to let in air, and shut one there to cut off a draft, as if there could be no tenderer consideration in life for him than her comfort. And he would talk of the river to her, explain the chart, pointing out eddies, whirlpools, shoals, depths, new beds, old beds, cut-offs, caving banks, and making banks, as exquisitely and respectfully as if she had been the River Commission.

It was his opinion that there was as great a river as the Mississippi flowing directly under it—an underself of a river, as much a counterpart of the other as the second story of a house is of the first; in fact, he said they were navigating through the upper story. Whirlpools were holes in the floor of the upper river, so to speak; eddies were rifts and cracks. And deep under the earth, hurrying toward the subterranean stream, were other streams, small and great, but all deep, hurrying to and from that great mother-stream underneath, just as the small and great overground streams hurry to and from their mother Mississippi. It was almost more than the little convent girl could take in: at least such was the expression of her eyes; for they opened as all eyes have to open at pilot stories. And he knew as much of astronomy as he did of hydrology, could call the stars by name, and define the shapes of the constellations; and she, who had studied astronomy at the convent, was charmed to find that it was all true what she had learned.

It was in the pilot-house, one night, that she forgot herself for the first time in her life, and stayed up until after nine o'clock at night. Although she appeared almost intoxicated at the wild pleasure, she was immediately overwhelmed at the wickedness of it, and observed much more rigidity of conduct thereafter. The engineer, the boiler-men, the firemen, the stokers, they all knew when the little convent girl was up in the pilot-house: the speaking-tube became so mild and gentle.

With all the delays of river and boat, however, there is an end to the journey from Cincinnati to New Orleans. The latter city, which at one time to the impatient seemed at the terminus of the never, began, all of a sudden, one day to make its nearingness felt; and from that period every other interest paled before the interest in the imminence of arrival into port, and the whole boat was seized with a panic of preparation, the little convent girl with the others. Although so immaculate was she in person and effects that she might have been struck with a landing, as some good people might be struck with death, at any moment without fear of results, her trunk was packed and repacked, her satchel arranged and rearranged, and, the last day, her hair was brushed and plaited and smoothed over and over again until the very last glimmer of a curl disappeared. Her dress was whisked, as if for microscopic inspection; her face was washed; and her finger-nails were scrubbed with the hard convent nail-brush, until the disciplined little tips ached with a pristine soreness. And still there were hours to wait, and still the boat added up delays. But she arrived at last, after all, with not more than the usual and expected difference between the actual and the advertised time of arrival.

There was extra blowing and extra ringing, shouting, commanding, rushing up the gangway and rushing down the gangway. The clerks, sitting behind tables on the first deck, were plied, in the twinkling of an eye, with estimates, receipts, charges, countercharges, claims, reclaims, demands, questions, accusations, threats, all at topmost voices. None but steamboat clerks could have stood it. And there were throngs composed of individuals every one of whom wanted to see the captain first and at once; and those who could not get to him shouted over the heads of the others; and as usual he lost his temper and politeness, and began to do what he termed "hustle."

"Captain! Captain!" a voice called him to where a hand plucked his sleeve, and a letter was thrust toward him. "The cross, and the name of the convent." He recognized the envelop of the mother superior. He read the duplicate of the letter given by the sisters. He looked at the woman—the mother—casually, then again and again.

The little convent girl saw him coming, leading some one toward her. She rose. The captain took her hand first, before the other greeting. "Good-by, my dear," he said. He tried to add something else, but seemed undetermined what. "Be a good little girl—" It was evidently all he could think of. Nodding to the woman behind him, he turned on his heel, and left.

One of the deck-hands was sent to fetch her trunk. He walked out behind them, through the cabin, and the crowd on deck, down the stairs, and out the gangway. The little convent girl and her mother went with hands tightly clasped. She did not turn her eyes to the right or left, or once (what all passengers do) look backward at the boat which, however slowly, had carried her surely over dangers that she wot not of. All looked at her as she passed. All wanted to say good-by to the little convent girl, to see the mother who had been deprived of her so long. Some expressed surprise in a whistle; some in other ways. All exclaimed audibly, or to themselves, "Colored!"

It takes about a month to make the round trip from New Orleans to Cincinnati and back, counting five days' stoppage in New Orleans. It was a month to a day when the steamboat came puffing and blowing up to the wharf again, like a stout dowager after too long a walk; and the same scene of confusion was enacted, as it had been enacted twelve times a year at almost the same wharf for twenty years; and the same calm, a death calmness by contrast, followed as usual the next morning.

The decks were quiet and clean; one cargo had just been delivered, part of another stood ready on the levee to be shipped. The captain was there waiting for his business to begin, the clerk was in his office getting his books ready, the voice of the mate could be heard below, mustering the old crew out and a new crew in; for if steamboat crews have a single principle,—and there are those who deny them any,— it is never to ship twice in succession on the same boat. It was too early yet for any but roustabouts, marketers, and church-goers; so early that even the river was still partly mist-covered; only in places could the swift, dark current be seen rolling swiftly along.

"Captain!" A hand plucked at his elbow, as if not confident that the mere calling would secure attention. The captain turned. The mother of the little convent girl stood there, and she held the little convent girl by the hand. "I have brought her to see you," the woman said. "You were so kind—and she is so quiet, so still, all the time, I thought it would do her a pleasure."

She spoke with an accent, and with embarrassment; otherwise one would have said that she was bold and assured enough.

"She don't go nowhere, she don't do nothing but make her crochet and her prayers, so I thought I would bring her for a little visit of 'How d' ye do' to you."

There was, perhaps, some inflection in the woman's voice that might have made known, or at least awakened, the suspicion of some latent hope or intention, had the captain's ear been fine enough to detect it. There might have been something in the little convent girl's face, had his eye been more sensitive,—a trifle paler, maybe, the lips a little tighter drawn, the blue ribbon a shade faded. He may have noticed that, but—And the visit of "How d' ye do" came to an end.

They walked down the stairway, the woman in front, the little convent girl—her hand released to shake hands with the captain—following, across the bared deck, out to the gangway, to the middle of it. No one was looking, no one saw more than a flutter of white petticoats, a show of white stockings, as the little convent girl went under the water.

The roustabout dived, as the roustabouts always do, after the drowning, even at the risk of their good-for-nothing lives. The mate himself jumped overboard; but she had gone down in a whirlpool. Perhaps, as the pilot had told her whirlpools always did, it may have carried her through to the underground river, to that vast, hidden, dark Mississippi that flows beneath the one we see; for her body was never seen again.

1893

AFRICAN AMERICAN FOLKTALES

Folktales provide a radical illustration of the principle that fictions are not the fixed texts that printed pages imply but interactions between authors and audiences, who bring to the meeting their own social and individual experiences. The printed texts of the folktales that follow are themselves products of a complex network of interactions. Though the process of collection, publication, and now selection gives them the appearance of a fixed identity, they are actually only moments in a continuous process of invention, adaptation, and performance—cupfuls dipped out of a river.

What goes into a published folktale? The structural elements of folktales are traditional tale types and motifs widespread in world folklore and classified by folk-lorists. The motifs of African American folktales come from both African and European tradition. Over time, storytellers have selected and adapted them to reflect their own social experience. For example, in European variants of the popular tale "Dividing Souls," here represented by John Blackamore's individualized "Old Boss Wants into Heaven," the two watchers are typically a parson and a sexton, but in most African American variants, they are a crippled master and the slave who carries him. The motif of the dependent master frightened into running on his own two feet becomes a metaphor for the un-warranted economic dependency of white on black in slavery. Blackamore's highly developed and pointed version of this tale calls attention to another component of the folktale, the individual storyteller's insight and imagination.

An oral story also involves interaction between the storyteller and the audience. The printed story, however, is the product of a different interaction, that between the storyteller and the folklore collector, who is at least to some extent an outsider to the folk group. Conventions of how to represent the folk storytelling situation and acknowledge the role of the collector have changed over the years. Early folklore popularizers often embedded the tales in a fictional framework and retold them in heightened language. "Brer Coon Gets His Meat" provides an example of exaggerated dialect as well as the mimicry and music of folk delivery. Zora Neale Hurston's "John Calls on the Lord" seems to reflect collaboration between storyteller and collector; here John addresses "the Lord" in language that Hurston, the daughter of a black lay preacher, had heard all her life and repeated with relish in her fiction. In the 1930s, Federal Writers Project teams collecting the reminiscences of the last generation of former slaves attempted to portray accurately the relationship between informants and collectors by describing the communities they visited, identifying individual informants, and recording their own role in eliciting the stories. They set the standard that subsequent collectors, notably Richard M. Dorson, have developed.

We cannot be sure to what extent collectors rather than storytellers have determined the history of the African American folktale repertoire. There is little doubt that the animal tales were told during slavery. However, tales of the contest of wits between the black man and the white first appear in collections between 1915 and 1919, and only gradually develop in the 1930s and 1940s into the cycle of episodes in the perpetual battle between John the unsubmissive slave and his Old Marster. Whether former slaves withheld these stories for fifty years after Emancipation, or early collectors intent on animal stories failed to seek them out, or they developed in the twentieth century as a commentary on the perpetuation of inequality, we don't know. What the published record does show is that, while African American folk narrative comes out of slavery, it is not an artifact of the slave period but a living tradition. In the twentieth century, as the selections below reflect, African American folktales became increasingly politically pointed and were adapted to the rhythms and concerns of an increasingly urban folk. Perhaps the clearest testimony to the continuing vitality of African American folk narrative is its importance in the fiction of such writers as Charles Chesnutt, Zora Neale Hurston, Langston Hughes, Ralph Ellison, and Toni Morrison.

The tales in this section have been chosen to represent some of the most commonly collected tales and a variety of narrative styles and collection principles. For more tales (including genres such as ghost stories and preacher jokes not included here), see the collections from which these are taken.

Susan L. Blake
Lafayette College

PRIMARY WORKS

In addition to the sources identified in the notes to the tales, see Bruce Jackson, *"Get Your Ass in the Water and Swim like Me": Narrative Poetry from Black Oral Tradition,* 1974; Daryl Cumber Dance, *Shuckin' and Jivin': Folklore from Contemporary Black Americans,* 1978; Roger D. Abrahams, *Afro-American Folktales: Stories from Black Traditions in the New World,* 1985; Linda Goss and Marian E. Barnes, *Talk That Talk: An Anthology of African-American Storytelling,* 1989.

Animal Tales

When Brer Deer and Brer Terrapin Runned a Race[1]

Brer Deer and Brer Terrapin was a-courting of Mr. Coon's daughter. Brer Deer was a peart chap, and have the airs of the quality, no put-on bigoty ways; Brer Deer am a right sure 'nough gentleman, that he is. Well, old Brer

[1]Emma Backus, "Animal Tales from North Carolina," *Journal of American Folk-Lore* 11(1898):284–85.

Terrapin am a poor, slow, old man; all the creeters wonder how the gal can smile on hisself when Mr. Deer flying round her, but them what knows tells how, when old man Terrapin lay hisself out, he have a mighty taking way with the gals, and the gals in the old times mighty like the gals these here times, and ain't got no sense nohow.

Well, old man Coon he favor Brer Deer, and he powerful set again Brer Terrapin, and he fault him to the gals constant; but the more Brer Coon fault Brer Terrapin, the more the hard-headed gal giggle and cut her eye when Brer Terrapin come 'bout; and old Brer Coon, he just nigh 'bout out-done with her foolishness, and he say he gwine set down on the fooling.

So he say, Brer Coon did, how Brer Deer and Brer Terrapin shall run a seven-mile race, and the one what get there first shall surely have the gal, 'cause he feel that sure in he mind, Brer Coon do, that Brer Deer nat'rally bound to outrun poor old Brer Terrapin.

But I tell you, sah, when old Brer Terrapin pull he head in he house, and shut up all the doors, and just give himself to study, when he do that there way, the old man ain't just dozing away the time. Don't you mind, sah, he have a mighty bright eye, Brer Terrapin have, sah.

Well, Brer Terrapin, he say he run the race, if he can run in the water, 'cause he 'low he mighty slow on the foots. And Brer Deer and Brer Coon, they talk it over to theyselves, and they 'low Brer Deer mighty slow in the water, and so they set the race 'long the river bank. Brer Deer, he gwine run seven miles on the bank, and Brer Terrapin, he gwine run 'long the shore in the water, and he say every mile he gwine raise he head out the water and say, "Oho! here I is."

Den Brer Deer and Brer Coon laugh to burst theyselves, 'cause they lay out for Brer Terrapin done pass the first mile, Brer Deer done win the race.

Well, sah, Brer Terrapin he have six brothers, and he set one in the water every mile, and he set one in the water at the starting-place, and the old man, he set hisself in the water at the seven-mile post. O my, massa, dat old Brer Terrapin, he got a head on hisself, he surely have.

Well, Brer Coon and Brer Deer, they come down to the water, and they see Brer Terrapin out there in the water, an' Brer Coon, he place Brer Deer, and tell him hold on till he get hisself there, 'cause he bound to see the end of the race. So he get on the horse and whip up, and directly Brer Deer and Brer Terrapin start out, and when Brer Deer come to the first milestone he stick his head out the water, and he say, "Oho, here I is!" and Brer Deer, he just set to faster, 'cause he know Brer Terrapin mighty short-winded, but when he git to the two-mile post, sure 'nough, there Brer Terrapin stick he head out and say, "Oho, here I is!" and Brer Deer, he that astonished he nigh 'bout break down, but he set to and do he best, and when he come to the three-mile post, 'fore God if there ain't Brer Terrapin's head come out the water, and he just holler out, "Oho, here I is!"

But Brer Deer he push on, and every mile that there bodacious old Brer Terrapin. Well, when Brer Deer come a-puffing and a-blowing up to the last-most post, and Brer Coon set there on the horse, and just 'fore Brer Deer come up, if there ain't sure 'nough old Brer Terrapin, just where he done been waiting all the time, and just 'fore Brer Deer fotch round *the* bend, he just stick up he head and say, "Oho, Brer Deer, here I is for yourself!"

But Brer Terrapin never tell the gals 'bout his management, and how he get there that soon.

1898

Why Mr. Dog Runs Brer Rabbit[2]

One morning, Mr. Buzzard he say he stomach just hungry for some fish, and he tell Mrs. Buzzard he think he go down to the branch, and catch some for breakfast. So he take he basket, and he sail along till he come to the branch.

He fish right smart, and by sun up he have he basket plum full. But Mr. Buzzard am a powerful greedy man, and he say to hisself, he did, I just catch one more. But while he done gone for this last one, Brer Rabbit he came along, clipity, clipity, and when he see basket plum full of fine whitefish he stop, and he say, "I 'clare to goodness, the old woman just gwine on up to the cabin, 'cause they got nothing for to fry for breakfast. I wonder what she think of this yer fish," and so he put the basket on he head, Brer Rabbit did, and make off to the cabin.

Direc'ly he meet up with Mr. Dog, and he ax him where he been fishing that early in the day, and Brer Rabbit he say how he done sot on the log 'longside of the branch, and let he tail hang in the water and catch all the fish, and he done tell Mr. Dog, the old rascal did, that he tail mighty short for the work, but that Mr. Dog's tail just the right sort for fishing.

So Mr. Dog, he teeth just ache for them whitefish, and he go set on the log and hang he tail in the water, and it mighty cold for he tail, and the fish don't bite, but he mouth just set for them fish, and so he just sot dar, and it turn that cold that when he feel he gin up, sure's you born, Mr. Dog, he tail froze fast in the branch, and he call he chillens, and they come and break the ice.

And then, to be sure, he start off to settle Ole Brer Rabbit, and he get on he track and he run the poor ole man to beat all, and directly he sight him he run him round and round the woods and holler, "Hallelujah! hallelujah!" and the puppies come on behind, and they holler, "Glory! glory!" and they make such a fuss, all the creeters in the woods, they run to see what the matter. Well, sah, from that day, Mr. Dog he run Brer Rabbit, and when they just get gwine on the swing in the big woods, you can hear ole Ben dar just letting hisself out, "Hallelujah! hallelujah!" and them pups just gwine "Glory! glory!" and it surely am the sound what has the music dar, it surely has the music dar.

1899

[2]Emma Backus, "Tales of the Rabbit from Georgia Negroes," *Journal of American Folk-Lore* 12 (1899):112–13.

How Sandy Got His Meat[3]

Brer Rabbit an Brer Coon wuz fishermuns. Brer Rabbit fished fur fish an Brer Coon fished fur f-r-o-g-s.

Arter while de frogs all got so wile Brer Coon couldent ketch em, an he hadn't hab no meat to his house an de chilluns wuz hongry an de ole oman beat em ober de haid wid de broom.

Brer Coon felt mighty bad an he went off down de rode wid he head down wundering what he gwine do. Des den ole Brer Rabbit wuz er skippin down de rode an he seed Brer Coon wuz worried an throwed up his years an say-ed:

"Mornin, Brer Coon."

"Mornin, Brer Rabbit."

"How is yer copperrosity segashuatin, Brer Coon?"

"Porely, Brer Rabbit, porely. De frogs haz all got so wile I caint ketch em an I aint got no meat to my house an de ole oman is mad an de chilluns hongry. Brer Rabbit, I'se got to hab help. Sumthin' haz got to be dun."

Old Brer Rabbit look away crost de ruver long time; den he scratch hiz year wid his hind foot, an say:

"I'll tole ye whut we do Brer Coon. We'll git eber one of dem frogs. You go down on de san bar an lie down an play des lack you wuz d-a-i-d. Don't yer mobe. Be jes as still, jest lack you wuz d-a-i-d."

Ole Brer Coon mosied on down to de ruver. De frogs hear-ed em er comin an de ole big frog say-ed:

"Yer better look er roun. Yer better look er roun. Yer better look er round."

Nother ole frog say-ed:

"Knee deep, knee deep, knee deep."

An "ker-chug" all de frogs went in de water.

But Ole Brer Coon lide down on de san an stretched out jest lack he wuz d-a-i-d. De flies got all ober em, but he never moobe. De sun shine hot, but he never moobe; he lie still jest lack he wuz d-a-i-d.

Drectly Ole Brer Rabbit cum er runnin tru de woods an out on de san bar an put his years up high an hollered out:

"Hay, de Ole Coon is d-a-i-d."

De ole big frog out in de ruver say-ed:

"I don't bleve it, I don't bleve it, I don't bleve it." And all de littul frogs roun de edge say-ed:

"I don't bleve it, I don't bleve it, I don't bleve it."

But de ole coon play jes lack he's d-a-i-d an all de frogs cum up out of de ruver an set er roun whare de ole coon lay.

Jes den Brer Rabbit wink his eye an say-ed:

"I'll tell yer what I'de do, Brer Frogs. I'de berry Old Sandy, berry em so deep he never could scratch out."

[3]A.W. Eddins, in *Round the Levee*, ed. Stith Thompson, Publications of the Texas Folk- Lore Society 1 (Austin: Texas Folk-Lore Society, 1916):47–49.

Den all de frogs gun to dig out de san, dig out de san from under de ole coon. When de had dug er great deep hole wid de ole coon in de middle of it, de frogs all got tired an de ole frog say-ed:

"Deep er nough,—deep er nough,—deep er nough."

An all de littul frogs say-ed:

"Deep er nough,—deep er nough,—deep er nough."

Ole Brer Rabbit was er takin er littul nap in der sun, and he woke up an say-ed:

"Kin you jump out?"

De ole big frog look up to de top of de hole an say-ed:

"Yes I kin. Yes I kin. Yes I kin."

An de littul frogs say-ed:

"Yes I kin. Yes I kin. Yes I kin."

Ole Brer Rabbit tole em:

"Dig it deeper."

Den all de frogs went to wuk an dug er great deep hole way down inside de san wid Old Brer Coon right in de middle jest lack he wuz d-a-i-d. De frogs wuz er gittin putty tired an de ole big frog sung out loud:—

"Deep er nough. Deep er nough. Deep er nough."

An all de littul frogs sung out too:—

"Deep er nough. Deep er nough. Deep er nough."

An Ole Brer Rabbit woke up er gin an axed em:—

"Kin yer jump out?"

"I bleve I kin. I bleve I kin. I bleve I kin."

Ole Brer Rabbit look down in de hole agin an say-ed:—

"Dig dat hole deeper."

Den all de frogs gin to wuk throwin out san, throwin out san, clear till most sun down and dey had er great deep hole way, way down in de san, wid de ole coon layin right in de middle. De frogs wuz plum clean tired out and de ole big frog say-ed:—

"Deep er nough. Deep er nough. Deep er nough."

An all de littul frogs say-ed:—

"Deep er nough. Deep er nough. Deep er nough."

Ole Brer Rabbit peeped down in de hole agin and say:—

"Kin yer jump out?"

An de ole frog say:—

"No I caint. No I caint. No I caint."

An all de littul frogs say:—

"No I caint. No I caint. No I caint."

Den Ole Brer Rabbit jump up right quick an holler out:—

"RISE UP SANDY AN GIT YOUR MEAT."

An Brer Coon had meat fer sepper dat nite.

1916

Who Ate Up the Butter?[4]

All the animals was farming a crop together. And they bought a pound of butter— they was in cahoots, all chipped in equally. So the next day they all goes to the field to work. All at once Brother Rabbit says, "Heya." All of them quits working, ask, "What is it, Brother Rabbit?"

"It's my wife, she's calling me, I ain't got time to fool with her." All of them together say, "Well you better go on, Brother Rabbit, and see what it is she wants." Off he goes to the house to see what his wife wants.

Twenty minutes he was back. They say, "What did your wife want, Brother Rabbit?" "Well she got a new baby up there." So they slapped Brother Rabbit on the back, said "Good, good. You named him yet?" "Yes, I named him Quarter Gone."

So they begin to work again. About thirty minutes more Brother Rabbit begins to holler again, "What do you want?" They say, "What was that, who you talking to?" "That was my wife, didn't you hear her calling?" "Well, you better go see what she wants." The Rabbit said, "I'm working, I haven't got time to fool with her." They said, "You'd better go on, Brother Rabbit."

So he goes on to the house to see what she wants. In about twenty more minutes he was back again. "What's the trouble this time, Brother Rabbit, what did your wife want?" "Same thing, another baby." They all said, "Good, good, what was it?" Said, "It was a boy." "What did you name him?" Said, "Oh, Half Gone." Said, "That sure is a pretty name." So he goes back hard to work.

After a while he hollers again, "Oooh, I ain't studying about you." They said, "What you hollering about, what you studying about, we ain't seed no one. Who was it?" "It was my wife." (She'd been calling him all morning.) "Well, why don't you go on Brother Rabbit, and see what she wants." "No, we'll never get nothing done if I just keep running to the house; no, I'm not going." The animals said, "That's all right, Brother Rabbit, it's only a little time, we don't mind, go on."

So Brother Rabbit goes on to the house. Well, he was there about forty minutes this time. "Brother Rabbit, what was your trouble this time?" "My wife had twins." "Good, good, good." They just rejoiced over it. "You'll have to set 'em up when we go to town this time." He said, "Well, the reason I was gone so long I was studying what to name those two twins so it would sound nearly alike." They asked, "What did you name them, Brother Rabbit?" They'd never heard tell of twins before, or of the rabbit having four. "Three Quarters Gone and All Gone." They insist on "Let's go see 'em." He says, "Well, we'll just work on till noon, then we'll have plenty of time, no need to hurry."

So he sent Brother Terrapin into the house to get some water. Well, he drank the water. Then he wanted a match, he wanted a smoke bad. So he said to Brother Deer, "Brother Terrapin is too slow, you run up there and bring those matches." Told Brother Fox, "You run on and drive the horses

[4]Told by J. D. Suggs, in Richard M. Dorson, *American Negro Folktales* (Greenwich, CT: Fawcett, 1967):68–71. Dorson collected the tales in this volume in Arkansas, Mississippi, and Michigan in 1952 and 1953.

to the barn, we think we're going to plow this evening. We'll be home 'gainst you get there." So he taken off to drive the horses. When Brother Fox got out of sight good, Brother Rabbit said, "Well, we'll go." So they had to go slow, 'cause Brother Terrapin poked along, and they all walked together with him. When they got to the house, Brother Fox was sitting on the front porch waiting for them. He said, "Mens, I sure is hungry, let's wash up and get in the kitchen."

In a few seconds, they was all washed up and in the kitchen they'd go. Brother Rabbit was the first one in there; he says, "Well, where's the butter? The butter's all gone!" *(Loud)* The first one they accused was Brother Rabbit. "Remember when he came by the house to see about his wife and them babies?"

He says, "No, I didn't even think about the butter. Now listen, you remember more than me come to the house, Brother Terrapin and Brother Deer and Brother Fox, and I'd be afraid to 'cuse them, for I know I didn't and I wouldn't say they did. But I got a plan and we can soon find out who done it, I or him or whom."

They all agreed to hear about Brother Rabbit's plan—they was confused and mad and forgot about being hungry, and said, "His plan always did work."

Now Brother Rabbit told them, "We'll make a big log heap and set fire to it, and run and jump, and the one that falls in it, he ate the butter." So they made the log heap and put the fire in it. The fire begins to burn and smoke, smoke and burn. "All right, we're ready to jump."

They were all lined up. Brother Deer taken the first jump. Brother Rabbit said, "Well, Brother Terrapin, guess I better take the next one." He done jump. Terrapin was waiting for the wind to turn. He was so short he knew he couldn't jump far. The wind started blowing the smoke down to the ground, on both sides of the log heap. So Brother Terrapin said, "Well, I guess it's my jump." He ran around the heap and turned somersault on the other side. Brother Rabbit and Brother Deer were looking way up in the smoke to see the others coming over; they weren't looking low, and thought he had jumped over. They said, "Well, Brother Terrapin he made it."

So all the rest of them they jumped it clear, Brother Fox, and Brother Bear, and that made everybody on the other side. "Well, Brother Deer, it's your jump again." So the three they jump over again, and only Brother Bear and Brother Terrapin is left. Brother Terrapin says, "Step here, Brother Bear, before you jump." Said, "I hear you can jump high across that fire, cross your legs and pull your teat out and show it to 'em (his back teat), stop in space, and then jump from there onto the other side. I don't know if you can, I only heard it." Brother Bear says, "O, yes I can." So Brother Terrapin was glad he was making that deal, for he didn't know if the smoke would be in his favor going back.

The Bear says, "Stand back, Mr. Terrapin, let me jump first this time, you can see this." *(Deep, gruff)* The Bear backed further, further than ever to get speed up to stop and cross his legs. He calls out, "Here goes Brother Bear," and takes off. In the middle he tries to cross his leg, and down he went, into the fire. Brother Rabbit said, "Push the fire on him, push the fire on him."

(Excited) "He's the one that eat the butter." So all of them go to the end, and begin to shove the chunks on Brother Bear. They all give Brother Rabbit credit for being the smart one to find the guilty fellow what eat the butter.

None of them ever thought Brother Bear was the only one never went to the house. Just like in a law case many men are convicted from showing evidence against them where there isn't any. They get a smart lawyer to show you was there when you wasn't there at all, trap you with his questions, get you convicted and behind the bars. Then they say, "He's a smart lawyer."

1967

Fox and Rabbit in the Well[5]

The Fox was after the Rabbit to kill him. So Ber Fox was about to catch Brother Rabbit. There was a well down in the flat between the two hills. It had two water buckets, one on each end of the rope. When you let one down, you'd be pulling one bucket of water up. Brother Rabbit jumped in the bucket was up. Down he went, the other bucket come up. The moon was shining right in the well. It looked like a round hoop of cheese. Ber Rabbit didn't know how he was goin' git back up after he was down there. He commenced hollering for Mr. Fox to come here quick.

Mr. Fox goes up to the well and looked down in there, says "What you want, Brother Rabbit?"

"See this big old hoop of cheese I got down in here?"

Says "Man, it sure is good."

Ber Fox says, "How did you get down in there?"

Says "Git in that bucket up there," says "That's the way I come down." Mr. Fox jumped in that bucket was up, Brother Rabbit jumped in the one was down. Down goes Mr. Fox, up come Brother Rabbit. Brother Rabbit passed Brother Fox. "Hey Brother Fox, this the way the world goes, some going and some coming."

My sister'd been watching round that well and she left a bar of soap. I stepped on it, and I skated on back home.[6]

1967

The Signifying Monkey[7]

Deep down in the jungle so they say
There's a signifying motherfucker down the way.
There hadn't been no disturbin' in the jungle for quite a bit,

---

[5]Suggs, Dorson 97–98.

[6]A formulaic closing.

[7]Roger D. Abrahams, *Deep Down in the Jungle: Negro Narrative Folklore from the Streets of Philadelphia* (Hatboro, PA: Folklore Associates, 1964): 149–51. This variant of "The Signifying Monkey"

is a toast, a narrative poem improvised in performance from a store of themes, conventions, and formulas. Other common toast subjects are the badman Stackolee and the sinking of the Titanic.

For up jumped the monkey in the tree one day and laughed, "I guess I'll start some shit." 5
Now the lion come through the jungle one peaceful day,
When the signifying monkey stopped him and this what he started to say.
He said, "Mr. Lion," he said, "A bad-assed motherfucker down your way." 10
He said, "Yeah! The way he talks about your folks is a certain shame.
I even heard him curse when he mentioned your grandmother's name."
The lion's tail shot back like a forty-four, 15
When he went down the jungle in all uproar.
He was pushing over mountains, knocking down trees.
In the middle of a pass he met an ape.
He said, "I ought to beat your ass just to get in shape."
He met the elephant in the shade of a tree. 20
"Come on long-eared motherfucker, it's gonna be you and me."
Now the elephant looked up out the corner of his eye,
Said, "Go on bird-shit, fight somebody your size."
Then the lion jumped back and made a hell of a pass.
The elephant side-stepped and kicked him dead on his ass. 25
Now he knocked in his teeth, fucked-up his eye,
Kicked in his ribs, tied-up his face,
Tied his tail in knots, stretched his tail out of place.
Now they fought all that night, half the next day.
I'll be damned if I can see how the lion got away. 30
When they was fussing and fighting, lion came back through the jungle more dead than alive,
When the monkey started some more of that signifying jive.
He said, "Damn, Mr. Lion, you went through here yesterday, the jungle rung.
Now you come back today, damn near hung." 35
He said, "Now you come by here when me and my wife trying to get a little bit,
T' tell me that 'I rule' shit."
He said, "Shut up, motherfucker, you better not roar 40
'Cause I'll come down there and kick your ass some more."
The monkey started getting panicked and jumped up and down,
When his feet slipped and his ass hit the ground.
Like a bolt of lightning, a stripe of white heat,
The lion was on the monkey with all four feet. 45
The monkey looked up with a tear in his eyes,
He said, "Please, Mr. Lion, I apologize."
He said, "You lemme get my head out the sand
Ass out the grass, I'll fight you like a natural man."

The lion jumped back and squared for a fight.   50
The motherfucking monkey jumped clear out of sight.
He said, "Yeah, you had me down, you had me last,
But you left me free, now you can still kiss my ass."
Again he started getting panicked and jumping up and down.
His feet slipped and his ass hit the ground.   55
Like a bolt of lightning, stripe of white heat,
Once more the lion was on the monkey with all four feet.
Monkey looked up again with tears in his eyes.
He said, "Please, Mr. Lion, I apologize."
Lion said, "Ain't gonna be no apologizing.   60
I'ma put an end to his motherfucking signifying."
Now when you go through the jungle, there's a tombstone so they
    say,
"Here the Signifying Monkey lay,
Who got kicked in the nose, fucked-up in the eyes,   65
Stomped in the ribs, kicked in the face,
Drove backwards to his ass-hole, knocked his neck out of place."
That's what I say.

"Kid"
1964

Memories of Slavery

Malitis[1]

... I remember Mammy told me about one master who almost starved his slaves. Mighty stingy, I reckon he was.

Some of them slaves was so poorly thin they ribs would kinda rustle against each other like corn stalks a-drying in the hot winds. But they gets even one hog-killing time, and it was funny, too, Mammy said.

They was seven hogs, fat and ready for fall hog-killing time. Just the day before Old Master told off they was to be killed, something happened to all them porkers. One of the field boys found them and come a-telling the master: "The hogs is all died, now they won't be any meats for the winter."

When the master gets to where at the hogs is laying, they's a lot of Negroes standing round looking sorrow-eyed at the wasted meat. The master asks: "What's the illness with 'em?"

"Malitis," they tells him, and they acts like they don't want to touch the hogs. Master says to dress them anyway for they ain't no more meat on the place.

---

[1]Told by Mrs. Josie Jordan, in B. A. Botkin, ed., *Lay My Burden Down: A Folk History of Slavery* (Chicago: U of Chicago P, 1945):4–5.
This volume contains excerpts from the Slave Narrative Collection of the Federal Writers' Project, compiled during the 1930s.

He says to keep all the meat for the slave families, but that's because he's afraid to eat it hisself account of the hogs' got malitis.

"Don't you all know what is malitis?" Mammy would ask the children when she was telling of the seven fat hogs and seventy lean slaves. And she would laugh, remembering how they fooled Old Master so's to get all them good meats.

"One of the strongest Negroes got up early in the morning," Mammy would explain, "long 'fore the rising horn called the slaves from their cabins. He skitted to the hog pen with a heavy mallet in his hand. When he tapped Mister Hog 'tween the eyes with that mallet, 'malitis' set in mighty quick, but it was a uncommon 'disease,' even with hungry Negroes around all the time."

1945

The Flying Africans[2]

A.

Prince [Sneed] proved to be an interesting talker, much of his knowledge having been gleaned from conversations by the fireside with his grandfather. The following narrative was still fresh in his memory:

"Muh gran say ole man Waldburg down on St. Catherine own some slabes wut wuzn climatize an he wuk um hahd an one day dey wuz hoein in duh fiel an duh dribuh come out an two ub um wuz unuh a tree in duh shade, an duh hoes wuz wukin by demsef. Duh dribuh say 'Wut dis?' an dey say, 'Kum buba yali kum buba tambe, Kum kunka yali kum kunka tambe,' quick like. Den dey rise off duh groun an fly away. Nobody ebuh see um no mo. Some say dey fly back tuh Africa. Muh gran see dat wid he own eye."

B.

We asked the old man [Wallace Quatermain] if he remembered any slaves that were real Africans.

"Sho I membuhs lots ub um. Ain I sees plenty ub um? I membuhs one boatload uh seben aw eight wut come down frum Savannah. Dat wuz jis a lill befo duh waw. Robbie McQueen wuz African an Katie an ole man Jacob King, dey's all African. I membuhs um all. Ole man King he lib till he ole, lib till I hep bury um. But yuh caahn unduhstan much wut deze people say. Dey caahn unduhstan yo talk an you caahn unduhstan dey talk. Dey go 'quack, quack, quack,' jis as fas as a hawse kin run, an muh pa say, 'Ain no good tuh lissen tuh um.' Dey git long all right but yuh know dey wuz a lot ub um wut ain stay down yuh."

[2]Two of more than two dozen variants recorded in *Drums and Shadows: Survival Studies among the Georgia Coastal Negroes* (Athens: U of Georgia P, 1940):78–79, 150–51.

Did he mean the Ibos[3] on St. Simons who walked into the water?

"No, ma'am, I ain mean dem. Ain yuh heah bout um? Well, at dat time Mr. Blue he wuz duh obuhseeuh an Mr. Blue put um in duh fiel, but he couldn do nuttn wid um. Dey gabble, gabble, gabble, an nobody couldn unduhstan um an dey didn know how tuh wuk right. Mr. Blue he go down one mawnin wid a long whip fuh tuh whip um good."

"Mr. Blue was a hard overseer?" we asked.

"No, ma'am, he ain hahd, he jis caahn make um unduhstan. Dey's foolish actin. He got tuh whip um, Mr. Blue, he ain hab no choice. Anyways, he whip um good an dey gits tuhgedduh an stick duh hoe in duh fiel an den say 'quack, quack, quack,' an dey riz up in duh sky an tun hesef intuh buzzuds an fly right back tuh Africa."

At this, we exclaimed and showed our astonishment.

"Wut, you ain heah bout um? Ebrybody know bout um. Dey sho lef duh hoe stannin in duh fiel an dey riz right up an fly right back tuh Africa."

Had Wallace actually seen this happen, we asked.

"No, ma'am, I ain seen um. I bin tuh Skidaway, but I knowd plenty wut did see um, plenty wut wuz right deah in duh fiel wid um an seen duh hoe wut dey lef stickin up attuh dey done fly way."

1940

Conjure Stories

Two Tales from Eatonville, Florida[1]

A.

Aunt Judy Cox was Old Man Massey's rival. She thought so anyway. Massey laughed at the very thought, but things finally got critical. She began to boast about being able to "throw back" his work on him. They had quit speaking.

One evening before sundown, Aunt Judy went fishing. That was something strange. She never fished. But she made her grandchildren fix her up a bait pole and a trout pole and set out to Blue Sink alone.

When it got good and dark and she did not come home, her folks got bothered about her. Then one of the village men said he had heard a woman cry out as he passed along the road near the lake. So they went to look for her.

They found her lying in the lake in shallow water having a hard time holding her old neck above the water for so long a time. She couldn't get up.

---

[3] A group of slaves from the Ibo tribe refused to submit to slavery. Led by their chief and singing tribal songs, they walked into the water and were drowned at a point on Dunbar Creek later named Ebo (Ibo) Landing. [Note in original.]

[1] Zora Neale Hurston, "Hoodoo in America: Conjure Stories," *Journal of American Folk-Lore* 44 (1931):404–05.

So they lifted her and carried her home. A large alligator was lying beside her, but dived away when the lantern flashed in his face.

Aunt Judy said that she hadn't wanted to go fishing to begin with, but that something had commanded her to go. She couldn't help herself. She had fished until the sun got very low; she started to come home, but somehow she couldn't, even though she was afraid to be down on the lake after dark. Furthermore, she was afraid to walk home when she couldn't see well for fear of snakes. *But she couldn't leave the lake.* When it was finally dark, she said some force struck her like lightning and threw her into the water. She screamed and called for help, holding her head above the water by supporting the upper part of her body with her hands.

Then the whole surface of the lake lit up with a dull blue light with a red path across it, and Old Man Massey walked to her upon the lake and thousands upon thousands of alligators swam along on each side of him as he walked down this red path of light to where she was and spoke.

"Hush!" he commanded. "Be quiet, or I'll make an end of you right now."

She hushed. She was too scared to move her tongue. Then he asked her: "Where is all that power you make out you got? I brought you to the lake and made you stay here till I got ready for you. I throwed you in, and you can't come out till I say so. When you acknowledge to yourself that I am your top-superior, then you can come out the water. I got to go about my business, but I'm going to leave a watchman, and the first time you holler he'll tear you to pieces. The minute you change your mind— I'll send help to you."

He vanished and the big 'gator slid up beside her. She didn't know how long she had been in the water, but it seemed hours. But she made up her mind to give up root-working all together before she was rescued. The doctor from Orlando said that she had had a stroke. She recovered to the point where she crept about her yard and garden, but she never did any more "work".

B.

But Aunt Judy was not unsung. The people had not forgotten how she fixed Horace Carter.

Horace was a husband eternally searching for love outside his home. He spent every cent he could rake and scrape on his clothes, on hair pomades and walking sticks, and the like.

When he brutally impressed his wife with the fact that there was nothing, absolutely nothing she could do about it, she said to him one Sunday in desperation: "Horace, if you don't mind your ways I'm going to take your case to Aunt Judy."

He laughed. "Tell her, sell her; turn her up and smell her." He went on about his business.

She did tell Aunt Judy and it is said she laid a hearing on Mr. Horace. He had a new suit in the post office. (It is customary to order clothes C.O.D. from mail-order houses, and they remain in the post office until paid out.)

He was bragging about how swell he would look in it. An out-of-town girl was coming over the first Sunday after he got his suit out to help him switch it around. That was the next Sunday after he had laughed at his wife and Aunt Judy.

So he got his suit out. He had a hat, shoes and everything to match.

He put the suit on and strolled over to the depot to meet the train, but before it came he took sick. He seemed to be vomiting so violently that it was running out of his nose as well as his mouth. His clothes were ruined and a great swarm of flies followed him. Before he could reach home, it was discovered that he was defecating through his mouth and nose. This kept up, off and on, for six months. He couldn't tell when it would start, nor stop. Se he kept himself hidden most of the time.

Aunt Judy said, "The dirty puppy! I'll show him how to talk under *my* clothes! Turn me up and smell me, hunh? I'll turn *him* up, and they'll sho smell him."

They say he paid her to take it off him after a while.

1931

John and Old Marster

Master Disguised[1]

Was his mahster's chicken-raiser. Mahster trust him. His mahster went away, so he give a big party. Mahster changed his clothes and blacked his face. Came an' knocked at de do'. John came to de do', said, "Whatshyer want here?" Mahster said, "Ise looking for Mister Johnson's plantation. Ise got lost." John said, "Come in heah, make yourself sca'se, too. Sit down here, eat dis. I'll show you where to go. I wantshyer to get out of heah, too." Mahster went home. Nex' day Mahster call him: "John, what did you steal my chicken fo'?"—"Mahster, let me tell you dishyere one t'ing. I done saw in de Bible dat de man had to reab whey he labor. Mahster, I done labor raisin' dose chickens."

1919

The Diviner[2]

The body-servant of a white man, Mr. Crum, he went out one night to see his girl, and took his master's horse. On his way home he turned the horse loose in the woods and walked home, so his master wouldn' know he had that horse. Next morning his master went to the stable, the horse wasn't

[1]Portia Smiley, "Folk-Lore from Virginia, South Carolina, Georgia, Alabama, and Florida," *Journal of American Folk-Lore* 32 (1919):362.   [2]Smiley 370.

there. He called John and told him about it. John said next morning at four o'clock the horse would come at the gate. Next morning at four o'clock John called his master. The horse was at the gate. "Yes, I told you so." Mr. Crum went to one of his neighbors, and said he had one of the smartest niggers in the country, could tell anything, do anything. The neighbor's name was Simmons, and Simmons said he bet he could do something he couldn't tell. He went out and caught a coon, and dug a hole and put in the coon, and a barrel over the hole. And they bet a thousand dollars against a thousand dollars, he couldn't tell what was under that barrel. Mr. Crum said he was going to give the negro his freedom if he could tell, and he'd beat him if he couldn't tell. He got his cards and threw 'em down, spit on his sticks, threw them down, made a cross-mark in his hand, picked up his cards, threw a stick and then a card. Now he made a motion with his body, raised himself up, picked up his cards and sticks, scratched the back of his head, and said, "Marstah, you got dis here coon at las'!" Mr. Simmons kicked over the barrel with an oath, and the coon jumped out.

1919

Massa and the Bear[3]

During slavery time, you know, Ole Massa had a nigger named John and he was a faithful nigger and Ole Massa lakted John a lot too.

One day Ole Massa sent for John and tole him, says: "John, somebody is stealin' my corn out de field. Every mornin' when I go out I see where they done carried off some mo' of my roastin' ears. I want you to set in de corn patch tonight and ketch whoever it is."

So John said all right and he went and hid in de field.

Pretty soon he heard somethin' breakin' corn. So John sneaked up behind him wid a short stick in his hand and hollered: "Now, break another ear of Ole Massa's corn and see what *Ah'll* do to you."

John thought it was a man all dis time, but it was a bear wid his arms full of roastin' ears. He throwed down de corn and grabbed John. And him and dat bear!

John, after while got loose and got de bear by the tail wid de bear tryin' to git to him all de time. So they run around in a circle all night long. John was so tired. But he couldn't let go of de bear's tail, do de bear would grab him in de back.

After a stretch they quit runnin' and walked. John swingin' on to de bear's tail and de bear's nose 'bout to touch him in de back.

Daybreak, Ole Massa come out to see 'bout John and he seen John and de bear walkin' 'round in de ring. So he run up and says: "Lemme take holt of 'im, John, whilst you run git help!"

John says: "All right, Massa. Now you run in quick and grab 'im just so."

[3]Hurston, *Mules* 100–01.

Ole Massa run and grabbed holt of de bear's tail and said: "Now, John you make haste to git somebody to help us."

John staggered off and set down on de grass and went to fanning hisself wid his hat.

Ole Massa was havin' plenty trouble wid dat bear and he looked over and see John settin' on de grass and he hollered:

"John, you better g'wan git help or else I'm gwinter turn dis bear aloose!"

John says: "Turn 'im loose, then. Dat's whut Ah tried to do all night long but Ah couldn't."

1935

Baby in the Crib[4]

John stole a pig from Old Marsa. He was on his way home with him and his Old Marsa seen him. After John got home he looked out and seen his Old Marsa coming down to the house. So he put this pig in a cradle they used to rock the babies in in them days (some people called them cribs), and he covered him up. When his Old Marster come in John was sitting there rocking him.

Old Marster says, "What's the matter with the baby, John?" "The baby got the measles." "I want to see him." John said, "Well you can't; the doctor said if you uncover him the measles will go back in on him and kill him." So his Old Marster said, "It doesn't matter; I want to see him, John." He reached down to uncover him.

John said, "If that baby is turned to a pig now, don't blame me."

1967

John Steals a Pig and a Sheep[5]

Old Marster had some sheep, and a fellow named John living on the place, a tenant there, he got hungry and he stole the meat from Old Boss. Then he got tired of the sheep meat and stole him a pig. Old Marster come down night after he stole the pig, to get him to play a piece on the banjo. Old Marster knocked on the door, when John had just got through putting the pig away. So Old Marster come in and say, "Play me a piece on the banjo." John started to pick a piece on the banjo; while he's playing he looked around and sees a pig's foot sticking out, so he sings, "Push that pig's foot further back under the bed." (He was talking to his wife.)

When he got tired of that pig meat he turned around and killed him another sheep. So he went back down to the barn and told Old Marster, "Another sheep dead, can't I have him?" Old Marster give him that sheep and he took that one home and ate it up. That made two that Old Marster

---

[4]Told by E. L. Smith, Dorson 138.   [5]Told by Ray Brooks, Dorson 138–39.

had given him, so Old Marster got a watch out for him. John killed another one and went and told Old Marster again that a sheep had died. Old Marster told him, "You killed that sheep. What did you kill my sheep for?" John says, "Old Marster, I'll tell you; I won't let nobody's sheep bite me."

1967

Talking Bones[6]

They used to carry the slaves out in the woods and leave them there, if they killed them—just like dead animals. There wasn't any burying then. It used to be a secret, between one plantation and another, when they beat up their hands and carried them off.

So John was walking out in the woods and seed a skeleton. He says: "This looks like a human. I wonder what he's doing out here." And the skeleton said, "Tongue is the cause of my being here." So John ran back to Old Marster and said, "The skeleton at the edge of the woods is talking." Old Marster didn't believe him and went to see. And a great many people came too. They said, "Make the bones talk." But the skeleton wouldn't talk. So they beat John to death, and left him there. And then the bones talked. They said, "Tongue brought us here, and tongue brought you here."

1967

Old Boss Wants into Heaven[7]

Old Boss he was a big plantation owner, but he was paralyzed and he couldn't even walk. So every time he was ready to move he'd call Mac up, to carry him around on his back and push him around in his wheel chair. This was back in slavery times, and Mac was his servant, his slave. Old Boss had a whole lot of slaves working for him, but Mac was the main attraction.

Every time the Boss had Mac carry him on his back, Mac figured he was being done wrong, since Boss had a wheel chair. He got to talking to himself about it out loud: "O Lord, these days ain't going to be much longer; God almighty going to call us all in." Then he wouldn't have to carry Old Boss around no more, 'cause he'd be flying around with angels in heaven, and Old Boss'd be down in hell burning with brimstone. Quite a few times the Boss heard him say it; so finally he asked him what did he mean by that remark.

Mac tells him, "You-all know what the Good Book says?" So the Boss says: "What do you mean by that? If anybody's going to Heaven I'm going, because I got all the money I can use, I got a lot of land, I got all the slaves I want to work the land, so I got everything I need to get to Heaven."

"That's just how come you ain't going to Heaven," Mac answers. "The Good Book says so." But Old Boss he really thought because he had all the

[6]Told by Beulah Tate, Dorson 147–48.   [7]Told by John Blackamore, Dorson 158–61.

land and all the money and all the slaves he was fixed straight, that was all he needed. Mac was kind of afraid to speak up any more, being a slave, you know. He just said, "That's all right Boss, you'll see," and kind of walked off from him.

Old Boss couldn't sleep that night. He tried to brush it off his mind but it kept coming on back to him, what Mac had told him. Finally he decided that Mac didn't know what he was talking about, that he was an ignorant slave and didn't know no more than what he (Old Boss) said: "I'll give you a forty-acre farm and a team of mules, if you accept about what work to do." Finally he went on to sleep. Early next morning Mac gets up and starts about his chores. Boss heard him singing.

Soon I will be up in Heaven with the angels,

Having a good time enjoying eternal life.

So that thought kind of hit Old Boss again—he wanted to know how could a slave go to heaven, and he himself being rich and going to hell. That kind of lay on his mind all day. That was Saturday. Sunday morning Mac gets up singing another song. He got on his clean overalls, and a clean shirt, and he gave himself a shave with one of the Boss's old razors—he was barefooted even on Sunday, but he was still happy; he was going to church. The song he was singing was:

I'm going to the mourning bench this morning,

And praise my master up above.

Boss knew they had a church, but he'd never heard a song like that before; so he got curious. He gets his wheel chair, and kind of sneaks on down to the church where they were having the meeting. So when he got there service had already begun. The preacher is up in the pulpit asking did anybody want anything explained to them. Mac raised his hand to let the preacher know he had a question. So he told him about his discussion with Old Boss. Since he could not read, he asked the preacher to explain it to him. The preacher gets his textbook, and gives Mac the book and the chapter and the verse, and then he read it to him. (Some of them could read and some of 'em could not.) So he read, "It's easier for a camel to go through the eye of a needle than it is for a rich man to go to Heaven." (In the meantime Old Boss is outside the window listening, taking it all in.) So he says, "Sisters and Brothers, there only two places to go after you die, and that is Heaven or Hell. And since Old Boss can't go to Heaven, there's no other place for him to go but to Hell."

Old Boss heard enough then. He wheels his chair on back home, he sets down on the porch, and calls his wife to bring him the Bible. He remembered the book and the chapter and the verse and he wanted to see if they knew what they were talking about. When he turns to the page, he found there in big red letters just what the preacher had read. That kind of worried him; he felt uneasy all day Sunday. Mac was away so he couldn't talk to him. Night came; still no Mac. So he decided to set up and wait for him.

On the way home from church Mac had to pass a graveyard. This being Sunday night, a couple of fellows had gone into Old Boss's cornfield and had stole a sack of corn. They went in to get two sacks of corn, but when they heard Mac coming they thought it might be Old Boss, and jumped over the fence into the graveyard. In getting over the fence they dropped a couple of ears. Mac heard them and that kind of scared him, because he thought they was hants, and so he hid behind a big tomb-stone.

One of the fellows said, "Well, since we didn't get but one sackful we're going to have to divide it." Mac didn't know what they were talking about, so he sat and listened. The two fellows started counting the corn. They figured they didn't have time to count all the ears together and then separate them; so they started counting off, "One for you and one for me." And they kept that up for quite a while.

Mac said, "O Lord, Judgment Day done come. I better go tell the Boss." So he struck out to running. When he gets to the house Old Boss is sitting on the porch smoking his pipe uneasily. Boss was glad to see Mac, and kind of scared for him too, 'cause he was running so hard. Before he could ask Mac how to get to Heaven, Mac fell upon the porch, almost out of breath. "I told you Judgment Day would be soon here; I sure told you!"

Old Boss says: "Well calm yourself. Tell me what this is all about." Mac tells him, "God and the Devil is down there in the graveyard separating the souls." Old Boss doesn't believe it. "Well, that couldn't be true, you know you're just lying." So Mac tells him, "Well if you think I am lying, I'll take you down there and prove it to you."

So he carries Old Boss down to the graveyard on his back. When Old Boss gets there he hears him counting, "One for you and one for me." So he wants to get a closer look; he wants to see what God and the Devil look like. It was dark out there, and the two fellows had moved around to the other side of the fence, where they'd dropped the corn. But when Old Boss gets around there he can't make out who it was because each of them had a great white cotton sack; that was all he could see, that cotton sack. Mac says, "See Boss, I told you so, they're down there sacking up souls." So one of the guys said, "Well, one for you and one for me." T'other pointed over to the fence where they had dropped the two ears, and he said, "There's two over there by the fence—you can have the big one and I'll take the little one."

Old Boss didn't want to hear no more. Mac was scared too. In fact Mac was too scared to move; he froze there in his tracks for a minute. Since Mac wasn't moving fast enough to carry Old Boss, Old Boss jumped down and run. And Mac looked around to see what had happened to Old Boss. Old Boss was out of sight. He figured 'cause Old Boss couldn't walk they must have sacked him up. So Mac run for Old Boss's house to tell Old Missy what happened. When he gets to the house he falls on the porch again, calling Old Missy.

Old Boss come out, without his wheel chair. Mac went to tell him what had happened to Old Boss. Then he realized it was Old Boss he was talking to. He froze again, so Old Boss asked him, "What happened after you left?" Mac told him, and asked Old Boss what happened to him. Boss said, "Well, you weren't moving fast enough; so I decided I'd come on without you." And he's been walking ever since.

Then Old Boss gave all his slaves an equal share in his kingdom that he had already built. He didn't want to get caught in that predicament no more.

1967

■ JOEL CHANDLER HARRIS ■
1848–1908

The conflicts between the values of the Old and New South were vividly illustrated in the journalistic and literary career of Joel Chandler Harris.

Born in Eatonton, Putnam County, Georgia, in 1848, Harris was the son of a poor white mother and an Irish day laborer who deserted his family shortly after Harris's birth. His mother supported the family through her work as a seamstress, but at thirteen Harris set out on his own, becoming an apprentice to Joseph Addison Turner, who published a newspaper on his plantation, Turnwold. It was from the slaves on this plantation that Harris first heard the African American folktales that were to make him famous.

Following the Civil War he worked on other newspapers in New Orleans and throughout Georgia, culminating in 1876 in his appointment to the editorial staff of the Atlanta *Constitution*. The *Constitution* was run by Henry Woodfin Grady (1850–1889), Georgia's most enthusiastic promoter of the "New South," an industrialized, urbanized, "Yankeefied" society totally reconciled to its restoration to the Union. Harris too was a believer in both sectional reconciliation and the commercial development of the region, and he produced numerous editorials supporting Grady's vision. In addition, however, he fulfilled a quite different assignment for the paper as he returned to the world of his youth in the retelling of the slave stories through a black character called Uncle Remus. Modeled after some of the slaves he had encountered at Turnwold, Uncle Remus in the earliest sketches was presented in an urban setting and used to express harsh critiques of the ex-slaves, particularly those who sought political power and formal education. This character evolved into the Remus with whom contemporary readers are familiar: the gentle old man who transfixes a little white boy night after night with stories about small, seemingly defenseless animals whose cunning outwits stronger but less intelligent beasts.

Reprinted in newspapers throughout the nation, the Uncle Remus stories were an immediate success, appealing to a reading public already receptive to the image of the antebellum South as an idyllic land where master and slave lived in harmony and older slaves considered the master's children their own. In 1880 Harris published his first collection, *Uncle Remus: His Songs and Sayings*, followed in 1883 by *Nights With Uncle Remus*. As the demand for more stories intensified, he was hard-pressed to come up with them and had to turn to the recollections of others; inevitably these later stories lacked the immediacy and vividness of those in the 1880 edition.

Harris was not unaware of the psychological implications of the stories he retold; he knew why the slaves, with few or no means at hand for effective physical resistance, celebrated the successes of weak but clever creatures like Brer Tarrypin and Brer Rabbit over the stronger but slower Brer Fox, Brer Bear, and Brer Wolf. He never told the stories to his own children, because in so many of them the punishments doled out to the smaller creatures' enemies (boiling, skinning alive, and burning) are so brutal. Nonetheless, in essays and rare public appearances he persisted in depicting the African American as gentle, compassionate, and eager for reconciliation with whites.

Harris became prolific in the 1880s and 1890s, producing such short story collections as *Mingo and Other Sketches in Black and White* (1884) and *Free Joe, and Other Georgia Sketches* (1887). He also wrote several novels and a collection of sketches built around a poor white homespun philosopher called Uncle Billy Sanders. However, it was for Uncle Remus that Harris is best remembered.

A shy, self-effacing man, Harris thought of himself as a "cornfield journalist" whose chief contribution was as compiler rather than creator. But his picturesque recollections and his marvelous ear for dialect have won him well-deserved praise. Harris unquestionably sentimentalized the lives of slaves in his sketches, and even in "Free Joe," where he reveals an awareness of the cruel side of race relations in the antebellum South, he has written a story that many critics see as supporting mainstream southern claims that blacks were better off in slavery. In judging Harris's work, however, we must recall that he was writing at a time when the South's most virulent spokespeople, in literature and in politics, were painting for a gullible public a picture of African Americans as vicious and bestial. Whatever his deficiencies in bridging the gap between races, Harris's nostalgic black portraits did serve to awaken white readers to the richness of African American folklore, a treasure they would have otherwise not encountered.

George Friedman
Towson State University

PRIMARY WORKS

Uncle Remus: His Songs and His Sayings, 1880; *Mingo, and Other Sketches in Black and White*, 1884; *Free Joe, and Other Georgian Sketches*, 1887; *Gabriel Tolliver: A Story of Reconstruction*, 1902; *The Complete Tales of Uncle Remus*, 1955.

from **Uncle Remus: His Songs and His Sayings**

II. The Wonderful Tar-Baby Story

"Didn't the fox *never* catch the rabbit, Uncle Remus?" asked the little boy the next evening. "He come mighty nigh it, honey, sho's you bawn—Brer Fox did. One day atter Brer[1] Rabbit fool 'im wid dat calamus root, Brer Fox

---

[1] Brother; used in the same way members of a
church congregation refer to each other.

went ter wuk en got 'im some tar, en mix it wid some turkentime, en fix up a contrapshun wat he call a Tar-Baby, en he tuck dish yer Tar-Baby en he sot 'er in de big road, en den he lay off in de bushes fer ter see wat de news wuz gwineter be. En he didn't hatter wait long, nudder, kaze[2] bimeby[3] here come Brer Rabbit pacin' down de road—lippity-clippity, clippity-lippity—dez ez sassy ez a jay-bird. Brer Fox, he lay low. Brer Rabbit come prancin' 'long twel he spy de Tar-Baby, en den he fotch up on his behime legs like he wuz 'stonished. De Tar-Baby, she sot dar, she did, en Brer Fox, he lay low.

"'Mawnin'!' sez Brer Rabbit, sezee—'nice wedder dis mawnin',' sezee.

"Tar-Baby ain't sayin' nuthin', en Brer Fox, he lay low.

"'How duz yo' sym'tums seem ter segashuate?'[4] sez Brer Rabbit, sezee.

"Brer Fox, he wink his eye slow, en lay low, en de Tar-Baby, she ain't sayin' nuthin'.

"'How you come on, den? Is you deaf?' sez Brer Rabbit, sezee. 'Kaze if you is, I kin holler louder,' sezee.

"Tar-Baby stay still, en Brer Fox, he lay low.

"'Youer stuck up, dat's w'at you is,' says Brer Rabbit, sezee, 'en I'm gwineter kyore you, dat's w'at I'm a gwineter do,' sezee.

"Brer Fox, he sorter chuckle in his stummuck, he did, but Tar-Baby ain't sayin' nuthin'.

"'I'm gwineter larn you howter talk ter 'specttubble fokes ef hit's de las' ack,' sez Brer Rabbit, sezee. 'Ef you don't take off dat hat en tell me howdy, I'm gwineter bus' you wide open,' sezee.

"Tar-Baby stay still, en Brer Fox, he lay low.

"Brer Rabbit keep on axin' 'im, en de Tar-Baby, she keep on sayin' nuthin', twel present'y Brer Rabbit draw back wid his fis', he did, en blip he tuck 'er side er de head. Right dar's whar he broke his merlasses jug. His fis' stuck, en he can't pull loose. De tar hilt 'im. But Tar-Baby, she stay still, en Brer Fox, he lay low.

"'Ef you don't lemme loose, I'll knock you agin,' sez Brer Rabbit, sezee, en wid dat he fotch 'er a wipe wid de udder han', en dat stuck. Tar-Baby, she ain't sayin' nuthin', en Brer Fox, he lay low.

"'Tu'n me loose, fo' I kick de natal stuffin' outen you,' sez Brer Rabbit, sezee, but de Tar-Baby, she ain't sayin' nuthin'. She des hilt on, en den Brer Rabbit lose de use er his feet in de same way. Brer Fox, he lay low. Den Brer Rabbit squall out dat ef de Tar-Baby don't tu'n 'im loose he butt 'er crank-sided. En den he butted, en his head got stuck. Den Brer Fox, he sa'ntered fort', lookin' des ez innercent ez wunner yo' mammy's mockin'-birds.

"'Howdy, Brer Rabbit,' sez Brer Fox, sezee. 'You look sorter stuck up dis mawnin',' sezee, en den he rolled on de groun', en laft en laft twel he couldn't laff no mo'. 'I speck you'll take dinner wid me dis time, Brer Rabbit. I done laid in some calamus root, en I ain't gwineter take no skuse,' sez Brer Fox, sezee."

---

[2]Because.
[3]By and by.

[4]*I.e.*, how are you feeling today?

Here Uncle Remus paused, and drew a two-pound yam out of the ashes.

"Did the fox eat the rabbit?" asked the little boy to whom the story had been told.

"Dat's all de fur de tale goes," replied the old man. "He mout, en den agin he mountent. Some say Jedge B'ar come 'long en loosed 'im—some say he didn't. I hear Miss Sally callin'. You better run 'long."

IV. How Mr. Rabbit Was Too Sharp for Mr. Fox

"Uncle Remus," said the little boy one evening, when he had found the old man with little or nothing to do, "did the fox kill and eat the rabbit when he caught him with the Tar-Baby?"

"Law, honey, ain't I tell you 'bout dat?" replied the old darkey, chuckling slyly. "I 'clar ter grashus I ought er tole you dat, but ole man Nod wuz ridin' on my eyeleds 'twel a leetle mo'n I'd a dis'member'd my own name, en den on to dat here come yo' mammy hollerin' atter you.

"W'at I tell you w'en I fus' begin? I tole you Brer Rabbit wuz a monstus soon beas'; leas'ways dat's w'at I laid out fer ter tell you. Well, den, honey, don't you go en make no udder kalkalashuns, kaze in dem days Brer Rabbit en his fambly wuz at de head er de gang w'en enny racket wuz on han', en dar dey stayed. 'Fo' you begins fer ter wipe yo' eyes 'bout Brer Rabbit, you wait en see whar'bouts Brer Rabbit gwineter fetch up at. But dat's needer yer ner dar.

"W'en Brer Fox fine Brer Rabbit mixt up wid de Tar-Baby, he feel mighty good, en he roll on de groun' en laff. Bimeby he up'n say, sezee:

"'Well, I speck I got you dis time, Brer Rabbit,' sezee; 'maybe I ain't, but I speck I is. You been runnin' roun' here sassin' atter me a mighty long time, but I speck you done come ter de een' er de row. You bin cuttin' up yo' capers en bouncin' 'roun' in dis naberhood ontwel you come ter b'leeve yo'se'f de boss er de whole gang. En den youer allers some'rs whar you got no bizness,' sez Brer Fox, sezee. 'Who ax you fer ter come en strike up a 'quaintence wid dish yer Tar-Baby? En who stuck you up dar whar you iz? Nobody in de roun' worril. You des tuck en jam yo'se'f on dat Tar-Baby widout waitin' fer enny invite,' sez Brer Fox, sezee, 'en dar you is, en dar you'll stay twel I fixes up a bresh-pile and fires her up, kaze I'm gwineter bobbycue you dis day, sho,' sez Brer Fox, sezee.

"Den Brer Rabbit talk mighty 'umble.

"'I don't keer w'at you do wid me, Brer Fox,' sezee, 'so you don't fling me in dat brier-patch. Roas' me, Brer Fox,' sezee, 'but don't fling me in dat brier-patch,' sezee.

"'Hit's so much trouble fer ter kindle a fire,' sez Brer Fox, sezee, 'dat I speck I'll hatter hang you,' sezee.

"'Hang me des ez high ez you please, Brer Fox,' sez Brer Rabbit, sezee, 'but do fer de Lord's sake don't fling me in that brier-patch,' sezee.

"'I ain't got no string,' sez Brer Fox, sezee, 'en now I speck I'll hatter drown you,' sezee.

"'Drown me des ez deep ez you please, Brer Fox,' sez Brer Rabbit, sezee, 'but do don't fling me in dat brier-patch,' sezee.

"'Dey ain't no water nigh,' sez Brer Fox, sezee, 'en now I speck I'll hatter skin you,' sezee.

"'Skin me, Brer Fox,' sez Brer Rabbit, sezee, 'snatch out my eyeballs, t'ar out my years by de roots, en cut off my legs,' sezee, 'but do please, Brer Fox, don't fling me in dat brier-patch,' sezee.

"Co'se Brer Fox wanter hurt Brer Rabbit bad ez he kin, so he cotch 'im by de behime legs en slung 'im right in de middle er de brier-patch. Dar was a considerbul flutter whar Brer Rabbit struck de bushes, en Brer Fox sorter hang 'roun' fer ter see w'at wuz gwineter happen. Bimeby he hear somebody call 'im, en way up de hill he see Brer Rabbit settin' cross-legged on a chinka-pin log koamin' de pitch outen his har wid a chip. Den Brer Fox know dat he bin swop off mighty bad. Brer Rabbit wuz bleedzed[1] fer ter fling back some er his sass, en he holler out:

"'Bred en bawn in a brier-patch, Brer Fox—bred en bawn in a brier-patch!' en wid dat he skip out des ez lively ez a cricket in de embers."

1880

Free Joe and the Rest of the World

The name of Free Joe strikes humorously upon the ear of memory. It is impossible to say why, for he was the humblest, the simplest, and the most serious of all God's living creatures, sadly lacking in all those elements that suggest the humorous. It is certain, moreover, that in 1850 the sober-minded citizens of the little Georgian village of Hillsborough were not inclined to take a humorous view of Free Joe, and neither his name nor his presence provoked a smile. He was a black atom, drifting hither and thither without an owner, blown about by all the winds of circumstance, and given over to shiftlessness.

The problems of one generation are the paradoxes of a succeeding one, particularly if war, or some such incident, intervenes to clarify the atmos-phere and strengthen the understanding. Thus, in 1850, Free Joe repre-sented not only a problem of large concern, but, in the watchful eyes of Hillsborough, he was the embodiment of that vague and mysterious danger that seemed to be forever lurking on the outskirts of slavery, ready to sound a shrill and ghostly signal in the impenetrable swamps, and steal forth under the midnight stars to murder, rapine, and pillage,—a danger always threatening, and yet never assuming shape; intangible, and yet real; impossi-ble, and yet not improbable. Across the serene and smiling front of safety, the pale outlines of the awful shadow of insurrection sometimes fell. With this invisible panorama as a background, it was natural that the figure of Free Joe, simple and humble as it was, should assume undue proportions.

[1]Obliged.

Go where he would, do what he might, he could not escape the finger of observation and the kindling eye of suspicion. His lightest words were noted, his slightest actions marked.

Under all the circumstances it was natural that his peculiar condition should reflect itself in his habits and manners. The slaves laughed loudly day by day, but Free Joe rarely laughed. The slaves sang at their work and danced at their frolics, but no one ever heard Free Joe sing or saw him dance. There was something painfully plaintive and appealing in his attitude, something touching in his anxiety to please. He was of the friendliest nature, and seemed to be delighted when he could amuse the little children who had made a playground of the public square. At times he would please them by making his little dog Dan perform all sorts of curious tricks, or he would tell them quaint stories of the beasts of the field and birds of the air; and frequently he was coaxed into relating the story of his own freedom. That story was brief, but tragical.

In the year of our Lord 1840, when a negro-speculator of a sportive turn of mind reached the little village of Hillsborough on his way to the Mississippi region, with a caravan of likely negroes of both sexes, he found much to interest him. In that day and at that time there were a number of young men in the village who had not bound themselves over to repentance for the various misdeeds of the flesh. To these young men the negro-speculator (Major Frampton was his name) proceeded to address himself. He was a Virginian, he declared; and, to prove the statement, he referred all the festively inclined young men of Hillsborough to a barrel of peach-brandy in one of his covered wagons. In the minds of these young men there was less doubt in regard to the age and quality of the brandy than there was in regard to the negro-trader's birthplace. Major Frampton might or might not have been born in the Old Dominion,—that was a matter for consideration and inquiry,—but there could be no question as to the mellow pungency of the peach-brandy.

In his own estimation, Major Frampton was one of the most accomplished of men. He had summered at the Virginia Springs; he had been to Philadelphia, to Washington, to Richmond, to Lynchburg, and to Charleston, and had accumulated a great deal of experience which he found useful. Hillsborough was hid in the woods of Middle Georgia, and its general aspect of innocence impressed him. He looked on the young men who had shown their readiness to test his peach-brandy, as overgrown country boys who needed to be introduced to some of the arts and sciences he had at his command. Thereupon the major pitched his tents, figuratively speaking, and became, for the time being, a part and parcel of the innocence that characterized Hillsborough. A wiser man would doubtless have made the same mistake.

The little village possessed advantages that seemed to be providentially arranged to fit the various enterprises that Major Frampton had in view. There was the auction-block in front of the stuccoed court-house, if he desired to dispose of a few of his negroes; there was a quarter-track, laid out to his hand and in excellent order, if he chose to enjoy the pleasures of horse-racing; there were secluded pine thickets within easy reach, if he desired to indulge in the exciting pastime of cock-fighting; and various lonely and unoccupied rooms in the second story of the tavern, if he cared to challenge the chances of dice or cards.

Major Frampton tried them all with varying luck, until he began his famous game of poker with Judge Alfred Wellington, a stately gentleman with a flowing white beard and mild blue eyes that gave him the appearance of a benevolent patriarch. The history of the game in which Major Frampton and Judge Alfred Wellington took part is something more than a tradition in Hillsborough, for there are still living three or four men who sat around the table and watched its progress. It is said that at various stages of the game Major Frampton would destroy the cards with which they were playing, and send for a new pack, but the result was always the same. The mild blue eyes of Judge Wellington, with few exceptions, continued to overlook "hands" that were invincible—a habit they had acquired during a long and arduous course of training from Saratoga to New Orleans. Major Frampton lost his money, his horses, his wagons, and all his negroes but one, his body-servant. When his misfortune had reached this limit, the major adjourned the game. The sun was shining brightly, and all nature was cheerful. It is said that the major also seemed to be cheerful. However this may be, he visited the courthouse, and executed the papers that gave his body-servant his freedom. This being done, Major Frampton sauntered into a convenient pine thicket, and blew out his brains.

The negro thus freed came to be known as Free Joe. Compelled, under the law, to choose a guardian, he chose Judge Wellington, chiefly because his wife Lucinda was among the negroes won from Major Frampton. For several years Free Joe had what may be called a jovial time. His wife Lucinda was well provided for, and he found it a comparatively easy matter to provide for himself; so that, taking all the circumstances into consideration, it is not matter for astonishment that he became somewhat shiftless.

When Judge Wellington died, Free Joe's troubles began. The judge's negroes, including Lucinda, went to his half-brother, a man named Calderwood, who was a hard master and a rough customer generally,—a man of many eccentricities of mind and character. His neighbors had a habit of alluding to him as "Old Spite"; and the name seemed to fit him so completely, that he was known far and near as "Spite" Calderwood. He probably enjoyed the distinction the name gave him, at any rate, he never resented it, and it was not often that he missed an opportunity to show that he deserved it. Calderwood's place was two or three miles from the village of Hillsborough, and Free Joe visited his wife twice a week, Wednesday and Saturday nights.

One Sunday he was sitting in front of Lucinda's cabin, when Calderwood happened to pass that way.

"Howdy, marster?" said Free Joe, taking off his hat.

"Who are you?" exclaimed Calderwood abruptly, halting and staring at the negro.

"I'm name' Joe, marster. I'm Lucindy's ole man."

"Who do you belong to?"

"Marse John Evans is my gyardeen, marster."

"Big name—gyardeen. Show your pass."

Free Joe produced that document, and Calderwood read it aloud slowly, as if he found it difficult to get at the meaning:

To whom it may concern: This is to certify that the boy Joe Frampton has my permission to visit his wife Lucinda.

This was dated at Hillsborough, and signed *"John W. Evans."*

Calderwood read it twice, and then looked at Free Joe, elevating his eyebrows, and showing his discolored teeth.

"Some mighty big words in that there. Evans own this place, I reckon. When's he comin' down to take hold?"

Free Joe fumbled with his hat. He was badly frightened.

"Lucindy says she speck you wouldn't min' my comin', long ez I behave, marster."

Calderwood tore the pass in pieces and flung it away.

"Don't want no free niggers 'round here," he exclaimed. "There's the big road. It'll carry you to town. Don't let me catch you here no more. Now, mind what I tell you."

Free Joe presented a shabby spectacle as he moved off with his little dog Dan slinking at his heels. It should be said in behalf of Dan, however, that his bristles were up, and that he looked back and growled. It may be that the dog had the advantage of insignificance, but it is difficult to conceive how a dog bold enough to raise his bristles under Calderwood's very eyes could be as insignificant as Free Joe. But both the negro and his little dog seemed to give a new and more dismal aspect to forlornness as they turned into the road and went toward Hillsborough.

After this incident Free Joe appeared to have clearer ideas concerning his peculiar condition. He realized the fact that though he was free he was more helpless than any slave. Having no owner, every man was his master. He knew that he was the object of suspicion, and therefore all his slender resources (ah! how pitifully slender they were!) were devoted to winning, not kindness and appreciation, but toleration; all his efforts were in the direction of mitigating the circumstances that tended to make his condition so much worse than that of the negroes around him,—negroes who had friends because they had masters.

So far as his own race was concerned, Free Joe was an exile. If the slaves secretly envied him his freedom (which is to be doubted, considering his miserable condition), they openly despised him, and lost no opportunity to treat him with contumely. Perhaps this was in some measure the result of the attitude which Free Joe chose to maintain toward them. No doubt his instinct taught him that to hold himself aloof from the slaves would be to invite from the whites the toleration which he coveted, and without which even his miserable condition would be rendered more miserable still.

His greatest trouble was the fact that he was not allowed to visit his wife; but he soon found a way out of this difficulty. After he had been ordered away from the Calderwood place, he was in the habit of wandering as far in that direction as prudence would permit. Near the Calderwood place, but not on Calderwood's land, lived an old man named Micajah Staley and his sister Becky Staley. These people were old and very poor. Old Micajah had a palsied arm and hand; but, in spite of this, he managed to earn a precarious living with his turning-lathe.

When he was a slave Free Joe would have scorned these representatives of a class known as poor white trash, but now he found them sympathetic and helpful in various ways. From the back door of their cabin he could hear the Calderwood negroes singing at night, and he sometimes fancied he could distinguish Lucinda's shrill treble rising above the other voices. A large poplar grew in the woods some distance from the Staley cabin, and at the foot of this tree Free Joe would sit for hours with his face turned toward Calderwood's. His little dog Dan would curl up in the leaves near by, and the two seemed to be as comfortable as possible.

One Saturday afternoon Free Joe, sitting at the foot of this friendly poplar, fell asleep. How long he slept, he could not tell; but when he awoke little Dan was licking his face, the moon was shining brightly, and Lucinda his wife stood before him laughing. The dog, seeing that Free Joe was asleep, had grown somewhat impatient, and he concluded to make an excursion to the Calderwood place on his own account. Lucinda was inclined to give the incident a twist in the direction of superstition.

"I'uz settin' down front er de fireplace," she said, "cookin' me some meat, w'en all of a sudden I year sumpin at de do'—scratch, scratch. I tuck'n tu'n de meat over, en make out I aint year it. Bimeby it come dar 'gin—scratch, scratch. I up en open de do', I did, en, bless de Lord! dar wuz little Dan, en it look like ter me dat his ribs done grow tergeer. I gin 'im some bread, en den, w'en he start out, I tuck'n foller 'im, kaze, I say ter myse'f, maybe my nigger man mought be some'rs 'roun'. Dat ar little dog got sense, mon."

Free Joe laughed and dropped his hand lightly on Dan's head. For a long time after that he had no difficulty in seeing his wife. He had only to sit by the poplar-tree until little Dan could run and fetch her. But after a while the other negroes discovered that Lucinda was meeting Free Joe in the woods, and information of the fact soon reached Calderwood's ears. Calderwood was what is called a man of action. He said nothing; but one day he put Lucinda in his buggy, and carried her to Macon, sixty miles away. He carried her to Macon, and came back without her; and nobody in or around Hillsborough, or in that section, ever saw her again.

For many a night after that Free Joe sat in the woods and waited. Little Dan would run merrily off and be gone a long time, but he always came back without Lucinda. This happened over and over again. The "willis-whistlers"[1] would call and call, like phantom huntsmen wandering on a far-off shore; the screech-owl would shake and shiver in the depths of the woods; the night-hawks, sweeping by on noiseless wings, would snap their beaks as though they enjoyed the huge joke of which Free Joe and little Dan were the victims; and the whip-poor-wills would cry to each other through the gloom. Each night seemed to be lonelier than the preceding, but Free Joe's patience was proof against loneliness. There came a time, however, when little Dan refused to go after Lucinda. When Free Joe motioned him in the direction of the Cal-derwood place, he would simply move about uneasily and whine; then he would curl up in the leaves and make himself comfortable.

One night, instead of going to the poplar-tree to wait for Lucinda, Free Joe went to the Staley cabin, and, in order to make his welcome good, as he expressed it, he carried with him an armful of fat-pine splinters. Miss Becky Staley had a great reputation in those parts as a fortune-teller, and the schoolgirls, as well as older people, often tested her powers in this direction, some in jest and some in earnest. Free Joe placed his humble offering of light-wood in the chimney-corner, and then seated himself on the steps, dropping his hat on the ground outside.

"Miss Becky," he said presently, "whar in de name er gracious you reckon Lucindy is?"

"Well, the Lord he'p the nigger!" exclaimed Miss Becky, in a tone that seemed to reproduce, by some curious agreement of sight with sound, her general aspect of peakedness. "Well, the Lord he'p the nigger! haint you been a-seein' her all this blessed time? She's over at old Spite Calderwood's, if she's anywheres, I reckon."

"No'm, dat I aint, Miss Becky. I aint seen Lucindy in now gwine on mighty nigh a mont'."

"Well, it haint a-gwine to hurt you," said Miss Becky, somewhat sharply. "In my day an' time it wuz allers took to be a bad sign when niggers got to honeyin' 'roun' an' gwine on."

"Yessum," said Free Joe, cheerfully assenting to the proposition—"yes-sum, dat's so, but me an' my ole 'oman, we 'uz raise tergeer, en dey aint bin many days w'en we 'uz 'way fum one 'n'er like we is now."

"Maybe she's up an' took up wi' some un else," said Micajah Staley from the corner. "You know what the sayin' is, 'New master, new nigger.'"

"Dat's so, dat's de sayin', but tain't wid my ole 'oman like 'tis wid yuther niggers. Me en her wuz des natally raise up tergeer. Dey's lots likelier nig-gers dan w'at I is," said Free Joe, viewing his shabbiness with a critical eye, "but I knows Lucindy mos' good ez I does little Dan dar—dat I does."

There was no reply to this, and Free Joe continued,

"Miss Becky, I wish you please, ma'am, take en run yo' kyards en see sump'n n'er 'bout Lucindy; kaze ef she sick, I'm gwine dar. Dey ken take en take me up en gimme a stroppin', but I'm gwine dar."

[1] The willet, a bird with a loud whistle.

Miss Becky got her cards, but first she picked up a cup, in the bottom of which were some coffee-grounds. These she whirled slowly round and round, ending finally by turning the cup upside down on the hearth and allowing it to remain in that position.

"I'll turn the cup first," said Miss Becky, "and then I'll run the cards and see what they say."

As she shuffled the cards the fire on the hearth burned low, and in its fitful light the gray-haired, thin-featured woman seemed to deserve the weird reputation which rumor and gossip had given her. She shuffled the cards for some moments, gazing intently in the dying fire; then, throwing a piece of pine on the coals, she made three divisions of the pack, disposing them about in her lap. Then she took the first pile, ran the cards slowly through her fingers, and studied them carefully. To the first she added the second pile. The study of these was evidently not satisfactory. She said nothing, but frowned heavily; and the frown deepened as she added the rest of the cards until the entire fifty-two had passed in review before her. Though she frowned, she seemed to be deeply interested. Without changing the relative position of the cards, she ran them all over again. Then she threw a larger piece of pine on the fire, shuffled the cards afresh, divided them into three piles, and subjected them to the same careful and critical examination.

"I can't tell the day when I've seed the cards run this a-way," she said after a while. "What is an' what aint, I'll never tell you; but I know what the cards sez."

"W'at does dey say, Miss Becky?" the negro inquired, in a tone the solemnity of which was heightened by its eagerness.

"They er runnin' quare.[2] These here that I'm a-lookin' at," said Miss Becky, "they stan' for the past. Them there, they er the present; and the t'others, they er the future. Here's a bundle,"—tapping the ace of clubs with her thumb,—"an' here's a journey as plain as the nose on a man's face. Here's Lucinda"—

"Whar she, Miss Becky?"

"Here she is—the queen of spades."

Free Joe grinned. The idea seemed to please him immensely.

"Well, well, well!" he exclaimed. "Ef dat don't beat my time! De queen er spades! W'en Lucindy year dat hit'll tickle 'er, sho'!"

Miss Becky continued to run the cards back and forth through her fingers.

"Here's a bundle an' a journey, and here's Lucinda. An' here's ole Spite Calderwood."

She held the cards toward the negro and touched the king of clubs.

"De Lord he'p my soul!" exclaimed Free Joe with a chuckle. "De faver's dar.[3] Yesser, dat's him! W'at de matter 'long wid all un um, Miss Becky?"

The old woman added the second pile of cards to the first, and then the third, still running them through her fingers slowly and critically. By this

[2]Queer.

[3]*I.e.*, It looks like him.

time the piece of pine in the fireplace had wrapped itself in a mantle of flame illuminating the cabin and throwing into strange relief the figure of Miss Becky as she sat studying the cards. She frowned ominously at the cards and mumbled a few words to herself. Then she dropped her hands in her lap and gazed once more into the fire. Her shadow danced and capered on the wall and floor behind her, as if, looking over her shoulder into the future, it could behold a rare spectacle. After a while she picked up the cup that had been turned on the hearth. The coffee-grounds, shaken around, presented what seemed to be a most intricate map.

"Here's the journey," said Miss Becky, presently; "here's the big road, here's rivers to cross, here's the bundle to tote." She paused and sighed. "They haint no names writ here, an' what it all means I'll never tell you. Cajy, I wish you'd be so good as to han' me my pipe."

"I haint no hand wi' the kyards," said Cajy, as he handed the pipe, "but I reckon I can patch out your misinformation, Becky, bekaze the other day, whiles I was a-finishin' up Mizzers Perdue's rollin'-pin, I hearn a rattlin' in the road. I looked out, an' Spite Calderwood was a-drivin' by in his buggy an' thar sot Lucinda by him. It'd in-about drapt out er my min'."

Free Joe sat on the door-sill and fumbled at his hat, flinging it from one hand to the other.

"You aint see um gwine back, is you, Mars Cajy?" he asked after a while.

"Ef they went back by this road," said Mr. Staley, with the air of one who is accustomed to weigh well his words, "it must 'a' bin endurin' of the time whiles I was asleep, bekaze I haint bin no furder from my shop than to yon bed."

"Well, sir!" exclaimed Free Joe in an awed tone, which Mr. Staley seemed to regard as a tribute to his extraordinary powers of statement.

"Ef it's my beliefs you want," continued the old man, "I'll pitch 'em at you fair and free. My beliefs is that Spite Calderwood is gone an' took Lucindy outen the county. Bless your heart and soul! when Spite Calderwood meets the Old Boy[4] in the road they'll be a turrible scuffle. You mark what I tell you."

Free Joe, still fumbling with his hat, rose and leaned against the door-facing. He seemed to be embarrassed. Presently he said,

"I speck I better be gittin' 'long. Nex' time I see Lucindy, I'm gwine tell 'er w'at Miss Becky say 'bout de queen er spades—dat I is. Ef dat don't tickle 'er, dey ain't no nigger 'oman never bin tickle'."

He paused a moment, as though waiting for some remark or comment, some confirmation of misfortune, or, at the very least, some endorsement of his suggestion that Lucinda would be greatly pleased to know that she had figured as the queen of spades; but neither Miss Becky nor her brother said any thing.

"One minnit ridin' in the buggy 'longside er Mars Spite, en de nex' high-falutin' 'roun' playin' de queen er spades. Mon, deze yer nigger gals gittin' up in de pictur's; dey sholy is."

[4]The devil.

With a brief "Good-night, Miss Becky, Mars Cajy," Free Joe went out into the darkness, followed by little Dan. He made his way to the poplar, where Lucinda had been in the habit of meeting him, and sat down. He sat there a long time; he sat there until little Dan, growing restless, trotted off in the direction of the Calderwood place. Dozing against the poplar, in the gray dawn of the morning Free Joe heard Spite Calderwood's fox-hounds in full cry a mile away.

"Shoo!" he exclaimed, scratching his head, and laughing to himself, "dem ar dogs is des a-warmin' dat old fox up."

But it was Dan the hounds were after, and the little dog came back no more. Free Joe waited and waited, until he grew tired of waiting. He went back the next night and waited, and for many nights thereafter. His waiting was in vain, and yet he never regarded it as in vain. Careless and shabby as he was, Free Joe was thoughtful enough to have his theory. He was convinced that little Dan had found Lucinda, and that some night when the moon was shining brightly through the trees, the dog would rouse him from his dreams as he sat sleeping at the foot of the poplar-tree, and he would open his eyes and behold Lucinda standing over him, laughing merrily as of old; and then he thought what fun they would have about the queen of spades.

How many long nights Free Joe waited at the foot of the poplar-tree for Lucinda and little Dan, no one can ever know. He kept no account of them, and they were not recorded by Micajah Staley nor by Miss Becky. The season ran into summer and then into fall. One night he went to the Staley cabin, cut the two old people an armful of wood, and seated himself on the door-steps, where he rested. He was always thankful—and proud, as it seemed—when Miss Becky gave him a cup of coffee, which she was sometimes thoughtful enough to do. He was especially thankful on this particular night.

"You er still layin' off for to strike up wi' Lucindy out thar in the woods, I reckon," said Micajah Staley, smiling grimly. The situation was not without its humorous aspects.

"Oh, dey er comin', Mars Cajy, dey er comin', sho," Free Joe replied. "I boun' you dey'll come; en w'en dey does come, I'll des take en fetch um yer, whar you kin see um wid your own eyes, you en Miss Becky."

"No," said Mr. Staley, with a quick and emphatic gesture of disapproval. "Don't! don't fetch 'em anywheres. Stay right wi' 'em as long as may be."

Free Joe chuckled, and slipped away into the night, while the two old people sat gazing in the fire. Finally Micajah spoke.

"Look at that nigger; look at 'im. He's pine-blank as happy now as a kill-dee[5] by a mill-race. You can't 'faze 'em. I'd in-about give up my t'other hand ef I could stan' flat-footed, an' grin at trouble like that there nigger."

"Niggers is niggers," said Miss Becky, smiling grimly, "an' you can't rub it out; yit I lay I've seed a heap of white people lots meaner'n Free Joe. He

---

[5] The killdeer.

grins,—an' that's nigger,—but I've ketched his under jaw a-trimblin' when Lucindy's name uz brung up. An' I tell you," she went on, bridling up a little, and speaking with almost fierce emphasis, "the Old Boy's done sharpened his claws for Spite Calderwood. You'll see it."

"Me, Rebecca?" said Mr. Staley, hugging his palsied arm; "me? I hope not."

"Well, you'll know it then," said Miss Becky, laughing heartily at her brother's look of alarm.

The next morning Micajah Staley had occasion to go into the woods after a piece of timber. He saw Free Joe sitting at the foot of the poplar, and the sight vexed him somewhat.

"Git up from there," he cried, "an' go an' arn your livin'. A mighty purty pass it's come to, when great big buck niggers can lie a-snorin' in the woods all day, when t'other folks is got to be up an' a-gwine. Git up from there!"

Receiving no response, Mr. Staley went to Free Joe, and shook him by the shoulder; but the negro made no response. He was dead. His hat was off, his head was bent, and a smile was on his face. It was as if he had bowed and smiled when death stood before him, humble to the last. His clothes were ragged; his hands were rough and callous; his shoes were literally tied together with strings; he was shabby in the extreme. A passer-by, glancing at him, could have no idea that such a humble creature had been summoned as a witness before the Lord God of Hosts.

1887

■ **THOMAS NELSON PAGE** ■
1853–1922

Thomas Nelson Page can be said to be the founder of the postbellum plantation school of Southern fiction, a genre that presented a nostalgic and idealized view of the Old South. Page was born on a family plantation near the village of Beaverdam, Virginia. Both the Nelsons and the Pages were among the First Families of Virginia, John Page having been a founder of Williamsburg and Thomas Nelson a settler in Yorktown. Like many young members of Southern aristocracy, young Page grew up reading the works of Walter Scott and Alfred Tennyson and learning the codes of chivalry and paternalism. The Civil War and Reconstruction devastated the wealth of both families, meaning that young Page was unable to complete his education at Washington College (now Washington and Lee University), where Robert E. Lee was president. In order to earn money to complete his schooling, he moved to Louisville, Kentucky, to tutor the children of his cousins. He later attended and received his degree from the University of Virginia School of Law. He set up a law practice in Richmond in 1876, where he remained until 1893. He married Anne Seddon Bruce in 1886; she was a descendant of one of the wealthiest men in the state. She died after two years of marriage. Five years later, he married again, this time to Florence Lathrop Field, the widow of Henry Field of the Marshall Field family of department store fame. Shortly after this marriage, he gave up his law practice and moved to Washington, D.C., to become a full-time writer. From 1913 to 1919, he served as ambassador to Italy under Woodrow Wilson. He died in 1922 at the ancestral family home known as Oakland, which he had been able to restore with his earnings from his literary work.

He began his writing career while at the University of Virginia as a member of the Jefferson Literary Society. His first significant publication came in 1877 with a dialect poem, "Uncle Gabe's White Folks," which appeared in *Scribner's Monthly*. This piece established his successful formula of using an African American vernacular voice to tell about the glories of Southern society before the war; while the dialect is difficult for modern readers, Page claimed that it was based on the actual speech of eastern Virginia blacks. He soon focused on short fiction. "Marse Chan," his first and most famous story, was published in 1884. When it appeared in the collection *In Ole Virginia* (1887), his reputation was made. The story and others like it combine the regional emphasis of local color writing with nostalgia for an antebellum world that had never actually existed. It was a world of beautiful women, chivalrous men, contented and loyal slaves, a code of honor, and a civilization superior to that which was developing in the New South of post-Reconstruction America. It was the world Page wanted to believe existed during his early childhood.

Recognition and reward from this work enabled him to eventually retire from the practice of law to write novels, children's books, biography, social commentary, popular history, and literary essays. He had a profound effect on a generation of Southern writers, including Grace King, Joel Chandler Harris, and George Washington Cable. That influence was not broken until the emergence of the more critical perspective of Ellen Glasgow, William Faulkner, and other members of the Southern Renaissance.

Keith Byerman
Indiana State University

PRIMARY WORKS

In Ole Virginia, or Marse Chan and Other Stories, 1887; *The Old South: Essays Social and Political*, 1892; *Red Rock*, 1898; *Gordon Keith*, 1903; *The Negro: The Southerner's Problem*, 1904; *Robert E. Lee, The Southerner*, 1908; *John Marvel, Assistant*, 1910; *The Red Riders*, 1924.

Marse Chan

A Tale of Old Virginia

One afternoon, in the autumn of 1872, I was riding leisurely down the sandy road that winds along the top of the water-shed between two of the smaller rivers of eastern Virginia. The road I was travelling, following "the ridge" for miles, had just struck me as most significant of the character of the race whose only avenue of communication with the outside world it had formerly been. Their once splendid mansions, now fast falling to decay, appeared to view from time to time, set back far from the road, in proud seclusion, among groves of oak and hickory, now scarlet and gold with the early frost. Distance was nothing to this people; time was of no consequence to them. They desired but a level path in life, and that they had, though the way was longer, and the outer world strode by them as they dreamed.

I was aroused from my reflections by hearing some one ahead of me calling, "Heah!—heah—whoo-oop, heah!"

Turning the curve in the road, I saw just before me a negro standing, with a hoe and a watering-pot in his hand. He had evidently just gotten over the "worm-fence"[1] into the road, out of the path which led zigzag across the "old field" and was lost to sight in the dense growth of sassafras. When I rode up, he was looking anxiously back down this path for his dog. So engrossed was he that he did not even hear my horse, and I reined in to wait until he should turn around and satisfy my curiosity as to the handsome old place half a mile off from the road.

The numerous out-buildings and the large barns and stables told that it had once been the seat of wealth, and the wild waste of sassafras that covered the broad fields gave it an air of desolation that greatly excited my interest. Entirely oblivious of my proximity, the negro went on calling "Whooo-oop, heah!" until along the path, walking very slowly and with great dignity, appeared a noble-looking old orange and white setter, gray with age, and corpulent with excessive feeding. As soon as he came in sight, his master began:

"Yes, dat you! You gittin' deaf as well as bline, I s'pose! Kyarnt heah me callin', I reckon? Whyn't yo' come on, dawg?"

The setter sauntered slowly up to the fence and stopped, without even deigning a look at the speaker, who immediately proceeded to take the rails down, talking meanwhile:

"Now, I got to pull down de gap, I s'pose! Yo' so sp'ilt yo' kyahn hardly walk. Jes'ez able to git over it as I is! Jes' like white folks—think 'cuz you's white and I's black, I got to wait on yo' all de time. Ne'm mine, I ain' gwi' do it!"

The fence having been pulled down sufficiently low to suit his dogship, he marched sedately through, and, with a hardly perceptible lateral movement of his tail, walked on down the road. Putting up the rails carefully, the negro turned and saw me.

"Sarvent, marster," he said, taking his hat off. Then, as if apologetically for having permitted a stranger to witness what was merely a family affair, he added: "He know I don' mean nothin' by what I sez. He's Marse Chan's

---

[1]A fence made of crossed rail that forms a zig-zag pattern.

dawg, an' he's so ole he kyahn git long no pearter. He know I'se jes' prod-jickin' wid 'im."

"Who is Marse Chan?" I asked; "and whose place is that over there, and the one a mile or two back—the place with the big gate and the carved stone pillars?"

"Marse Chan," said the darky, "he's Marse Channin'—my young mar-ster; an' dem places—dis one's Weall's, an' de one back dyar wid de rock gate-pos's is ole Cun'l Chahmb'lin's. Dey don' nobody live dyar now, 'cep' niggers. Arfter de war some one or nurr bought our place, but his name done kind o' slipped me. I nuver hearn on 'im befo'; I think dey's half-strainers[2] I don' ax none on 'em no odds. I lives down de road heah, a little piece, an' I jes' steps down of a evenin' and looks arfter de graves."

"Well, where is Marse Chan?" I asked.

"Hi! don' you know? Marse Chan, he went in de army. I was wid im. Yo' know he warn' gwine an' lef' Sam."

"Will you tell me all about it? "I said, dismounting.

Instantly, and as if by instinct, the darky stepped forward and took my bridle. I demurred a little; but with a bow that would have honored old Sir Roger,[3] he shortened the reins, and taking my horse from me, led him along.

"Now tell me about Marse Chan," I said.

"Lawd, marster, hit's so long ago, I'd a'most forgit all about it, ef I hedn' been wid him ever sence he wuz born. Ez 'tis, I remembers it jes' like 'twuz yistiddy. Yo' know Marse Chan an' me—we wuz boys togerr. I wuz older'n he wuz, jes' de same ez he wuz whiter'n me. I wuz born plantin' corn time, de spring arfter big Jim an' de six steers got washed away at de upper ford right down dyar b'low de quarters ez he wuz a bringin' de Chris'mas things home; an' Marse Chan, he warn' born tell mos' to de harves' arfter my sister Nancy married Cun'l Chahmb'lin's Torm, 'bout eight years arfterwoods.

"Well, when Marse Chan wuz born, dey wuz de grettes' doin's at home you ever did see. De folks all hed holiday, jes' like in de Chris'mas. Ole mar-ster (we didn' call 'im *ole* marster tell arfter Marse Chan wuz born—befo' dat he wuz jes' de marster, so)—well, ole marster, his face fyar shine wid pleasure, an' all de folks wuz mighty glad, too, 'cause dey all loved ole mar-ster, and aldo' dey did step aroun' right peart when ole marster was lookin' at 'em, dyar warn' nyar han' on de place but what, ef he wanted anythin', would walk up to de back poach, an' say he warn' to see de marster. An' ev'y-body wuz talkin' 'bout de young marster, an' de maids an' de wimmens 'bout de kitchen wuz sayin' how 'twuz de purties' chile dey ever see; an' at dinner-time de mens (all on 'em hed holiday) come roun' de poach an' ax how de missis an' de young marster wuz, an' ole marster come out on de poach an' smile wus'n a 'possum, an' sez, 'Thankee! Bofe doin' fust rate, boys;' an' den he stepped back in de house, sort o' laughin' to hisse'f, an' in a minute he

---

[2] Poor whites with ambitions to rise in society.
[3] Possibly Roger Robshart, mentioned in Walter Scott's *Kenilworth*.

come out ag'in wid de baby in he arms, all wrapped up in flannens[4] an' things, an' sez, 'Heah he is, boys.' All de folks den, dey went up on de poach to look at 'im, drappin' dey hats on de steps, an' scrapin' dey feets ez dey went up. An' pres'n'y ole marster, lookin' down at we all chil'en all packed togerr down dyah like a parecel o' sheep-burrs, cotch sight o' *me* (he knowed my name, 'cause I use' to hole he hoss fur 'im sometimes; but he didn' know all de chil'en by name, dey wuz so many on 'em), an' he sez, 'Come up heah.' So up I goes tippin', skeered like, an' old marster sez, 'Ain' you Mymie's son?' 'Yass, seh,' sez I. 'Well,' sez he, 'I'm gwine to give you to yo' young Marse Channin' to be his body-servant,' an' he put de baby right in my arms (it's de truth I'm tellin' yo'!), an' yo' jes' ought to a-heard de folks sayin', 'Lawd! marster, dat boy'll drap dat chile!' 'Naw, he won't,' sez marster; 'I kin trust 'im.' And den he sez: 'Now, Sam, from dis time you belong to yo' young Marse Channin'; I wan' you to tek keer on 'im ez long ez he lives. You are to be his boy from dis time. An' now,' he sez, 'carry 'im in de house.' An' he walks arfter me an' opens de do's fur me, an' I kyars 'im in my arms, an' lays 'im down on de bed. An from dat time I was tooken in de house to be Marse Channin's body-servant.

"Well, you nuver see a chile grow so. Pres'n'y he growed up right big, an' ole marster sez he must have some edication. So he sont 'im to school to ole Miss Lawry down dyar, dis side o' Cun'l Chahmb'lin's, an' I use' to go 'long wid 'im an' tote he books an' we all's snacks; an' when he larnt to read an' spell right good, an' got 'bout so-o big, ole Miss Lawry she died, an' ole marster said he mus' have a man to teach 'im an' trounce 'im. So we all went to Mr. Hall, whar kep' de school-house beyant de creek, an' dyar we went ev'y day, 'cep Sat'd'ys of co'se, an' sich days ez Marse Chan din' warn' go, an' ole missis begged 'im off.

"Hit wuz down dyar Marse Chan fust took notice o' Miss Anne. Mr. Hall, he taught gals ez well ez boys, an' Cun'l Chahmb'lin he sont his daughter (dat's Miss Anne I'm talkin' about). She wuz a leetle bit o' gal when she fust come. Yo' see, her ma wuz dead, an' ole Miss Lucy Chahmb'lin, she lived wid her brurr an' kep' house for 'im; an' he wuz so busy wid politics, he didn' have much time to spyar, so he sont Miss Anne to Mr. Hall's by a 'ooman wid a note. When she come dat day in de school-house, an' all de chil'en looked at her so hard, she tu'n right red, an' tried to pull her long curls over her eyes, an' den put bofe de backs of her little han's in her two eyes, an' begin to cry to herse'f. Marse Chan he was settin' on de een' o' de bench nigh de do', an' he jes' reached out an' put he arm roun' her an' drawed her up to 'im. An' he kep' whisperin' to her, an' callin' her name, an' coddlin' her; an' pres'n'y she took her han's down an' begin to laugh.

"Well, dey 'peared to tek' a gre't fancy to each urr from dat time. Miss Anne she warn' nuthin' but a baby hardly, an' Marse Chan he wuz a good big boy 'bout mos' thirteen years ole, I reckon. Hows'ever, dey sut'n'y wuz sot on each urr an' (yo' heah me!) ole marster an' Cun'l Chahmb'lin dey

[4]Flannel blankets.

'peared to like it 'bout well ez de chil'en. Yo' see, Cun'l Chahmb'lin's place j'ined ourn, an' it looked jes' ez natural fur dem two chil'en to marry an' mek it one plantation, ez it did fur de creek to run down de bottom from our place into Cun'l Chahmb'lin's. I don' rightly think de chil'en thought 'bout gittin' *married*, not den, no mo'n I thought 'bout marryin' Judy when she wuz a little gal at Cun'l Chahmb'lin's, runnin' 'bout de house, huntin' fur Miss Lucy's spectacles; but dey wuz good frien's from de start. Marse Chan he use' to kyar Miss Anne's books fur her ev'y day, an' ef de road wuz muddy or she wuz tired, he use' to tote her; an' 'twarn' hardly a day passed dat he didn' kyar her some'n' to school—apples or hick'y nuts, or some'n. He wouldn' let none o' de chil'en tease her, nurr. Heh! One day, one o' de boys poked he finger at Miss Anne, and arfter school Marse Chan he axed 'im 'roun' hine de school-house out o' sight, an' ef he didn' whop 'im!

"Marse Chan, he wuz de peartes' scholar ole Mr. Hall hed, an' Mr. Hall he wuz mighty proud o' 'im. I don' think he use' to beat 'im ez much ez he did de urrs, aldo' he wuz de head in all debilment dat went on, jes' ez he wuz in sayin' he lessons.

"Heh! one day in summer, jes' fo' de school broke up, dyah come up a storm right sudden, an' riz de creek (dat one yo' cross' back yonder), an Marse Chan he toted Miss Anne home on he back. He ve'y off'n did dat when de parf wuz muddy. But dis day when dey come to de creek, it had done washed all de logs 'way. 'Twuz still mighty high, so Marse Chan he put Miss Anne down, an' he took a pole an' waded right in. Hit took 'im long up to de shoulders. Den he waded back, an' took Miss Anne up on his head an' kyared her right over. At fust she wuz skeered; but he tol' her he could swim an' wouldn' let her git hu't, an' den she let 'im kyar her 'cross, she hol'in' his han's. I warn' 'long dat day, but he sut'n'y did dat thing.

"Ole marster he wuz so pleased 'bout it, he giv' Marse Chan a pony; an' Marse Chan rode 'im to school de day arfter he come, so proud, an' sayin' how he wuz gwine to let Anne ride behine 'im; an' when he come home dat evenin' he wuz walkin'. 'Hi! where's yo' pony?' said ole marster. 'I give 'im to Anne,' says Marse Chan. 'She liked 'im, an'—I kin walk.' 'Yes,' sez ole marster, laughin', 'I s'pose you's already done giv' her yo'se'f, an' nex' thing I know you'll be givin' her this plantation and all my niggers.'

"Well, about a fortnight[5] or sich a matter arfter dat, Cun'l Chahmb'lin sont over an' invited all o' we all over to dinner, an' Marse Chan wuz 'spressly named in de note whar Ned brought; an' arfter dinner he made ole Phil, whar wuz his ker'ige-driver, bring roun' Marse Chan's pony wid a little side-saddle on 'im, an' a beautiful little hoss wid a bran'-new saddle an' bridle on 'im; an' he gits up an' meks Marse Chan a gre't speech, an' presents 'im de little hoss; an' den he calls Miss Anne, an' she comes out on de poach in a little ridin' frock, an' dey puts her on her pony, an' Marse Chan mounts his hoss, an' dey goes to ride, while de grown folks is a-laughin' an' chattin' an' smokin' dey cigars.

[5]Two weeks.

"Dem wuz good ole times, marster—de bes' Sam ever see! Dey wuz, in fac'! Niggers didn' hed nothin' 't all to do—jes' hed to 'ten' to de feedin' an' cleanin' de hosses, an' doin' what de marster tell 'em to do; an' when dey wuz sick, dey had things sont 'em out de house, an' de same doctor come to see 'em whar 'ten' to de white folks when dey wuz po'ly. Dyar warn' no trouble nor nothin'.

"Well, things tuk a change arfter dat. Marse Chan he went to de bo'din' school, whar he use' to write to me constant. Ole missis use' to read me de letters, an' den I'd git Miss Anne to read 'em ag'in to me when I'd see her. He use' to write to her too, an' she use' to write to him too. Den Miss Anne she wuz sont off to school too. An' in de summer time dey'd bofe come home, an' yo' hardly knowed whether Marse Chan lived at home or over at Cun'l Chahmb'lin's. He wuz over dyah constant. 'Twuz always ridin' or fishin' down dyah in de river; or sometimes he' go over dyah, an' 'im an' she'd go out an' set in de yard onder de trees; she settin' up mekin' out she wuz knittin' some sort o' bright-cullored some'n', wid de grarss growin all up 'g'inst her, an' her hat th'owed back on her neck, an' he readin' to her out books; an' sometimes dey'd bofe read out de same book, fust one an' den todder. I use' to see 'em! Dat wuz when dey wuz growin' up like.

"Den ole marster he run for Congress, an' ole Cun'l Chahmb'lin he wuz put up to run 'g'inst ole marster by de Dimicrats; but ole marster he beat 'im. Yo' know he wuz gwine do dat! Co'se he wuz! Dat made ole Cun'l Chahmb'lin mighty mad, and dey stopt visitin' each urr reg'lar, like dey had been doin' all 'long. Den Cun'l Chahmb'lin he sort o' got in debt, an' sell some o' he niggers, an' dat's de way de fuss begun. Dat's whar de lawsuit cum from. Ole marster he didn' like nobody to sell niggers, an' knowin' dat Cun'l Chahmb'lin wuz sell-in' o' his, he writ an' offered to buy his M'ria an' all her chil'en, 'cause she hed married our Zeek'yel. An' don' yo' think, Cun'l Chahmb'lin axed ole marster mo' 'n th'ee niggers wuz wuth fur M'ria! Befo' old marster bought her, dough, de sheriff cum an' levelled on M'ria an' a whole parecel o' urr niggers. Ole marster he went to de sale, an' bid for 'em; but Cun'l Chahmb'lin he got some one to bid 'g'inst ole marster. Dey wuz knocked out to ole marster dough, an' den dey hed a big lawsuit, an' ole marster wuz agwine to co't, off an' on, fur some years, till at lars' de co't decided dat M'ria belonged to ole marster. Ole Cun'l Chahmb'lin den wuz so mad he sued ole marster for a little strip o' lan' down dyah on de line fence, whar he said belonged to 'im. Evy'body knowed hit belonged to ole marster. Ef yo' go down dyah now, I kin show it to yo', inside de line fence, whar it hed done bin ever since long befo' Cun'l Chahmb'lin wuz born. But Cun'l Chahmb'lin wuz a mons'us perseverin' man, an' ole marster he wouldn' let nobody run over im. No, dat he wouldn'! So dey wuz agwine down to co't about dat, fur I don' know how long, till ole marster beat 'im.

"All dis time, yo' know, Marse Chan wuz agoin' back'ads an' for'ads to college, an' wuz growed up a ve'y fine young man. He wuz a ve'y likely gent' man! Miss Anne she hed done mos' growed up too—wuz puttin' her hyar up like ole missis use' to put hers up, an' 't wuz jes' ez bright ez de sorrel's mane when de sun cotch on it, an' her eyes wuz gre't big dark eyes, like her pa's, on'y bigger an' not so fierce, an' 'twarn' none o' de young ladies ez purty ez she wuz. She an' Marse Chan still set a heap o' sto' by one 'nurr, but I don' think dey wuz easy wid each urr ez when he used to tote her home from school on his back. Marse Chan he use' to love de ve'y groun' she walked on, dough, in my 'pinion. Heh! His face 'twould light up whenever she come into chu'ch, or anywhere, jes' like de sun hed come th'oo a chink on it suddenly.

"Den ole marster lost he eyes. D' yo' ever heah 'bout dat? Heish! Didn' yo'? Well, one night de big barn cotch fire. De stables, yo' know, wuz under de big barn, an' all de hosses wuz in dyah. Hit 'peared to me like 'twarn' no time befo' all de folks an' de neighbors dey come, an' dey wuz a-totin' water, an' a-tryin' to save de po' critters, and dey got a heap on 'em out; but de ker'ige-hosses dey wouldn' come out, an' dey wuz a-runnin' back'ads an' for'ads inside de stalls, a-nikerin' an' a-screamin', like dey knowed dey time hed come. Yo' could heah 'em so pitiful, an' pres'n'y old marster said to Ham Fisher (he wuz de ker'ige-driver), 'Go in dyah an' try to save 'em; don' let 'em bu'n to death.' An' Ham he went right in. An' jest arfter he got in, de shed whar it hed fus' cotch fell in, an' de sparks shot 'way up in de air; an' Ham didn' come back, an' de fire begun to lick out under de eaves over whar de ker'ige hosses' stalls wuz, an' all of a sudden ole marster tu'ned an' kissed ole missis, who wuz standin' nigh him, wid her face jes' ez white ez a sper'it's, an', befo' anybody knowed what he wuz gwine do, jumped right in de do', an' de smoke come po'in' out behine 'im. Well, seh, I nuver 'spects to heah tell Judgment sich a soun' ez de folks set up! Ole missis she jes' drapt down on her knees in de mud an' prayed out loud. Hit 'peared like her pra'r wuz heard; for in a minit, right out de same do', kyarin' Ham Fisher in his arms, come ole marster, wid his clo's all blazin'. Dey flung water on 'im, an' put 'im out; an', ef you b'lieve me, yo' wouldn' a-knowed 'twuz ole marster. Yo' see, he hed find Ham Fisher done fall down in de smoke right by the ker'ige-hoss' stalls, whar he sont him, an' he hed to tote 'im back in his arms th'oo de fire what hed done cotch de front part o' de stable, and to keep de flame from gittin' down Ham Fisher's th'ote he hed tuk off his own hat and mashed it all over Ham Fisher's face, an' he hed kep' Ham Fisher from bein' so much bu'nt; but he wuz bu'nt dreadful! His beard an' hyar wuz all nyawed off, an' his face an' han's an' neck wuz scorified terrible. Well, he jes' laid Ham Fisher down, an' then he kind o' staggered for'ad, an' ole missis ketch' 'im in her arms. Ham Fisher, he warn' bu'nt so bad, an' he got out in a month or two; an' arfter a long time, ole marster he got well, too; but he wuz always stone blind arfter that. He nuver could see none from dat night.

"Marse Chan he comed home from college toreckly, an' he sut'n'y did nuss ole marster faithful—jes' like a 'ooman. Den he took charge of de plantation arfter dat; an' I use' to wait on 'im jes' like when we wuz boys togedder; an' sometimes we'd slip off an' have a fox-hunt, an' he'd be jes' like he wuz in ole times, befo' ole marster got bline, an' Miss Anne Chahmb'lin stopt comin' over to our house, an' settin' onder de trees, readin' out de same book.

"He sut'n'y wuz good to me. Nothin' nuvef made no diffunce 'bout dat. He nuver hit me a lick in his life—an' nuver let nobody else do it, nurr.

"I 'members one day, when he wuz a leetle bit o' boy, ole marster hed done tole we all chil'en not to slide on de straw-stacks; an' one day me an' Marse Chan thought ole marster hed done gone 'way from home. We watched him git on he hoss an' ride up de road out o' sight, an' we wuz out in de field a-slidin' an a-slidin', when up comes ole marster. We started to run; but he hed done see us, an' he called us to come back; an' sich a whuppin' ez he did gi' us!

"Fust he took Marse Chan, an' den he teched me up. He nuver hu't me, but in co'se I wuz a-hollerin' ez hard ez I could stave it, 'cause I knowed. dat wuz gwine mek him stop. Marse Chan he hed'n open he mouf long ez ole marster wuz tunin' 'im; but soon ez he commence warmin' me an' I begin to holler, Marse Chan he bu'st out cryin', an' stept right in befo' ole marster, an' ketchin' de whup, sed:

"'Stop, seh! Yo' shan't whup 'im; he b'longs to me, an' ef you hit 'im another lick I'll set 'im free!'

"I wish yo' hed see ole marster. Marse Chan he warn' mo'n eight years ole, an' dyah dey wuz—old marster stan'in' wid he whup raised up, an' Marse Chan red an' cryin', hol'in' on to it, an' sayin' I b'longst to 'im.

"Ole marster, he raise' de whup, an' den he drapt it, an' broke out in a smile over he face, an' he chuck' Marse Chan onder de chin, an' tu'n right roun' an' went away, laughin' to hisse'f, an' I heah' 'im tellin' ole missis dat evenin', an' laughin' 'bout it.

"'Twan' so mighty long arfter dat when dey fust got to talkin' 'bout de war. Dey wuz a-dictatin' back'ads an' for'ds 'bout it fur two or th'ee years 'fo' it come sho' nuff, you know. Ole marster, he was a Whig,[6] an' of co'se Marse Chan he tuk after he pa. Cun'l Chahmb'lin, he wuz a Dimicrat. He wuz in favor of de war, an' ole marster and Marse Chan dey wuz agin' it. Dey wuz a-talkin' 'bout it all de time, an' purty soon Cun'l Chahmb'lin he went about ev'vywhar speakin' an' noratin' 'bout Ferginia ought to secede; an' Marse Chan he wuz picked up to talk agin' 'im. Dat wuz de way dey come to fight de duil. I sut'n'y wuz skeered fur Marse Chan dat mawnin', an' he was jes' ez cool! Yo' see, it happen so: Marse Chan he wuz a-speakin' down at de Deep Creek Tavern, an' he kind o' got de bes' of ole Cun'l Chahmb'lin. All de white folks laughed an' hoorawed, an' ole Cun'l Chahmb'lin—my Lawd! I t'ought he'd 'a' bu'st, he was so mad. Well, when it come to his time to speak, he jes' light into Marse Chan. He call 'im a traitor, an' a ab'litionis', an' I don' know what all. Marse Chan, he jes' kep' cool till de ole Cun'l light into he pa. Ez soon ez he name ole marster, I seen Marse Chan sort o' lif' up he head. D' yo' ever see a hoss rar he head up right sudden at night when he see somethin' comin' to'ds 'im from de side an' he don' know what 'tis? Ole Cun'l Chahmb'lin he went right on.

[6]Political party operating 1830s to mid-1850s that opposed the policies of Andrew Jackson. Elements of it were absorbed into the Republican Party.

He said ole marster hed taught Marse Chan; dat ole marster wuz a wuss ab'litionis' dan he son. I looked at Marse Chan, an' sez to myse'f: 'Fo' Gord! old Cun'l Chahmb'lin better min', an' I hedn' got de wuds out, when ole Cun'l Chahmb'lin 'cuse' old marster o' cheatin' 'im out o' he niggers, an' stealin' piece o' he lan'—dat's de lan' I tole you 'bout. Well, seh, nex' thing I knowed, I heahed Marse Chan—hit all happen right 'long togerr, like lightnin' and thunder when they hit right at you—I heah 'im say:

"'Cun'l Chahmb'lin, what you say is false, an' yo' know it to be so. You have wilfully slandered one of de pures' an' nobles' men Gord ever made, an' nothin' but yo' gray hyars protects you.'

"Well, ole Cun'l Chahmb'lin, he ra'ed an' he pitch'd. He said he wan' too ole, an' he'd show 'im so.

"'Ve'y well,' says Marse Chan.

"De meetin broke up den. I wuz hol'in' de hosses out dyar in de road by de een' o' de poach, an' I see Marse Chan talkin' an' talkin' to Mr. Gordon an' anudder gent'man, and den he come out an' got on de sorrel an' galloped off. Soon ez he got out o' sight he pulled up, an' we walked along tell we come to de road whar leads off to'ds Mr. Barbour's. He wuz de big lawyer o' de country. Dar he tu'ned off. All dis time he hedn' sed a wud, 'cep' to kind o' mumble to hisse'f now and den. When we got to Mr. Barbour's, he got down an' went in. Dat wuz in de late winter; de folks wuz jes' beginnin' to plough fur corn. He stayed dyar 'bout two hours, an' when he come out Mr. Barbour come out to de gate wid 'im an' shake han's arfter he got up in de saddle. Den we all rode off. 'Twuz late den—good dark; an' we rid ez hard ez we could, tell we come to de ole school-house at ole Cun'l Chahmb'lin's gate. When we got dar, Marse Chan got down an' walked right slow 'roun' de house. Arfter lookin' roun' a little while an' tryin' de do' to see ef it wuz shet, he walked down de road tell he got to de creek. He stop' dyar a little while an' picked up two or three little rocks an' frowed 'em in, an' pres'n'y he got up an' we come on home. Ez he got down, he tu'ned to me an', rubbin' de sorrel's nose, said: 'Have 'em well fed, Sam; I'll want 'em early in de mawnin'.'

"Dat night at supper he laugh an' talk, an' he set at de table a long time. Arfter ole marster went to bed, he went in de charmber an' set on de bed by 'im talkin' to 'im an' tellin' 'im 'bout de meetin' an' e'vything; but he nuver mention ole Cun'l Chahmb'lin's name. When he got up to come out to de office in de yard, whar he slept, he stooped down an' kissed 'im jes' like he wuz a baby layin' dyar in de bed, an' he'd hardly let ole missis go at all. I knowed some'n wuz up, an' nex mawnin' I called 'im early befo' light, like he tole me, an' he dressed an' come out pres'n'y jes' like he wuz goin' to church. I had de hosses ready, an' we went out de back way to'ds de river. Ez we rode along, he said:

"'Sam, you an' I wuz boys togedder, wa'n't we?'

"'Yes,' sez I,' Marse Chan, dat we wuz.'

"'You have been ve'y faithful to me,' sez he, 'an' I have seen to it that you are well provided fur. You want to marry Judy, I know, an' you'll be able to buy her ef you want to.'

"Den he tole me he wuz goin' to fight a duil, an' in case he should git shot, he had set me free an' giv' me nuff to tek keer o' me an' my wife ez long ez we lived. He said he'd like me to stay an' tek keer o' ole marster an' ole missis ez long ez dey lived, an' he said it wouldn' be very long, he reckoned. Dat wuz de on'y time he voice broke—when he said dat; an' I couldn' speak a wud, my th'oat choked me so.

"When we come to de river, we tu'ned right up de bank, an' arfter ridin' 'bout a mile or sich a matter, we stopped whar dey wuz a little clearin' wid elder bushes on one side an' two big gum-trees on de urr, an' de sky wuz all red, an' de water down to'ds whar the sun wuz comin' wuz jes' like de sky.

"Pres'n'y Mr. Gordon he come, wid a 'hogany box 'bout so big 'fore 'im, an' he got down, an' Marse Chan tole me to tek all de hosses an' go 'roun' behine de bushes whar I tell you 'bout—off to one side; an' 'fore I got 'roun' dar, ole Cun'l Chahmb'lin an' Mr. Hennin an' Dr. Call come ridin' from t'urr way, to'ds ole Cun'l Chahmb'lin's. When dey hed tied dey hosses, de urr gent'mens went up to whar Mr. Gordon wuz, an' arfter some chattin' Mr. Hennin step' off 'bout fur ez 'cross dis road, or mebbe it mout be a little furder; an' den I seed 'em th'oo de bushes loadin' de pistils, an' talk a little while; an' den Marse Chan an' ole Cun'l Chahmb'lin walked up wid de pistils in dey han's, an' Marse Chan he stood wid his face right to'ds de sun. I seen it shine on him jes' ez it come up over de low groun's, an' he look like he did sometimes when he come out of church. I wuz so skeered I couldn' say nothin'. Ole Cun'l Chahmb'lin could shoot fust rate, an' Marse Chan he never missed.

"Den I heared Mr. Gordon say, 'Gent'mens, is yo' ready?' and bofe of 'em sez, 'Ready,' jes' so.

"An' he sez, 'Fire, one, two' — an' ez he said 'one,' ole Cun'l Chahmb'lin raised he pistil an' shot right at Marse Chan. De ball went th'oo his hat. I seen he hat sort o' settle on he head ez de bullit hit it, an' *he* jes' tilted his pistil up in de a'r an' shot—*bang*; an' ez de pistil went *bang*, he sez to Cun'l Chahmb'lin, 'I mek you a present to yo' fam'ly, seh!'

"Well, dey had some talkin' arfter dat. I didn't git rightly what it wuz; but it 'peared like Cun'l Chahmb'lin he warn't satisfied, an' wanted to have anurr shot. De seconds dey wuz talkin', an' pres'n'y dey put de pistils up, an' Marse Chan an' Mr. Gordon shook han's wid Mr. Hennin an' Dr. Call, an' come an' got on dey hosses. An' Cun'l Chahmb'lin he got on his horse an' rode away wid de urr gent'mens, lookin' like he did de day befo' when all de people laughed at 'im.

"I b'lieve ole Cun'l Chahmb'lin wan' to shoot Marse Chan, anyway!

"We come on home to breakfast, I totin' de box wid de pistils befo' me on de roan. Would you b'lieve me, seh, Marse Chan he nuver said a wud 'bout it to ole marster or nobody. Ole missis didn' fin' out 'bout it for mo'n a month, an' den, Lawd! how she did cry and kiss Marse Chan; an' ole marster, aldo' he never say much, he wuz jes' ez please' ez ole missis. He call' me in de room an' made me tole 'im all 'bout it, an' when I got th'oo he gi' me five dollars an' a pyar of breeches.

"But ole Cun'l Chahmb'lin he nuver did furgive Marse Chan, an' Miss Anne she got mad too. Wimmens is mons'us onreasonable nohow. Dey's jes' like a catfish: you can n' tek hole on 'em like udder folks, an' when you gits 'm yo' can n' always hole 'em.

"What meks me think so? Heaps o' things—dis: Marse Chan he done gi' Miss Anne her pa jes' ez good ez I gi' Marse Chan's dawg sweet 'taters, an' she git mad wid 'im ez if he hed kill 'im 'stid o' sen'in' 'im back to her dat mawnin' whole an' soun'. B'lieve me! she wouldn' even speak to him arfter dat!

"Don' I 'member dat mawnin'!

"We wuz gwine fox-huntin', 'bout six weeks or sich a matter arfter de duil, an' we met Miss Anne ridin' 'long wid anurr lady an' two gent'mens whar wuz stayin' at her house. Dyar wuz always some one or nurr dyar co't-ing her. Well, dat mawnin' we meet 'em right in de road. 'Twuz de fust time Marse Chan had see her sence de duil, an' he raises he hat ez he pahss, an' she looks right at 'im wid her head up in de yair like she nuver see 'im befo' in her born days; an' when she comes by me, she sez, 'Good-mawnin', Sam!' Gord! I nuver see nuthin' like de look dat come on Marse Chan's face when she pahss 'im like dat. He gi' de sorrel a pull dat fotch 'im back settin' down in de san' on he hanches. He ve'y lips wuz white. I tried to keep up wid 'im, but 'twarn' no use. He sont me back home pres'n'y, an' he rid on. I sez to myself, 'Cun'l Chahmb'lin, don' yo' meet Marse Chan dis mawnin'. He ain' bin lookin' 'roun' de ola school-house, whar he an' Miss Anne use' to go to school to ole Mr. Hall together, fur nuffin'. He won' stan' no prodjickin' to-day.'

"He nuver come home dat night tell 'way late, an' ef he'd been fox-hun-tin' it mus' ha' been de ole red whar lives down in de greenscum mashes he'd been chasin'. De way de sorrel wuz gormed up wid sweat an' mire sut'n'y did hu't me. He walked up to de stable wid he head down all de way, an' I'se seen 'im go eighty miles of a winter day, an' prance into de stable at night ez fresh ez ef he hed jes' cantered over to ole Cun'l Chahmb'lin's to supper. I nuver seen a hoss beat so sence I knowed de fetlock from de fo'lock, an' bad ez he wuz he wan' ez bad ez Marse Chan.

"Whew! he didn' git over dat thing, seh—he nuver did git over it.

"De war come on jes' den, an Marse Chan wuz elected cap'n; but he wouldn' tek it. He said Firginia hadn' seceded, an' he wuz gwine stan' by her. Den dey 'lected Mr. Gordon cap'n.

"I sut'n'y did wan' Marse Chan to tek de place, cuz I knowed he wuz gwine tek me wid 'im. He wan' gwine widout Sam. An' beside, he look so po' an' thin, I thought he wuz gwine die.

"Of co'se, ole missis she heared 'bout it, an' she met Miss Anne in de road, an' cut her jes' like Miss Anne cut Marse Chan.

"Ole missis, she wuz proud ez anybody! So we wuz mo' strangers dan ef we hadn' live' in a hunderd miles of each urr. An' Marse Chan he wuz gittin' thinner an' thinner, an' Firginia she come out, an' den Marse Chan he went to Richmond an' 'listed, an' come back an' sey he wuz a private, an' he didn' know whe'r he could tek me or not. He writ to Mr. Gordon, hows'ever, an' 'twuz 'cided dat when he went I wuz to go 'long an' wait on him an' de cap'n too. I didn' min' dat, yo' know, long ez I could go wid Marse Chan, an' I like' Mr. Gordon, anyways.

"Well, one night Marse Chan come back from de offis wid a telegram dat say, 'Come at once,' so he wuz to start nex' mawnin'. He uniform wuz all ready, gray wid yaller trimmin's, an' mine wuz ready too, an' he had ole marster's sword, whar de State gi' 'im in de Mexikin war; an' he trunks wuz all packed wid ev'rything in 'em, an' my chist was packed too, an' Jim Rasher he druv 'em over to de depo' in de waggin, an' we wuz to start nex' mawnin' 'bout light. Dis wuz 'bout de las' o' spring, you know. Dat night ole missis made Marse Chan dress up in he uniform, an' he sut'n'y did look splendid, wid he long mustache an' he wavin' hyar an' he tall figger.

"Arfter supper he come down an' sez: 'Sam, I wan' you to tek dis note an' kyar it over to Cun'l Chahmb'lin's, an' gi' it to Miss Anne wid yo' own han's, an' bring me wud what she sez. Don' let any one know 'bout it, or know why you've gone.' 'Yes, seh,' sez I.

"Yo' see, I knowed Miss Anne's maid over at ole Cun'l Chahmb'lin's—dat wuz Judy whar is my wife now—an' I knowed I could wuk it. So I tuk de roan an' rid over, an' tied 'im down de hill in de cedars, an' I wen' 'roun' to de back yard. 'Twuz a right blowy sort o' night; de moon wuz jes' risin', but de clouds wuz so big it didn' shine 'cep' th'oo a crack now an' den. I soon foun' my gal, an' arfter tellin' her two or three lies 'bout herse'f, I got her to go in an' ax Miss Anne to come to de do'. When she come, I gi' her de note, an' arfter a little while she bro't me anurr, an' I tole her good-by, an' she gi' me a dollar, an' I come home an' gi' de letter to Marse Chan. He read it, an' tole me to have de hosses ready at twenty minits to twelve at de corner of de garden. An' jes' befo' dat he come out ez ef he wuz gwine to bed, but instid he come, an' we all struck out to'ds Cun'l Chahmb'lin's. When we got mos' to de gate, de hosses got sort o' skeered, an' I see dey wuz some'n or somebody standin' jes' inside; an' Marse Chan he jumpt off de sorrel an' flung me de bridle and he walked up.

"She spoke fust ('twuz Miss Anne had done come out dyar to meet Marse Chan), an' she sez, jes' ez cold ez a chill, 'Well, seh, I granted your favor. I wished to relieve myse'f of de obligations you placed me under a few months ago, when you made me a present of my father, whom you fust insulted an then prevented from gittin' satisfaction.'

"Marse Chan he didn' speak fur a minit, an' den he said: 'Who is with you?' (Dat wuz ev'y wud.)

"'No one,' sez she; 'I came alone.'

"'My God!' sez he, 'you didn' come all through those woods by yourse'f at this time o' night?'

"'Yes, I'm not afraid,' sez she. (An' heah dis nigger! I don' b'lieve she wuz.)

"De moon come out, an' I cotch sight o' her stan'in' dyar in her white dress, wid de cloak she had wrapped herse'f up in drapped off on de groun', an' she didn' look like she wuz 'feared o' nuthin'. She wuz mons'us purty ez she stood dyar wid de green bushes behine her, an' she hed jes' a few flowers in her breas'—right hyah—and some leaves in her sorrel hyar; an' de moon come out an' shined down on her hyar an' her frock, an' 'peared like de light wuz jes' stan'in' off it ez she stood dyar lookin' at Marse Chan wid her head tho'd back, jes' like dat mawnin' when she pahss Marse Chan in de road widout speakin' to 'im, an' sez to me, 'Good mawnin', Sam.'

"Marse Chan, he den tole her he hed come to say good-by to her, ez he wuz gwine 'way to de war nex' mawnin'. I wuz watchin' on her, an' I tho't, when Marse Chan tole her dat, she sort o' started an' looked up at 'im like she wuz mighty sorry, an' 'peared like she didn' stan' quite so straight arfter dat Den Marse Chan he went on talkin' right fars to her; an' he tole her how he had loved her ever sence she wuz a little bit o' baby mos', an' how he nuver 'membered de time when he hedn' 'spected to marry her. He tole her it wuz his love for her dat hed made 'im stan' fust at school an' collige, an' hed kep' 'im good an' pure; an' now he wuz gwine 'way, wouldn' she let it be like 'twuz in ole times, an' ef he come back from de war wouldn' she try to think on him ez she use' to do when she wuz a little guirl?

"Marse Chan he had done been talkin' so serious, he hed done tuk Miss Anne's han', an' wuz lookin' down in her face like he wuz list'nin' wid his eyes.

"Arfter a minit Miss Anne she said somethin', an' Marse Chan he cotch her urr han' an' sez:

"'But if you love me, Anne?'

"When he said dat, she tu'ned her head 'way from 'im, an' wait' a minit, an' den she said—right clear:

"'But I don' love yo'.' (Jes' dem th'ee wuds!) De wuds fall right slow—like dirt falls out a spade on a coffin when yo's buryin' anybody, an' seys, 'Uth to uth.' Marse Chan he jes' let her hand drap, an' he stiddy hisse'f 'g'inst de gate-pos', an' he didn' speak torekly. When he did speak, all he sez wuz:

"'I mus' see you home safe.'

"I 'clar, marster, I didn' know 'twuz Marse Chan's voice tell I look at 'im right good. Well, she wouldn' let 'im go wid her. She jes' wrap' her cloak 'roun' her shoulders, an' wen' 'long back by herse'f, widout doin' more'n jes' look up once at Marse Chan leanin' dyah 'g'inst de gate-pos' in he sodger clo's, wid he eyes on de groun'. She said 'Good-by' sort o' sorf, an' Marse Chan, widout lookin' up, shake han's wid her, an' she wuz done gone down de road. Soon ez she got 'mos' 'roun de curve, Marse Chan he followed her, keepin' under de trees so ez not to be seen, an' I led de hosses on down de road behine 'im. He kep' 'long behine her tell she wuz safe in de house, an' den he come an' got on he hoss, an' we all come home.

"Nex' mawnin' we all come off to j'ine de army. An' dey wuz a-drillin' an' a-drillin' all 'bout for a while an' dey went 'long wid all de res' o' de army, an' I went wid Marse Chan an' clean he boots, an' look arfter de tent, an' tek keer o' him an' de hosses. An' Marse Chan, he wan' a bit like he use' to be. He wuz so solum an' moanful all de time, at leas' 'cep' when dyah wuz gwine to be a fight. Den he'd peartin' up, an' he alwuz rode at de head o' de company, 'cause he wuz tall; an' hit wan' on'y in battles whar all his company wuz dat *he* went, but he use' to volunteer whenever de cun'l wanted anybody to fine out anythin', an' 'twuz so dangersome he didn' like to mek one man go no sooner'n anurr, yo' know, an' ax'd who'd volunteer. *He* 'peared to like to go prowlin' aroun' 'mong dem Yankees, an' he use' to tek me wid 'im whenever he could. Yes, seh, he sut'n'y wuz a good sodger! He didn' mine bullets no more'n he did so many draps o' rain. But I use' to be pow'ful skeered sometimes. It jes' use' to 'pear like fun to 'im. In camp he use' to be so sorrerful he'd hardly open he mouf. You'd 'a' tho't he wuz seekin', he used to look so moanful; but jes' le' 'im git into danger, an' he use' to be like ole times—jolly an' laughin' like when he wuz a boy.

"When Cap'n Gordon got he leg shot off, dey mek Marse Chan cap'n on de spot, 'cause one o' de lieutenants got kilt de same day, an' turr one (named Mr. Ronny) wan' no 'count, an' all de company said Marse Chan wuz de man.

"An' Marse Chan he wuz jes' de same. He didn' never mention Miss Anne's name, but I knowed he wuz thinkin' on her constant. One night he wuz settin' by de fire in camp, an' Mr. Ronny—he wuz de secon' lieutenant—got to talkin' 'bout ladies, an' he say all sorts o' things 'bout 'em, an' I see Marse Chan kinder lookin' mad; an' de lieutenant mention Miss Anne's name. He hed been courtin' Miss Anne 'bout de time Marse Chan fit de duil wid her pa, an' Miss Anne hed kicked 'im, dough he wuz mighty rich, 'cause he warn' nuthin' but a half-strainer, an' 'cause she like Marse Chan, I believe dough she didn' speak to 'im; an' Mr. Ronny he got drunk, an' 'cause Cun'l Chahmb'lin tole 'im not to come dyah no more, he got mighty mad. An' dat evenin' I'se tellin' yo' 'bout, he wuz talkin', an' he mention' Miss Anne's name. I see Marse Chan tu'n he eye 'roun' on 'im an' keep it on he face, and pres'n'y Mr. Ronny said he wuz gwine hev some fun dyah yit. He didn' mention her name dat time;' but he said dey wuz all on 'em a parecel of stuck-up 'risticrats, an' her pa wan' no gent'man anyway, an'—— I don' know what he wuz gwine say (he nuver said it), fur ez he got dat far Marse Chan riz up an' hit 'im a crack, an' he fall like he hed been hit wid a fence-rail. He challenged Marse Chan to fight a duil, an' Marse Chan he excepted de challenge, an' dey wuz gwine fight; but some on 'em tole 'im Marse Chan wan' gwine mek a present o' him to his fam'ly, an' he got somebody to bre'k up de duil; twan' nuthin' dough, but he wuz 'fred to fight Marse Chan. An' purty soon he lef de comp'ny.

"Well, I got one o' de gent'mens to write Judy a letter for me, an' I tole her all 'bout de fight, an' how Marse Chan knock Mr. Ronny over fur speakin' discontemptuous o' Cun'l Chahmb'lin, an' I tole her how Marse Chan wuz a-dyin' fur love o' Miss Anne. An' Judy she gits Miss Anne to read de letter fur her. Den Miss Anne she tells her pa, an'—you mind, Judy tells me all dis arfterwards, an' she say when Cun'l Chahmb'lin hear 'bout it, he wuz settin' on de poach, an' he set still a good while, an' den he sey to hisse'f:

"'Well, he earn' he'p bein' a Whig.'

"An' den he gits up an' walks up to Miss Anne an' looks at her right hard; an' Miss Anne she hed done tu'n away her haid an' wuz makin' out she wuz fixin' a rose-bush 'g'inst de poach; an' when her pa kep' lookin' at her, her face got jes' de color o' de roses on de bush, and pres'n'y her pa sez:

"'Anne!'

"An' she tu'ned roun', an' he sez:

"'Do yo' want 'im?'

"An' she sez, 'Yes,' an' put her head on he shoulder an' begin to cry; an' he sez:

"'Well, I won' stan' between yo' no longer. Write to 'im an' say so.'

"We didn' know nuthin' 'bout' dis den. We wuz a-fightin' an' a-fightin' all dat time; an' come one day a letter to Marse Chan, an' I see 'im start to read it in his tent, an' he face hit look so cu'ious, an he han's trembled so I couldn' mek out what wuz de matter wid 'im. An' he fol' de letter up an' wen' out an' wen' way down 'hine de camp, an' stayed dyah 'bout nigh an hour. Well, seh, I wuz on de lookout for 'im when he come back, an', fo' Gord, ef he face didn' shine like a angel's! I say to myse'f, 'Um'm! ef de glory o' Gord ain' done shine on 'im!' An' what yo' 'spose 'twuz?

"He tuk me wid 'im dat evenin', an' he tell me he hed done git a letter from Miss Anne, an' Marse Chan he eyes look like gre't big stars, an' he face wuz jes' like 'twuz dat mawnin' when de sun riz up over de low groun', an' I see 'im stan'in' dyah wid de pistil in he han', lookin' at it, an' not knowin' but what it mout be de lars' time, an' he done mek up he mine not to shoot ole Cun'l Chahmb'lin fur Miss Anne's sake, what writ 'im de letter.

"He fol' de letter wha' was in his han' up, an' put it in he inside pocket—right dyar on de lef side; an' den he tole me he tho't mebbe we wuz gwine hev some warm wuk in de nex' two or th'ee days, an' arfter dat ef Gord speared 'im he'd git a leave o' absence fur a few days, an' we'd go home.

"Well, dat night de orders come, an' we all hed to git over to'ds Romney; an' we rid all night till 'bout light; an' we halted right on a little creek, an' we stayed dyah till mos' breakfas' time, an' I see Marse Chan set down on de groun' 'hine a bush an' read dat letter over an' over. I watch 'im, an' de battle wuz a-goin' on, but we had orders to stay 'hine de hill, an' ev'y now an' den de bullets would cut de limbs o' de trees right over us, an' one o' dem big shells what goes 'Awhar—awhar—awhar!' would fall right 'mong us; but Marse Chan he didn' mine it no mo'n nuthin'! Den it 'peared to git closer an' thicker, and Marse Chan he calls me, an' I crep' up, an' he sez:

"'Sam, we'se goin' to win in dis battle, an' den we'll go home an' git married; an' I'se goin' home wid a star on my collar.' An' den he sez, 'Ef I'm wounded, kyar me home, yo' hear?' An' I sez, 'Yes, Marse Chan.'

"Well, jes' den dey blowed boots an' saddles, 'an we mounted; an' de orders come to ride 'roun' de slope, an' Marse Chan's comp'ny wuz de secon', an' when we got 'roun' dyah, we wuz right in it. Hit wuz de wust place ever dis nigger got in. An' dey said, 'Charge 'em!' an' my king! ef ever you see bullets fly, dey did dat day. Hit wuz jes' like hail; an' we wen' down de slope (I long wid de res') an' up de hill right to'ds de cannons, an' de fire wuz so strong dyar (dey hed a whole rigiment o' infintrys layin' down dyar onder de cannons) our lines sort o' broke an' stop; de cun'l was kilt, an' I b'lieve dey wuz jes' 'bout to bre'k all to pieces, when Marse Chan rid up an' cotch hol' de fleg an' hollers, 'Foller me!' an' rid strainin' up de hill 'mong de cannons. I seen 'im when he went, de sorrel four good lengths ahead o' ev'y urr hoss, jes' like he use' to be in a fox-hunt, an' de whole rigiment right arfter 'im. Yo' ain' nuver hear thunder! Fust thing I knowed, de roan roll' head over heels an' flung me up 'g'inst de bank, like yo' chuck a nubbin over 'g'inst de foot o' de corn pile. An dat's what kep' me from bein' kilt, I 'spects. Judy she say she think 'twuz Providence, but I think 'twuz de bank. O' co'se, Providence put de bank dyah, but how come Providence nuver saved Marse Chan? When I look' 'roun', de roan wuz layin' dyah by me, stone dead, wid a cannon-ball gone 'mos' th'oo him, an our men hed done swep' dem on t'urr side from de top o' de hill. 'Twan' mo'n a minit, de sorrel come gallupin' back wid his mane flyin', an' de rein hangin' down on one side to his knee. 'Dyar!' says I, 'fo' Gord! I 'specks dey done kill Marse Chan, an' I promised to tek care on him.'

"I jumped up an' run over de bank, an' dyar, wid a whole lot o' dead men, an' some not dead yit, onder one o' de guns wid de fleg still in he han', an' a bullet right th'oo he body, lay Marse Chan. I tu'n 'im over an' call 'im, 'Marse Chan!' but 'twan' no use, he wuz done gone home, sho' 'nuff. I pick' 'im up in my arms wid de fleg still in he han's, an' toted 'im back jes' like I did dat day when he wuz a baby, an' ole marster gin 'im to me in my arms, an' sez he could trus' me, an' tell me to tek keer on 'im long ez he lived. I kyar'd 'im 'way off de battlefiel' out de way o' de balls, an' I laid 'im down onder a big tree till I could git somebody to ketch de sorrel for me. He wuz cotched arfter a while, an' I hed some money, so I got some pine plank an' made a coffin dat evenin', an' wrapt Marse Chan's body up in de fleg, an' put 'im in de coffin; but I didn' nail de top on strong, 'cause I knowed ole missis wan' see 'im; an' I got a' ambulance an' set out for home dat night. We reached dyar de nex' evein', arfter travellin' all dat night an' all nex' day.

"Hit 'peared like somethin' hed tole ole missis we wuz comin' so; for when we got home she wuz waitin' for us—done drest up in her best Sunday-clo'es, an' stan'n' at de head o' de big steps, an' ole marster settin' in his big cheer—ez we druv up de hill to'ds de house, I drivin' de ambulance an' de sorrel leadin' 'long behine wid de stirrups crost over de saddle.

"She come down to de gate to meet us. We took de coffin out de ambulance an' kyar'd it right into de big parlor wid de pictures in it, whar dey use' to dance in ole times when Marse Chan wuz a schoolboy, an' Miss Anne Chahmb'lin use' to come over, an' go wid ole missis into her chamber an' tek her things off. In dyar we laid de coffin on two o' de cheers, an' ole missis nuver said a wud; she jes' looked so ole an' white.

"When I had tell 'em all 'bout it, I tu'ned right 'roun' an' rid over to Cun'l Chahmb'lin's, 'cause I knowed dat wuz what Marse Chan he'd 'a' wanted me to do. I didn' tell nobody whar I wuz gwine, 'cause yo' know none on 'em hadn' nuver speak to Miss Anne, not sence de duil, an' dey didn' know 'bout de letter.

"When I rid up in de yard, dyar wuz Miss Anne a-stan'in' on de poach watchin' me ez I rid up. I tied my hoss to de fence, an' walked up de parf. She knowed by de way I walked dyar wuz soma thin' de motter, an' she wuz mighty pale. I drapt my cap down on de een' o' de steps an' went up. She nuver opened her mouf; jes' stan' right still an' keep her eyes on my face. Fust, I couldn' speak; den I cotch my voice, an' I say, 'Marse Chan, he done got he furlough.'

"Her face was mighty ashy, an' she sort o' shook, but she didn' fall. She tu'ned roun' an' said, 'Git me de ker'ige!' Dat wuz all.

"When de ker'ige come 'roun', she hed put on her bonnet, an' wuz ready. Ez she got in, she sey to me, 'Hev yo' brought him home?' an' we drove 'long, I ridin' behine.

"When we got home, she got out, an' walked up de big walk—up to de poach by herse'f. Ole missis hed done fin' de letter in Marse Chan's pocket, wid de love in it, while I wuz 'way, an' she wuz a-waitin' on de poach. Dey sey dat wuz de fust time ole missis cry when she find de letter, an' dat she sut'n'y did cry over it, pintedly.

"Well, seh, Miss Anne she walks right up de steps, mos' up to ole missis stan'in' dyar on de poach, an' jes' falls right down mos' to her, on her knees fust, an' den flat on her face right on de flo', ketchin' at ole missis' dress wid her two han's—so.

"Ole missis stood for 'bout a minit lookin' down at her, an' den she drapt down on de flo' by her, an' took her in bofe her arms.

"I couldn' see, I wuz cryin' so myse'f, an' ev'y'body wuz cryin'. But dey went in arfter a while in de parlor, an' shet de do'; an' I heahd 'em say, Miss Anne she tuk de coffin in her arms an' kissed it, an' kissed Marse Chan, an' call 'im by his name, an' her darlin', an' ole missis lef' her cryin' in dyar tell some on 'em went in, an' found her done faint on de flo'.

"Judy (she's my wife) she tell me she heah Miss Anne when she axed ole missis mout she wear mo'nin' fur 'im. I don' know how dat is; but when we buried 'im nex' day, she wuz de one whar walked arfter de coffin, holdin' ole marster, an' ole missis she walked next to 'em.

"Well, we buried Marse Chan dyar in de ole grabeyard, wid de fleg wrapped roun' 'im, an' he face lookin' like it did dat mawnin' down in de low groun's, wid de new sun shinin' on it so peaceful.

"Miss Anne she nuver went home to stay arfter dat; she stay wid ole marster an' ole missis ez long ez dey lived. Dat warn' so mighty long, 'cause ole marster he died dat fall, when dey wuz fallerin' fur wheat—I had jes' married Judy den—an' ole missis she warn' long behine him. We buried her by him next summer. Miss Anne she went in de hospitals toreckly arfter ole missis died; an' jes' fo' Richmond fell she come home sick wid de fever. Yo' nuver would 'a' knowed her fur de same ole Miss Anne. She wuz light ez a piece o' peth, an' so white, 'cep her eyes an' her sorrel hyar, an' she kep' on gittin' whiter an' weaker. Judy she sut'n'y did nuss her faithful. But she nuver got no betterment! De fever an' Marse Chan's bein' kilt hed done strain her, an' she died jes' fo' de folks wuz sot free.

"So we buried Miss Anne right by Marse Chan, in a place whar ole missis hed tole us to leave, an' dey's bofe on 'em sleep side by side over in de ole grabeyard at home.

"An' will yo' please tell me, marster? Dey tells me dat de Bible sey dyar won' be marryin' nor givin' in marriage in heaven, but I don' b'lieve it signifies dat—does you?"

I gave him the comfort of my earnest belief in some other interpretation, together with several spare "eighteen-pences," as he called them, for which he seemed humbly grateful. And as I rode away I heard him calling across the fence to his wife, who was standing in the door of a small whitewashed cabin, near which we had been standing for some time:

"Judy, have Marse Chan's dawg got home?"

1884

CHARLES WADDELL CHESNUTT
1858–1932

Charles W. Chesnutt was born in Cleveland, Ohio, the son of free blacks who had emigrated from Fayetteville, North Carolina. When he was eight years old, his parents returned to Fayetteville, where Charles worked in the family grocery store and attended a school founded by the Freedmen's Bureau. Financial necessity required that he begin a teaching career while still a teenager. By 1880 he had become principal of the Fayetteville State Normal School for Negroes. Seeking broader economic opportunity and a chance to hone the literary skills that he had begun to develop in his private journals, Chesnutt moved to the North in 1883, settling his family in Cleveland in 1884. There he passed the state bar examination and founded his own court-reporting firm. His business success and prominence in civic affairs made him one of Cleveland's most respected citizens.

"The Goophered Grapevine" was Chesnutt's first nationally recognized work of fiction. Written in black dialect and set in the Old South, "The Goophered Grapevine" appeared to be another contribution to the popular "plantation literature" of late-nineteenth-century America, in which slavery and the plantation system of the antebellum South were sentimentalized. But this story, like all of Chesnutt's "conjure" tales, displayed an unusually intimate knowledge of black southern folk culture and an appreciation of the importance of voodoo practices to the slave community. The teller of the conjure tales, Uncle Julius, is also a unique figure in southern plantation literature, a former slave who recalls the past not to celebrate it but to exploit white people's sentimentality about it. The publication of "The Goophered Grapevine" marked the first time that a short story by an African American had appeared in the prestigious *Atlantic Monthly*. After subsequent tales in this vein were accepted by other magazines, Chesnutt reached an agreement with Houghton Mifflin to publish his first work of fiction, *The Conjure Woman*, a collection of stories. Its reception was positive enough to convince the Boston firm to publish a second collection of Chesnutt's short fiction, *The Wife of His Youth and Other Stories of the Color Line*. This volume treated a broader range of southern and northern racial experience than any previous delineator of black American life in literature had attempted. Typical of Chesnutt's interest in life on the color line in the North is "A Matter of Principle," a satiric study of racial prejudice within the light-skinned, aspiring black middle class of Cleveland. "The Passing of Grandison" debunks the myth of the faithful slave retainer of the Old South, revealing beneath the mask of the docile slave a crafty and determined individual much more committed to the welfare of his family and himself than to his supposedly beloved master.

Chesnutt's short story collections provided his entering wedge into the world of professional authorship. In 1900 Houghton Mifflin published his first novel, *The House Behind the Cedars*, the story of two African Americans who pass for white in the postwar South. The novel testifies to Chesnutt's sensitivity to the psychological and social dilemmas that faced persons of mixed blood. His second novel, *The Marrow of Tradition*, is based on the Wilmington, North Carolina, racial massacre of 1898. Hoping to create the *Uncle Tom's Cabin* of his generation, Chesnutt wrote into his book a plea for racial justice that impressed the noted critic William Dean Howells and roused considerable controversy among reviewers. However, when *The Marrow of Tradition* did not sell widely, Chesnutt was forced to give up the effort he began two years earlier to support his family as a man of letters. The last novel published during his lifetime, *The Colonel's Dream* (1905), portrays an idealist's attempt to uplift a North Carolina town mired in economic depression and social injustice. The tragic outcome of the Colonel's program did not appeal to the few reviewers who commented on the novel.

Chesnutt continued to write and he did publish occasional short stories, but he was largely eclipsed in the 1920s by the writers of the New Negro Renaissance. Nevertheless, he was awarded the Spingarn Medal in 1928 by the National Association for the Advancement of Colored People for his pioneering literary efforts on behalf of the African American struggle. Since the late 1970s, Chesnutt has been recognized as a major innovator in the tradition of African American fiction. He showed his literary successors new ways of writing about black folk culture in the South and the embryonic black middle class in the North. His fiction participated in the deromanticizing of southern life that made possible a realistic literary tradition in the South. Perhaps most important, he recognized the genuinely comic potential of the black writer as manipulator of and ironic commentator on the myths and presumptions of the mainstream American reader.

William L. Andrews
University of North Carolina–Chapel Hill

PRIMARY WORKS

The Conjure Woman, 1899; *The Wife of His Youth and Other Stories of the Color Line*, 1899; *The House Behind the Cedars*, 1900; *The Marrow of Tradition*, 1901; *The Colonel's Dream*, 1905; *Mandy Oxendine*, 1997; *Paul Marchand*, 1999; *The Quarry*, 1999; *Essays and Speeches*, 1999; *A Business Career* (first published 2005); *Evelyn's Husband* (first published 2005).

What Is a White Man?[1]

The fiat having gone forth from the wise men of the South that "all-pervading, all-conquering Anglo-Saxon race" must continue forever to exercise exclusive control and direction of the government of this so-called Republic, it becomes important to every citizen who values his birthright to know who are included in this grandiloquent term. It is of course perfectly obvious that the writer or speaker who used this expression—perhaps Mr. Grady of Georgia—did not say what he meant. It is not probable that he meant to exclude from full citizenship the Celts and Teutons and Gauls and Slavs who make up so large a proportion of our population; he hardly meant to exclude the Jews, for even the most ardent fire-eater would hardly venture to advocate the disfranchisement of the thrifty race whose mortgages cover so large a portion of Southern soil. What the eloquent gentleman really meant by this high-sounding phrase was simply the white race; and the substance of the argument of that school of Southern writers to which he belongs, is simply that for the good of the country the Negro should have no voice in directing the government or public policy of the Southern States or of the nation.[2]

But is evident that where the intermingling of the races has made such progress as it has in this country, the line which separates the races must in many instances have been practically obliterated. And there has arisen in the United States a very large class of the population who are certainly not Negroes in an ethnological sense, and whose children will be no nearer Negroes than themselves. In view, therefore, of the very positive ground taken by the white leaders of the South, where most of these people reside, it becomes in the highest degree important to them to know what race they belong to. It ought to be also a matter of serious concern to the Southern white people; for if their zeal for good government is so great that they contemplate the practical overthrow of the Constitution and laws of the United States to secure it, they ought at least to be sure that no man entitled to it by their own argument, is robbed of a right so precious as that of free citizenship; the "all-pervading, all conquering Anglo-Saxon" ought to set as high a value on American citizenship as the all-conquering Roman placed upon

---

[1]*The Independent* [New York], May 30, 1889.
[2]Henry Woodfin Grady (1850–1889). From 1880 until his death on December 23, 1889, Grady was an editor of the *Atlanta Constitution* and the most visible and eloquent spokesman for the idea of a "new," recon- structed South. He defined the movement in the speech entitled "The New South," pre- sented in New York on December 22, 1886, at the annual dinner of the New England So- ciety. [Notes by Sally Ann H. Ferguson.]

the franchise of his State two thousand years ago. This discussion would of course be of little interest to the genuine Negro, who is entirely outside of the charmed circle, and must content himself with the acquisition of wealth, the pursuit of learning and such other privileges as his "best friends" may find it consistent with the welfare of the nation to allow him; but to every other good citizen the inquiry ought to be a momentous one, What is a white man?

In spite of the virulence an universality of race prejudice in the United States, the human intellect long ago revolted at the manifest absurdity of classifying men fifteen-sixteenths white as black men; and hence there grew up a number of laws in different states of the Union defining the limit which separated the white and colored races, which was, when these laws took their rise and is now to a large extent, the line which separated freedom and opportunity from slavery or hopeless degradation. Some of these laws are of legislative origin; others are judge-made laws, brought out by the exigencies of special cases which came before the courts for determination. Some day they will, perhaps, become mere curiosities of jurisprudence: the "black laws" will be bracketed with the "blue laws," and will be at best but landmarks by which to measure the progress of the nation.[3] But today these laws are in active operation, and they are, therefore, worthy of attention; for every good citizen ought to know the law, and, if possible, to respect it: and if not worthy of respect, it should be changed by the authority which enacted it. Whether any of the laws referred to here have been in any manner changed by very recent legislation the writer cannot say, but they are certainly embodied in the latest editions of the revised statutes of the states referred to.

The colored people were divided, in most of the Southern States, into two classes, designated by law as Negroes and mulattoes respectively. The term Negro was used in its ethnological sense, and needed no definition; but the term "mulatto" was held by legislative enactment to embrace all persons of color not Negroes. The words "quadroon" and "mestizo" are employed in some of the law books, tho not defined; but the term "octoroon," as indicating a person having one-eighth Negro blood, is not used at all, so far as the writer has been able to observe.

The states vary slightly in regard to what constitutes a mulatto or person of color, and as to what proportion of white blood should be sufficient to remove the disability of color. As a general rule, less than one-fourth of Negro blood left the individual white—in theory; race questions being, however, regulated very differently in practice. In Missouri, by the code of 1855, still in operation, so far as not inconsistent with the Federal Constitution and laws, "any person other than a Negro, any one of whose grandmothers

---

[3]The black codes were legal restrictions enacted to control African Americans politically, socially, and economically in Georgia, Alabama, South Carolina, North Carolina, Virginia, Florida, Louisiana, Tennessee, and several northern states. With these statutes, insecure whites sought to regain power lost over black-skinned people after Emancipation and the Civil War.

or grandfathers is or shall have been a Negro, tho all of his or her progentors except those descended from the Negro may have been white persons, shall be deemed a mulatto."[4] Thus the color-line is drawn at one-fourth of Negro blood, and persons with only one-eighth are white.

By the Mississippi code of 1880, the color-line is drawn at one-fourth of Negro blood, all persons having less being theoretically white.[5]

Under the *code noir* of Lousiana, the descendant of a white and a quadroon is white, thus drawing the line at one-eighth of Negro blood. The code of 1876 abolished all distinctions of color; as to whether they have been re-enacted since the Republican Party went out of power in that state the writer is not informed.[6]

Jumping to the extreme North, persons are white within the meaning of the Constitution of Michigan who have less than one-fourth of Negro blood.[7]

In Ohio the rule, as established by numerous decisions of the Supreme Court, was that a preponderance of white blood constituted a person a white man in the eye of the law, and entitled him to the exercise of all the civil rights of a white man. By a retrogressive step the color-line was extended in 1861 in the case of marriage, which by statute was forbidden between a person of pure white blood and one having a visible admixture of African blood. But by act of legislature, passed in the spring of 1887, all laws establishing or permitting distinctions of color were repealed. In many parts

---

[4]The exact code reads: "Every person other than a Negro, any one of whose grandfathers or grandmothers is, or shall have been a Negro, although all his or her other progenitors, except those descending from the Negro, may have been white persons, shall be deemed a mulatto; and every such person, who shall have one-fourth or more Negro blood, shall in like manner, be deemed a mulatto" (*Revised Statutes of the State of Missouri,* 2:1093–94).

[5]The *Revised Code of the Statute Laws of the State of Mississippi* states: "The marriage of a white person and a Negro or mulatto or person who shall have one-fourth or more of Negro blood, shall be unlawful, and such marriage shall be incestuous and void; and any party thereto, on conviction, shall be punished as for a marriage . . . and any attempt to evade this section by marrying out of this state, and returning to it shall be held to be within it." *The Annotated Code of the General Statute Laws of the State of Mississippi* is even more rigid: "The marriage of a white person and a Negro or mulatto or person who shall have one-eighth or more of Negro blood, or with a Mongolian or a person who shall have one-eighth or more Mongolian blood, shall be unlawful, and such marriage shall be unlawful and void . . ." (677).

[6]*Code noir* ("black code") derives from the "Edict Concerning the Negro Slaves in Louisiana," issued in March 1724 by Louis XV and enacted in Louisiana on September 10, 1724, by Governor Jean Baptiste Le Moyne Sieur de Bienville. The code consisted of fifty-four articles fixing the legal status of slaves and imposing specific obligations and prohibitions on slave owners. Its essential provisions were eventually integrated into the American black codes (*Dictionary of American History* 2:9). The 1876 code reads: "The said right of making private or religious marriages legal, valid and binding, as aforesaid, shall apply to marriages of all persons of whatever race or color, as well as to marriages formerly prohibited by article ninety-five of the Civil Code of Louisiana, or by any other article of said Code, or by any law of the State" (*Revised Statutes of the State of Louisiana,* 575).

[7]The *General Statutes of the State of Michigan* states: "All marriages heretofore contracted between white persons and those wholly or in part of African descent are hereby declared valid and effectual in law for all purposes, and the issue of such marriages shall be deemed and taken legitimate as to such issue and as to both of the parents" (1619).

of the state these laws were always ignored, and they would doubtless have been repealed long ago but for the sentiment of the southern counties, separated only by the width of the Ohio River from a former slave-holding state.[8] There was a bill introduced in the legislature during the last session to re-enact the "black laws," but it was hopelessly defeated; the member who introduced it evidently mistook his latitude; he ought to be a member of the Georgia legislature.

But the state which, for several reasons, one might expect to have the strictest laws in regard to the relations of the races, has really the loosest. Two extracts from decisions of the Supreme Court of South Carolina will make clear the law of that state in regard to the color line.

> The definition of the term mulatto, as understood in this state, seems to be vague, signifying generally a person of mixed white or European and Negro parentage, in whatever proportions the blood of the two races may be mingled in the individual. But it is not invariably applicable to every admixture of African blood with the European, nor is one having all the features of a white to be ranked with the degraded class designated by the laws of this state as persons of color, because of some remote taint of the Negro race. The line of distinction, however, is not ascertained by any rule of law.... Juries would probably be justified in holding a person to be white in whom the admixture of African blood did not exceed the proportion of one-eighth. But it is in all cases a question for the jury, to be determined by them upon the evidence of features and complexion afforded by inspection, the evidence of reputation as to parentage, and the evidence of the rank and station in society occupied by the party. The only rule which can be laid down by the courts is that where there is a distinct and visible admixture of Negro blood, the individual is to be denominated a mulatto or person of color.

In a later case the court held:

> The question whether persons are colored or white, where color or feature are doubtful, is for the jury to decide by reputation, by reception into society, and by their exercise of the privileges of the white man, as well as by admixture of blood.[9]

It is an interesting question why such should have been, and should still be, for that matter, the law of South Carolina, and why there should exist in that state a condition of public opinion which would accept such a law. Perhaps it may be attributed to the fact that the colored population of South

[8]Bishop Benjamin Arnett's bill to repeal school segregation and antimarriage laws, the last of Ohio's black codes, passed the Ohio Senate February 16, 1887. Because black Arnett had promised his mostly white constituents that he would take no initiative on such legislation, he was soon turned out of office.
[9]*State v. Thomas B. Davis; Same v. William Dana.* These were indictments under the bastardy act of 1795, tried before Justice Evans during the fall term held in Columbia, December 1831 (*Report of Cases Argued and Determined in The Supreme Court of South Carolina ... Book 8* 257–59). This decision was upheld in 1835 in the case of *State v. Vinson J. Cantey* and several other later decisions (*Reports of Cases Argued and Determined in The Supreme Court of South Carolina ... Book 9* 334–35).

Carolina always outnumbered the white population, and the eagerness of the latter to recruit their ranks was sufficient to overcome in some measure their prejudice against the Negro blood. It is certainly true that the color-line is, in practice as in law, more loosely drawn in South Carolina than in any other Southern State, and that no inconsiderable element of the population of that state consists of these legal white persons, who were either born in the state, or, attracted thither by this feature of the laws, have come in from surrounding states, and, forsaking home and kindred, have taken their social position as white people. A reasonable degree of reticence in regard to one's antecedents is, however, usual in such cases.

Before the [Civil] War the color-line, as fixed by law, regulated in theory the civil and political status of persons of color. What the status was, was expressed in the Dred Scott decision.[10] But since the War, or rather since the enfranchisement of the colored people, these laws have been mainly confined—in theory, be it always remembered—to the regulation of the intercourse of the races in schools and in the marriage relation. The extension of the color-line to places of public entertainment and resort, to inns and public highways, is in most states entirely a matter of custom. A colored man can sue in the courts of any Southern State for the violation of his common-law rights, and recover damages of say fifty cents without costs. A colored minister who sued a Baltimore steamboat company a few weeks ago for refusing him first-class accommodation, he having paid first-class fare, did not even meet with that measure of success: the learned judge, a Federal judge by the way, held that the plaintiff's rights had been invaded, and that he had suffered humiliation at the hands of the defendant company, but that "the humiliation was not sufficient to entitle him to damages." And the learned judge dismissed the action without costs to either party.

Having thus ascertained what constitutes a white man, the good citizen may be curious to know what steps have been taken to preserve the purity of the white race, Nature, by some unaccountable oversight having to some extent neglected a matter so important to the future prosperity and progress of mankind. The marriage laws referred to here are in active operation, and cases under them are by no means infrequent. Indeed, instead of being behind the age, the marriage laws in the Southern States are in advance of public opinion; for very rarely will a Southern community stop to figure on the pedigree of the contracting parties to a marriage where one is white and the other is known to have any strain of Negro blood.

In Virginia, under the title "Offenses against Morality," the law provides that "any white person who shall intermarry with a Negro shall be confined to jail not more than one year and fined not exceeding one hundred dollars." In a marginal note on the statute-book, attention is called to the fact that "a similar penalty is not imposed on the Negro"—a stretch of

[10]In 1857, a majority of the Supreme Court decided that Dred Scott, a Missouri slave whose owner had taken him to live in the free state of Illinois and subsequently to a fort in the northern part of the Louisiana Purchase, was not a citizen and therefore could not sue in court.

magnanimity to which the laws of other states are strangers. A person who performs the ceremony of marriage in such a case is fined two hundred dollars, one-half of which goes to the informer.

In Maryland, a minister who performs the ceremony of marriage between a Negro and a white person is liable to a fine of one hundred dollars.

In Mississippi, code of 1880, it is provided that "the marriage of a white person to a Negro or mulatto or person who shall have one-fourth or more of Negro blood, shall be unlawful"; and as this prohibition does not seem sufficiently emphatic, it is further declared to be "incestuous and void," and is punished by the same penalty prescribed for marriage within the forbidden degrees of consanguinity.

But it is Georgia, the *alma genetrix* of the chain-gang, which merits the questionable distinction of having the harshest set of color laws. By the law of Georgia the term "person of color" is defined to mean "all such as have an admixture of Negro blood; and the term 'Negro,' includes mulattoes." This definition is perhaps restricted somewhat by another provision, by which "all Negroes, mestizoes, and their descendants, having one-eighth of Negro or mulatto blood in their veins, shall be known in this State as persons of color." A colored minister is permitted to perform the ceremony of marriage between colored persons only, tho white ministers are not forbidden to join persons of color in wedlock. It is further provided that "the marriage relation between white persons and persons of African descent is forever prohibited, and such marriages shall be null and void." This is a very sweeping provision; it will be noticed that the term "persons of color," previously defined, is not employed, the expression "persons of African descent" being used instead. A court which was so inclined would find no difficulty in extending this provision of the law to the remotest strain of African blood. The marriage relation is forever prohibited. Forever is a long time. There is a colored woman in Georgia said to be worth $300,000—an immense fortune in the poverty stricken South.[11] With a few hundred such women in that state, possessing a fair degree of good looks, the color-line would shrivel up like a scroll in the heat of competition for their hands in marriage. The penalty for the violation of the law against intermarriage is the same sought to be imposed by the defunct Glenn Bill for violation of its provisions: *i.e.*, a fine not to exceed one thousand dollars, and imprisonment not to exceed six months, or twelve months in the chain-gang.[12]

[11]In its October 23, 1886, weekly Saturday column about African American life entitled "The Colored Race," the *Cleveland Gazette* named Amanda (Mandy) Eubanks of Rome, Georgia, whose white father left her $400,000 in his will, the richest African American woman in the South (1). A June 26, 1886, issue of the paper had listed Eubanks as still living in Alabama (1).

[12]On July 11, 1887, Representative W. C. Glenn of Dalton introduced a bill in the state legislature to cut off $8,000 allocated annually to Atlanta University as part of the Morrill Act of 1882. Glenn mainly sought to punish white faculty who refused to stop sending their children to, and thus integrating, the school. The Glenn Bill passed both the House and the Senate August 2, 1887, and was signed by Governor John B. Gordon. It became moot after the state established the State College of Industry for Colored Youth in Savannah in October 1891 and transferred the funds to it.

Whatever the wisdom or justice of these laws, there is one objection to them which is not given sufficient prominence in the consideration of the subject, even where it is discussed at all; they make mixed blood a *prima-facie* proof of illegitimacy. It is a fact that at present, in the United States, a colored man or woman whose complexion is white or nearly white is presumed, in the absence of any knowledge of his or her antecedents, to be the offspring of a union not sanctified by law. And by a curious but not uncommon process, such persons are not held in the same low estimation as white people in the same position. The sins of their fathers are not visited upon the children, in that regard at least; and their mothers' lapses from virtue are regarded either as misfortunes or as faults excusable under the circumstances. But in spite of all this, illegitimacy is not a desirable distinction, and is likely to become less so as these people of mixed blood advance in wealth and social standing. This presumption of illegitimacy was once, perhaps, true of the majority of such persons; but the times have changed. More than half of the colored people of the United States are of mixed blood; they marry and are given in marriage, and they beget children of complexions similar to their own. Whether or not, therefore, laws which stamp these children as illegitimate, and which by indirection establish a lower standard of morality for a large part of the population than the remaining part is judged by, are wise laws; and whether or not the purity of the white race could not be as well preserved by the exercise of virtue, and the operation of those natural laws which are so often quoted by Southern writers as the justification of all sorts of Southern "policies"—are questions which the good citizen may at least turn over in his mind occasionally, pending the settlement of other complications which have grown out of the presence of the Negro on this continent.

1889

The Goophered Grapevine

Some years ago my wife was in poor health, and our family doctor, in whose skill and honesty I had implicit confidence, advised a change of climate. I shared, from an unprofessional standpoint, his opinion that the raw winds, the chill rains, and the violent changes of temperature that characterized the winters in the region of the Great Lakes tended to aggravate my wife's difficulty, and would undoubtedly shorten her life if she remained exposed to them. The doctor's advice was that we seek, not a temporary place of sojourn, but a permanent residence, in a warmer and more equable climate. I was engaged at the time in grape-culture in northern Ohio, and, as I liked the business and had given it much study, I decided to look for some other locality suitable for carrying it on. I thought of sunny France, of sleepy Spain, of Southern California, but there were objections to them all. It occurred to me that I might find what I wanted in some one of our own Southern States. It was a sufficient time after the war for conditions in the

South to have become somewhat settled; and I was enough of a pioneer to start a new industry, if I could not find a place where grape-culture had been tried. I wrote to a cousin who had gone into the turpentine business in central North Carolina. He assured me, in response to my inquiries, that no better place could be found in the South than the State and neighborhood where he lived; the climate was perfect for health, and, in conjunction with the soil, ideal for grape-culture; labor was cheap, and land could be bought for a mere song. He gave us a cordial invitation to come and visit him while we looked into the matter. We accepted the invitation, and after several days of leisurely travel, the last hundred miles of which were up a river on a sidewheel steamer, we reached our destination, a quaint old town, which I shall call Patesville, because, for one reason, that is not its name. There was a red brick market-house in the public square, with a tall tower, which held a four-faced clock that struck the hours, and from which there pealed out a curfew at nine o'clock. There were two or three hotels, a court-house, a jail, stores, offices, and all the appurtenances of a county seat and a commercial emporium; for while Patesville numbered only four or five thousand inhabitants, of all shades of complexion, it was one of the principal towns in North Carolina, and had a considerable trade in cotton and naval stores. This business activity was not immediately apparent to my unaccustomed eyes. Indeed, when I first saw the town, there brooded over it a calm that seemed almost sabbatic in its restfulness, though I learned later on that underneath its somnolent exterior the deeper currents of life—love and hatred, joy and despair, ambition and avarice, faith and friendship—flowed not less steadily than in livelier latitudes.

We found the weather delightful at that season, the end of summer, and were hospitably entertained. Our host was a man of means and evidently regarded our visit as a pleasure, and we were therefore correspondingly at our ease, and in a position to act with the coolness of judgment desirable in making so radical a change in our lives. My cousin placed a horse and buggy at our disposal, and himself acted as our guide until I became somewhat familiar with the country.

I found that grape-culture, while it had never been carried on to any great extent, was not entirely unknown in the neighborhood. Several planters thereabouts had attempted it on a commercial scale, in former years, with greater or less success; but like most Southern industries, it had felt the blight of war and had fallen into desuetude.

I went several times to look at a place that I thought might suit me. It was a plantation of considerable extent, that had formerly belonged to a wealthy man by the name of McAdoo. The estate had been for years involved in litigation between disputing heirs, during which period shiftless cultivation had well-nigh exhausted the soil. There had been a vineyard of some extent on the place, but it had not been attended to since the war, and had lapsed into utter neglect. The vines—here partly supported by decayed and broken-down trellises, there twining themselves among the branches of the slender saplings which had sprung up among them—grew in wild and unpruned luxuriance, and the few scattered grapes they bore were the undisputed prey of the first comer. The site was admirably adapted to grape-raising; the soil, with a little attention, could not have been better; and with the native grape, the luscious scuppernong, as my main reliance in the beginning, I felt sure that I could introduce and cultivate successfully a number of other varieties.

One day I went over with my wife to show her the place. We drove out of the town over a long wooden bridge that spanned a spreading mill-pond, passed the long whitewashed fence surrounding the county fair-ground, and struck into a road so sandy that the horse's feet sank to the fetlocks. Our route lay partly up hill and partly down, for we were in the sand-hill county; we drove past cultivated farms, and then by abandoned fields grown up in scrub-oak and short-leaved pine, and once or twice through the solemn aisles of the virgin forest, where the tall pines, well-nigh meeting over the narrow road, shut out the sun, and wrapped us in cloistral solitude. Once, at a cross-roads, I was in doubt as to the turn to take, and we sat there waiting ten minutes—we had already caught some of the native infection of restfulness—for some human being to come along, who could direct us on our way. At length a little negro girl appeared, walking straight as an arrow, with a piggin[1] full of water on her head. After a little patient investigation, necessary to overcome the child's shyness, we learned what we wished to know, and at the end of about five miles from the town reached our destination.

We drove between a pair of decayed gateposts—the gate itself had long since disappeared—and up a straight sandy lane, between two lines of rotting rail fence, partly concealed by jimsonweeds and briers, to the open space where a dwelling-house had once stood, evidently a spacious mansion, if we might judge from the ruined chimneys that were still standing, and the brick pillars on which the sills rested. The house itself, we had been informed, had fallen a victim to the fortunes of war.

We alighted from the buggy, walked about the yard for a while, and then wandered off into the adjoining vineyard. Upon Annie's complaining of weariness I led the way back to the yard, where a pine log, lying under a spreading elm, afforded a shady though somewhat hard seat. One end of the log was already occupied by a venerable-looking colored man. He held on his knees a hat full of grapes, over which he was smacking his lips with great gusto, and a pile of grape-skins near him indicated that the performance was no new thing. We approached him at an angle from the rear, and were close to him before he perceived us. He respectfully rose as we drew near, and was moving away, when I begged him to keep his seat.

"Don't let us disturb you," I said. "There is plenty of room for us all."

He resumed his seat with somewhat of embarrassment. While he had been standing, I had observed that he was a tall man, and, though slightly bowed by the weight of years, apparently quite vigorous. He was not entirely black, and this fact, together with the quality of his hair, which was about

---

[1] A wooden pail.

six inches long and very bushy, except on the top of his head, where he was quite bald, suggested a slight strain of other than negro blood. There was a shrewdness in his eyes, too, which was not altogether African, and which, as we afterwards learned from experience, was indicative of a corresponding shrewdness in his character. He went on eating the grapes, but did not seem to enjoy himself quite so well as he had apparently done before he became aware of our presence.

"Do you live around here?" I asked, anxious to put him at his ease.

"Yas, suh. I lives des ober yander, behine de nex' san'-hill, on de Lumberton plank-road."

"Do you know anything about the time when this vineyard was cultivated?"

"Lawd bless you, suh, I knows all about it. Dey ain' na'er a man in dis settlement w'at won' tell you ole Julius McAdoo 'uz bawn en raise' on dis yer same plantation. Is you de Norv'n gemman w'at 's gwine ter buy de ole vimya'd?"

"I am looking at it," I replied; "but I don't know that I shall care to buy unless I can be reasonably sure of making something out of it."

"Well, suh, you is a stranger ter me, en I is a stranger ter you, en we is bofe strangers ter one anudder, but 'f I 'uz in yo' place, I wouldn' buy dis vimya'd."

"Why not?" I asked.

"Well, I dunno whe'r you b'lieves in cunj'in' er not,—some er de w'ite folks don't, er says dey don't,—but de truf er de matter is dat dis yer ole vimya'd is goophered."

"Is what?" I asked, not grasping the meaning of this unfamiliar word.

"Is goophered,—cunju'd, bewitch'."

He imparted this information with such solemn earnestness, and with such an air of confidential mystery, that I felt somewhat interested, while Annie was evidently much impressed, and drew closer to me.

"How do you know it is bewitched?" I asked.

"I wouldn' spec' fer you ter b'lieve me 'less you know all 'bout de fac's. But ef you en young miss dere doan' min' lis'nin' ter a ole nigger run on a minute er two w'ile you er restin', I kin 'splain to you how it all happen'."

We assured him that we would be glad to hear how it all happened, and he began to tell us. At first the current of his memory—or imagination— seemed somewhat sluggish; but as his embarrassment wore off, his language flowed more freely, and the story acquired perspective and coherence. As he became more and more absorbed in the narrative, his eyes assumed a dreamy expression, and he seemed to lose sight of his auditors, and to be living over again in monologue his life on the old plantation.

"Ole Mars Dugal' McAdoo," he began, "bought dis place long many years befo' de wah, en I 'member well w'en he sot out all dis yer part er de plantation in scuppernon's. De vimes growed monst'us fas', en Mars Dugal' made a thousan' gallon er scuppernon' wine eve'y year.

"Now, ef dey's an'thing a nigger lub, nex' ter 'possum, en chick'n, en wattermillyums, it's scuppernon's. Dey ain' nuffin dat kin stan' up side'n de scuppernon' fer sweetness; sugar ain't a suckumstance ter scuppernon'. W'en de season is nigh 'bout ober, en de grapes begin ter swivel up des a little wid de wrinkles er ole age,—w'en de skin git sof' en brown,—den de scuppernon' make you smack yo' lip en roll yo' eye en wush fer mo'; so I reckon it ain' very 'stonishin' dat niggers lub scuppernon'.

"Dey wuz a sight er niggers in de naberhood er de vimya'd. Dere wuz ole Mars Henry Brayboy's niggers, en ole Mars Jeems McLean's niggers, en Mars Dugal's own niggers; den dey wuz a settlement er free niggers en po' buckrahs[2] down by de Wim'l'ton Road, en Mars Dugal' had de only vimya'd in de naberhood. I reckon it ain' so much so nowadays, but befo' de wah, in slab'ry times, a nigger didn' mine goin' fi' er ten mile in a night, w'en dey wuz sump'n good ter eat at de yuther een'.

"So atter a w'ile Mars Dugal' begin ter miss his scuppernon's. Co'se he 'cuse' de niggers er it, but dey all 'nied it ter de las'. Mars Dugal' sot spring guns en steel traps, en he en de oberseah sot up nights once't er twice't, tel one night Mars Dugal'—he 'uz a monst'us keerless man—got his leg shot full er cow-peas. But somehow er nudder dey could n' nebber ketch none er de niggers. I dunner how it happen, but it happen des like I tell you, en de grapes kep' on a-goin' des de same.

"But bimeby ole Mars Dugal' fix' up a plan ter stop it. Dey wuz a cunjuh 'oman livin' down 'mongs' de free niggers on de Wim'l'ton Road, en all de darkies fum Rockfish ter Beaver Crick wuz feared er her. She would wuk de mos' powerfulles' kin' er goopher,—could make people hab fits, er rheumatiz, er make 'em des dwinel away en die; en dey say she went out ridin' de niggers at night, fer she wuz a witch 'sides bein' a cunjuh 'oman. Mars Dugal' hearn 'bout Aun' Peggy's doin's, en begun ter 'flect whe'r er no he couldn' git her ter he'p him keep de niggers off'n de grape vimes. One day in de spring er de year, ole miss pack' up a basket er chick'n en poun'-cake, en a bottle er scuppernon' wine, en Mars Dugal' tuk it in his buggy en driv ober ter Aun' Peggy's cabin. He tuk de basket in, en had a long talk wid Aun' Peggy.

"De nex' day Aun' Peggy come up ter de vimya'd. De niggers seed her slippin' 'round', en dey soon foun' out what she 'uz doin' dere. Mars Dugal' had hi'ed her ter goopher de grapevimes. She sa'ntered 'roun' 'mongs' de vimes, en tuk a leaf fum dis one, en a grape-hull fum dat one, en a grape-seed fum anudder one; en den a little twig fum here, en a little pinch er dirt fum dere,—en put it all in a big black bottle, wid a snake's toof en a speckle' hen's gall en some ha's fum a black cat's tail, en den fill' de bottle wid scuppernon' wine. W'en she got de goopher all ready en fix', she tuk 'n went out in de woods en buried it under de root uv a red oak tree, en den come back en tole one er de niggers she done goopher de grapevimes, en a'er a nigger w'at eat dem grapes 'ud be sho ter die inside'n twel' mont's.

---

[2] Whites regarded as of the lowest class by blacks.

"Atter dat de niggers let de scuppernon's 'lone, en Mars Dugal' didn' hab no 'casion ter fine no mo' fault; en de season wuz mos' gone, w'en a strange gemman stop at de plantation one night ter see Mars Dugal' on some business; en his coachman, seein' de scuppernon's growin' so nice en sweet, slip 'roun' behine de smokehouse, en et all de scuppernon's he could hole. Nobody didn' notice it at de time, but dat night, on de way home, de gemman's hoss runned away en kill' de coachman. W'en we hearn de noos, Aun' Lucy, de cook, she up'n say she seed de strange nigger eat'n' er de scuppernon's behine de smokehouse; en den we knowed de goopher had b'en er wukkin'. Den one er de nigger chilluns runned away fum de quarters one day, en got in de scuppernon's, en died de nex' week. W'ite folks say he die' er de fevuh, but de niggers knowed it wuz de goopher. So you k'n be sho de darkies didn' hab much ter do wid dem scuppernon' vimes.

"W'en de scuppernon' season 'uz ober fer dat year, Mars Dugal' foun' he had made fifteen hund'ed gallon er wine; en one er de niggers hearn him laffin' wid de oberseah fit ter kill, en sayin' dem fifteen hund'ed gallon er wine wuz monst'us good intrus' on de ten dollars he laid out on de vimya'd. So I 'low ez he paid Aun' Peggy ten dollars fer to goopher de grapevimes.

"De goopher didn' wuk no mo' tel de nex' summer, w'en 'long to'ds de middle er de season one er de fiel' han's died; en ez dat lef' Mars Dugal' sho't er han's, he went off ter town fer ter buy anudder. He fotch de noo nigger home wid 'im. He wuz er ole nigger, er de color er a gingy-cake, en ball ez a hoss-apple on de top er his head. He wuz a peart ole nigger, do', en could do a big day's wuk.

"Now it happen dat one er de niggers on de nex' plantation, one er ole Mars Henry Brayboy's niggers, had runned away de day befo', en tuk ter de swamp, en ole Mars Dugal' en some er de yuther nabor w'ite folks had gone out wid dere guns en dere dogs fer ter he'p 'em hunt fer de nigger; en de han's on our own plantation wuz all so flusterated dat we fuhgot ter tell de noo han' 'bout de goopher on de scuppernon' vimes. Co'se he smell de grapes en see de vimes, an atter dahk de fus' thing he done wuz ter slip off ter de grapevimes 'dout sayin' nuffin ter nobody. Nex' mawnin' he tole some er de niggers 'bout de fine bait er scuppernon' he et de night befo'.

"W'en dey tole 'im 'bout de goopher on de grapevimes, he 'uz dat tarrified dat he turn pale, en look des like he gwine ter die right in his tracks. De oberseah come up en axed w'at 'uz de matter; en w'en dey tole 'im Henry be'n eatin' er de scuppernon's, en got de goopher on 'im, he gin Henry a big drink er w'iskey, en 'low dat de nex' rainy day he take 'im ober ter Aun' Peggy's, en see ef she wouldn' take de goopher off'n him, seein' ez he didn' know nuffin erbout it tel he done et de grapes.

"Sho nuff, it rain de nex' day, en de oberseah went ober ter Aun' Peggy's wid Henry. En Aun' Peggy say dat bein' ez Henry didn' know 'bout de goopher, en et de grapes in ign'ance er de conseq'ences, she reckon she mought be able fer ter take de goopher of'n him. So she fotch out er bottle wid some cunjuh medicine in it, en po'd some out in a go'd fer Henry ter drink. He manage ter git it down; he say it tas'e like whiskey wid sump'n bitter in it.

She 'lowed dat 'ud keep de goopher off'n him tel de spring; but w'en de sap begin ter rise in de grapevimes he ha' ter come en see her ag'in, en she tell him w'at e's ter do.

"Nex' spring, w'en de sap commence' ter rise in de scuppernon' vime, Henry tuk a ham one night. Whar'd he git de ham? *I* doan know; dey wa'n't no hams on de plantation 'cep'n' w'at 'uz in de smoke-house, but *I* never see Henry 'bout de smoke-house. But ez I wuz a-sayin', he tuk de ham ober ter Aun' Peggy's; en Aun' Peggy tole 'im dat w'en Mars Dugal' begin ter prune de grapevimes, he mus' go en take 'n scrape off de sap whar it ooze out'n de cut een's er de vimes, en 'n'int his ball head wid it; en ef he do dat once't a year de goopher wouldn' wuk agin 'im long ez he done it. En bein' ez he fotch her de ham, she fix' it so he kin eat all de scuppernon' he want.

"So Henry 'n'int his head wid de sap out'n de big grapevime des ha'fway 'twix' de quarters en de big house, en de goopher nebber wuk again him dat summer. But de beatenes' thing you eber see happen ter Henry. Up ter dat time he wuz ez ball ez a sweeten' 'tater, but des ez soon ez de young leaves begun ter come out on de grapevimes, de ha'r begun ter grow out on Henry's head, en by de middle er de summer he had de bigges' head er ha'r on de plantation. Befo' dat, Henry had tol'able good ha'r 'roun' de aidges, but soon ez de young grapes begun ter come, Henry's ha'r begun to quirl all up in little balls, des like dis yer reg'lar grapy ha'r, en by de time de grapes got ripe his head look des like a bunch er grapes. Combin' it didn' do no good; he wuk at it ha'f de night wid er Jim Crow,[3] en think he git it straighten' out, but in de mawnin' de grapes 'ud be dere des de same. So he gin it up, en tried ter keep de grapes down by havin' his ha'r cut sho't.

"But dat wa'n't de quares' thing 'bout de goopher. When Henry come ter de plantation, he wuz gittin' a little ole an stiff in de j'ints. But dat summer he got des ez spry en libely ez any young nigger on de plantation; fac', he got so biggity dat Mars Jackson, de oberseah, ha' ter th'eaten ter whip 'im, ef he didn' stop cuttin' up his didos en behave hisse'f. But de mos' cur'ouses' thing happen' in de fall, when de sap begin ter go down in de grapevimes. Fus', when de grapes 'uz gethered, de knots begun ter straighten out'n Henry's ha'r; en w'en de leaves begin ter fall, Henry's ha'r 'mence' ter drap out; en when de vimes 'uz bar', Henry's head wuz baller 'n it wuz in de spring, en he begin ter git ole en stiff in de j'ints ag'in, en paid no mo' 'tention ter de gals dyoin' er de whole winter. En nex' spring, w'en he rub de sap on ag'in, he got young ag'in, en so soopl en libely dat none er de young niggers on de planta-tion couldn' jump, ner dance, ner hoe ez much cotton ez Henry. But in de fall er de year his grapes 'mence' ter straighten out, en his j'ints ter git stiff, en his ha'r drap off, en de rheumatiz begin ter wrastle wid 'im.

"Now, ef you 'd 'a' knowed ole Mars Dugal' McAdoo, you'd 'a' knowed dat it ha' ter be a mighty rainy day when he couldn' fine sump'n fer his nig-gers ter do, en it ha' ter be a mighty little hole he couldn' crawl thoo, en ha'

---

[3]"A small card, resembling a currycomb in construction, and used by negroes in the ru-ral districts instead of a comb." [Chesnutt's note.]

ter be a monst'us cloudy night when a dollar git by him in de dahkness; en w'en he see how Henry git young in de spring en ole in de fall, he 'lowed ter hisse'f ez how he could make mo' money out'n Henry dan by wukkin' him in de cotton-fiel'. 'Long de nex' spring, atter de sap 'mence' ter rise, en Henry 'n'int 'is head en sta'ted fer ter git young en soopl, Mars Dugal' up 'n tuk Henry ter town, en sole 'im fer fifteen hunder' dollars. Co'se de man w'at bought Henry didn' know nuffin 'bout de goopher, en Mars Dugal' didn' see no 'casion fer ter tell 'im. Long to'ds de fall, w'en de sap went down, Henry begin ter git ole ag'in same ez yuzhal, en his noo marster begin ter git skeered les'n he gwine ter lose his fifteen-hunder'-dollar nigger. He sent fer a mighty fine doctor, but de med'cine didn' 'pear ter do no good; de goopher had a good holt. Henry tole de doctor 'bout de goopher, but de doctor des laff at 'im.

"One day in de winter Mars Dugal' went ter town, en wuz santerin' 'long de Main Street, when who should he meet but Henry's noo marster. Dey said 'Hoddy,' en Mars Dugal' ax 'im ter hab a seegyar; en atter dey run on awhile 'bout de craps en de weather, Mars Dugal' ax 'im, sorter keerless, like ez ef he des thought of it,—

"'How you like de nigger I sole you las' spring?'

"Henry's marster shuck his head en knock de ashes off'n his seegyar.

"'Spec' I made a bad bahgin when I bought dat nigger. Henry done good wuk all de summer, but sence de fall set in he 'pears ter be sorter pinin' away. Dey ain' nuffin pertickler de matter wid 'im—leastways de doctor say so—'cep'n' a tech er de rheumatiz; but his ha'r is all fell out, en ef he don't pick up his strenk mighty soon, I spec' I'm gwine ter lose 'im.'

"Dey smoked on awhile, en bimeby ole mars say, 'Well, a bahgin 's a bahgin, but you en me is good fren's, en I doan wan' ter see you lose all de money you paid fer dat nigger; en ef w'at you say is so, en I ain't 'sputin' it, he ain't wuf much now. I 'spec's you wukked him too ha'd dis summer, er e'se de swamps down here don't agree wid de san'-hill nigger. So you des lemme know, en ef he gits any wusser I'll be willin' ter gib yer five hund'ed dollars fer 'im, en take my chances on his livin'.'

"Sho 'nuff, when Henry begun ter draw up wid de rheumatiz en it look like he gwine ter die fer sho, his noo marster sen' fer Mars Dugal', en Mars Dugal' gin him what he promus, en brung Henry home ag'in. He tuk good keer uv 'im dyoin' er de winter,—give 'im w'iskey ter rub his rheumatiz, en terbacker ter smoke, en all he want ter eat,—'caze a nigger w'at he could make a thousan' dollars a year off'n didn' grow on eve'y huckleberry bush.

"Nex' spring, w'en de sap ris en Henry's ha'r commence' ter sprout, Mars Dugal' sole 'im ag'in, down in Robeson County dis time; en he kep' dat sellin' business up fer five year er mo'. Henry nebber say nuffin 'bout de goopher ter his noo marsters, 'caze he know he gwine ter be tuk good keer uv de nex' winter, w'en Mars Dugal' buy him back. En Mars Dugal' made 'nuff money off'n Henry ter buy anudder plantation ober on Beaver Crick.

"But 'long 'bout de een' er dat five year dey come a stranger ter stop at de plantation. De fus' day he 'uz dere he went out wid Mars Dugal' en spent all de mawnin' lookin' ober de vimya'd, en atter dinner dey spent all de evenin' playing' kya'ds. De niggers soon 'skiver' dat he wuz a Yankee, en dat he come down ter Norf C'lina fer ter l'arn de w'ite folks how to raise grapes en make wine. He promus Mars Dugal' he c'd make de grapevimes b'ar twice't ez many grapes, en dat de noo winepress he wuz asellin' would make mo' d'n twice't ez many gallons er wine. En ole Mars Dugal' des drunk it all in, des 'peared ter be bewitch' wid dat Yankee. W'en de darkies see dat Yankee runnin' 'roun' de vimya'd en diggin' under de grapevimes, dey shuk dere heads, en 'lowed dat dey feared Mars Dugal' losin' his min'. Mars Dugal' had all de dirt dug away fum under de roots er all de scuppernon' vimes, an' let 'em stan' dat away fer a week er mo'. Den dat Yankee made de niggers fix up a mixtry er lime en ashes en manyo, en po' it 'roun' de roots er de grapevimes. Den he 'vise Mars Dugal' fer ter trim de vimes close't, en Mars Dugal' tuck 'n done eve'ything de Yankee tole him ter do. Dyoin' all er dis time, mind yer, dis yer Yankee wuz libbin' off'n de fat er de lan', at de big house, en playin' kya'ds wid Mars Dugal' eve'y night; en dey say Mars Dugal' los' mo'n a thousan' dollars dyoin' er de week dat Yankee wuz a-ruinin' de grapevimes.

"W'en de sap ris nex' spring, ole Henry 'n'inted his head ez yuzhal, en his ha'r 'mence' ter grow des de same ez it done eve'y year. De scuppernon' vimes growed monst's fas', en de leaves wuz greener en thicker dan dey eber be'n dyoin' my rememb'ance; en Henry's ha'r growed out thicker dan eber, en he 'peared ter git younger 'n younger, en soopler 'n soopler; en seein' ez he wuz sho't er han's dat spring, havin' tuk in consid'able noo groun', Mars Dugal' 'cluded he wouldn' sell Henry 'tel he git de crap in en de cotton chop'. So he kep' Henry on de plantation.

"But 'long 'bout time fer de grapes ter come on de scuppernon' vimes, dey 'peared ter come a change ober 'em; de leaves withered en swivel' up, en de young grapes turn' yaller, en bimeby eve'ybody on de plantation could see dat de whole vimya'd wuz dyin'. Mars Dugal' tuk 'n water de vimes en done all he could, but 't wa'n' no use: dat Yankee had done bus' de watermillyum. One time de vimes picked up a bit, en Mars Dugal' 'lowed dey wuz gwine ter come out ag'in; but dat Yankee done dug too close under de roots, en prune de branches too close ter de vime, en all dat lime en ashes done burn' de life out'n de vimes, en dey des kep' a-with'in' en a-swivelin'.

"All dis time de goopher wuz a-wukkin'. When de vimes sta'ted ter wither, Henry 'mence' ter complain er his rheumatiz; en when de leaves begin ter dry up, his ha'r 'mence' ter drap out. When de vimes fresh' up a bit, Henry'd git peart ag'in, en when de vimes wither' ag'in, Henry'd git ole ag'in, en des kep' gittin' mo' en mo' fitten fer nuffin; he des pined away, en pined away, en fine'ly tuk ter his cabin; en when de big vimes whar he got de sap ter 'n'int his head withered en turned yaller en died, Henry died too,—des went out sorter like a cannel. Dey didn't 'pear ter be nuffin de matter wid 'im, 'cep'n' de rheumatiz, but his strenk des dwinel' away 'tel he didn' hab ernuff lef' ter draw his bref. De goopher had got de under holt, en th'owed Henry dat time fer good en all.

"Mars Dugal' tuk on might'ly 'bout losin' his vimes en his nigger in de same year; en he swo' dat ef he could git holt er dat Yankee he'd wear 'im ter a frazzle, en den chaw up de frazzle; en he'd done it, too, for Mars Dugal' 'uz a monst'us brash man w'en he once git started. He sot de vimya'd out ober ag'in, but it wuz th'ee er fo' year befo' de vimes got ter b'arin' any scuppernon's.

"W'en de wah broke out, Mars Dugal' raise' a comp'ny, en went off ter fight de Yankees. He say he wuz mighty glad dat wah come, en he des want ter kill a Yankee fer eve'y dollar he los' 'long er dat grape-raisin' Yankee. En I 'spec' he would 'a' done it, too, ef de Yankees hadn' s'picioned sump'n, en killed him fus'. Atter de s'render ole miss move' ter town, de niggers all scat-tered 'way fum de plantation, en de vimya'd ain' be'n cultervated sence."

"Is that story true?" asked Annie doubtfully, but seriously, as the old man concluded his narrative.

"It's des ez true ez I'm a-settin' here, miss. Dey's a easy way ter prove it: I kin lead de way right ter Henry's grave ober yander in de plantation buryin'-groun'. En I tell yer w'at, marster, I wouldn' 'vise you to buy dis yer ole vimya'd, 'caze de goopher's on it yit, en dey ain' no tellin' w'en it's gwine ter crap out."

"But I thought you said all the old vines died."

"Dey did 'pear ter die, but a few un 'em come out ag'in, en is mixed in 'mongs' de yuthers. I ain' skeered ter eat de grapes, 'caze I knows de old vimes fum de noo ones; but wid strangers dey ain' no tellin' w'at mought happen. I wouldn' 'vise yer ter buy dis vimya'd."

I bought the vineyard, nervertheless, and it has been for a long time in a thriving condition, and is often referred to by the local press as a striking illustration of the opportunities open to Northern capital in the develop-ment of Southern industries. The luscious scuppernong holds first rank among our grapes, though we cultivate a great many other varieties, and our income from grapes packed and shipped to the Northern markets is quite considerable. I have not noticed any developments of the goopher in the vineyard, although I have a mild suspicion that our colored assistants do not suffer from want of grapes during the season.

I found, when I bought the vineyard, that Uncle Julius had occupied a cabin on the place for many years, and derived a respectable revenue from the product of the neglected grapevines. This, doubtless, accounted for his advice to me not to buy the vineyard, though whether it inspired the goopher story I am unable to state. I believe, however, that the wages I paid him for his services as coachman, for I gave him employment in that capacity, were more than an equivalent for anything he lost by the sale of the vineyard.

1899

Po' Sandy

On the northeast corner of my vineyard in central North Carolina, and fronting on the Lumberton plank-road, there stood a small frame house, of the simplest construction. It was built of pine lumber, and contained but one room, to which one window gave light and one door admission. Its weather-beaten sides revealed a virgin innocence of paint. Against one end of the house, and occupying half its width, there stood a huge brick chimney: the crumbling mortar had left large cracks between the bricks; the bricks themselves had begun to scale off in large flakes, leaving the chimney sprinkled with unsightly blotches. These evidences of decay were but partially concealed by a creeping vine, which extended its slender branches hither and thither in an ambitious but futile attempt to cover the whole chimney. The wooden shutter, which had once protected the unglazed window, had fallen from its hinges, and lay rotting in the rank grass and jimsonweeds beneath. This building, I learned when I bought the place, had been used as a schoolhouse for several years prior to the breaking out of the war, since which time it had remained unoccupied, save when some stray cow or vagrant hog had sought shelter within its walls from the chill rains and nipping winds of winter.

One day my wife requested me to build her a new kitchen. The house erected by us, when we first came to live upon the vineyard, contained a very conveniently arranged kitchen; but for some occult reason my wife wanted a kitchen in the back yard, apart from the dwelling-house, after the usual Southern fashion. Of course I had to build it.

To save expense, I decided to tear down the old schoolhouse, and use the lumber, which was in a good state of preservation, in the construction of the new kitchen. Before demolishing the old house, however, I made an estimate of the amount of material contained in it, and found that I would have to buy several hundred feet of lumber additional, in order to build the new kitchen according to my wife's plan.

One morning old Julius McAdoo, our colored coachman, harnessed the gray mare to the rockaway,[1] and drove my wife and me over to the sawmill from which I meant to order the new lumber. We drove down the long lane which led from our house to the plank-road; following the plank-road for about a mile, we turned into a road running through the forest and across the swamp to the sawmill beyond. Our carriage jolted over the half-rotted corduroy road[2] which traversed the swamp, and then climbed the long hill leading to the sawmill. When we reached the mill, the foreman had gone over to a neighboring farmhouse, probably to smoke or gossip, and we were compelled to await his return before we could transact our business. We remained seated in the carriage, a few rods from the mill, and watched the leisurely movements of the mill-hands. We had not waited long before a huge pine log was placed in position, the machinery of the mill was set in motion, and the circular saw began to eat its way through the log, with a loud whir which resounded throughout the vicinity of the mill. The sound rose and fell in a sort of rhythmic cadence, which, heard from where we sat, was not unpleasing, and not loud enough to prevent conversation. When

---

[1] A four-wheeled carriage with two seats and a standing top.

[2] Made of logs laid together transversely.

the saw started on its second journey through the log, Julius observed, in a lugubrious tone, and with a perceptible shudder:—

"Ugh! but dat des do cuddle my blood!"

"What's the matter, Uncle Julius?" inquired my wife, who is of a very sympathetic turn of mind. "Does the noise affect your nerves?"

"No, Mis' Annie," replied the ole man, with emotion, "I ain' narvous; but dat saw, a-cuttin' en grindin' thoo dat stick er timber, en moanin', en groanin,' en sweekin', kyars my 'memb'ance back ter ole times, en 'min's me er po' Sandy." The pathetic intonation with which he lengthened out the "po' Sandy" touched a responsive chord in our own hearts.

"And who was poor Sandy?" asked my wife, who takes a deep interest in the stories of plantation life which she hears from the lips of the older colored people. Some of these stories are quaintly humorous; others wildly extravagant, revealing the Oriental cast of the negro's imagination; while others, poured freely into the sympathetic ear of a Northern-bred woman, disclose many a tragic incident of the darker side of slavery.

"Sandy," said Julius, in reply to my wife's question, "was a nigger w'at useter b'long ter old Mars Marrabo McSwayne. Mars Marrabo's place wuz on de yuther side'n de swamp, right nex' ter yo' place. Sandy wuz a monst'us good nigger, en could do so many things erbout a plantation, en alluz 'ten' ter his wuk so well, dat w'en Mars Marrabo's chilluns growed up en married off, dey all un 'em wanted dey daddy fer ter gin 'em Sandy fer a weddin' present. But Mars Marrabo knowed de res' wouldn' be satisfied ef he gin Sandy ter a'er one un 'em; so w'en dey wuz all done married, he fix it by 'lowin' one er his chilluns ter take Sandy fer a mont' er so, en den ernudder for a mont' er so, en so on dat erway tel dey had all had 'im de same lenk er time; en den dey would all take him roun' ag'in, 'cep'n' oncet in a w'ile w'en Mars Marrabo would len' 'im ter some er his yuther kinfolks 'roun' de country, w'en dey wuz short er han's; tel bimeby it got so Sandy didn' hardly knowed whar he wuz gwine ter stay fum one week's een' ter de yuther.

"One time w'en Sandy wuz lent out ez yushal, a spekilater come erlong wid a lot er niggers, en Mars Marrabo swap' Sandy's wife off fer a noo 'oman. W'en Sandy come back, Mars Marrabo gin 'im a dollar, en 'lowed he wuz monst'us sorry fer ter break up de fambly, but de spekilater had gin 'im big boot,[3] en times wuz hard en money skase, en so he wuz bleedst ter make de trade. Sandy tuk on some 'bout losin' his wife, but he soon seed dey want no use cryin' ober spilt merlasses; en bein' ez he lacked de looks er de noo 'oman, he tuk up wid her atter she'd be'n on de plantation a mont' er so.

"Sandy en his noo wife got on mighty well tergedder, en de niggers all 'mence' ter talk about how lovin' dey wuz. W'en Tenie wuz tuk sick oncet, Sandy useter set up all night wid 'er, en den go ter wuk in de mawnin' des lack he had his reg'lar sleep; en Tenie would 'a' done anythin' in de worl' for her Sandy.

"Sandy en Tenie hadn' be'n libbin' tergedder fer mo' d'n two mont's befo' Mars Marrabo's old uncle, w'at libbed down in Robeson County, sent

[3]Special, unexpected value.

up ter fin' out ef Mars Marrabo couldn' len' 'im er hire 'im a good han' fer a mont' er so. Sandy's marster wuz one er dese yer easy-gwine folks w'at wanter please eve'ybody, en he says yas, he could len' 'im Sandy. En Mars Marrabo tol' Sandy fer ter git ready ter go down ter Robeson nex' day, fer ter stay a mont' er so.

"It wuz monst'us hard on Sandy fer ter take 'im 'way fum Tenie. It wuz so fur down ter Robeson dat he didn' hab no chance er comin' back ter see her tel de time wuz up; he would n' 'a' mine comin' ten er fifteen mile at night ter see Tenie, but Mars Marrabo's uncle's plantation wuz mo' d'n forty mile off. Sandy wuz mighty sad en cas' down atter w'at Mars Marrabo tol' 'im, en he says ter Tenie, sezee:—

"'I'm gittin' monst'us ti'ed er dish yer gwine roun' so much. Here I is lent ter Mars Jeems dis mont', en I got ter do so-en-so; en ter Mars Archie de nex' mont', en I got ter do so-en-so; den I got ter go ter Miss Jinnie's: en hit 's Sandy dis en Sandy dat, en Sandy yer en Sandy dere, tel it 'pears ter me I ain' got no home, ner no marster, ner no mistiss, ner no nuffin. I can't eben keep a wife: my yuther ole 'oman wuz sol' away widout my gittin' a chance fer ter tell her good-by; en now I got ter go off en leab you, Tenie, en I dunno whe'r I'm eber gwine ter see you ag'in er no. I wisht I wuz a tree, er a stump, er a rock, er sump'n w'at could stay on de plantation fer a w'ile.'

"Atter Sandy got thoo talkin', Tenie didn' say naer word, but des sot dere by de fier, studyin' en studyin'. Bimeby she up'n' says:—

"'Sandy, is I eber tol' you I wuz a cunjuh 'oman?'

"Co'se Sandy hadn' ebber dremp' er nuffin lack dat, en he made a great 'miration w'en he hear w'at Tenie say. Bimeby Tenie went on:—

"'I ain't goophered nobody, ner done no cunjuh wuk, fer fifteen year er mo'; en w'en I got religion I made up my mine I wouldn' wuk no mo' goopher. But dey is some things I doan b'lieve it's no sin fer ter do; en ef you doan wanter be sent roun' fum pillar ter pos', en ef you doan wanter go down ter Robeson, I kin fix things so you won't haf ter. Ef you'll des say de word, I kin turn you ter w'ateber you wanter be, en you kin stay right whar you wanter, ez long ez you mineter.'

"Sandy say he doan keer; he's willin' fer ter do anythin' fer ter stay close ter Tenie. Den Tenie ax 'im ef he doan wanter be turnt inter a rabbit.

"Sandy say, 'No, de dogs mought git atter me.'

"'Shill I turn you ter a wolf?' sez Tenie.

"'No, eve'ybody's skeered er a wolf, en I doan want nobody ter be skeered er me.'

"'Shill I turn you ter a mawkin'-bird?'

"'No, a hawk mought ketch me. I wanter be turnt inter sump'n w'at'll stay in one place.'

"'I kin turn you ter a tree,' sez Tenie. 'You won't hab no mouf ner years, but I kin turn you back oncet in a w'ile, so you kin git sump'n ter eat, en hear w'at's gwine on.'

"Well, Sandy say dat'll do. En so Tenie tuk 'im down by de aidge er de swamp, not fur fum de quarters, en turnt 'im inter a big pine-tree, en sot 'im out 'mongs' some yuther trees. En de nex' mawnin', ez some er de fiel' han's wuz gwine long dere, dey seed a tree w'at dey didn' 'member er habbin' seed befo'; it wuz monst'us quare, en dey wuz bleedst ter 'low dat dey hadn' 'membered right, er e'se one er de saplin's had be'n growin' monst'us fas'.

"W'en Mars Marrabo 'skiver' dat Sandy wuz gone, he 'lowed Sandy had runned away. He got de dogs out, but de las' place dey could track Sandy ter wuz de foot er dat pine-tree. En dere de dogs stood en barked, en bayed, en pawed at de tree, en tried ter climb up on it; en w'en dey wuz tuk roun' thoo de swamp ter look fer de scent, dey broke loose en made fer dat tree ag'in. It wuz de beatenis' thing de w'ite folks eber hearn of, en Mars Marrabo 'lowed dat Sandy must 'a' clim' up on de tree en jump' off on a mule er sump'n, en rid fur ernuff fer ter spile de scent. Mars Marrabo wanted ter 'cuse some er de yuther niggers er heppin' Sandy off, but dey all 'nied it ter de las'; en eve'ybody knowed Tenie sot too much sto' by Sandy fer ter he'p 'im run away whar she couldn' nebber see 'im no mo'.

"W'en Sandy had be'n gone long ernuff fer folks ter think he done got clean away, Tenie useter go down ter de woods at night en turn 'im back, en den dey'd slip up ter de cabin en set by de fire en talk. But dey ha' ter be monst'us keerful, er e'se somebody would 'a' seed 'em, en dat would 'a' spile' de whole thing; so Tenie alluz turnt Sandy back in de mawnin' early, befo' anybody wuz a-stirrin'.

"But Sandy didn' git erlong widout his trials en tribberlations. One day a woodpecker come erlong en 'mence' ter peck at de tree; en de nex' time Sandy wuz turnt back he had a little roun' hole in his arm, des lack a sharp stick be'n stuck in it. Atter dat Tenie sot a sparrer-hawk fer ter watch de tree; en w'en de woodpecker come erlong nex' mawnin' fer ter finish his nes', he got gobble' up mos' 'fo' he stuck his bill in de bark.

"Nudder time, Mars Marrabo sent a nigger out in de woods fer ter chop tuppentime boxes. De man chop a box in dish yer tree, en hack' de bark up two er th'ee feet, fer ter let de tuppentime run. De nex' time Sandy wuz turnt back he had a big skyar on his lef' leg, des lack it be'n skunt; en it tuk Tenie nigh 'bout all night fer ter fix a mixtry ter kyo it up. Atter dat, Tenie sot a hawnet fer ter watch de tree; en w'en de nigger come back ag'in fer ter cut ernudder box on de yuther side'n de tree, de hawnet stung 'im so hard dat de ax slip en cut his foot nigh 'bout off.

"W'en Tenie see so many things happenin' ter de tree, she 'cluded she'd ha' ter turn Sandy ter sump'n e'se; en atter studyin' de matter ober, en talkin' wid Sandy one ebenin', she made up her mine fer ter fix up a goopher mixtry w'at would turn herse'f en Sandy ter foxes, er sump'n, so dey could run away en go some'rs whar dey could be free en lib lack w'ite folks.

"But dey ain' no tellin' w'at 's gwine ter happen in dis worl'. Tenie had got de night sot fer her en Sandy ter run away, w'en dat ve'y day one er Mars Marrabo's sons rid up ter de big house in his buggy, en say his wife wuz monst'us sick, en he want his mammy ter len' 'im a 'oman fer ter nuss his wife. Tenie's mistiss say sen' Tenie; she wuz a good nuss. Young mars wuz in a tarrible hurry fer ter git back home. Tenie wuz washin' at de big house dat day, en her mistiss say she should go right 'long wid her young marster. Tenie tried ter make some 'scuse fer ter git away en hide 'tel night, w'en she would have eve'ything fix' up fer her en Sandy; she say she wanter go ter her cabin fer ter git her bonnet. Her mistiss say it doan matter 'bout de bonnet; her head-hankcher wuz good ernuff. Den Tenie say she wanter git her bes' frock; her mistiss say no, she doan need no mo' frock, en w'en dat one got dirty she could git a clean one whar she wuz gwine. So Tenie had ter git in de buggy en go 'long wid young Mars Dunkin ter his planta- tion, w'ich wuz mo' d'n twenty mile away; en dey wa'n't no chance er her seein' Sandy no mo' 'tel she come back home. De po' gal felt monst'us bad 'bout de way things wuz gwine on, en she knowed Sandy mus' be a wond'rin' why she didn' come en turn 'im back no mo'.

"W'iles Tenie wuz away nussin' young Mars Dunkin's wife, Mars Mar- rabo tuk a notion fer ter buil' 'im a noo kitchen; en bein' ez he had lots er timber on his place, be begun ter look 'roun' fer a tree ter hab de lumber sawed out'n. En I dunno how it come to be so, but he happen fer ter hit on de ve'y tree w'at Sandy wuz turnt inter. Tenie wuz gone, en dey wa'n't nobody ner nuffin fer ter watch de tree.

"De two men w'at cut de tree down say dey nebber had sech a time wid a tree befo': dey axes would glansh off, en didn' 'pear ter make no prMgress thoo de wood; en of all de creakin', en shakin', en wobblin' you eber see, dat tree done it w'en it commence' ter fall. It wuz de beatenis' thing!

"W'en dey got de tree all trim' up, dey chain it up ter a timber waggin, en start fer de sawmill. But dey had a hard time gittin' de log dere: fus' dey got stuck in de mud w'en dey wuz gwine crosst de swamp, en it wuz two er th'ee hours befo' dey could git out. W'en dey start' on ag'in, de chain kep' a- comin' loose, en dey had ter keep a-stoppin' en a-stoppin' fer ter hitch de log up ag'in. W'en dey commence' ter climb de hill ter de sawmill, de log broke loose, en roll down de hill en in 'mongs' de trees, en hit tuk nigh 'bout half a day mo' ter git it haul' up ter de sawmill.

"De nex' mawnin' atter de dey de tree wuz haul' ter de sawmill, Tenie come home. W'en she got back ter her cabin, de fus' thing she done wuz ter run down ter de woods en see how Sandy wuz gittin' on. W'en she seed de stump standin' dere, wid de sap runnin' out'n it, en de limbs layin' scattered roun', she nigh 'bout went out'n her min'. She run ter her cabin, en got her goopher mixtry, en den follered de track er de timber waggin ter de sawmill. She knowed Sandy couldn' lib mo' d'n a minute er so ef she turnt him back, fer he wuz all chop' up so he'd 'a' be'n bleedst ter die. But she wanted ter turn 'im back long ernuff fer ter 'splain ter 'im dat she hadn' went off a-pur- pose, en lef' 'im ter be chop' down en sawed up. She didn' want Sandy ter die wid no hard feelin's to'ds her.

"De han's at de sawmill had des got de big log on de kerridge, en wuz startin' up de saw, w'en dey seed a 'oman runnin' up de hill, all out er bref, cryin' en gwine on des lack she wuz plumb 'stracted. It wuz Tenie; she come right inter de mill, en th'owed herse'f on de log, right in front er de saw, a- hollerin' en cryin' ter her Sandy ter fergib her, en not ter think hard er her, fer it wa'n't no fault er hern. Den Tenie 'membered de tree didn' hab no years, en she wuz gittin' ready fer ter wuk her goopher mixtry so ez ter turn Sandy back, w'en de mill-hands kotch holt er her en tied her arms wid a rope, en fasten' her to one er de posts in de sawmill; en den dey started de saw up ag'in, en cut de log up inter bo'ds en scantlin's right befo' her eyes. But it wuz mighty hard wuk; fer of all de sweekin', en moanin', en groanin', dat log done it w'iles de saw wuz a-cuttin' thoo it. De saw wuz one er dese yer oletimey, up-en-down saws, en hit tuk longer dem days ter saw a log 'en it do now. Dey greased de saw, but dat didn' stop de fuss; hit kep' right on, tel fin'ly dey got de log all sawed up.

"W'en de oberseah w'at run de sawmill come fum breakfas', de han's up en tell him 'bout de crazy 'oman—ez dey s'posed she wuz—w'at had come runnin' in de sawmill, a-hollerin' en gwine on, en tried ter th'ow herse'f befo' de saw. En de oberseah sent two er th'ee er de han's fer ter take Tenie back ter her marster's plantation.

"Tenie 'peared ter be out'n her min' fer a long time, en her marster ha' ter lock her up in de smoke-'ouse 'tel she got ober her spells. Mars Marrabo wuz monst'us mad, en hit would 'a' made yo' flesh crawl fer ter hear him cuss, 'caze he say de speki-later w'at he got Tenie fum had fooled 'im by wukkin' a crazy 'oman off on him. W'iles Tenie wuz lock up in de smoke-'ouse, Mars Marrabo tuk 'n' haul de lumber fum de sawmill, en put up his noo kitchen.

"W'en Tenie got quiet' down, so she could be 'lowed ter go 'roun' de plantation, she up'n' tole her marster all erbout Sandy en de pine-tree; en w'en Mars Marrabo hearn it, he 'lowed she wuz de wuss 'stracted nigger he eber hearn of. He did n' know w'at ter do wid Tenie: fus' he thought he'd put her in de po'-house; but fin'ly, seein' ez she didn' do no harm ter nobody ner nuffin, but des went 'roun' moanin', en groanin', en shakin' her head, he 'cluded ter let her stay on de plantation en nuss de little nigger chilluns w'en dey mammies wuz ter wuk in de cotton-fiel'.

"De noo kitchen Mars Marrabo buil' wuzn' much use, fer it hadn' be'n put up long befo' de niggers 'mence' ter notice quare things erbout it. Dey could hear sump'n moanin' en groanin' 'bout de kitchen in de night-time, en w'en de win' would blow dey could hear sump'n a-hollerin' en sweekin' lack it wuz in great pain en sufferin'. En it got so atter a w'ile dat it wuz all Mars Marrabo's wife could do ter git a 'oman ter stay in de kitchen in de daytime long ernuff ter do de cookin'; en dey wa'n't naer nigger on de plantation w'at wouldn' rudder take forty dan ter go 'bout dat kitchen atter dark,—dat is, 'cep'n' Tenie; she didn' 'pear ter min' de ha'nts.[4] She useter slip 'roun' at night, en set on de kitchen steps, en lean up agin de do'-jamb, en run on ter herse'f wid some kine er foolishness w'at nobody couldn' make out; fer Mars Marrabo had th'eaten' ter sen' her off'n de plantation ef she say anything ter any er de yuther niggers 'bout de pine-tree. But somehow er 'nudder de niggers foun' out all erbout it, en dey all knowed de kitchen wuz ha'nted by

[4]Ghosts.

Sandy's sperrit. En bimeby hit got so Mars Marrabo's wife herse'f wuz skeered ter go out in de yard atter dark.

"W'en it come ter dat, Mars Marrabo tuk en to' de kitchen down, en use' de lumber fer ter buil' dat ole school'ouse w'at you er talkin' 'bout pullin' down. De school'ouse wuzn' use' 'cep'n' in de daytime, en on dark nights folks gwine 'long de road would hear quare soun's en see quare things. Po' ole Tenie useter go down dere at night, en wander 'roun' de school'ouse; en de niggers all 'lowed she went fer ter talk wid Sandy's sperrit. En one winter mawnin', w'en one er de boys went ter school early fer ter start de fire, w'at should he fin' but po' ole Tenie, layin' on de flo', stiff, en col', en dead. Dere didn''pear ter be nuffin pertickler de matter wid her,—she had des grieve' herse'f ter def fer her Sandy. Mars Marrabo did n' shed no tears. He thought Tenie wuz crazy, en dey wa'n't no tellin' w'at she mought do nex'; en dey ain' much room in dis worl' fer crazy w'ite folks, let 'lone a crazy nigger.

"Hit wa'n't long atter dat befo' Mars Marrabo sol' a piece er his track er lan' ter Mars Dugal' McAdoo,—*my* ole marster,—en dat's how de ole school'ouse happen to be on yo' place. W'en de wah broke out, de school stop', en de ole school'ouse be'n stannin' empty ever sence,—dat is, 'cep'n' fer de ha'nts. En folks sez dat de ole school'ouse, er any yuther house w'at got any er dat lumber in it w'at wuz sawed out'n de tree w'at Sandy wuz turnt inter, is gwine ter be ha'nted tel de las' piece er plank is rotted en crumble' inter dus'."

Annie had listened to this gruesome narrative with strained attention.

"What a system it was," she exclaimed, when Julius had finished, "under which such things were possible!"

"What things?" I asked, in amazement. "Are you seriously considering the possibility of a man's being turned into a tree?"

"Oh, no," she replied quickly, "not that;" and then she murmured absently, and with a dim look in her fine eyes, "Poor Tenie!"

We ordered the lumber, and returned home. That night, after we had gone to bed, and my wife had to all appearances been sound asleep for half an hour, she startled me out of an incipient doze by exclaiming suddenly,—

"John, I don't believe I want my new kitchen built out of the lumber in that old schoolhouse."

"You wouldn't for a moment allow yourself," I replied, with some asperity, "to be influenced by that absurdly impossible yarn which Julius was spinning to-day?"

"I know the story is absurd," she replied dreamily, "and I am not so silly as to believe it. But I don't think I should ever be able to take any pleasure in that kitchen if it were built out of that lumber. Besides, I think the kitchen would look better and last longer if the lumber were all new."

Of course she had her way. I bought the new lumber, though not without grumbling. A week or two later I was called away from home on business. On my return, after an absence of several days, my wife remarked to me,—

"John, there has been a split in the Sandy Run Colored Baptist Church, on the temperance question. About half the members have come out from the main body, and set up for themselves. Uncle Julius is one of the seceders, and he came to me yesterday and asked if they might not hold their meetings in the old schoolhouse for the present."

"I hope you didn't let the old rascal have it," I returned, with some warmth. I had just received a bill for the new lumber I had bought.

"Well," she replied, "I couldn't refuse him the use of the house for so good a purpose."

"And I'll venture to say," I continued, "that you subscribed something toward the support of the new church?"

She did not attempt to deny it.

"What are they going to do about the ghost?" I asked, somewhat curious to know how Julius would get around this obstacle.

"Oh," replied Annie, "Uncle Julius says that ghosts never disturb religious worship, but that if Sandy's spirit *should* happen to stray into meeting by mistake, no doubt the preaching would do it good."

1899

The Passing of Grandison

I

When it is said that it was done to please a woman, there ought perhaps to be enough said to explain anything; for what a man will not do to please a woman is yet to be discovered. Nevertheless, it might be well to state a few preliminary facts to make it clear why young Dick Owens tried to run one of his father's negro men off to Canada.

In the early fifties, when the growth of anti-slavery sentiment and the constant drain of fugitive slaves into the North had so alarmed the slave-holders of the border States as to lead to the passage of the Fugitive Slave Law,[1] a young white man from Ohio, moved by compassion for the sufferings of a certain bondman who happened to have a "hard master," essayed to help the slave to freedom. The attempt was discovered and frustrated; the abductor was tried and convicted for slave-stealing, and sentenced to a term of imprisonment in the penitentiary. His death, after the expiration of only a small part of the sentence, from cholera contracted while nursing stricken fellow prisoners, lent to the case a melancholy interest that made it famous in anti-slavery annals.

Dick Owens had attended the trial. He was a youth of about twenty-two, intelligent, handsome, and amiable, but extremely indolent, in a graceful and gentlemanly way; or, as old Judge Fenderson put it more than once, he was lazy as the Devil,—a mere figure of speech, of course, and not one

[1]Enacted by Congress as part of the Compromise of 1850, the Fugitive Slave Act provided for the return of escaped slaves in the North to their Southern owners.

that did justice to the Enemy of Mankind. When asked why he never did anything serious, Dick would good-naturedly reply, with a well-modulated drawl, that he didn't have to. His father was rich; there was but one other child, an unmarried daughter, who because of poor health would probably never marry, and Dick was therefore heir presumptive to a large estate. Wealth or social position he did not need to seek, for he was born to both. Charity Lomax had shamed him into studying law, but notwithstanding an hour or so a day spent at old Judge Fenderson's office, he did not make remarkable headway in his legal studies.

"What Dick needs," said the judge, who was fond of tropes, as became a scholar, and of horses, as was befitting a Kentuckian, "is the whip of necessity, or the spur of ambition. If he had either, he would soon need the snaffle to hold him back."

But all Dick required, in fact, to prompt him to the most remarkable thing he accomplished before he was twenty-five, was a mere suggestion from Charity Lomax. The story was never really known to but two persons until after the war, when it came out because it was a good story and there was no particular reason for its concealment.

Young Owens had attended the trial of this slave-stealer, or martyr,—either or both,—and, when it was over, had gone to call on Charity Lomax, and, while they sat on the veranda after sundown, had told her all about the trial. He was a good talker, as his career in later years disclosed, and described the proceedings very graphically.

"I confess," he admitted, "that while my principles were against the prisoner, my sympathies were on his side. It appeared that he was of good family, and that he had an old father and mother, respectable people, dependent upon him for support and comfort in their declining years. He had been led into the matter by pity for a negro whose master ought to have been run out of the county long ago for abusing his slaves. If it had been merely a question of old Sam Briggs's negro, nobody would have cared anything about it. But father and the rest of them stood on the principle of the thing, and told the judge so, and the fellow was sentenced to three years in the penitentiary."

Miss Lomax had listened with lively interest.

"I've always hated old Sam Briggs," she said emphatically, "ever since the time he broke a negro's leg with a piece of cordwood. When I hear of a cruel deed it makes the Quaker blood that came from my grandmother assert itself. Personally I wish that all Sam Briggs's negroes would run away. As for the young man, I regard him as a hero. He dared something for humanity. I could love a man who would take such chances for the sake of others."

"Could you love me, Charity, if I did something heroic?"

"You never will, Dick. You're too lazy for any use. You'll never do anything harder than playing cards or fox-hunting."

"Oh, come now, sweetheart! I've been courting you for a year, and it's the hardest work imaginable. Are you never going to love me?" he pleaded.

His hand sought hers, but she drew it back beyond his reach.

"I'll never love you, Dick Owens, until you have done something. When that time comes, I'll think about it."

"But it takes so long to do anything worth mentioning, and I don't want to wait. One must read two years to become a lawyer, and work five more to make a reputation. We shall both be gray by then."

"Oh, I don't know," she rejoined. "It doesn't require a lifetime for a man to prove that he is a man. This one did something, or at least tried to."

"Well, I'm willing to attempt as much as any other man. What do you want me to do, sweetheart? Give me a test."

"Oh, dear me!" said Charity, "I don't care what you *do*, so you do *something*. Really, come to think of it, why should I care whether you do anything or not?"

"I'm sure I don't know why you should, Charity," rejoined Dick humbly, "for I'm aware that I'm not worthy of it."

"Except that I do hate," she added, relenting slightly, "to see a really clever man so utterly lazy and good for nothing."

"Thank you, my dear; a word of praise from you has sharpened my wits already. I have an idea! Will you love me if *I* run a negro off to Canada?"

"What nonsense!" said Charity scornfully. "You must be losing your wits. Steal another man's slave, indeed, while your father owns a hundred!"

"Oh, there'll be no trouble about that," responded Dick lightly; "I'll run off one of the old man's; we've got too many anyway. It may not be quite as difficult as the other man found it, but it will be just as unlawful, and will demonstrate what I am capable of."

"Seeing's believing," replied Charity. "Of course, what you are talking about now is merely absurd. I'm going away for three weeks, to visit my aunt in Tennessee. If you're able to tell me, when I return, that you've done something to prove your quality, I'll—well, you may come and tell me about it."

II

Young Owens got up about nine o'clock next morning, and while making his toilet put some questions to his personal attendant, a rather bright looking young mulatto of about his own age.

"Tom," said Dick.

"Yas, Mars Dick," responded the servant.

"I'm going on a trip North. Would you like to go with me?"

Now, if there was anything that Tom would have liked to make, it was a trip North. It was something he had long contemplated in the abstract, but had never been able to muster up sufficient courage to attempt in the concrete. He was prudent enough, however, to dissemble his feelings.

"I wouldn't min' it, Mars Dick, ez long ez you'd take keer er me an' fetch me home all right."

Tom's eyes belied his words, however, and his young master felt well assured that Tom needed only a good opportunity to make him run away.

Having a comfortable home, and a dismal prospect in case of failure, Tom was not likely to take any desperate chances; but young Owens was satisfied that in a free State but little persuasion would be required to lead Tom astray. With a very logical and characteristic desire to gain his end with the least necessary expenditure of effort, he decided to take Tom with him, if his father did not object.

Colonel Owens had left the house when Dick went to breakfast, so Dick did not see his father till luncheon.

"Father," he remarked casually to the colonel, over the fried chicken, "I'm feeling a trifle run down. I imagine my health would be improved somewhat by a little travel and change of scene."

"Why don't you take a trip North?" suggested his father. The colonel added to paternal affection a considerable respect for his son as the heir of a large estate. He himself had been "raised" in comparative poverty, and had laid the foundations of his fortune by hard work; and while he despised the ladder by which he had climbed, he could not entirely forget it, and unconsciously manifested, in his intercourse with his son, some of the poor man's deference toward the wealthy and well-born.

"I think I'll adopt your suggestion, sir," replied the son, "and run up to New York; and after I've been there awhile I may go on to Boston for a week or so. I've never been there, you know."

"There are some matters you can talk over with my factor in New York," rejoined the colonel, "and while you are up there among the Yankees, I hope you'll keep your eyes and ears open to find out what the rascally abolitionists are saying and doing. They're becoming altogether too active for our comfort, and entirely too many ungrateful niggers are running away. I hope the conviction of that fellow yesterday may discourage the rest of the breed. I'd just like to catch any one trying to run off one of my darkeys. He'd get short shrift; I don't think any Court would have a chance to try him."

"They are a pestiferous lot," assented Dick, "and dangerous to our institutions. But say, father, if I go North I shall want to take Tom with me."

Now, the colonel, while a very indulgent father, had pronounced views on the subject of negroes, having studied them, as he often said, for a great many years, and, as he asserted oftener still, understanding them perfectly. It is scarcely worth while to say, either, that he valued more highly than if he had inherited them the slaves he had toiled and schemed for.

"I don't think it safe to take Tom up North," he declared, with promptness and decision. "He's a good enough boy, but too smart to trust among those low-down abolitionists. I strongly suspect him of having learned to read, though I can't imagine how. I saw him with a newspaper the other day, and while he pretended to be looking at a woodcut, I'm almost sure he was reading the paper. I think it by no means safe to take him."

Dick did not insist, because he knew it was useless. The colonel would have obliged his son in any other matter, but his negroes were the outward and visible sign of his wealth and station, and therefore sacred to him.

"Whom do you think it safe to take?" asked Dick. "I suppose I'll have to have a body-servant."

"What's the matter with Grandison?" suggested the colonel. "He's handy enough, and I reckon we can trust him. He's too fond of good eating, to risk losing his regular meals; besides, he's sweet on your mother's maid, Betty, and I've promised to let 'em get married before long. I'll have Grandison up, and we'll talk to him. Here, you boy Jack," called the colonel to a yellow youth in the next room who was catching flies and pulling their wings off to pass the time, "go down to the barn and tell Grandison to come here."

"Grandison," said the colonel, when the negro stood before him, hat in hand. "Yas, marster."

"Haven't I always treated you right?"

"Yas, marster."

"Haven't you always got all you wanted to eat?"

"Yas, marster."

"And as much whiskey and tobacco as was good for you, Grandison?"

"Y-a-s, marster."

"I should just like to know, Grandison, whether you don't think yourself a great deal better off than those poor free negroes down by the plank road, with no kind master to look after them and no mistress to give them medicine when they're sick and—and"—

"Well, I sh'd jes' reckon I is better off, suh, dan dem low-down free niggers, suh! Ef anybody ax 'em who dey b'long ter, dey has ter say nobody, er e'se lie erbout it. Anybody ax me who I b'longs ter, I ain' got no 'casion ter be shame' ter tell 'em, no, suh, 'deed I ain', suh!"

The colonel was beaming. This was true gratitude, and his feudal heart thrilled at such appreciative homage. What cold-blooded, heartless monsters they were who would break up this blissful relationship of kindly protection on the one hand, of wise subordination and loyal dependence on the other! The colonel always became indignant at the mere thought of such wickedness.

"Grandison," the colonel continued, "your young master Dick is going North for a few weeks, and I am thinking of letting him take you along. I shall send you on this trip, Grandison, in order that you may take care of your young master. He will need some one to wait on him, and no one can ever do it so well as one of the boys brought up with him on the old plantation. I am going to trust him in your hands, and I'm sure you'll do your duty faithfully, and bring him back home safe and sound—to old Kentucky."

Grandison grinned. "Oh yas, marster, I'll take keer er young Mars Dick."

"I want to warn you, though, Grandison," continued the colonel impressively, "against these cussed abolitionists, who try to entice servants from their comfortable homes and their indulgent masters, from the blue skies, the green fields, and the warm sunlight of their southern home, and send them away off yonder to Canada, a dreary country, where the woods are full of wildcats and wolves and bears, where the snow lies up to the eaves of the houses for six months of the year, and the cold is so severe that it freezes your breath and curdles your blood; and where, when runaway niggers get sick and can't work, they are turned out to starve and die, unloved and uncared for. I reckon, Grandison, that you have too much sense to permit yourself to be led astray by any such foolish and wicked people."

"'Deed, suh, I wouldn' low none er dem cussed, low-down abolitioners ter come nigh me, suh. I'd—I'd—would I be 'lowed ter hit 'em, suh?"

"Certainly, Grandison," replied the colonel, chuckling, "hit 'em as hard as you can. I reckon they'd rather like it. Begad, I believe they would! It would serve 'em right to be hit by a nigger!"

"Er ef I didn't hit 'em, suh," continued Grandison reflectively, "I'd tell Mars Dick, en *he'd* fix 'em. He'd smash de face off'n 'em, suh, I jes' knows he would."

"Oh yes, Grandison, your young master will protect you. You need fear no harm while he is near."

"Dey won't try ter steal me, will dey, marster?" asked the negro, with sudden alarm.

"I don't know, Grandison," replied the colonel, lighting a fresh cigar. "They're a desperate set of lunatics, and there's no telling what they may resort to. But if you stick close to your young master, and remember always that he is your best friend, and understands your real needs, and has your true interests at heart, and if you will be careful to avoid strangers who try to talk to you, you'll stand a fair chance of getting back to your home and your friends. And if you please your master Dick, he'll buy you a present, and a string of beads for Betty to wear when you and she get married in the fall."

"Thanky, marster, thanky, suh," replied Grandison, oozing gratitude at every pore; "you is a good marster, to be sho', suh; yas, 'deed you is. You kin jes' bet me and Mars Dick gwine git 'long jes' lack I wuz own boy ter Mars Dick. En it won't be my fault ef he don' want me fer his boy all de time, w'en we come back home ag'in."

"All right, Grandison, you may go now. You needn't work any more to-day, and here's a piece of tobacco for you off my own plug."

"Thanky, marster, thanky, marster! You is de bes' marster any nigger ever had in dis worl'." And Grandison bowed and scraped and disappeared round the corner, his jaws closing around a large section of the colonel's best tobacco.

"You may take Grandison," said the colonel to his son. "I allow he's abolitionist-proof."

III

Richard Owens, Esq., and servant, from Kentucky, registered at the fashionable New York hostelry for Southerners in those days, a hotel where an atmosphere congenial to Southern institutions was sedulously maintained. But there were negro waiters in the dining-room, and mulatto bell-boys, and Dick had no doubt that Grandison, with the native gregariousness and garrulousness of his race, would foregather and palaver with them sooner or later, and Dick hoped that they would speedily inoculate him with the virus of freedom. For it was not Dick's intention to say anything to his servant about his plan to free him, for obvious reasons. To mention one of them, if Grandison should go away, and by legal process be recaptured, his young master's part in the matter would doubtless become known, which would be embarrassing to Dick, to say the least. If, on the other hand, he should merely give Grandison sufficient latitude, he had no doubt he would eventually lose him. For while not exactly skeptical about Grandison's perfervid loyalty, Dick had been a somewhat keen observer of human nature, in his own indolent way, and based his expectations upon the force of the example and argument that his servant could scarcely fail to encounter. Grandison should have a fair chance to become free by his own initiative; if it should become necessary to adopt other measures to get rid of him, it would be time enough to act when the necessity arose; and Dick Owens was not the youth to take needless trouble.

The young master renewed some acquaintances and made others, and spent a week or two very pleasantly in the best society of the metropolis, easily accessible to a wealthy, well-bred young Southerner, with proper introductions. Young women smiled on him, and young men of convivial habits pressed their hospitalities; but the memory of Charity's sweet, strong face and clear blue eyes made him proof against the blandishments of the one sex and the persuasions of the other. Meanwhile he kept Grandison supplied with pocket-money, and left him mainly to his own devices. Every night when Dick came in he hoped he might have to wait upon himself, and every morning he looked forward with pleasure to the prospect of making his toilet unaided. His hopes, however, were doomed to disappointment, for every night when he came in Grandison was on hand with a bootjack, and a nightcap mixed for his young master as the colonel had taught him to mix it, and every morning Grandison appeared with his master's boots blacked and his clothes brushed, and laid his linen out for the day.

"Grandison," said Dick one morning, after finishing his toilet, "this is the chance of your life to go around among your own people and see how they live. Have you met any of them?"

"Yas, suh, I's seen some of 'em. But I don' keer nuffin fer 'em, suh. Dey're diffe'nt f'm de niggers down ou' way. Dey 'lows dey're free, but dey ain' got sense 'nuff ter know dey ain' half as well off as dey would be down Souf, whar dey'd be 'preciated."

When two weeks had passed without any apparent effect of evil example upon Grandison, Dick resolved to go on to Boston, where he thought the atmosphere might prove more favorable to his ends. After he had been at the Revere House for a day or two without losing Grandison, he decided upon slightly different tactics.

Having ascertained from a city directory the addresses of several well-known abolitionists, he wrote them each a letter something like this:—

DEAR FRIEND AND BROTHER:—

> *A wicked slaveholder from Kentucky, stopping at the Revere House, has dared to insult the liberty-loving people of Boston by bringing his slave into their midst. Shall this be tolerated? Or shall steps be taken in the name of liberty to rescue a fellow-man from bondage? For obvious reasons I can only sign myself,*
>
> A FRIEND OF HUMANITY.

That his letter might have an opportunity to prove effective, Dick made it a point to send Grandison away from the hotel on various errands. On one of these occasions Dick watched him for quite a distance down the street. Grandison had scarcely left the hotel when a long-haired, sharp-featured man came out behind him, followed him, soon overtook him, and kept along beside him until they turned the next corner. Dick's hopes were roused by this spectacle, but sank correspondingly when Grandison returned to the hotel. As Grandison said nothing about the encounter, Dick hoped there might be some self-consciousness behind this unexpected reticence, the results of which might develop later on.

But Grandison was on hand again when his master came back to the hotel at night, and was in attendance again in the morning, with hot water, to assist at his master's toilet. Dick sent him on further errands from day to day, and upon one occasion came squarely up to him—inadvertently of course—while Grandison was engaged in conversation with a young white man in clerical garb. When Grandison saw Dick approaching, he edged away from the preacher and hastened toward his master, with a very evident expression of relief upon his countenance.

"Mars Dick," he said, "dese yer abolitioners is jes' pesterin' de life out er me tryin' ter git me ter run away. I don' pay no 'tention ter 'em, but dey riles me so sometimes dat I'm feared I'll hit some of 'em some er dese days, an' dat mought git me inter trouble. I ain' said nuffin' ter you 'bout it, Mars Dick, fer I didn' wanter 'sturb yo' min'; but I don' like it, suh; no, suh, I don'! Is we gwine back home 'fo' long, Mars Dick?"

"We'll be going back soon enough," replied Dick somewhat shortly, while he inwardly cursed the stupidity of a slave who could be free and would not, and registered a secret vow that if he were unable to get rid of Grandison without assassinating him, and were therefore compelled to take him back to Kentucky, he would see that Grandison got a taste of an article of slavery that would make him regret his wasted opportunities. Meanwhile he determined to tempt his servant yet more strongly.

"Grandison," he said next morning, "I'm going away for a day or two, but I shall leave you here. I shall lock up a hundred dollars in this drawer and give you the key. If you need any of it, use it and enjoy yourself,—spend it all if you like,—for this is probably the last chance you'll have for some time to be in a free State, and you'd better enjoy your liberty while you may."

When he came back a couple of days later and found the faithful Grandi-son at his post, and the hundred dollars intact, Dick felt seriously annoyed. His vexation was increased by the fact that he could not express his feelings adequately. He did not even scold Grandison; how could he, indeed, find fault with one who so sensibly recognized his true place in the economy of civilization, and kept it with such touching fidelity?

"I can't say a thing to him," groaned Dick. "He deserves a leather medal, made out of his own hide tanned. I reckon I'll write to father and let him know what a model servant he has given me."

He wrote his father a letter which made the colonel swell with pride and pleasure. "I really think," the colonel observed to one of his friends, "that Dick ought to have the nigger interviewed by the Boston papers, so that they may see how contented and happy our darkeys really are."

Dick also wrote a long letter to Charity Lomax, in which he said, among many other things, that if she knew how hard he was working, and under what difficulties, to accomplish something serious for her sake, she would no longer keep him in suspense, but overwhelm him with love and admiration.

Having thus exhausted without result the more obvious methods of get-ting rid of Grandison, and diplomacy having also proved a failure, Dick was forced to consider more radical measures. Of course he might run away him-self, and abandon Grandison, but this would be merely to leave him in the United States, where he was still a slave, and where, with his notions of loy-alty, he would speedily be reclaimed. It was necessary, in order to accom-plish the purpose of his trip to the North, to leave Grandison permanently in Canada, where he would be legally free.

"I might extend my trip to Canada," he reflected, "but that would be too palpable. I have it! I'll visit Niagara Falls on the way home, and lose him on the Canadian side. When he once realizes that he is actually free, I'll warrant that he'll stay."

So the next day saw them westward bound, and in due course of time, by the somewhat slow conveyances of the period, they found themselves at Niagara. Dick walked and drove about the Falls for several days, taking Grandison along with him on most occasions. One morning they stood on the Canadian side, watching the wild whirl of the waters below them.

"Grandison," said Dick, raising his voice above the roar of the cataract, "do you know where you are now?"

"I's wid you, Mars Dick; dat's all I keers."

"You are now in Canada, Grandison, where your people go when they run away from their masters. If you wished, Grandison, you might walk away from me this very minute, and I could not lay my hand upon you to take you back."

Grandison looked around uneasily.

"Let's go back ober de ribber, Mars Dick. I's feared I'll lose you ovuh heah, an' den I won' hab no marster, an' won't nebber be able to git back home no mo'."

Discouraged, but not yet hopeless, Dick said, a few minutes later,—

"Grandison, I'm going up the road a bit, to the inn over yonder. You stay here until I return. I'll not be gone a great while."

Grandison's eyes opened wide and he looked somewhat fearful.

"Is dey any er dem dadblasted abolitioners roun' heah, Mars Dick?"

"I don't imagine that there are," replied his master, hoping there might be. "But I'm not afraid of *your* running away, Grandison. I only wish I were," he added to himself.

Dick walked leisurely down the road to where the whitewashed inn, built of stone, with true British solidity, loomed up through the trees by the roadside. Arrived there he ordered a glass of ale and a sandwich, and took a seat at a table by a window, from which he could see Grandison in the distance. For a while he hoped that the seed he had sown might have fallen on fertile ground, and that Grandison, relieved from the restraining power of a master's eye, and finding himself in a free country, might get up and walk away; but the hope was vain, for Grandison remained faithfully at his post, awaiting his master's return. He had seated himself on a broad flat stone, and, turning his eyes away from the grand and awe-inspiring spectacle that lay close at hand, was looking anxiously toward the inn where his master sat cursing his ill-timed fidelity.

By and by a girl came into the room to serve his order, and Dick very naturally glanced at her; and as she was young and pretty and remained in attendance, it was some minutes before he looked for Grandison. When he did so his faithful servant had disappeared.

To pay his reckoning and go away without the change was a matter quickly accomplished. Retracing his footsteps toward the Falls, he saw, to his great disgust, as he approached the spot where he had left Grandison, the familiar form of his servant stretched out on the ground, his face to the sun, his mouth open, sleeping the time away, oblivious alike to the grandeur of the scenery, the thunderous roar of the cataract, or the insidious voice of sentiment.

"Grandison," soliloquized his master, as he stood gazing down at his ebony encumbrance, "I do not deserve to be an American citizen; I ought not to have the advantages I possess over you; and I certainly am not worthy of Charity Lomax, if I am not smart enough to get rid of you. I have an idea! You shall yet be free, and I will be the instrument of your deliverance. Sleep on, faithful and affectionate servitor, and dream of the blue grass and the bright skies of old Kentucky, for it is only in your dreams that you will ever see them again!"

Dick retraced his footsteps towards the inn. The young woman chanced to look out of the window and saw the handsome young gentleman she had waited on a few minutes before, standing in the road a short distance away, apparently engaged in earnest conversation with a colored man employed as hostler for the inn. She thought she saw something pass from the white man to the other, but at that moment her duties called her away from the window, and when she looked out again the young gentleman had disappeared, and the hostler, with two other young men of the neighbor-hood, one white and one colored, were walking rapidly towards the Falls.

IV

Dick made the journey homeward alone, and as rapidly as the conveyances of the day would permit. As he drew near home his conduct in going back without Grandison took on a more serious aspect than it had borne at any previous time, and although he had prepared the colonel by a letter sent several days ahead, there was still the prospect of a bad quarter of an hour with him; not, indeed, that his father would upbraid him, but he was likely to make searching inquiries. And notwithstanding the vein of quiet reckless-ness that had carried Dick through his preposterous scheme, he was a very poor liar, having rarely had occasion or inclination to tell anything but the truth. Any reluctance to meet his father was more than offset, however, by a stronger force drawing him homeward, for Charity Lomax must long since have returned from her visit to her aunt in Tennessee.

Dick got off easier than he had expected. He told a straight story, and a truthful one, so far as it went.

The colonel raged at first, but rage soon subsided into anger, and anger moderated into annoyance, and annoyance into a sort of garrulous sense of injury. The colonel thought he had been hardly used; he had trusted this ne-gro, and he had broken faith. Yet, after all, he did not blame Grandison so much as he did the abolitionists, who were undoubtedly at the bottom of it.

As for Charity Lomax, Dick told her, privately of course, that he had run his father's man, Grandison, off to Canada, and left him there.

"Oh, Dick," she had said with shuddering alarm, "what have you done? If they knew it they'd send you to the penitentiary, like they did that Yankee."

"But they don't know it," he had replied seriously; adding, with an injured tone, "you don't seem to appreciate my heroism like you did that of the Yankee; perhaps it's because I wasn't caught and sent to the peniten-tiary. I thought you wanted me to do it."

"Why, Dick Owens!" she exclaimed. "You know I never dreamed of any such outrageous proceeding.

"But I presume I'll have to marry you," she concluded, after some insist-ence on Dick's part, "if only to take care of you. You are too reckless for any-thing; and a man who goes chasing all over the North, being entertained by New York and Boston society and having negroes to throw away, needs some one to look after him."

"It's a most remarkable thing," replied Dick fervently, "that your views correspond exactly with my profoundest convictions. It proves beyond ques-tion that we were made for one another."

They were married three weeks later. As each of them had just returned from a journey, they spent their honeymoon at home.

A week after the wedding they were seated, one afternoon, on the piazza of the colonel's house, where Dick had taken his bride, when a negro from the yard ran down the lane and threw open the big gate for the colonel's buggy to enter. The colonel was not alone. Beside him, ragged and travel-stained, bowed with weariness, and upon his face a haggard look that told of hardship and privation, sat the lost Grandison.

The colonel alighted at the steps.

"Take the lines, Tom," he said to the man who had opened the gate, "and drive round to the barn. Help Grandison down,—poor devil, he's so stiff he can hardly move!—and get a tub of water and wash him and rub him down, and feed him, and give him a big drink of whiskey, and then let him come round and see his young master and his new mistress."

The colonel's face wore an expression compounded of joy and indignation,—joy at the restoration of a valuable piece of property; indignation for reasons he proceeded to state.

"It's astounding, the depths of depravity the human heart is capable of! I was coming along the road three miles away, when I heard some one call me from the roadside. I pulled up the mare, and who should come out of the woods but Grandison. The poor nigger could hardly crawl along, with the help of a broken limb. I was never more astonished in my life. You could have knocked me down with a feather. He seemed pretty far gone,—he could hardly talk above a whisper,—and I had to give him a mouthful of whiskey to brace him up so he could tell his story. It's just as I thought from the beginning, Dick; Grandison had no notion of running away; he knew when he was well off, and where his friends were. All the persuasions of abolition liars and runaway niggers did not move him. But the desperation of those fanatics knew no bounds; their guilty consciences gave them no rest. They got the notion somehow that Grandison belonged to a nigger-catcher, and had been brought North as a spy to help capture ungrateful runaway servants. They actually kidnaped him—just think of it!—and gagged him and bound him and threw him rudely into a wagon, and carried him into the gloomy depths of a Canadian forest, and locked him in a lonely hut, and fed him on bread and water for three weeks. One of the scoundrels wanted to kill him, and persuaded the others that it ought to be done; but they got to quarreling about how they should do it, and before they had their minds made up Grandison escaped, and, keeping his back steadily to the North Star, made his way, after suffering incredible hardships, back to the old plantation, back to his master, his friends, and his home. Why, it's as good as one of Scott's novels![2] Mr. Simms[3] or some other one of our Southern authors ought to write it up."

[2]Sir Walter Scott (1771–1832), British histori-cal novelist immensely popular in both the United States and Great Britain.

[3]William Gilmore Simms (1806–1870), per-haps the antebellum South's most admired author, glorified the history and aristocratic traditions of his region in novels, magazines, histories, and biographies centering on his native South Carolina.

"Don't you think, sir," suggested Dick, who had calmly smoked his cigar throughout the colonel's animated recital, "that that kidnaping yarn sounds a little improbable? Isn't there some more likely explanation?"

"Nonsense, Dick; it's the gospel truth! Those infernal abolitionists are capable of anything—everything! Just think of their locking the poor, faithful nigger up, beating him, kicking him, depriving him of his liberty, keeping him on bread and water for three long, lonesome weeks, and he all the time pining for the old plantation!"

There were almost tears in the colonel's eyes at the picture of Grandison's sufferings that he conjured up. Dick still professed to be slightly skeptical, and met Charity's severely questioning eye with bland unconsciousness.

The colonel killed the fatted calf for Grandison, and for two or three weeks the returned wanderer's life was a slave's dream of pleasure. His fame spread throughout the county, and the colonel gave him a permanent place among the house servants, where he could always have him conveniently at hand to relate his adventures to admiring visitors.

About three weeks after Grandison's return the colonel's faith in sable humanity was rudely shaken, and its foundations almost broken up. He came near losing his belief in the fidelity of the negro to his master,—the servile virtue most highly prized and most sedulously cultivated by the colonel and his kind. One Monday morning Grandison was missing. And not only Grandison, but his wife, Betty the maid; his mother, aunt Eunice; his father, uncle Ike; his brothers, Tom and John, and his little sister Elsie, were likewise absent from the plantation; and a hurried search and inquiry in the neighborhood resulted in no information as to their whereabouts. So much valuable property could not be lost without an effort to recover it, and the wholesale nature of the transaction carried consternation to the hearts of those whose ledgers were chiefly bound in black. Extremely energetic measures were taken by the colonel and his friends. The fugitives were traced, and followed from point to point, on their northward run through Ohio. Several times the hunters were close upon their heels, but the magnitude of the escaping party begot unusual vigilance on the part of those who sympathized with the fugitives, and strangely enough, the underground railroad seemed to have had its tracks cleared and signals set for this particular train. Once, twice, the colonel thought he had them, but they slipped through his fingers.

One last glimpse he caught of his vanishing property, as he stood, accompanied by a United States marshal, on a wharf at a port on the south shore of Lake Erie. On the stern of a small steamboat which was receding rapidly from the wharf, with her nose pointing toward Canada, there stood a group of familiar dark faces, and the look they cast backward was not one of longing for the fleshpots of Egypt.[4] The colonel saw Grandison point him out to one of the crew of the vessel, who waved his hand derisively toward the colonel. The latter shook his fist impotently—and the incident was closed.

1899

---

[4]See Exodus 16:2–3.

The Wife of His Youth

I

Mr. Ryder was going to give a ball. There were several reasons why this was an opportune time for such an event.

Mr. Ryder might aptly be called the dean of the Blue Veins. The original Blue Veins were a little society of colored persons organized in a certain Northern city shortly after the war. Its purpose was to establish and maintain correct social standards among a people whose social condition presented almost unlimited room for improvement. By accident, combined perhaps with some natural affinity, the society consisted of individuals who were, generally speaking, more white than black. Some envious outsider made the suggestion that no one was eligible for membership who was not white enough to show blue veins. The suggestion was readily adopted by those who were not of the favored few, and since that time the society, though possessing a longer and more pretentious name, had been known far and wide as the "Blue Vein Society," and its members as the "Blue Veins."

The Blue Veins did not allow that any such requirement existed for admission to their circle, but, on the contrary, declared that character and culture were the only things considered; and that if most of their members were light-colored, it was because such persons, as a rule, had had better opportunities to qualify themselves for membership. Opinions differed, too, as to the usefulness of the society. There were those who had been known to assail it violently as a glaring example of the very prejudice from which the colored race had suffered most; and later, when such critics had succeeded in getting on the inside, they had been heard to maintain with zeal and earnestness that the society was a life-boat, an anchor, a bulwark and a shield,—a pillar of cloud by day and of fire by night, to guide their people through the social wilderness. Another alleged prerequisite for Blue Vein membership was that of free birth; and while there was really no such requirement, it is doubtless true that very few of the members would have been unable to meet it if there had been. If there were one or two of the older members who had come up from the South and from slavery, their history presented enough romantic circumstances to rob their servile origin of its grosser aspects.

While there were no such tests of eligibility, it is true that the Blue Veins had their notions on these subjects, and that not all of them were equally liberal in regard to the things they collectively disclaimed. Mr. Ryder was one of the most conservative. Though he had not been among the founders of the society, but had come in some years later, his genius for social leadership was such that he had speedily become its recognized adviser and head, the custodian of its standards, and the preserver of its traditions. He shaped its social policy, was active in providing for its entertainment, and when the interest fell off, as it sometimes did, he fanned the embers until they burst again into a cheerful flame.

There were still other reasons for his popularity. While he was not as white as some of the Blue Veins, his appearance was such as to confer distinction upon them. His features were of a refined type, his hair was almost straight; he was always neatly dressed; his manners were irreproachable, and his morals above suspicion. He had come to Groveland a young man, and obtaining employment in the office of a railroad company as messenger had in time worked himself up to the position of stationery clerk, having charge of the distribution of the office supplies for the whole company. Although the lack of early training had hindered the orderly development of a naturally fine mind, it had not prevented him from doing a great deal of reading or from forming decidedly literary tastes. Poetry was his passion. He could repeat whole pages of the great English poets; and if his pronunciation was sometimes faulty, his eye, his voice, his gestures, would respond to the changing sentiment with a precision that revealed a poetic soul and disarmed criticism. He was economical, and had saved money; he owned and occupied a very comfortable house on a respectable street. His residence was handsomely furnished, containing among other things a good library, especially rich in poetry, a piano, and some choice engravings. He generally shared his house with some young couple, who looked after his wants and were company for him; for Mr. Ryder was a single man. In the early days of his connection with the Blue Veins he had been regarded as quite a catch, and young ladies and their mothers had manœuvred with much ingenuity to capture him. Not, however, until Mrs. Molly Dixon visited Groveland had any woman ever made him wish to change his condition to that of a married man.

Mrs. Dixon had come to Groveland from Washington in the spring, and before the summer was over she had won Mr. Ryder's heart. She possessed many attractive qualities. She was much younger than he; in fact, he was old enough to have been her father, though no one knew exactly how old he was. She was whiter than he, and better educated. She had moved in the best colored society of the country, at Washington, and had taught in the schools of that city. Such a superior person had been eagerly welcomed to the Blue Vein Society, and had taken a leading part in its activities. Mr. Ryder had at first been attracted by her charms of person, for she was very good looking and not over twenty-five; then by her refined manners and the vivacity of her wit. Her husband had been a government clerk, and at his death had left a considerable life insurance. She was visiting friends in Groveland, and, finding the town and the people to her liking, had prolonged her stay indefinitely. She had not seemed displeased at Mr. Ryder's attentions, but on the contrary had given him every proper encouragement; indeed, a younger and less cautious man would long since have spoken. But he had made up his mind, and had only to determine the time when he would ask her to be his wife. He decided to give a ball in her honor, and at some time during the evening of the ball to offer her his heart and hand. He had no special fears about the outcome, but, with a little touch of romance, he wanted the surroundings to be in harmony with his own feelings when he should have received the answer he expected.

Mr. Ryder resolved that this ball should mark an epoch in the social history of Groveland. He knew, of course,—no one could know better,—the entertainments that had taken place in past years, and what must be done to surpass them. His ball must be worthy of the lady in whose honor it was to be given, and must, by the quality of its guests, set an example for the future. He had observed of late a growing liberality, almost a laxity, in social matters, even among members of his own set, and had several times been forced to meet in a social way persons whose complexions and callings in life were hardly up to the standard which he considered proper for the society to maintain. He had a theory of his own.

"I have no race prejudice," he would say, "but we people of mixed blood are ground between the upper and the nether millstone. Our fate lies between absorption by the white race and extinction in the black. The one does n't want us yet, but may take us in time. The other would welcome us, but it would be for us a backward step. 'With malice towards none, with charity for all,'[1] we must do the best we can for ourselves and those who are to follow us. Self-preservation is the first law of nature."

His ball would serve by its exclusiveness to counteract leveling tendencies, and his marriage with Mrs. Dixon would help to further the upward process of absorption he had been wishing and waiting for.

II

The ball was to take place on Friday night. The house had been put in order, the carpets covered with canvas, the halls and stairs decorated with palms and potted plants; and in the afternoon Mr. Ryder sat on his front porch, which the shade of a vine running up over a wire netting made a cool and pleasant lounging place. He expected to respond to the toast "The Ladies" at the supper, and from a volume of Tennyson—his favorite poet—was fortifying himself with apt quotations. The volume was open at "A Dream of Fair Women." His eyes fell on these lines, and he read them aloud to judge better of their effect:—

> At length I saw a lady within call,
>   Stiller than chisell'd marble, standing there;
> A daughter of the gods, divinely tall,
>   And most divinely fair.[2]

He marked the verse, and turning the page read the stanza beginning,—

> O sweet pale Margaret,
>   O rare pale Margaret.[3]

He weighed the passage a moment, and decided that it would not do. Mrs. Dixon was the palest lady he expected at the ball, and she was of a rather

[1]Abraham Lincoln, Second Inaugural Address (March 4, 1865). The full citation is, "With malice towards none, with charity for all, with firmness in the right, as God gives us to see."

[2]Alfred Lord Tennyson (1809–1892), "A Dream of Fair Women" (1832), stanza xxii, lines 85–88.

[3]Tennyson, "Margaret" (1833), lines 1–2.

ruddy complexion, and of lively disposition and buxom build. So he ran over the leaves until his eye rested on the description of Queen Guinevere:—

> *She seem'd a part of joyous Spring:*
> *A gown of grass-green silk she wore,*
> *Buckled with golden clasps before;*
> *A light-green tuft of plumes she bore*
> *Closed in a golden ring.*
> . . . .
> *She look'd so lovely, as she sway'd*
> *The rein with dainty finger-tips,*
> *A man had given all other bliss,*
> *And all his worldly worth for this,*
> *To waste his whole heart in one kiss*
> *Upon her perfect lips.*[4]

As Mr. Ryder murmured these words audibly, with an appreciative thrill, he heard the latch of his gate click, and a light foot-fall sounding on the steps. He turned his head, and saw a woman standing before his door.

She was a little woman, not five feet tall, and proportioned to her height. Although she stood erect, and looked around her with very bright and restless eyes, she seemed quite old; for her face was crossed and recrossed with a hundred wrinkles, and around the edges of her bonnet could be seen protruding here and there a tuft of short gray wool. She wore a blue calico gown of ancient cut, a little red shawl fastened around her shoulders with an old-fashioned brass brooch, and a large bonnet profusely ornamented with faded red and yellow artificial flowers. And she was very black,—so black that her toothless gums, revealed when she opened her mouth to speak, were not red, but blue. She looked like a bit of the old plantation life, summoned up from the past by the wave of a magician's wand, as the poet's fancy had called into being the gracious shapes of which Mr. Ryder had just been reading.

He rose from his chair and came over to where she stood.

"Good-afternoon, madam," he said.

"Good-evenin', suh," she answered, ducking suddenly with a quaint curtsy. Her voice was shrill and piping, but softened somewhat by age. "Is dis yere whar Mistuh Ryduh lib, suh?" she asked, looking around her doubt-fully, and glancing into the open windows, through which some of the preparations for the evening were visible.

"Yes," he replied, with an air of kindly patronage, unconsciously flattered by her manner, "I am Mr. Ryder. Did you want to see me?"

"Yas, suh, ef I ain't 'sturbin' of you too much."

"Not at all. Have a seat over here behind the vine, where it is cool. What can I do for you?"

---

[4]Tennyson, "Sir Lancelot and Queen Guinevere" (1842), lines 23–27, 40–45.

"'Scuse me, suh," she continued, when she had sat down on the edge of a chair, "'scuse me, suh, I 's lookin' for my husban'. I heerd you wuz a big man an' had libbed heah a long time, an' I 'lowed you would n't min' ef I 'd come roun' an' ax you ef you'd ever heerd of a merlatter man by de name er Sam Taylor 'quirin' roun' in de chu'ches ermongs' de people fer his wife 'Liza Jane?"

Mr. Ryder seemed to think for a moment.

"There used to be many such cases right after the war," he said, "but it has been so long that I have forgotten them. There are very few now. But tell me your story, and it may refresh my memory."

She sat back farther in her chair so as to be more comfortable, and folded her withered hands in her lap.

"My name's 'Liza," she began, "'Liza Jane. W'en I wuz young I us'ter b'long ter Marse Bob Smif, down in old Missoura. I wuz bawn down dere. W'en I wuz a gal I wuz married ter a man named Jim. But Jim died, an' after dat I married a merlatter man named Sam Taylor. Sam wuz free-bawn, but his mammy and daddy died, an' de w'ite folks 'prenticed him ter my marster fer ter work fer 'im 'tel he wuz growed up. Sam worked in de fiel', an' I wuz de cook. One day Ma'y Ann, ole miss's maid, came rushin' out ter de kitchen, an' says she, "Liza Jane, ole marse gwine sell yo' Sam down de ribber.'

"'Go way f'm yere,' says I; 'my husban' 's free!'

"'Don' make no diff'ence. I heerd ole marse tell ole miss he wuz gwine take yo' Sam 'way wid 'im ter-morrow, fer he needed money, an' he knowed whar he could git a t'ousan' dollars fer Sam an' no questions axed.'

"W'en Sam come home f'm de fiel' dat night, I tole him 'bout ole marse gwine steal 'im, an' Sam run erway. His time wuz mos' up, an' he swo' dat w'en he wuz twenty-one he would come back an' he'p me run erway, er else save up de money ter buy my freedom. An' I know he'd 'a' done it, fer he thought a heap er me, Sam did. But w'en he come back he did n' find me, fer I wuz n' dere. Ole marse had heerd dat I warned Sam, so he had me whip' an' sol' down de ribber.

"Den de wah broke out, an' w'en it wuz ober de cullud folks wuz scattered. I went back ter de ole home; but Sam wuz n' dere, an' I could n' l'arn nuffin' 'bout 'im. But I knowed he'd be'n dere to look fer me an' had n' foun' me, an' had gone erway ter hunt fer me.

"I 's be'n lookin' fer 'im eber sence," she added simply, as though twenty-five years were but a couple of weeks, "an' I knows he 's be'n lookin' fer me. Fer he sot a heap er sto' by me, Sam did, an' I know he 's be'n huntin' fer me all dese years,— 'less'n he 's be'n sick er sump'n, so he could n' work, er out'n his head, so he could n' 'member his promise. I went back down de ribber, fer I 'lowed he'd gone down dere lookin' fer me. I 's be'n ter Noo Orleens, an' Atlanty, an' Chalreston, an' Rich-mon'; an' w'en I'd be'n all ober de Souf I come ter de Norf. Fer I knows I'll fin' 'im some er dese days," she added softly, "er he 'll fin' me, an' den we 'll bofe be as happy in freedom as we wuz in de ole days befo' de wah." A smile stole over her withered countenance as she paused a moment, and her bright eyes softened into a faraway look.

This was the substance of the old woman's story. She had wandered a little here and there. Mr. Ryder was looking at her curiously when she finished.

"How have you lived all these years?" he asked.

"Cookin', suh. I 's a good cook. Does you know anybody w'at needs a good cook, suh? I 's stoppin' wid a cullud fam'ly roun' de corner yonder 'tel I kin git a place."

"Do you really expect to find your husband? He may be dead long ago."

She shook her head emphatically. "Oh no, he ain' dead. De signs an' de tokens tells me. I dremp three nights runnin' on'y dis las' week dat I foun' him."

"He may have married another woman. Your slave marriage would not have prevented him, for you never lived with him after the war, and without that your marriage does n't count."

"Would n' make no diff'ence wid Sam. He would n' marry no yuther 'ooman 'tel he foun' out 'bout me. I knows it," she added. "Sump'n 's be'n tellin' me all dese years dat I 's gwine fin' Sam 'fo' I dies."

"Perhaps he's outgrown you, and climbed up in the world where he would n't care to have you find him."

"No, indeed, suh," she replied, "Sam ain' dat kin' er man. He wuz good ter me, Sam wuz, but he wuz n' much good ter nobody e'se, fer he wuz one er de triflin'es' han's on de plantation. I 'spec's ter haf ter suppo't 'im w'en I fin' 'im, fer he nebber would work 'less'n he had ter. But den he wuz free, an' he did n' git no pay fer his work, an' I don' blame 'im much. Mebbe he's done better sence he run erway, but I ain' 'spectin' much."

"You may have passed him on the street a hundred times during the twenty-five years, and not have known him; time works great changes."

She smiled incredulously. "I'd know 'im 'mong's a hund'ed men. Fer dey wuz n' no yuther merlatter man like my man Sam, an' I could n' be mistook. I 's toted his picture roun' wid me twenty-five years."

"May I see it?" asked Mr. Ryder. "It might help me to remember whether I have seen the original."

As she drew a small parcel from her bosom he saw that it was fastened to a string that went around her neck. Removing several wrappers, she brought to light an old-fashioned daguerreotype in a black case. He looked long and intently at the portrait. It was faded with time, but the features were still distinct, and it was easy to see what manner of man it had represented.

He closed the case, and with a slow movement handed it back to her.

"I don't know of any man in town who goes by that name," he said, "nor have I heard of any one making such inquiries. But if you will leave me your address, I will give the matter some attention, and if I find out anything I will let you know."

She gave him the number of a house in the neighborhood, and went away, after thanking him warmly.

He wrote the address on the fly-leaf of the volume of Tennyson, and, when she had gone, rose to his feet and stood looking after her curiously. As she walked down the street with mincing step, he saw several persons whom she passed turn and look back at her with a smile of kindly amusement. When she had turned the corner, he went upstairs to his bedroom, and stood for a long time before the mirror of his dressing-case, gazing thoughtfully at the reflection of his own face.

III

At eight o'clock the ballroom was a blaze of light and the guests had begun to assemble; for there was a literary programme and some routine business of the society to be gone through with before the dancing. A black servant in evening dress waited at the door and directed the guests to the dressing-rooms.

The occasion was long memorable among the colored people of the city; not alone for the dress and display, but for the high average of intelligence and culture that distinguished the gathering as a whole. There were a number of school-teachers, several young doctors, three or four lawyers, some professional singers, an editor, a lieutenant in the United States army spending his furlough in the city, and others in various polite callings; these were colored, though most of them would not have attracted even a casual glance because of any marked difference from white people. Most of the ladies were in evening costume, and dress coats and dancing pumps were the rule among the men. A band of string music, stationed in an alcove behind a row of palms, played popular airs while the guests were gathering.

The dancing began at half past nine. At eleven o'clock supper was served. Mr. Ryder had left the ballroom some little time before the intermission, but reappeared at the supper-table. The spread was worthy of the occasion, and the guests did full justice to it. When the coffee had been served, the toast-master, Mr. Solomon Sadler, rapped the order. He made a brief introductory speech, complimenting host and guests, and then presented in their order the toasts of the evening. They were responded to with a very fair display of after-dinner wit.

"The last toast," said the toast-master, when he reached the end of the list, "is one which must appeal to us all. There is no one of us of the sterner sex who is not at some time dependent upon woman,—in infancy for protection, in manhood for companionship, in old age for care and comforting. Our good host has been trying to live alone, but the fair faces I see around me to-night prove that he too is largely dependent upon the gentler sex for most that makes life worth living,—the society and love of friends,—and rumor is at fault if he does not soon yield entire subjection to one of them. Mr. Ryder will now respond to the toast,—The Ladies."

There was a pensive look in Mr. Ryder's eyes as he took the floor and adjusted the eye-glasses. He began by speaking of woman as the gift of Heaven to man, and after some general observations on the relations of the sexes he said: "But perhaps the quality which most distinguishes woman is her fidelity and devotion to those she loves. History is full of examples, but has recorded none more striking than one which only to-day came under my notice."

He then related, simply but effectively, the story told by his visitor of the afternoon. He gave it in the same soft dialect, which came readily to his lips, while the company listened attentively and sympathetically. For the story had awakened a responsive thrill in many hearts. There were some present who had seen, and others who had heard their fathers and grandfathers tell, the wrongs and sufferings of this past generation, and all them still felt, in their darker moments, the shadow hanging over them. Mr. Ryder went on:—

"Such devotion and confidence are rare even among women. There are many who would have searched a year, some who would have waited five years, a few who might have hoped ten years; but for twenty-five years this woman has retained her affection for and her faith in a man she has not seen or heard of in all that time.

"She came to me to-day in the hope that I might be able to help her find this long-lost husband. And when she was gone I gave my fancy rein, and imagined a case I will put to you.

"Suppose that this husband, soon after his escape, had learned that his wife had been sold away, and that such inquiries as he could make brought no information of her whereabouts. Suppose that he was young, and she much older than he; that he was light, and she was black; that their marriage was a slave marriage, and legally binding only if they chose to make it so after the war. Suppose, too, that he made his way to the North, as some of us have done, and there, where he had larger opportunities, had improved them, and had in the course of all these years grown to be as different from the ignorant boy who ran away from fear of slavery as the day is from the night. Suppose, even, that he had qualified himself, by industry, by thrift, and by study, to win the friendship and be considered worthy the society of such people as these I see around me to-night, gracing my board and filling my heart with gladness; for I am old enough to remember the day when such a gathering would not have been possible in this land. Suppose, too, that, as the years went by, this man's memory of the past grew more and more indistinct, until at last it was rarely, except in his dreams, that any image of this bygone period rose before his mind. And then suppose that accident should bring to his knowledge the fact that the wife of his youth, the wife he had left behind him,—not one who had walked by his side and kept pace with him in his upward struggle, but one upon whom advancing years and a laborious life had set their mark,—was alive and seeking him, but that he was absolutely safe from recognition or discovery, unless he chose to reveal himself. My friends, what would the man do? I will presume that he was one who loved honor, and tried to deal justly with all men. I will even carry the case further, and suppose that perhaps he had set his heart upon another, whom he had hoped to call his own. What would he do, or rather what ought he to do, in such a crisis of a lifetime?

"It seemed to me that he might hesitate, and I imagined that I was an old friend, a near friend, and that he had come to me for advice; and I argued the case with him. I tried to discuss it impartially. After we had looked upon the matter from every point of view, I said to him, in words that we all know:—

> *This above all: to thine own self be true,*
> *And it must follow, as the night the day,*
> *Thou canst not then be false to any man.*[5]

Then, finally, I put the question to him, 'Shall you acknowledge her?'

"And now, ladies and gentlemen, friends and companions, I ask you, what should he have done?"

There was something in Mr. Ryder's voice that stirred the hearts of those who sat around him. It suggested more than mere sympathy with an imaginary situation; it seemed rather in the nature of a personal appeal. It was observed, too, that his look rested more especially upon Mrs. Dixon, with a mingled expression of renunciation and inquiry.

She had listened, with parted lips and streaming eyes. She was the first to speak: "He should have acknowledged her."

"Yes," they all echoed, "he should have acknowledged her."

"My friends and companions," responded Mr. Ryder. "I thank you, one and all. It is the answer I expected, for I knew your hearts."

He turned and walked toward the closed door of an adjoining room, while every eye followed him in wondering curiosity. He came back in a moment, leading by the hand his visitor of the afternoon, who stood startled and trembling at the sudden plunge into this scene of brilliant gayety. She was neatly dressed in gray, and wore the white cap of an elderly woman.

"Ladies and gentlemen," he said, "this is the woman, and I am the man, whose story I have told you. Permit me to introduce to you the wife of my youth."

1898

The Doll[1]

When Tom Taylor, proprietor of the Wyandot Hotel barber shop, was leaving home, after his noonday luncheon, to return to his work, his daughter, a sprightly, dimunitive brown maid, with very bright black eyes and very curly black hair, thrust into his coat pocket a little jointed doll somewhat the worse for wear.

"Now, don't forget, papa," she said, in her shrill childish treble, "what's to be done to her. Her arms won't work, and her legs won't work, and she can't hold her head up. Be sure and have her mended this afternoon, and

[5]William Shakespeare (1564–1616), *Hamlet,* act 1, scene 3, lines 78–80.

[1]*The Crisis,* April 1912.

bring her home when you come to supper; for she's afraid of the dark, and always sleeps with me. I'll meet you at the corner at half-past six—and don't forget, whatever you do."

"No, Daisy, I'll not forget," he replied as he lifted her to the level of his lips and kissed her.

Upon reaching the shop he removed the doll from his pocket and hung it on one of the gilded spikes projecting above the wire netting surrounding the cashier's desk, where it would catch his eye. Some time during the afternoon he would send it to a toy shop around the corner for repairs. But the day was a busy one, and when the afternoon was well advanced he had not yet attended to it.

Colonel Forsyth had come up from the South to attend a conference of Democratic leaders to consider presidential candidates and platforms. He had put up at the Wyandot Hotel, but had been mainly in the hands of Judge Beeman, chairman of the local Jackson club, who was charged with the duty of seeing that the colonel was made comfortable and given the freedom of the city. It was after a committee meeting, and about four in the afternoon, that the two together entered the lobby of the Wyandot. They were discussing the platforms to be put forward by the two great parties in the approaching campaign.

"I reckon, judge," the colonel was saying, "that the Republican party will make a mistake if it injects the Negro question into its platform. The question is primarily a local one, and if the North will only be considerate about the matter, and let us alone, we can settle it to our entire satisfaction. The Negro's place is defined by nature, and in the South he knows it and gives us no trouble."

"The Northern Negroes are different," returned the judge.

"They are just the same," rejoined the colonel. "It is you who are different. You pamper them and they take liberties with you. But they are all from the South, and when they meet a Southerner they act accordingly. They are born to serve and to submit. If they had been worthy of equality they would never have endured slavery. They have no proper self-respect; they will neither resent an insult, nor defend a right, nor avenge a wrong."

"Well, now, colonel, aren't you rather hard on them? Consider their past."

"Hard? Why, no, bless your heart! I've got nothing against the nigger. I like him—in his place. But what I say is the truth. Are you in a hurry?"

"Not at all."

"Then come downstairs to the barber shop and I'll prove what I say."

The shop was the handsomest barber shop in the city. It was in the basement, and the paneled ceiling glowed with electric lights. The floor was of white tile, the walls lined with large mirrors. Behind ten chairs, of the latest and most comfortable design, stood as many colored barbers, in immaculate white jackets, each at work upon a white patron. An air of discipline and good order pervaded the establishment. There was no loud talking by patrons, no unseemly garrulity on the part of the barbers. It was very obviously a well-conducted barber shop, frequented by gentlemen who could afford to pay liberally for superior service. As the judge and the colonel entered, a customer vacated the chair served by the proprietor.

"Next gentleman," said the barber.

The colonel removed his collar and took his seat in the vacant chair, remarking, as he ran his hand over his neck, "I want a close shave, barber."

"Yes, sir; a close shave."

The barber was apparently about forty, with a brown complexion, clean-cut features and curly hair. Committed by circumstances to a career of personal service, he had lifted it by intelligence, tact and industry to the dignity of a successful business. The judge, a regular patron of the shop, knew him well and had often, while in his chair, conversed with him concerning his race—a fruitful theme, much on the public tongue.

"As I was saying," said the colonel, while the barber adjusted a towel about his neck, "the Negro question is a perfectly simple one."

The judge thought it hardly good taste in the colonel to continue in his former strain. Northern men might speak slightingly of the Negro, but seldom in his presence. He tried a little diversion.

"The tariff," he observed, "is a difficult problem."

"Much more complicated, suh, than the Negro problem, which is perfectly simple. Let the white man once impress the Negro with his superiority; let the Negro see that there is no escape from the inevitable, and that ends it. The best thing about the Negro is that, with all his limitations, he can recognize a finality. It is the secret of his persistence among us. He has acquired the faculty of evolution, suh—by the law of the survival of the fittest. Long ago, when a young man, I killed a nigger to teach him his place. One who learns a lesson of that sort certainly never offends again, nor fathers any others of his breed."

The barber, having lathered the colonel's face, was stropping his razor with long, steady strokes. Every word uttered by the colonel was perfectly audible to him, but his impassive countenance betrayed no interest. The colonel seemed as unconscious of the barber's presence as the barber of the colonel's utterance. Surely, thought the judge, if such freedom of speech were the rule in the South the colonel's contention must be correct, and the Negroes thoroughly cowed. To a Northern man the situation was hardly comfortable.

"The iron and sugar interests of the South," persisted the judge, "will resist any reduction of the tariff."

The colonel was not to be swerved from the subject, nor from his purpose, whatever it might be.

"Quite likely they will; and we must argue with them, for they are white men and amenable to reason. The nigger, on the other hand, is the creature of instinct; you cannot argue with him; you must order him, and if he resists shoot him, as I did."

"Don't forget, barber," said the colonel, "that I want a close shave."

"No, sir," responded the barber, who having sharpened his razor, now began to pass it, with firm and even hand, over the colonel's cheek.

"It must have been," said the judge, "an aggravated case, to justify so extreme a step."

"Extreme, suh? I beg yo' pardon, suh, but I. can't say I had regarded my conduct in that light. But it was an extreme case so far as the nigger was concerned. I am not boasting about my course; it was simply a disagreeable necessity. I am naturally a kind-hearted man, and don't like to kill even a fly. It was after the war, suh, and just as the Reconstruction period was drawing to a close. My mother employed a Negro girl, the child of a former servant of hers, to wait upon her."

The barber was studying the colonel's face as the razor passed over his cheek. The colonel's eyes were closed, or he might have observed the sudden gleam of interest that broke through the barber's mask of self-effacement, like a flash of lightning from a clouded sky. Involuntarily the razor remained poised in midair, but, in less time than it takes to say it, was moving again, swiftly and smoothly, over the colonel's face. To shave a talking man required a high degree of skill, but they were both adept, each in his own trade—the barbed at shaving, the colonel at talking.

"The girl was guilty of some misconduct, and my mother reprimanded her and sent her home. She complained to her father, and he came to see my mother about it. He was insolent, offensive and threatening. I came into the room and ordered him to leave it. Instead of obeying, he turned on me in a rage, suh, and threatened me. I drew my revolver and shot him. The result was unfortunate; but he and his people learned a lesson. We had no further trouble with bumptious niggers in our town."

"And did you have no trouble in the matter?" asked the judge.

"None, suh, to speak of. There were proceedings, but they were the merest formality. Upon my statement, confirmed by that of my mother, I was discharged by the examining magistrate, and the case was never even reported to the grand jury. It was a clear case of self-defense."

The barber had heard the same story, with some details ignored or forgotten by the colonel. It was the barber's father who had died at the colonel's hand, and for many long years the son had dreamed of this meeting.

He remembered the story in this wise: His father had been a slave. Freed by the Civil War, he had entered upon the new life with the zeal and enthusiasm of his people at the dawn of liberty, which seem, in the light of later discouragements, so pathetic in the retrospect. The chattel aspired to own property; the slave, forbidden learning, to educate his children. He had worked early and late, had saved his money with a thrift equal to that of a German immigrant and had sent his children regularly to school.

The girl—the barber remembered her very well—had been fair of feature, soft of speech and gentle of manner, a pearl among pebbles. One day her father's old mistress had met him on the street and, after a kindly inquiry about his family, had asked if she might hire his daughter during the summer, when there was no school. Her own married daughter would be visiting her, with a young child, and they wanted some neat and careful girl to nurse the infant.

"Why, yas ma'am," the barber's father had replied. "I reckon it might be a good thing fer Alice. I wants her ter be a teacher; but she kin l'arn things from you, ma'am, that no teacher kin teach her. She kin l'arn manners, ma'am, an' white folks' ways, and nowhere better than in yo' house."

So Alice had gone to the home of her father's former mistress to learn white folks' ways. The lady had been kind and gracious. But there are ways and ways among all people.

When she had been three weeks in her new employment her mistress's son—a younger brother of the colonel—came home from college. Some weeks later Alice went home to her father. Who was most at fault the barber never knew. A few hours afterward the father called upon the lady. There was a stormy interview. Things were said to which the ears of white ladies were unaccustomed from the lips of black men. The elder son had entered the room and interfered. The barber's father had turned to him and exclaimed angrily:

"Go 'way from here, boy, and don't talk ter me, or I'm liable ter harm you."

The young man stood his ground. The Negro advanced menacingly toward him. The young man drew his ready weapon and fatally wounded the Negro—he lived only long enough, after being taken home, to gasp out the facts to his wife and children.

The rest of the story had been much as the colonel had related it. As the barber recalled it, however, the lady had not been called to testify, but was ill at the time of the hearing, presumably from the nervous shock.

That she had secretly offered to help the family the barber knew, and that her help had been rejected with cold hostility. He knew that the murderer went unpunished, and that in later years he had gone into politics, and became the leader and mouthpiece of his party. All the world knew that he had ridden into power on his hostility to Negro rights.

The barber had been a mere boy at the time of his father's death, but not too young to appreciate the calamity that had befallen the household. The family was broken up. The sordid details of its misfortunes would not be interesting. Poverty, disease and death had followed them, until he alone was left. Many years had passed. The brown boy who had wept beside his father's bier, and who had never forgotten nor forgiven, was now the grave-faced, keen-eyed, deft-handed barber, who held a deadly weapon at the throat of his father's slayer.

How often he had longed for this hour! In his dreams he had killed this man a hundred times, in a dozen ways. Once, when a young man, he had gone to meet him, with the definite purpose of taking his life, but chance had kept them apart. He had imagined situations where they might come face to face; he would see the white man struggling in the water; he would have only to stretch forth his hand to save him; but he would tell him of his hatred and let him drown. He would see him in a burning house, from which he might rescue him; and he would call him murderer and let him burn! He would see him in the dock for murder of a white man, and only his testimony could save him, and he would let him suffer the fate that he doubly deserved! He saw a vision of his father's form, only an hour before thrilling with hope and energy, now stiff and cold in death; while under his keen razor lay the neck of his enemy, the enemy, too, of his race, sworn to degrade them, to teach them, if need be, with the torch and with the gun, that their place was at the white man's feet, his heel upon their neck; who held them in such contempt that he could speak as he had spoken in the presence of one of them. One stroke of the keen blade, a deflection of half an inch in its course, and a murder would be avenged, an enemy destroyed!

For the next sixty seconds the barber heard every beat of his own pulse, and the colonel, in serene unconsciousness, was nearer death than he had even been in the course of a long and eventful life. He was only a militia colonel, and had never been under fire, but his turbulent political career had been passed in a community where life was lightly valued, where hot words were often followed by rash deeds, and murder was tolerated as a means of private vengeance and political advancement. He went on talking, but neither the judge nor the barber listened, each being absorbed in his own thoughts.

To the judge, who lived in a community where Negroes voted, the colonel's frankness was a curious revelation. His language was choice, though delivered with the Southern intonation, his tone easy and conversational, and, in addressing the barber directly, his manner had been courteous enough. The judge was interested, too, in watching the barber, who, it was evident, was repressing some powerful emotion. It seemed very probable to the judge that the barber might resent this cool recital of murder and outrage. He did not know what might be true of the Negroes in the South, but he had been judge of a police court in one period of his upward career, and had found colored people prone to sudden rages, when under the influence of strong emotion, handy with edged tools, and apt to cut thick and deep, nor always careful about the color of the cuticle. The barber's feelings were plainly stirred, and the judge, a student of human nature, was curious to see if he would be moved to utterance. It would have been no novelty—patrons of the shop often discussed race questions with the barber. It was evident that the colonel was trying an experiment to demonstrate his contention in the lobby above. But the judge could not know the barber's intimate relation to the story, nor did it occur to him that the barber might conceive any deadly purpose because of a purely impersonal grievance. The barber's hand did not even tremble.

In the barber's mind, however, the whirlwind of emotions had passed lightly over the general and settled upon the particular injury. So strong, for the moment, was the homicidal impulse that it would have prevailed already had not the noisy opening of the door to admit a patron diverted the barber's attention and set in motion a current of ideas which fought for the colonel's life. The barber's glance toward the door, from force of habit, took in the whole shop. It was a handsome shop, and had been to the barber a matter of more than merely personal pride. Prominent among a struggling people, as yet scarcely beyond the threshold of citizenship, he had long been looked upon, and had become accustomed to regard himself, as a representative man, by whose failure or success his race would be tested. Should he slay this man now beneath his hand, this beautiful shop would be lost to his people. Years before the whole trade had been theirs. One by one the colored master barbers, trained in the slovenly old ways, had been forced to the wall by white competition, until his shop was one of the few good ones remaining in the hands of men of his race. Many an envious eye had been cast upon it. The lease had only a year to run. Strong pressure, he knew, had been exerted by a white rival to secure the reversion. The barber had the hotel proprietor's promise of a renewal; but he knew full well that should he lose the shop no colored man would succeed him; a center of industry, a medium of friendly contact with white men, would be lost to his people—many a good turn had the barber been able to do for them while he had the ear—literally had the ear—of some influential citizen, or held some aspirant for public office by the throat. Of the ten barbers in the shop all but one were married, with families dependent upon them for support. One was sending a son to college; another was buying a home. The unmarried one was in his spare hours studying a profession, with the hope of returning to practice it among his people in a Southern state. Their fates were all, in a measure, dependent upon the proprietor of the shop. Should he yield to the impulse which was swaying him, their livelihood would be placed in jeopardy. For what white man, while the memory of this tragic event should last, would trust his throat again beneath a Negro's razor?

Such, however, was the strength of the impulse against which the barber was struggling that these considerations seemed likely not to prevail. Indeed, they had presented themselves to the barber's mind in a vague, remote, detached manner, while the dominant idea was present and compelling, clutching at his heart, drawing his arm, guiding his fingers. It was by their mass rather than by their clearness that these restraining forces held the barber's arm so long in check—it was society against self, civilization against the primitive instinct typifying, more fully than the barber could realize, the great social problem involved in the future of his race.

He had now gone once over the colonel's face, subjecting that gentleman to less discomfort than he had for a long time endured while undergoing a similar operation. Already he had retouched one cheek and had turned the colonel's head to finish the other. A few strokes more and the colonel could be released with a close shave—how close he would never know!—or, one stroke, properly directed, and he would never stand erect again! Only the day before, the barber had read, in the newspapers, the account of a ghastly lynching in a Southern state, where, to avenge a single provoked murder, eight Negroes had bit the dust and a woman had been burned at the stake for no other crime than that she was her husband's wife. One stroke and there would be one less of those who thus wantonly played with human life!

The uplifted hand had begun the deadly downward movement—when one of the barbers dropped a shaving cup, which was smashed to pieces on the marble floor. Fate surely fought for the colonel—or was it for the barber? Involuntarily the latter stayed his hand—instinctively his glance went toward the scene of the accident. It was returning to the upraised steel, and its uncompleted task, when it was arrested by Daisy's doll, hanging upon the gilded spike where he had left it.

If the razor went to its goal he would not be able to fulfill his promise to Daisy! She would wait for him at the corner, and wait in vain! If he killed the colonel he himself could hardly escape, for he was black and not white, and this was North and not South, and personal vengeance was not accepted by the courts as a justification for murder. Whether he died or not, he would be lost to Daisy. His wife was dead, and there would be no one to take care of Daisy. His own father had died in defense of his daughter; he must live to protect his own. If there was a righteous God, who divided the evil from the good, the colonel would some time get his just deserts. Vengeance was God's; it must be left to Him to repay!

The jointed doll had saved the colonel's life. Whether society had conquered self or not may be an open question, but it had stayed the barber's hand until love could triumph over hate!

The barber laid aside the razor, sponged off the colonel's face, brought him, with a movement of the chair, to a sitting posture, brushed his hair, pulled away the cloths from around his neck, handed him a pasteboard check for the amount of his bill, and stood rigidly by his chair. The colonel adjusted his collar, threw down a coin equal to double the amount of his bill and, without waiting for the change, turned with the judge to leave the shop. They had scarcely reached the door leading into the hotel lobby when the barber, overwrought by the long strain, collapsed heavily into the nearest chair.

"Well, judge," said the colonel, as they entered the lobby, "that was a good shave. What a sin it would be to spoil such a barber by making him a postmaster! I didn't say anything to him, for it don't do to praise a nigger much—it's likely to give him the big head—but I never had," he went on, running his hand appreciatively over his cheek, "I never had a better shave in my life. And I proved my theory. The barber is the son of the nigger I shot."

The judge was not sure that the colonel had proved his theory, and was less so after he had talked, a week later, with the barber. And, although the colonel remained at the Wyandot for several days, he did not get shaved again in the hotel barber shop.

1912

FRANCES ELLEN WATKINS HARPER
1825–1911

Frances Ellen Watkins Harper's life spanned the tumultuous period from the first third of the nineteenth century to the first decade of the twentieth, an era of tremendous social and political change, especially for African Americans, including women, and for women more generally. Harper was active in both the antislavery struggle and the first-wave feminism that it spawned in the nineteenth century, and she remained committed to both movements in their antilynching and women's suffrage incarnations in the early twentieth century. Her political investments in race and gender equality were directly reflected in her writing, which embraced major literary genres: the novel, the short story, poetry, the essay, and speeches. Her literary accomplishments bear the mark of her accomplishments as an orator. She gave speeches and lectures on a variety of political and religious topics, and her novel *Iola Leroy* interpolates several of these, while much of her poetry has a powerfully oral quality. Her writing and oratory, and her activism as well, were suffused with the deep religious sentiment that informed her intellectual and personal life.

Frances Ellen Watkins was born free in Baltimore in 1825. Orphaned at three years of age, she was raised by her maternal uncle, William Watkins, who ran an academy for Negro youth. The rigorous curriculum for the academy—which included daily study of the Bible, history, geography, mathematics, English, natural philosophy, Greek, Latin, music, and rhetoric—was more than adequate to stimulate her inquisitive spirit and driving intellect. She was also inspired by her family's opposition to slavery. William Watkins was active in antislavery causes, and his son, William J. Watkins, assisted Frederick Douglass with his abolitionist paper, *The North Star*. Although Frances Watkins worked as a domestic in her teens, she put her education to good use, securing teaching positions at Union Seminary in Wilberforce, Ohio, and a school in Little York, Pennsylvania in 1850–1852. In 1854 her volume *Poems on Miscellaneous Subjects* was published in Boston. Around this time she also began a long career as a speaker, joining the antislavery lecture circuit and traveling throughout Massachusetts, Pennsylvania, New York, New Jersey, Ohio, and Maine.

Frances Watkins married Fenton Harper in 1860, and their daughter, Mary, was born in 1862. (Fenton Harper had three children from a previous marriage.) They settled on a farm in Columbus, Ohio; but after being widowed in 1864, she returned to Baltimore in 1865. She also returned to public speaking. Two Reconstruction lecture tours—in 1867-69 and 1869–1871—took Harper to Georgia, Florida, Alabama, Mississippi, Louisiana, North Carolina, Virginia, Kentucky, Tennessee, Missouri, Delaware, and Maryland. She drew heavily on her experiences during these travels in her most famous work, the novel *Iola Leroy, or Shadows Uplifted* (1892). In 1871 Harper settled in Pennsylvania with her daughter, Mary, who preceded her in death in 1909. Harper died in Pennsylvania in 1911.

Although most of the critical attention on Harper has focused on *Iola Leroy*, poetry was the genre in which she initially published, and during her lifetime her best-loved and most acclaimed work was poetry. At first glance, it is easy to dismiss Harper's writing, particularly her poetry, as sentimental and conventional. However, like many African American poets, from Phillis Wheatley to later Harlem Renaissance authors Countee Cullen and Claude McKay, Harper used formal poetic conventions of her time but infused them with new content. "The Slave Mother," for example, versifies the image of family separations during slavery—a core argument against slavery—using sentimentality to forge a connection between the reader and the subject of the text. Her antebellum poems often explicate complex theological arguments that were part of the public debate over the Bible and slavery or cast in verse graphic stories of injustice and brutality; "The Tennessee Hero" and "Free Labor" are two examples of the latter. After the Civil War, she continued to use poetic form to represent gritty topics in the news of the day, as she does in "Aunt Chloe's Politics" and "The Martyr of Alabama."

Likewise Harper's nonfiction prose is conventional in style while taking on difficult, even controversial, issues. In "The Colored People in America" she writes in the tradition of another African American woman, Maria W. Stewart, using rhetorical questions to critique current conditions and prophesy the future of African American people. Similarly, in "Women's Political Future" she writes, "O women of America! Into your hands God has pressed one of the sublimest opportunities that ever came into the hands of the women of any race or people." The positioning of her literary persona as female prophet and visionary places Harper in a tradition of African American women writers and orators like Stewart, Jarena Lee, Ann Plato, Sojourner Truth, and Anna Julia Cooper.

Harper's accomplishments include the short story "The Two Offers," which appeared in the *Anglo-African Magazine* in 1859 and was probably the first short story published in the United States by an African American. A tale most explicitly concerned with morality, it demonstrates her flair for dialogue and for representing dramatic relationships. Moreover, as subsequent commentary highlights, it challenges contemporary ideology that held that women could only attain happiness as wives and mothers. Most of Harper's speeches, which were famous in her lifetime, are unfortunately unavailable to posterity because she did not deliver them from written texts. What we have of her oratory was recorded by listeners, in this resembling the "Ain't I a Woman?" speech of Sojourner Truth, who never learned how to read or write (Truth's speech was re-created, some argue re-shaped, by Frances Gage). Like Truth, Harper was reported to be a dynamic speaker who could hold an audience's attention for as much as two hours. Like other black women who entered the male-dominated arena of public speaking, she was often subjected to hecklers who doubted her femininity and, at times, her race. Although we can never recover her oratory, Harper's surviving canon—a novel, parts of four serialized shorter novels, four volumes of poetry, a short story, and written correspondence—is more than representative of her long and prolific career.

Katherine Clay Bassard
Virginia Commonwealth University

PRIMARY WORKS

Poems on Miscellaneous Subjects, 1854; "The Two Offers," 1859; *Sketches of Southern Life*, 1872; *Iola Leroy, of Shadows Uplifted*, 1892; *The Martyr of Alabama and Other Poems*, 1894; *Complete Poems of Frances E. W. Harper*, ed. Maryemma Graham, 1988; *A Brighter Coming Day: A France Ellen Watkins Harper Reader*, ed. Frances Smith Foster, 1990; *Minnie's Sacrifice, Sowing and Reaping, Trial and Triumph: Three Rediscovered Novels*, ed. Frances Smith Foster, 1994.

Aunt Chloe's Politics

Of course, I don't know very much
   About these politics,
But I think that some who run 'em,
   Do mighty ugly tricks.

I've seen 'em honey-fugle round,   5
   And talk so awful sweet,
That you'd think them full of kindness,
   As an egg is full of meat.

Now I don't believe in looking
   Honest people in the face,   10
And saying when you're doing wrong,
   That "I haven't sold my race."

When we want to school our children,
   If the money isn't there,
Whether black or white have took it,[1]   15
   The loss we all must share.

And this buying up each other
   Is something worse than mean,[2]
Though I thinks a heap of voting,[3]
   I go for voting clean.   20

1872

[1]One of the major issues in the South was whether or not public funds should be expended on the education of children, black or white. In some cases, black politicians had been accused, rightly or wrongly, of diverting such funds to their own or other uses.

[2]The period about which Aunt Chloe is speaking was notable for political corruption. New York's "Boss" Tweed had been exposed in 1871, and the Credit Mobilier scandal broke in 1872.

[3]While it would be almost half a century before the Woman's Suffrage amendment to the Con-

stitution would pass, in 1872 the idea of women's voting did not seem so remote. The amendment had first been introduced into Congress in 1868 and had been given considerable visibility in 1871 by Victoria Wood-hull's Congressional testimony. Women had gone to the polls in Wyoming and Utah in 1870 and in 1871. In 1872, after women had tried to vote in ten states and the District of Columbia, Susan B. Anthony had tried to cast her ballot in the presidential election.

Learning to Read

Very soon the Yankee teachers
  Came down and set up school;
But, oh! how the Rebs did hate it,—
  It was agin' their rule.

Our masters always tried to hide 5
  Book learning from our eyes;
Knowledge didn't agree with slavery—
  'Twould make us all too wise.

But some of us would try to steal
  A little from the book, 10
And put the words together,
  And learn by hook or crook.

I remember Uncle Caldwell,
  Who took pot liquor fat

And greased the pages of his book, 15
  And hid it in his hat.

And had his master ever seen
  The leaves upon his head,
He'd have thought them greasy papers,
  But nothing to be read. 20

And there was Mr. Turner's Ben,
  Who heard the children spell,
And picked the words right up by heart,
  And learned to read 'em well.

Well, the Northern folks kept sending 25
  The Yankee teachers down;
And they stood right up and helped us,
  Though Rebs did sneer and frown.

And I longed to read my Bible,
  For precious words it said; 30
But when I begun to learn it,
  Folks just shook their heads,

And said there is no use trying,
  Oh! Chloe, you're too late;

But as I was rising sixty,
  I had no time to wait.

So I got a pair of glasses,
  And straight to work I went,
And never stopped till I could read
  The hymns and Testament.

Then I got a little cabin—
  A place to call my own—
And I felt as independent
  As the queen upon her throne.

1873

35

40

The Martyr of Alabama

[The following news item appeared in the newspapers throughout the country, issue of December 27th, 1894:

"Tim Thompson, a little negro boy, was asked to dance for the amusement of some white toughs. He refused, saying he was a church member. One of the men knocked him down with a club and then danced upon his prostrate form. He then shot the boy in the hip. The boy is dead; his murderer is still at large."][1]

He lifted up his pleading eyes,
  And scanned each cruel face,
Where cold and brutal cowardice
  Had left its evil trace.

It was when tender memories
  Round Beth'lem's manger lay,
And mothers told their little ones
  Of Jesu's natal day.

And of the Magi from the East
  Who came their gifts to bring,
And bow in rev'rence at the feet
  Of Salem's new-born King.

And how the herald angels sang
  The choral song of peace,
That war should close his wrathful lips,
  And strife and carnage cease.

5

10

15

[1]This text in brackets following the title appeared in the original publication.

At such an hour men well may hush
   Their discord and their strife,
And o'er that manger clasp their hands
   With gifts to brighten life.   20

Alas! that in our favored land,
   That cruelty and crime
Should cast their shadows o'er a day,
   The fairest pearl of time.

A dark-browed boy had drawn anear   25
   A band of savage men,
Just as a hapless lamb might stray
   Into a tiger's den.

Cruel and dull, they saw in him
   For sport an evil chance,   30
And then demanded of the child
   To give to them a dance.

"Come dance for us," the rough men said;
   "I can't," the child replied,
"I cannot for the dear Lord's sake,   35
   Who for my sins once died."

Tho' they were strong and he was weak,
   He wouldn't his Lord deny.
His life lay in their cruel hands,
   But he for Christ could die.   40

Heard they aright? Did that brave child
   Their mandates dare resist?
Did he against their stern commands
   Have courage to resist?

Then recklessly a man (?) arose,   45
   And dealt a fearful blow.
He crushed the portals of that life,
   And laid the brave child low.

And trampled on his prostrate form,
   As on a broken toy;
Then danced with careless, brutal feet,   50
   Upon the murdered boy.

Christians! behold that martyred child!
　His blood cries from the ground;
Before the sleepless eye of God,　　　　　　　　　　　55
　He shows each gaping wound.

Oh! Church of Christ arise! arise!
　Lest crimson stain thy hand,
When God shall inquisition make
　For blood shed in the land.　　　　　　　　　　　60

Take sackcloth of the darkest hue,
　And shroud the pulpits round;
Servants of him who cannot lie
　Sit mourning on the ground.

Let holy horror blanch each brow,　　　　　　　　　65
　Pale every cheek with fears,
And rocks and stones, if ye could speak,
　Ye well might melt to tears.

Through every fane send forth a cry,
　Of sorrow and regret,　　　　　　　　　　　　　70
Nor in an hour of careless ease
　Thy brother's wrongs forget.

Veil not thine eyes, nor close thy lips,
　Nor speak with bated breath;
This evil shall not always last,—　　　　　　　　　75
　The end of it is death.

Avert the doom that crime must bring
　Upon a guilty land;
Strong in the strength that God supplies,
　For truth and justice stand.　　　　　　　　　　80

For Christless men, with reckless hands,
　Are sowing round thy path
The tempests wild that yet shall break
　In whirlwinds of God's wrath.

　　　　　　　　　　　　　　　　　　　　　　　1895

A Double Standard

Do you blame me that I loved him?
　If when standing all alone

I cried for bread a careless world
  Pressed to my lips a stone.

Do you blame me that I loved him,   5
  That my heart beat glad and free,
When he told me in the sweetest tones
  He loved but only me?

Can you blame me that I did not see
  Beneath his burning kiss   10
The serpent's wiles, nor even hear
  The deadly adder hiss?

Can you blame me that my heart grew cold
  That the tempted, tempter turned;
When he was feted and caressed   15
  And I was coldly spurned?

Would you blame him, when you draw from me
  Your dainty robes aside,
If he with gilded baits should claim
  Your fairest as his bride?   20

Would you blame the world if it should press
  On him a civic crown;
And see me struggling in the depth
  Then harshly press me down?

Crime has no sex and yet to-day   25
  I wear the brand of shame;
Whilst he amid the gay and proud
  Still bears an honored name.

Can you blame me if I've learned to think
  Your hate of vice a sham,   30
When you so coldly crushed me down
  And then excused the man?

Would you blame me if to-morrow
  The coroner should say,
A wretched girl, outcast, forlorn,   35
  Has thrown her life away?

Yes, blame me for my downward course,
  But oh! remember well,

Within your homes you press the hand
   That led me down to hell.   40

I'm glad God's ways are not our ways,
   He does not see as man;
Within His love I know there's room
   For those whom others ban.

I think before His great white throne,   45
   His throne of spotless light,
That whited sepulchres shall wear
   The hue of endless night.

That I who fell, and he who sinned,
   Shall reap as we have sown;   50
That each the burden of his loss
   Must bear and bear alone.

No golden weights can turn the scale
   Of justice in His sight;
And what is wrong in woman's life   55
   In man's cannot be right.

                                   1895

Songs for the People

Let me make the songs for the people,
   Songs for the old and young;
Songs to stir like a battle-cry
   Wherever they are sung.

Not for the clashing of sabres,   5
   For carnage nor for strife;
But songs to thrill the hearts of men
   With more abundant life.

Let me make the songs for the weary,
   Amid life's fever and fret,   10
Till hearts shall relax their tension,
   And careworn brows forget.

Let me sing for little children,
   Before their footsteps stray,
Sweet anthems of love and duty,   15
   To float o'er life's highway.

I would sing for the poor and aged,
  When shadows dim their sight;
Of the bright and restful mansions,
  Where there shall be no night.   20

Our world, so worn and weary,
  Needs music, pure and strong,
To hush the jangle and discords
  Of sorrow, pain, and wrong.

Music to soothe all its sorrow,   25
  Till war and crime shall cease;
And the hearts of men grown tender
  Girdle the world with peace.

1895

Woman's Political Future

If before sin had cast its deepest shadows or sorrow had distilled its bitter-est tears, it was true that it was not good for man to be alone, it is no less true, since the shadows have deepened and life's sorrows have increased, that the world has need of all the spiritual aid that woman can give for the social advancement and moral development of the human race. The tend-ency of the present age, with its restlessness, religious upheavals, failures, blunders, and crimes, is toward broader freedom, an increase of knowledge, the emancipation of thought, and a recognition of the brotherhood of man; in this movement woman, as the companion of man, must be a sharer. So close is the bond between man and woman that you can not raise one with-out lifting the other. The world can not move without woman's sharing in the movement, and to help give a right impetus to that movement is wom-an's highest privilege.

If the fifteenth century discovered America to the Old World, the nine-teenth is discovering woman to herself. Little did Columbus imagine, when the New World broke upon his vision like a lovely gem in the coronet of the universe, the glorious possibilities of a land where the sun should be our en-graver, the winged lightning our messenger, and steam our beast of burden. But as mind is more than matter, and the highest ideal always the true real, so to woman comes the opportunity to strive for richer and grander discov-eries than ever gladdened the eye of the Genoese mariner.

Not the opportunity of discovering new worlds, but that of filling this old world with fairer and higher aims than the greed of gold and the lust of power, is hers. Through weary, wasting years men have destroyed, dashed in pieces, and overthrown, but to-day we stand on the threshold of woman's era, and woman's work is grandly constructive. In her hand are possibilities whose use or abuse must tell upon the political life of the nation, and send their influence for good or evil across the track of unborn ages.

As the saffron tints and crimson flushes of morn herald the coming day, so the social and political advancement which woman has already gained bears the promise of the rising of the full-orbed sun of emancipation. The result will be not to make home less happy, but society more holy; yet I do not think the mere extension of the ballot a panacea for all the ills of our national life. What we need to-day is not simply more voters, but better voters. To-day there are red-handed men in our republic, who walk unwhipped of justice, who richly deserve to exchange the ballot of the freeman for the wristlets of the felon; brutal and cowardly men, who torture, burn, and lynch their fellow-men, men whose defenselessness should be their best defense and their weakness an ensign of protection. More than the changing of institutions we need the development of a national conscience, and the upbuilding of national character. Men may boast of the aristocracy of blood, may glory in the aristocracy of talent, and be proud of the aristocracy of wealth, but there is one aristocracy which must ever outrank them all, and that is the aristocracy of character; and it is the women of a country who help to mold its character, and to influence if not determine its destiny; and in the political future of our nation woman will not have done what she could if she does not endeavor to have our republic stand foremost among the nations of the earth, wearing sobriety as a crown and righteousness as a garment and a girdle. In coming into her political estate woman will find a mass of illiteracy to be dispelled. If knowledge is power, ignorance is also power. The power that educates wickedness may manipulate and dash against the pillars of any state when they are undermined and honeycombed by injustice.

I envy neither the heart nor the head of any legislator who has been born to an inheritance of privileges, who has behind him ages of education, dominion, civilization, and Christianity, if he stands opposed to the passage of a national education bill, whose purpose is to secure education to the children of those who were born under the shadow of institutions which made it a crime to read.

To-day women hold in their hands influence and opportunity, and with these they have already opened doors which have been closed to others. By opening doors of labor woman has become a rival claimant for at least some of the wealth monopolized by her stronger brother. In the home she is the priestess, in society the queen, in literature she is a power, in legislative halls law-makers have responded to her appeals, and for her sake have humanized and liberalized their laws. The press has felt the impress of her hand. In the pews of the church she constitutes the majority; the pulpit has welcomed her, and in the school she has the blessed privilege of teaching children and youth. To her is apparently coming the added responsibility of political power; and what she now possesses should only be the means of preparing her to use the coming power for the glory of God and the good of mankind; for power without righteousness is one of the most dangerous forces in the world.

Political life in our country has plowed in muddy channels, and needs the infusion of clearer and cleaner waters. I am not sure that women are naturally so much better than men that they will clear the stream by the virtue of their womanhood; it is not through sex but through character that the best influence of women upon the life of the nation must be exerted.

I do not believe in unrestricted and universal suffrage for either men or women. I believe in moral and educational tests. I do not believe that the most ignorant and brutal man is better prepared to add value to the strength and durability of the government than the most cultured, upright, and intelligent woman. I do not think that willful ignorance should swamp earnest intelligence at the ballot box, nor that educated wickedness, violence, and fraud should cancel the votes of honest men. The unsteady hands of a drunkard can not cast the ballot of a freeman. The hands of lynchers are too red with blood to determine the political character of the government for even four short years. The ballot in the hands of woman means power added to influence. How well she will use that power I can not foretell. Great evils stare us in the face that need to be throttled by the combined power of an upright manhood and an enlightened womanhood; and I know that no nation can gain its full measure of enlightenment and happiness if one-half of it is free and the other half is fettered. China compressed the feet of her women and thereby retarded the steps of her men. The elements of a nation's weakness must ever be found at the hearthstone.

More than the increase of wealth, the power of armies, and the strength of fleets is the need of good homes, of good fathers, and good mothers.

The life of a Roman citizen was in danger in ancient Palestine, and men had bound themselves with a vow that they would eat nothing until they had killed the Apostle Paul. Pagan Rome threw around that imperiled life a bulwark of living clay consisting of four hundred and seventy human hearts, and Paul was saved.[1] Surely the life of the humblest American citizen should be as well protected in America as that of a Roman citizen was in heathen Rome. A wrong done to the weak should be an insult to the strong. Woman coming into her kingdom will find enthroned three great evils, for whose overthrow she should be as strong in a love of justice and humanity as the warrior is in his might. She will find intemperance sending its flood of shame, and death, and sorrow to the homes of men, a fretting leprosy in our politics, and a blighting curse in our social life; the social evil sending to our streets women whose laughter is sadder than their tears, who slide from the paths of sin and shame to the friendly shelter of the grave; and lawlessness enacting in our republic deeds over which angels might weep, if heaven knows sympathy.

---

[1]This is a somewhat romanticized version of the biblical story (Acts 24) in which the Apostle Paul is rescued from enemies who have sworn to kill him. His rescuers are four hundred and seventy soldiers sent to defend him because he was a Roman citizen.

How can any woman send petitions to Russia against the horrors of Siberian prisons if, ages after the Inquisition has ceased to devise its tortures, she has not done all she could by influence, tongue, and pen to keep men from making bonfires of the bodies of real or supposed criminals?

O women of America! into your hands God has pressed one of the sublimest opportunities that ever came into the hands of the women of any race or people. It is yours to create a healthy public sentiment; to demand justice, simple justice, as the right of every race; to brand with everlasting infamy the lawless and brutal cowardice that lynches, burns, and tortures your own countrymen.

To grapple with the evils which threaten to undermine the strength of the nation and to lay magazines to powder under the cribs of future generations is no child's play.

Let the hearts of the women of the world respond to the song of the herald angels of peace on earth and good will to men. Let them throb as one heart unified by the grand and holy purpose of uplifting the human race, and humanity will breathe freer, and the world grow brighter. With such a purpose Eden would spring up in our path, and Paradise be around our way.

1894

■ ANNA JULIA COOPER ■
1858?–1964

Born in North Carolina to a slave named Hannah Stanley Haywood and Haywood's white master, Anna Julia Cooper rose from these unpromising beginnings to establish herself as one of the leading black scholars and teachers of her day. Her remarkable career in education began quite early, when at nine she was offered a scholarship to attend St. Augustine's Normal School, an institution founded to train teachers for service among the ex-slaves. Cooper stayed there for roughly fourteen years, eventually joining the school's faculty. It was while teaching at St. Augustine's that Anna Haywood married George Cooper, a Bahamas-born Greek instructor. In September of 1879, however, her husband died, and Cooper remained single for the remainder of her life.

In 1881 Cooper entered Oberlin College, graduating in 1884 with two other black women, one of whom, Mary Church (Terrell), would gain considerable celebrity as an important activist of the time. After teaching briefly at Wilberforce, Cooper returned to St. Augustine's in 1885. In 1887 she received a master's degree in mathematics from Oberlin based largely on her teaching experience. Later that same year, she moved to Washington, D.C., where she began a long and at times stormy tenure at Washington Colored High School, also known as the M Street School. After teaching mathematics and science there for over a

decade, Cooper became principal in 1902 of what was perhaps the most distinguished black high school in the country, one that produced many well-known
African American politicians, artists, and professionals.

The 1890s constituted an especially productive and politically active period
for Cooper. In June 1892, she helped to organize the Colored Woman's League
of Washington, D.C.; the following year, she and two other black leaders, Fannie
Barrier Williams and Fannie Jackson Coppin, addressed the Women's Congress
in Chicago, convened during the Columbian Exposition held in that city. Cooper
spoke on "The Needs and the Status of Black Women." In 1895 she played an
active role in the first meeting of the National Conference of Colored Women,
and in 1900 she traveled to London, where she participated in the Pan-African
Conference along with W.E.B. Du Bois, who had been instrumental in setting up
the event. Cooper also found time during these years to help edit *The Southland*,
a magazine founded in 1890 by Joseph C. Price, the head of Livingstone College
in North Carolina. More importantly, Cooper published *A Voice from the South:
By a Black Woman of the South* in 1892, a collection of essays in which she
addresses a wide range of issues concerning black women at the end of the nineteenth century.

The conceptual core of *A Voice from the South* is Cooper's contention that "the
fundamental agency under God in the regeneration, the re-training of the race, as
well as the ground work and starting point of its progress upward, must be the
black woman." Or, as Cooper put it, "Only the BLACK WOMAN can say 'when and
where I enter, in the quiet, undisputed dignity of my womanhood, without violence and without suing or special patronage, then and there the whole *Negro race
enters with me*.'" The dominant position that Cooper accords the black woman in
her vision of racial progress reflects, in part, the influence of nineteenth-century
bourgeois ideals of "true womanhood," which assumed that women constituted
the heart and conscience—the moral center, as it were—of a society. At the same
time, Cooper consistently argued for the unique position of black women in particular. Both as women in a male-dominated society and as blacks in racist society,
black women brought to bear on contemporary problems a special and invaluable
perspective forged in the crucible of multiple and intersecting oppressions. Therefore, to develop their talents and capacities to the fullest—especially through formal education, Cooper argued—would be of inestimable value not just to women
or blacks generally but to the nation as a whole. It also follows that no one could
or should speak for the black woman; to Cooper, it was critical that the black
woman's voice be raised on her own behalf.

By the mid-1890s, Cooper had come to be recognized as an important member of the black intelligentsia. She was a member of the Bethel Literary and Historical Association in Washington, D.C., and she even received an invitation to
join the American Negro Academy, the previously male-only organization of
such leading black thinkers as W.E.B. Du Bois, Kelly Miller, Arthur Schomburg,
Francis Grimke, Alexander Crummell, and Carter Woodson. Cooper's distinguished record as a scholar and teacher, however, did not protect her from scandal, as she became embroiled in 1904 in what became known as the "M Street
School controversy." Under fire for allegedly condoning smoking and drinking
on the part of her students and morally questionable behavior on the part of
her teachers, she herself was the target of rumors linking her romantically with

a member of the school's faculty whom she happened to have raised in her house. Despite the support of many blacks in the Washington, D.C., community, Cooper was dismissed in 1906. After teaching in Missouri, she returned in 1910 to the M Street School (known as Paul Laurence Dunbar High School after 1916), where she worked until her retirement in 1930.

The remainder of Cooper's life was marked by academic achievement and a commitment to ensuring the welfare of the black community through education and social service organizations. After studying at Columbia University, Cooper earned her Ph.D. in French from the University of Paris in 1925 despite extraordinary obstacles (including the lack of support on the part of her employers). During this time, she continued her efforts to improve conditions within the local black community as well, taking a leadership role in the Colored Settlement House in Washington, D.C., and in the local Colored Young Women's Christian Association. This involvement culminated in 1930 in her accepting the presidency of Frelinghuysen University, a school founded in 1917 to serve black Washington, D.C., residents (especially working people) who might otherwise have little access to higher education. At one point, in an attempt to save the school, Cooper even moved its operations into her home. Anna Julia Cooper's educational and community activities continued to the end of her life, one as long and rich and full of dedicated service to her race as that of her far-better known contemporary W. E. B. Du Bois, whom she outlived by exactly six months.

Richard Yarborough
University of California, Los Angeles

PRIMARY WORK

A Voice from the South, 1892.

SECONDARY WORKS

Bert James Loewenberg and Ruth Bogin, eds., *Black Women in Nineteenth-Century American Life: Their Words, Their Thoughts, Their Feelings*, 1976; Sharon Harley and Rosalyn Terborg-Penn, eds., *The Afro-American Woman: Struggles and Images*, 1978; Louise Daniel Hutchinson, *Anna J. Cooper: A Voice from the South*, 1981; Dorothy Sterling, *We Are Your Sisters: Black Women in the Nineteenth Century*, 1984; Mary Helen Washington, Introduction, *A Voice from the South*, rpt. 1988; Ann Allen Shockley, ed., *Afro-American Women Writers, 1746–1933: An Anthology and Critical Guide*, 1989.

from **A Voice from the South**

Our Raison d'Être[1]

In the clash and clatter of our American Conflict, it has been said that the South remains Silent. Like the Sphinx[2] she inspires vociferous disputation, but herself takes little part in the noisy controversy. One muffled strain in

---

[1]French: reason for being, rationale.
[2]In Greek mythology, a creature with a lion's body and woman's head that asked travelers a riddle and devoured them if they answered it incorrectly.

the Silent South, a jarring chord and a vague and uncomprehended cadenza has been and still is the Negro. And of that muffled chord, the one mute and voiceless note has been the sadly expectant Black Woman,

> An infant crying in the night,
> An infant crying for the light;
> And with *no language—but a cry.*[3]

The colored man's inheritance and apportionment is still the sombre crux, the perplexing *cul de sac*[4] of the nation,—the dumb skeleton in the closet provoking ceaseless harangues, indeed, but little understood and seldom consulted. Attorneys for the plaintiff and attorneys for the defendant, with bungling *gaucherie*[5] have analyzed and dissected, theorized and synthesized with sublime ignorance or pathetic misapprehension of counsel from the black client. One important witness has not yet been heard from. The summing up of the evidence deposed, and the charge to the jury have been made—but no word from the Black Woman.

It is because I believe the American people to be conscientiously committed to a fair trial and ungarbled evidence, and because I feel it essential to a perfect understanding and an equitable verdict that truth from *each* standpoint be presented at the bar,—that this little Voice has been added to the already full chorus. The "other side" has not been represented by one who "lives there." And not many can more sensibly realize and more accurately tell the weight and the fret of the "long dull pain" than the open-eyed but hitherto voiceless Black Woman of America.

The feverish agitation, the perfervid energy, the busy objectivity of the more turbulent life of our men serves, it may be, at once to cloud or color their vision somewhat, and as well to relieve the smart and deaden the pain for them. Their voice is in consequence not always temperate and calm, and at the same time radically corrective and sanatory. At any rate, as our Caucasian barristers are not to blame if they cannot *quite* put themselves in the dark man's place, neither should the dark man be wholly expected fully and adequately to reproduce the exact Voice of the Black Woman.

Delicately sensitive at every pore to social atmospheric conditions, her calorimeter may well be studied in the interest of accuracy and fairness in diagnosing what is often conceded to be a "puzzling" case. If these broken utterances can in any way help to a clearer vision and a truer pulse-beat in studying our Nation's Problem, this Voice by a Black Woman of the South will not have been raised in vain.

TAWAWA CHIMNEY CORNER
SEPT. 17, 1892

---

[3]Alfred, Lord Tennyson, "In Memoriam A.H.H.," LIV. Cooper has added the dash and italics.
[4]French: dead end.
[5]French: awkwardness.

Woman versus the Indian

In the National Woman's Council convened at Washington in February 1891, among a number of thoughtful and suggestive papers read by eminent woman, was one by the Rev. Anna Shaw,[6] bearing the above title.

That Miss Shaw is broad and just and liberal in principal is proved beyond contradiction. Her noble generosity and womanly firmness are unimpeachable. The unwavering stand taken by herself and Miss Anthony[7] in the subsequent color ripple in Wimodaughsis ought to be sufficient to allay forever any doubts as to the pure gold of these two women.

Of Wimodaughsis (which, being interpreted for the uninitiated, is a woman's culture club whose name is made up of the first few letters of the four words wives, mothers, daughters, and sisters) Miss Shaw is president, and a lady from the Blue Grass State *was* secretary.

Pandora's box is opened in the ideal harmony of this modern Eden without an Adam when a colored lady, a teacher in one of our schools, applies for admission to its privileges and opportunities.

The Kentucky secretary, a lady zealous in good works and one who, I can't help imagining, belongs to that estimable class who daily thank the Lord that He made the earth that they may have the job of superintending its rotations, and who really would like to help "elevate" the colored people (in her own way of course and so long as they understand their places) is filled with grief and horror that any persons of Negro extraction should aspire to learn type-writing or languages or to enjoy any other advantages offered in the sacred halls of Wimodaughsis. Indeed, she had not calculated that there were any wives, mothers, daughters, and sisters, except white ones; and she is really convinced that *Whimodaughsis* would sound just as well, and then it need mean just *white mothers, daughters and sisters.* In fact, so far as there is anything in a name, nothing would be lost by omitting for the sake of euphony, from this unique mosaic, the letters that represent wives. *Whiwimodaughsis* might be a little startling, and on the whole wives would better yield to white; since clearly all women are not wives, while surely all wives are daughters. The daughters therefore could represent the wives and this immaculate assembly for propagating liberal and progressive ideas and disseminating a broad and humanizing culture might be spared the painful possibility of the sight of a black man coming in the future to escort from an evening class this solitary cream-colored applicant. Accordingly the Kentucky secretary took the cream-colored applicant aside, and, with emotions befitting such an epochmaking crisis, told her, "as kindly as she could," that colored people were not admitted to the classes, at the same time refunding the money which said cream-colored applicant had paid for lessons in type-writing.

---

[6]Anna Shaw (1847–1919), American minister, physician, and activist in the women's suffrage and temperance movements.

[7]Susan B. Anthony (1820–1906), American leader of the woman's suffrage and temperance movements.

When this little incident came to the knowledge of Miss Shaw, she said firmly and emphatically, NO. As a minister of the gospel and as a Christian woman, she could not lend her influence to such unreasonable and uncharitable discrimination; and she must resign the honor of president of Wimodaughsis if persons were to be proscribed solely on account of their color.

To the honor of the board of managers, be it said, they sustained Miss Shaw; and the Kentucky secretary, and those whom she succeeded in inoculating with her prejudices, resigned.

'Twas only a ripple,—some bewailing of lost opportunity on the part of those who could not or would not seize God's opportunity for broadening and enlarging their own souls—and then the work flowed on as before.

Susan B. Anthony and Anna Shaw are evidently too noble to be held in thrall by the provincialisms of women who seem never to have breathed the atmosphere beyond the confines of their grandfathers' plantations. It is only from the broad plateau of light and love that one can see petty prejudice and narrow priggishness in their true perspective; and it is on this high ground, as I sincerely believe, these two grand women stand.

As leaders in the woman's movement of today, they have need of clearness of vision as well as firmness of soul in adjusting recalcitrant forces, and wheeling into line the thousand and one none-such, never-to-be modified, won't-be-dictated-to banners of their somewhat mottled array.

The black woman and the southern woman, I imagine, often get them into the predicament of the befuddled man who had to take singly across a stream a bag of corn, a fox and a goose. There was no one to help, and to leave the goose with the fox was death—with the corn, destruction. To re-christen the animals, the lion could not be induced to lie down with the lamb unless the lamb would take the inside berth.

The black woman appreciates the situation and can even sympathize with the actors in the serio-comic dilemma.

But, may it not be that, as women, the very lessons which seem hardest to master now, are possibly the ones most essential for our promotion to a higher grade of work?

We assume to be leaders of thought and guardians of society. Our country's manners and morals are under our tutoring. Our standards are law in our several little worlds. However tenaciously men may guard some prerogatives, they are our willing slaves in that sphere which they have always conceded to be woman's. Here, no one dares demur when her fiat has gone forth. The man would be mad who presumed, however inexplicable and past finding out any reason for her action might be, to attempt to open a door in her kingdom officially closed and regally sealed by her.

The American woman of to-day not only gives tone directly to her immediate world, but her tiniest pulsation ripples out and out, down and down, till the outermost circles and the deepest layers of society feel the vibrations. It is pre-eminently an age of organizations. The "leading woman," the preacher, the reformer, the organizer "enthuses" her lieutenants and captains, the literary women, the thinking women, the strong, earnest, irresistible women; these in turn touch their myriads of church clubs, social clubs, culture clubs, pleasure clubs and charitable clubs, till the same lecture has been duly administered to every married man in the land (not to speak of sons and brothers) from the President in the White House to the stone-splitter of the ditches. And so woman's lightest whisper is heard as in Dionysius'[8] ear, by quick relays and endless reproductions, through every recess and cavern as well as on every hilltop and mountain in her vast domain. And her mandates are obeyed. When she says "thumbs up," woe to the luckless thumb that falters in its rising. They may be little things, the amenities of life, the little nothings which cost nothing and come to nothing, and yet can make a sentient being so comfortable or so miserable in this life, the oil of social machinery, which we call the courtesies of life, all are under the magic key of woman's permit.

The American woman then is responsible for American manners. Not merely the right ascension and declination of the satellites of her own drawing room; but the rising and the setting of the pestilential or life-giving orbs which seem to wander afar in space, all are governed almost wholly through her magnetic polarity. The atmosphere of street cars and parks and boulevards, of cafes and hotels and steamboats is charged and surcharged with her sentiments and restrictions. Shop girls and serving maids, cashiers and accountant clerks, scribblers and drummers, whether wage earner, salaried toiler, or proprietress, whether laboring to instruct minds, to save souls, to delight fancies, or to win bread,—the working women of America in whatever station or calling they may be found, are subjects, officers, or rulers of a strong centralized government, and bound together by a system of codes and countersigns, which, though unwritten, forms a network of perfect subordination and unquestioning obedience as marvelous as that of the Jesuits. At the head and center in this regime stands the Leading Woman in the principality. The one talismanic word that plays along the wires from palace to cook-shop, from imperial Congress to the distant plain, is *Caste*. With all her vaunted independence, the American woman of today is as fearful of losing caste as a Brahmin in India. That is the law under which she lives, the precepts which she binds as frontlets between her eyes and writes on the door-posts of her homes, the lesson which she instills into her children with their first baby breakfasts, the injunction she lays upon husband and lover with direst penalties attached.

The queen of the drawing room is absolute ruler under this law. Her pose gives the cue. The microscopic angle at which her pencilled brows are elevated, signifies who may be recognized and who are beyond the pale. The delicate intimation is, quick as electricity, telegraphed down. Like the wonderful transformation in the House that Jack Built (or regions thereabouts) when the rat began to gnaw the rope, the rope to hang the butcher, the

[8]Greek soldier and tyrant of Syracuse (405–367 B.C.). Not to be confused with the Greek god Dionysus.

butcher to kill the ox, the ox to drink the water, the water to quench the fire, the fire to burn the stick, the stick to beat the dog, and the dog to worry the cat, and on, and on, and on,—when miladi[9] causes the inner arch over her matchless orbs to ascend the merest trifle, *presto*! the Miss at the notions counter grows curt and pert, the dress goods clerk becomes indifferent and taciturn, hotel waiters and ticket dispensers look the other way, the Irish street laborer snarles and scowls, conductors, policemen and park superintendents jostle and push and threaten, and society suddenly seems transformed into a band of organized adders, snapping, and striking and hissing just because they like it on general principles. The tune set by the head singer, sung through all keys and registers, with all qualities of tone,— the smooth, flowing, and gentle, the creaking, whizzing, grating, screeching, growling—according to ability, taste, and temperament of the singers. Another application of like master, like man. In this case, like mistress, like nation.

It was the good fortune of the Black Wo[man] of the South to spend some weeks, not long since, in a land over which floated the Union Jack. The Stars and Stripes were not the only familiar experiences missed. A uniform, matter-of-fact courtesy, a genial kindliness, quick perception of opportunities for rendering any little manly assistance, a readiness to give information to strangers,—a hospitable, thawing-out atmosphere everywhere—in shops and waiting rooms, on cars and in the streets, actually seemed to her chilled little soul to transform the commonest boor in the service of the public into one of nature's noblemen, and when the old whipped-cur feeling was taken up and analyzed she could hardly tell whether it consisted mostly of self pity for her own wounded sensibilities, or of shame for her country and mortification that her countrymen offered such an unfavorable contrast.

Some American girls, I noticed recently, in search of novelty and adventure, were taking an extended trip through our country unattended by gentlemen friends; their wish was to write up for a periodical or lecture the ease and facility, the comfort and safety of American travel, even for the weak and unprotected, under our well-nigh perfect railroad systems and our gentlemanly and efficient corps of officials and public servants. I have some material I could furnish these young ladies, though possibly it might not be just on the side they wish to have illuminated. The Black Woman of the South has to do considerable travelling in this country, often unattended. She thinks she is quiet and unobtrusive in her manner, simple and inconspicuous in her dress, and can see no reason why in any chance assemblage of *ladies*, or even a promiscuous gathering of ordinarily well-bred and dignified individuals, she should be signaled out for any marked consideration. And yet she has seen these same "gentlemanly and efficient" railroad conductors, when their cars had stopped at stations having no raised platforms,

[9]A woman regarded as having fashionable or expensive tastes.

making it necessary for passengers to take the long and trying leap from the car step to the ground or step on the narrow little stool placed under by the conductor, after standing at their posts and handing woman after woman from the steps to the stool, thence to the ground, or else relieving her of satchels and bags and enabling her to make the descent easily, deliberately fold their arms and turn round when the Black Woman's turn came to alight—bearing her satchel, and bearing besides another unnamable burden inside the heaving bosom and tightly compressed lips. The feeling of slighted womanhood is unlike every other emotion of the soul. Happily for the human family, it is unknown to many and indescribable to all. Its poignancy, compared with which even Juno's *spretae injuria formae*[10] is earthly and vulgar, is holier than that of jealousy, deeper than indignation, tenderer than rage. Its first impulse of wrathful protest and proud self vindication is checked and shamed by the consciousness that self assertion would outrage still further the same delicate instinct. Were there a brutal attitude of hate or of ferocious attack, the feminine response of fear or repulsion is simple and spontaneous. But when the keen sting comes through the finer sensibilities, from a hand which, by all known traditions and ideals of propriety, should have been trained to reverence and respect them, the condemnation of man's inhumanity to woman is increased and embittered by the knowledge of personal identity with a race of beings so fallen.

I purposely forbear to mention instances of personal violence to colored women travelling in less civilized sections of our country, where women have been forcibly ejected from cars, thrown out of seats, their garments rudely torn, their person wantonly and cruelly injured. America is large and must for some time yet endure its outof-the-way jungles of barbarism as Africa its uncultivated tracts of marsh and malaria. There are murderers and thieves and villains in both London and Paris. Humanity from the first has had its vultures and sharks, and representatives of the fraternity who prey upon mankind may be expected no less in America than elsewhere. That this virulence breaks out most readily and commonly against colored persons in this country, is due of course to the fact that they are, generally speaking, weak and can be imposed upon with impunity. Bullies are always cowards at heart and may be credited with a pretty safe instinct in scenting their prey. Besides, society, where it has not exactly said to its dogs "s-s-sik him!" has at least engaged to be looking in another direction or studying the rivers on Mars. It is not of the dogs and their doings, but of society holding the leash that I shall speak. It is those subtile exhalations of atmospheric odors for which woman is accountable, the indefinable, unplaceable aroma which seems to exude from the very pores in her finger tips like the delicate sachet so dexterously hidden and concealed in her linens; the essence of her teaching, guessed rather than read, so adroitly is the lettering and wording

[10]Latin: Virgil, *Aeneid*, I, 26: "the wrong offered
her slighted beauty" by the Judgment of Paris.
Spoken by Juno, queen of the gods.

manipulated; it is the undertones of the picture laid finely on by woman's own practiced hand, the reflection of the lights and shadows on her own brow; it is, in a word, the reputation of our nation for general politeness and good manners and of our fellow citizens to be somewhat more than cads or snobs that shall engage our present study. There can be no true test of national courtesy without travel. Impressions and conclusions based on provincial traits and characteristics can thus be modified and generalized. Moreover, the weaker and less influential the experimenter, the more exact and scientific the deductions. Courtesy "for revenue only" is not politeness, but diplomacy. Any rough can assume civilty toward those of "his set," and does not hesitate to carry it even to servility toward those in whom he recognizes a possible patron or his master in power, wealth, rank, or influence. But, as the chemist prefers distilled H_2O in testing solutions to avoid complications and unwarranted reactions, so the Black Woman holds that her femininity linked with the impossibility of popular affinity or unexpected attraction through position and influence in her case makes her a touchstone of American courtesy exceptionally pure and singularly free from extraneous modifiers. The man who is courteous to her is so, not because of anything he hopes or fears or sees, but because *he is a gentleman.*

I would eliminate also from the discussion all uncharitable reflections upon the orderly execution of laws existing in certain states of this Union, requiring persons known to be colored to ride in one car, and persons supposed to be white in another. A good citizen may use his influence to have existing laws and statutes changed or modified, but a public servant must not be blamed for obeying orders. A railroad conductor is not asked to dictate measures, nor to make and pass laws. His bread and butter are conditioned on his managing his part of the machinery as he is told to do. If therefore, I found myself in that compartment of a train designated by the sovereign law of the state for presumable Caucasians, and for colored persons only when traveling in the capacity of nurses and maids, should a conductor inform me, as a gentleman might, that I had made a mistake, and offer to show me the proper car for black ladies; I might wonder at the expensive arrangements of the company and of the state in providing special and separate accommodations for the transportation of the various hues of humanity, but I certainly could not take it as a want of courtesy on the conductor's part that he gave the information. It is true, public sentiment precedes and begets all laws, good or bad; and on the ground I have taken, our women are to be credited largely as teachers and moulders of public sentiment. But when a law has passed and received the sanction of the land, there is nothing for our officials to do but enforce it till repealed; and I for one, as a loyal American citizen, will give those officials cheerful support and ready sympathy in the discharge of their duty. But when a great burly six feet of masculinity with sloping shoulders and unkempt beard swaggers in, and, throwing a roll of tobacco into one corner of his jaw, growls out 'n dis kyar 'f yer don't, I'll put yer out,"—my mental annotation is *Here's an American citizen who has been badly trained. He is sadly lacking in both* 'sweetness' and 'light'; and when in the same section of our enlightened and progressive country, I see from the car window, working on private estates, convicts from the state penitentiary, among them squads of boys from four- teen to eighteen years of age in a chain-gang, their feet chained together and heavy blocks attached—not in 1850, but in 1890, '91 and '92, I make a note on the flyleaf of my memorandum, *The women in this section should organize a Society for the Prevention of Cruelty to Human Beings, and dissemi- nate civilizing tracts, and send throughout the region apostles of anti-barbarism for the propagation of humane and enlightened ideas.* And when farther on in the same section our train stops at a dilapidated station, rendered yet more unsightly by dozens of loafers with their hands in their pockets while a pro- ductive soil and inviting climate beckon in vain to industry; and when, look- ing a little more closely, I see two dingy little rooms with "FOR LADIES" swinging over one and "FOR COLORED PEOPLE" over the other; while wondering under which head I come, I notice a little way off the only hotel proprietor of the place whittling a pine stick as he sits with one leg thrown across an empty goods box; and as my eye falls on a sample room next door which seems to be driving the only wide-awake and popular business of the commonwealth, I cannot help ejaculating under my breath, "What a field for the missionary woman." I know that if by any fatality I should be obliged to lie over at that station, and, driven by hunger, should be compelled to seek refreshments or the bare necessities of life at the only public accommoda- tion in the town, that same stick-whittler would coolly inform me, without looking up from his pine splinter, "We doan uccommodate no niggers hyur." And yet we are so scandalized at Russia's barbarity and cruelty to the Jews! We pay a man a thousand dollars a night just to make us weep, by a recital of such heathenish inhumanity as is practiced on Slavonic soil. . . .

Now, am I right in holding the American Woman responsible? Is it true that the exponents of woman's advancement, the leaders in woman's thought, the preachers and teachers of all woman's reforms, can teach this nation to be courteous, to be pitiful, having compassion one of another, not rendering evil for inoffensiveness, and railing in proportion to the improbability of being struck back; but contrariwise, being *all* of one mind, to love as brethren?

I think so.

It may require some heroic measures, and like all revolutions will call for a determined front and a courageous, unwavering, stalwart heart on the part of the leaders of the reform.

The "*all*" will inevitably stick in the throat of the Southern woman. She must be allowed, please, to except the 'darkey' from the 'all'; it is too bitter a pill with black people in it. You must get the Revised Version to put it, "*love all white people* as breathren." She really could not enter any society on earth, or in heaven above, or in—the waters under the earth, on such unpa- latable conditions.

The Black Woman has tried to understand the Southern woman's diffi- culties; to put herself in her place, and to be as fair, as charitable, and as free from prejudice in judging her antipathies, as she would have others in regard to her own. She has honestly weighed the apparently sincere excuse, "But you must remember that these people were once our slaves"; and that other, "But civility towards the Negroes will bring us on *social equality* with them."

These are the two bugbears; or rather, the two humbugbears: for, though each is founded on a most glaring fallacy, one would think they were words to conjure with, so potent and irresistible is their spell as an argument at the North as well as in the South.

One of the most singular facts about the unwritten history of this country is the consummate ability with which Southern influence, Southern ideas and Southern ideals, have from the very beginning even up to the present day, dictated to and domineered over the brain and sinew of this nation. Without wealth, without education, without inventions, arts, sciences, or industries, without well-nigh every one of the progressive ideas and impulses which have made this country great, prosperous and happy, personally indolent and practically stupid, poor in everything but bluster and self-esteem, the Southerner has nevertheless with Italian finesse and exquisite skill, uniformly and invariably, so manipulated Northern sentiment as to succeed sooner or later in carrying his point and shaping the policy of this government to suit his purposes. Indeed, the Southerner is a magnificent manager of men, a born educator. For two hundred and fifty years he trained to his hand a people whom he made absolutely his own, in body, mind, and sensibility. He so insinuated differences and distinctions among them, that their personal attachment for him was stronger than for their own brethren and fellow sufferers. He made it a crime for two or three of them to be gathered together in Christ's name without a white man's supervision, and a felony for one to teach them to read even the Word of Life; and yet they would defend his interest with their life blood; his smile was their happiness, a pat on the shoulder from him their reward. The slightest difference among themselves in condition, circumstances, opportunities, became barriers of jealousy and disunion. He sowed his blood broadcast among them, then pitted mulatto against black, bond against free, house slave against plantation slave, even the slave of one clan against like slave of another clan; till, wholly oblivious of their ability for mutual succor and defense, all became centers of myriad systems of repellent forces, having but one sentiment in common, and that their entire subjection to that master hand.

And he not only managed the black man, he also hoodwinked the white man, the tourist and investigator who visited his lordly estates. The slaves were doing well, in fact couldn't be happier,—plenty to eat, plenty to drink, comfortably housed and clothed—they wouldn't be free if they could; in short, in his broad brimmed plantation hat and easy aristocratic smoking gown, he made you think him a veritable patriarch in the midst of a lazy, well fed, good natured, over-indulged tenantry.

Then, too, the South represented blood—not red blood, but blue blood. The difference is in the length of the stream and your distance from its source. If your own father was a pirate, a robber, a murderer, his hands are dyed in red blood, and you don't say very much about it. But if your great great great grandfather's grandfather stole and pillaged and slew, and you can prove it, your blood has become blue and you are at great pains to establish the relationship. So the South had neither silver nor gold, but she had blood; and she paraded it with so much gusto that the substantial little Puritan maidens of the North, who had been making bread and canning currants and not thinking of blood the least bit, began to hunt up the records of the Mayflower to see if some of the passengers thereon could not claim the honor of having been one of William the Conqueror's brigands, when he killed the last of the Saxon kings and, red-handed, stole his crown and his lands. Thus the ideal from out the Southland brooded over the nation and we sing less lustily than of yore

> Kind hearts are more than coronets
> And simple faith than Norman blood.[11]

In politics, the two great forces, commerce and empire, which would otherwise have shaped the destiny of the country, have been made to pander and cater to Southern notions. "Cotton is King" meant the South must be allowed to dictate or there would be no fun. Every statesman from 1830 to 1860 exhausted his genius in persuasion and compromises to smooth out her ruffled temper and gratify her petulant demands. But like a sullen younger sister, the South has pouted and sulked and cried: "I won't play with you now; so there!" and the big brother at the North has coaxed and compromised and given in, and—ended by letting her have her way. Until 1860 she had as her pet an institution which it was death by the law to say anything about, except that it was divinely instituted, inaugurated by Noah, sanctioned by Abraham, approved by Paul, and just ideally perfect in every way. And when, to preserve the autonomy of the family arrangements, in '61, '62 and '63, it became necessary for the big brother to administer a little wholesome correction and set the obstreperous Miss vigorously down in her seat again, she assumed such an air of injured innocence, and melted away so lugubriously, the big brother has done nothing since but try to sweeten and pacify and laugh her back into a companionable frame of mind.

Father Lincoln did all he could to get her to repent of her petulance and behave herself. He even promised she might keep her pet, so disagreeable to all the neighbors and hurtful even to herself, and might manage it at home to suit herself, if she would only listen to reason and be just tolerably nice. But, no—she was going to leave and set up for herself; she didn't propose to be meddled with; and so, of course, she had to be spanked. Just a little at first—didn't mean to hurt, merely to teach her who was who. But she grew so ugly, and kicked and fought and scratched so outrageously, and seemed

---

[11]Alfred, Lord Tennyson, "Lady Clara Vere de Vere," 11. 55–56.

so determined to smash up the whole business, the head of the family got red in the face, and said: "Well, now, he couldn't have any more of that foolishness. Arabella must just behave herself or take the consequences." And after the spanking, Arabella sniffed and whimpered and pouted, and the big brother bit his lip, looked half ashamed, and said: "Well, I didn't want to hurt you. You needn't feel so awfully bad about it, I only did it for your good. You know I wouldn't do anything to displease you if I could help it; but you would insist on making the row, and so I just had to. Now, there—there—let's be friends!" and he put his great strong arms about her and just dared anybody to refer to that little unpleasantness—he'd show them a thing or two. Still Arabella sulked,—till the rest of the family decided she might just keep her pets, and manage her own affairs and nobody should interfere.

So now, if one intimates that some clauses of the Constitution are a dead letter at the South and that only the name and support of that pet institution are changed while the fact and essence, minus the expense and responsibility, remain, he is quickly told to mind his own business and informed that he is waving the bloody shirt....

... Not even the chance traveller from England or Scotland escapes. The arch-manipulator takes him under his special watchcare and training, uses up his stock arguments and gives object lessons with his choicest specimens of Negro depravity and worthlessness; take him through what, in New York, would be called "the slums," and would predicate there nothing but the duty of enlightened Christians to send out their light and emulate their Master's aggressive labors of love; but in Georgia is denominated "our terrible problem, which people of the North so little understand, yet vouchsafe so much gratuitous advice about." With an injured air he shows the stupendous and atrocious mistake of reasoning about these people as if they were just ordinary human beings, and amenable to the tenets of the Gospel; and not long after the inoculation begins to work, you hear this old-time friend of the oppressed delivering himself something after this fashion: "Ah, well, the South must be left to manage the Negro. She is most directly concerned and must understand her problem better than outsiders. We must not meddle. We must be very careful not to widen the breaches. The Negro is not worth a feud between brothers and sisters."

Lately a great national and international movement characteristic of this age and country, a movement based on the inherent right of every soul to its own highest development, I mean the movement making for Woman's full, free, and complete emancipation, has, after much courting, obtained the gracious smile of the Southern woman—I beg her pardon—the Southern *lady*.

She represents blood, and of course could not be expected to leave that out; and firstly and foremostly she must not, in any organization she may deign to grace with her presence, be asked to associate with "these people who were once her slaves."

Now the Southern woman (I may be pardoned, being one myself) was never renowned for her reasoning powers, and it is not surprising that just a little picking will make her logic fall to pieces even here.

In the first place she imagines that because her grandfather had slaves who were black, all the blacks in the world of every shade and tint were once in the position of her slaves. This is as bad as the Irishman who was about to kill a peaceable Jew in the streets of Cork,—having just learned that Jews slew his Redeemer. The black race constitutes one-seventh the known population of the globe; and there are representatives of it here as elsewhere who were never in bondage at any time to any man,—whose blood is as blue and lineage as noble as any, even that of the white lady of the South. That her slaves were black and she despises her slaves, should no more argue antipathy to all dark people and peoples, than that Guiteau,[12] an assassin, was white, and I hate assassins, should make me hate all persons more or less white. The objection shows a want of clear discrimination.

The second fallacy in the objection grows out of the use of an ambiguous middle, as the logicians would call it, or assigning a double signification to the term "*Social equality.*"

Civility to the Negro implies social equality. I am opposed to *associating* with dark persons on terms of social equality. Therefore, I abrogate civility to the Negro. This is like

> Light is opposed to darkness.
> Feathers are light.
> *Ergo,* Feathers are opposed to darkness.

The "social equality" implied by civility to the Negro is a very different thing from forced association with him socially. Indeed it seems to me that the mere application of a little cold common sense would show that uncongenial social environments could by no means be forced on any one. I do not, and cannot be made to associate with all dark persons, simply on the ground that I am dark; and I presume the Southern lady can imagine some whose faces are white, with whom she would no sooner think of chatting unreservedly than, were it possible, with a veritable 'darkey.' Such things must and will always be left to individual election. No law, human or divine, can legislate for or against them. Like seeks like; and I am sure with the Southern lady's antipathies at their present temperature, she might enter ten thousand organizations besprinkled with colored women without being any more deflected by them than by the proximity of a stone. The social equality scare then is all humbug, conscious or unconscious, I know not which. And were it not too bitter a thought to utter here, I might add that the overtures for forced association in the past history of these two races were not made by the manacled black man, nor by *the silent and suffering black woman!*

---

[12]The assassin of President James Garfield.

When I seek food in a public café or apply for first-class accommodations on a railway train, I do so because my physical necessities are identical with those of other human beings of like constitution and temperament, and crave satisfaction. I go because I want food, or I want comfort—not because I want association with those who frequent these places; and I can see no more "social equality" in buying lunch at the same restaurant, or riding in a common car, than there is in paying for dry goods at the same counter or walking on the same street.

The social equality which means forced or unbidden association would be as much deprecated and as strenuously opposed by the circle in which I move as by the most hide-bound Southerner in the land. Indeed I have been more than once annoyed by the inquisitive white interviewer, who, with spectacles on nose and pencil and notebook in hand, comes to get some "points" about *your people.* My "people" are just like other people—indeed, too like for their own good. They hate, they love, they attract and repel, they climb or they grovel, struggle or drift, aspire or despair, endure in hope or curse in vexation, exactly like all the rest of unregenerate humanity. Their likes and dislikes are as strong; their antipathies—and prejudices too I fear, are as pronounced as you will find anywhere; and the entrance to the inner sanctuary of their homes and hearts is as jealously guarded against profane intrusion.

What the dark man wants then is merely to live his own life, in his own world, with his own chosen companions, in whatever of comfort, luxury, or emoluments his talent or his money can in an impartial market secure. Has he wealth, he does not want to be forced into inconvenient or unsanitary sections of cities to buy a home and rear his family. Has he art, he does not want to be cabined and cribbed into emulation with the few who merely happen to have his complexion. His talent aspires to study without proscription the masters of all ages and to rub against the broadest and fullest movements of his own day.

Has he religion, he does not want to be made to feel that there is a white Christ and a black Christ, a white Heaven and a black Heaven, a white Gospel and a black Gospel,—but the one ideal of perfect manhood and womanhood, the one universal longing for development and growth, the one desire for being, and being better, the one great yearning, aspiring, outreaching, in all the heartthrobs of humanity in whatever race or clime.

A recent episode in the Corcoran art gallery at the American capital is to the point. A colored woman who had shown marked ability in drawing and coloring, was advised by her teacher, himself an artist of no mean rank, to apply for admission to the Corcoran school in order to study the models and to secure other advantages connected with the organization. She accordingly sent a written application accompanied by specimens of her drawings, the usual *modus operandi* in securing admission.

The drawings were examined by the best critics and pronounced excellent, and a ticket of admission was immediately issued together with a highly complimentary reference to her work.

The next day my friend, congratulating her country and herself that at least in the republic of art no caste existed, presented her ticket of admission *in propria persona*.[13] There was a little preliminary side play in Delsarte[14] pantomine,—aghast—incredulity—wonder; then the superintendent told her in plain unartistic English that of course he had not dreamed a colored person could do such work, and had he suspected the truth he would never have issued the ticket of admission; that, to be right frank, the ticket would have to be cancelled,—she could under no condition be admitted to the studio.

Can it be possible that even art in America is to be tainted by this shrivelling caste spirit? If so, what are we coming to? Can any one conceive a Shakespeare, a Michael Angelo, or a Beethoven putting away any fact of simple merit because the thought, or the suggestion, or the creation emanated from a soul with an unpleasing exterior? . . .

. . . No true artist can allow himself to be narrowed and provincialized by deliberately shutting out any class of facts or subjects through prejudice against externals. And American art, American science, American literature can never be founded in truth, the universal beauty; can never learn to speak a language intelligible in all climes and for all ages, till this paralyzing grip of caste prejudice is loosened from its vitals, and the healthy sympathetic eye is taught to look out on the great universe as holding no favorites and no black beasts, but bearing in each plainest or loveliest feature the handwriting of its God.

And this is why, as it appears to me, woman in her lately acquired vantage ground for speaking an earnest helpful word, can do this country no deeper and truer and more lasting good than by bending all her energies to thus broadening, humanizing, and civilizing her native land.

"Except ye become as little children" is not a pious precept, but an inexorable law of the universe. God's kingdoms are all sealed to the seedy, mossgrown mind of self-satisfied maturity. Only the little child in spirit, the simple, receptive, educable mind can enter. Preconceived notions, blinding prejudices, and shrivelling antipathies must be wiped out, and the cultivable soul made a *tabula rasa*[15] for whatever lesson great Nature has to teach.

This, too, is why I conceive the subject to have been unfortunately worded which was chosen by Miss Shaw at the Woman's Council and which stands at the head of this chapter.

Miss Shaw is one of the most powerful of our leaders, and we feel her voice should give no uncertain note. Woman should not, even by inference, or for the sake of argument, seem to disparage what is weak. For woman's cause is the cause of the weak; and when all the weak shall have received their due consideration, then woman will have her "rights," and the Indian will have his rights, and the Negro will have his rights, and all the strong will have learned at last to deal justly, to love mercy, and to walk humbly;

---

[13]Latin; literally in her own person, *i.e.*, physically.
[14]French musician and teacher.
[15]Latin: blank slate.

and our fair land will have been taught the secret of universal courtesy which is after all nothing but the art, the science, and the religion of regarding one's neighbor as one's self, and to do for him as we would, were conditions swapped, that he do for us.

It cannot seem less than a blunder, whenever the exponents of a great reform or the harbingers of a noble advance in thought and effort allow themselves to seem distorted by a narrow view of their own aims and principles. All prejudices, whether of race, sect or sex, class pride and caste distinctions are the belittling inheritance and badge of snobs and prigs.

The philosophic mind sees that its own "rights" are the rights of humanity. That in the universe of God nothing trivial is or mean; and the recognition it seeks is not through the robber and wild beast adjustment of the survival of the bullies but through the universal application ultimately of the Golden Rule....

The cause of freedom is not the cause of a race or a sect, a party or a class,—it is the cause of human kind, the very birthright of humanity. Now unless we are greatly mistaken the Reform of our day, known as the Woman's Movement, is essentially such an embodiment, if its pioneers could only realize it, of the universal good. And specially important is it that there be no confusion of ideas among its leaders as to its scope and universality. All mists must be cleared from the eyes of woman if she is to be a teacher of morals and manners: the former strikes its roots in the individual and its training and pruning may be accomplished by classes; but the latter is to lubricate the joints and minimize the friction of society, and it is important and fundamental that there be no chromatic or other aberration when the teacher is settling the point, "Who is my neighbor?"

It is not the intelligent woman vs. the ignorant woman; nor the white woman vs. the black, the brown, and the red,—it is not even the cause of woman vs. man. Nay, 'tis woman's strongest vindication for speaking that *the world needs to hear her voice*. It would be subversive of every human interest that the cry of one-half the human family be stifled. Woman in stepping from the pedestal of statue-like inactivity in the domestic shrine, and daring to think and move and speak,—to undertake to help shape, mold, and direct the thought of her age, is merely completing the circle of the world's vision. Hers is every interest that has lacked an interpreter and a defender. Her cause is linked with that of every agony that has been dumb— every wrong that needs a voice.

It is no fault of man's that he has not been able to see truth from her standpoint. It does credit both to his head and heart that no greater mistakes have been committed or even wrongs perpetrated while she sat making tatting and snipping paper flowers. Man's own innate chivalry and the mutual interdependence of their interests have insured his treating her cause, in the main at least, as his own. And he is pardonably surprised and even a little chagrined, perhaps, to find his legislation not considered "perfectly lovely" in every respect. But in any case his work is only impoverished by her remaining dumb. The world has had to limp along with the wobbling gait and one-sided hesitancy of a man with one eye. Suddenly the bandage is removed from the other eye and the whole body is filled with light. It sees a circle where before it saw a segment. The darkened eye restored, every member rejoices with it.

What a travesty of its case for this eye to become plaintiff in a suit, *Eye vs. Foot.* "There is that dull clod, the foot, allowed to roam at will, free and untrammelled; while I, the source and medium of light, brilliant and beautiful, am fettered in darkness and doomed to desuetude." The great burly black man, ignorant and gross and depraved, is allowed to vote; while the franchise is withheld from the intelligent and refined, the pure-minded and lofty souled white woman. Even the untamed and untamable Indian of the prairie, who can answer nothing but 'ugh' to great economic and civic questions, is thought by some worthy to wield the ballot which is still denied the Puritan maid and the first lady of Virginia.

Is not this hitching our wagon to something much lower than a star? Is not woman's cause broader, and deeper, and grander, than a blue stocking debate or an aristocratic pink tea? Why should woman become plaintiff in a suit versus the Indian, or the Negro or any other race or class who have been crushed under the iron heel of Anglo-Saxon power and selfishness? If the Indian has been wronged and cheated by the puissance of this American government, it is woman's mission to plead with her country to cease to do evil and to pay its honest debts. If the Negro has been deceitfully cajoled or inhumanly cuffed according to selfish expediency or capricious antipathy, let it be woman's mission to plead that he be met as a man and honestly given half the road. If woman's own happiness has been ignored or misunderstood in our country's legislating for bread winners, for rum sellers, for property holders, for the family relations, for any or all the interests that touch her vitally, let her rest her plea, not on Indian inferiority, nor on Negro depravity, but on the obligation of legislators to do for her as they would have others do for them were relations reversed. Let her try to teach her country that every interest in this world is entitled at least to a respectful hearing, that every sentiency is worthy of its own gratification, that a helpless cause should not be trampled down, nor a bruised reed broken; and when the right of the individual is made sacred, when the image of God in human form, whether in marble or in clay, whether in alabaster or in ebony, is consecrated and inviolable, when men have been taught to look beneath the rags and grime, the pomp and pageantry of mere circumstance and have regard unto the celestial kernel uncontaminated at the core,—when race, color, sex, condition, are realized to be the accidents, not the substance of life, and consequently as not obscuring or modifying the inalienable title to life, liberty, and pursuit of happiness,—then is mastered the science of politeness, the art of courteous contact, which is naught but the practical application of the principle of benevolence, the back bone and marrow of all religion; then woman's lesson is taught and woman's cause is won—not the white woman nor the black woman nor the red woman, but the cause of every man or woman who has writhed silently under a mighty wrong. The pleading of the American woman for the right and the opportunity to employ the American method of influencing the disposal to be made of herself, her property, her children in civil, economic, or domestic relations is thus seen to be based on a principle as broad as the human race and as old as human society. Her wrongs are thus indissolubly linked with all undefended woe, all helpless suffering, and the plenitude of her "rights" will mean the final triumph of all right over might, the supremacy of the moral forces of reason and justice and love in the government of the nation.

God hasten the day.

1892

OUTSIDE/INSIDE U.S.A.: EXPANSION AND IMMIGRATION

IN FOCUS

Expansion and Immigration

WHEN DID THE UNITED STATES BECOME AN IMPORTANT ACTOR ON THE WORLD stage? The Spanish-American War is sometimes seen as the turning point. However, it is more accurately regarded as a tipping point, for the nation had long been expanding geographically, commercially, culturally, and in other ways.

By 1898, the year of the war, the United States had been increasing its geographic size by means of purchases (the Louisiana Purchase, the purchase of Alaska), military action (most notably against Native peoples), war (with Mexico), and annexation (of the Republic of Texas). Before the Civil War, some Southerners who wanted to secede from the United States to create a slaveholding confederation wanted to expand into Cuba and Latin America. For decades, the United States had also been moving into the world beyond its borders, new and old. U.S. merchants and those with other commercial interests had long been making their way into the Far East, Caribbean, Pacific Islands, and Latin America. Missionaries dedicated to spreading Christianity in the Far East and Africa brought Euro-American culture and education with them and established organizational networks. Whether deliberately or not, their efforts facilitated an increased U.S. economic and military presence there, too.

The nation was also moving beyond its physical borders militarily and politically. It gained naval bases in Samoa (1878) and naval rights to Pearl Harbor, in Hawai'i (1887), and formally annexed Hawai'i in 1898. U.S. foreign policy asserted that the nation's sphere of influence was even broader than all of this suggests. During the last decade of the century, the Monroe Doctrine, which held that European nations were not to interfere in independent nations of the Americas, was reformulated as a proclamation that the United States was "practically sovereign on this continent." Its "fiat is law upon the subjects to which it confines its interposition," declared Secretary of State Richard Olney to the British when they seemed on the verge of military defense of British Guiana in a border dispute with Venezuela. Olney's threat was successful: Britain backed down.

But the United States was far from alone in pursuing expansion. In fact, the United States was a latecomer in what has been called "the age of empire." The principle imperialist European nation in the nineteenth century was Great Britain; others included Belgium, Germany, Portugal, Spain, France, and the Netherlands. It is not surprising that, by the 1890s, sentiment within the United States in support of the nation's assumption of its place as a global power had gathered steam. Supporters came from all segments of the population—elected officials, government policy makers, businessmen, newspaper editors, intellectuals, and ordinary people. This support drew on and intensified the rhetoric of expansion that had been set forth in the Monroe Doctrine. Indeed, in the years preceding the Spanish-American War, that rhetoric became increasingly militant and increasingly widespread. By April 25, 1898, when the United States declared war on Spain, a discourse of militant expansion pervaded the environment of phrases and arguments, images and music, in which U.S. residents lived.

This discourse circulated everywhere—in newspapers, magazines, political speeches, sermons, sheet music, and everyday talk. William Dean Howells' short story "Editha" (in the Howells section of Volume C) calls attention to several of the discourse's prominent motifs: associating manliness with war, characterizing peoples of color as inferior beings in need of whites' protection, defining patriotism as the championing of national policy. "Editha" also references newspaper articles and songs that stirred support for the war.

Another key feature of the discourse (although it is not alluded to in "Editha") was the visual image. Technological advances had made drawings and photographs relatively inexpensive and easy to reproduce, and newspapers and magazines included many of both. The "yellow press"—jingoistic newspapers like William Randolph Hearst's New York Journal and Joseph Pulitzer's New York World—was adroit in using visual images to promote going to war with Spain and, once war was under way, to fuel support for it. Probably the most powerful of these images was the spectacle of the wreck of the battleship U.S.S. Maine, which exploded off the coast of Cuba in February 1898, killing more than 275 crew members. Although the cause of the explosion has never been definitively established, it was widely attributed to Spain, especially by the press. Demanding war against Spain, the World featured picture after picture of the Maine in ruins; other newspapers and magazines did so as well. A slogan—"Remember the Maine, To hell with Spain"—also emerged in short order. Originating in a reporter's account of a remark he heard in a tavern, the phrase was reiterated by politicians and editorial page writers and invoked at rallies. Complemented by the visual image of the Maine, it became a watchword for waging war with Spain and then for winning it.

The discourse of expansion and war was passionately enthusiastic, but that did not rule out debate and critique. Consider the diverse uses to which another catch phrase associated with the Spanish-American War, "the white man's burden," was put. The phrase was given currency by a poem of that title published by British writer Rudyard Kipling in support of the U.S. victory in the Philippines. "The White Man's Burden" appeared in McClure's, an American magazine with a national circulation, only six days after Congress, following heated debate, ratified the Treaty of Paris, which established the global status of the United States. (The Treaty mandated that Spain cede Puerto Rico and several other Caribbean islands, Guam, and the Philippine Islands to the United States and that the United States occupy Cuba until the Spanish departed.) A number of factors combined to secure a larger readership for the poem—Kipling's rhetorical and technical skill, the poem's timeliness, the prominence of the writer and of *McClure's*. Its viewpoint did not go unchallenged, however. In fact, it served as a flashpoint. As two other poems we reprint here suggest, the phrasing and structure of Kipling's poem were mimicked to critique its core argument that the United States had gone to war to defend the rights of Cubans and Filipinos against Spanish oppression. How long, asks an anonymous versifier, would America have to bear such burdens?

How hypocritical, insists feminist physician Anna Manning Comfort, to claim to advance democracy abroad when U.S. citizens are denied their rights at home. One of Comfort's targets is the widespread abuse of African Americans. In 1898 she could not know it, but the war would lead to new forms of that abuse, for although African American divisions fought in Cuba and Puerto Rico with courage and success, African American military men were subjected to insult and dismissal once the war was won. Even the navy, the branch that had been most receptive to black servicemen, edged blacks out. In 1906 President Theodore Roosevelt, who had praised black troops' bravery during the battle of San Juan hill, accepted the decision of the Secretary of War to disband a black regiment rather than incense whites in the area of Texas where it was to be quartered with the rest of its battalion. The cartoon we reprint from *The Voice of the Negro* is one among many expressions of blacks' anger at this move and at the general surge in racism after the war. For some observers, moreover, the war and its aftermath also cast relationships between racism within the United States and U.S. foreign policy in high relief. In *The Marrow of Tradition* (1901), Charles W. Chesnutt ties national acceptance of the intensification of southern whites' reign of terror against blacks to racial rationalizations of America's economic and military control of people of color elsewhere.

Resistance to racism and to empire had little effect on U.S. interventions abroad, however. In 1902, after a three-year war, the United States ousted an independent Philippine republic that had been established after the Filipinos declared their independence from Spain. U.S. troops occupied the country until 1912. (For an influential justification of the U.S. occupation of the Philippines, see the speech that President William McKinley reportedly made to members of the General Missionary Committee of the Methodist Episcopal Church who visited him at the White House in 1899; it was not published until 1903, two years after his assassination, and its veracity has been disputed.) Between the turn of the century and World War I, U.S. troops were sent to Haiti, Mexico, Panama, Cuba, Nicaragua, and the Dominican Republic. While many Americans were enthusiastic about these activities, some were not, and the American Anti-Imperialist League was organized in 1898 to oppose U.S. annexation of Hawai'i and U.S. military action against Filipino self-government. As the petition we include here indicates, women as well as men were active in the League. The League included many well-known figures, among them Jane Addams, Andrew Carnegie, and several writers whose work appears in this volume—Ambrose Bierce, Finley Peter Dunne, William Dean Howells, and Mark Twain. Twain served as the League's vice president from 1901 until his death in 1910 and wrote a number of critiques of war and imperialism. His scathing essay "To the Person Sitting in Darkness" exposes the continuity between the conduct and rhetoric of imperialist nations and those of the United States. The rationale that his essay tears apart—that Western nations are bringing civilization to "the person sitting in darkness"—is a close relative of the motif of the white man's burden.

Other pieces in this section speak to the world's presence in the United States in the form of immigration. Immigrants from southern Italy, eastern Europe, Ireland, Germany, and the Scandinavian countries came to the United States in record numbers in the last three decades of the nineteenth century and the first two of the twentieth. Poverty, violence, political oppression, religious bigotry, ethnic bigotry, absence of opportunity for education or economic improvement—these were among the reasons they came. To be sure, neither immigration nor many of these motives were of recent origin. The forebears of most U.S. citizens were immigrants from Europe, many of whom had come seeking opportunity of one kind or another. Their immigration had not been restricted, although the Irish—one of the largest groups of immigrants between 1800 and 1880—were met with considerable hostility and some violence, fueled by anti-Catholicism.

Chinese immigrants, however, faced virulent racism and exclusionary laws soon after they began to arrive. Chinese labor had been essential to U.S. development, most memorably in the laying of the transcontinental railroad (completed in 1869), but increasingly they were viewed as a menace to the nation— "the yellow peril." Violence against them erupted as early as 1849. In 1875 Congress passed the Page Act, which restricted immigration from China, Japan, and "any [other] Oriental country," and in 1882 it passed the first of several Chinese Exclusion Acts. Speaking in support of such legislation, Maine Senator James G. Blaine expressed the widely held belief that the Chinese were an alien race. "Asiatics" cannot come to the United States and "make a homogeneous element" "with our population," Blair proclaimed, for to the Chinese, family and home are foreign concepts. "There is not a peasant cottage inhabited by a Chinaman. There is not a hearthstone, in the sense we understand it, of an American home, or an English home, or an Irish, or German, or French home."

Blaine was charactering the Chinese as uncivilizable—barbarians, as the thinking of the era had it—but the hatred and violence to which the Chinese were subjected did not serve civilization in the United States itself. In *Driven Out: The Forgotten War Against Chinese Americans* (2007), Jean Pfaelzer documents the pogroms, purges, round-ups, and other actions against Chinese Americans that occurred in the Pacific Northwest and California throughout the second half of the century. She also details how resourceful and organized the Chinese were in fighting back, using the courts, economic actions, and other legal means. And from the start, some U.S. citizens regarded the Chinese Exclusion Act, not the Chinese, as a desecration of the nation. Thomas Nast's 1882 cartoon "*E Pluribus Unum* (Except the Chinese)" pictures the Act as invalidating the U.S. national slogan *E Pluribus Unum* (out of many, one). What the Act achieves, the cartoon shows, is to catapult the nation back into the middle ages by violating the commitment to liberty on which it was founded.

Although immigrants from Europe were not subject to federal restrictions until Congress established immigration quotas in 1921, their reception in the United States was often far from favorable. To be sure, some welcomed them with a humanitarianism captured in Emma Lazarus' famous sonnet, "The New

Colossus." Written in 1883 to raise funds for a pedestal for the Statue of Liberty—which quickly became the most important visual icon of the welcome America extended to immigrants—the poem was largely forgotten until the early twentieth century, when it was engraved on a plaque that was affixed to the statue's base. However, anti-immigration feelings ran very strong, and they underwrote organizations that advocated restrictions on immigration. One of the most visible was the Anti-Immigration League, founded in Boston in 1894. It included among its members the powerful senior senator from Massachusetts, Henry Cabot Lodge, a friend of President McKinley and an influential supporter of U.S. expansion, and Thomas Bailey Aldrich, editor of the prestigious *Atlantic Monthly Magazine* from 1880 to 1890. Aldrich's poem "Strait are the Gates" imagines with horror the aliens who pour into the nation and overwhelm the white race. His "Liberty" is not a statue welcoming huddled masses but a "white goddess" whom he implores to preserve the supremacy of real—that is, Anglo-Saxon—Americans. The similarity of the tropes the two poems use in response to the same general circumstances, as well as their formal similarities, testify that, like expansion, immigration was a vital part of the nation's discourse by the last decades of the nineteenth century.

Sandra A. Zagarell
Oberlin College

■   # WILLIAM McKINLEY   ■
1843–1901

from **Interview with President McKinley**

By General James F. Rusling

I would like to say just a word about the Philippine business. I have been criticised a good deal about the Philippines, but don't deserve it. The truth is I didn't want the Philippines, and when they came to us, as a gift from the gods, I did not know what to do with them. When the Spanish war broke out Dewey was at Hongkong, and I ordered him to go to Manila and to capture or destroy the Spanish fleet, and he had to; because, if defeated, he had no place to refit on that side of the globe, and if the Done were victorious they would likely cross the Pacific and ravage our Oregon and California coasts. And so he had to destroy the Spanish fleet, and did it! But that was as far as I thought then.

"When next I realized that the Philippines had dropped into our laps I confess I did not know what to do with them. I sought counsel from all sides—Democrats as well as Republicans—but got little help. I thought first we would take only Manila; then Luzon; then other islands perhaps also. I walked the floor of the White House night after night until midnight; and I am not ashamed to tell you, gentlemen, that I went down on my knees and prayed Almighty God for light and guidance more than one night. And one night late it came to me this way—I don't know how it was, but it came: (1) That we could not give them back to Spain—that would be cowardly and dishonorable; (2) that we could not turn them over to France or Germany— our commercial rivals in the Orient—that would be bad business and discreditable; (3) that we could not leave them to themselves—they were unfit for self-government—and they would soon have anarchy and misrule over there worse than Spain's was; and (4) that there was nothing left for us to do but to take them all, and to educate the Filipinos, and uplift and civilize and Christianize them, and by God's grace do the very best we could by them, as our fellow-men for whom Christ also died. And then I went to bed, and went to sleep, and slept soundly, and the next morning I sent for the chief engineer of the War Department (our map-maker), and I told him to put the Philippines on the map of the United States [pointing to a large map on the wall of his office], and there they are, and there they will stay while I am President!"

1903

RUDYARD KIPLING
1865–1936

The White Man's Burden[1]

Take up the White Man's burden—
Send forth the best ye breed—
Go, bind your sons to exile
To serve your captives' need;
To wait, in heavy harness,   5
On fluttered folk and wild—
Your new-caught sullen peoples,
Half devil and half child.

Take up the White Man's burden—
In patience to abide,   10
To veil the threat of terror
And check the show of pride;
By open speech and simple,
An hundred times made plain,
To seek another's profit   15
And work another's gain.

[1]*McClure's Magazine* 12 (February 1899).

Take up the White Man's burden—
The savage wars of peace—
Fill full the mouth of Famine,
And bid the sickness cease;   20
And when your goal is nearest
(The end for others sought)
Watch sloth and heathen folly
Bring all your hope to nought.

Take up the White Man's burden—   25
No iron rule of kings,
But toil of serf and sweeper—
The tale of common things.
The ports ye shall not enter,
The roads ye shall not tread,   30
Go, make them with your living
And mark them with your dead.

Take up the White Man's burden
And reap his old reward—
The blame of those ye better   35
The hate of those ye guard—
The cry of hosts ye humour
(Ah, slowly!) toward the light:—
"Why brought ye us from bondage,
Our loved Egyptian night?"   40

Take up the White Man's burden—
Ye dare not stoop to less—
Nor call too loud on Freedom
To cloak your weariness.
By all ye will or whisper,   45
By all ye leave or do,
The silent sullen peoples
Shall weigh your God and you.

Take up the White Man's burden!
Have done with childish days—   50
The lightly-proffered laurel,
The easy ungrudged praise:
Comes now, to search your manhood
Through all the thankless years,
Cold, edged with dear-bought wisdom,   55
The judgment of your peers.

1899

■ ANONYMOUS IN THE NEW YORK WORLD ■

We've Taken Up the White Man's Burden[1]

We've taken up the white man's burden
Of ebony and brown;
Now will you kindly tell us, Rudyard,
How we may put it down?

July 15, 1899

■ ANNA MANNING COMFORT ■
1845–1931

Home Burdens of Uncle Sam[1']

"Take up the white man's burden,"—
Yes, Uncle Sam, oh do!
But why seek other countries
Your burdens to renew?
Great questions here confront you.   5
Then, too, we have a past—
Don't pose as a reformer!
Why, nations look aghast!

"Take up the white man's burden,"—
But try to lift more true.   10
Recall the poor wild Indian
Whom ruthlessly you slew.
Ignoble was our treatment,
Ungenerous we dealt
With him and his hard burden,   15
'Tis known from belt to belt.

"Take up the white man's burden,"—
The negro, once our slave!
Boast lightly of his freedom,

[1]Reprinted in *The Public* 2 (July 15, 1899).   [1']*The Public* 2 (May 13, 1899).

This problem still is grave.   20
We scoff and shoot and lynch him,
And yet, because he's black,
We shove him out from office
And crowd him off the track.

"Take up the white man's burden,"—   25
Yes, one of them is sex.
Enslaved are your brave women,
No ballot, while you tax!
Your labors and your conflicts
Columbia's daughters share,   30
Yet still denied the franchise,
Quick give! be just! deal fair!

"Take up the white man's burden,"—
Start in with politics.
Clean out the rotten platform,   35
Made up of tricks and tricks,—
Our politics disgraceful,
In church and school and state.
We have no "ruling bosses,"
Oh, no! the country's great.   40

"Take up the white man's burden,"—
But, oh, if you are wise
You'll seek not "motes" far distant,
With "beams" in your own eyes.
Why fight the foreign despots,   45
Or Filipino isles?
Come, "scrap it" with "home tyrants!"
And politicians' wiles.

"Take up the white man's burden,"—
Right here in our own times.   50
Give justice, 'tis demanded
This side of distant climes.
Yes, take the white man's burden,
But take it here at home;
With self, oh, Samuel, wrestle,   55
And cease the seas to roam!

                              1899

■ *from* THE VOICE OF THE NEGRO ■

Buster Brown in a New Role (1906)

BUSTER BROWN IN A NEW ROLE— Courtesy of the *Chicago Republic*

Columbia—I consider it most unjust and unworthy of you, Buster, to treat your colored soldiers in that way.

Buster—But you see, mother, it pleases Tige,—that's the point.

THE WOMEN'S AUXILIARY OF THE ANTI-IMPERIALIST LEAGUE

In Behalf of the Foundation Principles of the Republic

To the Women of the United States:

Believing that, in this national crisis, it is the duty of every American citizen, woman no less than man, to uphold the principles of the Declaration of Independence, and believing that the noble work of the anti-imperialist league should be heartily supported by all true patriots, we invite all women of the United States to join us in helping on that work by sending at once to Miss F. L. Abbot, 43 Larch street, Cambridge, Mass., their signatures (with the names of their town or city and state) for the following petition:—

Mrs. Thomas Wentworth Higginson, Mrs. Lewis G. Janes, Alice Freeman Palmer, Margaret Storer Warner, D.A.R.; Sarah Sherman Storer, Annie Longfellow Thorp, Harriet E. Brooks, Mrs. William James, Sarah E. Hunt, D.R.; Fannie L. Abbot, D.R.

Petition

To the President of the United States:

We, women of the United States, earnestly protest against the war of conquest into which our country has been plunged in the Philippine islands. We appeal to the Declaration of Independence, which is the moral foundation of the constitution you have sworn to defend, and we reaffirm its weighty words:

> We hold these truths to be self-evident that all men are created equal [before the law], that they are endowed by their Creator with certain inalienable rights, that among these are life, liberty and the pursuit of happiness; that, to secure these rights, governments are instituted among men, deriving their just powers from the consent of the governed; that, whenever any form of government becomes destructive of those ends, it is the right of the people to alter or abolish it, and to institute new government, laying its foundation on such principles and organizing its powers in such form as to them shall seem most likely to effect their safety and happiness.

And we unqualifiedly approve and support these resolutions of the anti-imperialist league:

> First. That our government shall take immediate steps toward a suspension of hostilities in the Philippines and a conference with the Philippine leaders with a view to preventing further bloodshed, upon the basis of a recognition of their freedom and independence as soon as proper guarantees can be had for order and protection of property.

*Second. That the government of the United States shall tender an offi-
cial assurance to the inhabitants of the Philippine islands that they will encourage and assist in the organization of such a government in the islands as
the people thereof shall prefer, and that upon its organization in stable manner, the United States, in accordance with its traditional and prescriptive
policy in such cases, will recognize the independence of the Philippines and
its equality among nations, and gradually withdraw all military and naval
forces.*

In those eternal truths of the Declaration of Independence lie the principles which we firmly believe ought to govern your action as a faithful servant of the American people. In those resolutions of the anti-imperialist
league lies the clear application of those principles to the duty of the hour.
In the name of justice, freedom, and humanity, and in the spirit of George
Washington and Abraham Lincoln, we urge you to obey those principles,
and cease at once this war of "criminal aggression" against a brave people
fighting for their independence just as our forefathers fought for theirs
and ours.

May 30, 1899

MARK TWAIN
1835–1910

from **To the Person Sitting in Darkness**[1]

[Twain comments on a leading Protestant missionary's report that he had
obtained payment from destitute Chinese peasants in retribution for murders
of missionaries during the Boxer Rebellion in China, and he quotes a newspaper
correspondent's statement that the Japanese feel "that the missionary
organizations constitute a constant menace to peaceful international relations."
He then raises these questions:]

[S]hall we go on conferring our Civilization upon the peoples that sit in
darkness, or shall we give those poor things a rest? Shall we bang right
ahead in our old-time, loud, pious way, and commit the new century to the
game; or shall we sober up and sit down and think it over first? Would it
not be prudent to get our Civilization-tools together, and see how much
stock is left on hand in the way of Glass Beads and Theology, and Maxim

[1]*North American Review* (February 1901).

Guns and Hymn Books, and Trade-Gin and Torches of Progress and Enlightenment (patent adjustable ones, good to fire villages with, upon occasion), and balance the books, and arrive at the profit and loss, so that we may intelligently decide whether to continue the business or sell out the property and start a new Civilization Scheme on the proceeds?

Extending the Blessings of Civilization to our Brother who Sits in Darkness has been a good trade and has paid well, on the whole; and there is money in it yet, if carefully worked—but not enough, in my judgement, to make any considerable risk advisable. The People that Sit in Darkness are getting to be too scarce—too scarce and too shy. And such darkness as is now left is really of but an indifferent quality, and not dark enough for the game. The most of those People that Sit in Darkness have been furnished with more light than was good for them or profitable for us. We have been injudicious.

The Blessings-of-Civilization Trust, wisely and cautiously administered, is a Daisy. There is more money in it, more territory, more sovereignty, and other kinds of emolument, than there is in any other game that is played. But Christendom has been playing it badly of late years, and must certainly suffer by it, in my opinion. She has been so eager to get every stake that appeared on the green cloth, that the People who Sit in Darkness have noticed it—they have noticed it, and have begun to show alarm. They have become suspicious of the Blessings of Civilization. More—they have begun to examine them. This is not well. The Blessings of Civilization are all right, and a good commercial property; there could not be a better, in a dim light. In the right kind of a light, and at a proper distance, with the goods a little out of focus, they furnish this desirable exhibit to the Gentlemen who Sit in Darkness:

LOVE,	LAW AND ORDER,
JUSTICE,	LIBERTY,
GENTLENESS,	EQUALITY,
CHRISTIANITY,	HONORABLE DEALING,
PROTECTION TO THE WEAK,	MERCY,
TEMPERANCE,	EDUCATION,
—and so on.	

There. Is it good? Sir, it is pie. It will bring into camp any idiot that sits in darkness anywhere. But not if we adulterate it. It is proper to be emphatic upon that point. This brand is strictly for Export—apparently. Apparently. Privately and confidentially, it is nothing of the kind. Privately and confidentially, it is merely an outside cover, gay and pretty and attractive, displaying the special patterns of our Civilization which we reserve for Home Consumption, while inside the bale is the Actual Thing that the Customer Sitting in Darkness buys with his blood and tears and land and liberty. That Actual Thing is, indeed, Civilization, but it is only for Export. Is there a difference between the two brands? In some of the details, yes.

We all know that the Business is being ruined. The reason is not far to seek. It is because our Mr. McKinley, and Mr. Chamberlain, and the Kaiser, and the Czar and the French have been exporting the Actual Thing with the outside cover left off.[2] This is bad for the Game. It shows that these new players of it are not sufficiently acquainted with it.

It is a distress to look on and note the mismoves, they are so strange and so awkward. Mr. Chamberlain manufactures a war out of materials so inadequate and so fanciful that they make the boxes grieve and the gallery laugh, and he tries hard to persuade himself that it isn't purely a private raid for cash, but has a sort of dim, vague respectability about it somewhere, if he could only find the spot; and that, by and by, he can scour the flag clean again after he has finished dragging it through the mud, and make it shine and flash in the vault of heaven once more as it had shone and flashed there a thousand years in the world's respect until he laid his unfaithful hand upon it. It is bad play—bad. For it exposes the Actual Thing to Them that Sit in Darkness, and they say: "What! Christian against Christian? And only for money? Is this a case of magnanimity, forbearance, love, gentleness, mercy, protection of the weak—this strange and over-showy onslaught of an elephant upon a nest of field-mice, on the pretext that the mice had squeaked an insolence at him—conduct which 'no self-respecting government could allow to pass unavenged?' as Mr. Chamberlain said.... Is this Civilization and Progress? Is it something better than we already possess? These harryings and burnings and desert-makings in the Transvaal—is this an improvement on our darkness? Is it, perhaps, possible that there are two kinds of Civilization—one for home consumption and one for the heathen market?" ...

[After further detailing British imperialism in South Africa and then the activities of Germany, Twain takes up Russia.] And, next, Russia must go and play the game injudiciously. She affronts England once or twice—with the Person Sitting in Darkness observing and noting; by moral assistance of France and Germany, she robs Japan of her hard-earned spoil, all swimming in Chinese blood—Port Arthur—with the Person again observing and noting; then she seizes Manchuria, raids its villages, and chokes its great river with the swollen corpses of countless massacred peasants—that astonished Person still observing and noting. And perhaps he is saying to himself: "It is yet another Civilized Power, with its banner of the Prince of Peace in one hand and its loot-basket and its butcher-knife in the other. Is there no salvation for us but to adopt Civilization and lift ourselves down to its level?"

And by and by comes America, and our Master of the Game plays it badly—plays it as Mr. Chamberlain was playing it in South Africa. It was a

[2]William McKinley was elected U.S. president in 1896. He was assassinated in September 1901. British Member of Parliament and leader of the Liberal Party Joseph Chamber- lain (1836–1914) was an outspoken imperialist; he strongly supported the British war with the Boers in South Africa.

mistake to do that; also, it was one which was quite unlooked for in a Master who was playing it so well in Cuba. In Cuba, he was playing the usual and regular American game, and it was winning, for there is no way to beat it. The Master, contemplating Cuba, said: "Here is an oppressed and friendless little nation which is willing to fight to be free; we go partners, and put up the strength of seventy million sympathizers and the resources of the United States: play!" Nothing but Europe combined could call that hand: and Europe cannot combine on anything. There, in Cuba, he was following our great traditions in a way which made us very proud of him, and proud of the deep dissatisfaction which his play was provoking in Continental Europe. Moved by a high inspiration, he threw out those stirring words which proclaimed that forcible annexation would be "criminal aggression;" and in that utterance fired another "shot heard round the world." The memory of that fine saying will be outlived by the remembrance of no act of his but one—that he forgot it within the twelvemonth, and its honorable gospel along with it.

For, presently, came the Philippine temptation. It was strong; it was too strong, and he made that bad mistake: he played the European game, the Chamberlain game. It was a pity, it was a great pity, that error; that one grievous error, that irrevocable error. For it was the very place and time to play the American game again. And at no cost. Rich winnings to be gathered in, too; rich and permanent; indestructible; a fortune transmissible forever to the children of the flag. Not land, not money, not dominion—no, something worth many times more than that dross: our share, the spectacle of a nation of long harassed and persecuted slaves set free through our influence; our posterity's share, the golden memory of that fair deed. The game was in our hands. If it had been played according to the American rules, Dewey would have sailed away from Manila as soon as he had destroyed the Spanish fleet—after putting up a sign on shore guaranteeing foreign property and life against damage by the Filipinos, and warning the Powers that interference with the emancipated patriots would be regarded as an act unfriendly to the United States.[3] The Powers cannot combine, in even a bad cause, and the sign would not have been molested.

Dewey could have gone about his affairs elsewhere, and left the competent Filipino army to starve out the little Spanish garrison and send it home, and the Filipino citizens to set up the form of government they might prefer, and deal with the friars and their doubtful acquisitions according to Filipino ideas of fairness and justice—ideas which have since been tested and found to be of as high an order as any that prevail in Europe or America.

But we played the Chamberlain game, and lost the chance to add another Cuba and another honorable deed to our good record.

The more we examine the mistake, the more clearly we perceive that it is going to be bad for the Business. The Person Sitting in Darkness is almost sure

[3]George Dewey (1837–1917), admiral of the U.S. Navy. He led the navy to victory against Spain in the Battle of Manila Bay (1898) without any American losses, though one American died of heat stroke.

to say: "There is something curious about this—curious and unaccountable. There must be two Americas: one that sets the captive free, and one that takes a once-captive's new freedom away from him, and picks a quarrel with him with nothing to found it on; then kills him to get his land."

The truth is, the Person Sitting in Darkness is saying things like that; and for the sake of the Business we must persuade him to look at the Philippine matter in another and healthier way. We must arrange his opinions for him. I believe it can be done; for Mr. Chamberlain has arranged England's opinion of the South African matter, and done it most cleverly and successfully. He presented the facts—some of the facts—and showed those confiding people what the facts meant. He did it statistically, which is a good way. He used the formula: "Twice 2 are 14, and 2 from 9 leaves 35." Figures are effective; figures will convince the elect.

Now, my plan is a still bolder one than Mr. Chamberlain's, though apparently a copy of it. Let us be franker than Mr. Chamberlain; let us audaciously present the whole of the facts, shirking none, then explain them according to Mr. Chamberlain's formula. This daring truthfulness will astonish and dazzle the Person Sitting in Darkness, and he will take the Explanation down before his mental vision has had time to get back into focus. Let us say to him:

"Our case is simple. On the 1st of May, Dewey destroyed the Spanish fleet. This left the Archipelago in the hands of its proper and rightful owners, the Filipino nation. Their army numbered 30,000 men, and they were competent to whip out or starve out the little Spanish garrison; then the people could set up a government of their own devising. Our traditions required that Dewey should now set up his warning sign, and go away. But the Master of the Game happened to think of another plan—the European plan. He acted upon it. This was, to send out an army—ostensibly to help the native patriots put the finishing touch upon their long and plucky struggle for independence, but really to take their land away from them and keep it. That is, in the interest of Progress and Civilization. The plan developed, stage by stage, and quite satisfactorily. We entered into a military alliance with the trusting Filipinos, and they hemmed in Manila on the land side, and by their valuable help the place, with its garrison of 8,000 or 10,000 Spaniards, was captured—a thing which we could not have accomplished unaided at that time. We got their help by—by ingenuity. We knew they were fighting for their independence, and that they had been at it for two years. We knew they supposed that we also were fighting in their worthy cause—just as we had helped the Cubans fight for Cuban independence— and we allowed them to go on thinking so. Until Manila was ours and we could get along without them. Then we showed our hand. Of course, they were surprised—that was natural; surprised and disappointed; disappointed and grieved. To them it looked un-American; un-characteristic; foreign to our established traditions. And this was natural, too; for we were only playing the American Game in public—in private it was the European. It was neatly done, very neatly, and it bewildered them. They could not understand it; for we had been so friendly—so affectionate, even—with those simple-minded patriots! We, our own selves, had brought back out of exile their leader, their hero, their hope, their Washington—Aguinaldo; brought him in a warship, in high honor, under the sacred shelter and hospitality of the flag; brought him back and restored him to his people, and got their moving and eloquent gratitude for it.[4] Yes, we had been so friendly to them, and had heartened them up in so many ways! We had lent them guns and ammunition; advised with them; exchanged pleasant courtesies with them; placed our sick and wounded in their kindly care; entrusted our Spanish prisoners to their humane and honest hands; fought shoulder to shoulder with them against "the common enemy" (our own phrase); praised their courage, praised their gallantry, praised their mercifulness, praised their fine and honorable conduct; borrowed their trenches, borrowed strong positions which they had previously captured from the Spaniard; petted them, lied to them—officially proclaiming that our land and naval forces came to give them their freedom and displace the bad Spanish Government—fooled them, used them until we needed them no longer; then derided the sucked orange and threw it away. We kept the positions which we had beguiled them of; by and by, we moved a force forward and overlapped patriot ground—a clever thought, for we needed trouble, and this would produce it. A Filipino soldier, crossing the ground, where no one had a right to forbid him, was shot by our sentry. The badgered patriots resented this with arms, without waiting to know whether Aguinaldo, who was absent, would approve or not. Aguinaldo did not approve; but that availed nothing. What we wanted, in the interest of Progress and Civilization, was the Archipelago, unencumbered by patriots struggling for independence; and War was what we needed. We clinched our opportunity. It is Mr. Chamberlain's case over again—at least in its motive and intention; and we played the game as adroitly as he played it himself.... [Twain recounts the pretense for the American attack on the Filipinos after Spain is defeated and discusses the Americans' conduct during the war. He then takes on reports by General Arthur MacArthur, who led American forces in the Philippines].

Of course, we must not venture to ignore our General MacArthur's reports—oh, why do they keep on printing those embarrassing things?—we must drop them trippingly from the tongue and take the chances:

During the last ten months our losses have been 268 killed and 750 wounded; Filipino loss, three thousand, two hundred and twenty-seven killed, and 694 wounded."

We must stand ready to grab the Person Sitting in Darkness, for he will swoon away at this confession, saying: "Good God, those 'niggers' spare their wounded, and the Americans massacre theirs!"

[4]Emilio Aguinaldo y Famy (March 22, 1869–February 6, 1964), leader in the Philippine fight for independence and first president of the independent Philippines. He was a U.S. ally during the war against Spain but was later deemed an enemy. His 1901 capture by Americans and subsequent declaration of loyalty to the United States (for which his life was spared) ended the First Republic of the Philippines.

We must bring him to, and coax him and coddle him, and assure him that the ways of Providence are best, and that it would not become us to find fault with them; and then, to show him that we are only imitators, not originators, we must read the following passage from the letter of an American soldier-lad in the Philippines to his mother, published in *Public Opinion,* of Decorah, Iowa, describing the finish of a victorious battle:

"WE NEVER LEFT ONE ALIVE. IF ONE WAS WOUNDED, WE WOULD RUN OUR BAYONETS THROUGH HIM."

Having now laid all the historical facts before the Person Sitting in Darkness, we should bring him to again, and explain them to him. We should say to him:

"They look doubtful, but in reality they are not. There have been lies; yes, but they were told in a good cause. We have been treacherous; but that was only in order that real good might come out of apparent evil. True, we have crushed a deceived and confiding people; we have turned against the weak and the friendless who trusted us; we have stamped out a just and intelligent and well-ordered republic; we have stabbed an ally in the back and slapped the face of a guest; we have bought a Shadow from an enemy that hadn't it to sell; we have robbed a trusting friend of his land and his liberty; we have invited our clean young men to shoulder a discredited musket and do bandit's work under a flag which bandits have been accustomed to fear, not to follow; we have debauched America's honor and blackened her face before the world; but each detail was for the best. We know this. The Head of every State and Sovereignty in Christendom and ninety per cent. of every legislative body in Christendom, including our Congress and our fifty State Legislatures, are members not only of the church, but also of the Blessings-of-Civilization Trust. This world-girdling accumulation of trained morals, high principles, and justice, cannot do an upright thing, an unfair thing, an ungenerous thing, an unclean thing. It knows what it is about. Give yourself no uneasiness; it is all right."

Now then, that will convince the Person. You will see. It will restore the Business. Also, it will elect the Master of the Game to the vacant place in the Trinity of our national gods; and there on their high thrones the Three will sit, age after age, in the people's sight, each bearing the Emblem of his service: Washington, the Sword of the Liberator; Lincoln, the Slave's Broken Chains; the Master, the Chains Repaired.

It will give the Business a splendid new start. You will see.

Everything is prosperous, now; everything is just as we should wish it. We have got the Archipelago, and we shall never give it up. Also, we have every reason to hope that we shall have an opportunity before very long to slip out of our Congressional contract with Cuba and give her something better in the place of it. It is a rich country, and many of us are already beginning to see that the contract was a sentimental mistake. But now—right now—is the best time to do some profitable rehabilitating work—work that will set us up and make us comfortable, and discourage gossip. We cannot conceal from ourselves that, privately, we are a little troubled about our uniform. It is one of our prides; it is acquainted with honor; it is familiar with great deeds and noble; we love it, we revere it; and so this errand it is on makes us uneasy. And our flag—another pride of ours, our chiefest! We have worshipped it so; and when we have seen it in far lands—glimpsing it unexpectedly in that strange sky, waving its welcome and benediction to us—we have caught our breath, and uncovered our heads, and couldn't speak, for a moment, for the thought of what it was to us and the great ideals it stood for. Indeed, we must do something about these things; we must not have the flag out there, and the uniform. They are not needed there; we can manage in some other way. England manages, as regards the uniform, and so can we. We have to send soldiers—we can't get out of that—but we can disguise them. It is the way England does in South Africa. Even Mr. Chamberlain himself takes pride in England's honorable uniform, and makes the army down there wear an ugly and odious and appropriate disguise, of yellow stuff such as quarantine flags are made of, and which are hoisted to warn the healthy away from unclean disease and repulsive death. This cloth is called khaki. We could adopt it. It is light, comfortable, grotesque, and deceives the enemy, for he cannot conceive of a soldier being concealed in it.

And as for a flag for the Philippine Province, it is easily managed. We can have a special one—our States do it: we can have just our usual flag, with the white stripes painted black and the stars replaced by the skull and cross-bones.

And we do not need that Civil Commission out there. Having no powers, it has to invent them, and that kind of work cannot be effectively done by just anybody; an expert is required. Mr. Croker can be spared.[5] We do not want the United States represented there, but only the Game. By help of these suggested amendments, Progress and Civilization in that country can have a boom, and it will take in the Persons who are Sitting in Darkness, and we can resume Business at the old stand.

1901

■ UNITED STATES CONGRESS ■

from **The Page Act**

The Page Act (1875), which restricted Chinese immigration to the U.S., was the first federal law to specify classes of people of a particular race and to

---

[5]Richard Croker (1841–1922), corrupt and powerful New York City political figure.

deny them entry into the U.S. Reflecting contemporary anti-Chinese stereotypes, the law singled out contract laborers, or "coolies," women seeking to enter "for lewd and immoral purposes" (i.e., prostitution) and people convicted of a felony or prostitution in any Northeast Asian country.

From The Page Act. FORTY-THIRD CONGRESS. SESS. II. CH. 141. 1875. CHAP. 141.-An act supplementary to the acts in relation to immigration.

Be it enacted by the Senate and House of Representatives of the United States of America in Congress assembled, That in determining whether the immigration of any subject of China, Japan, or any Oriental country, to the United States, is free and voluntary... it shall be the duty of the consul-general or consul of the United States residing at the port from which it is proposed to convey such subjects, in any vessels enrolled or licensed in the United States, or any port within the same, before delivering to the masters of any such vessels the permit or certificate provided for in such section, to ascertain whether such immigrant has entered into a contract or agreement for a term of service within the United States, for lewd and immoral purposes; and if there be such contract or agreement, the said consul-general or consul shall not deliver the required permit or certificate.

SEC. 2. That if any citizen of the United States, or other person amenable to the laws of the United States shall take, or cause to be taken or transported, to or from the United States any subject of China, Japan, or any Oriental country, without their free and voluntary consent, for the purpose of holding them to a term of service, such citizen or other person shall be liable to be indicted therefore....

SEC. 3. That the importation into the United States of women for the purposes of prostitution is hereby forbidden; and all contracts and agreements in relation thereto, made in advance or in pursuance of such illegal importation and purposes, are hereby declared void; and whoever shall knowingly and willfully import, or cause any importation of, women into the United States for the purposes of prostitution, or shall knowingly or willfully hold, or attempt to hold, any woman to such purposes, in pursuance of such illegal importation and contract or agreement, shall be deemed guilty of a felony, and, on conviction thereof, shall be imprisoned not exceeding five years and pay a fine not exceeding five thousand dollars.

SEC. 4. That if any person shall knowingly and willfully contract, or attempt to contract, in advance or in pursuance of such illegal importation, to supply to another the labor of any cooly or other person brought into the United States in violation of section two thousand one hundred and fifty-eight of the Revised Statutes, or of any other section of the laws prohibiting the cooly-trade or of this act, such person shall be deemed guilty of a felony, and, upon conviction thereof, in any United States court, shall be fined in a sum not exceeding five hundred dollars and imprisoned for a term not exceeding one year.

SEC. 5. That it shall be unlawful for aliens of the following classes to immigrate into the United States, namely, persons who are undergoing a sentence for conviction in their own country of felonious crimes other than political or growing out of or the result of such political offenses, or whose sentence has been remitted on condition of their emigration, and women "imported for the purposes of prostitution." Every vessel arriving in the United States may be inspected under the direction of the collector of the port at which it arrives, if he shall have reason to believe that any such obnoxious persons are on board; and the officer making such inspection shall certify the result thereof to the master or other person in charge of such vessel, designating in such certificate the person or persons, if any there be, ascertained by him to be of either of the classes whose importation is hereby forbidden. When such inspection is required by the collector as aforesaid, it shall be unlawful without his permission, for any alien to leave any such vessel arriving in the United States from a foreign country until the inspection shall have been had and the result certified as herein provided; and at no time thereafter shall any alien certified to by the inspecting officer as being of either of the classes whose immigration is forbidden by this section, be allowed to land in the United States, except in obedience to a judicial process issued pursuant to law. If any person shall feel aggrieved by the certificate of such inspecting officer stating him or her to be within either of the classes whose immigration is forbidden by this section, and shall apply for release or other remedy to any proper court or judge, then it shall be the duty of the collector at said port of entry to detain said vessel until a hearing and determination of the matter are had, to the end that if the said inspector shall be found to be in accordance with this section and sustained, the obnoxious person or persons shall be returned on board of said vessel, and shall not thereafter be permitted to land, unless the master, owner or consignee of the vessel shall give bond and security, to be approved by the court or judge hearing the cause, in the sum of five hundred dollars for each such person permitted to land, conditioned for the return of such person, within six months from the date thereof, to the country whence his or her emigration shall have taken place, or unless the vessel bringing such obnoxious person or persons shall be forfeited, in which event the proceeds of such forfeiture shall be paid over to the collector of the port of arrival, and applied by him, as far as necessary, to the return of such person or persons to his or her own country within the said period of six months. And for all violations of this act, the vessel, by the acts, omissions, or connivance of the owners, master, or other custodian, or the consignees of which the same are committed, shall be liable to forfeiture, and may be proceeded against as in cases of frauds against the revenue laws, for which forfeiture is prescribed by existing law.

Approved March 3, 1875.

▪ UNITED STATES CONGRESS ▪

from **Chinese Exclusion Act: An Act to Execute Certain Treaty Stipulations Relating to Chinese**

Whereas, in the opinion of the Government of the United States the coming of Chinese laborers to this country endangers the good order of certain localities within the territory thereof: Therefore,

Be it enacted by the Senate and House of Representatives of the United States of America in Congress assembled, That from and after the expiration of ninety days next after the passage of this act, and until the expiration of ten years next after the passage of this act, the coming of Chinese laborers to the United States be, and the same is hereby, suspended; and during such suspension it shall not be lawful for any Chinese laborer to come, or, having so come after the expiration of said ninety days, to remain within the United States....

That for the purpose of properly identifying Chinese laborers who were in the United States on the seventeenth day of November, eighteen hundred and eighty, or who shall have come into the same before the expiration of ninety days next after the passage of this act, and in order to furnish them with the proper evidence of their right to go from and come to the United States of their free will and accord, as provided by the treaty between the United States and China dated November 17, 1880, the collector of customs of the district from which any such Chinese laborer shall depart from the United States shall, in person or by deputy, go on board each vessel having on board any such Chinese laborer and cleared or about to sail from his district for a foreign port, and on such vessel make a list of all such Chinese laborers....

That in order to the faithful execution of articles one and two of the treaty in this act before mentioned, every Chinese person other than a laborer who may be entitled by said treaty and this act to come within the United States, and who shall be about to come to the United States, shall be identified as so entitled by the Chinese Government in each case, such identity to be evidenced by a certificate issued under the authority of said government, which certificate shall be in the English language or (if not in the English language) accompanied by a translation into English, stating such right to come, and which certificate shall state the name, title, or official rank, if any, the age, height, and all physical peculiarities, former and present occupation or profession, and place of residence in China of the person to whom the certificate is issued and that such person is entitled conformably to the treaty in this act mentioned to come within the United States....

That hereafter no State court or court of the United States shall admit Chinese to citizenship; and all laws in conflict with this act are hereby repealed.

May 6, 1882

THOMAS NAST
1840–1902

E Pluribus Unum (Except the Chinese)

E PLURIBUS UNUM (EXCEPT THE CHINESE).

EMMA LAZARUS
1849–1887

The New Colossus

Not like the brazen giant of Greek fame,
With conquering limbs astride from land to land;
Here at our sea-washed, sunset gates shall stand
A mighty woman with a torch, whose flame
Is the imprisoned lightning, and her name   5
Mother of Exiles. From her beacon-hand
Glows world-wide welcome; her mild eyes command
The air-bridged harbor that twin cities frame.
"Keep, ancient lands, your storied pomp!" cries she
With silent lips. "Give me your tired, your poor,   10
Your huddled masses yearning to breathe free,
The wretched refuse of your teeming shore.
Send these, the homeless, tempest-tost to me,
I lift my lamp beside the golden door!"

1883

THOMAS BAILEY ALDRICH
1836–1907

Unguarded Gates[1]

Wide open and unguarded stand our gates
And through them presses a wild, motley throng—
Men from the Volga and the Tartar steppes,
Featureless figures of the Hoang-Ho,
Malayan, Scythian, Teuton, Kelt, and Slav,   5
Flying the Old World's poverty and scorn;
These bringing with them unknown gods and rites,

---

[1]*The Atlantic Monthly* 75 (March 1895).

Those, tiger passions, here to stretch their claws.
In the street and alley what strange tongues are loud,
Accents of menace alien to our air,   10
Voices that once the Tower of Babel knew!

O Liberty, white Goddess! is it well
To leave the gates unguarded? On thy breast
Fold Sorrow's children, soothe the hurts of hate,
Lift the down-trodden, but with hands of steel   15
Stay those who to thy sacred portals come
To waste the gifts of freedom. Have a care
Lest from thy brow the clustered stars be torn
And trampled in the dust. For so of old
The thronging Goth and Vandal trampled Rome,   20
And where the temples of the Caesars stood
The lean wolf unmolested made her lair.

1894

FINLEY PETER DUNNE
1867–1936

Born to Irish immigrants on Chicago's West Side in 1867, Finley Peter Dunne began a career as a newspaperman in the city in 1884. After working on six different dailies, he settled in as the precocious editorial chair at the *Chicago Evening Post* in 1892. There, he imagined himself into the character of Martin Dooley, whose 750-word monologues (delivered to genial politician John McKenna or long-suffering millworker Malachi Hennessy) became a Chicago tradition. The last in a series of dialect experiments by his creator, Mr. Dooley succeeded Dunne's Colonel Malachi McNeery, a fictional downtown Chicago barkeeper who had become a popular *Post* feature during the World's Fair of 1893. Unlike the cosmopolitan McNeery, Mr. Dooley was placed on Chicago's South Side, in the Irish working-class neighborhood known as Bridgeport.

Between 1893 and 1900, when Dunne moved on to New York and a different sort of career as a satirist of our national life, some 300 Dooley pieces appeared in Chicago newspapers. Taken together, they form a coherent body of work, in which a vivid, detailed world comes into existence—that of Bridgeport, a self-contained immigrant culture with its own set of customs and ceremonies, and a social structure rooted in family, geography, and occupation.

The Chicago Dooley pieces contain valuable chunks of social history and pioneering contributions to the development of literary realism in America. Dunne takes the late-nineteenth-century journalistic phenomenon of urban local color and extends it, through his feeling for place and community, to evoke Bridgeport as the most solidly realized ethnic neighborhood in nineteenth-century American literature. He takes the realist's faith in the common man as literary subject and creates sympathetic, dignified, even heroic characters, plausibly placed in a working-class immigrant neighborhood. And finally, place, community, and character are all embodied in the vernacular voice of a sixty-year-old, smiling public-house man, the first such dialect voice to transcend the stereotypes of "stage-Irish" ethnic humor. Throughout the 1890s, Mr. Dooley gave Chicagoans a weekly example of the potential for serious fiction of common speech and everyday life. In his way, Dunne was as much a trail-blazer into the American city as a setting for literature as Theodore Dreiser or Stephen Crane. Actually, he adds a dimension lacking in the work of both of these better known writers. Unlike those archetypal lost souls in the alien city, Dreiser's Carrie Meeber and Crane's Maggie, Mr. Dooley is relatively comfortable in Bridgeport. He proves that the city can be a home.

Dunne's career took a sharp turn in 1898, when Mr. Dooley's satirical coverage of the Spanish-American War brought him to the attention of readers outside Chicago. Beginning with his scoop of "Cousin George" Dewey's victory at Manila, Mr. Dooley's reports of military and political bungling during the "splendid little war" were widely reprinted, and national syndication soon followed. By the time Dunne moved to New York in 1900, Mr. Dooley was the most popular figure in American journalism. From this point until World War I,

Dunne's gadfly mind ranged over the spectrum of newsworthy events and characters, both national and international: from Teddy Roosevelt's health fads to Andrew Carnegie's passion for libraries; from the invariable silliness of politics to society doings at Newport; from the Boer and Boxer Rebellions abroad to the so-called Negro, Indian, and immigration problems in the United States.

Mr. Dooley's perspective was consistently skeptical and critical. The salutary effect of most pieces was the exposure of affectation and hypocrisy through under-cutting humor and common sense. The most frequently quoted Dooley-isms indicate this thrust. Teddy Roosevelt's egocentric account of the Rough Riders is retitled, "Alone in Cuba." The rationale of American imperialists becomes "Hands acrost th' sea an' into somewan else's pocket." High Court solemnity is undercut with a memorable phrase: "America follows th' flag, but th' Supreme Court follows th' illiction returns." A fanatic is defined as "a man that does what he thinks th' Lord wud do if He knew th' facts iv th' case." Although he joined Ida Tarbell and Lincoln Steffens in taking over the *American Magazine* in 1906, Dunne was not himself a progressive reformer. He viewed the world as irrevocably fallen and unimprovable, and many Dooley pieces reflect their author's tendency toward fatalism. More pronounced in the early Chicago work than in the lighter national commentary, Dunne's darker side may be explained by his roots in the oppressed, colonized culture of Ireland and his journalist's education into the harsh realities of nineteenth-century urban life.

The pieces in this selection represent both Dunne's Chicago work—his pioneering realistic sketches of an urban ethnic community—and his national phase, which includes some of the best social and political commentary ever written in America.

Charles Fanning
Southern Illinois University at Carbondale

PRIMARY WORKS

Mr. Dooley in Peace and in War, 1898; *Mr. Dooley in the Hearts of His Countrymen*, 1899; *Mr. Dooley's Philosophy*, 1900; *Mr. Dooley's Opinions*, 1901; *Observations by Mr. Dooley*, 1902; *Dissertations by Mr. Dooley*, 1906; *Mr. Dooley Says*, 1910; *Mr. Dooley on Making a Will and Other Necessary Evils*, 1919; *Mr. Dooley and the Chicago Irish*, ed. Charles Fanning, 1987.

The Wanderers

[Mr. Dooley's version of the archetypal crossing narrative balances humor and pathos in a memorable short piece, a prose poem of the trauma of immigration by sea.

Dunne attempts to render Mr. Dooley's Irish brogue or accent by spelling words phonetically. Here is a brief key to some words he uses that may confuse a contemporary American reader: *iv* = of; *dure* = door; *sthrapping* = strapping; *dhrink* = drink; *say* = sea; *aise* = ease; *ivry* = every; *on'y* = only.]

"Poor la-ads, poor la-ads," said Mr. Dooley, putting aside his newspaper and rubbing his glasses. "'Tis a hard lot theirs, thim that go down into th' say in ships, as Shakespeare says. Ye niver see a storm on th' ocean? Iv coorse ye didn't. How cud ye, ye that was born away fr'm home? But I have, Jawn. May th' saints save me fr'm another! I come over in th' bowels iv a big crazy balloon iv a propeller, like wan iv thim ye see hooked up to Dempsey's dock, loaded with lumber an' slabs an' Swedes. We watched th' little ol' island fadin' away behind us, with th' sun sthrikin' th' white house-tops iv Queens-town[1] an' lightin' up th' chimbleys iv Martin Hogan's liquor store. Not wan iv us but had left near all we loved behind, an' sare a chance that we'd iver spoon th' stirabout out iv th' pot above th' ol' peat fire again. Yes, by dad, there was wan,—a lad fr'm th' County Roscommon.[2] Divvle th' tear he shed. But, whin we had parted fr'm land, he turns to me, an' says, 'Well, we're on our way,' he says. 'We are that,' says I. 'No chanst f'r thim to turn around an' go back,' he says. 'Divvle th' fut,' says I. 'Thin,' he says, raisin' his voice, 'to 'ell with th' Prince iv Wales,'[3] he says. 'To 'ell with him' he says.

"An' that was th' last we see of sky or sun f'r six days. That night come up th' divvle's own storm. Th' waves tore an' walloped th' ol' boat, an' th' wind howled, an' ye cud hear th' machinery snortin' beyant. Murther, but I was sick. Wan time th' ship 'd be settin' on its tail, another it'd be standin' on its head, thin rollin' over cow-like on th' side; an' ivry time it lurched me stummick lurched with it, an' I was tore an' rint an' racked till, if death come, it 'd found me willin'. An' th' Roscommon man,—glory be, but he was disthressed. He set on th' flure, with his hands on his belt an' his face as white as stone, an' rocked to an' fro. 'Ahoo,' he says, 'ahoo, but me insides has torn loose,' he says, 'an' are tumblin' around,' he says. 'Say a pather an' avy,'[4] says I, I was that mad f'r th' big bosthoon[5] f'r his blatherin' on th' flure. 'Say a pather an' avy,' I says; 'f'r ye're near to death's dure, avick.[6]' 'Am I?' says he, raising up. 'Thin,' he says, 'to 'ell with the whole rile fam'ly,' he says. Oh, he was a rebel!

"Through th' storm there was a babby cryin'. 'Twas a little wan, no more thin a year ol'; an' 'twas owned be a Tipp'rary man[7] who come fr'm near Clonmel,[8] a poor, weak, scarey-lookin' little divvle that lost his wife, an' see th' bailiff walk off with th' cow, an' thin see him come back again with th' process servers. An' so he was comin' over with th' babby, an' bein' mother an' father to it. He'd rock it be th' hour on his knees, an' talk dam nonsense to it, an' sing it songs, 'Aha, 'twas there I met a maiden down be th' tanyard side,' an' 'Th' Wicklow Mountaineer,' an' 'Th' Rambler fr'm Clare,' an' 'O'Donnel Aboo,'[9] croonin' thim in th' little babby's ears, an' payin' no attintion to th' poorin' thunder above his head, day an' night, day an' night, poor

---

[1] Harbor village outside Cork City from which emigrant ships embarked. Original name was Cobh; renamed by the British in honor of Queen Victoria. Now called Cobh again.
[2] Irish county in the west midlands.
[3] Member of British royal family, traditionally heir to the throne.
[4] A Pater Noster (Our Father) and an Ave Maria (Hail Mary).

[5] A blunderer (Irish).
[6] My son (Irish).
[7] A man from County Tipperary in the southeast of Ireland.
[8] A town in County Tipperary.
[9] Traditional Irish songs.

soul. An' th' babby cryin' out his heart, an' him settin' there with his eyes as red as his hair, an' makin' no kick, poor soul.

"But wan day th' ship settled down steady, an' ragin' stummicks with it; an' th' Roscommon man shakes himself, an' says, 'to 'ell with th' Prince iv Wales an' th' Dook iv Edinboroo,'[10] an' goes out. An' near all th' steerage followed; f'r th' storm had done its worst, an' gone on to throuble those that come afther, an' may th' divvle go with it. 'Twill be rest f'r that little Tipp'rary man; f'r th' waves was r-runnin' low an' peaceful, an' th' babby have sthopped cryin'.

"He had been settin' on a stool, but he come over to me. 'Th' storm,' says I, 'is over.' 'Yis,' says he, "tis over.' 'Twas wild while it lasted,' says I. 'Ye may say so,' says he. 'Well, please Gawd,' says I, 'that it left none worse off thin us.' 'It blew ill f'r some an' aise f'r others,' says he. 'Th' babby is gone.'

"An' so it was, Jawn, f'r all his rockin' an' singin'. An' in th' avnin' they burried it over th' side into th' say, an' th' little Tipp'rary man wint up an' see them do it. He see them do it."

1895

The Popularity of Firemen

[A Chicago fire-fighting tragedy prompted this piece that opens with
Mr. Dooley naming the four firemen who had died the day before in a
downtown factory and warehouse blaze.]

"O'Donnell, Sherrick, Downs, Prendergast," Mr. Dooley repeated slowly. "Poor laads. Poor la-ads. Plaze Gawd, they wint to th' long home like thrue min. 'Tis good to read th' names, Jawn. Thanks be, we're not all in th' council.

"I knowed a man be th' name iv Clancy wanst, Jawn. He was fr'm th' County May-o,[1] but a good man f'r all that; an' whin he'd growed to be a big, sthrappin' fellow, he wint on to th' fire departmint. They'se an Irishman 'r two on th' fire departmint an' in th' army, too, Jawn, though ye'd think be hearin' some talk they was all runnin' prim'ries an' thryin' to be cinthral comitymen.[2] So ye wud. Ye niver hear iv thim on'y whin they die; an' thin, murther, what funerals they have!

"Well, this Clancy wint on th' fire departmint, an' they give him a place in thruck twinty-three. All th' r-road was proud iv him, an' faith he was proud iv himsilf. He r-rode free on th' sthreet ca-ars, an' was th' champeen handball player f'r miles around. Ye shud see him goin' down th' sthreet, with his blue shirt an' his blue coat with th' buttons on it, an' his cap on his ear. But ne'er a cap or coat'd he wear whin they was a fire. He might be shiv'rin' be th' stove in th' ingine house with a buffalo robe over his head; but, whin th' gong sthruck, 'twas off with coat an' cap an' buffalo robe, an' out come me brave Clancy, bare-headed an' bare hand, dhrivin' with wan line an' spillin' th' hose cart on wan wheel at ivry jump iv th' horse. Did anny wan iver see a fireman

---

[10]Member of British royalty.

[1]Irish county on the west coast.

[2]Central committeeman; an important post in the ward system of city government.

with his coat on or a polisman with his off? Why, wanst, whin Clancy was standin' up f'r Grogan's eighth,[3] his son come runnin' in to tell him they was a fire in Vogel's packin' house. He dhropped th' kid at Father Kelly's feet, an' whipped off his long coat an' wint tearin' f'r th' dure, kickin' over th' poorbox an' buttin' ol' Mis' O'Neill that'd come in to say th' stations. 'Twas lucky 'twas wan iv th' Grogans. They're a fine family f'r falls. Jawn Grogan was wurrukin' on th' top iv Metzri an' O'Connell's brewery wanst, with a man be th' name iv Dorsey. He slipped an' fell wan hundherd feet. Whin they come to see if he was dead, he got up, an' says he: 'Lave me at him.' 'At who?' says they. 'He's deliryous,' they says. 'At Dorsey,' says Grogan. 'He thripped me.' So it didn't hurt Grogan's eighth to fall four 'r five feet.

"Well, Clancy wint to fires an' fires. Whin th' big organ facthry burnt, he carrid th' hose up to th' fourth story an' was squirtin' whin th' walls fell. They dug him out with pick an' shovel, an' he come up fr'm th' brick an' boards an' saluted th' chief. 'Clancy,' says th' chief, 'ye betther go over an' get a dhrink.' He did so, Jawn. I heerd it. An' Clancy was that proud!

"Whin th' Hogan flats on Halsted Sthreet[4] took fire, they got all th' people out but wan; an' she was a woman asleep on th' fourth flure. 'Who'll go up?' says Bill Musham. 'Sure, sir,' says Clancy. 'I'll go'; an' up he wint. His captain was a man be th' name iv O'Connell, fr'm th' County Kerry;[5] an' he had his fut on th' ladder whin Clancy started. Well, th' good man wint into th' smoke, with his wife faintin' down below. 'He'll be kilt,' says his brother. 'Ye don't know him,' says Bill Musham. An' sure enough, whin ivry wan'd give him up, out comes me brave Clancy, as black as a Turk, with th' girl in his arms. Th' others wint up like monkeys, but he shtud wavin' thim off, an' come down th' ladder face forward. 'Where'd ye larn that?' says Bill Musham. 'I seen a man do it at th' Lyceem[6] whin I was a kid,' says Clancy. 'Was it all right?' 'I'll have ye up before th' ol' man,' says Bill Musham. 'I'll teach ye to come down a laddher as if ye was in a quadhrille, ye horse-stealin', ham-sthringin' May-o man,' he says. But he didn't. Clancy wint over to see his wife. 'O Mike,' says she, "twas fine,' she says. 'But why d'ye take th' risk?' she says. 'Did ye see th' captain?' he says with a scowl. 'He wanted to go. Did ye think I'd follow a Kerry man with all th' ward lukkin' on?' he says.

"Well, so he wint dhrivin' th' hose-cart on wan wheel, an' jumpin' whin he heerd a man so much as hit a glass to make it ring. All th' people looked up to him, an' th' kids followed him down th' sthreet; an' 'twas th' gr-reatest priv'lige f'r anny wan f'r to play dominos with him near th' joker. But about a year ago he come in to see me, an' says he, 'Well, I'm goin' to quit.' 'Why,' says I, 'ye'er a young man yet,' I says. 'Faith,' he says, 'look at me hair,' he says,—'young heart, ol' head. I've been at it these twinty year, an' th' good woman's wantin' to see more iv me thin blowin' into a saucer iv coffee,' he says. 'I'm goin' to

---

[3] Being a godfather at a new child's baptism in church.

[4] A major north-south Chicago street and one of the main streets in the Bridgeport neighborhood.

[5] Irish county on the southwest coast.

[6] Lyceum; a hall in which public performances are presented.

quit,' he says, 'on'y I want to see wan more good fire,' he says. 'A rale good ol' hot wan,' he says, 'with th' win' blowin' f'r it an' a good dhraft in th' ilivator-shaft, an' about two stories, with pitcher-frames an' gasoline an' excelsior, an' to hear th' chief yellin': "Play 'way, sivinteen. What th' hell an' damnation are ye standin' aroun' with that pipe f'r? Is this a fire 'r a dam livin' pitcher? I'll break ivry man iv eighteen, four, six, an' chem'cal five to-morra mornin' befure breakfast." Oh,' he says, bringin' his fist down, 'wan more, an' I'll quit.'

"An' he did, Jawn. Th' day th' Carpenter Brothers' box factory burnt. 'Twas wan iv thim big, fine-lookin' buildings that pious men built out iv cel-luloid an' plasther iv Paris. An' Clancy was wan iv th' men undher whin th' wall fell. I seen thim bringin' him home; an' th' little woman met him at th' dure, rumplin' her apron in her hands."

1895

The Piano in the Parlor

[In 1890 Edward Harrigan produced a popular musical, *Reilly and the Four Hundred,* about the social pretensions of the "lace curtain" Irish of the new middle class. The show's hit song applies to this Dooley piece: "There's an organ in the parlor, to give the house a tone,/ And you're welcome every evening at Maggie Murphy's home." Here the family conflict between traditional Irish music and tonier classical music indicates the gulf between old and new ways.]

"Ol' man Donahue bought Molly a pianny las' week," Mr. Dooley said in the course of his conversation with Mr. McKenna. "She'd been takin' lessons fr'm a Dutchman down th' sthreet, an' they say she can play as aisy with her hands crossed as she can with wan finger. She's been whalin' away iver since, an' Donahue is dhrinkin' again.

"Ye see th' other night some iv th' la-ads wint over f'r to see whether they cud smash his table in a frindly game iv forty-fives. I don't know what possessed Donahue. He niver asked his frinds into the parlor befure. They used to set in th' dining-room; an', whin Mrs. Donahue coughed at iliven o'clock, they'd toddle out th' side dure with their hats in their hands. But this here night, whether 'twas that Donahue had taken on a tub or two too much or not, he asked thim all in th' front room, where Mrs. Donahue was settin' with Molly. 'I've brought me frinds,' he says, 'f'r to hear Molly take a fall out iv th' music-box,' he says. 'Let me have ye'er hat, Mike,' he says. 'Ye'll not feel it whin ye go out,' he says.

"At anny other time Mrs. Donahue'd give him th' marble heart. But they wasn't a man in th' party that had a pianny to his name, an' she knew they'd be throuble whin they wint home an' tould about it. "Tis a melodjious insthrument,' says she. 'I cud sit here be the hour an' listen to Bootoven and Choochooski,'[1] she says.

---

[1]Beethoven and Tchaikovsky, composers.

"'What did thim write?' says Cassidy. 'Chunes,'[2] says Donahue, 'chunes. Molly,' he says, 'fetch 'er th' wallop to make th' gintlemen feel good,' he says. 'What'll it be, la-ads?' 'D'ye know "The Rambler fr'm Clare"?'[3] says Slavin. 'No,' says Molly. 'It goes like this,' says Slavin. 'A-ah, din yadden, yooden a-yadden, arrah yadden ay-a.' 'I dinnaw it,' says th' girl. "Tis a low chune, annyhow,' says Mrs. Donahue. 'Misther Slavin ividintly thinks he's at a polis picnic,' she says. 'I'll have no come-all-ye's in this house,' she says. 'Molly, give us a few ba-ars fr'm Wagner.'[4] 'What Wagner's that?' says Flanagan. 'No wan ye know,' says Donahue; 'he's a German musician.' 'Thim Germans is hot people fr music,' says Cassidy. 'I knowed wan that cud play th' "Wacht am Rhine"[5] on a pair iv cymbals,' he says. 'Whisht!' says Donahue. 'Give th' girl a chanst.'

"Slavin tol' me about it. He says he niver heerd th' like in his born days. He says she fetched th' pianny two or three wallops that made Cassidy jump out iv his chair, an' Cassidy has charge iv th' steam whistle at th' quarry at that. She wint at it as though she had a gredge at it. First 'twas wan hand an' thin th' other, thin both hands, knuckles down; an' it looked, says Slavin, as if she was goin' to leap into th' middle iv it with both feet, whin Donahue jumps up. 'Hol' on!' he says. 'That's not a rented pianny, ye daft girl,' he says. 'Why, pap-pah,' says Molly, 'what d'ye mean?' she says. 'That's Wag-ner,' she says. "Tis th' music iv th' future,' she says. 'Yes,' says Donahue, 'but I don't want me hell on earth. I can wait fr it,' he says, 'with th' kind per-mission iv Mrs. Donahue,' he says. 'Play us th' "Wicklow Mountaineer,"'[6] he says, 'an' threat th' masheen kindly,' he says. 'She'll play no "Wicklow Moun-taineer,"' says Mrs. Donahue. 'If ye want to hear that kind iv chune, ye can go down to Finucane's Hall,'[7] she says, 'an' call in Crowley, th' blind piper,' she says. 'Molly,' she says, 'give us wan iv thim Choochooski things,' she says. 'They're so ginteel.'

"With that Donahue rose up. 'Come on,' says he. 'This is no place fr us,' he says. Slavin, with th' politeness iv a man who's gettin' even, turns at th' dure. 'I'm sorry I can't remain,' he says. 'I think th' wurruld an' all iv Choo-chooski,' he says. 'Me brother used to play his chunes,' he says,—'me brother Mike, that run th' grip ca-ar,' he says. 'But there's wan thing missin' fr'm Molly's playin',' he says. 'And what may that be?' says Mrs. Donahue. 'An ax,' says Slavin, backin' out.

"So Donahue has took to dhrink."

1895

---

[2]Tunes (dialect).
[3]Traditional Irish song.
[4]Richard Wagner, German composer (1813–1883).
[5]Popular German patriotic anthem.

[6]Traditional Irish song.
[7]A real hall in the Bridgeport neighborhood where many public meetings were held. Owned by the Finucane family.

Immigration

[Senator Henry Cabot Lodge was a vocal advocate of immigration restrictions. As a first step in this direction, he proposed a literacy test for immigrants as early as 1896.]

"Well, I see Congress has got to wurruk again," said Mr. Dooley.

"The Lord save us fr'm harm," said Mr. Hennessy.

"Yes, sir," said Mr. Dooley, "Congress has got to wurruk again, an' manny things that seems important to a Congressman 'll be brought up befure thim. 'Tis sthrange that what's a big thing to a man in Wash'nton, Hinnissy, don't seem much account to me. Divvle a bit do I care whether they dig th' Nicaragoon Canal[1] or cross th' Isthmus in a balloon; or whether th' Monroe docthrine[2] is enfoorced or whether it ain't; or whether th' thrusts is abolished as Teddy Rosenfelt wud like to have thim or encouraged to go on with their neefaryous but magnificent entherprises as th' Prisidint wud like; or whether th' water is poured into th' ditches to reclaim th' arid lands iv th' West or th' money f'r thim to fertilize th' arid pocket-books iv th' conthractors; or whether th' Injun is threated like a depindant an' miserable thribesman or like a free an' indepindant dog; or whether we restore th' merchant marine to th' ocean or whether we lave it to restore itsilf. None iv these here questions inthrests me, an' be me I mane you an' be you I mane ivrybody. What we want to know is, ar-re we goin' to have coal enough in th' hod whin th' cold snap comes; will th' plumbin' hold out, an' will th' job last.

"But they'se wan question that Congress is goin' to take up that you an' me are intherested in. As a pilgrim father that missed th' first boats, I must raise me claryon voice again' th' invasion iv this fair land be th' paupers an' arnychists iv effete Europe. Ye bet I must—because I'm here first. 'Twas diff'rent whin I was dashed high on th' stern an' rockbound coast. In thim days America was th' refuge iv th' oppressed iv all th' wurruld. They cud come over here an' do a good job iv oppressin' thimsilves. As I told ye I come a little late. Th' Rosenfelts an' th' Lodges[3] bate me be at laste a boat lenth, an' be th' time I got here they was stern an' rockbound thimsilves. So I got a gloryous rayciption as soon as I was towed off th' rocks. Th' stars an' sthripes whispered a welcome in th' breeze an' a shovel was thrust into me hand an' I was pushed into a sthreet excyvatin' as though I'd been born here. Th' pilgrim father who bossed th' job was a fine ol' puritan be th' name iv Doherty, who come over in th' Mayflower about th' time iv th' potato rot in Wexford, an' he made me think they was a hole in th' breakwather iv th'

---

[1] In 1901 a U.S. Canal Commission decided that a route through Nicaragua was the most practical. In 1903 the route through the Isthmus of Panama was chosen instead. Work on the Panama Canal began in 1905.

[2] President James Monroe in 1823 declared U.S. opposition to European political interference in the Americas.

[3] Powerful Massachusetts political family. Henry Cabot Lodge (1850–1924) was a U.S. Senator during this period who supported immigration restriction.

haven iv refuge an' some iv th' wash iv th' seas iv opprission had got through. He was a stern an' rockbound la-ad himsilf, but I was a good hand at loose stones an' wan day—but I'll tell ye about that another time.

"Annyhow, I was rayceived with open arms that sometimes ended in a clinch. I was afraid I wasn't goin' to assimilate with th' airlyer pilgrim fathers an' th' instichoochions iv th' counthry, but I soon found that a long swing iv th' pick made me as good as another man an' it didn't require a greart intellect, or sometimes anny at all, to vote th' dimmycrat ticket, an' befure I was here a month, I felt enough like a native born American to burn a witch. Wanst in a while a mob iv intilligint collajeens, whose grandfathers had bate me to th' dock, wud take a shy at me Pathrick's Day procission[4] or burn down wan iv me churches, but they got tired iv that befure long; 'twas too much like wurruk.

"But as I tell ye, Hinnissy, 'tis diff'rent now. I don't know why 'tis diff'rent but 'tis diff'rent. 'Tis time we put our back again' th' open dure an' keep out th' savage horde. If that cousin iv ye'ers expects to cross, he'd betther tear f'r th' ship. In a few minyits th' gates 'll be down an' whin th' oppressed wurruld comes hikin' acrost to th' haven iv refuge, they'll do well to put a couplin' pin undher their hats, f'r th' Goddess iv Liberty 'll meet thim at th' dock with an axe in her hand. Congress is goin' to fix it. Me frind Shaughnessy says so. He was in yisterdah an' says he: "Tis time we done something to make th' immigration laws sthronger,' says he. 'Thrue f'r ye, Miles Standish,'[5] says I; 'but what wud ye do?' 'I'd keep out th' offscourin's iv Europe,' says he. 'Wud ye go back?' says I. 'Have ye'er joke,' says he. "Tis not so seeryus as it was befure ye come,' says I. 'But what ar-re th' immygrants doin' that's roonous to us?' I says. 'Well,' says he, 'they're arnychists,'[6] he says; 'they don't assymilate with th' counthry,' he says. 'Maybe th' counthry's digestion has gone wrong fr'm too much rich food,' says I; 'perhaps now if we'd lave off thryin' to digest Rockyfellar an' thry a simple diet like Schwartzmeister, we wudden't feel th' effects iv our vittels,' I says. 'Maybe if we'd season th' immygrants a little or cook thim thurly, they'd go down betther,' I says.

"'They're arnychists, like Parsons,'[7] he says. 'He wud've been an immygrant if Texas hadn't been admitted to th' Union,' I says. 'Or Snolgosh,'[8] he says. 'Has Mitchigan seceded?' I says. 'Or Gittoo,'[9] he says. 'Who come fr'm th' effete monarchies iv Chicago, west iv Ashland Av'noo,'[10] I says. 'Or what's-his-name, Wilkes Booth,'[11] he says. 'I don't know what he was—

[4]Oppose the St. Patrick's Day parade by force.
[5]A military and political leader of the 1620 Pilgrim settlement at Plymouth, Massachusetts.
[6]Anarchists. A late nineteenth-century movement holding the belief that the political state should be abolished and that society should be governed by voluntary groups. The movement's violent wing came to the fore in the 1886 Haymarket Square bombing in Chicago and in the 1901 assassination of President William McKinley.

[7]Albert Parsons, American anarchist, hanged for his role in the Haymarket bombing in which seven policemen died.
[8]Leon Czolgosz, anarchist and the assassin of President McKinley in September 1901.
[9]Charles J. Guiteau, a disappointed office-seeker who fatally wounded President James A. Garfield in July 1881.
[10]Ashland Avenue, a major Chicago north-south street.
[11]John Wilkes-Booth, assassin of President Abraham Lincoln in 1865.

maybe a Boolgharyen,' says I. 'Well, annyhow,' says he, 'they're th' scum iv th' earth.' 'They may be that,' says I; 'but we used to think they was th' cream iv civilization,' I says. 'They're off th' top annyhow. I wanst believed 'twas th' best men iv Europe come here, th' la-ads that was too sthrong and indipindant to be kicked around be a boorgomasther at home an' wanted to dig out f'r a place where they cud get a chanst to make their way to th' money. I see their sons fightin' into politics an' their daughters tachin' young American idee how to shoot too high in th' public school, an' I thought they was all right. But I see I was wrong. Thim boys out there towin' wan heavy foot afther th' other to th' rowlin' mills is all arnychists. There's warrants out f'r all names endin' in 'inski, an' I think I'll board up me windows, f'r,' I says, 'if immygrants is as dangerous to this counthry as ye an' I an' other pilgrim fathers believe they are, they'se enough iv thim sneaked in already to make us aborigines about as infloointial as the prohibition vote in th' Twenty-ninth Ward.[12] They'll dash again' our stern an' rock-bound coast till they bust it,' says I.

"'But I ain't so much afraid as ye ar-re. I'm not afraid iv me father an' I'm not afraid iv mesilf. An' I'm not afraid iv Schwartzmeister's father or Hinnery Cabin Lodge's grandfather. We all come over th' same way, an' if me ancestors were not what Hogan calls rigicides, 'twas not because they were not ready an' willin', on'y a king niver come their way. I don't believe in killin' kings, mesilf. I niver wud've sawed th' block off that curly-headed potintate that I see in th' pitchers down town, but, be hivins, Presarved Codfish Shaughnessy,[13] if we'd begun a few years ago shuttin' out folks that wudden't mind handin' a bomb to a king, they wudden't be enough people in Mattsachoosetts to make a quorum f'r th' Anti-Impeeryal S'ciety,' says I. 'But what wud ye do with th' offscourin' iv Europe?' says he. 'I'd scour thim some more,' says I.

"An' so th' meetin' iv th' Plymouth Rock Assocyation come to an end. But if ye wud like to get it together, Deacon Hinnissy, to discuss th' immygration question, I'll sind out a hurry call f'r Schwartzmeister[14] an' Mulcahey an' Ignacio Sbarbaro an' Nels Larsen an' Petrus Gooldvink, an' we 'll gather to-night at Fanneilnoviski Hall[15] at th' corner iv Sheridan an' Sigel sthreets. All th' pilgrim fathers is rayquested f'r to bring interpreters."

"Well," said Mr. Hennessy, "divvle th' bit I care, on'y I'm here first, an' I ought to have th' right to keep th' bus fr'm bein' overcrowded."

"Well," said Mr. Dooley, "as a pilgrim father on me gran' nephew's side, I don't know but ye're right. An' they'se wan sure way to keep thim out."

"What's that?" asked Mr. Hennessy.

"Teach thim all about our instichoochions befure they come," said Mr. Dooley.

1902

<hr>

[12] Voters in favor of the amendment prohibiting sale of alcoholic beverages.

[13] A playful juxtaposition of parodic WASP names with an Irish last name.

[14] A mix of names illustrating the ethnic diversity of Chicago.

[15] Connotes the Europeanization of Faneuil Hall, the Boston cradle of liberty.

■ EDITH MAUD EATON (SUI SIN FAR) ■
1865–1914

Between the late 1890s and 1914, short stories and articles signed "Sui Sin Far" appeared in such popular and prominent national magazines as *Overland, Century,* the *Independent, Good Housekeeping,* and *New England Magazine,* and Americans of Chinese ancestry began to have a literary voice in the United States. Hatred and fear of the Chinese had spread throughout the nation, culminating in the Chinese Exclusion Act of 1882. The courageous pen of Sui Sin Far, the first person of Chinese ancestry to write in defense of the Chinese in America, countered beliefs widely held at the time that the Chinese were unassimilable, morally corrupt, and corrupting. Sui Sin Far demonstrated that the Chinese were human, like everyone else, but victimized by the laws of the land.

Born in Macclesfield, England, in 1865, Edith Maud Eaton was the eldest daughter and second child of fourteen surviving children of an unusual and romantic couple: Grace Trefusius, a Chinese woman adopted by an English couple and reared in England, and Edward Eaton, an Englishman and struggling landscape painter. According to *Me,* the autobiography of Edith's sister, novelist Winnifred Eaton, who used the pseudonym Onoto Watanna, the Eaton household was bohemian artistic and poverty-stricken, offering fertile ground for self-expression. Their mother read them Tennyson's *Idylls of the King,* and the children would act out the characters. Artistic endeavors, as well as early financial independence, were encouraged. While still in their teens, Edith and Winnifred began publishing poems, stories, and articles for the local newspaper, becoming the first Asian American writers of fiction.

Edith Eaton's autobiographical essay, "Leaves from the Mental Portfolio of an Eurasian," focuses on the education in race relations of an Eurasian in Caucasian-dominated societies. The essay emphasizes the pain endured by a person considered socially unacceptable on two counts: her race and her single state. Yet the essay also reveals her courageous spirit: her willingness to confront wrongs done to herself and others and to right those wrongs. Though her facial features did not betray her ancestry, Edith boldly asserted her Chinese identity. Though single women were mocked, she remained unmarried, channeling her energies and her income into the care of her numerous siblings and of Chinese people in need. Her stories were collected in one volume, *Mrs. Spring Fragrance,* originally published in 1912 and recently reprinted. Set in Seattle or San Francisco, these stories show the struggles and joys in the daily lives of Chinese families in North America. Particularly poignant are the stories delineating the cultural conflicts of Eurasians and recent immigrants. In the ironically titled "In the Land of the Free," Sui Sin Far shows the suffering caused by discriminatory immigration laws, while "The Wisdom of the New" contemplates the personal and cultural consequences for those who are accepted as immigrants.

Edith Eaton died April 7, 1914, in Montreal and is buried in the Protestant Cemetery there. In gratitude for her work on their behalf, the Chinese community erected a special headstone on her tomb inscribed with the characters "Yi bu wang hua" ("The righteous one does not forget China").

Amy Ling
Late of University of Wisconsin, Madison

King-Kok Cheung
University of California, Los Angeles

Dominika Ferens
University of Wroclaw, Poland

PRIMARY WORKS

"Leaves from the Mental Portfolio of an Eurasian," *Independent* (January 21, 1909), 125–132; "The Persecution and Oppression of Me," *Independent* (August 24, 1911), 421–424; *Mrs. Spring Fragrance* (1912, 1995).

Leaves from the Mental Portfolio of an Eurasian

When I look back over the years I see myself, a little child of scarcely four years of age, walking in front of my nurse, in a green English lane, and listening to her tell another of her kind that my mother is Chinese. "Oh, Lord!" exclaims the informed. She turns me around and scans me curiously from head to foot. Then the two women whisper together. Tho the word "Chinese" conveys very little meaning to my mind, I feel that they are talking about my father and mother and my heart swells with indignation. When we reach home I rush to my mother and try to tell her what I have heard. I am a young child. I fail to make myself intelligible. My mother does not understand, and when the nurse declares to her, "Little Miss Sui is a story-teller," my mother slaps me.

Many a long year has past over my head since that day—the day on which I first learned that I was something different and apart from other children, but tho my mother has forgotten it, I have not.

I see myself again, a few years older. I am playing with another child in a garden. A girl passes by outside the gate. "Mamie," she cries to my companion. "I wouldn't speak to Sui if I were you. Her mamma is Chinese."

"I don't care," answers the little one beside me. And then to me, "Even if your mamma is Chinese, I like you better than I like Annie."

"But I don't like you," I answer, turning my back on her. It is my first conscious lie.

I am at a children's party, given by the wife of an Indian officer whose children were schoolfellows of mine. I am only six years of age, but have attended a private school for over a year, and have already learned that China is a heathen country, being civilized by England. However, for the time being, I am a merry romping child. There are quite a number of grown people present. One, a white haired old man, has his attention called to me by the hostess. He adjusts his eyeglasses and surveys me critically. "Ah, indeed!" he exclaims, "Who would have thought it at first glance. Yet now I see the difference between her and other children. What a peculiar coloring! Her mother's eyes and hair and her father's features, I presume. Very interesting little creature!"

I had been called from my play for the purpose of inspection. I do not return to it. For the rest of the evening I hide myself behind a hall door and refuse to show myself until it is time to go home.

My parents have come to America. We are in Hudson City, N.Y., and we are very poor. I am out with my brother, who is ten months older than myself. We pass a Chinese store, the door of which is open. "Look!" says Charlie, "Those men in there are Chinese!" Eagerly I gaze into the long low room. With the exception of my mother, who is English bred with English ways and manner of dress, I have never seen a Chinese person. The two men within the store are uncouth specimens of their race, drest in working blouses and pantaloons with queues hanging down their backs. I recoil with a sense of shock.

"Oh, Charlie," I cry, "Are we like that?"

"Well, we're Chinese, and they're Chinese, too, so we must be!" returns my seven-year-old brother.

"Of course you are," puts in a boy who has followed us down the street, and who lives near us and has seen my mother: "Chinky, Chinky, Chinaman, yellow-face, pigtail, rat-eater." A number of other boys and several little girls join in with him.

"Better than you," shouts my brother, facing the crowd. He is younger and smaller than any there, and I am even more insignificant than he; but my spirit revives.

"I'd rather be Chinese than anything else in the world," I scream.

They pull my hair, they tear my clothes, they scratch my face, and all but lame my brother; but the white blood in our veins fights valiantly for the Chinese half of us. When it is all over, exhausted and bedraggled, we crawl home, and report to our mother that we have "won the battle."

"Are you sure?" asks my mother doubtfully.

"Of course. They ran from us. They were frightened," returns my brother.

My mother smiles with satisfaction.

"Do you hear?" she asks my father.

"Umm," he observes, raising his eyes from his paper for an instant. My childish instinct, however, tells me that he is more interested than he appears to be.

It is tea time, but I cannot eat. Unobserved I crawl away. I do not sleep that night. I am too excited and I ache all over. Our opponents had been so very much stronger and bigger than we. Toward morning, however, I fall into a doze from which I awake myself, shouting:

> *Sound the battle cry;*
> *See the foe is nigh.*

My mother believes in sending us to Sunday school. She has been brought up in a Presbyterian college.

The scene of my life shifts to Eastern Canada. The sleigh which has carried us from the station stops in front of a little French Canadian hotel. Immediately we are surrounded by a number of villagers, who stare curiously at my mother as my father assists her to alight from the sleigh. Their curiosity, however, is tempered with kindness, as they watch, one after another, the little black heads of my brothers and sisters and myself emerge out of the buffalo robe, which is part of the sleigh's outfit. There are six of us, four girls and two boys; the eldest, my brother, being only seven years of age. My father and mother are still in their twenties. "Les pauvres enfants," the inhabitants murmur, as they help to carry us into the hotel. Then in lower tones: "Chinoise, Chinoise."

For some time after our arrival, whenever we children are sent for a walk, our footsteps are dogged by a number of young French and English Canadians, who amuse themselves with speculations as to whether, we being Chinese, are susceptible to pinches and hair pulling, while older persons pause and gaze upon us, very much in the same way that I have seen people gaze upon strange animals in a menagerie. Now and then we are stopt and plied with questions as to what we eat and drink, how we go to sleep, if my mother understands what my father says to her, if we sit on chairs or squat on floors, etc., etc., etc.

There are many pitched battles, of course, and we seldom leave the house without being armed for conflict. My mother takes a great interest in our battles, and usually cheers us on, tho I doubt whether she understands the depth of the troubled waters thru which her little children wade. As to my father, peace is his motto, and he deems it wisest to be blind and deaf to many things.

School days are short, but memorable. I am in the same class with my brother, my sister next to me in the class below. The little girl whose desk my sister shares shrinks close against the wall as my sister takes her place. In a little while she raises her hand.

"Please, teacher!"

"Yes, Annie."

"May I change my seat?"

"No, you may not!"

The little girl sobs. "Why should she have to sit beside a———"

Happily my sister does not seem to hear, and before long the two little girls become great friends. I have many such experiences.

My brother is remarkably bright; my sister next to me has a wonderful head for figures, and when only eight years of age helps my father with his night work accounts. My parents compare her with me. She is of sturdier build than I, and, as my father says, "Always has her wits about her." He thinks her more like my mother, who is very bright and interested in every little detail of practical life. My father tells me that I will never make half the woman that my mother is or that my sister will be. I am not as strong as my sisters, which makes me feel somewhat ashamed, for I am the eldest little girl, and more is expected of me. I have no organic disease, but the strength of my feelings seems to take from me the strength of my body. I am prostrated at times with attacks of nervous sickness. The doctor says that my heart is unusually large; but in the light of the present I know that the cross of the Eurasian bore too heavily upon my childish shoulders. I usually hide my weakness from the family until I cannot stand. I do not understand myself, and I have an idea that the others will despise me for not being as strong as they. Therefore, I like to wander away alone, either by the river or in the bush. The green fields and flowing water have a charm for me. At the age of seven, as it is today, a bird on the wing is my emblem of happiness.

I have come from a race on my mother's side which is said to be the most stolid and insensible to feeling of all races, yet I look back over the years and see myself so keenly alive to every shade of sorrow and suffering that it is almost a pain to live.

If there is any trouble in the house in the way of a difference between my father and mother, or if any child is punished, how I suffer! And when harmony is restored, heaven seems to be around me. I can be sad, but I can also be glad. My mother's screams of agony when a baby is born almost drive me wild, and long after her pangs have subsided I feel them in my own body. Sometimes it is a week before I can get to sleep after such an experience.

A debt owing by my father fills me with shame. I feel like a criminal when I pass the creditor's door. I am only ten years old. And all the while the question of nationality perplexes my little brain. Why are we what we are? I and my brothers and sisters. Why did God make us to be hooted and stared at? Papa is English, mamma is Chinese. Why couldn't we have been either one thing or the other? Why is my mother's race despised? I look into the faces of my father and mother. Is she not every bit as dear and good as he? Why? Why? She sings us the songs she learned at her English school. She tells us tales of China. Tho a child when she left her native land she remembers it well, and I am never tired of listening to the story of how she was stolen from her home. She tells us over and over again of her meeting with my father in Shanghai and the romance of their marriage. Why? Why?

I do not confide in my father and mother. They would not understand. How could they? He is English, she is Chinese. I am different to both of them—a stranger, tho their own child. "What are we?" I ask my brother. "It doesn't matter, sissy," he responds. But it does. I love poetry, particularly heroic pieces. I also love fairy tales. Stories of everyday life do not appeal to me. I dream dreams of being great and noble; my sisters and brothers also. I glory in the idea of dying at the stake and a great genie arising from the flames and declaring to those who have scorned us: "Behold, how great and glorious and noble are the Chinese people!"

My sisters are apprenticed to a dressmaker; my brother is entered in an office. I tramp around and sell my father's pictures, also some lace which I make myself. My nationality, if I had only known it at that time, helps to make sales. The ladies who are my customers call me "The Little Chinese Lace Girl." But it is a dangerous life for a very young girl. I come near to "mysteriously disappearing" many a time. The greatest temptation was in the thought of getting far away from where I was known, to where no mocking cries of "Chinese!" "Chinese!" could reach.

Whenever I have the opportunity I steal away to the library and read every book I can find on China and the Chinese. I learn that China is the oldest civilized nation on the face of the earth and a few other things. At eighteen years of age what troubles me is not that I am what I am, but that others are ignorant of my superiority. I am small, but my feelings are big—and great is my vanity.

My sisters attend dancing classes, for which they pay their own fees. In spite of covert smiles and sneers, they are glad to meet and mingle with other young folk. They are not sensitive in the sense that I am. And yet they understand. One of them tells me that she overheard a young man say to another that he would rather marry a pig than a girl with Chinese blood in her veins.

In course of time I too learn shorthand and take a position in an office. Like my sister, I teach myself, but, unlike my sister, I have neither the perseverance nor the ability to perfect myself. Besides, to a temperament like mine, it is torture to spend the hours in transcribing other people's thoughts. Therefore, altho I can always earn a moderately good salary, I do not distinguish myself in the business world as does she.

When I have been working for some years I open an office of my own. The local papers patronize me and give me a number of assignments, including most of the local Chinese reporting. I meet many Chinese persons, and when they get into trouble am often called upon to fight their battles in the papers. This I enjoy. My heart leaps for joy when I read one day an article signed by a New York Chinese in which he declares "The Chinese in America owe an everlasting debt of gratitude to Sui Sin Far for the bold stand she has taken in their defense."

The Chinaman who wrote the article seeks me out and calls upon me. He is a clever and witty man, a graduate of one of the American colleges and as well a Chinese scholar. I learn that he has an American wife and several children. I am very much interested in these children, and when I meet them my heart throbs in sympathetic tune with the tales they relate of their experiences as Eurasians. "Why did papa and mamma born us?" asks one. Why?

I also meet other Chinese men who compare favorably with the white men of my acquaintance in mind and heart qualities. Some of them are quite handsome. They have not as finely cut noses and as well developed chins as the white men, but they have smoother skins and their expression is more serene; their hands are better shaped and their voices softer.

Some little Chinese women whom I interview are very anxious to know whether I would marry a Chinaman. I do not answer No. They clap their hands delightedly, and assure me that the Chinese are much the finest and best of all men. They are, however, a little doubtful as to whether one could be persuaded to care for me, full-blooded Chinese people having a prejudice against the half white.

Fundamentally, I muse, all people are the same. My mother's race is as prejudiced as my father's. Only when the whole world becomes as one family will human beings be able to see clearly and hear distinctly. I believe that some day a great part of the world will be Eurasian. I cheer myself with the thought that I am but a pioneer. A pioneer should glory in suffering.

"You were walking with a Chinaman yesterday," accuses an acquaintance.

"Yes, what of it?"

"You ought not to. It isn't right."

"Not right to walk with one of my mother's people? Oh, indeed!"

I cannot reconcile his notion of righteousness with my own.

I am living in a little town away off on the north shore of a big lake. Next to me at the dinner table is the man for whom I work as a stenographer. There are also a couple of business men, a young girl and her mother.

Some one makes a remark about the cars full of Chinamen that past [sic] that morning. A transcontinental railway runs thru the town.

My employer shakes his rugged head. "Somehow or other," says he, "I cannot reconcile myself to the thought that the Chinese are humans like ourselves. They may have immortal souls, but their faces seem to be so utterly devoid of expression that I cannot help but doubt."

"Souls," echoes the town clerk. "Their bodies are enough for me. A Chinaman is, in my eyes, more repulsive than a nigger."

"They always give me such a creepy feeling," puts in the young girl with a laugh.

"I wouldn't have one in my house," declares my landlady.

"Now, the Japanese are different altogether. There is something bright and likeable about those men," continues Mr. K.

A miserable, cowardly feeling keeps me silent. I am in a Middle West town. If I declare what I am, every person in the place will hear about it the next day. The population is in the main made up of working folks with strong prejudices against my mother's countrymen. The prospect before me is not an enviable one—if I speak. I have no longer an ambition to die at the stake for the sake of demonstrating the greatness and nobleness of the Chinese people.

Mr. K. turns to me with a kindly smile.

"What makes Miss Far so quiet?" he asks.

"I don't suppose she finds the 'washee washee men' particularly interesting subjects of conversation," volunteers the young manager of the local bank.

With a great effort I raise my eyes from my plate. "Mr. K.," I say, addressing my employer, "the Chinese people may have no souls, no expression on their faces, be altogether beyond the pale of civilization, but whatever they are, I want you to understand that I am—I am a Chinese."

There is silence in the room for a few minutes. Then Mr. K. pushes back his plate and standing up beside me, says:

"I should not have spoken as I did. I know nothing whatever about the Chinese. It was pure prejudice. Forgive me!"

I admire Mr. K.'s moral courage in apologizing to me; he is a conscientious Christian man, but I do not remain much longer in the little town.

I am under a tropic sky, meeting frequently and conversing with persons who are almost as high up in the world as birth, education and money can set them. The environment is peculiar, for I am also surrounded by a race of people, the reputed descendants of Ham, the son of Noah, whose offspring, it was prophesied, should be the servants of the sons of Shem and Japheth. As I am a descendant, according to the Bible, of both Shem and Japheth, I have a perfect right to set my heel upon the Ham people; but tho I see others around me following out the Bible suggestion, it is not in my nature to be arrogant to any but those who seek to impress me with their superiority, which the poor black maid who has been assigned to me by the hotel certainly does not. My employer's wife takes me to task for this. "It is unnecessary," she says, "to thank a black person for a service."

The novelty of life in the West Indian island is not without its charm. The surroundings, people, manner of living, are so entirely different from what I have been accustomed to up North that I feel as if I were "born again." Mixing with people of fashion, and yet not of them, I am not of sufficient importance to create comment or curiosity. I am busy nearly all day and often well into the night. It is not monotonous work, but it is certainly strenuous. The planters and business men of the island take me as a matter of course and treat me with kindly courtesy. Occasionally an Englishman will warn me against the "brown boys" of the island, little dreaming that I too am of the "brown people" of the earth.

When it begins to be whispered about the place that I am not all white, some of the "sporty" people seek my acquaintance. I am small and look much younger than my years. When, however, they discover that I am a very serious and sober-minded spinster indeed, they retire quite gracefully, leaving me a few amusing reflections.

One evening a card is brought to my room. It bears the name of some naval officer. I go down to my visitor, thinking he is probably some one who, having been told that I am a reporter for the local paper, has brought me an item of news. I find him lounging in an easy chair on the veranda of the hotel—a big, blond, handsome fellow, several years younger than I.

"You are Lieutenant——?" I inquire.

He bows and laughs a little. The laugh doesn't suit him somehow—and it doesn't suit me, either.

"If you have anything to tell me, please tell it quickly, because I'm very busy." "Oh, you don't really mean that," he answers, with another silly and offensive laugh. "There's always plenty of time for good times. That's what I am here for. I saw you at the races the other day and twice at King's House. My ship will be here for——weeks."

"Do you wish that noted?" I ask.

"Oh, no! Why—I came just because I had an idea that you might like to know me. I would like to know you. You look such a nice little body. Say, wouldn't you like to go out for a sail this lovely night? I will tell you all about the sweet little Chinese girls I met when we were at Hong Kong. They're not so shy!"

I leave Eastern Canada for the Far West, so reduced by another attack of rheumatic fever that I only weigh eighty-four pounds. I travel on an advertising contract. It is presumed by the railway company that in some way or other I will give them full value for their transportation across the continent. I have been ordered beyond the Rockies by the doctor, who declares that I will never regain my strength in the East. Nevertheless, I am but two days in San Francisco when I start out in search of work. It is the first time that I have sought work as a stranger in a strange town. Both of the other positions away from home were secured for me by home influence. I am quite surprised to find that there is no demand for my services in San Francisco and that no one is particularly interested in me. The best I can do is to accept an offer from a railway agency to typewrite their correspondence for $5 a month. I stipulate, however, that I shall have the privilege of taking in outside work and that my hours shall be light. I am hopeful that the sale of a story or newspaper article may add to my income, and I console myself with the reflection that, considering that I still limp and bear traces of sickness, I am fortunate to secure any work at all.

The proprietor of one of the San Francisco papers, to whom I have a letter of introduction, suggests that I obtain some subscriptions from the people of Chinatown, that district of the city having never been canvassed. This suggestion I carry out with enthusiasm, tho I find that the Chinese merchants and people generally are inclined to regard me with suspicion. They have been imposed upon so many times by unscrupulous white people. Another drawback—save for a few phrases, I am unacquainted with my mother tongue. How, then, can I expect these people to accept me as their own countrywoman? The Americanized Chinamen actually laugh in my face when I tell them that I am of their race. However, they are not all "doubting Thomases." Some little women discover that I have Chinese hair, color of eyes and complexion, also that I love rice and tea. This settles the matter for them—and for their husbands.

My Chinese instincts develop. I am no longer the little girl who shrunk against my brother at the first sight of a Chinaman. Many and many a time, when alone in a strange place, has the appearance of even an humble laundryman given me a sense of protection and made me feel quite at home. This fact of itself proves to me that prejudice can be eradicated by association.

I meet a half Chinese, half white girl. Her face is plastered with a thick white coat of paint and her eyelids and eyebrows are blackened so that the shape of her eyes and the whole expression of her face is changed. She was born in the East, and at the age of eighteen came West in answer to an advertisement. Living for many years among the working class, she had heard little but abuse of the Chinese. It is not difficult, in a land like California, for a half Chinese, half white girl to pass as one of Spanish or Mexican origin. This the poor child does, tho she lives in nervous dread of being "discovered." She becomes engaged to a young man, but fears to tell him what she is, and only does so when compelled by a fearless American girl friend. This girl, who knows her origin, realizing that the truth sooner or later must be told, and better soon than late, advises the Eurasian to confide in the young man, assuring her that he loves her well enough not to allow her nationality to stand, a bar sinister, between them. But the Eurasian prefers to keep her secret, and only reveals it to the man who is to be her husband when driven to bay by the American girl, who declares that if the halfbreed will not tell the truth she will. When the young man hears that the girl he is engaged to has Chinese blood in her veins, he exclaims: "Oh, what will my folks say?" But that is all. Love is stronger than prejudice with him, and neither he nor she deems it necessary to inform his "folks."

The Americans, having for many years manifested a much higher regard for the Japanese than for the Chinese, several half Chinese young men and women, thinking to advance themselves, both in a social and business sense, pass as Japanese. They continue to be known as Eurasians; but a Japanese Eurasian does not appear in the same light as a Chinese Eurasian. The unfortunate Chinese Eurasians! Are not those who compel them to thus cringe more to be blamed than they?

People, however, are not all alike. I meet white men, and women, too, who are proud to mate with those who have Chinese blood in their veins, and think it a great honor to be distinguished by the friendship of such. There are also Eurasians and Eurasians. I know of one who allowed herself to become engaged to a white man after refusing him nine times. She had discouraged him in every way possible, had warned him that she was half Chinese; that her people were poor, that every week or month she sent home a certain amount of her earnings, and that the man she married would have to do as much, if not more; also, most uncompromising truth of all, that she did not love him and never would. But the resolute and undaunted lover swore that it was a matter of indifference to him whether she was a Chinese or a Hottentot, that it would be his pleasure and privilege to allow her relations double what it was in her power to bestow, and as to not loving him—that did not matter at all. He loved her. So, because the young woman had a married mother and married sisters, who were always picking at her and gossiping over her independent manner of living, she finally consented to marry him, recording the agreement in her diary thus:

"I have promised to become the wife of —— —— on —— ——, 189-, because the world is so cruel and sneering to a single woman—and for no other reason."

Everything went smoothly until one day. The young man was driving a pair of beautiful horses and she was seated by his side, trying very hard to imagine herself in love with him, when a Chinese vegetable gardener's cart came rumbling along. The Chinaman was a jolly-looking individual in blue cotton blouse and pantaloons, his rakish looking hat being kept in place by a long queue which was pulled upward from his neck and wound around it. The young woman was suddenly possest with the spirit of mischief. "Look!" she cried, indicating the Chinaman, "there's my brother. Why don't you salute him?"

The man's face fell a little. He sank into a pensive mood. The wicked one by his side read him like an open book.

"When we are married," said she. "I intend to give a Chinese party every month."

No answer.

"As there are very few aristocratic Chinese in this city, I shall fill up with the laundrymen and vegetable farmers. I don't believe in being exclusive in democratic America, do you?"

He hadn't a grain of humor in his composition, but a sickly smile contorted his features as he replied:

"You shall do just as you please, my darling. But—but—consider a moment. Wouldn't it be just a little pleasanter for us if, after we are married, we allowed it to be presumed that you were—er—Japanese? So many of my friends have inquired of me if that is not your nationality. They would be so charmed to meet a little Japanese lady."

"Hadn't you better oblige them by finding one?"

"Why—er—what do you mean?"

"Nothing much in particular. Only—I am getting a little tired of this," taking off his ring.

"You don't mean what you say! Oh, put it back, dearest! You know I would not hurt your feelings for the world!"

"You haven't. I'm more than pleased. But I do mean what I say."

That evening the "ungrateful" Chinese Eurasian diaried, among other things, the following:

"Joy, oh, joy! I'm free once more. Never again shall I be untrue to my own heart. Never again will I allow any one to 'hound' or 'sneer' me into matrimony."

I secure transportation to many California points. I meet some literary people, chief among whom is the editor of the magazine who took my first Chinese stories. He and his wife give me a warm welcome to their ranch. They are broad-minded people, whose interest in me is sincere and intelligent, not affected and vulgar. I also meet some funny people who advise me to "trade" upon my nationality. They tell me that if I wish to succeed in literature in America I should dress in Chinese costume, carry a fan in my hand, wear a pair of scarlet beaded slippers, live in New York, and come of high birth. Instead of making myself familiar with the Chinese-Americans around me, I should discourse on my spirit acquaintance with Chinese ancestors and quote in between the "Good mornings" and "How d'ye dos" of editors.

"Confucius, Confucius, how great is Confucius, Before Confucius, there never was Confucius. After Confucius, there never came Confucius," etc., etc., etc.,

or something like that, both illuminating and obscuring, don't you know. They forget, or perhaps they are not aware that the old Chinese sage taught "The way of sincerity is the way of heaven."

My experiences as an Eurasian never cease; but people are not now as prejudiced as they have been. In the West, too, my friends are more advanced in all lines of thought than those whom I know in Eastern Canada—more genuine, more sincere, with less of the form of religion, but more of its spirit.

So I roam backward and forward across the continent. When I am East, my heart is West. When I am West, my heart is East. Before long I hope to be in China. As my life began in my father's country it may end in my mother's.

After all I have no nationality and am not anxious to claim any. Individuality is more than nationality. "You are you and I am I," says Confucius. I give my right hand to the Occidentals and my left to the Orientals, hoping that between them they will not utterly destroy the insignificant "connecting link." And that's all.

1909

from **Mrs. Spring Fragrance**

In the Land of the Free[1]

I

"See, Little One—the hills in the morning sun. There is thy[2] home for years to come. It is very beautiful and thou wilt be very happy there."

The Little One looked up into his mother's face in perfect faith. He was engaged in the pleasant occupation of sucking a sweetmeat; but that did not prevent him from gurgling responsively.

"Yes, my olive bud; there is where thy father is making a fortune for thee. Thy father! Oh, wilt thou not be glad to behold his dear face. 'Twas for thee I left him."

The Little One ducked his chin sympathetically against his mother's knee. She lifted him on to her lap. He was two years old, a round, dimple-cheeked boy with bright brown eyes and a sturdy little frame.

"Ah! Ah! Ah! Ooh! Ooh! Ooh!" puffed he, mocking a tugboat steaming by.

[1]This story was initially published in the progressive New York magazine, *Independent* 67, 3170 (September 2, 1909) 504–508, in the third decade of the Chinese Exclusion Act when legal harassment of Chinese was still prevalent.

[2]The use of *thy* and *thou* is not to be associated with sixteenth-century usage or nine-

teenth-century Quakers. Sui Sin Far's intent here is to convey a tone of familiarity and intimacy, as well as a slight foreignness, in this Chinese mother's remarks, supposedly in Chinese, to her two-year-old child.

San Francisco's waterfront was lined with ships and steamers, while other craft, large and small, including a couple of white transports from the Philippines, lay at anchor here and there off shore. It was some time before the *Eastern Queen* could get docked, and even after that was accomplished, a lone Chinaman who had been waiting on the wharf for an hour was detained that much longer by men with the initials U.S.C. on their caps, before he could board the steamer and welcome his wife and child.

"This is thy son," announced the happy Lae Choo.

Hom Hing lifted the child, felt of his little body and limbs, gazed into his face with proud and joyous eyes; then turned inquiringly to a customs officer at his elbow.

"That's a fine boy you have there," said the man. "Where was he born?"

"In China," answered Hom Hing, swinging the Little One on his right shoulder, preparatory to leading his wife off the steamer.

"Ever been to America before?"

"No, not he," answered the father with a happy laugh.

The customs officer beckoned to another.

"This little fellow," said he, "is visiting America for the first time."

The other customs officer stroked his chin reflectively.

"Good day," said Hom Hing.

"Wait!" commanded one of the officers. "You cannot go just yet."

"What more now?" asked Hom Hing.

"I'm afraid," said the first customs officer, "that we cannot allow the boy to go ashore. There is nothing in the papers that you have shown us— your wife's papers and your own—having any bearing upon the child."

"There was no child when the papers were made out," returned Hom Hing. He spoke calmly; but there was apprehension in his eyes and in his tightening grip on his son.

"What is it? What is it?" quavered Lae Choo, who understood a little English.

The second customs officer regarded her pityingly.

"I don't like this part of the business," he muttered.

The first officer turned to Hom Hing and in an official tone of voice, said:

"Seeing that the boy has no certificate entitling him to admission to this country you will have to leave him with us."

"Leave my boy!" exclaimed Hom Hing.

"Yes; he will be well taken care of, and just as soon as we can hear from Washington he will be handed over to you."

"But," protested Hom Hing, "he is my son."

"We have no proof," answered the man with a shrug of his shoulders; "and even if so we cannot let him pass without orders from the Government."

"He is my son," reiterated Hom Hing, slowly and solemnly. "I am a Chinese merchant and have been in business in San Francisco for many years. When my wife told to me one morning that she dreamed of a green tree with spreading branches and one beautiful red flower growing thereon, I answered her that I wished my son to be born in our country, and for her to prepare to go to China. My wife complied with my wish. After my son was born my mother fell sick and my wife nursed and cared for her; then my father, too, fell sick, and my wife also nursed and cared for him. For twenty moons my wife care for and nurse the old people, and when they die they bless her and my son, and I send for her to return to me. I had no fear of trouble. I was a Chinese merchant and my son was my son."

"Very good, Hom Hing," replied the first officer. "Nevertheless, we take your son."

"No, you not take him; he my son too."

It was Lae Choo. Snatching the child from his father's arms she held and covered him with her own.

The officers conferred together for a few moments; then one drew Hom Hing aside and spoke in his ear.

Resignedly Hom Hing bowed his head, then approached his wife. "'Tis the law," said he, speaking in Chinese, "and 'twill be but for a little while—until tomorrow's sun arises."

"You, too," reproached Lae Choo in a voice eloquent with pain. But accustomed to obedience she yielded the boy to her husband, who in turn delivered him to the first officer. The Little One protested lustily against the transfer; but his mother covered her face with her sleeve and his father silently led her away. Thus was the law of the land complied with.

II

Day was breaking. Lae Choo, who had been awake all night, dressed herself, then awoke her husband.

"'Tis the morn," she cried. "Go, bring our son."

The man rubbed his eyes and arose upon his elbow so that he could see out of the window. A pale star was visible in the sky. The petals of a lily in a bowl on the windowsill were unfurled.

"'Tis not yet time," said he, laying his head down again.

"Not yet time. Ah, all the time that I lived before yesterday is not so much as the time that has been since my little one was taken from me."

The mother threw herself down beside the bed and covered her face.

Hom Hing turned on the light, and touching his wife's bowed head with a sympathetic hand inquired if she had slept.

"Slept!" she echoed, weepingly. "Ah, how could I close my eyes with my arms empty of the little body that has filled them every night for more than twenty moons! You do not know—man—what it is to miss the feel of the little fingers and the little toes and the soft round limbs of your little one. Even in the darkness his darling eyes used to shine up to mine, and often have I fallen into slumber with his pretty babble at my ear. And now, I see him not; I touch him not; I hear him not. My baby, my little fat one!"

"Now! Now! Now!" consoled Hom Hing, patting his wife's shoulder reassuringly; "there is no need to grieve so; he will soon gladden you again. There cannot be any law that would keep a child from its mother!"

Lae Choo dried her tears.

"You are right, my husband," she meekly murmured. She arose and stepped about the apartment, setting things to rights. The box of presents she had brought for her California friends had been opened the evening before; and silks, embroideries, carved ivories, ornamental lacquer-ware, brasses, camphorwood boxes, fans, and chinaware were scattered around in confused heaps. In the midst of unpacking the thought of her child in the hands of strangers had overpowered her, and she had left everything to crawl into bed and weep.

Having arranged her gifts in order she stepped out on to the deep balcony.

The star had faded from view and there were bright streaks in the western sky. Lae Choo looked down the street and around. Beneath the flat occupied by her and her husband were quarters for a number of bachelor Chinamen, and she could hear them from where she stood, taking their early morning breakfast. Below their dining-room was her husband's grocery store. Across the way was a large restaurant. Last night it had been resplendent with gay colored lanterns and the sound of music. The rejoicings over "the completion of the moon,"[3] by Quong Sum's first-born, had been long and loud, and had caused her to tie a handkerchief over her ears. She, a bereaved mother, had it not in her heart to rejoice with other parents. This morning the place was more in accord with her mood. It was still and quiet. The revellers had dispersed or were asleep.

A roly-poly woman in black sateen, with long pendant earrings in her ears, looked up from the street below and waved her a smiling greeting. It was her old neighbor, Kuie Hoe, the wife of the gold embosser, Mark Sing. With her was a little boy in yellow jacket and lavender pantaloons. Lae Choo remembered him as a baby. She used to like to play with him in those days when she had no child of her own. What a long time ago that seemed! She caught her breath in a sigh, and laughed instead.

"Why are you so merry?" called her husband from within.

"Because my Little One is coming home," answered Lae Choo. "I am a happy mother—a happy mother."

She pattered into the room with a smile on her face.

The noon hour had arrived. The rice was steaming in the bowls and a fragrant dish of chicken and bamboo shoots was awaiting Hom Hing. Not for one moment had Lae Choo paused to rest during the morning hours; her activity had been ceaseless. Every now and again, however, she had

[3]The Chinese traditionally give banquets to celebrate the completion of an infant boy's first month.

raised her eyes to the gilded clock on the curiously carved mantelpiece. Once, she had exclaimed:

"Why so long, oh! why so long?" Then apostrophizing herself: "Lae Choo, be happy. The Little One is coming! The Little One is coming!" Several times she burst into tears and several times she laughed aloud.

Hom Hing entered the room; his arms hung down by his side.

"The Little One!" shrieked Lae Choo.

"They bid me call tomorrow."

With a moan the mother sank to the floor.

The noon hour passed. The dinner remained on the table.

III

The winter rains were over: the spring had come to California, flushing the hills with green and causing an ever-changing pageant of flowers to pass over them. But there was no spring in Lae Choo's heart, for the Little One remained away from her arms. He was being kept in a mission. White women were caring for him, and though for one full moon he had pined for his mother and refused to be comforted he was now apparently happy and contented. Five moons or five months had gone by since the day he had passed with Lae Choo through the Golden Gate; but the great Government at Washington still delayed sending the answer which would return him to his parents.

Hom Hing was disconsolately rolling up and down the balls in his abacus box when a keen-faced young man stepped into his store.

"What news?" asked the Chinese merchant.

"This!" The young man brought forth a typewritten letter. Hom Hing read the words:

"Re Chinese child, alleged to be the son of Hom Hing, Chinese merchant, doing business at 425 Clay street, San Francisco.

"Same will have attention as soon as possible."

Hom Hing returned the letter, and without a word continued his manipulation of the counting machine.

"Have you anything to say?" asked the young man.

"Nothing. They have sent the same letter fifteen times before. Have you not yourself showed it to me?"

"True!" The young man eyed the Chinese merchant furtively. He had a proposition to make and he was pondering whether or not the time was opportune.

"How is your wife?" he inquired solicitously—and diplomatically.

Hom Hing shook his head mournfully.

"She seems less every day," he replied. "Her food she takes only when I bid her and her tears fall continually. She finds no pleasure in dress or flowers and cares not to see her friends. Her eyes stare all night. I think before another moon she will pass into the land of spirits."

"No!" exclaimed the young man, genuinely startled.

"If the boy not come home I lose my wife sure," continued Hom Hing with bitter sadness.

"It's not right," cried the young man indignantly. Then he made his proposition. The Chinese father's eyes brightened exceedingly.

"Will I like you to go to Washington and make them give you the paper to restore my son?" cried he. "How can you ask when you know my heart's desire?"

"Then," said the young fellow, "I will start next week. I am anxious to see this thing through if only for the sake of your wife's peace of mind."

"I will call her. To hear what you think to do will make her glad," said Hom Hing.

He called a message to Lae Choo upstairs through a tube in the wall.

In a few moments she appeared, listless, wan, and hollow-eyed; but when her husband told her the young lawyer's suggestion she became as one electrified; her form straightened, her eyes glistened; the color flushed to her cheeks.

"Oh," she cried, turning to James Clancy, "You are a hundred man good!"

The young man felt somewhat embarrassed; his eyes shifted a little under the intense gaze of the Chinese mother.

"Well, we must get your boy for you," he responded. "Of course"—turning to Hom Hing—"it will cost a little money. You can't get fellows to hurry the Government for you without gold in your pocket."

Hom Hing stared blankly for a moment. Then: "How much do you want, Mr. Clancy?" he asked quietly.

"Well, I will need at least five hundred to start with."

Hom Hing cleared his throat.

"I think I told to you the time I last paid you for writing letters for me and seeing the Custom boss here that nearly all I had was gone!"

"Oh, well then we won't talk about it, old fellow. It won't harm the boy to stay where he is, and your wife may get over it all right."

"What that you say?" quavered Lae Choo.

James Clancy looked out of the window.

"He says," explained Hom Hing in English, "that to get our boy we have to have much money."

"Money! Oh, yes."

Lae Choo nodded her head.

"I have not got the money to give him."

For a moment Lae Choo gazed wonderingly from one face to the other; then, comprehension dawning upon her, with swift anger, pointing to the lawyer, she cried: "You not one hundred man good; you just common white man."

"Yes, ma'am," returned James Clancy, bowing and smiling ironically.

Hom Hing pushed his wife behind him and addressed the lawyer again: "I might try," said he, "to raise something; but five hundred—it is not possible."

"What about four?"

"I tell you I have next to nothing left and my friends are not rich."

"Very well!"

The lawyer moved leisurely toward the door, pausing on its threshold to light a cigarette.

"Stop, white man; white man, stop!"

Lae Choo, panting and terrified, had started forward and now stood beside him, clutching his sleeve excitedly.

"You say you can go to get paper to bring my Little One to me if Hom Hing give you five hundred dollars?"

The lawyer nodded carelessly; his eyes were intent upon the cigarette which would not take the fire from the match.

"Then you go get paper. If Hom Hing not can give you five hundred dollars—I give you perhaps what more that much."

She slipped a heavy gold bracelet from her wrist and held it out to the man. Mechanically he took it.

"I go get more!"

She scurried away, disappearing behind the door through which she had come.

"Oh, look here, I can't accept this," said James Clancy, walking back to Hom Hing and laying down the bracelet before him.

"It's all right," said Hom Hing, seriously, "pure China gold. My wife's parent give it to her when we married."

"But I can't take it anyway," protested the young man.

"It is all same as money. And you want money to go to Washington," replied Hom Hing in a matter of fact manner.

"See, my jade earrings—my gold buttons—my hairpins—my comb of pearl and my rings—one, two, three, four, five rings; very good—very good—all same much money. I give them all to you. You take and bring me paper for my Little One."

Lae Choo piled up her jewels before the lawyer.

Hom Hing laid a restraining hand upon her shoulder. "Not all, my wife," he said in Chinese. He selected a ring—his gift to Lae Choo when she dreamed of the tree with the red flower. The rest of the jewels he pushed toward the white man.

"Take them and sell them," said he. "They will pay your fare to Washington and bring you back with the paper."

For one moment James Clancy hesitated. He was not a sentimental man; but something within him arose against accepting such payment for his services.

"They are good, good," pleadingly asserted Lae Choo, seeing his hesitation.

Whereupon he seized the jewels, thrust them into his coat pocket, and walked rapidly away from the store.

IV

Lae Choo followed after the missionary woman through the mission nursery school. Her heart was beating so high with happiness that she could scarcely breathe. The paper had come at last—the precious paper which gave Hom Hing and his wife the right to the possession of their own child. It was ten months now since he had been taken from them—ten months since the sun had ceased to shine for Lae Choo.

The room was filled with children—most of them wee tots, but none so wee as her own. The mission woman talked as she walked. She told Lae Choo that little Kim, as he had been named by the school, was the pet of the place, and that his little tricks and ways amused and delighted every one. He had been rather difficult to manage at first and had cried much for his mother; "but children so soon forget, and after a month he seemed quite at home and played around as bright and happy as a bird."

"Yes," responded Lae Choo. "Oh, yes, yes!"

But she did not hear what was said to her. She was walking in a maze of anticipatory joy.

"Wait here, please," said the mission woman, placing Lae Choo in a chair. "The very youngest ones are having their breakfast."

She withdrew for a moment—it seemed like an hour to the mother— then she reappeared leading by the hand a little boy dressed in blue cotton overalls and white-soled shoes. The little boy's face was round and dimpled and his eyes were very bright.

"Little One, ah, my Little One!" cried Lae Choo.

She fell on her knees and stretched her hungry arms toward her son.

But the Little One shrunk from her and tried to hide himself in the folds of the white woman's skirt.

"Go'way, go'way!" he bade his mother.

1909

The Wisdom of the New

I

Old Li Wang, the peddler, who had lived in the land beyond the sea, was wont to declare: "For every cent that a man makes here, he can make one hundred there."

"Then, why," would ask Sankwei, "do you now have to move from door to door to fill your bowl with rice?"

And the old man would sigh and answer:

"Because where one learns how to make gold, one also learns how to lose it."

"How to lose it!" echoed Wou Sankwei. "Tell me all about it."

So the old man would tell stories about the winning and the losing, and the stories of the losing were even more fascinating than the stories of the winning.

"Yes, that was life," he would conclude. "Life, life."

At such times the boy would gaze across the water with wistful eyes. The land beyond the sea was calling to him.

The place was a sleepy little south coast town where the years slipped by monotonously. The boy was the only son of the man who had been the town magistrate.

Had his father lived, Wou Sankwei would have been sent to complete his schooling in another province. As it was he did nothing but sleep, dream, and occasionally get into mischief. What else was there to do? His mother and sister waited upon him hand and foot. Was he not the son of the house? The family income was small, scarcely sufficient for their needs; but there was no way by which he could add to it, unless, indeed, he disgraced the name of Wou by becoming a common fisherman. The great green waves lifted white arms of foam to him, and the fishes gleaming and lurking in the waters seemed to beseech him to draw them from the deep; but his mother shook her head.

"Should you become a fisherman," said she, "your family would lose face. Remember that your father was a magistrate."

When he was about nineteen there returned to the town one who had been absent for many years. Ching Kee, like old Li Wang, had also lived in the land beyond the sea; but unlike old Li Wang he had accumulated a small fortune.

"'Tis a hard life over there," said he, "but 'tis worth while. At least one can be a man, and can work at what work comes his way without losing face." Then he laughed at Wou Sankwei's flabby muscles, at his soft, dark eyes, and plump, white hands.

"If you lived in America," said he, "you would learn to be ashamed of such beauty."

Whereupon Wou Sankwei made up his mind that he would go to America, the land beyond the sea. Better any life than that of a woman man.

He talked long and earnestly with his mother. "Give me your blessing," said he. "I will work and save money. What I send home will bring you many a comfort, and when I come back to China, it may be that I shall be able to complete my studies and obtain a degree. If not, my knowledge of the foreign language which I shall acquire, will enable me to take a position which will not disgrace the name of Wou."

His mother listened and thought. She was ambitious for her son whom she loved beyond all things on earth. Moreover, had not Sik Ping, a Canton merchant, who had visited the little town two moons ago, declared to Hum Wah, who traded in palm leaves, that the signs of the times were that the son of a cobbler, returned from America with the foreign language, could easier command a position of consequence than the son of a school-teacher unacquainted with any tongue but that of his motherland?

"Very well," she acquiesced; "but before you go I must find you a wife. Only your son, my son, can comfort me for your loss."

II

Wou Sankwei stood behind his desk, busily entering figures in a long yellow book. Now and then he would thrust the hair pencil with which he worked behind his ears and manipulate with deft fingers a Chinese counting machine. Wou Sankwei was the junior partner and bookkeeper of the firm of Leung Tang Wou & Co. of San Francisco. He had been in America seven years and had made good use of his time. Self-improvement had been his object and ambition, even more than the acquirement of a fortune, and who, looking at his fine, intelligent face and listening to his careful English, could say that he had failed?

One of his partners called his name. Some ladies wished to speak to him. Wou Sankwei hastened to the front of the store. One of his callers, a motherly looking woman, was the friend who had taken him under her wing shortly after his arrival in America. She had come to invite him to spend the evening with her and her niece, the young girl who accompanied her.

After his callers had left, Sankwei returned to his desk and worked steadily until the hour for his evening meal, which he took in the Chinese restaurant across the street from the bazaar. He hurried through with this, as before going to his friend's house, he had a somewhat important letter to write and mail. His mother had died a year before, and the uncle, to whom he was writing, had taken his wife and son into his home until such time as his nephew could send for them. Now the time had come.

Wou Sankwei's memory of the woman who was his wife was very faint. How could it be otherwise? She had come to him but three weeks before the sailing of the vessel had brought him to America, and until then he had not seen her face. But she was his wife and the mother of his son. Ever since he had worked in America he had sent money for her support, and she had proved a good daughter to his mother.

As he sat down to write he decided that he would welcome her with a big dinner to his countrymen.

"Yes," he replied to Mrs. Dean, later on in the evening, "I have sent for my wife."

"I am so glad," said the lady. "Mr. Wou"—turning to her niece—"has not seen his wife for seven years."

"Deary me!" exclaimed the young girl. "What a lot of letters you must have written!"

"I have not written her one," returned the young man somewhat stiffly.

Adah Charlton looked up in surprise. "Why—" she began.

"Mr. Wou used to be such a studious boy when I first knew him," interrupted Mrs. Dean, laying her hand affectionately upon the young man's shoulder. "Now, it is all business. But you won't forget the concert on Saturday evening."

"No, I will not forget," answered Wou Sankwei.

"He has never written to his wife," explained Mrs. Dean when she and her niece were alone, "because his wife can neither read nor write."

"Oh, isn't that sad!" murmured Adah Charlton, her own winsome face becoming pensive.

"They don't seem to think so. It is the Chinese custom to educate only the boys. At least it has been so in the past. Sankwei himself is unusually bright. Poor boy! He began life here as a laundryman, and you may be sure that it must have been hard on him, for, as the son of a petty Chinese Government official, he had not been accustomed to manual labor. But Chinese character is wonderful; and now after seven years in this country, he enjoys a reputation as a business man amongst his countrymen, and is as up to date as any young American."

"But, Auntie, isn't it dreadful to think that a man should live away from his wife for so many years without any communication between them whatsoever except through others."

"It is dreadful to our minds, but not to theirs. Everything with them is a matter of duty. Sankwei married his wife as a matter of duty. He sends for her as a matter of duty."

"I wonder if it is all duty on her side," mused the girl.

Mrs. Dean smiled. "You are too romantic, Adah," said she. "I hope, however, that when she does come, they will be happy together. I think almost as much of Sankwei as I do of my own boy."

III

Pau Lin, the wife of Wou Sankwei, sat in a corner of the deck of the big steamer, awaiting the coming of her husband. Beside her, leaning his little queued head against her shoulder, stood her six-year-old son. He had been ailing throughout the voyage, and his small face was pinched with pain. His mother, who had been nursing him every night since the ship had left port, appeared very worn and tired. This, despite the fact that with a feminine desire to make herself fair to see in the eyes of her husband, she had arrayed herself in a heavily embroidered purple costume, whitened her forehead and cheeks with powder, and tinted her lips with carmine.

He came at last, looking over and beyond her. There were two others of her country-women awaiting the men who had sent for them, and each had a child, so that for a moment he seemed somewhat bewildered. Only when the ship's officer pointed out and named her, did he know her as his. Then he came forward, spoke a few words of formal welcome, and, lifting the child in his arms, began questioning her as to its health.

She answered in low monosyllables. At his greeting she had raised her patient eyes to his face—the face of the husband whom she had not seen for seven long years—then the eager look of expectancy which had crossed her own faded away, her eyelids drooped, and her countenance assumed an almost sullen expression.

"Ah, poor Sankwei!" exclaimed Mrs. Dean, who with Adah Charlton stood some little distance apart from the family group.

"Poor wife!" murmured the young girl. She moved forward and would have taken in her own white hands the ringed ones of the Chinese woman, but the young man gently restrained her. "She cannot understand you," said he. As the young girl fell back, he explained to his wife the presence of the stranger women. They were there to bid her welcome; they were kind and good and wished to be her friends as well as his.

Pau Lin looked away. Adah Charlton's bright face, and the tone in her husband's voice when he spoke to the young girl, aroused a suspicion in her

mind—a suspicion natural to one who had come from a land where friendship between a man and woman is almost unknown.

"Poor little thing! How shy she is!" exclaimed Mrs. Dean.

Sankwei was glad that neither she nor the young girl understood the
meaning of the averted face.

Thus began Wou Sankwei's life in America as a family man. He soon
became accustomed to the change, which was not such a great one after all.
Pau Lin was more of an accessory than a part of his life. She interfered not
at all with his studies, his business, or his friends, and when not engaged in
housework or sewing, spent most of her time in the society of one or the
other of the merchants' wives who lived in the flats and apartments around
her own. She kept up the Chinese custom of taking her meals after her husband or at a separate table, and observed faithfully the rule laid down for
her by her late mother-in-law: to keep a quiet tongue in the presence of her
man. Sankwei, on his part, was always kind and indulgent. He bought her
silk dresses, hair ornaments, fans, and sweetmeats. He ordered her favorite
dishes from the Chinese restaurant. When she wished to go out with her
women friends, he hired a carriage, and shortly after her advent erected
behind her sleeping room a chapel for the ancestral tablet and gorgeous goddess which she had brought over seas with her.

Upon the child both parents lavished affection. He was a quaint, serious
little fellow, small for his age and requiring much care. Although naturally
much attached to his mother, he became also very fond of his father who,
more like an elder brother than a parent, delighted in playing all kinds of
games with him, and whom he followed about like a little dog. Adah Charlton took a great fancy to him and sketched him in many different poses for
a book on Chinese children which she was illustrating.

"He will be strong enough to go to school next year," said Sankwei to
her one day. "Later on I intend to put him through an American college."

"What does your wife think of a Western training for him?" inquired
the young girl.

"I have not consulted her about the matter," he answered. "A woman
does not understand such things."

"A woman, Mr. Wou," declared Adah, "understands such things as well
as and sometimes better than a man."

"An American woman, maybe," amended Sankwei; "but not a Chinese."

From the first Pau Lin had shown no disposition to become Americanized, and Sankwei himself had not urged it.

"I do appreciate the advantages of becoming westernized," said he to
Mrs. Dean whose influence and interest in his studies in America had helped
him to become what he was, "but it is not as if she had come here as I came,
in her learning days. The time for learning with her is over."

One evening, upon returning from his store, he found the little Yen sobbing pitifully.

"What!" he teased, "A man—and weeping."

The boy tried to hide his face, and as he did so, the father noticed that his little hand was red and swollen. He strode into the kitchen where Pau Lin was preparing the evening meal.

"The little child who is not strong—is there anything he could do to merit the infliction of pain?" he questioned.

Pau Lin faced her husband. "Yes, I think so," said she.

"What?"

"I forbade him to speak the language of the white women, and he disobeyed me. He had words in that tongue with the white boy from the next street."

Sankwei was astounded.

"We are living in the white man's country," said he. "The child will have to learn the white man's language."

"Not my child," answered Pau Lin.

Sankwei turned away from her. "Come, little one," said he to his son, "we will take supper tonight at the restaurant, and afterwards Yen shall see a show."

Pau Lin laid down the dish of vegetables which she was straining and took from a hook a small wrap which she adjusted around the boy.

"Now go with thy father," said she sternly.

But the boy clung to her—to the hand which had punished him. "I will sup with you," he cried, "I will sup with you."

"Go," repeated his mother, pushing him from her. And as the two passed over the threshold, she called to the father: "Keep the wrap around the child. The night air is chill."

Late that night, while father and son were peacefully sleeping, the wife and mother arose, and lifting gently the unconscious boy, bore him into the next room where she sat down with him in a rocker. Waking, he clasped his arms around her neck. Backwards and forwards she rocked him, passionately caressing the wounded hand and crooning and crying until he fell asleep again.

The first chastisement that the son of Wou Sankwei had received from his mother, was because he had striven to follow in the footsteps of his father and use the language of the stranger.

"You did perfectly right," said old Sien Tau the following morning, as she leaned over her balcony to speak to the wife of Wou Sankwei. "Had I again a son to rear, I should see to it that he followed not after the white people."

Sien Tau's son had married a white woman, and his children passed their grandame on the street without recognition.

"In this country, she is most happy who has no child," said Lae Choo, resting her elbow upon the shoulder of Sien Tau. "A Toy, the young daughter of Lew Wing, is as bold and free in her ways as are the white women, and her name is on all the men's tongues. What prudent man of our race would take her as wife?"

"One needs not to be born here to be made a fool of," joined in Pau Lin, appearing at another balcony door. "Think of Hum Wah. From sunrise till midnight he worked for fourteen years, then a white man came along and persuaded from him every dollar, promising to return doublefold within the moon. Many moons have risen and waned, and Hum Wah still waits on this side of the sea for the white man and his money. Meanwhile, his father and mother, who looked long for his coming, have passed beyond returning."

"The new religion—what trouble it brings!" exclaimed Lae Choo. "My man received word yestereve that the good old mother of Chee Ping—he who was baptized a Christian at the last baptizing in the Mission around the corner—had her head secretly severed from her body by the steadfast people of the village, as soon as the news reached there. 'Twas the first violent death in the records of the place. This happened to the mother of one of the boys attending the Mission corner of my street."

"No doubt, the poor old mother, having lost face, minded not so much the losing of her head," sighed Pau Lin. She gazed below her curiously. The American Chinatown held a strange fascination for the girl from the seacoast village. Streaming along the street was a motley throng made up of all nationalities. The sing-song voices of girls whom respectable merchants' wives shudder to name, were calling to one another from high balconies up shadowy alleys. A fat barber was laughing hilariously at a drunken white man who had fallen into a gutter; a withered old fellow, carrying a bird in a cage, stood at the corner entreating passersby to have a good fortune told; some children were burning punk on the curbstone. There went by a stalwart Chief of the Six Companies engaged in earnest confab with a yellow-robed priest from the joss house. A Chinese dressed in the latest American style and a very blonde woman, laughing immoderately, were entering a Chinese restaurant together. Above all the hubbub of voices was heard the clang of electric cars and the jarring of heavy wheels over cobblestones.

Pau Lin raised her head and looked her thoughts at the old woman, Sien Tau.

"Yes," nodded the dame, "'tis a mad place in which to bring up a child."

Pau Lin went back into the house, gave little Yen his noonday meal, and dressed him with care. His father was to take him out that afternoon. She questioned the boy, as she braided his queue, concerning the white women whom he visited with his father.

It was evening when they returned—Wou Sankwei and his boy. The little fellow ran up to her in high glee. "See, mother," said he, pulling off his cap, " I am like father now. I wear no queue."

The mother looked down upon him—at the little round head from which the queue, which had been her pride, no longer dangled.

"Ah!" she cried. "I am ashamed of you; I am ashamed!"

The boy stared at her, hurt and disappointed.

"Never mind, son," comforted his father. "It is all right."

Pau Lin placed the bowls of seaweed and chickens' liver before them and went back to the kitchen where her own meal was waiting. But she did not eat. She was saying within herself: "It is for the white woman he has done this; it is for the white woman!"

Later, as she laid the queue of her son within the trunk wherein lay that of his father, long since cast aside, she discovered a picture of Mrs. Dean, taken when the American woman had first become the teacher and benefactress of the youthful laundryman. She ran over with it to her husband. "Here," said she; "it is a picture of one of your white friends." Sankwei took it from her almost reverently, "That woman," he explained, "has been to me as a mother."

And the young woman—the one with eyes the color of blue china—is she also as a mother?" inquired Pau Lin gently.

But for all her gentleness, Wou Sankwei flushed angrily.

"Never speak of her," he cried. "Never speak of her!"

"Ha, ha, ha! Ha, ha, ha!" laughed Pau Lin. It was a soft and not unmelodious laugh, but to Wou Sankwei it sounded almost sacrilegious.

Nevertheless, he soon calmed down. Pau Lin was his wife, and to be kind to her was not only his duty but his nature. So when his little boy climbed into his lap and besought his father to pipe him a tune, he reached for his flute and called to Pau Lin to put aside work for that night. He would play her some Chinese music: And Pau Lin, whose heart and mind, undiverted by change, had been concentrated upon Wou Sankwei ever since the day she had become his wife, smothered, for the time being, the bitterness in her heart, and succumbed to the magic of her husband's playing—a magic which transported her in thought to the old Chinese days, the old Chinese days whose impression and influence ever remain with the exiled sons and daughters of China.

IV

That a man should take to himself two wives, or even three, if he thought proper, seemed natural and right in the eyes of Wou Pau Lin. She herself had come from a home where there were two broods of children and where her mother and her father's other wife had eaten their meals together as sisters. In that home there had not always been peace; but each woman at least, had the satisfaction of knowing that her man did not regard or treat the other woman as her superior. To each had fallen the common lot—to bear children to the man, and the man was master of all.

But, oh! the humiliation and shame of bearing children to a man who looked up to another woman—and a woman of another race—as a being above the common uses of women. There is a jealousy of the mind more poignant than any mere animal jealousy.

When Wou Sankwei's second child was two weeks old, Adah Charlton and her aunt called to see the little one, and the young girl chatted brightly with the father and played merrily with Yen, who was growing strong and merry. The American women could not, of course, converse with the Chinese; but Adah placed beside her a bunch of beautiful flowers, pressed her hand, and looked down upon her with radiant eyes. Secure in the difference of race, in the love of many friends, and in the happiness of her chosen work, no suspicion whatever crossed her mind that the woman whose husband was her aunt's protégé tasted everything bitter because of her.

After the visitors had gone, Pau Lin, who had been watching her husband's face while the young artist was in the room, said to him:

"She can be happy who takes all and gives nothing."

"Takes all and gives nothing," echoed her husband. "What do you mean?"

"She has taken all your heart," answered Pau Lin, "but she has not given you a son. It is I who have had that task."

"You are my wife," answered Wou Sankwei. "And she—oh! how can you speak of her so? She, who is as a pure water-flower—a lily!"

He went out of the room, carrying with him a little painting of their boy, which Adah Charlton had given to him as she bade him goodbye and which he had intended showing with pride to the mother.

It was on the day that the baby died that Pau Lin first saw the little picture. It had fallen out of her husband's coat pocket when he lifted the tiny form in his arms and declared it lifeless. Even in that first moment of loss Pau Lin, stooping to pick up the portrait, had shrunk back in horror, crying: "She would cast a spell! She would cast a spell!"

She set her heel upon the face of the picture and destroyed it beyond restoration.

"You know not what you say and do," sternly rebuked Sankwei. He would have added more, but the mystery of the dead child's look forbade him.

"The loss of a son is as the loss of a limb," said he to his childless partner, as under the red glare of the lanterns they sat discussing the sad event.

"But you are not without consolation," returned Leung Tsao. "Your first-born grows in strength and beauty."

"True," assented Wou Sankwei, his heavy thoughts becoming lighter.

And Pau Lin, in her curtained balcony overhead, drew closer her child and passionately cried:

"Sooner would I, O heart of my heart, that the light of thine eyes were also quenched, than that thou shouldst be contaminated with the wisdom of the new."

V

The Chinese women friends of Wou Pau Lin gossiped among themselves, and their gossip reached the ears of the American woman friend of Pau Lin's husband. Since the days of her widowhood Mrs. Dean had devoted herself earnestly and wholeheartedly to the betterment of the condition and the uplifting of the young work-ingmen of Chinese race who came to America. Their appeal and need, as she had told her niece, was for closer acquaintance with the knowledge of the Western people, and *that* she had undertaken to give them, as far as she was able. The rewards and satisfactions of her work had been rich in some cases. Witness Wou Sankwei.

But the gossip had reached and much perturbed her. What was it that they said Wou Sankwei's wife had declared—that her little son should not go to an American school nor learn the American learning. Such bigotry and narrow-mindedness! How sad to think of! Here was a man who had benefited and profited by living in America, anxious to have his son receive the benefits of a Western education—and here was this man's wife opposing him with her ignorance and hampering him with her unreasonable jealousy.

Yes, she had heard that too. That Wou Sankwei's wife was jealous—jealous—and her husband the most moral of men, the kindest and the most generous.

"Of what is she jealous?" she questioned Adah Charlton. Other Chinese men's wives, I have known, have had cause to be jealous, for it is true some of them are dreadfully immoral and openly support two or more wives. But not Wou Sankwei. And this little Pau Lin. She has everything that a Chinese woman could wish for."

A sudden flash of intuition came to the girl, rendering her for a moment speechless. When she did find words, she said:

"Everything that a Chinese woman could wish for, you say. Auntie, I do not believe there is any real difference between the feelings of a Chinese wife and an American wife. Sankwei is treating Pau Lin as he would treat her were he living in China. Yet it cannot be the same to her as if she were in their own country, where he would not come in contact with American women. A woman is a woman with intuitions and perceptions, whether Chinese or American, whether educated or uneducated, and Sankwei's wife must have noticed, even on the day of her arrival, her husband's manner towards us, and contrasted it with his manner towards her. I did not realize this before you told me that she was jealous. I only wish I had. Now, for all her ignorance, I can see that the poor little thing became more of an American in that one half hour on the steamer than Wou Sankwei, for all your pride in him, has become in seven years."

Mrs. Dean rested her head on her hand. She was evidently much perplexed.

"What you say may be, Adah," she replied after a while; "but even so, it is Sankwei whom I have known so long, who has my sympathies. He has much to put up with. They have drifted seven years of life apart. There is no bond of interest or sympathy between them, save the boy. Yet never the slightest hint of trouble has come to me from his own lips. Before the coming of Pau Lin, he would confide in me every little thing that worried him, as if he were my own son. Now he maintains absolute silence as to his private affairs."

"Chinese principles," observed Adah, resuming her work. "Yes, I admit Sankwei has some puzzles to solve. Naturally, when he tries to live two lives—that of a Chinese and that of an American."

"He is compelled to that," retorted Mrs. Dean. "Is it not what we teach these Chinese boys—to become Americans? And yet, they are Chinese, and must, in a sense, remain so."

Adah did not answer.

Mrs. Dean sighed. "Poor, dear children, both of them," mused she. "I feel very low-spirited over the matter. I suppose you wouldn't care to come down town with me. I should like to have another chat with Mrs. Wing Sing."

"I shall be glad of the change," replied Adah, laying down her brushes.

Rows of lanterns suspended from many balconies shed a mellow, moonshiny radiance. On the walls and doors were splashes of red paper inscribed with hieroglyphics. In the narrow streets, booths decorated with flowers, and banners and screens painted with immense figures of josses diverted the eye; while bands of musicians in gaudy silks, shrilled and banged, piped and fluted.

Everybody seemed to be out of doors—men, women, and children—and nearly all were in holiday attire. A couple of priests, in vivid scarlet and yellow robes, were kotowing before an altar covered with a rich cloth, embroidered in white and silver. Some Chinese students from the University of California stood looking on with comprehending, half-scornful interest; three girls lavishly dressed in colored silks, with their black hair plastered back from their faces and heavily bejewelled behind, chirped and chattered in a gilded balcony above them like birds in a cage. Little children, their hands full of half-moon-shaped cakes, were pattering about, with eyes, for all the hour, as bright as stars.

Chinatown was celebrating the Harvest Moon Festival,[1] and Adah Charlton was glad that she had an opportunity to see something of the celebration before she returned East. Mrs. Dean, familiar with the Chinese people and the mazes of Chinatown, led her around fearlessly, pointing out this and that object of interest and explaining to her its meaning. Seeing that it was a gala night, she had abandoned her idea of calling upon the Chinese friend.

Just as they turned a corner leading up to the street where Wou Sankwei's place of business and residence was situated, a pair of little hands grasped Mrs. Dean's skirt and a delighted little voice piped: "See me! See me!" It was little Yen, resplendent in mauve-colored pantaloons and embroidered vest and cap. Behind him was a tall man whom both women recognized.

"How do you happen to have Yen with you?" Adah asked.

"His father handed him over to me as a sort of guide, counsellor, and friend. The little fellow is very amusing."

"See over here," interrupted Yen. He hopped over the alley to where the priests stood by the altar. The grown people followed him.

"What is that man chanting?" asked Adah. One of the priests had mounted a table, and with arms outstretched towards the moon sailing high in the heavens, seemed to be making some sort of an invocation.

Her friend listened for some moments before replying:

---

[1] A traditional Chinese harvest festival celebrated in midautumn.

"It is a sort of apotheosis of the moon. I have heard it on a like occasion in Hankow, and the Chinese *bonze*[2] who officiated gave me a translation. I almost know it by heart. May I repeat it to you?"

Mrs. Dean and Yen were examining the screen with the big josses.

"Yes, I should like to hear it," said Adah.

"Then fix your eyes upon Diana."

"Dear and lovely moon, as I watch thee pursuing thy solitary course o'er the silent heavens, heart-easing thoughts steal o'er me and calm my passionate soul. Thou art so sweet, so serious, so serene, that thou causest me to forget the stormy emotions which crash like jarring discords across the harmony of life, and bringest to my memory a voice scarce ever heard amidst the warring of the world—love's low voice.

"Thou art so peaceful and so pure that it seemth as if naught false or ignoble could dwell beneath thy gentle radiance, and that earnestness—even the earnestness of genius—must glow within the bosom of him on whose head thy beams fall like blessings.

"The magic of thy sympathy disburtheneth me of many sorrows, and thoughts, which, like the songs of the sweetest sylvan singer, are too dear and sacred for the careless ears of day, gush forth with unconscious eloquence when thou art the only listener.

"Dear and lovely moon, there are some who say that those who dwell in the sunlit fields of reason should fear to wander through the moonlit valleys of imagination; but, I, who have ever been a pilgrim and a stranger in the realm of the wise, offer to thee the homage of a heart which appreciates that thou graciously shinest—even on the fool."

"Is that really Chinese?" queried Adah.

"No doubt about it—in the main. Of course, I cannot swear to it word for word."

"I should think that there would be some reference to the fruits of the earth—the harvest. I always understood that the Chinese religion was so practical."

"Confucianism is. But the Chinese mind requires two religions. Even the most commonplace Chinese has yearnings for something above everyday life. Therefore, he combines with his Confucianism, Buddhism—or, in this country, Christianity."

"Thank you for the information. It has given me a key to the mind of a certain Chinese in whom Auntie and I are interested."

"And who is this particular Chinese in whom you are interested."

"The father of the little boy who is with us tonight."

"Wou Sankwei! Why, here he comes with Lee Tong Hay. Are you acquainted with Lee Tong Hay?"

"No, but I believe Aunt is. Plays and sings in vaudeville, doesn't he?"

---

[2]Monk of the Mahayana sect of Buddhism.

"Yes; he can turn himself into a German, a Scotchman, an Irishman, or an American, with the greatest ease, and is as natural in each character as he is as a Chinaman. Hello, Lee Tong Hay."

"Hello, Mr. Stimson."

While her friend was talking to the lively young Chinese who had answered his greeting, Adah went over to where Wou Sankwei stood speaking to Mrs. Dean.

"Yen begins school next week," said her aunt, drawing her arm within her own. It was time to go home.

Adah made no reply. She was settling her mind to do something quite out of the ordinary. Her aunt often called her romantic and impractical. Perhaps she was.

VI

Auntie went out of town this morning," said Adah Charlton. "I, 'phoned for you to come up, Sankwei, because I wished to have a personal and private talk with you."

"Any trouble, Miss Adah," inquired the young merchant. "Anything I can do for you?"

Mrs. Dean often called upon him to transact little business matters for her or to consult with him on various phases of her social and family life.

"I don't know what I would do without Sankwei's head to manage for me," she often said to her niece.

"No," replied the girl, "you do too much for us. You always have, ever since I've known you. It's a shame for us to have allowed you."

"What are you talking about, Miss Adah? Since I came to America your aunt has made this house like a home to me, and, of course, I take an interest in it and like to do anything for it that a man can. I am always happy when I come here."

"Yes, I know you are, poor old boy," said Adah to herself.

Aloud she said: "I have something to say to you which I would like you to hear. Will you listen, Sankwei?"

"Of course I will," he answered.

"Well then," went on Adah, "I asked you to come here today because I have heard that there is trouble at your house and that your wife is jealous of you."

"Would you please not talk about that, Miss Adah. It is a matter which you cannot understand."

"You promised to listen and heed. I do understand, even though I cannot speak to your wife nor find out what she feels and thinks. I know you, Sankwei, and I can see just how the trouble has arisen. As soon as I heard that your wife was jealous I knew why she was jealous."

"Why?" he queried.

"Because," she answered unflinchingly, "you are thinking far too much of other women."

"Too much of other women?" echoed Sankwei dazedly. "I did not know that."

"No, you didn't. That is why I am telling you. But you are, Sankwei. And you are becoming too Americanized. My aunt encourages you to become so, and she is a good woman, with the best and highest of motives; but we are all liable to make mistakes, and it is a mistake to try and make a Chinese man into an American—if he has a wife who is to remain as she always has been. It would be different if you were not married and were a man free to advance. But you are not."

"What am I to do then, Miss Adah? You say that I think too much of other women besides her, and that I am too much Americanized. What can I do about it now that it is so?"

"First of all you must think of your wife. She has done for you what no American woman would do—came to you to be your wife, love you and serve you without even knowing you—took you on trust altogether. You must remember that for many years she was chained in a little cottage to care for your ailing and aged mother—a hard task indeed for a young girl. You must remember that you are the only man in the world to her, and that you have always been the only one that she has ever cared for. Think of her during all the years you are here, living a lonely hard-working life—a baby and an old woman her only companions. For this, she had left all her own relations. No American woman would have sacrificed herself so.

"And, now, what has she? Only you and her housework. The white woman reads, plays, paints, attends concerts, entertainments, lectures, absorbs herself in the work she likes, and in the course of her life thinks of and cares for a great many people. She has much to make her happy besides her husband. The Chinese woman has him only."

"And her boy."

"Yes, her boy," repeated Adah Charlton, smiling in spite of herself, but lapsing into seriousness the moment after. "There's another reason for you to drop the American for a time and go back to being a Chinese. For sake of your darling little boy, you and your wife should live together kindly and cheerfully. That is much more important for his welfare than that he should go to the American school and become Americanized."

"It is my ambition to put him through both American and Chinese schools."

"But what he needs most of all is a loving mother."

"She loves him all right."

"Then why do you not love her as you should? If I were married I would not think my husband loved me very much if he preferred spending his evenings in the society of other women than in mine, and was so much more polite and deferential to other women than he was to me. Can't you understand now why your wife is jealous?"

Wou Sankwei stood up.

"Goodbye," said Adah Charlton, giving him her hand.

"Goodbye," said Wou Sankwei.

Had he been a white man, there is no doubt that Adah Charlton's little lecture would have had a contrary effect from what she meant it to have. At least, the lectured would have been somewhat cynical as to her sincerity. But Wou Sankwei was not a white man. "He was a Chinese, and did not see any reason for insincerity in a matter as important as that which Adah Charlton had brought before him. He felt himself exiled from Paradise, yet it did not occur to him to question, as a white man would have done, whether the angel with the flaming sword had authority for her action. Neither did he lay the blame for things gone wrong upon any woman. He simply made up his mind to make the best of what was.

VII

It had been a peaceful week in the Wou household—the week before little Yen was to enter the American school. So peaceful indeed that Wou Sankwei had begun to think that his wife was reconciled to his wishes with regard to the boy. He whistled softly as he whittled away at a little ship he was making for him. Adah Charlton's suggestions had set coursing a train of thought which had curved around Pau Lin so closely that he had decided that, should she offer any further opposition to the boy's attending the American school, he would not insist upon it. After all, though the American language might be useful during this century, the wheel of the world would turn again, and then it might not be necessary at all. Who could tell? He came very near to expressing himself thus to Pau Lin.

And now it was the evening before the morning that little Yen was to march away to the American school. He had been excited all day over the prospect, and to calm him, his father finally told him to read aloud a little story from the Chinese book which he had given him on his first birthday in America and which he had taught him to read. Obediently the little fellow drew his stool to his mother's side and read in his childish sing-song the story of an irreverent lad who came to great grief because he followed after the funeral of his grandfather and regaled himself on the crisply roasted chickens and loose-skinned oranges which were left on the grave for the feasting of the spirit.

Wou Sankwei laughed heartily over the story. It reminded him of some of his own boyish escapades. But Pau Lin stroked silently the head of the little reader, and seemed lost in reverie.

A whiff of fresh salt air blew in from the Bay. The mother shivered, and Wou Sankwei, looking up from the fastening of the boat's rigging, bade Yen close the door. As the little fellow came back to his mother's side, he stumbled over her knee.

"Oh, poor mother!" he exclaimed with quaint apology. "'Twas the stupid feet, not Yen."

"So," she replied, curling her arm around his neck, "'tis always the feet. They are to the spirit as the cocoon to the butterfly. Listen, and I will sing you the song of the Happy Butterfly."

She began singing the old Chinese ditty in a fresh birdlike voice. Wou Sankwei, listening, was glad to hear her. He liked having everyone around him cheerful and happy. That had been the charm of the Dean household.

The ship was finished before the little family retired. Yen examined it, critically at first, then exultingly. Finally, he carried it away and placed it carefully in the closet where he kept his kites, balls, tops, and other treasures. "We will set sail with it tomorrow after school," said he to his father, hugging gratefully that father's arm.

Sankwei rubbed the little round head. The boy and he were great chums.

What was that sound which caused Sankwei to start from his sleep? It was just on the border land of night and day, an unusual time for Pau Lin to be up. Yet, he could hear her voice in Yen's room. He raised himself on his elbow and listened. She was softly singing a nursery song about some little squirrels and a huntsman. Sankwei wondered at her singing in that way at such an hour. From where he lay he could just perceive the child's cot and the silent child figure lying motionless in the dim light. How very motionless! In a moment Sankwei was beside it.

The empty cup with its dark dregs told the tale.

The thing he loved the best in all the world—the darling son who had crept into his heart with his joyousness and beauty—had been taken from him—by her who had given.

Sankwei reeled against the wall. The kneeling figure by the cot arose. The face of her was solemn and tender.

"He is saved," smiled she, "from the Wisdom of the New."

In grief too bitter for words the father bowed his head upon his hands.

"Why! Why!" queried Pau Lin, gazing upon him bewilderedly. "The child is happy. The butterfly mourns not o'er the shed cocoon."

Sankwei put up his shutters and wrote this note to Adah Charlton:

I have lost my boy through an accident. I am returning to China with my wife whose health requires a change.

1912

■　YONE NOGUCHI (NOGUCHI YONEJIRŌ)　■
1875–1947

Following in the footsteps of American writers like Lafcadio Hearn, Ernest Fenollosa, and less well-known but equally influential Japanese scholars like Okakura Tenshin, Yone Noguchi heralded a new generation of writers who formed and packaged Japanese art and culture for the Western world and filtered the Western world for Japan. Although he became best known for his essays and critiques, Noguchi began his literary career as a poet, and his photo appeared in Marianne Moore's *Poetry Magazine*.

Yonejiro Noguchi was born in 1875 near Nagoya and later moved to Tokyo to further his English education. In 1893, at the age of eighteen, Noguchi traveled to the United States with a few dollars in his pocket. Arriving in San Francisco, he became a "school boy," a name that referred to the many young Japanese men who earned their tuition by working as domestic servants in wealthy American homes. Eager to further his education, Noguchi sought out, worked for, and finally made friends with Joachim Miller, the so-called Poet of the Sierras, who lived as a semi-recluse in the Oakland hills. Here Noguchi reinvented himself as a poet affiliated with a group of San Francisco bohemians called Les Jeunes. In *The Octopus*, Frank Norris humorously paints a young, affected Japanese character (unmistakably Noguchi) who dramatically dons a silk kimono while spouting his own poetry at the most fashionable San Francisco literary salons. By 1898 he received praise from Willa Cather, who enthusiastically described his verses as "naïve, ... fragile," and "conspicuously Oriental." However, other critical and commercial failures ultimately led him to travel ever farther east.

In 1903 Noguchi arrived in London, where he mailed his self-published collection of poetry to the most eminent English literary figures. Here he finally secured his reputation through the support of W. B. Yeats, Thomas Hardy, and others. Although Noguchi returned to Japan in 1904 to take a teaching position at Keio University, he continued to publish extensively in English throughout his life. He never returned to the United States but visited Oxford University in 1913 to give a lecture at the invitation of poet laureate Robert Bridges.

During his ten years in the United States, Noguchi led an extraordinary life. He fathered (but was not much of a father to) the modernist sculptor Isamu Noguchi. The elder Noguchi allegedly had sexual affairs with old, wealthy, influential writers like Charles Warren Stoddard and young, independent women like the *Washington Post* reporter Ethel Ames. He left his long-suffering American wife and long-time editor Leonore Gilmore and married a Japanese woman after he returned to Japan. Noguchi's melodramatic life makes it tempting to disparage his literary works as the scribbles of an ambitious charmer who was cashing in on his Asian exoticism. However, Noguchi's cultural hustling and aesthetic acrobatics during his long career followed a core belief in the beauty of Japanese art and the potential for hybridity *avant la letter*. In 1904, at least a decade before Pound's famous imagist poem "In the Station of the Metro," Noguchi published an article in *Reader* magazine imploring American poets to incorporate the *hokku*, an early version of the haiku, to create a new American poetics. Although his own works may read more as Keats or Poe than Bassho, they nonetheless attest to a commitment to intertwining poetic forms and traditions. Like his contemporary Winnifred Eaton (Otono Watanna), he clearly welcomed and survived on Japanophilia at the turn of the century. (Japan's popularity was not just an extension of the *Japonisme* that the impressionists nurtured; Japan's rise in military power and victories in the Sino-Japanese War and Russo-Japanese War made the Japanese especially popular in America at this time.) But his works nonetheless resist Orientalist pandering. For example, Noguchi often incorporates Japanese cultural references without ethnographic translations, as if to disorient the reader's sense of mastery of the material. Though "I Hail

Myself as I Do Homer" mimics Whitman, the reverence for nature also alludes to a long history of nature imagery in Japanese and Chinese poetry.

Noguchi published only two "novels" during his career—*The American Diary of a Japanese Girl* (1902) and its sequel, *The American Letters of a Japanese Parlor Maid* (1905). Both were written as nonfictional pieces in the guise of intimate observations penned by a young, wealthy, Japanese girl named Miss Morning Glory. Both were dismal commercial and critical failures. Ironically, the plotless, stylistically breezy, seemingly frivolous or opportunistically Orientalist fictional diary, *The American Diary*, offers one of the most formally experimental innovations in existence of the kind that he so prophetically encouraged. Indeed, although *American Diary*'s content roughly follows Noguchi's own autobiographical experiences, the novel's seemingly Orientalist style functions as both a literary allusion and a veil that obscures his attempts to incorporate Japanese aesthetic forms into American contexts.

American Diary recalls canonical, classical Japanese travelogues from the Heian period (794–1185) like *Tosa Nikki* (*Tosa Diary*), written by a male aristocrat in the voice of a lady in waiting. These travelogues are notable for the lack of a strong narrative plot and a preponderance of wandering reflections and poetic fragments. Thus, although Noguchi's wealthy, flighty Japanese female protagonist, Miss Morning Glory, clearly resonates with contemporaneous stereotypes of tittering, ornamental Japanese women, his formal choice signifies far richer political implications.

The allusion contained in this form is especially noteworthy because at the turn of the twentieth century, Japan's transformation into a modern nation-state included dramatic changes in the literary canon. Whereas Chinese literature and poetry had historically been revered as the most aesthetically refined and intellectually accomplished works, the Meiji period heralded a cultural nationalism that newly idealized indigenous Japanese literature.

Curiously, because writing was rigorously gendered during the Heian period, official, "intellectual" work was written exclusively by men in Chinese. Women were relegated to writing "uneducated," affective prose, stories, and personal diaries in *kana*, the indigenous Japanese script. Consequently, Japan's literary canon now includes many works by women, including *The Tale of Genji* by Lady Muraskai and *The Pillow Book* by Sei Shonagon. *Tosa Nikki* is written by Ki no Tsurayuki, a famous male *waka* poet (a poet who writes in Japanese, not Chinese). In this context, *American Diary* appeases and twists the Orientalist fantasy to offer instead formal interventions that introduce indigenous Japanese literary forms into American literature.

Although Noguchi himself never became an American citizen, his works mark one of the first instances of poetry and fiction written and published in English in the United States by a Japanese man, arguably making his works among the earliest Asian American texts. Near the end of his life, in the 1930s and 1940s, Noguchi, like many of his countrymen, rejected the idyllic trans-Pacific aesthetic crossings to embrace a more fascistic cultural nationalism instead. However, his life and works attest to an important but still largely unattended voice in studies of modernism, Asian American studies, and American studies.

Mayumi Takada
Independent Scholar

PRIMARY WORKS

Seen and Unseen: Or, Monologues of a Homeless Snail (1897); *The American Diary of a Japanese Girl* (1902); *The American Letters of a Japanese Parlor-Maid* (1905); *Through the Torii* (1914); *The Spirit of Japanese Poetry* (1914); *Hiroshige* (1940).

SECONDARY WORKS

Masayo Duus, *The Life of Isamu Noguchi: Journey without Borders*, trans. Peter Duus (Princeton, NJ: Princeton University Press, 2004); Laura E. Franey, introduction to *The American Diary of a Japanese Girl: An Annotated Edition* (Philadelphia: Temple University Press, 2007), vii–xx; Yoshinobu Hakutani, ed., introduction to *Selected English Writings of Yone Noguchi: An East-West Literary Assimilation* (Madison, NJ: Fairleigh Dickinson University Press, 1992); Edward Marx, afterword for *The American Diary of a Japanese Girl: An Annotated Edition* (Philadelphia: Temple University Press, 2007), 131–52.

I Hail Myself as I Do Homer[1]

The heart of God, the unpretending heaven, concealing the midnight
    stars in glassing the day of earth,
Showers of his brooding love upon the green-crowned goddess, May
    Earth, in the heart-lulling mirth.
O Poet, begin thy flight by singing of the hidden soul in vaporous
    harmony;
Startle thy lazy noon drowsing in the full-flowing tide of the
    sunbeams nailing thy chants in Eternity!
The melody breathing peace in the name of Spring, calms tear to
    smile, envy to rest.   5
Ah thou, world of this day, sigh not of the poets who have deserted
    thee—aye, I hail myself as I do Homer!
Behold, a baby flower hymns the creation of the universe in the
    breeze, charming my soul as the lover-moon!
O Yone,—a ripple of the vanity-water, a raindrop from the vanity-
    cloud,—lay thy body under the sun-enameled shade of the trees
As a heathen idol in an untrodden path awakening in spirit sent by
    the unseen genius of the sphere!
The earth, a single-roomed hermitage for mortals, shows not unto
    me a door to Death on the joy-carpeted floor—   10
Aye, I call the once dead light of the day from the dark-breasted
    slumber of night!—
I repose in the harmonious difference of the divine Sister and
    Brother,— Voice and Silence in Time.
O Yone, return to Nature in the woodland,—thy home, where
    Wisdom and Laughter entwine their arms!

[1]From *The Voice of the Valley* (San Francisco:
Doxey Press, 1897).

Ah Cities, scorning the order of the world, ye plunder rest from night,
    paint day with snowy vice,—
Alas, the smoke-dragon obscures the light of God; the
    sky-measuring steeple speaks of discontent unto the Heaven!   15
O Yone, wander not city-ward—there thou art sentenced to veil they
    tears with smiles!
Behold, the cloud hides the sins of the cities—regiments of redwood-
    giants guard the holy gates of the woodland against the shames!
Chant of Nature, O Yone,—sing thy destiny—hymn of darkness for
    the ivory-browned dawn—
Behold, the deathless Deity blesses thee in silence from the thousand
    temples of the stars above!

                                                1897

O Hana San[1]

It was many and many a year ago,
In a garden of the cherry-blossom
Of a far-off isle you may know
By the fairy name of Nippon,[2]
That a maiden who was dressing her hair   5
Against the mirror of a shining spring,
Casting over me her sudden heavenly glance,
Entreated me to break a beautiful branch
Of the cherry-tree: I cannot forget.
I was a boy on the way home   10
From my school; I threw aside
All my books and slate, and I climbed
Up the tree, and looked down
Over her little anxious butterfly face:
Oh, how the wind blew fanning me   15
With a love that was more than earthly love,
In a garden of the cherry-blossom
Of a far-off isle you may know
By the fairy name of Nippon!
I broke a branch, slowly dropped it   20
To her up-raised hands that God shaped
With best art and pain; she smiled
Toward me an angel smile; she,
Speaking no word, ran away as a breeze,

[1]From *From the Eastern Sea* (London: self-published, January 1903; expanded versions London: Unicorn Press, March 1903; Tokyo: Fuzanbo, October 1903). *O Hana San* translates as Miss Hana. *O* is a common prefix to nouns, especially native Japanese nouns, that implies a level of politeness or deference. *San* is a nongendered honorific.
[2]Phonetically accurate Japanese appellation for Japan.

Leaving behind the silver evening moon,   25
And hid from me in the shadow of a pine-tree
In a garden of the cherry-blossom
Of a far-off isle you may know
By the fairy name of Nippon.
I stole toward her on tiptoe,   30
As a silent moonbeam to a sleeping flower,
And frightened her with a shout of "Mitsuketa wa,"[3]
And I ran away from her, smiling and blushing,
In a garden of the cherry-blossom
Of a far-off isle you may know   35
By the fairy name of Nippon.
And I hid me beneath the gate of a temple,
That was a pathway to the heavens.
She stepped softly as the night,
Found me and looked upon me witha smile like a star.   40
Tapped my head with the branch,
Speaking fondly, 'My Sweetest one!'
I had no answer but a glad laugh
That was taught by the happy wind
In a garden of the cherry-blossom   45
Of a far-off isle you may know
By the fairy name of Nippon.
And that maiden who was known
By the pretty name of O Hana San,
Ran away gracefully as a Spring cloud   50
Into the heavens, blushing and smiling,
Then I followed O Hana's steps,
Into, into the realm of Love

                                                        1903

The Lotus Worshippers[1]

From dale and hill the worshipers steal
In whitest robes: yea, with whitest souls.
They sit around the holy pond, the lotus home,
Their finger-tips folded like the hushing lotus-buds
Thrust through the water and twilight, nun-like,   5
And they pray (the silent prayer that is higher than the prayer of speech).
The stars and night suddenly cease their song,

---

[3]I found you.
[1]From *The Pilgrimage* (Kamakura: Valley Press;
London: Elkin Mathews, 1909).

The air and birds begin to stir.
(O Resurrection, Resurrection of World and Life!)
Lo, Sun ascend! The lotus buds flash with hearts parted,   10
With one chant "Namu, Amida!"[2]
The stars disappear, nay, they fall in their hearts.
The worshipers turn their silent steps toward their homes,
Learning the stars will fall in their truthful souls,
And[3] the road of sunlight is the road of prayer,   15
And for Paradise.
Their faces shining under the sun's blessing gold,
They chant the divine name along the woodland.

                                                                    1909

from **Japanese Hokkus**[1]

12

Leaves blown,
Birds flown away.

I wander in and out the Hall of Autumn

16

Are the fallen stars
Returning up the sky?—
The dews on the grass.

36

But the march to Life . . .
Break song to sing the new song!
Clouds leap, flowers bloom.

71

The nightingales under the boughs,
Sighing now white, now red,
Sing a pearl song
Over the greyness of earth.

                                                                    1920

[2]Buddhist chant that literally translates to "In the name of Amida," or "Praise to Amida," and is a shortened part of the chant "Namu Amida Butsu" (Name of Amida Buddha).

[3]*That* in later versions.
[1]From *Japanese Hokkus* (Boston: Four Seas, 1920).

from **The American Diary of a Japanese Girl**

[After a dedication "To Her Majesty Haruko, Empress of Japan" explaining her intent to "publish my simple diary of my American journey," the narrative begins with Miss Morning Glory in Tokyo, awaiting her departure.]

Before I Sailed[1]

Tokyo, Sept. 23rd

My new page of life is dawning.

A trip beyond the seas—Merken Kenbutsu[2]—it's not an ordinary event.

It is verily the first event in our family history that I could trace back for six centuries.

My to-day's dream of America—dream of a butterfly sipping on golden dews—was rudely broken by the artless chirrup of a hundred sparrows in my garden.

"Chui, chui! Chui, chui, chui!"[3]

Bad sparrows!

My dream was silly but splendid.

Dream is no dream without silliness which is akin to poetry.

If my dream ever comes true!

24th—The song of gay children scattered over the street had subsided. The harvest moon shone like a yellow halo of "Nono Sama."[4] All things in blessed Mitsuho No Kuni[5]—the smallest ant also—bathed in sweet inspiring beams of beauty. The soft song that is not to be heard but to be felt, was in the air.

'Twas a crime, I judged, to squander lazily such a gracious graceful hour within doors.

I and my maid strolled to the Konpira shrine.[6]

Her red stout fingers—like sweet potatoes—didn't appear so bad tonight, for the moon beautified every ugliness.

Our Emperor should proclaim forbidding woman to be out at any time except under the moonlight.

Without beauty woman is nothing. Face is the whole soul. I prefer death if I am not given a pair of dark velvety eyes.

What a shame even woman must grow old!

One stupid wrinkle on my face would be enough to stun me.

My pride is in my slim fingers of satin skin.

I'll carefully clean my roseate finger-nails before I'll land in America.

---

[1]Noguchi divides *The American Diary of a Japanese Girl* into three sections. Of these, the first two ("Before I Sailed" and "On the Ocean") take up only the first thirty-two pages, while the majority of the 260-page novel is dedicated to the section entitled "In Amerikey."

[2]*Merikan* is a shortening of *American. Kenbutsu* means sightseeing.

[3]Phonetic noise of sparrows in Japanese.

[4]A child's phrasing for spirits of the dead, Buddha, and the Shinto gods; a general reference to god.

[5]Literally, the country of rice shoots. The phrase is a self-consciously poetic term for Japan.

[6]A famous shrine located on Mount Zozu, a steep mountain in Shikoku region. It is known as a protector of ventures at sea.

Our wooden clogs sounded melodious, like a rhythmic prayer unto the sky. Japs fit themselves to play music even with footgear. Every house with a lantern at its entrance looked a shrine cherishing a thousand idols within.

I kneeled to the Konpira god.

I didn't exactly see how to address him, being ignorant what sort of god he was.

I felt thirsty when I reached home. Before I pulled a bucket from the well, I peeped down into it. The moonbeams were beautifully stealing into the waters.

My tortoise-shell comb from my head dropped into the well.

The waters from far down smiled, heartily congratulating me on going to Amerikey.

25th—I thought all day long how I'll look in 'Merican dress.

26th—My shoes and six pairs of silk stockings arrived.

How I hoped they were Nippon silk![7]

One pair's value is 4 yens.

Extravagance! How dear!

I hardly see any bit of reason against bare feet.

Well, of course, it depends on how they are shaped.

A Japanese girl's feet are a sweet little piece. Their flatness and archlessness manifest their pathetic womanliness.

Feet tell as much as palms.

I have taken the same laborious care with my feet as with my hands. Now they have to retire into the heavy constrained shoes of America.

It's not so bad, however, to slip one's feet into gorgeous silk like that.

My shoes are of superior shape. They have a small high heel.

I'm glad they make me much taller.

A bamboo I set some three Summers ago cast its unusually melancholy shadow on the round paper window of my room, and whispered, "Sara! Sara! Sara!"[8]

It sounded to me like a pallid voice of sayonara.[9]

(By the way, the profuse tips of my bamboo are like the ostrich plumes of my new American hat.)

"Sayonara" never sounded before more sad, more thrilling.

My good-bye to "home sweet home" amid the camellias and white chrysanthemums is within ten days.[10] The steamer "Belgic" leaves Yokohama on

---

[7]That is, Japanese silk.

[8]In Japanese, onomatopoetic sound of leaves rustling in the wind.

[9]Goodbye.

[10]In Japan, camellias are one of the first flowers to bloom, symbolizing the end of winter and the beginning of spring. However, the camellia is less a harbinger of spring than a melancholic reminder of the end of winter. While chrysan-themums in general symbolize autumn, white chrysanthemums are correlated more specifically with funerary arrangements and thus death. Because it's clear that Miss Morning Glory leaves Japan on October 6, these floral references symbolize metaphorical, rather than literal, seasons, reflecting her conflicted feelings in leaving her homeland.

the sixth of next month. My beloved uncle is chaperon during my American journey....

> [Miss Morning Glory arrives in San Francisco with her Uncle chaperone. She stays at the Palace Hotel and meets Miss Ada, a socialite living on the fashionable Van Ness Avenue.]

28th—How old is she?

I could never suggest the age of a Meriken woman.

That Miss Ada was a beauty.

It's becoming clearer to me now why California puts so much pride in her own girls.

Ada was a San Franciscan whom Mrs. Consul presented to me.

What was her family name?

Never mind! It is an extra to remember it for girls. We don't use it.

How envious I was of her long eyelashes lacing around the large eyes of brown hue!

Brown was my preference for the velvet hanao[11] of my wooden clogs.

Long eyelashes are a grace, like the long skirt.

I know that she is a clever young thing.

She was learned in the art of raising and dropping her curtain of eye-lashes. That is the art of being enchanting. I had said that nothing could beat the beauty of my black eyes. But I see there are other pretty eyes in this world.

Everything doesn't grow in Japan. Noses particularly.

My sweet Ada's nose was an inspiration, like the snow-capped peak of O Fuji San.[12] It rose calmly—how symmetrically!—from between her eyebrows.

I had thought that 'Merican nose was rugged, big of bone.

I see an exception in Ada.

She must be the pattern of Meriken beauty.

I felt that I was so very homely.

I stole a sly glance into the looking-glass, and convinced myself that I was a beauty also, but Oriental.

We had different attractions.

She may be Spring white sunshine, while I am yellow Autumn moon-beams. One is animation, and the other sweetness.

I smiled.

She smiled back promptly.

We promised love in our little smile.

She placed her hand on my shoulder. How her diamond ring flashed! She praised the satin skin of my face.

She was very white, with a few sprinkles of freckles. Their scattering added briskness to the face in her case. (But doesn't San Francisco produce

---

[11]The straps on the geta, or Japanese sandal-like shoe.

[12]Mount Fuji. *O* is a common prefix to nouns, especially native Japanese nouns, that implies a level of politeness or deference. *San* is a nongendered honorific.

too many freckles in woman?) The texture of Ada's skin wasn't fine. Her face was like a ripe peach with powdery hair.

Is it true that dark skin is gaining popularity in American society?

The Japanese type of beauty is coming to the front then, I am happy.

I repaid her compliment, praising her elegant set of teeth.

Ada is the free-born girl of modern Amerikey.

She need never fear to open her mouth wide.

She must have been using special tooth-powder three times a day.

"We are great friends already, aren't we?" I said.

And I extended my finger-tips behind her, and pulled some wisps of her chestnut hair.

"Please, don't!" she said, and raised her sweetly accusing eyes. Then our friendship was confirmed.

Girls don't take much time to exchange their faith.

I was uneasy at first, thinking that Ada might settle herself in a *tête-à-tête* with me, in the chit-chat of poetry. I tried to recollect how the first line of the "Psalm of Life" went, for Longfellow would of course be the first one to encounter.

Alas, I had forgotten it all.

I was glad that her query did not roam from the remote corner of poesy.

"Do you play golf?" she asked.

She thinks the same things are going on in Japan.

Ada! Poor Ada!

The honourable consul and my uncle looked stupid at the lunch table.

I thought they were afraid of being given some difficult question by the Meriken ladies.

Mrs. Consul and Ada ate like hungry pigs. (I beg their pardon!)

"You eat like a pussy!" is no adequate compliment to pay to a Meriken woman.

I found out that their English was neither Macaulay's nor Irving's....

[Miss Morning Glory sits alone in her room at the Palace Hotel, obliquely critiquing American commercialism. Two days later, on the 12th, Miss Morning Glory decides to move to a boarding house on California Street, in the posh area of Nob Hill.]

10th—I yawned.

Nothing is more unbecoming to a woman than yawning.

I think it no offence to swear once in a while in one's closet.

I was alone.

I tore to pieces my "Things Seen in the Street," and fed the waste-paper basket with them.

The basket looked so hungry without any rubbish. An unkept basket is more pleasing, like a soiled autograph-book.

"I didn't come to Amerikey to be critical, that is, to act mean, did I?" I said.

I must remain an Oriental girl, like a cherry blossom smiling softly in the Spring moonlight.

But afterwards I felt sorry for my destruction.

I thrust my hand into the basket. I plucked them up. They were illegibly as follows:

> women coursing like a 'rikisha[13] of 'Hama[14]
>   their children crying at home   left somewhere their
> womanliness   gentleman with stove-pipe hat   blowing nose
> with his fingers   young lady   kept busy chewing gum while
> walking. If you once show such a grace at Tokio, you shall wait fruitlessly for the
> marriage offer.
>   old grandma in gay red skirt
> aged man arm-in-arm with wife so young   What a martyrdom to marry
> for G-O-L-D!   policeman has no
>   San Francisco is a beautiful city, but 'vertisements of "The Girl From Paris"
>   W——d's Beer
> with the watches hanging on their breasts
>   God bless you, red necktie gentleman
>   woman at the corner chattering like a street politician.

And I missed some other hundred lines. . . .

[After arriving at the boarding house Miss Morning Glory begins exploring her immediate surroundings.]

17th—I went to the gallery of the photographer Taber,[15] and posed in Nippon "pera pera."[16]

The photographer spread before me many pictures of the actress in the part of "Geisha."

She was absurd.

I cannot comprehend where 'Mericans get the conception that Jap girls are eternally smiling puppets.

Are we crazy to smile without motive?

What an untidy presence!

She didn't even fasten the front of her kimono.

Charm doesn't walk together with disorder under the same Japanese parasol.

And I had the honour to be presented to an extraordinary mode in her hair.

---

[13]A rickshaw, a two-wheeled cart or cab pulled by a man.

[14]A shortening of Yokohama, a lively international port town in Japan.

[15]A famous and prolific photographer of both landscapes and portraits in California in the nineteenth and early twentieth centuries.

[16]Onomatopoetic Japanese word for a flimsy or fluttery garment. There is a connotation of a literal and metaphorical looseness also.

It might be entitled "ghost style."[17] It suggested an apparition in the "Botan Toro"[18] played by kikugoro.[19]

The photographer handed me a fan.

Alas! It was a Chinese fan in a crude mixture of colour.

He urged me to carry it.

I declined, saying:

"Nobody fans in cool November!"

[After a short interlude in Los Angeles, Miss Morning Glory returns to San Francisco. Upon invitation from the poet, Mr. Heine, she and her Uncle visit the Heights, the name of his rustic Oakland home. The entire interlude is clearly based on Noguchi's time with Joachim Miller at "the Heights." Miss Morning Glory composes a series of sketches from the perspective of a squirrel, which she entitles "The Cave Journal," divided into sections from A to S.

20th—The squirrel by my window shows a great fancy for me. He honoured me three times already this morning. He bore a somewhat scholarly air. A retired professor, I reckon.

Is he regular with his diary?

Possibly he is idle with a pen, like any other professor.

Let me scribble for him to-day!

My one bottle of ink has some time to dry up yet.

I will name it "The Cave Journal." I will leave it to the Professor for a souvenir upon my sayonara to this hill.

A

Where are my spectacles?

B

Upon my soul, I believe that some mischief is raging. I can never trust even the poet abode. Who stole my two-cent stamp?

God bless you, my precious daughter at Sierra Nevada!

By and by I will erect my private telegraph between us.

---

[17]In contradistinction to contemporaneous Western hairstyles that romanticized loose tresses, in Japan only ghosts, harlots, and the poor or insane appeared with wisps of hair falling from updo hairstyles.

[18]Literally translated *Peony Lantern*, it was a hit kabuki play in the late nineteenth century and centered on a ghost story. Famously, Onoe Kikugoro V played three roles at once, including that of a female ghost.

[19]The surname of a kabuki acting dynasty. In the late nineteenth century, Onoe Kikugoro V began acting in kabuki plays dressed in both western and traditional Japanese clothing. In the eighteenth century, Onoe Kikugoro III distinguished himself by being the first kabuki actor to break from the tradition of playing only one type of role (villain, woman, hero) to instead play many. The Kikugoro name continues to this day.

C

The idea of an idiotic spider tying his net across my front gate!

How ever could he be so ambitious as even to incline to arrest me!

He may very likely be a detective. A railroad brigand is hiding in these Heights,[20] *I suppose.*

The world is running worse every day.

How shocking!

It was a fundamental error of God, to create that adventuress Eve. The offspring of a crow can't be other than a crow.

Our squirrel history is not blotted by any criminal. I feel a bit conceited in speaking about it. How can I help it?

The trouble with God is that he was awfully vain to express his own ability by so many useless things.

Rifle, for instance.

My poor wife!

D

To-day is the anniversary of my beloved. She was shot by one two-legged barbarian.

I appealed to the police. American police are rotten, through and through. The murderer bribed them, I fancy.

I found my wife, but she was only a skin.

How often did I tell her that she was risking too much in sporting around! But she didn't mind me, insisting that sight-seeing was a better education.

I carried her skin into my home.

I cleansed it, and altered its form a trifle, because it was a lady's. I am still keeping it for church-wear.

I feel dreadful, thinking of her.

E

A butterfly passed by my cavern, a hundred times.

Each time she threw me a vulgar laugh.

Her face was thickly powdered in yellow. Does she think herself charming? I should say that I would prefer a girl in tights from a saloon-stage to her indecency.

Such a flirt!

I suppose that she wanted me to marry her.

No!

Am I not old enough to avoid running into such foolishness?

---

[20]The home of Mr. Heine, the fictionalized name of Joachim Miller.

F

Rainy day!

I sat in a memorial corner of my cave, with an unfinished novel of my wife's.

I do judge she had flashes of genius. She was so deep, like the sky. I never suspected that she could gracefully have beaten George Eliot, if she had only survived.

Poor girl!

One tenderly loved by God passes away young.

I have fallen into the habit of crying unmanfully nowadays.

I cannot help it, can I?

G

One thing I must furnish is a bathroom.

Cleanliness is the first rule of heaven, I am told.

I went to the lily pond to take a gracious bath.

O such water gamins! Dirty-handed frogs!

How could I dip me in the turbid water?

The frogs ought to go to a reformatory school. They have no culture, whatever.

H

Camera hunters are thick as fogs.

To-day I came near being a victim.

No, sir!

I can't permit my picture to be seen with those of cheap matinee idols. I must keep some dignity.

Americans are too commercial altogether. The pictures of our race are in demand, I imagine.

I

Beautiful moon, last night!

I filled my stomach with the divine water from a creek.

My face waved in the water. I flattered myself that I was a pretty handsome gentleman.

I sang an ancient Chinese song:

"Come 'long, to-morrow moon,
Carrying a harp!"

J

Stop your empty noise, meadow-larks!

Silence is the first study of this hill and the last, don't you know?

I am absorbed in my grave work, "The Secret of the World."

K

My neighbouring Jap girl is rather attractive, isn't she?
I heard a few scratches of her native bubbling.
The pagan speech is not so bad as I thought.

L

If there is one thing I cannot endure, it is ignorance.
What is the state of your roses, old boy?
The poet Heine is utterly alien to rose culture. Shall I order "How to Raise Roses" from a London publisher?

M

I went up the hill to pray to God. The higher the nearer.
When I came back, my honourable vestibule was blocked, I found, by the dirt. The poet was ditching close by my residence.
I couldn't blame his conduct, however, because no one could see my home. I don't hang out a sign like a quack doctor.
It occurred to me that I would strike into his cottage, and snatch the best poems from his drawer, and sell them with my name.
"I must secure the international copyright," I said.
But I couldn't dare it, my impulse being thwarted.
I am no wicked reporter, don't you see?
I hid me in his historical iron pot all day.

N

Heine was posting around the following card:

No Shooting.

I venture to say that he is the only one civilised Two-Legged in the whole world.

O

Where is my napkin?
Chinese laundry isn't punctual in delivery.

P

I think I must learn how to swear for a pastime.

Q

My fellow brother Mr.——was shot this morning.

The paper says that there is a possibility of war between Russian and Japan. A preacher prophesies the disappearance of the universe.

Everything is precarious in the extreme.

I will not poke around outside during the day. I will loaf in the poet's orchard under the breezy moonlight.

Poetical existence is just enough. I will withdraw me to the sanctuary of the Muses.

R

Heaven be with my soul! Amen!

S

Good-bye, my dear old world! . . .

[After her arrival in New York City, Miss Morning Glory's narrative takes a more overt ethnographic turn. The novel ends by firmly setting up the premise of the sequel, *The American Letters of a Japanese Parlor-Maid*.]

16th—It seems to me a recent style that New York ladies discard their babies to leave them in the hands of European immigrants (very likely they want them to learn an ungrammatical hodge-podge, as respectableness is old-fashioned) and accompany a dog with mighty affection.

O my dear "chin"[21] that I left at home!

Shall I call it to Amerikey?

Little loyal thing, pathetic, clinging!

I am sure it would beat any other in a dog contest.

17th—I never saw such hungry eyes in my life as those of an organ-grinder, set upon the windows for a dropping penny.

To an artist they would hint of a prisoner's bloodshot eyes numbed by useless gazing toward the light of the world.

Poor Italians!

They don't know one thing but turning the handle.

The last two days they placed their organ—read their sign, "Garibaldi & Co."—under my apartment at the same hour for my bit money.

I thought one of them might be a grandson of the renowned Italian patriot. How interesting it would be to be told of his shipwreck in life!

---

[21]A breed of Japanese dog but also often a generic name for any dog.

Now three o'clock.

There's one more hour before their frolic music will gush.

I must wrap some money in paper for them.

God bless them—simple creatures who work hard!

18th—Mr. Consul—an old man who sips the grayness of celibacy—never strays out from his official duty. He calls society and novels two recent pieces of foolery.

The family of Uncle's intimate is off in Europe.

The possibility of a nice time for me is verily illegible. Tsumaranai![22]

Last night I sketched an adventure of enlisting in the band of domestics.

"Capital idea to examine a New York household!" I said, when I left my breakfast table.

I humbled myself to a newspaper office with the following shamefaced advertisement:

"Jap girl, nineteen, good-looking, longs for a place in a family of the first rank."

I used every kind of oratory to bring my uncle to agree to my two weeks of freedom.

19th—Two letters were waiting me at the office.

One from No. 296 of a certain part.

296?

Unfortunately it sounds like "nikumu" in Japanese, meaning hatred.

And the other was from Fifth Avenue.

Parlour maid.

Twelve dollars for a month.

I shall accept it, since it is the proper quarter for seeing the high-toned New Yorker.

I feel already a servant feeling.

I am sorry that I didn't discipline myself before in dusting.

I will style me an honest worker for awhile. "Toiling for my daily bread," does ring an American sound, doesn't it?

"Domestic girl has no right, I think, to sit with Messrs. Consul and Secretary," I said, moving my dinner plate to the kitchen table.

Morning Glory, isn't it time you changed the book of your diary?

Really, sir!

Let me close now with a ceremonious bow!

My next book shall be entitled:

"The Diary of a Parlour Maid."

1905

---

[22]What a bore!

ABRAHAM CAHAN
1860–1951

Abraham Cahan has been described as the single most influential personality in the cultural life of well over two million Jewish immigrants and their families during his lifetime. As a journalist and writer, his unique ability to mediate among the various sensibilities and languages of the Lower East Side in New York City placed him at the center of American Jewish culture and Jewish writing. His major fictional works, *Yekl* (1896) and *The Rise of David Levinsky* (1917), are widely recognized as classic accounts of the immigrant experience of Americanization.

Born in Podberezy, Russia, Cahan was educated at traditional Jewish cheders and also studied at the Vilna Teachers Institute, a Russian government school for Jewish teachers. After graduating in 1881, he began teaching and at the same time became deeply involved in radical, underground anti-czarist activities. Forced to flee, he joined a group of immigrants bound for America and arrived in Philadelphia on June 5, 1882. The next day he reached New York, where his religious training proved useless and secular success beckoned. In 1890 he became editor of the weekly *Arbeiter Zeitung*, the paper of the United Hebrew Trades. Using the pseudonym "Proletarian Preacher" he wrote columns that mixed Russian fables, Talmudic parables, and Marxist ideas to convey his socialist critique of capitalism.

National prominence came to Cahan in 1896, when his novella, *Yekl: A Tale of the New York Ghetto*, was published in English. Like many of his contemporaries—Dreiser, Crane, and Norris, for example—Cahan was probing the impact of America's social and economic forces, their power to influence acculturation and assimilation. In *Yekl*, Jake compromises his religion, values, dress, behavior, and family to become an "American" (that is, not a greenhorn) and to acquire money and a new identity. "The Imported Bridegroom" turns on the many kinds of generational and cultural changes, some of them unexpected, that the Americanization of eastern European Jews could entail.

During the decade that followed Cahan published *The Imported Bridegroom and Other Stories* (1898), *The White Terror and the Red: A Novel of Revolutionary Russia* (1905), as well as stories in *Cosmopolitan*. In 1913 he published a four-part series for *McClure's* magazine, "The Autobiography of an American Jew." Enthusiastically received, this work was the genesis of the novel that appeared four years later, Cahan's masterpiece, *The Rise of David Levinsky*. The story of an immigrant who becomes a successful cloak manufacturer, the novel probed deeply into the tensions and conflicts involved in pursuing the American dream of success that had begun to surface in *Yekl*.

Cahan paralleled his career as a novelist and short-story writer with a long, distinguished career as a newspaperman and editor. From 1903 to 1946 he served as editor of the Jewish *Daily Forward*, a socialist paper that he transformed into a mass circulation pacesetter for the Yiddish press. Originally a political radical, Cahan became a pragmatic socialist, influenced by the forces of

Americanization so evident in his fiction and journalism. His dynamic leadership, his use of conversational instead of literary Yiddish, and his pioneering "Bintel Brief," a Yiddish "Dear Abby" column, endeared him to his fellow immigrants and placed him at the center of American Jewish culture and writing. Under Cahan's guidance the *Forward* developed into a powerful national voice in journalism, and he gained influence in American society, especially in liberal and progressive circles.

Cahan's five volumes of memoirs, *Bleter fun mein Leben (Leaves from My Life)*, published from 1926 to 1931, spanned the decades from the 1860s in Russia to the beginning of World War I. When he died in 1951, Abraham Cahan was revered in both Yiddish- and English-speaking communities as an immigrant who had succeeded in the New World but had never forgotten the Old.

Daniel Walden
Pennsylvania State University

PRIMARY WORKS

Yekl and *The Imported Bridegroom and Other Stories*, 1895, 1898; *The Rise of David Levinsky*, 1917.

The Imported Bridegroom

I

Flora was alone in the back parlor, which she had appropriated for a sort of boudoir. She sat in her rocker, in front of the parlor stove, absorbed in *Little Dorrit*. Her well-groomed girlish form was enveloped in a kindly warmth whose tender embrace tinged her interest in the narrative with a triumphant consciousness of the snowstorm outside.

Little by little the rigid afternoon light began to fade into a melancholy gray. Dusk was creeping into the room in almost visible waves. Flora let the book rest on her lap and fixed her gaze on the twinkling scarlet of the stove-glass. The thickening twilight, the warmth of the apartment, and the atmosphere of the novel blended together, and for some moments Flora felt far away from herself.

She was the only girl of her circle who would read Dickens, Scott, or Thackeray in addition to the *Family Story Paper* and the *Fireside Companion*, which were the exclusive literary purveyors to her former classmates at the Chrystie Street Grammar School. There were a piano and a neat little library in her room.

She was rather tall and well formed. Her oblong ivory face, accentuated by a mass of unruly hair of a lusterless black, was never deserted by a faint glimmer of a smile, at once pensive and arch. When she broke into one of her hearty, good-natured laughs, her deep, dark, appealing eyes would seem filled with grief. Her nose, a trifle too precipitous, gave an unexpected tone to the extreme picturesqueness of the whole effect, and, when she walked, partook of the dignity of her gait.

A month or two before we make Flora's acquaintance she had celebrated her twentieth birthday, having been born in this little private house on Mott Street, which was her father's property.

A matchmaker had recently called, and he had launched into a eulogy of a young Jewish physician; but old Stroon had cut him short, in his blunt way: his only child was to marry a God-fearing business man, and no fellow deep in Gentile lore and shaving his beard need apply. As to Flora, she was burning to be a doctor's wife. A rising young merchant, a few years in the country, was the staple matrimonial commodity in her set. Most of her married girl friends, American-born themselves, like Flora, had husbands of this class—queer fellows, whose broken English had kept their own sweethearts chuckling. Flora hated the notion of marrying as the other Mott or Bayard Street girls did. She was accustomed to use her surroundings for a background, throwing her own personality into high relief. But apart from this, she craved a more refined atmosphere than her own, and the vague ideal she had was an educated American gentleman, like those who lived uptown.

Accordingly, when the word "doctor" had left the match-maker's lips, she seized upon it as a great discovery. In those days—the early eighties—a match of this kind was an uncommon occurrence in the New York Ghetto.

Flora pictured a clean-shaven, high-hatted, spectacled gentleman jumping out of a buggy, and the image became a fixture in her mind. "I won't marry anybody except a doctor," she would declare, with conscious avoidance of bad grammar, as it behooved a doctor's wife.

But what was to be done with father's opposition? Asriel Stroon had never been the man to yield, and now that he grew more devout every day, her case seemed hopeless. But then Flora was her father's daughter, and when she took a resolve she could not imagine herself otherwise than carrying it out, sooner or later.

Flora's thoughts were flowing in this direction when her father's gruff voice made itself heard from the dining room below. It was the anniversary of his father's death. In former years he would have contented himself with obit services, at the synagogue; this time, however, he had passed the day in fasting and chanting psalms at home, in addition to lighting his own candle in front of the cantor's desk and reciting *Kaddish*[1] for the departed soul, at the house of prayer. It touched Flora's heart to think of him fasting and praying all day, and, with her book in her hand, she ran down to meet him.

"Just comin' from the synagogue, papa?" she greeted him affectionately, in English. "This settles your fast, don't it?"

"It is not so easy to settle with Him, my daughter," he returned, in Yiddish, pointing to the ceiling. "You can never be through serving the Uppermost. Hurry up, Tamara!" he added, in the direction of the adjoining kitchen.

"You ain' goin' to say more Thilim[2] tonight, are you, pa?"

"Why, does it cost you too much?" he snarled good humoredly.

---

[1]A prayer recited by mourners.   [2]Psalms.

"Yes it does—your health. I won't let you sing again. You are weak and you got enough."

"Hush! It is not potato soup; you can never have enough of it." He fell to tugging nervously at his white beard, which grew in a pair of tiny imperials. "Tamara! It's time to break the fast, isn't it?"

"You can wash your hands. Supper is ready," came the housekeeper's pleasant voice.

He took off his brown derby, and covered his steel-gray hair with a velvet skullcap; and as he carried his robust, middle-sized body into the kitchen, to perform his ablutions, his ruddy, gnarled face took on an air of piety.

When supper was over and Asriel and Tamara were about to say grace, Flora resumed the reading of her novel.

"Off with that lump of Gentile nastiness while holy words are being said!" the old man growled.

Flora obeyed, in amazement. Only a few months before she had seldom seen him intone grace at all. She was getting used to his new habits, but such rigor as he now displayed was unintelligible to her, and she thought it unbearable.

"You can read your book a little after. The wisdom of it will not run away," chimed in Tamara, with good-natured irony. She was a poor widow of forty. Asriel had engaged her for her piety and for the rabbinical learning of her late husband, as much as for her culinary fame in the Ghetto.

Asriel intoned grace in indistinct droning accents. By degrees, however, as he warmed up to the Hebrew prayer, whose words were a conglomeration of incomprehensible sounds to him, he fell to swaying to and fro, and his voice broke into an exalted, heart-rending singsong, Tamara accompanying him in whispers, and dolefully nodding her bewigged head[3] all the while.

Flora was moved. The scene was novel to her, and she looked on with the sympathetic reverence of a Christian visiting a Jewish synagogue on the Day of Atonement.

At last the fervent tones died away in a solemn murmur. Silence fell over the cozy little room. Asriel sat tugging at his scanty beard as if in an effort to draw it into a more venerable growth.

"Flora!" he presently growled. "I am going to Europe."

When Asriel Stroon thought he spoke, and when he spoke he acted.

"Goin' to Europe! Are you crazy, papa? What are you talkin' about?"

"Just what you hear. After Passover I am going to Europe. I must take a look at Pravly."

"But you ain't been there over thirty-five years. You don't remember not'in' at all."

---

[3]In the Jewish Orthodox tradition, women are forbidden to wear their hair loose and exposed in the street. In the nineteenth century, women obeyed this law by shaving their heads and wearing wigs.

"I don't remember Pravly? Better than Mott Street; better than my nose. I was born there, my daughter," he added, as he drew closer to her and began to stroke her glossless black hair. This he did so seldom that the girl felt her heart swelling in her throat. She was yearning after him in advance.

Tamara stared in beaming amazement at the grandeur of the enterprise. "Are you really going?" she queried, with a touch of envy.

"What will you do there?—It's so far away!" Flora resumed, for want of a weightier argument at hand.

"Never mind, my child; I won't have to walk all the way."

"But the Russian police will arrest you for stayin' away so long. Didn't you say they would?"

"The kernel of a hollow nut!" he replied, extemporizing an equivalent of "fiddlesticks!" Flora was used to his metaphors, although they were at times rather vague, and set one wondering how they came into his head at all. "The kernel of a hollow nut! Show a *treif*[4] gendarme a *kosher*[5] coin, and he will be shivering with ague. Long live the American dollar!"

She gave him a prolonged, far-away look, and said, peremptorily: "Mister, you am' goin' nowheres."

"Tamara, hand me my Psalter, will you?" the old man grumbled.

When the girl was gone, the housekeeper inquired: "And Flora—will you take her along?"

"What for? That she might make fun of our ways there, or that the pious people should point their fingers at her and call her Gentile girl, hey? She will stay with you and collect rent. I did not have her in Pravly, and I want to be there as I used to. I feel like taking a peep at the graves of my folks. It is pulling me by the heart, Tamara," he added, in a grave undertone, as he fell to turning over the leaves of his Psalter.

II

When Asriel Stroon had retired from business, he suddenly grew fearful of death. Previously he had had no time for that. What with his flour store, two bakeries, and some real estate, he had been too busy to live, much less to think of death. He had never been seen at the synagogue on weekdays; and on the Sabbath, when, enveloped in his praying-shawl, he occupied a seat at the East Wall, he would pass the time drowsing serenely and nodding unconscious approval of the cantor's florid improvisations, or struggling to keep flour out of his mind, where it clung as pertinaciously as it did to his long Sabbath coat.

The first sermon that failed to lull him to sleep was delivered by a newly landed preacher, just after Asriel had found it more profitable to convert his entire property into real estate. The newcomer dwelt, among other things, upon the fate of the wicked after death and upon their forfeited share in the World to Come. As Asriel listened to the fiery exhortation it suddenly burst upon him that he was very old and very wicked. "I am as full of sins as a watermelon is of

---

[4]Impure.   [5]Pure.

seeds," he said to himself, on coming out of the synagogue. "You may receive notice to move at any time, Asriel. And where is your baggage? Got anything to take along to the other world, as the preacher said, hey?"

Alas! he had been so taken up with earthly title deeds that he had given but little thought to such deeds as would entitle him to a "share in the World-to-Come"; and while his valuable papers lay secure between the fireproof walls of his iron safe, his soul was left utterly exposed to the flames of Sheol.[6]

Then it was that he grew a pair of bushy sidelocks, ceased trimming his twin goatees, and, with his heart divided between yearning after the business he had sold and worrying over his sins, spent a considerable part of his unlimited leisure reading psalms.

What a delight it was to wind off chapter after chapter! And how smoothly it now came off, in his father's (peace upon him!) singsong, of which he had not even thought for more than thirty years, but which suddenly came pouring out of his throat, together with the first verse he chanted! Not that Asriel Stroon could have told you the meaning of what he was so zestfully intoning, for in his boyhood he had scarcely gone through the Pentateuch[7] when he was set to work by his father's side, at flax heckling. But then the very sounds of the words and the hereditary intonation, added to the consciousness that it was psalms he was reciting, "made every line melt like sugar in his mouth," as he once described it to the devout housekeeper.

He grew more pious and exalted every day, and by degrees fell prey to a feeling to which he had been a stranger for more than three decades.

Asriel Stroon grew homesick.

It was thirty-five years since he had left his birthplace; thirty years or more since, in the whirl of his American successes, he had lost all interest in it. Yet now, in the fifty-eighth year of his life, he suddenly began to yearn and pine for it.

Was it the fervor of his religious awakening which resoldered the long-broken link? At all events, numerous as were the examples of piety within the range of his American acquaintance, his notion of genuine Judaism was somehow inseparably associated with Pravly. During all the years of his life in New York he had retained a vague but deep-rooted feeling that American piety was as tasteless an article as American cucumbers and American fish— the only things in which his ecstasy over the adopted country admitted its hopeless inferiority to his native town.

III

On a serene afternoon in May, Asriel drove up to Pravly in a peasant's wagon. He sat listlessly gazing at the unbroken line of wattle-fences and running an imaginary stick along the endless zigzag of their tops. The activity of his senses seemed suspended.

[6]The underworld.
[7]The five books of Moses, which comprise the
Hebrew Bible, or Torah.

Presently a whiff of May aroma awakened his eye to a many-colored waving expanse, and his ear to the languorous whisper of birds. He recognized the plushy clover knobs in the vast array of placid magnificence, and the dandelions and the golden buttercups, although his poor mother tongue could not afford a special name for each flower, and he now addressed them collectively as *tzatzkes*[8]—a word he had not used for thirty-five years. He looked at the tzatzkes, as they were swaying thoughtfully hither and thither, and it somehow seemed to him that it was not the birds but the clover blossoms which did the chirping. The whole scene appealed to his soul as a nodding, murmuring congregation engrossed in the solemnity of worship. He felt as though there were no such flowers in America, and that he had not seen any since he had left his native place.

Echoes of many, many years ago called to Asriel from amid the whispering host. His soul burst into song. He felt like shutting his eyes and trusting himself to the caressing breath of the air, that it might waft him whithersoever it chose. His senses were in confusion: he beheld a sea of fragrance; he inhaled heavenly music; he listened to a symphony of hues.

"What a treat to breathe! What a paradise!" he exclaimed in his heart. "The cholera take it, how delicious! Do you deserve it, old sinner you? Ten plagues you do! But hush! the field is praying—"

With a wistful babyish look he became absorbed in a gigantic well-sweep suspended from the clear sky, and then in the landscape it overhung. The woody mass darkling in the distance was at once racing about and standing still. Fleecy clouds crawled over a hazy hilltop. And yonder—behold! a long, broad streak of silver gleaming on the horizon! Is it a lake? Asriel's eyes are riveted and memories stir in his breast. He recalls not the place itself, but he can remember his reminiscences of it. During his first years in America, at times when he would surrender himself to the sweet pangs of homesickness and dwell, among other things, on the view that had seen him off to the unknown land, his mind would conjure up something like the effect now before his eyes. As a dream does it comes back to him now. The very shadows of thirty-five years ago are veiled.

Asriel gazes before him in deep reverence. The sky is letting itself down with benign solemnity, its measureless trough filled with melody, the peasant's wagon creaking an accompaniment to it all—to every speck of color, as well as to every sound of the scene.

At one moment he felt as though he had strayed into the other world; at another, he was seized with doubt as to his own identity. "Who are you?" he almost asked himself, closing and reopening his hand experimentally. "Who or what is that business which you call life? Are you alive, Asriel?" Whereupon he somehow remembered Flora's photograph, and, taking it out of his bosom pocket, fell to contemplating it.

The wagon turned into a side road, and the Polish peasant, leaning forward, cursed and whipped the animal into a peevish trot. Presently something

---

[8]Trinkets, ornaments.

gray hove in sight. Far away, below, hazy blotches came creeping from behind the sky. The wagon rolls downhill. Asriel is in a flurry. He feels like one on the eve of a great event, he knows not exactly what.

The wagon dashes on. Asriel's heart is all of a flutter. Suddenly—O Lord of the Universe! Why, there glistens the brook—what do you call it? "'Repka?'" he asks the driver.

"Repka!" the other replies, without facing about.

"Repka, a disease into her heart! Repka, dear, may she live long! Who could beat Asriel in swimming?" Over there, on the other side, it was where Asriel's father once chased him for bathing during Nine Days.[9] He bumped his head against the angle of a rock, did the little scamp, and got up with a deep, streaming gash in his lower lip. The mark is still there, and Asriel delights to feel it with his finger now. As he does so the faces of some of his playmates rise before him. Pshaw! he could whip every one of them! Was he not a daredevil of a loafer! But how many of those fellow truants of his will he find alive? he asks himself, and the question wrings his heart.

Asriel strains his eyes at the far distance till, behold! smoke is spinning upward against the blue sky. He can make out the chimney pots. His soul overflows. Sobs choke his breath. "Say!" he begins, addressing himself to the driver. But "say" is English. "*Sloukhai!*"[10] he shouts, with delight in the Polish word. He utters the names of the surrounding places, and the dull peasant's nods of assent thrill him to the core. He turns this way and that, and in his paroxysm of impatience all but leaps out of the wagon. The rambling groups of houses define their outlines. Asriel recognizes the Catholic church. His heart bounds with joy. "Hush, wicked thing! It's a church of Gentiles."[11] But the wicked thing surreptitiously resumes its greeting. And over there, whitening at some distance from the other dwellings—what is it? "The nobleman's palace, as sure as I am a Jew!" He had forgotten all about it, as sure as he was a Jew! But what is the nobleman's name? Is he alive?—And there is the mill—the same mill! "I'll swoon away!" he says to himself audibly.

Asriel regains some composure.

Half an hour later he made his entry into his native town. Here he had expected his agitation to pass the bounds of his physical strength; but it did not. At this moment he was solemnly serene.

The town had changed little, and he recognized it at once. Every spot greeted him, and his return of the salutation was a speechless devotional pathos. He found several things which had faded out of his enshrined picture of the place, and the sight of these moved his soul even more powerfully than those he had looked forward to. Only in one instance was he taken aback. Sure enough, this is Synagogue Lane, as full of puddles as ever; but

---

[9]The nine days that occur between two Jewish holidays, the Feast of Tabernacles and Simhat Torah.

[10]Listen! Cahan gives the transliteration for the Ukrainian word. The Polish word is pronounced and transliterated slightly differently.

[11]People who are not Jewish.

what has come over him? He well remembers that little alley in the rear; and yet it runs quite the other way. Length has turned into width.

And here is Leizer Poisner's inn. "But how rickety it has become!" Asriel's heart exclaims with a pang, as though at sight of a friend prematurely aged and run to seed. He can almost smell the stable occupying the entire length of the little building, and he remembers every room. Hello! The same market place, the same church with the bailiff's office by its side! The sparse row of huts on the river bank, the raft bridge, the tannery—everything was the same as he had left it; and yet it all had an odd, mysterious, far-away air—like things seen in a cyclorama. It was Pravly and at the same time it was not; or, rather, it certainly was the same dear old Pravly, but added to it was something else, through which it now gazed at Asriel. Thirty-five years lay wrapped about the town.

Still, Stroon feels like Asrielke Thirteen Hairs, as his nickname had been here. Then he relapses into the Mott Street landlord, and for a moment he is an utter stranger in his birthplace. Why, he could buy it all up now! He could discount all the rich men in town put together; and yet there was a time when he was of the meanest hereabout. An overpowering sense of triumph surged into his breast. Hey, there! Where are your bigbugs[12]—Zorach Latozky, Reb[13] Lippe, Reb Nochum? Are they alive? Thirty-five years ago Asrielke considered it an honor to shake their palm branch on the Feast of Tabernacles,[14] while now out with your purses, you proud magnates, measure fortunes with Asrielke the heckler, if you dare! His heart swells with exultation. And yet—the black year take it!—it yearns and aches, does Asriel's heart. He looks at Pravly, and his soul is pining for Pravly—for the one of thirty-five years ago, of which this is only a reflection—for the one in which he was known as a crack-brained rowdy of a mechanic, a poor devil living on oatmeal and herring.

With the townspeople of his time Asriel's experience was somewhat different from what he felt in the case of inanimate Pravly. As he confronted them some faces lighted up with their identity at once; and there were even some younger people in whom he instantly recognized the transcribed images of their deceased parents. But many a countenance was slow to catch the reflection of the past which shone out of his eyes; and in a few instances it was not until the name was revealed to Asriel that the retrospective likeness would begin to struggle through the unfamiliar features before him.

"Shmulke!" he shrieked, the moment he caught sight of an old crony, as though they had been parted for no more than a month. Shmulke is not the blooming, sprightly young fellow of yore. He has a white beard and looks somewhat decrepit. Asriel, however, feels as if the beard were only glued to the smooth face he had known. But how Asriel's heart does shrink in his bosom! The fever of activity in which he had passed the thirty-five years had

---

[12]Big shots.
[13]Rabbi or, in some cases, mister.

[14]Palm branches are customarily carried at the Feast of Tabernacles, the Jewish harvest festival.

kept him deaf to the departing footsteps of Time. Not until recently had he realized that the words "old man" applied to him; but even then the fact never came home to him with such convincing, with such terrible force, as it did now that he stood face to face with Shmulke. Shmulke was his mirror.

"Shmulke, Angel of Death, an inflammation into your bones!" he shouted, as he suddenly remembered his playmate's byname and fell on his shoulder.

Shmulke feels awkward. He is ashamed of the long-forgotten nickname, and is struggling to free himself from the unwelcome embrace; but Asriel is much the stronger of the two, and he continues to squeeze him and pat him, grunting and puffing for emotion as he does so.

Aunt Sarah-Rachel, whom Asriel had left an elderly but exceedingly active and clever tradeswoman, he found a bag of bones and in her dotage.

"Don't you know me, auntie?" he implored her. She made no reply, and went on munching her lips. "Can it be that you don't know Asrielke, who used to steal raisins from your grocery?"

"She does not understand anything!" Asriel whispered, in consternation.

IV

Asriel's first Sabbath in the native place he was revisiting was destined to be a memorable day in the annals of that peaceful little town.

At the synagogue, during the morning service, he was not the only object of interest. So far as the furtive glances that came through the peep-holes of the women's compartment were concerned, a much younger guest, from a hamlet near by, had even greater magnetism than he. Reb Lippe, for forty years the "finest householder" of the community, expected to marry his youngest daughter to an *Illoui*,[15] and he now came to flaunt him, and the five-thousand rouble dowry he represented, before the congregation.

Only nineteen and a poor orphan, the fame of the prospective bridegroom, as a marvel of acumen and memory, reached far and wide. Few of the subtlest rabbinical minds in the district were accounted his match in debate, and he was said to have some two thousand Talmudical folios literally at his finger's ends. This means that if you had placed the tip of your finger on some word of a volume, he could have told you the word which came under your pressure on any other page you might name. As we shall have to cultivate the young man's acquaintance, let it be added that he was quite boyish of figure, and that had it not been for an excess of smiling frankness, his pale, blue-eyed face would have formed the nearest Semitic approach to the current portraits of Lord Byron. His admirers deplored his lack of staidness. While visiting at Pravly, in a manner, as the guest of the town, he was detected giving snuff to a pig, and then participating with much younger boys in a race over the bridge.

---

[15]A prodigy of Talmudic lore.

His betrothment to Reb Lippe's daughter was still the subject of negotiation, and there were said to be serious obstacles in the way. The prodigy's relatives were pleased with Reb Lippe's pedigree and social rank, but thought that the boy could marry into a wealthier family and get a prettier girl into the bargain. Nevertheless Reb Lippe's manner at the synagogue was as though the engagement were an accomplished fact, and he kept the young man by his side, his own seat being next the rabbi's, which was by the Holy Ark.[16]

Asriel, as a newcomer, and out of respect for his fabulous wealth, was also accorded a seat of honor on the other side of the Ark. Before he had expatriated himself his place used to be near the door—a circumstance which was fresh in the mind of Reb Lippe, who chafed to see him divert attention from the prodigy and his purchaser. Now Reb Lippe was a proud old gentleman, too jealous of the memory of his rabbinical ancestry and of his own time-honored dignity to give way to a mere boor of a heckler, no matter how much American gold he had to atone for his antecedents. Accordingly, when his fellow trustee suggested that the American ought to be summoned to the reading of the Third Section[17] in the week's portion of the Pentateuch—the highest honor connected with the reading of the Law, and one for which the visiting nabob was sure to pay a liberal donation—the venerable countenance turned crimson.

"Let the sections be auctioned off!" he jerked out.

The proceeding was seldom practiced on an ordinary Sabbath; but Rep Lippe's will was law, as peremptory and irresistible as the Law of Moses, with which it was now concerned. And so the worshippers presently found themselves converted into so many eyewitnesses of a battle of purses.

"Five gildens for the Third!" called out the weazen-faced little sexton from the reading platform, in the traditional sing-song that became his draggling black beard so well. As a bona-fide business transaction is not allowed on the holy day, even though the house of God be the sole gainer by it, the sexton's figures were fictitious—in so far, at least, as they were understood to represent double the actual amount to be paid to the synagogue by the purchaser of the good deed.

"Six gildens for the Third!" he went on in interpretation of a frowning nod from Reb Lippe.

A contemptuous toss of Asriel's head threw another gilden on top of the sum. Two other members signaled to the auctioneer, and, warming up to his task, he sang out with gusto, "Eight gildens for the Third!"

Then came in rapid succession: "Nine gildens for the Third! Ten gildens for the Third! Eleven gildens, twelve, thirteen, fourteen gildens for the Third!"

The other bidders, one by one, dropped out of the race, and when the sum reached sixty gildens the field was left to Reb Lippe and Asriel.

---

[16]The closet or chest in a synagogue that holds the Torah scrolls that are used for public worship.

[17]A designated portion of the Torah is read at communal services, and the weekly portions are divided into sections.

The congregation was spellbound. Some with gaping mouths, others with absorbed simpers on their faces, but all with sportsman-like fire in their eyes, the worshipers craned their necks in the direction of the two contestants alternately.

The prodigy had edged away from his seat to a coign of vantage. He was repeatedly called back by winks from his uncle, but was too deeply interested in the progress of the auction to heed them.

"Seventy gildens for the Third! Seventy-one, seventy-two, three, four, five, seventy-six, seventy-seven, eight, nine, eighty gildens for the Third!"

The skirmish waxed so hot, shots flew so thick and so fast, that the perspiring sexton, and with him some of the spectators, was swiveling his head from right to left and from left to right with the swift regularity of gymnastic exercise.

It must be owned that so far as mute partisanship was concerned, Asriel had the advantage of his adversary, for even some of Reb Lippe's staunchest friends and admirers had a lurking relish for seeing it brought home to their leading citizen that there were wealthier people than he in the world.

The women, too, shared in the excitement of the morning. Their windows were glistening with eyes, and the reports of their lucky occupants to the anxious knots in the rear evoked hubbubs of conflicting interjections which came near involving the matronly assemblage in civil war.

The Third Section brought some twenty-eight rubles, net. Asriel was certain that the last bid had been made by him, and that the honor and the good deed were accordingly his. When it came to the reading, however, and the Third Section was reached, the reader called out Reb Lippe's name.

Asriel was stupefied.

"Hold on! That won't do!" he thundered, suddenly feeling himself an American citizen. "I have bought it and I mean to have it." His face was fire; his eyes looked havoc.

A wave of deprecation swept over the room. Dozens of reading desks were slapped for order. Reb Lippe strode up to the platform, pompous, devout, resplendent in the gold lace of his praying-shawl and the flowing silver of his beard, as though the outburst of indignation against Asriel were only an ovation to himself. He had the cunning of a fox, the vanity of a peacock, and the sentimentality of a woman during the Ten Days of Penance.[18] There were many skeptics as to the fairness of the transaction, but these were too deeply impressed by the grandeur of his triumphal march to whisper an opinion. The prodigy alone spoke his mind.

"Why, I do think the other man was the last to nod—may I be ill if he was not," the *enfant terrible* said quite audibly, and was hushed by his uncle.

"Is he really going to get it?" Asriel resumed, drowning all opposition with his voice. "Milk a billy goat! You can't play that trick on me! Mine was the last bid. Twenty-eight scurvy rubles! Pshaw! I am willing to pay a

[18]The ten days between the Jewish New Year
and the Day of Atonement.

hundred, two hundred, five hundred. I can buy up all Pravly, Reb Lippe, his gold lace and all, and sell him at a loss, too!" He made a dash at the reading platform, as if to take the Third Section by force, but the bedlam which his sally called forth checked him.

"Is this a market place?" cried the second trustee, with conscious indignation.

"Shut the mouth of that boor!" screamed a member, in sincere disgust.

"Put him out!" yelled another, with relish in the scene.

"If he can't behave in a holy place let him go back to his America!" exclaimed a third, merely to be in the running. But his words had the best effect: they reminded Asriel that he was a stranger and that the noise might attract the police.

At the same moment he saw the peaked face of the aged rabbi by his side. Taking him by the arm, the old man begged him not to disturb the Sabbath.

Whether the mistake was on Asriel's side or on the sexton's, or whether there was any foul play in the matter, is not known; but Asriel relented and settled down at his desk to follow the remainder of the reading in his Pentateuch, although the storm of revenge which was raging in his breast soon carried off his attention, and he lost track.

The easy success of his first exhortation brought the rabbi to Asriel's side once again.

"I knew your father—peace upon him! He was a righteous Jew," he addressed him in a voice trembling and funereal with old age. "Obey me, my son, ascend the platform, and offer the congregation a public apology. The Holy One—blessed be He will help you."

The rabbi's appeal moved Asriel to tears, and tingling with devout humility he was presently on the platform, speaking in his blunt, gruff way.

"Do not take it hard, my rabbis! I meant no offense to any one, though there was a trick—as big as a fat bull. Still, I donate two hundred rubles, and let the cantor recite 'God full of Mercy' for the souls of my father and mother—peace upon them."

It was quite a novel way of announcing one's contribution, and the manner of his apology, too, had at once an amusing and a scandalizing effect upon the worshipers, but the sum took their breath away and silenced all hostile sentiment.

The reading over, and the scrolls restored, amid a tumultuous acclaim, to the Holy Ark, the cantor resumed his place at the Omud,[19] chanting a hurried *Half-Kaddish*.[20] "And say ye Amen!" he concluded abruptly, as if startled, together with his listeners, into sudden silence.

Nodding or shaking their heads, or swaying their forms to and fro, some, perhaps mechanically, others with composed reverence, still others in a convulsion of religious fervor, the two or three hundred men were joined

---

[19]The pulpit; sometimes transliterated as *ammud*.

[20]A prayer recited to demarcate one section of a religious service from another.

in whispering chorus, offering the solemn prayer of *Mussaff*.[21] Here and there a sigh made itself heard amid the monotony of speechless, gesticulating ardor; a pair of fingers snapped in an outburst of ecstasy, a sob broke from some corner, or a lugubrious murmur from the women's room. The prodigy, his eyes shut, and his countenance stern with unfeigned rapture, was violently working his lips as if to make up for the sounds of the words which they dared not utter. Asriel was shaking and tossing about. His face was distorted with the piteous, reproachful mien of a neglected child about to burst into tears, his twin imperials dancing plaintively to his whispered intonations. He knew not what his lips said, but he did know that his soul was pouring itself forth before Heaven, and that his heart might break unless he gave way to his restrained sobs.

At last the silent devotions were at an end. One after another the worshipers retreated, each three paces from his post. Only three men were still absorbed in the sanctity of the great prayer: the rabbi, for whom the cantor was respectfully waiting with the next chant, Reb Lippe, who would not "retreat" sooner than the rabbi, and Asriel, who, in his frenzy of zeal, was repeating the same benediction for the fifth time.

When Asriel issued forth from the synagogue he found Pravly completely changed. It was as if, while he was praying and battling, the little town had undergone a trivializing process. All the poetry of thirty-five years' separation had fled from it, leaving a heap of beggarly squalor. He felt as though he had never been away from the place, and were tired to death of it, and at the same time his heart was contracted with homesickness for America. The only interest the town now had for him was that of a medium to be filled with the rays of his financial triumph. "I'll show them who they are and who Asriel is," he comforted himself.

The afternoon service was preceded by a sermon. The "town preacher" took his text, as usual, from the passage in the "Five Books" which had been read in the morning. But he contrived to make it the basis of an allusion to the all-absorbing topic of gossip. Citing the Talmud and the commentaries with ostentatious profuseness, he laid particular stress on the good deed of procuring a scholar of sacred lore for one's son-in-law.

"It is a well-known saying in tractate *Psohim*,"[22] he said, "that one should be ready to sell his all in order to marry his daughter to a scholar.' On the other hand, 'to give your daughter in marriage to a boor is like giving her to a lion.' Again, in trac-tate *Berochath*[23] we learn that 'to give shelter to a scholar bent upon sacred studies, and to sustain him from your estates, is like offering sacrifices to God'; and 'to give wine to such a student is,' according to a passage in tractate *Sota*,[24] 'tantamount to pouring it out on an altar.'"

Glances converged on Reb Lippe and the prodigy by his side.

---

[21]Additional prayers given at services during Sabbaths and other select holidays.
[22]A Torah portion.

[23]A Torah portion.
[24]A Torah portion.

Proceeding with his argument, the learned preacher, by an ingenious chain of quotations and arithmetical operations upon the numerical value of letters, arrived at the inference that compliance with the above teachings was one of the necessary conditions of securing a place in the Garden of Eden.

All of which filled Asriel's heart with a new dread of the world to come and with a rankling grudge against Reb Lippe. He came away from the synagogue utterly crushed, and when he reached his inn the prodigy was the prevailing subject of his chat with the landlord.

V

In the evening of the same day, at the conclusion of the Sabbath, the auction of another good deed took place, and once more the purses of Reb Lippe and Asriel clashed in desperate combat.

This time the good deed assumed the form of a prodigy of Talmudic learning in the character of a prospective son-in-law.

The room (at the residence of one of the young man's uncles) was full of bearded Jews, tobacco smoke, and noise. There were Shaya, the prodigy himself, his two uncles, Reb Lippe, his eldest son, and two of his lieutenants, Asriel, his landlord, and a matchmaker. A live broad-shouldered samovar, its air-holes like so many glowing eyes, stood in the center of the table. Near it lay Flora's photograph, representing her in all the splendor of Grand Street millinery.

The youthful hero of the day eyed the portrait with undisguised, open-mouthed curiosity, till, looked out of countenance by the young lady's doleful, penetrating eyes, he turned from it, but went on viewing it with furtive interest.

His own formula of a bride was a hatless image. The notion, therefore, of this princess becoming his wife both awed him and staggered his sense of decorum. Then the smiling melancholy of the Semitic face upset his image of himself in his mind and set it afloat in a haze of phantasy. "I say you need not look at me like that," he seemed to say to the picture. "Pshaw! you are a Jewish girl after all, and I am not afraid of you a bit. But what makes you so sad? Can I do anything for you? Why don't you answer? Do take off that hat, will you?"

Reb Lippe's daughter did not wear a hat, but she was not to his liking, and he now became aware of it. On the other hand, the word "America" had a fascinating ring, and the picture it conjured was a blend of Talmudic and modern glory.

Reb Lippe's venerable beard was rippled with a nervous smile.

"Yes, I am only a boor!" roared Asriel, with a touch of Bounderby ostentation.[25]

---

[25]In Charles Dickens's novel *Hard Times* (1854), Josiah Bounderby is a wealthy manufacturer who falsely presents himself as having been abandoned and homeless as a child and to have risen despite these obstacles.

"But you know it is not myself I want the boy to marry. Twenty thousand rubles, spot cash, then, and when the old boor takes himself off, Shaya will inherit ten times as much. She is my only child, and when I die—may I be choked if I take any of my houses into the grave. Worms don't eat houses, you know."

The quality of his unhackneyed phrase vexed the sedate old talmudists, and one of them remarked, as he pointed a sarcastic finger at the photograph: "Your girl looks like the daughter of some titled Gentile. Shaya is a Jewish boy."

"You don't like my girl, don't you?" Asriel darted back. "And why, pray? Is it because she is not a lump of ugliness and wears a hat? The grand rabbi of Wilna is as pious as any of you, isn't he? Well, when I was there, on my way here, I saw his daughter, and she also wore a hat and was also pretty. Twenty thousand rubles!"

By this time the prodigy was so absorbed in the proceedings that he forgot the American photograph, as well as the bearing which the auction in progress had upon himself. Leaning over the table as far as the samovar would allow, and propping up his face with both arms, he watched the scene with thrilling but absolutely disinterested relish.

After a great deal of whispering and suppressed excitement in the camp of Asriel's foe, Reb Lippe's son announced: "Ten thousand rubles and five years' board." This, added to Reb Lippe's advantages over his opponent by virtue of his birth, social station, and learning, as well as of his residing in Russia, was supposed to exceed the figure named by Asriel. In point of fact, everybody in the room knew that the old talmudist's bid was much beyond his depth; but the assemblage had no time to be surprised by his sum, for no sooner had it been uttered than Asriel yelled out, with impatient sarcasm: "Thirty thousand rubles, and life-long board, and lodging, and bath money, and stocking darning, and cigarettes, and matches, and mustard, and soap—and what else?"

The prodigy burst into a chuckle, and was forthwith pulled down to his chair. He took a liking to the rough-and-ready straightforwardness of the American.

There was a pause. Shaya and his uncles were obviously leaning toward the "boor." Asriel was clearly the master of the situation.

At last Reb Lippe and his suite rose from their seats.

"You can keep the bargain!" he said to Asriel, with a sardonic smile.

"And be choked with it!" added his son.

"What is your hurry, Reb Lippe?" said one of the uncles, rushing to the old man's side with obsequious solicitude. "Why, the thing is not settled yet. We don't know whether—"

"You don't, but I do. I won't take that boy if _he_ brings twenty thousand rubles to _his_ marriage portion. Good-night!"

"Good-night and good-year!" Asriel returned. "Why does the cat hate the cream? Because it is locked up."

An hour afterward the remainder of the gathering were touching glasses and interchanging *mazol-tovs*[26] upon the engagement of Flora Stroon to Shaya Golub.

"And now receive my *mazol-tov!*" said Asriel, pouncing upon the prodigy and nearly crushing him in his mighty embrace. "*Mazol-tov* to you, Flora's bridegroom! *Mazol-tov* to you, Flora's predestined one! My child's dear little bridegroom!" he went on, hiding his face on the young man's shoulder. "I am only a boor, but you shall be my son-in-law. I'll dine you and wine you, as the preacher commanded, pearls will I strew on your righteous path, a crown will I place on your head—I am only a boor!"

Sobs rang in the old man s voice. The bystanders looked on in smiling, pathetic silence.

"A boor, but an honest man," some one whispered to the uncles.

"A heart of gold!" put in the innkeeper.

"And what will Flora say?" something whispered to Asriel, from a corner of his overflowing heart. "Do you mean to tell me that the American young lady will marry this old-fashioned, pious fellow?" "Hold your tongue, fool you!" Asriel snarled inwardly. "She will have to marry him, and that settles it, and don't you disturb my joy. It's for her good as well as for mine."

With a sudden movement he disengaged his arms, and, taking off his enormous gold watch and chain, he put it on Shaya, saying: "Wear it in good health, my child. This is your first present from your sweetheart. But wait till we come to America!"

The next morning Asriel visited the cemetery, and was overawed by its size. While living Pravly had increased by scarcely a dozen houses, the number of dwellings in silent Pravly had nearly doubled.

The headstones, mostly of humble size and weatherworn, were a solemn minority in a forest of plain wooden monuments, from which hung, for identification, all sorts of unceremonious tokens, such as old tin cans, bottomless pots, cast-off hats, shoes, and what not. But all this, far from marring the impressiveness of the place, accentuated and heightened the inarticulate tragedy of its aspect. The discarded utensils or wearing apparel seemed to be brooding upon the days of their own prime, when they had participated in the activities of the living town yonder. They had an effect of mysterious muteness, as of erstwhile animated beings—comrades of the inmates of the overgrown little mounds underneath, come to join them in the eternal rest of the city of death.

"Father! Father!" Asriel began, in a loud synagogue intonation, as he prostrated himself upon an old grave, immediately after the cantor had concluded his prayer and withdrawn from his side. "It is I, Asriel, your son—do you remember? I have come all the way from America to ask you to pray for me and my child. She is a good girl, father, and I am trying to lead her on the path of righteousness. She is about to marry the greatest scholar of

[26]Congratulations.

God's Law hereabouts. Do pray that the boy may find favor in her eyes, father! You know, father dear, that I am only a boor, and woe is me! I am stuffed full of sins. But now I am trying to make up and to be a good Jew. Will you pray the Uppermost to accept my penance?" he besought, with growing pathos in his voice. "You are near Him, father, so do take pity upon your son and see to it that his sins are forgiven. Will you pray for me? Will you? But, anyhow, I care more for Flora—Bloome, her Yiddish name is. What am I? A rusty lump of nothing. But Flora—she is a flower. Do stand forth before the High Tribunal and pray that no ill wind blow her away from me, that no evil eye injure my treasure. She lost her mother when she was a baby, poor child, and she is the only consolation I have in the world. But you are her grandfather—do pray for her!"

Asriel's face shone, his heavy voice rang in a dismal, rapturous, devotional singsong. His eyes were dry, but his soul was full of tears and poetry, and he poured it forth in passionate, heart-breaking cadences.

"What is the difference between this grass blade and myself?" he asked, a little after. "Why should you give yourself airs, Asriel? Don't kick, be good, be pious, carry God in your heart, and make no fuss! Be as quiet as this grass, for hark! the hearse is coming after you, the contribution boxes are jingling, the Angel of Death stands ready with his knife—Oh, do pray for your son, father!" he shrieked, in terror.

He paused. A bee, droning near by, seemed to be praying like himself, and its company stirred Asriel's heart.

"Oh, father! I have not seen you for thirty-five years. Thirty-five years!" he repeated in deliberate tones and listening to his own voice.

"We are the thirty-five?" some distant tombstones responded, and Asriel could not help pausing to look about, and then he again repeated, "Thirty-five years! Can I never see you again, father? Can't I see your dear face and talk to you, as of old, and throw myself into fire or water for you? Can't I? Can't I? Do you remember how you used to keep me on your knees or say prayers with me at the synagogue, and box my ears so that the black year took me when you caught me skipping in the prayer book? Has it all flown away? Has it really?"

He paused as though for an answer, and then resumed, with a bitter, malicious laugh at his own expense: "Your father is silent, Asriel! Not a word, even if you tear yourself to pieces. All is gone, Asrielke! All, all, all is lost forever!"

His harsh voice collapsed. His speech died away in a convulsion of subdued sobbing. His soul went on beseeching his father to admit him to the restful sanctity of his company.

When Asriel rose to his feet and his eye fell upon a tombstone precisely like his father's, he frowned upon it, with a sense of jealousy. On his way to his mother's grave, in the older part of the cemetery, he ever and anon turned to look back. His father's tombstone was rapidly becoming merged in a forest of other monuments. His dead father, his poor father, was losing his individuality, till he was a mere speck in this piebald medley of mounds, stones, boards, and all sorts of waste. Asriel felt deeply hurt. He retraced his steps till his father's resting place once more became the center of the world.

Then he went to pay his respects and tears to the graves of his mother, sisters, brothers, uncles. At last, completely exhausted, he took to walking among the other headstones. As he stopped to make out their Hebrew inscriptions, he would now hang his head, in heart-wringing reminiscence, now heave a sigh, or clap his hands, in grievous surprise.

The tombstones and tomb-boards were bathed in the reddish gold of the late afternoon sun. Asriel had not yet broken his fast, but although shattered in body and spirit he felt no hunger and was reluctant to leave the graveyard. He found here more of his contemporaries that he well remembered, more of the Pravly of his time, than in the town a verst or two away. The place asserted a stronger claim upon him and held him by the force of its unearthly fascination.

When he reached town at last, he felt newborn. Pravly was again dear to his heart, although Flora and America drew him to them with more magnetism than ever. He strove to speak in soft accents, and went about the houses of his relatives and the poor of the town, distributing various sums and begging the recipients of his gifts "to have pity and not to thank him," lest it should detract from the value of his good deed.

Then he went to make peace with Reb Lippe.

"You are going to stay here, so you can get another prodigy," he pleaded humbly. "But one cannot get such goods in America. Besides, you can read Talmud yourself, while I am only a boor, and what have I done to make sure of my share in the world to come? Here are three hundred rubles for charity. Do forgive me, Reb Lippe, will you? What will you lose by it?"

There were others in the room, and the unique pathos of the plea touched and amused them at once. Reb Lippe was moved to the point of tears. Moreover, the present situation took the venom out of his defeat.

"I forgive you with all my heart," he said impulsively, patting "the boor" as he would a child. "Be seated. May the Uppermost bring you home in peace and bless the union. There is another young man who is worthy of my daughter; and Shaya—may the Holy One—blessed be He—grant him the will and the power to spread His Law in America. The Jews there want a young man like him, and I am glad he is going with you. You are taking a precious stone with you, Reb Asriel. Hold it dear."

"You bet I will," Asriel replied gleefully.

VI

The nearer Asriel, with the prodigy in tow, came to New York, the deeper did Pravly sink into the golden mist of romance, and the more real did the great American city grow in his mind. Every mile added detail to the picture, and every new bit of detail made it dearer to his heart.

He was going home. He felt it more keenly, more thrillingly every day, every hour, every minute.

Sandy Hook[27] hove in sight.

Can there be anything more beautiful, more sublime, and more uplifting than the view, on a clear summer morning, of New York harbor from an approaching ship? Shaya saw in the enchanting effect of sea, verdure, and sky a new version of his visions of paradise, where, ensconced behind luxuriant foliage, the righteous—venerable old men with silvery beards—were nodding and swaying over gold-bound tomes of the Talmud. Yet, overborne with its looming grandeur, his heart grew heavy with suspense, and he clung close to Asriel.

All was bustle and expectation on board. The little deck engines never ceased rumbling, and the passengers, spruced up as if for church, were busy about their baggage, or promenading with a festive, nervous air.

Asriel twitched and bit his lip in rapture.

"Oh, how blue the water is!" said Shaya wistfully.

"America is a fine country, is it not?" the old man rejoined. "But it can't hold a candle to Flora. Wait till you see her. You just try to be a good boy," he kept murmuring; "stick to your Talmud, and don't give a peper[28] for anything else, and all God has given me shall be yours. I have no son to say Kaddish[29] for my soul when I am dead. Will you be my Kaddish, Shaya? Will you observe the anniversary of my death?" he queried, in a beseeching tone which the young man had never heard from him.

"Of course I will," Shaya returned, like a dutiful child.

"Will you? May you live long for it. In palaces will I house you, like the eye in my head will I cherish you. I am only a boor, but she is my daughter, my only child, and my whole life in this world."

Asriel kept Flora unadvised as to the name of the steamer or the date of his arrival. Upon landing he did not go directly to his residence, but first took his importation into a large "clothing and gents' furnishing store" on Broadway, from which the *illoui* emerged completely transformed. Instead of his uncouth cap and the draggling coat which had hidden his top boots from view, he was now arrayed in the costliest "Prince Albert," the finest summer derby, and the most elegant button shoes the store contained. This and a starched shirt-front, a turned-down collar, and a gaudy puff-tie set into higher relief the Byronic effect of his intellectual, winsome face.

Asriel snapped his fingers for delight. He thought him easily the handsomest and best-dressed man on Broadway. "It is the Divine Presence shining upon him!" he murmured to himself, dragging the young man by the hand, as if he were a truant schoolboy. Barring the prodigy's sidelocks,[30] which were tightly curled into two little cushions in front of his ears, he now thought him thoroughly Americanized.

---

[27]A barrier peninsula on the coast of New Jersey.
[28]Pepper.
[29]A central prayer in the Jewish prayer service that is used also in funerals and memorial

services. "Saying Kaddish" denotes the ritual of mourning.
[30]Signs of divine learning and piety.

The prodigy, however, felt tied and fettered in the garb of Gentile civilization, and as he trudged along by his convoy's side, he viewed his transformed self in the store windows, or stared, rabbit-like, at the lumbering stagecoaches and the hurrying noblemen.

Asriel let himself and his charge in noiselessly with the latch-key, which had accompanied him, together with a bunch of other keys, on his tour. They entered the hallway on tiptoe.

The little house rang with the voluminous tones of Flora's piano, through which trickled the doleful tremolo of her subdued contralto. Since her father had left her pining for his return, "Home, Sweet Home" had become her favorite tune.

Flora was alone in the house, and her unconscious welcome was all the sweeter to Asriel's soul for the grieving note which ran through it. His heart throbbed with violence. Shaya's sank in awe. He had never heard a piano except through the window of some nobleman's house.

"Hush! Do you hear?" the old man whispered. "That's your predestined bride." With that he led the way downstairs. There they paused to kiss the divine name on the *Mezuzah* of the doorpost.[31]

"Tamara!" Asriel called, under his breath, looking for the pious housekeeper in the dining room and in the kitchen. "She is not in. Must be out marketing or about her good deeds. A dear soul she! Oh, it's her fast day; she fasts Mondays and Thursdays."

Then he stepped up in front of a tin box that was nailed to one of the kitchen doors and took out his pocketbook. It was one of the contribution-boxes of the "Meyer-the-Wonder-worker Fund," which is devoted to the support of pious old European Jews who go to end their days in the Land of Israel. Every orthodox Jew in the world keeps a similar box in his house and drops a coin into it whenever he escapes some danger. Asriel had safely crossed the wide ocean, and his offering was a handful of silver.

Well, you stay here, Shaya, and don't budge till you are called," he said; and leaving the young man to his perplexity he betook himself upstairs, to surprise his daughter.

Flora burst into tears of joy, and hugged him again and again, while he stroked her black hair or stood scowling and grinning for admiration.

"Ah, you dear, cranky papa!" she burst out, for the fourth time realizing that he was actually come back to her, and for the fourth time attacking him.

At last he thought they had had enough. He was dying to protract the scene, but there was that troublesome job to get rid of, and Asriel was not the man to put such things off. Whenever he felt somewhat timid he would grow facetious. This was the case at the present juncture.

---

[31]A parchment that is inscribed with verses from the Torah, rolled up like a scroll, and placed inside a wooden or metal case that is affixed to doorposts. It is customary to touch the mezuzah and recite a prayer after passing through the door.

"Well, Flora, guess what sort of present your papa has brought you," he said, reddening to his ears. "I'll bet you you won't hit if you keep on guessing till tomorrow. No girl has ever got such a present as long as America is America."

Flora's eyes danced with joyous anticipation. Her mind was ablaze with diamonds, rubies, emeralds, sapphires, pearls.

"I have got a bridegroom for you—a fifteen-thousand-dollar one. Handsomest and smartest fellow on earth. He is an *illoui*."

"A what?" she asked, in amazement.

"Oh, a wonderful chap, you know, deep in the Talmud and the other holy books. He could knock all the rabbis of Europe to smithereens. The biggest bug in Pravly was after him, but I beat him clean out of his boots. Shaya! Come right up!"

The girl gazed at her father in bewilderment. Was he joking or was he in dead, terrific earnest?

Shaya made his appearance, with his eyes on the floor, and wringing the index finger of his right hand, as he was wont to do whenever he felt ill at ease, which was seldom, however.

Flora's brain was in a whirl.

"This is your predestined bridegroom, my daughter. A fine present, is it not? Did you ever expect such a raisin of a sweetheart, hey? Well, children, I must go around to see about the baggage. Have a chat and be acquainted." With that he advanced to the door.

"Papa! Papa!" Flora frantically called to him. But he never turned his head and went his way.

In her despair she rushed at the young stranger, who was still wringing his finger, as he stood in the middle of the parlor, eyeing the carpet, and snapped out: — "Mister, you had better go. If you think you are going to be my bridegroom, you are sadly mistaken."

She spoke in Yiddish, but her pronunciation, particularly of the letter "r," was so decidedly American that to Shaya it sounded at once like his native tongue and the language of Gentiles. However, it was Yiddish enough, and the fact of this imposing young lady speaking it gave him the feeling of being in the presence of a Jewish princess of biblical times.

"Where shall I go? I don't know anybody here." He said it with an air of naïve desperation which touched the girl's heart. "Where is my fault?" he added pleadingly.

She gave him a close look, and, taking him by his clean-cut beardless chin, opened her eyes wide at him, and broke into a hearty laugh.

"My father has really brought you over to marry me?" she questioned, for the first time awakening to the humorous side of the situation, and again she burst out laughing.

Shaya blushed and took hold of his finger, but he forthwith released it and also broke into a giggle. Her merriment set him at his ease, and her labored Yiddish struck him as the prattle of a child.

Flora was amused and charmed as with a baby. Shaya felt as if he were playing with another boy.

Of all the immigrants who had married or were engaged to marry some of her girlfriends, none had, just after landing, been so presentable, so sweet-faced, and so droll as this scholarly looking fellow. There would have been nothing odd in her marrying him a year or two later, after he had picked up some broken English and some of the customs of the country. But then her mind was firmly made up, and she had boasted to her friends that she was bound to marry a doctor, and here this boy was not even going to be a business man, but an orthodox rabbi or something of the sort. The word "rabbi" was associated in her mind with the image of an unkempt, long-skirted man who knew nothing of the world, took snuff, and made life a nuisance to himself and to others. Is she going to be a *rabbitzen?*[32] No! No! No! Come what may, none but a refined American gentleman shall lead her under the nuptial canopy! And in her rage she fled from the parlor and went to nurse her misery on the dining room lounge.

Presently, as she lay with her hands clasped under her head, abandoned to her despair and fury, and yet unable to realize that it was all in real earnest, a fretting sensation settled somewhere in her heart. At first it was only like a grain of sand, but it kept growing till it lay a heavy, unbearable lump. She could not stand the idea of that poor, funny dear being left alone and scared out of his wits. Still, she would not stir. Let papa take him away or she will leave the house and go to work in a factory.

"Tamara!" she suddenly raised herself to say, the moment the housekeeper came into the room. "There is a man upstairs. He must be hungry."

"Then why don't you give him something to eat?" Tamara responded tartly. "You know it is Monday and I am faint. But who is he and what is he doing upstairs? Let him come down."

"Go and see him for yourself," snapped Flora. "You will find him one of your set—a Talmudical scholar, a pious soul," she added, with a venomous laugh.

Tamara bent upon her a look full of resentment as well as of devout reproach, and betook herself upstairs.

When Asriel came he explained that Shaya was not going to be a rabbi, nor dress otherwise than as an American gentleman, but that he would lead a life of piety and spend his time studying the Talmud, partly at home and partly at some synagogue. "What, then, have I worked all my life for?" he pleaded. "I am only a boor, my daughter, and how long does a fellow live? Don't darken my days, Flora."

Tamara kept nodding pious assent. "In the old country a girl like you would be glad to marry such a child of the Law," she expostulated with the girl. "It is only here that we are sinners and girls marry none but worldly men. May every daughter of Israel be blessed with such a match."

"Mind your own business!" Flora exploded. She understood her father's explanation but vaguely, and it had the opposite of the desired effect upon her. "Leave her alone. The storm will blow over," Asriel whispered.

* * *

---

[32]A rabbi's wife.

When Asriel's baggage arrived it proved to include a huge box full of Hebrew books. They were of various sizes, but twenty-five of them were large, uniform, leather-bound folio volumes, portly and resplendent in a superabundance of gilding and varnish. Of these, twenty contained the whole of the Babylonian Talmud together with the various commentaries, the remaining five comprising the Alphos. After a little a walnut bookcase made its appearance. It was accorded a place of honor in the front parlor, and Asriel, Tamara, and Shaya busied themselves with arranging the sacred books on its shelves.

Flora sat eyeing them sarcastically, till, sobs rising to her throat, she retired to the seclusion of her bedroom, on the top floor, and burst out crying as if her heart would break. The contents of all those books, which her father had imported as accessories of her would-be bridegroom, were Chinese to her. She had never seen so many of them nor given a moment's attention to the occasional talks which she had chanced to overhear concerning such books and the men who spent their lives reading them. They now frightened her, as if they were filled with weird incantations and Shaya were the master of some uncanny art.

The prodigy was busy arranging his library, now and then opening a book to examine its print. Presently, as he was squatting down before a chair upon which he was turning over the leaves of a bulky volume, his attention was arrested by a celebrated passage. Without changing his posture, he proceeded to glance it over, until, completely absorbed, he fell to humming the words, in that peculiar singsong, accompanied by indescribable controversial gesticulations, which seem to be as indispensable in reading Talmud as a pair of eyes.

"Look, look!" Tamara nudged Asriel, whom she was helping to transfer the remaining books to the marble table. Asriel turned his head toward the prodigy, and for a few moments the two stood staring at the odd, inspiring spectacle with gaping admiration. Then the housekeeper and her employer exchanged a glance of intelligence, she nodding her bewigged head piously, as much as to say: "What a find Heaven has placed in your way!"

"The Uppermost has blessed you," she added in whispers.

"May he enjoy long life with us!" Asriel returned, with a sigh.

"Flora does not know what a treasure the Lord of the Universe has sent her."

"She will," he rejoined curtly.

VII

It was at the head of a dozen venerable Talmudists, including the rabbi of the congregation, that Asriel returned from the synagogue next Saturday morning. The learned company was entertained with wine, cold fish, and some of the lemon pie and genuine Yiddish pastry for which Tamara was famous.

"Here is life, Mr. Stroon! Here is life, Shaya!" each of the guests said, raising his glass.

"Life and peace! Life and peace!" was the uniform response. "God bless the union and let them live a hundred and twenty years," pursued Reb

Mendele, a little man with luxuriant red sidelocks, as he reached for a piece of Sabbath cake.

"And grant that they give birth to children and bring them up to the Law, the Bridal Canopy, and deeds of righteousness," chimed in another, whose ear-locks were two sorry corkscrew-like appendages, as he held up a slice of fish on the points of his fork.

"And Shaya continue a child of the Law and study it with never-failing zeal," came from between a dangling pair of tubes.

"That's the point!" emphasized a chorus of munching mouths.

"But where is the bride?" somebody demanded. "She must show herself! she must show herself!"

"That's right," Reb Mendele seconded heartily. "Out with the bride! 'And the daughters of Jerusalem come out dancing,'" he quoted; "'and what do they say? "Lift thine eyes, young man, and behold the maiden thou choosest. Do not set thine eye on beauty—.""'" He broke off abruptly, reddening. The remainder of the quoted passage runs as follows: "Set thine eye (the maidens say to the young man) on good family connections, as is written in Proverbs: 'False is grace and vain is beauty: a woman that feareth the Lord shall indeed be praised.'" It would have been anything but appropriate to the occasion, and while the Chaldaic[33] and the Hebrew of the citation were Greek to Asriel, there was the prodigy to resent it.

Another hoary-headed child of the Law interposed: "'Go forth and look, O ye daughters of Zion, on King Solomon, with the crown wherewith his mother hath crowned him on the day of the joy of his espousals, and on the day of the joy of his heart.' Saith the Talmud: 'By "the day of his espousals" is meant the day of the Giving of the Law.' Accordingly, when Shaya's wedding takes place, if God be pleased, it will be an espousal in the literal as well as in the Talmudic sense, for is he not full of Law? It will therefore be the Giving of the Law in marriage to Reb Asriel's daughter, will it not?"

"Never mind blushing, Shaya," said the rabbi, although the prodigy, engrossed with the "paradise taste" of the lemon pie—a viand he had never dreamed of—and keeping a sharp eye on the dwindling contents of the tart-dish, was too busy to blush. Flora was in her bedroom, the place of her voluntary exile most of the time that her compulsory sweetheart was in the house. Her father was kind and attentive to her, as usual, and never mentioned Shaya's name to her. But she knew that he was irrevocably bent upon the marriage, and her mood often verged on suicide. Could it really be that after all her cherished dreams of afternoon drives in Central Park, in a doctor's buggy and with the doctor himself by her side, she was doomed to be the wife of that clumsy rustic, who did not even know how to shake hands or to bow to a lady, and who could not say a word without performing some grotesque gesture or curling his horrid sidelocks? Oh, what would the girls

[33]Referring to an ancient language of southern Mesopotamia that is one of the languages of the Talmud.

say! She had twitted them on the broken English of their otherwise wordly and comparatively well-mannered sweethearts, and now she herself was matched with that wretch of a holy soul!

And yet Shaya was never in her mind invested in the image of a "clumsy rustic" nor of a "holy soul." Whenever she saw him she would screw up a frown, but on one occasion, when their eyes met across the supper table, they could not help smiling to each other, like children at church.

"Flora dear, I want to speak to you," Asriel said, knocking at the locked door of her hiding-place.

"Leave me alone, papa, will you? I've got a headache," she responded.

"That's all right, but unlock the door. I won't eat you up."

She was burning to have her father broach the painful subject, so that she might have it out with him. With that end in view, she set her teeth and turned the key. But Asriel came in so unaggressive, so meek, in a pleading attitude so utterly unlike him, that he took her by surprise, as it were, and she stood completely disarmed.

"I beg you, my daughter, do not shorten my days, and come down-stairs," he entreated with heartfelt ardor. "I have so little to live, and the Uppermost has sent me a piece of comfort so that I may die a righteous Jew—will you take it away from me? Will you put me to shame before God and man?"

The words and the pathos with which they were delivered so oddly con-trasted with all she knew of her father that she felt as if he were really pray-ing for his life. She was deeply touched and dazed, and before she knew what she was about, found herself in the crowded little dining room below.

"Good Sabbath, Flora, good Sabbath!" the venerable assemblage greeted her.

"Good Sabbath!" she returned, bowing gracefully, and blushing.

"May your guest be pleasing to you," one of the company went on in time-honored phrase; "and, if God be pleased, we shall live to make merry at your wedding."

Flora's face turned a deeper red.

Several of the Talmudists were itching for some banter at the expense of the young pair, but the American girl's dignified bearing and her com-manding figure and dress bore down every tendency in that direction, so that the scholarly old gentlemen turned their overflowing spirits in other channels.

"Give us some Law, Shaya!" said Reb Mendele, with a Talmudic wave of both hands.

"That's right," the others concurred. "Your prospective father-in-law is feasting us upon fare of the earth, and it is meet that you should regale us with Words of Law."

Shaya, his face as red as Flora's, was eyeing the tablecloth as he mur-mured, "'No conversing during repast.'"

"Words of Law are no converse," Reb Mendele retorted. "The Commen-tary adds: 'Not so much as to quote the precept about silence during repast,'" Shaya rejoined reluctantly, without raising his eyes. "Now the precept is

Words of the Law, is it not? Which means that the prohibition does extend to Words of Law."

Apart from his embarrassment, the prodigy was somehow loath to engage in a spiritual discussion in the presence of the stylish young lady.

"Why did you quote it then?" Reb Mendele pursued aggressively. He referred to two other passages, in support of his position; and Shaya, with his eyes still on the tablecloth, and refraining from all gesticulation, could not help showing the irrelevance of both. It was a "knock-out blow," but his red-bearded opponent cleverly extricated himself from the ignominy of his defeat by assuming an amused air, as if it had all been mere bait to decoy the prodigy to a display of his erudition and mental powers; and retaining his smile against further emergency, Reb Mendele hazarded another assault. Some of the other Talmudists took a hand. The battle waxed hot, though Shaya, fighting single-handed against half a dozen elders, remained calm, and parried their blows with a shamefaced but contemptuous look, never raising a finger nor his eyes from the tablecloth. Once in the fray, he would not have Flora see him get the worst of it.

She, on her part, could not help a growing interest in the debate, and finally accepted the chair which Tamara had tenderly placed by her side five minutes before. To be sure, she understood not a word of the controversy. To her it was something like a boxing-match, with every exciting element of the sport, but without any of its violence (which alone kept Flora from attending pugilistic performances), though the arms and fingers of our venerable combatants were even more active than are the arms and fists of two athletes in a modern ring. As she watched the progress of the discussion she became conscious of a decided partisan feeling in favor of the younger man. "It ain't fair a bit!" she said to herself. "Six old-timers against one boy—I declare!"

Asriel and Tamara, to both of whom the contest was as unintelligible as it was to Flora, were so abandoned to their admiration of the youthful disputant that they omitted to notice the girl's undisguised interest in the scene and to congratulate themselves upon it. The host followed the controversy with a sheepish look of reverence, as if the company were an assemblage of kings. The housekeeper looked on with a beaming face, and every time one of the patriarchs made a bold attack, she would nod her head as if she understood it all, and conceded the strength of his contention.

Egged on by Flora's presence as well as by the onslaughts of his adversaries, Shaya gradually warmed up to the debate, until, having listened, with sardonic patience, to a lengthy and heated argument by a fleshy child of the Law, he suddenly leaped upon his man.

"Is this the way you understand the passage?" he shouted, with a vicious chuckle. Then, thrusting his curly head in his opponent's face, and savagely gesticulating, he poured forth a veritable cataract of the most intricate syllogisms and quotations.

It was quite a new Shaya. His blue eyes flashed fire, his whole countenance gleamed, his singsong rang with tuneful ferocity.

"But it seems to me that Rabbi Yohanon does not say that," the portly Talmudist objected. "I am afraid you have misquoted him."

It was the drowning man's straw. Even Flora, who understood the Yiddish of the retort, could see that; and her heart bounded with cruel delight.

"Have I? You are sure, are you?" Shaya demanded, with boyish virulence. "All right. We shall see!" With which he darted out of the room and upstairs.

"The boy is a *gaon*,"[34] the corpulent old man remarked humbly. "What a head! What a memory, what a *chariff!*"[35]

"Yes, and what a *bokki!*"[36] chimed in the rabbi. "One cannot help wondering when he had time to study up so much."

"He'll just take a peep at a book and then he knows it all by heart," put in Asriel. "He licked all the rabbis around Pravly."

The boorish remark disposed some of the listeners to laugh, but they did not.

"You have got a treasure, Mr. Stroon," said Reb Mendele.

"You bet!" the host answered with a blissful simper, as he took to stroking his daughter's hair.

"You know what the Talmud says, Mr. Stroon?" resumed the rabbi. "That he who supports a scholar of the Law is like unto him who offers sacrifices."

"I know," Asriel returned exultingly. At the Pravly synagogue the preacher had applied the same quotation to Reb Lippe.

Presently Shaya returned with a pile of huge volumes in his arms. His citation proved correct, and meeting with no further opposition, but too far carried away by the subject to quit it so soon, he volunteered an extemporaneous discourse. His face was now wrapped in genial, infantile ecstasy and his intonation was a soft, impassioned melody. The old man followed him with paternal admiration.

When he concluded and leaned back in his chair, he gave Flora a triumphant smile. The color mounted to her cheeks and she dropped her gaze. At the same moment Asriel flung himself upon the young hero.

"Oh, you dear little sparrow!" he exclaimed, lifting Shaya in his arms like a baby, and passionately kissing him.

Tamara wiped her eyes with her apron. Flora had a mind to flee for safety, but she forthwith saw herself out of danger, for her father seemed unmindful of her presence, and the first thing he did as he let the prodigy down was to invite his guests upstairs to show them the newly imported library.

As the patriarchal company was filing out of the dining room, Shaya, passing by Flora, said to her gleefully: "I gave it to them, didn't I?"

"Tell me now," said Tamara, when the two women found themselves alone in the room; "ought you not to thank God for such a treasure of a sweetheart?"

"He is nothing of the kind to me," Flora burst out, "and he never will be, either. I don't care how long papa is going to keep him in the house."

---

[34]A genius.
[35]Acute intellect.

[36]A serious student.

VIII

"Oh, papa!" sobbed Flora; "will you ever put an end to it? You know I'll never marry him."

"Do I compel you to?" he replied. "What do you care if he is in the house? He does not take away your dinner, does he? Imagine that he is your brother and don't bother your head about him. The boy has become so dear to me that I feel as if he were my own son. Will *you* recite Kaddish for my soul? Will you play for me at the anniversary of my death? God thought I was not good enough to have a son, but he sent me this holy child to take the place of one. As I hear him read his holy books," he went on, with mounting pathos, "it melts like ice cream in my heart. It pleased the Uppermost to make a boor of your papa. Well, I suppose He knows his business, and I am not going to poke my nose in, and ask questions; but He seems to have taken pity on me after all, and in my old age he has sent me an angel, so that I may get the credit of supporting him. Did you hear what the wise men said? That to support a man who does nothing but study sacred books is as good as offering sacrifices. Yes, my daughter, God has put this boy in my hands; He sent me all the way to Pravly for him—all to give me a chance to make up for my sins. Do you want me to kick him out? Not if New York turned upside down."

"But, father—"

"Hold on! Let me talk the heart out of myself. It's no use asking me to send him away. He is God's gift. He is as holy as a Purity.[37] You are my daughter, and he is my son. I don't chase you under the bridal canopy with a strap, do I? If God does not wish the match, it won't come off, that's all."

The conversation took place about a fortnight after the great debate. Asriel lived in the hope that when Shaya had learned some English and the ways of Flora's circle, she would get to like him. He could not see how it was possible to withstand the charms of the young man whom he sincerely thought the handsomest fellow in the Jewish colony. He provided him with a teacher, and trusted the rest to time and God.

"Just fix him up in English and a little figuring, and that's all," he instructed the teacher. "But mind you, don't take him too far into those Gentile books of yours. He does not want any of the monkey tricks they teach the children at college. Do you understand?"

Flora was getting used to Shaya's presence in the house, as if he actually were a newly discovered brother of hers, brought up in a queer way which she could not understand, and it was only occasionally and at growing intervals that the situation would burst upon her, and she would plead with her father as she had done.

The two young people frequently found themselves alone. The door between the front parlor, which was now Shaya's study, and Flora's boudoir was most of the time open. They often talked together, and she quizzed him about his manners, and once or twice even went over his English lessons

[37]Refers to the scrolls of the Talmud.

with him, laughing at his mispronunciations, and correcting them in the imposing manner of her former schoolteachers.

"Why do you work your fingers like that?" she once said, with a pained look. "Can't you try and read without them?"

"I am used to it from the Talmud—he—he—he!" he tittered, as if acknowledging a compliment.

Her piano did not disturb him in his studies, for in the synagogues, where he had grown up, he had been used to read in a turmoil of other voices; but he loved the instrument, and he would often pause to listen to Flora's energetic strokes through the door. When the tune was a melancholy one its first accords would make him start, with a thrill; and as he proceeded to listen his heart would contract with a sharp feeling of homesickness, and at the same time he would be longing for still more familiarity in the performer's manner toward him. Sometimes he would cross over to her room and quietly stand behind her while she was playing.

"Ah, it is so nice!" he once said, feeling himself in a paradise on earth.

"What are you doing here?" she exclaimed, facing about toward him, in affected surprise. "Music ain't for a 'holy child' like yourself." She mocked a favorite expression of her father's.

"Don't say that," he reproached her. "You always like to tease me. Why don't I tease you?"

Upon the whole, Shaya took the situation quite recklessly. He studied his Talmud and his English, let Tamara cloy him with all sorts of tidbits, and roamed about the streets and public buildings. In less than six months he knew the city and its suburbs much better than Flora, and could tell the meaning of thousands of printed English words, although he neither knew how to use them himself nor recognized them in the speech of others. Flora was amazed by his rapid progress, and the facility with which he mastered his Arithmetic and English Grammar in neither of which she had been strong at school—even piqued her ambition. It was as if she had been beaten by the "holy soul" on her own ground.

The novelty of studying things so utterly out of his rut was like a newly discovered delicacy to his mental palate. He knew by heart a considerable part of the English translation in his Hebrew prayer book and Old Testament, and his greatest pleasure, when Asriel was not about, was to do arithmetical problems. But the problems were all child's play to him, and he craved some higher grade of intellectual food in the same Gentile line. This he knew from his Talmud to be contained in the "Wisdom of Measuring," which he had learned of his teacher to call Geometry.

"Bring me a Geometry, please," he whispered to his instructor.

"I will, but don't say a word to Mr. Stroon about it."

The forbidden fruit was furnished, and the prodigy of sacred lore applied himself to it with voracity.

"How cunning!" he said to the teacher, in a transport of enthusiasm. "Of course, it is not as deep as Talmud, but I never dreamed there were such subtle things in the Gentile books at all—may I be ill if I did."

"This is only the beginning of it," the other returned, in whispered exultation. "Wait till you get deeper into it. And then there are other books, far more interesting."

"Say, young fellow!" Asriel said to Shaya's teacher a week or so later; "you need not trouble your righteous legs to bring you here any more. You are getting too thick with the boy."

Shaya now found no difficulty in plodding through the theorems and problems unaided. But he yearned after his teacher and friend, and for several days could relish neither his Talmud nor his contraband Geometry. He grew restless. His soul was languishing with thirst.

"Guess where I have been," he confidentially said to Flora, coming from the street one afternoon. He spoke in Yiddish, and she answered in English, interspersed with the same dialect.

"Not in the synagogue, studying?" she queried.

"No—at the Astor Library," he whispered. "They have such a lot of books there, Flora! Upstairs and downstairs—large rooms like rich synagogues, with shelves all over the walls, and all full of books. Have you ever been there, Flora?"

"N—no!" she owned, with reluctance. The "holy soul" was clearly forging ahead of her in a world which she considered all her own; and she hated the idea of it, and liked it at the same time. "What did you there?"

"I just looked at the books—oh, what a lot!—and then I found out how to get a Geometry—they have everything in the world, I tell you—and I did some problems. Don't tell your father I was there."

"Of course I won't," she said intimately. "Can ladies come in?"

"Certainly; they have a separate place for them, though; will you go there with me?"

"Some day," she rejoined evasively.

"Will you? Oh, it's so nice to be sitting and reading there! Only you must sit still. I forgot myself, and as I was figuring out some nice point, I began to reason aloud, so a fine old gentleman stepped up to my side and touched me on the shoulder. Oh, I got so scared, Flora! But he did not do me anything—may I be ill if he did. He only told me to be quiet."

Flora burst out laughing.

"I'll bet you, you was singing in that funny way you have when you are studying the Talmud."

"Yes," he admitted joyfully.

"And working your hands and shaking the life out of yourself," she pursued, mimicking his gestures.

"No, I was not—may I not live till tomorrow if I was," he protested vehemently, with a touch of resentment. "Oh, it is so nice to be there! I never knew there were so many Gentile books in the world at all. I wonder what they are all about. Only I am so troubled about my English." He interrupted himself, with a distressed air. "When I asked them for the book, and how to get it, they could not understand me."

"I can understand everything you say when you speak English. You're all right," she comforted him. His troubled, childlike smile and his shining clear blue eyes, as he spoke, went to her heart.

"You can, but other people can't. I so wish I could speak it like you, Flora. Do read a page or two with me, will you? I'll get my Reader—shall I?"

"What's your hurry? Can't you wait?"

He could not wait. He was in a fever of impatience to inhale the whole of the Gentile language—definitions, spelling, pronunciation, and all—with one desperate effort. It was the one great impediment that seemed to stand between him and the enchanted new world that had revealed itself to him.

"Oh, do hear me read—may you live long, Flora! It somehow draws me as with a kind of impure force. Will you?"

"All right," she yielded, with kindly curiosity at the fervor of his request, and feeling flattered.

He had been reading perhaps a quarter of an hour when he grew absent-minded.

"You must have skipped a line again," she said, in an awkward undertone.

"Oh, yes!"

They were seated at a respectful distance, with the corner of the marble table between them, her full, well-modeled bust erect and stately against the pier-glass. She wore a waist of dark-blue silk, trimmed with red, and there was a red ribbon in her shock of inky hair. Presently she leaned forward to see a mispronounced word for herself. Their heads found themselves close together. Her ivory cheek almost touched his.

"Where is it?" she questioned, under her breath.

He made no reply. His glance was riveted to her raven eyelashes. A dash of scarlet lurking under her chin dazed his brain. After a slight pause he said, as he timidly stroked her burning cheek: "It is so smooth!"

She had an impulse to withdraw her face, but felt benumbed. He went on patting her, until, meeting with no resistance, his lips touched her cheek, in a gingerly kiss. Both lowered their eyes. They were silent, but their hearts, each conscious of the other's beatings, throbbed wildly.

"Bad boy!" she then whispered, without raising her head.

After another silence, as their eyes met, they burst into a subdued nervous titter.

"You must not do that again," she said. "Is this the kind of pious man you are?"

"Don't say that, Flora—pray don't. You know it hurts my feelings when you speak like that," he implored her. And impelled by the embarrassed, affectionate sadness of her mien, he seized her hand and fell to kissing first her fingers and then her eyes, as though beseeching them to reveal the meaning of their somber look. Their lips met and clung together in a trance of passion. When they parted Shaya felt ten years older, and as his eye fell upon the bookcase, he wondered what those glittering, massive tomes were doing there.

"Will you tell your father that you want to be my sweetheart?" he asked after a while.

His voice and his features appeared to her in a novel aspect.

"How do you know I do?" she said, with playful defiance, hiding a burst of admiration which was lost upon the unworldly young man.

"Why—don't you?" he demanded solicitously.

Then, a sudden light of inspiration coming in her eyes, Flora said, "Hol' on! How would you like to be a doctor, Shayie?"

"But your father would turn me out if I began to study for it."

She grew thoughtful. "But suppose he had no objection?" she queried, her bashfulness suddenly returning to her face.

"Oh, then I should be dying to study doctor books—any kind of Gentile books you wanted me to, Flora. But Reb Asriel won't let me."

"Listen! Can you keep a secret?" she asked like a conspiring little schoolgirl.

"You mean about your being my sweetheart?"

"No!" she rejoined impatiently. "I mean the other thing—your studyin'. Papa needn't get wind of it till it's too late—you understand? If you are smart, we can fix that."

"That's all right. I am awful clever at keeping a secret," he boasted.

"Well, I want you to be a doctor, Shayie," she resumed, with matronly tenderness. "If you are, I'll care for you, and you'll be my birdie boy, an' all; if not, you won't. Oh, won't it be lovely when everybody knows that you go to college and study together with nice, educated uptown fellows! We would go to theaters together and read different books. You'll make a daisy of a college boy, too—you bet. Would you like to wear a high hat, and spec's, and ride in a buggy with a driver? Would you, would you, bad boy, you? Hello, Doctor Golub! How are you?"

She presented her lips, and they kissed again and again.

"You know what, Shayie? When papa comes I'll go out somewheres, so you can tell him—you know what I mean. It'll make it so much easier to fool him. Will you tell him?"

"I am ashamed."

"I won't tell him."

"Don't be angry—I will. I shall always do everything you tell me, Flora," he said, looking into her black gleaming eyes—"always, always!" And in the exuberance of his delight he once again felt himself a little boy, and broke out into a masterly imitation of the crow of a cock, jumping up and flapping his arms for a pair of wings.

When Asriel and Shaya were alone in the parlor, the young man said, as he fell to wringing his index finger, "Flora wants me to tell you that she is satisfied."

"Satisfied with what?" the old man demanded, leaping to his feet.

"To be my sweetheart."

"Is she? Did she say so? When? Tamara!" he yelled, rushing downstairs and dragging the prodigy along, "Tamara! May you live long! The Uppermost has taken pity upon me after all. Floraly[38] has come around—blessed be the Uppermost."

---

[38]An affectionate diminutive.

"Blessed be the Uppermost!" Tamara echoed, her pleasant, swarthy face beaming with heartfelt delight. "When He wills, walls of iron must give way. It is a divine match—any one can see it is. May they live a hundred and twenty years together. Mazol-tov!"

"Mazol-tov to you and to all of us," Asriel responded. "But where is Flora? Fetch some drink, Tamara."

He stepped up to the "Wonder-worker box," and deposited a silver coin for the support of the pilgrims at Palestine, saying as he did so: "I thank and praise thee, O Lord of the Universe, for thy mercy toward me. Mayest Thou grant the children long years, and keep up in Shaya his love for thy sacred Law. You know the match is all of your own making, and you must take care of it. I am only your slave, that's all."

IX

"Is Shayaly in?" inquired old Asriel on entering Flora's room one morning in midsummer. It was four months after his daughter's betrothment to the Talmudist had been celebrated by a solemn ceremony and a sumptuous feast, the wedding having been set for a later date. The crowning glory of his achievement Stroon postponed, like a rare bottle of wine, for some future day. He dreaded to indulge himself in such a rapid succession of This World joys lest he might draw upon his Share in the World-to-come. Will the Uppermost let him live to see his daughter and the "holy child," standing side by side under the Canopy? Asriel was now confident that He would. "Is Shayaly in?"

"Of course he is—papa," Flora answered, raising her face from her book. Her "papa" was added aloud, and as if upon afterthought.

The parlor door stood ajar. Asriel stationed himself near by and listened to the young man's habitual singsong. The old man's face gradually became radiant with bliss.

"My crown, my Messiah, my Kaddish! My Share in the World-to-come!" he muttered.

"Did you have breakfast, papa?" Flora demanded, speaking still louder than before.

At this moment Shaya's singsong broke out with fresh enthusiasm and his Hebrew words became distinct. Asriel waved her away fiercely. After a little he remarked in a subdued voice, as he pointed to the front parlor, "*This* is my breakfast. This is for the soul, my child; the worms of the grave cannot touch it, and you take it along to the other world. Everything else is a lot of rubbish."

He made to leave, but could not help pausing, in fresh admiration, and then, softly opening the parlor door he entered the sanctum, on tiptoe, in order to feast his eye as well as his ear on the thrilling scene. He found Shaya rapturously swaying and singing over a Talmud volume. Flora watched her father with roguish delight.

"I am afraid I must not be gloating over him like this," Asriel rebuked himself in his heart. "I may give him the evil eye." When he regained the back parlor he said, under his breath: "Floraly, I am afraid your company may disturb him sometimes. A pretty sweetheart is apt to stir a fellow's brains, you know, and take him away from the Law. He had better study more at the synagogues."

The girl blushed to her charcoal hair and dropped her glance. But her father had scarcely gained his room, on the floor above, when she flew into the front parlor with a ringing giggle.

"Now you can go right on, dearie," she said, encircling Shaya's neck with one arm, and producing with the other an English textbook on Natural Philosophy, which had lain open under the huge Hebrew volume.

"You heard me holler, didn't you?"

"Of course I did," Shaya answered beamingly. "He interrupted me in the middle of such a cunning explanation!"

"Did he? What was it about? All about sounds—the same as before?"

"Yes, but it is even more brainy than what I told you."

He proceeded to expound, in Yiddish, what he had been reading on Acoustics, she listening to his enthusiastic popularization with docile, loving inattention.

The young man made a pretense of spending his afternoons, and sometimes also mornings, at the various synagogues of the Jewish quarter. His proud guardian encouraged this habit, in order that his "daughter's bridegroom" might disseminate his sacred knowledge among other congregations than his own. "Your learning is the gift of God, Shayaly," he would say, "and you needn't be ashamed to peddle it around. Reb Lippe said America wanted a man like you to spread the holy Law here. Go and do it, my son, and the Uppermost will help us all for your sake."

The prodigy and his importer were the talk of the orthodox colony, and nothing was more pleasing to Asriel than to hear the praises of his daughter's fiancé sounded by the Talmudists. There came a time, however, when, in his own synagogue, at least, these encomiums ceased. Asriel missed them keenly and pestered the learned men of the congregation with incessant talks about Shaya, for the purpose of worrying out some acknowledgment of his phenomenal talents. But the concession was mostly made in a half-hearted way, and poor Asriel would be left hungrier than ever. Particularly was his heart longing for the warm eulogies of Reb Tzalel, a poor, sickly old peddler, who was considered one of the most pious and learned men in the neighborhood. Asriel liked the man for his nervous sincerity and uncompromising self-respect. He often asked him to his house, but the tattered, underfed peddler invariably declined the invitation.

"What will I do there, Reb Asriel?" he would say, with the pained sort of smile which would light up his ghastly old face whenever he spoke. "Look at your costly carpet and furniture, and bear in mind that you are a landlord and I a poor peddler! At the synagogue I like you better, for here we are equals. Saith the verse in the Book of Job: 'Whereas He is one that shows no favor to chieftains, and distinguishes not the rich before the indigent, for all of them are the work of his hands.'" Reb Tzalel translated the verse into Yiddish for the benefit of his listener, whereupon Asriel felt a much wealthier man than he was, and at the same time he had a sense of humiliation, as though his money were something to be ashamed of.

This man's unusual reticence on the point of Shaya's merits chagrined Asriel sorely, and his mind even began to be troubled by some vague misgivings on that score.

One evening Asriel sat by Reb Tzalel's side in the study rooms of his synagogue. It was in the latter part of November, and Shaya's wedding was to take place during the Feast of Hanuccah, some few weeks later. The evening services, which on week days were held in these rooms, were over, and the "learners" could now give themselves to their divine studies undisturbed, save for the possible and unwelcome advent of some belated Ten Worshipers.[39] The two spacious, dingy rooms, their connecting doors wide open, were dimly lighted with candles placed upon the plain long deal tables[40] ranged against their discolored walls. The open bookcases were filled with dilapidated old volumes, many more being in use or strewn about, in chaotic heaps, on the tables, benches, or window sills.

In one room, around one of the long tables, were gathered the members of the daily Mishnah[41] class. There were about a dozen of them, mostly poor peddlers or artisans—a humble, seedy, pitiable lot, come after a hard day's work or freezing, to "take a holy word into their mouths." Hardly one of these was up to the Gemarah[42] part of the Talmud, and even the Mishnah only few could brave single-handed. They sat at their open books following their voluntary teacher, a large, heavy, middle-aged man—a mass of unkempt beard, flesh, and rags, ablaze with the intellectual fury of his enormous black eyes. He was reading aloud, with ferocious appetite, swaying and jerking his disheveled bulk, as he ever and anon tossed up his head to interpret the Mishnah to his pupils, and every little while breaking off in the middle of a sentence, or even a word, to let his class shout the other half as a guaranty of proficiency. Some of his listeners plodded along the lines of their books, in humble silence, with their index fingers for fescues; the brighter ones boldly interrupted the ponderous man, joyously anticipating his explanations or pointing out some discrepancy; one old dissembler repeated unintelligible half-sentences with well-acted gusto; another little old fellow betrayed the fog in his mind by timid nods of assent, while still another was bravely kept from dozing off on his holy book by frequent neighborly nudges from the man next him. Standing behind the members of

---

[39]In Judaism, communal prayer requires a quorum of ten people, called a *minyan*.

[40]A table that is made of fir or pine boards.

[41]A section of the Talmud; a transcription of orally transmitted law.

[42]A section of the Talmud; an exposition of the Mishnah.

the class were some envying "boors," like our poor Asriel, to whom even the Mishnah was a luxury beyond their intellectual means.

One of the long tables in the adjoining room was covered with the open folios of the daily Gemarah class—some fifteen men of all ages and economical conditions from the doddering apple-vender, to whom the holy books are the only source of pleasure in this life as well as in the other, to the well-fed, over-dressed young furniture-dealer, with whom the Talmud is a second nature, contracted in the darker days of his existence in Russia. There were several "keen brains" in the group, and a former "prodigy" or two, like Shaya. The class needed no guide, but one old man with a boyish face framed in snow-white hair, and wearing a sea of unstarched linen collar about his emaciated neck, was their chosen reader. He also left many sentences un-uttered, but he did it merely because he thought them too well-known to need repetition. Whenever he had something to add to the text, he would address himself to the man by his side, snapping his fingers at him genially, and at times all but pinching him for ecstasy. The others participated now by a twirl of a finger, now by the swift repetition of a whole syllogism, now by an indescribable system of gestures, enacting, in dumb show, the whole logical process involved in a nice point. All at once the whole class would burst into a bedlam of voices and gesticulations. When the whirlwind of enthusiasm subsided, it might be followed by a bit of pleasantry from the exuberance of good spirits at having got the better of a difficult point—and upon the whole the motley company looked like a happy family at the Sabbath table.

The other long tables in both rooms were occupied by lomdim,[43] each intent upon the good deed of studying "for study's sake" by himself: some humming to their musty folios melodiously; others smiling and murmuring to them, like a fond mother to her babe; still others wailing or grumbling or expostulating with their books, or slapping them and yelling for delight, or roaring like a lion in a cage. A patriarch teaching his ten-year-old grandson and both shouting at the top of their voices, in an entanglement of pantomime; a swarthy little grammar-school boy going it on his own hook over a volume bigger than himself; a "fine householder" in reduced circumstances dignifiedly swinging his form and twirling his sidelock as if he were confiding a secret to his immense golden beard; one or two of the hollow-voiced *prooshim*,[44] who had come to America in search of fortune, but who were now supported by the congregation for giving all their time to "the law and the service"; a knot of men engaged in a mixed discussion of "words of laws" and "words of every-day life"—all these voices and murmurs mingled in one effervescence of the sublime and the ridiculous, with tragedy for a keynote—twenty centuries thrown pellmell in a chaos of sound and motion.

---

[43]Learned men.

[44]The name given to the disciples of Rabbi Elijah ben Solomon Zalman, who settled in Palestine in the late eighteenth and early nineteenth centuries; more commonly transliterated as *perushim*.

Asriel could have lived on the spectacle, and although unable to participate in it himself, he now, since the advent of the prodigy, looked upon it as
a world in which he was not without a voice. He was seated in a remote corner of the Gemarah room, now watching the noisy scenes with open-mouthed
reverence, now turning to admire Reb Tzalel by his side. The cadaverous face
and burning eyes of the peddler were sneering at the drab-colored page before
him, while his voice sounded melancholy, like a subdued bugle call.

Presently Reb Tzalel paused, and the two engaged in converse. As Asriel
was boasting of Shaya's genius and kindliness of disposition, vainly courting
his friend for a word of assent, the peddler, suddenly reddening in the face,
interrupted him:

"What's the use of playing cat and rat, Mr. Stroon?" he burst out with
his ghastly smile. "I may as well tell you what lies like a heavy stone on my
heart. Your Shaya is going to the bad. He is an *appikoros*."[45]

"An appikoros!" Asriel demanded, as if the word had suddenly acquired
a new meaning.

"Yes, an appikoros, and a Jeroboam the son of Nebat—he sins, and
leads others to sin," the Talmudist declared tartly. "I hated to cause you the
pain, Mr. Stroon, but he has gone too far in Gentile books, and when he is
here and you are not about he talks to everybody he can get hold of concerning the way the world swings around the sun, how rain and thunder,
day and night—everything—an be explained as a matter of common sense,
and that there is no God in heaven, and all that sort of vile stuff that you
hear from every appikoros—may they all be hurled from one end of the
world to the other! Everything can be explained—may the Angel of Death
explain it to them, may they—"

"Hold on, Reb Tzalel!" Asriel shouted: "You need not curse him: you
don't feed him, do you? And what you say is a lie! —as big a lie as Og the
King of Bashan!"[46] he concluded with calm ferocity, raising his burly figure
from the bench.

"A lie, is it? Very well, then—you shall know all. Little Mendele saw your
imported decoration smoking a cigarette last Sabbath."

"Shaya smoke on the Sabbath!" Asriel echoed. The practical, concrete nature
of this sin came home to him with a more forceful blow than all the peddler
had said about Shaya's ungodly theories. "Begone!" the surrounding chaos
seemed to say to the "boor." "From now on you have nothing to do here!"

"Shaya smoke a cigarette on the Sabbath!" he repeated. "Well, and I have
this to say, that Mendele, and yourself, and the whole lot of you are nothing
but a set of first-class liars and begrudging gossip-mongers. It must give
him a belly-ache to think that he could not afford such a bridegroom for his
girl and that I could. Well, I have got a prodigy for my daughter and he has
licked the whole lot of you learned fellows to ground coffee. I have got

---

[45]An epicurean, an atheist.
[46]According to the Old Testament, Og was the
ancient Amorite king of Bashan, who, along
with his army, was slain by Joshua at the battle of Edrei. *Og* means "gigantic" in Hebrew;
presumably this is what Cahan is punning on.

him—see?—and let all my enemies and the boy's enemies burst for envy."
He clicked his tongue and snapped his fingers, and for a moment stood glaring witheringly at his interlocutor.

"Well, I am not going to argue with a boor," said Reb Tzalel, in utter disgust.

His words were drowned in the noise, but the "boor" reached Asriel's ear and touched him on the raw. "Shut up, Reb Tzalel!"" he said, paling.

"Why should I? This is not your house. It is God's dwelling. Here I am richer than you. I only wanted to say that it is not you I pity. You have been a boor, and that's what you are and will be. But the boy was about to become a great man in Israel, and you have brought him over here for bedeviled America to turn him into an appikoros. Woe! woe! woe!"

"Keep still, Reb Tzalel; take pity," Asriel implored, in a squeaking voice. "Don't spill any salt over my wounds. Forgive me—you know I am a boor. Do take pity and say no more; but all you have said—they have said—is a lie—the cholera choke me if it is not." And gasping for breath, he ran out of the synagogue.

When he found himself in the street he was conscious of some terrific blow having just been dealt him, but did not clearly realize its full meaning; and what had transpired a minute before, between him and Reb Tzalel, seemed to have occurred in the remote past. The clamor of the street peddlers, and the whole maze of squalor and noise through which he was now scurrying, he appeared to hear and to view at a great distance, as if it all were on the other side of a broad river, he hurrying on his lonely way along the deserted bank opposite.

"An appikoros! an appikoros!" he said to himself, vainly trying to grasp the meaning of the word which he knew but too well. "An appikoros, smoking on the Sabbath!" The spectacle smote him in cold blood. "Shaya smoke on the holy Sabbath! It's a lie!"

He started in the direction of Mendele's residence, bent upon thrashing the redhaired talebearer to death. Soon, however, he halted and turned homeward. The courage failed Asriel Stroon to face the man who had seen his daughter's fiancé smoke a cigarette on a Saturday. Then Shaya appeared to his mind as something polluted, sacrilegious, and although this something had nothing in common with his beloved prodigy, save the name, and the young man whitened in the distance, pure and lovely as ever, Asriel's rage surged in the direction of his home, and he mended pace to storm the house as soon as he could get there.

When he collected his wits he decided to wait till he found out everything for himself. For the first time, perhaps, he felt himself a coward. He quailed before the thought that what he had heard from the learned peddler might prove true, and he cringingly begged his own mind to put off the culminating agony of believing it.

Nevertheless, when he saw Shaya, at the supper table, his heart whispered to him, in dismay: "An appikoros!" and the unuttered word enveloped the prodigy in a forbidding, sinister atmosphere.

He now hated Shaya; he felt as though he feared him.

"Where have you been so late, papa?" Flora inquired.

"Deep in the earth. You care much where your papa is, do you?" he snarled.

"Papa!" she said deprecatingly; "are you mad?"

He made no response.

"Have you been to the Mariv service?"[47] Shaya intervened. "I studied at the Souvalk Synagogue today."

Asriel remained grimly uncommunicative.

The young people, reinforced by Tamara, made several other attempts at conversation, but the dogged taciturnity of the head of the family cast a spell of misery over them all, and the meal passed in unsupportable silence.

"See if papa ain't getting on to what you are doing, Shayie," Flora said, when the two were alone.

"Pshaw! is it the first time you see him out of humor? He must have had some trouble with a tenant or janitor."

"He must have," she assented gloomily. "But what if he gets wind? I'm worrying the life out of myself about it."

"So am I. I love your father just the same as if he were my own papa. I wish the wedding were over, don't you?" he asked in his childish way.

X

On the following morning Asriel repaired to the Souvalk Synagogue to attend the service (his usual place of worship he had not the heart to visit), and, incidentally, to ascertain how Shaya had spent his time there the day before.

To his consternation he learned that his "daughter's bridegroom" had not been seen there for weeks.

Asriel held his counsel, and took to shadowing the young man.

He now had no doubt as to the accuracy of Reb Tzalel's story. But it gave him no pain. It was Shaya no longer; it was not his daughter's bridegroom; it was not the prodigy he had imported—it was an appikoros. But then Asriel's heart withered at the notion of being the victim of systematic deception. Shaya was an appikoros and a secret, sneaking enemy.

"That youngster trick Asriel Stroon!" He panted with hatred and thrilled with a detective-like passion to catch Shaya in the act of some grave violation of the Mosaic Law.[48]

He went about the various synagogues where the young man was supposed to study the Talmud, with a keen foretaste of his vicious joy at finding that he had been playing truant. Yet each time his fervent expectations were realized he would, instead of triumph, experience an overpowering sense of defeat.

"You have been cheated out of your boots by a stripling, Asrielke—woe to your foolish head!" he tortured himself, reveling in an agony of fury. "Ah, a cholera into him! I'll show him how to fool Asriel Stroon!"

[47]The evening service.

[48]The Jewish laws revealed by God to Moses
and outlined in the five books of the Torah.

He discovered that Shaya's frequent companion was his former teacher of English, whom he often visited in his attic room on Clinton Street, and he impatiently awaited the next Saturday to raid the atheistic resort and to overtake Shaya smoking or writing on the holy day. But the climax came a day or two sooner.

After tracing Shaya to the Clinton Street house Asriel stood waiting around a corner, at a vantage point from which he could see the windows of the two garret rooms one of which was the supposed scene of the young man s ungodly pursuits. He had no definite purpose in view, for it was not Sabbath, and he would not spoil his game by apprehending his man in the mere act of reading Gentile books. Yet he was rooted to the place, and remained aimlessly waiting, with his eyes riveted to the windows which they could not penetrate. Tired at last, and overcome with a sense of having been engaged in a fool's errand, he returned home, and, reaching his bedroom, sank on the bed in a prostration of hurt pride and impotent rage.

On the following morning he returned to his post. The attic windows drew him like the evil one, as he put it to himself.

He had been keeping watch for some minutes when, to his fierce joy, Shaya and his accomplice sallied forth into the street. He dogged their steps to Grand Street, and thence, through the Bowery, to Lafayette Place, where they disappeared behind the massive doors of an imposing structure, apparently neither a dwelling place nor an office building.

"Dis a choych?" Asriel asked a passerby.

"A church? No, it's a library—the Astor Library," the stranger explained.

"Ah, a lot of Gentile books!" he exclaimed to himself, disappointed in one way and triumphant in another. The accustomed neighborhood and the novelty of his impressions increased the power of the "evil one" over him. He took up a position whence he could observe without being observed, and waited for the two young men to come out. What he would gain by tracing them back to the Jewish quarter he never asked himself. He waited because the "evil one" would not let him stir from the spot.

An hour passed. He was growing faint with hunger; yet he never moved. "He has not had his lunch, either," he thought. "Still, he can stand it. It's the witchcraft of the Gentile books—may he be burned to death!—keeping up his strength. They'll come out in a minute or two."

Many more minutes elapsed, and still Asriel waited. At last "Here, they are, the convert Jews! Look at them—how jolly! It's the Black Year shining out of their faces—may they shine on their death-beds! That beggar of a teacher I shall have arrested."

He followed them through Fourth Street back to the Bowery and down the rumbling thoroughfare, till—"a lamentation!" they entered a Christian restaurant!

A terrific pang smote Asriel's heart. It was as if he saw his temple, the embodiment of many years of labor, the object of his fondest cares, just completed and ready to be dedicated, suddenly enveloped in flames. The prodigy, *his* prodigy, his Kaddish, his glory in this and the other world, plunged into the very thick of impurity!

He made to rush after them, but checked himself to wait till the treife food was served them. A few minutes later he made his entry, cool and collected as a regular customer.

Each of the two young men was bent on a veal cutlet. The collegian was dispatching his with the nonchalant appetite and ease of manner of an habitué, whereas poor Shaya looked like one affecting to relish his first plate of raw oysters. The smells proceeding from the kitchen made him dizzy, and the cutlet itself, partly because he was accustomed to meat of a better quality, but mainly through the consciousness of eating treife, inclined him to nausea.

Asriel took a vacant chair at the same table.

"Bless the sitter,[49] Shaya!" he said.

The two young men were petrified.

"How is the pork—does it taste well?" Asriel pursued.

"It is not pork. It is veal cutlet," the teacher found tongue to retort.

"I am not speaking to you, am I?" Asriel hissed out. Murder was swelling in his heart. But at this point the waiter came up to his side.

"Vot'll ye have?"

"Notink!" Asriel replied, suddenly rising from his seat and rushing out, as if this were the most terrible sort of violence he could conceive.

XI

Asriel found his daughter playing.

"Stop that or I'll smash your Gentile piano to pieces!" he commanded her, feeling as though the instrument had all along been in the conspiracy and were now bidding him defiance.

"Why, what's the matter?" she questioned, getting up from her stool in stupefaction.

"Matter? Bluff a dead rooster, not me—my head is still on my shoulders. Here it is, you see?" he added, taking himself by the head. "It's all up, Flora."

"What do you mean?" she made out to inquire.

"I mean that if Shayke[50] ever enters this house I'll murder both of you. You thought your papa was a fool, didn't you? Well, you are a poor hand at figuring, Flora. I knew everything, but I wanted some particulars. I have got them all now here, in my pocket, and a minute ago I took the pleasure of bidding him 'bless the sitter' in a Gentile restaurant—may he be choked with his treife gorge!"

"You've got no business to curse him like that!" she flamed out, coloring violently.

"*I* have no business? And who is to stop me, pray?"

---

[49]A form of address when the host is at the dinner table. [50]A contemptuous diminutive.

"*I* am. It ain't my fault. You know I did not care at first."

The implication that he had only himself to blame threw him into a new frenzy. But he restrained himself, and said with ghastly deliberation: "Flora, you are not going to marry him."

"I *am*. I can't live without him," she declared with quiet emphasis.

Asriel left her room.

"It's all gone, Tamara! My candle is blown out," he said, making his way from the dining room to the kitchen. "There is no Shaya any longer."

"A weeping, a darkness to me! Has an accident—mercy and peace!—befallen the child?"

"Yes, he is 'dead and buried, and gone from the market place.' Worse than that: a convert Jew is worse than a dead one. It's all gone, Tamara!" he repeated gravely. "I have just seen him eating treife in a Gentile restaurant. America has robbed me of my glory."

"Woe is me!" the housekeeper gasped, clutching at her wig. "Treife! Does he not get enough to eat here?" She then burst out, "Don't I serve him the best food there is in the world? Any king would be glad to get such dinners."

"Well, it seems treife tastes better," Asriel rejoined bitterly. "A calamity upon my sinful head! We must have evil-eyed the child; we have devoured him with our admiring looks."

While Asriel was answering her volley of questions, Flora stealthily left the house.

When Stroon missed her he hurried off to Clinton Street. There he learned of the landlady that her lodger had left a short while before, in the company of his friend and a young lady whom the two young men had found waiting in her parlor. In his despair Asriel betook himself to the Astor Library, to some of Flora's friends, and even to the Bowery restaurant.

When he reached home, exhausted with fatigue and rage, he found his daughter in her room.

"Where have you been?" he demanded, sternly.

"I'll tell you where, but don't aggravate yourself, papaly," she replied in beseeching, tearful accents.

"Where have you been?"

"I am going to tell you, but don't blame Shaya. He is awful fond of you. It's all my fault. He didn't want to go, but I couldn't help it, papaly. We've been to the city court and got married by a judge. Shaya didn't want to."

"You married!"

"Yes, but don't be angry, papaly darlin'. We'll do everything to please you. If you don't want him to be a doctor, he won't."

"A doctor!" he resumed, still speaking like one in a daze. "Is that what you have been up to? I see—you have got the best of me, after all. You married, Flora?" he repeated, unable to apply the meaning of the word to his daughter. "In court—without Canopy and Dedication—like Gentiles? What have you done, Flora?" He sank into a chair, gnashing his teeth and tearing at his sidelocks.

"Papaly, papaly, don't!" she sobbed, hugging and kissing him. "You know I ain't to blame for it all."

It dawned upon him that no serious wrong had been committed, after all, and that it could all be mended by a Jewish marriage ceremony; and so great was his relief at the thought that it took away all his anger, and he even felt as if he were grateful to his daughter for not being guilty of a graver transgression than she was.

"I know you are not to blame," he said, tragic in his calmness. "America has done it all. But what is the use talking! It's gone, and I am not going to take another sin upon my soul. I won t let you be his wife without Canopy and Dedication. Let the Jewish wedding come off at once—this week—tomorrow. You have got the best of me and I don't kick, do I? It seems God does not want Asrielke the boor to have some joy in his old age, nor a Kaddish for his soul, when the worms will be feasting upon his silly bones—"

"Oh, don't say that, papa. It'll break my heart if you do. You know Shaya is as good as a son to you.

"An appikoros my son? An appikoros my Kaddish? No," he rejoined, shaking his head pensively.

As he said it he felt as if Flora, too, were a stranger to him. He descended to the basement in a state of mortal indifference. "I have lost everything, Tamara," he said. "I have no daughter, either. I am all alone in the world—alone as a stone."

He had no sooner closed the kitchen door behind him, than Flora was out and away to Clinton Street to surprise her bridegroom with the glad news of her father's surrender.

The housekeeper was in the kitchen, sewing upon some silk vestments for the scrolls of her synagogue. Asriel stood by her side, leaning against the cupboard door, in front of the Palestine box.[51] Speaking in a bleak, resigned undertone, he told her of Flora's escapade and of his determination to make the best of it by precipitating the Jewish ceremony. A gorgeous celebration was now, of course, out of the question. The proposed fête which was to have been the talk of the synagogues and which had been the center of his sweetest dreams had suddenly turned in his imagination to something like a funeral feast. Tamara bade him be of good cheer, and cited Rabbi Nochum And-This-Too, who would hail the severest blows of fate with the words: "And this, too, is for the best." But Asriel would not be comforted.

"Yes, Tamara, it is gone, all gone," he murmured forlornly. "It was all a dream—a last year's lemon pie. It has flown away and you can't catch it. Gone, and that's all. You know how I feel? As if some fellow had played a joke on me."

The pious woman was moved.

"But it is a sin to take things so close to heart," she said impetuously. "You must take care of your health. Bear up under your affliction like a righteous

---

[51]Charity boxes that were placed in Orthodox synagogues and homes to collect funds for indigent Jews in Palestine and those who wished to make pilgrimages there.

Jew, Reb Asriel. Trust to the Uppermost, and you will live to rejoice in your child and in her children, if God be pleased."

Asriel heaved a sigh and fell silent. He stood with his eyes upon the pilgrim box, listening to the whisper of her needle.

"You know what; let us go to the Land of Israel," he presently said, as though continuing an interrupted sentence. "They have got the best of me. I cannot change the world. Let them live as they please and be responsible to the Uppermost for themselves. I don't care the kernel of a hollow nut. I shall give Flora half my property and the rest I'll sell. You are a righteous woman, Tamara. Why not marry and end our days serving God in the Holy Land together?"

Tamara plied her needle with redoubled zeal. He could see only her glossy black wig and the flaming dusk of her cheek.

"We'll have a comfortable living and plenty of money for deeds of charity," he pursued. "I know I am only a boor. Do I say I am not? But is a boor no human being at all? Can't I die a righteous Jew?" he pleaded piteously.

The glossy wig bent lower and the silk rustled busily.

"You know that I have on my tongue what I have on my lung, Tamara. I mean what I say, and we want no matchmakers. America is now treife to me. I can't show my head. The world is dark and empty to me. All is gone, gone, gone. I am a little baby, Tamara. Come, take pity. I shall see Flora married according to the laws of Moses and Israel, and then let us put up a canopy and set out on our journey. I want to be born again. Well?"

There was no response.

"Well, Tamara?"

"Since it is the will of God," she returned resignedly, without raising her head from the vestments.

XII

Flora was all of a flutter with impatience to share her joy with Shaya, and yearning for his presence. She had not seen him since he had become her legal husband, and the two or three hours seemed a week.

When the German landlady of the little Clinton Street house told her that neither her lodger nor his friend were in the attic room the young woman's heart sank within her. Her message seemed to be bubbling over and her over-wrought mind too weak to bear it another minute. She mentally berated her absent bridegroom, and not knowing whither to bend her steps in quest of him she repaired to some girl friends to while away the time and to deliver herself of part of her burden to them.

"When he comes tell him he da's not leave for one second till I come back. Tell him I've got some grand news for him," she instructed the landlady, struggling hard against a wild temptation to unbosom herself to the stranger.

It was about eight o'clock when she returned. Shaya met her in the hallway.

"Well?" he inquired anxiously.

"Well?" she mocked him. "You are a daisy! Why didn't you wait? Couldn't you guess I'd come?"

"How should I? But tell me what your father says. Why should you torment me?"

"He says he don't want you," she replied. But her look told even a more encouraging tale than the one she had to deliver, and they flew into mutual embrace in an outburst of happiness which seemed to both of them unlike any they had ever experienced before.

"A life into your little eyes! A health into your little hands and feet!" he muttered, stroking her arm sheepishly. "You shall see how fine it will all come out. You don't know me yet. I tell you you don't begin to know me," he kept repeating with some braggadocio and without distinctly knowing what he meant.

They were to return home at once and to try to pacify Asriel as best they could. When Flora pressed him to take his hat and overcoat, however, he looked reluctant and then said:

"Floraly, you know what; come upstairs for just one minute. We are reading the nicest book you ever saw, and there is a lot of such nice gentlemen there!—several genuine Americans—Christians. Do come, Floraly." He drew her up the two flights of stairs almost by force. "Don't be afraid: the landlady knows all about it," he whispered. "You'll see what nice people. I tell you they are so educated, and they love Jews so much! A Jew is the same as a Gentile to them—even better."

Flora felt a lump growing in her heart. The notion of Shaya being at this minute interested in anything outside of herself and their mutual happiness literally dazed her, and before she had time to recover from her shock she was in the over-crowded attic.

There were some ten or twelve men in the room, some seated—two on chairs, two on the host's trunk, and three on his bed—the others standing by the window or propping the sloping wall with their heads. They were clustered about a round table, littered with books, papers, and cigarette stumps. A tin can was hissing on the flat top of a little parlor stove, and some of the company were sipping Russian tea from tumblers, each with a slice of lemon floating in it. The group was made up of a middle-aged man with a handsome and intensely intellectual Scotch face, who was a laborer by day and a philosopher by night; a Swedish tailor with the face of a Catholic priest; a Zurich Ph.D. in blue eyeglasses; a young Hindoo who eked out a wretched existence by selling first-rate articles to second- rate weeklies, and several Russian Jews, all of them insatiable debaters and most of them with university or gymnasium diplomas. The group met every Thursday to read and discuss Harriet Martineau's *Auguste Comte,* under the guidance of the Scotchman, who was a leading spirit in positivist circles.

The philosopher surrendered his chair to the lady, in a flurry of chivalry, but a seat was made for him on the trunk, and he forthwith resumed his reading with well-bred impetuosity, the kerosene lamp in the center of the table casting a halo upon his frank, pleasant face.

His auditors were now listening with conscious attention, some of the younger men affecting an absorbed mien or interrupting the reader with unnecessary questions. Shaya's eyes were traveling between Flora and the Scotchman's audience. "Did you ever see such a beautiful and stylish young lady?" he seemed to be saying. "She is my bride—mine and nobody else's in the world," and, "Look at these great men, Flora—I am their chum." Presently, however, he became engrossed in the reading; and only half-conscious of Flora's presence, he sat leaning forward, his mouth wide open, his face rapt, and his fingers quietly reproducing the mental gymnastics of Comte's system in the air.

The young woman gazed about her in perplexity. The Scotchman and his reading inspired her with respect, but the rest of the company and the *tout ensemble* of the scene impressed her as the haunt of queer individuals, meeting for some sinister purpose. It was anything but the world of intellectual and physical elegance into which she had dreamed to be introduced by marriage to a doctor. Any society of "custom peddlers" was better dressed than these men, who appeared to her more like some of the grotesque and uncouth characters in Dickens's novels than an assemblage of educated people. For a moment even Shaya seemed a stranger and an enemy. Overcome by the stuffy, overheated atmosphere of the misshapen apartment, she had a sense of having been kidnaped into the den of some terrible creatures, and felt like crying for help. Next she was wondering what her Shaya could have in common with these shabby beings and what it all had to do with becoming a doctor and riding in a buggy.

"Shaya!" she whispered, tugging him by the coat-sleeve.

"Just one moment, Floraly," he begged her. "Ah, it's so deep!"

A discussion engaged itself. The Russians fell to greedily. One of them, in particular, a young man with a dignified bass, was hateful to Flora. She could not have told you why, but his voice, coupled with the red embroidery of his Little-Russian shirt front, cut her to the quick.

The room was full of smoke and broken English.

Shaya was brimful of arguments and questions which he had not the courage to advance; and so he sat, now making a vehement gesture of despair at somebody else's absurdities, now nodding violent approval, and altogether fidgeting about in a St. Vitus's dance of impotent pugnacity.

"Shaya, it is getting late, and papa—"

"One second, do please, Floraly, may you live long," he implored her, with some irritation; and taking the book from the Scotchman's hand, he fell to turning over its leaves in a feverish search of what struck him as a misinterpreted passage.

Flora was going to protest and to threaten to leave without him, but she could neither speak nor stir from her seat. A nightmare of desolation and jealousy choked her—jealousy of the Scotchman's book, of the Little-Russian shirt, of the empty tea-glasses with the slices of lemon on their bottoms, of the whole excited crowd, and of Shaya's entire future, from which she seemed excluded.

1898

MARY ANTIN
1881–1949

Mary Antin was born in Polotzk in the Pale of Settlement, the area of czarist Russia in which Jews were allowed to live. Even when young, she became aware of how restricted life in Russia was for Jews. The Russian government allowed them few options in terms of where they could live and what work they could do. They had few of the rights of the poorest peasants. In Polotzk, their religious options were limited, and their lives were thoroughly controlled by Jewish Orthodoxy.

After experiencing serious illnesses, Antin's parents lost their modest fortune. When Mary was eleven, her father, Israel, went to America seeking affluence but, more important, hoping to live with freedom and dignity. Shortly after his family arrived in Boston in 1894, Israel proudly enrolled his three younger children in public school. Later, Mary pictured the public schools as the immigrant child's road to Americanization. Thriving in the public schools of Boston, she went from first to fifth grade in half a year.

Her abilities as a writer appeared early. At fifteen, she published her first poem in the *Boston Herald*. In 1899, Antin's first book, *From Plotzk* [sic] *to Boston*, was published; it briefly recounts her trip from Russia through Germany to Boston. With the appearance of this book, Mary, eighteen at the time, was hailed as a child prodigy. The material in this volume became the basis of her masterpiece, *The Promised Land*.

After attending Girls Latin School in Boston, she attended Teachers College of Columbia University from 1901 to 1902 and Barnard College from 1902 to 1904. In college, she met and married Amadeus W. Grabau, a geologist, one-time Columbia professor, and non-Jew, thus putting into action her belief that religious differences are irrelevant to life in America. While living in New York, she also became friends with Emma Lazarus, who encouraged her to write *The Promised Land* and to whom Antin dedicated the book. Appearing in serial form in the *Atlantic Monthly* in 1911 to 1912, *The Promised Land* was published in book form in 1912. Immediately hailed as a masterpiece, it is still regarded as a classic work of immigrant autobiography.

Antin wrote one more book, *They Who Knock at the Gates*, in which she argues in favor of immigration for all but criminals and declares that the best people of Europe crowd the steerage compartments of ships steaming toward America. For several more years, she published articles and short stories in magazines and did social work. From 1913 to 1918, she lectured throughout the United States. Although her marriage fell apart when, in 1920, her husband left her and settled in China, she retained her ardent faith in America and in the eventual Americanization of the immigrants.

Antin is remembered today for *The Promised Land*. Many critics view the book as a naive, overly optimistic hymn of praise for Americanization and total assimilation. Others, however, view it as a sensitive, truthful account of a

Jewish girl's odyssey from an essentially medieval life in Russia to a modern life in America.

Richard Tuerk
Texas A&M University–Commerce

PRIMARY WORKS

From Plotzk to Boston, 1899; *The Promised Land*, 1912; *They Who Knock at the Gates: A Complete Gospel of Immigration*, 1914.

from **The Promised Land**

from Chapter IX

... Anybody who knows Boston knows that the West and North Ends are the wrong ends of that city. They form the tenement district, or, in the newer phrase, the slums of Boston. Anybody who is acquainted with the slums of any American metropolis knows that that is the quarter where poor immigrants foregather, to live, for the most part, as unkempt, half-washed, toiling, unaspiring foreigners; pitiful in the eyes of social missionaries, the despair of boards of health, the hope of ward politicians, the touchstone of American democracy. The well-versed metropolitan knows the slums as a sort of house of detention for poor aliens, where they live on probation till they can show a certificate of good citizenship.

He may know all this and yet not guess how Wall Street, in the West End, appears in the eyes of a little immigrant from Polotzk.[1] What would the sophisticated sight-seer say about Union Place, off Wall Street, where my new home waited for me? He would say that it is no place at all, but a short box of an alley. Two rows of three-story tenements are its sides, a stingy strip of sky is its lid, a littered pavement is the floor, and a narrow mouth its exit.

But I saw a very different picture on my introduction to Union Place. I saw two imposing rows of brick buildings, loftier than any dwelling I had ever lived in. Brick was even on the ground for me to tread on, instead of common earth or boards. Many friendly windows stood open, filled with uncovered heads of women and children. I thought the people were interested in us, which was very neighborly. I looked up to the topmost row of windows, and my eyes were filled with the May blue of an American sky!

In our days of affluence in Russia we had been accustomed to upholstered parlors, embroidered linen, silver spoons and candlesticks, goblets of gold, kitchen shelves shining with copper and brass. We had feather-beds heaped halfway to the ceiling; we had clothes presses dusky with velvet and silk and fine woollen. The three small rooms into which my father now ushered us, up one flight of stairs, contained only the necessary beds, with lean mattresses; a few wooden chairs; a table or two; a mysterious iron structure,

---

[1] The town in Russia where Antin lived.

which later turned out to be a stove; a couple of unornamental kerosene lamps; and a scanty array of cooking-utensils and crockery. And yet we were all impressed with our new home and its furniture. It was not only because we had just passed through our seven lean years, cooking in earthen vessels, eating black bread on holidays and wearing cotton; it was chiefly because these wooden chairs and tin pans were American chairs and pans that they shone glorious in our eyes. And if there was anything lacking for comfort or decoration we expected it to be presently supplied—at least, we children did. Perhaps my mother alone, of us newcomers, appreciated the shabbiness of the little apartment, and realized that for her there was as yet no laying down of the burden of poverty.

Our initiation into American ways began with the first step on the new soil. My father found occasion to instruct or correct us even on the way from the pier to Wall Street, which journey we made crowded together in a rickety cab. He told us not to lean out of the windows, not to point, and explained the word "greenhorn."[2] We did not want to be "greenhorns," and gave the strictest attention to my father's instructions. I do not know when my parents found opportunity to review together the history of Polotzk in the three years past, for we children had no patience with the subject; my mother's narrative was constantly interrupted by irrelevant questions, interjections, and explanations.

The first meal was an object lesson of much variety. My father produced several kinds of food, ready to eat, without any cooking, from little tin cans that had printing all over them. He attempted to introduce us to a queer, slippery kind of fruit, which he called "banana," but had to give it up for the time being. After the meal, he had better luck with a curious piece of furniture on runners, which he called "rocking-chair." There were five of us newcomers, and we found five different ways of getting into the American machine of perpetual motion, and as many ways of getting out of it. One born and bred to the use of a rocking-chair cannot imagine how ludicrous people can make themselves when attempting to use it for the first time. We laughed immoderately over our various experiments with the novelty, which was a wholesome way of letting off steam after the unusual excitement of the day.

In our flat we did not think of such a thing as storing the coal in the bathtub. There was no bathtub. So in the evening of the first day my father conducted us to the public baths. As we moved along in a little procession, I was delighted with the illumination of the streets. So many lamps, and they burned until morning, my father said, and so people did not need to carry lanterns. In America, then, everything was free, as we had heard in Russia. Light was free; the streets were as bright as a synagogue on a holy day.

[2] A term, often derogatory, for a newly arrived immigrant. It implies that one has not yet adapted to life in America.

Music was free; we had been serenaded, to our gaping delight, by a brass band of many pieces, soon after our installation on Union Place.

Education was free. That subject my father had written about repeatedly, as comprising his chief hope for us children, the essence of American opportunity, the treasure that no thief could touch, not even misfortune or poverty. It was the one thing that he was able to promise us when he sent for us; surer, safer than bread or shelter. On our second day I was thrilled with the realization of what this freedom of education meant. A little girl from across the alley came and offered to conduct us to school. My father was out, but we five between us had a few words of English by this time. We knew the word school. We understood. This child, who had never seen us till yesterday, who could not pronounce our names, who was not much better dressed than we, was able to offer us the freedom of the schools of Boston! No application made, no questions asked, no examinations, rulings, exclusions; no machinations, no fees. The doors stood open for every one of us. The smallest child could show us the way.

This incident impressed me more than anything I had heard in advance of the freedom of education in America. It was a concrete proof—almost the thing itself. One had to experience it to understand it.

It was a great disappointment to be told by my father that we were not to enter upon our school career at once. It was too near the end of the term, he said, and we were going to move to Crescent Beach in a week or so. We had to wait until the opening of the schools in September. What a loss of precious time—from May till September!

Not that the time was really lost. Even the interval on Union Place was crowded with lessons and experiences. We had to visit the stores and be dressed from head to foot in American clothing; we had to learn the mysteries of the iron stove, the wash-board, and the speaking-tube; we had to learn to trade with the fruit peddler through the window, and not to be afraid of the policeman; and, above all, we had to learn English.

The kind people who assisted us in these important matters form a group by themselves in the gallery of my friends. If I had never seen them from those early days till now, I should still have remembered them with gratitude. When I enumerate the long list of my American teachers, I must begin with those who came to us on Wall Street and taught us our first steps. To my mother, in her perplexity over the cook-stove, the woman who showed her how to make the fire was an angel of deliverance. A fairy godmother to us children was she who led us to a wonderful country called "uptown," where, in a dazzlingly beautiful palace called a "department store," we exchanged our hateful homemade European costumes, which pointed us out as "greenhorns" to the children on the street, for real American machine-made garments, and issued forth glorified in each other's eyes.

With our despised immigrant clothing we shed also our impossible Hebrew names. A committee of our friends, several years ahead of us in American experience, put their heads together and concocted American names for us all. Those of our real names that had no pleasing American equivalents they ruthlessly discarded, content if they retained the initials. My mother, possessing a name that was not easily translatable, was punished with the undignified nickname of Annie. Fetchke, Joseph, and Deborah issued as Frieda, Joseph, and Dora, respectively. As for poor me, I was simply cheated. The name they gave me was hardly new. My Hebrew name being Maryashe in full, Mashke for short, Russianized into Marya (*Mar-ya*), my friends said that it would hold good in English as *Mary*; which was very disappointing, as I longed to possess a strange-sounding American name like the others.

I am forgetting the consolation I had, in this matter of names, from the use of my surname, which I have had no occasion to mention until now. I found on my arrival that my father was "Mr. Antin" on the slightest provocation, and not, as in Polotzk, on state occasions alone. And so I was "Mary Antin," and I felt very important to answer to such a dignified title. It was just like America that even plain people should wear their surnames on week days....

The apex of my civic pride and personal contentment was reached on the bright September morning when I entered the public school. That day I must always remember, even if I live to be so old that I cannot tell my name. To most people their first day at school is a memorable occasion. In my case the importance of the day was a hundred times magnified, on account of the years I had waited, the road I had come, and the conscious ambitions I entertained.

I am wearily aware that I am speaking in extreme figures, in superlatives. I wish I knew some other way to render the mental life of the immigrant child of reasoning age. I may have been ever so much an exception in acuteness of observation, powers of comparison, and abnormal self-consciousness; none the less were my thoughts and conduct typical of the attitude of the intelligent immigrant child toward American institutions. And what the child thinks and feels is a reflection of the hopes, desires, and purposes of the parents who brought him overseas, no matter how precocious and independent the child may be. Your immigrant inspectors will tell you what poverty the foreigner brings in his baggage, what want in his pockets. Let the overgrown boy of twelve, reverently drawing his letters in the baby class, testify to the noble dreams and high ideals that may be hidden beneath the greasy caftan of the immigrant. Speaking for the Jews, at least, I know I am safe in inviting such an investigation.

Who were my companions on my first day at school? Whose hand was in mine, as I stood, overcome with awe, by the teacher's desk, and whispered my name as my father prompted? Was it Frieda's steady, capable hand? Was it her loyal heart that throbbed, beat for beat with mine, as it had done through all our childish adventures? Frieda's heart did throb that day, but not with my emotions. My heart pulsed with joy and pride and ambition; in her heart longing fought with abnegation. For I was led to the schoolroom, with its sunshine and its singing and the teacher's cheery smile; while she was led to the workshop, with its foul air, care-lined faces, and the foreman's stern command. Our going to school was the fulfilment of my father's best promises to us, and Frieda's share in it was to fashion and fit the calico frocks in which the baby sister and I made our first appearance in a public schoolroom.

I remember to this day the gray pattern of the calico, so affectionately did I regard it as it hung upon the wall—my consecration robe awaiting the beatific day. And Frieda, I am sure, remembers it, too, so longingly did she regard it as the crisp, starchy breadths of it slid between her fingers. But whatever were her longings, she said nothing of them; she bent over the sewing-machine humming an Old-World melody. In every straight, smooth seam, perhaps, she tucked away some lingering impulse of childhood; but she matched the scrolls and flowers with the utmost care. If a sudden shock of rebellion made her straighten up for an instant, the next instant she was bending to adjust a ruffle to the best advantage. And when the momentous day arrived, and the little sister and I stood up to be arrayed, it was Frieda herself who patted and smoothed my stiff new calico; who made me turn round and round, to see that I was perfect; who stooped to pull out a disfiguring basting-thread. If there was anything in her heart besides sisterly love and pride and good-will, as we parted that morning, it was a sense of loss and a woman's acquiescence in her fate; for we had been close friends, and now our ways would lie apart. Longing she felt, but no envy. She did not grudge me what she was denied. Until that morning we had been children together, but now, at the fiat of her destiny, she became a woman, with all a woman's cares; whilst I, so little younger than she, was bidden to dance at the May festival of untroubled childhood.

I wish, for my comfort, that I could say that I had some notion of the difference in our lots, some sense of the injustice to her, of the indulgence to me. I wish I could even say that I gave serious thought to the matter. There had always been a distinction between us rather out of proportion to the difference in our years. Her good health and domestic instincts had made it natural for her to become my mother's right hand, in the years preceding the emigration, when there were no more servants or dependents. Then there was the family tradition that Mary was the quicker, the brighter of the two, and that hers could be no common lot. Frieda was relied upon for help, and her sister for glory. And when I failed as a milliner's apprentice, while Frieda made excellent progress at the dressmaker's, our fates, indeed, were sealed. It was understood, even before we reached Boston, that she would go to work and I to school. In view of the family prejudices, it was the inevitable course. No injustice was intended. My father sent us hand in hand to school, before he had ever thought of America. If, in America, he had been able to support his family unaided, it would have been the culmination of his best hopes to see all his children at school, with equal advantages at home. But when he had done his best, and was still unable to provide even bread and shelter for us all, he was compelled to make us children self-supporting as fast as it was practicable. There was no choosing possible; Frieda was the oldest, the strongest, the best prepared, and the only one who was of legal age to be put to work.

My father has nothing to answer for. He divided the world between his children in accordance with the laws of the country and the compulsion of his circumstances. I have no need of defending him. It is myself that I would like to defend, and I cannot. I remember that I accepted the arrangements made for my sister and me without much reflection, and everything that was planned for my advantage I took as a matter of course. I was no heartless monster, but a decidedly self-centered child. If my sister had seemed unhappy it would have troubled me; but I am ashamed to recall that I did not consider how little it was that contented her. I was so preoccupied with my own happiness that I did not half perceive the splendid devotion of her attitude towards me, the sweetness of her joy in my good luck. She not only stood by approvingly when I was helped to everything; she cheerfully waited on me herself. And I took everything from her hand as if it were my due.

The two of us stood a moment in the doorway of the tenement house on Arlington Street, that wonderful September morning when I first went to school. It was I that ran away, on winged feet of joy and expectation; it was she whose feet were bound in the treadmill of daily toil. And I was so blind that I did not see that the glory lay on her, and not on me.

Father himself conducted us to school. He would not have delegated that mission to the President of the United States. He had awaited the day with impatience equal to mine, and the visions he saw as he hurried us over the sun-flecked pavements transcended all my dreams. Almost his first act on landing on American soil, three years before, had been his application for naturalization. He had taken the remaining steps in the process with eager promptness, and at the earliest moment allowed by the law, he became a citizen of the United States. It is true that he had left home in search of bread for his hungry family, but he went blessing the necessity that drove him to America. The boasted freedom of the New World meant to him far more than the right to reside, travel, and work wherever he pleased; it meant the freedom to speak his thoughts, to throw off the shackles of superstition, to test his own fate, unhindered by political or religious tyranny. He was only a young man when he landed—thirty-two; and most of his life he had been held in leading-strings. He was hungry for his untasted manhood.

Three years passed in sordid struggle and disappointment. He was not prepared to make a living even in America, where the day laborer eats wheat instead of rye. Apparently the American flag could not protect him against the pursuing Nemesis of his limitations; he must expiate the sins of his fathers who slept across the seas. He had been endowed at birth with a poor constitution, a nervous, restless temperament, and an abundance of hindering prejudices. In his boyhood his body was starved, that his mind might be stuffed with useless learning. In his youth this dearly gotten learning was sold, and the price was the bread and salt which he had not been trained to earn for himself. Under the wedding canopy he was bound for life to a girl whose features were still strange to him; and he was bidden to multiply himself, that sacred learning might be perpetuated in his sons, to the glory of the God of his fathers. All this while he had been led about as a creature without a will, a chattel, an instrument. In his maturity he awoke, and found himself poor in health, poor in purse, poor in useful knowledge, and hampered on all sides. At the first nod of opportunity he broke away from his prison, and strove to atone for his wasted youth by a life of useful labor; while at the same time he sought to lighten the gloom of his narrow scholarship by freely partaking of modern ideas. But his utmost endeavor still left him far from his goal. In business, nothing prospered with him. Some fault of hand or mind or temperament led him to failure where other men found success. Wherever the blame for his disabilities be placed, he reaped their bitter fruit. "Give me bread!" he cried to America. "What will you do to earn it?" the challenge came back. And he found that he was master of no art, of no trade; that even his precious learning was of no avail, because he had only the most antiquated methods of communicating it.

So in his primary quest he had failed. There was left him the compensation of intellectual freedom. That he sought to realize in every possible way. He had very little opportunity to prosecute his education, which, in truth, had never been begun. His struggle for a bare living left him no time to take advantage of the public evening school; but he lost nothing of what was to be learned through reading, through attendance at public meetings, through exercising the rights of citizenship. Even here he was hindered by a natural inability to acquire the English language. In time, indeed, he learned to read, to follow a conversation or lecture; but he never learned to write correctly, and his pronunciation remains extremely foreign to this day.

If education, culture, the higher life were shining things to be worshipped from afar, he had still a means left whereby he could draw one step nearer to them. He could send his children to school, to learn all those things that he knew by fame to be desirable. The common school, at least, perhaps high school; for one or two, perhaps even college! His children should be students, should fill his house with books and intellectual company; and thus he would walk by proxy in the Elysian Fields of liberal learning. As for the children themselves, he knew no surer way to their advancement and happiness.

So it was with a heart full of longing and hope that my father led us to school on that first day. He took long strides in his eagerness, the rest of us running and hopping to keep up.

At last the four of us stood around the teacher's desk; and my father, in his impossible English, gave us over in her charge, with some broken word of his hopes for us that his swelling heart could no longer contain. I venture to say that Miss Nixon was struck by something uncommon in the group we made, something outside of Semitic features and the abashed manner of the alien. My little sister was as pretty as a doll, with her clear pink-and-white face, short golden curls, and eyes like blue violets when you caught them looking up. My brother might have been a girl, too, with his cherubic contours of face, rich red color, glossy black hair, and fine eyebrows. Whatever secret fears were in his heart, remembering his former teachers, who had taught with the rod, he stood up straight and uncringing before the American teacher, his cap respectfully doffed. Next to him stood a starved-looking girl with eyes ready to pop out, and short dark curls that would not have made much of a wig for a Jewish bride.

All three children carried themselves rather better than the common run of "green" pupils that were brought to Miss Nixon. But the figure that challenged attention to the group was the tall, straight father, with his earnest face and fine forehead, nervous hands eloquent in gesture, and a voice full of feeling. This foreigner, who brought his children to school as if it were an act of consecration, who regarded the teacher of the primer class with reverence, who spoke of visions, like a man inspired, in a common schoolroom, was not like other aliens, who brought their children in dull obedience to the law; was not like the native fathers, who brought their unmanageable boys, glad to be relieved of their care. I think Miss Nixon guessed what my father's best English could not convey. I think she divined that by the simple act of delivering our school certificates to her he took possession of America.

1912

■

A Latino Chorus for Social Change

To speak of a Latino chorus of change suggests that the term *Latino* might have been functioning in the late nineteenth-century United States to include Cubans, Puerto Ricans, Peruvians, Ecuadorans, Mexicans, and others who sought to establish themselves in either the continental United States or regions that the United States came to describe as being within its borders. However, that was not the case at all. Rather than sharing an understanding of Latin America or Latino or Latinidad as ideas, the various activist intellectuals who began to publish their calls for social, political, and economic changes at the turn of the nineteenth century shared a sense of a relay between and among languages, colonization, industrial expansion, and widening U.S. imperial practices.

Indeed, leaders such as Raphael Serra and Sotero Figueroa more clearly envisioned, as historian Nancy Raquel Mirabal argues, an Antillean commonwealth or, as followers of the anarchist, revolutionary, and organic intellectual Ricardo Flores Magón proposed, a new multiracial nation that would provide an opportunity for liberation and peace. For readers in the early twenty-first century, the term *Latino/a* offers an opportunity to learn about and a means to make connections between and among activist intellectuals that have often been absent or excluded from the accounts of many national histories.

Part of what has kept many of these once-prominent writers from ongoing fame has been that their venues of publication were newspapers with small press runs. But most of these writers published in one of the Americas' major languages, Spanish, which few scholars of American literature were willing to work in until recently. The ephemeral nature of many of these newspapers was also a problem. Few were systematically collected and archived, and so what is available to historians, especially in the U.S. Southwest, is idiosyncratic. Yet across the continent, newspapers were a crucial tool for organizing communities and establishing networks of interpretation and influence as places to call for change at the broadest level.

During the nineteenth century, Puerto Rican and Cuban activists often joined forces in New York City to work together to end Spain's colonial rule. While many were nervous that the departure of Spain would lead to the arrival of U.S. governance, they nevertheless actively developed broad organizations to assist exiles with the transition from the islands to the United States, where Caribbean activists began to organize broad networks either in support of extending U.S. influence in the region or in opposition to Spain's continued colonial rule as well as to U.S. empire building. The Cuban community in New York during the nineteenth century was so significant, Silvio Torres-Saillant argues, that we cannot easily distinguish Cuban American writing and the texts that form the core of the Cuban national canon from one another.

While anticolonial activity joined exiles together, U.S. practices of racial segregation threatened their coalitions. Afro-Cuban and black Puerto Rican activists and residents found themselves faced with the complexities of navigating both their escape from colonial rule and their entrance into the segregated norms of the northern United States. To navigate such complexities, Afro-Cuban Rafael Serra (1858–1909) worked with others to establish a number of independent newspapers and to form *La liga de instrución,* a group focused on offering educational opportunities to Cubans and Puerto Ricans of color in New York. Worrying that U.S. industrial expansion depended to a degree on racial segregation, Serra and others argued that education would prove crucial to a social transformation that countered the business elites' seeming reliance on degradation and exploitation to manage profits.

Many Cuban and Puerto Rican activists of color found much to admire in the writings of anarchists and union organizers, as did white Puerto Rican labor activists such as Luisa Capetillo. Capetillo (1879–1922) is often described as Puerto Rico's first or pioneer feminist. For many years, she worked as a reader (*lectora*) in cigar factories in Puerto Rico before becoming a union organizer in Puerto Rico and Miami as well as a suffragist, advocate for free love, essayist, and playwright. Highly influenced by anarchist theories emerging from Europe, Capetillo, like Serra, became a strong voice for the importance of education to equalize class divisions and eliminate poverty. As an advocate for completely egalitarian societies, Capetillo was highly critical of the exploitative tendencies of industrial wage labor as well as organized religion—which she saw as protecting the wealthy and ensuring the ignorance of workers. She extended her criticism to politicians of all stripes because they, too, she argued, helped maintain a social system that thrived on radical economic inequality.

As Puerto Rican and Cuban criticism of Spain moved toward full-scale war, Mexican radicals began to intensify their critique of Porfirio Díaz's dictatorial reign in Mexico and of U.S. corporate support of his militaristic policies. Writing at nearly the same time as Capetillo was the little-known poet and labor activist Sara Estella Ramirez, who would also later be termed a founding feminist because of her insistence that gender equality be a part of any revolutionary platform. Born in Coahuila, Mexico, in 1881, she ultimately moved to Laredo, Texas, where she became an active supporter of socialist and union mobilization efforts. Her newspaper, *La Corregidora*, political letters, poetry, and close involvement with revolutionary leaders such as Ricardo Flores Magón and others gained her a long-standing reputation as a crucial intellectual force in the trans-frontier revolutionary effort, although her poetry has been less well recognized. Her achievements as a revolutionary intellectual are all the more to be admired given that she died at age twenty-nine.

Ramirez's journalistic activities were part of a larger southwestern effort that A. Gabriel Meléndez describes as a broad and impressive effort to create a print culture that would express "opposition to Anglo-American political, social, and cultural hegemony in the Southwest after 1848." As Meléndez astutely notes, early newspapers in the Southwest have more in common with the contemporary political tract than with their more recent role as logs that claim to objectively record current events. This earlier role helps explain "the urgency of their purpose and intent." Such newspapers included long analytical and historical essays as well as poetry and plays. They reported on wagon trains moving through the region and tracked the development of the railroad lines and mines.

However, they also attempted, as the anonymous author of "Collaboration" suggests, to promote a sense of cultural pride that would distinguish itself from what many saw as the excesses of the Anglo-Protestant work ethic and industrialization more generally. In this early effort to assail a cultural transformation that many saw as dangerous, what fueled the early Arizona press was not union agitation but a Catholic-inspired moralism that would indeed be repudiated by many radicals across the borderlands a mere twenty-five years later.

For if the anonymous author of "Collaboration" in 1877 worried about the impact of Anglo rule in southern Arizona, by the second decade of the twentieth century, those fears had largely proved prophetic. In the period after 1910, thousands of Mexican Americans, particularly Tejanos, were lynched as Anglo vigilantes sought to forcibly appropriate Tejanos' land and capital, eliminate what political power they had, and severely limit their claims to enfranchisement and citizenship. The Plan de San Diego should be initially understood as an early and prescient index of the sort of racialized hatred that would lead to the mass executions of Tejano/as, the ongoing harassment of nearly all Mexicanos in south Texas and parts of California, and their forced relocation from ranches they had held for generations to cities, towns, and the migrant labor circuit.

In some sense, the deliberately provocative Plan de San Diego in calling for a race war was indeed naming the de facto racialized politics in the United States—but with a difference. The plan called for a collaborative revolution that would draw together all those who had been aggressively harmed by U.S. policies. Imagining in a sense a new nation, perhaps modeled on the early vision of Liberia as a haven for freed slaves, the plan proposed a limit on U.S. expansion and a restoration of lands previously lost. As radical and violent as the plan might appear today, its authors could see no alternative to the violence of vigilantism and mass executions.

Mary Pat Brady
Cornell University

PRIMARY SOURCES

Many thanks to Armando Garcia and Alicia Munoz for their English translations of these works.
Anonymous, "Colaboracion," *Las Dos Republicas* (Tucson, AZ, July 1877); Luisa Capetillo, *Ensayos libertarios* (Arecibo: Imprenta Unión Obrera, 1907); "Plan de San Diego" (Archives of the State of Texas); Sara Estela Ramirez, "21 de Marzo: A Juarez," *El Demócrata Fronterizo* (Mexico City; Laredo, TX; San Antonio, TX, 9 May 1908); Rafael Serra, *Ensayos politicos, sociales y económicos*, 3rd ed. (New York: Howes, 1899).

■ RAFAEL SERRA ■
1858–1909

from ***Nuestro Periódico (Our Newspaper)***

It is understood that a country's forms of government will accommodate themselves to their natural elements; that the absolute ideas, so as not to fail because of an error in the form, will put themselves in forms relative to themselves; that liberty, to be viable, must be full and sincere; that if the Republic does not open its arms to everyone and advance with everyone, the Republic dies.

Strategy is politics. The people will have to live criticizing themselves because criticism is health but with a single chest and a single mind.

There should be faith in the best of man but no confidence in the worst of him. Opportunity must be given to his best so it may reveal itself and prevail over the worst. If not, the worst prevails.

The people must have a pillory for whoever urges them toward useless hatreds and another for whoever does not tell them the truth in time.

—*José Martí*

Our newspaper does not set a tone of discord, nor is it a symbol of a political faction, nor the work of cowardly passion carved by mysterious and invisible hands. It is the exact reflection of our character, which cannot be swayed by political swiveling to the ease of compromise, without the torment of conscience, with God and the devil.

This newspaper will not for one second sway from its firm goal and, sanctioned by our conviction, is the resulting work of our solid experience, acquired by the harsh blows that have torn our country, by the evident and constant fighting so that neither right, nor liberty, nor justice be adulterated in Cuba. This newspaper is the resulting work of our lived experience, acquired by the pains and sufferings with which man's egotism has filled the world and of which evil we have been the most direct and defenseless victims. For this reason, this newspaper, which we do not publish as a profitable venture or to flatter vanities or unhealthy passions or to please the whole world, because that would be impossible, is solely, like our love, our sincerity, and our lives, entirely at the service of Cuba.

1897

from Sin justicia no hay unión (Without Justice There Is No Unity)

Much is spoken about unity, but it is not known what type of unity we are being invited to. There is temporary unity and stable unity.

That which is verified by calculation, speculation, and the narrowness of some difficult circumstance and that which makes itself splendorous and spontaneous, without more stimulus than the practice of love and justice that must be produced between men. A marriage contracted by calculation, by speculation, and by the narrowness of circumstance cannot be a happy marriage.

Humanity is tired of the vagueness and inefficiency of philanthropy by the book. It is time that it be repaired and benefit from philanthropy of the heart.

In our eyes, unity should create itself with the effusive and ceaseless example of moral wisdom. It is dementia, naïveté, or craftiness trying to find elsewhere what does not exist in morality. That is why there are so many people with merits that displease and others that please with faults.

Those that only particularly and extremely care about their own being, despite the fullness of their talent, can wrongly be the living reflection of the common well-being.

Those that cannot fight against their own defects, where shall they have moral strength to, with advantage, correct the defects of others?

We the laborers of *The Doctrine* can speak about unity because we have worked and will always work for it. We can speak about unity because we are willing and absolutely determined to fight so that justice may reign in our land. We can speak about unity because we are not ashamed to recognize and correct our defects and because we will not deny our competition to those who of better faith desire to work for respectable, indissoluble, and positive unity. But they cannot speak about unity who want their own desires to be tended to; without sarcasm, they [cannot speak about unity] who do not prove, with constant valor against all injustices, their full conviction of the need for unity to exist. Those who are deceived by the erroneous theory of the old school, who do not want to understand that times have changed and that yesterday's naive ones are today skilled in the art of recognizing the deceivers: they cannot speak about unity. Egotists who want everything for themselves and nothing for others cannot speak about unity. Those arrogant ones who, with despotic force, tend to humiliate anyone who does not declare himself in rebellion cannot speak about unity. Those who publicly preach unity and condemn it in private with dismal doctrines cannot speak about unity. Those weak in spirit cannot speak about unity because without control of one's passions one can wrongly hurt the works of those that *are* strong. Pretentious beings who consider good only the delicacies derived from their own intellect and direction cannot speak about unity. Those who morally accept the unjust differences and distinctions established by the iniquity of tyrants cannot speak about unity.

1897

■ LUISA CAPETILLO ■
1879–1922

Anarquismo y espiritismo (Anarchy and Spiritualism)

Fellow workers, brothers in socialist, spiritualist, and anarchist ideas: many ignorant ones will ask how I aspire to unite anarchists and spiritualists. Do anarchists not have a soul, or is theirs constituted in a different manner? Many so-called spiritualists would desire to be like many true anarchists, who are the most united, equitable, humane men and women, loyal friends and comrades in spite of the distances. Brave and determined defendants of universal brotherhood. Because of their known ideas, they carry the risk of losing their lives for the good of their brothers. Read *The Anarchist Philosophy, The Conquest of Bread, God and the State,* and *The Psychology of the Socialist Anarchist.*

Having strayed from the point that I was going to discuss—and that is, comrades, that no worker and no one who considers himself a free man or aspires to be one should allow entry into their homes any brother belonging to dogmatic sects, who may with sermons darken the little clarity that free modern thought has been able to introduce:

Comrades, do not baptize your children. Consider that if it were necessary, it is stupid that there are millions who do not believe in it.

It is a system of exploitation in order to live without great troubles. Independent of all rites and dogma, which are ridiculous in this century: Do not work for idle or ignorant beings. Do not help support with your vote the current state of tyranny, maintaining in power men who go against the worker after having exploited him, who if he does not find work and seizes a roll of bread or any needed object and is hence called a thief and incarcerated in a dark prison, his wife and children finding themselves in misery and unprotected because of this.

Educate yourselves, since one can never be sufficiently wise. You will always learn something new, and you will see the pile of errors in which humanity is enveloped because of its laws. Know that an unfortunate being who allows himself to be defeated by rage and commits homicide because of ignorance is punished with a penalty of death. Down with the death penalty! It is as stupid as those who approved it, and nevertheless, to these madmen go honors and glory.

1908

Situación del trabajador puertorriqueño
(The Situation of the Puerto Rican Worker)

Let us work in the struggle so that everyone has what belongs to him. It is unjust that we watch with indifference, that after a life of hard labor, like the one carried out by the workers on the farms, they have as a result to beg for money or go to the hospital in clothing worth admiring, and this in the towns where there *is* a hospital. Let us eradicate these customs in this growing generation so that it does not become used to that exploitative system. They should be practicing Christians but not in foreign ways carrying out rituals and accepting stupid and ridiculous dogmas that hinder their thinking, and by going to the church they already believe themselves Christians, confess to the priest, receive Holy Communion or attend mass....

Christ prayed amid nature. This is his true temple, worthy and beautiful to elevate our thoughts and to think about those who hold such beliefs in the future, even though we should all think since we will have to go there, and we must be prepared. Here is the reason that it is necessary to fight to improve our material life, educating ourselves to perfect ourselves and to prevent the opposite case, as we will have observed, of a worker who asks for a raise in salary and becomes the owner but then tries to lower the salary of his coworkers from before.

This reveals how little men appreciate each other and that selfishness dominates the feelings of brotherhood.

It is necessary to fight and energize the organizing movement, since the more salaries they have, the more abundance in their homes, the fewer hours of work, the more education, and the less likely they will commit errors. In a home that lacks necessities, blasphemy occurs, they despair, there is skepticism, atheism, indifference, envy, rage, grudges. In a family where domestic work is excessive and work outside the home contributes to this to secure food, meet the house payment, and buy clothing, existence is terrible, it is exasperating, it leads to suicide. This condition brings horrible consequences for body and soul.

The mother becomes easily enraged. She beats her children in a stupid and savage manner and degenerates their brain. Due to the insufficient food and excessive work and since she cannot tend to her children (since to secure food, she needs to spend all week tied to a batea, wet, dirty, under-nourished), and her children go here and there, dirty and with torn clothes, speaking in bad language. They do not go to school since their mother does not dare send them dirty and barefoot and she cannot afford shoes with her salary. Well, a great many misfortunes, and we call ourselves Christians. And we observe from a balcony a woman perfumed and en-wrapped in high-quality laces, instead of paying a miserable coal miner 15 cents for his little sack of coal. Let us suppose that the sack of coal is not even worth 10. But what do these unfortunate people live on? ... And that woman, forgetting these details, tries to pay 10 or 12 cents for one sack and does not make amends when she goes to a store and buys high-quality, wide laces of two, three, and five dollars and bottles of good Tinaud or Rigaud perfume for her toilette. Oh! humanity, your own tyrant; what a derision! And you go to temples to worship images, pagan cult. Christ prohibited the adoration of idols, and the Roman Church demands it. Christ built a cult—love for one's fellow man, and he practiced it in his life, forgiving his executioners and slanderers. We do the contrary: if someone slanders our name, we take revenge; and if someone laughs at us, we laugh back; and if they offend us with insults, we denounce them.

1908

SARA ESTELA RAMIREZ
1881–1910

21 de marzo (March 21)

To Benito Juárez

It is true that my homeland, which I adore,
Has counted in thousands its feats
And counted its heroes in thousands.
How many golden pages
In that story of epic songs!
How many sublime verses in those pages
In which Liberty etched its name
With clear, indelible, red letters!

5

Sweet truth that I evoke with pride:
How many times has the arrogant eagle   10
Of that sacred flag
Been raised to celebrate a son of hers?
Whether for a hero fallen with honor,
Whether for a laurel fitted with honor,
See how she flies grandly and beautifully,   15
Recalling for the homeland an epic poem,
A joyful day, the memorable day
When that Liberator who, without fortune,
At the rocks of Ixtlán had a cradle
That a king's descendants would envy.   20

How many titans, how many gladiators
With their arms of steel destroying
The thrones of the crude oppressors!
How many ardent lives sacrificed
On the fields of struggle,   25
Upholding their honor with swords!

Of all of them the past speaks to us
And all of them are—who would believe it!—
A sublime and unresolved prologue
Of the hidden and sought after paradise   30
Called Redemption, which awaits us still.

All of those heroic deeds,
Cheers that the mountains repeat
Like an echo from God, drive us mad:
And that is why as they travel from mouth to mouth,   35
From heart to heart. One forgets
That the glory of the present is small,
And the work of good is unfinished.

Is it the fault of chance? It does not guess!
Is it the fault of destiny? I don't think so!   40
It is only the fault of human effort.
May it forgive me if I find it guilty!

I know well that it is not an instant venture,
The conquest of good that man yearns for,
It is an enormous and difficult task   45
That begins behind school walls
And continues to be very distant from us.

Oh! Yesterday's pages, blessed, holy,
You are a pedestal of glory
Which our footsteps follow.   50
    Let us move forward with persistence,
Now that we have guardian gods,
Like the undefeated Juárez,
That guide our step.
Oh, Juárez! When the name of the athlete   55
Rises to my lips with divine accent,
I am happy because I feel
My heart shouts like a prophet:
You, the indomitable Mexican race,
You look toward the past and think of tomorrow,   60
You are still too distant from the goal.

1908

■   ANONYMOUS   ■

from **Las Dos Republicas**
Colaboración (Collaboration)

Light is born from dialogue.

We have seen, then, in the previous articles that, between the two peoples
that occupy the continent of América, those of the North enjoy a strong
government, an industry and venture without equal, and all the material
advantages of European civilization.

But all of this lacks soul, the invigorating principle of a moral system.
Thus, in the midst of its prosperity, every now and then the fatal indications of barbarism are discovered. The religions of spiritualism, the "Free
Love" of the Mormons, the "Women's Rights" party, the practice of divorce:
all of this indicates that morally the Anglo-Saxon does not have the power
to perpetuate the patrimony of civilization he inherited from Christianity
and even less power to engender it in other regions.

On the contrary, we are not the rich heirs of a civilization but the architects, through Christianity, of our own social progress; and for that same
reason, our construction is incomplete, but there exist the new and firm
foundations of our good customs and of our faith.

In the clash of these two societies, our physical power is futile, but the
Latin civilization will succeed in the end, because of the strength of our
superior morality, and our efforts should be aimed at reinforcing the principles that have saved us to this day and not to destroy them like some

supporters of this idea are trying to do. This would be surrendering at the discretion of the enemy.

But something more than this is necessary to gain victory in the social battle in which we find ourselves. It could be that the Saxon will adopt our good customs and thus heal the evils that afflict him; whereas we, if we do not adopt his industries or learn to govern ourselves or to take advantage of the circumstances around us, the consequences will be that they throw us out of our native country, that our race and our language disappear.

The battle that we sustain here in Arizona in this war of the races is first moral and second physical. Our good customs depend on the first one, and our existence on the second.

The United States' system of government is the best in the world for those who take advantage of its laws and the worst for those who do not.

This government assures peace, and an industrious one prospers and accumulates possessions, and these give him an estate and social status and from these the opportunity to educate himself and his children. Now the government is in the hands of the citizens, and an individual's freedom, the protection of his properties, and his very life depend on the people who elect those who govern.

From here, emerge two consequences for those who spurn industry and politics. The idle being must fall into poverty and insignificance, and whoever refuses to participate in political matters must suffer insults in silence and without appeal. This is what it means to suffer slavery at the hands of a free government.

We are here, then, as the skilled guards of Latin civilization in America, and our duty is to hold our position against the attack of Northern hordes. Our duty is (1) to maintain our faith, our customs, and our language; (2) to cultivate our knowledge, arise from the lethargy of indolence, and rival the Saxon in industry and accumulate a fortune; (3) to dispute the empire of the state and ensure that laws that conform to our interests be dictated and that men who look after our well-being be put in power.

It would be good if it weren't true, but the case is that the United States has already taken a large portion of Mexico. For this reason, should we abandon the land and retract step by step until they cast us into the ocean like they did with the indigenous? No, sir, let us learn from the Confederates who accepted the military trial and surrendered but only to change their tactics from the battleground to politics and the halls of Congress. Similarly, if by strength they defeat us, we should take refuge in our strong points, and by seizing their own arms we shall finally defeat the victor. Our customs, our faith, our language, activity, industry, education; taking part in politics, influencing legislation, and naming those who govern: these are the arms with which the Latin civilization must defeat the Saxon civilization.

1877

■ ANONYMOUS ■

from **Plan de San Diego**

Provisional Directorate of the Plan of San Diego, Tex.
Plan (Plot) of San Diego, State of Texas, January 6th, 1915.

We who in turn sign our names, assembled in the REVOLUTIONARY PLOT OF SAN DIEGO, TEXAS, solemnly promise each other, on our word of honor, that we will fulfill, and cause to be fulfilled and complied with, all the clauses and provisions stipulated in this document, and execute the orders and the wishes emanating from the PROVISIONAL DIRECTORATE of this movement, and recognize as military Chief of the name, Mr. Augustin S. GARZA, guaranteeing with our lives the faithful accomplishment of what is here agreed upon.

1. On the 20th day of February, 1915, at two o'clock in the morning, we will arise in arms against the Government and Country of the United States of North America, ONE AS ALL AND ALL AS ONE, proclaiming the liberty of the individuals of the black race and its independence of Yankee tyranny which has held us in iniquitous slavery since remote times; and at the same time and in the same manner we will proclaim the independence and segregation of the States bordering upon the Mexican Nation, which are: TEXAS, NEW MEXICO, ARIZONA, COLORADO, and UPPER CALIFORNIA, of which States the REPUBLIC OF MEXICO was robbed in a most perfidious manner by North American imperialism.

2. In order to render the foregoing clause effective the necessary army corps will be formed, under the immediate command of military leaders named by the SUPREME REVOLUTIONARY CONGRESS of SAN DIEGO, TEXAS, which shall have full power to designate a SUPREME CHIEF, who shall be at the head of said army. The banner which shall guide us in this enterprise shall be red, with a white diagonal fringe, and bearing the following inscription: "EQUALITY AND INDEPENDENCE" and none of the subordinate leaders or subalterns shall use any other flag (except only the white flag for signals). The aforesaid army shall be known by the name of: "LIBERATING ARMY FOR RACES AND PEOPLES."

1915

■ ONOTO WATANNA (WINNIFRED EATON) ■
1875–1954

Growing up in Montreal, Canada, as the eighth of twelve children born to a Chinese woman missionary and an English merchant-artist-turned-factory clerk, Winnifred Eaton was understandably interested in such stories of inter-racial love as Pierre Loti's *Madame Chrysanthème* (1893) and John Luther Long's "Madame Butterfly" (1895). Until 1894, Eaton's mother, Grace, was the only Chinese woman in Montreal, and her children drew many curious gazes. Eaton's first known article, "A Half Caste" (1898), focused on the plight of Eurasian children fathered by white Orientalists. She ended it by saying that the half-Japanese children of the literary celebrities Lafcadio Hearn and Sir Edwin Arnold might "prove exceptions, as they will doubtless have the protection and love of these great men." The article suggests that her own father had not been equal to raising his large biracial family in Sinophobic Canada.

Without much of an education, parental protection, or a dowry, Winnifred Eaton came to rely on her spunk and storytelling talent. Her oldest sister, Edith Eaton, faced Sinophobia head on. Throughout her adult life, she published stories and articles about the Chinese in North America under the pen name Sui Sin Far, though she barely managed to support herself as a typist. Winnifred, by contrast, evaded Sinophobia by learning to exploit the Western fad for things Japanese. Rather than tackling interracial relations in North America, she removed them to an imaginary Japan. Using the pen name Onoto Watanna, she borrowed freely from the writings of Pierre Loti, Lafcadio Hearn, and John Luther Long, treating them as field workers who supplied the raw materials for her ethnographic fiction. However, her ambitions went well beyond the publication of a dozen "Japanese" romances. During the course of her astounding career, which lasted more than thirty years, she reinvented herself repeatedly, starting out as a newspaper reporter in Jamaica at 21, becoming the kimono-clad half-Japanese writer Onoto Watanna in Chicago at 22; an exotic New York celebrity who drove her own car and lived on Long Island at 28; a wife and mother of three, focused on writing to support her family, a Reno divorcee, Canadian rancher's wife, and author of prairie novels in her forties; a prolific Hollywood screen-writer in her fifties; and a patron of the arts in Calgary when she retired.

As Onoto Watanna, she knowingly recycled recognizable formulas of popular fiction. The narrator of her anonymously published autobiographical novel, *Me: A Book of Remembrance* (1915), confesses: "My success was founded upon a cheap and popular device." Yet because she reproduced Orientalist narratives as a woman of color with serious ideological problems to resolve, her plots attempted to erode long-established truths: that the white race is intellectually, morally, and physically superior to all others; that biracial people are degenerate; that culture is racially determined; that Asians are incapable of higher feelings; and that, as Havelock Ellis claimed, "people do not tend to fall in love with those who are in racial respects a contrast to themselves." While inscribing herself in the Orientalist tradition, she worked hard to subvert it.

If we consider that Onoto Watanna made her name during the McKinley and Roosevelt presidencies, when the Anti-Asiatic League was at its most vocal and eugenics was institutionalized through immigration policies, her involving miscegenation plots seem anything but formulaic. Can we call conventional a story of a white American woman who seduces a Japanese student on shipboard on his way home from the United States (*Miss Nume of Japan*)? How conventional is a romance that begins with the marriage of a widowed Japanese businessman to a white American widow, who cheerfully assimilates into Japanese culture (*A Japanese Blossom*)? Or a story in which a white middle-aged sex tourist in Japan falls in love with a teahouse dancer who turns out to be the child he fathered on a previous trip ("A Half Caste")? Each of these plots was a skeleton straight out of the American race closet. It is the drapery around the skeletons that is conventional: Onoto Watanna's Japanese heroines speak pidgin English, and "Japan" (a country she never visited) is constructed out of iconic images lifted from tourist guidebooks, fans, and lacquer trays. But only by catering to such reader expectations was Eaton able to rattle the bones of the skeletons.

"A Half Caste" (1899), included in this volume, can be read as an ironic anti-Orientalist sequel to the fictions of "loving, leaving, and grieving" popularized by Pierre Loti's novel *Madame Chrysanthème* (1893). Watanna's story foregrounds the problem of economic exchange, which was often displaced from the travel narratives. Kiku, the heroine, works as a teahouse entertainer not because the Japanese traditionally indenture their daughters to brothel and teahouse owners, as some Americans claimed, but because Westerners have created jobs in the new tourist industry at precisely the moment when modernization has left large segments of the population destitute. This is one of Onoto Watanna's bolder stories, one that denounces the objectification and exploration of Asians by white Westerners with an interest in the exotic. Some of her later work is more conciliatory in tone.

Dominika Ferens
University of Wroclaw, Poland

PRIMARY WORKS

Miss Nume: A Japanese-American Romance, 1899, reprinted in *A Japanese Nightingale*, 1901; *The Heart of Hyacinth*, 1903, reprinted in 2000; *The Wooing of Wistaria*, 1903; *The Daughters of Nijo: A Romance of Japan*, 1904; *The Love of Azalea*, 1904; *A Japanese Blossom*, 1906; *The Diary of Delia: Being a Veracious Chronicle of the Kitchen with Some Side-Lights on the Parlour*, 1907; *Tama*, 1910; *The Honorable Miss Moonlight*, 1912; *Chinese-Japanese Cook Book* (with Sara Bosse), 1914; *Me: A Book of Remembrance*, 1915, reprinted in 1997; *Marion: The Story of an Artist's Model*, 1916; *Sunny-San*, 1922; *Cattle*, 1924; *His Royal Nibs*, 1925; "A Half Caste" and Other Writings, eds. Linda Trinh Moser and Elizabeth Rooney, 2003.

A Half Caste

A miscellaneous crowd of men, women and children jostled each other on the wharf, some of them going perilously near the end of it in their eagerness to watch the passengers on the *Empress of India,* which had just arrived.

Norman Hilton stood on deck, his hands thrust deep in his trousers pockets. He seemed in no hurry to leave the boat, but leaned against the guardrail, watching the surging crowd on the wharf beneath.

"Shall you go ashore to-night?"

He started from the moody dream into which he had drifted, then answered, absently, pushing his cap far back on his head: "Well, I don't know. Fact is, now the journey is over—I feel—er—just a trifle nervous."

His friend looked at him keenly.

"Second trip for you, I believe?"

"Yes."

"Fifth for me," his companion continued. "Rather be here than any-where else."

"Why?" Hilton looked at him curiously.

The other laughed, waving his hand lightly toward the city.

"You know my weakness—and, for that matter your own—women. I like the Japanese style, too—artless, jolly, pretty—er—. Agree with me?"

"Perhaps."

Hilton put a cigar between his teeth and began smoking it. He broke a silence that fell between them with the information that on his former voy-age he had married a Japanese girl—in Japanese fashion—adding, with unconcealed grim contempt for himself, that of course he had left her in American fashion.

"Expect to see her again?"

"No, she's dead!" He paused for a moment, and then added, a trifle hesi-tatingly: "There was a child. I want it."

"Ah!"

Hilton finished smoking his cigar and threw the stub into the bay.

"I have a hard job before me," he said nervously, "as I have little or no clew to the child's whereabouts. It was nearly sixteen years ago, you know." He paused again, ruminating, and took a few slow strides across the deck. "I am alone in the world. She is about all the kin I have, in fact. It sounds bru-tal, I suppose, but during all these years I have made no inquiry about her whatever. I forgot the fact of her birth almost as I forgot the mother's exis-tence. I don't know what possessed me to come now, anyhow. One of my unconquerable impulses, I suppose. You know how they affect me."

His friend made no remark whatever. Hilton had always seemed to him so young a man that it was hard for him to realize for the moment that he was actually the father of a girl of fifteen. He was an extremely handsome man, with a keen, clever face, hair slightly tinged with gray, and a fine athletic figure. He dressed well, and he had the appearance of a man of the world, one who was in the habit, perhaps, of putting himself always first and best.

In his early youth Hilton had gone the pace of most young men of fashion and wealth in a foreign land. Divorced from his American wife scarcely a year after his marriage to her, he had lived alone ever since. His wife had remarried long ago. Now, at the age of forty, Hilton had found himself altogether alone in the world, with a strong weariness of his own companionship and an un-conquerable longing to have someone with him who actually belonged to him. Then, one day, there came a memory of a little Japanese woman who had once really loved him for himself. Hilton's hard eyes had softened a trifle. He was suddenly keenly alive to the fact that he was a father; that he owed his first duty in life to the one being in the world who belonged to him—his little Japanese daughter, whom he had never seen, for she had been born after he had left Japan. He could not account for the vague yearning and longing for his own child that now suddenly possessed him.

Okikusan (Miss Chrysanthemum) was in trouble again. This time she had offended her master by refusing to dance for the American who threw his money so lavishly about. He had specially asked that the girl with the red cheeks, large eyes and white skin be asked to dance for him.

The dancing mats were thrown, the music started, and Kiku had thrust forward one little foot and had curtsied to the four corners of the earth. Then she twirled clear around on the tips one little foot, her hand tapering out towards the American. She had started dancing without once glancing at the visitor. By chance her eye happened to fall on him, and with a sudden whim she paused in her steps and subsided to the mats, her little feet drawn under her.

The proprietor of the garden came toward her in amazement.

"What does this mean?" he asked in a terrible voice of suppressed anger.

"That I will *not* dance for the foreign devil!" she said defiantly.

Takahashi, the proprietor, looked in trepidation at his customer as she spoke, fearing that he had overheard her, and perhaps understood the language. The American was watching the girl with amused eyes. Then he crossed to where she sat on the ground.

"Why did you stop dancing?" he asked her in fairly good Japanese.

She answered him in broken English.

"Tha's account I nod lig' to danze for you!" she told him candidly.

"Why?"

Takahashi answered hastily for her.

"She is mos' rude. I beg your augustness to pardon her. She is the most miserably rude girl in the tea-house. Deign to permit me to furnish you with someone who is more amiable to dance for you. I will dismiss this one."

"Ah and if you do I will never come here again," the American told him, for Kiku-san was the prettiest thing he had ever seen, far prettier than all the other geisha girls. If she would not dance for him he would not insist. In fact, he was content to simply look at her.

Takahashi made some abject apologies for her, volunteering the information that he never could understand the girl's unreasonable dislike for foreigners. Then he left the two together.

The girl sat still on the mat, looking straight out before her, her face unreadable in its cold indifference. Hilton could not understand her. She was so unlike any Japanese girl he had ever met, for they generally were so willing and eager to please. After a time he broke the somewhat strained silence to say, in his soft, drawling fashion:

"Would you not like something—er—to drink? Shall I fetch something for you?"

The question was so absurd that the girl's studied indifference broke down.

"Tha's nod your place to waid on me!" she said, loftily, rising to her feet. "I thing thad you lig something to dring. Yes? That I git paid to worg here. I thing I bedder bring you something to dring," she added stiffly. "But I no lig to waid on you. I prefer vaery much waid on Japanese gents."

There was a sibilant softness to her voice that was bewildering in its charm and sweetness, and her broken English was prettier than anything he had ever heard.

When she brought the hot saké back to him her face was smiling above the dainty tray, and as she knelt at his feet while he drank it, he could see that her former petulant mood was gone, and that she was now using every effort to please and conciliate him.

"Now you look like a Japanese sunbeam," he told her softly, looking unutterable things at her out of his deep gray eyes.

"Tha's account I 'fraid gitting discharged," she told him, calmly, still smiling. "Mr. Takahashi tell me if I nod vaery kin' to you he goin' to send me a long way from here."

"Ah, I see. Then you are only pretending to smile?"

She shrugged her little shoulders.

"Yes," she said indifferently. "Tha's worg' for geisha girl. Whad do you thing we goin' to git paid for. Account we frown? Or account we laugh? I thing that's account we laugh. Thad is my worg. You nod onderstand? *You* worg, *I* worg, *aeverybody* worg. All different ways. Geisha girl *mus'* be always gay—always dance, laugh, sing; laugh mos' of all—to mek you laugh too, so that you pay the money, mek us reech. I nod lig vaery much thees worg, but whad kin I do? Thad I nod worgin' I goin' to starve. Tha's bedder I worg foraever. Whad you thing?"

"That you are a philosopher," he told her, smiling, and added: "But what a cynic, too! I didn't expect to find it among Japanese women—cynicism."

The girl smiled a trifle bitterly.

"Oa!" she said, "you nod fin thad 'mong Japanese—only me! I different from aeverybody else." She set the tray on the ground and sat down at his feet.

Takahashi strolled across the grounds and passed them slowly, giving the girl a quick, stern, almost threatening look, and beaming at the American in a fashion that annoyed him.

Okikusan began to speak in a panic to the American, raising her voice so that the words would reach Takahashi:

"But I lig you. My! *how* nize I thing you are!"

Hilton stared at her in amazement. The moment Takahashi had passed out of sight, she rose impatiently to her feet.

"Tha's a liar," she said with quiet scorn. "You thing I mean thad?—that I lig you? I only spik thad for please Takahashi-sama."

The soft outlines of her face had suddenly hardened and surprised him with a look of shrewd understanding, such as he had never seen on a Japanese woman's face before.

"*You* are lig this," she said, making a sweeping gesture with her hands, "so fool conceit. Tha's way all big mans come from the West. They thing my! we so *nize*! Thing, we foolin' with liddle Japanese women thad don' know much."

"How old are you?" Hilton asked her curiously?

"Twenty-two," she told him.

"You look like a child."

It was two weeks later. With a restless fascination he could not understand, Hilton went every day to the little tea-house on the hill. Always he sought out Okikusan, and would spend the entire day with her, totally oblivious to almost all else save the girl's beauty and charm. It was her shrewdness and cleverness that had first attracted him to her. Formerly he had delighted in the Japanese women because of that artlessness which is so original and refreshing in them. Kiku was anything but artless. She said things that no American girl would say, and that few Japanese girls would understand, and in spite of this she was a charming individual. And Hilton forgot his mission in Japan, forgot that Japanese women had always merely been the playthings of the moment; that he had tired of life—everything save the delightful, irresistible feelings that had awakened in him. What was it? Hilton was in love, and with a Japanese woman! Years ago he had married one in Japanese fashion, and had left her. She had been a gentle, clinging woman, with whom he had passed a dreamy, sleepy summer. What could he do with Kiku? She was unlike any Japanese woman he had ever known—unlike any woman he had met. She was the one woman in the world he had loved during all his long, checkered career—a life spent in idle pursuit of his own pleasures.

Hilton's friend, who had accompanied him on the voyage, was beginning to feel anxious about him, for, in spite of his admission of his own weakness for Japanese women, he was far more alive to and quick to scent real danger than Hilton, who followed his extravagant impulses only, while the cooler man kept a level head in the midst of his pleasures.

"My dear boy," he said to Hilton, "you've got the fever, I believe?"

Hilton laughed weakly.

"Nonsense!"

"You are in love with some Japanese girl!" his friend continued. "You want to look out for them, you know."

Hilton rose to his feet and began pacing the room in long, irregular strides.

"Don't you suppose I am old enough to be proof against such things?"

"Well, I don't know, Hilton, to tell you the truth. You see, Japanese women are different. You're only human, after all. I'd advise you to marry her—for a while, of course, as you did the other one."

"I have an idea," Hilton said with some hesitancy, "that I am too old for another affair of that kind. I thought of settling down—that is, I intended returning to America, and—er—marrying."

"What are you waiting for, then? The child died, did it not?"

"So they say."

He flung himself restlessly across a couch, staring moodily at the fusuma.

"What do you say to our leaving next week?"

"Good."

"Better keep away from the tea-house in the meanwhile," his friend advised.

Hilton did not answer.

He did not go near the tea-house, however, all the next day. By evening he was seized with a fit of unconquerable restlessness and blues. He was awake the entire night, tossing from side to side.

He kept up his resolution all the next morning, but about the middle of the afternoon threw it up, and almost rushed across the rice-fields to the lit-tle tea-garden. He found her in a field blazing with a vivid burning glory of natan and azalea blossoms. She saw him coming, and stooped down among the grasses to hide from him. The man was intoxicated with his hunger for her, and caught her in his arms with all his pent-up love and passion.

"Kiku," he whispered, "I tried to stay away. I could not. Don't you understand?" He was holding her close to him now, and covering her face with a passion of kisses. "I love you! I love you! I love you!" he began, mur-muring in her ear.

The girl's eyes were fixed full on his face. He caught the elfish, searching full gaze, and for a moment released her. She stooped to pick up the scat-tered blossoms that had fallen.

"Go 'way!" she said pettishly. "I nod lig you. You mus' *nod* do thad," she continued, as he tried to draw her into his arms again. "Tha's nod ride! Tha's—"

"It *is* right, Kiku-san," he whispered, "because I love you!" His words hurried over each other. "I am going to take you away with me, Kiku-san—to my home. We will be married. I cannot live without you, and—"

The girl shivered, and her face suddenly grew white.

"Go 'way!" she repeated, this time with an almost imploring note in her voice. "I don' wanter tell you. I thing it bes' nod. No, I nod tell you—aevery-thing. Besides, I nod lig you vaery much. Jus' a liddle bit now. At first I hate—hate with all my heart! Now I ver' sawry thad, thad I bin unkin'. Tha's account you unkin' too."

"I unkind!" he repeatedly stupidly. "I don't understand, Kiku-san."

"No, you nod onderstan'," she said in despair. "What kin I do? Oh, pitiful Kwannon! help me! I thing I tell you. I bin mos vaery onhappy long time now, because aeverybody hate me. Account I loog lig American. You no onderstand? No? My fadder"—she paused a moment—"he leave my modder. We vaery onhappy so thad she goin' to die. Then w'enn she die I worg, worg hard at the factory, an' here. Nobody lig me account my father American, an' I thing account that I goin' hate all Americans foraever, because my fadder vaery wigged, because he mek my modder suffer. And me? I suffer too."

A grayness crept over Hilton's face. He felt suddenly weak and old.

"You still nod onderstand?" she asked. Her hands had fallen from his now, and he staggered back a few paces.

"Not yet!" he said faintly.

"Then I tell you," she said firmly. "I nod lig you because w'en you come here someone that know my mother w'en she alive point at you and say, '*Thad* you' fadder!'"

The silence that was between them now was horrible. It suddenly assumed a savage mockery by the wild singing of a nightingale which flew over their heads and trilled aloud its song of gladness.

The man could not speak. He stood looking out in front of him with a pitiful look of horror, and only half comprehension on his face.

After a while the girl continued:

"Firs' I thing I will tell you. Then I remember my modder and how onhappy she be, and how hard I worg all these years w'ile you have so much rich, an' then I hate you foraever and bury all sawry for you in my heart, an' I hate all the mens from the West, foraever so fool of conceit. Tha's a liar thad I say I twenty-two years old. I thing now thad my time come to fool. I thing I revenge my modder? I think I mek you suffer lig her. You nod onderstan? Always she have pain here!" She clasped her hand over her heart, and then continued wearily: "Tha's account you tich her to luf you. I nod onderstan thad liddle word vaery much. Aeverybody say I nod have aeny heart. All hard dead. Tha's account I luf only my modder, an' she die. An' I also hate you thad you kill that modder."

Through the mists of pain and horror that had overcome him the memories of dead days were coming back to Hilton. He could not think of Kiku-san now as his own child—his very own blood—he could not!

"You must be mistaken!" His voice sounded strange, even to his own ears. "My child died—they told me so."

The girl laughed bitterly.

"Tha's bedder I daed. I going away. Aeverybody thinging I daed 'cept me. I know always. You thing I loog lig Japanese girl?"

She suddenly loosened her hair, and it fell down around her in thick, shining brown curls.

"Thad lig Japanese girl?—thad?—thad?—thad? Thad?"

She pushed back the sleeves and showed him the white purity of her arms.

Then she turned and left him, with the same still look of despair on his face and the pitiless sun beating down on the golden fields.

1899

■

Empire, Independence, and Self-Definition: Voices from the Philippines

On December 10, 1898, as part of the terms that officially ended the Spanish-American War, the United States acquired control over Cuba, Puerto Rico, and, in exchange for 20 million dollars, the Philippines. This transaction ended Spain's four centuries of colonial rule and significantly altered U.S. foreign policy for the fifty years that the archipelago remained a U.S. territory. With the acquisition of the Philippines, the United States gained a strategic access point in the Asia-Pacific region that President William McKinley and subsequent administrations were unwilling to relinquish until after World War II. U.S.–Philippine relations were quite volatile in the first two decades of the twentieth century, when Filipino independence debates were contentious and unresolved, and an active Philippine resistance movement attempted to win control of the islands. However, the battlegrounds were also the pages of American and Philippine periodicals, lecture rooms, and the floors of Congress, as U.S. politicians attempted to justify the occupation to American and Filipino audiences. Responding with their own speeches and published works, Filipino and Filipina authors in both countries quickly became involved in these discursive skirmishes.

This section collects some key contributions to the fraught discussion of empire, independence, national self-definition, and gender in the early twentieth-century Philippines and the United States. Many of these texts also represent the first works of English literature published by Filipinas and Filipinos in the United States. Despite the importance of the U.S. occupation of the Philippines and the key role that literary discourse played in debates over Philippine independence, we do not know much about early Filipino and Filipina literary production. The essays and columns featured in the following pages are deeply vested in campaigning for Philippine independence; in documenting the experiences of Filipinos abroad; in negotiating the terms of national, political, and cultural identity during the U.S. occupation, and in examining the differences in Filipino masculinity and Filipino femininity after contact with the United States.

In part, it was U.S. foreign policy that catalyzed the rapid appearance of English literature in the Philippines. From the initial days of the occupation, the American government couched its objectives in ambivalent terms. The United States refused to officially recognize the Philippines as an independent nation, but the McKinley administration also maintained that its interest in the islands was not colonial. Despite the unresolved conflict in the Philippines (which U.S. officials called an insurrection rather than a war) and persistent campaigns for independence, the official word was that occupation was a necessary and beneficial venture for both countries. McKinley and others argued that Filipinos were not capable of self-government and needed the civilizing benefits of colonial tutelage. According to McKinley, the U.S. "mission" was not one of colonialism or invasion, but the "benevolent assimilation" of America's "little brown brothers" (a term coined by future president William Howard Taft, then Governor-General of the Philippines).

To facilitate the so-called benevolent assimilation of the Philippines, the United States launched a multifaceted platform that included the institution of English as a national language, the rapid establishment of a public school system, and the widespread instruction of English by teachers exported from the States. In 1903, the *Pensionado* Act inaugurated a venture that sponsored a select group of Filipinos and Filipinas for the pursuit of advanced degrees at U.S. universities. Made possible in part by Filipinos' unique, ambiguous classification as U.S. nationals—neither citizens nor aliens—the *pensionado* program ostensibly encouraged the education of model Filipinas and Filipinos who would eventually return to the Philippines to spread the principles of American democracy. Although citizens of other Asian nations were subject to strict immigration restrictions, Filipinas and Filipinos who could afford the price of passage (appointees to political commissions, U.S.-appointed representatives, or members of other elite groups) were also able to travel between the Philippines and the United States.

The first decade of the U.S. occupation saw the remarkably rapid appearance of English language material authored by Filipinos and Filipinas, whose familiarity with the language was facilitated by their travels or university experiences in the States. From the turn of the century to the end of the Great War, Filipino and Filipina authors produced essays, editorials, or news columns in three primary sites—U.S. magazines and newspapers; small, Filipino-produced periodicals, or, in rare cases, book format. Many of the first published works advocated for the Philippines right to independence. At the turn of the century, Sixto Lopez began touring the United States as a representative of the Philippine cause, and his speeches (translated by his secretary) appeared regularly in U.S. newspapers. A decade later, Filipinos and Filipinas were fluent enough to compose works in English without the aid of a translator. Like his predecessor Lopez, Manuel Quezon, who eventually became President of the Philippine Republic, also supplemented his speaking tours with published essays. As the appointed Resident Commissioner of the Philippines, in Washington D.C., Quezon published and circulated *The Filipino People*. On the West Coast, Filipino and Filipina students at the University of California, Berkeley, produced *The Filipino Students' Magazine*, which collected articles from *pensionados* who were scattered at universities across the United States. Book publication by Filipinos was a less viable option; Maximo Kalaw's *The Case for the Filipinos* and *Self Government in the Philippines* are exceptional.

Filipina- and Filipino-authored English works written in the early twentieth century display a rhetorical dexterity and complexity that underscore the authors' awareness of multiple reading audiences. Accessibility, education, language, and location determined Filipina and Filipino readership; most Filipino and Filipina readers of literature in English would have been part of the expatriate community. Quezon attempted to widen his readership by publishing *The Filipino People* in English and Spanish. This bilingual translation addressed the linguistic diversity of the Filipino upper class, many of whom still spoke, read, and conducted business in Spanish. However, writers like Kalaw, Lopez, and Quezon also crafted their treatises for a larger American readership that was interested in Philippine independence debates or in learning more about the islands. In addition to disseminating developments in U.S.–Philippine politics, periodicals like *The Filipino People* or books like Kalaw's *The Case for the Filipinos* worked hard to circumvent and critique representations of the Philippines and Filipinos that circulated in the mainstream press or that were propagated by U.S. politicians. The exhibits of tribes from the Philippines in the 1904 St. Louis World's' Fair did much to further an American perception of Filipinos and Filipinas as uncivilized. Authors thus often directly responded to a wide variety of texts, ranging from newspaper coverage of U.S. congressional debates to the publication of book-length studies of the Philippines. While Kalaw's *Self Government in the Philippines* is quite serous in its objective of altering American misconceptions, the parody "Who Are the Original Dog-eaters" takes a more humorous approach in playfully critiquing the U.S. circulation of Filipinos stereotypes.

Filipino and Filipina writers had to tread carefully the uneasy ground between overtly criticizing U.S. imperial policy and persuading American readers to support the independence movement. These authors negotiate with a U.S. audience by appealing to moral, democratic principles and, in later texts, by stressing that the Philippines had successfully achieved a model of democracy fashioned after that of the United States. Writers persistently incorporated language that mimicked familiar phrases from the Declaration of Independence and the U.S. constitution; Sixto Lopez, for example, asks his reader to recognize the "self-evident" truth of Philippine rights and compares the U.S.–Philippine solution to the conflict between England and the thirteen colonies. As elites who ostensibly spoke for the country as a whole, many Filipino and Filipina authors also elided complex class and regional differences in the islands to ground their claims that the Philippines was a unified nation. The drawn-out debate over Philippine independence also affected later works. As the years passed without the successful ratification of a bill that would explicitly provide for Philippine independence, Filipino authors adjusted their strategies to address the longstanding influence of the occupation. Earlier writers, including Lopez, phrased their critique of the United States much more aggressively than authors who produced works in the later period.

Constructions of masculinity and femininity were also crucial components of the U.S.–Philippine debate. Filipino writers often used tropes of masculinity to ground their arguments. One frequent strain implored Americans to recognize that Filipinos were men, and that no real man could allow his country to remain subjugated to the will of another nation. This emphasis on independence as a right accorded to men addressed constructions of U.S. imperialism as the destined project of white, red-blooded, and virile American men, with its accompanying counter-construct of Filipinos as uncivilized "little brown brothers." However, the trope of Filipino masculinity in U.S.–Philippine independence debates also dovetailed with the increasingly vexed discussions about Filipina and American women's suffrage. Filipina suffrage complicated the issue of Philippine independence. Certain Filipino politicians argued that the extension of the vote to women should not be included in the terms for independence, while others, like Kalaw, supported the women's movement. In the United States, American suffrage activists faced a related conundrum. Although many suffragists early included their Filipina sisters within a broad campaign for women's rights, others balked at the prospect that Philippine independence might take precedence over women's suffrage in the United States.

Women such as Emma Sarepta Yule (a white American who moved to the Philippines and had a long career in Philippine academia) and Filipina author M. P. de Veyra carefully constructed Eastern and white American femininity and responded to the vexed intersections of Filipina and American women's suffrage. The confluence of debates over U.S. women's suffrage and Philippine independence contributed to a growing curiosity about Filipina women. Addressing these interests, Filipino periodicals and U.S. publications such as *Scribner's* printed essays that described Filipinas to American readers. Many of these texts idealize domestic femininity and present the Filipina as a woman who is devoted to the home and family, yet still desires education and independence. Filipina writers who lived or traveled in the United States praised the American people for valuing equality between men and women. According to many of these works, Filipinas were unlike other models of Asian femininity with which a U.S. audience might be more familiar. Writing as a supporter of Filipina feminism, Yule carefully differentiates Filipinas from "the category of 'oriental woman,'" who was embodied by Japanese and Chinese femininity: "While custom and religion were drawing tighter the bonds of restriction about her Asiatic sisters, the Philippine woman was widening her sphere of thought and action under the influence which Western control brought to bear on the social development of her country." Yule and de Veyra's essays thus complicate the easy rhetoric of transnational sisterhood that was often employed in global women's suffrage debates.

Ultimately, appeals for Philippine independence and Filipina suffrage would remain unanswered for much of the first half of the twentieth century. Provisions for Philippine independence were not established until the passage of the Tydings-McDuffie Act (1934), which established a commonwealth and ten-year transition to an independent republic that was interrupted by the outbreak of World War II and the Japanese occupation of the Philippines. The Americans would not officially recognize the Philippines as an independent republic until 1946. Filipinas were granted the vote in 1937. The texts in this section provide important, previously unstudied views of a crucial, transitional moment in relations between the Philippines and the United States and in the histories of both nations.

Denise Cruz
Indiana University–Bloomington

SIXTO LOPEZ
1863–1947

The Philippine Problem: A Proposition for a Solution[1]

[Mr. Sixto Lopez is an authoritative though not an official representative of the Filipino people in the United States. He is, like a very large body of his fellow-countrymen, a man not only of native intelligence but of education, cultivation, and agreeable personality. One has only to read his article to see that he possesses a clear mind and a reasoning faculty of unusual logical power. At our request Mr. Lopez has undertaken to state the basis on which he believes his countrymen would cheerfully acquiesce in American control of the Philippine Islands. We think his article deserves wide reading and careful consideration. We comment more fully on it in another column— The Editors.]

"What form of government, exercised by the United States would the Filipinos acquiesce in, so as to put an end to the war and pave the way for a peaceful and an intelligent conference on the question of final independence?"

This question, which has been put to me by the editors of The Outlook, is one that comes from many other sources. It is a question which can be answered in one sentence: The Filipinos would accept the same or any similar form of government or control as that exercised over Cuba during the interregnum between cession by Spain and final independence. Nay, more, the Filipinos would accept any form of government, any form of despotism, government by caprice or by the will of any one with or without benevolent intentions, provided that they be given a similar promise to that given to the Cubans. Any form of government, or government without any form, would be preferable to the present indescribable horror under which honest men are not allowed to express their opinions; by which the best of our people are driven through swamp and jungle and shot down in the proportion, according to official reports, of five killed to one wounded; and during which the honor of our women, in outlying districts, is at the mercy of common soldiers' passion. There never has been any dispute or objection, as far as the Filipinos are concerned, as to what form of government they are prepared to temporarily accept. They have already accepted the arbitrament of war, and war is the worst condition conceivable, especially when waged by an Anglo Saxon race which despises its opponent as an alien or inferior people. Yet the Filipinos accepted it with a full knowledge of its horror and of the sacrifices in life and property which they knew they would be called upon to make.

It is therefore unnecessary to inquire if the Filipinos would be prepared to accept a less horrible condition of affairs, coupled with the understanding

[1]*Outlook,* April 13, 1901.

that there was to be "a peaceful and an intelligent conference on the question of final independence." The whole trouble lies in the fact that the Filipinos have never been promised or offered a conference upon the question of final independence. If they had been offered such a conference, the war would have ceased at once. But when Aguinaldo's emissaries came to confer with the Schurman Commission, they were told that the question of American sovereignty (which was the negation of Philippine independence) had been settled and could not, therefore, be discussed. The Bacon resolution and other similar resolutions have been rejected by Congress, and the only official statement of America's intention with regard to the Philippines is the proclamation of the President annexing the whole of the archipelago and demanding unconditional and apparently perpetual submission to American sovereignty.

Every fair-minded man will see, and many will admit, that the Filipinos have never been treated as though they were human beings possessing rights and aspirations of their own. They have been required to submit to American authority without a promise or a guarantee that the question of final independence would ever be discussed in an intelligent or any other kind of conference. On the contrary, they have been told that the question was one which could not be discussed at all. The question of independence has never been referred to in any official utterance. The only assurances that the Filipinos have received—and these not from Congress but from the President, whose decision Congress may or may not sustain—are that they shall have such personal liberty and such a share in the government of their own country "as is consistent with American interests and the discharge of American obligations." But, worse than this, America is to be the sole judge of the Filipinos' fitness for taking any part in the government of their own country. They are to be given only such things as America may choose to give them, not as a matter of right, but in the form of benevolence. Their rights are thus to become privileges, and everything that they are permitted to enjoy will be due to the benevolence of a foreign master who, whilst giving, has yet the power to withhold. It ought to be plain to the meanest intellect that this is a wholly one-sided arrangement, which would never have been offered except under the consciousness of overwhelming power to enforce it. It is a thousand times less liberal than the conditions imposed by England upon the Transvaal, and yet, presumably, American sympathies generally are with the latter. One can imagine with what scorn Washington and Jefferson and Patrick Henry would have refused such terms had they been offered by George III. And every one knows with what derision the English potentate's proclamation was met when he declared that he was "desirous of restoring to them [the American colonists] the blessings of law, which they have fatally and desperately exchanged for the calamities of war and the arbitrary *tyranny of their chiefs.*"

Now, the above truthfully and fairly represents the actual condition of affairs—a condition to which the Filipinos will never submit, and which is causing a prolongation of the war with all its attendant horrors; and yet I confess that it does not truthfully represent the desires and intentions of the American people generally. I am aware that there are those in America, as in every country in the world, who desire to lay hands upon everything within reach, irrespective of the laws relating to *meum* and *tuum*. But they constitute only a minority. I am convinced that a large majority of the American people desire to treat the Filipinos fairly, as human beings possessing certain rights; and that they do not intend to deny ultimate independence to a people who once fought side by side with American soldiers and rendered all the assistance in their power against "a common enemy." And here we reach the essence of the whole difficulty. This same majority of American people have placed in power those who do not, or who will not, in their official utterances, declare to the Filipinos the real intention of this majority. Yet the Filipinos, if they submit at all, must do so, not to the conditions required by this majority, which presuppose and include final independence, but to the conditions which I have explained above, and in which no mention is made of final independence.

It is, therefore, clear that the solution of the Philippine problem lies in the bringing of official assurances into line with the desire and intention of the majority of the American people. If this can be achieved, the Filipinos will not continue, or *desire* to continue, the strife for one day longer.

It may be premised that the Filipinos are not unreasonable in their desires. Indeed, under present conditions they would naturally be disposed to accept terms which might be regarded as somewhat unreasonable. On the other hand, America ought to admit that the Filipinos do possess certain rights, and that flat-footed power is neither a just nor a practicable means of settling the difficulty.

There are also certain propositions which, if not admitted as self-evident, ought to receive at least some attention. A people capable of civilized government is capable of self-government. Fitness lies not so much in the ability of the few men deputed to make and administer the laws as in the nature of the people themselves, in their deference to properly constituted authority, and in their social, domestic, and personal virtues. The best administrators will never succeed in governing a bad people, but indifferent administrators may succeed in governing a good people. Colonial government, unless it be what is termed responsible government, has never proved a conspicuous success. Representative government is the only sure means of securing purity in administration.

These propositions show that if the Filipinos are capable of being governed by America, they are capable of governing themselves, and that American rule would be neither as good nor as suitable for the Filipinos as their own rule. It is necessary to approach the subject with at least an open mind upon this question of fitness, or, at any rate, it should not be concluded, a priori, that the Filipinos are unfit.

With these tentative premises, and leaving out of the question for the moment all acts and utterances which have aroused resentment on both sides, let both parties approach the problem with a determination to be fair.

The Filipinos are, and always have been, prepared to yield, under an understanding as to final independence, all that America can possibly gain by force of arms. In details, the Filipinos are willing to yield to America: (*a*) The right and the means to fulfill all obligations to other nations. (*b*) The right and the means to protect life and property—foreign and native—and to conserve any and every interest possessed in the Philippines. (*c*) The right of American citizens to embark in missionary or educational enterprise if they so desire. (*d*) Bases of trade and military operations for the Far East. (*e*) Coaling stations. (*f*) Repayment of the $20,000,000 paid to Spain, if demanded; and (*g*) trade concessions, or any other reasonable demand not included in the foregoing list.

The yielding of these rights and concessions implies that America would have the right to retain troops in the islands, to demand suitable guarantees from the Filipinos, and to appoint a Customs Commissioner in order to secure the fulfillment of such guarantees. But these implied rights need not be, and ought not to be, made perpetual.

These rights, express and implied, do not necessitate American sovereignty in the Philippines, and they are not incompatible with present partial, and complete final, independence.

As, therefore, the American people do not intend to deny final independence to the Filipinos, and as the Filipinos are ready to yield all that America is demanding or can obtain by force of arms, what is it that is causing a continuance of the war? Is it not abundantly clear that it is due to the fact that the intention of the American people has never been officially expressed? From the time of the cession under the Treaty of Paris, up to the present moment, the Filipinos have never been officially informed, and therefore do not know, what their fate is to be—whether they are to become citizens, subjects, or ciphers. They are required to give up the one inalienable right that God gave to man, and to trust entirely to the will and the benevolence of the President. If this is not imperialism, make the *least* of it!

It is true that the American people do not make this demand, but they have placed in power those who do not make it clear that such is *not* their demand.

Thus, the solution of the problem lies in the official expression of the intentions of the American people with regard to the final independence of the Philippines.

I sincerely hope that the President and Congress will see the wisdom of giving such an expression of policy. One sentence, "It is not the intention of America to exercise permanent jurisdiction, sovereignty, or control over the Philippines," would restore peace, put an end to all this misery and untold sorrow, and save the lives of thousands of Americans and tens of thousands of Filipinos. All details as to the how and when could be arranged by friendly negotiation. The difficulty is not in the arranging, but in the agreeing to arrange. And if the Filipinos finally desired to remain under American rule, as many Americans hope and believe, though personally I do not, they would be at liberty to do so if America also desired it.

1901

MARIA GUADALUPE GUTIERREZ QUINTERO DE JOSEPH
(UNKNOWN DATES)

American and Filipino Women[1]

[The following contribution was written primarily for publication in *El Renacimiento*, a Filipino newspaper of Manila, by a young Filipino woman who during the past year was connected with the Philippine exhibit at St. Louis. Aside from its discussion of the "sphere of women" from a Spanish-Filipino point of view, it is interesting as showing that the Filipinos can pick flaws in us as well as we in them. In connection with some of the harsher expressions about American women it should be borne in mind that the writer would doubtless tone her criticisms somewhat if writing directly for an American audience, and also that she appears to have had a limited view of American women and, one must conclude, has been unduly influenced by some of a certain type whom she has seen in St. Louis. Perhaps also the joke columns and some of the sensational features of a certain kind of newspaper that flourishes in the United States have misled the writer with regard to American social conditions.—Editor.]

When the chrysalis breaks the prison that during so long a time has held it, there are in the nature now flooded by the light of the sun of springtime explosions of joy, which, uniting in concert, intone a hymn to life and love. And when a people which from very remote ages has lived a latent life, growing powerful wings to plow, in the flight of a giant, the joyous skies of civilization and progress, spreads those wings in the attitude of lifting itself in flight, ought not the other peoples, themselves butterflies which some time before have flown upward, to salute with joy their new and graceful companion, who for a longer time was held prisoner in the shades of austere mysticism and who is therefore more eager to see the sun from near at hand?

Such is the dreamer-nation that opens its eyes to the light and its brain to the life of intelligence at the present historic moment. The Philippines rises from its lethargic sleep of centuries.

It suffices to cast a glance at the newspapers of the country to be convinced that the sap accumulating during so long a time overflows now into a splendid flowering of noble and vigorous ideas of humanity and progress. And the consciousnesses held subject, prisoners in the gloomy dungeons wherein the friars confined them, shake off the atrophy into which three centuries and a half of obscurantism had plunged them and begin to discern the radiance of the new idea, a redeeming idea, the symbol of future felicity.

---

[1]*The Independent*, June 22, 1905.

The thinking minds of the country have comprehended and have inculcated in the mind of the people the idea that advancement of peoples in greatness depends upon the education and cultivation of the feminine element, which, if formerly the obstacle to progress on account of its blindness, will in a short time be the element that, bearing on the victorious standard of civilization, will bequeath the prize of civilization to its children for the benefit of future generations.

The American people, which now plants its feet insecurely on Oriental soil, perhaps only for a short time, will wish to make of our women faithful likenesses of its daughters, hybrid beings with all the defects and weaknesses of woman, without any of her delicate qualities, but with many others peculiar to man, who only aspires to an egoistic end. And our woman, timid and a dreamer, accustomed to the semi-obscurity of the temples, and to see her ideal through thick clouds of incense, is still very tender and very much a being of submission to pass at one blow from the temple to the parliament, to exchange the sewing room for the office, and her graceful and undulant feminine garb for the short skirt that is anything but esthetic, and the collars and cuffs that so well befit the features unlit by smiles of the American women. No, the Filipino woman is still very delicate for this ill-befitting and violent as well as unjust change. There are those who maintain that woman, constituted like man, has the same rights and, finally, is destined to the same labors. Admitting this, which is incontrovertible in principle, yet practical life demonstrates daily the contrary, to be necessary, to which of the two should be intrusted the labors of a delicate sort, the fantastic productions of the needle, the sweetnesses and tendernesses of the home? Either these last must be eliminated from human life, and we must make of all peoples an American people, among whom the children take care of themselves and grow up without affection or die most frequently in their tender years, burned, asphyxiated and even poisoned, while the mother goes to the shop, the factory of the office, or, merely impelled by her adventure-seeking character, sallies forth into the street to enjoy, under one pretext or another, the rights which have been conceded to her equally with man; or else the day will have to come—as has already occurred in America—when the man or the woman indifferently, according to his or her taste, takes up the delicate labors and the care of the home.

Will it not be more fitting to make of woman a practical, useful and intelligent being, developing in her, along with her intelligence, her heart, making her adapted to the physiological tasks for which nature has destined her and to the moral responsibility to which her position with reference to her children holds her subject? For it is not the father, as we in the Latin countries have wrongly understood, to whom the education of the children is intrusted, but the mother. She, according to nature, is more intimately bound to the child; it is she who first inculcates in him her ideas and transmits to his ductile and sensitive young soul her own impressions and sentiments, even without being aware of it. Why, then, not prepare her so that in place of thrusting herself forth into life in search of the dollar she may continue her educative work upon the future citizen, upon the society of the future? It often occurs in our countries that when the child emerges from the stage of early infancy the father thinks he ought now to go to school. Here arises the first struggle, the mother oftentimes opposing, while the child, accustomed to find in her an easy compliance to all his caprices and a being ready to sacrifice herself foolishly for him, meets with the first contradictions to his will, and unconsciously sets up a comparison between his mother and his master, to her disadvantage. This brings the relaxation of domestic discipline, with the consciousness on the part of the child that the mother does not count intellectually as of much force; the father stands at one side by himself, unknown, hardly ever seen and much feared by the child, and the mother is a useless martyr, upon whom weighs the tacit disregard of the father and the children. This is the Latin woman, a poor creature overborne by her own abnegation and joyless, born to suffer and involuntarily to hinder civilization. But, on the other hand, the opposing type is not the one to be taken for a model, but rather one made up from an advantageous mixture of Latinism and Saxonism, which will produce not the ideal being born to languish, covered with luxuries, in the harem, nor the delicate type, the nun of marble pallor, nor much less the coarse being with blowsy face and felt hat, who leaves every morning on the seven o'clock train to attend to business in an office, but instead a type—ideal, yes; but not yet perceived—of woman, strong physically and morally, well instructed, intelligent, full of faith in the future, who, balancing the heart and the head, shall fulfil her educative and redemptive mission and shall be equal to man, but without invading his territory—equal in the fulfilment of her mission as the air and the plant alike fulfil their missions, the former to nourish the latter, and the latter to purify the former. This is what they plan to make the Filipino woman, an achievement which, once accomplished, will make powerful and great the Filipino people, who, finally, fulfilling an unescapable law of social biology, will at last take a seat long vacant at the banquet of the sovereign peoples.

Thee, beautiful butterfly of the Oriental skies, my native land, eagle of America, I salute!

1905

■ THE FILIPINO STUDENTS' MAGAZINE ■

Who Were the Original Dog-Eaters?[1]

A few days ago one of our Filipino friends was approached by an inquisitive young American on the question of dog-eating in the Philippines, and the following dialogue was heard:

[1]*Filipino Students' Magazine* 1:3 (September 1905), 20.

American—Mr. L., is it true that the mountain tribes of Luzon eat dog meat at their meals?

Filipino—"Yes it is very true. Why, don't you believe it?"

"Yes, I believe it all right, but I wonder how in the world it originated?"

"Why, don't you know?"

"No, siree; I don't know. How the deuce would I know?"

"Why, when the Americans went over to the islands a few years ago the Spaniards told the ignorant Igorrotes in the mountains of Northern Luzon that the Americans—red, white and negroes—were all very fond of dog meat, and that when they had a big feast the principal dish at the supper table was not a chicken nor a turkey, but a good, fat, tender, well roasted pup. Whereupon the Igorrotes, who were then very very anxious to be *Americanized*, made a fearful scramble for dog meat. In a few minutes all the tribes of several villages were out, and inside an hour there was not a single dog in sight that was not captured and cooked. Every householder had a dog feast consisting of:

Soup a la Poodle;
Entree a la Pup;
Roast dog a la Americana,

and various other side dishes.

"The master of each house then made a speech, in which the principle sentences were: 'Now we are true Americanos,' 'Nothing can beat Yankee Poodle,' etc., etc.

1905

▪ MANUEL L. QUEZON ▪
1878–1944

The Philippines—What They Are and What They Would Be[1]

[Editor's Note: Part of a recent, but hitherto unpublished, address.]

The Philippines are an archipelago lying between latitudes 21° North and 4° North and between meridians 116° and 127° East longitude. On these Islands Nature has bestowed with generous hand and in harmonious combination her riches and her beauties. More than 73,000,000 acres are farm land, where numerous classes of products abound, and of these, only 7,000,000 acres are already private property. Cotton, cocoa, coffee,

[1]*The Filipino People* (November 1913).

sugarcane, tobacco, cocoanuts, rice, hemp, sisal and other articles are being produced today and can be grown in practically unlimited quantities with but a reasonable amount of effort. Rubber could also readily become one of our principal products. Forests untrodden by the foot of man are found on every side, the Philippines being the sixth country in the world in wealth of forest products. In no other place are woods of such richness and variety to be had, with their remarkable coloring, size and durability, and it has been declared by experts in these matters that the amount of wood now growing, at the present price, is worth easily six and one-half billions of dollars. In various parts of the archipelago there are valuable mines of gold and silver and rich deposits of lead, iron, coal and petroleum. The Pacific Ocean and the China Sea, which bathe our shores on the east and on the west, contain unnumbered species of food fish and in the Sulu Sea are found shells and pearls in large commercial quantities. The Islands are traversed by many mighty rivers which could be converted into motive power sufficient to supply immense industries in every town. Our imports and exports are already attaining important figures.

For the tourist who seeks charming views and beautiful panoramas we have sunsets superior to any other in the world, moonlight scenes and stormy nights of which the most ambitious painter could not even dream, much less succeed in reproducing.... Cascades, precipices, lakes, valleys, rivers, mountains and volcanoes with which Nature has prepared her scenery there demand the admiration of every one who is fortunate enough to see them.

Ancient Civilization

And on all sides one sees the stamp of an ancient European civilization—churches and cathedrals of beautiful and solid architecture; stone bridges which have stood the ravages of centuries; colleges and universities. Of more recent construction we have roads and tram-ways, railroads, telegraphs, telephone systems, harbors, lighthouses, docks, schools, in every village, where over 600,000 Filipino youths get the benefit of free, public education—in a word, all that is necessary for the rapid development of modern commerce, industry, science and intellectual training. An excellent system of sanitation with splendid hospitals and laboratories has been established. Public order throughout the Islands is maintained, and the local governments, administered by Filipinos elected by the people, are a complete and gratifying success.

This country is inhabited by a people of the Malay race, over 8,000,000 in number, and all Christians with the exception of some half million, who are Mohammedans in the Island of Mindanao, and other non-Christians in one or two of the northern provinces.

What my countrymen of all classes, ages and walks in life most fervently desire is the right to govern themselves and to become, without restriction of any kind, a free and independent nation. Whether this result shall be most expedited by an international agreement providing for the neutralization of the Islands or whether the speedier course would be through the establishment of an American protectorate I do not here pretend to say, but whatever the method selected to bring about this result, the fact remains that the Filipino people look confidently forward to the early realization of their most cherished ideals. Fortunately this most legitimate aspiration is in perfect accord with the democratic interests, with the liberal and humanitarian theories, and with the history of the American people. Since the days when the American fleet first entered the harbor of Manila and American troops first landed on the shores of those Islands the Filipino people have regarded the fulfillment of the pledge then held out to them as a matter of honor on the part of this nation and as the only means for permanently realizing their happiness and material well-being.

Prosperity Hampered

The Filipino people cannot be content so long as their future is wrapped in impenetrable doubt whether they are to be sold to some other nation, kept in perpetuity as a colonial possession, or disposed of in some other manner than the one to which they aspire. Is it too much to say that the material development and prosperity of the Islands is today seriously handicapped by the uncertainty and doubt regarding the policy of this government toward them? ...

Capacity of Filipinos

We have all heard the statement frequently made that the Filipino people are not capable of maintaining a free and independent government, were it to be conceded to them in the near future. It is, of course, easy to say a thing of this kind. It has been said about the United States and even after 134 years of tremendous development in national success there are those petrified minds in Europe who still pretend to believe that the American people cannot maintain their republican institutions and remain a great world power. Americans smile at this and well may, because as Americans they know themselves, their weaknesses and their powers better than any outsider could possibly know them. For the same reason I and my countrymen, who know our people, smile also at this statement that we would be unable to maintain and administer a free and independent government in the Philippines. If it be asked what demonstration of this fitness we have given, I answer that we have demonstrated the fact to exactly the extent and in precisely the same measure as the opportunity to do so has been afforded us by the American government. More than that no people can do; but of what we have done in the past ten years, under most peculiarly difficult conditions, I must leave the world to judge, pointing only to the unbroken testimony of every American Governor General who has served in these Islands from President Taft down, as shown by their statements along this line made in numerous official reports. The Filipino Assembly which was regarded with something akin to horror by the conservative element in this country, and among the Americans and foreigners in the Philippines, has demonstrated that from the very outset a body of Filipino citizens, elected by the direct vote of the people, is capable of playing a prominent part in the conduct of their affairs with skill, dignity, firmness and, above all, with unswerving loyalty to the ideals of their fellow-citizens.

Gratitude to the United States

There is one point concerning the advantage to the United States of granting the independence of my people on which I wish to touch. I have said that my countrymen regard that concession as a matter of honor with the American people. If that pledge shall be fulfilled at an early date, there will be a great practical benefit to this country, for the Filipinos will naturally and properly feel a heavy debt of gratitude for that boon, and with the political and international situation as it is in the Orient today, it might well become a matter of no little moment to America to be at once relieved of the expense of maintaining her sovereignty in the Philippine Islands and at the same time be assured of the loyal support and assistance of the entire Filipino people in the case of those eventualitics which ought not to, but which sometimes do, occur.

Is it too much, then, to hope that today, though a century and a third have rolled by, American ears and hearts are still open to the cry of a weaker and distant people, whose foremost desire is to breathe that same air of freedom in which the United States and its people have grown so great and so strong?

1913

■ ## MAXIMO M. KALAW ■
(UNKNOWN DATES)

from The Case for the Filipinos[1]

Preface

In this volume I have sought to present the so-called Philippine question as it appears to a Filipino and from an angle rather different from that at which other books on the subject have regarded it. The ordinary course taken in the discussion of the Philippine problem is this: If the writer be

[1]Maximo M. Kalaw, *The Case for the Filipinos* (New York: Century, 1916).

an advocate of Philippine retention, after hastily disposing, in his first few pages, of Philippine acquisition as an inevitable God-sent incident of the Spanish-American War, he usually devotes the rest of his work to an exhaustive discussion of American achievements in the Islands, the improvements in education, roads, and public buildings, the extension of sanitary measures, and the fostering of commerce and industry; belittling, ignoring, or denying the coöperation given by the Filipinos in accomplishing these results; often depicting them in the darkest colors, if not, indeed, flagrantly misrepresenting them, ridiculing their characteristics, exploiting their supposed ignorance, and exaggerating, if not entirely creating new, native vices and shortcomings. He, too, often takes the greatest pains to expose the mistakes of some locality or the crimes of some individual, and, by adroit innuendoes, indicates them as the prevailing tendencies of the Filipinos. Nothing in such volumes is spared to prejudice the American people against the Filipinos, so that he may close the volume with the conclusion that American domination must continue indefinitely and that Philippine independence, if any such thing ever be possible, is yet a long way off. On the other hand, if the writer be an advocate of independence, he takes the opposite view, and after making a much more appreciative study of the Philippine Government, established at Malolos, he enumerates in detail the unmistakable signs of capacity manifested by the Filipinos during American occupation, and then urges the granting of independence without any further delay. This discussion has been going on for well-nigh seventeen years, volumes enough to fill a library have already been written on the subject, and yet through this very confusion of authorities the American people are perhaps more hazy now as to Philippine conditions than ever before.

It is not, however, necessary for the American nation to know—and she can never thoroughly know—the minute details of Philippine conditions, in order to be able to settle, once and for all, the Philippine question. She did not have to know the characteristics and the skulls of the people of Santiago de Cuba, or whether the city of Havana could honestly use the Australian ballot, before she declared that Cuba should be free and independent. It was enough to realize that an entire people were desperately fighting for liberty and that for that cause thousands were starving in *reconcentrado* camps. Without stopping to learn the racial differences separating the inhabitants of the Island or the great ignorance of the masses— much greater than in the Philippines—and even before they had been rescued from tyranny, the principle to be adopted toward that people had been proclaimed to the world—that they were and of right ought to be free and independent.

One fact must be conceded in studying the Philippine question: the Filipinos are *a people*, like the Cubans or the Irish or the French—a distinct political entity, with a consciousness of kind and with national feelings and aspirations, no matter how poorly developed they may be in some directions. Once this fact is conceded, the real issue to be dealt with then becomes not the success or failure of American experiments in the Islands or the fitness or unfitness of the Filipinos to establish American institutions, but the relations that should exist between the American people and the Filipino people. What is the present political status of the Philippines? How did they come to be under American rule? What do they now ask of America? Can it be granted without impairing American interests in the Islands?

It is the purpose of the present volume to review American relations with the Filipino people—the acquisition of the Philippines by America, the motives underlying that acquisition, the frame of mind of the American people at the time, the vain protests of the Filipinos against their forcible subjection, the refusal of the American Congress to make a declaration of its purpose towards them, the publicity campaign carried on by the advocates of retention, the appeals of the Filipino people, and the factors that have brought about the recent legislative attempt to liberate the Islands. The passage in the Senate of the United States of a bill granting independence to the Philippines within four years closes a very interesting chapter in the history of Filipino-American relations.

This book, however, is not intended solely for Americans. It is hoped that through this volume the Filipino people may have a glimpse of the drama of their national future as it is staged in America—the attitude of the American people toward them, the continuous struggle for their rights as a people, the efforts of many Americans in behalf of their cause, the work done by the deadly foes of their national freedom, and the concessions that are being made to the Filipinos themselves. Such knowledge is necessary not only because it is a part of their history as a nation, but also because it is indispensable to them in their present task of developing their country and preparing it for the ever-widening opportunities of the future.

1916

from Self-Government in the Philippines[1]

The Promise of the Philippines . . .

Prophets of disaster have pictured a dark and gloomy future for the Philippines after the attainment of their independence. They see a weak, half-developed country in the midst of mysterious Asia, steeped in everlasting intrigues and deceit, and in their mental picture they behold the Islands immediately gobbled up or partitioned by selfish powers, or running headlong towards internal chaos and anarchy. As the Filipinos see it, the future of their country is not as dark as that. Even though we belong to a continent which has always been associated in the minds of Occidentals with mystery and intrigue, we see a brighter prospect for our people. In the first place, we have no frontier problems, which are the most fertile source of international friction and difficulties and about which most of the wars in history have

[1]Maximo M. Kalaw, *Self-Government in the Philippines* (New York: Century, 1919).

been waged. The knottiest problems before the Paris Peace Conference related to these very questions. Asia has suffered from the same malady. Siam, India and China have their frontiers constantly changed because of the oscillating interests that from time to time predominate on either side of their boundary lines. China had to yield Kowloon, because the security of Hongkong as an English possession demanded it. She may have to relinquish even her slight hold on Manchuria, which has been a bone of contention between her two northern neighbors. Japan's proximity to Korea facilitated annexation of that territory, because Korea in the hands of any other foreign power would be a menace to Japan. Similarly, the Liaotung Peninsula has twice changed foreign masters because of its propinquity to Russia and Japan. Siam has had to submit to changes in her frontiers many times and has suffered each time a considerable interference in her domestic affairs.

The Philippines are geographically more fortunately situated than other oriental countries. Our frontiers are determined by God Himself through the tremendous waterways that separate us from the mainland of Asia. Although the Archipelago is composed of thousands of islands, the possession of a single one of them is of little use unless it is accompanied by the possession of the whole group. America found this out at the Treaty of Paris of 1898. At first she wanted Luzon alone, but the closeness of the islands to one another made her decide to take over all or none. The problem of the international relations of the Philippines with the neighboring countries would also be simplified by the geographical position of the Islands. We hear of the so-called Japanese menace. In fact, danger from Japan is the most serious argument advanced against the independence of the Philippines. Japan is pictured as a land-hungry nation, awaiting only the withdrawal of American power from the Philippines for the opportunity to take over the Islands. If we examine the question calmly, we shall arrive at certain facts which will help us to consider the question on its own merit. In the first place, it is doubtful if Japan would find it to her advantage completely to colonize the Islands. The task of converting the ten million Christian Filipinos into unwilling Japanese subjects would be fraught with much greater difficulty than that encountered by Japan in the subjugation of other peoples....

Granting, then—at least for the sake of argument—that Japan will not endeavor to colonize the Philippines, what are the principles upon which sound and friendly Filipino-Japanese relations can be built? Japan will surely find the Philippine Republic a friendly neighbor and sister. The Filipinos themselves have nothing but admiration and good wishes for an Asiatic people who, by their own strength, have won the recognition of a hitherto doubting world and have carved their proud name in the council-chamber of the great nations. The Philippines are asking only for an opportunity for free and unhampered development of their people and natural resources, so that they can, in their humble way, contribute to the civilization and progress of mankind. This desire cannot be of any possible damage to Japan. On the contrary, what Japan desires of her neighbors is the least possible interference by western nations. She told that to China many times, and that was the main reason she gave for annexing Korea.

Is it not, therefore, clear that both the Japanese and Filipino nations can work in harmony toward the furtherance of their common interests?

The problem of government in the Philippines is relatively much simpler than that in any other tropical country of Asia. The Filipino people are already a unified mass, loyal to a centralized government. They have no institutions of royalty, nobility or blood distinctions, which make republican institutions for the time being impossible in Java, the Malay States and the protectorate of Indo-China. Even the strongest opponents of our independence concede us that advantage....

No better material can be found in Asia for the development of a democratic state than the Philippines. The twenty years of American occupation have accomplished wonders in the development of this potential democracy into a practical representative government....

In spirit the Philippines are today the most democratic country of the Far East. It is for this reason that upon the outbreak of the European War, even before the entry of the United States, the Filipinos were already in spirit with the Allies, for they instinctively felt that democracy was on the side of the Allies, while autocracy was with the Central Powers. They do not, like the Japanese, offer blind obedience to a Mikado, a political attitude which, despite its recognized advantages, is an enduring obstacle to the establishment of democracy in Japan....

A survey of the promise of the Philippines would not be complete without saying something of the Filipino woman. The position of the Filipino woman in the Orient is unique. "Midway geographically between the kimono maiden of Japan and the veiled lady of India," says an American writer,[2] "and alongside of the 'lily-footed' dame of China is the woman of the Philippines, a woman unique in the Orient, a woman in whose development there has been neither seclusion, nor oppression, nor servitude." Even before the coming of the Spaniards four centuries ago, the Filipino woman held a relatively high position. The Spanish discoverers found the Filipino woman sharing equally with her husband the rights and duties of the home, and in case of his death inheriting half of their joint gains. Sometimes the position of the chief official of a town, upon his death, fell to the widow when there was no male heir. Christian ideals strengthened the position of the Filipino woman and gave her even greater freedom and power. Today she is the mistress of the home and the safe keeper of the family funds. Through her hold in the home she wields a strong influence in the outside world. In business she is the equal, if not the superior, of her mate; and politically, though she does not enjoy popular suffrage, she has proved, to quote the American writer again, "in more than one case, indeed in very many, that she is an active campaigner of no mean order."

[2]Emma Sarepta Yule, in the *Philippines Monthly,* 1915.

The education of the Filipino woman has broadened her scope in life and is making her more interested in the civic activities of the Philippines. In 1917 there were enrolled in the primary and intermediate grades of the public schools 234,905 girls. Filipino women are now occupying positions in the Bureau of Education and the University of the Philippines. While there is no strong agitation for suffrage, it is doubtful whether, when they demand it, their brothers will deny it to them. There have been established over fifty women's clubs in the Philippines, engaged in social settlement work, the improvement of health conditions, and the prevention of infant mortality. Writers on the Philippines and observers of Philippine conditions have time and again testified to the superiority of women in the Philippines, and to the tremendous influence that they are bearing, and will continue to bear, upon the country and the people. "Possibly ... on these lovely isles where the lotos blooms and the cocoanut lifts high its green-crowned head there may evolve the Altruria of the vision of the suffragette, a land of perfect sex equality with chivalry tipping the scale in favor of lovely woman." That was the promise pictured by the American writer who has paid such a pleasing tribute to the Filipino women. . . .

Is it any wonder, therefore, that the Filipino people should have such a splendid optimism as regards their country's future? They are convinced that in a modest way they have a manifest destiny to fulfil. This destiny cannot be realized unless they are independent of all foreign control, free to develop their country and their genius in their own way. It must be confessed that the domestic autonomy which they now enjoy fails to satisfy them completely. It is simply a privilege conceded them, the United States still continuing to be the absolute arbiter of their destiny. The Filipino people have no voice in their foreign affairs, and thus they have to limit their activities to purely local matters and cannot participate in those world enterprises which are, in these days of international intercourse and communication, the greatest factors in the growth and progress of nations. Even in the final disposition and development of their natural resources, such as timber, mining concessions, and public lands, as well as in other important matters, they must first obtain sanction of the President of the United States. The American flag still symbolizes to them the sovereignty of a foreign people, no matter how lightly or generously exercised that sovereignty may be. The United States Congress can take away any rights or privileges that have been granted to them. Their Bill of Rights can be taken away at any moment. The Supreme Court has held that the Filipino people enjoy only such civil and political rights as the American Congress is willing to give them. . . .

The ten million Filipinos are not such a very small people. Their desire for freedom is no mere passing whim. It was written in blood during those dark days of 1896–1898, when they overthrew the tyrannous yoke of Spain. It was rebaptized in those gloomy years of 1899–1902 when, although convinced that they would be defeated in the end, they gave up thousands of lives to show the American people that they would not lightly exchange political masters and that they were willing to die if need be for the independence of their country. Secluded as they are from Asia, protected by tremendous waterways, with no frontier problems or large vested foreign interests, save those of the United States, to vex them, united by a strong tie of nationality, inspired by democratic ideals, with untold economic possibilities at their command, they feel that they have a good chance to work out their own destiny. Weaker and smaller nations, beset by graver problems, have taken a more hazardous chance at freedom.

In the opinion of many observers, the Filipino people have progressed much more remarkably than the Japanese in a similar space of time. This progress has been made, inspired by the promises of the United States that they would in due time enjoy the blessings of complete freedom. Nations, like individuals, accomplish more when they encounter difficulties and look ahead to a sublime ideal for their guide. Under a flag of their own, as a member of the concert of free nations, confronted by greater problems and even much greater difficulties—who can foretell what further strides the Filipino people may not make and what greater surprises they may not give the expectant world? Sixty years ago Commodore Perry opened to the world an Oriental country ignorant of the ways of civilization, living in a mist of medievalism, and in that brief space of time they have forged ahead, put on the garb of the Occident, bridged the chasm of centuries which separated them from the modern world and secured for themselves a place among the great powers of the earth. The Philippines, though a smaller country, have been under the influence of Christianity for three hundred years and have had the tutorship of the greatest and most enlightened republic for twenty years. Who can foretell the fate that the Supreme Arbiter of the destiny of nations has reserved for them?

1919

■ EMMA SAREPTA YULE ■
1863–1939

The Woman Question in the Philippines[1]

It is an impressionistic vision that the phrase "Oriental woman" conjures up in the Westerner's mind. Vague figures appear in the haze, some wrapped in mysterious veils through which gleam lustrous eyes, others with pitiful "lily-feet" showing below mannish silken trouser legs, while kneeling or standing with modest mien is "Japan's most esthetic product," quaint, flower-like.

[1]The Philippines Monthly, December 1915.

Back in the deeper shadows are the half-clad barbarous creatures of Java, Borneo, the Philippines and other out-of-the-way regions, the inhabitants of which the world has become familiar with through the "highly educative" exhibits at international expositions. These are the types that have served as an emergency magazine of rhetorical ammunition for the woman's rights platform speaker for half a century or more. But the onward swing of events in the East indicates that the "oriental woman" brand of shrapnel shell that has rattled so harmlessly on tyrant man's armor in the past will soon not be available, and forensic fervor will have to go elsewhere for fuel to warm the feminine Laodicean into action.

Midway geographically between the dainty kimono maiden of Japan and the veiled lady of India and alongside of the "lily-footed" dame of China is the woman of the Philippines, a woman unique in the orient. A woman in whose development there has been neither seclusion, nor compression, nor servitude. A woman who is not and has never been in the category of "oriental woman" as popularly and fairly correctly conceived.

Effect of Christianity

It is accepted as a truism that the position and freedom of western woman as compared with her eastern sister is largely the result of the influence of the Christian religion. We may call St. Paul a crusty old bachelor in these days of the militant swashbuckler suffragette, but we cannot deny that the home and not the harem has gone with his teachings, and, though he commanded that the talking in meeting should be left to the men, he did not forbid women the enjoyment of the open air, the golden sunlight. He left them free to travel the open road of life with the "jolly heaven above and the byway nigh them." So the unique position of the Philippine woman among oriental women must very largely be attributed to the fact that she is the only eastern mother who teaches "Our Father" to her little ones. It must not be overlooked, however, that the Spaniards found the woman of the Philippines sharing equally with her husband the rights and duties of the home and in case of his death inheriting half of their joint gains. Respect and consideration were accorded her and her influence was great in the tribal communities. Sometimes when a chief official in a small town died, the position fell to the widow when there were no male heirs. The doctrines of Christianity, taught by the Spanish, fostered and strengthened this recognition of woman's freedom and power. While custom and religion were drawing tighter the bonds of restriction about her Asiatic sisters, the Philippine woman was widening her sphere of thought and action under the influence which Western control brought to bear on the social development of her country....

Wage-Earning Women

Among the bulk of the population, the masses, one cannot use the term, middle class, in its accurate sense, as that class is only evolving, or rather under American influence is beginning to evolve; the wife and mother is usually more than the home-keeper—she is a definite wage-earner, literally the help-meet of her husband. She has time to aid in getting the living for the family as her housekeeping duties are light, exceedingly light and not very well performed according to our western ideas, but Filipino life is simple and free from many of the non-essentials that are so dear to the western housewife.

If the husband be a farmer, and that is the chief occupation of the Filipino, the wife helps in many parts of the work. She aids in transplanting the rice, in harvesting it, in threshing when this is done by stamping the grain out with the feet. Husking the rice by pounding it out in a mortar, winnowing it by means of hand-woven baskets and mats are tasks performed by the wife and daughters, though often the whole family work together. It may be remarked that the farmer's wife does not work for, but with her husband in pleasant comradeship. If the crop be coconut, sugar, or hemp, here again her hands give willing aid in the lighter parts of the work. In tobacco-growing more than in any other crop the work of woman is of value. One thing is noteworthy that the Filipino woman is rarely, almost never, seen performing heavy work, carrying burdensome loads, fit only for animals, as may be seen in China and Japan and some other countries in Europe. She is not seen working on roads, around docks, neither does she dig or plow the soil on the farm.

As a shopkeeper and in the market stall she excels. To quote a Filipino: "Women are the best merchants, as they are great talkers and have such captivating manners and winning ways that people cannot help buying." The revenue from her tienda, or little shop, which she tends in addition to her home duties, adds many pesos to the family income....

But what about her in things not so material? Socially, she ranks equal with man, or, to express it another way, she holds relatively the same position in the community that the American cousins across the Pacific do, with this difference, that she is less prominent after marriage than before. Here the tinge of the East is apparent. Her instinct, created by custom, is to sink into the background in the social life of her home and of the community when she assumes the dignity of matron. When her husband has guests, she hies to the kitchen to superintend the preparation of food which plays so important a part in the hospitality of the Filipino. Frequently a daughter, a mere girl in early teens, will act as hostess at the dinner or luncheon table when her father entertains friends. This is not due to want of admiration for the mother nor to want of respect, nor is she a household drudge; it is simply a custom which is more nearly allied to the custom in Japanese homes than to that in western homes. Were the guests friends of the son or daughter, the mother would probably not appear unless it were in the capacity of a chaperone. But this custom aside, woman, collectively and individually, is of influence and wields power in the part of the community life that comes under the head of social.

Political Status

Politically, though popular suffrage is so new a thing in the country and woman has not the right of ballot, she has proven in more than one case, indeed in very many, that she is an active campaigner of no mean order. She is a power that is reckoned with by the wise political aspirant. Without as yet taking actively to the stump and platform, in various capacities in a more limited arena, she has demonstrated that she possesses a power of forensic eloquence that would make her no weak adversary in an oratorical combat. Like her brothers she has a freedom for self-consciousness that seems to be a trait of the oriental.

As a moral force one may make the assertion and be far within the bounds of truth, that woman outranks man in *Las Islas Filipinas.* Quoting a Filipino lad: "Much can be said in pro of her in this connection and little can be mentioned in con of her." She is the guiding, moulding influence in her son's as well as her daughter's life. One cannot talk for long with a Filipino youth and not be impressed with the value he places on his mother; though he may not often speak of her, the esteem is which he holds her and her judgment is apparent. The friends and family of a wayward young man often feel relief and shift the responsibility when he marries. The right of the wife to hold a good firm check rein on her husband is recognized and very often she holds it with skill as well as strength. Ambition to stand well, to accumulate, to give the children opportunities, is greater, usually, in the wife than in the husband. Custom as well as character gives her the right to be the dictator on the home "ways and means committee." She is usually the keeper of the family treasury. All revenue, no matter by whom earned, is given to the wife, and she it is who has the final say as to how it is to be spent. It must not be inferred, far from it, that family finances are never wrecked at the cockpit and in other useless extravagances. But the thought of the "wife Kate" at home "nursing her wrath" and the Filipino Kate has a tongue as well as wrath, has sent more than one Filipino "Tam O'Shanter" home when he would fain have bided a bit longer with some "Souter Johnny."

Love of Home

One of the most beautiful characteristics in the Filipino is a remarkably strong love for home. Looking at the little cramped, cheerless shack of a home, one wonders why he loves it, what the force is that created his attachment. It does not speak of beauty, comfort, aught that means "homelike" to the westerner. One can but conclude that the mother's love is the occult force that holds the affection of the family. The shelter is such a temporary affair, family possessions are so few and of so ephemeral a nature that the love of home does not signify, as often with the Westerner, love of building some particular piece of furniture, some remembered vista from a doorway, a bit of sky or a tree or vine from the "little window where the sun came peeping in at morn," the old swing, the blush rose bush, but rather human affection. That the Filipino's love for home should be so devoted, so beautiful, testifies to the power, the tenderness, the sheltering strength of the affection that surrounds his youthful years.

In business, it is the verdict of the foreigners in the islands that they would rather deal with the women than the men. It is conceded that they are keener, far more to be relied on to keep their word as to time, materials, and other essentials. That is, they do business more nearly on western principles. There are many Filipino women who are property holders and who manage their holdings and business with shrewdness and decided ability. Marriage does not mean the yielding up of the management of inherited or acquired property to the control of the husband. Not at all. The typical Filipino woman would never think of such a thing. On the contrary, more than one case could be cited where the husband having brought the family property close to the abyss of bankruptcy, the wife assumed control and by economy, good sense and industry not only saved the property, but put the business on a sound basis again. . . .

Personal Traits

Admitting the Filipino woman to be an industrial factor of value, the logical query is: What sort of a woman is she? Has she charm of personality, is she feminine? Or is she that terrible ogre, a mannish woman? Assuredly the Filipino woman has much feminine charm. The matron as well as the maiden has natural grace, poise, a personality that is attractive if not altogether winning. Even when driving a hard bargain she is gracious. Assurance she does not lack; every movement of her body from the poise of her head to the not particularly graceful swing of her body expresses self-confidence. She looks the whole world in the face with a fearlessness of expression born of an inner consciousness of being perfectly able to cope with anything that offers. The lack of hesitancy, the quiet, cool assumption of capability are almost disconcerting to a stranger. Yet she is not noisy or bold in manner; she is simply confident, the woman unafraid.

The Filipino woman has all the love of personal adornment that belongs to the normal daughter of Eve. After one has become accustomed to the native dress, it is realized that she is neat and particular about her attire. The stiff, wide sleeves and specially folded wide collar, the most individual feature of her costume, are always fresh, never mussed or wrinkled. The same may be said of her long sweeping starched skirt. Her straight black hair is simply dressed and is invariably smooth and neat. Exception must be made to the woman engaged in manual labor, who is certainly not always a tidy looking creature. Often she looks as though she took pieces of cloth and wrapped them around her without much regard to grace of line or fit. And of course the really dirty slovenly woman is not an unknown quantity, far from it. But on the whole the Filipino woman is neat and careful as to her personal appearance.

The woman of the Philippines demands and receives from the masculine sex courteous attentions and almost slavish consideration. In the case of a young lady, particularly, the chivalry is accompanied, impregnated with all the perfervid sentimentality that results from a Latin graft on a tropical plant.

"Womans' Rights" Movements

It would seem as though there were little need for Woman's Equal Rights clubs in the Philippines, but Manila boasts of two, "The Woman's League" and "The Modern Woman," with a large membership. In a parade recently in Manila, the floats of these two clubs decorated with banners bearing the old familiar legends: "Strike off our oppressors' chains," "Give us Equal Rights," could but make the foreign onlooker smile. It was quite unnecessary for the president of the American National Suffrage Association when travelling in the orient to come to the Philippines as a suffragette propagandist. The Filipino woman as a militant is in advance of the country's onward march.

What of the future? With popular education sweeping the girls out of the homes into all the productive occupations, with already more than the usual share of responsibility resting on woman's shoulders, with her imperious demands upon man and from him, it would seem well to cry, not for the Filipino woman but for the Filipino man: "Watchman, what of the night?" What sort of a nation can be founded where man weakly shifts his responsibility as bread winner, home builder, tamely surrenders authority, submits to absurd demands, for, with all her capability, the Filipino woman is femininely capricious? It is not in industrial competition alone that the danger signal flies but in the mental attitude that accords undue homage to woman and smilingly accepts her anomalous assumption of burdens that should rest on man's shoulders. This condition cannot bring forth men of the fiber that makes a strong people. In the world's smelter the "life ore" from such a people will never yield returns of the useful metals large enough to be worth recording, or of the precious metals to form an amalgam.

Possibly, who knows, it is written in the book of destiny that under the Stars and Stripes on these lovely isles where the lotos blooms and the coconut lifts high its green-crowned head there may evolve the altruria of the vision of the suffragette, a land of perfect sex equality with chivalry tipping the scale in *favor* of lovely woman.

1916

■   # M. P. DE VEYRA   ■

UNKNOWN DATES

The Filipino Woman[1]

Often times erroneous ideas remain in the minds of the readers after the perusal of a paper by observant visitors, relating to our women. They are, as

[1] *The Filipino Students' Magazine*, October 1906.

a mater of fact, honest and capable of picturing out our mothers and sisters, but on the other hand, frequently, ignorant to our customs and civilization. Lack of information, and not seldom viviated errors, strong preconceived ideas and malevolent attitude toward the Filipinos are the case; this mistake regardless of their position.

The following is intended to check out these conceptions and meet the request of many friends who are intensely interested to know "something" of the "Filipino Woman." The credit is Senor Katigbak's, who before a ladies' society in Maine, in speaking about our women, read as follows:

"One of the most picturesque types of women in the Far East, rivaling even the well-known Japanese woman of today, is the Filipino woman. She is interesting not only for her graceful and becoming attire and the softened complexion with which nature has enriched her, but also for the personality she presents which makes her a distinct and unique type.

The Filipino women have kept the old manners of their mothers alongside their modern education. This does not imply however, unrefined customs, on the contrary, by being conservative on the one hand and equipped with a thorough modem education on the other, they have reaped the advantages of both and rid themselves of those traits of western civilization which were not suitable to their natural environment, and so although every nation claims for its women the most perfect contentment with their lot in life, even the Mohammedans whose women are mere creatures of their will and passion—yet as regards real happiness the Filipino woman have nothing to envy in any other women in the world.

From time immemorial the Filipino people have been very careful in the bringing up of their daughters. From her tenderest years until her marriage she is under the constant care and strict vigilance of her mother. Her mother is not only her inseparable companies, her confidant and true friend, but often times her only teacher.

The characteristic of the Filipino woman's education lies in the special care of the mother in moulding her sentiments in a certain direction, that is, to love her home and the duties she will have to perform in her future life. From the early days of her girlhood her interest is absorbed in housekeeping, she is taught how to sew, how to weave, how to cook, how to keep everything in the house clean and in good order, and how to exercise supervision over the servants.

An ordinary Filipino girl seldom goes out of the house and if she does she is always accompanied by her mother, a friend or a servant girl. It is not proper for a Filipino girl to go out without a chaperon even in the day time, and going only a short distance. Of invitations to parties, parents are first notified and they decide on their acceptance or non-acceptance. This untiring vigilance of the mother is carried to such a point that even those engaegd to be married can never go alone anywhere without sufficient cause.

"It will appear to strangers that this protection of the maternal wing is too restrictive, yet it becomes a second nature to the youthful maiden who is dependent on it for her own happiness. From the protection of her mother she passed to the protection of her husband; hence self-reliance and independence of character are not so well developed in her as in the women of the Occident. But on the other hand she still possesses high qualities, such as moral sensitiveness, soundness of principles, cleanliness of heart, piety and devotion to home.

Brought up in charge of the domestic affairs and expenses, the Filipino girl is given special opportunities to develop a commercial and practical judgment. This explains the fact that in many cases the wife of a financier helps her husband most effectively. She sits at his desk, keeps accounts and transacts business as if she had been pursuing a business profession all her life.

"Then, too, the artistic proclivities of the Filipino woman are remarkably great. Poetry, music, singing, painting and embroidery are natural gifts to her, and she learns these arts with ease and not infrequently entirely by herself.

"From the foregoing statements it may be thought that while Filipino girls are given the most scrupulous care, their freedom of action is very much hampered. Not so. They are free to do whatever women of other nations do, the only difference being that their parents must always be consulted, and this, moreover, not to restrict their freedom, but to check any undue expansion of youth which lacks experience in life. The ethics of the Filipinos in this line are based on a certain definite principle, namely, to bring up the girl in such a way as to make of her later a good wife and a good mother.

To be a good mother is the ideal of the Filipino woman, and to the acquisition of such qualities as becomes her no sacrifice of her parents is spared. The result of such procedure is most gratifying. To it is to be attributed the increase of our population, the healthy growth of our families., the perfect harmony between wives and husbands and the happiness of the home which to a Filipino woman is not her castle, but rather her earthly paradise.

1906

■

Confronting Frontier and Industrial Violence: Latino Narratives

The short fictional narratives included here were published in Spanish-language periodicals in the United States during the final decades of the nineteenth century. These texts are significant for at least two reasons: first, they exemplify how writers we would now identify as Latino/a understood new conditions of the modern world, including violent conflict, disenfranchisement, and industrial capitalism. With the reverberations of the Mexican-American War still ringing in their ears, these writers felt anew the threat of U.S. imperialism, which would produce the Spanish-American War of 1898. Second, these narratives revise conventional literary histories of American short fiction, demonstrating the dynamic transnational literary culture in which a proto-Latino/a identity fermented. Spanish-language periodical culture in the United States provided a laboratory in which writers experimented with the combination of North and Latin American narrative forms. Far from following the movement that has been conventionally, if too simply, plotted from romanticism to realism to naturalism to modernism, Spanish-language short fiction develops out of the peculiar genre known as *costumbrismo*. The *cuadro de costumbres* (literally, "sketch of customs or manners"), or *costumbrista* sketch, was by far the most popular short narrative form in Spain and Latin American during the nineteenth century. The Spanish short story as we know it today emerged when the *costumbrista* sketch was abandoned in favor of the aesthetic experimentation of *modernismo*, which is itself a very different artistic movement than Anglo-American or European modernism.

The writers included here demonstrate a transnational aesthetic as they synthesize generic movements of Latin America with those of the United States. For example, Carlos F. Galán's "Recuerdos de California" experiments with the *costumbrista* sketch while maintaining an awareness of how regional realist writers such as Bret Harte cast Mexican Americans as the villains in the ongoing melodrama of Manifest Destiny. Only a few biographical details remain about Galán (1831–??), who was born in Spain and moved to Mexico in 1845 to attend the military academy at Chapultepec in Mexico City, going on to fight with the Mexican army during the Mexican-American War (1846–1848). He spent time working in the gold fields of California during the early 1850s, but found working and living conditions for Mexicans shocking and unbearable. Well-educated, he edited several newspapers in the Mexican states of Baja California and Sinaloa before serving briefly as governor of Baja California (1867–1868). He moved back to California in the 1870s and in 1881 became editor of *La Voz del Nuevo Mundo*, one of the most influential and longest-running Spanish-language periodicals on the West coast. After editing the paper for a year, he left California and apparently returned to Mexico.

Galán's transnational movement did not prevent him from forming a strong identification with California Latinos, including *californios* (longtime inhabitants who became U.S. citizens after the Mexican-American War) as well as newly immigrated Mexicans, Chileans, Peruvians, and others. His editing of *La Voz del Nuevo Mundo* shows him to have been an avid proponent of *costumbrismo*, as he republished sketches by such literary stars as Ricardo Palma and Ramón de Mesonero Romanos. He also published a series of his own sketches under the title "Recuerdos de California" that showcases the evolution of the brief narrative in Spanish. *Costumbrismo* is notoriously difficult to define as a genre, combining elements of short fiction, journalism, and history, usually under the guidance of a narrator whose presence is strongly asserted in the narrative itself. The *costumbrista* sketch takes many different forms, from romantic social narratives such as Argentine writer Esteban Echevarría's "El matadero" (1871) to imaginative recountings of episodes from colonial or indigenous history, as in Peruvian Ricardo Palma's *Tradiciones peruanas* (1872–1910). Across these varied manifestations, a strong narratorial presence creates works in which story is often second in priority to subjective reflection. Such is certainly the case with the first two installments of Galán's "Recuerdos de California," in which Galán narrates events he personally witnessed in the mining camps of Sonora, California. The sketch included here is the third installment in the series, published in *La Voz del Nuevo Mundo* on June 11, 1881, and is particularly significant for its representation of an actual historical event that took place thirty years earlier, the lynching of a Mexican woman named Josefa Segovia in Downieville, California, in 1851. The history behind the story suggests the generic mixture of the *costumbrista* sketch; so too does the fictionalizing, which includes changing the name of the victim—she becomes Josefa Juvera in the story—as well as many of the details of her alleged crime and punishment. In contrast to earlier installments in the series, however, the narrator is a relatively soft presence in this sketch until the final paragraph, where he breaks forth in an impassioned condemnation of American frontier justice. Even then, the narrator never intrudes as a character in the story itself, allowing the brutality of Josefa's murder to speak for itself. This is a departure from the *cuadro de costumbres* proper. The sketch's strong central narrative also sets it apart from other *costumbrista* narratives, suggesting that in "Recuerdos de California" we glimpse the beginning of the genre's evolution into the modern short story.

The second narrative included here exemplifies the transformations in Latino narrative under the auspices of *modernismo*, which began as a movement with the publication of Nicaraguan poet Ruben Darío's groundbreaking book *Azul* (1888). "La historia de un guante" was written by Nicanor Bolet Peraza, one of the foremost Venezuelan writers of the period and a forerunner of twentieth-century U.S. Latino/a writers. Bolet Peraza was born in Caracas and raised in Barcelona, Venezuela. Encouraged by his father to pursue a career as a writer, Bolet Peraza assisted in editing the literary review *Oasis* (the first major periodical ever published in his home state of Anzoátegui) at a young age, but his writing career was interrupted by the Federal War in 1859, a five-year civil war between Conservative and Liberal factions over the issue of federalism and state power. Against his father's advice, Bolet Peraza entered the military, rising to the rank of General for the Liberals. An early supporter of President Antonio Guzmán Blanco, who rose to power under the auspices of the Liberal party, Bolet Peraza eventually came to oppose that regime's immense centralization of power and became an editor of *La Tribuna Liberal*, an important opposition newspaper, in 1877. Shortly thereafter Guzmán Blanco departed in exile for Europe, but upon Guzmán Blanco's return in an 1879 coup, Bolet Peraza became a political target, and he moved with his family to New York, where he would live until his death in 1906. In New York, Bolet Peraza participated in a thriving Spanish-language literary culture. He was close friends with Juan Antonio Pérez Bonalde and José Martí, founding La Sociedad Literaria Hispano-Americana de Nueva York, an intellectual salon famous for hosting a talk by Martí in 1889 that would evolve into the essay "Nuestra América." In New York, Bolet Peraza also edited two lavishly illustrated periodicals in the 1890s, *La Revista Ilustrada*, where "Nuestra América" was first published in 1891, and *Las Tres Américas*. Bolet Peraza was literally at the center of a hemispheric intellectual ferment focused on responding to the threat of U.S. imperialism.

Bolet Peraza is known as a *costumbrista* writer, but stories such as "La historia de un guante" clearly show a shift to the aesthetics of *modernismo*. Although the word *modernismo* is a cognate for *modernism* in English, it is important to acknowledge the differences between the artistic movements that go under these names. Both are responses to what appeared as new conditions of existence at the turn of the twentieth century. However, where English-language modernism used dense allusiveness and fragmentation to recover a sense of authenticity from the modern world's urban, industrial landscapes, *modernismo* in Latin America harnessed the bold metaphors and revolutionary meters of French Symbolism and Parnassianism to declare the existence of an organically *American* spirit. In this respect, while Darío's *Azul* announces the advent of *modernismo* in poetry, Martí's "Nuestra América" (1891) and Uruguayan writer José Enrique Rodó's *Ariel* (1900) delineate the movement's aesthetic and spiritual concerns, especially its opposition to the conformity and materialism of the United States and the Old World. "La historia de un guante" manifests these *modernista* concerns in the glove's story of its own manufacture, a litany of tortures that provides a ready critique of the dehumanization attendant on industrial modernization. The story is significant for tackling these concerns in a peculiar fashion, however, with its introduction of the talking glove. One might see in this plotline the influence of Edgar Allen Poe, who was immensely popular in Latin America. As in Poe, the story's baroque aesthetics are inextricable from its fantastic narrative. It is interesting to note how the narrator's verbose description of being enraptured by the glove parallels the glove's magniloquent description of feeling the electricity of his mistress's romantic encounter at the ball. The glove becomes a tactile representation of the narrator's radical solipsism, as suggested in the story's ironic epilogue, implying that the narrator's isolation begins in the material conditions of the industrialized, modern world.

"La historia de un guante" demonstrates how the aesthetic experiments of *modernismo* flourished in U.S. Spanish-language periodical culture. The story was published in *Las Tres Américas* in 1895, but it had appeared before then, published in 1892 in two different newspapers in the Southwest: *El Hispano-Américano* of Las Vegas, New Mexico, and *Las Dos Repúblicas* of Los Angeles. Both of these papers likely acquired the story through exchanges with Mexican newspapers, evincing the liveliness of hemispheric print culture. By the same token, the appearance of "Recuerdos de California" in *La Voz del Nuevo Mundo* alongside established *costumbrista* writers such as Ricardo Palma and Ramón de Mesonero Romanos indicates that Galán and his fellow travelers in the periodical trade experienced hemispheric literary culture as continuous, not fragmented by the national boundaries that have come to rule American literary histories. Galán, Bolet Peraza, and their fellow travelers show the hemispheric consciousness underpinning Latino/a narrative aesthetics at the turn of the twentieth century. Responding to the new conditions of American modernity—the threat of imperialism and its violent imposition, as well as the dehumanization of industrial capitalism—these writers worked in syncretic narrative forms that anticipate the hybrid aesthetics of Latino/a writers of later generations.

John Alba Cutler
Northwestern University

■ # CARLOS F. GALÁN ■
1831–?

Recuerdos de California, 11 June 1881 (in Spanish)

En el invierno de 1850 á 1851, el antiguo pueblo de San José, en California, fue el punto de reunión de gran parte de los aventureros que de todas partes concurrieron, en busca del *vil* metal. Como acontece en esas grandes y hetereogéneas reuniones, había mucho malo y algo bueno, y como rara vez sucede, escaseaba el sexo débil, y los pocos representantes que de él había, no brillaban por la moralidad de sus costumbres, haciéndose notar, como era consiguiente, las virtuosas.

Entre éstas, descollaba por su hermosura, patriotismo y finos modales, una joven de Atotonilco el Alto, en el estado de Jalisco, Méjico, Josefa Juvera, y era por tales razones el objeto de las amorosas ánsias y enamorados suspiros de casi todos los que la conocían. Participando al fin de los sentimientos que inspiraba, hizo la felicidad de un joven sinaloense, jurándole eterna fidelidad ante la competente autoridad, y ambos fueron á ocultar su dicha de profanas miradas, al retirado placer de Downieville, en el condado de Yuba.

Allí fabricaron su choza, ó casa de troncos de pino, como era uso y costumbre de los mineros, y el recién casado, por so separarse de su cara mitad, dedicóse al comercio, en vez de hacer como la generalidad de sus compatriotas, ir a buscar el oro en las vertientes de la Sierra. Un año de felicidad habían gozado, entre los turbulentos habitantes de aquel campo minero, sin mas que ligeras nubecillas producidas por los sentimientos que la hermosura de Josefa excitaba en aquellos toscos gambusinos y que no manifestaban con muy corteses palabras ni muy finos ademanes.

Josefa estaba en la situación que las mujeres que aman a sus maridos desean, y esperaba en breve estrechar en sus brazos el fruto de sus amores. Se aproximaba el aniversario de la declaración de la independencia de las colonias inglesas de la metrópoli, y por todas partes se hacían preparativos para celebrarlo dignamente. Aconteció estar allí, el representante de California en el Congreso General, el Hon. J. W. McKibben, y algunas otras personas de buena posición social, y todos se aprestaban a oír los discursos y alocuciones propios del día. Se erigió una plataforma y se tomaron medidas para que los mineros de los campos vecinos no tuvieran sed—de licores, por lo menos.

Llegó por fin el día, y centenares de tiros de fusil, rifle y pistola saludaron sus primeros albores: la música—no muy armoniosa, por cierto—hacia resonar las monótonas melodías de *Yankee Doodle* y *Hail Columbia*, y poco después había llegado el entusiasmo a su colmo, ausiliado en parte con sendas libaciones de whiskey. Ya no se bebía en vasos, sino en baldes, en cubos, y se hubiera bebido en tinas, a haberlas tenido a la mano. Vinieron los discursos y después los entusiastas hurras a la independencia, y comenzaron a retirarse a sus campos la parte sensata de la reunión. Quedaron, como sucede generalmente, los más viciosos—la hez de la sociedad—bebiendo y haciendo locuras bien ajenas ya del día que celebraban.

Los Estados Unidos de América, acojen bajo la protección de su pabellón de listas estrellado, a los hijos de todas las naciones del globo. Aprovechándose del privilegio, multitud de irlandeses cambiaron el nombre de súbditos de la reina de Inglaterra por el de ciudadanos de Norte América, pero muchos de ellos comprendían muy poco las obligaciones y deberes que su nueva condición les imponía. Más papistas que el Papa, tomaban del americano todos sus odios, muchas de sus preocupaciones y muy pocas de sus virtudes.

La guerra de los Estados Unidos con Méjico estaba muy reciente todavía y aun no cesaba la exaltación de los ánimos. El oro de California, que los mejicanos encontraban con la mayor facilidad, les suscitaba envidia y mala voluntad de los menos afortunados, que eran especialmente los irlandeses, y el término de *greaser*, aplicado indistintamente a todos los de raza española, era para estos un sangriento insulto.

Josefa y su marido, habían permanecido en su casa, sin tomar parte alguna en las festividades temerosos ambos de los desmanes de aquella gente casi enloquecida por los espíritus del alcohol. Acostáronse temprano, y como a media noche, oyeron golpes en la débil puerta que los separaba de la calle, y enérgicas demandas por licor. Alarmados pensaban en huir, cuando oyeron que algunos vecinos intervenían con los alborotadores y los persuadieron al fin que se retirasen.

En la madrugada repitiéronse de nuevo los golpes y los más horribles juramentos pronunciados por una porción de los que entonces se llamaban *galgos*, y que a voz en cuello pedían entrar o echarían abajo la casa. Levantóse el marido de Josefa e invitó a ésta que hiciera lo mismo, pero la desvelada y su estado de gravidez le habían causado una excitación nerviosa que le impedía moverse. Cedió por fin la puerta a los repetidos golpes y aquella jauría se precipitó en el interior de la casa y aproximó a la cama en que yacía casi inmóvil la infortunada Josefa. Un *galgo* más audaz o más ébrio que los demás, se subió a la cama e intentó meter la mano bajo los cobertores, mientras que cargando todo el peso de su cuerpo sobre Josefa, le impedía hacer el menor movimiento en defensa de su honor que aquel infame intentaba arrebatarle. Su marido, aprisionado por el resto de aquellos malvados, pugnaba en vano por desasirse y volar al socorro de su mujer y se desgañitaba pidiendo ausilio, sin que nadie atendiera sus gritos. En medio de su agonía, recordó que había un cuchillo debajo de la almohada y le gritó a su mujer que se defendiera: ésta pudo alcanzarlo y sin volverse a mirar siquiera, hirió con él en el cuello al miserable raptor.

Al grito despavorido de éste sucedió un momento de silencio que terminó con una escena de horror. Sin cerciorarse siquiera del estado del herido, se lanzaron furiosos sobre la media desnuda Josefa y la arrancaron de su lecho arrastrándola hasta la calle, y allí la amarraron a su marido, codo con codo. En seguida, despertaron a cuantos amigos y parciales tenían en el campo y les comunicaron lo sucedido, pintándolo a su manera: no era preciso mucha exageración: había un individuo de la raza anglo-sajona muerto o herido por un *greaser*; no era menester más para que el entusiasmo cundiese y por todas partes se pidiera su muerte.

Para mengua de la autoridad judicial, hubo un juez de paz, un alcalde de barrio, que sin más jurisdicción que para conocer de asuntos civiles en

cantidad menor de cien pesos, y en criminales tan solo para practicar la aver-
iguación sumaria, tomó sobre sí juzgar a Josefa, por homicidio, sin cercio-
narse siquiera de la existencia del cuerpo del delito.

Reunió una docena de individuos de entre los mismos asaltantes y los
llamó jurado: y erigiéndose en el tribunal, examinaron los testigos que les
parecieron convenientes, y sin darle un defensor a la acusada, y sin oírla ni
quererla oir, fallaron su condenación a la última pena. Tal veredicto fue reci-
bido con ahullidos de frenético placer y en el acto, convertidos los jueces en
verdugos, con la misma rapidez que de agresores se habían convertido en
jueces, procedieron a arreglar el cadahalso en que debía expiar la infortunada
Josefa el delito de haber defendido su honor.

La plataforma que horas antes se habían proclamado los sacros e inalien-
ables derechos del hombre, el juicio por jurados, dos instancias para los juic-
ios criminales, etc. etc., fue el lugar escogido para patíbulo. Allí en un
momento, colgaron una cuerda de la rama de un árbol y se arreglaron de
modo, que sujeto el dogal al cuello de la víctima empujasen a esta a la plataforma y la caída bastara a desnucarla.

Cuando estaba todo preparado, el Sr. McKibben y algunos americanos,
que hubieron de saber algo de lo que pasaba, llegaron al lugar de la ejecución
y el primero, subiéndose en un cajón vacío, arengó a aquella horda de bandi-
dos adjurándoles por cuanto estimaran santo, no se mancharan con tal crí-
men, ni hicieran recaer sobre el Estado de California, que acababa de
ingresar a la Union, infamia tal.

Nada había sagrado para aquellos bárbaros y ni la vida de su representa-
tate lo hubiera sido, si este permanece allí algunos minutos más. Sus amigos
lo pusieron en salvo, incapaces de oponerse a la turba multa de verdugos,
que les eran superiores en número.

Josefa al notar los inútiles esfuerzos de su improvisado defensor, se
encomendó al Defensor Universal y colocó con sus delicadas manos en su
blanco y mórbido cuello el tosco dogal de que no habían podido libertarla.
Ni su hermosura podía afectar a aquellos caníbales.

Aun entonces, a la undécima hora, un neoyorkino, doctor en medicina,
hizo observar el estado de gravidez de la sentencia y les aseguró a sus jueces,
que las leyes del los Estados Unidos y las de toda la tierra, prohibían el sacrifi-
cio del inocente y lo era a todas luces el aun no nacido hijo de Josefa. También
el doctor tuvo que huir para no ser víctima. Y apresurándose cuanto era posible, lanzaron por fin de la plataforma a Josefa que murió momentos después.

Pero aun no estaba saciada la sed insana de los bárbaros. Notó uno de
ellos, que el feto se movía en las entrañas de la madre sacrificada, y a pata-
das le quitaron la vida, que sin ellas hubiera perdido muy pronto.

[Muchos años después, y cuando la Comisión Mista en Washington oía
las reclamaciones por atentados de autoridades americanas, presentó el
viudo de Josefa la suya, que fue rechazada a instancias del comisionado
mejicano, porque no se había probado debidamente el matrimonio. Así es
que por tal razón, lo que sufrió este mal aventurado, fue solo una broma.
¡Tal es la justicia de los hombres!]

Memories of California, 11 June 1881 (in English)[1]

In the winter of 1850 to 1851, the old town of San Jose, California was the site of a gathering of a great number of those adventurers who came from all parts in search of filthy lucre. As often happens in these large and diverse gatherings, there was much bad and some good, and as sometimes is the case, the weaker sex was scarce, and the few representatives there could not be called beacons of morality, making the truly virtuous stand out as a result.

Among these was Josefa Juvera, a maiden from Atotonilco el Alto, in the state of Jalisco, Mexico, who distinguished herself for her beauty, patriotism, and fine manners, and for these reasons became the object of the heartsick yearnings and loving sighs of almost every man who met her. Partaking at last of the very feelings she inspired, she made a young man from Sinaloa very happy, swearing her eternal fidelity to him before the appropriate authority, and the pair left to hide their happiness from profane looks in Downieville, a delightful, remote town in Yuba County.

There they made their home, a house of pine logs, as was the tradition and practice of the miners, and the newlyweds, so as not to be separated from their better halves, went into business instead of looking for gold in the slopes of the Sierra Nevada like the majority of their compatriots. They had enjoyed a year of happiness among the roughshod inhabitants of that mining camp, suffering only the merest slights produced by the passions excited in those coarse golddiggers[2] by Josefa's beauty, passions not expressed in the politest words or most refined gestures.

Josefa was in that situation desired by women who love their husbands, and expected soon to cradle in her arms the fruit of their love. The anniversary of the declaration of independence of the English colonies from the home country was fast approaching, and everywhere preparations were being made to celebrate it worthily. The California representative to Congress, the Honorable J.W. McKibben, happened to be there, along with other individuals of high social standing, and everyone prepared to hear the speeches and recitations appropriate to the day. A platform was built and measures were taken so that miners from neighboring camps would suffer no thirst—for liquor, at least.

The day at last arrived, and hundreds of musket, rifle, and pistol shots greeted its first dawning: the music—not so sonorous, to be certain—echoed back the monotonous melodies of *Yankee Doodle* and *Hail Columbia*, and shortly thereafter the general enthusiasm had arrived at its climax, aided in part by abundant libations of whiskey. It was no longer drunk from cups, but from pails or buckets, and would have been drunk from bathtubs if they had been had at hand. The speeches came, followed by enthusiastic hurrahs for independence, and then the sober portion of the gathering began to retire. As usually happens, the more depraved remained—the dregs of society—drinking and enacting follies far removed from the day being celebrated.

---

[1]Translated by John Alba Cutler, Northwestern University.

[2]"Gambusinos": Slang for miners who went north during the California gold rush in the nineteenth century.

The United States of America welcomes beneath the protection of its starry pavilion children from every nation of the globe. Taking advantage of the privilege, a multitude of Irishmen had exchanged the name of subjects of the queen of England for that of citizens of North America, but many of them little comprehended the obligations and duties imposed upon them by their new status. More Catholic than the Pope,[3] they took from the American all of his prejudices, many of his worries, and very few of his virtues.

The war of the United States with Mexico had very recently ended and the heightened emotions still had not ebbed. The gold of California, which the Mexicans were most adept at finding, provoked envy and bad will against them from the less fortunate, especially the Irish, and the term *greaser*, used indiscriminately against all those of the Spanish race, became for them a cruel insult.

Josefa and her husband had remained in their house, not taking any part in the festivities, both of them frightened by the excesses of all those people driven made by the demon rum. They retired early, and around midnight heard fists pounding on the fragile door that separated them from the street, along with emphatic demands for liquor. Alarmed, they considered fleeing, when they heard some neighbors intervene with the troublemakers and persuade them to withdraw.

In the morning the fist-pounding resumed, along with the most horrible oaths sworn by those known at that time as *greyhounds*,[4] who at the top of their voices demanded to be let in or they would tear the house down. Josefa's husband arose and beckoned her to do likewise, but the sleepless night and her pregnant state had excited her nerves and prevented her from moving. The door finally gave way to the repeated blows and that pack of dogs entered the interior of the house and approached the bed where the unfortunate Josefa was sprawled immobile. One *greyhound*, more bold or drunk than the others, got up on the bed and attempted to thrust his hand beneath the covers. Keeping the weight of his body on Josefa, the villain prevented her from making the slightest move to defend that honor of which he intended to rob her. Her husband, restrained by the rest of the scoundrels, fought in vain to free himself and fly to his wife's aid, shouting himself hoarse for help, but no one listened to his cries. Amidst his agony, he remembered that there was a knife beneath the pillow and he shouted to his wife to defend herself: she managed to reach it and, without looking, buried it in the neck of her miserable attacker.

His shocking cry was followed by a moment of silence that ended with a scene of horror. Without even assessing the state of the wounded man, they launched themselves furiously upon the half-naked Josefa and tore her from

---

[3]"Más papistas que el Papa": literally, "more popish than the Pope," but intending to convey that a person is overly zealous in his or her regard for a custom or law, or in this case, that the Irish have become more zealously American than natural-born citizens.

[4]"Galgos": it is unclear whether the Irishmen were called *galgos* by the Spanish-speaking population or more generally.

her sickbed, dragging her into the street, where they bound her to her husband, elbow to elbow. Straightaway they awoke some friends and allies that they had in the camp and related what had happened, after their own manner. Not much exaggeration was needed: an individual of the Anglo-Saxon race had been killed or wounded by a *greaser*; nothing more was necessary for the mania to spread and all quarters to call for her death.

As a show of judicial authority there was a justice of the peace, a ward magistrate with jurisdiction to hear civil suits only of one hundred dollars or less, and in criminal matters empowered only to hear arraignments, who took upon himself the authority to convict Josefa of homicide without even examining the body in question.

The platform from which hours earlier the sacred and inalienable rights of man had been proclaimed—trial by jury, two appeals for criminal judgments, etc. etc.—was the place chosen for the gallows. There, after a moment, a rope hung from a tree limb, arranged in such a way that when the victim's neck was put in the noose and her body pushed from the platform, the fall would suffice to snap her neck.

When everything was prepared, Mr. McKibben and some other Americans, who must have known what was happening, arrived at the execution spot and the former, alighting on an empty box, harangued that mob of bandits, exhorting them by all that they held holy not to sully themselves with such a crime, nor to cause infamy to redound to the State of California, which had only just been admitted to the Union.

Nothing was sacred to those barbarians, not even the life of their congressman had he remained a few minutes more. His friends helped him to safety, unable to oppose the rowdy mob of executioners, who were superior in number.

Josefa, upon noting the fruitless efforts of her impromptu defender, yielded herself to the Universal Defender and with her own dainty hands placed around her white and delicate neck the coarse noose from which he had been unable to free her. Not even her beauty could affect those cannibals.

Even then, at the final hour, a New Yorker, a medical doctor, observed the gravity of the sentence and swore to the judges that the laws of the United States and of all the earth forbade the murder of innocents, and the unborn child of Josefa was innocent by all rights. The doctor had to flee as well to avoid becoming the next victim. Hastening as fast as they could, they threw Josefa's body at last from the platform and she died moments later.

But even then the bloodlust of the barbarians was not satiated. One of them noted that the fetus still moved within the dead mother's womb, and they kicked it until it was dead, which would have happened soon anyway.

[Many years later, when the Bilateral Commission in Washington heard the claims of outrages committed by Americans, and the widower of Josefa presented his, it was rejected by the Mexican commissioner because sufficient proof of the marriage was not given. Thus it is that the sufferings of this terrible nightmare were reduced to a jest. Such is the justice of men!]

La Voz del Nuevo Mundo, 11 June 1881

N. Bolet Peraza
1838–1906

Historia de un guante (in Spanish)

Recuerdos de la mocedad

Habia llegado ya la hora del cansancio, del fastidio y del sueño. Las bujías habían sido cambiadas tres veces, el "buffet" estaba agotado; los músicos exhaus-
tos, los trajes femeninos en desorden, los peinados desmayados, los lindos
rizos que la bandolina sostuvo hasta le fue humanamente posible, caían sobre
los ojos medio dormidos haciendo en ellos el estorboso efecto de las moscas;
la concurrencia comenzaba a desfilar por delante de los dueños de la casa,
ensayando cada cual una sonrisa de despedida, una mueca de trasnochado.

Una dama de las que salían y que seguramente comenzaba a dormirse
por partes, dejó caer uno de sus guantes. La mano estaba ya en su primer
sueño. Yo recogí aquella prenda. Como sucede con todo hallazgo, al cual se
examina para ver si por insignificante ha de devolverse a su dueño o si por
valioso ha de guardarse, no examiné yo el guante, pues todos los guantes
son iguales, sino que miré la cara de la dama que lo había perdido. Era bella,
y lo guardé. Si hubiera sido fea, me precio de galante. Era hermosa y caí . . .

Los niños se llevan a la boca los objetos que se les dan o que atrapan.
Los jóvenes ejecutan este mismo instintivo movimiento con diferencia de
una pulgada. En siendo artículo de mujer lo primero que hacen es llevarlo a
la nariz. Yo era joven entonces y el sentido del olfato me gritó con imperio:
"¡dame a oler ese guante!"

—Pues huele, respondí para mis adentros, y me tapé las dos ventanillas
del órgano con la suave piel de cabrito.

Aquella olía a gloria—¿A que huele la gloria? A mujer bonita debe ser.

Yo he visitado todas las perfumerías buscando aquel aroma. La flor que
le produce no es de este planeta; la retorta en que se destila debe estar en
algún hornillo atizado por ángeles disfrazado de benedictinos.

Metíme aquel guante en el bolsillo del corazón. Desde allí me llegaban
sus deliciosos efluvios y la entraña comenzó a palpitar con inquietud, con
impertinencia, como gritándome: "si no me la quitas de encima te rompo el
pecho y me salgo." El pobre corazón se imaginaba lo mismo que yo me di a
imaginar, a saber: que lo que llevaba allí prisionero, no era un guante de una
mujer, sino la mujer misma.

Al llegar a casa, afuera el frae y afuera el cautivo. ¡Pobrecito! Estaba hecho
una miseria: arrugado, plegado, contraído, como si se hubiese refugiado en el rin-
cón del bolsillo, contando con que allí no lo encontrarían mis codiciosos dedos.

Le volví a oler y torné a sentir el mismo mareito celestial de la vez primera. No me acuerdo si lo besé. ¿Qué creen los muchachos de veinte años?
lo besaría?

Despues de besarlo, lo estiré suavemente, como se estiran los miembros de un niño encontrado en un altosano a media noche. ¡Qué piel tan suave! ¡Qué formas tan lindas! Cada dedito era una cosa monísima. Yo quería conocer la propia figura de la mano que había llevado aquella postiza epidermis. La abotoné bien, me la acerqué a los labios y soplé! ¡Santo Dios! Si alguien me hubiese estado atisbando por el hueco de la cerradura, ¡qué vergüenza! Soplaba y luego apuñaba, apuñazaba, "apurruñaba," como hacen los niños, como hacen los micos. Era una cosa ridícula, sí señor, muy ridícula! tan ridícula cuanto ustedes quieran, pero estaba a un negro de uña del sublime!

Todavía estaría allí, a medio vestir, o mejor dicho, a medio desnudar, y tira y jala y sopla y aprieta del infeliz guante a no ser que de mi mujaderia me sacara un sutilísimo suspiro, una especie de quejido que de la misteriosa prenda escuché que salía.

¿Quién dijo miedo? No señor. Audacia fue lo que me entró en aquel instante. Para mí no existía delante de mis ojos el tal guante; sino su dueña encantadora, o a lo menos un pedazo de ella, su mano angelical.

—Dime, prenda de otra prenda, le dije: ¿Sientes y hablas?

—Hablo y siento, me contestó con esa voz cercana y distante a la vez con que se expresa el fonógrafo.

—¿Quieres contarme tu historia?

—Si me ofreces devolverme a mi dueña.

Tales fueron sus palabras. Las recuerdo por la circunstancia de que no dijo dueño sino dueña. Esta falta de propiedad en el lenguaje me afligió. El guante debió ser de alguna dama cursi.

—Te lo prometo.

—Júralo.

—Lo juro.

—¿Por qué lo juras?

Estaban entonces muy de moda los dramas de Echegaray y contesté con firmeza:

—Lo juro sobre el puño de la espada.

—Has de saber, pues, dijo el guante, que mi madre fue una cabrita infeliz.

—No te aflijas por lo humilde de la cuna. Vivimos en épocas democráticas en que el mérito es quien da la estirpe.

—Un curtidor, después de mil atomias me zabulló; me dio a comer alumbre, una cosa que frunce y da carraspera; me ahogó en tinta gris perla, me prensó y aplanchó, y me entregó a un cortador que me despedazó, y de allí me tomó una costurera que me acribilló a puntadas.

En la tienda estaba yo con otros compañeros, cuando llegó una dama de manos divinas. Al verla, "me salió el cabrito." Me enamoré de ella. Yo no sé como fue aquello, pero me di mis artes para que la dama me tomara. Y me prefirió a los otros que en la caja estaban. Al punto se me calzó. Yo me sentía en mis glorias. Aquella misma noche debíamos asistir al baile; es decir, anoche, porque ya va siendo de día. Varias parejas danzaron con mi dueña. Yo conocía en que grado estimaba ella a cada uno. Al darle la mano cierto primo majadero, cierto jactancioso trincapiñones muy vano, sentí que sus nervios le repelían; luego vino un solterón maduro, y al tomarla para el vals, sentí que la mano se le volvía un pedazo de hielo. Yo tuve frío. El siguiente fue un militar de negros mostachos.

A cada roce de la charretera sobre la mano de mi señora, y a cada apretoncillo de la otra del galán, las venitas delicadas se inflaban, un cierto calor de niño sano las animaba, y el pulso iba aumentando su natural celeridad.

Al llegar a unos ochenta latidos por minuto no subió más, y comenzó a bajar. Yo me dije, para mi sayo: este es un amante pretérito. Luego tocó su turno a un mozo guapísimo, de no sé que Embajada que en aquellos momentos estaba en subida. Al tocarse ambas manos, experimenté un choque eléctrico terrible, dos corrientes magnéticas poderosas me atravesaron, un gran calor se desarrolló, un temblor extraordinario se apoderó de la diestra de ella y de a siniestra de él, y yo no pude menos que preguntar al guante del caballero, ¿qué pasa por esos mundos, camarada?; a lo que él, un guante muy amable y fino, me respondió: tormenta tenemos. Comenzaron a bailar y rompieron a conversar los dos pichones. La electricidad seguía aumentando. Yo sentí que las costuras del guante del joven estallaban; las mías estaban en un tris de hacer un disparate. Aquello ardía, aquello era inaguantable. Yo no podía oír lo que decián los amantes, pero choques iban y choques venían, y por cada dedo de la niña y por cada dedo del pareja pasaba un despacho telegráfico derecho al corazón. Uno de estos telegramas atravesó como un rayo mi pobre piel. No sé cómo no me achicharró aquella descarga. El despacho decía: ¿me amas? Y allí mismo una centella encendida pasó a través de mis poros; era un sí apasionado y ardiente.

—Me estorba tu guante, exclamó el joven. Quitémonsos estos enojosos intermedios y dejemos que libre se ame nuestra sangre, se besen nuestros nervios, que nuestra carne se confunda, como se confunden nuestras almas.

Y ¡zas! de un tirón me arrojó al suelo la exaltada hermosura. De allí me recogisteis vos, atolondrado joven, me olisteis y me besaisteis; y yo entretanto me reía de vuestros trasportes. El perfume que en mí encontrasteis y que os embriagaba, no es el aroma de una mujer linda, como creisteis, es la deliciosa fragancia del botón divino del amor!

¿Qué hice con aquel guante locuas y cruel?

Todavía lo conservo para el prosaico oficio de limpiar mis gafas de cincuentón. Cuando la vista se me empaña no veo las cosas bien claras, paso su fina piel por los cristales y me parece que veo más y mejor.

El Hispano-Americano (1892), *Las Dos Repúblicas* (1892), *Las Tres Américas* (1895)

The Tale of a Glove, Or, a Youth Remembers (in English)[1]

The hour of fatigue, ennui, and sleepiness had already arrived. The candles had been changed three times, the "buffet" was empty, the musicians exhausted, the women's dress in disorder, their coiffures failed. The delicate

[1]Translated by John Alba Culter, Northwestern University.

curls that the bandolín had sustained as long as humanly possible fell over half-closed eyes, making them as annoying as flies. The crowd began to shuffle out before their hosts, everyone making a half-hearted smile of farewell, a sign of their exhaustion.

One of these ladies, already half-asleep, dropped one of her gloves. Her hand had already fallen to sleep. I recovered that treasure. As happens with every discovery, which must be examined to see if it is insignificant enough to return to its owner or precious enough to keep, I did not examine the glove, since every glove is the same, but rather looked at the face of the lady who had lost it. She was beautiful, and I kept it. If she had been ugly, I pride myself on my gallantry. But she was beautiful and I fell ...

Children immediately put things that they find or have given to them in their mouths. Adolescent boys execute the same instinctive maneuver with the difference of an inch. When it is something of a woman's, the first thing they do is bring it to their noses. I was young then and my olfactory organ shouted at me imperiously: "Let me smell that glove!"

"Smell then," I responded within, and I covered the two windows of the organ with the soft goat leather.

It smelled of glory. What does glory smell like? Like a beautiful woman.

I have visited every perfumer's shop in the city searching for that scent. The flower that produces it is not of this world; the beaker in which it is distilled must be in some fire kept by angels disguised as Benedictines.

I thrust the glove into my coat pocket near my heart. Its delicious emanations teased me from there and my heart began to beat wildly, impertinently, as if shouting at me, "If you don't remove that glove from me I will burst from your chest and depart." My poor heart imagined the same thing as I did: that what I held prisoner there was not the glove of a woman, but the woman herself.

When I arrive at home, I removed my dress coat and took out the glove. Poor thing! She looked disgraceful: wrinkled, folded, shrunken, as if she had taken refuge in the corner of the pocket, hoping to evade there my hungry fingers.

I smelled her again and was flooded with the same heavenly scent as the first time. I do not remember if I kissed it. What do you young men of twenty years say? Would you kiss it?

After kissing it, I stretched it out softly, the way you would stretch out the body of a child found sleeping on a hillock at midnight. What soft skin! What perfect shapes! Every finger was gorgeous. I yearned to know the actual figure of the hand that had worn this artificial skin. I buttoned it up tight, brought it to my lips and blew! Oh God! If someone had been spying on me through the keyhole, I would have been humiliated! I blew and then seized it, struck it, and scandalized it, as children do, as monkeys do.[2] It was

---

[2]Bolet Peraza uses an alliterative catalogue here, "Soplaba y luego apuñaba, apuñazaba, "apurruñaba," como hacen los niños...." The quotation marks around "apurruñaba," a verb used mainly in the Caribbean and meaning to maltreat or handle roughly, could signal Bolet Peraza's understanding of the word as having only regional currency.

a ridiculous thing, yes sir, ridiculous! Just as ridiculous as you like, but it was only a sliver of a fingernail away from the sublime!

I would still be there, half-dressed, or half-naked rather, wringing and growling and pinching and squeezing the poor glove if I had not been wrenched from my hysteria by the subtlest sigh, the merest hint of complaint which I heard escape from the token I held in hand.

Was I afraid. No sir. Boldness was what I felt in that instant. For me it was a not a glove I held before my eyes, but an enchanting mistress, or at least a piece of her, her angelic hand.

"Tell me, O token of another token," I said. "Do you feel and speak?"

"I speak and feel," it answered me with a voice like a phonograph's, near and distant at once.

"Will you tell me your story?"

"If you offer to return me to my mistress."

Such were her words. I remember them because she did not say "master" but rather "mistress." This lack of propriety in language grieved me. The glove must belong to some pretentious lady.

"I promise you."

"Swear it."

"I swear it."

"On what do you swear?"

During that time the plays of Echegaray were very much in fashion, and I answered firmly, "I swear by edge of the sword."[3]

"You must know, then," said the glove, "that my mother was an unfortunate goat."

"Don't be distressed by the humility of your birth. We live in democratic times in which merit determines the stock."

"A tanner, after a thousand indecencies, washed me clean. He gave me alum to eat, which made me wretch and grow hoarse. He drowned me in pearl gray dye and ironed me, and then delivered me to a leatherworker who cut me in pieces, and from there took me to a seamstress who pierced me everywhere with stitches.

"I was in the store with my other companions when a lady arrived with beatific hands. When I saw her I almost jumped out of my skin![4] I fell in love with her. I don't know how I did it, but I used all my art so that the lady would pick me. And she did choose me over all the others in the box. She put me on immediately. I was euphoric. That same night we were to attend the ball; that is to say, last night, as day is already coming on. My mistress danced with several different partners. I knew precisely the degree of esteem she held for each one. When she gave her hand to some idiot cousin or some vain, swaggering drunk, I felt her nerves reject him. Then she was approached by

[3] José Echegaray (1832–1916) was one of the leading Spanish dramatists of the late nineteenth century, famous for his melodramatic, Romantic flourishes.

[4] The Spanish idiom used here is "me salió el cabrito," which means something like "the kid (goat) got away from me," with an obvious ironic reference to the glove's provenance from a goat.

an old bachelor, and when he took her for the waltz, I felt her hand turn to ice. I was chilled. Next up was a soldier with a black moustache.

"Each time my lady's hand rubbed against the epaulets of his uniform, and at each little squeeze from his hand, her delicate veins swelled, the warmth of a healthy child rushed through them, and her pulse quickened from its natural pace.

"When it arrived at some eighty beats per minute it stopped rising and began to lower. I said to myself, in my mind: this is a past lover. Then a handsome young bachelor took his turn, a man from I don't remember which Embassy that was at the moment up-and-coming. As their hands touched I felt a terrible electric shock, two magnetic currents cut through me, an intense heat arose, a violent shaking took hold of her right hand and his left, and I could not help myself from asking the gentleman's glove, "What in the world is happening, my friend?" To which he, a very fine and amiable glove, responded, "What we have here is a storm." They began to dance and broke into conversation like two lovebirds. The electricity continued to increase. I felt the seams of the young man's glove begin to burst; my own were a moment away from disaster themselves. It burned. It was unbearable. I could not hear what the two lovers said, but the shocks came and went, telegraph dispatches passing through each finger of the girl and each finger of her companion, straight to their hearts. One of these telegrams cut through my poor skin like a lightning bolt. I don't know how the discharge failed to scorch me. The dispatch said: "Do you love me?" And right there a spark passed through my pores. It was an impassioned and ardent yes.

"Your glove annoys me," exclaimed the young man. "Let us remove these irksome intermediaries and allow our blood to make love, our nerves to kiss, our flesh to commingle, as our souls have commingled."

And bang! At once the young beauty threw me to the ground. From there you picked me up, oh thoughtless youth, smelling me and kissing me. And I all the meanwhile laughed at your insanities. The perfume that you smelled on me, that made you drunk with love, is not the scent of a beautiful women, as you believed. It is the delicious fragrance of love in divine bloom!

What did I do with that garrulous and cruel glove?

I still keep it for the prosaic office of cleaning my spectacles. When my now-aging sight begins to fail and I do not see things clearly, I pass her fine leather over the lenses and it seems to me that I see more and more.

El Hispano-Americano (1892), *Las Dos Repúblicas* (1892), *Las Tres Américas* (1895)

JOSÉ MARTÍ
1853–1895

The date: January 1880. A few weeks before he turned twenty-seven, José Martí arrived in New York City as yet another Cuban immigrant displaced by the long war for independence on his native island. Already a recognized writer, patriot (who at seventeen was sentenced to a labor camp for his revolutionary activities against Spanish rule), and talented orator, Martí was welcomed as a leader in the community of exiled Cubans in the Northeast. At night he strolled through the streets of lower Manhattan and, in an essay for the newspaper the *Hour*, described the misery of the "shoeless and foodless" unemployed whom he encountered on one of his nocturnal walks in Madison Square. During a brief stay the following year in Caracas, Venezuela, Martí worked as a teacher and founded a journal to promote his vision of a greater "America" in which north and south are unified by mutual respect and understanding.

In the last fourteen years of his life Martí worked in New York as a translator, teacher, and regular correspondent for newspapers in Venezuela, Argentina, and Mexico. He also wrote articles for the *New York Sun* and frequent letters to the editors of other local newspapers. He was a private tutor and a volunteer teacher of working-class pupils of all colors. Martí wrote poignant essays on the North American cultural and political scene for Spanish American readers. In them he offered the first portraits of Whitman, Emerson, and General Ulysses S. Grant, and he interpreted contemporary events on subjects as diverse as impressionist painting, monetary policy, college education, ethnic conflicts, labor strife, earthquakes, floods, and universal suffrage. In early 1890 Martí founded, with Rafael Serra, La Liga, a center for Cubans and Puerto Ricans of color. Martí admired three women—Clara Barton, Harriet Beecher Stowe, and Helen Hunt Jackson—for their social and humanitarian commitments. He translated Jackson's novel *Ramona* as well as textbooks on agriculture, logic, and the classical world. He published two books of poetry and a novel, directed several journals, and edited a children's magazine. Most of all, however, Martí worked to unite the rival factions of the independence movement under the Cuban Revolutionary Party. He traveled from New York to Key West and to Central America, Mexico, and the Caribbean, to promote Cuba's long quest for freedom, which was eventually renewed on the battlefield in 1895. This armed struggle sought to gain independence from Spain *and* from the United States, to build a just society based on racial equality, without social inequalities. José Martí was killed on the battlefield, in eastern Cuba, on the afternoon of May 19, 1895.

His essay "Our America" is required reading in our days of compulsion for world order, when geopolitical concerns shift from deposits of funds to funds of information, when imperialist expansions emphasize cultural transformations. Martí's ultimate concern is for one "America" based on its Native American uniqueness, without racial hatred, an America that distances itself from Europe and creates requited appreciation (North and South) based on peaceful coexistence and mutual knowledge and respect.

Martí identified the United States as "Anglo-Saxon America," a threat to full Spanish American independence. Martí saw especially during the last two decades of the nineteenth century the developing strategy for the economic and political control of all of America that was taking shape in Washington under the direction of Secretary of State James G. Blaine. For many decades the United States had expressed an interest in buying or, if necessary, gently taking Cuba from Spain. Southern states had been particularly interested in gaining territory farther south that would strengthen the rationale for slavery. In the 1850s, filibuster William Walker had invaded Nicaragua, declared himself its president, established English as the official language, and even reinstated slavery for the Nicaraguans, all in the quest of a manifest destiny south of the border.

Martí saw in Blaine's Pan-American Conference of 1889–1890 not an opportunity for cooperation among American republics but a United States plan to inherit the previous Spanish colonies as new markets for surplus products. His greatest apprehension was that this economic and political domination would be in place before Cuba and Puerto Rico won their independence. Thus, he wrote profusely about the consequences of this brand of Pan-Americanism and what he perceived as Blaine's real objective: political control of the Americas. If Spanish America was to be absorbed economically, politically, and culturally before it had relished the opportunity to gain its true independence by recognizing its indigenous roots, multiracial identity, and knowledge of itself, Martí's greater "America" would be in danger. If the government of the United States proceeded thoughtlessly, without attempting to study the true nature of its neighbors, Martí's greater "America" would be lost. For America could only be one if all its constituents understood and knew one another and all consented to be part of a greater "America."

Such is the invitation to read José Martí's "Our America," the best of his works and one whose timeliness persists.

Enrique Sacerio-Garí
Bryn Mawr College

PRIMARY WORKS

Ismaelillo, 1882; *Versos libres*, 1882; *Amistad funesta*, 1885; *La edad de oro*, 1889; *Versos sencillos*, 1891.

Our America[1]

[**TRANSLATOR'S NOTE:** José Martí, like many other writers in exile, became a translator. It was a way of earning a living in his interlingual landscapes, exploring thoughts with new words. His first translation was very carefully selected. It was a translation of Victor Hugo's *Mes Fils* ("My Sons"), published in Mexico in 1875, the year of his return to America, by way of Paris, after his first period of exile in Spain. In *Mes Fils*, Hugo summarizes his life, especially his life in exile and how his two sons helped him during this arduous experience. In England, one of his sons became a

[1]Translation © Enrique Sacerio-Garí, 2000. All rights reserved. *Nuestra América* was published in *La Revista Ilustrada de Nueva York* (January 10, 1891) and then in Mexico in *El Partido Liberal* (January 30, 1891).

translator of Shakespeare into French. Hugo devotes a significant portion of *Mes Fils* to comments on the importance of translation and the sorrows of life as an exile. A greater pain awaited Hugo when he returned to France, after nineteen years of exile: the death of both of his sons. *Mes Fils* is the story of this loss and the hope and desire to be reunited with them after death.

Translators often meet texts after death. Martí, then, translated a text about the art of translation and the life of an exile like himself. He becomes partially identified with Hugo's son by planning to translate *Hamlet*, a project he did not complete. He says in the introduction to his translation that he has chosen to translate Victor Hugo and not Victor Hugo's French because "Victor Hugo does not write in French, [and] he can not be translated into Spanish . . . because Victor Hugo writes in Victor Hugo." He wants to translate "a mind." He adds that he finds himself wherever he finds ideas and that "if all lofty ideas are concentrated in [Hugo's] snowy head, I am either his son or his brother, I live in that head."

I offer a new translation of *Nuestra América* into an English that must be read as José Martí: a syntax whose interstitial twists and turns will hopefully place you within his tropical head.]

The presumptuous villager believes that the whole world is his village, and as long as he stays as mayor or can torture the rival who took his girlfriend or keep his savings growing in the bank, he declares the universal order good, unaware of the giants with overdeveloped boots who can crush him or of the competing comets in the sky, moving through drowsy space, devouring worlds. What remains of the provincial village in America must awake. These are not times for covering one's head, but rather for weapons as pillows, like Juan de Castellanos' illustrious men.[2] Mind warfare conquers all other weapons. Trenches of ideas are better than trenches of stone.

There is no prow that can cut through a cloud of ideas. An energetic idea, unfurled in time before the world, can stop a battleship squadron, like the mystical banner of judgment day. Nations that do not know each other should do so quickly, as allies before a common enemy. Those who shake their fists at each other, like jealous brothers who covet the same land, or the one with a small house who envies the one with a mansion, should join hands and be one. Those who, protected by a criminal tradition, served the lands of their brother, with a sword stained with their own blood, must return the lands to the conquered brother, who has been punished enough, if they do not want the people to call them thieves. The honest man does not settle debts of honor by receiving money at so much a slap. We can no longer be the people of leaves up in the air, treetops heavy with flowers, creaking or rustling at the whim of a caring light, or thrashed and uprooted by the tempests: the trees must close ranks to keep the overdeveloped giant from passing! It is the time to review the lines and to march united. We must advance tightly organized, like silver at the roots of the Andes.

Only those whose birth is premature will lack courage. Those who do not have faith in their homeland are premature men. Because they lack

[2]Juan de Castellanos (1522–1607), Spanish poet, author of an elegy that celebrates the deeds of illustrious men from the "New World."

courage, they deny it to others. Their weak limbs cannot reach the difficult tree, limbs adorned with painted nails and braclets, Madrid or Paris limbs; and they insist the tree cannot be climbed. We must load the ships with these destructive insects, which gnaw the very bone of the fatherland that nourishes them. If they are from Paris or Madrid, let them prance along the Prado, or stop at Tortoni's for sherbet. Those carpenter's sons who are ashamed that their fathers are carpenters! Those born in America who are ashamed of the Indian apron and the mother who raised them, and disown their sick mother, the indolent good-for-nothings, who desert a mother on her sickbed! Then, who is man, the real man? The one who stays at his mother's side to heal her, or the one who puts her to work out of sight and lives off her toil in rotten lands, sporting a wormy tie, cursing the womb that carried him, displaying the sign of a traitor on the back of his paper frockcoat? These children of our America, an ever-improving America that will be saved by its Indians, or these deserters who bear arms in the armies of North America and its worsening conditions that drown its Indians in blood! These delicate creatures, who are men but do not want to do the work of men! Did Washington, who made them this land, go to live with the English, precisely at the time he saw them moving against his homeland? These men of *incredible* honor, who drag their honor crawling on foreign soil, like the *incroyables* in the French Revolution, dancing haughtily, dragging and rolling their *rs*!

For in what native lands can a man take greater pride than in our suffering American republics, to the sounds of battle between the book and the high processional candle, republics uplifted among the silent Indian masses by the bleeding arms of a hundred apostles. Never before have such advanced and unified nations been forged in less time from such splintered elements. The haughty character believes that the earth was created to serve as his pedestal because he can easily handle his pen or colorful speech, and he accuses his native land of being worthless and irreparable because its virgin forests do not continuously grant him the means to travel abroad, driving Persian ponies through champagne trails, as if he owned the world. The in-capacity does not reside with the emerging country, searching for appropriate forms and a useful greatness, but rather with those who attempt to rule different nations, uniquely composed of their own character and singular violence, with a legacy of laws freely exercised during four centuries in the United States and nineteen centuries of monarchy in France. A decree by Hamilton[3] does not stop the charging colts of the *Ilaneros*.[4] A phrase of Sieyès[5] does nothing to release the stagnant blood of the Indian race. In

[3]Alexander Hamilton (1757–1804), secretary of the treasury in George Washington's cabinet. He strongly favored centralized government and the strengthening of federal control at the expense of the states.

[4]*Llaneros,* famous horsemen from the plains of Venezuela who fought alongside Simón

Bolívar under the command of José Antonio Páez.

[5]Emmanuel Joseph Sieyès (1748–1836), French revolutionary and priest who edited the *Declaration of Rights of Man* (1789) and the Constitution of 1791.

order to govern well one must face commitments as they truly are in the land. The good ruler in America is not the one who knows how government functions in France or Germany, but one who knows the elements that form his country and how to lead them in unsion in order to reach, using methods and institutions that have risen from within the country, that desirable state where every man may attain and engage self-knowledge, where all men may enjoy the abundance that Nature bestowed for everyone in the nation they enrich with their labor and defend with their lives. The government should be born from the country itself. The spirit of the government should be the same as that of the country. The form of government must agree with the inherent constitution of the country. True government is nothing more than the balance of a country's natural elements.

That is why the imported book has been defeated in America by the natural man. Natural men have defeated the artificial learned men. The native people of mixed race have defeated the exotic Creoles. The battle is not between barbarism and civilization,[6] but between false erudition and Nature. The natural man is good and he abides by and rewards superior intelligence as long as it does not take advantage of his submission to harm him; as long as he is not offended by being disregarded, the one thing he does not forgive, the natural man is always prepared to regain by force the respect of whoever wounds his sensitivity or harms his interests. Tyrants in America have risen to power in accordance with these scorned natural elements, and have fallen the moment they betrayed them. Republics have suffered in tyrannies their inability to recognize the true elements of their countries, to derive from them the form of government, and govern with them. Ruler, in a new country, means creator.

In nations composed of cultured and uncultured elements, the uncultured will govern, because it is their habit to attack and resolve all doubts by force, wherever the cultured fail to learn the art of government. The uncultured masses are lazy and timid in the realms of intelligence. They want to be governed well. But if it hurts them, they get rid of government and govern themselves. How can the universities produce a governing subject, if there is not a single university in America that teaches the rudimentary basics of the art of government, to wit, the analysis of the elements peculiar to the peoples of America? Like guesswork, out in the world wearing Yankee or French spectacles, young men aspire to govern a nation they do not know. In the political race, we should ban all those who are ignorant of the basic rudiments of politics. The prize in literary contests should not be awarded to the best ode, but to the best study of the country's political factors. Newspapers, universities, and academies should undertake the study of the real factors that influence the country. To know them is enough, with eyes open and without beating around the bush. Whoever sets aside, by

[6]Allusion to Argentinean statesman Domingo Faustino Sarmiento (1811–1888), author of *Facundo, or Civilization and Barbarity,* and supporter of European models of education and development. He blamed the uncultured *gauchos* for the violence that characterized Argentina's tyrannical governments.

choice or oversight, any part of the truth is doomed to fall under the truth that is lacking, that grows in a context of negligence and brings down whatever was erected without it. After knowing all the elements of a problem it is easier to solve it than not knowing them. Along comes the natural man, outraged and strong, and brings down all justice built on books because justice was not served according to the obvious needs of the country. To know is to act with resolution. To know one's country, and to govern it based on that knowledge, is the only way to free it from tyrannies. The European university must yield to the American university. The history of America, from the Incas to the present, must be taught inside out, even if the archons of Greece are not taught at all. Our Greece is preferable over the Greece that is not our own.[7] We need it more. Nationalist politicians must replace exotic politicians. Let the world be grafted onto our republics, but the trunk must be our own. And let the defeated pedant hold his tongue: for there is no native land in which a man can take greater pride than in our suffering American republics.

Bearing the rosary, our head white and our multicolored bodies, Indian and Creole, we unflaggingly entered the world of nations. We set out to conquer freedom under the banner of the Virgin. A priest,[8] a handful of lieutenants, and a woman[9] raised the Mexican Republic onto the shoulders of the Indians. A Spanish cleric, beneath his priestly veneer, instructed in French liberty a few heroic students, who supported a Spanish general against the rule of Spain. In monarchic garb and chest uplifted by the sun, Venezuelans from the north and Argentineans from the south set out and began to build nations. When the two heroes clashed, and the continent was about to tremble, one of them, and not the lesser of the two, turned and rode back.[10] And since heroism in times of peace is rare by being less glorious than during wars, it is easier for men to die with honor than to think logically. It is more feasible to govern when sentiments are exalted and united than to lead the mind after the battle when diverse, arrogant, exotic, or ambitious thoughts emerge. The authorities that were crushed in this epic onslaught undermined, with expected feline cunning and by the weight of reality, the edifice that held high the flag of nations, nations nurtured by the sap of a continuous practice of reason and freedom in government, a flag that was raised throughout the crude and singular regions of our mixed America, at

[7]Eight years before, under contract with D. Appleton and Company, Martí translated into Spanish *Roman Antiquities* by A. S. Wilkins and *Greek Antiquities* by J. P. Mahaffy.

[8]Miguel Hidalgo y Costilla (1753–1811), Mexican patriot and priest, leader of the *Grito de Dolores* (1810), which marked the beginning of the Mexican revolt against Spain. He was captured, tried, and shot by the Spaniards.

[9]María Josefa Ortiz de Domínguez (?–1829), known as "La Corregidora de Querétaro." Although her husband was chief magistrate (*corregidor*) of Querétaro, she risked her life

(and was imprisoned for) conspiring with Father Hidalgo in favor of the revolution.

[10]Refers to a meeting in Guayaquil, Ecuador, between Simón Bolívar and José de San Martín. San Martín had successfully crossed the Andes from Argentina to Chile and, after several significant victories over the Spanish, was about to enter Peru. At the meeting with Bolívar, who was moving from the north to Peru, he agreed to let Bolívar assume control of the subsequent critical battles.

the towns of people with bare legs and those with frock coats from Paris. The hierarchical constitution of the colonies resisted the democratic organization of the republics.[11] The bow tie capital cities would keep in the vestibule the open country of colt leather boots. The bookish redeemers did not realize that the revolution that triumphed with the soul of the land, once unleashed from the voice of the savior, had to govern with that soul of the land, and not against it or without it. America began to suffer, and still suffers, from the fatigue of trying to reconcile the discordant and hostile elements it inherited from a despotic and perverse colonizer, and the imported ideas and modes which have been delaying logical government because of their lack of local reality. The continent, dislocated for three centuries by a power that denied men the right to use their reason, disregarding or closing its ears to the illiterate hordes that help it, attained its redemption, embarked on a form of government based on reason, a reason belonging to everyone for everyone's concerns, not a university reason over a country reason. The problem of independence entailed not a change of forms but a change of spirit.

A common cause had to be made with the oppressed, in order to consolidate the new system opposed to the interests and habits of power of the oppressors. The tiger, frightened by the outburst of gunpowder, returns and haunts the prey at night. It dies: flames shooting from its eyes, paws in the air. It cannot be heard as it approaches, for it moves on velvet paws. When the prey awakens, the tiger is already on top. The colony remained alive in the republic, and our America is saving itself from its greatest errors—the arrogance of its capital cities, the blind triumph of the scorned peasants, the excessive influx of other people's ideas and formulas, the wicked, impolitic and disdainful treatment of the aboriginal race—by exercising a higher virtue, fertilized with necessary blood, of the republic that struggles against the colony. The tiger waits behind each tree, curled up at every junction. It will die: paws in the air, flames shooting from its eyes.

But "these countries will be saved," as Rivadavia[12] announced, the Argentinean whose sin was a predilection for refinement in crude times; a machete does not go well in a silk scabbard, nor can one leave behind the lance in a country won by the lance, for it becomes angry, and presents itself at the door of Iturbide's congress[13] de manding that "the blond one be made emperor." These countries will be saved because with a genius for moderation that seems to prevail—due to Nature's imperturbable harmony in the continent of

---

[11]Thus begins Martí's presentation of residual colonial structures with feline qualities, a dangerous tiger "behind every tree" within the republic. Martí's intertextual struggles with Sarmiento's *Facundo*, where the tiger is a symbol of *gaucho* individual violence transformed into the violence of the state, surfaces again.

[12]Bernardino Rivadavia (1780–1845), first president of Argentina (1826). He resigned under pressure for carelessly negotiating peace with Brazil.

[13]Agustín de Iturbide (1783–1824), Mexican conservative leader who initially opposed the war for independence against Spain. After the *Tratado de Córdoba* he entered Mexico City and was later proclaimed Emperor Agustín I. He left for Europe after being deposed by General Antonio López de Santa Anna but returned in 1824 and was then executed.

light and a surge of critical reading that had replaced the previous European generation's mode, so imbued with a reading based on trial and error and phalanstery—a truly real man is born for America during these real times.

We were a spectacle with the chest of an athlete, the hands of a dandy, and the head of a child. We were masked: English trousers, Parisian vest, North American jacket and Spanish cap. The Indian, silenced, was round-about us, and would go to the mountains to baptize his children. The Negro, looked down upon, poured out at night the music of his heart, alone and unknown among the waves and the wild. With blind indignation, the peasant, the creator, turned on the disdainful city and his own child. We wore epaulets and academic gown in countries that came into the world with hemp sandals and Indian headbands. Our true character would have been to join in brotherhood, with the charity of heart and daring of the founding father, the Indian headband and the academic gown, to rescue the Indian from stagnation, to open spaces for the able Negro, to fit liberty to the body of those who rose up and triumphed in its name. We were left with the judge, the general, the scholar and the privileged. The angelic youth tossed their heads upwards toward Heaven, crowned with clouds, only to drop back in sterile glory, as if from the tentacles of an octopus. The natural people, driven by instinct and blinded by victory, overwhelmed the staffs of gold. Neither the European nor the Yankee book could solve the Hispanic-American riddle. Hate was tried, and the countries came further down in the world, year by year. Exhausted by this senseless hate, by the resistance of the book against the lance, of reason against the high processional candle, of the city against the country, of the impossible imperial domination of divided urban ranks over the natural nation, whether tempestuous or inert, we begin almost unknowingly to try love. Then, the nations stand up and greet each other. "What (and how) are we?" they ask themselves, and they begin to tell themselves what (and how) they are. When a problem arises in Cojimar, they do not look for the solution in Danzig. The frock coats are still French, but thought begins to be from America. The youth of America roll up their sleeves and bury their hands into the dough and make it rise with the yeast of their brows. They understand that there is too much imitation, and that salvation is to be found in creation. "Create" is the keyword of this generation. The wine is made from plantains, and even if it turns out sour, it is our wine! It is understood that the forms of government of a country must be in keeping with its natural elements; that absolute ideas must be stated in relative forms to avoid mistakes of form; that liberty, to be viable, must be sincere and complete; that the republic dies if it does not open its arms to all, and make progress with all. The tiger within lets itself in through a crevice, and the tiger from without. The general holds his cavalry to a pace that suits his infantry. The enemy surrounds the cavalry if the infantry is left in the rear. Strategy equals politics. Nations must live in a context of mutual and self-criticism, because criticism is healthy but always with one heart and one mind. Reach down to the wretched and lift them up in your arms! Dissolve the clots of America with the fire of your heart! Let the natural blood of the nations run boiling and throbbing through the veins! On their feet, with happy workingmen eyes, the new Americans greet each other people to people. The natural statesmen emerge from their direct study of Nature. They read to apply what is read, not to copy mindlessly. Economists study the problems at their origin. Orators begin to restrain their rhetoric. Dramatists bring native characters to the stage. Academies discuss feasible topics. Poetry shears off its romantic Zorrilla locks and hangs its red vest on the glorious tree. Prose, sifted and sparkling expression, is charged with ideas. Those who govern Indian republics, learn Indian languages.

America begins to escape all its dangers. Above some republics still lies the octopus in its sleep. Others, in turn and in balance, set sail with furious and sublime haste to make up for lost centuries. Some, forgetting that Juárez[14] rode in a mule-drawn carriage, hitch their carriage to the wind with soap bubbles coachmen. Poisonous luxury, the enemy of freedom, corrupts the frivolous and opens the door to the foreigner. Others, with the epic spirit of a threatened independence, refine the virile character. Others, in rapacious wars against their neighbors, breed unruly soldiers who could devour them. But our America is facing another danger that does not come from itself but from the difference in origins, methods, and interests between the two halves of the continent. The time is near at hand when our America will be approached by an enterprising and booming nation demanding close relations, although it does not know our America and, indeed, despises it. And since potent countries, self-made by shotgun and law, love strong countries, only strong countries; since the time of unbridled recklessness and ambition (from which North America could perhaps be freed by the predominance of what is purest in its blood, or on which it may be thrown by its vengeful and sordid masses, its tradition of expansion, or the interests of a clever leader) is not so near at hand even to the most startled eye that there is not time to put it to the test of continuous and discreet dignity that could approach and dissuade it; since its honor as a republic in the eyes of the world's attentive nations places a restraint on North America that would not be eliminated even by the puerile provocation, or ostentatious arrogance, or parricidal discords of our America, the urgent duty for our America is to show itself as it is, one in soul and purpose, swift defeater of a suffocating tradition, stained only by the copious blood sapped from hands by the struggle to clear away ruins, and dripping from our veins, cut by our masters. The scorn of the formidable neighbor, who does not know our America, is the greatest danger for our America. It is imperative, since the day of the visit is at hand, for our neighbors to know our America, and to know it soon, so they stop disdaining it. Through ignorance, they might go so far as to covet it. Out of respect, once they know us, they would remove their hands. One must have faith in the

---

[14]Benito Juárez (1806–1872), Mexican politician, governor of Oaxaca and president of Mexico in 1867 and 1871. He successfully led the fight against the French intervention and captured the "Mexican" Emperor Maximilian at Querétaro.

best in men and distrust the worst. One must promote the best so that it be revealed and prevails over the worst. Otherwise, the worst prevails. Nations should have a pillory for whoever arouses useless hates and another one for whoever does not tell them the truth in time.

There can be no racial hate, because there are no races. The feeble thinkers, the detached thinkers, rattle off and reheat library-collected races, which the just traveler and the cordial observer seek in vain in Nature's justice, where what stands out, within a triumphant love and turbulent hunger for life, is the universal identity of man. The soul emanates, equal and eternal, from bodies of different shapes and colors.[15] Whoever foments and spreads confrontation and hate between races, sins against Humanity. But in its formative years, a nation among other different nations condenses particular and characteristic ideas and habits, of expansion and conquest, of vanity and greed, which could, during a period of internal disorder or alacrity of its accumulated character, turn from the latent state of national concerns into a serious threat to the neighboring lands, isolated and weak, which the strong country considers perishable and inferior. Thinking is serving. But one should not presuppose, by antagonistic small-mindedness, a fatal and innate wickedness in the blond nation of the continent, because it does not speak our language or does not see particulars as we do, nor resemble us in its political stigmas, so different from ours, nor does it favorably deem the short-tempered, dark-skinned people, nor does it look charitably from its still uncertain eminence on those less favored by History, who climb every heroic stretch of the way of the republics. The patently obvious facts of the problem should not be hidden, for proper study and the tacit and urgent union of the continental soul can settle this matter peacefully for ever and ever. A unanimous hymn is already resounding! The present generation lifts hard-working America on its shoulders and takes it along the fertile road of the sublime fathers; from the Rio Grande to the Straits of Magellan, the Great Semi,[16] bore by the condor, scattered the seed of the new America throughout the romantic nations of the continent and the sorrowful islands of the sea!

1891

---

[15]Martí spent the last years of his life fighting against racism among Cubans and writing about issues of race and ethnicity in the United States and Spanish America. See Martí's *Inside the Monster* (New York: Monthly Review Press, 1975), pp. 209–42.

[16]Martí's figure of "the Great Semi" is based on an Arawak (Taíno) deity called a "cemí." During his first journey to this hemisphere, Columbus met the peaceful Taínos ("the noble ones") and the Caribes ("the strong ones"). The latter Columbus called "caní-

bales"—that is, cannibals, a word of uncertain origin that was, nevertheless, the source of Shakespeare's character Caliban in *The Tempest*. Martí hopes the seed of his Great Semi will break forth into a lasting peace for a new America. For the Taínos, see José Juan Arrom's *Mitología y artes prehispánicas en las Antillas* (1975), Mercedes López-Baralt's *El mito taíno: Levi-Strauss en las Antillas* (1985) and Irving Rouse's *The Tainos: Rise and Decline of the People Who Greeted Columbus* (1992).

ON THE CUSP OF A NEW CENTURY

F or decades the literature of the late nineteenth century seemed to conform to the middle term of an orderly sequence from realism to naturalism to modernism. However, as our understanding of American literature has expanded, the categories we had used to organize that understanding have come to seem severely restricted. As the first section of Volume C suggested, realism was actually *realisms*, and although the focus, form, philosophy, and style of particular literary works may have been realistic and the post–Civil War era saw the emergence of a self-consciously "realist" movement, realist writing was too varied and too persistent to permit realism to serve as a temporal marker—to characterize a period of literary expression. No more does naturalism characterize literature at the turn into the twentieth century. Naturalism has often been regarded as an outgrowth of realism that was influenced by evolutionary thought and presented humans as determined by larger force—biological, social, economic, or cosmic. The concept is appropriate for the fiction of Frank Norris, an example of which is included elsewhere in Volume C, and naturalism's imprint is evident in *The Open Boat* (1897), *The Awakening* (1899), *The Jungle* (1906), and other writing of the era. However, as we now recognize, U.S. literature at the turn into the twentieth century was so various that it far exceeded "naturalism" or any other single classification. More useful than trying to fit it into categories is to see its congruence with the accelerating pace and widening reach of the changes that were apparent in virtually every aspect of life in the United States.

Change was everywhere. Not only were scientific theory and knowledge, technology, politics, economics, religion, education, and the very composition and geography of the country transforming, but so too were what had once seemed natural conditions: gender, race, sex, family, and home, for example. Expressive culture was no exception. New media were emerging (Thomas Edison invented the phonograph cylinder in 1877); the numbers and kinds of writers and readers were increasing; opportunities for publishing continued to expand. Not surprisingly, it is a *sense* of change—and a sense that change might continue to prevail—that marks American literature at the cusp of the new century.

That sense of change registers in both subject and form. Some writers, seeking to characterize the changes underway, wrote what we might term cultural criticism. Henry Adams famously does so in a kind of auto-ethnography that is fueled by apprehension about his own irrelevance in a world whose changes alarm him. In prose fiction, writers like Charlotte Perkins Gilman and Kate Chopin devised forms and styles that highlighted the unacceptable constraints of ordinary conditions—marriage, the limitations of gender—and the potential for alteration. Stephen Crane combined journalistic techniques, symbolism, understatement, abrupt shifts in perspective, and fragmented sequencing in fiction that featured nondescript characters who are confronted with extraordinary situations such as being afloat in dangerous waters in a fragile lifeboat (*The Open Boat*). Jack London customized the short story to accommodate contemporary subjects such as class conflicts and consequences for native peoples of the U.S. takeover of Hawai'i. Poetry, too, was multiform. Paul Laurence Dunbar adapted the popular mode of dialect poetry to African American "folks" who articulated their experiences and observations in the vernacular (white readers' non-receptiveness to his writing in other forms made dialect poetry a painful restriction for him as well as an opportunity). Sadakichi Hartmann wrote intensely aesthetic and sometimes sensuous poetry in a variety of forms, including Japanese-derived *haikai* (later known as haiku). Sophie Jewett wrote lyrically of lesbian love. Alice Dunbar-Nelson experimented with both free verse and the sketch form.

This is only to begin to take the measure of literature at the end of our period. The selections in this section, along with contemporary selections in other sections of this volume, demonstrate how rich and how diverse this writing was. As the context section on "Literature and Aesthetics" shows, views about the definition of literature were also enormously varied. Not only was literature on the cusp of a new century commensurate with the multifariousness of its era, in so being it points forward to the literature created in the United States during the hundred years and more that have followed.

Sandra A. Zagarell
Oberlin College

Literature and Aesthetics

TOO OFTEN WE DON'T RECOGNIZE THAT OUR OWN SENSE OF WHAT COUNTS AS literature—and what does not—is historically and culturally inflected. Rather, we tend to assume that we are responding to intrinsic merits of individual works. The writing in this section suggests, however, that postbellum American conceptions of what constitutes literature, its importance, and the criteria used to judge it were particular to America during that period. That in some ways these conceptions and criteria resemble contemporary ones can best be understood as an index of continuities between the late nineteenth century and our own day rather than a confirmation that literature and aesthetics rise above history.

In America, the very concept of literature as a distinct kind of writing initially took shape in the postbellum era. Until then, "literature" was an inchoate, fairly catchall term encompassing a broad range of writing that included poetry, novels, essays, sermons, travel sketches, memoirs, and much else. As a remunerative undertaking, it was at best unreliable. By the 1850s, however, written works were becoming profitable commodities, produced and distributed by the increasingly powerful publishers of books and magazines, and authorship was on its way to being a financially viable vocation, and a respected one. In the decades after the war, distinctions were also instituted among *kinds* of writing. These, too, were partly market driven. In conjunction with the publishing industry, editors, reviewers, and critics, along with authors, were instrumental in dividing expressive culture, including literature, into particular cultural zones—and market niches—each tied to a distinct segment of the population.

Scholars have often cast these distinctions in polarized terms, as elite and popular or highbrow and lowbrow, assigning "literature" to the elite pole. In practice, postbellum literature was actually more dynamic and various than this dichotomizing terminology proposes, but the concept of highbrow literature usefully registers the important role that culture played in cementing social distinctions in a population that was undergoing extensive change. For the upper and upper-middle classes, which were both expanding and consolidating, genteel culture was a marker of their difference from the far more rapidly expanding pool of laborers—skilled and unskilled, agricultural and urban—whose ranks were swelled by the influx of immigrants during the same period. For elites and those who identified with them, association with refined culture was a visible index of social status; (highbrow) literature, along with its counterparts in the visual arts, music, interior design, personal attire, manners, decorum, and taste in general, was an integral element of this culture.

Elite literature was much more than a market niche or a sign of status, however. Qualities and criteria were being articulated that established literature as an art. Although some antebellum writers and editors (notably Edgar Allen Poe, who was both) had sought to establish criteria for artistic writing, only in the postbellum era did literature take shape as a specific kind of writing that was annealed in the crucible of its creator's imagination yet was governed by articulable standards of craft, execution, appeal, and for some, subject matter. It also engaged certain kinds of material. Assessments of literary works centered on their integrity of form and style, and on the vision that informed them, in terms that presumed artistic quality as something free-standing, independent of social or commercial coordinates. And it was as an art in this sense that many readers responded to literature. In letters and journals, they testify to the experience of reading as elevating, even spiritual, and often deeply personal. Along similar lines, the identification of authors as artists, Romantic in origin, was gaining wider recognition. This is the premise of Constance Fennimore Woolson's "Miss Grief," which celebrates the artistic genius of its protagonist, Aronna Moncrief, while deriding the publishing industry for rejecting her work. Woolson's friend Henry James, in his important essay "The Art of Fiction," insists on the imaginative integrity that must be granted to authors who qualify as artists and, though on grounds different than Woolson's, also maintains that true art is and must be free of commercial entanglement. (See the Woolson and James sections of this volume.)

The influence of the era's most important man of letters, William Dean Howells, helps us understand how literature could be both an art and a sociocultural institution. As editor of the *Atlantic Monthly* and then of *Harper's*, Howells penned countless reviews and columns that educated readers—and writers—in the essentials of "good" literature, thereby guiding how people actually read. As an editor, Howells also had considerable influence on what was published and what was not. He was, that is, both a tastemaker and a gatekeeper. In both these capacities, he was deeply committed to democracy. He was instrumental in establishing realism as the major kind of fiction of the day, and realism, as he characterized it, was democratic. It featured the lives of ordinary Americans in ordinary situations, confronted with ordinary dilemmas, in all the country's many regions; moreover, it was written in the language Americans actually spoke. It also (democratically) respected readers' capabilities. Howells censured literature that told readers what to think or feel and favored literature that allowed readers to draw their own moral and political inferences; as the critic Brook Thomas has shown, Howells's own novels were written to encourage this kind of reading.

But the parameters of Howellsian realism also functioned as restraints. Not only did they attribute artistic merit to certain kinds of writing but not others, they set limits on what should be included under the rubric of quotidian American life. For some years, Howells maintained that American life itself was harmonious (or "smiling," as he put it in an 1886 *Harper's* column that we include here) and that American writing should reflect that. His outlook became less sanguine, and he began to turn his attention to injustices within America and to American expansionism (see his letters to the *New-York Tribune* and his short story "Editha," both in the Howells section), but he nevertheless did not welcome writing whose criticism was too sharp-edged.

Forceful challenges to the status quo—racial, sexual, political, or creative—made him deeply anxious. Thus he termed Charles W. Chesnutt's brilliant *Marrow of Tradition* (1901), a searing indictment of white violence against African Americans in race riots in Wilmington, North Carolina, unpalatably "bitter." Likewise, while he was an enthusiastic supporter of fiction by many white women and championed work by several African American writers—Chesnutt's early fiction, Paul Laurence Dunbar's dialect poetry—Howells was often oblivious to departures from his own expectations. He did not pick up on the subversive undercurrents in the work of writers like Mary E. Wilkins Freeman, for instance. More dramatically, his presumption that dialect poetry was the appropriate mode for African Americans led him to ignore the many poems Dunbar wrote in "standard" English and to guide the reading public toward Dunbar's dialect poetry only.

Whatever Howells's limitations, his unceasing support of literature and his prominence contributed to making literature a key part of Americans' lives. Our excerpts from personal writing by Chesnutt and Sarah Orne Jewett indicate how deeply literature was interwoven into the ways in which they thought about themselves and the world; these excerpts also reflect habits of mind shared by many Americans who were not authors or would-be authors (it warrants notice that Howells assisted the careers of both Jewett and Chesnutt).

When Chesnutt was a largely self-educated man of twenty-two, living in obscurity in Fayetteville, North Carolina, the writing in his journals reflects his regard for both reading and writing as personally fulfilling and socially significant, and he imagines himself an author. Along lines that comport with Howells's critical criteria, Chesnutt expresses what would be a lifelong conviction that literature's fusion of imagination, thought, and emotion make it an extraordinarily effective way to reach people. He dedicates himself to the "high and holy purpose" of writing fiction about southern African American life (one facet of ordinary American life) that will dislodge white readers' prejudices and lead them to recognize the humanity of African Americans. Thus he hopes to effect his readers' transformation "imperceptibly," rather than trying to tell them what to think.

For Jewett, the shared appreciation of literature was an essential element of her personal relationships; she wrote often about books and magazines in letters to friends and to her companion, Annie Fields. The letter to Fields that we excerpt reflects her belief that the best literature expresses the common condition of humankind. Admiring the nuanced portrayal of the thwarted, tawdry romanticism of Emma Bovary, the country protagonist of French novelist Gustav Flaubert's *Madame Bovary*, Jewett writes of rural life as an intricate web of relationships. As her empathic tone suggests, the web of quotidian life extends to everyone, including Fields and Jewett herself, even though their cosmopolitanism also sets them apart from ordinary country people.

Like Chesnutt and Jewett, many Americans responded to literature as though its value were innate, and they associated that value with its capacity to explore a variety of people, and significant questions, imaginatively and with integrity. What imagination and integrity actually entailed, however, was open to debate. Some writers, Henry James among them, sought to protect what they regarded as literature's integrity by undercutting writing that did not meet the grade.

As a book reviewer, James often used his ideas about imaginative integrity to denigrate not just the individual work he was reviewing, but also certain *kinds* of writing. In the 1867 review that we excerpt, he lambastes a collection of short stories by Rebecca Harding Davis, a progressive writer in the then-poplar affective mode, criticizing it not, he says, because she wrote about the poor but because she did so with an emotionalism that was self-indulgent and false. His derision of sentimentalism extended to the work of many other widely read writers of the day, many of whom were also women. As he disparages sentimentality, James also clears a path for the kind of fiction he himself undertook, which he deems both intelligent ("a study ... or [an] intelligent inspection") and daring, in the sense that it engages with "truth" rather than airing preconceived convictions. Journalist, activist, and fiction writer Victoria Earle Matthews also embraced the integrity of engaging with truth, but the truth she had in mind was the particular character of African Americans' lives. In her 1895 speech "The Value of Race Literature," she maintains that African Americans had always been subjected to prejudice and oppression, but had not lost their resilience. A long tradition of African American literature (which, following *Webster's*, she defines as fiction, poetry, history, speeches, journalism, memoir, and other forms) has reflected on the specific character of African American lives, she says, urging her audience to be familiar with this literature and to support current and future literature that builds on it. Then, she predicts, "race literature" ... will "stand out preeminent, not only in the limited history of colored people, but in the broader field of universal literature."

If Earle Matthews's concepts of literature and integrity run counter to James's, other writers held that artistic integrity was incompatible with tastefulness. Jack London, who allied himself with the working classes, excoriates taste for being synonymous with bourgeois self-protectiveness and the cautiousness of publishers. These, he maintains, have resulted in the privileging of superficial literature—as he characterizes the kind of ordinary life Howells celebrates—and the marginalization of literature which explores primitive and enduring aspects of human nature—fear and terror. Yet another perspective was taken by writers who affirmed that literature was an incomparable means of confronting people with political and social realities they might wish to ignore. Pauline Hopkins's preface to her 1899 novel, *Contending Forces*, identifies fiction as an effective medium for informing Americans about horrific circumstances of contemporary African American life—the widespread lynching and rape of African Americans in the South, which were rooted in slavery and were underwriting the post-Reconstruction reinstatement of white supremacy—and for honoring northern African Americans' "hard struggles to obtain a respectable living and a partial education" in the face of entrenched northern racism. Her concept of fiction bears some resemblance to that of Harding Davis—for one thing, it openly solicits readers' emotions for a standpoint she already embraces—and, like James and Chesnutt, and Harding Davis as well, she has enormous faith in the power of literature to enter readers' being and to alter it.

To see the postbellum era as a time during which many Americans were reading widely, taking part in lively, often impassioned conversations about literature, and responding to it in ways that seemed personal, even if those responses were anchored in their culture, is to perceive only part of the picture, however. By the end of the century, literature and art in general were becoming subjects of more specialized forms of attention: they were emerging as academic subjects. With men like Harvard professor Barrett Wendall seeking to establish "the" American literary tradition, American literature was beginning to become a field of study. Like literature, philosophy was also being institutionalized as an academic discipline, with aesthetics beginning to take form as a discrete subject within philosophy.

One of the first major American works on aesthetics (many term it the first) was *The Sense of Beauty*, published by Harvard philosophy professor George Santayana in 1896. Our selections from *The Sense of Beauty* suggest that to some extent Santayana's thinking in this seminal book overlapped with the attitudes toward literature of many critics and writers. For him, as for Jewett, James, and others, a sense of beauty and a moral sense were defining human characteristics. However, *The Sense of Beauty* entailed a radical shift in emphasis in thinking about art, including literature, and about human beings. As Santayana's title suggests, his primary focus is beauty, and unlike the writers and critics we excerpt in this In Focus section, he separates beauty from morality and ethics. He characterizes beauty as something unique; moreover, he aligns it with pleasure, explaining that the sense of beauty is the experience of pleasure. Moreover, Santayana conceives of beauty in subjective terms—not as the property of, say, works of art or literature or of a sunset, but as something that exists in individuals' experience of such phenomena. He is commonly said to define beauty as objectified pleasure, for he explains that while we feel that beauty inheres in what inspires our pleasure, in actuality we are projecting the quality of our experience onto what has given rise to it.

The pleasure (or "delight") that Santayana discusses is uplifting, even spiritual. He distinguishes it from sensory pleasures and would have found many twenty-first-century notions of pleasure hedonistic. However, its location in individuals' sense of it—not in any objective reality—implicitly questions the status of art, literature included, as something distinct. If anything can be an occasion for pleasure, on what grounds can we assume that literature has special qualities? The links he suggests between the aesthetic and the spiritual were also tenuous, and he would soon revisit his thinking and associate the aesthetic firmly with the spiritual-religious. He would also affirm that the aesthetic suffused all of life. Yet his early teaching and work marked the thinking and writing of some of the young men who studied at Harvard while he was there and would become important modernist writers, including T. S. Eliot and Wallace Stevens. Eliot, in particular, felt that the vulgarity and materialism of modern life put the very capacity to experience beauty—or to express it—at risk. He and some of the other modernists recast "literature" as something much more rarified, more elite, than was literature as understood by Howells, Jewett, Chesnutt, and their cohort.

To be sure, this was only one of the directions that modernism would follow (the poetry of E. A. Robinson, who was at Harvard when Eliot and Stevens were, followed a very different path, for instance). Moreover, Americans, whether ordinary or elite, politically progressive, apolitical, or conservative, continued to read, write, and discuss literature that reflected them to themselves and sometimes literature that sought to lead them "imperceptibly" (as Chesnutt put it) to the goal of improving the common life. Still, by early in the twentieth century, the terms of the conversation about literature were changing, and the venues in which conversations took place were becoming more compartmentalized than were those of postbellum America. What counted as literature was altering as well. All these changes would continue to play out throughout the twentieth century, as they do today. An awareness of such changes returns us to the historical particularity of what literature is; it also points to the continuing vitality of literature itself.

Sandra A. Zagarell
Oberlin College

■ HENRY JAMES ■
1843–1916

Review of *Waiting for the Verdict*

Mrs. Davis has written a number of short stories, chiefly of country life in Virginia and Pennsylvania, all distinguished by a certain severe and uncultured strength, but all disfigured by an injudicious straining after realistic effects which leave nature and reality at an infinite distance behind and beside them. The author has made herself the poet of poor people—laborers, farmers, mechanics, and factory hands. She has attempted to reproduce in dramatic form their manners and habits and woes and wants. The intention has always been good, but the execution has, to our mind, always been monstrous. The unfortunate people whom she transfers into her stories are as good material for the story-teller's art as any other class of beings, but not a bit better. They come no nearer doing the work for themselves and leaving the writer to amuse himself than the best-housed and the best-fed and the best-clad classes in the community. They are worth reading about only so long as they are studied with a keen eye versed in the romance of human life, and described in the same rational English which we exact from writers on other subjects. Mrs. Davis's manner is in direct oppugnancy to this truth. She drenches the whole field beforehand with a flood of lachrymose sentimentalism, and riots in the murky vapors which rise in consequence of the act. It is impossible to conceive of a method of looking at people and things less calculated to elicit the truth—less in the nature of a sturdy or of intelligent inspection. The author is oppressed with the conviction that there exists in the various departments of human life some logical correlative to that luxurious need for tears and sighs and sad-colored imagery of all kinds which dwells in the mind of all those persons, whether men or women, who pursue literature under the sole guidance of sentimentality, and consider it a sufficient outlet for the pursuit. Nothing is more respectable on the part of a writer—a novelist—than the intelligent sadness which forces itself upon him on the completion of a dramatic scheme which is in strict accordance with human life and its manifold miseries. But nothing is more trivial than that intellectual temper which, for ever dissolved in the melting mood, goes dripping and trickling over the face of humanity, and washing its honest lineaments out of all recognition. It is enough to make one forswear for ever all decent reflection and honest compassion, and take refuge in cynical jollity and elegant pococurantism. Spontaneous pity is an excellent emotion, but there is nothing so hardening as to have your pity for ever tickled and stimulated, and nothing so debasing as to become an agent between the supply and demand of the commodity. This is the function which the author of the present work seems to have taken upon her, and we need no better proof of our assertion than the pernicious effect it has wrought upon her style. We know of no style among story-tellers more utterly difficult to read. In her desire to impart such reality to her characters as shall make them appeal successfully to our feelings, she emphasizes their movements and gestures to that degree that all vocal sounds, all human accents, are lost to the ear, and nothing is left but a crowd of ghastly, frowning, grinning automatons. The reader, exhausted by the constant strain upon his moral sensibilities, cries aloud for the good, graceful old nullities of the "fashionable novel."

Nation, November 21, 1867

WILLIAM DEAN HOWELLS
1837–1920

from **Criticism and Fiction**

It used to be one of the disadvantages of the practice of romance in America, which Hawthorne more or less whimsically lamented, that there were so few shadows and inequalities in our broad level of prosperity; and it is one of the reflections suggested by Dostoievsky's novel, "The Crime and the Punishment," that whoever struck a note so profoundly tragic in American fiction would do a false and mistaken thing—as false and as mistaken in its way as dealing in American fiction with certain nudities which the Latin peoples seem to find edifying. Whatever their deserts, very few American novelists have been led out to be shot, or finally exiled to the rigors of a winter at Duluth; and in a land where journeymen carpenters and plumbers strike for four dollars a day the sum of hunger and cold is comparatively small, and the wrong from class to class has been almost inappreciable, though all this is changing for the worse. Our novelists, therefore, concern themselves with the more smiling aspects of life, which are the more American, and seek the universal in the individual rather than the social interests. It is worth while, even at the risk of being called commonplace, to be true to our well-to-do actualities; the very passions themselves seem to be softened and modified by conditions which formerly at least could not be said to wrong any one, to cramp endeavor, or to cross lawful desire. Sin and suffering and shame there must always be in the world, I suppose, but I believe that in this new world of ours it is still mainly from one to another one, and oftener still from one to one's self. We have death, too, in America, and a great deal of disagreeable and painful disease, which the multiplicity of our patent medicines does not seem to cure; but this is tragedy that comes in the very nature of things, and is not peculiarly American, as the large, cheerful average of health and success and happy life is. It will not do to boast, but it is well to be true to the facts, and to see that, apart from these purely mortal troubles, the race here has enjoyed conditions in which most of the ills that have darkened its annals might be averted by honest work and unselfish behavior.

1891

VICTORIA EARLE MATTHEWS
1861–1907

---

from **The Value of Race Literature**

If the black man carries in his bosom an indispensable element of a new and coming civilization, for the sake of that element, no money, nor strength, nor circumstance can hurt him; he will survive and play his part. . . . If you have man, black or white is an insignificance. The intellect—that is miraculous who has it, has the talisman. His skin and bones, though they were the color of night, are transparent, and the everlasting stars shine through with attractive beams.

—RALPH WALDO EMERSON

Literature, according to Webster, is learning: acquaintance with books or letters: the collective body of literary productions, embracing the entire results of knowledge and fancy, preserved in writing, also the whole body of literature, productions or writings upon any given subject, or in reference to a particular science, a branch of knowledge, as the Literature of Biblical Customs, the Literature of Chemistry, etc.

In the light of this definition, many persons may object to the term Race Literature, questioning seriously the need, doubting if there be any, or indeed whether there can be a Race Literature in a country like ours apart from the general American Literature. Others may question the correctness of the term American Literature, since our civilization in its essential features is a reproduction of all that is most desirable in the civilizations of the Old World. English being the language of America, they argue in favor of the general term English Literature.

While I have great respect for the projectors of this theory, yet it is a limited definition; it does not express the idea in terms sufficiently clear.

The conditions which govern the people of African descent in the United States have been and still are, such as create a very marked difference in the limitations, characteristics, aspirations, and ambitions of this class of people, in decidedly strong contrast with the more or less powerful races which dominate it.

Laws were enacted denying and restricting their mental development in such pursuits, which engendered servility and begot ox-like endurance; and though statutes were carefully, painstakingly prepared by the most advanced and learned American jurists to perpetuate ignorance, yet they were powerless to keep all the race out from the Temple of Learning. Many though in chains mastered the common rudiments and others possessing talent of higher order—like the gifted Phyllis Wheatley, who dared to express her meditations in poetic elegance which won recognition in England and America, from persons distinguished in letters and statesmanship—dared to seek the sources of knowledge and wield a pen....

The prejudice of color! Not condition, not character, not capacity for artistic development, not the possibility of emerging from savagery into Christianity, not these but the "Prejudice of Color." Washington Irving's *Life of Columbus* contains a translation from the contemporaries of Las Casas, in which this prejudice is plainly evident. Since our reception on this continent, men have cried out against this inhuman prejudice; granting that, a man may improve his condition, accumulate wealth, become wise and upright, merciful and just as an infidel or Christian, but they despair because he can not change his color, as if it were possible for the victim to change his organic structure, and impossible for the oppressor to change his wicked heart.

But all this impious wrong has made a Race Literature a possibility, even a necessity to dissipate the odium conjured up by the term "colored" persons, not originally perhaps designed to humiliate, but unfortunately still used to express not only an inferior order, but to accentuate and call unfavorable attention to the most ineradicable difference between the race....

When the literature of our race is developed, it will of necessity be different in all essential points of greatness, true heroism and real Christianity from what we may at the present time, for convenience, call American Literature. When some master hand writes the stories as Dr. Dvorak[1] has caught

---

[1]Antonin Dvorak (1841–1904) was a celebrated Czech composer with an interest in folk music who spent several years in the United States. He was deeply impressed with traditional African American music, on which he drew for his ninth symphony, "From the New World." George Eliot was the pen name of Mary Ann Evans (1819–1880), a leading British humanist novelist and intellectual.

the melodies when, amid the hearts of the people, there shall live a George Eliot, moving this human world by the simple portrayal of the scenes of our ordinary existence; or when the pure, ennobling touch of a black Hannah Moore[2] shall rightly interpret our unappreciated contribution to Christianity and make it into universal literature, such writers will attain and hold imperishable fame.

The novelists most read at the present time in this country find a remunerative source for their doubtful literary productions based upon the wrongly interpreted and too often grossly exaggerated frailties. This is patent to all intelligent people. The Negro need not envy such reputation, nor feel lost at not revelling in its ill-gotten wealth or repute. We are the only people most distinctive from those who have civilized and governed this country, who have become typical Americans, and we rank next to the Indians in originality of soil, and yet remain a distinct people....

Though Race Literature be founded upon the traditionary history of a people yet its fullest and largest development ought not to be circumscribed by the narrow limits of race or creed for the simple reason that literature in its loftiest development reaches out to the utmost limits of soul enlargement and outstrips all earthly limitations. Our history and individuality as a people not only provides material for masterly treatment, but would seem to make a Race Literature a necessity as an outlet for the unnaturally suppressed inner lives which our people have been compelled to lead....

When the foundations of such a literature shall have been properly laid, the benefit to be derived will be at once apparent. There will be a revelation to our people, and it will enlarge our scope, make us better known wherever real lasting culture exists, will undermine and utterly drive out the traditional Negro in dialect,—the subordinate, the servant as the type representing a race whose numbers are now far into the millions. It would suggest to the world the wrong and contempt with which the lion viewed the picture that the hunter and famous painter besides, had drawn of the King of the Forest....

We cannot afford any more than any other people to be indifferent to the fact that the surest road to real fame is through literature. Who is so well known and appreciated by the cultured minds as Dumas of France, and Pushkin of Russia?[3] I need not say to this thoughtful and intelligent gathering that, any people without a literature is valued lightly the world round. Who knows or can judge of our intrinsic worth without actual evidence of our breadth of mind, our boundless humanity? Appearing well and weighted

---

[2]Hannah Moore (1745–1833) was a prominent British playwright, poet, religious writer, and opponent of the slave trade.

[3]French writer Alexandre Dumas (1805–1870) was best known in the United States for *The Three Musketeers* (1844) and *The Count of Monte Cristo* (1845–1846). Russian Alexander Pushkin (1799–1837) remains Russia's best-loved writer. Both were descended from both their country's aristocracy and from people of color. Dumas's paternal grandmother was a Haitian slave and his grandfather a member of the French nobility. Pushkin's maternal great-grandfather was African; his father was a member of the Russian nobility and his mother was descended from Scandinavian and German nobility.

with many degrees of titles, will not raise us in our own estimation while color is the white elephant in America. Yet, America is but a patch on the universe: if she ever produces a race out of her cosmopolitan population that can look beyond mere money-getting to more permanent qualities of true greatness as a nation, it will call this age her unbalanced stage....

"While we of to-day view with increasing dissatisfaction the trend of the literary productions of this country, concerning us, yet are we standing squarely on the foundation laid for us by our immediate predecessors?

This is the question I would bring to your minds. Are we adding to the structure planned for us by our pioneers? Do we know our dwelling and those who under many hardships, at least, gathered the material for its upbuilding? Knowing them do we honor—do we love them—what have they done that we should love? Your own Emerson says—"To judge the production of a people you must transplant the spirit of the times in which they lived."

In the ten volumes of American Literature edited by H. L. Stoddard only Phyllis [sic] Wheatley and George W. Williams find a place. This does not show that we have done nothing in literature; far from it, but it does show that we have done nothing so brilliant, so effective, so startling as to attract the attention of these editors. Now it is a fact that thoughtful, scholarly white people do not look for literature in its highest sense from us any more than they look for high scholarship, profound and critical learning on any one point, nor for any eminent judicial acumen or profound insight into causes and effects.

These are properly regarded as the results only of matured intellectual growth or abundant leisure and opportunity, when united with exceptional talents, and this is the world's view and it is in the main a correct one. Even the instances of precocious geniuses and the rare examples of extraordinary talent appearing from humble and unpromising parentage and unfortuitous surroundings, are always recognized as brilliant, sporadic cases, exceptions.

Consequently our success in Race Literature will be looked upon with curiosity and only a series of projected enterprises in various directions—history, poetry, novel writing, speeches, orations, forensic effort, sermons, and so on, will have the result of gaining for us recognition....

And now comes the question, What part shall we women play in the Race Literature of the future? I shall best answer that question by calling your attention to the glorious part which they have already performed in the columns of The Woman's Era, edited by Josephine St. P. Ruffin.

Here within the compass of one small journal we have struck out a new line of departure—a journal, a record of Race interests gathered from all parts of the United States, carefully selected, moistened, winnowed, and garnered by the ablest intellects of educated colored women, shrinking at no lofty theme, shirking no serious duty, aiming at every possible excellence, and determined to do their part in the future uplifting of the race.

If twenty women, by their concentrated efforts in one literary movement, can meet with such success as has engendered, planned out, and so successfully consummated this convention, what much more glorious results, what wider spread success, what grander diffusion of mental light will not come forth at the bidding of the enlarged hosts of women writers, already called into being by the stimulus of your efforts?

And here let me speak one word for my journalistic sisters who have already entered the broad arena of journalism. Before *The Woman's Era* had come into existence, no one except themselves can appreciate the bitter experience and sore disappointments under which they have at all times been compelled to pursue their chosen vocations.

If their brothers of the press have had their difficulties to contend with, I am here as a sister journalist to state, from the fullness of knowledge, that their task has been an easy one compared with that of the colored woman in journalism. . . .

The lesson to be drawn from this cursory glance at what I may call the past, present, and future of our Race Literature, apart from its value as first beginnings, not only to us as a people but literature in general, is that unless earnest and systematic effort be made to procure and preserve for transmission to our successors, the records, books, and various publications already produced by us, not only will the sturdy pioneers who paved the way and laid the foundation for our Race Literature be robbed of their just due, but an irretrievable wrong will be inflicted upon the generations that shall come after us.

1895

JACK LONDON
1876–1916

The Terrible and Tragic in Fiction

[London opens this essay by discussing publishers' and editors' reluctance to publish the fiction of Edgar Allen Poe during Poe's lifetime despite the chord his writing struck in many of his readers.]

Yet the conditions which obtained in Poe's time obtain just as inexorably today. No self-respecting editor with an eye to the subscription-list can be bribed or bullied into admitting a terrible or tragic story into his magazine; while the reading public, when it does chance upon such stories in one way or another,—and it manages to chance upon them somehow,—says it does not care for them.

A person reads such a story, lays it down with a shudder, and says: "It makes my blood run cold. I never want to read anything like that again."

Yet he or she will read something like that again, and again, and yet again, and return and read them over again. Talk with the average man or woman of the reading public and it will be found that they have read all, or nearly all, of the terrible and horrible tales which have been written. Also, they will shiver, express a dislike for such tales, and then proceed to discuss them with a keenness and understanding as remarkable as it is surprising.

When it is considered that so many condemn these tales and continue to read them (as is amply proved by heart-to-heart experience and by the book sales such as Poe's), the question arises: Are folk honest when they shudder and say they do not care for the terrible, the horrible, and the tragic? Do they really not like to be afraid? Or are they afraid that they do like to be afraid?

Deep down in the roots of the race is fear. It came first into the world, and it was the dominant emotion in the primitive world. Today, for that matter, it remains the most firmly seated of the emotions. But in the primitive world people were uncomplex, not yet self-conscious, and they frankly delighted in terror-inspiring tales and religions. Is it true that the complex, self-conscious people of to-day do not delight in the things which inspire terror? or is it true that they are ashamed to make known their delight?

What is it that lures boys to haunted houses after dark, compelling them to fling rocks and run away with their hearts going so thunderously pit-a-pat as to drown the clatter of their flying feet? What is it that grips a child, forcing it to listen to ghost stories which drive it into ecstasies of fear, and yet forces it to beg for more and more? Is it a baleful thing? a thing his instinct warns him as unhealthy and evil the while his desire leaps out to it? Or, again, what is it that sends the heart fluttering up and quickens the feet of the man or woman who goes alone down a long, dark hall or up a winding stair? Is it a stirring of the savage in them?—of the savage who has slept, but never died since the time the river-folk crouched over the fires of their squatting-places, or the tree-folk bunched together and chattered in the dark?

Whatever the thing is, and whether it be good or evil, it is a thing and it is real. It is a thing Poe rouses in us, scaring us in broad day and throwing us into "admired disorders." It is rarely that the grown person who is afraid of the dark will make confessions. It does not seem to them proper to be afraid of the dark, and they are ashamed. Perhaps people feel that it is not proper to delight in stories that arouse fear and terror. They may feel instinctively that it is bad and injurious to have such emotions aroused, and because of this are impelled to say that they do not like such stories, while in actuality they do like them.

The great emotion exploited by Dickens was fear.... The militant nobility seemed to possess an excess of courage and to respond more readily to things courageous. On the other hand, the rising bourgeoisie, the timid merchant-folk and city-dwellers, fresh from the oppressions and robberies of their rough-handed lords, seemed to possess an excess of fear, and to respond more readily to things fearsome. For this reason they greedily de-voured Dickens's writings, for he was as peculiarly their spokesman as Scott was the spokesman of the old and dying nobility.

But since Dickens's day, if we may judge by the editorial attitude and by the dictum of the reading public, a change seems to have taken place. In Dickens's day, the bourgeoisie, as a dominant class being but newly risen, had fear still strong upon it, much as a negro mammy, a couple of genera-tions from Africa, stands in fear of the Voodoo. But to-day it would seem that this same bourgeoisie, firmly seated and triumphant, is ashamed of its old terror, which it remembers dimly, as it might a bad nightmare. When fear was strong upon it, it loved nothing better than fear-exciting things; but with fear far removed, no longer menaced and harassed, it has become afraid of fear. By this is meant that the bourgeoisie has become self-conscious, much in the same fashion that the black slave, freed and con-scious of the stigma attached to "black," calls himself a colored gentleman, though in his heart of hearts he feels himself black nigger still. So the bour-geoisie may feel in a dim, mysterious way the stigma attached to the fear of its cowardly days, and, self-conscious, brands as improper all fear-exciting things, while deep down in its secret being it delights in them still. . . .

Putting the horror-story outside the pale, can any story be really great, the theme of which is anything but tragic or terrible? Can the sweet common-places of life be made into anything else than sweetly commonplace stories?

It would not seem so. The great short stories in the world's literary treasure-house seem all to depend upon the tragic and terrible for their strength and greatness. Not half of them deal with love at all; and when they do, they derive their greatness, not from the love itself, but from the tragic and terrible with which the love is involved. . . .

The editors of the magazines have very good reasons for refusing admis-sion to the terrible and tragic. Their readers say they do not like the terrible and tragic, and that is enough, without going farther. But either their read-ers prevaricate most shamelessly or delude themselves into believing they tell the truth, or else the people who read the magazines are not the people who continue to buy, say, the works of Poe.

In the circumstances, there being a proved demand for the terrible and tragic, is there not room in the otherwise crowded field for a magazine devoted primarily to the terrible and tragic? A magazine such as Poe dreamed of, about which there shall be nothing namby-pamby, yellowish, or emasculated, and which will print stories that are bids for place and perma-nence rather than for the largest circulation?

On the face of it two things appear certain: That enough of that portion of the reading public which cares for the tragic and terrible would be suffi-ciently honest to subscribe; and that the writers of the land would be capa-ble of supplying the stories. The only reason why such stories are not written to-day is that there is no magazine to buy them, and that the writer-folk are busy turning out the stuff, mainly ephemeral, which the mag-azines will buy. The pity of it is that the writer-folk are writing for bread first and glory after; and that their standard of living goes up as fast as their capacity for winning bread increases,—so that they never get around to glory,—the ephemeral flourishes, and the great stories remain unwritten.

1903

SARAH ORNE JEWETT
1849–1909

Letter to Annie Fields, October 12, 1890

It is quite wonderful how great a book Flaubert makes of [*Madame Bovary*]. People talk about dwelling upon trivialities and commonplaces in life, but a master writer gives everything weight, and makes you feel the distinction and importance of it, and count it upon the right or the wrong side of a life's account. That is one reason why writing about simple country people takes my time and thought. But I should make too long a letter for this short morning. Flaubert, who sees so far into the shadows of life, may "dwell" and analyze and reflect as much as he pleases with the trivial things of life; the woes of Hamlet absorb our thoughts no more than the silly wavering gait of this Madame Bovary, who is uninteresting, ill-bred, and without the attraction of rural surroundings. But the very great pathos of the book to me, is not the sin of her, but the thought, all the time, if she *could* have had a little brightness and prettiness of taste in the dull doctor, if she could have taken what there was in that dull little village! She is such a lesson to dwellers in country towns, who drift out of relation to their surroundings, not only social, but the very companionships of nature, unknown to them.

1890

CHARLES WADDELL CHESNUTT
1858–1932

from Journal

May 29, 1880 . . . I think I must write a book. I am almost afraid to undertake a book so early and with so little experience in composition. But it has been my cherished dream, and I feel an influence that I cannot resist calling me to the task. Besides, I do not know but I am as well prepared as some other successful writers. A fair knowledge of the classics, a speaking acquaintance with the modern languages, an intimate friendship with literature, etc.; seven years experience in the school room, two years of married life, and a habit of studying character have I think, left me not entirely unprepared to write even a book. Fifteen years of life in the South, in one of the most eventful eras of its history; among a people whose life is rich in the elements of romance; under conditions calculated to stir one's soul to the very depths—I think there is here a fund of experience, a supply of material, which a skillful pers[on] could work up with tremendous effect. Besides, If I do write, I shall write for a purpose, a high, holy purpose, and this will inspire me to greater effort. The object of my writings would be not so much the elevation of the colored people as the elevation of the whites—for I consider the unjust spirit of caste which is so insidious as to pervade a whole nation, and so powerful as to subject a whole race and all connected with it to scorn and social ostracism—I consider this a barrier to the moral progress of the American people; and I would be one of the first to head a determined, organized crusade against it. Not a fierce indiscriminate onslaught; not an appeal to force, for this is something that force can but slightly affect; but a moral revolution which must be brought about in a different manner. The Abolition[ist]s stirred up public opinion in behalf of the slave, by appealing in trumpet tones to those principles of justice and humanity which were only lying dormant in the northern heart. The iron hand of power set the slave free from personal bondage, and by admitting him to all the rights of citizenship—the ballot, education—is fast freeing him from the greater bondage of ignorance. But the subtle almost indefinable feeling of repulsion toward the negro, which is common to most Americans—and easily enough accounted for— cannot be stormed and taken by assault; the garrison will not capitulate: so their position must be mined, and we will find ourselves in their midst before they think it.

This work is of a twofold character. The negro's part is to prepare himself for social recognition and equality; and it is the province of literature to open the way for him to get it—to accustom the public mind to the idea; and while amusing them to lead them on imperceptibly, unconsciously step by step to the desired state of feeling. If I can do anything to further this work, and can see any likelihood of obtaining success in it, I would gladly devote my life to the work.

1880

■ PAULINE ELIZABETH HOPKINS ■
1859–1930

from **Contending Forces: A Romance Illustrative of**
Negro Life North and South

Preface

In giving this little romance expression in print, I am not actuated by a desire for notoriety or for profit, but to do all that I can in an humble way to raise the stigma of degradation from my race.

While I make no apology for my somewhat abrupt and daring venture within the wide field of romantic literature, I ask the kind indulgence of the generous public for the many crudities which I know appear in the work, and their approval of whatever may impress them as being of value to the Negro race and to the world at large.

The colored race has historians, lecturers, ministers, poets, judges and lawyers,—men of brilliant intellects who have arrested the favorable attention of this busy, energetic nation. But, after all, it is the simple, homely tale, unassumingly told, which cements the bond of brotherhood among all classes and all complexions.

Fiction is of great value to any people as a preserver of manners and customs—religious, political and social. It is a record of growth and development from generation to generation. *No one will do this for us; we must ourselves develop the men and women who will faithfully portray the inmost thoughts and feelings of the Negro with all the fire and romance which lie dormant in our history*, and, as yet, unrecognized by writers of the Anglo-Saxon race....

In these days of mob violence, when lynch-law is raising its head like a venomous monster, more particularly in the southern portion of the great American republic, the retrospective mind will dwell upon the history of the past, seeking there a solution of these monstrous outbreaks under a government founded upon the greatest and brightest of principles for the elevation of mankind. While we ponder the philosophy of cause and effect, the world is horrified by a fresh outbreak, and the shocked mind wonders that in this—the brightest epoch of the Christian era—*such things are.*

Mob-law is nothing new. Southern sentiment has not been changed; the old ideas close in analogy to the spirit of the buccaneers, who formed in many instances the first settlers of the Southland, still prevail, and break forth clothed in new forms to force the whole republic to an acceptance of its principles.

"Rule or ruin" is the motto which is committing the most beautiful portion of our glorious country to a cruel revival of piratical methods; and, finally, to the introduction of *Anarchy.* Is this not so? Let us compare the happenings of one hundred—two hundred years ago, with those of today. The difference between then and now, if any there be, is so slight as to be scarcely worth mentioning. The atrocity of the acts committed one hundred years ago are duplicated today, when slavery is supposed no longer to exist.

I have tried to tell an impartial story, leaving it to the reader to draw conclusions. I have tried to portray our hard struggles here in the North to obtain a respectable living and partial education. I have presented both sides of the dark picture—lynching and concubinage—truthfully and without vituperation, pleading for that justice of heart and mind for my people which the Anglo-Saxon in America never withholds from suffering humanity.

In Chapter XIII. I have used for the address of the Hon. Herbert Clapp the statements and accusations made against the Negro by ex-Governor Northern of Georgia, in his memorable address before the Congregational Club at Tremont Temple, Boston, Mass., May 22, 1899. In Chapter XV. I have made Will Smith's argument in answer to the Hon. Herbert Clapp a combination of the best points made by well-known public speakers in the United States—white and black—in defense of the Negro.[1] I feel my own deficiencies too strongly to attempt original composition on this subject at this crisis in the history of the Negro in the United States. I have introduced enough of the exquisitely droll humor peculiar to the Negro (a work like this would not be complete without it) to give a bright touch to an otherwise gruesome subject.

The Author.
1901

GEORGE SANTAYANA
1863–1952

from **The Sense of Beauty**

[Santayana says that aesthetics, his subject, "is concerned with the perception of values."]

We may ... at once assert this axiom, important for all moral philosophy and fatal to certain stubborn incoherences of thought, that there is no value apart from some appreciation of it, and no good apart from some preference of it before its absence or its opposite. In appreciation, in preference, lies the root and essence of all excellence. Or, as Spinoza clearly expresses it, we desire nothing because it is good, but it is good only because we desire it. . . .

---

[1]The Honorable Herbert Clapp and Will Smith are fictional characters in *Contending Forces*.

It is evident that beauty is a species of value, and what we have said of value in general applies to this particular kind. A first approach to a definition of beauty has therefore been made by the exclusion of all intellectual judgments, all judgments of matter of fact or of relation. To substitute judgments of fact for judgments of value, is a sign of a pedantic and borrowed criticism. If we approach a work of art or nature scientifically, for the sake of its historical connexions or proper classification, we do not approach it aesthetically. The discovery of its date or of its author may be otherwise interesting; it only remotely affects our aesthetic appreciation by adding to the direct effect certain associations. If the direct effect were absent, and the object in itself uninteresting, the circumstances would be immaterial. Molière's *Misanthrope* says to the court poet who commends his sonnet as written in a quarter of an hour,

Voyons, monsieur, le temps ne fait rien à l'affaire,[1]

and so we might say to the critic that sinks into the archæologist, show us the work, and let the date alone.

In an opposite direction the same substitution of facts for values makes its appearance, whenever the reproduction of fact is made the sole standard of artistic excellence. Many half-trained observers condemn the work of some naïve or fanciful masters with a sneer, because, as they truly say, it is out of drawing. The implication is that to be correctly copied from a model is the prerequisite of all beauty. Correctness is, indeed, an element of effect and one which, in respect to familiar objects, is almost indispensable, because its absence would cause a disappointment and dissatisfaction incompatible with enjoyment. We learn to value truth more and more as our love and knowledge of nature increase. But fidelity is a merit only because it is in this way a factor in our pleasure. It stands on a level with all other ingredients of effect. When a man raises it to a solitary pre-eminence and becomes incapable of appreciating anything else, he betrays the decay of æsthetic capacity. The scientific habit in him inhibits the artistic.

That facts have a value of their own, at once complicates and explains this question. We are naturally pleased by every perception, and recognition and surprise are particularly acute sensations. When we see a striking truth in any imitation, we are therefore delighted, and this kind of pleasure is very legitimate, and enters into the best effects of all the representative arts. Truth and realism are therefore æsthetically good, but they are not all-sufficient, since the representation of everything is not equally pleasing and effective. The fact that resemblance is a source of satisfaction justifies the critic in demanding it, while the æsthetic insufficiency of such veracity shows the different value of truth in science and in art. Science is the response to the demand for information, and in it we ask for the whole truth and nothing but the truth. Art is the response to the demand for

---

[1]French. "But, sir, time has nothing to do with
   this matter."

entertainment, for the stimulation of our senses and imagination, and truth enters into it only as it subserves these ends....

But as impersonal thoughts are such only in their object, not in their subject or agent, since all thoughts are the thoughts of somebody: so also unselfish interests have to be somebody's interests. If we were not interested in beauty, if it were of no concern to our happiness whether things were beautiful or ugly, we should manifest not the maximum, but the total absence of æsthetic faculty. The distinterestedness of this pleasure is, therefore, that of all primitive and intuitive satisfactions, which are in no way conditioned by a reference to an artificial general concept, like that of the self, all the potency of which must itself be derived from the independent energy of its component elements. I care about myself because "myself" is a name for the things I have at heart. To set up the verbal figment of personality and make it an object of concern apart from the interests which were its content and substance, turns the moralist into a pedant, and ethics into a superstition. The self which is the object of *amour propre* is an idol of the tribe, and needs to be disintegrated into the primitive objective interests that underlie it before the cultus of it can be justified by reason.

1896

HENRY ADAMS
1838–1918

At his birth Henry Brooks Adams, the grandson and great-grandson of American presidents, entered a privileged world. Along with his political name, he also inherited a special responsibility: to bear witness, through writing, to the complexity of life. Today Adams owes his popular reputation to a single record of that kind, *The Education of Henry Adams*, which won a Pulitzer Prize in 1919. Yet over a long and productive career as a writer, he also produced a substantial body of essays, biographies, novels, letters, and histories, which largely reward our attention.

Adams's earliest publications, dating from his undergraduate years at Harvard University, from 1854 to 1858, pointed directions for his later work. As he wrote of men, architecture, and books, the young Adams testified to the high seriousness of his concern for human experience as a field of lifelong investigation. Yet he knew his preparation to be incomplete. After graduation and a tour of Europe, first he settled in Germany, where he mastered German historical method, the most rigorous type of scholarship available at the time. Then, at the behest of his father, Charles Francis Adams, elected to Congress in 1860, Henry moved to Washington to serve as a private secretary (and as a secret correspondent for the *Boston Daily Advertiser*). In 1861 Henry went to London, spending the years of the Civil War there while his father served as President Lincoln's Minister to the Court of St. James's. From this diplomatic outpost the son wrote letters, dispatches, and essays, honing his thoughts on politics, history, science, and English and American culture—in writings that display the intellectual skills of a critic.

Back in Washington after the war, Adams enlisted his literary talents in the service of political reform, writing essays and reviews in support of such causes as the establishment of the federal civil service system. However, the disillusionment caused by the administration of President Ulysses Grant and the growing corruption of American politics quickly foreclosed Adams's personal interest in political service. In 1870 he returned to Boston and Harvard to begin a joint career as a teacher of history and editor of the prestigious *North American Review*. By 1872 he had married Marian "Clover" Hooper, whose suicide in 1885 Adams would come to regard as the end of his life in the world. During the 1870s, he also introduced German historical techniques, including the use of original documentary sources and the seminar method, into graduate studies at Harvard.

Adams's own research focused on the medieval period in Europe and on medieval women in various early civilizations. This special interest led him, in December 1876, to deliver a seminal public address on "The Primitive Rights of Women." Later, he would investigate the situation of contemporary American women in two novels, *Democracy* (1880) and *Esther* (1884). Neither book proposed a solution to the practical problems of being a woman in nineteenth-century America, but both were sympathetic in recognizing how their lack of control over circumstance handicapped women and reduced their effectiveness in human activities. Already, Adams was approaching his far more ambitious theory of feminine force—the important hypothesis developed in his two most celebrated works, *Mont-Saint-Michel and Chartres* and *The Education of Henry Adams*. In both, Adams drew upon his long study of ancient and modern, "primitive" and "civilized" societies, to conclude that, on the basis of all historical evidence, women—rather than men—represented both the highest standard of moral behavior and the greatest source of human energy. In the figure of the Virgin, for example, woman had exercised her power by inspiring the building of a great cathedral at Chartres. In his own time, however, Adams saw the force of the Virgin superseded by new scientific forces, symbolized by the modern dynamo. History, in Adams's view, traced the path between the two.

Long before he fixed on the technology of the dynamo and the scientific laws that explained its operation as a way of interpreting human history, Adams had considered the possibilities of a more conventional history—as a narrative of events that emphasized the roles played by great men. His classic nine-volume *History of the United States during the Administrations of Thomas Jefferson and James Madison* (1888–1891) used Germanic scholarly methods to examine American life from 1800 to 1816. It failed, however, to locate any convenient key in the American past that could be used predictively—to lay out an American future. Increasingly as he grew older, and as the closing chapters of *The Education* reveal, Adams sought to find such a key, in history, literature, science, and personal experience. But he never succeeded, at least to his own satisfaction.

Mont-Saint-Michel and Chartres (privately printed in 1904 and published in 1913) was less an attempt to write conventional history than a compelling invitation to sample the joys of medieval life, including medieval architecture, in which the Virgin is a unifying force. As autobiography, *The Education of Henry Adams* (privately printed in 1907 and published in 1918 after the author's death) is also unconventional, using the third person point of view and preserving complete silence about Adams's wife and married life. *The Education* tells Adams's story as both unique and representative. As a member of a presidential family, his experience was special. However, as a man living at a time when the eighteenth-century qualities of civic virtue and service (which had made the Adams name) no longer seem useful, a time that offered the individual only marginal control over the impersonal forces at work in the world, Adams treats his failure as typical. Modern science and technology have brought unforeseen results, and Adams, lacking sufficient explanation, has been reduced to the same diminutive role played by the nineteenth-century woman. Unless his readers, alive in the twentieth and twenty-first centuries, can learn to educate themselves more efficiently, Adams argues, their experience will be no better than his.

Earl N. Harbert
Independent scholar/editor

PRIMARY WORKS

The Life of Albert Gallatin, 1879; *Democracy: An American Novel* (anon.), 1880, 1882; *John Randolph*, 1882, rev. 1883; *Esther: A Novel* (as Frances Snow Compton), 1884,

1885; *History of the United States of America During the Administrations of Thomas Jefferson and James Madison*, 1884, 1885, 1888, 1889, 1890, 1891; *Historical Essays*, 1891; *Mont-Saint-Michel and Chartres* (anon.), 1904, rev. 1912, 1913, 1914; *The Education of Henry Adams*, 1907, 1918, 1919; *Sketches for the North American Review* (ed. Edward Chalfant), 1986.

from Mont-Saint-Michel and Chartres

Chapter VI. The Virgin of Chartres

[Henry Adams's *Mont-Saint-Michel and Chartres* drew from his deep appreciation of medieval culture, especially of the vital role that the Virgin Mary played in religious belief and practice. The book is structured as a tour of medieval France, expertly guided by its author. Along the route the two most memorable points of interest are the impressive fortress abbey, Mont-Saint-Michel, just off the coast of France, and the beautiful cathedral at Chartres, fifty-five miles from Paris. As Chapter VI illustrates, Adams uses his own vast knowledge to encourage the reader's understanding of complexity and power in medieval life. The distant past, in this author's view, should not be considered inferior to the present.]

We must take ten minutes to accustom our eyes to the light, and we had better use them to seek the reason why we come to Chartres rather than to Rheims or Amiens or Bourges,[1] for the cathedral that fills our ideal. The truth is, there are several reasons; there generally are, for doing the things we like; and after you have studied Chartres to the ground, and got your reasons settled, you will never find an antiquarian to agree with you; the architects will probably listen to you with contempt; and even these excellent priests, whose kindness is great, whose patience is heavenly, and whose good opinion you would so gladly gain, will turn from you with pain, if not with horror. The Gothic is singular in this; one seems easily at home in the Renaissance; one is not too strange in the Byzantine; as for the Roman, it is ourselves; and we could walk blindfolded through every chink and cranny of the Greek mind; all these styles[2] seem modern, when we come close to them; but the Gothic gets away.

No two men think alike about it, and no woman agrees with either man. The Church itself never agreed about it, and the architects agree even less than the priests. To most minds it casts too many shadows; it wraps itself in mystery; and when people talk of mystery, they commonly mean fear. To others, the Gothic seems hoary with age and decrepitude, and its shadows mean death. What is curious to watch is the fanatical conviction of the Gothic enthusiast, to whom the twelfth century means exuberant youth, the eternal child of Wordsworth, over whom its immortality broods like the

---

[1]French cities in which cathedrals are located.
[2]Adams refers to various historical styles of architecture.

day; it is so simple and yet so complicated; it sees so much and so little; it loves so many toys and cares for so few necessities; its youth is so young, its age so old, and its youthful yearning for old thought is so disconcerting, like the mysterious senility of the baby that—

> Deaf and silent, reads the eternal deep,
> Haunted forever by the eternal mind.[3]

One need not take it more seriously than one takes the baby itself. Our amusement is to play with it, and to catch its meaning in its smile; and whatever Chartres may be now, when young it was a smile. To the Church, no doubt, its cathedral here has a fixed and administrative meaning, which is the same as that of every other bishop's seat and with which we have nothing whatever to do. To us, it is a child's fancy; a toy-house to please the Queen of Heaven,—to please her so much that she would be happy in it,—to charm her till she smiled.

The Queen Mother was as majestic as you like; she was absolute; she could be stern; she was not above being angry; but she was still a woman, who loved grace, beauty, ornament,—her toilette, robes, jewels;—who considered the arrangements of her palace with attention, and liked both light and colour; who kept a keen eye on her Court, and exacted prompt and willing obedience from king and archbishops as well as from beggars and drunken priests. She protected her friends and punished her enemies. She required space, beyond what was known in the Courts of kings, because she was liable at all times to have ten thousand people begging her for favours—mostly inconsistent with law—and deaf to refusal. She was extremely sensitive to neglect, to disagreeable impressions, to want of intelligence in her surroundings. She was the greatest artist, as she was the greatest philosopher and musician and theologist, that ever lived on earth, except her Son, Who, at Chartres, is still an Infant under her guardianship. Her taste was infallible; her silence eternally final. This church was built for her in this spirit of simple-minded, practical, utilitarian faith,—in this singleness of thought, exactly as a little girl sets up a doll-house for her favourite blonde doll. Unless you can go back to your dolls, you are out of place here. If you can go back to them, and get rid of one small hour of the weight of custom, you shall see Chartres in glory.

The palaces of earthly queens were hovels compared with these palaces of the Queen of Heaven at Chartres, Paris, Laon, Noyon, Rheims, Amiens, Rouen, Bayeux, Coutances,—a list that might be stretched into a volume. The nearest approach we have made to a palace was the Merveille at Mont-Saint-Michel, but no Queen had a palace equal to that. The Merveille was built, or designed, about the year 1200; toward the year 1500, Louis XI built a great castle at Loches in Touraine, and there Queen Anne de Bretagne had apartments which still exist, and which we will visit. At Blois you shall see

---

[3] From "Ode: Intimations of Immortality from Recollections of Early Childhood" (VIII) by William Wordsworth (1770–1852).

the residence which served for Catherine de Medicis till her death in 1589. Anne de Bretagne was trebly queen, and Catherine de Medicis took her standard of comfort from the luxury of Florence. At Versailles you can see the apartments which the queens of the Bourbon line occupied through their century of magnificence. All put together, and then trebled in importance, could not rival the splendour of any single cathedral dedicated to Queen Mary in the thirteenth century; and of them all, Chartres was built to be peculiarly and exceptionally her delight.

One has grown so used to this sort of loose comparison, this reckless waste of words, that one no longer adopts an idea unless it is driven in with hammers of statistics and columns of figures. With the irritating demand for literal exactness and perfectly straight lines which lights up every truly American eye, you will certainly ask when this exaltation of Mary began, and unless you get the dates, you will doubt the facts. It is your own fault if they are tiresome; you might easily read them all in the "Iconographie de la Sainte Vierge," by M. Rohault de Fleury, published in 1878. You can start at Byzantium with the Empress Helena in 326, or with the Council of Ephesus in 431. You will find the Virgin acting as the patron saint of Constantinople and of the Imperial residence, under as many names as Artemis or Aphrodite had borne. As Godmother ($\Theta\epsilon o\mu\eta\tau\eta\rho$), Deipara ($\Theta\epsilon\tau o\kappa o$), Pathfinder ($O\delta o\eta\gamma\eta\tau\rho\iota\alpha$), she was the chief favourite of the Eastern Empire, and her picture was carried at the head of every procession and hung on the wall of every hut and hovel, as it is still wherever the Greek Church goes. In the year 610, when Heraclius sailed from Carthage to de-throne Phocas at Constantinople, his ships carried the image of the Virgin at their mast-heads.[4] In 1143, just before the flèche on the Chartres clocher was begun, the Basileus[5] John Comnenus died, and so devoted was he to the Virgin that, on a triumphal entry into Constantinople, he put the image of the Mother of God in his chariot, while he himself walked. In the Western Church the Virgin had always been highly honoured, but it was not until the crusades that she began to overshadow the Trinity itself. Then her miracles became more frequent and her shrines more frequented, so that Chartres, soon after 1100, was rich enough to build its western portal with Byzantine splendour. A proof of the new outburst can be read in the story of Citeaux. For us, Citeaux means Saint Bernard, who joined the Order[6] in 1112, and in 1115 founded his Abbey of Clairvaux in the territory of Troyes. In him, the religious emotion of the half-century between the first and second crusades (1095–1145) centred as in no one else. He was a French precursor of Saint Francis of Assisi who lived a century later. If we were to plunge into the story of Citeaux and Saint Bernard we should never escape, for Saint Bernard incarnates what we are trying to understand, and his mind is further

---

[4]Adams traces early appearances of the Virgin in pre-medieval history, beginning with Byzantium and concluding just before Chartres was begun, before the spire (flèche) on the tower (clocher) was started.

[5]King.

[6]A group of monks.

from us than the architecture. You would lose hold of everything actual, if you could comprehend in its contradictions the strange mixture of passion and caution, the austerity, the self-abandonment, the vehemence, the restraint, the love, the hate, the miracles, and the scepticism of Saint Bernard. The Cistercian Order, which was founded in 1098, from the first put all its churches under the special protection of the Virgin, and Saint Bernard in his time was regarded as the apple of the Virgin's eye. Tradition as old as the twelfth century, which long afterwards gave to Murillo[7] the subject of a famous painting, told that once, when he was reciting before her statue the "Ave Maris Stella,"[8] and came to the words, "Monstra te esse Matrem,"[9] the image, pressing its breast, dropped on the lips of her servant three drops of the milk which had nourished the Saviour. The same miracle, in various forms, was told of many other persons, both saints and sinners; but it made so much impression on the mind of the age that, in the fourteenth century, Dante, seeking in Paradise[10] for some official introduction to the foot of the Throne, found no intercessor with the Queen of Heaven more potent than Saint Bernard. You can still read Bernard's hymns to the Virgin, and even his sermons, if you like. To him she was the great mediator. In the eyes of a culpable humanity, Christ was too sublime, too terrible, too just, but not even the weakest human frailty could fear to approach his Mother. Her attribute was humility; her love and pity were infinite. "Let him deny your mercy who can say that he has ever asked it in vain."

Saint Bernard was emotional and to a certain degree mystical, like Adam de Saint-Victor, whose hymns were equally famous, but the emotional saints and mystical poets were not by any means allowed to establish exclusive rights to the Virgin's favour. Abélard was as devoted as they were, and wrote hymns as well. Philosophy claimed her, and Albert the Great, the head of scholasticism, the teacher of Thomas Aquinas, decided in her favour the question: "Whether the Blessed Virgin possessed perfectly the seven liberal arts." The Church at Chartres had decided it a hundred years before by putting the seven liberal arts next her throne, with Aristotle himself to witness; but Albertus[11] gave the reason: "I hold that she did, for it is written, 'Wisdom has built herself a house, and has sculptured seven columns.' That house is the blessed Virgin; the seven columns are the seven liberal arts. Mary, therefore, had perfect mastery of science." Naturally she had also perfect mastery of economics, and most of her great churches were built in economic centres. The guilds were, if possible, more devoted to her than the monks; the bourgeoisie of Paris, Rouen, Amiens, Laon, spent money by millions to gain her favour. Most surprising of all, the great military class was perhaps the most vociferous. Of all inappropriate haunts for the gentle, courteous, pitying Mary, a field of

---

[7]Bartolomé Murillo (1617–1682), a Spanish painter of religious subjects.
[8]"Hail, Star of the Sea."
[9]"Show thou art the Mother."
[10]Dante Alighieri (1265–1321), Italian poet who wrote about Paradise in *The Divine Comedy*.

[11]Adams uses these early spokesmen of religion and philosophy to demonstrate widespread interest in the Virgin.

battle seems to be the worst, if not distinctly blasphemous; yet the greatest French warriors insisted on her leading them into battle, and in the actual mêlée when men were killing each other, on every battlefield in Europe, for at least five hundred years, Mary was present, leading both sides. The battle-cry of the famous Constable du Guesclin was "Notre-Dame-Guesclin"; "Notre-Dame-Coucy" was the cry of the great Sires de Coucy; "Notre-Dame-Auxerre"; "Notre-Dame-Sancerre"; "Notre-Dame-Hainault"; "Notre-Dame-Gueldres"; "Notre-Dame-Bourbon"; "Notre-Dame-Bearn";—all well-known battle-cries. The King's own battle at one time cried, "Notre-Dame-Saint-Denis-Montjoie"; the Dukes of Burgundy cried, "Notre-Dame-Bourgogne"; and even the soldiers of the Pope were said to cry, "Notre-Dame-Saint-Pierre."

The measure of this devotion, which proves to any religious American mind, beyond possible cavil, its serious and practical reality, is the money it cost. According to statistics, in the single century between 1170 and 1270, the French built eighty cathedrals and nearly five hundred churches of the cathedral class, which would have cost, according to an estimate made in 1840, more than five thousand millions to replace. Five thousand million francs is a thousand million dollars, and this covered only the great churches of a single century. The same scale of expenditure had been going on since the year 1000, and almost every parish in France had rebuilt its church in stone; to this day France is strewn with the ruins of this architecture, and yet the still preserved churches of the eleventh and twelfth centuries, among the churches that belong to the Romanesque and Transition period, are numbered by hundreds until they reach well into the thousands. The share of this capital which was—if one may use a commercial figure—invested in the Virgin cannot be fixed, any more than the total sum given to religious objects between 1000 and 1300; but in a spiritual and artistic sense, it was almost the whole, and expressed an intensity of conviction never again reached by any passion, whether of religion, of loyalty, of patriotism, or of wealth; perhaps never even paralleled by any single economic effort, except in war. Nearly every great church of the twelfth and thirteenth centuries belonged to Mary, until in France one asks for the church of Notre Dame as though it meant cathedral; but, not satisfied with this, she contracted the habit of requiring in all churches a chapel of her own, called in English the "Lady Chapel," which was apt to be as large as the church but was always meant to be handsomer; and there, behind the high altar, in her own private apartment, Mary sat, receiving her innumerable suppliants, and ready at any moment to step up upon the high altar itself to support the tottering authority of the local saint.

Expenditure like this rests invariably on an economic idea. Just as the French of the nineteenth century invested their surplus capital in a railway system in the belief that they would make money by it in this life, in the thirteenth they trusted their money to the Queen of Heaven because of their belief in her power to repay it with interest in the life to come. The investment was based on the power of Mary as Queen rather than on any orthodox Church conception of the Virgin's legitimate station. Papal Rome never greatly loved Byzantine empresses or French queens. The Virgin of Chartres was never wholly sympathetic to the Roman Curia.[12] To this day the Church writers—like the Abbé Bulteau or M. Rohault de Fleury—are singularly shy of the true Virgin of majesty, whether at Chartres or at Byzantium or wherever she is seen. The fathers Martin and Cahier at Bourges alone left her true value. Had the Church controlled her, the Virgin would perhaps have remained prostrate at the foot of the Cross. Dragged by a Byzantine Court, backed by popular insistence and impelled by overpowering self-interest, the Church accepted the Virgin throned and crowned, seated by Christ, the Judge throned and crowned; but even this did not wholly satisfy the French of the thirteenth century who seemed bent on absorbing Christ in His Mother, and making the Mother the Church, and Christ the Symbol.

The Church had crowned and enthroned her almost from the beginning, and could not have dethroned her if it would. In all Christian art—sculpture or mosaic, painting or poetry—the Virgin's rank was expressly asserted. Saint Bernard, like John Comnenus, and probably at the same time (1120–40), chanted hymns to the Virgin as Queen:—

O Salutaris Virgo Stella Maris	O saviour Virgin, Star of Sea,
Generans prolem, Æquitatis solem,	Who bore for child the Son of Justice,
Lucis auctorem, Retinens pudorem,	The source of Light, Virgin always
Suscipe laudem!	Hear our praise!
Celi Regina Per quam medicina	Queen of Heaven who have given
Datur aegrotis, Gratia devotis,	Medicine to the sick, Grace to the devout,
Gaudium molstis, Mundo lux coelestis,	Joy to the sad, Heaven's light to the world
Spesque salutis;	And hope of salvation;
Aula regalis, Virgo specialis,	Court royal, Virgin typical,
Posce medelam Nobis et tutelam,	Grant us cure and guard,
Suscipe vota, Precibusque cuncta	Accept our vows, and by prayers
Pelle molesta!	Drive all griefs away!

As the lyrical poet of the twelfth century, Adam de Saint-Victor seems to have held rank higher if possible than that of Saint Bernard, and his hymns on the Virgin are certainly quite as emphatic an assertion of her majesty:—

Imperatrix supernorum!	Empress of the highest,
Superatrix infernorum!	Mistress over the lowest,
Eligenda via coeli,	Chosen path of Heaven,
Retinenda spe fideli,	Held fast by faithful hope,
Separatos a te longe	Those separated from you far,
Revocatos ad te junge	Recalled to you, unite
Tuorum collegio!	In your fold!

[12]The administrative organization of the Catholic Church.

To delight in the childish jingle of the mediaeval Latin is a sign of a futile mind, no doubt, and I beg pardon of you and of the Church for wasting your precious summer day on poetry which was regarded as mystical in its age and which now sounds like a nursery rhyme; but a verse or two of Adam's hymn on the Assumption of the Virgin completes the record of her rank, and goes to complete also the documentary proof of her majesty at Chartres:—

Salve, Mater Salvatoris!	Mother of our Saviour, hail!
Vas electum! Vas honoris!	Chosen vessel! Sacred Grail!
Vas coelestis Gratiæ!	Font of celestial grace!
Ab æterno Vas provisum!	From eternity forethought!
Vas insigne! Vas excisum	By the hand of Wisdom wrought!
Manu sapientiæ!	Precious, faultless Vase!
Salve, Mater pietatis,	Hail, Mother of Divinity!
Et totius Trinitatis	Hail, Temple of the Trinity!
Nobile Triclinium!	Home of the Triune God!
Verbi tamen incarnati	In whom the Incarnate Word hath birth,
Speciale majestati	The King! to whom you gave on earth
Præparans hospitium!	Imperial abode.
O Maria! Stella maris!	Oh, Maria! Constellation!
Dignitate singularis,	Inspiration! Elevation!
Super omnes ordinaris	Rule and Law and Ordination
Ordines coelestium!	Of the angels' host!
In supremo sita poli	Highest height of God's Creation,
Nos commenda tuæ proli,	Pray your Son's commiseration,
Ne terrores sive doli	Lest, by fear or fraud, salvation
Nos supplantent hostium!	For our souls be lost!

Constantly—one might better say at once, officially, she was addressed in these terms of supreme majesty: "Imperatrix supernorum!" "Cœli Regina!" "Aula regalis!"[13] but the twelfth century seemed determined to carry the idea out to its logical conclusion in defiance of dogma. Not only was the Son absorbed in the Mother, or represented as under her guardianship, but the Father fared no better, and the Holy Ghost followed. The poets regarded the Virgin as the "Templum Trinitatis"; "totius Trinitatis nobile Triclinium." She was the refectory of the Trinity—the "Triclinium"—because the refectory was the largest room and contained the whole of the members, and was divided in three parts by two rows of columns. She was the "Templum Trinitatis," the Church itself, with its triple aisle. The Trinity was absorbed in her.

---

[13]"Empress of the highest," "Queen of Heaven," "Regal Power."

This is a delicate subject in the Church, and you must feel it with delicacy, without brutally insisting on its necessary contradictions. All theology and all philosophy are full of contradictions quite as flagrant and far less sympathetic. This particular variety of religious faith is simply human, and has made its appearance in one form or another in nearly all religions; but though the twelfth century carried it to an extreme, and at Chartres you see it in its most charming expression, we have got always to make allowances for what was going on beneath the surface in men's minds, consciously or unconsciously, and for the latent scepticism which lurks behind all faith. The Church itself never quite accepted the full claims of what was called Mariolatry. One may be sure, too, that the bourgeois capitalist and the student of the schools, each from his own point of view, watched the Virgin with anxious interest. The bourgeois had put an enormous share of his capital into what was in fact an economical speculation, not unlike the South Sea Scheme,[14] or the railway system of our own time; except that in one case the energy was devoted to shortening the road to Heaven; in the other, to shortening the road to Paris; but no serious schoolman could have felt entirely convinced that God would enter into a business partnership with man, to establish a sort of joint-stock society for altering the operation of divine and universal laws. The bourgeois cared little for the philosophical doubt if the economical result proved to be good, but he watched this result with his usual practical sagacity, and required an experience of only about three generations (1200–1300) to satisfy himself that relics were not certain in their effects; that the Saints were not always able or willing to help; that Mary herself could not certainly be bought or bribed; that prayer without money seemed to be quite as efficacious as prayer with money; and that neither the road to Heaven nor Heaven itself had been made surer or brought nearer by an investment of capital which amounted to the best part of the wealth of France. Economically speaking, he became satisfied that his enormous money-investment had proved to be an almost total loss, and the reaction on his mind was as violent as the emotion. For three hundred years it prostrated France. The efforts of the bourgeoisie and the peasantry to recover their property, so far as it was recoverable, have lasted to the present day and we had best take care not to get mixed in those passions.

If you are to get the full enjoyment of Chartres, you must, for the time, believe in Mary as Bernard and Adam did, and feel her presence as the architects did, in every stone they placed, and every touch they chiselled. You must try first to rid your mind of the traditional idea that the Gothic is an intentional expression of religious gloom. The necessity for light was the motive of the Gothic architects. They needed light and always more light, until they sacrificed safety and common sense in trying to get it. They converted their walls into windows, raised their vaults, diminished their piers,

---

[14]Between 1711 and 1720 a giant financial speculation involving South Sea trade dominated London gossip. Investments experienced the extremes of boom and bust during this period.

until their churches could no longer stand. You will see the limits at Beauvais; at Chartres we have not got so far, but even here, in places where the Virgin wanted it,—as above the high altar,—the architect has taken all the light there was to take. For the same reason, fenestration[15] became the most important part of the Gothic architect's work, and at Chartres was uncommonly interesting because the architect was obliged to design a new system, which should at the same time satisfy the laws of construction and the taste and imagination of Mary. No doubt the first command of the Queen of Heaven was for light, but the second, at least equally imperative, was for colour. Any earthly queen, even though she were not Byzantine in taste, loved colour; and the truest of queens—the only true Queen of Queens—had richer and finer taste in colour than the queens of fifty earthly kingdoms, as you will see when we come to the immense effort to gratify her in the glass of her windows. Illusion for illusion,—granting for the moment that Mary was an illusion,—the Virgin Mother in this instance repaid to her worshippers a larger return for their money than the capitalist has ever been able to get, at least in this world, from any other illusion of wealth which he has tried to make a source of pleasure and profit.

The next point on which Mary evidently insisted was the arrangement for her private apartments, the apse, as distinguished from her throne-room, the choir; both being quite distinct from the hall, or reception-room of the public, which was the nave with its enlargements in the transepts. This arrangement marks the distinction between churches built as shrines for the deity and churches built as halls of worship for the public. The difference is chiefly in the apse, and the apse of Chartres is the most interesting of all apses from this point of view.

The Virgin required chiefly these three things, or, if you like, these four: space, light, convenience, and colour decoration to unite and harmonize the whole. This concerns the interior; on the exterior she required statuary, and the only complete system of decorative sculpture that existed seems to belong to her churches:—Paris, Rheims, Amiens, and Chartres. Mary required all this magnificence at Chartres for herself alone, not for the public. As far as one can see into the spirit of the builders, Chartres was exclusively intended for the Virgin, as the Temple of Abydos[16] was intended for Osiris. The wants of man, beyond a mere roof-cover, and perhaps space to some degree, enter to no very great extent into the problem of Chartres. Man came to render homage or to ask favours. The Queen received him in her palace, where she alone was at home, and alone gave commands.

The artist's second thought was to exclude from his work everything that could displease Mary; and since Mary differed from living queens only in infinitely greater majesty and refinement, the artist could admit only what pleased the actual taste of the great ladies who dictated taste at the Courts of France and England, which surrounded the little Court of the

---

[15]The placement of windows and doors in a structure.   [16]An ancient Egyptian city near the Nile River.

Counts of Chartres. What they were—these women of the twelfth and thirteenth centuries—we shall have to see or seek in other directions; but Chartres is perhaps the most magnificent and permanent monument they left of their taste, and we can begin here with learning certain things which they were not.

In the first place, they were not in the least vague, dreamy, or mystical in a modern sense;—far from it! They seemed anxious only to throw the mysteries into a blaze of light; not so much physical, perhaps,—since they, like all women, liked moderate shadow for their toilettes,—but luminous in the sense of faith. There is nothing about Chartres that you would think mystical, who know your Lohengrin, Siegfried, and Parsifal.[17] If you care to make a study of the whole literature of the subject, read M. Mâle's "Art Religieux du XIIIe Siècle en France," and use it for a guide-book. Here you need only note how symbolic and how simple the sculpture is, on the portals and porches. Even what seems a grotesque or an abstract idea is no more than the simplest child's personification. On the walls you may have noticed the *Ane qui vielle*,—the ass playing the lyre; and on all the old churches you can see "bestiaries," as they were called, of fabulous animals, symbolic or not; but the symbolism is as simple as the realism of the oxen at Laon. It gave play to the artist in his effort for variety of decoration, and it amused the people,—probably the Virgin also was not above being amused;—now and then it seems about to suggest what you would call an esoteric meaning, that is to say, a meaning which each one of us can consider private property reserved for our own amusement, and from which the public is excluded; yet, in truth, in the Virgin's churches the public is never excluded, but invited. The Virgin even had the additional charm of the public that she was popularly supposed to have no very marked fancy for priests as such; she was a queen, a woman, and a mother, functions, all, which priests could not perform. Accordingly, she seems to have had little taste for mysteries of any sort, and even the symbols that seem most mysterious were clear to every old peasant-woman in her church. The most pleasing and promising of them all is the woman's figure you saw on the front of the cathedral in Paris; her eyes bandaged; her head bent down; her crown falling; without cloak or royal robe; holding in her hand a guidon or banner with its staff broken in more than one place. On the opposite pier stands another woman, with royal mantle, erect and commanding. The symbol is so graceful that one is quite eager to know its meaning; but every child in the Middle Ages would have instantly told you that the woman with the falling crown meant only the Jewish Synagogue, as the one with the royal robe meant the Church of Christ.

Another matter for which the female taste seemed not much to care was theology in the metaphysical sense. Mary troubled herself little about theology except when she retired into the south transept with Pierre de Dreux.[18]

---

[17]Three legendary heroes, the subjects of operas by the German composer Richard Wagner.

[18]A Duke of Brittany who built the south porch of Chartres.

Even there one finds little said about the Trinity, always the most meta-physical subtlety of the Church. Indeed, you might find much amusement here in searching the cathedral for any distinct expression at all of the Trinity as a dogma recognized by Mary. One cannot take seriously the idea that the three doors, the three portals, and the three aisles express the Trinity, because, in the first place, there was no rule about it; churches might have what portals and aisles they pleased; both Paris and Bourges have five; the doors themselves are not allotted to the three members of the Trinity, nor are the portals; while another more serious objection is that the side doors and aisles are not of equal importance with the central, but mere adjuncts and dependencies, so that the architect who had misled the ignorant public in accepting so black a heresy would have deserved the stake, and would probably have gone to it. Even this suggestion of Trinity is wanting in the transepts, which have only one aisle, and in the choir, which has five, as well as five or seven chapels, and, as far as an ignorant mind can penetrate, no triplets whatever. Occasionally, no doubt, you will discover in some sculpture or window, a symbol of the Trinity, but this discovery itself amounts to an admission of its absence as a controlling idea, for the ordinary worshipper must have been at least as blind as we are, and to him, as to us, it would have seemed a wholly subordinate detail. Even if the Trinity, too, is anywhere expressed, you will hardly find here an attempt to explain its meta-physical meaning—not even a mystic triangle.

The church is wholly given up to the Mother and the Son. The Father seldom appears; the Holy Ghost still more rarely. At least, this is the impression made on an ordinary visitor who has no motive to be orthodox; and it must have been the same with the thirteenth-century worshipper who came here with his mind absorbed in the perfections of Mary. Chartres represents, not the Trinity, but the identity of the Mother and Son. The Son represents the Trinity, which is thus absorbed in the Mother. The idea is not orthodox, but this is no affair of ours. The Church watches over its own.

The Virgin's wants and tastes, positive and negative, ought now to be clear enough to enable you to feel the artist's sincerity in trying to satisfy them; but first you have still to convince yourselves of the people's sincerity in employing the artists. This point is the easiest of all, for the evidence is express. In the year 1145 when the old flèche was begun,—the year before Saint Bernard preached the second crusade at Vézelay,—Abbot Haimon, of Saint-Pierre-sur-Dives in Normandy, wrote to the monks of Tutbury Abbey in England a famous letter to tell of the great work which the Virgin was doing in France and which began at the Church of Chartres. "Hujus sacræ institutionis ritus apud Carnotensem, ecclesiam est inchoatus."[19] From Chartres it had spread through Normandy, where it produced among other things the beautiful spire which we saw at Saint-Pierre-sur-Dives. "Postremo per totam fere Normanniam longe lateque convaluit ac loca per singula

---

[19]"This holy institutional work was begun at the church of Chartres."

Matri misericordiæ dicata præcipue occupavit."[20] The movement affected especially the places devoted to Mary, but ran through all Normandy, far and wide. Of all Mary's miracles, the best attested, next to the preservation of her church, is the building of it; not so much because it surprises us as because it surprised even more the people of the time and the men who were its instruments. Such deep popular movements are always surprising, and at Chartres the miracle seems to have occurred three times, coinciding more or less with the dates of the crusades, and taking the organization of a crusade, as Archbishop Hugo of Rouen described it in a letter to Bishop Thierry of Amiens. The most interesting part of this letter is the evident astonishment of the writer, who might be talking to us to-day, so modern is he:—

> The inhabitants of Chartres have combined to aid in the construction of their church by transporting the materials; our Lord has rewarded their humble zeal by miracles which have roused the Normans to imitate the piety of their neighbours.... Since then the faithful of our diocese and of other neighbouring regions have formed associations for the same object; they admit no one into their company unless he has been to confession, has renounced enmities and revenges, and has reconciled himself with his enemies. That done, they elect a chief, under whose direction they conduct their waggons in silence and with humility.

The quarries at Berchères-l'Evêque are about five miles from Chartres. The stone is excessively hard, and was cut in blocks of considerable size, as you can see for yourselves; blocks which required great effort to transport and lay in place. The work was done with feverish rapidity, as it still shows, but it is the solidist building of the age, and without a sign of weakness yet. The Abbot told, with more surprise than pride, of the spirit which was built into the cathedral with the stone:—

> Who has ever seen!—Who has ever heard tell, in times past, that powerful princes of the world, that men brought up in honour and in wealth, that nobles, men and women, have bent their proud and haughty necks to the harness of carts, and that, like beasts of burden, they have dragged to the abode of Christ these waggons, loaded with wines, grains, oil, stone, wood, and all that is necessary for the wants of life, or for the construction of the church? But while they draw these burdens, there is one thing admirable to observe; it is that often when a thousand persons and more are attached to the chariots,—so great is the difficulty,—yet they march in such silence that not a murmur is heard, and truly if one did not see the thing with one's eyes, one might believe that among such a multitude there was hardly a person present. When they halt on the road, nothing is heard but the confession of sins, and pure and suppliant prayer to God to obtain pardon. At the voice of the priests who exhort their hearts to peace, they forget all hatred, discord is thrown far aside, debts are remitted, the unity of hearts is established. But

---

[20]"Finally it became established far and wide through almost all Normandy, and especially it took hold in certain places dedicated to the Mother of Mercy."

if any one is so far advanced in evil as to be unwilling to pardon an offender, or if he rejects the counsel of the priest who has piously advised him, his offering is instantly thrown from the wagon as impure, and he himself ignominiously and shamefully excluded from the society of the holy. There one sees the priests who preside over each chariot exhort every one to penitence, to confession of faults, to the resolution of better life! There one sees old people, young people, little children, calling on the Lord with a suppliant voice, and uttering to Him, from the depth of the heart, sobs and sighs with words of glory and praise! After the people, warned by the sound of trumpets and the sight of banners, have resumed their road, the march is made with such ease that no obstacle can retard it.... When they have reached the church they arrange the wagons about it like a spiritual camp, and during the whole night they celebrate the watch by hymns and canticles. On each waggon they light tapers and lamps; they place there the infirm and sick, and bring them the precious relics of the Saints for their relief. Afterwards the priests and clerics close the ceremony by processions which the people follow with devout heart, imploring the clemency of the Lord and of his Blessed Mother for the recovery of the sick.

Of course, the Virgin was actually and constantly present during all this labour, and gave her assistance to it, about you would get no light on the architecture from listening to an account of her miracles, nor do they heighten the effect of popular faith. Without the conviction of her personal presence, men would not have been inspired; but, to us, it is rather the inspiration of the art which proves the Virgin's presence, and we can better see the conviction of it in the work than in the words. Every day, as the work went on, the Virgin was present, directing the architects, and it is this direction that we are going to study, if you have now got a realizing sense of what it meant. Without this sense, the church is dead. Most persons of a deeply religious nature would tell you emphatically that nine churches out of ten actually were dead-born, after the thirteenth century, and that church architecture became a pure matter of mechanism and mathematics; but that is a question for you to decide when you come to it; and the pleasure consists not in seeing the death, but in feeling the life.

Now let us look about!

1904

from **The Education of Henry Adams**

Chapter XXV. The Dynamo and the Virgin

[In *The Education of Henry Adams* the author organizes a perceptive commentary on his own times around the facts of his autobiography. Unlike many other autobiographers, however, Adams always resists frank revelation; he does not bare his soul to the reader. His individual experience, distanced through his use of the third person, becomes a sample used to measure the results of human evolution, as Adams compares and

contrasts his own life and time with the distant past. That connection
between present and past becomes explicit in the very title of Chapter XXV
of the *Education*, where both the dynamo and the Virgin share the
representative value of force or energy sufficient to get work done in the
world. By placing them side by side Adams suggests that the religious faith
of the medieval past has been replaced by the forces of modern science and
industry, as seen in the electrical power that the dynamo can generate.]

Until the Great Exposition of 1900 closed its doors in November, Adams
haunted it, aching to absorb knowledge, and helpless to find it.[1] He would
have liked to know how much of it could have been grasped by the best-
informed man in the world. While he was thus meditating chaos, Langley
came by, and showed it to him. At Langley's[2] behest, the Exhibition dropped
its superfluous rags and stripped itself to the skin, for Langley knew what to
study, and why, and how; while Adams might as well have stood outside in
the night, staring at the Milky Way. Yet Langley said nothing new, and
taught nothing that one might not have learned from Lord Bacon, three
hundred years before; but though one should have known the "Advancement
of Science"[3] as well as one knew the "Comedy of Errors,"[4] the literary knowledge counted for nothing until some teacher should show how to apply it.
Bacon took a vast deal of trouble in teaching King James I and his subjects,
American or other, towards the year 1620, that true science was the development or economy of forces; yet an elderly American in 1900 knew neither
the formula nor the forces; or even so much as to say to himself that his historical business in the Exposition concerned only the economies of developments of force since 1893, when he began the study at Chicago.[5]

Nothing in education is so astonishing as the amount of ignorance it
accumulates in the form of inert facts. Adams had looked at most of the
accumulations of art in the storehouses called Art Museums; yet he did not
know how to look at the art exhibits of 1900. He had studied Karl Marx and
his doctrines of history with profound attention, yet he could not apply
them at Paris. Langley, with the ease of a great master of experiment, threw
out of the field every exhibit that did not reveal a new application of force,
and naturally threw out, to begin with, almost the whole art exhibit.
Equally, he ignored almost the whole industrial exhibit. He led his pupil
directly to the forces. His chief interest was in new motors to make his air-
ship feasible, and he taught Adams the astonishing complexities of the new
Daimler motor, and of the automobile, which, since 1893, had become a
nightmare at a hundred kilometres an hour, almost as destructive as the
electric tram which was only ten years older; and threatening to become as
terrible as the locomotive steam-engine itself, which was almost exactly
Adams's own age.

---

[1]The Paris Exposition opened on April 15, 1900, and lasted for seven months.

[2]Samuel Pierpont Langley (1834–1906), as-
tronomer and pioneer in aerodynamical
experiments. A friend and mentor to Adams.

[3]Adams may have mistaken the title of Francis
Bacon's *The Advancement of Learning* (1605).

[4]A play by Shakespeare.

[5]The World's Columbian Exposition held at
Chicago in 1893.

Then he showed his scholar the great hall of dynamos, and explained how little he knew about electricity or force of any kind, even of his own special sun, which spouted heat in inconceivable volume, but which, as far as he knew, might spout less or more, at any time, for all the certainty he felt in it. To him, the dynamo itself was but an ingenious channel for conveying somewhere the heat latent in a few tons of poor coal hidden in a dirty engine-house carefully kept out of sight; but to Adams the dynamo became a symbol of infinity. As he grew accustomed to the great gallery of machines, he began to feel the forty-foot dynamos as a moral force, much as the early Christians felt the Cross. The planet itself seemed less impressive, in its old-fashioned, deliberate, annual or daily revolution, than this huge wheel, revolving within arm's-length at some vertiginous speed, and barely murmuring—scarcely humming an audible warning to stand a hair's-breadth further for respect of power—while it would not wake the baby lying close against its frame. Before the end, one began to pray to it; inherited instinct taught the natural expression of man before silent and infinite force. Among the thousand symbols of ultimate energy, the dynamo was not so human as some, but it was the most expressive.

Yet the dynamo, next to the steam-engine, was the most familiar of exhibits. For Adams's objects its value lay chiefly in its occult mechanism. Between the dynamo in the gallery of machines and the engine-house outside, the break of continuity amounted to abysmal fracture for a historian's objects. No more relation could he discover between the steam and the electric current than between the Cross and the cathedral. The forces were interchangeable if not reversible, but he could see only an absolute *fiat* in electricity as in faith. Langley could not help him. Indeed, Langley seemed to be worried by the same trouble, for he constantly repeated that the new forces were anarchical, and especially that he was not responsible for the new rays, that were little short of parricidal in their wicked spirit towards science. His own rays, with which he had doubled the solar spectrum, were altogether harmless and beneficent; but Radium denied its God—or, what was to Langley the same thing, denied the truths of his Science. The force was wholly new.

A historian who asked only to learn enough to be as futile as Langley or Kelvin,[6] made rapid progress under this teaching, and mixed himself up in the tangle of ideas until he achieved a sort of Paradise of ignorance vastly consoling to his fatigued senses. He wrapped himself in vibrations and rays which were new, and he would have hugged Marconi and Branly[7] had he met them, as he hugged the dynamo; while he lost his arithmetic in trying to figure out the equation between the discoveries and the economies of force. The economies, like the discoveries, were absolute, super-sensual, occult; incapable of expression in horse-power. What mathematical equivalent could

[6]Lord Kelvin (1824–1907), famous British scientist.
[7]Guglielmo Marconi (1834–1937) and Edouard Branly (1846–1940) played important roles in the development of radio and the understanding of sound waves.

he suggest as the value of a Branly coherer? Frozen air, or the electric furnace, had some scale of measurement, no doubt, if somebody could invent a thermometer adequate to the purpose; but X-rays had played no part whatever in man's consciousness, and the atom itself had figured only as a fiction of thought. In these seven years man had translated himself into a new universe which had no common scale of measurement with the old. He had entered a supersensual world, in which he could measure nothing except by chance collisions of movements imperceptible to his senses, perhaps even imperceptible to his instruments, but perceptible to each other, and so to some known ray at the end of the scale. Langley seemed prepared for anything, even for an indeterminable number of universes interfused—physics stark mad in metaphysics.

Historians undertake to arrange sequences,—called stories, or histories—assuming in silence a relation of cause and effect. These assumptions, hidden in the depths of dusty libraries, have been astounding, but commonly unconscious and childlike; so much so, that if any captious critic were to drag them to light, historians would probably reply, with one voice, that they had never supposed themselves required to know what they were talking about. Adams, for one, had toiled in vain to find out what he meant. He had even published a dozen volumes of American history for no other purpose than to satisfy himself whether, by the severest process of stating, with the least possible comment, such facts as seemed sure, in such order as seemed rigorously consequent, he could fix for a familiar moment a necessary sequence of human movement. The result had satisfied him as little as at Harvard College. Where he saw sequence, other men saw something quite different, and no one saw the same unit of measure. He cared little about his experiments and less about his statesmen, who seemed to him quite as ignorant as himself and, as a rule, no more honest; but he insisted on a relation of sequence, and if he could not reach it by one method, he would try as many methods as science knew. Satisfied that the sequence of men led to nothing and that the sequence of their society could lead no further, while the mere sequence of time was artificial, and the sequence of thought was chaos, he turned at last to the sequence of force; and thus it happened that, after ten years' pursuit, he found himself lying in the Gallery of Machines at the Great Exposition of 1900, his historical neck broken by the sudden irruption of forces totally new.

Since no one else showed much concern, an elderly person without other cares had no need to betray alarm. The year 1900 was not the first to upset schoolmasters. Copernicus and Galileo[8] had broken many professional necks about 1600; Columbus had stood the world on its head towards 1500; but the nearest approach to the revolution of 1900 was that of 310, when Constantine set up the Cross.[9] The rays that Langley disowned, as well as those which he fathered, were occult, supersensual, irrational; they were a revelation of

---

[8]Copernicus (1473–1543) and Galileo (1564–1642), astronomers who helped to establish belief in the sun, rather than the earth, as the center of the universe.

[9]Adams treats 310 as the beginning of Christianity in the Roman Empire under Constantine I.

mysterious energy like that of the Cross; they were what, in terms of mediae-val science, were called immediate modes of the divine substance.

The historian was thus reduced to his last resources. Clearly if he was bound to reduce all these forces to a common value, this common value could have no measure but that of their attraction on his own mind. He must treat them as they had been felt; as convertible, reversible, inter-changeable attractions on thought. He made up his mind to venture it; he would risk translating rays into faith. Such a reversible process would vastly amuse a chemist, but the chemist could not deny that he, or some of his fel-low physicists, could feel the force of both. When Adams was a boy in Bos-ton, the best chemist in the place had probably never heard of Venus except by way of scandal, or of the Virgin except as idolatry; neither had he heard of dynamos or automobiles or radium; yet his mind was ready to feel the force of all, though the rays were unborn and the women were dead.

Here opened another totally new education, which promised to be by far the most hazardous of all. The knife-edge along which he must crawl, like Sir Lancelot[10] in the twelfth century, divided two kingdoms of force which had nothing in common but attraction. They were as different as a magnet is from gravitation, supposing one knew what a magnet was, or gravitation, or love. The force of the Virgin was still felt at Lourdes, and seemed to be as potent as X-rays; but in America neither Venus nor Virgin ever had value as force—at most as sentiment. No American had ever been truly afraid of either.

This problem in dynamics gravely perplexed an American historian. The Woman had once been supreme; in France she still seemed potent, not merely as a sentiment, but as a force. Why was she unknown in America? For evidently America was ashamed of her, and she was ashamed of herself, otherwise they would not have strewn fig-leaves so profusely all over her. When she was a true force, she was ignorant of fig-leaves, but the monthly-magazine-made American female had not a feature that would have been recognized by Adam.[11] The trait was notorious, and often humorous, but any one brought up among Puritans knew that sex was sin. In any previous age, sex was strength. Neither art nor beauty was needed. Every one, even among Puritans, knew that neither Diana of the Ephesians[12] nor any of the Oriental goddesses was worshipped for her beauty. She was goddess because of her force; she was the animated dynamo; she was reproduction—the greatest and most mysterious of all energies; all she needed was to be fe-cund. Singularly enough, not one of Adams's many schools of education had ever drawn his attention to the opening lines of Lucretius, though they were perhaps the finest in all Latin literature, where the poet invoked Venus exactly as Dante invoked the Virgin:—

Quae quoniam rerum naturam *sola* gubernas."[13]

[10]A legendary hero of chivalric tales.
[11]In "Genesis," after the Fall, Eve and Adam cov-ered their genitals with fig leaves, as a sign of shame. Popular ("monthly-magazine") litera-ture especially avoided dealing with sexuality.

[12]Goddess of the moon and of the hunt.
[13]From *De Rerum Natura*, "Since you [Venus] alone govern the nature of things."

The Venus of Epicurean philosophy survived in the Virgin of the Schools:—

> Donna, sei tanto grande, e tanto vali,
> Che qual vuol grazia, e a te non ricorre,
> Sua disianza vuol volar senz' ali."[14]

All this was to American thought as though it had never existed. The true American knew something of the facts, but nothing of the feelings; he read the letter, but he never felt the law. Before this historical chasm, a mind like that of Adams felt itself helpless; he turned from the Virgin to the Dynamo as though he were a Branly coherer. On one side, at the Louvre and at Chartres, as he knew by the record of work actually done and still before his eyes, was the highest energy ever known to man, the creator of four-fifths of his noblest art, exercising vastly more attraction over the human mind than all the steam-engines and dynamos ever dreamed of; and yet this energy was unknown to the American mind. An American Virgin would never dare command; an American Venus would never dare exist.

The question, which to any plain American of the nineteenth century seemed as remote as it did to Adams, drew him almost violently to study, once it was posed; and on this point Langleys were as useless as though they were Herbert Spencers[15] or dynamos. The idea survived only as art. There one turned as naturally as though the artist were himself a woman. Adams began to ponder, asking himself whether he knew of any American artist who had ever insisted on the power of sex, as every classic had always done; but he could think only of Walt Whitman; Bret Harte, as far as the magazines would let him venture; and one or two painters, for the fleshtones. All the rest had used sex for sentiment, never for force; to them, Eve was a tender flower, and Herodias[16] an un-feminine horror. American art, like the American language and American education, was as far as possible sexless. Society regarded this victory over sex as its greatest triumph, and the historian readily admitted it, since the moral issue, for the moment, did not concern one who was studying the relations of unmoral force. He cared nothing for the sex of the dynamo until he could measure its energy.

Vaguely seeking a clue, he wandered through the art exhibit, and, in his stroll, stopped almost every day before St. Gaudens's General Sherman,[17] which had been given the central post of honor. St. Gaudens himself was in Paris, putting on the work his usual interminable last touches, and listening to the usual contradictory suggestions of brother sculptors. Of all the American artists who gave to American art whatever life it breathed in the

---

[14]From Dante, *Divine Comedy* ("Paradiso"), "Lady [Virgin Mary], thou art so great and hast such worth, that if there be one who would have grace yet who has not betaken himself to thee, his longing seeketh to fly without wings."

[15]Herbert Spencer (1820–1903), popularizer of Darwinism in England and America.

[16]King Herod's wife, who ordered that John the Baptist be slain.

[17]A statue by Augustus Saint-Gaudens (1848–1907), now located in Central Park, New York City. It was then in Paris.

seventies, St. Gaudens was perhaps the most sympathetic, but certainly the most inarticulate. General Grant or Don Cameron[18] had scarcely less instinct of rhetoric than he. All the others—the Hunts, Richardson, John La Farge, Stanford White—were exuberant; only St. Gaudens could never discuss or dilate on an emotion, or suggest artistic arguments for giving to his work the forms that he felt. He never laid down the law, or affected the despot, or became brutalized like Whistler by the brutalities of his world. He required no incense; he was no egoist; his simplicity of thought was excessive; he could not imitate, or give any form but his own to the creations of his hand. No one felt more strongly than he the strength of other men, but the idea that they could affect him never stirred an image in his mind.

This summer his health was poor and his spirits were low. For such a temper, Adams was not the best companion, since his own gaiety was not *folle*;[19] but he risked going now and then to the studio on Mont Parnasse to draw him out for a stroll in the Bois de Boulogne,[20] or dinner as pleased his moods, and in return St. Gaudens sometimes let Adams go about in his company.

Once St. Gaudens took him down to Amiens, with a party of Frenchmen, to see the cathedral. Not until they found themselves actually studying the sculpture of the western portal, did it dawn on Adams's mind that, for his purposes, St. Gaudens on that spot had more interest to him than the cathedral itself. Great men before great monuments express great truths, provided they are not taken too solemnly. Adams never tired of quoting the supreme phrase of his idol Gibbon, before the Gothic cathedrals: "I darted a contemptuous look on the stately monuments of superstition." Even in the footnotes of his history, Gibbon had never inserted a bit of humor more human than this, and one would have paid largely for a photograph of the fat little historian, on the background of Notre Dame of Amiens, trying to persuade his readers—perhaps himself—that he was darting a contemptuous look on the stately monument, for which he felt in fact the respect which every man of his vast study and active mind always feels before objects worthy of it; but besides the humor, one felt also the relation. Gibbon ignored the Virgin, because in 1789 religious monuments were out of fashion. In 1900 his remark sounded fresh and simple as the green fields to ears that had heard a hundred years of other remarks, mostly no more fresh and certainly less simple. Without malice, one might find it more instructive than a whole lecture of Ruskin. One sees what one brings, and at that moment Gibbon brought the French Revolution. Ruskin brought reaction against the Revolution. St. Gaudens had passed beyond all. He liked the stately monuments much more than he liked Gibbon or Ruskin;[21] he loved their dignity; their unity; their scale; their lines; their lights and shadows;

---

[18]James Donald Cameron (1833–1918), U.S. Senator and Secretary of War under President Grant.

[19]"Wild" or "mad."

[20]Mont Parnasse and the Bois de Boulogne are well-known sections of Paris.

[21]John Ruskin (1819–1900), English critic of art and architecture.

their decorative sculpture; but he was even less conscious than they of the force that created it all—the Virgin, the Woman—by whose genius "the stately monuments of superstition" were built, through which she was expressed. He would have seen more meaning in Isis[22] with the cow's horns, at Edfoo, who expressed the same thought. The art remained, but the energy was lost even upon the artist.

Yet in mind and person St. Gaudens was a survivor of the 1500s; he bore the stamp of the Renaissance, and should have carried an image of the Virgin round his neck, or stuck in his hat, like Louis XI. In mere time he was a lost soul that had strayed by chance into the twentieth century, and forgotten where it came from. He writhed and cursed at his ignorance, much as Adams did at his own, but in the opposite sense. St. Gaudens was a child of Benvenuto Cellini,[23] smothered in an American cradle. Adams was a quintessence of Boston, devoured by curiosity to think like Benvenuto. St. Gaudens's art was starved from birth, and Adams's instinct was blighted from babyhood. Each had but half of a nature, and when they came together before the Virgin of Amiens they ought both to have felt in her the force that made them one; but it was not so. To Adams she became more than ever a channel of force; to St. Gaudens she remained as before a channel of taste.

For a symbol of power, St. Gaudens instinctively preferred the horse, as was plain in his horse and Victory of the Sherman monument. Doubtless Sherman also felt it so. The attitude was so American that, for at least forty years, Adams had never realized that any other could be in sound taste. How many years had he taken to admit a notion of what Michael Angelo and Rubens were driving at? He could not say; but he knew that only since 1895 had he begun to feel the Virgin or Venus as force, and not everywhere even so. At Chartres—perhaps at Lourdes—possibly at Cnidos if one could still find there the divinely naked Aphrodite of Praxiteles[24]—but otherwise one must look for force to the goddesses of Indian mythology. The idea died out long ago in the German and English stock. St. Gaudens at Amiens was hardly less sensitive to the force of the female energy than Matthew Arnold at the Grande Chartreuse.[25] Neither of them felt goddesses as power—only as reflected emotion, human expression, beauty, purity, taste, scarcely even as sympathy. They felt a railway train as power; yet they, and all other artists, constantly complained that the power embodied in a railway train could never be embodied in art. All the steam in the world could not, like the Virgin, build Chartres.

Yet in mechanics, whatever the mechanicians might think, both energies acted as interchangeable forces on man, and by action on man all known force may be measured. Indeed, few men of science measured force in any other way. After once admitting that a straight line was the shortest

---

[22]Adams had seen a statue of the goddess Isis during a trip along the Nile River, at Edfu (or "Edfoo") in Egypt.

[23]Cellini (1500–1571) was an Italian artist who wrote a famous autobiography.

[24]A Greek sculptor (4th century B.C.) who created a famous statue of Venus (Aphrodite).

[25]Arnold (1822–1888) wrote "Stanzas from the Grande Chartreuse," an English poem about the loss of medieval religious faith.

distance between two points, no serious mathematician cared to deny anything that suited his convenience, and rejected no symbol, unproved or unproveable, that helped him to accomplish work. The symbol was force, as a compass-needle or a triangle was force, as the mechanist might prove by losing it, and nothing could be gained by ignoring their value. Symbol or energy, the Virgin had acted as the greatest force the Western world ever felt, and had drawn man's activities to herself more strongly than any other power, natural or supernatural, had ever done; the historian's business was to follow the track of the energy; to find where it came from and where it went to; its complex source and shifting channels; its values, equivalents, conversions. It could scarcely be more complex than radium; it could hardly be deflected, diverted, polarized, absorbed more perplexingly than other radiant matter. Adams knew nothing about any of them, but as a mathematical problem of influence on human progress, though all were occult, all reacted on his mind, and he rather inclined to think the Virgin easiest to handle.

The pursuit turned out to be long and tortuous, leading at last into the vast forests of scholastic science. From Zeno to Descartes, hand in hand with Thomas Aquinas, Montaigne, and Pascal, one stumbled as stupidly as though one were still a German student of 1860.[26] Only with the instinct of despair could one force one's self into this old thicket of ignorance after having been repulsed at a score of entrances more promising and more popular. Thus far, no path had led anywhere, unless perhaps to an exceedingly modest living. Forty-five years of study had proved to be quite futile for the pursuit of power; one controlled no more force in 1900 than in 1850, although the amount of force controlled by society had enormously increased. The secret of education still hid itself somewhere behind ignorance, and one fumbled over it as feebly as ever. In such labyrinths, the staff is a force almost more necessary than the legs; the pen becomes a sort of blind-man's dog, to keep him from falling into the gutters. The pen works for itself, and acts like a hand, modelling the plastic material over and over again to the form that suits it best. The form is never arbitrary, but is a sort of growth like crystallization, as any artist knows too well; for often the pencil or pen runs into side-paths and shapelessness, loses its relations, stops or is bogged. Then it has to return on its trail, and recover, if it can, its line of force. The result of a year's work depends more on what is struck out than on what is left in; on the sequence of the main lines of thought, than on their play or variety. Compelled once more to lean heavily on this support, Adams covered more thousands of pages with figures as formal as though they were algebra, laboriously striking out, altering, burning, experimenting, until the year had expired, the Exposition had long been closed, and winter drawing to its end, before he sailed from Cherbourg, on January 19, 1901, for home.

1907

[26]Adams refers to his study of Greek, medieval, and seventeenth- and eighteenth-century phi-losophers, and his studies in Germany, 1858–1860.

KATE CHOPIN
1851–1904

The Awakening's depiction of its upper-class white heroine's discovery of herself and her sexuality may seem tame by today's standards, but reviewers were shocked and offended at its publication in 1899. Chopin's exploration of female identity—especially the focus on the erotic and the maternal—put her in the midst of the turn-of-the-century debates about gender roles. At the same time, because of her stories' insistence that the erotic and the maternal are shaped by the specifics of region, race, ethnicity, and class, her work must also be contextualized within late-nineteenth-century debates about national identity.

The daughter of Thomas and Eliza (Faris) O'Flaherty, Chopin was raised in St. Louis in the context of her mother's extended French family. Her wealthy Roman Catholic slaveowning family had Kate educated at the Academy of the Sacred Heart, and in 1870, two years after graduating, she married Oscar Chopin, a French Creole businessman from Louisiana. During the next nine years, Chopin bore six children and fulfilled the heavy social obligations of the wife of a seemingly successful New Orleans cotton broker. However, in 1879 Oscar's business failed, and the family moved from New Orleans to Cloutierville, Nachitoches Parish, where Kate and Oscar operated a plantation and a store owned by his family. Oscar died in 1882, leaving Kate a thirty-two-year-old widow with six children and limited financial resources. In 1884 she moved her family back to St. Louis, where she lived for the rest of her life.

Chopin began writing in earnest in 1889 and within a decade had produced and published the bulk of her work, including twenty poems, ninety-five short stories, two novels, one play, and eight essays of literary criticism. She is best known for her fiction, which is wide-ranging but focuses particularly on tracing the complexities of Louisiana culture in the second half of the nineteenth century. From the publication of her first stories in 1889, Chopin was understood by critics as part of the regional fiction championed by William Dean Howells: like Alice Dunbar-Nelson, Grace King, Charles Chesnutt, and George Washington Cable, Chopin was read as chronicling the South. But like the stories of so many women regional writers (Sarah Orne Jewett, Mary Noailles Murfree, and Mary Austen, among others), Chopin's portraits of specific communities serve not to consolidate simplified notions of a unified nation but rather to complicate them.

Her characters range from wealthy plantation owners to poor rural Cajuns; from white Creoles to Creoles of color to African Americans to Native Americans to Cajuns both white and of color; from urban New Orleans residents to rural farmers; from "French" Catholics to "American" Protestants. That her characters are economically, racially, ethnically, geographically, and religiously marked, both to the reader and to other characters in the story, allows Chopin to disrupt homogenizing notions of the "South." When combined with her focus on female identity, this focus on the multiple layers of Louisiana society also reveals the links among gendered identity, regional identity, and national identity. In this way, Chopin's explorations of southern womanhood can be seen as central to broad cultural issues of the post-Reconstruction period: racial relations, regional relations, and gender roles in a rapidly modernizing society.

Her early stories—"Wiser Than a God," "A Point at Issue," and "The Story of an Hour," for instance—introduce a theme central to Chopin's fiction: the struggle for female selfhood, especially in relation to the conventional female roles of wife and mother. As *The Awakening* would do later, these early stories frequently represent women as constrained by social norms.

A similar willingness to confront controversial topics is evident in *At Fault* (1890), Chopin's first novel. Featuring a young but unusually strong widow as its protagonist, this novel treats both alcoholism and divorce, daring subjects for the time, and goes so far as to offer a sympathetic portrait of an alcoholic wife abandoned by her husband. The boldness that would offend critics nine years later was thus present in Chopin's work from the start but went unremarked, in part because her work was read as local color fiction, which, by definition, was always seen as focused on the quaint, the exotic, or the marginal.

Chopin's first stories were published in local periodicals in the St. Louis and New Orleans areas, but she soon began publishing in important eastern magazines with national readerships. Her 1894 short story collection, *Bayou Folk*, was followed in 1897 by *A Night in Acadie*, with a final volume, *A Vocation and a Voice*, remaining unpublished until 1991, many years after her death.

A number of Chopin's stories take as their starting point the then-shocking premise that white women experienced erotic desire. Published in 1897, *A Night in Acadie*, for instance, offers a representation of a heroine who actively recognizes her desire and seeks to determine its outcome in the choice of a husband. However, like *The Awakening*, this story offers a critique of gender norms while simultaneously reinforcing racial stereotypes of the period.

Motherhood as a central category of female identity came under examination in Chopin's fiction as well. Chopin challenges the meaning of motherhood by offering various versions demonstrating that the maternal is defined by the specifics of race, ethnicity, region, and class. In "Athénaïse" (1896), for instance, the incipient motherhood of the newly wedded protagonist reconciles her to marriage and consolidates her position as plantation mistress. "La Belle Zoraïde" (1894), in contrast, offers a representation of an enslaved woman as mother, demonstrating the ways in which slavery forcibly redefines the meaning of motherhood for both the enslaved black woman and the white mistress.

Chopin's thematizing of "blood" and miscegenation in "Désirée's Baby" links this story not only to other works in her canon but also to earlier U.S. narratives such as Stowe's *Uncle Tom's Cabin* (1852) and Harriet Jacobs's *Incidents in the Life of a Slave Girl* (1861), narratives that protested slavery on the basis of its disruption of the mother–child bond. Because of its use of the "tragic mulatto" plot, "Désirée's Baby" can also be read as in conversation with texts by writers such as Charles Chesnutt, Pauline Hopkins, and Frances E.W. Harper. However, where these writers challenge the system of racial binaries that condemns the "tragic mulatto" to death, Chopin's story can be read as confirming it, both in her heroine's end and in the narrative's offer of sympathy for Désirée's plight but not for La Blanche's.

This same movement between challenging and reinforcing regional, racial, and gender stereotypes can be seen in *The Awakening*, the text that many believe to be Chopin's masterpiece. Mrs. Pontellier's discovery of herself and her rebellion against the constriction of marriage and motherhood was indeed radical for its day, even as the novel reinscribed stereotypical images of sexually knowledgeable women of color. In her own day, readers and critics condemned Chopin not because of her representation of racial hierarchies but because she allowed her protagonist to take control of her own life without criticizing her for doing so. Even Mrs. Pontellier's end did not satisfy the critics, who accused Chopin of writing immoral and decadent fiction and compared her to very un-American French writers such as Emile Zola.

For many years, twentieth-century critics dismissed Chopin as a local color writer, but after her *Complete Works* appeared, this viewpoint became untenable, and critics began to assess her work more seriously. The influence of Hawthorne, Whitman, Henry James, and especially Maupassant on Chopin's work has been documented. Other critics have traced elements of romanticism, Transcendentalism, realism, and naturalism in her work, placing her in the mainstream of nineteenth-century U.S. literary currents. More recently, critics have explored Chopin's contributions to late-nineteenth-century discourses of national identity. Informed by U.S. literary and cultural contexts, Chopin drew on both to open a new arena of fiction, offering readers a complex portrait of late-nineteenth-century womanhood.

Kate McCullough
Cornell University

PRIMARY WORKS

At Fault, 1890; *Bayou Folk*, 1894; *A Night in Acadie*, 1897; *The Awakening*, 1899; *The Complete Works*, ed. Per Seyersted, 1969; *A Kate Chopin Miscellany*, ed. Per Seyersted and Emily Toth, 1979; *A Vocation and a Voice*, 1991.

Désirée's Baby

As the day was pleasant, Madame Valmondé drove over to L'Abri to see Désirée and the baby.

It made her laugh to think of Désirée with a baby. Why, it seemed but yesterday that Désirée was little more than a baby herself; when Monsieur in riding through the gateway of Valmondé had found her lying asleep in the shadow of the big stone pillar.

The little one awoke in his arms and began to cry for "Dada." That was as much as she could do or say. Some people thought she might have strayed there of her own accord, for she was of the toddling age. The prevailing belief was that she had been purposely left by a party of Texans, whose canvas-covered wagon, late in the day, had crossed the ferry that Coton Maïs kept, just below the plantation. In time Madame Valmondé abandoned every speculation but the one that Désirée had been sent to her by a beneficent Providence to be the child of her affection, seeing that she was without child of the flesh. For the girl grew to be beautiful and gentle, affectionate and sincere,—the idol of Valmondé.

It was no wonder, when she stood one day against the stone pillar in whose shadow she had lain asleep, eighteen years before, that Armand Aubigny riding by and seeing her there, had fallen in love with her. That was the way all the Aubignys fell in love, as if struck by a pistol shot. The wonder was that he had not loved her before; for he had known her since his father brought him home from Paris, a boy of eight, after his mother died there. The passion that awoke in him that day, when he saw her at the gate, swept along like an avalanche, or like a prairie fire, or like anything that drives headlong over all obstacles.

Monsieur Valmondé grew practical and wanted things well considered: that is, the girl's obscure origin. Armand looked into her eyes and did not care. He was reminded that she was nameless. What did it matter about a name when he could give her one of the oldest and proudest in Louisiana? He ordered the *corbeille*[1] from Paris, and contained himself with what patience he could until it arrived; then they were married.

Madame Valmondé had not seen Désirée and the baby for four weeks. When she reached L'Abri she shuddered at the first sight of it, as she always did. It was a sad looking place, which for many years had not known the gentle presence of a mistress, old Monsieur Aubigny having married and buried his wife in France, and she having loved her own land too well ever to leave it. The roof came down steep and black like a cowl, reaching out beyond the wide galleries that encircled the yellow stuccoed house. Big, solemn oaks grew close to it, and their thick-leaved, far-reaching branches shadowed it like a pall. Young Aubigny's rule was a strict one, too, and under it his negroes had forgotten how to be gay, as they had been during the old master's easy-going and indulgent lifetime.

The young mother was recovering slowly, and lay full length, in her soft white muslins and laces, upon a couch. The baby was beside her, upon her arm, where he had fallen asleep, at her breast. The yellow nurse woman sat beside a window fanning herself.

Madame Valmondé bent her portly figure over Désirée and kissed her, holding her an instant tenderly in her arms. Then she turned to the child.

"This is not the baby!" she exclaimed, in startled tones. French was the language spoken at Valmondé in those days.

"I knew you would be astonished," laughed Désirée, "at the way he has grown. The little *cochon de lait*![2] Look at his legs, mamma, and his hands and fingernails,— real finger-nails. Zandrine had to cut them this morning. Isn't it true, Zandrine?"

The woman bowed her turbaned head majestically, "Mais si,[3] Madame."

"And the way he cries," went on Désirée, "is deafening. Armand heard him the other day as far away as La Blanche's cabin."

Madame Valmondé had never removed her eyes from the child. She lifted it and walked with it over to the window that was lightest. She

---

[1]Wedding presents.   [3]Yes, indeed!
[2]Suckling pig.

scanned the baby narrowly, then looked as searchingly at Zandrine, whose face was turned to gaze across the fields.

"Yes, the child has grown, has changed," said Madame Valmondé, slowly, as she replaced it beside its mother. "What does Armand say?"

Désirée's face became suffused with a glow that was happiness itself.

"Oh, Armand is the proudest father in the parish, I believe, chiefly because it is a boy, to bear his name; though he says not,—that he would have loved a girl as well. But I know it isn't true. I know he says that to please me. And mamma," she added, drawing Madame Valmondé's head down to her, and speaking in a whisper, "he hasn't punished one of them— not one of them—since baby is born. Even Négrillon, who pretended to have burnt his leg that he might rest from work—he only laughed, and said Négrillon was a great scamp. Oh, mamma, I'm so happy; it frightens me."

What Désirée said was true. Marriage, and later the birth of his son had softened Armand Aubigny's imperious and exacting nature greatly. This was what made the gentle Désirée so happy, for she loved him desperately. When he frowned she trembled, but loved him. When he smiled, she asked no greater blessing of God. But Armand's dark, handsome face had not often been disfigured by frowns since the day he fell in love with her.

When the baby was about three months old, Désirée awoke one day to the conviction that there was something in the air menacing her peace. It was at first too subtle to grasp. It had only been a disquieting suggestion; an air of mystery among the blacks; unexpected visits from far-off neighbors who could hardly account for their coming. Then a strange, an awful change in her husband's manner, which she dared not ask him to explain. When he spoke to her, it was with averted eyes, from which the old love-light seemed to have gone out. He absented himself from home; and when there, avoided her presence and that of her child, without excuse. And the very spirit of Satan seemed suddenly to take hold of him in his dealings with the slaves. Désirée was miserable enough to die.

She sat in her room, one hot afternoon, in her *peignoir*,[4] listlessly drawing through her fingers the strands of her long, silky brown hair that hung about her shoulders. The baby, half naked, lay asleep upon her own great mahogany bed, that was like a sumptuous throne, with its satin-lined half-canopy. One of La Blanche's little quadroon boys—half naked too—stood fanning the child slowly with a fan of peacock feathers. Désirée's eyes had been fixed absently and sadly upon the baby, while she was striving to penetrate the threatening mist that she felt closing about her. She looked from her child to the boy who stood beside him, and back again; over and over. "Ah!" It was a cry that she could not help; which she was not conscious of having uttered. The blood turned like ice in her veins, and a clammy moisture gathered upon her face.

She tried to speak to the little quadroon boy; but no sound would come, at first. When he heard his name uttered, he looked up, and his mistress

[4]A lady's loose dressing gown.

was pointing to the door. He laid aside the great, soft fan, and obediently stole away, over the polished floor, on his bare tiptoes.

She stayed motionless, with gaze riveted upon her child, and her face the picture of fright.

Presently her husband entered the room, and without noticing her, went to a table and began to search among some papers which covered it.

"Armand," she called to him, in a voice which must have stabbed him, if he was human. But he did not notice. "Armand," she said again. Then she rose and tottered towards him. "Armand," she panted once more, clutching his arm, "look at our child. What does it mean? tell me."

He coldly but gently loosened her fingers from about his arm and thrust the hand away from him. "Tell me what it means!" she cried despairingly.

"It means," he answered lightly, "that the child is not white; it means that you are not white."

A quick conception of all that this accusation meant for her nerved her with un-wonted courage to deny it. "It is a lie; it is not true, I am white! Look at my hair, it is brown; and my eyes are gray, Armand, you know they are gray. And my skin is fair," seizing his wrist. "Look at my hand; whiter than yours, Armand," she laughed hysterically.

"As white as La Blanche's," he returned cruelly; and went away leaving her alone with their child.

When she could hold a pen in her hand, she sent a despairing letter to Madame Valmondé.

"My mother, they tell me I am not white. Armand has told me I am not white. For God's sake tell them it is not true. You must know it is not true. I shall die. I must die. I cannot be so unhappy, and live."

The answer that came was as brief:

"My own Désirée: Come home to Valmondé; back to your mother who loves you. Come with your child."

When the letter reached Désirée she went with it to her husband's study, and laid it open upon the desk before which he sat. She was like a stone image; silent, white, motionless after she placed it there.

In silence he ran his cold eyes over the written words. He said nothing. "Shall I go, Armand?" she asked in tones sharp with agonized suspense.

"Yes, go."

"Do you want me to go."

"Yes, I want you to go."

He thought Almighty God had dealt cruelly and unjustly with him; and felt, somehow, that he was paying Him back in kind when he stabbed thus into his wife's soul. Moreover he no longer loved her, because of the unconscious injury she had brought upon his home and his name.

She turned away like one stunned by a blow, and walked slowly towards the door, hoping he would call her back.

"Good-by, Armand," she moaned.

He did not answer her. That was his last blow at fate.

Désirée went in search of her child. Zandrine was pacing the sombre gallery with it. She took the little one from the nurse's arms with no word of explanation, and descending the steps, walked away, under the live-oak branches.

It was an October afternoon; the sun was just sinking. Out in the still fields the negroes were picking cotton.

Désirée had not changed the thin white garment nor the slippers which she wore. Her hair was uncovered and the sun's rays brought a golden gleam from its brown meshes. She did not take the broad, beaten road which led to the far-off plantation of Valmondé. She walked across a deserted field, where the stubble bruised her tender feet, so delicately shod, and tore her thin gown to shreds.

She disappeared among the reeds and willows that grew thick along the banks of the deep, sluggish bayou; and she did not come back again.

Some weeks later there was a curious scene enacted at L'Abri. In the centre of the smoothly swept back yard was a great bonfire. Armand Aubigny sat in the wide hallway that commanded a view of the spectacle; and it was he who dealt out to a half dozen negroes the material which kept this fire ablaze.

A graceful cradle of willow, with all its dainty furbishings, was laid upon the pyre, which had already been fed with the richness of a priceless *layette*.[5] Then there were silk gowns, and velvet and satin ones added to these; laces, too, and embroideries; bonnets and gloves; for the *corbeille* had been of rare quality.

The last thing to go was a tiny bundle of letters; innocent little scribblings that Désirée had sent to him during the days of their espousal. There was the remnant of one back in the drawer from which he took them. But it was not Désirée's; it was part of an old letter from his mother to his father. He read it. She was thanking God for the blessing of her husband's love:—

"But, above all," she wrote, "night and day, I thank the good God for having so arranged our lives that our dear Armand will never know that his mother, who adores him, belongs to the race that is cursed with the brand of slavery."

1892

The Storm

A Sequel to "At the 'Cadian Ball"[1]

I

The leaves were so still that even Bibi thought it was going to rain. Bobinôt, who was accustomed to converse on terms of perfect equality with his little son, called the child's attention to certain sombre clouds that were rolling

---

[5]A complete outfit for a newborn baby, including clothes, bedding, and accessories.
[1]"At the 'Cadian Ball" was a story Chopin wrote July 15–17, 1892, in which Calixta and Alcee Laballiere chose spouses from their own social classes despite their strong sexual attraction for each other.

with sinister intention from the west, accompanied by a sullen, threatening roar. They were at Friedheimers store and decided to remain there till the storm had passed. They sat within the door on two empty kegs. Bibi was four years old and looked very wise.

"Mama'll be 'fraid, yes," he suggested with blinking eyes.

"She'll shut the house. Maybe she got Sylvie helpin' her this evenin',' Bobinôt responded reassuringly.

"No; she ent got Sylvie. Sylvie was helpin' her yistiday," piped Bibi.

Bobinôt arose and going across to the counter purchased a can of shrimps, of which Calixta was very fond. Then he returned to his perch on the keg and sat stolidly holding the can of shrimps while the storm burst. It shook the wooden store and seemed to be ripping great furrows in the distant field. Bibi laid his little hand on his father's knee and was not afraid.

II

Calixta, at home, felt no uneasiness for their safety. She sat at a side window sewing furiously on a sewing machine. She was greatly occupied and did not notice the approaching storm. But she felt very warm and often stopped to mop her face on which the perspiration gathered in beads. She unfastened her white sacque[2] at the throat. It began to grow dark, and suddenly realizing the situation she got up hurriedly and went about closing windows and doors.

Out on the small front gallery she had hung Bobinôt's Sunday clothes to air and she hastened out to gather them before the rain fell. As she stepped outside, Alcée Laballière rode in at the gate. She had not seen him very often since her marriage, and never alone. She stood there with Bobinôt's coat in her hands, and the big rain drops began to fall. Alcée rode his horse under the shelter of a side projection where the chickens had huddled and there were plows and a harrow piled up in the corner.

"May I come and wait on your gallery till the storm is over, Calixta?" he asked.

"Come 'long in, M'sieur Alcée."

His voice and her own startled her as if from a trance, and she seized Bobinôt's vest. Alcée, mounting to the porch, grabbed the trousers and snatched Bibi's braided jacket that was about to be carried away by a sudden gust of wind. He expressed an intention to remain outside, but it was soon apparent that he might as well have been out in the open: the water beat in upon the boards in driving sheets, and he went inside, closing the door after him. It was even necessary to put something beneath the door to keep the water out.

"My! what a rain! It's good two years since it rain' like that," exclaimed Calixta as she rolled up a piece of bagging and Alcée helped her to thrust it beneath the crack.

[2]A short, loose-fitting woman's jacket.

She was a little fuller of figure than five years before when she married; but she had lost nothing of her vivacity. Her blue eyes still retained their melting quality; and her yellow hair, dishevelled by the wind and rain, kinked more stubbornly than ever about her ears and temples.

The rain beat upon the low, shingled roof with a force and clatter that threatened to break an entrance and deluge them there. They were in the dining room—the sitting room—the general utility room. Adjoining was her bed room, with Bibi's couch along side her own. The door stood open, and the room with its white, monumental bed, its closed shutters, looked dim and mysterious.

Alcée flung himself into a rocker and Calixta nervously began to gather up from the floor the lengths of a cotton sheet which she had been sewing.

"If this keeps up, *Dieu sait*[3] if the levees goin' to stan' it!" she exclaimed.

"What have you got to do with the levees?"

"I got enough to do! An' there's Bobinôt with Bibi out in that storm—if he only didn' left Friedheimer's!"

"Let us hope, Calixta, that Bobinôt's got sense enough to come in out of a cyclone."

She went and stood at the window with a greatly disturbed look on her face. She wiped the frame that was clouded with moisture. It was stifingly hot. Alcée got up and joined her at the window, looking over her shoulder. The rain was coming down in sheets obscuring the view of far-off cabins and enveloping the distant wood in a gray mist. The playing of the lightning was incessant. A bolt struck a tall chinaberry tree at the edge of the field. It filled all visible space with a blinding glare and the crash seemed to invade the very boards they stood upon.

Calixta put her hands to her eyes, and with a cry, staggered backward. Alcée's arm encircled her, and for an instant he drew her close and spasmodically to him.

"*Bonté!*"[4] she cried, releasing herself from his encircling arm and retreating from the window, "the house'll go next! If I only knew w'ere Bibi was!" She would not compose herself; she would not be seated. Alcée clasped her shoulders and looked into her face. The contact of her warm, palpitating body when he had unthinkingly drawn her into his arms, had aroused all the old-time infatuation and desire for her flesh.

"Calixta," he said, "don't be frightened. Nothing can happen. The house is too low to be struck, with so many tall trees standing about. There! aren't you going to be quiet? say, aren't you?" He pushed her hair back from her face that was warm and steaming. Her lips were as red and moist as pomegranate seed. Her white neck and a glimpse of her full, firm bosom disturbed him powerfully. As she glanced up at him the fear in her liquid blue eyes had given place to a drowsy gleam that unconsciously betrayed a sensuous desire. He looked down into her eyes and there was nothing for him to do but to gather her lips in a kiss. It reminded him of Assumption.

---

[3]God knows.   [4]Goodness!

"Do you remember—in Assumption, Calixta?" he asked in a low voice broken by passion. Oh! she remembered; for in Assumption he had kissed her and kissed and kissed her; until his senses would well nigh fail, and to save her he would resort to a desperate flight. If she was not an immaculate dove in those days, she was still inviolate; a passionate creature whose very defenselessness had made her defense, against which his honor forbade him to prevail. Now—well, now—her lips seemed in a manner free to be tasted, as well as her round, white throat and her whiter breasts.

They did not heed the crashing torrents, and the roar of the elements made her laugh as she lay in his arms. She was a revelation in that dim, mysterious chamber as white as the couch she lay upon. Her firm, elastic flesh that was knowing for the first time its birthright, was like a creamy lily that the sun invites to contribute its breath and perfume to the undying life of the world.

The generous abundance of her passion, without guile or trickery, was like a white flame which penetrated and found response in depths of his own sensuous nature that had never yet been reached.

When he touched her breasts they gave themselves up in quivering ecstasy, inviting his lips. Her mouth was a fountain of delight. And when he possessed her, they seemed to swoon together at the very borderland of life's mystery.

He stayed cushioned upon her, breathless, dazed, enervated, with his heart beating like a hammer upon her. With one hand she clasped his head, her lips lightly touching his forehead. The other hand stroked with a soothing rhythm his muscular shoulders.

The growl of the thunder was distant and passing away. The rain beat softly upon the shingles, inviting them to drowsiness and sleep. But they dared not yield.

The rain was over; and the sun was turning the glistening green world into a palace of gems. Calixta, on the gallery, watched Alcée ride away. He turned and smiled at her with a beaming face; and she lifted her pretty chin in the air and laughed aloud.

III

Bobinôt and Bibi, trudging home, stopped without at the cistern to make themselves presentable.

"My! Bibi, w'at will yo' mama say! You ought to be ashame'. You oughtn' put on those good pants. Look at 'em! An' that mud on yo' collar! How you got that mud on yo' collar, Bibi? I never saw such a boy!" Bibi was the picture of pathetic resignation. Bobinôt was the embodiment of serious solicitude as he strove to remove from his own person and his son's the signs of their tramp over heavy roads and through wet fields. He scraped the mud off Bibi's bare legs and feet with a stick and carefully removed all traces from his heavy brogans. Then, prepared for the worst—the meeting with an over-scrupulous housewife, they entered cautiously at the back door.

Calixta was preparing supper. She had set the table and was dripping coffee at the hearth. She sprang up as they came in.

"Oh, Bobinôt! You back! My! but I was uneasy. W'ere you been during the rain? An' Bibi? he ain't wet? he ain't hurt?" She had clasped Bibi and was kissing him effusively. Bobinôt's explanations and apologies which he had been composing all along the way, died on his lips as Calixta felt him to see if he were dry, and seemed to express nothing but satisfaction at their safe return.

"I brought you some shrimps, Calixta," offered Bobinôt, hauling the can from his ample side pocket and laying it on the table.

"Shrimps! Oh, Bobinôt! you too good fo' anything!" and she gave him a smacking kiss on the cheek that resounded. "*J'vous réponds,*[5] we'll have a feas' to night! umph-umph!"

Bobinôt and Bibi began to relax and enjoy themselves, and when the three seated themselves at table they laughed much and so loud that anyone might have heard them as far away as Laballière's.

IV

Alcée Laballière wrote to his wife, Clarisse, that night. It was a loving letter, full of tender solicitude. He told her not to hurry back, but if she and the babies liked it at Biloxi, to stay a month longer. He was getting on nicely; and though he missed them, he was willing to bear the separation a while longer—realizing that their health and pleasure were the first things to be considered.

V

As for Clarisse, she was charmed upon receiving her husband's letter. She and the babies were doing well. The society was agreeable; many of her old friends and acquaintances were at the bay. And the first free breath since her marriage seemed to restore the pleasant liberty of her maiden days. Devoted as she was to her husband, their intimate conjugal life was something which she was more than willing to forego for a while.

So the storm passed and every one was happy.

1898

The Story of an Hour

Knowing that Mrs. Mallard was afflicted with a heart trouble, great care was taken to break to her as gently as possible the news of her husband's death.

It was her sister Josephine who told her, in broken sentences; veiled hints that revealed in half concealing. Her husband's friend Richards was there, too, near her. It was he who had been in the newspaper office when

---

[5]A colloquial expression meaning "You bet!" or "no kidding!"

intelligence of the railroad disaster was received, with Brently Mallard's name leading the list of "killed." He had only taken the time to assure himself of its truth by a second telegram, and had hastened to forestall any less careful, less tender friend in bearing the sad message.

She did not hear the story as many women have heard the same, with a paralyzed inability to accept its significance. She wept at once, with sudden, wild abandonment, in her sister's arms. When the storm of grief had spent itself she went away to her room alone. She would have no one follow her.

There stood, facing the open window, a comfortable, roomy armchair. Into this she sank, pressed down by a physical exhaustion that haunted her body and seemed to reach into her soul.

She could see in the open square before her house the tops of the trees that were all aquiver with the new spring life. The delicious breath of rain was in the air. In the street below a peddler was crying his wares. The notes of a distant song which some one was singing reached her faintly, and countless sparrows were twittering in the eaves.

There were patches of blue sky showing here and there through the clouds that had met and piled one above the other in the west facing her window.

She sat with her head thrown back upon the cushion of the chair, quite motionless, except when a sob came up into her throat and shook her, as a child who has cried itself to sleep continues to sob in its dreams.

She was young, with a fair, calm face, whose lines bespoke repression and even a certain strength. But now there was a dull stare in her eyes, whose gaze was fixed away off yonder on one of those patches of blue sky. It was not a glance of reflection, but rather indicated a suspension of intelligent thought.

There was something coming to her and she was waiting for it, fearfully. What was it? She did not know; it was too subtle and elusive to name. But she felt it, creeping out of the sky, reaching toward her through the sounds, the scents, the color that filled the air.

Now her bosom rose and fell tumultuously. She was beginning to recognize this thing that was approaching to possess her, and she was striving to beat it back with her will—as powerless as her two white slender hands would have been.

When she abandoned herself a little whispered word escaped her slightly parted lips. She said it over and over under her breath: "free, free, free!" The vacant stare and the look of terror that had followed it went from her eyes. They stayed keen and bright. Her pulses beat fast, and the coursing blood warmed and relaxed every inch of her body.

She did not stop to ask if it were or were not a monstrous joy that held her. A clear and exalted perception enabled her to dismiss the suggestion as trivial.

She knew that she would weep again when she saw the kind, tender hands folded in death; the face that had never looked save with love upon her, fixed and gray and dead. But she saw beyond that bitter moment a long procession of years to come that would belong to her absolutely. And she opened and spread her arms out to them in welcome.

There would be no one to live for her during those coming years; she would live for herself. There would be no powerful will bending hers in that blind persistence with which men and women believe that have a right to impose a private will upon a fellow-creature. A kind intention or a cruel intention made the act seem no less a crime as she looked upon it in that brief moment of illumination.

And yet she loved him—sometimes. Often she had not. What did it matter! What could love, the unsolved mystery, count for in face of this possession of self-assertion which she suddenly recognized as the strongest impulse of her being!

"Free! Body and soul free!" she kept whispering.

Josephine was kneeling before the closed door with her lips to the keyhole, imploring for admission. "Louise, open the door! I beg; open the door—you will make yourself ill. What are you doing, Louise? For heaven's sake open the door."

"Go away. I am not making myself ill." No; she was drinking in a very elixir of life through that open window.

Her fancy was running riot along those days ahead of her. Spring days, and summer days, and all sorts of days that would be her own. She breathed a quick prayer that life might be long. It was only yesterday she had thought with a shudder that life might be long.

She arose at length and opened the door to her sister's importunities. There was a feverish triumph in her eyes, and she carried herself unwittingly like a goddess of Victory. She clasped her sister's waist, and together they descended the stairs. Richards stood waiting for them at the bottom.

Some one was opening the front door with a latchkey. It was Brently Mallard who entered, a little travel-stained, composedly carrying his gripsack and umbrella. He had been far from the scene of the accident, and did not even know there had been one. He stood amazed at Josephine's piercing cry; at Richards' quick motion to screen him from the view of his wife.

But Richards was too late.

When the doctors came they said she had died of heart disease—of joy that kills.

1894

The Awakening

I

A green and yellow parrot, which hung in a cage outside the door, kept repeating over and over:

"*Allez vous-en! Allez vous-en! Sapristi!*[1] That's all right!"

---

[1]French: "Go away! Go away! Heavens!"

He could speak a little Spanish, and also a language which nobody understood, unless it was the mocking-bird that hung on the other side of the door, whistling his fluty notes out upon the breeze with maddening persistence.

Mr. Pontellier, unable to read his newspaper with any degree of comfort, arose with an expression and an exclamation of disgust. He walked down the gallery and across the narrow "bridges" which connected the Lebrun cottages one with the other. He had been seated before the door of the main house. The parrot and the mocking-bird were the property of Madame Lebrun, and they had the right to make all the noise they wished. Mr. Pontellier had the privilege of quitting their society when they ceased to be entertaining.

He stopped before the door of his own cottage, which was the fourth one from the main building and next to the last. Seating himself in a wicker rocker which was there, he once more applied himself to the task of reading the newspaper. The day was Sunday; the paper was a day old. The Sunday papers had not yet reached Grand Isle.[2] He was already acquainted with the market reports, and he glanced restlessly over the editorials and bits of news which he had not had time to read before quitting New Orleans the day before.

Mr. Pontellier wore eye-glasses. He was a man of forty, of medium height and rather slender build; he stooped a little. His hair was brown and straight, parted on one side. His beard was neatly and closely trimmed.

Once in a while he withdrew his glance from the newspaper and looked about him. There was more noise than ever over at the house. The main building was called "the house," to distinguish it from the cottages. The chattering and whistling birds were still at it. Two young girls, the Farival twins, were playing a duet from "Zampa"[3] upon the piano. Madame Lebrun was bustling in and out, giving orders in a high key to a yard-boy whenever she got inside the house, and directions in an equally high voice to a dining-room servant whenever she got outside. She was a fresh, pretty woman, clad always in white with elbow sleeves. Her starched skirts crinkled as she came and went. Farther down, before one of the cottages, a lady in black was walking demurely up and down, telling her beads.[4] A good many persons of the *pension*[5] had gone over to the *Chênière Caminada*[6] in Beaudelet's lugger[7] to hear mass. Some young people were out under the water-oaks playing croquet. Mr. Pontellier's two children were there—sturdy little fellows of four and five. A quadroon[8] nurse followed them about with a far-away, meditative air.

[2]A popular resort island.
[3]A romantic opera (1831) by Louis Hérold.
[4]The act of manipulating a string of beads to count out the recitation of a series of prayers.
[5]French: boarding house.
[6]Another coastal island between Grande Isle and Louisiana.

[7]A small boat.
[8]A person of one-quarter black ancestry; thus, someone whose grandparent is African American.

Mr. Pontellier finally lit a cigar and began to smoke, letting the paper drag idly from his hand. He fixed his gaze upon a white sunshade that was advancing at snail's pace from the beach. He could see it plainly between the gaunt trunks of the water-oaks and across the stretch of yellow camomile. The gulf looked far away, melting hazily into the blue of the horizon. The sunshade continued to approach slowly. Beneath its pink-lined shelter were his wife, Mrs. Pontellier, and young Robert Lebrun. When they reached the cottage, the two seated themselves with some appearance of fatigue upon the upper step of the porch, facing each other, each leaning against a supporting post.

"What folly! to bathe at such an hour in such heat!" exclaimed Mr. Pontellier. He himself had taken a plunge at daylight. That was why the morning seemed long to him.

"You are burnt beyond recognition," he added, looking at his wife as one looks at a valuable piece of personal property which has suffered some damage. She held up her hands, strong, shapely hands, and surveyed them critically drawing up her lawn sleeves above the wrists. Looking at them reminded her of her rings, which she had given to her husband before leaving for the beach. She silently reached out to him, and he, understanding, took the rings from his vest pocket and dropped them into her open palm. She slipped them upon her fingers; then clasping her knees, she looked across at Robert and began to laugh. The rings sparkled upon her fingers. He sent back an answering smile.

"What is it?" asked Pontellier, looking lazily and amused from one to the other. It was some utter nonsense; some adventure out there in the water, and they both tried to relate it at once. It did not seem half so amusing when told. They realized this, and so did Mr. Pontellier. He yawned and stretched himself. Then he got up, saying he had half a mind to go over to Klein's hotel[9] and play a game of billiards.

"Come go along, Lebrun," he proposed to Robert. But Robert admitted quite frankly that he preferred to stay where he was and talk to Mrs. Pontellier.

"Well, send him about his business when he bores you, Edna," instructed her husband as he prepared to leave.

"Here, take the umbrella," she exclaimed, holding it out to him. He accepted the sunshade, and lifting it over his head descended the steps and walked away.

"Coming back to dinner?" his wife called after him. He halted a moment and shrugged his shoulders. He felt in his vest pocket; there was a ten-dollar bill there. He did not know; perhaps he would return for the early dinner and perhaps he would not. It all depended upon the company which he found over at Klein's and the size of "the game." He did not say this, but she understood it, and laughed, nodding good-by to him.

Both children wanted to follow their father when they saw him starting out. He kissed them and promised to bring them back bonbons and peanuts.

---

[9]A popular resort hotel.

II

Mrs. Pontellier's eyes were quick and bright; they were a yellowish brown, about the color of her hair. She had a way of turning them swiftly upon an object and holding them there as if lost in some inward maze of contemplation or thought.

Her eyebrows were a shade darker than her hair. They were thick and almost horizontal, emphasizing the depth of her eyes. She was rather handsome than beautiful. Her face was captivating by reason of a certain frankness of expression and a contradictory subtle play of features. Her manner was engaging.

Robert rolled a cigarette. He smoked cigarettes because he could not afford cigars, he said. He had a cigar in his pocket which Mr. Pontellier had presented him with, and he was saving it for his after-dinner smoke.

This seemed quite proper and natural on his part. In coloring he was not unlike his companion. A clean-shaved face made the resemblance more pronounced than it would otherwise have been. There rested no shadow of care upon his open countenance. His eyes gathered in and reflected the light and languor of the summer day.

Mrs. Pontellier reached over for a palmleaf fan that lay on the porch and began to fan herself, while Robert sent between his lips light puffs from his cigarette. They chatted incessantly: about the things around them; their amusing adventure out in the water—it had again assumed its entertaining aspect; about the wind, the trees, the people who had gone to the *Chênière*; about the children playing croquet under the oaks, and the Farival twins, who were now performing the overture to "The Poet and the Peasant."[10]

Robert talked a good deal about himself. He was very young, and did not know any better. Mrs. Pontellier talked a little about herself for the same reason. Each was interested in what the other said. Robert spoke of his intention to go to Mexico in the autumn, where fortune awaited him. He was always intending to go to Mexico, but some way never got there. Meanwhile he held on to his modest position in a mercantile house in New Orleans, where an equal familiarity with English, French and Spanish gave him no small value as a clerk and correspondent.

He was spending his summer vacation, as he always did, with his mother at Grand Isle. In former times, before Robert could remember, "the house" had been a summer luxury of the Lebruns. Now, flanked by its dozen or more cottages, which were always filled with exclusive visitors from the *"Quartier Français,"*[11] it enabled Madame Lebrun to maintain the easy and comfortable existence which appeared to be her birthright.

[10]A comic operetta by Franz Von Suppé (1819–1895).

[11]The French Quarter, New Orleans's oldest neighborhood, settled by the French in the early eighteenth century.

Mrs. Pontellier talked about her father's Mississippi plantation and her girlhood home in the old Kentucky blue-grass country. She was an American woman, with a small infusion of French which seemed to have been lost in dilution. She read a letter from her sister, who was away in the East, and who had engaged herself to be married. Robert was interested, and wanted to know what manner of girls the sisters were, what the father was like, and how long the mother had been dead.

When Mrs. Pontellier folded the letter it was time for her to dress for the early dinner.

"I see Léonce isn't coming back," she said, with a glance in the direction whence her husband had disappeared. Robert supposed he was not, as there were a good many New Orleans club men over at Klein's.

When Mrs. Pontellier left him to enter her room, the young man descended the steps and strolled over toward the croquet players, where, during the half-hour before dinner, he amused himself with the little Pontellier children, who were very fond of him.

III

It was eleven o'clock that night when Mr. Pontellier returned from Klein's hotel. He was in an excellent humor, in high spirits, and very talkative. His entrance awoke his wife, who was in bed and fast asleep when he came in. He talked to her while he undressed, telling her anecdotes and bits of news and gossip that he had gathered during the day. From his trousers pockets he took a fistful of crumpled bank notes and a good deal of silver coin, which he piled on the bureau indiscriminately with keys, knife, handkerchief, and whatever else happened to be in his pockets. She was overcome with sleep, and answered him with little half utterances.

He thought it very discouraging that his wife, who was the sole object of his existence, evinced so little interest in things which concerned him and valued so little his conversation.

Mr. Pontellier had forgotten the bonbons and peanuts for the boys. Notwithstanding he loved them very much, and went into the adjoining room where they slept to take a look at them and make sure that they were resting comfortably. The result of his investigation was far from satisfactory. He turned and shifted the youngsters about in bed. One of them began to kick and talk about a basket full of crabs.

Mr. Pontellier returned to his wife with the information that Raoul had a high fever and needed looking after. Then he lit a cigar and went and sat near the open door to smoke it.

Mrs. Pontellier was quite sure Raoul had no fever. He had gone to bed perfectly well, she said, and nothing had ailed him all day. Mr. Pontellier was too well acquainted with fever symptoms to be mistaken. He assured her the child was consuming at that moment in the next room.

He reproached his wife with her inattention, her habitual neglect of the children. If it was not a mother's place to look after children, whose on earth was it? He himself had his hands full with his brokerage business. He could not be in two places at once; making a living for his family on the street, and staying at home to see that no harm befell them. He talked in a monotonous, insistent way.

Mrs. Pontellier sprang out of bed and went into the next room. She soon came back and sat on the edge of the bed, leaning her head down on the pillow. She said nothing, and refused to answer her husband when he questioned her. When his cigar was smoked out he went to bed, and in half a minute he was fast asleep.

Mrs. Pontellier was by that time thoroughly awake. She began to cry a little, and wiped her eyes on the sleeve of her *peignoir*.[12] Blowing out the candle, which her husband had left burning, she slipped her bare feet into a pair of satin *mules* at the foot of the bed and went out on the porch, where she sat down in the wicker chair and began to rock gently to and fro.

It was then past midnight. The cottages were all dark. A single faint light gleamed out from the hallway of the house. There was no sound abroad except the hooting of an old owl in the top of a water-oak, and the everlasting voice of the sea, that was not uplifted at that soft hour. It broke like a mournful lullaby upon the night.

The tears came so fast to Mrs. Pontellier's eyes that the damp sleeve of her *peignoir* no longer served to dry them. She was holding the back of her chair with one hand; her loose sleeve had slipped almost to the shoulder of her uplifted arm. Turning, she thrust her face, steaming and wet, into the bend of her arm, and she went on crying there, not caring any longer to dry her face, her eyes, her arms. She could not have told why she was crying. Such experiences as the foregoing were not uncommon in her married life. They seemed never before to have weighed much against the abundance of her husband's kindness and a uniform devotion which had come to be tacit and self-understood.

An indescribable oppression, which seemed to generate in some unfamiliar part of her consciousness, filled her whole being with a vague anguish. It was like a shadow, like a mist passing across her soul's summer day. It was strange and unfamiliar; it was a mood. She did not sit there inwardly upbraiding her husband, lamenting at Fate, which had directed her footsteps to the path which they had taken. She was just having a good cry all to herself. The mosquitoes made merry over her, biting her firm, round arms and nipping at her bare insteps.

The little stinging, buzzing imps succeeded in dispelling a mood which might have held her there in the darkness half a night longer.

The following morning Mr. Pontellier was up in good time to take the rockaway[13] which was to convey him to the steamer at the wharf. He was returning to the city to his business, and they would not see him again at the Island till the coming Saturday. He had regained his composure, which

---

[12]French: robe.   [13]A carriage.

seemed to have been somewhat impaired the night before. He was eager to be gone, as he looked forward to a lively week in Carondelet Street.[14]

Mr. Pontellier gave his wife half the money which he had brought away from Klein's hotel the evening before. She liked money as well as most women, and accepted it with no little satisfaction.

"It will buy a handsome wedding present for Sister Janet!" she exclaimed, smoothing out the bills as she counted them one by one.

"Oh! we'll treat Sister Janet better than that, my dear," he laughed, as he prepared to kiss her good-by.

The boys were tumbling about, clinging to his legs, imploring that numerous things be brought back to them. Mr. Pontellier was a great favorite, and ladies, men, children, even nurses, were always on hand to say good-by to him. His wife stood smiling and waving, the boys shouting, as he disappeared in the old rockaway down the sandy road.

A few days later a box arrived for Mrs. Pontellier from New Orleans. It was from her husband. It was filled with *friandises*,[15] with luscious and toothsome bits—the finest of fruits, *patés*,[16] a rare bottle or two, delicious syrups, and bonbons in abundance.

Mrs. Pontellier was always very generous with the contents of such a box; she was quite used to receiving them when away from home. The *patés* and fruit were brought to the dining-room; the bonbons were passed around. And the ladies, selecting with dainty and discriminating fingers and a little greedily, all declared that Mr. Pontellier was the best husband in the world. Mrs. Pontellier was forced to admit that she knew of none better.

IV

It would have been a difficult matter for Mr. Pontellier to define to his own satisfaction or any one else's wherein his wife failed in her duty toward their children. It was something which he felt rather than perceived, and he never voiced the feeling without subsequent regret and ample atonement.

If one of the little Pontellier boys took a tumble whilst at play, he was not apt to rush crying to his mother's arms for comfort; he would more likely pick himself up, wipe the water out of his eyes and the sand out of his mouth, and go on playing. Tots as they were, they pulled together and stood their ground in childish battles with doubled fists and uplifted voices, which usually prevailed against the other mother-tots. The quadroon nurse was looked upon as a huge encumbrance, only good to button up waists and panties and to brush and part hair; since it seemed to be a law of society that hair must be parted and brushed.

In short, Mrs. Pontellier was not a mother-woman. The mother-women seemed to prevail that summer at Grand Isle. It was easy to know them, fluttering about with extended, protecting wings when any harm, real or imaginary, threatened their precious brood. They were women who idolized

---

[14]New Orleans's center for commercial exchange.   [16]French: pastries.
[15]French: candy.

their children, worshiped their husbands, and esteemed it a holy privilege to efface themselves as individuals and grow wings as ministering angels.

Many of them were delicious in the rôle; one of them was the embodiment of every womanly grace and charm. If her husband did not adore her, he was a brute, deserving of death by slow torture. Her name was Adèle Ratignolle. There are no words to describe her save the old ones that have served so often to picture the bygone heroine of romance and the fair lady of our dreams. There was nothing subtle or hidden about her charms; her beauty was all there, flaming and apparent: the spun-gold hair that comb nor confining pin could restrain; the blue eyes that were like nothing but sapphires; two lips that pouted, that were so red one could only think of cherries or some other delicious crimson fruit in looking at them. She was growing a little stout, but it did not seem to detract an iota from the grace of every step, pose, gesture. One would not have wanted her white neck a mite less full or her beautiful arms more slender. Never were hands more exquisite than hers, and it was a joy to look at them when she threaded her needle or adjusted her gold thimble to her taper middle finger as she sewed away on the little night-drawers or fashioned a bodice or a bib.

Madame Ratignolle was very fond of Mrs. Pontellier, and often she took her sewing and went over to sit with her in the afternoons. She was sitting there the afternoon of the day the box arrived from New Orleans. She had possession of the rocker, and she was busily engaged in sewing upon a diminutive pair of night-drawers.

She had brought the pattern of the drawers for Mrs. Pontellier to cut out—a marvel of construction, fashioned to enclose a baby's body so effectually that only two small eyes might look out from the garment, like an Eskimo's. They were designed for winter wear, when treacherous drafts came down chimneys and insidious currents of deadly cold found their way through key-holes.

Mrs. Pontellier's mind was quite at rest concerning the present material needs of her children, and she could not see the use of anticipating and making winter night garments the subject of her summer meditations. But she did not want to appear un-amiable and uninterested, so she had brought forth newspapers which she spread upon the floor of the gallery, and under Madame Ratignolle's directions she had cut a pattern of the impervious garment.

Robert was there, seated as he had been the Sunday before, and Mrs. Pontellier also occupied her former position on the upper step, leaning listlessly against the post. Beside her was a box of bonbons, which she held out at intervals to Madame Ratignolle.

That lady seemed at a loss to make a selection, but finally settled upon a stick of nugat, wondering if it were not too rich; whether it could possibly hurt her. Madame Ratignolle had been married seven years. About every two years she had a baby. At that time she had three babies, and was beginning to think of a fourth one. She was always talking about her "condition." Her "condition" was in no way apparent, and no one would have known a thing about it but for her persistence in making it the subject of conversation.

Robert started to reassure her, asserting that he had known a lady who had subsisted upon nugat during the entire—but seeing the color mount into Mrs. Pontellier's face he checked himself and changed the subject.

Mrs. Pontellier, though she had married a Creole,[17] was not thoroughly at home in the society of Creoles; never before had she been thrown so intimately among them. There were only Creoles that summer at Lebrun's. They all knew each other, and felt like one large family, among whom existed the most amicable relations. A characteristic which distinguished them and which impressed Mrs. Pontellier most forcibly was their entire absence of prudery. Their freedom of expression was at first incomprehensible to her, though she had no difficulty in reconciling it with a lofty chastity which in the Creole woman seems to be inborn and unmistakable.

Never would Edna Pontellier forget the shock with which she heard Madame Ratignolle relating to old Monsieur Farival the harrowing story of one of her *accouchements*,[18] withholding no intimate detail. She was growing accustomed to like shocks, but she could not keep the mounting color back from her cheeks. Oftener than once her coming had interrupted the droll story with which Robert was entertaining some amused group of married women.

A book had gone the rounds of the *pension*. When it came her turn to read it, she did so with profound astonishment. She felt moved to read the book in secret and solitude, though none of the others had done so—to hide it from view at the sound of approaching footsteps. It was openly criticised and freely discussed at table. Mrs. Pontellier gave over being astonished, and concluded that wonders would never cease.

V

They formed a congenial group sitting there that summer afternoon—Madame Ratignolle sewing away, often stopping to relate a story or incident with much expressive gesture of her perfect hands; Robert and Mrs. Pontellier sitting idle, exchanging occasional words, glances or smiles which indicated a certain advanced stage of intimacy and *camaraderie*.

He had lived in her shadow during the past month. No one thought anything of it. Many had predicted that Robert would devote himself to Mrs. Pontellier when he arrived. Since the age of fifteen, which was eleven years before, Robert each summer at Grand Isle had constituted himself the devoted attendant of some fair dame or damsel. Sometimes it was a young girl, again a widow; but as often as not it was some interesting married woman.

For two consecutive seasons he lived in the sunlight of Mademoiselle Duvigné's presence. But she died between summers; then Robert posed

[17]In Chopin's usage, aristocrats of French and Spanish ancestry.   [18]French: childbirths.

as an inconsolable, prostrating himself at the feet of Madame Ratignolle for whatever crumbs of sympathy and comfort she might be pleased to vouchsafe.

Mrs. Pontellier liked to sit and gaze at her fair companion as she might look upon a faultless Madonna.

"Could any one fathom the cruelty beneath that fair exterior?" murmured Robert. She knew that I adored her once, and she let me adore her. It was 'Robert, come; go; stand up; sit down; do this; do that; see if the baby sleeps; my thimble, please, that I left God knows where. Come and read Daude[19] to me while I sew.'"

"*Par exemple!*[20] I never had to ask. You were always there under my feet, like a troublesome cat."

"You mean like an adoring dog. And just as soon as Ratignolle appeared on the scene, then it *was* like a dog. '*Passez! Adieu! Allez vous-en!*'"[21]

"Perhaps I feared to make Alphonse jealous," she interjoined, with excessive naïveté. That made them all laugh. The right hand jealous of the left! The heart jealous of the soul! But for that matter, the Creole husband is never jealous; with him the gangrene passion is one which has become dwarfed by disuse.

Meanwhile Robert, addressing Mrs. Pontellier, continued to tell of his one time hopeless passion for Madame Ratignolle; of sleepless nights, of consuming flames till the very sea sizzled when he took his daily plunge. While the lady at the needle kept up a little running, contemptuous comment:

"*Blagueur—farceur—gros bête, va!*"[22]

He never assumed this serio-comic tone when alone with Mrs. Pontellier. She never knew precisely what to make of it; at that moment it was impossible for her to guess how much of it was jest and what proportion was earnest. It was understood that he had often spoken words of love to Madame Ratignolle, without any thought of being taken seriously. Mrs. Pontellier was glad he had not assumed a similar rôle toward herself. It would have been unacceptable and annoying.

Mrs. Pontellier had brought her sketching materials, which she sometimes dabbled with in an unprofessional way. She liked the dabbling. She felt in it satisfaction of a kind which no other employment afforded her.

She had long wished to try herself on Madame Ratignolle. Never had that lady seemed a more tempting subject than at that moment, seated there like some sensuous Madonna, with the gleam of the fading day enriching her splendid color.

Robert crossed over and seated himself upon the step below Mrs. Pontellier, that he might watch her work. She handled her brushes with a certain ease and freedom which came, not from long and close acquaintance with them, but from a natural aptitude. Robert followed her work with close

---

[19]Alphonse Daudet (1840–1897), French novelist noted for his naturalism.
[20]French: "For God's sake!"

[21]French: "Go on! Goodbye! Go away!"
[22]French: "Joker—mischief-maker—fool, come off it!"

attention, giving forth little ejaculatory expressions of appreciation in French, which he addressed to Madame Ratignolle.

"Mais ce n'est pas mal! Elle s'y connait, elle a de la force, oui."[23]

During his oblivious attention he once quietly rested his head against Mrs. Pontellier's arm. As gently she repulsed him. Once again he repeated the offense. She could not but believe it to be thoughtlessness on his part; yet that was no reason she should submit to it. She did not remonstrate, except again to repulse him quietly but firmly. He offered no apology.

The picture completed bore no resemblance to Madame Ratignolle. She was greatly disappointed to find that it did not look like her. But it was a fair enough piece of work, and in many respects satisfying.

Mrs. Pontellier evidently did not think so. After surveying the sketch critically she drew a broad smudge of paint across its surface, and crumpled the paper between her hands.

The youngsters came tumbling up the steps, the quadroon following at the respectful distance which they required her to observe. Mrs. Pontellier made them carry her paints and things into the house. She sought to detain them for a little talk and some pleasantry. But they were greatly in earnest. They had only come to investigate the contents of the bonbon box. They accepted without murmuring what she chose to give them, each holding out two chubby hands scoop-like, in the vain hope that they might be filled; and then away they went.

The sun was low in the west, and the breeze soft and languorous that came up from the south, charged with the seductive odor of the sea. Children, freshly befurbelowed were gathering for their games under the oaks. Their voices were high and penetrating.

Madame Ratignolle folded her sewing, placing thimble, scissors and thread all neatly together in the roll, which she pinned securely. She complained of faintness. Mrs. Pontellier flew for the cologne water and a fan. She bathed Madame Ratignolle's face with cologne, while Robert plied the fan with unnecessary vigor.

The spell was soon over, and Mrs. Pontellier could not help wondering if there were not a little imagination responsible for its origin, for the rose tint had never faded from her friend's face.

She stood watching the fair woman walk down the long line of galleries with the grace and majesty which queens are sometimes supposed to possess. Her little ones ran to meet her. Two of them clung about her white skirts, the third she took from its nurse and with a thousand endearments bore it along in her own fond, encircling arms. Though, as everybody well knew, the doctor had forbidden her to lift so much as a pin!

"Are you going bathing?" asked Robert of Mrs. Pontellier. It was not so much a question as a reminder.

---

[23]French: "Not bad at all! She knows what she is doing, she has talent!"

"Oh, no," she answered, with a tone of indecision. "I'm tired; I think not." Her glance wandered from his face away toward the Gulf, whose sonorous murmur reached her like a loving but imperative entreaty.

"Oh, come!" he insisted. "You mustn't miss your bath. Come on. The water must be delicious; it will not hurt you. Come."

He reached up for her big, rough straw hat that hung on a peg outside the door, and put it on her head. They descended the steps, and walked away together toward the beach. The sun was low in the west and the breeze was soft and warm.

VI

Edna Pontellier could not have told why, wishing to go to the beach with Robert, she should in the first place have declined, and in the second place have followed in obedience to one of the two contradictory impulses which impelled her.

A certain light was beginning to dawn dimly within her,—the light which, showing the way, forbids it.

At that early period it served but to bewilder her. It moved her to dreams, to thoughtfulness, to the shadowy anguish which had overcome her the midnight when she had abandoned herself to tears.

In short, Mrs. Pontellier was beginning to realize her position in the universe as a human being, and to recognize her relations as an individual to the world within and about her. This may seem like a ponderous weight of wisdom to descend upon the soul of a young woman of twenty-eight— perhaps more wisdom than the Holy Ghost is usually pleased to vouchsafe to any woman.

But the beginning of things, of a world especially, is necessarily vague, tangled, chaotic, and exceedingly disturbing. How few of us ever emerge from such beginning! How many souls perish in its tumult!

The voice of the sea is seductive; never ceasing, whispering, clamoring, murmuring, inviting the soul to wander for a spell in abysses of solitude; to lose itself in mazes of inward contemplation.

The voice of the sea speaks to the soul. The touch of the sea is sensuous, enfolding the body in its soft, close embrace.

VII

Mrs. Pontellier was not a woman given to confidences, a characteristic hitherto contrary to her nature. Even as a child she had lived her own small life all within herself. At a very early period she had apprehended instinctively the dual life—that outward existence which conforms, the inward life which questions.

That summer at Grand Isle she began to loosen a little the mantle of reserve that had always enveloped her. There may have been—there must have been—influences, both subtle and apparent, working in their several ways to induce her to do this; but the most obvious was the influence of

Adèle Ratignolle. The excessive physical charm of the Creole had first attracted her, for Edna had a sensuous susceptibility to beauty. Then the candor of the woman's whole existence, which every one might read, and which formed so striking a contrast to her own habitual reserve—this might have furnished a link. Who can tell what metals the gods use in forging the subtle bond which we call sympathy, which we might as well call love.

The two women went away one morning to the beach together, arm in arm, under the huge white sunshade. Edna had prevailed upon Madame Ratignolle to leave the children behind, though she could not induce her to relinquish a diminutive roll of needlework, which Adèle begged to be allowed to slip into the depths of her pocket. In some unaccountable way they had escaped from Robert.

The walk to the beach was no inconsiderable one, consisting as it did of a long, sandy path, upon which a sporadic and tangled growth that bordered it on either side made frequent and unexpected inroads. There were acres of yellow camomile reaching out on either hand. Further away still, vegetable gardens abounded, with frequent small plantations of orange or lemon trees intervening. The dark green clusters glistened from afar in the sun.

The women were both of goodly height, Madame Ratignolle possessing the more feminine and matronly figure. The charm of Edna Pontellier's physique stole insensibly upon you. The lines of her body were long, clean and symmetrical; it was a body which occasionally fell into splendid poses; there was no suggestion of the trim, stereotyped fashion-plate about it. A casual and indiscriminating observer, in passing, might not cast a second glance upon the figure. But with more feeling and discernment he would have recognized the noble beauty of its modeling, and the graceful severity of poise and movement, which made Edna Pontellier different from the crowd.

She wore a cool muslin that morning—white, with a waving vertical line of brown running through it; also a white linen collar and the big straw hat which she had taken from the peg outside the door. The hat rested any way on her yellow-brown hair, that waved a little, was heavy, and clung close to her head.

Madame Ratignolle, more careful of her complexion, had twined a gauze veil about her head. She wore dogskin gloves, with gauntlets that protected her wrists. She was dressed in pure white, with a fluffiness of ruffles that became her. The draperies and fluttering things which she wore suited her rich, luxuriant beauty as a greater severity of line could not have done.

There were a number of bath-houses along the beach, of rough but solid construction, built with small, protecting galleries facing the water. Each house consisted of two compartments, and each family at Lebrun's possessed a compartment for itself, fitted out with all the essential paraphernalia of the bath and whatever other conveniences the owners might desire. The two women had no intention of bathing; they had just strolled down to the beach for a walk and to be alone and near the water. The Pontellier and Ratignolle compartments adjoined one another under the same roof.

Mrs. Pontellier had brought down her key through force of habit. Unlocking the door of her bath-room she went inside, and soon emerged, bringing a rug, which she spread upon the floor of the gallery, and two huge hair pillows covered with crash, which she placed against the front of the building.

The two seated themselves there in the shade of the porch, side by side, with their backs against the pillows and their feet extended. Madame Ratignolle removed her veil, wiped her face with a rather delicate handkerchief, and fanned herself with the fan which she always carried suspended somewhere about her person by a long, narrow ribbon. Edna removed her collar and opened her dress at the throat. She took the fan from Madame Ratignolle and began to fan both herself and her companion. It was very warm, and for a while they did nothing but exchange remarks about the heat, the sun, the glare. But there was a breeze blowing, a choppy stiff wind that whipped the water into froth. It fluttered the skirts of the two women and kept them for a while engaged in adjusting, readjusting, tucking in, securing hair-pins and hat-pins. A few persons were sporting some distance away in the water. The beach was very still of human sound at that hour. The lady in black was reading her morning devotions on the porch of a neighboring bath-house. Two young lovers were exchanging their hearts' yearnings beneath the children's tent, which they had found unoccupied.

Edna Pontellier, casting her eyes about had finally kept them at rest upon the sea. The day was clear and carried the gaze out as far as the blue sky went; there were a few white clouds suspended idly over the horizon. A lateen sail was visible in the direction of Cat Island, and others to the south seemed almost motionless in the far distance.

"Of whom—of what are you thinking?" asked Adèle of her companion, whose countenance she had been watching with a little amused attention, arrested by the absorbed expression which seemed to have seized and fixed every feature into a statuesque repose.

"Nothing," returned Mrs. Pontellier, with a start, adding at once: "How stupid! But it seems to me it is the reply we make instinctively to such a question. Let me see," she went on, throwing back her head and narrowing her fine eyes till they shone like two vivid points of light. "Let me see. I was really not conscious of thinking of anything, but perhaps I can retrace my thoughts."

"Oh! never mind!" laughed Madame Ratignolle. "I am not quite so exacting. I will let you off this time. It is really too hot to think, especially to think about thinking."

"But for the fun of it," persisted Edna. "First of all, the sight of the water stretching so far away, those motionless sails against the blue sky, made a delicious picture that I just wanted to sit and look at. The hot wind beating in my face made me think—without any connection that I can trace—of a summer day in Kentucky, of a meadow that seemed as big as the ocean to the very little girl walking through the grass, which was higher than her waist. She threw out her arms as if swimming when she walked, beating the tall grass as one strikes out in the water. Oh, I see the connection now!"

"Where were you going that day in Kentucky, walking through the grass?"

"I don't remember now. I was just walking diagonally across a big field. My sunbonnet obstructed the view. I could see only the stretch of green before me, and I felt as if I must walk on forever, without coming to the end of it. I don't remember whether I was frightened or pleased. I must have been entertained.

"Likely as not it was Sunday," she laughed; "and I was running away from prayers, from the Presbyterian service, read in a spirit of gloom by my father that chills me yet to think of."

"And have you been running away from prayers ever since, *ma chère?*"[24] asked Madame Ratignolle, amused.

"No! oh, no!" Edna hastened to say. "I was a little unthinking child in those days, just following a misleading impulse without question. On the contrary, during one period of my life religion took a firm hold upon me; after I was twelve and until—until—why, I suppose until now, though I never thought much about it—just driven along by habit. But do you know," she broke off, turning her quick eyes upon Madame Ratignolle and leaning forward a little so as to bring her face quite close to that of her companion, "sometimes I feel this summer as if I were walking through the green meadow again; idly, aimlessly, unthinking and unguided."

Madame Ratignolle laid her hand over that of Mrs. Pontellier, which was near her. Seeing that the hand was not withdrawn, she clasped it firmly and warmly. She even stroked it a little, fondly, with the other hand, murmuring in an undertone, "*Pauvre chérie.*"[25]

The action was at first a little confusing to Edna, but she soon lent herself readily to the Creole's gentle caress. She was not accustomed to an outward and spoken expression of affection, either in herself or in others. She and her younger sister, Janet, had quarreled a good deal through force of unfortunate habit. Her older sister, Margaret, was matronly and dignified, probably from having assumed matronly and house-wifely responsibilities too early in life, their mother having died when they were quite young. Margaret was not effusive; she was practical. Edna had had an occasional girl friend, but whether accidentally or not, they seemed to have been all of one type—the self-contained. She never realized that the reserve of her own character had much, perhaps everything, to do with this. Her most intimate friend at school had been one of rather exceptional intellectual gifts, who wrote fine-sounding essays, which Edna admired and strove to imitate; and with her she talked and glowed over the English classics, and sometimes held religious and political controversies.

Edna often wondered at one propensity which sometimes had inwardly disturbed her without causing any outward show or manifestation on her

---

[24]French: "my dear." [25]French: "Poor dear."

part. At a very early age—perhaps it was when she traversed the ocean of waving grass—she remembered that she had been passionately enamored of a dignified and sad-eyed cavalry officer who visited her father in Kentucky. She could not leave his presence when he was there, nor remove her eyes from his face, which was something like Napoleon's, with a lock of black hair falling across the forehead. But the cavalry officer melted imperceptibly out of her existence.

At another time her affections were deeply engaged by a young gentleman who visited a lady on a neighboring plantation. It was after they went to Mississippi to live. The young man was engaged to be married to the young lady, and they sometimes called upon Margaret, driving over of afternoons in a buggy. Edna was a little miss, just merging into her teens; and the realization that she herself was nothing, nothing, nothing to the engaged young man was a bitter affliction to her. But he, too, went the way of dreams.

She was a grown young woman when she was overtaken by what she supposed to be the climax of her fate. It was when the face and figure of a great tragedian[26] began to haunt her imagination and stir her senses. The persistence of the infatuation lent it an aspect of genuineness. The hopelessness of it colored it with the lofty tones of a great passion.

The picture of the tragedian stood enframed upon her desk. Any one may possess the portrait of a tragedian without exciting suspicion or comment. (This was a sinister reflection which she cherished.) In the presence of others she expressed admiration for his exalted gifts, as she handed the photograph around and dwelt upon the fidelity of the likeness. When alone she sometimes picked it up and kissed the cold glass passionately.

Her marriage to Léonce Pontellier was purely an accident, in this respect resembling many other marriages which masquerade as the decrees of Fate. It was in the midst of her secret great passion that she met him. He fell in love, as men are in the habit of doing, and pressed his suit with an earnestness and an ardor which left nothing to be desired. He pleased her; his absolute devotion flattered her. She fancied there was a sympathy of thought and taste between them, in which fancy she was mistaken. Add to this the violent opposition of her father and her sister Margaret to her marriage with a Catholic, and we need seek no further for the motives which led her to accept Monsieur Pontellier for her husband.

The acme of bliss, which would have been a marriage with the tragedian, was not for her in this world. As the devoted wife of a man who worshiped her, she felt she would take her place with a certain dignity in the world of reality, closing the portals forever behind her upon the realm of romance and dreams.

But it was not long before the tragedian had gone to join the cavalry officer and the engaged young man and a few others; and Edna found herself face to face with the realities. She grew fond of her husband, realizing with some unaccountable satisfaction that no trace of passion or excessive and fictitious warmth colored her affection, thereby threatening its dissolution.

[26]Actor.

She was fond of her children in an uneven, impulsive way. She would sometimes gather them passionately to her heart; she would sometimes forget them. The year before they had spent part of the summer with their grandmother Pontellier in Iberville. Feeling secure regarding their happiness and welfare, she did not miss them except with an occasional intense longing. Their absence was a sort of relief, though she did not admit this, even to herself. It seemed to free her of a responsibility which she had blindly assumed and for which Fate had not fitted her.

Edna did not reveal so much as all this to Madame Ratignolle that summer day when they sat with faces turned to the sea. But a good part of it escaped her. She had put her head down on Madame Ratignolle's shoulder. She was flushed and felt intoxicated with the sound of her own voice and the unaccustomed taste of candor. It muddled her like wine, or like a first breath of freedom.

There was the sound of approaching voices. It was Robert, surrounded by a troop of children, searching for them. The two little Pontelliers were with him, and he carried Madame Ratignolle's little girl in his arms. There were other children beside, and two nursemaids followed, looking disagreeable and resigned.

The women at once rose and began to shake out their draperies and relax their muscles. Mrs. Pontellier threw the cushions and rug into the bath-house. The children all scampered off to the awning, and they stood there in a line, gazing upon the intruding lovers, still exchanging their vows and sighs. The lovers got up, with only a silent protest, and walked slowly away somewhere else.

The children possessed themselves of the tent, and Mrs. Pontellier went over to join them.

Madame Ratignolle begged Robert to accompany her to the house; she complained of cramp in her limbs and stiffness of the joints. She leaned draggingly upon his arm as they walked.

VIII

"Do me a favor, Robert," spoke the pretty woman at his side, almost as soon as she and Robert had started on their slow, homeward way. She looked up in his face, leaning on his arm beneath the encircling shadow of the umbrella which he had lifted.

"Granted; as many as you like," he returned, glancing down into her eyes that were full of thoughtfulness and some speculation.

"I only ask for one; let Mrs. Pontellier alone."

"*Tiens!*" he exclaimed, with a sudden, boyish laugh. "*Voilà que Madame Ratignolle est jalouse!*"[27]

"Nonsense! I'm in earnest; I mean what I say. Let Mrs. Pontellier alone."

"Why?" he asked; himself growing serious at his companion's solicitation.

[27]French: "So! Madame Ratignolle is jealous!"

"She is not one of us; she is not like us. She might make the unfortunate blunder of taking you seriously."

His face flushed with annoyance, and taking off his soft hat he began to beat it impatiently against his leg as he walked. "Why shouldn't she take me seriously?" he demanded sharply. "Am I a comedian, a clown, a jack-in-the-box? Why shouldn't she? You Creoles! I have no patience with you! Am I always to be regarded as a feature of an amusing programme? I hope Mrs. Pontellier does take me seriously. I hope she has discernment enough to find in me something besides the *blagueur*. If I thought there was any doubt—"

"Oh, enough, Robert!" she broke into his heated outburst. "You are not thinking of what you are saying. You speak with about as little reflection as we might expect from one of those children down there playing in the sand. If your attentions to any married women here were ever offered with any intention of being convincing, you would not be the gentleman we all know you to be, and you would be unfit to associate with the wives and daughters of the people who trust you."

Madame Ratignolle had spoken what she believed to be the law and the gospel. The young man shrugged his shoulders impatiently.

"Oh! well! That isn't it," slamming his hat down vehemently upon his head. "You ought to feel that such things are not flattering to say to a fellow."

"Should our whole intercourse consist of an exchange of compliments? *Ma foi!*"[28]

"It isn't pleasant to have a woman tell you—" he went on, unheedingly, but breaking off suddenly: "Now if I were like Arobin—you remember Alcée Arobin and that story of the consul's wife at Biloxi?"[29] And he related the story of Alcée Arobin and the consul's wife; and another about the tenor of the French Opera, who received letters which should never have been written; and still other stories, grave and gay, till Mrs. Pontellier and her possible propensity for taking young men seriously was apparently forgotten.

Madame Ratignolle, when they had regained her cottage, went in to take the hour's rest which she considered helpful. Before leaving her, Robert begged her pardon for the impatience—he called it rudeness—with which he had received her well-meant caution.

"You made one mistake, Adèle," he said, with a light smile; "there is no earthly possibility of Mrs. Pontellier ever taking me seriously. You should have warned me against taking myself seriously. Your advice might then have carried some weight and given me subject for some reflection. *Au revoir.*[30] But you look tired," he added, solicitously. "Would you like a cup of bouillon? Shall I stir you a toddy? Let me mix you a toddy with a drop of Angostura."

She acceded to the suggestion of bouillon, which was grateful and acceptable. He went himself to the kitchen, which was a building apart from

---

[28]French: "For heaven's sake!"
[29]A resort on the coast of Mississippi.
[30]French: "Goodbye."

the cottages and lying to the rear of the house. And he himself brought her the golden-brown bouillon, in a dainty Sèvres cup, with a flaky cracker or two on the saucer.

She thrust a bare, white arm from the curtain which shielded her open door, and received the cup from his hands. She told him he was a *bon garçon*,[31] and she meant it. Robert thanked her and turned away toward "the house."

The lovers were just entering the grounds of the *pension*. They were leaning toward each other as the water-oaks bent from the sea. There was not a particle of earth beneath their feet. Their heads might have been turned upside-down, so absolutely did they tread upon blue ether. The lady in black, creeping behind them, looked a trifle paler and more jaded than usual. There was no sign of Mrs. Pontellier and the children. Robert scanned the distance for any such apparition. They would doubtless remain away till the dinner hour. The young man ascended to his mother's room. It was situated at the top of the house, made up of odd angles and a queer, sloping ceiling. Two broad dormer windows looked out toward the Gulf, and as far across it as a man's eye might reach. The furnishings of the room were light, cool, and practical.

Madame Lebrun was busily engaged at the sewing-machine. A little black girl sat on the floor, and with her hands worked the treadle of the machine. The Creole woman does not take any chances which may be avoided of imperiling her health.

Robert went over and seated himself on the broad sill of one of the dormer windows. He took a book from his pocket and began energetically to read it, judging by the precision and frequency with which he turned the leaves. The sewing-machine made a resounding clatter in the room; it was of a ponderous, by-gone make. In the lulls, Robert and his mother exchanged bits of desultory conversation.

"Where is Mrs. Pontellier?"

"Down at the beach with the children."

"I promised to lend her the Goncourt.[32] Don't forget to take it down when you go; it's there on the bookshelf over the small table." Clatter, clatter, clatter, bang! for the next five or eight minutes.

"Where is Victor going with the rockaway?"

"The rockaway? Victor?"

"Yes; down there in front. He seems to be getting ready to drive away somewhere."

"Call him." Clatter, clatter!

Robert uttered a shrill, piercing whistle which might have been heard back at the wharf.

"He won't look up."

---

[31]French: a good boy.

[32]A novel by Edward Goncourt (1822–1896),
   a French realist.

Madame Lebrun flew to the window. She called "Victor!" She waved a handkerchief and called again. The young fellow below got into the vehicle and started the horse off at a gallop.

Madame Lebrun went back to the machine, crimson with annoyance. Victor was the younger son and brother—a *tête montée*,[33] with a temper which invited violence and a will which no ax could break.

"Whenever you say the word I'm ready to thrash any amount of reason into him that he's able to hold."

"If your father had only lived!" Clatter, clatter, clatter, clatter, bang! It was a fixed belief with Madame Lebrun that the conduct of the universe and all things pertaining thereto would have been manifestly of a more intelligent and higher order had not Monsieur Lebrun been removed to other spheres during the early years of their married life.

"What do you hear from Montel?" Montel was a middle-aged gentleman whose vain ambition and desire for the past twenty years had been to fill the void which Monsieur Lebrun's taking off had left in the Lebrun household. Clatter, clatter, bang, clatter!

"I have a letter somewhere," looking in the machine drawer and finding the letter in the bottom of the work-basket. "He says to tell you he will be in Vera Cruz the beginning of next month"—clatter, clatter!—"and if you still have the intention of joining him"—bang! clatter, clatter, bang!

"Why didn't you tell me so before, mother? You know I wanted—" Clatter, clatter, clatter!

"Do you see Mrs. Pontellier starting back with the children? She will be in late to luncheon again. She never starts to get ready for luncheon till the last minute." Clatter, clatter! "Where are you going?"

"Where did you say the Goncourt was?"

IX

Every light in the hall was ablaze; every lamp turned as high as it could be without smoking the chimney or threatening explosion. The lamps were fixed at intervals against the wall, encircling the whole room. Some one had gathered orange and lemon branches and with these fashioned graceful festoons between. The dark green of the branches stood out and glistened against the white muslin curtains which draped the windows, and which puffed, floated, and flapped at the capricious will of a stiff breeze that swept up from the Gulf.

It was Saturday night a few weeks after the intimate conversation held between Robert and Madame Ratignolle on their way from the beach. An unusual number of husbands, fathers, and friends had come down to stay over Sunday; and they were being suitably entertained by their families, with the material help of Madame Lebrun. The dining tables had all been removed to one end of the hall, and the chairs ranged about in rows and in

---

[33]French: an impulsive character.

clusters. Each little family group had had its say and exchanged its domestic gossip earlier in the evening. There was now an apparent disposition to relax; to widen the circle of confidences and give a more general tone to the conversation.

Many of the children had been permitted to sit up beyond their usual bedtime. A small band of them were lying on their stomachs on the floor looking at the colored sheets of the comic papers which Mr. Pontellier had brought down. The little Pontellier boys were permitting them to do so, and making their authority felt.

Music, dancing, and a recitation or two were the entertainments furnished, or rather, offered. But there was nothing systematic about the programme, no appearance of prearrangement nor even premeditation.

At an early hour in the evening the Farival twins were prevailed upon to play the piano. They were girls of fourteen, always clad in the Virgin's colors, blue and white, having been dedicated to the Blessed Virgin at their baptism. They played a duet from "Zampa," and at the earnest solicitation of every one present followed it with the overture to "The Poet and the Peasant."

"Allez vous-en! Sapristi!" shrieked the parrot outside the door. He was the only being present who possessed sufficient candor to admit that he was not listening to these gracious performances for the first time that summer. Old Monsieur Farival, grandfather of the twins, grew indignant over the interruption, and insisted upon having the bird removed and consigned to regions of darkness. Victor Lebrun objected; and his decrees were as immutable as those of Fate. The parrot fortunately offered no further interruption to the entertainment, the whole venom of his nature apparently having been cherished up and hurled against the twins in that one impetuous outburst.

Later a young brother and sister gave recitations, which every one present had heard many times at winter evening entertainments in the city.

A little girl performed a skirt dance in the center of the floor. The mother played her accompaniments and at the same time watched her daughter with greedy admiration and nervous apprehension. She need have had no apprehension. The child was mistress of the situation. She had been properly dressed for the occasion in black tulle and black silk tights. Her little neck and arms were bare, and her hair, artificially crimped, stood out like fluffy black plumes over her head. Her poses were full of grace, and her little black-shod toes twinkled as they shot out and upward with a rapidity and suddenness which were bewildering.

But there was no reason why every one should not dance. Madame Ratignolle could not, so it was she who gaily consented to play for the others. She played very well, keeping excellent waltz time and infusing an expression into the strains which was indeed inspiring. She was keeping up her music on account of the children, she said; because she and her husband both considered it a means of brightening the home and making it attractive.

Almost every one danced but the twins, who could not be induced to separate during the brief period when one or the other should be whirling around the room in the arms of a man. They might have danced together, but they did not think of it.

The children were sent to bed. Some went submissively; others with shrieks and protests as they were dragged away. They had been permitted to sit up till after the ice-cream, which naturally marked the limit of human indulgence.

The ice-cream was passed around with cake—gold and silver cake arranged on platters in alternate slices; it had been made and frozen during the afternoon back of the kitchen by two black women, under the supervision of Victor. It was pronounced a great success—excellent if it had only contained a little less vanilla or a little more sugar, if it had been frozen a degree harder, and if the salt might have been kept out of portions of it. Victor was proud of his achievement, and went about recommending it and urging every one to partake of it to excess.

After Mrs. Pontellier had danced twice with her husband, once with Robert, and once with Monsieur Ratignolle, who was thin and tall and swayed like a reed in the wind when he danced, she went out on the gallery and seated herself on the low window-sill, where she commanded a view of all that went on in the hall and could look out toward the Gulf. There was a soft effulgence in the east. The moon was coming up, and its mystic shimmer was casting a million lights across the distant, restless water.

"Would you like to hear Mademoiselle Reisz play?" asked Robert, coming out on the porch where she was. Of course Edna would like to hear Mademoiselle Reisz play; but she feared it would be useless to entreat her.

"I'll ask her," he said. "I'll tell her that you want to hear her. She likes you. She will come." He turned and hurried away to one of the far cottages, where Mademoiselle Reisz was shuffling away. She was dragging a chair in and out of her room, and at intervals objecting to the crying of a baby, which a nurse in the adjoining cottage was endeavoring to put to sleep. She was a disagreeable little woman, no longer young, who had quarreled with almost every one, owing to a temper which was self-assertive and a disposition to trample upon the rights of others. Robert prevailed upon her without any too great difficulty.

She entered the hall with him during a lull in the dance. She made an awkward, imperious little bow as she went in. She was a homely woman, with a small weazened face and body and eyes that glowed. She had absolutely no taste in dress, and wore a batch of rusty black lace with a bunch of artificial violets pinned to the side of her hair.

"Ask Mrs. Pontellier what she would like to hear me play," she requested of Robert. She sat perfectly still before the piano, not touching the keys, while Robert carried her message to Edna at the window. A general air of surprise and genuine satisfaction fell upon every one as they saw the pianist enter. There was a settling down, and a prevailing air of expectancy everywhere. Edna was a trifle embarrassed at being thus signaled out for the imperious little woman's favor. She would not dare to choose, and begged that Mademoiselle Reisz would please herself in her selections.

Edna was what she herself called very fond of music. Musical strains, well rendered, had a way of evoking pictures in her mind. She sometimes liked to sit in the room of mornings when Madame Ratignolle played or practiced. One piece which that lady played Edna had entitled "Solitude." It was a short, plaintive, minor strain. The name of the piece was something else, but she called it "Solitude." When she heard it there came before her imagination the figure of a man standing beside a desolate rock on the sea-shore. He was naked. His attitude was one of hopeless resignation as he looked toward a distant bird winging its flight away from him.

Another piece called to her mind a dainty young woman clad in an Empire gown, taking mincing dancing steps as she came down a long avenue between tall hedges. Again, another reminded her of children at play, and still another of nothing on earth but a demure lady stroking a cat.

The very first chords which Mademoiselle Reisz struck upon the piano sent a keen tremor down Mrs. Pontellier's spinal column. It was not the first time she had heard an artist at the piano. Perhaps it was the first time she was ready, perhaps the first time her being was tempered to take an impress of the abiding truth.

She waited for the material pictures which she thought would gather and blaze before her imagination. She waited in vain. She saw no pictures of solitude, of hope, of longing, or of despair. But the very passions themselves were aroused within her soul, swaying it, lashing it, as the waves daily beat upon her splendid body. She trembled, she was choking, and the tears blinded her.

Mademoiselle had finished. She arose, and bowing her stiff, lofty bow, she went away, stopping for neither thanks nor applause. As she passed along the gallery she patted Edna upon the shoulder.

"Well, how did you like my music?" she asked. The young woman was unable to answer; she pressed the hand of the pianist convulsively. Mademoiselle Reisz perceived her agitation and even her tears. She patted her again upon the shoulder as she said:

"You are the only one worth playing for. Those others? Bah!" and she went shuffling and sidling on down the gallery toward her room.

But she was mistaken about "those others." Her playing had aroused a fever of enthusiasm. "What passion!" "What an artist!" "I have always said no one could play Chopin[34] like Mademoiselle Reisz!" "That last prelude! Bon Dieu! It shakes a man!"

It was growing late, and there was a general disposition to disband. But some one, perhaps it was Robert, thought of a bath at that mystic hour and under that mystic moon.

[34]Frederic François Chopin (1810–1849), Polish composer and pianist of the early Romantic period.

X

At all events Robert proposed it, and there was not a dissenting voice. There was not one but was ready to follow when he led the way. He did not lead the way, however, he directed the way; and he himself loitered behind with the lovers, who had betrayed a disposition to linger and hold themselves apart. He walked between them, whether with malicious or mischievous intent was not wholly clear, even to himself.

The Pontelliers and Ratignolles walked ahead; the women leaning upon the arms of their husbands. Edna could hear Robert's voice behind them, and could sometimes hear what he said. She wondered why he did not join them. It was unlike him not to. Of late he had sometimes held away from her for an entire day, redoubling his devotion upon the next and the next, as though to make up for hours that had been lost. She missed him the days when some pretext served to take him away from her, just as one misses the sun on a cloudy day without having thought much about the sun when it was shining.

The people walked in little groups toward the beach. They talked and laughed; some of them sang. There was a band playing down at Klein's hotel, and the strains reached them faintly, tempered by the distance. There were strange, rare odors abroad—a tangle of the sea smell and of weeds and damp, new-plowed earth, mingled with the heavy perfume of a field of white blossoms somewhere near. But the night sat lightly upon the sea and the land. There was no weight of darkness; there were no shadows. The white light of the moon had fallen upon the world like the mystery and the softness of sleep.

Most of them walked into the water as though into a native element. The sea was quiet now, and swelled lazily in broad billows that melted into one another and did not break except upon the beach in little foamy crests that coiled back like slow, white serpents.

Edna had attempted all summer to learn to swim. She had received instructions from both the men and women; in some instances from the children. Robert had pursued a system of lessons almost daily; and he was nearly at the point of discouragement in realizing the futility of his efforts. A certain ungovernable dread hung about her when in the water, unless there was a hand near by that might reach out and reassure her.

But that night she was like the little tottering, stumbling, clutching child, who of a sudden realizes its powers, and walks for the first time alone, boldly and with over-confidence. She could have shouted for joy. She did shout for joy, as with a sweeping stroke or two she lifted her body to the surface of the water.

A feeling of exultation overtook her, as if some power of significant import had been given her soul. She grew daring and reckless, overestimating her strength. She wanted to swim far out, where no woman had swum before.

Her unlooked-for achievement was the subject of wonder, applause, and admiration. Each one congratulated himself that his special teachings had accomplished this desired end.

"How easy it is!" she thought. "It is nothing," she said aloud; "why did I not discover before that it was nothing. Think of the time I have lost splashing about like a baby!" She would not join the groups in their sports and bouts, but intoxicated with her newly conquered power, she swam out alone.

She turned her face seaward to gather in an impression of space and solitude, which the vast expanse of water, meeting and melting with the moonlit sky, conveyed to her excited fancy. As she swam she seemed to be reaching out for the unlimited in which to lose herself.

Once she turned and looked toward the shore, toward the people she had left there. She had not gone any great distance—that is, what would have been a great distance for an experienced swimmer. But to her unaccustomed vision the stretch of water behind her assumed the aspect of a barrier which her unaided strength would never be able to overcome.

A quick vision of death smote her soul, and for a second of time appalled and enfeebled her senses. But by an effort she rallied her staggering faculties and managed to regain the land.

She made no mention of her encounter with death and her flash of terror, except to say to her husband, "I thought I should have perished out there alone."

"You were not so very far, my dear; I was watching you," he told her.

Edna went at once to the bath-house, and she had put on her dry clothes and was ready to return home before the others had left the water. She started to walk away alone. They all called to her and shouted to her. She waved a dissenting hand, and went on, paying no further heed to their renewed cries which sought to detain her.

"Sometimes I am tempted to think that Mrs. Pontellier is capricious," said Madame Lebrun, who was amusing herself immensely and feared that Edna's abrupt departure might put an end to the pleasure.

"I know she is," assented Mr. Pontellier; "sometimes, not often."

Edna had not traversed a quarter of the distance on her way home before she was overtaken by Robert.

"Did you think I was afraid?" she asked him, without a shade of annoyance.

"No; I knew you weren't afraid."

"Then why did you come? Why didn't you stay out there with the others?"

"I never thought of it."

"Thought of what?"

"Of anything. What difference does it make?"

"I'm very tired," she uttered, complainingly.

"I know you are."

"You don't know anything about it. Why should you know? I never was so exhausted in my life. But it isn't unpleasant. A thousand emotions have swept through me to-night. I don't comprehend half of them. Don't mind what I'm saying; I am just thinking aloud. I wonder if I shall ever be stirred again as Mademoiselle Reisz's playing moved me to-night. I wonder if any night on earth will ever again be like this one. It is like a night in a dream. The people about me are like some uncanny, half-human beings. There must be spirits abroad to-night."

"There are," whispered Robert. "Didn't you know this was the twenty-eighth of August?"

"The twenty-eighth of August?"

"Yes. On the twenty-eighth of August, at the hour of midnight, and if the moon is shining—the moon must be shining—a spirit that has haunted these shores for ages rises up from the Gulf. With its own penetrating vision the spirit seeks some one mortal worthy to hold him company, worthy of being exalted for a few hours into realms of the semi-celestials. His search has always hitherto been fruitless, and he has sunk back, disheartened, into the sea. But tonight he found Mrs. Pontellier. Perhaps he will never wholly release her from the spell. Perhaps she will never again suffer a poor, unworthy earthling to walk in the shadow of her divine presence."

"Don't banter me," she said, wounded at what appeared to be his flippancy. He did not mind the entreaty, but the tone with its delicate note of pathos was like a reproach. He could not explain; he could not tell her that he had penetrated her mood and understood. He said nothing except to offer her his arm, for, by her own admission, she was exhausted. She had been walking alone with her arms hanging limp, letting her white skirts trail along the dewy path. She took his arm, but she did not lean upon it. She let her hand lie listlessly, as though her thoughts were elsewhere—somewhere in advance of her body, and she was striving to overtake them.

Robert assisted her into the hammock which swung from the post before her door out to the trunk of a tree.

"Will you stay out here and wait for Mr. Pontellier?" he asked.

"I'll stay out here. Good-night."

"Shall I get you a pillow?"

"There's one here," she said, feeling about, for they were in the shadow.

"It must be soiled; the children have been tumbling it about."

"No matter." And having discovered the pillow, she adjusted it beneath her head. She extended herself in the hammock with a deep breath of relief. She was not a supercilious or an over-dainty woman. She was not much given to reclining in the hammock, and when she did so it was with no cat-like suggestion of voluptuous ease, but with a beneficent repose which seemed to invade her whole body.

"Shall I stay with you till Mr. Pontellier comes?" asked Robert, seating himself on the outer edge of one of the steps and taking hold of the hammock rope which was fastened to the post.

"If you wish. Don't swing the hammock. Will you get my white shawl which I left on the window-sill over at the house?"

"Are you chilly?"

"No; but I shall be presently."

"Presently?" he laughed. "Do you know what time it is? How long are you going to stay out here?"

"I don't know. Will you get the shawl?"

"Of course I will," he said, rising. He went over to the house, walking along the grass. She watched his figure pass in and out of the strips of moonlight. It was past midnight. It was very quiet.

When he returned with the shawl she took it and kept it in her hand. She did not put it around her.

"Did you say I should stay till Mr. Pontellier came back?"

"I said you might if you wished to."

He seated himself again and rolled a cigarette, which he smoked in silence. Neither did Mrs. Pontellier speak. No multitude of words could have been more significant than those moments of silence, or more pregnant with the first-felt throbbings of desire.

When the voices of the bathers were heard approaching, Robert said good-night. She did not answer him. He thought she was asleep. Again she watched his figure pass in and out of the strips of moonlight as he walked away.

XI

"What are you doing out here, Edna? I thought I should find you in bed," said her husband, when he discovered her lying there. He had walked up with Madame Lebrun and left her at the house. His wife did not reply.

"Are you asleep?" he asked, bending down close to look at her.

"No." Her eyes gleamed bright and intense, with no sleepy shadows, as they looked into his.

"Do you know it is past one o'clock? Come on," and he mounted the steps and went into their room.

"Edna!" called Mr. Pontellier from within, after a few moments had gone by.

"Don't wait for me," she answered. He thrust his head through the door.

"You will take cold out there," he said, irritably. "What folly is this? Why don't you come in?"

"It isn't cold; I have my shawl."

"The mosquitoes will devour you."

"There are no mosquitoes."

She heard him moving about the room; every sound indicating impatience and irritation. Another time she would have gone in at his request. She would, through habit, have yielded to his desire; not with any sense of submission or obedience to his compelling wishes, but unthinkingly, as we walk, move, sit, stand, go through the daily treadmill of the life which has been portioned out to us.

"Edna, dear, are you not coming in soon?" he asked again, this time fondly, with a note of entreaty.

"No; I am going to stay out here."

"This is more than folly," he blurted out. "I can't permit you to stay out there all night. You must come in the house instantly."

With a writhing motion she settled herself more securely in the hammock. She perceived that her will had blazed up, stubborn and resistant.

She could not at that moment have done other than denied and resisted. She wondered if her husband had ever spoken to her like that before, and if she had submitted to his command. Of course she had; she remembered that she had. But she could not realize why or how she should have yielded, feeling as she then did.

"Léonce, go to bed," she said. "I mean to stay out here. I don't wish to go in, and I don't intend to. Don't speak to me like that again; I shall not answer you."

Mr. Pontellier had prepared for bed, but he slipped on an extra garment. He opened a bottle of wine, of which he kept a small and select supply in a buffet of his own. He drank a glass of the wine and went out on the gallery and offered a glass to his wife. She did not wish any. He drew up the rocker, hoisted his slippered feet on the rail, and proceeded to smoke a cigar. He smoked two cigars; then he went inside and drank another glass of wine. Mrs. Pontellier again declined to accept a glass when it was offered to her. Mr. Pontellier once more seated himself with elevated feet, and after a reasonable interval of time smoked some more cigars.

Edna began to feel like one who awakens gradually out of a dream, a delicious, grotesque, impossible dream, to feel again the realities pressing into her soul. The physical need for sleep began to overtake her; the exuberance which had sustained and exalted her spirit left her helpless and yielding to the conditions which crowded her in.

The stillest hour of the night had come, the hour before dawn, when the world seems to hold its breath. The moon hung low, and had turned from silver to copper in the sleeping sky. The old owl no longer hooted, and the water-oaks had ceased to moan as they bent their heads.

Edna arose, cramped from lying so long and still in the hammock. She tottered up the steps, clutching feebly at the post before passing into the house.

"Are you coming in, Léonce?" she asked, turning her face toward her husband.

"Yes, dear," he answered, with a glance following a misty puff of smoke. "Just as soon as I have finished my cigar."

XII

She slept but a few hours. They were troubled and feverish hours, disturbed with dreams that were intangible, that eluded her, leaving only an impression upon her half-awakened senses of something unattainable. She was up and dressed in the cool of the early morning. The air was invigorating and steadied somewhat her faculties. However, she was not seeking refreshment or help from any source, either external or from within. She was blindly following whatever impulse moved her, as if she had placed herself in alien hands for direction, and freed her soul of responsibility.

Most of the people at that early hour were still in bed and asleep. A few, who intended to go over to the *Chênière* for mass, were moving about. The lovers, who had laid their plans the night before, were already strolling toward the wharf. The lady in black, with her Sunday prayer book, velvet and gold-clasped, and her Sunday silver beads, was following them at no great distance. Old Monsieur Farival was up, and was more than half inclined to do anything that suggested itself. He put on his big straw hat, and taking his umbrella from the stand in the hall, followed the lady in black, never overtaking her.

The little negro girl who worked Madame Lebrun's sewing-machine was sweeping the galleries with long, absent-minded strokes of the broom. Edna sent her up into the house to awaken Robert.

"Tell him I am going to the *Chênière*. The boat is ready; tell him to hurry."

He had soon joined her. She had never sent for him before. She had never asked for him. She had never seemed to want him before. She did not appear conscious that she had done anything unusual in commanding his presence. He was apparently equally unconscious of anything extraordinary in the situation. But his face was suffused with a quiet glow when he met her.

They went together back to the kitchen to drink coffee. There was no time to wait for any nicety of service. They stood outside the window and the cook passed them their coffee and a roll, which they drank and ate from the window-sill. Edna said it tasted good. She had not thought of coffee nor of anything. He told her he had often noticed that she lacked forethought.

"Wasn't it enough to think of going to the *Chênière* and waking you up?" she laughed. "Do I have to think of everything?—as Léonce says when he's in a bad humor. I don't blame him; he'd never be in a bad humor if it weren't for me."

They took a short cut across the sands. At a distance they could see the curious procession moving toward the wharf—the lovers, shoulder to shoulder, creeping; the lady in black, gaining steadily upon them; old Monsieur Farival, losing ground inch by inch, and a young barefooted Spanish girl, with a red kerchief on her head and a basket on her arm, bringing up the rear.

Robert knew the girl, and he talked to her a little in the boat. No one present understood what they said. Her name was Mariequita. She had a round, sly, piquant face and pretty black eyes. Her hands were small, and she kept them folded over the handle of her basket. Her feet were broad and coarse. She did not strive to hide them. Edna looked at her feet, and noticed the sand and slime between her brown toes.

Beaudelet grumbled because Mariequita was there, taking up so much room. In reality he was annoyed at having old Monsieur Farival, who considered himself the better sailor of the two. But he would not quarrel with so old a man as Monsieur Farival, so he quarreled with Mariequita. The girl was deprecatory at one moment, appealing to Robert. She was saucy the next, moving her head up and down, making "eyes" at Robert and making "mouths" at Beaudelet.

The lovers were all alone. They saw nothing, they heard nothing. The lady in black was counting her beads for the third time. Old Monsieur

Farival talked incessantly of what he knew about handling a boat, and of what Beaudelet did not know on the same subject.

Edna liked it all. She looked Mariequita up and down, from her ugly brown toes to her pretty black eyes, and back again.

"Why does she look at me like that?" inquired the girl of Robert.

"Maybe she thinks you are pretty. Shall I ask her?"

"No. Is she your sweetheart?"

"She's a married lady, and has two children."

"Oh! well! Francisco ran away with Sylvano's wife, who had four children. They took all his money and one of the children and stole his boat."

"Shut up!"

"Does she understand?"

"Oh, hush!"

"Are those two married over there—leaning on each other?"

"Of course not," laughed Robert.

"Of course not," echoed Mariequita, with a serious, confirmatory bob of the head.

The sun was high up and beginning to bite. The swift breeze seemed to Edna to bury the sting of it into the pores of her face and hands. Robert held his umbrella over her.

As they went cutting sidewise through the water, the sails bellied taut, with the wind filling and overflowing them. Old Monsieur Farival laughed sardonically at something as he looked at the sails, and Beaudelet swore at the old man under his breath.

Sailing across the bay to the *Chênière Caminada*, Edna felt as if she were being borne away from some anchorage which had held her fast, whose chains had been loosening—had snapped the night before when the mystic spirit was abroad, leaving her free to drift whithersoever she chose to set her sails. Robert spoke to her incessantly; he no longer noticed Mariequita. The girl had shrimps in her bamboo basket. They were covered with Spanish moss. She beat the moss down impatiently, and muttered to herself sullenly.

"Let us go to Grande Terre[35] to-morrow?" said Robert in a low voice.

"What shall we do there?"

"Climb up the hill to the old fort and look at the little wriggling gold snakes, and watch the lizards sun themselves."

She gazed away toward Grande Terre and thought she would like to be alone there with Robert, in the sun, listening to the ocean's roar and watching the slimy lizards writhe in and out among the ruins of the old fort.

"And the next day or the next we can sail to the Bayou Brulow,"[36] he went on. "What shall we do there?"

"Anything—cast bait for fish."

[35]An island near Grand Isle.
[36]A village near Grande Isle built upon a platform in the bayou.

"No; we'll go back to Grande Terre. Let the fish alone."

"We'll go wherever you like," he said. "I'll have Tonie come over and help me patch and trim my boat. We shall not need Beaudelet nor any one. Are you afraid of the pirogue?"[37]

"Oh, no."

"Then I'll take you some night in the pirogue when the moon shines. Maybe your Gulf spirit will whisper to you in which of these islands the treasures are hidden— direct you to the very spot, perhaps."

"And in a day we should be rich!" she laughed. "I'd give it all to you, the pirate gold and every bit of treasure we could dig up. I think you would know how to spend it. Pirate gold isn't a thing to be hoarded or utilized. It is something to squander and throw to the four winds, for the fun of seeing the golden specks fly."

"We'd share it, and scatter it together," he said. His face flushed.

They all went together up to the quaint little Gothic church of Our Lady of Lourdes, gleaming all brown and yellow with paint in the sun's glare.

Only Beaudelet remained behind, tinkering at his boat, and Mariequita walked away with her basket of shrimps, casting a look of childish ill-humor and reproach at Robert from the corner of her eye.

XIII

A feeling of oppression and drowsiness overcame Edna during the service. Her head began to ache, and the lights on the altar swayed before her eyes. Another time she might have made an effort to regain her composure; but her one thought was to quit the stifling atmosphere of the church and reach the open air. She arose, climbing over Robert's feet with a muttered apology. Old Monsieur Farival, flurried, curious, stood up, but upon seeing that Robert had followed Mrs. Pontellier, he sank back into his seat. He whispered an anxious inquiry of the lady in black, who did not notice him or reply, but kept her eyes fastened upon the pages of her velvet prayerbook.

"I felt giddy and almost overcome," Edna said, lifting her hands instinctively to her head and pushing her straw hat up from her forehead. "I couldn't have stayed through the service." They were outside in the shadow of the church. Robert was full of solicitude.

"It was folly to have thought of going in the first place, let alone staying. Come over to Madame Antoine's; you can rest there." He took her arm and led her away, looking anxiously and continuously down into her face,

How still it was, with only the voice of the sea whispering through the reeds that grew in the salt-water pools! The long line of little gray, weather-beaten houses nestled peacefully among the orange trees. It must always have been God's day on that low, drowsy island, Edna thought. They stopped, leaning over a jagged fence made of sea-drift, to ask for water. A youth, a mild-faced Acadian,[38] was drawing water from the cistern, which

---

[37]A boat similar to a canoe.   [38]A person of French Canadian descent.

was nothing more than a rusty buoy, with an opening on one side, sunk in the ground. The water which the youth handed to them in a tin pail was not cold to taste, but it was cool to her heated face, and it greatly revived and refreshed her.

Madame Antoine's cot was at the far end of the village. She welcomed them with all the native hospitality, as she would have opened her door to let the sunlight in. She was fat, and walked heavily and clumsily across the floor. She could speak no English, but when Robert made her understand that the lady who accompanied him was ill and desired to rest, she was all eagerness to make Edna feel at home and to dispose of her comfortably.

The whole place was immaculately clean, and the big, four-posted bed, snow-white, invited one to repose. It stood in a small side room which looked out across a narrow grass plot toward the shed, where there was a disabled boat lying keel upward.

Madame Antoine had not gone to mass. Her son Tonie had, but she supposed he would soon be back, and she invited Robert to be seated and wait for him. But he went and sat outside the door and smoked. Madame Antoine busied herself in the large front room preparing dinner. She was boiling mullets[39] over a few red coals in the huge fireplace.

Edna, left alone in the little side room, loosened her clothes, removing the greater part of them. She bathed her face, her neck and arms in the basin that stood between the windows. She took off her shoes and stockings and stretched herself in the very center of the high, white bed. How luxurious it felt to rest thus in a strange, quaint bed, with its sweet country odor of laurel lingering about the sheets and mattress! She stretched her strong limbs that ached a little. She ran her fingers through her loosened hair for a while. She looked at her round arms as she held them straight up and rubbed them one after the other, observing closely, as if it were something she saw for the first time, the fine, firm quality and texture of her flesh. She clasped her hands easily above her head, and it was thus she fell asleep.

She slept lightly at first, half awake and drowsily attentive to the things about her. She could hear Madame Antoine's heavy, scraping tread as she walked back and forth on the sanded floor. Some chickens were clucking outside the windows, scratching for bits of gravel in the grass. Later she half heard the voices of Robert and Tonie talking under the shed. She did not stir. Even her eyelids rested numb and heavily over her sleepy eyes. The voices went on—Tonie's slow, Acadian drawl, Robert's quick, soft, smooth French. She understood French imperfectly unless directly addressed, and the voices were only part of the other drowsy, muffled sounds lulling her senses.

When Edna awoke it was with the conviction that she had slept long and soundly. The voices were hushed under the shed. Madame Antoine's step was no longer to be heard in the adjoining room. Even the chickens had gone elsewhere to scratch and cluck. The mosquito bar was drawn over

---

[39]An edible spiny-finned fish.

her; the old woman had come in while she slept and let down the bar. Edna arose quietly from the bed, and looking between the curtains of the window, she saw by the slanting rays of the sun that the afternoon was far advanced. Robert was out there under the shed, reclining in the shade against the sloping keel of the overturned boat. He was reading from a book. Tonie was no longer with him. She wondered what had become of the rest of the party. She peeped out at him two or three times as she stood washing herself in the little basin between the windows.

Madame Antoine had laid some coarse, clean towels upon a chair, and had placed a box of *poudre de riz*[40] within easy reach. Edna dabbed the powder upon her nose and cheeks as she looked at herself closely in the little distorted mirror which hung on the wall above the basin. Her eyes were bright and wide awake and her face glowed.

When she had completed her toilet she walked into the adjoining room. She was very hungry. No one was there. But there was a cloth spread upon the table that stood against the wall, and a cover was laid for one, with a crusty brown loaf and a bottle of wine beside the plate. Edna bit a piece from the brown loaf, tearing it with her strong, white teeth. She poured some of the wine into the glass and drank it down. Then she went softly out of doors, and plucking an orange from the low-hanging bough of a tree, threw it at Robert, who did not know she was awake and up.

An illumination broke over his whole face when he saw her and joined her under the orange tree.

"How many years have I slept?" she inquired. "The whole island seems changed. A new race of beings must have sprung up, leaving only you and me as past relics. How many ages ago did Madame Antoine and Tonie die? and when did our people from Grand Isle disappear from the earth?"

He familiarly adjusted a ruffle upon her shoulder.

"You have slept precisely one hundred years. I was left here to guard your slumbers; and for one hundred years I have been out under the shed reading a book. The only evil I couldn't prevent was to keep a broiled fowl from drying up."

"If it had turned to stone, still will I eat it," said Edna, moving with him into the house. "But really, what has become of Monsieur Farival and the others?"

"Gone hours ago. When they found that you were sleeping they thought it best not to awake you. Any way, I wouldn't have let them. What was I here for?"

"I wonder if Léonce will be uneasy!" she speculated, as she seated herself at table.

"Of course not; he knows you are with me," Robert replied, as he busied himself among sundry pans and covered dishes which had been left standing on the hearth.

"Where are Madame Antoine and her son?" asked Edna.

[40]French: a cosmetic powder made of rice.

"Gone to Vespers,[41] and to visit some friends, I believe. I am to take you back in Tonie's boat whenever you are ready to go."

He stirred the smoldering ashes till the broiled fowl began to sizzle afresh. He served her with no mean repast, dripping the coffee anew and sharing it with her. Madame Antoine had cooked little else than the mullets, but while Edna slept Robert had foraged the island. He was childishly gratified to discover her appetite, and to see the relish with which she ate the food which he had procured for her.

"Shall we go right away?" she asked, after draining her glass and brushing together the crumbs of the crusty loaf.

"The sun isn't as low as it will be in two hours," he answered.

"The sun will be gone in two hours."

"Well, let it go; who cares!"

They waited a good while under the orange trees, till Madame Antoine came back, panting, waddling, with a thousand apologies to explain her absence. Tonie did not dare to return. He was shy, and would not willingly face any woman except his mother.

It was very pleasant to stay there under the orange trees, while the sun dipped lower and lower, turning the western sky to flaming copper and gold. The shadows lengthened and crept out like stealthy, grotesque monsters across the grass.

Edna and Robert both sat upon the ground—that is, he lay upon the ground beside her, occasionally picking at the hem of her muslin gown.

Madame Antoine seated her fat body, broad and squat, upon a bench beside the door. She had been talking all the afternoon, and had wound herself up to the storytelling pitch.

And what stories she told them! But twice in her life she had left the *Chênière Caminada*, and then for the briefest span. All her years she had squatted and waddled there upon the island, gathering legends of the Bartarians[42] and the sea. The night came on, with the moon to lighten it. Edna could hear the whispering voices of dead men and the click of muffled gold.

When she and Robert stepped into Tonie's boat, with the red lateen sail, misty spirit forms were prowling in the shadows and among the reeds, and upon the water were phantom ships, speeding to cover.

XIV

The youngest boy, Etienne, had been very naughty, Madame Ratignolle said, as she delivered him into the hands of his mother. He had been unwilling to go to bed and had made a scene; whereupon she had taken charge of him and pacified him as well as she could. Raoul had been in bed and asleep for two hours.

The youngster was in his long white nightgown, that kept tripping him up as Madame Ratignolle led him along by the hand. With the other chubby

[41]Evening prayer.
[42]The pirates who plundered the region of Barataria Bay.

fist he rubbed his eyes, which were heavy with sleep and ill humor. Edna took him in her arms, and seating herself in the rocker, began to coddle and caress him, calling him all manner of tender names, soothing him to sleep.

It was not more than nine o'clock. No one had yet gone to bed but the children.

Léonce had been very uneasy at first, Madame Ratignolle said, and had wanted to start at once for the *Chênière*. But Monsieur Farival had assured him that his wife was only overcome with sleep and fatigue, that Tonie would bring her safely back later in the day; and he had thus been dissuaded from crossing the bay. He had gone over to Klein's, looking up some cotton broker whom he wished to see in regard to securities, exchanges, stocks, bonds, or something of the sort, Madame Ratignolle did not remember what. He said he would not remain away late. She herself was suffering from heat and oppression, she said. She carried a bottle of salts and a large fan. She would not consent to remain with Edna, for Monsieur Ratignolle was alone, and he detested above all things to be left alone.

When Etienne had fallen asleep Edna bore him into the back room, and Robert went and lifted the mosquito bar that she might lay the child comfortably in his bed. The quadroon had vanished. When they emerged from the cottage Robert bade Edna goodnight.

"Do you know we have been together the whole livelong day, Robert— since early this morning?" she said at parting.

"All but the hundred years when you were sleeping. Good-night."

He pressed her hand and went away in the direction of the beach. He did not join any of the others, but walked alone toward the Gulf.

Edna stayed outside, awaiting her husband's return. She had no desire to sleep or to retire; nor did she feel like going over to sit with the Ratignolles, or to join Madame Lebrun and a group whose animated voices reached her as they sat in conversation before the house. She let her mind wander back over her stay at Grand Isle; and she tried to discover wherein this summer had been different from any and every other summer of her life. She could only realize that she herself—her present self—was in some way different from the other self. That she was seeing with different eyes and making the acquaintance of new conditions in herself that colored and changed her environment, she did not yet suspect.

She wondered why Robert had gone away and left her. It did not occur to her to think he might have grown tired of being with her the livelong day. She was not tired, and she felt that he was not. She regretted that he had gone. It was so much more natural to have him stay, when he was not absolutely required to leave her.

As Edna waited for her husband she sang low a little song that Robert had sung as they crossed the bay. It began with "Ah! *Si tu savais*," and every verse ended with "*si tu savais*."[43]

---

[43]"Couldst Thou but Know," a refrain from a song of the same name written by Michael William Balfe (1808–1870), an Irish composer and baritone.

Robert's voice was not pretentious. It was musical and true. The voice, the notes, the whole refrain haunted her memory.

XV

When Edna entered the dining-room one evening a little late, as was her habit, an unusually animated conversation seemed to be going on. Several persons were talking at once, and Victor's voice was predominating, even over that of his mother. Edna had returned late from her bath, had dressed in some haste, and her face was flushed. Her head, set off by her dainty white gown, suggested a rich, rare blossom. She took her seat at table between old Monsieur Farival and Madame Ratignolle.

As she seated herself and was about to begin to eat her soup, which had been served when she entered the room, several persons informed her simultaneously that Robert was going to Mexico. She laid her spoon down and looked about her bewildered. He had been with her, reading to her all the morning, and had never even mentioned such a place as Mexico. She had not seen him during the afternoon; she had heard some one say he was at the house, upstairs with his mother. This she had thought nothing of, though she was surprised when he did not join her later in the afternoon, when she went down to the beach.

She looked across at him, where he sat beside Madame Lebrun, who presided. Edna's face was a blank picture of bewilderment, which she never thought of disguising. He lifted his eyebrows with the pretext of a smile as he returned her glance. He looked embarrassed and uneasy.

"When is he going?" she asked of everybody in general, as if Robert were not there to answer for himself.

"To-night!" "This very evening!" "Did you ever!" "What possesses him!" were some of the replies she gathered, uttered simultaneously in French and English.

"Impossible!" she exclaimed. "How can a person start off from Grand Isle to Mexico at a moment's notice, as if he were going over to Klein's or to the wharf or down to the beach?"

"I said all along I was going to Mexico; I've been saying so for years!" cried Robert, in an excited and irritable tone, with the air of a man defending himself against a swarm of stinging insects.

Madame Lebrun knocked on the table with her knife handle.

"Please let Robert explain why he is going, and why he is going to-night," she called out. "Really, this table is getting to be more and more like Bedlam[44] every day, with everybody talking at once. Sometimes—I hope God will forgive me—but positively sometimes I wish Victor would lose the power of speech."

---

[44]An insane asylum.

Victor laughed sardonically as he thanked his mother for her holy wish, of which he failed to see the benefit to anybody, except that it might afford her a more ample opportunity and license to talk herself.

Monsieur Farival thought that Victor should have been taken out in mid-ocean in his earliest youth and drowned. Victor thought there would be more logic in thus disposing of old people with an established claim for making themselves universally obnoxious. Madame Lebrun grew a trifle hysterical; Robert called his brother some sharp, hard names.

"There's nothing much to explain, mother," he said; though he explained, nevertheless—looking chiefly at Edna—that he could only meet the gentleman whom he intended to join at Vera Cruz by taking such and such a steamer, which left New Orleans on such a day; that Beaudelet was going out with his lugger-load of vegetables that night, which gave him an opportunity of reaching the city and making his vessel in time.

"But when did you make up your mind to all this?" demanded Monsieur Farival.

"This afternoon," returned Robert, with a shade of annoyance.

"At what time this afternoon?" persisted the old gentleman, with nagging determination, as if he were cross-questioning a criminal in a court of justice.

"At four o'clock this afternoon, Monsieur Farival," Robert replied, in a high voice and with a lofty air, which reminded Edna of some gentleman on the stage.

She had forced herself to eat most of her soup, and now she was picking the flaky bits of a *court bouillon*[45] with her fork.

The lovers were profiting by the general conversation on Mexico to speak in whispers of matters which they rightly considered were interesting to no one but themselves. The lady in black had once received a pair of prayer-beads of curious workmanship from Mexico, with very special indulgence attached to them, but she had never been able to ascertain whether the indulgence extended outside the Mexican border. Father Fochel of the Cathedral had attempted to explain it; but he had not done so to her satisfaction. And she begged that Robert would interest himself, and discover, if possible, whether she was entitled to the indulgence accompanying the remarkably curious Mexican prayer-beads.

Madame Ratignolle hoped that Robert would exercise extreme caution in dealing with the Mexicans, who, she considered, were a treacherous people, unscrupulous and revengeful. She trusted she did them no injustice in thus condemning them as a race. She had known personally but one Mexican, who made and sold excellent tamales, and whom she would have trusted implicitly, so softspoken was he. One day he was arrested for stabbing his wife. She never knew whether he had been hanged or not.

---

[45]French: fish broth.

Victor had grown hilarious, and was attempting to tell an anecdote about a Mexican girl who served chocolate one winter in a restaurant in Dauphine Street.[46] No one would listen to him but old Monsieur Farival, who went into convulsions over the droll story.

Edna wondered if they had all gone mad, to be talking and clamoring at that rate. She herself could think of nothing to say about Mexico or the Mexicans.

"At what time do you leave?" she asked Robert.

"At ten," he told her. "Beaudelet wants to wait for the moon."

"Are you all ready to go?"

"Quite ready. I shall only take a handbag, and shall pack my trunk in the city."

He turned to answer some question put to him by his mother, and Edna, having finished her black coffee, left the table.

She went directly to her room. The little cottage was close and stuffy after leaving the outer air. But she did not mind; there appeared to be a hundred different things demanding her attention indoors. She began to set the toilet-stand to rights, grumbling at the negligence of the quadroon, who was in the adjoining room putting the children to bed. She gathered together stray garments that were hanging on the backs of chairs, and put each where it belonged in closet or bureau drawer. She changed her gown for a more comfortable and commodious wrapper. She rearranged her hair, combing and brushing it with unusual energy. Then she went in and assisted the quadroon in getting the boys to bed.

They were very playful and inclined to talk—to do anything but lie quiet and go to sleep. Edna sent the quadroon away to her supper and told her she need not return. Then she sat and told the children a story. Instead of soothing it excited them, and added to their wakefulness. She left them in heated argument, speculating about the conclusion of the tale which their mother promised to finish the following night.

The little black girl came in to say that Madame Lebrun would like to have Mrs. Pontellier go and sit with them over at the house till Mr. Robert went away. Edna returned answer that she had already undressed, that she did not feel quite well, but perhaps she would go over to the house later. She started to dress again, and got as far advanced as to remove her *peignoir*. But changing her mind once more she resumed the *peignoir*, and went outside and sat down before her door. She was over-heated and irritable, and fanned herself energetically for a while. Madame Ratignolle came down to discover what was the matter.

"All that noise and confusion at the table must have upset me," replied Edna, "and moreover, I hate shocks and surprises. The idea of Robert starting off in such a ridiculously sudden and dramatic way! As if it were a matter of life and death! Never saying a word about it all morning when he was with me."

[46]A street located in the French Quarter.

"Yes," agreed Madame Ratignolle. "I think it was showing us all—you especially—very little consideration. It wouldn't have surprised me in any of the others; those Lebruns are all given to heroics. But I must say I should never have expected such a thing from Robert. Are you not coming down? Come on, dear, it doesn't look friendly."

"No," said Edna, a little sullenly. "I can't go to the trouble of dressing again; I don't feel like it."

"You needn't dress; you look all right; fasten a belt around your waist. Just look at me!"

"No," persisted Edna; "but you go on. Madame Lebrun might be offended if we both stayed away."

Madame Ratignolle kissed Edna good-night, and went away, being in truth rather desirous of joining in the general and animated conversation which was still in progress concerning Mexico and the Mexicans.

Somewhat later Robert came up, carrying his hand-bag.

"Aren't you feeling well?" he asked,

"Oh, well enough. Are you going right away?"

He lit a match and looked at his watch. "In twenty minutes," he said. The sudden and brief flare of the match emphasized the darkness for a while. He sat down upon a stool which the children had left out on the porch.

"Get a chair," said Edna.

"This will do," he replied. He put on his soft hat and nervously took it off again, and wiping his face with his handkerchief, complained of the heat.

"Take the fan," said Edna, offering it to him.

"Oh, no! Thank you. It does no good; you have to stop fanning some time, and feel all the more uncomfortable afterward."

"That's one of the ridiculous things which men always say. I have never known one to speak otherwise of fanning. How long will you be gone?"

"Forever, perhaps. I don't know. It depends upon a good many things."

"Well, in case it shouldn't be forever, how long will it be?"

"I don't know."

"This seems to me perfectly preposterous and uncalled for. I don't like it. I don't understand your motive for silence and mystery, never saying a word to me about it this morning." He remained silent, not offering to defend himself. He only said, after a moment:

"Don't part from me in an ill-humor. I never knew you to be out of patience with me before."

"I don't want to part in any ill-humor," she said. "But can't you understand? I've grown used to seeing you, to having you with me all the time, and your action seems unfriendly, even unkind. You don't even offer an excuse for it. Why, I was planning to be together, thinking of how pleasant it would be to see you in the city next winter."

"So was I," he blurted. "Perhaps that's the—" He stood up suddenly and held out his hand. "Good-by, my dear Mrs. Pontellier; good-by. You won't— I hope you won't completely forget me." She clung to his hand, striving to detain him.

"Write to me when you get there, won't you, Robert?" she entreated.

"I will, thank you. Good-by."

How unlike Robert! The merest acquaintance would have said something more emphatic than "I will, thank you; good-by," to such a request.

He had evidently already taken leave of the people over at the house, for he descended the steps and went to join Beaudelet, who was out there with an oar across his shoulder waiting for Robert. They walked away in the darkness. She could only hear Beaudelet's voice; Robert had apparently not even spoken a word of greeting to his companion.

Edna bit her handkerchief convulsively, striving to hold back and to hide, even from herself as she would have hidden from another, the emotion which was troubling—tearing—her. Her eyes were brimming with tears.

For the first time she recognized anew the symptoms of infatuation which she felt incipiently as a child, as a girl in her earliest teens, and later as a young woman. The recognition did not lessen the reality, the poignancy of the revelation by any suggestion or promise of instability. The past was nothing to her; offered no lesson which she was willing to heed. The future was a mystery which she never attempted to penetrate. The present alone was significant; was hers, to torture her as it was doing then with the biting conviction that she had lost that which she had held, that she had been denied that which her impassioned, newly awakened being demanded.

XVI

"Do you miss your friend greatly?" asked Mademoiselle Reisz one morning as she came creeping up behind Edna, who had just left her cottage on her way to the beach. She spent much of her time in the water since she had acquired finally the art of swimming. As their stay at Grand Isle drew near its close, she felt that she could not give too much time to a diversion which afforded her the only real pleasurable moments that she knew. When Mademoiselle Reisz came and touched her upon the shoulder and spoke to her, the woman seemed to echo the thought which was ever in Edna's mind; or, better, the feeling which constantly possessed her.

Robert's going had some way taken the brightness, the color, the meaning out of everything. The conditions of her life were in no way changed, but her whole existence was dulled, like a faded garment which seems to be no longer worth wearing. She sought him everywhere—in others whom she induced to talk about him. She went up in the mornings to Madame Lebrun's room, braving the clatter of the old sewing-machine. She sat there and chatted at intervals as Robert had done. She gazed around the room at the pictures and photographs hanging upon the wall, and discovered in some corner an old family album, which she examined with the keenest interest, appealing to Madame Lebrun for enlightenment concerning the many figures and faces which she discovered between its pages.

There was a picture of Madame Lebrun with Robert as a baby, seated in her lap, a round-faced infant with a fist in his mouth. The eyes alone in the baby suggested the man. And that was he also in kilts, at the age of five, wearing long curls and holding a whip in his hand. It made Edna laugh, and she laughed, too, at the portrait in his first long trousers; while another interested her, taken when he left for college, looking thin, long-faced, with eyes full of fire, ambition and great intentions. But there was no recent picture, none which suggested the Robert who had gone away five days ago, leaving a void and wilderness behind him.

"Oh, Robert stopped having his pictures taken when he had to pay for them himself! He found wiser use for his money, he says," explained Madame Lebrun. She had a letter from him, written before he left New Orleans. Edna wished to see the letter, and Madame Lebrun told her to look for it either on the table or the dresser, or perhaps it was on the mantelpiece.

The letter was on the bookshelf. It possessed the greatest interest and attraction for Edna; the envelope, its size and shape, the postmark, the handwriting. She examined every detail of the outside before opening it. There were only a few lines, setting forth that he would leave the city that afternoon, that he had packed his trunk in good shape, that he was well, and sent her his love and begged to be affectionately remembered to all. There was no special message to Edna except a postscript saying that if Mrs. Pontellier desired to finish the book which he had been reading to her, his mother would find it in his room, among other books there on the table. Edna experienced a pang of jealousy because he had written to his mother rather than to her.

Every one seemed to take for granted that she missed him. Even her husband, when he came down the Saturday following Robert's departure, expressed regret that he had gone.

"How do you get on without him, Edna?" he asked.

"It's very dull without him," she admitted. Mr. Pontellier had seen Robert in the city, and Edna asked him a dozen questions or more. Where had they met? On Carondelet Street, in the morning. They had gone "in" and had a drink and a cigar together. What had they talked about? Chiefly about his prospects in Mexico, which Mr. Pontellier thought were promising. How did he look? How did he seem—grave, or gay, or how? Quite cheerful, and wholly taken up with the idea of his trip, which Mr. Pontellier found altogether natural in a young fellow about to seek fortune and adventure in a strange, queer country.

Edna tapped her foot impatiently, and wondered why the children persisted in playing in the sun when they might be under the trees. She went down and led them out of the sun, scolding the quadroon for not being more attentive.

It did not strike her as in the least grotesque that she should be making of Robert the object of conversation and leading her husband to speak of him. The sentiment which she entertained for Robert in no way resembled that which she felt for her husband, or had ever felt, or ever expected to feel. She had all her life long been accustomed to harbor thoughts and emotions which never voiced themselves. They had never taken the form of struggles. They belonged to her and were her own, and she entertained the conviction that she had a right to them and that they concerned no one but herself. Edna had once told Madame Ratignolle that she would never sacrifice herself for her children, or for any one. Then had followed a rather heated argument; the two women did not appear to understand each other or to be talking the same language. Edna tried to appease her friend, to explain.

"I would give up the unessential; I would give my money, I would give my life for my children; but I wouldn't give myself. I can't make it more clear; it's only something which I am beginning to comprehend, which is revealing itself to me."

"I don't know what you would call the essential, or what you mean by the unessential," said Madame Ratignolle, cheerfully; "but a woman who would give her life for her children could do no more than that—your Bible tells you so. I'm sure I couldn't do more than that."

"Oh, yes you could!" laughed Edna.

She was not surprised at Mademoiselle Reisz's question the morning that lady, following her to the beach, tapped her on the shoulder and asked if she did not greatly miss her young friend.

"Oh, good morning, Mademoiselle; it is you? Why, of course I miss Robert. Are you going down to bathe?"

"Why should I go down to bathe at the very end of the season when I haven't been in the surf all summer?" replied the woman, disagreeably.

"I beg your pardon," offered Edna, in some embarrassment, for she should have remembered that Mademoiselle Reisz's avoidance of the water had furnished a theme for much pleasantry. Some among them thought it was on account of her false hair, or the dread of getting the violets wet, while others attributed it to the natural aversion for water sometimes believed to accompany the artistic temperament. Mademoiselle offered Edna some chocolates in a paper bag, which she took from her pocket, by way of showing that she bore no ill feeling. She habitually ate chocolates for their sustaining quality; they contained much nutriment in small compass, she said. They saved her from starvation, as Madame Lebrun's table was utterly impossible; and no one save so impertinent a woman as Madame Lebrun could think of offering such food to people and requiring them to pay for it.

"She must feel very lonely without her son," said Edna, desiring to change the subject. "Her favorite son, too. It must have been quite hard to let him go."

Mademoiselle laughed maliciously.

"Her favorite son! Oh, dear! Who could have been imposing such a tale upon you? Aline Lebrun lives for Victor, and for Victor alone. She has spoiled him into the worthless creature he is. She worships him and the ground he walks on. Robert is very well in a way, to give up all the money he can earn to the family, and keep the barest pittance for himself. Favorite son, indeed! I miss the poor fellow myself, my dear. I liked to see him and to hear him about the place—the only Lebrun who is worth a pinch of salt.

He comes to see me often in the city. I like to play to him. That Victor! hanging would be too good for him. It's a wonder Robert hasn't beaten him to death long ago."

"I thought he had great patience with his brother," offered Edna, glad to be talking about Robert, no matter what was said.

"Oh! he thrashed him well enough a year or two ago," said Mademoiselle. "It was about a Spanish girl, whom Victor considered that he had some sort of claim upon. He met Robert one day talking to the girl, or walking with her, or bathing with her, or carrying her basket—I don't remember what;—and he became so insulting and abusive that Robert gave him a thrashing on the spot that has kept him comparatively in order for a good while. It's about time he was getting another."

"Was her name Mariequita?" asked Edna.

"Mariequita—yes, that was it; Mariequita. I had forgotten. Oh, she's a sly one, and a bad one, that Mariequita!"

Edna looked down at Mademoiselle Reisz and wondered how she could have listened to her venom so long. For some reason she felt depressed, almost unhappy. She had not intended to go into the water; but she donned her bathing suit, and left Mademoiselle alone, seated under the shade of the children's tent. The water was growing cooler as the season advanced. Edna plunged and swam about with an abandon that thrilled and invigorated her. She remained a long time in the water, half hoping that Mademoiselle Reisz would not wait for her.

But Mademoiselle waited. She was very amiable during the walk back, and raved much over Edna's appearance in her bathing suit. She talked about music. She hoped that Edna would go to see her in the city, and wrote her address with the stub of a pencil on a piece of card which she found in her pocket.

"When do you leave?" asked Edna.

"Next Monday; and you?"

"The following week," answered Edna, adding, "It has been a pleasant summer, hasn't it, Mademoiselle?"

"Well," agreed Mademoiselle Reiz, with a shrug, "rather pleasant, if it hadn't been for the mosquitoes and the Farival twins."

XVII

The Pontelliers possessed a very charming home on Esplanade Street[47] in New Orleans. It was a large, double cottage, with a broad front veranda, whose round, fluted columns supported the sloping roof. The house was painted a dazzling white; the outside shutters, or jalousies, were green. In the yard, which was kept scrupulously neat, were flowers and plants of every description which flourishes in South Louisiana. Within doors the appointments were perfect after the conventional type. The softest carpets and rugs

[47]A street in New Orleans's most elite neighborhood.

covered the floors; rich and tasteful draperies hung at doors and windows. There were paintings, selected with judgment and discrimination, upon the walls. The cut glass, the silver, the heavy damask which daily appeared upon the table were the envy of many women whose husbands were less generous than Mr. Pontellier.

Mr. Pontellier was very fond of walking about his house examining its various appointments and details, to see that nothing was amiss. He greatly valued his possessions, chiefly because they were his, and derived genuine pleasure from contemplating a painting, a statuette, a rare lace curtain—no matter what—after he had bought it and placed it among his household gods.

On Tuesday afternoons—Tuesday being Mrs. Pontellier's reception day[48]—there was a constant stream of callers—women who came in carriages or in the street cars, or walked when the air was soft and distance permitted. A light-colored mulatto boy, in dress coat and bearing a diminutive silver tray for the reception of cards, admitted them. A maid, in white fluted cap, offered the callers liqueur, coffee, or chocolate, as they might desire. Mrs. Pontellier, attired in a handsome reception gown, remained in the drawing-room the entire afternoon receiving her visitors. Men sometimes called in the evening with their wives.

This had been the programme which Mrs. Pontellier had religiously followed since her marriage, six years before. Certain evenings during the week she and her husband attended the opera or sometimes the play.

Mr. Pontellier left his home in the mornings between nine and ten o'clock, and rarely returned before half-past six or seven in the evening—dinner being served at half-past seven.

He and his wife seated themselves at table on Tuesday evening, a few weeks after their return from Grand Isle. They were alone together. The boys were being put to bed; the patter of their bare, escaping feet could be heard occasionally, as well as the pursuing voice of the quadroon, lifted in mild protest and entreaty. Mrs. Pontellier did not wear her usual Tuesday reception gown; she was in ordinary house dress. Mr. Pontellier, who was observant about such things, noticed it, as he served the soup and handed it to the boy in waiting.

"Tired out, Edna? Whom did you have? Many callers?" he asked. He tasted his soup and began to season it with pepper, salt, vinegar, mustard—everything within reach.

"There were a good many," replied Edna, who was eating her soup with evident satisfaction. "I found their cards when I got home; I was out."

"Out!" exclaimed her husband, with something like genuine consternation in his voice as he laid down the vinegar cruet and looked at her through

---

[48]Women of the upper class were expected to receive visitors on one designated day of the week.

his glasses. "Why, what could have taken you out on Tuesday? What did you have to do?"

"Nothing. I simply felt like going out, and I went out."

"Well, I hope you left some suitable excuse," said her husband, somewhat appeased, as he added a dash of cayenne pepper to the soup.

"No, I left no excuse. I told Joe to say I was out, that was all."

"Why, my dear, I should think you'd understand by this time that people don't do such things; we've got to observe *les convenances*[49] if we ever expect to get on and keep up with the procession. If you felt that you had to leave home this afternoon, you should have left some suitable explanation for your absence.

"This soup is really impossible; it's strange that woman hasn't learned yet to make a decent soup. Any free-lunch stand in town serves a better one. Was Mrs. Belthrop here?"

"Bring the tray with the cards, Joe. I don't remember who was here."

The boy retired and returned after a moment, bringing the tiny silver tray, which was covered with ladies' visiting cards. He handed it to Mrs. Pontellier.

"Give it to Mr. Pontellier," she said.

Joe offered the tray to Mr. Pontellier, and removed the soup.

Mr. Pontellier scanned the names of his wife's callers, reading some of them aloud, with comments as he read.

"'The Misses Delasidas.' I worked a big deal in futures[50] for their father this morning; nice girls; it's time they were getting married. 'Mrs. Belthrop.' I tell you what it is, Edna; you can't afford to snub Mrs. Belthrop. Why, Belthrop could buy and sell us ten times over. His business is worth a good, round sum to me. You'd better write her a note. 'Mrs. James Highcamp.' Hugh! the less you have to do with Mrs. Highcamp, the better. 'Madame Laforcé.' Came all the way from Carrolton, too, poor old soul. 'Miss Wiggs,' 'Mrs. Eleanor Boltons.'" He pushed the cards aside.

"Mercy!" exclaimed Edna, who had been fuming. "Why are you taking the thing so seriously and making such a fuss over it?"

"I'm not making any fuss over it. But it's just such seeming trifles that we've got to take seriously; such things count."

The fish was scorched. Mr. Pontellier would not touch it. Edna said she did not mind a little scorched taste. The roast was in some way not to his fancy, and he did not like the manner in which the vegetables were served.

"It seems to me," he said, "we spend money enough in this house to procure at least one meal a day which a man could eat and retain his self-respect."

"You used to think the cook was a treasure," returned Edna, indifferently.

[49]French: social conventions.
[50]A contract for a specific commodity bought or sold for delivery at a future date.

"Perhaps she was when she first came; but cooks are only human. They need looking after, like any other class of persons that you employ. Suppose I didn't look after the clerks in my office, just let them run things their own way; they'd soon make a nice mess of me and my business."

"Where are you going?" asked Edna, seeing that her husband arose from table without having eaten a morsel except a taste of the highly-seasoned soup.

"I'm going to get my dinner at the club. Good night." He went into the hall, took his hat and stick from the stand, and left the house.

She was somewhat familiar with such scenes. They had often made her very unhappy. On a few previous occasions she had been completely deprived of any desire to finish her dinner. Sometimes she had gone into the kitchen to administer a tardy rebuke to the cook. Once she went to her room and studied the cookbook during an entire evening, finally writing out a menu for the week, which left her harassed with a feeling that, after all, she had accomplished no good that was worth the name.

But that evening Edna finished her dinner alone, with forced deliberation. Her face was flushed and her eyes flamed with some inward fire that lighted them. After finishing her dinner she went to her room, having instructed the boy to tell any other callers that she was indisposed.

It was a large, beautiful room, rich and picturesque in the soft, dim light which the maid had turned low. She went and stood at an open window and looked out upon the deep tangle of the garden below. All the mystery and witchery of the night seemed to have gathered there amid the perfumes and the dusky and tortuous outlines of flowers and foliage. She was seeking herself and finding herself in just such sweet, half-darkness which met her moods. But the voices were not soothing that came to her from the darkness and the sky above and the stars. They jeered and sounded mournful notes without promise, devoid even of hope. She turned back into the room and began to walk to and fro down its whole length, without stopping, without resting. She carried in her hands a thin handkerchief, which she tore into ribbons, rolled into a ball, and flung from her. Once she stopped, and taking off her wedding ring, flung it upon the carpet. When she saw it lying there, she stamped her heel upon it, striving to crush it. But her small boot heel did not make an indenture, not a mark upon the little glittering circlet.

In a sweeping passion she seized a glass vase from the table and flung it upon the tiles of the hearth. She wanted to destroy something. The crash and clatter were what she wanted to hear.

A maid, alarmed at the din of breaking glass, entered the room to discover what was the matter.

"A vase fell upon the hearth," said Edna. "Never mind; leave it till morning."

"Oh! you might get some of the glass in your feet, ma'am," insisted the young woman, picking up bits of the broken vase that were scattered upon the carpet. "And here's your ring, ma'am, under the chair."

Edna held out her hand, and taking the ring, slipped it upon her finger.

XVIII

The following morning Mr. Pontellier, upon leaving for his office, asked Edna if she would not meet him in town in order to look at some new fixtures for the library.

"I hardly think we need new fixtures, Léonce. Don't let us get anything new; you are too extravagant. I don't believe you ever think of saving or putting by."

"The way to become rich is to make money, my dear Edna, not to save it," he said. He regretted that she did not feel inclined to go with him and select new fixtures. He kissed her good-by, and told her she was not looking well and must take care of herself. She was unusually pale and very quiet.

She stood on the front veranda as he quitted the house, and absently picked a few sprays of jessamine[51] that grew upon a trellis near by. She inhaled the odor of the blossoms and thrust them into the bosom of her white morning gown. The boys were dragging along the banquette[52] a small "express wagon," which they had filled with blocks and sticks. The quadroon was following them with little quick steps, having assumed a fictitious animation and alacrity for the occasion. A fruit vender was crying his wares in the street.

Edna looked straight before her with a self-absorbed expression upon her face. She felt no interest in anything about her. The street, the children, the fruit vender, the flowers growing there under her eyes, were all part and parcel of an alien world which had suddenly become antagonistic.

She went back into the house. She had thought of speaking to the cook concerning her blunders of the previous night; but Mr. Pontellier had saved her that disagreeable mission, for which she was so poorly fitted. Mr. Pontellier's arguments were usually convincing with those whom he employed. He left home feeling quite sure that he and Edna would sit down that evening, and possibly a few subsequent evenings, to a dinner deserving of the name.

Edna spent an hour or two in looking over some of her old sketches. She could see their shortcomings and defects, which were glaring in her eyes. She tried to work a little, but found she was not in the humor. Finally she gathered together a few of the sketches—those which she considered the least discreditable; and she carried them with her when, a little later, she dressed and left the house. She looked handsome and distinguished in her street gown. The tan of the seashore had left her face, and her forehead was smooth, white, and polished beneath her heavy, yellow-brown hair. There were a few freckles on her face, and a small, dark mole near the under lip and one on the temple, half-hidden in her hair.

As Edna walked along the street she was thinking of Robert. She was still under the spell of her infatuation. She had tried to forget him, realizing the inutility of remembering. But the thought of him was like an obsession,

---

[51]French: jasmine.   [52]French: sidewalk.

ever pressing itself upon her. It was not that she dwelt upon details of their acquaintance, or recalled in any special or peculiar way his personality; it was his being, his existence, which dominated her thought, fading sometimes as if it would melt into the mist of the forgotten, reviving again with an intensity which filled her with an incomprehensible longing.

Edna was on her way to Madame Ratignolle's. Their intimacy, begun at Grand Isle, had not declined, and they had seen each other with some frequency since their return to the city. The Ratignolles lived at no great distance from Edna's home, on the corner of a side street, where Monsieur Ratignolle owned and conducted a drug store which enjoyed a steady and prosperous trade. His father had been in the business before him, and Monsieur Ratignolle stood well in the community and bore an enviable reputation for integrity and clear-headedness. His family lived in commodious apartments over the store, having an entrance on the side within the *porte cochère*.[53] There was something which Edna thought very French, very foreign, about their whole manner of living. In the large and pleasant salon which extended across the width of the house, the Ratignolles entertained their friends once a fortnight with a *soirée musicale*,[54] sometimes diversified by card-playing. There was a friend who played upon the cello. One brought his flute and another his violin, while there were some who sang and a number who performed upon the piano with various degrees of taste and agility. The Ratignolles' *soirées musicales* were widely known, and it was considered a privilege to be invited to them.

Edna found her friend engaged in assorting the clothes which had returned that morning from the laundry. She at once abandoned her occupation upon seeing Edna, who had been ushered without ceremony into her presence.

"'Cité can do it as well as I; it is really her business," she explained to Edna, who apologized for interrupting her. And she summoned a young black woman, whom she instructed, in French, to be very careful in checking off the list which she handed her. She told her to notice particularly if a fine linen handkerchief of Monsieur Ratignolle's, which was missing last week, had been returned; and to be sure to set to one side such pieces as required mending and darning.

Then placing an arm around Edna's waist, she led her to the front of the house, to the salon, where it was cool and sweet with the odor of great roses that stood upon the hearth in jars.

Madame Ratignolle looked more beautiful than ever there at home, in a negligé which left her arms almost wholly bare and exposed the rich, melting curves of her white throat.

"Perhaps I shall be able to paint your picture some day," said Edna with a smile when they were seated. She produced the roll of sketches and started to unfold them. "I believe I ought to work again. I feel as if I wanted to be doing something. What do you think of them? Do you think it worth

---

[53]French: carriage entrance.   [54]French: an evening of music.

while to take it up again and study some more? I might study for a while with Laidpore."

She knew that Madame Ratignolle's opinion in such a matter would be next to valueless, that she herself had not alone decided, but determined; but she sought the words and praise and encouragement that would help her to put heart into her venture.

"Your talent is immense, dear!"

"Nonsense!" Protested Edna, well pleased.

"Immense, I tell you," persisted Madame Ratignolle, surveying the sketches one by one, at close range, then holding them at arm's length, narrowing her eyes, and dropping her head on one side. "Surely, this Bavarian peasant is worthy of framing; and this basket of apples! never have I seen anything more lifelike. One might almost be tempted to reach out a hand and take one."

Edna could not control a feeling which bordered upon complacency at her friend's praise, even realizing, as she did, its true worth. She retained a few of the sketches, and gave all the rest to Madame Ratignolle, who appreciated the gift far beyond its value and proudly exhibited the pictures to her husband when he came up from the store a little later for his midday dinner.

Mr. Ratignolle was one of those men who are called the salt of the earth. His cheerfulness was unbounded, and it was matched by his goodness of heart, his broad charity, and common sense. He and his wife spoke English with an accent which was only discernible through its un-English emphasis and a certain carefulness and deliberation. Edna's husband spoke English with no accent whatever. The Ratignolles understood each other perfectly. If ever the fusion of two human beings into one has been accomplished on this sphere it was surely in their union.

As Edna seated herself at table with them she thought, "Better a dinner of herbs,"[55] though it did not take her long to discover that was no dinner of herbs, but a delicious repast, simple, choice, and in every way satisfying.

Monsieur Ratignolle was delighted to see her, though he found her looking not so well as at Grand Isle, and he advised a tonic. He talked a good deal on various topics, a little politics, some city news and neighborhood gossip. He spoke with an animation and earnestness that gave an exaggerated importance to every syllable he uttered. His wife was keenly interested in everything he said, laying down her fork the better to listen, chiming in, taking the words out of his mouth.

Edna felt depressed rather than soothed after leaving them. The little glimpse of domestic harmony which had been offered her, gave her no regret, no longing. It was not a condition of life which fitted her, and she could see in it but an appalling and hopeless ennui. She was moved by a kind of commiseration for Madame Ratignolle,—a pity for that colorless

[55]Allusion to Proverbs 15:17: "Better is a dinner of herbs where love is, than a stalled ox and hatred therewith."

existence which never uplifted its possessor beyond the region of blind contentment, in which no moment of anguish ever visited her soul, in which she would never have the taste of life's delirium. Edna vaguely wondered what she meant by "life's delirium." It had crossed her thought like some unsought, extraneous impression.

XIX

Edna could not help but think that it was very foolish, very childish, to have stamped upon her wedding ring and smashed the crystal vase upon the tiles. She was visited by no more outbursts, moving her to such futile expedients. She began to do as she liked and to feel as she liked. She completely abandoned her Tuesdays at home, and did not return the visits of those who had called upon her. She made no ineffectual efforts to conduct her household *en bonne ménagère*,[56] going and coming as it suited her fancy, and, so far as she was able, lending herself to any passing caprice.

Mr. Pontellier had been a rather courteous husband so long as he met a certain tacit submissiveness in his wife. But her new and unexpected line of conduct completely bewildered him. It shocked him. Then her absolute disregard for her duties as a wife angered him. When Mr. Pontellier became rude, Edna grew insolent. She had resolved never to take another step backward.

"It seems to me the utmost folly for a woman at the head of a household, and the mother of children, to spend in an atelier[57] days which would be better employed contriving for the comfort of her family."

"I feel like painting," answered Edna. "Perhaps I shan't always feel like it."

"Then in God's name paint! but don't let the family go to the devil. There's Madame Ratignolle; because she keeps up her music, she doesn't let everything else go to chaos. And she's more of a musician than you are a painter."

"She isn't a musician, and I'm not a painter. It isn't on account of painting that I let things go."

"On account of what, then?"

"Oh! I don't know. Let me alone; you bother me."

It sometimes entered Mr. Pontellier's mind to wonder if his wife were not growing a little unbalanced mentally. He could see plainly that she was not herself. That is, he could not see that she was becoming herself and daily casting aside that fictitious self which we assume like a garment with which to appear before the world.

Her husband let her alone as she requested, and went away to his office. Edna went up to her atelier—a bright room in the top of the house. She was working with great energy and interest, without accomplishing anything, however, which satisfied her even in the smallest degree. For a time she had the whole household enrolled in the service of art. The boys posed

---

[56]French: as a good housewife. [57]French: studio.

for her. They thought it amusing at first, but the occupation soon lost its attractiveness when they discovered that it was not a game arranged especially for their entertainment. The quadroon sat for hours before Edna's palette, patient as a savage, while the housemaid took charge of the children, and the drawing-room went undusted. But the house-maid, too, served her term as model when Edna perceived that the young woman's back and shoulders were molded on classic lines, and that her hair, loosened from its confining cap, became an inspiration. While Edna worked she sometimes sang low the little air, "Ah! *si tu savais!*"

It moved her with recollections. She could hear again the ripple of the water, the flapping sail. She could see the glint of the moon upon the bay, and could feel the soft, gusty beating of the hot south wind. A subtle current of desire passed through her body, weakening her hold upon the brushes and making her eyes burn.

There were days when she was very happy without knowing why. She was happy to be alive and breathing, when her whole being seemed to be one with the sunlight, the color, the odors, the luxuriant warmth of some perfect Southern day. She liked then to wander alone into strange and unfamiliar places. She discovered many a sunny, sleepy corner, fashioned to dream in. And she found it good to dream and to be alone and unmolested.

There were days when she was unhappy, she did not know why,—when it did not seem worth while to be glad or sorry, to be alive or dead; when life appeared to her like a grotesque pandemonium and humanity like worms struggling blindly toward inevitable annihilation. She could not work on such a day, nor weave fancies to stir her pulses and warm her blood.

XX

It was during such a mood that Edna hunted up Mademoiselle Reisz. She had not forgotten the rather disagreeable impression left upon her by their last interview; but she nevertheless felt a desire to see her—above all, to listen while she played upon the piano. Quite early in the afternoon she started upon her quest for the pianist. Unfortunately she had mislaid or lost Mademoiselle Reisz's card, and looking up her address in the city directory, she found that the woman lived on Bienvilles Street,[58] some distance away. The directory which fell into her hands was a year or more old, however, and upon reaching the number indicated, Edna discovered that the house was occupied by a respectable family of mulattoes who had *chambres garnies*[59] to let. They had been living there for six months, and knew absolutely nothing of a Mademoiselle Reisz. In fact, they knew nothing of any of their neighbors; their lodgers were all people of the highest distinction, they assured Edna. She did not linger to discuss class distinctions with Madame Pouponne, but hastened to a neighboring grocery store, feeling sure that Mademoiselle would have left her address with the proprietor.

---

[58]A street near New Orleans's shipyards.   [59]French: furnished rooms.

He knew Mademoiselle Reisz a good deal better than he wanted to know her, he informed his questioner. In truth, he did not want to know her at all, anything concerning her—the most disagreeable and unpopular woman who ever lived in Bienville Street. He thanked heaven she had left the neighborhood, and was equally thankful that he did not know where she had gone.

Edna's desire to see Mademoiselle Reisz had increased tenfold since these unlooked-for obstacles had arisen to thwart it. She was wondering who could give her the information she sought, when it suddenly occurred to her that Madame Lebrun would be the one most likely to do so. She knew it was useless to ask Madame Ratignolle, who was on the most distant terms with the musician, and preferred to know nothing concerning her. She had once been almost as emphatic in expressing herself upon the subject as the corner grocer.

Edna knew that Madame Lebrun had returned to the city, for it was the middle of November. And she also knew where the Lebruns lived, on Chartres Street.

Their home from the outside looked like a prison, with iron bars before the door and lower windows. The iron bars were a relic of the old *régime*,[60] and no one had ever thought of dislodging them. At the side was a high fence enclosing the garden. A gate or door opening upon the street was locked. Edna rang the bell at this side garden gate, and stood upon the banquette, waiting to be admitted.

It was Victor who opened the gate for her. A black woman, wiping her hands upon her apron, was close at his heels. Before she saw them Edna could hear them in altercation, the woman—plainly an anomaly—claiming the right to be allowed to perform her duties, one of which was to answer the bell.

Victor was surprised and delighted to see Mrs. Pontellier, and he made no attempt to conceal either his astonishment or his delight. He was a dark-browed, good-looking youngster of nineteen, greatly resembling his mother, but with ten times her impetuosity. He instructed the black woman to go at once and inform Madame Lebrun that Mrs. Pontellier desired to see her. The woman grumbled a refusal to do part of her duty when she had not been permitted to do it all, and started back to her interrupted task of weeding the garden. Whereupon Victor administered a rebuke in the form of a volley of abuse, which owing to its rapidity and incoherence, was all but incomprehensible to Edna. Whatever it was, the rebuke was convincing, for the woman dropped her hoe and went mumbling into the house.

Edna did not wish to enter. It was very pleasant there on the side porch, where there were chairs, a wicker lounge, and a small table. She seated herself, for she was tired from her long tramp; and she began to rock gently and smooth out the folds of her silk parasol. Victor drew up his chair beside her. He at once explained that the black woman's offensive conduct was all

[60]The Spanish regime (1766–1803).

due to imperfect training, as he was not there to take her in hand. He had only come up from the island the morning before, and expected to return next day. He stayed all winter at the island; he lived there, and kept the place in order and got things ready for the summer visitors.

But a man needed occasional relaxation, he informed Mrs. Pontellier, and every now and again he drummed up a pretext to bring him to the city. My! but he had had a time of it the evening before! He wouldn't want his mother to know, and he began to talk in a whisper. He was scintillant with recollections. Of course, he couldn't think of telling Mrs. Pontellier all about it, she being a woman and not comprehending such things. But it all began with a girl peeping and smiling at him through the shutters as he passed by. Oh! but she was a beauty! Certainly he smiled back, and went up and talked to her. Mrs. Pontellier did not know him if she supposed he was one to let an opportunity like that escape him. Despite herself, the youngster amused her. She must have betrayed in her look some degree of interest or entertainment. The boy grew more daring, and Mrs. Pontellier might have found herself, in a little while, listening to a highly colored story but for the timely appearance of Madame Lebrun.

That lady was still clad in white, according to her custom of the summer. Her eyes beamed an effusive welcome. Would not Mrs. Pontellier go inside? Would she partake of some refreshment? Why had she not been there before? How was that dear Mr. Pontellier and how were those sweet children? Has Mrs. Pontellier ever known such a warm November?

Victor went and reclined on the wicker lounge behind his mother's chair, where he commanded a view of Edna's face. He had taken her parasol from her hands while he spoke to her, and he now lifted it and twirled it above him as he lay on his back. When Madame Lebrun complained that it was *so* dull coming back to the city; that she saw *so* few people now; that even Victor, when he came up from the island for a day or two, had *so* much to occupy him and engage his time; then it was that the youth went into contortions on the lounge and winked mischievously at Edna. She somehow felt like a confederate in crime, and tried to look severe and disapproving.

There had been but two letters from Robert, with little in them, they told her. Victor said it was really not worth while to go inside for the letters, when his mother entreated him to go in search of them. He remembered the contents, which in truth he rattled off very glibly when put to the test.

One letter was written from Vera Cruz and the other from the City of Mexico. He had met Montel, who was doing everything toward his advancement. So far, the financial situation was no improvement over the one he had left in New Orleans, but of course the prospects were vastly better. He wrote of the City of Mexico, the buildings, the people and their habits, the conditions of life which he found there. He sent his love to the family. He inclosed a check to his mother, and hoped she would affectionately remember him to all his friends. That was about the substance of the two letters. Edna felt that if there had been a message for her, she would have received it. The despondent frame of mind in which she had left home began again to overtake her, and she remembered that she wished to find Mademoiselle Reisz.

Madame Lebrun knew where Mademoiselle Reisz lived. She gave Edna the address, regretting that she would not consent to stay and spend the remainder of the afternoon, and pay a visit to Mademoiselle Reisz some other day. The afternoon was already well advanced.

Victor escorted her out upon the banquette, lifted her parasol, and held it over her while he walked to the car with her. He entreated her to bear in mind that the disclosures of the afternoon were strictly confidential. She laughed and bantered him a little, remembering too late that she should have been dignified and reserved.

"How handsome Mrs. Pontellier looked!" said Madame Lebrun to her son.

"Ravishing!" he admitted. "The city atmosphere has improved her. Some way she doesn't seem like the same woman."

XXI

Some people contended that the reason Mademoiselle Reisz always chose apartments up under the roof was to discourage the approach of beggars, peddlars and callers. There were plenty of windows in her little front room. They were for the most part dingy, but as they were nearly always open it did not make so much difference. They often admitted into the room a good deal of smoke and soot; but at the same time all the light and air that there was came through them. From her windows could be seen the crescent of the river, the masts of ships and the big chimneys of the Mississippi steamers. A magnificent piano crowded the apartment. In the next room she slept, and in the third and last she harbored a gasoline stove on which she cooked her meals when disinclined to descend to the neighboring restaurant. It was there also that she ate, keeping her belongings in a rare old buffet, dingy and battered from a hundred years of use.

When Edna knocked at Mademoiselle Reisz's front room door and entered, she discovered that person standing beside the window, engaged in mending or patching an old prunella gaiter.[61] The little musician laughed all over when she saw Edna. Her laugh consisted of a contortion of the face and all the muscles of the body. She seemed strikingly homely, standing there in the afternoon light. She still wore the shabby lace and the artificial bunch of violets on the side of her head.

"So you remembered me at last," said Mademoiselle. "I had said to myself, 'Ah, bah! she will never come.'"

"Did you want me to come?" asked Edna with a smile.

"I had not thought much about it," answered Mademoiselle. The two had seated themselves on a little bumpy sofa which stood against the wall. "I am glad, however, that you came. I have the water boiling back there, and was just about to make some coffee. You will drink a cup with me. And how

---

[61]A shoe with a twill upper section.

is *la belle dame?*[62] Always handsome! always healthy! always contented!" She took Edna's hand between her strong wiry fingers, holding it loosely without warmth, and executing a sort of double theme upon the back and palm.

"Yes," she went on; "I sometimes thought: 'She will never come. She promised as those women in society always do, without meaning it. She will not come.' For I really don't believe you like me, Mrs. Pontellier."

"I don't know whether I like you or not," replied Edna, gazing down at the little woman with a quizzical look.

The candor of Mrs. Pontellier's admission greatly pleased Mademoiselle Reisz. She expressed her gratification by repairing forthwith to the region of the gasoline stove and rewarding her guest with the promised cup of coffee. The coffee and the biscuit accompanying it proved very acceptable to Edna, who had declined refreshment at Madame Lebrun's and was now beginning to feel hungry. Mademoiselle set the tray which she brought in upon a small table near at hand, and seated herself once again on the lumpy sofa.

"I have had a letter from your friend," she remarked, as she poured a little cream into Edna's cup and handed it to her.

"My friend?"

"Yes, your friend Robert. He wrote to me from the City of Mexico."

"Wrote to *you?*" repeated Edna in amazement, stirring her coffee absently.

"Yes, to me. Why not? Don't stir all the warmth out of your coffee; drink it. Though the letter might as well have been sent to you; it was nothing but Mrs. Pontellier from beginning to end."

"Let me see it," requested the young woman, entreatingly.

"No; a letter concerns no one but the person who writes it and the one to whom it is written."

"Haven't you just said it concerned me from beginning to end?"

"It was written about you, not to you. 'Have you seen Mrs. Pontellier? How is she looking?' he asks. 'As Mrs. Pontellier says,' or 'as Mrs. Pontellier once said!' 'If Mrs. Pontellier should call upon you, play for her that Impromptu of Chopin's, my favorite. I heard it here a day or two ago, but not as you play it. I should like to know how it affects her,' and so on, as if he supposed we were constantly in each other's society."

"Let me see the letter."

"Oh, no."

"Have you answered it?"

"No."

"Let me see the letter."

"No, and again, no."

"Then play the Impromptu for me."

"It is growing late; what time do you have to be home?"

"Time doesn't concern me. Your question seems a little rude. Play the Impromptu."

---

[62]French: "my beautiful friend."

"But you have told me nothing of yourself. What are you doing?"

"Painting!" laughed Edna. "I am becoming an artist. Think of it!"

"Ah! an artist! You have pretensions, Madame."

"Why pretensions? Do you think I could not become an artist?"

"I do not know you well enough to say. I do not know your talent or your temperament. To be an artist includes much; one must possess many gifts—absolute gifts—which have not been acquired by one's own effort. And, moreover, to succeed, the artist must possess the courageous soul."

"What do you mean by the courageous soul?"

"Courageous, *ma foi*! The brave soul. The soul that dares and defies."

"Show me the letter and play for me the Impromptu. You see that I have persistence. Does that quality count for anything in art?"

"It counts with a foolish old woman whom you have captivated," replied Mademoiselle, with her wriggling laugh.

The letter was right there at hand in the drawer of the little table upon which Edna had just placed her coffee cup. Mademoiselle opened the drawer and drew forth the letter, the topmost one. She placed it in Edna's hands, and without further comment arose and went to the piano.

Mademoiselle played a soft interlude. It was an improvisation. She sat low at the instrument, and the lines of her body settled into ungraceful curves and angles that gave it an appearance of deformity. Gradually and imperceptibly the interlude melted into the soft opening minor chords of the Chopin Impromptu.

Edna did not know when the Impromptu began or ended. She sat in the sofa corner reading Robert's letter by the fading light. Mademoiselle had glided from the Chopin into the quivering lovenotes of Isolde's song,[63] and back again to the Impromptu with its soulful and poignant longing.

The shadows deepened in the little room. The music grew strange and fantastic—turbulent, insistent, plaintive and soft with entreaty. The shadows grew deeper. The music filled the room. It floated out upon the night, over the housetops, the crescent of the river, losing itself in the silence of the upper air.

Edna was sobbing, just as she had wept one midnight at Grand Isle when strange, new voices awoke in her. She arose in some agitation to take her departure. "May I come again, Mademoiselle?" she asked at the threshold.

"Come whenever you feel like it. Be careful; the stairs and landings are dark; don't stumble."

Mademoiselle reëntered and lit a candle. Robert's letter was on the floor. She stooped and picked it up. It was crumpled and damp with tears. Mademoiselle smoothed the letter out, restored it to the envelope, and replaced it in the table drawer.

---

[63]Refers to German composer Richard Wagner's (1813–1883) tragic opera *Tristan and Isolde* (1865); in particular, to the song "Liebestod" ("Love-death"), which Isolde sings as she dies in her dead lover's arms.

XXII

One morning on his way into town Mr. Pontellier stopped at the house of his old friend and family physician, Doctor Mandelet. The Doctor was a semi-retired physician, resting, as the saying is, upon his laurels. He bore a reputation for wisdom rather than skill—leaving the active practice of medicine to his assistants and younger contemporaries—and was much sought for in matters of consultation. A few families, united to him by bonds of friendship, he still attended when they required the services of a physician. The Pontelliers were among these.

Mr. Pontellier found the Doctor reading at the open window of his study. His house stood rather far back from the street, in the center of a delightful garden, so that it was quiet and peaceful at the old gentleman's study window. He was a great reader. He stared up disapprovingly over his eye-glasses as Mr. Pontellier entered, wondering who had the temerity to disturb him at that hour of the morning.

"Ah, Pontellier! Not sick, I hope. Come and have a seat. What news do you bring this morning?" He was quite portly, with a profusion of gray hair, and small blue eyes which age had robbed of much of their brightness but none of their penetration.

"Oh! I'm never sick, Doctor. You know that I come of tough fiber—of that old Creole race of Pontelliers that dry up and finally blow away. I came to consult—no, not precisely to consult—to talk to you about Edna. I don't know what ails her."

"Madame Pontellier not well?" marveled the Doctor. "Why, I saw her—I think it was a week ago—walking along Canal Street, the picture of health, it seemed to me."

"Yes, yes; she seems quite well," said Mr. Pontellier, leaning forward and whirling his stick between his two hands; "but she doesn't act well. She's odd, she's not like herself. I can't make her out, and I thought perhaps you'd help me."

"How does she act?" inquired the doctor.

"Well, it isn't easy to explain," said Mr. Pontellier, throwing himself back in his chair. "She lets the housekeeping go to the dickens."

"Well, well; women are not all alike, my dear Pontellier. We've got to consider—"

"I know that; I told you I couldn't explain. Her whole attitude—toward me and everybody and everything—has changed. You know I have a quick temper, but I don't want to quarrel or be rude to a woman, especially my wife; yet I'm driven to it, and feel like ten thousand devils after I've made a fool of myself. She's making it devilishly uncomfortable for me," he went on nervously. "She's got some sort of notion in her head concerning the eternal rights of women; and—you understand—we meet in the morning at the breakfast table."

The old gentleman lifted his shaggy eyebrows, protruded his thick nether lip, and tapped the arms of his chair with his cushioned finger-tips.

"What have you been doing to her, Pontellier?"

"Doing! *Parbleu!*"[64]

"Has she," asked the Doctor, with a smile, "has she been associating of late with a circle of pseudo-intellectual women—super-spiritual superior beings? My wife has been telling me about them."

"That's the trouble," broke in Mr. Pontellier, "she hasn't been associating with any one. She has abandoned her Tuesdays at home, has thrown over all her acquaintances, and goes tramping about by herself, moping in the street-cars, getting in after dark. I tell you she's peculiar. I don't like it; I feel a little worried over it."

This was a new aspect for the Doctor. "Nothing hereditary?" he asked, seriously. "Nothing peculiar about her family antecedents, is there?"

"Oh, no, indeed! She comes of sound old Presbyterian Kentucky stock. The old gentleman, her father, I have heard, used to atone for his week-day sins with his Sunday devotions. I know for a fact, that his race horses literally ran away with the prettiest bit of Kentucky farming land I ever laid eyes upon. Margaret—you know Margaret—she has all the Presbyterianism undiluted. And the youngest is something of a vixen. By the way, she gets married in a couple of weeks from now."

"Send your wife up to the wedding," exclaimed the Doctor, foreseeing a happy solution. "Let her stay among her own people for a while; it will do her good."

"That's what I want her to do. She won't go to the marriage. She says a wedding is one of the most lamentable spectacles on earth. Nice thing for a woman to say to her husband!" exclaimed Mr. Pontellier, fuming anew at the recollection.

"Pontellier," said the Doctor, after a moment's reflection, "let your wife alone for a while. Don't bother her, and don't let her bother you. Woman, my dear friend, is a very peculiar and delicate organism—a sensitive and highly organized woman, such as I know Mrs. Pontellier to be, is especially peculiar. It would require an inspired psychologist to deal successfully with them. And when ordinary fellows like you and me attempt to cope with their idiosyncrasies the result is bungling. Most women are moody and whimsical. This is some passing whim of your wife, due to some cause or causes which you and I needn't try to fathom. But it will pass happily over, especially if you let her alone. Send her around to see me."

"Oh! I couldn't do that; there'd be no reason for it," objected Mr. Pontellier.

"Then I'll go around and see her," said the Doctor. "I'll drop in to dinner some evening *en bon ami.*"[65]

"Do! by all means," urged Mr. Pontellier. "What evening will you come? Say Thursday. Will you come Thursday?" he asked, rising to take his leave.

"Very well; Thursday. My wife may possibly have some engagement for me Thursday. In case she has, I shall let you know. Otherwise, you may expect me."

---

[64]French: "Good Lord!"   [65]French: "as a friend."

Mr. Pontellier turned before leaving to say:

"I am going to New York on business very soon. I have a big scheme on hand, and want to be on the field proper to pull the ropes and handle the ribbons.[66] We'll let you in on the inside if you say so, Doctor," he laughed.

"No, I thank you, my dear sir," returned the Doctor. "I leave such ventures to you younger men with the fever of life still in your blood."

"What I wanted to say," continued Mr. Pontellier, with his hand on the knob; "I may have to be absent a good while. Would you advise me to take Edna along?"

"By all means, if she wishes to go. If not, leave her here. Don't contradict her. The mood will pass, I assure you. It may take a month, two, three months—possibly longer, but it will pass; have patience."

"Well, good-by, *à jeudi*,"[67] said Mr. Pontellier, as he let himself out.

The Doctor would have liked during the course of conversation to ask, "Is there any man in the case?" but he knew his Creole too well to make such a blunder as that.

He did not resume his book immediately, but sat for a while meditatively looking out into the garden.

XXIII

Edna's father was in the city, and had been with them several days. She was not very warmly or deeply attached to him, but they had certain tastes in common, and when together they were companionable. His coming was in the nature of a welcome disturbance; it seemed to furnish a new direction for her emotions.

He had come to purchase a wedding gift for his daughter, Janet, and an outfit for himself in which he might make a creditable appearance at her marriage. Mr. Pontellier had selected the bridal gift, as every one immediately connected with him always deferred to his taste in such matters. And his suggestions on the question of dress—which too often assumes the nature of a problem—were of inestimable value to his father-in-law. But for the past few days the old gentleman had been upon Edna's hands, and in his society she was becoming acquainted with a new set of sensations. He had been a colonel in the Confederate army, and still maintained, with the title, the military bearing which had always accompanied it. His hair and mustache were white and silky, emphasizing the rugged bronze of his face. He was tall and thin, and wore his coats padded, which gave a fictitious breadth and depth to his shoulders and chest. Edna and her father looked very distinguished together, and excited a good deal of notice during their perambulations. Upon his arrival she began by introducing him to her atelier and making a sketch of him. He took the whole matter very seriously. If her talent had been ten-fold greater than it was, it would not have surprised him, convinced as he was that he had bequeathed to all of his daughters the

---

[66]To be in charge.   [67]French: "until Thursday."

germs of a masterful capability, which only depended upon their own efforts to be directed toward successful achievement.

Before her pencil he sat rigid and unflinching, as he had faced the cannon's mouth in days gone by. He resented the intrusion of the children, who gaped with wondering eyes at him, sitting so stiff up there in their mother's bright atelier. When they drew near he motioned them away with an expressive action of the foot, loath to disturb the fixed lines of his countenance, his arms, or his rigid shoulders.

Edna, anxious to entertain him, invited Mademoiselle Reisz to meet him, having promised him a treat in her piano playing; but Mademoiselle declined the invitation. So together they attended a *soirée musicale* at the Ratignolle's. Monsieur and Madame Ratignolle made much of the Colonel, installing him as the guest of honor and engaging him at once to dine with them the following Sunday, or any day which he might select. Madame coquetted with him in the most captivating and naive manner, with eyes, gestures, and a profusion of compliments, till the Colonel's old head felt thirty years younger on his padded shoulders. Edna marveled, not comprehending. She herself was almost devoid of coquetry.

There were one or two men whom she observed at the *soirée musicale*; but she would never have felt moved to any kittenish display to attract their notice—to any feline or feminine wiles to express herself toward them. Their personality attracted her in an agreeable way. Her fancy selected them, and she was glad when a lull in the music gave them an opportunity to meet her and talk with her. Often on the street the glance of strange eyes had lingered in her memory, and sometimes had disturbed her.

Mr. Pontellier did not attend these *soirées musicales*. He considered them *bourgeois*,[68] and found more diversion at the club. To Madame Ratignolle he said the music dispensed at her *soirées* was too "heavy," too far beyond his untrained comprehension. His excuse flattered her. But she disapproved of Mr. Pontellier's club, and she was frank enough to tell Edna so.

"It's a pity Mr. Pontellier doesn't stay home more in the evenings. I think you would be more—well, if you don't mind my saying it—more united, if he did."

"Oh! dear no!" said Edna, with a blank look in her eyes. "What should I do if he stayed home? We wouldn't have anything to say to each other."

She had not much of anything to say to her father, for that matter; but he did not antagonize her. She discovered that he interested her, though she realized that he might not interest her long; and for the first time in her life she felt as if she were thoroughly acquainted with him. He kept her busy serving him and ministering to his wants. It amused her to do so. She would not permit a servant or one of the children to do anything for him which she might do herself. Her husband noticed, and thought it was the expression of a deep filial attachment which he had never suspected.

---

[68]French: middle-class, boorish.

The Colonel drank numerous "toddies" during the course of the day, which left him, however, imperturbed. He was an expert at concocting strong drinks. He had even invented some, to which he had given fantastic names, and for whose manufacture he required diverse ingredients that it devolved upon Edna to procure for him.

When Doctor Mandelet dined with the Pontelliers on Thursday he could discern in Mrs. Pontellier no trace of that morbid condition which her husband had reported to him. She was excited and in a manner radiant. She and her father had been to the race course, and their thoughts when they seated themselves at table were still occupied with the events of the afternoon, and their talk was still of the track. The Doctor had not kept pace with turf affairs. He had certain recollections of racing in what he called "the good old times" when the Lecompte stables[69] flourished, and he drew upon this fund of memories so that he might not be left out and seem wholly devoid of the modern spirit. But he failed to impose upon the Colonel, and was even far from impressing him with this trumped-up knowledge of bygone days. Edna had staked her father on his last venture, with the most gratifying results to both of them. Besides, they had met some very charming people, according to the Colonel's impressions. Mrs. Mortimer Merriman and Mrs. James Highcamp, who were there with Alcée Arobin, had joined them and had enlivened the hours in a fashion that warmed him to think of.

Mr. Pontellier himself had no particular leaning toward horseracing, and was even rather inclined to discourage it as a pastime, especially when he considered the fate of that blue-grass farm in Kentucky. He endeavored, in a general way, to express a particular disapproval, and only succeeded in arousing the ire and opposition of his father-in-law. A pretty dispute followed, in which Edna warmly espoused her father's cause and the Doctor remained neutral.

He observed his hostess attentively from under his shaggy brows, and noted a subtle change which had transformed her from the listless woman he had known into a being who, for the moment, seemed palpitant with the forces of life. Her speech was warm and energetic. There was no repression in her glance or gesture. She reminded him of some beautiful, sleek animal waking up in the sun.

The dinner was excellent. The claret was warm and the champagne was cold, and under their beneficent influence the threatened unpleasantness melted and vanished with the fumes of the wine.

Mr. Pontellier warmed up and grew reminiscent. He told some amusing plantation experiences, recollections of old Iberville and his youth, when he hunted 'possum in company with some friendly darky; thrashed the pecan trees, shot the grosbec,[70] and roamed the woods and fields in mischievous idleness.

---

[69]These stables were integral to the races that were so popular in New Orleans during the antebellum period.

[70]French: a game bird with a large beak.

The Colonel, with little sense of humor and of the fitness of things, related a somber episode of those dark and bitter days, in which he had acted a conspicuous part and always formed a central figure. Nor was the Doctor happier in his selection, when he told the old, ever new and curious story of the waning of a woman's love, seeking strange, new channels, only to return to its legitimate source after days of fierce unrest. It was one of the many little human documents which had been un-folded to him during his long career as a physician. The story did not seem especially to impress Edna. She had one of her own to tell, of a woman who paddled away with her lover one night in a pirogue and never came back. They were lost amid the Baratarian Islands, and no one ever heard of them or found trace of them from that day to this. It was a pure invention. She said that Madame Antoine had related it to her. That, also, was an invention. Perhaps it was a dream she had had. But every glowing word seemed real to those who listened. They could feel the hot breath of the Southern night; they could hear the long sweep of the pirogue through the glistening moonlit water, the beating of birds' wings, rising startled from among the reeds in the salt-water pools; they could see the faces of the lovers, pale, close together, rapt in oblivious forgetfulness, drifting into the unknown.

The champagne was cold, and its subtle fumes played fantastic tricks with Edna's memory that night.

Outside, away from the glow of the fire and the soft lamplight, the night was chill and murky. The Doctor doubled his old-fashioned cloak across his breast as he strode home through the darkness. He knew his fellow-creatures better than most men; knew that inner life which so seldom unfolds itself to unanointed eyes. He was sorry he had accepted Pontellier's invitation. He was growing old, and beginning to need rest and an imperturbed spirit. He did not want the secrets of other lives thrust upon him.

"I hope it isn't Arobin," he muttered to himself as he walked. "I hope to heaven it isn't Alcée Arobin."

XXIV

Edna and her father had a warm, and almost violent dispute upon the subject of her refusal to attend her sister's wedding. Mr. Pontellier declined to interfere, to interpose either his influence or his authority. He was following Doctor Mandelet's advice, and letting her do as she liked. The Colonel reproached his daughter for her lack of filial kindness and respect, her want of sisterly affection and womanly consideration. His arguments were labored and unconvincing. He doubted if Janet would accept any excuse— forgetting that Edna had offered none. He doubted if Janet would ever speak to her again, and he was sure Margaret would not.

Edna was glad to be rid of her father when he finally took himself off with his wedding garments and his bridal gifts, with his padded shoulders, his Bible reading, his "toddies" and ponderous oaths.

Mr. Pontellier followed him closely. He meant to stop at the wedding on his way to New York and endeavor by every means which money and love could devise to atone somewhat for Edna's incomprehensible action.

"You are too lenient, too lenient by far, Léonce," asserted the Colonel. "Authority, coercion are what is needed. Put your foot down good and hard; the only way to manage a wife. Take my word for it."

The Colonel was perhaps unaware that he had coerced his own wife into her grave. Mr. Pontellier had a vague suspicion of it which he thought it needless to mention at that late day.

Edna was not so consciously gratified at her husband's leaving home as she had been over the departure of her father. As the day approached when he was to leave her for a comparatively long stay, she grew melting and affectionate, remembering his many acts of consideration and his repeated expressions of an ardent attachment. She was solicitous about his health and his welfare. She bustled around, looking after his clothing, thinking about heavy underwear, quite as Madame Ratignolle would have done under similar circumstances. She cried when he went away, calling him her dear, good friend, and she was quite certain she would grow lonely before very long and go to join him in New York.

But after all, a radiant peace settled upon her when she at last found herself alone. Even the children were gone. Old Madame Pontellier had come herself and carried them off to Iberville with their quadroon. The old madame did not venture to say she was afraid they would be neglected during Léonce's absence; she hardly ventured to think so. She was hungry for them—even a little fierce in her attachment. She did not want them to be wholly "children of the pavement," she always said when begging to have them for a space. She wished them to know the country, with its streams, its fields, its woods, its freedom, so delicious to the young. She wished them to taste something of the life their father had lived and known and loved when he, too, was a little child.

When Edna was at last alone, she breathed a big, genuine sigh of relief. A feeling that was unfamiliar but very delicious came over her. She walked all through the house, from one room to another, as if inspecting it for the first time. She tried the various chairs and lounges, as if she had never sat and reclined upon them before. And she perambulated around the outside of the house, investigating, looking to see if windows and shutters were secure and in order. The flowers were like new acquaintances; she approached them in a familiar spirit, and made herself at home among them. The garden walks were damp, and Edna called to the maid to bring out her rubber sandals. And there she stayed, and stooped, digging around the plants, trimming, picking dead, dry leaves. The children's little dog came out, interfering, getting in her way. She scolded him, laughing at him, played with him. The garden smelled so good and looked so pretty in the afternoon sunlight. Edna plucked all the bright flowers she could find, and went into the house with them, she and the little dog.

Even the kitchen assumed a sudden interesting character which she had never before perceived. She went in to give directions to the cook, to say that the butcher would have to bring much less meat, that they would require only half their usual quantity of bread, of milk and groceries. She told the cook that she herself would be greatly occupied during Mr. Pontellier's absence, and she begged her to take all thought and responsibility of the larder upon her own shoulders.

That night Edna dined alone. The candelabra, with a few candles in the center of the table, gave all the light she needed. Outside the circle of light in which she sat, the large dining-room looked solemn and shadowy. The cook, placed upon her mettle, served a delicious repast—a luscious tenderloin broiled à point. The wine tasted good; the marron glacé[71] seemed to be just what she wanted. It was so pleasant, too, to dine in a comfortable peignoir.

She thought a little sentimentally about Léonce and the children, and wondered what they were doing. As she gave a dainty scrap or two to the doggie, she talked intimately to him about Etienne and Raoul. He was beside himself with astonishment and delight over these companionable advances, and showed his appreciation by his little quick, snappy barks and a lively agitation.

Then Edna sat in the library after dinner and read Emerson[72] until she grew sleepy. She realized that she had neglected her reading, and determined to start anew upon a course of improving studies, now that her time was completely her own to do with as she liked.

After a refreshing bath, Edna went to bed. And as she snuggled comfortably beneath the eiderdown a sense of restfulness invaded her, such as she had not known before.

XXV

When the weather was dark and cloudy Edna could not work. She needed the sun to mellow and temper her mood to the sticking point. She had reached a stage when she seemed to be no longer feeling her way, working, when in the humor, with sureness and ease. And being devoid of ambition, and striving not toward accomplishment, she drew satisfaction from the work in itself.

On rainy or melancholy days Edna went out and sought the society of the friends she had made at Grand Isle. Or else she stayed indoors and nursed a mood with which she was becoming too familiar for her own comfort and peace of mind. It was not despair; but it seemed to her as if life were passing by, leaving its promise broken and unfulfilled. Yet there were other days when she listened, was led on and deceived by fresh promises which her youth held out to her.

She went again to the races, and again. Alcée Arobin and Mrs. Highcamp called for her one bright afternoon in Arobin's drag.[73] Mrs. Highcamp was a worldly but unaffected, intelligent, slim, tall blonde woman in the forties,

---

[71]French: chestnuts glazed with sugar.

[72]Ralph Waldo Emerson (1803–1882), American philosopher in the forefront of the Transcendental movement.

[73]A coach.

with an indifferent manner and blue eyes that stared. She had a daughter who served her as a pretext for cultivating the society of young men of fashion. Alcée Arobin was one of them. He was a familiar figure at the race course, the opera, the fashionable clubs. There was a perpetual smile in his eyes, which seldom failed to awaken a corresponding cheerfulness in any one who looked into them and listened to his good-humored voice. His manner was quiet, and at times a little insolent. He possessed a good figure, a pleasing face, not overburdened with depth of thought or feeling; and his dress was that of the conventional man of fashion.

He admired Edna extravagantly, after meeting her at the races with her father. He had met her before on other occasions, but she had seemed to him unapproachable until that day. It was at his instigation that Mrs. Highcamp called to ask her to go with them to the Jockey Club[74] to witness the turf event of the season.

There were possibly a few track men out there who knew the race horse as well as Edna, but there was certainly none who knew it better. She sat between her two companions as one having authority to speak. She laughed at Arobin's pretensions, and deplored Mrs. Highcamp's ignorance. The race horse was a friend and intimate associate of her childhood. The atmosphere of the stables and the breath of the blue grass paddock revived in her memory and lingered in her nostrils. She did not perceive that she was talking like her father as the sleek geldings ambled in review before them. She played for very high stakes, and fortune favored her. The fever of the game flamed in her cheeks and eyes, and it got into her blood and into her brain like an intoxicant. People turned their heads to look at her, and more than one lent an attentive ear to her utterances, hoping thereby to secure the elusive but ever-desired "tip." Arobin caught the contagion of excitement which drew him to Edna like a magnet. Mrs. Highcamp remained, as usual, unmoved, with her indifferent stare and uplifted eyebrows.

Edna stayed and dined with Mrs. Highcamp upon being urged to do so. Arobin, also remained and sent away his drag.

The dinner was quiet and uninteresting, save for the cheerful efforts of Arobin to enliven things. Mrs. Highcamp deplored the absence of her daughter from the races, and tried to convey to her what she had missed by going to the "Dante[75] reading" instead of joining them. The girl held a geranium leaf up to her nose and said nothing, but looked knowing and noncommittal. Mr. Highcamp was a plain, bald-headed man, who only talked under compulsion. He was unresponsive. Mrs. High-camp was full of delicate courtesy and consideration toward her husband. She addressed most of her conversation to him at table. They sat in the library after dinner and read the evening papers together under the drop-light;[76] while the younger people went into the drawing-room near by and talked. Miss Highcamp played

---

[74]A local elite club.

[75]Dante Alighieri (1265–1321), Italian poet and author of *The Divine Comedy*.

[76]A gas lamp.

some selections from Grieg upon the piano. She seemed to have apprehended all of the composer's coldness and none of his poetry. While Edna
listened she could not help wondering if she had lost her taste for music.

When the time came for her to go home, Mr. Highcamp grunted a lame
offer to escort her, looking down at his slippered feet with tactless concern.
It was Arobin who took her home. The car ride was long, and it was late
when they reached Esplanade Street. Arobin asked permission to enter for a
second to light his cigarette—his match safe[77] was empty. He filled his
match safe, but did not light his cigarette until he left her, after she had
expressed her willingness to go to the races with him again.

Edna was neither tired nor sleepy. She was hungry again, for the Highcamp dinner, though of excellent quality, had lacked abundance. She rummaged in the larder and brought forth a slice of "Gruyère"[78] and some
crackers. She opened a bottle of beer which she found in the ice-box. Edna
felt extremely restless and excited. She vacantly hummed a fantastic tune as
she poked at the wood embers on the hearth and munched a cracker.

She wanted something to happen—something, anything; she did not
know what. She regretted that she had not made Arobin stay a half hour to
talk over the horses with her. She counted the money she had won. But
there was nothing else to do, so she went to bed, and tossed there for hours
in a sort of monotonous agitation.

In the middle of the night she remembered that she had forgotten to
write her regular letter to her husband; and she decided to do so next day
and tell him about her afternoon at the Jockey Club. She lay wide awake
composing a letter which was nothing like the one which she wrote next
day. When the maid awoke her in the morning Edna was dreaming of Mr.
Highcamp playing the piano at the entrance of a music store on Canal
Street, while his wife was saying to Alcée Arobin, as they boarded an Esplanade Street car:

"What a pity that so much talent has been neglected! but I must go."

When, a few days later, Alcée Arobin again called for Edna in his drag,
Mrs. Highcamp was not with him. He said they would pick her up. But as
that lady had not been apprised of his intention of picking her up, she was
not at home. The daughter was just leaving the house to attend the meeting
of a branch Folk Lore Society, and regretted that she could not accompany
them. Arobin appeared nonplused, and asked Edna if there were any one
else she cared to ask.

She did not deem it worth while to go in search of any of the fashionable acquaintances from whom she had withdrawn herself. She thought of
Madame Ratignolle, but knew that her fair friend did not leave the house,
except to take a languid walk around the block with her husband after
nightfall. Mademoiselle Reisz would have laughed at such a request from
Edna. Madame Lebrun might have enjoyed the outing, but for some reason
Edna did not want her. So they went alone, she and Arobin.

---

[77]A box designed to contain friction matches.   [78]A type of cheese.

The afternoon was intensely interesting to her. The excitement came back upon her like a remittent fever. Her talk grew familiar and confidential. It was no labor to become intimate with Arobin. His manner invited easy confidence. The preliminary stage of becoming acquainted was one which he always endeavored to ignore when a pretty and engaging woman was concerned.

He stayed and dined with Edna. He stayed and sat beside the wood fire. They laughed and talked; and before it was time to go he was telling her how different life might have been if he had known her years before. With ingenuous frankness he spoke of what a wicked, ill-disciplined boy he had been, and impulsively drew up his cuff to exhibit upon his wrist the scar from a saber cut which he had received in a duel outside of Paris when he was nineteen. She touched his hand as she scanned the red cicatrice on the inside of his white wrist. A quick impulse that was somewhat spasmodic impelled her fingers to close in a sort of clutch upon his hand. He felt the pressure of her pointed nails in the flesh of his palm.

She arose hastily and walked toward the mantel.

"The sight of a wound or scar always agitates and sickens me," she said. "I shouldn't have looked at it."

"I beg your pardon," he entreated, following her; "it never occurred to me that it might be repulsive."

He stood close to her, and the effrontery in his eyes repelled the old, vanishing self in her, yet drew all her awakening sensuousness. He saw enough in her face to impel him to take her hand and hold it while he said his lingering good night.

"Will you go to the races again?" he asked.

"No," she said. "I've had enough of the races. I don't want to lose all the money I've won, and I've got to work when the weather is bright, instead of—"

"Yes; work; to be sure. You promised to show me your work. What morning may I come up to your atelier? To-morrow?"

"No!"

"Day after?"

"No, no."

"Oh, please don't refuse me! I know something of such things. I might help you with a stray suggestion or two."

"No. Good night. Why don't you go after you have said good night? I don't like you," she went on in a high, excited pitch, attempting to draw away her hand. She felt that her words lacked dignity and sincerity, and she knew that he felt it.

"I'm sorry you don't like me. I'm sorry I offended you. How have I offended you? What have I done? Can't you forgive me?" And he bent and pressed his lips upon her hand as if he wished never more to withdraw them.

"Mr. Arobin," she complained, "I'm greatly upset by the excitement of the afternoon; I'm not myself. My manner must have misled you in some way. I wish you to go, please." She spoke in a monotonous, dull tone. He took his hat from the table, and stood with eyes turned from her, looking into the dying fire. For a moment or two he kept an impressive silence.

"Your manner has not misled me, Mrs. Pontellier," he said finally. "My own emotions have done that. I couldn't help it. When I'm near you, how could I help it? Don't think anything of it, don't bother, please. You see, I go when you command me. If you wish me to stay away, I shall do so. If you let me come back, I—oh! you will let me come back?"

He cast one appealing glance at her, to which she made no response. Alcée Arobin's manner was so genuine that it often deceived even himself.

Edna did not care or think whether it were genuine or not. When she was alone she looked mechanically at the back of her hand which he had kissed so warmly. Then she leaned her head down on the mantelpiece. She felt somewhat like a woman who in a moment of passion is betrayed into an act of infidelity, and realizes the significance of the act without being wholly awakened from its glamour. The thought was passing vaguely through her mind, "What would he think?"

She did not mean her husband; she was thinking of Robert Lebrun. Her husband seemed to her now like a person whom she had married without love as an excuse.

She lit a candle and went up to her room. Alcée Arobin was absolutely nothing to her. Yet his presence, his manners, the warmth of his glances, and above all the touch of his lips upon her hand had acted like a narcotic upon her.

She slept a languorous sleep, interwoven with vanishing dreams.

XXVI

Alcée Arobin wrote Edna an elaborate note of apology, palpitant with sincerity. It embarrassed her; for in a cooler, quieter moment it appeared to her absurd that she should have taken his action so seriously, so dramatically. She felt sure that the significance of the whole occurrence had lain in her own self-consciousness. If she ignored his note it would give undue importance to a trivial affair. If she replied to it in a serious spirit it would still leave in his mind the impression that she had in a susceptible moment yielded to his influence. After all, it was no great matter to have one's hand kissed. She was provoked at his having written the apology. She answered in as light and bantering a spirit as she fancied it deserved, and said she would be glad to have him look in upon her at work whenever he felt the inclination and his business gave him the opportunity.

He responded at once by presenting himself at her home with all his disarming naïveté. And then there was scarcely a day which followed that she did not see him or was not reminded of him. He was prolific in pretexts. His attitude became one of good-humored subservience and tacit adoration. He was ready at all times to submit to her moods, which were as often kind as they were cold. She grew accustomed to him. They became intimate and friendly by imperceptible degrees, and then by leaps. He sometimes talked

in a way that astonished her at first and brought the crimson into her face;
in a way that pleased her at last, appealing to the animalism that stirred
impatiently within her.

There was nothing which so quieted the turmoil of Edna's senses as a
visit to Mademoiselle Reisz. It was then, in the presence of that personality
which was offensive to her, that the woman, by her divine art, seemed to
reach Edna's spirit and set it free.

It was misty, with heavy, lowering atmosphere, one afternoon, when
Edna climbed the stairs to the pianist's apartments under the roof. Her
clothes were dripping with moisture. She felt chilled and pinched as she
entered the room. Mademoiselle was poking at a rusty stove that smoked a
little and warmed the room indifferently. She was endeavoring to heat a pot
of chocolate on the stove. The room looked cheerless and dingy to Edna as
she entered. A bust of Beethoven, covered with a hood of dust, scowled at
her from the Mantelpiece.

"Ah! here comes the sunlight!" exclaimed Mademoiselle, rising from her
knees before the stove. "Now it will be warm and bright enough; I can let
the fire alone."

She closed the stove door with a bang, and approaching, assisted in
removing Edna's dripping mackintosh.

"You are cold; you look miserable. The chocolate will soon be hot. But
would you rather have a taste of brandy? I have scarcely touched the bottle
which you brought me for my cold." A piece of red flannel was wrapped around
Mademoiselle's throat; a stiff neck compelled her to hold her head on one side.

"I will take some brandy," said Edna, shivering as she removed her
gloves and overshoes. She drank the liquor from the glass as a man would
have done. Then flinging herself upon the uncomfortable sofa she said, "Mademoiselle, I am going to move away from my house on Esplanade Street."

"Ah!" ejaculated the musician, neither surprised nor especially interested. Nothing ever seemed to astonish her very much. She was endeavoring
to adjust the bunch of violets which had become loose from its fastening in
her hair. Edna drew her down upon the sofa, and taking a pin from her own
hair, secured the shabby artificial flowers in their accustomed place.

"Aren't you astonished?"

"Passably. Where are you going? To New York? to Iberville? to your father in Mississippi? where?"

"Just two steps away," laughed Edna, "in a little four-room house
around the corner. It looks so cozy, so inviting and restful, whenever I pass
by; and it's for rent. I'm tired looking after that big house. It never seemed
like mine, anyway—like home. It's too much trouble. I have to keep too
many servants. I am tired bothering with them.

"That is not your true reason, *ma belle*. There is no use in telling me lies.
I don't know your reason, but you have not told me the truth." Edna did
not protest or endeavor to justify herself.

"The house, the money that provides for it, are not mine. Isn't that
enough reason?"

"They are your husband's," returned Mademoiselle, with a shrug and a malicious elevation of the eyebrows.

"Oh! I see there is no deceiving you. Then let me tell you: It is a caprice. I have a little money of my own from my mother's estate, which my father sends me by driblets. I won a large sum this winter on the races, and I am beginning to sell my sketches. Laidpore is more and more pleased with my work; he says it grows in force and individuality. I cannot judge of that myself, but I feel that I have gained in ease and confidence. However, as I said, I have sold a good many through Laidpore. I can live in the tiny house for little or nothing, with one servant. Old Celestine, who works occasionally for me, says she will come stay with me and do my work. I know I shall like it, like the feeling of freedom and independence."

"What does your husband say?"

"I have not told him yet. I only thought of it this morning. He will think I am demented, no doubt. Perhaps you think so."

Mademoiselle shook her head slowly. "Your reason is not yet clear to me," she said.

Neither was it quite clear to Edna herself; but it unfolded itself as she sat for a while in silence. Instinct had prompted her to put away her husband's bounty in casting off her allegiance. She did not know how it would be when he returned. There would have to be an understanding, an explanation. Conditions would some way adjust themselves, she felt; but whatever came, she had resolved never again to belong to another than herself.

"I shall give a grand dinner before I leave the old house!" Edna exclaimed. "You will have to come to it, Mademoiselle. I will give you everything that you like to eat and to drink. We shall sing and laugh and be merry for once." And she uttered a sigh that came from the very depths of her being.

If Mademoiselle happened to have received a letter from Robert during the interval of Edna's visits, she would give her the letter unsolicited. And she would seat herself at the piano and play as her humor prompted her while the young woman read the letter.

The little stove was roaring; it was red-hot, and the chocolate in the tin sizzled and sputtered. Edna went forward and opened the stove door, and Mademoiselle rising, took a letter from under the bust of Beethoven and handed it to Edna.

"Another! so soon!" she exclaimed, her eyes filled with delight. "Tell me, Mademoiselle, does he know that I see his letters?"

"Never in the world! He would be angry and would never write to me again if he thought so. Does he write to you? Never a line. Does he send you a message? Never a word. It is because he loves you, poor fool, and is trying to forget you, since you are not free to listen to him or to belong to him."

"Why do you show me his letters, then?"

"Haven't you begged for them? Can I refuse you anything? Oh! you cannot deceive me," and Mademoiselle approached her beloved instrument and began to play. Edna did not at once read the letter. She sat holding it in her hand, while the music penetrated her whole being like an effulgence, warming and brightening the dark places of her soul. It prepared her for joy and exultation.

"Oh!" she exclaimed, letting the letter fall to the floor. "Why did you not tell me?" She went and grasped Mademoiselle's hands up from the keys. "Oh! unkind! malicious! Why did you not tell me?"

"That he was coming back? No great news, *ma foi*.[79] I wonder he did not come long ago."

"But when, when?" cried Edna, impatiently. "He does not say when."

"He says 'very soon.' You know as much about it as I do; it is all in the letter."

"But why? Why is he coming? Oh, if I thought—" and she snatched the letter from the floor and turned the pages this way and that way, looking for the reason, which was left untold.

"If I were young and in love with a man," said Mademoiselle, turning on the stool and pressing her wiry hands between her knees as she looked down at Edna, who sat on the floor holding the letter, "it seems to me he would have to be some *grand esprit*; a man with lofty aims and ability to reach them; one who stood high enough to attract the notice of his fellowmen. It seems to me if I were young and in love I should never deem a man of ordinary caliber worthy of my devotion."

"Now it is you who are telling lies and seeking to deceive me, Mademoiselle; or else you have never been in love, and know nothing about it. Why," went on Edna, clasping her knees and looking up into Mademoiselle's twisted face, "do you suppose a woman knows why she loves? Does she select? Does she say to herself: 'Go to! Here is a distinguished statesman with presidential possibilities; I shall proceed to fall in love with him.' Or, 'I shall set my heart upon this musician, whose fame is on every tongue?' Or, 'This financier, who controls the world's money markets?'"

"You are purposely misunderstanding me, *ma reine*.[80] Are you in love with Robert?"

"Yes," said Edna. It was the first time she had admitted it, and a glow overspread her face, blotching it with red spots.

"Why?" asked her companion. "Why do you love him when you ought not to?"

Edna, with a motion or two, dragged herself on her knees before Mademoiselle Reisz, who took the glowing face between her two hands.

"Why? Because his hair is brown and grows away from his temples; because he opens and shuts his eyes, and his nose is a little out of drawing; because he has two lips and a square chin, and a little finger which he can't straighten from having played baseball too energetically in his youth. Because—"

"Because you do, in short," laughed Mademoiselle. "What will you do when he comes back?" she asked.

"Do? Nothing, except feel glad and happy to be alive."

---

[79]French: "in fact."   [80]French: "my queen" or "my lovely."

She was already glad and happy to be alive at the mere thought of his return. The murky, lowering sky, which had depressed her a few hours before, seemed bracing and invigorating as she splashed through the streets on her way home.

She stopped at a confectioner's and ordered a huge box of bonbons for the children in Iberville. She slipped a card in the box, on which she scribbled a tender message and sent an abundance of kisses.

Before dinner in the evening Edna wrote a charming letter to her husband, telling him of her intention to move for a while into the little house around the block, and to give a farewell dinner before leaving, regretting that he was not there to share it, to help her out with the menu and assist her in entertaining the guests. Her letter was brilliant and brimming with cheerfulness.

XXVII

"What is the matter with you?" asked Arobin that evening. "I never found you in such a happy mood." Edna was tired by that time, and was reclining on the lounge before the fire.

"Don't you know the weather prophet has told us we shall see the sun pretty soon?"

"Well, that ought to be reason enough," he acquiesced. "You wouldn't give me another if I sat here all night imploring you." He sat close to her on a low tabouret, and as he spoke his fingers lightly touched the hair that fell a little over her forehead. She liked the touch of his fingers through her hair, and closed her eyes sensitively.

"One of these days," she said, "I'm going to pull myself together for a while and think—try to determine what character of a woman I am; for, candidly I don't know. By all the codes which I am acquainted with, I am a devilishly wicked specimen of the sex. But some way I can't convince myself that I am. I must think about it."

"Don't. What's the use? Why should you bother thinking about it when I can tell you what manner of woman you are." His fingers strayed occasionally down to her warm, smooth cheeks and firm chin, which was growing a little full and double.

"Oh, yes! You will tell me that I am adorable; everything that is captivating. Spare yourself the effort."

"No; I shan't tell you anything of the sort, though I shouldn't be lying if I did."

"Do you know Mademoiselle Reisz?" she asked irrelevantly.

"The pianist? I know her by sight. I've heard her play."

"She says queer things sometimes in a bantering way that you don't notice at the time and you find yourself thinking about afterward."

"For instance?"

"Well, for instance, when I left her today, she put her arms around me and felt my shoulder blades, to see if my wings were strong, she said. 'The bird that would soar above the level plain of tradition and prejudice must have strong wings. It is a sad spectacle to see the weaklings bruised, exhausted, fluttering back to earth.'"

"Whither would you soar?"

"I'm not thinking of any extraordinary flights. I only half comprehend her."

"I've heard she's partially demented," said Arobin.

"She seems to me wonderfully sane," Edna replied.

"I'm told she's extremely disagreeable and unpleasant. Why have you introduced her at a moment when I desired to talk of you?"

"Oh! talk of me if you like," cried Edna, clasping her hands beneath her head; "but let me think of something else while you do."

"I'm jealous of your thoughts to-night. They're making you a little kinder than usual; but some way I feel as if they were wandering, as if they were not here with me." She only looked at him and smiled. His eyes were very near. He leaned upon the lounge with an arm extended across her, while the other hand still rested upon her hair. They continued silently to look into each other's eyes. When he leaned forward and kissed her, she clasped his head, holding his lips to hers.

It was the first kiss of her life to which her nature had really responded. It was a flaming torch that kindled desire.

XXVIII

Edna cried a little that night after Arobin left her. It was only one phase of the multitudinous emotions which had assailed her. There was with her an overwhelming feeling of irresponsibility. There was the shock of the unexpected and the unaccustomed. There was her husband's reproach looking at her from the external things around her which he had provided for her external existence. There was Robert's reproach making itself felt by a quicker, fiercer, more overpowering love, which had awakened within her toward him. Above all, there was understanding. She felt as if a mist had been lifted from her eyes, enabling her to look upon and comprehend the significance of life, that monster made up of beauty and brutality. But among the conflicting sensations which assailed her, there was neither shame nor remorse. There was a dull pang of regret because it was not the kiss of love which had inflamed her, because it was not love which had held this cup of life to her lips.

XXIX

Without even waiting for an answer from her husband regarding his opinion or wishes in the matter, Edna hastened her preparations for quitting her home on Esplanade Street and moving into the little house around the block. A feverish anxiety attended her every action in that direction. There was no moment of deliberation, no interval of repose between the thought and its fulfillment. Early upon the morning following those hours passed in

Arobin's society, Edna set about securing her new abode and hurrying her arrangements for occupying it. Within the precincts of her home she felt like one who has entered and lingered within the portals of some forbidden temple in which a thousand muffled voices bade her begone.

Whatever was her own in the house, everything which she had acquired aside from her husband's bounty, she caused to be transported to the other house, supplying simple and meager deficiencies from her own resources.

Arobin found her with rolled sleeves, working in company with the house-maid when he looked in during the afternoon. She was splendid and robust, and had never appeared handsomer than in the old blue gown, with a red silk handkerchief knotted at random around her head to protect her hair from the dust. She was mounted upon a high step-ladder, unhooking a picture from the wall when he entered. He had found the front door open, and had followed his ring by walking in unceremoniously.

"Come down!" he said. "Do you want to kill yourself?" She greeted him with affected carelesness, and appeared absorbed in her occupation.

If he had expected to find her languishing, reproachful, or indulging in sentimental tears, he must have been greatly surprised.

He was no doubt prepared for any emergency, ready for any one of the foregoing attitudes, just as he bent himself easily and naturally to the situation which confronted him.

"Please come down," he insisted, holding the ladder and looking up at her.

"No," she answered; "Ellen is afraid to mount the ladder. Joe is working over at the 'pigeon house'—that's the name Ellen gives it, because it's so small and looks like a pigeon house[81]—and some one has to do this."

Arobin pulled off his coat, and expressed himself ready and willing to tempt fate in her place. Ellen brought him one of her dustcaps, and went into contortions of mirth, which she found it impossible to control, when she saw him put it on before the mirror as grotesquely as he could. Edna herself could not refrain from smiling when she fastened it at his request. So it was he who in turn mounted the ladder, un-hooking pictures and curtains, and dislodging ornaments as Edna directed. When he had finished he took off his dust-cap and went out to wash his hands.

Edna was sitting on the tabouret,[82] idly brushing the tips of a feather duster along the carpet when he came in again.

"Is there anything more you will let me do?" he asked.

"That is all," she answered. "Ellen can manage the rest." She kept the young woman occupied in the drawing-room, unwilling to be left alone with Arobin.

"What about the dinner?" he asked; "the grand event, the *coup d'état?*"

"It will be day after to-morrow. Why do you call it the '*coup d'état?*' Oh! it will be very fine; all my best of everything—crystal, silver and gold, Sèvres, flowers, music, and champagne to swim in. I'll let Léonce pay the bills. I wonder what he'll say when he sees the bills."

---

[81]A dovecote; a house for domesticated pigeons.   [82]French: stool.

"And you ask me why I call it a *coup d'état?*" Arobin had put on his coat, and he stood before her and asked if his cravat[83] was plumb. She told him it was, looking no higher than the tip of his collar.

"When do you go to the 'pigeon house?'—with all due acknowledgment to Ellen."

"Day after to-morrow, after the dinner. I shall sleep there."

"Ellen, will you very kindly get me a glass of water?" asked Arobin. "The dust in the curtains, if you will pardon me for hinting such a thing, has parched my throat to a crisp."

"While Ellen gets the water," said Edna, rising, "I will say good-by and let you go. I must get rid of this grime, and I have a million things to do and think of."

"When shall I see you?" asked Arobin, seeking to detain her, the maid having left the room.

"At the dinner, of course. You are invited."

"Not before?—not to-night or to-morrow morning or to-morrow noon or night? or the day after morning or noon? Can't you see yourself, without my telling you, what an eternity it is?"

He had followed her into the hall and to the foot of the stairway, looking up at her as she mounted with her face half turned to him.

"Not an instant sooner," she said. But she laughed and looked at him with eyes that at once gave him courage to wait and made it torture to wait.

XXX

Though Edna had spoken of the dinner as a very grand affair, it was in truth a very small affair and very select, in so much as the guests invited were few and were selected with discrimination. She had counted upon an even dozen seating themselves at her round mahogany board, forgetting for the moment that Madame Ratignolle was to the last degree *souffrante*[84] and unpresentable, and not foreseeing that Madame Lebrun would send a thousand regrets at the last moment. So there were only ten, after all, which made a cozy, comfortable number.

There were Mr. and Mrs. Merriman, a pretty, vivacious little woman in the thirties; her husband, a jovial fellow, something of a shallow pate,[85] who laughed a good deal at other people's witticisms, and had thereby made himself extremely popular. Mrs. Highcamp had accompanied them. Of course, there was Alcée Arobin; and Mademoiselle Reisz had consented to come. Edna had sent her a fresh bunch of violets with black lace trimmings for her hair. Monsieur Ratignolle brought himself and his wife's excuses. Victor Lebrun, who happened to be in the city, bent upon relaxation, had accepted with alacrity. There was a Miss Mayblunt, no longer in her teens, who looked at the world through lorgnettes[86] and with the keenest interest. It was thought and said that she was intellectual; it was suspected of her that

---

[83]A necktie or scarf.
[84]French: ill.

[85]A clown.
[86]Eyeglasses attached to a handle.

she wrote under a *nom de guerre*.[87] She had come with a gentleman by the name of Gouvernail, connected with one of the daily papers, of whom nothing special could be said, except that he was observant and seemed quiet and inoffensive. Edna herself made the tenth, and at half-past eight they seated themselves at table, Arobin and Monsieur Ratignolle on either side of their hostess.

Mrs. Highcamp sat between Arobin and Victor Lebrun. Then came Mrs. Merriman, Mr. Gouvernail, Miss Mayblunt, Mr. Merriman, and Mademoiselle Reisz next to Monsieur Ratignolle.

There was something extremely gorgeous about the appearance of the table, an effect of splendor conveyed by a cover of pale yellow satin under strips of lace-work. There were wax candles in massive brass candelabra, burning softly under yellow silk shades; full, fragrant roses, yellow and red, abounded. There were silver and gold, as she had said there would be, and crystal which glittered like the gems which the women wore.

The ordinary stiff dining chairs had been discarded for the occasion and replaced by the most commodious and luxurious which could be collected throughout the house. Mademoiselle Reisz, being exceedingly diminutive, was elevated upon cushions, as small children are sometimes hoisted at table upon bulky volumes.

"'Something new, Edna?" exclaimed Miss Mayblunt, with lorgnette directed toward a magnificent cluster of diamonds that sparkled, that almost sputtered, in Edna's hair, just over the center of her forehead.

"Quite new; 'brand' new, in fact; a present from my husband. It arrived this morning from New York. I may as well admit that this is my birthday, and that I am twenty-nine. In good time I expect you to drink my health. Meanwhile, I shall ask you to begin with this cocktail, composed—would you say 'composed?'" with an appeal to Miss Mayblunt—"composed by my father in honor of Sister Janet's wedding."

Before each guest stood a tiny glass that looked and sparkled like a garnet gem.

"Then, all things considered," spoke Arobin, "it might not be amiss to start out by drinking the Colonel's health in the cocktail which he composed, on the birthday of the most charming of women—the daughter whom he invented."

Mr. Merriman's laugh at this sally was such a genuine outburst and so contagious that it started the dinner with an agreeable swing that never slackened.

Miss Mayblunt begged to be allowed to keep her cocktail untouched before her, just to look at. The color was marvelous! She could compare it to nothing she had ever seen, and the garnet lights which it emitted were unspeakably rare. She pronounced the Colonel an artist, and stuck to it.

Monsieur Ratignolle was prepared to take things seriously; the *mets*, the *entre-mets*,[88] the service, the decorations, even the people. He looked up from his pompono and inquired of Arobin if he were related to the

---

[87]French: pseudonym. [88]French: the main and side dishes.

gentleman of that name who formed one of the firm of Laitner and Arobin, lawyers. The young man admitted that Laitner was a warm personal friend, who permitted Arobin's name to decorate the firm's letterheads and to appear upon a shingle that graced Perdido Street.

"There are so many inquisitive people and institutions abounding," said Arobin, "that one is really forced as a matter of convenience these days to assume the virtue of an occupation if he has it not."

Monsieur Ratignolle stared a little, and turned to ask Mademoiselle Reisz if she considered the symphony concerts up to the standard which had been set the previous winter. Mademoiselle Reisz answered Monsieur Ratignolle in French, which Edna thought a little rude, under the circumstances, but characteristic. Mademoiselle had only disagreeable things to say of the symphony concerts, and insulting remarks to make of all the musicians of New Orleans, singly and collectively. All her interest seemed to be centered upon the delicacies placed before her.

Mr. Merriman said that Mr. Arobin's remark about inquisitive people reminded him of a man from Waco[89] the other day at the St. Charles Hotel— but as Mr. Merriman's stories were always lame and lacking point, his wife seldom permitted him to complete them. She interrupted him to ask if he remembered the name of the author whose book she had bought the week before to send to a friend in Geneva. She was talking "books" with Mr. Gouvernail and trying to draw from him his opinion upon current literary topics. Her husband told the story of the Waco man privately to Miss Mayblunt, who pretended to be greatly amused and to think it extremely clever.

Mrs. Highcamp hung with languid but unaffected interest upon the warm and impetuous volubility of her left-hand neighbor, Victor Lebrun. Her attention was never for a moment withdrawn from him after seating herself at table; and when he turned to Mrs. Merriman, who was prettier and more vivacious than Mrs. High-camp, she waited with easy indifference for an opportunity to reclaim his attention. There was the occasional sound of music, of mandolins, sufficiently removed to be an agreeable accompaniment rather than an interruption to the conversation. Outside the soft, monotonous splash of a fountain could be heard; the sound penetrated into the room with the heavy odor of jessamine that came through the open windows.

The golden shimmer of Edna's satin gown spread in rich folds on either side of her. There was a soft fall of lace encircling her shoulders. It was the color of her skin, without the glow, the myriad living tints that one may sometimes discover in vibrant flesh. There was something in her attitude, in her whole appearance when she leaned her head against the high-backed chair and spread her arms, which suggested the regal woman, the one who rules, who looks on, who stands alone:

But as she sat there amid her guests, she felt the old ennui overtaking her; the hopelessness which so often assailed her, which came upon her like an obsession, like something extraneous, independent of volition. It was

---

[89]Waco, Texas.

something which announced itself; a chill breath that seemed to issue from some vast cavern wherein discords wailed. There came over her the acute longing which always summoned into her spiritual vision the presence of the beloved one, overpowering her at once with a sense of the unattainable.

The moments glided on, while a feeling of good fellowship passed around the circle like a mystic cord, holding and binding these people together with jest and laughter. Monsieur Ratignolle was the first to break the pleasant charm. At ten o'clock he excused himself. Madame Ratignolle was waiting for him at home. She was *bien souffrante*[90] and she was filled with vague dread, which only her husband's presence could allay.

Mademoiselle Reisz arose with Monsieur Ratignolle, who offered to escort her to the car. She had eaten well; she had tasted the good, rich wines, and they must have turned her head, for she bowed pleasantly to all as she withdrew from table. She kissed Edna upon the shoulder, and whispered: "*Bonne nuit, ma reine; soyez sage.*"[91] She had been a little bewildered upon rising, or rather, descending from her cushions, and Monsieur Ratignolle gallantly took her arm and led her away.

Mrs. Highcamp was weaving a garland of roses, yellow and red. When she had finished the garland, she laid it lightly upon Victor's black curls. He was reclining far back in the luxurious chair, holding a glass of champagne to the light.

As if a magician's wand had touched him, the garland of roses transformed him into a vision of Oriental beauty. His cheeks were the color of crushed grapes, and his dusky eyes glowed with a languishing fire.

"*Sapristi!*" exclaimed Arobin.

But Mrs. Highcamp had one more touch to add to the picture. She took from the back of her chair a white silken scarf, with which she had covered her shoulders in the early part of the evening. She draped it across the boy in graceful folds, and in a way to conceal his black, conventional evening dress. He did not seem to mind what she did to him, only smiled, showing a faint gleam of white teeth, while he continued to gaze with narrowing eyes at the light through his glass of champagne.

"Oh! to be able to paint in color rather than in words!" exclaimed Miss Mayblunt, losing herself in a rhapsodic dream as she looked at him.

"'There was a graven image of Desire
Painted with red blood on a ground of gold.'"[92]

murmured Gouvernail, under his breath.

The effect of the wine upon Victor was, to change his accustomed volubility into silence. He seemed to have abandoned himself to a reverie, and to be seeing pleasing visions in the amber bead.

"Sing," entreated Mrs. Highcamp. "Won't you sing to us?"

"Let him alone," said Arobin.

---

[90]French: very ill.
[91]French: "Good night, my queen; be good."

[92]An excerpt from the sonnet "A Cameo," by A. C. Swinburne (1837–1909).

"He's posing," offered Mr. Merriman; "let him have it out."

"I believe he's paralyzed," laughed Mrs. Merriman. And leaning over the youth's chair, she took the glass from his hand and held it to his lips. He sipped the wine slowly, and when he had drained the glass she laid it upon the table and wiped his lips with her little filmy handkerchief.

"Yes, I'll sing for you," he said, turning in his chair toward Mrs. Highcamp. He clasped his hands behind his head, and looking up at the ceiling began to hum a little, trying his voice like a musician tuning an instrument. Then, looking at Edna, he began to sing:

"Ah! si tu savais!"

"Stop!" she cried, "don't sing that. I don't want you to sing it," and she laid her glass so impetuously and blindly upon the table as to shatter it against a caraffe. The wine spilled over Arobin's legs and some of it trickled down upon Mrs. Highcamp's black gauze gown. Victor had lost all idea of courtesy, or else he thought his hostess was not in earnest, for he laughed and went on:

"Ah! si tu savais
Ce que tes yeux me disent"—

"Oh! you mustn't! you mustn't," exclaimed Edna, and pushing back her chair she got up, and going behind him placed her hand over his mouth. He kissed the soft palm that pressed upon his lips.

"No, no, I won't, Mrs. Pontellier. I didn't know you meant it," looking up at her with caressing eyes. The touch of his lips was like a pleasing sting to her hand. She lifted the garland of roses from his head and flung it across the room.

"Come, Victor; you've posed long enough. Give Mrs. Highcamp her scarf."

Mrs. Highcamp undraped the scarf from about him with her own hands. Miss Mayblunt and Mr. Gouvernail suddenly conceived the notion that it was time to say good night. And Mr. and Mrs. Merriman wondered how it could be so late.

Before parting from Victor, Mrs. Highcamp invited him to call upon her daughter, who she knew would be charmed to meet him and talk French and sing French songs with him. Victor expressed his desire and intention to call upon Miss Highcamp at the first opportunity which presented itself. He asked if Arobin were going his way. Arobin was not.

The mandolin players had long since stolen away. A profound stillness had fallen upon the broad, beautiful street. The voices of Edna's disbanding guests jarred like a discordant note upon the quiet harmony of the night.

XXXI

"Well?" questioned Arobin, who had remained with Edna after the others had departed.

"Well," she reiterated, and stood up, stretching her arms, and feeling the need to relax her muscles after having been so long seated.

"What next?" he asked.

"The servants are all gone. They left when the musicians did. I have dismissed them. The house has to be closed and locked, and I shall trot around to the pigeon house, and shall send Celestine over in the morning to straighten things up."

He looked around, and began to turn out some of the lights.

"What about upstairs?" he inquired.

"I think it is all right; but there may be a window or two unlatched. We had better look; you might take a candle and see. And bring me my wrap and hat on the foot of the bed in the middle room."

He went up with the light, and Edna began closing doors and windows. She hated to shut in the smoke and the fumes of the wine. Arobin found her cape and hat, which he brought down and helped her to put on.

When everything was secured and the lights put out, they left through the front door, Arobin locking it and taking the key, which he carried for Edna. He helped her down the steps.

"Will you have a spray of jessamine?" he asked, breaking off a few blossoms as he passed.

"No; I don't want anything."

She seemed disheartened, and had nothing to say. She took his arm, which he offered her, holding up the weight of her satin train with the other hand. She looked down, noticing the black line of his leg moving in and out so close to her against the yellow shimmer of her gown. There was the whistle of a railway train somewhere in the distance, and the midnight bells were ringing. They met no one in their short walk.

The "pigeon-house" stood behind a locked gate, and a shallow *parterre*[93] that had been somewhat neglected. There was a small front porch, upon which a long window and the front door opened. The door opened directly into the parlor; there was no side entry. Back in the yard was a room for servants, in which old Celestine had been ensconced.

Edna had left a lamp burning low upon the table. She had succeeded in making the room look habitable and homelike. There were some books on the table and a lounge near at hand. On the floor was a fresh matting, covered with a rug or two; and on the walls hung a few tasteful pictures. But the room was filled with flowers. These were a surprise to her. Arobin had sent them, and had had Celestine distribute them during Edna's absence. Her bedroom was adjoining, and across a small passage were the dining-room and kitchen.

Edna seated herself with every appearance of discomfort.

"Are you tired?" he asked.

"Yes, and chilled, and miserable. I feel as if I had been wound up to a certain pitch—too tight—and something inside of me had snapped." She rested her head against the table upon her bare arm.

---

[93]French: garden.

"You want to rest," he said, "and to be quiet. I'll go; I'll leave you and let you rest."

"Yes," she replied.

He stood up beside her and smoothed her hair with his soft, magnetic hand. His touch conveyed to her a certain physical comfort. She could have fallen quietly asleep there if he had continued to pass his hand over her hair. He brushed the hair upward from the nape of her neck.

"I hope you will feel better and happier in the morning," he said. "You have tried to do too much in the past few days. The dinner was the last straw; you might have dispensed with it."

"Yes," she admitted; "it was stupid."

"No, it was delightful; but it has worn you out." His hand had strayed to her beautiful shoulders, and he could feel the response of her flesh to his touch. He seated himself beside her and kissed her lightly upon the shoulder.

"I thought you were going away," she said, in an uneven voice.

"I am, after I have said good night."

"Good night," she murmured.

He did not answer, except to continue to caress her. He did not say good night until she had become supple to his gentle, seductive entreaties.

XXXII

When Mr. Pontellier learned of his wife's intention to abandon her home and take up her residence elsewhere, he immediately wrote her a letter of unqualified disapproval and remonstrance. She had given reasons which he was unwilling to acknowledge as adequate. He hoped she had not acted upon her rash impulse; and he begged her to consider first, foremost, and above all else, what people would say. He was not dreaming of scandal when he uttered this warning; that was a thing which would never have entered into his mind to consider in connection with his wife's name or his own. He was simply thinking of his financial integrity. It might get noised about that the Pontelliers had met with reverses, and were forced to conduct their *ménage*[94] on a humbler scale than heretofore. It might do incalculable mischief to his business prospects.

But remembering Edna's whimsical turn of mind of late, and foreseeing that she had immediately acted upon her impetuous determination, he grasped the situation with his usual promptness and handled it with his well-known business tact and cleverness.

The same mail which brought to Edna his letter of disapproval carried instructions—the most minute instructions—to a well-known architect concerning the remodeling of his home, changes which he had long contemplated, and which he desired carried forward during his temporary absence.

[94]French: household.

Expert and reliable packers and movers were engaged to convey the furniture, carpets, pictures—everything movable, in short—to places of security. And in an incredibly short time the Pontellier house was turned over to the artisans. There was to be an addition—a small snuggery;[95] there was to be frescoing, and hardwood flooring was to be put into such rooms as had not yet been subjected to this improvement.

Furthermore, in one of the daily papers appeared a brief notice to the effect that Mr. and Mrs. Pontellier were contemplating a summer sojourn abroad, and that their handsome residence on Esplanade Street was undergoing sumptuous alterations, and would not be ready for occupancy until their return. Mr. Pontellier had saved appearances!

Edna admired the skill of his maneuver, and avoided any occasion to balk his intentions. When the situation as set forth by Mr. Pontellier was accepted and taken for granted, she was apparently satisfied that it should be so.

The pigeon-house pleased her. It at once assumed the intimate character of a home, while she herself invested it with a charm which it reflected like a warm glow. There was with her a feeling of having descended in the social scale, with a corresponding sense of having risen in the spiritual. Every step which she took toward relieving herself from obligations added to her strength and expansion as an individual. She began to look with her own eyes; to see and to apprehend the deeper undercurrents of life. No longer was she content to "feed upon opinion" when her own soul had invited her.

After a little while, a few days, in fact, Edna went up and spent a week with her children in Iberville. They were delicious February days, with all the summer's promise hovering in the air.

How glad she was to see the children! She wept for very pleasure when she felt their little arms clasping her; their hard, ruddy cheeks pressed against her own glowing cheeks. She looked into their faces with hungry eyes that could not be satisfied with looking. And what stories they had to tell their mother! About the pigs, the cows, the mules! About riding to the mill behind Gluglu; fishing back in the lake with their Uncle Jasper; picking pecans with Lidie's little black brood, and hauling chips in their express wagon. It was a thousand times more fun to haul real chips for old lame Susie's real fire than to drag painted blocks along the banquette on Esplanade Street!

She went with them herself to see the pigs and the cows, to look at the darkies laying the cane, to thrash the pecan trees, and catch fish in the back lake. She lived with them a whole week long, giving them all of herself, and gathering and filling herself with their young existence. They listened, breathless, when she told them the house in Esplanade Street was crowded with workmen, hammering, nailing, sawing, and filling the place with clatter. They wanted to know where their bed was; what had been done with their rocking-horse; and where did Joe sleep, and where had Ellen gone, and

[95]A small, comfortable room.

the cook? But, above all, they were fired with a desire to see the little house around the block. Was there any place to play? Were there any boys next door? Raoul, with pessimistic foreboding, was convinced that there were only girls next door. Where would they sleep, and where would papa sleep? She told them the fairies would fix it all right.

The old Madame was charmed with Edna's visit, and showered all manner of delicate attentions upon her. She was delighted to know that the Esplanade Street house was in a dismantled condition. It gave her the promise and pretext to keep the children indefinitely.

It was with a wrench and a pang that Edna left her children. She carried away with her the sound of their voices and the touch of their checks. All along the journey homeward their presence lingered with her like the memory of a delicious song. But by the time she had regained the city the song no longer echoed in her soul. She was again alone.

<h2 style="text-align:center">XXXIII</h2>

It happened sometimes when Edna went to see Mademoiselle Reisz that the little musician was absent, giving a lesson or making some small necessary household purchase. The key was always left in a secret hiding-place in the entry, which Edna knew. If Mademoiselle happened to be away, Edna would usually enter and wait for her return.

When she knocked at Mademoiselle Reisz's door one afternoon there was no response; so unlocking the door, as usual, she entered and found the apartment deserted, as she had expected. Her day had been quite filled up, and it was for a rest, for a refuge, and to talk about Robert, that she sought out her friend.

She had worked at her canvas—a young Italian character study—all the morning, completing the work without the model; but there had been many interruptions, some incident to her modest housekeeping, and others of a social nature.

Madame Ratignolle had dragged herself over, avoiding the too public thoroughfares, she said. She complained that Edna had neglected her much of late. Besides, she was consumed with curiosity to see the little house and the manner in which it was conducted. She wanted to hear all about the dinner party; Monsieur Ratignolle had left so early. What had happened after he left? The champagne and grapes which Edna sent over were *too* delicious. She had so little appetite; they had refreshed and toned her stomach. Where on earth was she going to put Mr. Pontellier in that little house, and the boys? And then she made Edna promise to go to her when her hour of trial overtook her.

"At any time—any time of the day or night, dear," Edna assured her.

Before leaving Madame Ratignolle said:

"In some way you seem to me like a child, Edna. You seem to act without a certain amount of reflection which is necessary in this life. That is the reason I want to say you mustn't mind if I advise you to be a little careful while you are living here alone. Why don't you have some one come and stay with you? Wouldn't Mademoiselle Reisz come?"

"No; she wouldn't wish to come, and I shouldn't want her always with me."

"Well, the reason—you know how evil-minded the world is—some one was talking of Alcée Arobin visiting you. Of course, it wouldn't matter if Mr. Arobin had not such a dreadful reputation. Monsieur Ratignolle was telling me that his attentions alone are considered enough to ruin a woman's name."

"Does he boast of his successes?" asked Edna, indifferently, squinting at her picture.

"No, I think not. I believe he is a decent fellow as far as that goes. But his character is so well known among the men. I shan't be able to come back and see you; it was very, very imprudent today."

"Mind the step!" cried Edna.

"Don't neglect me," entreated Madame Ratignolle; "and don't mind what I said about Arobin, or having some one to stay with you."

"Of course not," Edna laughed. "You may say anything you like to me." They kissed each other good-bye. Madame Ratignolle had not far to go, and Edna stood on the porch a while watching her walk down the street.

Then in the afternoon Mrs. Merriman and Mrs. Highcamp had made their "party call." Edna felt that they might have dispensed with the formality. They had also come to invite her to play *vingt-et-un*[96] one evening at Mrs. Merriman's. She was asked to go early, to dinner, and Mr. Merriman or Mr. Arobin would take her home. Edna accepted in a half-hearted way. She sometimes felt very tired of Mrs. Highcamp and Mrs. Merriman.

Late in the afternoon she sought refuge with Mademoiselle Reisz, and stayed there alone, waiting for her, feeling a kind of repose invade her with the very atmosphere of the shabby, unpretentious little room.

Edna sat at the window, which looked out over the house-tops and across the river. The window frame was filled with pots of flowers, and she sat and picked the dry leaves from a rose geranium. The day was warm, and the breeze which blew from the river was very pleasant. She removed her hat and laid it on the piano. She went on picking the leaves and digging around the plants with her hat pin. Once she thought she heard Mademoiselle Reisz approaching. But it was a young black girl, who came in, bringing a small bundle of laundry, which she deposited in the adjoining room, and went away.

Edna seated herself at the piano, and softly picked out with one hand the bars of a piece of music which lay open before her. A half-hour went by. There was the occasional sound of people going and coming in the lower hall. She was growing interested in her occupation of picking out the aria, when there was a second rap at the door. She vaguely wondered what these people did when they found Mademoiselle's door locked.

[96]French: twenty-one, a card game.

"Come in," she called, turning her face toward the door. And this time it was Robert Lebrun who presented himself. She attempted to rise; she could not have done so without betraying the agitation which mastered her at sight of him, so she fell back upon the stool, only exclaiming, "Why, Robert!"

He came and clasped her hand, seemingly without knowing what he was saying or doing.

"Mrs. Pontellier! How do you happen—oh! how well you look! Is Mademoiselle Reisz not here? I never expected to see you."

"When did you come back?" asked Edna in an unsteady voice, wiping her face with her handkerchief. She seemed ill at ease on the piano stool, and he begged her to take the chair by the window. She did so, mechanically, while he seated himself on the stool.

"I returned day before yesterday," he answered, while he leaned his arm on the keys, bringing forth a crash of discordant sound.

"Day before yesterday!" she repeated, aloud; and went on thinking to herself, "day before yesterday," in a sort of an uncomprehending way. She had pictured him seeking her at the very first hour, and he had lived under the same sky since day before yesterday; while only by accident had he stumbled upon her. Mademoiselle must have lied when she said, "Poor fool, he loves you."

"Day before yesterday," she repeated, breaking off a spray of Mademoiselle's geranium; "then if you had not met me here to-day you wouldn't—when—that is, didn't you mean to come and see me?"

"Of course, I should have gone to see you. There have been so many things—" he turned the leaves of Mademoiselle's music nervously. "I started in at once yesterday with the old firm. After all there is as much chance for me here as there was there—that is, I might find it profitable some day. The Mexicans were not very congenial."

So he had come back because the Mexicans were not congenial; because business was as profitable here as there; because of any reason, and not because he cared to be near her. She remembered the day she sat on the floor, turning the pages of his letter, seeking the reason which was left untold.

She had not noticed how he looked—only feeling his presence; but she turned deliberately and observed him. After all, he had been absent but a few months, and was not changed. His hair—the color of hers—waved back from his temples in the same way as before. His skin was not more burned than it had been at Grand Isle. She found in his eyes, when he looked at her for one silent moment, the same tender caress, with an added warmth and entreaty which had not been there before—the same glance which had penetrated to the sleeping places of her soul and awakened them.

A hundred times Edna had pictured Robert's return, and imagined their first meeting. It was usually at her home, whither he had sought her out at once. She always fancied him expressing or betraying in some way his love for her. And here, the reality was that they sat ten feet apart, she at the window, crushing geranium leaves in her hand and smelling them, he twirling around on the piano stool, saying:

"I was very much surprised to hear of Mr. Pontellier's absence; it's a wonder Mademoiselle Reisz did not tell me; and your moving—mother told me yesterday. I should think you would have gone to New York with him, or to Iberville with the children, rather than be bothered here with housekeeping. And you are going abroad, too, I hear. We shan't have you at Grand Isle next summer, it won't seem—do you see much of Mademoiselle Reisz? She often spoke of you in the few letters she wrote."

"Do you remember that you promised to write to me when you went away?" A flush overspread his whole face.

"I couldn't believe that my letters would be of any interest to you."

"That is an excuse; it isn't the truth." Edna reached for her hat on the piano. She adjusted it, sticking the hat pin through the heavy coil of hair with some deliberation.

"Are you not going to wait for Mademoiselle Reisz?" asked Robert.

"No; I have found when she is absent this long, she is liable not to come back till late." She drew on her gloves, and Robert picked up his hat.

"Won't you wait for her?" asked Edna.

"Not if you think she will not be back till late," adding, as if suddenly aware of some discourtesy in his speech, "and I should miss the pleasure of walking home with you." Edna locked the door and put the key back in its hiding-place.

They went together, picking their way across muddy streets and sidewalks encumbered with the cheap display of small tradesmen. Part of the distance they rode in the car, and after disembarking, passed the Pontellier mansion, which looked broken and half torn asunder. Robert had never known the house, and looked at it with interest.

"I never knew you in your home," he remarked.

"I am glad you did not."

"Why?" She did not answer. They went on around the corner, and it seemed as if her dreams were coming true after all, when he followed her into the little house.

"You must stay and dine with me, Robert. You see I am all alone, and it is so long since I have seen you. There is so much I want to ask you."

She took off her hat and gloves. He stood irresolute, making some excuse about his mother who expected him; he even muttered something about an engagement. She struck a match and lit the lamp on the table; it was growing dusk. When he saw her face in the lamplight, looking pained, with all the soft lines gone out of it, he threw his hat aside and seated himself.

"Oh! you know I want to stay if you will let me!" he exclaimed. All the softness came back. She laughed, and went and put her hand on his shoulder.

"This is the first moment you have seemed like the old Robert. I'll go tell Celestine." She hurried away to tell Celestine to set an extra place. She even sent her off in search of some added delicacy which she had not thought of for herself. And she recommended great care in dripping the coffee and having the omelet done to a proper turn.

When she reëntered, Robert was turning over magazines, sketches, and things that lay upon the table in great disorder. He picked up a photograph, and exclaimed:

"Alcée Arobin! What on earth is his picture doing here?"

"I tried to make a sketch of his head one day," answered Edna, "and he thought the photograph might help me. It was at the other house. I thought it had been left there. I must have packed it up with my drawing materials."

"I should think you would give it back to him if you have finished with it."

"Oh! I have a great many such photographs. I never think of returning them. They don't amount to anything." Robert kept on looking at the picture.

"It seems to me—do you think his head worth drawing? Is he a friend of Mr. Pontellier's? You never said you knew him."

"He isn't a friend of Mr. Pontellier's; he's a friend of mine. I always knew him—that is, it is only of late that I know him pretty well. But I'd rather talk about you, and know what you have been seeing and doing and feeling out there in Mexico." Robert threw aside the picture.

"I've been seeing the waves and the white beach of Grand Isle; the quiet, grassy street of the *Chênière*; the old fort at Grande Terre. I've been working like a machine, and feeling like a lost soul. There was nothing interesting."

She leaned her head upon her hand to shade her eyes from the light.

"And what have you been seeing and doing and feeling all these days?" he asked.

"I've been seeing the waves and the white beach of Grand Isle; the quiet, grassy street of the *Chênière Caminada*; the old sunny fort at Grande Terre. I've been working with little more comprehension than a machine, and still feeling like a lost soul. There was nothing interesting."

"Mrs. Pontellier, you are cruel," he said, with feeling, closing his eyes and resting his head back in his chair. They remained in silence till old Celestine announced dinner.

XXXIV

The dining-room was very small. Edna's round mahogany would have almost filled it. As it was there was but a step or two from the little table to the kitchen, to the mantel, the small buffet, and the side door that opened out on the narrow brick-paved yard.

A certain degree of ceremony settled upon them with the announcement of dinner. There was no return to personalities. Robert related incidents of his sojourn in Mexico, and Edna talked of events likely to interest him, which had occurred during his absence. The dinner was of ordinary quality, except for the few delicacies which she had sent out to purchase. Old Celestine, with a bandana *tignon*[97] twisted about her head, hobbled in and out,

---

[97]A hair "bun."

taking a personal interest in everything; and she lingered occasionally to talk patois[98] with Robert, whom she had known as a boy.

He went out to a neighboring cigar stand to purchase cigarette papers, and when he came back he found that Celestine had served the black coffee in the parlor.

"Perhaps I shouldn't have come back," he said, "When you are tired of me, tell me to go."

"You never tire me. You must have forgotten the hours and hours at Grand Isle in which we grew accustomed to each other and used to being together."

"I have forgotten nothing at Grand Isle," he said, not looking at her, but rolling a cigarette. His tobacco pouch, which he laid upon the table, was a fantastic embroidered silk affair, evidently the handiwork of a woman.

"You used to carry your tobacco in a rubber pouch," said Edna, picking up the pouch and examining the needlework.

"Yes; it was lost."

"Where did you buy this one? In Mexico?"

"It was given to me by a Vera Cruz girl; they are very generous," he replied, striking a match and lighting his cigarette.

"They are very handsome, I suppose, those Mexican women; very picturesque, with their black eyes and their lace scarfs."

"Some are; others are hideous. Just as you find women everywhere."

"What was she like—the one who gave you the pouch? You must have known her very well."

"She was very ordinary. She wasn't of the slightest importance. I knew her well enough."

"Did you visit at her house? Was it interesting? I should like to know and hear about the people you met, and the impressions they made on you."

"There are some people who leave impressions not so lasting as the imprint of an oar upon the water."

"Was she such a one?"

"It would be ungenerous for me to admit that she was of that order and kind." He thrust the pouch back in his pocket, as if to put away the subject with the trifle which had brought it up.

Arobin dropped in with a message from Mrs. Merriman, to say that the card party was postponed on account of the illness of one of her children.

"How do you do, Arobin?" said Robert, rising from the obscurity.

"Oh! Lebrun. To be sure! I heard yesterday you were back. How did they treat you down in Mexique?"

"Fairly well."

"But not well enough to keep you there. Stunning girls, though, in Mexico. I thought I should never get away from Vera Cruz when I was down there a couple of years ago."

---

[98]A provincial or local dialect that blends several languages; in this case, a dialect spoken by Acadian descendants that combines French, English, Spanish, German, and Native American words and phrases.

"Did they embroider slippers and tobacco pouches and hat-bands and things for you?" asked Edna.

"Oh! my! no! I didn't get so deep in their regard. I fear they made more impression on me than I made on them."

"You were less fortunate than Robert, then."

"I am always less fortunate than Robert. Has he been imparting tender confidences?"

"I've been imposing myself long enough," said Robert, rising, and shaking hands with Edna. "Please convey my regards to Mr. Pontellier when you write."

He shook hands with Arobin and went away.

"Fine fellow, that Lebrun," said Arobin when Robert had gone. "I never heard you speak of him."

"I knew him last summer at Grand Isle," she replied. "Here is that photograph of yours. Don't you want it?"

"What do I want with it? Throw it away." She threw it back on the table.

"I'm not going to Mrs. Merriman's," she said. "If you see her, tell her so. But perhaps I had better write. I think I shall write now, and say that I am sorry her child is sick, and tell her not to count on me."

"It would be a good scheme," acquiesced Arobin. "I don't blame you; stupid lot!"

Edna opened the blotter, and having procured paper and pen, began to write the note. Arobin lit a cigar and read the evening paper, which he had in his pocket.

"What is the date?" she asked. He told her.

"Will you mail this for me when you go out?"

"Certainly." He read to her little bits out of the newspaper, while she straightened things on the table.

"What do you want to do?" he asked, throwing aside the paper. "Do you want to go out for a walk or a drive or anything? It would be a fine night to drive."

"No; I don't want to do anything but just be quiet. You go away and amuse yourself. Don't stay."

"I'll go away if I must; but I shan't amuse myself. You know that I only live when I am near you."

He stood up to bid her good night.

"Is that one of the things you always say to women?"

"I have said it before, but I don't think I ever came so near meaning it," he answered with a smile. There were no warm lights in her eyes; only a dreamy, absent look.

"Good night. I adore you. Sleep well," he said, and he kissed her hand and went away.

She stayed alone in a kind of reverie—a sort of stupor. Step by step she lived over every instant of the time she had been with Robert after he had entered Mademoiselle Reisz's door. She recalled his words, his looks. How few and meager they had been for her hungry heart! A vision—a transcendently seductive vision of a Mexican girl arose before her. She writhed with a jealous pang. She wondered when he would come back. He had not said he would come back. She had been with him, had heard his voice and touched his hand. But some way he had seemed nearer to her off there in Mexico.

XXXV

The morning was full of sunlight and hope. Edna could see before her no denial—only the promise of excessive joy. She lay in bed awake, with bright eyes full of speculation. "He loves you, poor fool." If she could but get that conviction firmly fixed in her mind, what mattered about the rest? She felt she had been childish and unwise the night before in giving herself over to despondency. She recapitulated the motives which no doubt explained Robert's reserve. They were not insurmountable; they would not hold if he really loved her; they could not hold against her own passion, which he must come to realize in time. She pictured him going to his business that morning. She even saw how he was dressed; how he walked down one street, and turned the corner of another; saw him bending over his desk, talking to people who entered the office, going to his lunch, and perhaps watching for her on the street. He would come to her in the afternoon or evening, sit and roll his cigarette, talk a little, and go away as he had done the night before. But how delicious it would be to have him there with her! She would have no regrets, nor seek to penetrate his reserve if he still chose to wear it.

Edna ate her breakfast only half dressed. The maid brought her a delicious printed scrawl from Raoul, expressing his love, asking her to send him some bonbons, and telling her they had found that morning ten tiny white pigs all lying in a row beside Lidie's big white pig.

A letter also came from her husband, saying he hoped to be back early in March, and then they would get ready for that journey abroad which he had promised her so long, which he felt now fully able to afford; he felt able to travel as people should, without any thought of small economies—thanks to his recent speculations in Wall Street.

Much to her surprise she received a note from Arobin, written at midnight from the club. It was to say good morning to her, to hope that she had slept well, to assure her of his devotion, which he trusted she in some faintest manner returned.

All these letters were pleasing to her. She answered the children in a cheerful frame of mind, promising them bonbons, and congratulating them upon their happy find of the little pigs.

She answered her husband with friendly evasiveness,—not with any fixed design to mislead him, only because all sense of reality had gone out of her life; she had abandoned herself to Fate, and awaited the consequences with indifference.

To Arobin's note she made no reply. She put it under Celestine's stove-lid.

Edna worked several hours with much spirit. She saw no one but a picture dealer, who asked her if it were true that she was going abroad to study in Paris.

She said possibly she might, and he negotiated with her for some Parisian studies to reach him in time for the holiday trade in December.

Robert did not come that day. She was keenly disappointed. He did not come the following day, nor the next. Each morning she awoke with hope, and each night she was a prey to despondency. She was tempted to seek him out. But far from yielding to the impulse, she avoided any occasion which might throw her in his way. She did not go to Mademoiselle Reisz's nor pass by Madame Lebrun's, as she might have done if he had still been in Mexico.

When Arobin, one night, urged her to drive with him, she went—out to the lake, on the Shell Road. His horses were full of mettle, and even a little unmanageable. She liked the rapid gait at which they spun along, and the quick, sharp sound of the horses' hoofs on the hard road. They did not stop anywhere to eat or to drink. Arobin was not needlessly imprudent. But they ate and they drank when they regained Edna's little dining-room—which was comparatively early in the evening.

It was late when he left her. It was getting to be more than a passing whim with Arobin to see her and be with her. He had detected the latent sensuality, which unfolded under his delicate sense of her nature's requirements like a torpid, torrid, sensitive blossom.

There was no despondency when she fell asleep that night; nor was there hope when she awoke in the morning.

XXXVI

There was a garden out in the suburbs; a small, leafy corner, with a few green tables under the orange trees. An old cat slept all day on the stone step in the sun, and an old *mulatresse*[99] slept her idle hours away in her chair at the open window, till some one happened to knock on one of the green tables. She had milk and cream cheese to sell, and bread and butter. There was no one who could make such excellent coffee or fry a chicken so golden brown as she.

The place was too modest to attract the attention of people of fashion, and so quiet as to have escaped the notice of those in search of pleasure and dissipation. Edna had discovered it accidentally one day when the high-board gate stood ajar. She caught sight of a little green table, blotched with the checkered sunlight that filtered through the quivering leaves overhead. Within she had found the slumbering *mulatresse*, the drowsy cat, and a glass of milk which reminded her of the milk she had tasted in Iberville.

She often stopped there during her perambulations; sometimes taking a book with her, and sitting an hour or two under the trees when she found the place deserted. Once or twice she took a quiet dinner there alone, having

[99]Woman of mixed racial origin.

instructed Celestine beforehand to prepare no dinner at home. It was the last place in the city where she would have expected to meet any one she knew.

Still she was not astonished when, as she was partaking of a modest dinner late in the afternoon, looking into an open book, stroking the cat, which had made friends with her—she was not greatly astonished to see Robert come in at the tall garden gate.

"I am destined to see you only by accident," she said, shoving the cat off the chair beside her. He was surprised, ill at ease, almost embarrassed at meeting her thus so unexpectedly.

"Do you come here often?" he asked.

"I almost live here," she said.

"I used to drop in very often for a cup of Catiche's good coffee. This is the first time since I came back."

"She'll bring you a plate, and you will share my dinner. There's always enough for two—even three." Edna had intended to be indifferent and as reserved as he when she met him; she had reached the determination by a laborious train of reasoning, incident to one of her despondent moods. But her resolve melted when she saw him before her, seated there beside her in the little garden, as if a designing Providence had led him into her path.

"Why have you kept away from me, Robert?" she asked, closing the book that lay open upon the table.

"Why are you so personal, Mrs. Pontellier? Why do you force me to idiotic subterfuges?" he exclaimed with sudden warmth. "I suppose there's no use telling you I've been very busy, or that I've been sick, or that I've been to see you and not found you at home. Please let me off with any one of these excuses."

"You are the embodiment of selfishness," she said. "You save yourself something—I don't know what—but there is some selfish motive, and in sparing yourself you never consider for a moment what I think, or how I feel your neglect and indifference. I suppose this is what you would call unwomanly; but I have got into a habit of expressing myself. It doesn't matter to me, and you may think me unwomanly if you like."

"No; I only think you cruel, as I said the other day. Maybe not intentionally cruel; but you seem to be forcing me into disclosures which can result in nothing; as if you would have me bare a wound for the pleasure of looking at it, without the intention or power of healing it."

"I'm spoiling your dinner, Robert; never mind what I say. You haven't eaten a morsel."

"I only came in for a cup of coffee." His sensitive face was all disfigured with excitement.

"Isn't this a delightful place?" she remarked. "I am so glad it has never actually been discovered. It is so quiet, so sweet, here. Do you notice there is scarcely a sound to be heard? It's so out of the way; and a good walk from the car. However, I don't mind walking. I always feel so sorry for women who don't like to walk; they miss so much—so many rare little glimpses of life; and we women learn so little of life on the whole.

"Catiche's coffee is always hot. I don't know how she manages it, here in the open air. Celestine's coffee gets cold bringing it from the kitchen to the dining-room. Three lumps! How can you drink it so sweet? Take some of the cress with your chop; it's so biting and crisp. Then there's the advantage of being able to smoke with your coffee out here. Now, in the city—aren't you going to smoke?"

"After a while," he said, laying a cigar on the table.

"Who gave it to you?" she laughed.

"I bought it. I suppose I'm getting reckless; I bought a whole box." She was determined not to be personal again and make him uncomfortable.

The cat made friends with him, and climbed into his lap when he smoked his cigar. He stroked her silky fur, and talked a little about her. He looked at Edna's book, which he had read; and he told her the end, to save her the trouble of wading through it, he said.

Again he accompanied her back to her home; and it was after dusk when they reached the little "pigeon-house." She did not ask him to remain, which he was grateful for, as it permitted him to stay without the discomfort of blundering through an excuse which he had no intention of considering. He helped her to light the lamp; then she went into her room to take off her hat and to bathe her face and hands.

When she came back Robert was not examining the pictures and magazines as before; he sat off in the shadow, leaning his head back on the chair as if in a reverie. Edna lingered a moment beside the table, arranging the books there. Then she went across the room to where he sat. She bent over the arm of his chair and called his name.

"Robert," she said, "are you asleep?"

"No," he answered, looking up at her.

She leaned over and kissed him—a soft, cool, delicate kiss, whose voluptuous sting penetrated his whole being—then she moved away from him. He followed, and took her in his arms, just holding her close to him. She put her hand up to his face and pressed his cheek against her own. The action was full of love and tenderness. He sought her lips again. Then he drew her down upon the sofa beside him and held her hand in both of his.

"Now you know," he said, "now you know what I have been fighting against since last summer at Grand Isle; what drove me away and drove me back again."

"Why have you been fighting against it?" she asked. Her face glowed with soft lights.

"Why? Because you were not free; you were Léonce Pontellier's wife. I couldn't help loving you if you were ten times his wife; but so long as I went away from you and kept away I could help telling you so." She put her free hand up to his shoulder, and then against his cheek, rubbing it softly. He kissed her again. His face was warm and flushed.

"There in Mexico I was thinking of you all the time, and longing for you."

"But not writing to me," she interrupted.

"Something put into my head that you cared for me; and I lost my senses. I forgot everything but a wild dream of your some way becoming my wife."

"Your wife!"

"Religion, loyalty, everything would give way if only you cared."

"Then you must have forgotten that I was Léonce Pontellier's wife."

"Oh! I was demented, dreaming of wild, impossible things, recalling men who had set their wives free, we have heard of such things."

"Yes, we have heard of such things."

"I came back full of vague, mad intentions. And when I got here—"

"When you got here you never came near me!" She was still caressing his cheek.

"I realized what a cur I was to dream of such a thing, even if you had been willing."

She took his face between her hands and looked into it as if she would never withdraw her eyes more. She kissed him on the forehead, the eyes, the cheeks, and the lips.

"You have been a very, very foolish boy, wasting your time dreaming of impossible things when you speak of Mr. Pontellier setting me free! I am no longer one of Mr. Pontellier's possessions to dispose of or not. I give myself where I choose. If he were to say, 'Here, Robert, take her and be happy; she is yours,' I should laugh at you both."

His face grew a little white. "What do you mean?" he asked.

There was a knock at the door. Old Celestine came in to say that Madame Ratignolle's servant had come around the back way with a message that Madame had been taken sick and begged Mrs. Pontellier to go to her immediately.

"Yes, yes," said Edna, rising; "I promised. Tell her yes—to wait for me. I'll go back with her."

"Let me walk over with you," offered Robert.

"No," she said; "I will go with the servant." She went into her room to put on her hat, and when she came in again she sat once more upon the sofa beside him. He had not stirred. She put her arms about his neck.

"Good-by, my sweet Robert. Tell me good-by." He kissed her with a degree of passion which had not before entered into his caress, and strained her to him.

"I love you," she whispered, "only you; no one but you. It was you who awoke me last summer out of a life-long, stupid dream. Oh! you have made me so unhappy with your indifference. Oh! I have suffered, suffered! Now you are here we shall love each other, my Robert. We shall be everything to each other. Nothing else in the world is of any consequence. I must go to my friend; but you will wait for me? No matter how late; you will wait for me, Robert?"

"Don't go; don't go! Oh! Edna, stay with me," he pleaded. "Why should you go? Stay with me, stay with me."

"I shall come back as soon as I can; I shall find you here." She buried her face in his neck, and said good-by again. Her seductive voice, together with his great love for her, had enthralled his senses, had deprived him of every impulse but the longing to hold her and keep her.

XXXVII

Edna looked in at the drug store. Monsieur Ratignolle was putting up a mixture himself, very carefully, dropping a red liquid into a tiny glass. He was grateful to Edna for having come; her presence would be a comfort to his wife. Madame Ratignolle's sister, who had always been with her at such trying times, had not been able to come up from the plantation, and Adèle had been inconsolable until Mrs. Pontellier so kindly promised to come to her. The nurse had been with them at night for the past week, as she lived a great distance away. And Dr. Mandelet had been coming and going all the afternoon. They were then looking for him any moment.

Edna hastened upstairs by a private stairway that led from the rear of the store to the apartments above. The children were all sleeping in a back room. Madame Ratignolle was in the salon, whither she had strayed in her suffering impatience. She sat on the sofa, clad in an ample white *peignoir*, holding a handkerchief tight in her hand with a nervous clutch. Her face was drawn and pinched, her sweet blue eyes haggard and unnatural. All her beautiful hair had been drawn back and plaited. It lay in a long braid on the sofa pillow, coiled like a golden serpent. The nurse, a comfortable looking *Griffe*[100] woman in white apron and cap, was urging her to return to her bedroom.

"There is no use, there is no use," she said at once to Edna. "We must get rid of Mandelet; he is getting too old and careless. He said he would be here at half-past seven; now it must be eight. See what time it is, Joséphine."

The woman was possessed of a cheerful nature, and refused to take any situation too seriously, especially a situation with which she was so familiar. She urged Madame to have courage and patience. But Madame only set her teeth hard into her under lip, and Edna saw the sweat gather in beads on her white forehead. After a moment or two she uttered a profound sigh and wiped her face with the handkerchief rolled in a ball. She appeared exhausted. The nurse gave her a fresh handkerchief, sprinkled with cologne water.

"This is too much!" she cried. "Mandelet ought to be killed! Where is Alphonse? Is it possible I am to be abandoned like this—neglected by every one?"

"Neglected, indeed!" exclaimed the nurse. Wasn't she there? And here was Mrs. Pontellier leaving, no doubt, a pleasant evening at home to devote to her? And wasn't Monsieur Ratignolle coming that very instant through the hall? And Joséphine was quite sure she had heard Doctor Mandelet's coupé. Yes, there it was, down at the door.

Adèle consented to go back to her room. She sat on the edge of a little low couch next to her bed.

[100]Descendant of a mulatto and an African American or Native American.

Doctor Mandelet paid no attention to Madame Ratignolle's upbraidings. He was accustomed to them at such times, and was too well convinced of her loyalty to doubt it.

He was glad to see Edna, and wanted her to go with him into the salon and entertain him. But Madame Ratignolle would not consent that Edna should leave her for an instant. Between agonizing moments, she chatted a little, and said it took her mind off her sufferings.

Edna began to feel uneasy. She was seized with a vague dread. Her own like experiences seemed far away, unreal, and only half remembered. She recalled faintly an ecstasy of pain, the heavy odor of chloroform, a stupor which had deadened sensation, and an awakening to find a little new life to which she had given being, added to the great unnumbered multitude of souls that come and go.

She began to wish she had not come; her presence was not necessary. She might have invented a pretext for staying away; she might even invent a pretext now for going. But Edna did not go. With an inward agony, with a flaming, outspoken revolt against the ways of Nature, she witnessed the scene [of] torture.

She was still stunned and speechless with emotion when later she leaned over her friend to kiss her and softly say good-by. Adèle, pressing her check, whispered in an exhausted voice: "Think of the children, Edna. Oh think of the children! Remember them!"

XXXVIII

Edna still felt dazed when she got outside in the open air. The Doctor's coupé had returned for him and stood before the *porte cochère*. She did not wish to enter the coupé, and told Doctor Mandelet she would walk; she was not afraid, and would go alone. He directed his carriage to meet him at Mrs. Pontellier's, and he started to walk home with her.

Up—away up, over the narrow street between the tall houses, the stars were blazing. The air was mild and caressing, but cool with the breath of spring and the night. They walked slowly, the Doctor with a heavy, measured tread and his hands behind him; Edna, in an absent-minded way, as she had walked one night at Grand Isle, as if her thoughts had gone ahead of her and she was striving to overtake them.

"You shouldn't have been there, Mrs. Pontellier," he said. "That was no place for you. Adèle is full of whims at such times. There were a dozen women she might have had with her, unimpressionable women. I felt that it was cruel, cruel. You shouldn't have gone."

"Oh, well!" she answered, indifferently. "I don't know that it matters after all. One has to think of the children some time or other; the sooner the better."

"When is Léonce coming back?"

"Quite soon. Some time in March."

"And you are going abroad?"

"Perhaps—no, I am not going. I'm not going to be forced into doing things. I don't want to go abroad. I want to be let alone. Nobody has any right—except children, perhaps—and even then, it seems to me—or it did seem—" She felt that her speech was voicing the incoherency of her thoughts, and stopped abruptly.

"The trouble is," sighed the Doctor, grasping her meaning intuitively, "that youth is given up to illusions. It seems to be a provision of Nature; a decoy to secure mothers for the race. And Nature takes no account of moral consequences, of arbitrary conditions which we create, and which we feel obliged to maintain at any cost."

"Yes," she said. "The years that are gone seem like dreams—if one might go on sleeping and dreaming—but to wake up and find—oh! well! perhaps it is better to wake up after all, even to suffer, rather than to remain a dupe to illusions all one's life."

"It seems to me, my dear child," said the Doctor at parting, holding her hand, "you seem to me to be in trouble. I am not going to ask for your confidence. I will only say that if ever you feel moved to give it to me, perhaps I might help you. I know I would understand, and I tell you there are not many who would—not many, my dear."

"Some way I don't feel moved to speak of things that trouble me. Don't think I am ungrateful or that I don't appreciate your sympathy. There are periods of despondency and suffering which take possession of me. But I don't want anything but my own way. That is wanting a good deal, of course, when you have to trample upon the lives, the hearts, the prejudices of others—but no matter—still, I shouldn't want to trample upon the little lives. Oh! I don't know what I'm saying, Doctor. Good night. Don't blame me for anything."

"Yes, I will blame you if you don't come and see me soon. We will talk of things you never have dreamt of talking about before. It will do us both good. I don't want you to blame yourself, whatever comes. Good night, my child."

She let herself in at the gate, but instead of entering she sat upon the step of the porch. The night was quiet and soothing. All the tearing emotion of the last few hours seemed to fall away from her like a somber, uncomfortable garment, which she had but to loosen to be rid of. She went back to that hour before Adèle had sent for her; and her senses kindled afresh in thinking of Robert's words, the pressure of his arms, and the feeling of his lips upon her own. She could picture at that moment no greater bliss on earth than possession of the beloved one. His expression of love had already given him to her in part. When she thought that he was there at hand, waiting for her, she grew numb with the intoxication of expectancy. It was so late; he would be asleep perhaps. She would awaken him with a kiss. She hoped he would be asleep that she might arouse him with her caresses.

Still, she remembered Adèle's voice whispering, "Think of the children; think of them." She meant to think of them; that determination had driven into her soul like a death wound—but not tonight. To-morrow would be time to think of everything.

Robert was not waiting for her in the little parlor. He was nowhere at hand. The house was empty. But he had scrawled on a piece of paper that lay in the lamplight:

"I love you. Good-by—because I love you."

Edna grew faint when she read the words. She went and sat on the sofa. Then she stretched herself out there, never uttering a sound. She did not sleep. She did not go to bed. The lamp sputtered and went out. She was still awake in the morning, when Celestine unlocked the kitchen door and came in to light the fire.

XXXIX

Victor, with hammer and nails and scraps of scantling, was patching a corner of one of the galleries. Mariequita sat near by, dangling her legs, watching him work, and handing him nails from the tool-box. The sun was beating down upon them. The girl had covered her head with her apron folded into a square pad. They had been talking for an hour or more. She was never tired of hearing Victor describe the dinner at Mrs. Pontellier's. He exaggerated every detail, making it appear a veritable Lucillean[101] feast. The flowers were in tubs, he said. The champagne was quaffed[102] from huge golden goblets. Venus rising from the foam[103] could have presented no more entrancing a spectacle than Mrs. Pontellier, blazing with beauty and diamonds at the head of the board, while the other women were all of them youthful houris[104] possessed of incomparable charms.

She got it into her head that Victor was in love with Mrs. Pontellier, and he gave her evasive answers, framed so as to confirm her belief. She grew sullen and cried a little, threatening to go off and leave him to his fine ladies. There were a dozen men crazy about her at the *Chênière*; and since it was the fashion to be in love with married people, why, she could run away any time she liked to New Orleans with Célina's husband.

Célina's husband was a fool, a coward, and a pig, and to prove it to her, Victor intended to hammer his head into a jelly the next time he encountered him. This assurance was very consoling to Mariequita. She dried her eyes, and grew cheerful at the prospect.

They were still talking of the dinner and the allurements of city life when Mrs. Pontellier herself slipped around the corner of the house. The two youngsters stayed dumb with amazement before what they considered to be an apparition. But it was really she in flesh and blood, looking tired and a little travel-stained.

"I walked up from the wharf," she said, "and heard the hammering. I supposed it was you, mending the porch. It's a good thing. I was always

---

[101]After the famously lavish banquets of Lucius Licinius Lucullus, a first-century Roman general.
[102]To drink deeply.

[103]The goddess of love and beauty, counterpart to the Greek Aphrodite.
[104]Nymphs.

tripping over those loose planks last summer. How dreary and deserted everything looks!"

It took Victor some little time to comprehend that she had come in Beaudelet's lugger, that she had come alone, and for no purpose but to rest.

"There's nothing fixed up yet, you see. I'll give you my room; it's the only place."

"Any corner will do," she assured him.

"And if you can stand Philomel's cooking," he went on, "though I might try to get her mother while you are here. Do you think she would come?" turning to Mariequita.

Mariequita thought that perhaps Philomel's mother might come for a few days, and money enough.

Beholding Mrs. Pontellier make her appearance, the girl had at once suspected a lovers' rendezvous. But Victor's astonishment was so genuine, and Mrs. Pontellier's indifference so apparent, that the disturbing notion did not lodge long in her brain. She contemplated with the greatest interest this woman who gave the most sumptuous dinners in America, and who had all the men in New Orleans at her feet.

"What time will you have dinner?" asked Edna. "I'm very hungry; but don't get anything extra."

"I'll have it ready in little or no time," he said, bustling and packing away his tools. "You may go to my room to brush up and rest yourself. Mariequita will show you."

"Thank you," said Edna. "But, do you know, I have a notion to go down to the beach and take a good wash and even a little swim, before dinner?"

"The water is too cold!" they both exclaimed. "Don't think of it."

"Well, I might go down and try—dip my toes in. Why, it seems to me the sun is hot enough to have warmed the very depths of the ocean. Could you get me a couple of towels? I'd better go right away, so as to be back in time. It would be a little too chilly if I waited till this afternoon."

Mariequita ran over to Victor's room, and returned with some towels, which she gave to Edna.

"I hope you have fish for dinner," said Edna, as she started to walk away; "but don't do anything extra if you haven't."

"Run and find Philomel's mother," Victor instructed the girl. "I'll go to the kitchen and see what I can do. By Gimminy! Women have no consideration! She might have sent me word."

Edna walked on down to the beach rather mechanically, not noticing anything special except that the sun was hot. She was not dwelling upon any particular train of thought. She had done all the thinking which was necessary after Robert went away, when she lay awake upon the sofa till morning.

She had said over and over to herself: "To-day it is Arobin; to-morrow it will be some one else. It makes no difference to me, it doesn't matter about Léonce Pontellier—but Raoul and Etienne!" She understood now clearly what she had meant long ago when she said to Adèle Ratignolle that she would give up the unessential, but she would never sacrifice herself for her children.

Despondency had come upon her there in the wakeful night, and had never lifted. There was no one thing in the world that she desired. There was no human being whom she wanted near her except Robert; and she even realized that the day would come when he, too, and the thought of him would melt out of her existence, leaving her alone. The children appeared before her like antagonists who had overcome her; who had over-powered and sought to drag her into the soul's slavery for the rest of her days. But she knew a way to elude them. She was not thinking of these things when she walked down to the beach.

The water of the Gulf stretched out before her, gleaming with the million lights of the sun. The voice of the sea is seductive, never ceasing, whispering, clamoring, murmuring, inviting the soul to wander in abysses of solitude. All along the white beach, up and down, there was no living thing in sight. A bird with a broken wing was beating the air above, reeling, fluttering, circling disabled down, down to the water.

Edna had found her old bathing suit still hanging, faded, upon its accustomed peg.

She put it on, leaving her clothing in the bath-house. But when she was there beside the sea, absolutely alone, she cast the unpleasant, pricking garments from her, and for the first time in her life she stood naked in the open air, at the mercy of the sun, the breeze that beat upon her, and the waves that invited her.

How strange and awful it seemed to stand naked under the sky! how delicious! She felt like some new-born creature, opening its eyes in a familiar world that it had never known.

The foamy wavelets curled up to her white feet, and coiled like serpents about her ankles. She walked out. The water was chill, but she walked on. The water was deep, but she lifted her white body and reached out with a long, sweeping stroke. The touch of the sea is sensuous, enfolding the body in its soft, close embrace.

She went on and on. She remembered the night she swam far out, and recalled the terror that seized her at the fear of being unable to regain the shore. She did not look back now, but went on and on, thinking of the blue-grass meadow that she had traversed when a little child, believing that it had no beginning and no end.

Her arms and legs were growing tired.

She thought of Léonce and the children. They were a part of her life. But they need not have thought that they could possess her, body and soul. How Mademoiselle Reisz would have laughed, perhaps sneered, if she knew! "And you call yourself an artist! What pretensions, Madame! The artist must possess the courageous soul that dares and defies."

Exhaustion was pressing upon and over-powering her.

"Good-by—because, I love you." He did not know; he did not understand. He would never understand. Perhaps Doctor Mandelet would have understood if she had seen him—but it was too late; the shore was far behind her, and her strength was gone.

She looked into the distance, and the old terror flamed up for an instant, then sank again. Edna heard her father's voice and her sister Margaret's. She heard the barking of an old dog that was chained to the sycamore tree. The spurs of the cavalry officer clanged as he walked across the porch. There was the hum of bees, and the musky odor of pinks filled the air.

1899

■ CHARLOTTE PERKINS GILMAN ■
1860–1935

Considered the leading intellectual in the woman's movement from the 1890s to 1920, Charlotte Perkins Gilman was widely known both in the United States and abroad for her incisive studies of woman's role and status in society. By the time of her death in 1935, all of her books were out of print, and in the intervening decades her ideas were largely forgotten. Since the 1970s her writings have been re-discovered, and her short story "The Yellow Wall-Paper" is regarded today as a classic of nineteenth-century literature.

Gilman was born in Hartford, Connecticut, in 1860 to Mary Westcott and Frederick Beecher Perkins; her childhood was a difficult one. Her father (through whom she was related to the famous Beecher clan, including Harriet Beecher Stowe) abandoned his family shortly after Charlotte's birth, and she, her mother, and brother moved constantly, often barely skirting poverty. Determined to be self-supporting, Gilman studied art and earned her living by teaching and by designing greeting cards. In 1884, after much hesitation—some of it due to her apprehension about the difficulties a woman faced in attempting to combine marriage and motherhood with professional work—she married a fellow artist, Charles Stetson. When the birth of a daughter a year after her marriage was followed by a severe depression, Gilman consulted the prominent nerve specialist Dr. S. Weir Mitchell and underwent his famous "rest cure"—a regimen of total bed rest, confinement, and isolation. Once at home, she attempted to follow Mitchell's advice: to devote herself to domestic work and her child and "never touch pen, brush, or pencil as long as you live." It drove her, she said, to the brink of "utter mental ruin." A trial separation from her husband and a trip to California restored her health, and eventually she and Stetson were amicably divorced. Gilman's second marriage, to a first cousin, George Houghton Gilman, in 1900, was deeply satisfying and endured until his death in 1934, a year before her own.

Establishing herself in California, Gilman began to write and lecture on suffrage and woman's rights and on the social reforms advocated by the Nationalist clubs inspired by Edward Bellamy's Utopian novel *Looking Backward* (1888).

In 1892 she published "The Yellow Wall-Paper." Based on her experience with Dr. Mitchell, it is an indictment of nineteenth-century medical attitudes toward women as well as a subtle analysis of the power politics of marriage. Rejected by the prestigious *Atlantic Monthly*, whose editor found it too personally distressing to publish, it appeared instead in the less widely circulated *New England Magazine*.

It was for her sociological studies, however, that Gilman became best known in her own lifetime. In 1898 she published *Women and Economics*, her comprehensive analysis of women's past and present subordination in society. An ambitious blend of history, sociology, anthropology, and psychology, it was Gilman's important contribution to the newly developing social sciences. Gilman's major thesis was that women's economic dependence inside marriage, their unpaid and therefore undervalued work in the home, determines their subordinate status. Her solution was to remove "women's work," and women themselves, from the home and to professionalize and socialize domestic work. Abolishing the sexual division of labor would free women to pursue work in the public world and become more productive members of society.

Women and Economics brought Gilman immediate fame. In the decades that followed she enjoyed an international reputation, lecturing extensively in the United States and abroad. She continued to develop her social analyses in a series of books, including *The Home* (1904), *Human Work* (1904), and *The Man-Made World* (1911), and in a magazine, *The Forerunner*, that she published from 1910 to 1916 and for which she wrote all the copy—articles, editorials, poems, short stories, and serialized novels—the equivalent, she estimated, of twenty-eight books in seven years. The total included three Utopian novels that presented ideal societies based on her reform principles. In one of these, *Herland* (1915), a Utopia of women without men, she wittily exposed American society's arbitrary assignment of "masculine" and "feminine" sex roles and behavioral traits. *Herland* is a society governed by principles of nurturing, in which children, raised collectively by trained specialists, are the most valuable resource.

In addition to "The Yellow Wall-Paper" Gilman wrote over two hundred short stories, most of them for *The Forerunner*. "Turned" is an example of this fiction, written to dramatize and offer solutions for the inequities in women's lives that Gilman's nonfiction works analyzed. "Turned" forthrightly treats marital infidelity, and its "solution" is as provocative as it is unexpected.

Elaine Hedges
late of Towson State University

PRIMARY WORKS

"The Yellow Wall-Paper," 1892; *Women and Economics 1898*; *Forerunner*, vols. 1–7, 1901–1916; *The Man-Made World*, 1911; *The Living of Charlotte Perkins Gilman: An Autobiography*, 1935; Barbara H. Solomon, ed., *"Herland" and Selected Stories by Charlotte Perkins Gilman*, 1992; Denise D. Knight, ed., *"The Yellow Wall-Paper" and Selected Stories of Charlotte Perkins Gilman*, 1994; idem, *The Diaries of Charlotte Perkins Gilman*, 2 vols., 1994; idem, *The Later Poetry of Charlotte Perkins Gilman*, 1996.

The Yellow Wall-Paper

It is very seldom that mere ordinary people like John and myself secure ancestral halls for the summer.

A colonial mansion, a hereditary estate, I would say a haunted house, and reach the height of romantic felicity—but that would be asking too much of fate!

Still I will proudly declare that there is something queer about it.

Else, why should it be let so cheaply? And why have stood so long untenanted?

John laughs at me, of course, but one expects that in marriage.

John is practical in the extreme. He has no patience with faith, an intense horror of superstition, and he scoffs openly at any talk of things not to be felt and seen and put down in figures.

John is a physician, and *perhaps*—(I would not say it to a living soul, of course, but this is dead paper and a great relief to my mind—) *perhaps* that is one reason I do not get well faster.

You see he does not believe I am sick!

And what can one do?

If a physician of high standing, and one's own husband, assures friends and relatives that there is really nothing the matter with one but temporary nervous depression—a slight hysterical tendency[1]—what is one to do?

My brother is also a physician, and also of high standing, and he says the same thing.

So I take phosphates or phosphites—whichever it is, and tonics, and journeys, and air, and exercise, and am absolutely forbidden to "work" until I am well again.

Personally, I disagree with their ideas.

Personally, I believe that congenial work, with excitement and change, would do me good.

But what is one to do?

I did write for a while in spite of them; but it *does* exhaust me a good deal—having to be so sly about it, or else meet with heavy opposition.

I sometimes fancy that in my condition if I had less opposition and more society and stimulus—but John says the very worst thing I can do is to think about my condition, and I confess it always makes me feel bad.

So I will let it alone and talk about the house.

The most beautiful place! It is quite alone, standing well back from the road, quite three miles from the village. It makes me think of English places that you read about, for there are hedges and walls and gates that lock, and lots of separate little houses for the gardeners and people.

There is a *delicious* garden! I never saw such a garden—large and shady, full of box-bordered paths, and lined with long grape-covered arbors with seats under them.

[1]Women's emotional problems from anxiety and depression to fatigue and nervousness were described as "hysteria" at this time.

There were greenhouses, too, but they are all broken now.

There was some legal trouble, I believe, something about the heirs and coheirs; anyhow, the place has been empty for years.

That spoils my ghostliness, I am afraid, but I don't care—there is something strange about the house—I can feel it.

I even said so to John one moonlight evening, but he said what I felt was a *draught*, and shut the window.

I get unreasonably angry with John sometimes. I'm sure I never used to be so sensitive. I think it is due to this nervous condition.

But John says if I feel so, I shall neglect proper self-control; so I take pains to control myself—before him, at least, and that makes me very tired.

I don't like our room a bit. I wanted one downstairs that opened on the piazza and had roses all over the window, and such pretty old-fashioned chintz hangings! but John would not hear of it.

He said there was only one window and not room for two beds, and no near room for him if he took another.

He is very careful and loving, and hardly lets me stir without special direction.

I have a schedule prescription for each hour in the day; he takes all care from me, and so I feel basely ungrateful not to value it more.

He said we came here solely on my account, that I was to have perfect rest and all the air I could get. "Your exercise depends on your strength, my dear," said he, "and your food somewhat on your appetite; but air you can absorb all the time." So we took the nursery at the top of the house.

It is a big, airy room, the whole floor nearly, with windows that look all ways, and air and sunshine galore. It was nursery first and then playroom and gymnasium, I should judge; for the windows are barred for little children, and there are rings and things in the walls.

The paint and paper look as if a boys' school had used it. It is stripped off—the paper—in great patches all around the head of my bed, about as far as I can reach, and in a great place on the other side of the room low down. I never saw a worse paper in my life.

One of those sprawling flamboyant patterns committing every artistic sin.

It is dull enough to confuse the eye in following, pronounced enough to constantly irritate and provoke study, and when you follow the lame uncertain curves for a little distance they suddenly commit suicide—plunge off at outrageous angles, destroy themselves in unheard of contradictions.

The color is repellant, almost revolting; a smouldering unclean yellow, strangely faded by the slow-turning sunlight.

It is a dull yet lurid orange in some places, a sickly sulphur tint in others.

No wonder the children hated it! I should hate it myself if I had to live in this room long.

There comes John, and I must put this away,—he hates to have me write a word.

* * *

We have been here two weeks, and I haven't felt like writing before, since that first day.

I am sitting by the window now, up in this atrocious nursery, and there is nothing to hinder my writing as much as I please, save lack of strength.

John is away all day, and even some nights when his cases are serious.

I am glad my case is not serious!

But these nervous troubles are dreadfully depressing.

John does not know how much I really suffer. He knows there is no *reason* to suffer, and that satisfies him.

Of course it is only nervousness. It does weigh on me so not to do my duty in any way!

I meant to be such a help to John, such a real rest and comfort, and here I am a comparative burden already!

Nobody would believe what an effort it is to do what little I am able,— to dress and entertain, and order things.

It is fortunate Mary is so good with the baby. Such a dear baby!

And yet I *cannot* be with him, it makes me so nervous.

I suppose John never was nervous in his life. He laughs at me so about this wall-paper!

At first he meant to repaper the room, but afterwards he said that I was letting it get the better of me, and that nothing was worse for a nervous patient than to give way to such fancies.

He said that after the wall-paper was changed it would be the heavy bedstead, and then the barred windows, and then that gate at the head of the stairs, and so on.

"You know the place is doing you good," he said, "and really, dear, I don't care to renovate the house just for a three months' rental."

"Then do let us go downstairs," I said, "there are such pretty rooms there."

Then he took me in his arms and called me a blessed little goose, and said he would go down cellar, if I wished, and have it whitewashed into the bargain.

But he is right enough about the beds and windows and things.

It is an airy and comfortable room as any one need wish, and, of course, I would not be so silly as to make him uncomfortable just for a whim.

I'm really getting quite fond of the big room, all but that horrid paper.

Out of one window I can see the garden, those mysterious deep-shaded arbors, the riotous old-fashioned flowers, and bushes and gnarly trees.

Out of another I get a lovely view of the bay and a little private wharf belonging to the estate. There is a beautiful shaded lane that runs down there from the house. I always fancy I see people walking in these numerous paths and arbors, but John has cautioned me not to give way to fancy in the least. He says that with my imaginative power and habit of story-making, a nervous weakness like mine is sure to lead to all manner of excited fancies, and that I ought to use my will and good sense to check the tendency. So I try.

I think sometimes that if I were only well enough to write a little it would relieve the press of ideas and rest me.

But I find I get pretty tired when I try.

It is so discouraging not to have any advice and companionship about my work. When I get really well, John says we will ask cousin Henry and Julia down for a long visit; but he says he would as soon put fireworks in my pillow-case as to let me have those stimulating people about now.

I wish I could get well faster.

But I must not think about that. This paper looks to me as if it *knew* what a vicious influence it had!

There is a recurrent spot where the pattern lolls like a broken neck and two bulbous eyes stare at you upside down.

I get positively angry with the impertinence of it and the everlastingness. Up and down and sideways they crawl, and those absurd, unblinking eyes are everywhere. There is one place where two breadths didn't match, and the eyes go all up and down the line, one a little higher than the other.

I never saw so much expression in an inanimate thing before, and we all know how much expression they have! I used to lie awake as a child and get more entertainment and terror out of blank walls and plain furniture than most children could find in a toy-store.

I remember what a kindly wink the knobs of our big, old bureau used to have, and there was one chair that always seemed like a strong friend.

I used to feel that if any of the other things looked too fierce I could always hop into that chair and be safe.

The furniture in this room is no worse than inharmonious, however, for we had to bring it all from downstairs. I suppose when this was used as a playroom they had to take the nursery things out, and no wonder! I never saw such ravages as the children have made here.

The wall-paper, as I said before, is torn off in spots, and it sticketh closer than a brother—they must have had perseverance as well as hatred.

Then the floor is scratched and gouged and splintered, the plaster itself is dug out here and there, and this great heavy bed which is all we found in the room, looks as if it had been through the wars.

But I don't mind it a bit—only the paper.

There comes John's sister. Such a dear girl as she is, and so careful of me! I must not let her find me writing.

She is a perfect and enthusiastic housekeeper, and hopes for no better profession. I verily believe she thinks it is the writing which made me sick!

But I can write when she is out, and see her a long way off from these windows.

There is one that commands the road, a lovely shaded winding road, and one that just looks off over the country. A lovely country, too, full of great elms and velvet meadows.

This wallpaper has a kind of subpattern in a different shade, a particularly irritating one, for you can only see it in certain lights, and not clearly then.

But in the places where it isn't faded and where the sun is just so—I can see a strange, provoking, formless sort of figure, that seems to skulk about behind that silly and conspicuous front design.

There's sister on the stairs!

Well, the Fourth of July is over! The people are all gone and I am tired out. John thought it might do me good to see a little company, so we just had mother and Nellie and the children down for a week.

Of course I didn't do a thing. Jennie sees to everything now.

But it tired me all the same.

John says if I don't pick up faster he shall send me to Weir Mitchell[2] in the fall.

But I don't want to go there at all. I had a friend who was in his hands once, and she says he is just like John and my brother, only more so!

Besides, it is such an undertaking to go so far.

I don't feel as if it was worth while to turn my hand over for anything, and I'm getting dreadfully fretful and querulous.

I cry at nothing, and cry most of the time.

Of course I don't when John is here, or anybody else, but when I am alone.

And I am alone a good deal just now. John is kept in town very often by serious cases, and Jennie is good and lets me alone when I want her to.

So I walk a little in the garden or down that lovely lane, sit on the porch under the roses, and lie down up here a good deal.

I'm getting really fond of the room in spite of the wallpaper. Perhaps *because* of the wall-paper.

It dwells in my mind so!

I lie here on this great immovable bed—it is nailed down, I believe—and follow that pattern about by the hour. It is as good as gymnastics, I assure you. I start, we'll say, at the bottom, down in the corner over there where it has not been touched, and I determine for the thousandth time that I *will* follow that pointless pattern to some sort of a conclusion.

I know a little of the principle of design, and I know this thing was not arranged on any laws of radiation, or alternation, or repetition, or symmetry, or anything else that I ever heard of.

It is repeated, of course, by the breadths, but not otherwise.

Looked at in one way each breadth stands alone, the bloated curves and flourishes—a kind of "debased Romanesque"[3] with *delirium tremens*—go waddling up and down in isolated columns of fatuity.

But, on the other hand, they connect diagonally, and the sprawling outlines run off in great slanting waves of optic horror, like a lot of wallowing seaweeds in full chase.

---

[2] Dr. S. Weir Mitchell (1829-1914), whose celebrated "rest cure" for "hysteria" Gilman had undergone.

[3] A style of architecture with profuse ornamentation.

The whole thing goes horizontally, too, at least it seems so, and I exhaust myself in trying to distinguish the order of its going in that direction.

They have used a horizontal breadth for a frieze, and that adds wonderfully to the confusion.

There is one end of the room where it is almost intact, and there, when the crosslights fade and the low sun shines directly upon it, I can almost fancy radiation after all,—the interminable grotesques seem to form around a common centre and rush off in headlong plunges of equal distraction.

It makes me tired to follow it. I will take a nap I guess.

I don't know why I should write this.

I don't want to.

I don't feel able.

And I know John would think it absurd. But I *must* say what I feel and think in some way—it is such a relief!

But the effort is getting to be greater than the relief.

But the effort is getting to be greater than the relief.

Half the time now I am awfully lazy, and lie down ever so much.

John says I mustn't lose my strength, and has me take cod liver oil and lots of tonics and things, to say nothing of ale and wine and rare meat.

Dear John! He loves me very dearly, and hates to have me sick. I tried to have a real earnest reasonable talk with him the other day, and tell him how I wish he would let me go and make a visit to Cousin Henry and Julia.

But he said I wasn't able to go, nor able to stand it after I got there; and I did not make out a very good case for myself, for I was crying before I had finished.

It is getting to be a great effort for me to think straight. Just this nervous weakness I suppose.

And dear John gathered me up in his arms, and just carried me upstairs and laid me on the bed, and sat by me and read to me till it tired my head.

He said I was his darling and his comfort and all he had, and that I must take care of myself for his sake, and keep well.

He says no one but myself can help me out of it, that I must use my will and self-control and not let any silly fancies run away with me.

There's one comfort, the baby is well and happy, and does not have to occupy this nursery with the horrid wallpaper.

If we had not used it, that blessed child would have! What a fortunate escape! Why, I wouldn't have a child of mine, an impressionable little thing, live in such a room for worlds.

I never thought of it before, but it is lucky that John kept me here after all, I can stand it so much easier than a baby, you see.

Of course I never mention it to them any more—I am too wise,—but I keep watch of it all the same.

There are things in that paper that nobody knows but me, or ever will.

Behind that outside pattern the dim shapes get clearer every day.

It is always the same shape, only very numerous.

And it is like a woman stooping down and creeping about behind that pattern. I don't like it a bit. I wonder—I begin to think—I wish John would take me away from here!

It is so hard to talk with John about my case, because he is so wise, and because he loves me so.

But I tried it last night.

It was moonlight. The moon shines in all around just as the sun does.

I hate to see it sometimes, it creeps so slowly, and always comes in by one window or another.

John was asleep and I hated to waken him, so I kept still and watched the moonlight on that undulating wallpaper till I felt creepy.

The faint figure behind seemed to shake the pattern, just as if she wanted to get out.

I got up softly and went to feel and see if the paper *did* move, and when I came back John was awake.

"What is it, little girl?" he said. "Don't go walking about like that—you'll get cold."

I thought it was a good time to talk, so I told him that I really was not gaining here, and that I wished he would take me away.

"Why, darling!" said he, "our lease will be up in three weeks, and I can't see how to leave before.

"The repairs are not done at home, and I cannot possibly leave town just now. Of course if you were in any danger, I could and would, but you really are better, dear, whether you can see it or not. I am a doctor, dear, and I know. You are gaining flesh and color, your appetite is better, I feel really much easier about you."

"I don't weigh a bit more," said I, "nor as much; and my appetite may be better in the evening when you are here, but it is worse in the morning when you are away!"

"Bless her little heart!" said he with a big hug, "she shall be as sick as she pleases! But now let's improve the shining hours[4] by going to sleep, and talk about it in the morning!"

"And you won't go away?" I asked gloomily.

"Why, how can I, dear? It is only three weeks more and then we will take a nice little trip of a few days while Jennie is getting the house ready. Really dear you are better!"

"Better in body perhaps—" I began, and stopped short, for he sat up straight and looked at me with such a stern, reproachful look that I could not say another word.

"My darling," said he, "I beg of you, for my sake and for our child's sake, as well as for your own, that you will never for one instant let that idea

---

[4]From a poem by Isaac Watts (1674–1748), "Against Idleness and Mischief," containing the lines: How doth the little busy bee/Improve each shining hour,/ And gather honey all the day/ From every opening flower!

enter your mind! There is nothing so dangerous, so fascinating, to a temperament like yours. It is a false and foolish fancy. Can you not trust me as a physician when I tell you so?"

So of course I said no more on that score, and we went to sleep before long. He thought I was asleep first, but I wasn't, and lay there for hours trying to decide whether that front pattern and the back pattern really did move together or separately.

On a pattern like this, by daylight, there is a lack of sequence, a defiance of law, that is a constant irritant to a normal mind.

The color is hideous enough, and unreliable enough, and infuriating enough, but the pattern is torturing.

You think you have mastered it, but just as you get well underway in following, it turns a back-somersault and there you are. It slaps you in the face, knocks you down, and tramples upon you. It is like a bad dream.

The outside pattern is a florid arabesque, reminding one of a fungus. If you can imagine a toadstool in joints, an interminable string of toadstools, budding and sprouting in endless convolutions—why, that is something like it.

That is, sometimes!

There is one marked peculiarity about this paper, a thing nobody seems to notice but myself, and that is that it changes as the light changes.

When the sun shoots in through the east window—I always watch for that first long, straight ray—it changes so quickly that I never can quite believe it.

That is why I watch it always.

By moonlight—the moon shines in all night when there is a moon—I wouldn't know it was the same paper.

At night in any kind of light, in twilight, candlelight, lamplight, and worst of all by moonlight, it becomes bars! The outside pattern I mean, and the woman behind it is as plain as can be.

I didn't realize for a long time what the thing was that showed behind, that dim sub-pattern, but now I am quite sure it is a woman.

By daylight she is subdued, quiet. I fancy it is the pattern that keeps her so still. It is so puzzling. It keeps me quiet by the hour.

I lie down ever so much now. John says it is good for me, and to sleep all I can.

Indeed he started the habit by making me lie down for an hour after each meal.

It is a very bad habit I am convinced, for you see I don't sleep.

And that cultivates deceit, for I don't tell them I'm awake—O no!

The fact is I am getting a little afraid of John.

He seems very queer sometimes, and even Jennie has an inexplicable look.

It strikes me occasionally, just as a scientific hypothesis,—that perhaps it is the paper!

I have watched John when he did not know I was looking, and come into the room suddenly on the most innocent excuses, and I've caught him several times *looking at the paper*! And Jennie too. I caught Jennie with her hand on it once.

She didn't know I was in the room, and when I asked her in a quiet, a very quiet voice, with the most restrained manner possible, what she was doing with the paper—she turned around as if she had been caught stealing, and looked quite angry—asked me why I should frighten her so!

Then she said that the paper stained everything it touched, that she had found yellow smooches on all my clothes and John's, and she wished we would be more careful!

Did not that sound innocent? But I know she was studying that pattern, and I am determined that nobody shall find it out but myself!

Life is very much more exciting now than it used to be. You see I have something more to expect, to look forward to, to watch. I really do eat better, and am more quiet than I was.

John is so pleased to see me improve! He laughed a little the other day, and said I seemed to be flourishing in spite of my wall-paper.

I turned it off with a laugh. I had no intention of telling him it was *because* of the wall-paper—he would make fun of me. He might even want to take me away.

I don't want to leave now until I have found it out. There is a week more, and I think that will be enough.

I'm feeling ever so much better! I don't sleep much at night, for it is so interesting to watch developments; but I sleep a good deal in the daytime.

In the daytime it is tiresome and perplexing.

There are always new shoots on the fungus, and new shades of yellow all over it. I cannot keep count of them, though I have tried conscientiously.

It is the strangest yellow, that wall-paper! It makes me think of all the yellow things I ever saw—not beautiful ones like buttercups, but old foul, bad yellow things.

But there is something else about that paper—the smell! I noticed it the moment we came into the room, but with so much air and sun it was not bad. Now we have had a week of fog and rain, and whether the windows are open or not, the smell is here.

It creeps all over the house.

I find it hovering in the dining-room, skulking in the parlor, hiding in the hall, lying in wait for me on the stairs.

It gets into my hair.

Even when I go to ride, if I turn my head suddenly and surprise it—there is that smell!

Such a peculiar odor, too! I have spent hours in trying to analyze it, to find what it smelled like.

It is not bad—at first, and very gentle, but quite the subtlest, most enduring odor I ever met.

In this damp weather it is awful, I wake up in the night and find it hanging over me. It used to disturb me at first. I thought seriously of burning the house—to reach the smell.

But now I am used to it. The only thing I can think of that it is like is the *color* of the paper! A yellow smell.

There is a very funny mark on this wall, low down, near the mopboard. A streak that runs round the room. It goes behind every piece of furniture, except the bed, a long, straight, even *smooch*, as if it had been rubbed over and over.

I wonder how it was done and who did it, and what they did it for. Round and round and round—round and round and round—it makes me dizzy!

I really have discovered something at last.

Through watching so much at night, when it changes so, I have finally found out.

The front pattern *does* move—and no wonder! The woman behind shakes it!

Sometimes I think there are a great many women behind, and sometimes only one, and she crawls around fast, and her crawling shakes it all over.

Then in the very bright spots she keeps still, and in the very shady spots she just takes hold of the bars and shakes them hard.

And she is all the time trying to climb through. But nobody could climb through that pattern—it strangles so; I think that is why it has so many heads.

They get through, and then the pattern strangles them off and turns them upside down, and makes their eyes white!

If those heads were covered or taken off it would not be half so bad.

I think that woman gets out in the daytime!

And I'll tell you why—privately—I've seen her!

I can see her out of every one of my windows!

It is the same woman, I know, for she is always creeping, and most women do not creep by daylight.

I see her in that long shaded lane, creeping up and down. I see her in those dark grape arbors, creeping all around the garden.

I see her on that long road under the trees, creeping along, and when a carriage comes she hides under the blackberry vines.

I don't blame her a bit. It must be very humiliating to be caught creeping by daylight!

I always lock the door when I creep by daylight. I can't do it at night, for I know John would suspect something at once.

And John is so queer now, that I don't want to irritate him. I wish he would take another room! Besides, I don't want anybody to get that woman out at night but myself.

I often wonder if I could see her out of all the windows at once.

But, turn as fast as I can, I can only see out of one at one time.

And though I always see her, she *may* be able to creep faster than I can turn!

I have watched her sometimes away off in the open country, creeping as fast as a cloud shadow in a high wind.

If only that top pattern could be gotten off from the under one! I mean to try it, little by little.

I have found out another funny thing, but I shan't tell it this time! It does not do to trust people too much.

There are only two more days to get this paper off, and I believe John is beginning to notice. I don't like the look in his eyes.

And I heard him ask Jennie a lot of professional questions about me. She had a very good report to give.

She said I slept a good deal in the daytime.

John knows I don't sleep very well at night, for all I'm so quiet!

He asked me all sorts of questions, too, and pretended to be very loving and kind.

As if I couldn't see through him!

Still, I don't wonder he acts so, sleeping under this paper for three months.

It only interests me, but I feel sure John and Jennie are secretly affected by it.

Hurrah! This is the last day, but it is enough. John to stay in town over night, and won't be out until this evening.

Jennie wanted to sleep with me—the sly thing! but I told her I should undoubtedly rest better for a night all alone.

That was clever, for really I wasn't alone a bit! As soon as it was moonlight and that poor thing began to crawl and shake the pattern, I got up and ran to help her.

I pulled and she shook, I shook and she pulled, and before morning we had peeled off yards of that paper.

A strip about as high as my head and half around the room.

And then when the sun came and that awful pattern began to laugh at me, I declared I would finish it to-day!

We go away to-morrow, and they are moving all my furniture down again to leave things as they were before.

Jennie looked at the wall in amazement, but I told her merrily that I did it out of pure spite at the vicious thing.

She laughed and said she wouldn't mind doing it herself, but I must not get tired.

How she betrayed herself that time!

But I am here, and no person touches this paper but me,—not *alive*!

She tried to get me out of the room—it was too patent! But I said it was so quiet and empty and clean now that I believed I would lie down again and sleep all I could; and not to wake me even for dinner—I would call when I woke.

So now she is gone, and the servants are gone, and the things are gone, and there is nothing left but that great bedstead nailed down, with the canvas mattress we found on it.

We shall sleep downstairs to-night, and take the boat home to-morrow.

I quite enjoy the room, now it is bare again.

How those children did tear about here!

This bedstead is fairly gnawed!

But I must get to work.

I have locked the door and thrown the key down into the front path.

I don't want to go out, and I don't want to have anybody come in, till John comes.

I want to astonish him.

I've got a rope up here that even Jennie did not find. If that woman does get out, and tries to get away, I can tie her!

But I forgot I could not reach far without anything to stand on!

This bed will *not* move!

I tried to lift and push it until I was lame, and then I got so angry I bit off a little piece at one corner—but it hurt my teeth.

Then I peeled off all the paper I could reach standing on the floor. It sticks horribly and the pattern just enjoys it! All those strangled heads and bulbous eyes and waddling fungus growths just shriek with derision!

I am getting angry enough to do something desperate. To jump out of the window would be admirable exercise, but the bars are too strong even to try.

Besides I wouldn't do it. Of course not. I know well enough that a step like that is improper and might be misconstrued.

I don't like to *look* out of the windows even—there are so many of those creeping women, and they creep so fast.

I wonder if they all come out of that wall-paper as I did?

But I am securely fastened now by my well-hidden rope—you don't get *me* out in the road there!

I suppose I shall have to get back behind the pattern when it comes night, and that is hard!

It is so pleasant to be out in this great room and creep around as I please!

I don't want to go outside. I won't, even if Jennie asks me to.

For outside you have to creep on the ground, and everything is green instead of yellow.

But here I can creep smoothly on the floor, and my shoulder just fits in that long smooch around the wall, so I cannot lose my way.

Why there's John at the door!

It is no use, young man, you can't open it!

How he does call and pound!

Now he's crying for an axe.

It would be a shame to break down that beautiful door!

"John dear!" said I in the gentlest voice, "the key is down by the front steps, under a plantain leaf!"

That silenced him for a few moments.

Then he said—very quietly indeed, "Open the door, my darling!"

"I can't," said I. "The key is down by the front door under a plantain leaf!"

And then I said it again, several times, very gently and slowly, and said it so often that he had to go and see, and he got it of course, and came in. He stopped short by the door.

"What is the matter?" he cried. "For God's sake, what are you doing!"

I kept on creeping just the same, but I looked at him over my shoulder.

"I've got out at last," said I, "in spite of you and Jane.[5] And I've pulled off most of the paper, so you can't put me back!"

Now why should that man have fainted? But he did, and right across my path by the wall, so that I had to creep over him every time!

1892

Turned

In her soft-carpeted, thick-curtained, richly furnished chamber, Mrs. Marroner lay sobbing on the wide, soft bed.

She sobbed bitterly, chokingly, despairingly; her shoulders heaved and shook convulsively; her hands were tight-clenched; she had forgotten her elaborate dress, the more elaborate bedcover; forgotten her dignity, her self-control, her pride. In her mind was an overwhelming, unbelievable horror, an immeasurable loss, a turbulent, struggling mass of emotion.

In her reserved, superior, Boston-bred life she had never dreamed that it would be possible for her to feel so many things at once, and with such trampling intensity.

She tried to cool her feelings into thoughts; to stiffen them into words; to control herself—and could not. It brought vaguely to her mind an awful moment in the breakers at York Beach, one summer in girlhood, when she had been swimming under water and could not find the top.

In her uncarpeted, thin-curtained, poorly furnished chamber on the top floor, Gerta Petersen lay sobbing on the narrow, hard bed.

She was of larger frame than her mistress, grandly built and strong; but all her proud young womanhood was prostrate, now, convulsed with agony, dissolved in tears. She did not try to control herself. She wept for two.

If Mrs. Marroner suffered more from the wreck and ruin of a longer love—perhaps a deeper one; if her tastes were finer, her ideals loftier; if she bore the pangs of bitter jealousy and outraged pride, Gerta had personal shame to meet, a hopeless future, and a looming present which filled her with unreasoning terror.

---

[5]Presumably another name for Jennie.

She had come like a meek young goddess into that perfectly ordered house, strong, beautiful, full of good will and eager obedience, but ignorant and childish—a girl of eighteen.

Mr. Marroner had frankly admired her, and so had his wife. They discussed her visible perfections and as visible limitations with that perfect confidence which they had so long enjoyed. Mrs. Marroner was not a jealous woman. She had never been jealous in her life—till now.

Gerta had stayed and learned their ways. They had both been fond of her. Even the cook was fond of her. She was what is called "willing," was unusually teachable and plastic; and Mrs. Marroner, with her early habits of giving instruction, tried to educate her somewhat.

"I never saw anyone so docile," Mrs. Marroner had often commented. "It is perfection in a servant, but almost a defect in character. She is so helpless and confiding."

She was precisely that; a tall, rosy-cheeked baby; rich womanhood without, helpless infancy within. Her braided wealth of dead-gold hair, her grave blue eyes, her mighty shoulders, and long, firmly moulded limbs seemed those of a primal earth spirit; but she was only an ignorant child, with a child's weakness.

When Mr. Marroner had to go abroad for his firm, unwillingly, hating to leave his wife, he had told her he felt quite safe to leave her in Gerta's hands—she would take care of her.

"Be good to your mistress, Gerta," he told the girl that last morning at breakfast. "I leave her to you to take care of. I shall be back in a month at latest."

Then he turned, smiling, to his wife. "And you must take care of Gerta, too," he said. "I expect you'll have her ready for college when I get back."

This was seven months ago. Business had delayed him from week to week, from month to month. He wrote to his wife, long, loving, frequent letters; deeply regretting the delay, explaining how necessary, how profitable it was; congratulating her on the wide resources she had; her well-filled, well-balanced mind; her many interests.

"If I should be eliminated from your scheme of things, by any of those 'acts of God' mentioned on the tickets, I do not feel that you would be an utter wreck," he said. "That is very comforting to me. Your life is so rich and wide that no one loss, even a great one, would wholly cripple you. But nothing of the sort is likely to happen, and I shall be home again in three weeks—if this thing gets settled. And you will be looking so lovely, with that eager light in your eyes and the changing flush I know so well—and love so well! My dear wife! We shall have to have a new honeymoon—other moons come every month, why shouldn't the mellifluous kind?"

He often asked after "little Gerta," sometimes enclosed a picture postcard to her, joked his wife about her laborious efforts to educate "the child"; was so loving and merry and wise——.

All this was racing through Mrs. Marroner's mind as she lay there with the broad, hemstitched border of fine linen sheeting crushed and twisted in one hand, and the other holding a sodden handkerchief.

She had tried to teach Gerta, and had grown to love the patient, sweet-natured child, in spite of her dullness. At work with her hands, she was clever, if not quick, and could keep small accounts from week to week. But to the woman who held a Ph.D., who had been on the faculty of a college, it was like baby-tending.

Perhaps having no babies of her own made her love the big child the more, though the years between them were but fifteen.

To the girl she seemed quite old, of course; and her young heart was full of grateful affection for the patient care which made her feel so much at home in this new land.

And then she had noticed a shadow on the girl's bright face. She looked nervous, anxious, worried. When the bell rang she seemed startled, and would rush hurriedly to the door. Her peals of frank laughter no longer rose from the area gate as she stood talking with the always admiring tradesmen.

Mrs. Marroner had labored long to teach her more reserve with men, and flattered herself that her words were at last effective. She suspected the girl of homesickness; which was denied. She suspected her of illness, which was denied also. At last she suspected her of something which could not be denied.

For a long time she refused to believe it, waiting. Then she had to believe it, but schooled herself to patience and understanding. "The poor child," she said. "She is here without a mother—she is so foolish and yielding—I must not be too stern with her." And she tried to win the girl's confidence with wise, kind words.

But Gerta had literally thrown herself at her feet and begged her with streaming tears not to turn her away. She would admit nothing, explain nothing; but frantically promised to work for Mrs. Marroner as long as she lived—if only she would keep her.

Revolving the problem carefully in her mind, Mrs. Marroner thought she would keep her, at least for the present. She tried to repress her sense of ingratitude in one she had so sincerely tried to help, and the cold, contemptuous anger she had always felt for such weakness.

"The thing to do now," she said to herself, "is to see her through this safely. The child's life should not be hurt any more than is unavoidable. I will ask Dr. Bleet about it—what a comfort a woman doctor is! I'll stand by the poor, foolish thing till it's over, and then get her back to Sweden somehow with her baby. How they do come where they are not wanted—and don't come where they are wanted!" And Mrs. Marroner, sitting alone in the quiet, spacious beauty of the house, almost envied Gerta.

Then came the deluge.

She had sent the girl out for needed air toward dark. The late mail came; she took it in herself. One letter for her—her husband's letter. She knew the postmark, the stamp, the kind of typewriting. She impulsively kissed it in the dim hall. No one would suspect Mrs. Marroner of kissing her husband's letters—but she did, often.

She looked over the others. One was for Gerta, and not from Sweden. It looked precisely like her own. This struck her as a little odd, but Mr. Marroner had several times sent messages and cards to the girl. She laid the letter on the hall table and took hers to her room.

"My poor child," it began. What letter of hers had been sad enough to warrant that?

"I am deeply concerned at the news you send." What news to so concern him had she written? "You must bear it bravely, little girl. I shall be home soon, and will take care of you, of course. I hope there is no immediate anxiety—you do not say. Here is money, in case you need it. I expect to get home in a month at latest. If you have to go, be sure to leave your address at my office. Cheer up—be brave—I will take care of you."

The letter was typewritten, which was not unusual. It was unsigned, which was unusual. It enclosed an American bill—fifty dollars. It did not seem in the least like any letter she had ever had from her husband, or any letter she could imagine him writing. But a strange, cold feeling was creeping over her, like a flood rising around a house.

She utterly refused to admit the ideas which began to bob and push about outside her mind, and to force themselves in. Yet under the pressure of these repudiated thoughts she went downstairs and brought up the other letter—the letter to Gerta. She laid them side by side on a smooth dark space on the table; marched to the piano and played, with stern precision, refusing to think, till the girl came back. When she came in, Mrs. Marroner rose quietly and came to the table. "Here is a letter for you," she said.

The girl stepped forward eagerly, saw the two lying together there, hesitated, and looked at her mistress.

"Take yours, Gerta. Open it, please."

The girl turned frightened eyes upon her.

"I want you to read it, here," said Mrs. Marroner.

"Oh, ma'am——No! Please don't make me!"

"Why not?"

There seemed to be no reason at hand, and Gerta flushed more deeply and opened her letter. It was long; it was evidently puzzling to her; it began "My dear wife." She read it slowly.

"Are you sure it is your letter?" asked Mrs. Marroner. "Is not this one yours? Is not that one—mine?"

She held out the other letter to her.

"It is a mistake," Mrs. Marroner went on, with a hard quietness. She had lost her social bearings somehow; lost her usual keen sense of the proper thing to do. This was not life, this was a nightmare.

"Do you not see? Your letter was put in my envelope and my letter was put in your envelope. Now we understand it."

But poor Gerta had no antechamber to her mind; no trained forces to preserve order while agony entered. The thing swept over her, resistless, overwhelming. She cowered before the outraged wrath she expected; and from some hidden cavern that wrath arose and swept over her in pale flame.

"Go and pack your trunk," said Mrs. Marroner. "You will leave my house tonight. Here is your money."

She laid down the fifty-dollar bill. She put with it a month's wages. She had no shadow of pity for those anguished eyes, those tears which she heard drop on the floor.

"Go to your room and pack," said Mrs. Marroner. And Gerta, always obedient, went.

Then Mrs. Marroner went to hers, and spent a time she never counted, lying on her face on the bed.

But the training of the twenty-eight years which had elapsed before her marriage; the life at college, both as student and teacher; the independent growth which she had made, formed a very different background for grief from that in Gerta's mind.

After a while Mrs. Marroner arose. She administered to herself a hot bath, a cold shower, a vigorous rubbing. "Now I can think," she said.

First she regretted the sentence of instant banishment. She went upstairs to see if it had been carried out. Poor Gerta! The tempest of her agony had worked itself out at last as in a child, and left her sleeping, the pillow wet, the lips still grieving, a big sob shuddering itself off now and then.

Mrs. Marroner stood and watched her, and as she watched she considered the helpless sweetness of the face; the defenseless, unformed character; the docility and habit of obedience which made her so attractive—and so easily a victim. Also she thought of the mighty force which had swept over her; of the great process now working itself out through her; of how pitiful and futile seemed any resistance she might have made.

She softly returned to her own room, made up a little fire, and sat by it, ignoring her feelings now, as she had before ignored her thoughts.

Here were two women and a man. One woman was a wife; loving, trusting, affectionate. One was a servant; loving, trusting, affectionate: a young girl, an exile, a dependent; grateful for any kindness; untrained, uneducated, childish. She ought, of course, to have resisted temptation; but Mrs. Marroner was wise enough to know how difficult temptation is to recognize when it comes in the guise of friendship and from a source one does not suspect.

Gerta might have done better in resisting the grocer's clerk; had, indeed, with Mrs. Marroner's advice, resisted several. But where respect was due, how could she criticize? Where obedience was due, how could she refuse—with ignorance to hold her blinded—until too late?

As the older, wiser woman forced herself to understand and extenuate the girl's misdeed and foresee her ruined future, a new feeling rose in her heart, strong, clear, and overmastering; a sense of measureless condemnation for the man who had done this thing. He knew. He understood. He could fully foresee and measure the consequences of his act. He appreciated to the full the innocence, the ignorance, the grateful affection, the habitual docility, of which he deliberately took advantage.

Mrs. Marroner rose to icy peaks of intellectual apprehension, from which her hours of frantic pain seemed far indeed removed. He had done this thing under the same roof with her—his wife. He had not frankly loved the younger woman, broken with his wife, made a new marriage. That would have been heart-break pure and simple. This was something else.

That letter, that wretched, cold, carefully guarded, unsigned letter: that bill—far safer than a check—these did not speak of affection. Some men can love two women at one time. This was not love.

Mrs. Marroner's sense of pity and outrage for herself, the wife, now spread suddenly into a perception of pity and outrage for the girl. All that splendid, clean young beauty, the hope of a happy life, with marriage and motherhood; honorable independence, even—these were nothing to that man. For his own pleasure he had chosen to rob her of her life's best joys.

He would "take care of her" said the letter? How? In what capacity?

And then, sweeping over both her feelings for herself, the wife, and Gerta, his victim, came a new flood, which literally lifted her to her feet. She rose and walked, her head held high. "This is the sin of man against woman," she said. "The offense is against womanhood. Against motherhood. Against—the child."

She stopped.

The child. His child. That, too, he sacrificed and injured—doomed to degradation.

Mrs. Marroner came of stern New England stock. She was not a Calvinist, hardly even a Unitarian, but the iron of Calvinism was in her soul: of that grim faith which held that most people had to be damned "for the glory of God."

Generations of ancestors who both preached and practiced stood behind her; people whose lives had been sternly moulded to their highest moments of religious conviction. In sweeping bursts of feeling they achieved "conviction," and afterward they lived and died according to that conviction.

When Mr. Marroner reached home, a few weeks later, following his letters too soon to expect an answer to either, he saw no wife upon the pier, though he had cabled; and found the house closed darkly. He let himself in with his latch-key, and stole softly upstairs, to surprise his wife.

No wife was there.

He rang the bell. No servant answered it.

He turned up light after light; searched the house from top to bottom; it was utterly empty. The kitchen wore a clean, bald, unsympathetic aspect. He left it and slowly mounted the stair, completely dazed. The whole house was clean, in perfect order, wholly vacant.

One thing he felt perfectly sure of—she knew.

Yet was he sure? He must not assume too much. She might have been ill. She might have died. He started to his feet. No, they would have cabled him. He sat down again.

For any such change, if she had wanted him to know, she would have written. Perhaps she had, and he, returning so suddenly, had missed the letter. The thought was some comfort. It must be so. He turned to the telephone, and again hesitated. If she had found out—if she had gone—utterly gone, without a word—should he announce it himself to friends and family?

He walked the floor; he searched everywhere for some letter, some word of explanation. Again and again he went to the telephone—and always stopped. He could not bear to ask: "Do you know where my wife is?"

The harmonious, beautiful rooms reminded him in a dumb, helpless way of her; like the remote smile on the face of the dead. He put out the lights; could not bear the darkness; turned them all on again.

It was a long night——

In the morning he went early to the office. In the accumulated mail was no letter from her. No one seemed to know of anything unusual. A friend asked after his wife—"Pretty glad to see you, I guess?" He answered evasively.

About eleven a man came to see him; John Hill, her lawyer. Her cousin, too. Mr. Marroner had never liked him. He liked him less now, for Mr. Hill merely handed him a letter, remarked, "I was requested to deliver this to you personally," and departed, looking like a person who is called on to kill something offensive.

"I have gone. I will care for Gerta. Good-bye. Marion."

That was all. There was no date, no address, no postmark; nothing but that.

In his anxiety and distress he had fairly forgotten Gerta and all that. Her name aroused in him a sense of rage. She had come between him and his wife. She had taken his wife from him. That was the way he felt.

At first he said nothing, did nothing; lived on alone in his house, taking meals where he chose. When people asked him about his wife he said she was traveling—for her health. He would not have it in the newspapers. Then, as time passed, as no enlightenment came to him, he resolved not to bear it any longer, and employed detectives. They blamed him for not having put them on the track earlier, but set to work, urged to the utmost secrecy.

What to him had been so blank a wall of mystery seemed not to embarrass them in the least. They made careful inquiries as to her "past," found where she had studied, where taught, and on what lines; that she had some little money of her own, that her doctor was Josephine L. Bleet, M.D., and many other bits of information.

As a result of careful and prolonged work, they finally told him that she had resumed teaching under one of her old professors; lived quietly, and apparently kept boarders; giving him town, street, and number, as if it were a matter of no difficulty whatever.

He had returned in early spring. It was autumn before he found her.

A quiet college town in the hills, a broad, shady street, a pleasant house standing in its own lawn, with trees and flowers about it. He had the address in his hand, and the number showed clear on the white gate. He walked up the straight gravel path and rang the bell. An elderly servant opened the door.

"Does Mrs. Marroner live here?"

"No, sir."

"This is number twenty-eight?"

"Yes, sir."

"Who does live here?"

"Miss Wheeling, sir."

Ah! Her maiden name. They had told him, but he had forgotten.

He stepped inside. "I would like to see her," he said.

He was ushered into a still parlor, cool and sweet with the scent of flowers, the flowers she had always loved best. It almost brought tears to his eyes. All their years of happiness rose in his mind again; the exquisite beginnings; the days of eager longing before she was really his; the deep, still beauty of her love.

Surely she would forgive him—she must forgive him. He would humble himself; he would tell her of his honest remorse—his absolute determination to be a different man.

Through the wide doorway there came in to him two women. One like a tall Madonna, bearing a baby in her arms.

Marion, calm, steady, definitely impersonal; nothing but a clear pallor to hint of inner stress.

Gerta, holding the child as a bulwark, with a new intelligence in her face, and her blue, adoring eyes fixed on her friend—not upon him.

He looked from one to the other dumbly.

And the woman who had been his wife asked quietly:

"What have you to say to us?"

1911

Why I Wrote "The Yellow Wallpaper"[1]

Many and many a reader has asked that. When the story first came out, in the *New England Magazine* about 1891, a Boston physician made protest in *The Transcript*. Such a story ought not to be written, he said; it was enough to drive anyone mad to read it.

Another physician, in Kansas I think, wrote to say that it was the best description of incipient insanity he had ever seen, and—begging my pardon—had I been there?

Now the story of the story is this:

For many years I suffered from a severe and continuous nervous breakdown tending to melancholia—and beyond. During about the third year of this trouble I went, in devout faith and some faint stir of hope, to a noted specialist in nervous diseases, the best known in the country. This wise man put me to bed and applied the rest cure, to which a still-good physique responded so promptly that he concluded there was nothing much the matter with me,

[1]*The Forerunner* (October 10, 1913).

and sent me home with solemn advice to "live as domestic a life as far as possible," to "have but two hours' intellectual life a day," and "never to touch pen, brush, or pencil again" as long as I lived. This was in 1887.

I went home and obeyed those directions for some three months, and came so near the borderline of utter mental ruin that I could see over.

Then, using the remnants of intelligence that remained, and helped by a wise friend, I cast the noted specialist's advice to the winds and went to work again—work, the normal life of every human being; work, in which is joy and growth and service, without which one is a pauper and a parasite—ultimately recovering some measure of power.

Being naturally moved to rejoicing by this narrow escape, I wrote "The Yellow Wallpaper," with its embellishments and additions, to carry out the ideal (I never had hallucinations or objections to my mural decorations) and sent a copy to the physician who so nearly drove me mad. He never acknowledged it.

The little book is valued by alienist[2] and as a good specimen of one kind of literature. It has, to my knowledge, saved one woman from a similar fate—so terrifying her family that they let her out into normal activity and she recovered.

But the best result is this. Many years later I was told that the great specialist had admitted to friends of his that he had altered his treatment of neurasthenia[3] since reading "The Yellow Wallpaper."

It was not intended to drive people crazy, but to save people from being driven crazy, and it worked.

1913

SADAKICHI HARTMANN
c. 1867–1944

Sadakichi Hartmann was born on an island in Japan's Nagasaki Harbor to a German father and a Japanese mother. His mother died in childbirth, and Hartmann was sent to relatives in Germany, where he lived until he ran away to Paris at the age of thirteen. His flight angered his father, who disinherited him and in 1882 shipped him off to relations in Philadelphia. Hartmann described his early years in Philadelphia as "the customary apprenticeship in the Academy of Hard Knocks," and he balanced days of menial labor with nights spent reading in the Mercantile Library. His self-education in literature and the arts led

---

[2]An alienist was a physician accepted by a court of law as an expert on the mental competence of principals or witnesses appearing before it.

[3]A term formerly used to describe a mental disorder with such symptoms as easy fatigability, lack of motivation, and feelings of inadequacy.

Hartmann to Camden, New Jersey, to seek out Walt Whitman—whom he visited regularly from 1884–1892—and eventually to a series of trips to Europe, where he met artistic luminaries like poet Stéphane Mallarmé and playwright Henrik Ibsen, whose works Hartmann championed in the United States.

Hartmann began his writing career with journalistic pieces on art published in newspapers in Philadelphia, Boston, and New York. While he supported himself with what he termed "occasional hack" for the papers, he made a sustained study of art history that culminated in his two-volume *A History of American Art* (1902), the first such study ever written, which became a standard textbook. For the next fifteen years, Hartmann was in demand as a lecturer in cities across the country, and throughout his life he fostered painters and photographers for whom his striking visage became a favorite subject. Alongside his myriad publications on art, Hartmann was a prolific artist in his own right: in 1893, he wrote a drama called *Christ*, a decadent fantasy that landed Hartmann in a Boston jail, and he went on to write a string of religious dramas—from *Buddha* in 1897 to the unpublished *Baker Eddy* (about the founder of Christian Science, Mary Baker Eddy) discovered posthumously among his papers. He published his first book of poetry, *Drifting Flowers of the Sea*, in 1904, and he continued to write verse in a range of forms, notably including the five-line tanka and three-line haiku, spare forms derived from classical Japanese verse. An extravagant writer who reveled in scandal, his poetry captured startling moments but also delighted in scenes of aesthetic reflection. Hartmann styled himself as an artistic bridge that spanned both the Atlantic and the Pacific: not only did he introduce modern European art to the American scene; he cultivated an appreciation of Japanese art and poetry in the United States. In addition to drama and poetry, Hartmann also published short stories and one novel, *The Last Thirty Days of Christ* (1920).

In 1915, Hartmann was dubbed the "King of Bohemia": he cut a flamboyant figure, marveled at by the cultural elite—James Gibbons Huneker called him "the man with the Hokusai profile and broad Teutonic culture"—as well as the literati—as in Ezra Pound's statement that "If one had not been oneself, it wd. have been worthwhile being Sadakichi." Hartmann, however, suffered from bouts of physical illness and depression. He met his first wife in the hospital—where she worked as a nurse—after a suicide attempt in 1891; in 1908 he abandoned his wife and family for a young artist. In the early 1920s, Hartmann held court in Hollywood society: he appeared as the court magician in the 1924 Douglas Fairbanks picture *The Thief of Bagdad*, seemingly playing himself—yet though he fascinated this crowd, to them he was more an improbable figure than a venerated one.

Hartmann continued writing and lecturing into the 1930s, but at the end of his life, he retreated to a shack adjacent to his daughter's house on the edge of the Morongo Indian Reservation in Banning, California. His gaunt figure made him first a mystery and then a perceived threat to the small town: after Pearl Harbor, his German–Japanese heritage—the source of his mystique in the past—became a bitter liability. Hartmann was hounded by FBI agents, and his artistic activities were cast under a pall of suspicion. Hartmann had been an American citizen since 1894, when he naturalized; he spent his final years incredulous that the author of *A History of American Art* should be so persecuted. When Sadakichi

Hartmann died in 1944, he was buried in a pauper's grave, and his works were largely forgotten. A small flurry of interest in Hartmann by art historians and Japanese critics in the late 1960s led two literary scholars, Harry Lawton and George Knox, to open the lid on the trunk of writing he left behind in his desert shack. Inside, they discovered pages of unpublished writing, including notes for an autobiography which reeled off a list of possible titles, including "A Mud-Bespattered Purist," "The First Eurasian," and "Singular Without a Plural."

Josephine Park
University of Pennsylvania

PRIMARY WORKS

Conversations with Walt Whitman, 1895; *Schopenhauer in the Air: Seven Stories*, 1899; *Shakespeare in Art*, 1901; *A History of American Art*, 1902; *Japanese Art*, 1904; *Drifting Flowers of the Sea*, 1904; *The Whistler Book*, 1910; *My Rubaiyat*, 1913; *Tanka and Hai-kai: Japanese Rhythms*, 1916; *Last Thirty Days of Christ*, 1920; *Seven Short Stories*, 1930; *Buddha, Confucius, Christ: Three Prophetic Plays*, ed. Harry Lawton and George Knox, 1971; *White Chrysanthemums: Literary Fragments and Pronouncements*, ed. Knox and Lawton, 1971.

Cathedral Sacrilege

A silken hose in a golden haze
An opening rose in a maze of lace
A color dream in a marmorean whiteness
A sensual gleam in subdued brightness
    And my languid soul   5
    In a mild vibration
    Embraces the nude
    In a wild violation

                              1892

Drifting Flowers of the Sea

Across the dunes, in the waning light,
The rising moon pours her amber rays,
Through the slumbrous air of the dim, brown night
The pungent smell of the seaweed strays—
    From vast and trackless spaces   5
    Where wind and water meet,
    White flowers, that rise from the sleepless deep,
    Come drifting to my feet.
They flutter the shore in a drowsy tune,
Unfurl their bloom to the lightlorn sky,   10
    Allow a caress to the rising moon,
    Then fall to slumber, and fade, and die.

White flowers, a-bloom on the vagrant deep,
Like dreams of love, rising out of sleep,
You are the songs, I dreamt but never sung,   15
Pale hopes my thoughts alone have known
Vain words ne'er uttered, though on the tongue,
That winds to the sibilant seas have blown.
  In you, I see the everlasting drift of years
    That will endure all sorrows, smiles and tears;   20
    For when the bell of time will ring the doom
      To all the follies of the human race,
        You still will rise in fugitive bloom
        And garland the shores of ruined space.

                                                              1904

Immaculate Conception

A maiden flower stands lonesome on a vast and
    desolate plain, in trembling fear that
    her longings for life and love prove vain.
But the passing breeze takes pity, it embraces
    some flowering plant and carries its golden   5
    riches to the bride of the desolate land.

Windstirred she tosses her clustering hair to the
    dust of golden glow, and flower-starred with
    the waxing morn the desolate meadows grow.

                                                              1904

To the "Flat Iron"[1,2]

On roof and street, on park and pier,
The springtide sun shines soft and white,
Where the "Flat Iron", gaunt, austere,
Lifts its huge tiers in limpid light.

    From the city's stir and madd'ning roar   5
    Your monstrous shape soars in massive flight,
    And 'mid the breezes the ocean bore
    Your windows flame in the sunset light.

---

[1]A triangular skyscraper in Manhattan, completed in 1902.

[2]Nickname for New York City, popularized in the nineteenth century.

Lonely and lithe, o'er the nocturnal city's
Flickering flames, you proudly tower,   10
Like some ancient, giant monolith,
Girt with the stars and mists that lower.

All else we see fade fast and disappear,
Only your prow-like form looms gaunt, austere,
As in a sea of fog, now veiled, now clear.   15

Iron structure of the time,
  Rich, in showing no pretense,
  Fair, in frugalness sublime,
Emblem staunch of common sense,
  Well may you smile over Gotham's vast domain,   20
  As dawn greets your pillars with roseate flame,
    For future ages will proclaim
      Your beauty, boldly,
        Without shame.

                                                            1904

Tanka VIII.

Of pleasures be mine
  As aeons and aeons roll by,
Why should I repine
  That under some future sky
  I may live as butterfly?   5

                                                            1915

Haikai[1] I.

White petals afloat
  On a winding woodland stream—
What else is life's dream?

                                                            1915

---

[1]"Haikai" and "hokku" were both terms used
to denote the Japanese verse form that was
standardized into "haiku" in the 1950s.

■   STEPHEN CRANE   ■
1871–1900

With the publication of his Civil War novel, *The Red Badge of Courage* (1895), when he was twenty-four years old, Stephen Crane became famous in the United States and England. Less than five years later he was dead of tuberculosis. In his brief life, however, he had published five novels, two volumes of poetry, and over three hundred sketches, reports, and short stories.

Crane was born in Newark, New Jersey, the fourteenth child of Jonathan Townley Crane, a Methodist minister, and Mary Helen Peck Crane, who was herself descended from a long line of Methodist clergy. Crane's formal education included a brief stay at a military school, where he gained the rank of adjutant and which may have had experiences that contributed to his later success in writing about war, the subject for which he became famous. In 1891 Crane went to work as a journalist in New York City. During this period he published *Maggie: A Girl of the Streets* (1893), a powerful portrayal of the blighted, poverty-stricken lives of the Bowery. Although few copies were sold, the book led to Crane's friendships with two of the leading figures in American literary realism, Hamlin Garland and William Dean Howells, both of whom publicly praised the book.

During his years in New York City he wrote many works about city life that reflected his interest in extreme environments. The sketches "An Experiment in Misery" and "An Experiment in Luxury" (1894), in which he described living in a flophouse and in a millionaire's mansion, recorded the effects of these experiences on his own consciousness. As experiments in perception, they anticipated the subjective "new journalism" of the 1960s, such as Norman Mailer's *Armies of the Night*.

Crane's interest in environmental determinism links him to late-nineteenth-century naturalistic writers such as Frank Norris, Jack London, and Theodore Dreiser, but he avoids their often heavy factual documentation; instead, he usually defines his characters with sharply focused comments and vivid images. Such compression and imagery and an intense concern with color have led numerous critics to see in his writing a literary parallel to impressionist painting. Crane is comparable to both naturalists and impressionists in his desire to shock readers with new and often disturbing ideas and perceptions.

In his poetry, collected in *The Black Riders and Other Lines* (1895) and *War Is Kind* (1900), he often aims rebukes at conventional piety while also revealing his preoccupation with questions that parallel the concerns of religion. Experimental in form, unconventional in rhyme, and brief often to the point of being cryptic, Crane's poems in some ways foreshadowed the *vers libre* of the early twentieth century and also bear resemblance to the koans of Zen Buddhist religious practice. When published, their brevity was comparable to that of Emily Dickinson's poems, but to a large degree they were unlike any poems written previously in the United States.

Crane's Civil War writings are imaginative reconstructions of events that took place before he was born. Historical writings and conversations with veterans contributed to his understanding of the war, but such sources do not fully explain his powerful rendering of the young recruit, Henry Fleming, and his consciousness in *The Red Badge of Courage* or equally powerful passages in "A Mystery of Heroism" (1895) and other works. The Civil War seems to have been an unusually provocative stimulus for Crane's imagination, enabling him to envision emotional and psychological struggles in nearly hallucinatory detail.

Crane sought a variety of experiences. In 1895, in the first flush of success of *The Red Badge of Courage*, he traveled in the American West and in Mexico. Later he expressed a desire to go to Alaska and to the Transvaal to report on the Boers. In 1897 he tried to slip into Cuba to observe the guerrilla insurgency. Later that same year he traveled to Europe to report the Greco-Turkish war. Crane drew upon these experiences for some of his most successful short stories, most notably "The Bride Comes to Yellow Sky" (1898), "The Blue Hotel" (1898), and "Death and the Child" (1898).

"The Open Boat" (1898), the story that many critics believe is Crane's best piece of work, is a remarkable fusion of his respect for the power of the external world and his intense concern with the mysterious inner world of emotions and fantasies. The story derives directly from his experience in a dinghy adrift at sea for thirty hours after the sinking of the *Commodore*, a steamship illegally bound for Cuba shortly before the Spanish–American War. In exploring the developing consciousness of the narrator, his growing awareness of nature, and his deepening relationships to other human beings, the story measures the vastness of human loneliness and defines a brotherhood of those who have encountered the sea. "The Open Boat" balances cosmic uncertainties with glimpses of human achievements in awareness, cooperation, and courage.

After his ordeal at sea, Crane was nursed back to health by Cora Taylor, the proprietor of a house of assignation in Jacksonville, Florida, whom he had met shortly before the ill-fated *Commodore* left port. They traveled together to Greece and then to England, where, early in 1898, they moved into an ancient manor house in Sussex, with the writers Henry James and Joseph Conrad for neighbors.

Crane seems to have first learned he was tubercular when he tried to enlist in the army in 1897 to go to Cuba. It appears he did little to regain his health. When he became very ill in April 1900, Cora took him in desperation to a sanitorium in the Black Forest in Germany, where he died on June 5.

Donald Vanouse
State University of New York
(College at Oswego)

PRIMARY WORKS

Maggie: A Girl of the Streets (1893), A Facsimile of the First Edition, ed. Donald Pizer, 1968; *The Works of Stephen Crane*, 12 vols., ed. Fredson Bowers, 1969–1976; *The Correspondence of Stephen Crane*, 2 vols., ed. Stanley Wertheim and Paul Sorrentino, 1987.

The Open Boat

A Tale Intended to Be after the Fact Being the Experience of Four Men from the Sunk Steamer Commodore

I

None of them knew the color of the sky. Their eyes glanced level, and were fastened upon the waves that swept toward them. These waves were of the hue of slate, save for the tops, which were of foaming white, and all of the men knew the colors of the sea. The horizon narrowed and widened, and dipped and rose, and at all times its edge was jagged with waves that seemed thrust up in points like rocks.

Many a man ought to have a bath-tub larger than the boat which here rode upon the sea. These waves were most wrongfully and barbarously abrupt and tall, and each froth-top was a problem in small boat navigation.

The cook squatted in the bottom and looked with both eyes at the six inches of gunwale which separated him from the ocean. His sleeves were rolled over his fat forearms, and the two flaps of his unbuttoned vest dangled as he bent to bail out the boat. Often he said: "Gawd! That was a narrow clip." As he remarked it he invariably gazed eastward over the broken sea.

The oiler, steering with one of the two oars in the boat, sometimes raised himself suddenly to keep clear of water that swirled in over the stern. It was a thin little oar and it seemed often ready to snap.

The correspondent, pulling at the other oar, watched the waves and wondered why he was there.

The injured captain, lying in the bow, was at this time buried in that profound dejection and indifference which comes, temporarily at least, to even the bravest and most enduring when, willy nilly, the firm fails, the army loses, the ship goes down. The mind of the master of a vessel is rooted deep in the timbers of her, though he command for a day or a decade, and this captain had on him the stern impression of a scene in the grays of dawn of seven turned faces, and later a stump of a top-mast with a white ball on it that slashed to and fro at the waves, went low and lower, and down. Thereafter there was something strange in his voice. Although steady, it was deep with mourning, and of a quality beyond oration or tears.

"Keep'er a little more south, Billie," said he.

"'A little more south,' sir," said the oiler in the stern.

A seat in this boat was not unlike a seat upon a bucking broncho, and, by the same token, a broncho is not much smaller. The craft pranced and reared, and plunged like an animal. As each wave came, and she rose for it, she seemed like a horse making at a fence outrageously high. The manner of her scramble over these walls of water is a mystic thing, and, moreover, at the top of them were ordinarily these problems in white water, the foam racing down from the summit of each wave, requiring a new leap, and a leap from the air. Then, after scornfully bumping a crest, she would slide, and race, and splash down a long incline and arrive bobbing and nodding in front of the next menace.

A singular disadvantage of the sea lies in the fact that after successfully surmounting one wave you discover that there is another behind it just as important and just as nervously anxious to do something effective in the way of swamping boats. In a ten-foot dingey one can get an idea of the resources of the sea in the line of waves that is not probable to the average experience, which is never at sea in a dingey. As each slaty wall of water approached, it shut all else from the view of the men in the boat, and it was not difficult to imagine that this particular wave was the final outburst of the ocean, the last effort of the grim water. There was a terrible grace in the move of the waves, and they came in silence, save for the snarling of the crests.

In the wan light, the faces of the men must have been gray. Their eyes must have glinted in strange ways as they gazed steadily astern. Viewed from a balcony, the whole thing would doubtlessly have been weirdly picturesque. But the men in the boat had no time to see it, and if they had had leisure there were other things to occupy their minds. The sun swung steadily up the sky, and they knew it was broad day because the color of the sea changed from slate to emerald-green, streaked with amber lights, and the foam was like tumbling snow. The process of the breaking day was unknown to them. They were aware only of this effect upon the color of the waves that rolled toward them.

In disjointed sentences the cook and the correspondent argued as to the difference between a life-saving station and a house of refuge. The cook had said: "There's a house of refuge just north of the Mosquito Inlet Light, and as soon as they see us, they'll come off in their boat and pick us up."

"As soon as who see us?" said the correspondent.

"The crew," said the cook.

"Houses of refuge don't have crews," said the correspondent. "As I understand them, they are only places where clothes and grub are stored for the benefit of shipwrecked people. They don't carry crews."

"Oh, yes, they do," said the cook.

"No, they don't," said the correspondent.

"Well, we're not there yet, anyhow," said the oiler, in the stern.

"Well," said the cook, "perhaps it's not a house of refuge that I'm thinking of as being near Mosquito Inlet Light. Perhaps it's a life-saving station."

"We're not there yet," said the oiler, in the stern.

II

As the boat bounced from the top of each wave, the wind tore through the hair of the hatless men, and as the craft plopped her stern down again the spray slashed past them. The crest of each of these waves was a hill, from the top of which the men surveyed, for a moment, a broad tumultuous expanse; shining and wind-riven. It was probably splendid. It was probably glorious, this play of the free sea, wild with lights of emerald and white and amber.

"Bully good thing it's an on-shore wind," said the cook. "If not, where would we be? Wouldn't have a show."

"That's right," said the correspondent.

The busy oiler nodded his assent.

Then the captain, in the bow, chuckled in a way that expressed humor, contempt, tragedy, all in one. "Do you think we've got much of a show, now, boys?" said he.

Whereupon the three were silent, save for a trifle of hemming and hawing. To express any particular optimism at this time they felt to be childish and stupid, but they all doubtless possessed this sense of the situation in their mind. A young man thinks doggedly at such times. On the other hand, the ethics of their condition was decidedly against any open suggestion of hopelessness. So they were silent.

"Oh, well," said the captain, soothing his children, "we'll get ashore all right."

But there was that in his tone which made them think, so the oiler quoth:

"Yes! If this wind holds!"

The cook was bailing: "Yes! If we don't catch hell in the surf."

Canton flannel gulls flew near and far. Sometimes they sat down on the sea, near patches of brown sea-weed that rolled over the waves with a movement like carpets on a line in a gale. The birds sat comfortably in groups, and they were envied by some in the dingey, for the wrath of the sea was no more to them than it was to a covey of prairie chickens a thousand miles inland. Often they came very close and stared at the men with black bead-like eyes. At these times they were uncanny and sinister in their unblinking scrutiny, and the men hooted angrily at them, telling them to be gone. One came, and evidently decided to alight on the top of the captain's head. The bird flew parallel to the boat and did not circle, but made short sidelong jumps in the air in chicken-fashion. His black eyes were wistfully fixed upon the captain's head. "Ugly brute," said the oiler to the bird. "You look as if you were made with a jackknife." The cook and the correspondent swore darkly at the creature. The captain naturally wished to knock it away with the end of the heavy painter,[1] but he did not dare do it, because anything resembling an emphatic gesture would have capsized this freighted boat, and so with his open hand, the captain gently and carefully waved the gull away. After it had been discouraged from the pursuit the captain breathed easier on account of his hair, and others breathed easier because the bird struck their minds at this time as being somehow grewsome and ominous.

[1]A rope attached to the bow used for tying up a boat.

In the meantime the oiler and the correspondent rowed. And also they rowed.

They sat together in the same seat, and each rowed an oar. Then the oiler took both oars; then the correspondent took both oars; then the oiler; then the correspondent. They rowed and they rowed. The very ticklish part of the business was when the time came for the reclining one in the stern to take his turn at the oars. By the very last star of truth, it is easier to steal eggs from under a hen than it was to change seats in the dingey. First the man in the stern slid his hand along the thwart and moved with care, as if he were of Sèvres.[2] Then the man in the rowing seat slid his hand along the other thwart. It was all done with the most extraordinary care. As the two sidled past each other, the whole party kept watchful eyes on the coming wave, and the captain cried: "Look out now! Steady there!"

The brown mats of sea-weed that appeared from time to time were like islands, bits of earth. They were travelling, apparently, neither one way nor the other. They were, to all intents, stationary. They informed the men in the boat that it was making progress slowly toward the land.

The captain, rearing cautiously in the bow, after the dingey soared on a great swell, said that he had seen the lighthouse at Mosquito Inlet. Presently the cook remarked that he had seen it. The correspondent was at the oars, then, and for some reason he too wished to look at the lighthouse, but his back was toward the far shore and the waves were important, and for some time he could not seize an opportunity to turn his head. But at last there came a wave more gentle than the others, and when at the crest of it he swiftly scoured the western horizon.

"See it?" said the captain.

"No," said the correspondent, slowly, "I didn't see anything."

"Look again," said the captain. He pointed. "It's exactly in that direction."

At the top of another wave, the correspondent did as he was bid, and this time his eyes chanced on a small still thing on the edge of the swaying horizon. It was precisely like the point of a pin. It took an anxious eye to find a lighthouse so tiny.

"Think we'll make it, captain?"

"If this wind holds and the boat don't swamp, we can't do much else," said the captain.

The little boat, lifted by each towering sea, and splashed viciously by the crests, made progress that in the absence of seaweed was not apparent to those in her. She seemed just a wee thing wallowing, miraculously, top-up, at the mercy of five oceans. Occasionally, a great spread of water, like white flames, swarmed into her.

"Bail her, cook," said the captain, serenely.

"All right, captain," said the cheerful cook.

[2]A delicate porcelain made in Sèvres, France.

III

It would be difficult to describe the subtle brotherhood of men that was here established on the seas. No one said that it was so. No one mentioned it. But it dwelt in the boat, and each man felt it warm him. They were a captain, an oiler, a cook, and a correspondent, and they were friends, friends in a more curiously ironbound degree than may be common. The hurt captain, lying against the waterjar in the bow, spoke always in a low voice and calmly, but he could never command a more ready and swiftly obedient crew than the motley three of the dingey. It was more than a mere recognition of what was best for the common safety. There was surely in it a quality that was personal and heartfelt. And after this devotion to the commander of the boat there was this comradeship that the correspondent, for instance, who had been taught to be cynical of men, knew even at the time was the best experience of his life. But no one said that it was so. No one mentioned it.

"I wish we had a sail," remarked the captain. "We might try my overcoat on the end of an oar and give you two boys a chance to rest." So the cook and the correspondent held the mast and spread wide the overcoat. The oiler steered, and the little boat made good way with her new rig. Sometimes the oiler had to scull sharply to keep a sea from breaking into the boat, but otherwise sailing was a success.

Meanwhile the light-house had been growing slowly larger. It had now almost assumed color, and appeared like a little gray shadow on the sky. The man at the oars could not be prevented from turning his head rather often to try for a glimpse of this little gray shadow.

At last, from the top of each wave the men in the tossing boat could see land. Even as the light-house was an upright shadow on the sky, this land seemed but a long black shadow on the sea. It certainly was thinner than paper. "We must be about opposite New Smyrna," said the cook, who had coasted this shore often in schooners. "Captain, by the way, I believe they abandoned that life-saving station there about a year ago."

"Did they?" said the captain.

The wind slowly died away. The cook and the correspondent were not now obliged to slave in order to hold high the oar. But the waves continued their old impetuous swooping at the dingey, and the little craft, no longer under way, struggled woundily over them. The oiler or the correspondent took the oars again.

Shipwrecks are *apropos* of nothing. If men could only train for them and have them occur when the men had reached pink condition, there would be less drowning at sea. Of the four in the dingey none had slept any time worth mentioning for two days and two nights previous to embarking in the dingey, and in the excitement of clambering about the deck of a foundering ship they had also forgotten to eat heartily.

For these reasons, and for others, neither the oiler nor the correspondent was fond of rowing at this time. The correspondent wondered ingenuously how in the name of all that was sane could there be people who

thought it amusing to row a boat. It was not an amusement; it was a diabolical punishment, and even a genius of mental aberrations could never conclude that it was anything but a horror to the muscles and a crime against
the back. He mentioned to the boat in general how the amusement of rowing struck him, and the weary-faced oiler smiled in full sympathy. Previously
to the foundering, by the way, the oiler had worked doublewatch in the
engine-room of the ship.

"Take her easy, now, boys," said the captain. "Don't spend yourselves. If
we have to run a surf you'll need all your strength, because we'll sure have
to swim for it. Take your time."

Slowly the land arose from the sea. From a black line it became a line of
black and a line of white, trees, and sand. Finally, the captain said that he
could make out a house on the shore. "That's the house of refuge, sure," said
the cook. "They'll see us before long, and come out after us."

The distant light-house reared high. "The keeper ought to be able to
make us out now, if he's looking through a glass," said the captain. "He'll
notify the life-saving people."

"None of those other boats could have got ashore to give word of the
wreck," said the oiler, in a low voice. "Else the life-boat would be out hunting us."

Slowly and beautifully the land loomed out of the sea. The wind came
again. It had veered from the northeast to the southeast. Finally, a new
sound struck the ears of the men in the boat. It was the low thunder of the
surf on the shore. "We'll never be able to make the light-house now," said
the captain. "Swing her head a little more north, Billie," said the captain.

"'A little more north,' sir," said the oiler.

Whereupon the little boat turned her nose once more down the wind,
and all but the oarsman watched the shore grow. Under the influence of this
expansion doubt and direful apprehension was leaving the minds of the
men. The management of the boat was still most absorbing, but it could not
prevent a quiet cheerfulness. In an hour, perhaps, they would be ashore.

Their back-bones had become thoroughly used to balancing in the boat
and they now rode this wild colt of a dingey like circus men. The correspondent thought that he had been drenched to the skin, but happening to
feel in the top pocket of his coat, he found therein eight cigars. Four of
them were soaked with sea-water; four were perfectly scatheless. After a
search, somebody produced three dry matches, and thereupon the four
waifs rode in their little boat, and with an assurance of an impending rescue
shining in their eyes, puffed at the big cigars and judged well and ill of all
men. Everybody took a drink of water.

IV

"Cook," remarked the captain, "there don't seem to be any signs of life
about your house of refuge."

"No," replied the cook. "Funny they don't see us!"

A broad stretch of lowly coast lay before the eyes of the men. It was of low dunes topped with dark vegetation. The roar of the surf was plain, and sometimes they could see the white lip of a wave as it spun up the beach. A tiny house was blocked out black upon the sky. Southward, the slim lighthouse lifted its little gray length.

Tide, wind, and waves were swinging the dingey northward. "Funny they don't see us," said the men.

The surf's roar was here dulled, but its tone was, nevertheless, thunderous and mighty. As the boat swam over the great rollers, the men sat listening to this roar.

"We'll swamp sure," said everybody.

It is fair to say here that there was not a life-saving station within twenty miles in either direction, but the men did not know this fact and in consequence they made dark and opprobrious remarks concerning the eyesight of the nation's life-savers. Four scowling men sat in the dingey and surpassed records in the invention of epithets.

"Funny they don't see us."

The light-heartedness of a former time had completely faded. To their sharpened minds it was easy to conjure pictures of all kinds of incompetency and blindness and, indeed, cowardice. There was the shore of the populous land, and it was bitter and bitter to them that from it came no sign.

"Well," said the captain, ultimately, "I suppose we'll have to make a try for ourselves. If we stay out here too long, we'll none of us have strength left to swim after the boat swamps."

And so the oiler, who was at the oars, turned the boat straight for the shore. There was a sudden tightening of muscles. There was some thinking.

"If we don't all get ashore—" said the captain. "If we don't all get ashore, I suppose you fellows know where to send news of my finish?"

They then briefly exchanged some addresses and admonitions. As for the reflections of the men, there was a great deal of rage in them. Perchance they might be formulated thus: "If I am going to be drowned—if I am going to be drowned—if I am going to be drowned, why, in the name of the seven mad gods who rule the sea, was I allowed to come thus far and contemplate sand and trees? Was I brought here merely to have my nose dragged away as I was about to nibble the sacred cheese of life? It is preposterous. If this old ninny-woman, Fate, cannot do better than this, she should be deprived of the management of men's fortunes. She is an old hen who knows not her intention. If she has decided to drown me, why did she not do it in the beginning and save me all this trouble. The whole affair is absurd.... But, no, she cannot mean to drown me. She dare not drown me. She cannot drown me. Not after all this work." Afterward the man might have had an impulse to shake his fist at the clouds: "Just you drown me, now, and then hear what I call you!"

The billows that came at this time were more formidable. They seemed always just about to break and roll over the little boat in a turmoil of foam. There was a preparatory and long growl in the speech of them. No mind unused to the sea would have concluded that the dingey could ascend these sheer heights in time. The shore was still afar. The oiler was a wily surfman. "Boys," he said, swiftly, "she won't live three minutes more and we're too far out to swim. Shall I take her to sea again, captain?"

"Yes! Go ahead!" said the captain.

This oiler, by a series of quick miracles, and fast and steady oarsmanship, turned the boat in the middle of the surf and took her safely to sea again.

There was a considerable silence as the boat bumped over the furrowed sea to deeper water. Then somebody in gloom spoke. "Well, anyhow, they must have seen us from the shore by now."

The gulls went in slanting flight up the wind toward the gray desolate east. A squall, marked by dingy clouds, and clouds brick-red, like smoke from a burning building, appeared from the southeast.

"What do you think of those life-saving people? Ain't they peaches?"

"Funny they haven't seen us."

"Maybe they think we're out here for sport! Maybe they think we're fishin'. Maybe they think we're damned fools."

It was a long afternoon. A changed tide tried to force them southward, but wind and wave said northward. Far ahead, where coast-line, sea, and sky formed their mighty angle, there were little dots which seemed to indicate a city on the shore.

"St. Augustine?"

The captain shook his head. "Too near Mosquito Inlet."

And the oiler rowed, and then the correspondent rowed. Then the oiler rowed. It was a weary business. The human back can become the seat of more aches and pains than are registered in books for the composite anatomy of a regiment. It is a limited area, but it can become the theatre of innumerable muscular conflicts, tangles, wrenches, knots, and other comforts.

"Did you ever like to row, Billie?" asked the correspondent.

"No," said the oiler. "Hang it."

When one exchanged the rowing-seat for a place in the bottom of the boat, he suffered a bodily depression that caused him to be careless of everything save an obligation to wiggle one finger. There was cold sea-water swashing to and fro in the boat, and he lay in it. His head, pillowed on a thwart, was within an inch of the swirl of a wave crest, and sometimes a particularly obstreperous sea came in-board and drenched him once more. But these matters did not annoy him. It is almost certain that if the boat had capsized he would have tumbled comfortably out upon the ocean as if he felt sure that it was a great soft mattress.

"Look! There's a man on the shore!"

"Where?"

"There! See 'im? See 'im?"

"Yes, sure! He's walking along."

"Now he's stopped. Look! He's facing us!"

"He's waving at us!"

"So he is! By thunder!"

"Ah, now, we're all right! Now we're all right! There'll be a boat out here for us in half an hour."

"He's going on. He's running. He's going up to that house there."

The remote beach seemed lower than the sea, and it required a searching glance to discern the little black figure. The captain saw a floating stick and they rowed to it. A bath-towel was by some weird chance in the boat, and, tying this on the stick, the captain waved it. The oarsman did not dare turn his head, so he was obliged to ask questions.

"What's he doing now?"

"He's standing still again. He's looking, I think.... There he goes again. Toward the house.... Now he's stopped again."

"Is he waving at us?"

"No, not now! he was, though."

"Look! There comes another man!"

"He's running."

"Look at him go, would you."

"Why, he's on a bicycle. Now he's met the other man. They're both waving at us. Look!"

"There comes something up the beach."

"What the devil is that thing?"

"Why, it looks like a boat."

"Why, certainly it's a boat."

"No, it's on wheels."

"Yes, so it is. Well, that must be the life-boat. They drag them along shore on a wagon."

"That's the life-boat, sure."

"No, by—, it's—it's an omnibus."

"I tell you it's a life-boat."

"It is not! It's an omnibus. I can see it plain. See? One of these big hotel omnibuses."

"By thunder, you're right. It's an omnibus, sure as fate. What do you suppose they are doing with an omnibus? Maybe they are going around collecting the life-crew, hey?"

"That's it, likely. Look! There's a fellow waving a little black flag. He's standing on the steps of the omnibus. There come those other two fellows. Now they're all talking together. Look at the fellow with the flag. Maybe he ain't waving it."

"That ain't a flag, is it? That's his coat. Why, certainly, that's his coat."

"So it is. It's his coat. He's taken it off and is waving it around his head. But would you look at him swing it."

"Oh, say, there isn't any life-saving station there. That's just a winter resort hotel omnibus that has brought over some of the boarders to see us drown."

"What's that idiot with the coat mean? What's he signaling, anyhow?"

"It looks as if he were trying to tell us to go north. There must be a life-saving station up there."

"No! He thinks we're fishing. Just giving us a merry hand. See? Ah, there, Willie."

"Well, I wish I could make something out of those signals. What do you suppose he means?"

"He don't mean anything. He's just playing."

"Well, if he'd just signal us to try the surf again, or to go to sea and wait, or go north, or go south, or go to hell—there would be some reason in it. But look at him. He just stands there and keeps his coat revolving like a wheel. The ass!"

"There come more people."

"Now there's quite a mob. Look! Isn't that a boat?"

"Where? Oh, I see where you mean. No, that's no boat."

"That fellow is still waving his coat."

"He must think we like to see him do that. Why don't he quit it. It don't mean anything."

"I don't know. I think he is trying to make us go north. It must be that there's a life-saving station there somewhere."

"Say, he ain't tired yet. Look at 'im wave."

"Wonder how long he can keep that up. He's been revolving his coat ever since he caught sight of us. He's an idiot. Why aren't they getting men to bring a boat out. A fishing boat—one of those big yawls—could come out here all right. Why don't he do something?"

"Oh, it's all right, now."

"They'll have a boat out here for us in less than no time, now that they've seen us."

A faint yellow tone came into the sky over the low land. The shadows on the sea slowly deepened. The wind bore coldness with it, and the men began to shiver.

"Holy smoke!" said one, allowing his voice to express his impious mood, "if we keep on monkeying out here! If we've got to flounder out here all night!"

"Oh, we'll never have to stay here all night! Don't you worry. They've seen us now, and it won't be long before they'll come chasing out after us."

The shore grew dusky. The man waving a coat blended gradually into this gloom, and it swallowed in the same manner the omnibus and the group of people. The spray, when it dashed uproariously over the side, made the voyagers shrink and swear like men who were being branded.

"I'd like to catch the chump who waved the coat. I feel like soaking him one, just for luck."

"Why? What did he do?"

"Oh, nothing, but then he seemed so damned cheerful."

In the meantime the oiler rowed, and then the correspondent rowed, and then the oiler rowed. Gray-faced and bowed forward, they mechanically, turn by turn, plied the leaden oars. The form of the light-house had vanished from the southern horizon, but finally a pale star appeared, just lifting from the sea. The streaked saffron in the west passed before the all-merging darkness, and the sea to the east was black. The land had vanished, and was expressed only by the low and drear thunder of the surf.

"If I am going to be drowned—if I am going to be drowned—if I am going to be drowned, why, in the name of the seven mad gods, who rule the sea, was I allowed to come thus far and contemplate sand and trees? Was I brought here merely to have my nose dragged away as I was about to nibble the sacred cheese of life?"

The patient captain, drooped over the water-jar, was sometimes obliged to speak to the oarsman.

"Keep her head up! Keep her head up!"

"'Keep her head up,' sir." The voices were weary and low.

This was surely a quiet evening. All save the oarsman lay heavily and listlessly in the boat's bottom. As for him, his eyes were just capable of noting the tall black waves that swept forward in a most sinister silence, save for an occasional subdued growl of a crest.

The cook's head was on a thwart, and he looked without interest at the water under his nose. He was deep in other scenes. Finally he spoke. "Billie," he murmured, dreamfully, "what kind of pie do you like best?"

V

"Pie," said the oiler and the correspondent, agitatedly. "Don't talk about those things, blast you!"

"Well," said the cook, "I was just thinking about ham sandwiches, and—"

A night on the sea in an open boat is a long night. As darkness settled finally, the shine of the light, lifting from the sea in the south, changed to full gold. On the northern horizon a new light appeared, a small bluish gleam on the edge of the waters. These two lights were the furniture of the world. Otherwise there was nothing but waves.

Two men huddled in the stern, and distances were so magnificent in the dingey that the rower was enabled to keep his feet partly warmed by thrusting them under his companions. Their legs indeed extended far under the rowing-seat until they touched the feet of the captain forward. Sometimes, despite the efforts of the tired oarsman, a wave came piling into the boat, an icy wave of the night, and the chilling water soaked them anew. They would twist their bodies for a moment and groan, and sleep the dead sleep once more, while the water in the boat gurgled about them as the craft rocked.

The plan of the oiler and the correspondent was for one to row until he lost the ability, and then arouse the other from his sea-water couch in the bottom of the boat.

The oiler plied the oars until his head drooped forward, and the overpowering sleep blinded him. And he rowed yet afterward. Then he touched a man in the bottom of the boat, and called his name. "Will you spell me for a little while?" he said, meekly.

"Sure, Billie," said the correspondent, awakening and dragging himself to a sitting position. They exchanged places carefully, and the oiler, cuddling down in the sea-water at the cook's side, seemed to go to sleep instantly.

The particular violence of the sea had ceased. The waves came without snarling. The obligation of the man at the oars was to keep the boat headed so that the tilt of the rollers would not capsize her, and to preserve her from filling when the crests rushed past. The black waves were silent and hard to be seen in the darkness. Often one was almost upon the boat before the oarsman was aware.

In a low voice the correspondent addressed the captain. He was not sure that the captain was awake, although this iron man seemed to be always awake. "Captain, shall I keep her making for that light north, sir?"

The same steady voice answered him. "Yes. Keep it about two points off the port bow."

The cook had tied a life-belt around himself in order to get even the warmth which this clumsy cork contrivance could donate, and he seemed almost stove-like when a rower, whose teeth invariably chattered wildly as soon as he ceased his labor, dropped down to sleep.

The correspondent, as he rowed, looked down at the two men sleeping under foot. The cook's arm was around the oiler's shoulders, and, with their fragmentary clothing and haggard faces, they were the babes of the sea, a grotesque rendering of the old babes in the wood.

Later he must have grown stupid at his work, for suddenly there was a growling of water, and a crest came with a roar and a swash into the boat, and it was a wonder that it did not set the cook afloat in his life-belt. The cook continued to sleep, but the oiler sat up, blinking his eyes and shaking with the new cold.

"Oh, I'm awful sorry, Billie," said the correspondent, contritely.

"That's all right, old boy," said the oiler, and lay down again and was asleep.

Presently it seemed that even the captain dozed, and the correspondent thought that he was the one man afloat on all the oceans. The wind had a voice as it came over the waves, and it was sadder than the end.

There was a long, loud swishing astern of the boat, and a gleaming trail of phosphorescence, like blue flame, was furrowed on the black waters. It might have been made by a monstrous knife.

Then there came a stillness, while the correspondent breathed with the open mouth and looked at the sea.

Suddenly there was another swish and another long flash of bluish light, and this time it was alongside the boat, and might almost have been reached with an oar. The correspondent saw an enormous fin speed like a shadow through the water, hurling the crystalline spray and leaving the long glowing trail.

The correspondent looked over his shoulder at the captain. His face was hidden, and he seemed to be asleep. He looked at the babes of the sea. They certainly were asleep. So, being bereft of sympathy, he leaned a little way to one side and swore softly into the sea.

But the thing did not then leave the vicinity of the boat. Ahead or astern, on one side or the other, at intervals long or short, fled the long sparkling streak, and there was to be heard the whiroo of the dark fin. The speed and power of the thing was greatly to be admired. It cut the water like a gigantic and keen projectile.

The presence of this biding thing did not affect the man with the same horror that it would if he had been a picnicker. He simply looked at the sea dully and swore in an undertone.

Nevertheless, it is true that he did not wish to be alone with the thing. He wished one of his companions to awaken by chance and keep him company with it. But the captain hung motionless over the water-jar and the oiler and the cook in the bottom of the boat were plunged in slumber.

VI

"If I am going to be drowned—if I am going to be drowned—if I am going to be drowned, why, in the name of the seven mad gods, who rule the sea, was I allowed to come thus far and contemplate sand and trees?"

During this dismal night, it may be remarked that a man would conclude that it was really the intention of the seven mad gods to drown him, despite the abominable injustice of it. For it was certainly an abominable injustice to drown a man who had worked so hard, so hard. The man felt it would be a crime most unnatural. Other people had drowned at sea since galleys swarmed with painted sails, but still——

When it occurs to a man that nature does not regard him as important, and that she feels she would not maim the universe by disposing of him, he at first wishes to throw bricks at the temple, and he hates deeply the fact that there are no bricks and no temples. Any visible expression of nature would surely be pelleted with his jeers.

Then, if there be no tangible thing to hoot he feels, perhaps, the desire to confront a personification and indulge in pleas, bowed to one knee, and with hands supplicant, saying: "Yes, but I love myself."

A high cold star on a winter's night is the word he feels that she says to him. Thereafter he knows the pathos of his situation.

The men in the dingey had not discussed these matters, but each had, no doubt, reflected upon them in silence and according to his mind. There was seldom any expression upon their faces save the general one of complete weariness. Speech was devoted to the business of the boat.

To chime the notes of his emotion, a verse mysteriously entered the correspondent's head. He had even forgotten that he had forgotten this verse, but it suddenly was in his mind.

> *A soldier of the Legion lay dying in Algiers,*
> *There was lack of woman's nursing, there was dearth of woman's tears;*
> *But a comrade stood beside him, and he took that comrade's hand*
> *And he said: "I shall never see my own, my native land."*[3]

---

[3]Crane has skillfully condensed the lines of "Bingen on the Rhine" (1883) by Caroline E. S. Norton.

In his childhood, the correspondent had been made acquainted with the fact that a soldier of the Legion lay dying in Algiers, but he had never regarded the fact as important. Myriads of his school-fellows had informed him of the soldier's plight, but the dinning had naturally ended by making him perfectly indifferent. He had never considered it his affair that a soldier of the Legion lay dying in Algiers, nor had it appeared to him as a matter for sorrow. It was less to him than breaking of a pencil's point.

Now, however, it quaintly came to him as a human, living thing. It was no longer merely a picture of a few throes in the breast of a poet, meanwhile drinking tea and warming his feet at the grate; it was an actuality—stern, mournful, and fine.

The correspondent plainly saw the soldier. He lay on the sand with his feet out straight and still. While his pale left hand was upon his chest in an attempt to thwart the going of his life, the blood came between his fingers. In the far Algerian distance, a city of low square forms was set against a sky that was faint with the last sunset hues. The correspondent, plying the oars and dreaming of the slow and slower movements of the lips of the soldier, was moved by a profound and perfectly impersonal comprehension. He was sorry for the soldier of the Legion who lay dying in Algiers.

The thing which had followed the boat and waited had evidently grown bored at the delay. There was no longer to be heard the slash of the cut-water, and there was no longer the flame of the long trail. The light in the north still glimmered, but it was apparently no nearer to the boat. Sometimes the boom of the surf rang in the correspondent's ears, and he turned the craft seaward then and rowed harder. Southward, someone had evidently built a watch-fire on the beach. It was too low and too far to be seen, but it made a shimmering, roseate reflection upon the bluff back of it, and this could be discerned from the boat. The wind came stronger, and sometimes a wave suddenly raged out like a mountain-cat and there was to be seen the sheen and sparkle of a broken crest.

The captain, in the bow, moved on his water-jar and sat erect. "Pretty long night," he observed to the correspondent. He looked at the shore. "Those life-saving people take their time."

"Did you see that shark playing around?"

"Yes, I saw him. He was a big fellow, all right."

"Wish I had known you were awake."

Later the correspondent spoke into the bottom of the boat.

"Billie!" There was a slow and gradual disentanglement. "Billie, will you spell me?"

"Sure," said the oiler.

As soon as the correspondent touched the cold comfortable sea-water in the bottom of the boat, and had huddled close to the cook's life-belt he was deep in sleep, despite the fact that his teeth played all the popular airs. This sleep was so good to him that it was but a moment before he heard a voice call his name in a tone that demonstrated the last stages of exhaustion. "Will you spell me?"

"Sure, Billie."

The light in the north had mysteriously vanished, but the correspondent took his course from the wide-awake captain.

Later in the night they took the boat farther out to sea, and the captain directed the cook to take one oar at the stern and keep the boat facing the seas. He was to call out if he should hear the thunder of the surf. This plan enabled the oiler and the correspondent to get respite together. "We'll give those boys a chance to get into shape again," said the captain. They curled down and, after a few preliminary chatterings and trembles, slept once more the dead sleep. Neither knew they had bequeathed to the cook the company of another shark, or perhaps the same shark.

As the boat caroused on the waves, spray occasionally bumped over the side and gave them a fresh soaking, but this had no power to break their repose. The ominous slash of the wind and the water affected them as it would have affected mummies.

"Boys," said the cook, with the notes of every reluctance in his voice, "she's drifted in pretty close. I guess one of you had better take her to sea again." The correspondent, aroused, heard the crash of the toppled crests.

As he was rowing, the captain gave him some whiskey and water, and this steadied the chills out of him. "If I ever get ashore and anybody shows me even a photograph of an oar—"

At last there was a short conversation.

"Billie.... Billie, will you spell me?"

"Sure," said the oiler.

VII

When the correspondent again opened his eyes, the sea and the sky were each of the gray hue of the dawning. Later, carmine and gold was painted upon the waters. The morning appeared finally, in its splendor, with a sky of pure blue, and the sunlight flamed on the tips of the waves.

On the distant dunes were set many little black cottages, and a tall white windmill reared above them. No man, nor dog, nor bicycle appeared on the beach. The cottages might have formed a deserted village.

The voyagers scanned the shore. A conference was held in the boat. "Well," said the captain, "if no help is coming, we might better try to run through the surf right away. If we stay out here much longer we will be too weak to do anything for ourselves at all." The others silently acquiesced in this reasoning. The boat was headed for the beach. The correspondent wondered if none ever ascended the tall wind-tower, and if then they never looked seaward. This tower was a giant, standing with its back to the plight of the ants. It represented in a degree, to the correspondent, the serenity of nature amid the struggles of the individual—nature in the wind, and nature in the vision of men. She did not seem cruel to him then, nor beneficent, nor treacherous, nor wise. But she was indifferent, flatly indifferent. It is, perhaps, plausible that a man in this situation, impressed with the unconcern of the universe, should see the innumerable flaws of his life and have them taste wickedly in his mind and wish for another chance. A distinction between right and wrong seems absurdly clear to him, then, in this new ignorance of the grave-edge, and he understands that if he were given another opportunity he would mend his conduct and his words, and be better and brighter during an introduction, or at a tea.

"Now, boys," said the captain, "she is going to swamp sure. All we can do is to work her in as far as possible, and then when she swamps, pile out and scramble for the beach. Keep cool now and don't jump until she swamps sure."

The oiler took the oars. Over his shoulders he scanned the surf. "Captain," he said, "I think I'd better bring her about, and keep her head-on to the seas and back her in."

"All right, Billie," said the captain. "Back her in." The oiler swung the boat then and, seated in the stern, the cook and the correspondent were obliged to look over their shoulders to contemplate the lonely and indifferent shore.

The monstrous inshore rollers heaved the boat high until the men were again enabled to see the white sheets of water scudding up the slanted beach. "We won't get in very close," said the captain. Each time a man could wrest his attention from the rollers, he turned his glance toward the shore, and in the expression of the eyes during this contemplation there was a singular quality. The correspondent, observing the others, knew that they were not afraid, but the full meaning of their glances was shrouded.

As for himself, he was too tired to grapple fundamentally with the fact. He tried to coerce his mind into thinking of it, but the mind was dominated at this time by the muscles, and the muscles said they did not care. It merely occurred to him that if he should drown it would be a shame.

There were no hurried words, no pallor, no plain agitation. The men simply looked at the shore. "Now, remember to get well clear of the boat when you jump," said the captain.

Seaward the crest of a roller suddenly fell with a thunderous crash, and the long white comber came roaring down upon the boat.

"Steady now," said the captain. The men were silent. They turned their eyes from the shore to the comber and waited. The boat slid up the incline, leaped at the furious top, bounced over it, and swung down the long back of the waves. Some water had been shipped and the cook bailed it out.

But the next crest crashed also. The tumbling boiling flood of white water caught the boat and whirled it almost perpendicular. Water swarmed in from all sides. The correspondent had his hands on the gunwale at this time, and when the water entered at that place he swiftly withdrew his fingers, as if he objected to wetting them.

The little boat, drunken with this weight of water, reeled and snuggled deeper into the sea.

"Bail her out, cook! Bail her out," said the captain.

"All right, captain," said the cook.

"Now, boys, the next one will do for us, sure," said the oiler. "Mind to jump clear of the boat."

The third wave moved forward, huge, furious, implacable. It fairly swallowed the dingey, and almost simultaneously the men tumbled into the sea. A piece of life-belt had lain in the bottom of the boat, and as the correspondent went overboard he held this to his chest with his left hand.

The January water was icy, and he reflected immediately that it was colder than he had expected to find it off the coast of Florida. This appeared to his dazed mind as a fact important enough to be noted at the time. The coldness of the water was sad; it was tragic. This fact was somehow mixed and confused with his opinion of his own situation that it seemed almost a proper reason for tears. The water was cold.

When he came to the surface he was conscious of little but the noisy water. Afterward he saw his companions in the sea. The oiler was ahead in the race. He was swimming strongly and rapidly. Off to the correspondent's left, the cook's great white and corked back bulged out of the water, and in the rear the captain was hanging with his one good hand to the keel of the overturned dingey.

There is a certain immovable quality to a shore, and the correspondent wondered at it amid the confusion of the sea.

It seemed also very attractive, but the correspondent knew that it was a long journey, and he paddled leisurely. The piece of life-preserver lay under him, and sometimes he whirled down the incline of a wave as if he were on a hand-sled.

But finally he arrived at a place in the sea where travel was beset with difficulty. He did not pause swimming to inquire what manner of current had caught him, but there his progress ceased. The shore was set before him like a bit of scenery on a stage, and he looked at it and understood with his eyes each detail of it.

As the cook passed, much farther to the left, the captain was calling to him, "Turn over on your back, cook! Turn over on your back and use the oar."

"All right, sir." The cook turned on his back, and, paddling with an oar, went ahead as if he were a canoe.

Presently the boat also passed to the left of the correspondent with the captain clinging with one hand to the keel. He would have appeared like a man raising himself to look over a board fence, if it were not for the extraordinary gymnastics of the boat. The correspondent marvelled that the captain could still hold to it.

They passed on, nearer to shore—the oiler, the cook, the captain—and following them went the water-jar, bouncing gayly over the seas.

The correspondent remained in the grip of this strange new enemy—a current. The shore, with its white slope of sand and its green bluff, topped with little silent cottages, was spread like a picture before him. It was very near to him then, but he was impressed as one who in a gallery looks at a scene from Brittany or Algiers.

He thought: "I am going to drown? Can it be possible? Can it be possible? Can it be possible? Perhaps an individual must consider his own death to be the final phenomenon of nature.

But later a wave perhaps whirled him out of this small deadly current, for he found suddenly that he could again make progress toward the shore. Later still, he was aware that the captain, clinging with one hand to the keel of the dingey, had his face turned away from the shore and toward him, and was calling his name. "Come to the boat! Come to the boat!"

In his struggle to reach the captain and the boat, he reflected that when one gets properly wearied, drowning must really be a comfortable arrangement, a cessation of hostilities accompanied by a large degree of relief, and he was glad of it, for the main thing in his mind for some moments had been horror of the temporary agony. He did not wish to be hurt.

Presently he saw a man running along the shore. He was undressing with most remarkable speed. Coat, trousers, shirt, everything flew magically off him.

"Come to the boat," called the captain.

"All right, captain." As the correspondent paddled, he saw the captain let himself down to bottom and leave the boat. Then the correspondent performed his one little marvel of the voyage. A large wave caught him and flung him with ease and supreme speed completely over the boat and far beyond it. It struck him even then as an event in gymnastics, and a true miracle of the sea. An overturned boat in the surf is not a plaything to a swimming man.

The correspondent arrived in water that reached only to his waist, but his condition did not enable him to stand for more than a moment. Each wave knocked him into a heap, and the under-tow pulled at him.

Then he saw the man who had been running and undressing, and undressing and running, come bounding into the water. He dragged ashore the cook, and then waded toward the captain, but the captain waved him away, and sent him to the correspondent. He was naked, naked as a tree in winter, but a halo was about his head, and he shone like a saint. He gave a strong pull, and a long drag, and a bully heave at the correspondent's hand. The correspondent, schooled in the minor formulae, said: "Thanks, old man." But suddenly the man cried: "What's that?" He pointed a swift finger. The correspondent said: "Go."

In the shallows, face downward, lay the oiler. His forehead touched sand that was periodically, between each wave, clear of the sea.

The correspondent did not know all that transpired afterward. When he achieved safe ground he fell, striking the sand with each particular part of his body. It was as if he had dropped from a roof, but the thud was grateful to him.

It seems that instantly the beach was populated with men with blankets, clothes, and flasks, and women with coffee-pots and all the remedies sacred to their minds. The welcome of the land to the men from the sea was warm and generous, but a still and dripping shape was carried slowly up the beach, and the land's welcome for it could only be the different and sinister hospitality of the grave.

When it came night, the white waves paced to and fro in the moonlight, and the wind brought the sound of the great sea's voice to the men on shore, and they felt that they could then be interpreters.

1897

The Bride Comes to Yellow Sky

I

The great Pullman was whirling onward with such dignity of motion that a glance from the window seemed simply to prove that the plains of Texas were pouring eastward. Vast flats of green grass, dull-hued spaces of mesquite and cactus, little groups of frame houses, woods of light and tender trees, all were sweeping into the east, sweeping over the horizon, a precipice.

A newly married pair had boarded this coach at San Antonio. The man's face was reddened from many days in the wind and sun, and a direct result of his new black clothes was that his brick-colored hands were constantly performing in a most conscious fashion. From time to time he looked down respectfully at his attire. He sat with a hand on each knee, like a man waiting in a barber's shop. The glances he devoted to other passengers were furtive and shy.

The bride was not pretty, nor was she very young. She wore a dress of blue cashmere, with small reservations of velvet here and there and with steel buttons abounding. She continually twisted her head to regard her puff sleeves, very stiff, straight, and high. They embarrassed her. It was quite apparent that she had cooked, and that she expected to cook, dutifully. The blushes caused by the careless scrutiny of some passengers as she had entered the car were strange to see upon this plain, under-class countenance, which was drawn in placid, almost emotionless lines.

They were evidently very happy. "Ever been in a parlor-car before?" he asked, smiling with delight.

"No," she answered. "I never was. It's fine, ain't it?"

"Great! And then after a while we'll go forward to the diner and get a big layout. Finest meal in the world. Charge a dollar."

"Oh, do they?" cried the bride. "Charge a dollar? Why, that's too much—for us—ain't it, Jack?"

"Not this trip, anyhow," he answered bravely. "We're going to go the whole thing."

Later, he explained to her about the trains. "You see, it's a thousand miles from one end of Texas to the other, and this train runs right across it and never stops but four times." He had the pride of an owner. He pointed out to her the dazzling fittings of the coach, and in truth her eyes opened wider as she contemplated the sea-green figured velvet, the shining brass, silver, and glass, the wood that gleamed as darkly brilliant as the surface of a pool of oil. At one end a bronze figure sturdily held a support for a separated chamber, and at convenient places on the ceiling were frescoes in olive and silver.

To the minds of the pair, their surroundings reflected the glory of their marriage that morning in San Antonio. This was the environment of their new estate, and the man's face in particular beamed with an elation that made him appear ridiculous to the negro porter. This individual at times surveyed them from afar with an amused and superior grin. On other occasions he bullied them with skill in ways that did not make it exactly plain to them that they were being bullied. He subtly used all the manners of the most unconquerable kind of snobbery. He oppressed them, but of this oppression they had small knowledge, and they speedily forgot that infrequently a number of travelers covered them with stares of derisive enjoyment. Historically there was supposed to be something infinitely humorous in their situation.

"We are due in Yellow Sky at 3.42," he said, looking tenderly into her eyes.

"Oh, are we?" she said, as if she had not been aware of it. To evince surprise at her husband's statement was part of her wifely amiability. She took from a pocket a little silver watch, and as she held it before her and stared at it with a frown of attention, the new husband's face shone.

"I bought it in San Anton' from a friend of mine," he told her gleefully.

"It's seventeen minutes past twelve," she said, looking up at him with a kind of shy and clumsy coquetry. A passenger, noting this play, grew excessively sardonic, and winked at himself in one of the numerous mirrors.

At last they went to the dining-car. Two rows of negro waiters, in glowing white suits, surveyed their entrance with the interest and also the equanimity of men who had been forewarned. The pair fell to the lot of a waiter who happened to feel pleasure in steering them through their meal. He viewed them with the manner of a fatherly pilot, his countenance radiant with benevolence. The patronage, entwined with the ordinary deference, was not plain to them. And yet, as they returned to their coach, they showed in their faces a sense of escape.

To the left, miles down a long purple slope, was a little ribbon of mist where moved the keening Rio Grande. The train was approaching it at an angle, and the apex was Yellow Sky. Presently it was apparent that, as the distance from Yellow Sky grew shorter, the husband became commensurately restless. His brick-red hands were more insistent in their prominence. Occasionally he was even rather absentminded and far-away when the bride leaned forward and addressed him.

As a matter of truth, Jack Potter was beginning to find the shadow of a deed weigh upon him like a leaden slab. He, the town marshal of Yellow Sky, a man known, liked, and feared in his corner, a prominent person, had gone to San Antonio to meet a girl he believed he loved, and there, after the usual prayers, had actually induced her to marry him, without consulting Yellow Sky for any part of the transaction. He was now bringing his bride before an innocent and unsuspecting community.

Of course, people in Yellow Sky married as it pleased them, in accordance with a general custom; but such was Potter's thought of his duty to his friends, or of their idea of his duty, or of an unspoken form which does not control men in these matters, that he felt he was heinous. He had committed an extraordinary crime. Face to face with this girl in San Antonio, and spurred by his sharp impulse, he had gone headlong over all the social hedges. At San Antonio he was like a man hidden in the dark. A knife to sever any friendly duty, any form, was easy to his hand in that remote city. But the hour of Yellow Sky, the hour of daylight, was approaching.

He knew full well that his marriage was an important thing to his town. It could only be exceeded by the burning of the new hotel. His friends could not forgive him. Frequently he had reflected on the advisability of telling them by telegraph, but a new cowardice had been upon him. He feared to do it. And now the train was hurrying him toward a scene of amazement, glee, and reproach. He glanced out of the window at the line of haze swinging slowly in towards the train.

Yellow Sky had a kind of brass band, which played painfully, to the delight of the populace. He laughed without heart as he thought of it. If the citizens could dream of his prospective arrival with his bride, they would parade the band at the station and escort them, amid cheers and laughing congratulations, to his adobe home.

He resolved that he would use all the devices of speed and plains-craft in making the journey from the station to his house. Once within that safe citadel, he could issue some sort of a vocal bulletin, and then not go among the citizens until they had time to wear off a little of their enthusiasm.

The bride looked anxiously at him. "What's worrying you, Jack?"

He laughed again, "I'm not worrying, girl. I'm only thinking of Yellow Sky."

She flushed in comprehension.

A sense of mutual guilt invaded their minds and developed a finer tenderness. They looked at each other with eyes softly aglow. But Potter often laughed the same nervous laugh. The flush upon the bride's face seemed quite permanent.

The traitor to the feelings of Yellow Sky narrowly watched the speeding landscape. "We're nearly there," he said.

Presently the porter came and announced the proximity of Potter's home. He held a brush in his hand and, with all his airy superiority gone, he brushed Potter's new clothes as the latter slowly turned this way and that way. Potter fumbled out a coin and gave it to the porter, as he had seen others do. It was a heavy and muscle-bound business, as that of a man shoeing his first horse.

The porter took their bag, and as the train began to slow they moved forward to the hooded platform of the car. Presently the two engines and their long string of coaches rushed into the station of Yellow Sky.

"They have to take water here," said Potter, from a constricted throat and in mournful cadence, as one announcing death. Before the train stopped, his eye had swept the length of the platform, and he was glad and astonished to see there was none upon it but the station-agent, who, with a slightly hurried and anxious air, was walking toward the water-tanks. When the train had halted, the porter alighted first and placed in position a little temporary step.

"Come on, girl," said Potter hoarsely. As he helped her down they each laughed on a false note. He took the bag from the negro, and bade his wife cling to his arm. As they slunk rapidly away, his hang-dog glance perceived that they were unloading the two trunks, and also that the station-agent far ahead near the baggage-car had turned and was running toward him, making gestures. He laughed, and groaned as he laughed, when he noted the first effect of his marital bliss upon Yellow Sky. He gripped his wife's arm firmly to his side, and they fled. Behind them the porter stood chuckling fatuously.

II

The California Express on the Southern Railway was due at Yellow Sky in twenty-one minutes. There were six men at the bar of the "Weary Gentleman" saloon. One was a drummer who talked a great deal and rapidly; three were Texans who did not care to talk at that time; and two were Mexican sheep-herders who did not talk as a general practice in the "Weary Gentleman" saloon. The barkeeper's dog lay on the board walk that crossed in front of the door. His head was on his paws, and he glanced drowsily here and there with the constant vigilance of a dog that is kicked on occasion. Across the sandy street were some vivid green grass plots, so wonderful in appearance amid the sands that burned near them in a blazing sun that they caused a doubt in the mind. They exactly resembled the grass mats used to represent lawns on the stage. At the cooler end of the railway station a man without a coat sat in a tilted chair and smoked his pipe. The fresh-cut bank of the Rio Grande circled near the town, and there could be seen beyond it a great, plum-colored plain of mesquite.

Save for the busy drummer and his companions in the saloon, Yellow Sky was dozing. The new-comer leaned gracefully upon the bar, and recited many tales with the confidence of a bard who has come upon a new field.

"——and at the moment that the old man fell down stairs with the bureau in his arms, the old woman was coming up with two scuttles of coal, and, of course—"

The drummer's tale was interrupted by a young man who suddenly appeared in the open door. He cried: "Scratchy Wilson's drunk, and has turned loose with both hands." The two Mexicans at once set down their glasses and faded out of the rear entrance of the saloon.

The drummer, innocent and jocular, answered: "All right, old man. S'pose he has. Come in and have a drink, anyhow."

But the information had made such an obvious cleft in every skull in the room that the drummer was obliged to see its importance. All had become instantly solemn. "Say," said he, mystified, "what is this?" His three companions made the introductory gesture of eloquent speech, but the young man at the door forestalled them.

"It means, my friend," he answered, as he came into the saloon, "that for the next two hours this town won't be a health resort."

The barkeeper went to the door and locked and barred it. Reaching out of the window, he pulled in heavy wooden shutters and barred them. Immediately a solemn, chapel-like gloom was upon the place. The drummer was looking from one to another.

"But, say," he cried, "what is this, anyhow? You don't mean there is going to be a gun-fight?"

"Don't know whether there'll be a fight or not," answered one man grimly. "But there'll be some shootin'—some good shootin'."

The young man who had warned them waved his hand. "Oh, there'll be a fight fast enough, if anyone wants it. Anybody can get a fight out there in the street. There's a fight just waiting."

The drummer seemed to be swayed between the interest of a foreigner and a perception of personal danger.

"What did you say his name was?" he asked.

"Scratchy Wilson," they answered in chorus.

"And will he kill anybody? What are you going to do? Does this happen often? Does he rampage around like this once a week or so? Can he break in that door?"

"No, he can't break down that door," replied the barkeeper. "He's tried it three times. But when he comes you'd better lay down on the floor, stranger. He's dead sure to shoot at it, and a bullet may come through."

Thereafter the drummer kept a strict eye upon the door. The time had not yet been called for him to hug the floor, but, as a minor precaution, he sidled near to the wall. "Will he kill anybody?" he said again.

The men laughed low and scornfully at the question.

"He's out to shoot, and he's out for trouble. Don't see any good in experimentin' with him."

"But what do you do in a case like this? What do you do?"

A man responded: "Why, he and Jack Potter—"

"But," in chorus, the other men interrupted, "Jack Potter's in San Anton'."

"Well, who is he? What's he got to do with it?"

"Oh, he's the town marshal. He goes out and fights Scratchy when he gets on one of these tears."

"Wow," said the drummer, mopping his brow. "Nice job he's got."

The voices had toned away to mere whisperings. The drummer wished to ask further questions which were born of an increasing anxiety and bewilderment; but when he attempted them, the men merely looked at him in irritation and motioned him to remain silent. A tense waiting hush was upon them. In the deep shadows of the room their eyes shone as they listened for sounds from the street. One man made three gestures at the

barkeeper, and the latter, moving like a ghost, handed him a glass and a bottle. The man poured a full glass of whisky, and set down the bottle noiselessly. He gulped the whisky in a swallow, and turned again toward the door
in immovable silence. The drummer saw that the barkeeper, without a
sound, had taken a Winchester from beneath the bar. Later he saw this individual beckoning to him, so he tiptoed across the room.

"You better come with me back of the bar."

"No, thanks," said the drummer, perspiring. "I'd rather be where I can
make a break for the back door."

Whereupon the man of bottles made a kindly but peremptory gesture.
The drummer obeyed it, and finding himself seated on a box with his head
below the level of the bar, balm was laid upon his soul at sight of various
zinc and copper fittings that bore a resemblance to armorplate. The barkeeper took a seat comfortably upon an adjacent box.

"You see," he whispered, "this here Scratchy Wilson is a wonder with a
gun—a perfect wonder—and when he goes on the war trail, we hunt our
holes—naturally. He's about the last one of the old gang that used to hang
out along the river here. He's a terror when he's drunk. When he's sober
he's all right—kind of simple— wouldn't hurt a fly—nicest fellow in town.
But when he's drunk—whoo!"

There were periods of stillness. "I wish Jack Potter was back from San
Anton'," said the barkeeper. "He shot Wilson up once—in the leg—and he
would sail in and pull out the kinks in this thing."

Presently they heard from a distance the sound of a shot, followed by
three wild yowls. It instantly removed a bond from the men in the darkened
saloon. There was a shuffling of feet. They looked at each other. "Here he
comes," they said.

III

A man in a maroon-colored flannel shirt, which had been purchased for purposes of decoration and made, principally, by some Jewish women on the
east side of New York, rounded a corner and walked into the middle of the
main street of Yellow Sky. In either hand the man held a long, heavy, blue-
black revolver. Often he yelled, and these cries rang through a semblance of
a deserted village, shrilly flying over the roofs in a volume that seemed to
have no relation to the ordinary vocal strength of a man. It was as if the
surrounding stillness formed the arch of a tomb over him. These cries of ferocious challenge rang against walls of silence. And his boots had red tops
with gilded imprints, of the kind beloved in winter by little sledding boys on
the hillsides of New England.

The man's face flamed in a rage begot of whisky. His eyes, rolling and
yet keen for ambush, hunted the still doorways and windows. He walked
with the creeping movement of the midnight cat. As it occurred to him, he
roared menacing information. The long revolvers in his hands were as easy

as straws; they were moved with an electric swiftness. The little fingers of each hand played sometimes in a musician's way. Plain from the low collar of the shirt, the cords of his neck straightened and sank, straightened and sank, as passion moved him. The only sounds were his terrible invitations. The calm adobes preserved their demeanor at the passing of this small thing in the middle of the street.

There was no offer of fight; no offer of fight. The man called to the sky. There were no attractions. He bellowed and fumed and swayed his revolvers here and everywhere.

The dog of the barkeeper of the "Weary Gentleman" saloon had not appreciated the advance of events. He yet lay dozing in front of his master's door. At sight of the dog, the man paused and raised his revolver humorously. At sight of the man, the dog sprang up and walked diagonally away, with a sullen head, and growling. The man yelled, and the dog broke into a gallop. As it was about to enter an alley, there was a loud noise, a whistling, and something spat the ground directly before it. The dog screamed, and, wheeling in terror, galloped headlong in a new direction. Again there was a noise, a whistling, and sand was kicked viciously before it. Fear-stricken, the dog turned and flurried like an animal in a pen. The man stood laughing, his weapons at his hips.

Ultimately the man was attracted by the closed door of the "Weary Gentleman" saloon. He went to it, and hammering with a revolver, demanded drink.

The door remaining imperturbable, he picked up a bit of paper from the walk and nailed it to the framework with a knife. He then turned his back contemptuously upon this popular resort, and walking to the opposite side of the street, and spinning there on his heel quickly and lithely, fired at the bit of paper. He missed it by a half inch. He swore at himself, and went away. Later, he comfortably fusilladed the windows of his most intimate friend. The man was playing with this town. It was a toy for him.

But still there was no offer of fight. The name of Jack Potter, his ancient antagonist, entered his mind, and he concluded that it would be a glad thing if he should go to Potter's house and by bombardment induce him to come out and fight. He moved in the direction of his desire, chanting Apache scalp-music.

When he arrived at it, Potter's house presented the same still front as had the other adobes. Taking up a strategic position, the man howled a challenge. But this house regarded him as might a great stone god. It gave no sign. After a decent wait, the man howled further challenges, mingling with them wonderful epithets.

Presently there came the spectacle of a man churning himself into deepest rage over the immobility of a house. He fumed at it as the winter wind attacks a prairie cabin in the North. To the distance there should have gone the sound of a tumult like the fighting of 200 Mexicans. As necessity bade him, he paused for breath or to reload his revolvers.

IV

Potter and his bride walked sheepishly and with speed. Sometimes they laughed together shamefacedly and low.

"Next corner, dear," he said finally.

They put forth the efforts of a pair walking bowed against a strong wind. Potter was about to raise a finger to point the first appearance of the new home when, as they circled the corner, they came face to face with a man in a maroon-colored shirt who was feverishly pushing cartridges into a large revolver. Upon the instant the man dropped his revolver to the ground, and, like lightning, whipped another from its holster. The second weapon was aimed at the bridegroom's chest.

There was a silence. Potter's mouth seemed to be merely a grave for his tongue. He exhibited an instinct to at once loosen his arm from the woman's grip, and he dropped the bag to the sand. As for the bride, her face had gone as yellow as old cloth. She was a slave to hideous rites gazing at the apparitional snake.

The two men faced each other at a distance of three paces. He of the revolver smiled with a new and quiet ferocity.

"Tried to sneak up on me," he said. "Tried to sneak up on me!" His eyes grew more baleful. As Potter made a slight movement, the man thrust his revolver venomously forward. "No, don't you do it, Jack Potter. Don't you move a finger toward a gun just yet. Don't you move an eyelash. The time has come for me to settle with you, and I'm goin' to do it my own way and loaf along with no interferin'. So if you don't want a gun bent on you, just mind what I tell you."

Potter looked at his enemy. "I ain't got a gun on me, Scratchy," he said. "Honest, I ain't." He was stiffening and steadying, but yet somewhere at the back of his mind a vision of the Pullman floated, the sea-green figured velvet, the shining brass, silver, and glass, the wood that gleamed as darkly brilliant as the surface of a pool of oil—all the glory of the marriage, the environment of the new estate. "You know I fight when it comes to fighting, Scratchy Wilson, but I ain't got a gun on me. You'll have to do all the shootin' yourself."

His enemy's face went livid. He stepped forward and lashed his weapon to and fro before Potter's chest. "Don't you tell me you ain't got no gun on you, you whelp. Don't tell me no lie like that. There ain't a man in Texas ever seen you without no gun. Don't take me for no kid." His eyes blazed with light, and his throat worked like a pump.

"I ain't takin' you for no kid," answered Potter. His heels had not moved an inch backward. "I'm takin' you for a——fool. I tell you I ain't got a gun, and I ain't. If you're goin' to shoot me up, you better begin now. You'll never get a chance like this again."

So much enforced reasoning had told on Wilson's rage. He was calmer. "If you ain't got a gun, why ain't you got a gun?" he sneered. "Been to Sunday-school?"

"I ain't got a gun because I've just come from San Anton' with my wife. I'm married," said Potter. "And if I'd thought there was going to be any galoots like you prowling around when I brought my wife home, I'd had a gun, and don't you forget it."

"Married!" said Scratchy, not at all comprehending.

"Yes, married. I'm married," said Potter distinctly.

"Married?" said Scratchy. Seemingly for the first time he saw the drooping, drowning woman at the other man's side. "No!" he said. He was like a creature allowed a glimpse of another world. He moved a pace backward, and his arm with the revolver dropped to his side. "Is this the lady?" he asked.

"Yes, this is the lady," answered Potter.

There was another period of silence.

"Well," said Wilson at last, slowly, "I s'pose it's all off now."

"It's all off if you say so, Scratchy. You know I didn't make the trouble." Potter lifted his valise.

"Well, I 'low it's off, Jack," said Wilson. He was looking at the ground. "Married!" He was not a student of chivalry; it was merely that in the presence of this foreign condition he was a simple child of the earlier plains. He picked up his starboard revolver, and placing both weapons in their holsters, he went away. His feet made funnel-shaped tracks in the heavy sand.

1898

from **The Black Riders and Other Lines**[1]

God Lay Dead in Heaven

God lay dead in Heaven;
Angels sang the hymn of the end;
Purple winds went moaning,
Their wings drip-dripping
With blood   5
That fell upon the earth.
It, groaning thing,
Turned black and sank.
Then from the far caverns
Of dead sins   10
Came monsters, livid with desire.
They fought,
Wrangled over the world,
A morsel.
But of all sadness this was sad,—   15

---

[1]In the two volumes of verse that he published, Crane chose to omit titles for individual poems. Poems in *The Black Riders and Other Lines* were identified by Roman numerals at the beginning of each poem. The decision to omit titles for individual poems reflects Crane's desire to present his innovative writing in an appropriately *avant garde* format. (Here the editors have included first lines as titles for reference purposes.)

A woman's arms tried to shield
The head of a sleeping man
From the jaws of the final beast.

1895

from **War Is Kind**

Do Not Weep, Maiden, for War Is Kind

Do not weep, maiden, for war is kind.
Because your lover threw wild hands toward the sky
And the affrighted steed ran on alone,
Do not weep.
War is kind.   5

    Hoarse, booming drums of the regiment
    Little souls who thirst for fight,
    These men were born to drill and die
    The unexplained glory flies above them
    Great is the battle-god, great, and his kingdom—   10
    A field where a thousand corpses lie.

Do not weep, babe, for war is kind.
Because your father tumbled in the yellow trenches,
Raged at his breast, gulped and died,
Do not weep.   15
War is kind.

    Swift, blazing flag of the regiment
    Eagle with crest of red and gold,
    These men were born to drill and die
    Point for them the virtue of slaughter   20
    Make plain to them the excellence of killing
    And a field where a thousand corpses lie.

Mother whose heart hung humble as a button
On the bright splendid shroud of your son,
Do not weep.   25
War is kind.

1896

The Impact of a Dollar upon the Heart

The impact of a dollar upon the heart
Smiles warm red light

Sweeping from the hearth rosily upon the white table,
With the hanging cool velvet shadows
Moving softly upon the door. 5
The impact of a million dollars
Is a crash of flunkeys
And yawning emblems of Persia
Cheeked against oak, France and a sabre,
The outcry of old Beauty 10
Whored by pimping merchants
To submission before wine and chatter.
Silly rich peasants stamp the carpets of men,
Dead men who dreamed fragrance and light
Into their woof, their lives; 15
The rug of an honest bear
Under the feet of a cryptic slave
Who speaks always of baubles
Forgetting place, multitude, work and state,
Champing and mouthing of hats, 20
Making ratful squeak of hats,
Hats.

1898

A Man Said to the Universe

A man said to the universe:
"Sir, I exist!"
"However," replied the universe,
"The fact has not created in me
"A sense of obligation." 5

1899

A Newspaper Is a Collection of Half-Injustices

A newspaper is a collection of half-injustices
Which, bawled by boys from mile to mile,
Spreads its curious opinion
To a million merciful and sneering men,
While families cuddle the joys of the fireside 5
When spurred by tale of dire lone agony.
A newspaper is a court
Where every one is kindly and unfairly tried
By a squalor of honest men.
A newspaper is a market 10

Where wisdom sells its freedom
And melons are crowned by the crowd.
A newspaper is a game
Where his error scores the player victory
While another's skill wins death.   15
A newspaper is a symbol;
It is fetless life's chronicle,
A collection of loud tales
Concentrating eternal stupidities,
That in remote ages lived unhaltered,   20
Roaming through a fenceless world.

                                                          1899

There Was a Man with Tongue of Wood

There was a man with tongue of wood
Who essayed to sing
And in truth it was lamentable
But there was one who heard
The clip-clapper of this tongue of wood   5
And knew what the man
Wished to sing
And with that the singer was content.

                                                          1899

from **Uncollected Poems**

Chant You Loud of Punishments

Chant you loud of punishments,
Of the twisting of the heart's poor strings
Of the crash of the lightning's fierce revenge.

Then sing I of the supple-souled men
And the strong, strong gods   5
That shall meet in times hereafter And the amaze of the gods
At the strength of the men. —The strong, strong gods—
    —And the supple-souled men—   10

                                                          1929

A Selection of Poetry by Late-Nineteenth-Century American Women

Except Emily Dickinson, whose assumed "difference" acts as a *cordon sanitaire* separating her from her peers, nineteenth-century women poets are the most maligned group of writers in American literary history. Defining themselves in terms of their resistance to nineteenth-century genteel poetics, early modernists treated nineteenth-century American poetry globally as an overly polite or, worse, excessively sentimental literature. Although the prestige of male poets such as Henry Wadsworth Longfellow and Oliver Wendell Holmes was diminished through this maneuver, their devaluation was slight in comparison to that suffered by their female peers. Made irresistibly comic by Twain's Emmeline Grangerford in *Huckleberry Finn*, the figure of the nineteenth-century "poetess" came to epitomize the worst of nineteenth-century versifying. Sentimental, foolish, addicted to clichés, and morbidly obsessed with death, the "poetess" joined the "old maid" and the "blue-stocking" as a butt for popular humor and a target for sometimes savage critical attack.

In recent years interest in nineteenth-century women's poetry has revived but focused mainly on poets from the first half of the century, such as Lydia Sigourney and Frances Osgood, who, like Harriet Beecher Stowe, explored the power of sentiment—or feeling—to sustain familial bonds and motivate socially progressive change. With a few exceptions (notably, Frances Ellen Watkins Harper and Emma Lazarus), little attention has been paid to poets writing after 1865. Though welcome, this new interest has continued to reinforce the critical misperception that nineteenth-century American women's poetry is the homogeneous product of northeastern white women writing in the "sentimental" tradition. Nothing could be farther from the truth. By the end of the nineteenth century, women poets came from every ethnic group, every walk of life, and every region of the country. What is more, they brought their differences with them.

To understand the development of late-nineteenth-century American women's poetry, one should turn first to the major venues in which it was marketed—newspapers and periodicals. Despised by the early modernists, who favored the avant-garde "little magazines," these venues were not without their virtues. In particular, they provided open spaces where new poets were all but guaranteed a hearing. Since, it seems, every special-interest group in society had its own newspaper or journal, from labor groups and Spiritualists to new immigrant populations and individual Native American tribes, the very diversity of these outlets also ensured that there would be diversity among contributors. If these media published a good deal of poorly crafted poetry, they also made poetry a highly accessible art form. Any woman (the message went) could write poetry; most women probably did.

Under such conditions, not surprisingly, serious women poets—as well as the Emmeline Grangerford variety—flourished. Taking advantage of the print media's rapacious need for fresh copy, these women filled the "poet's corner" of their local newspapers, as well as the better literary periodicals (*Harper's* and *Atlantic*, for instance), with their verse. For many of these women, as for Dickinson, poetry was a site for exploration and experimentation—not for reinforcing old truths. They used it as a vehicle by which to test possibilities for themselves and to address their social, political, and spiritual concerns, from matters of faith and doubt as in Celia Thaxter's "Wherefore" and Sarah B. Piatt's "We Two" to those of desire and disenchantment as in Jewett's "I Speak Your Name." Coming at the end of a century witnessing massive changes in women's social position and personal expectations, their poetry maps their evolution as emergent modern women or, as the nineteenth century itself put it, as "new women."

To bring together a collection of late-nineteenth-century American women's poetry, and to give Piatt her own section, is to present a group of very diverse voices. No selection this brief can possibly do justice to this diversity. However, certain myths about late-nineteenth-century American women's poetry—besides its homogeneity—can be laid to rest: the first and most important is that these writers were uniformly sentimental; the second, that their handling of poetic strategies was uniformly uninspired and conventional; and the third, often said of Dickinson herself, that all they wrote about was death (*pace* Emmeline).

It has been so taken for granted that nineteenth-century American women's writing is uniformly sentimental that even scholars seeking to retrieve it have spent most of their critical energy defending sentimentalism itself. Yet as Piatt's "His Mother's Way" suggests, many nineteenth-century women writers, especially in the latter part of the century, found sentimentalism problematic as a vehicle by which to hold families together or effect social change. Although the mother in this poem clearly has the high moral ground over her bullish mate (whose solution to the problem of the homeless is pistols and prison), her own power to affect him is radically undermined by her excessive reliance on tears. Along with critiquing the efficacy of excessive feeling, especially when isolated from other considerations (a modern parallel might be conservative responses to the "bleeding heart liberal"), Piatt's poem also suggests that by the second half of the century women had developed a good deal of irony about themselves and about the very capacity to feel with which they were socially identified. Poems such as Thaxter's "In Kittery Churchyard," Piatt's "Shapes of a Soul" and "The Palace-Burner," and Ella Wheeler Wilcox's "Illusion" all implicitly or explicitly use irony as a means of self-distancing. These are complex, sophisticated poems in which the speakers themselves approach their own emotional engagement suspiciously. As such, they are at the furthest remove from sentimentality.

If the uniform sentimentality of late-nineteenth-century American women's poetry turns out on closer inspection to be an unfair generalization, so does the charge that the poetry, like Emmeline Grangerford's, is badly or conventionally written. Alice Dunbar-Nelson, the wife of the well-known African American poet Paul Laurence Dunbar, for instance, experiments with free verse. Even when these poets used traditional forms, moreover, they did not necessarily treat them conventionally. On the contrary. By using multiple voices, fragmented narratives, and irregular and broken rhythms, Piatt, in particular, roughens the surface of her verse.

Finally, in terms of content, late-nineteenth-century women's poetry, far from being obsessed with death, turns out to be as diverse as the women who authored it. Born on a slave-holding plantation outside Lexington, Kentucky, in 1836 and marrying a northerner in 1861, Piatt, for instance, uses the Civil War as a dividing line between two worlds, two ways of life, both of which were profoundly alienating to her. Wilcox—a "flapper" before her time—was an internationally known poet whose writing was touched by scandal. Much of her poetry seems staid by today's standards, but her *Poems of Passion* (1883) was notorious in its own day.

Striking differences divide the New England poets reprinted here, but marginalization shapes the work of both Jewett, a teacher of medieval literature at Wellesley College and a lesbian, and Eastman, a Berkshire farm girl who married Dr. Charles Eastman (Ohiyesa) and spent much of her life in the Dakotas laboring among her husband's people. In each case the individual poets' content and approach were determined by their differing social and political commitments. Nor is this any less true of E. Pauline Johnson (Tekahionwake), a Canadian Mohawk, who explicitly used her poetry to bridge the social and racial groups that were her biological legacy, or Dunbar-Nelson, who wrote from the position of the "new," post-Reconstruction, black woman.

Each poet represented in this collection writes as much from her own personal subject position as she does from her position as social subject. As the poems indicate, by the last decade of the nineteenth century, the "new woman" had arrived—and she was a mercurial creature, given at times to passionate extremes yet also not at all averse to making fun of herself. Taken together, these poems suggest that what modernity gave these women was the latitude to be many, very different women writing in many, very different ways.

Paula Bennett
Professor Emerita, Southern Illinois
University at Carbondale

PRIMARY WORKS

Adah Menken, *Infelicia*, 1868; Celia Thaxter, *Poems*, 1872; Edith Thomas, *Selected Poems*, 1926; E. Pauline Johnson, *Flint and Feather*, 1912; Louise Imogen Guiney, *Happy Ending*, 1909 (2nd ed. 1927).

SECONDARY WORKS

Emily Stipes Watts, *The Poetry of American Women from 1632 to 1943*, 1978; Cheryl Walker, *The Nightingale's Burden: Women Poets and American Culture before 1900*, 1982; Gloria T. Hull, *Color, Sex, and Poetry: Three Women Writers of the Harlem Renaissance*, 1987; Paula Bennett, "Late Nineteenth-Century American Women's Nature Poetry and the Evolution of the Imagist Poem," *Legacy: A Journal of Nineteenth-Century American Women Writers* 9 (1992); Paula Bennett, "The Descent of the Angel: Interrogating Domestic Ideology in American Women's Poetry, 1858–1890," *American Literary History* 7 (1995); Paula Bennett, *Women in the Public Sphere: The Emancipatory Project of American Women's Poetry, 1800–1900* (2003); Mary Loeffelholz, *From School to Salon: Reading Nineteenth-Century American Women's Poetry*, 2004.

■ ADAH MENKEN ■
1835?–1868

Judith[1]

"Repent, or I will come unto thee quickly, and will fight thee with the sword of my mouth."

—*Revelations 2:16*

I

Ashkelon is not cut off with the remant of a valley.
Baldness dwells not upon Gaza.[2]
The field of the valley is mine, and it is clothed in verdue.
The steepness of Baal-perazim is mine;
And the Philistines spread themselves in the valley of Rephaim.[3]   5
They shall yet be delivered into my hands.
For the God of Battles has gone before me!
The sword of the mouth shall smite them to dust.
I have slept in the darkness—
But the seventh angel[4] woke me, and giving me a sword of flame,   10
    points to the blood-ribbed cloud, that lifts his reeking head
    above the mountain.
Thus am I the prophet.
I see the dawn that heralds to my waiting soul the advent of power.
Power that will unseal the thunders!   15
    Power that will give voice to graves!
    Graves of the living;
    Graves of the dying;
    Graves of the sinning;
Graves of the loving;   20
Graves of despairing;
And oh! graves of the deserted!
These shall speak, each as their voices shall be loosed.
And the day is dawning.

---

[1]In the *Apocrypha* Judith saves her people from Nebuchadnezzar's forces by stealing into the camp of his general, Holofernes, and beheading him.

[2]Ashkelon and Gaza are two cities in southwest Palestine.

[3]Baal-perazim and the Valley of Rephaim are sites where David conquered the Philistines in 2 Samuel 5:18–25.

[4]See Revelations 10:7–11.

II

Stand back, ye Philistines! 25
Practice what ye preach to me;
I heed ye not, for I know ye all.
Ye are living burning lies, and profanation to the garments which with
stately steps ye sweep your marble palaces.
Your palaces of Sin, around which the damning evidence of guilt
hangs like a reeking vapor. 30
Stand back!
I would pass up the golden road of the world.
A place in the ranks awaits me.
I know that ye are hedged on the borders of my path. 35
Lie and tremble, for ye well know that I hold with iron grasp the
battle axe.
Creep back to your dark tents in the valley.
Slouch back to your haunts of crime.
Ye do not know me, neither do ye see me. 40
But the sword of the mouth is unsealed, and ye coil yourselves in
slime and bitterness at my feet.
I mix your jeweled heads, and your gleaming eyes, and your hissing
tongues with the dust.
My garments shall bear no mark of ye. 45
When I shall return this sword to the angel, your foul blood will not
stain its edge.
It will glimmer with the light of truth, and the strong arm shall rest.

III

Stand back!
I am no Magdalene waiting to kiss the hem of your garment. 50
It is mid-day.
See ye not what is written on my forehead?
I am Judith!
I wait for the head of my Holofernes!
Ere the last tremble of the conscious death-agony shall have 55
shuddered, I will show it to ye with the long black hair clinging
to the glazed eyes, and the great mouth opened in search of
voice, and the strong throat all hot and reeking with blood, that
will thrill me with wild unspeakable joy as it courses down my
bare body and dabbles my cold feet! 60
My sensuous soul will quake with the burden of so much bliss.
Oh, what wild passionate kisses will I draw up from that bleeding
mouth!
I will strangle this pallid throat of mine on the sweet blood!
I will revel in my passion. 65

At midnight I will feast on it in the darkness.
For it was that which thrilled its crimson tides of reckless passion
    through the blue veins of my life, and made them leap up in the
    wild sweetness of Love and agony of Revenge!
I am starving for this feast.   70
Oh forget not that I am Judith!
And I know where sleeps Holoferness.

1868

CELIA THAXTER
1835–1894

In Kittery Churchyard[1]

*"Mary, wife of Charles Chauncy, died April 23, 1758, in the 24th year
of her age."*

Crushing the scarlet strawberries in the grass,
I kneel to read the slanting stone. Alas!
How sharp a sorrow speaks! A hundred years
And more have vanished, with their smiles and tears,
Since here was laid, upon an April day,   5
Sweet Mary Chauncy in the grave away,—
A hundred years since here her lover stood
Beside her grave in such despairing mood,
And yet from out the vanished past I hear
His cry of anguish sounding deep and clear,   10
And all my heart with pity melts, as though
To-day's bright sun were looking on his woe.
"Of such a wife, O righteous Heaven! bereft,
What joy for me, what joy on earth is left?
Still from my inmost soul the groans arise,   15
Still flow the sorrows ceaseless from mine eyes."
Alas, poor tortured soul! I look away
From the dark stone,—how brilliant shines the day!
A low wall, over which the roses shed
Their perfumed petals, shuts the quiet dead   20
Apart a little, and the tiny square

---

[1]Kittery, a seacoast town on the Maine–New
Hampshire border, settled in the late seventeenth century.

Stands in the broad and laughing field so fair,
And gay green vines climb o'er the rough stone wall,
And all about the wild birds flit and call,
And but a stone's throw southward, the blue sea   25
Rolls sparkling in and sings incessantly.
Lovely as any dream the peaceful place,
And scarcely changed since on her gentle face
For the last time on that sad April day
He gazed, and felt, for him, all beauty lay   30
Buried with her forever. Dull to him
Looked the bright world through eyes with tears so dim!
"I soon shall follow the same dreary way
That leads and opens to the coasts of day."
His only hope! But when slow time had dealt   35
Firmly with him and kindly, and he felt
The storm and stress of strong and piercing pain
Yielding at last, and he grew calm again,
Doubtless he found another mate before
He followed Mary to the happy shore!   40
But none the less his grief appeals to me
Who sit and listen to the singing sea
This matchless summer day, beside the stone
He made to echo with his bitter moan.
And in my eyes I feel the foolish tears   45
For buried sorrow, dead a hundred years!

1874

Wherefore

Black sea, black sky! A ponderous steamship driving
   Between them, laboring westward on her way,
And in her path a trap of Death's contriving
   Waiting remorseless for its easy prey.

Hundreds of souls within her frame lie dreaming,   5
   Hoping and fearing, longing for the light:
With human life and thought and feeling teeming,
   She struggles onward through the starless night.

Upon her furnace fires fresh fuel flinging,
   The swarthy firemen grumble at the dust   10
Mixed with the coal—when suddenly upspringing,
   Swift through the smoke-stack like a signal thrust,

Flares a red flame, a dread illumination!
   A cry,—a tumult! Slowly to her helm

The vessel yields, 'mid shouts of acclamation,   15
  And joy and terror all her crew o'erwhelm;

For looming from the blackness drear before them
  Discovered is the iceberg—hardly seen,
Its ghastly precipices hanging o'er them,
  Its reddened peaks, with dreadful chasms between,   20

Ere darkness swallows it again! and veering
  Out of its track the brave ship onward steers,
Just grazing ruin. Trembling still, and fearing,
  Her grateful people melt in prayers and tears.

Is it a mockery, their profound thanksgiving?   25
  Another ship goes shuddering to her doom
Unwarned, that very night, with hopes as living
  With freight as precious, lost amid the gloom,

With not a ray to show the apparition
  Waiting to slay her, none to cry "Beware!"   30
Rushing straight onward headlong to perdition,
  And for her crew no time vouchsafed for prayer.

Could they have stormed Heaven's gate with anguished praying,
  It would not have availed a feather's weight
Against their doom. Yet were they disobeying   35
  No law of God, to beckon such a fate.

And do not tell me the Almighty Master
  Would work a miracle to save the one,
And yield the other up to dire disaster,
  By merely human justice thus outdone!   40

Vainly we weep and wrestle with our sorrow—
  We cannot see his roads, they lie so broad;
But his eternal day knows no to-morrow,
  And life and death are all the same with God.

                                      1874

Two Sonnets

Not so! You stand as long ago a king[1]
  Stood on the seashore, bidding back the tide

---

[1]King Canute of England, Norway, and Denmark (995?–1035).

That onward rolled resistless still, to fling
  Its awful volume landward, wild and wide.
And just as impotent is your command   5
  To stem the tide that rises in my soul.
It ebbs not at the lifting of your hand,
  It owns no curb, it yields to no control;
Mighty it is, and of the elments,—
  Brother of winds and lightning, cold and fire,   10
Subtle as light, as steadfast and intense;
  Sweet as the music of Apollo's lyre.
You think to rule the ocean's ebb and flow
  With that soft woman's hand? Nay, love, not so.

And like the lighthouse on the rock you stand,   15
  And pierce the distance with your searching eyes;
Nor do you heed the waves that storm the land
  And endlessly about you fall and rise,
But seek the ships that wander night and day
  Within the dim horizon's shadowy ring;   20
And some with flashing glance you warn away,
  And some you beckon with sweet welcoming.
So steadfast still you keep your lofty place,
  Safe from the tumult of the restless tide,
Firm as the rock in your resisting grace,   25
  And strong through humble duty, not through pride.
While I—I cast my life before your feet,
And only live that I may love you, sweet!

                                        1896

■ LOUISE CHANDLER MOULTON ■
1835–1908

A Girl's Funeral in Milan

There in the strange old gilded hearse
  With a mound of paper-flowers on her breast,
Her life being over, for better or worse,
  They bore her on to her final rest.

And the women followed her, two by two,   5
  And talked of how young she was to die;

And the cold drops drenched them through and through,
  As under the pitiless, frowning sky

On they marched in the drizzling rain
  To the little old church in the Milan square,   10
Where the choir-boys chanted with shrill refrain,
  And the toothless Padre muttered his prayer;

Then straight to the waiting grave they went;
  And the rain rained on, and the wind was still;
Since, all her treasure of life being spent,   15
  It was time Death had of the girl his will.

And they left her there with the rain and the wind,
  Glad, I think, to have come to the end;
For the grave folds close, and the sod is kind,
  And thus do the friendless find a friend.   20

                                                    1891

Laus Veneris[1]

Pallid with too much longing,
  White with passion and prayer,
Goddess of love and beauty,
  She sits in the picture there—

Sits, with her dark eyes seeking   5
  Something more subtle still
Than the old delights of loving
  Her measureless days to fill.

She has loved and been loved so often,
  In her long, immortal years,   10
That she tires of the worn-out rapture,
  Sickens of hopes and fears.

No joys or sorrows moved her—
  Done with her ancient pride,
For her head she found too heavy   15
  The crown she has cast aside.

Clothed in her scarlet splendour,
  Bright with her glory of hair,

---

[1]In praise of Venus, or love. Moulton alternatively titled this poem "The Venus of Burne-Jones," after a work by the pre-Raphaelite artist.

Sad that she is not mortal,
   Eternally sad and fair,   20

Longing for joys she knows not,
   Athirst with a vain desire,
There she sits, in the picture,
   Daughter of foam and fire.

                                     1891

■   # ELLA WHEELER WILCOX
1850–1919   ■

Illusion

God and I in space alone,
   And nobody else in view.
And "Where are the people, O Lord," I said,
  "The earth below and the sky o'erhead
   And the dead whom once I knew?"   5

"That was a dream," God smiled and said:
  "A dream that seemed to be true.
There were no people living or dead,
There was no earth and no sky o'erhead—
  There was only Myself and you."   10

"Why do I feel no fear," I asked,
  Meeting YOU here this way?
"For I have sinned, I know full well;
And is there heaven, and is there hell,
  And is this the Judgment Day?"   15

"Nay! those were but dreams," the great God said;
  "Dreams that have ceased to be.
There are no such things as fear, or sin;
There is no you—you never have been—
  There is nothing at all but me!"   20

                                     1896

Goddess of Liberty,[1] Answer

Goddess of Liberty, listen! listen. I say, and look
To the sounds and sights of sorrow this side of Sandy Hook![2]
Your eye is searching the distance, you are holding your torch too high
To see the slaves who are fettered, though close at your feet they lie.
And the cry of the suffering stranger has reached your ear and your
    breast,   5
But you do not heed the wail that comes from the haunts of your own
    oppressed.

Goddess of Liberty, follow, follow me where I lead;
Come down into sweat-shops and look on the work of greed!   10
Look on the faces of children, old before they were born!
Look on the haggard women of all sex graces shorn!
Look on the men—God, help us! if this is what it means
To be men in the land of freedom and live like mere machines!

Goddess of Liberty, answer! how can the slaves of Spain   15
Find freedom under your banner, while your own still wear the chain?
Loud is the screech of your eagle and boastful the voice of your drums,
But they do not silence the wail of despair that rises out of your slums.
What will you do with your conquests, and how shall your hosts be fed,
While your streets are filled with desperate throngs, crying for work
    or bread?   20

                                                                1898

■   # MARY E. WILKINS FREEMAN   ■
1852–1930

Love and the Witches

It was a little, fearful maid,
    Whose mother left her all alone;
Her door with iron bolt she stayed,
    And 'gainst it rolled a lucky stone—

[1]The Statue of Liberty. This poem appears to be a response to Emma Lazarus's "The New Colossus."

[2]Sandy Hook, a spit of land on the New Jersey coast, opposite the south end of Manhattan. It marked the boundary beyond which lay the open ocean and Europe, source of the immigrant populations to whom Lazarus's poem is addressed.

For many a night she'd waked with fright   5
  When witches by the house had flown.

To piping lute in still midnight,
  Who comes a-singing at the door,—
That showeth seams of gold light,—
  "Ah, open, darling, I implore"?   10
She could not help knowing 't was Love,
  Although they'd never met before.

She swiftly shot the iron bar,
  And rolled the lucky stone away,
And careful set the door ajar—   15
  "Now enter in, Sir Love, I pray;
My mother knows it not, but I have watched
  For you this many a day."

With fan and roar of gloomy wings
  They gave the door a windy shove;   20
They perched on chairs and brooms and things;
  Like bats they beat around above—
Poor little maid, she'd let the witches in with Love.

1891

■   **EDITH THOMAS**   ■
1854–1925

The Torches of the Dawn

Beneath the rough, black verge where ledgy isle
  And serried wave and fragment cloud are hurled,
    Swift through the underworld—
Lo where the torchmen of the Dawn defile!

Unseen they march beneath the rough, black verge,   5
  Unseen, save from the torches which they bear,
    Smoke and a crimson flare,
Wind-blown one way, show where their course they urge!

1893

The Deep-Sea Pearl

The love of my life came not
 As love unto others is cast;
For mine was a secret wound—
 But the wound grew a pearl, at last.

The divers may come and go,   5
 The tides, they arise and fall;
The pearl in its shell lies sealed,
 And the Deep Sea covers all.

                1903

"Frost To-night"

Apple-green west and an orange bar;
And the crystal eye of a lone, one star ...
And, "Child, take the shears and cut what you will,
Frost to-night—so clear and dead-still."

Then I sally forth, half sad, half proud,   5
And I come to the velvet, imperial crowd,
The wine-red, the gold, the crimson, the pied,—
The dahlias that reign by the garden-side.

The dahlias I might not touch till to-night!
A gleam of shears in the fading light,   10
And I gathered them all,—the splendid throng,
And in one great sheaf I bore them along.

In my garden of Life with its all late flowers
I heed a Voice in the shrinking hours:
"Frost to-night—so clear and dead-still" ...   15
Half sad, half proud, my arms I fill.

                1926

To Walk Invisible

"We have the receipt of fern-seed; we walk invisible."[1]

I smile—yet better might I sigh than smile—
 At my young waywardness that wished to try
"Receipt of fern-seed"; for some little while
 To walk unseen of any prying eye.

[1] *1 Henry IV*, 2:1:12.

I said 'twas but detachment that I sought, 5
To better know my own good comrade, Thought.

I added, I had made, must keep, the tryst
  With Beauty, who had counseled Solitude—
I would be back again ere I was missed;
  Whoever loved me would indulge my mood, 10
Nor would they strive the veiling charm to break.
Nor turn aside my hidden path to take.

And then, I moved untroubled by the crowd.
  I softly stepped, and silence lapped me round.
I was but young—God knows I was not proud! 15
  My venture was to me enchanted ground
Where I might pass unseen, but, soon as fain,
Into my human world return again.

I went my way, I kept me far from sight,
  From jostling touch and ill-timed greeting free.... 20
I, who was more beholden to the night
  Than any charm that could sequester me!
Now, deeper night and elder solitude
Begin to close around my errant mood.

And when I walk invisible, indeed, 25
  Who knows, I may the genius be of all
Who out of trodden ways their spirit lead?
  Then I will answer to their lonely call
Who, straying, have strayed wider than they wist,
Who walk invisible—and are not missed. 30

1926

■ LIZETTE WOODWORTH REESE ■
1856–1935

Early September

The swallows have not left us yet, praise God!
And bees still hum, and gardens hold the musk
Of white rose and of red; firing the dusk

By the old wall, the hollyhocks do nod,
And pinks that send the sweet East down the wind.   5
And yet, a yellowing leaf shows here and there
Among the boughs, and through the smoky air—
That hints the frost at dawn—the wood looks thinned.
The little half-grown sumachs, all as green
As June last week, now in the crackling sedge,   10
Colored like wine burn to the water's edge.
We feel, at times, as we had come unseen
Upon the aging Year, sitting apart,
Grief in his eyes, some ache at his great heart.

                                                                    1887

Telling the Bees

(A Colonial Custom)[1]

Bathsheba came out to the sun,
Out to our wallèd cherry-trees;
The tears adown her cheek did run,
Bathsheba standing in the sun,
Telling the bees.   5

My mother had that moment died;
Unknowing, sped I to the trees,
And plucked Bathsheba's hand aside;
Then caught the name that there she cried
Telling the bees.   10

Her look I never can forget,
I that held her sobbing to her knees;
The cherry-boughs above us met;
I think I see Bathsheba yet
Telling the bees.   15

                                                                    1896

Drought

Silence—and in the air
A stare.
One bush, the color of rust,
Stands in the endless lane;

[1]Upon a death in the family, a household
member would, according to old New England
custom, "tell the bees" lest they fly away.

And farther on, hot, hard of pane,   5
With roof shrunk black,
Headlong against the sky
A house is thrust;
Betwixt the twain,
Like meal poured from a sack,   10
Stirless, foot high—
The dust.

                                                      1920

White Flags[1]

Now since they plucked them for your grave,
And left the garden bare
As a great house of candlelight,
Oh, nothing else so fair!
I knew before that they were white,   5
In April by a wall,
A dozen or more. That people died
I did not know at all.

                                                      1922

Emily

She had a garden full of herbs,
   And many another pleasant thing,
Like pink round asters in the fall,
   Blue flags, white flags a week in spring.

Housewives ran in each hour or so,   5
   For sprigs of thyme, mint, parsley too;
For pans to borrow, or some meal;
   She was the kindest thing they knew.

Tall, and half slender, slightly grey,
   With gay, thin lips, eyes flower-clear,   10
She bragged her stock was Puritan;
   Her usual mood was Cavalier.

[1]White iris.

Ample of deed; clipped, warm of speech,
   Each day in some large-flowered gown,
She went the rounds to sad, to sick   15
   Saint, humorist to the faded town.

She died at sixty. For a while
   They missed her in each intimate spot—
Tall, and half slender, slightly grey—
   They ate, drank, slept, and quite forgot.   20

                                              1923

Spring Ecstasy

Oh, let me run and hide,
   Let me run straight to God;
The weather is so mad with white
   From sky down to the clod!

If but one thing were so,   5
   Lilac, or thorn out there,
It would not be, indeed,
   So hard to bear.

The weather has gone mad with white;
   The cloud, the highway touch;   10
When lilac is enough;
   White thorn too much!

                                              1923

Crows

Earth is raw with this one note,
This battered making of a song
Narrowed down to a crow's throat,
Above the willow-trees that throng

The crooking field from end to end.   5
Fixed as the sun, the grass, that sound;
Of what the weather has to spend,
As much a part as sky, or ground.

The primal yellow of that flower,
That tansy making August plain,   10
And the stored wildness of this hour,
It sucks up like a bitter rain.

Miss it we would, were it not here;
Simple as water, rough as spring,
It hurls us, at the point of spear,   15
Back to some naked, early thing.

                                                       1927

SOPHIE JEWETT
1861–1909

Entre Nous[1]

I talk with you of foolish things and wise,
Of persons, places, books, desires and aims,
Yet all our words a silence underlies,
An earnest, vivid thought that neither names.

Ah! what to us were foolish talk or wise?   5
Were persons, places, books, desires or aims,
Without the deeper sense that underlies,
The sweet encircling thought that neither names?

                                            MS 1882, 1910

Armistice

The water sings along our keel,
  The wind falls to a whispering breath;
I look into your eyes and feel
  No fear of life or death;
So near is love, so far away   5
The losing strife of yesterday.

We watch the swallow skim and dip;
  Some magic bids the world be still;
Life stands with finger upon lip;
  Love hath his gentle will;   10
Though hearts have bled, and tears have burned,
The river floweth unconcerned.

---

[1]French for "between us."

We pray the fickle flag of truce
  Still float deceitfully and fair;
Our eyes must love its sweet abuse;   15
  This hour we will not care,
Though just beyond to-morrow's gate
Arrayed and strong, the battle wait.

1892

I Speak Your Name

I speak your name in alien ways, while yet
November smiles from under lashes wet.
  In the November light I see you stand
  Who love the fading woods and withered land,
Where Peace may walk, and Death, but not Regret.   5

The year is slow to alter or forget;
June's glow and autumn's tenderness are met.
  Across the months by this swift sunlight spanned,
    I speak your name.

Because I loved your golden hair, God set   10
His sea between our eyes. I may not fret,
  For, sure and strong, to meet my soul's demand,
  Comes your soul's truth, more near than hand in hand;
And low to God, who listens, Margaret,
    I speak your name.   15

MS 1892, 1910

■ E. PAULINE JOHNSON (TEKAHIONWAKE) ■
1861–1913

The Camper

Night 'neath the northern skies, lone, black, and grim:
Naught but the starlight lies 'twixt heaven, and him.

Of man no need has he, of God, no prayer;
He and his Deity are brothers there.

Above his bivouac the firs fling down 5
Through branches gaunt and black, their needles brown.

Afar some mountain streams, rockbound and fleet,
Sing themselves through his dreams in cadence sweet,

The pine trees whispering, the heron's cry,
The plover's wing, his lullaby. 10

And blinking overhead the white stars keep
Watch o'er his hemlock bed—his sinless sleep.

1895

The Corn Husker

Hard by the Indian lodges, where the bush
   Breaks in a clearing, through ill-fashioned fields,
She comes to labour, when the first still hush
   Of autumn follows large and recent yields.

Age in her fingers, hunger in her face, 5
   Her shoulders stooped with weight of work and years,
But rich in tawny colouring of her race,
   She comes a-field to strip the purple ears.

And all her thoughts are with the days gone by,
   Ere might's injustice banished from their lands 10
Her people, that to-day unheeded lie,
   Like the dead husks that rustle through her hands.

1903

The Indian Corn Planter

He needs must leave the trapping and the chase,
   For mating game his arrows ne'er despoil,
And from the hunter's heaven turn his face,
   To wring some promise from the dormant soil.

He needs must leave the lodge that wintered him, 5
   The enervating fires, the blanket bed—
The women's dulcet voices, for the grim
   Realities of labouring for bread.

So goes he forth beneath the planter's moon
   With sack of seed that pledges large increase, 10

His simple pagan faith knows night and noon,
   Heat, cold, seedtime and harvest shall not cease.

And yielding to his needs, this honest sod,
   Brown as the hand that tills it, moist with rain,
Teeming with ripe fulfillment, true as God,   15
   With fostering richness, mothers every grain.

                                         1912

LOUISE IMOGEN GUINEY
1861–1920

Hylas[1]

Jar in the arm, they bade him rove
Thro' the alder's long alcove,
Where the hid spring musically
Gushes to the ample valley.
(There's a bird on the under bough   5
Fluting evermore and now:
"Keep—young!" but who knows how?)

Down the woodland corridor,
Odors deepened more and more;
Blossomed dogwood, in the briers,   10
Struck her faint delicious fires;
Miles of April passed between
Crevices of closing green,
And the moth, the violet-lover,
By the wellside saw him hover.   15

Ah, the slippery sylvan dark!
Never after shall he mark
Noisy ploughmen drinking, drinking,
On his drownèd cheek down-sinking;

---

[1] In Greek mythology, a beautiful youth, beloved of Hercules. While serving as an Argonaut, he was sent to fetch water from a spring. There, the nymphs who lived in the spring, catching sight of his beauty, dragged him in and his body was never found.

Quit of serving is that wild,   20
Absent, and bewitchèd child,
Unto action, age, and danger,
Thrice a thousand years a stranger.

Fathoms low, the naiads[2] sing
In a birthday welcoming;[3]   25
Water-white their breasts, and o'er him;
Water-gray, their eyes adore him.
(There's a bird on the under bough
Fluting evermore and now;
"Keep—young!" but who knows how?)   30

                                                               1893

Monochrome

Shut fast again in Beauty's sheath
Where ancient forms renew,
The round world seems above, beneath,
One wash of faintest blue,

And air and tide so stilly sweet   5
In nameless union lie,
The little far-off fishing fleet
Goes drifting up the sky.

Secure of neither misted coast
Nor ocean undefined,   10
Our flagging sail is like the ghost
Of one that served mankind,

Who in the void, as we upon
This melancholy sea,
Finds labour and allegiance done,   15
And Self begin to be.

                                                               1896

[2]In Greek mythology, the nymphs inhabiting
streams, rivers, and lakes.
[3]Guiney appears to be suggesting that Hylas's
"death" in this life marked his rebirth (or
"birthday") in the next.

Charista Musing

Moveless, on the marge of a sunny cornfield,
Rapt in sudden revery while thou standest,
Like the sheaves, in beautiful Doric[1] yellow
Clad to the ankle,

Oft to thee with delicate hasty footstep   5
So I steal, and suffer because I find thee
Inly flown, and only a fallen feather
Left of my darling.

Give me back thy wakening breath, thy ringlets
Fragrant as the vine of the bean in blossom,   10
And those eyes of violet dusk and daylight
Under sea-water,

Eyes too far away, and too full of longing!
Yes: and go not heavenward where I lose thee,
Go not, go not whither I cannot follow,   15
Being but earthly.

Willing swallow poisèd upon my finger,
Little wild-wing ever from me escaping,
For the care thou art to me, I thy lover
Love thee, and fear thee.   20

1899

■   ELAINE GOODALE EASTMAN   ■
1863–1953

The Wood-Chopper to His Ax

My comrade keen, my lawless friend,
When will your savage temper mend?

---

[1]The Doric order (or style) was the oldest and simplest of the three major Greek architectural and musical modes. Guiney appears to want to associate Charista with classical Greek beauty and simplicity. Her name (Charista) derives from the ancient Greek for love (as does the modern English "charity"), and there may also be a pun on "musing" ("muse" or source of poetic inspiration, as in Greek mythology).

I wield you, powerless to resist;
I feel your weight bend back my wrist,
    Straighten the corded arm,   5
    Caress the hardened palm.

War on these forest tribes they made,
The men who forged your sapphire blade;
Its very substance thus renewed
Tenacious of the ancient feud,   10
    In crowding ranks uprose
    Your ambushed, waiting foes.

This helve, by me wrought out and planned,
By long use suited to this hand,
Was carved, with patient, toilsome art,   15
From stubborn hickory's milk-white heart;
    Its satin gloss makes plain
    The fineness of the grain.

When deeply sunk, an entering wedge,
The live wood tastes your shining edge;   20
When, strongly cleft from side to side,
You feel its shrinking heart divide,
    List not the shuddering sigh
    Of that dread agony.

Yon gaping mouth you need not miss,   25
But close it with a poignant kiss;
Nor dread to search, with whetted knife,
The naked mystery of life,
    And count on shining rings
    The ever-widening springs.   30

Hew, trenchant steel, the ivory core,
One mellow, resonant stroke the more!
Loudly the cracking sinews start,
Unwilling members wrenched apart—
    Dear ax, your 'complice I   35
    In love and cruelty!

                          1883

The Cross and the Pagan

As men in the forest, erect and free,
We prayed to God in the living tree;

You razed our shrine, to the wood-god's loss,
And out of the tree you fashioned a Cross!

You left us for worship one day in seven;   5
In exchange for our earth you offered us heaven;
Dizzy with wonder, and wild with loss,
We bent the knee to your awful Cross.

Your sad, sweet Christ—we called him Lord;
He promised us peace, but he brought a sword;   10
In shame and sorrow, in pain and loss,
We have drunk his cup;[1] we have borne his Cross!

                                                                           1912

ALICE DUNBAR-NELSON
1875–1935

I Sit and Sew

I sit and sew—a useless task it seems,
My hands grown tired, my head weighed down with dreams—
The panoply of war, the martial tred of men,
Grim-faced, stern-eyed, gazing beyond the ken
Of lesser souls, whose eyes have not seen Death,   5
Nor learned to hold their lives but as a breath—
But—I must sit and sew.

I sit and sew—my heart aches with desire—
That pageant terrible, that fiercely pouring fire
On wasted fields, and writhing grotesque things   10
Once men. My soul in pity flings
Appealing cries, yearning only to go
There in that holocaust of hell, those fields of woe—
But—I must sit and sew.

The little useless seam, the idle patch;   15
Why dream I here beneath my homely thatch,
When there they lie in sodden mud and rain,

---

[1]Communion cup; Christ's blood.

Pitifully calling me, the quick ones and the slain?
You need me, Christ! It is no roseate dream
That beckons me—this pretty futile seam   20
It stifles me—God, must I sit and sew?

                                                          1920

You! Inez!

Orange gleams athwart a crimson soul
Lambent flames; purple passion lurks
In your dusk eyes.
Red mouth; flower soft,
Your soul leaps up—and flashes   5
Star-like, white, flame-hot.
Curving arms, encircling a world of love.
You! Stirring the depths of passionate desire!

                                                      MS 1921

The Proletariat Speaks

I love beautiful things:
Great trees, bending green winged branches to a velvet lawn,
Fountains sparkling in white marble basins,
Cool fragrance of lilacs and roses and honeysuckle.
Or exotic blooms, filling the air with heart-contracting odors;   5
Spacious rooms, cool and gracious with statues and books,
Carven seats and tapestries, and old masters
Whose patina shows the wealth of centuries.

And so I work
In a dusty office, whose grimèd windows   10
Look out in an alley of unbelievable squalor,
Where mangy cats, in their degradation, spurn
Swarming bits of meat and bread;
Where odors, vile and breath taking, rise in fetid waves
Filling my nostrils, scorching my humid, bitter cheeks.   15

I love beautiful things:
Carven tables laid with lily-hued linen
And fragile china and sparkling iridescent glass;
Pale silver, etched with heraldies,
Where tender bits of regal dainties tempt,   20
And soft-stepped service anticipates the unspoken wish.

And so I eat
In the food-laden air of a greasy kitchen,
At an oil-clothed table:
Plate piled high with food that turns my head away,   25
Lest a squeamish stomach reject too soon
The lumpy gobs it never needed.
Or in a smoky cafeteria, balancing a slippery tray
To a table crowded with elbows
Which lately the bus boy wiped with a grimy rag.   30

I love beautiful things:
Soft linen sheets and silken coverlet,
Sweet coolth of chamber opened wide to fragrant breeze;
Rose shaded lamps and golden atomizers,
Spraying Parisian fragrance over my relaxed limbs,   35
Fresh from a white marble bath, and sweet cool spray.

And so I sleep
In a hot hall-room whose half-opened window,
Unscreened, refuses to budge another inch;
Admits no air, only insects, and hot choking gasps,   40
That make me writhe, nun-like, in sack-cloth sheets and lumps
    of straw.
And then I rise
To fight my way to a dubious tub,
Whose tiny, tepid stream threatens to make me late;
And hurrying out, dab my unrefreshed face   45
With bits of toiletry from the ten cent store.

                                                                       1929

PAUL LAURENCE DUNBAR
1872–1906

Paul Laurence Dunbar was one of the most prolific, versatile, and puzzling writers in the history of American literature. By the time he died just short of his
thirty-fourth birthday, he had published fourteen books of poetry, four books of
short stories, four novels, and numerous songs, dramatic works, short stories,
poems, and essays in several American periodicals. Beginning in the mid-1890s,
he became the first American author of African descent to be an international
phenomenon. Fellow writers and critics alike anointed him the literary laureate
of the black race, spurring the extraordinary commercial sales of his creative

writings and establishing the public terms by which other black writers of his era and thereafter were appreciated. Yet his career also suggested that he negotiated a personal crisis. Evidently, his creative loyalties were torn between, on the one hand, demonstrating his commitment to black political progress and, on the other hand, writing what prominent literary critics and publishers expected of him and of black writers in general. The standard biographies of Dunbar by Virginia Cunningham, Benjamin Brawley, Addison Gayle, Jr., Peter Revell, Felton O. Best, and Eleanor Alexander support this assessment, but a closer look at his writings may also reveal the nuances of his life and career.

Dunbar was born in the small town of Dayton, Ohio, the son of former Kentucky slaves whose tales of their antebellum experiences eventually inspired the vernacular language and themes of his creative writing. He grew up in a period known to white southerners as Redemption. In the mid-1870s, this group of whites spear-headed the national rollback of black civil rights that included political disenfranchisement and racial segregation of blacks in public life. In contrast, the social terror and political setbacks faced by blacks convinced scholars to call this period the Nadir. Blacks had enjoyed the Union victory in the Civil War and the formal mandates of Radical Reconstruction, which helped to emancipate them from slavery and protect their entitlements to national citizenship; they now realized that their racial progress faced a politically uphill and violent battle.

Dunbar responded to this atmosphere of racial unrest by publishing essays in local newspapers, such as the *Dayton Tattler*. One essay, which appeared in the *Tattler* in 1890, implored local black readers to buy the paper to "espouse the spirit of honest republicanism." Another essay, published in 1893 in the Chicago *Record*, argued that the black press facilitated black political progress, also known as racial uplift. Similarly themed essays—printed in the *Toledo Journal*, the *Philadelphia Times*, and the *New York Times*—appeared during the next decade. Dunbar's foray into political journalism illustrated his sensitivity to the conditions of black communities across the country. Yet the approach also anticipated the irony of his literary talent, critical reception, and commercial success, all of which often contradicted his original political sensibilities.

In the June 27, 1896, issue of *Harper's Weekly*, William Dean Howells, the preeminent critic of American literature and culture, effusively praised Dunbar's second collection of poetry, *Majors and Minors*. (Dunbar's first collection, *Oak and Ivy*, arrived without fanfare.) In response to Dunbar's frontispiece, Howells expressed his appreciation that the ostensibly dark-skinned author was "the pure African type." Howells also loved the poems written in dialect, which he felt represented exclusively black vernacular. Truth be told, the dialect poems reflected various regional and ethnic, not only black, dialects. The dialect poems also amounted to only a quarter of the book's poems; the other three-quarters were prayers, lyrics, odes, ballads, and sonnets in formal English. Nonetheless, to Howells the dialect poems represented when Dunbar was "most himself" and allowed readers to enjoy an authentic and transparent window into the black community. Coincidentally, the orthography of black dialect was a hallmark of popular American literature at the time, thanks mainly to the commercial success of white writers of the postbellum "plantation tradition," especially Joel Chandler Harris and Thomas Nelson Page.

Most critics reviewing *Majors and Minors* followed in Howells's influential footsteps. They similarly lauded Dunbar's dialect poems, contrary to the bulk of evidence—including *Oak and Ivy, Majors and Minors, Lyrics of Lowly Life, Lyrics of the Hearthside, Lyrics of Love and Laughter*, and *Lyrics of Sunshine and Shadow*—that the fledgling black writer was most interested in writing poems in formal English. The critical neglect of Dunbar's poems in formal English resulted from the overwhelming commercial popularity of the dialect poems included in these books and those that he published in magazines and performed in public. (To be fair, he did not exactly oppose the financial incentives of this popularity. He needed the money.) The dialect poems often painted senti-mental and romantic images of Negroes in the aesthetic tradition of mid- to late-nineteenth-century blackface minstrelsy, which appealed to many whites, who wanted to return to the antebellum culture of blacks' docility and subser-vience. Dunbar's dialect poems also ran counter to the prevailing signs of black political progress not only in the real world, but also in works of racial uplift that were written by Frances Ellen Watkins Harper, Pauline Hopkins, W.E.B. Du Bois, and, in some cases, Charles W. Chesnutt and Dunbar himself.

However, some of Dunbar's dialect poems belong to the literary tradition of racial uplift, because, even as they may have perpetuated black stereotypes to achieve a mass appeal, they criticized racial injustice in subtle ways. For exam-ple, a poem that Howells lauds in his review and that is included in this anthol-ogy, "When Malindy Sings," focuses on the extent that a woman's talent as a singer captivates anyone who hears her. Buried beneath the poem's dense dia-lect, sentimental aura, and minstrel imagery (such as the banjo player) is the ref-erence to Malindy's song, "Swing Low, Sweet Chariot." This "Negro spiritual" was first sung by slaves and passed down among blacks for generations as a mel-ody of religious hope and civil rights activism.

In the preface to a 1922 collection of African American poetry, James Wel-don Johnson bemoaned that the "qualities that gave [black dialect poetry] vogue—tenderness, sentimentality, homely humor, genial optimism—are the very qualities that now bring disparagement on it." Johnson assessed Dunbar's legacy in these terms to elbow him aside, to create room in the canon of African American poetry for himself, Langston Hughes, and Claude McKay, writers who became representatives of the Harlem, or New Negro, Renaissance. However, the allegation could not undermine the fact that Dunbar's orthographic dexter-ity with dialect and his thematic ironies inspired these and other writers of their generation to hone their skills in representing black vernacular while delivering subtle political messages.

In addition to poetry, Dunbar wrote or published in the second half of his life more than one hundred short stories, many of them in four books, *Folks from Dixie, The Strength of Gideon and Other Stories, In Old Plantation Days*, and *The Heart of Happy Hollow*. As the titles suggest, several stories in the books sympathize with antebellum racial politics and representations. Yet some also break from these themes, illustrating the cultural, political, and religious com-plexities of black communities and humanizing blacks in ways that the formal exigencies of Dunbar's poems may not have always permitted. Dunbar's four novels are equally experimental in examining the naturalistic impact of the envi-ronment on human agency. The first three—*The Uncalled, The Love of Landry*, and *The Fanatics*—use whites as main characters to tell stories about, respectively, spiritual regeneration and redemption, the stricture of social convention, and the morality of the Civil War. In contrast, the last novel, *The Sport of the Gods*, returns to the conventional form of African American literary realism by using a black protagonist to describe the cultural, regional, and ideological differences that fracture black communities.

The reviews of all these works were mixed, to say the least, showing the degree to which Dunbar's experiments with literary form and theme contradicted mainstream critical and commercial demands. One century after his death, however, many critics and scholars agree that his prodigious talent and versatility as a writer, and his sophistication and diplomacy in racial politics, deserve high admiration and both a contemporary readership and further academic study.

Gene Jarrett
Boston University

PRIMARY WORKS

Oak and Ivy, 1893; *Majors and Minors*, 1896; *Lyrics of Lowly Life*, 1896; *Folks from Dixie*, 1898; *The Uncalled*, 1898; *Lyrics of the Hearthside*, 1899; *The Strength of Gideon and Other Stories*, 1900; *The Love of Landry*, 1900; *The Fanatics*, 1901; *The Sport of the Gods*, 1902; *Lyrics of Love and Laughter*, 1903; *In Old Plantation Days*, 1903; *The Heart of Happy Hollow*, 1904; *Lyrics of Sunshine and Shadow*, 1905; *The Complete Stories of Paul Laurence Dunbar*, 2005.

from **Lyrics of Lowly Life**

Frederick Douglass

A hush is over all the teeming lists,
    And there is pause, a breath-space in the strife;
A spirit brave has passed beyond the mists
    And vapors that obscure the sun of life.
And Ethiopia, with bosom torn,   5
Laments the passing of her noblest born.

She weeps for him a mother's burning tears—
    She loved him with a mother's deepest love.
He was her champion thro' direful years,
    And held her weal all other ends above.   10
When Bondage held her bleeding in the dust,
He raised her up and whispered, "Hope and Trust."

For her his voice, a fearless clarion, rung
    That broke in warning on the ears of men;
For her the strong bow of his power he strung,   15
    And sent his arrows to the very den

Where grim Oppression held his bloody place
And gloated o'er the mis'ries of a race.

And he was no soft-tongued apologist;
   He spoke straightforward, fearlessly uncowed;   20
The sunlight of his truth dispelled the mist,
   And set in bold relief each dark-hued cloud;
To sin and crime he gave their proper hue,
And hurled at evil what was evil's due.

Through good and ill report he cleaved his way   25
   Right onward, with his face set toward the heights,
Nor feared to face the foeman's dread array,—
   The lash of scorn, the sting of petty spites.
He dared the lightning in the lightning's track,
And answered thunder with his thunder back.   30

When men maligned him, and their torrent wrath
   In furious imprecations o'er him broke,
He kept his counsel as he kept his path;
   'T was for his race, not for himself, he spoke.
He knew the import of his Master's call,   35
And felt himself too mighty to be small.

No miser in the good he held was he,—
   His kindness followed his horizon's rim.
His heart, his talents, and his hands were free
   To all who truly needed aught of him.   40
Where poverty and ignorance were rife,
He gave his bounty as he gave his life.

The place and cause that first aroused his might
   Still proved its power until his latest day.
In Freedom's lists and for the aid of Right   45
   Still in the foremost rank he waged the fray;
Wrong lived; his occupation was not gone.
He died in action with his armor on!

We weep for him, but we have touched his hand,
   And felt the magic of his presence nigh,   50
The current that he sent throughout the land,
   The kindling spirit of his battle-cry.
O'er all that holds us we shall triumph yet,
And place our banner where his hopes were set!

Oh, Douglass, thou hast passed beyond the shore,   55
   But still thy voice is ringing o'er the gale!
Thou'st taught thy race how high her hopes may soar,
   And bade her seek the heights, nor faint, nor fail.
She will not fail, she heeds thy stirring cry,
She knows thy guardian spirit will be nigh,   60
And, rising from beneath the chast'ning rod,
She stretches out her bleeding hands to God!

                                                1896

We Wear the Mask

We wear the mask that grins and lies,
   It hides our cheeks and shades our eyes,—
This debt we pay to human guile;
With torn and bleeding hearts we smile,
And mouth with myriad subtleties.   5

Why should the world be over-wise,
In counting all our tears and sighs?
Nay, let them only see us, while
   We wear the mask.

We smile, but, O great Christ, our cries   10
To thee from tortured souls arise.
We sing, but oh the clay is vile
Beneath our feet, and long the mile;
But let the world dream otherwise,
   We wear the mask!   15

                                                1896

When Malindy Sings

G'way an' quit dat noise, Miss Lucy—
   Put dat music book away;
What's de use to keep on tryin'?
   Ef you practise twell you're gray,
You cain't sta't no notes a-flyin'   5
   Lak de ones dat rants and rings
F'om de kitchen to de big woods
   When Malindy sings.
You ain't got de nachel o'gans
   Fu' to make de soun' come right,   10
You ain't got de tu'ns an' twistin's
   Fu' to make it sweet an' light.

Tell you one thing now, Miss Lucy,
   An' I'm tellin' you fu' true,
When hit comes to raal right singin',   15
   'T ain't no easy thing to do.

Easy 'nough fu' folks to hollah,
   Lookin' at de lines an' dots,
When dey ain't no one kin sence it,
   An' de chune comes in, in spots;   20
But fu' real melojous music,
   Dat jes' strikes yo' hea't and clings,
Jes' you stan' an' listen wif me
   When Malindy sings.

Ain't you nevah hyeahd Malindy?   25
   Blessed soul, tek up de cross!
Look hyeah, ain't you jokin', honey?
   Well, you don't know whut you los'.
Y' ought to hyeah dat gal a-wa'blin',
   Robins, la'ks, an' all dem things,   30
Heish dey moufs an' hides dey faces
   When Malindy sings.

Fiddlin' man jes' stop his fiddlin',
   Lay his fiddle on de she'f;
Mockin'-bird quit tryin' to whistle,   35
   'Cause he jes' so shamed hisse'f.
Folks a-playin' on de banjo
   Draps dey fingahs on de strings—
Bless yo' soul—fu'gits to move 'em,
   When Malindy sings.   40

She jes' spreads huh mouf and hollahs,
   "Come to Jesus," twell you hyeah
Sinnahs' tremblin' steps and voices,
   Timid-lak a-drawin' neah;
Den she tu'ns to "Rock of Ages,"   45
   Simply to de cross she clings,
An' you fin' yo' teahs a-drappin'
   When Malindy sings.

Who dat says dat humble praises
   Wif de Master nevah counts?   50
Heish yo' mouf, I hyeah dat music,
   Ez hit rises up an' mounts—

Floatin' by de hills an' valleys,
　　Way above dis buryin' sod,
Ez hit makes its way in glory　　　　　　　　　　　　55
　　To de very gates of God!

Oh, hit's sweetah dan de music
　　Of an edicated band;
An' hit's dearah dan de battle's
　　Song o' triumph in de lan'.　　　　　　　　　　　60
It seems holier dan evenin'
　　When de solemn chu'ch bell rings,
Ez I sit an' ca'mly listen
　　While Malindy sings.

Towsah, stop dat ba'kin', hyeah me!　　　　　　　　65
　　Mandy, mek dat chile keep still;
Don't you hyeah de echoes callin'
　　F'om de valley to de hill?
Let me listen, I can hyeah it,
　　Th'oo de bresh of angel's wings,　　　　　　　　70
Sof' an' sweet, "Swing Low, Sweet Chariot,"
　　Ez Malindy sings.

　　　　　　　　　　　　　　　　　　　　　　1896

from **Lyrics of the Hearthside**

Sympathy

I know what the caged bird feels, alas!
　　When the sun is bright on the upland slopes;
When the wind stirs soft through the springing grass,
And the river flows like a stream of glass;
　　When the first bird sings and the first bud opes,　　5
And the faint perfume from its chalice steals—
I know what the caged bird feels!

I know why the caged bird beats his wing
　　Till its blood is red on the cruel bars;
For he must fly back to his perch and cling　　　　　10
When he fain would be on the bough a-swing;
　　And a pain still throbs in the old, old scars
And they pulse again with a keener sting—
I know why he beats his wing!

I know why the caged bird sings, ah me,　　　　　　15
　　When his wing is bruised and his bosom sore,—

When he beats his bars and he would be free;
It is not a carol of joy or glee,
    But a prayer that he sends from his heart's deep core,
But a plea, that upward to Heaven he flings—   20
I know why the caged bird sings!

                            1899

Prometheus

Prometheus stole from Heaven the sacred fire
    And swept to earth with it o'er land and sea.
    He lit the vestal flames of poesy,
Content, for this, to brave celestial ire.

Wroth were the gods, and with eternal hate   5
    Pursued the fearless one who ravished Heaven
    That earth might hold in fee the perfect leaven
To lift men's souls above their low estate.

But judge you now, when poets wield the pen,
    Think you not well the wrong has been repaired?   10
    'T was all in vain that ill Prometheus fared:
The fire has been returned to Heaven again!

We have no singers like the ones whose note
    Gave challenge to the noblest warbler's song.
    We have no voice so mellow, sweet, and strong   15
As that which broke from Shelley's golden throat.

The measure of our songs is our desires:
    We tinkle where old poets used to storm
    We lack their substance tho' we keep their form:
We strum our banjo-strings and call them lyres.   20

                            19??

The Lynching of Jube Benson

Gordon Fairfax's library held but three men, but the air was dense with clouds of smoke. The talk had drifted from one topic to another much as the smoke wreaths had puffed, floated, and thinned away. Then Handon Gay, who was an ambitious young reporter, spoke of a lynching story in a recent magazine, and the matter of punishment without trial put new life into the conversation.

    "I should like to see a real lynching," said Gay rather callously.

    "Well, I should hardly express it that way," said Fairfax, "but if a real, live lynching were to come my way, I should not avoid it."

"I should," spoke the other from the depths of his chair, where he had been puffing in moody silence. Judged by his hair, which was freely sprinkled with gray, the speaker might have been a man of forty-five or fifty, but his face, though lined and serious, was youthful, the face of a man hardly past thirty.

"What, you, Dr. Melville? Why, I thought that you physicians wouldn't waken at anything."

"I have seen one such affair," said the doctor gravely, "in fact, I took a prominent part in it."

"Tell us about it," said the reporter, feeling for his pencil and note-book, which he was, nevertheless, careful to hide from the speaker.

The men drew their chairs eagerly up to the doctor's, but for a minute he did not seem to see them, but sat gazing abstractedly into the fire, then he took a long draw upon his cigar and began:

"I can see it all very vividly now. It was in the summer time and about seven years ago. I was practising at the time down in the little town of Bradford. It was a small and primitive place, just the location for an impecunious medical man, recently out of college.

"In lieu of a regular office, I attended to business in the first of two rooms which I rented from Hiram Daly, one of the more prosperous of the townsmen. Here I boarded and here also came my patients—white and black—whites from every section, and blacks from 'nigger town,' as the west portion of the place was called.

"The people about me were most of them coarse and rough, but they were simple and generous, and as time passed on I had about abandoned my intention of seeking distinction in wider fields and determined to settle into the place of a modest country doctor. This was rather a strange conclusion for a young man to arrive at, and I will not deny that the presence in the house of my host's beautiful young daughter, Annie, had something to do with my decision. She was a beautiful young girl of seventeen or eighteen, and very far superior to her surroundings. She had a native grace and a pleasing way about her that made everybody that came under her spell her abject slave. White and black who knew her loved her, and none, I thought, more deeply and respectfully than Jube Benson, the black man of all work about the place.

"He was a fellow whom everybody trusted; an apparently steady-going, grinning sort, as we used to call him. Well, he was completely under Miss Annie's thumb, and would fetch and carry for her like a faithful dog. As soon as he saw that I began to care for Annie, and anybody could see that, he transferred some of his allegiance to me and became my faithful servitor also. Never did a man have a more devoted adherent in his wooing than did I, and many a one of Annie's tasks which he volunteered to do gave her an extra hour with me. You can imagine that I liked the boy and you need not wonder any more that as both wooing and my practice waxed apace, I was content to give up my great ambitions and stay just where I was.

"It wasn't a very pleasant thing, then, to have an epidemic of typhoid break out in the town that kept me going so that I hardly had time for the courting that a fellow wants to carry on with his sweetheart while he is still young enough to call her his girl. I fumed, but duty was duty, and I kept to my work night and day. It was now that Jube proved how invaluable he was a coadjutor. He not only took messages to Annie, but brought sometimes little ones from her to me, and he would tell me little secret things that he had overheard her say that made me throb with joy and swear at him for repeating his mistress' conversation. But best of all, Jube was a perfect Cerberus, and no one on earth could have been more effective in keeping away or deluding the other young fellows who visited the Dalys. He would tell me of it afterwards, chuckling softly to himself. 'An', Doctah, I say to Mistah Hemp Stevens, "'Scuse us, Mistah Stevens, but Miss Annie, she des gone out," an' den he go outer de gate lookin' moughty lonesome. When Sam Elkins come, I say, "Sh, Mistah Elkins, Miss Annie, she done tuk down," an' he say, "What, Jube, you don' reckon hit de—" Den he stop an' look skeert, an' I say, "I feared hit is, Mistah Elkins," an' sheks my haid ez solemn. He goes outer de gate lookin' lak his bes' frien' done daid, an' all de time Miss Annie behine de cu'tain ovah de po'ch des' a laffin' fit to kill.'

"Jube was a most admirable liar, but what could I do? He knew that I was a young fool of hypocrite, and when I would rebuke him for these deceptions, he would give way and roll on the floor in an excess of delighted laughter until from very contagion I had to join him—and, well, there was no need of my preaching when there had been no beginning to his repentance and when there must ensue a continuance of his wrong-doing.

"This thing went on for over three months, and then, pouf! I was down like a shot. My patients were nearly all up, but the reaction from overwork made me an easy victim of the lurking germs. Then Jube loomed up as a nurse. He put everyone else aside, and with the doctor, a friend of mine from a neighbouring town, took entire charge of me. Even Annie herself was put aside, and I was cared for as tenderly as a baby. Tom, that was my physician and friend, told me all about it afterward with tears in his eyes. Only he was a big, blunt man and his expressions did not convey all that he meant. He told me how my nigger had nursed me as if I were a sick kitten and he my mother. Of how fiercely he guarded his right to be the sole one to 'do' for me, as he called it, and how, when the crisis came, he hovered, weeping, but hopeful, at my bedside, until it was safely passed, when they drove him, weak and exhausted, from the room. As for me, I knew little about it at the time, and cared less. I was too busy in my fight with death. To my chimerical vision there was only a black but gentle demon that came and went, alternating with a white fairy, who would insist on coming in on her head, growing larger and larger and then dissolving. But the pathos and devotion in the story lost nothing in my blunt friend's telling.

"It was during the period of a long convalescence, however, that I came to know my humble ally as he really was, devoted to the point of abjectness. There were times when for very shame at his goodness to me, I would beg him to go away, to do something else. He would go, but before I had time to realise that I was not being ministered to, he would be back at my side, grinning and pottering just the same. He manufactured duties for the joy of performing them. He pretended to see desires in me that I never had, because he liked to pander to them, and when I became entirely exasperated, and ripped out a good round oath, he chuckled with the remark, 'Dah, now, you sholy is gittin' well. Nevah did hyeah a man anywhaih nigh Jo'dan's sho' cuss lak dat.'

"Why, I grew to love him, love him, oh yes, I loved him as well—oh, what am I saying? All human love and gratitude are damned poor things; excuse me, gentlemen, this isn't a pleasant story. The truth is usually a nasty thing to stand.

"It was not six months after that that my friendship to Jube, which he had been at such great pains to win, was put to too severe a test.

"It was in the summer time again, and as business was slack, I had ridden over to see my friend, Dr. Tom. I had spent a good part of the day there, and it was past four o'clock when I rode leisurely into Bradford. I was in a particularly joyous mood and no premonition of the impending catastrophe oppressed me. No sense of sorrow, present or to come, forced itself upon me, even when I saw men hurrying through the almost deserted streets. When I got within sight of my home and saw a crowd surrounding it, I was only interested sufficiently to spur my horse into a jog trot, which brought me up to the throng, when something in the sullen, settled horror in the men's faces gave me a sudden, sick thrill. They whispered a word to me, and without a thought, save for Annie, the girl who had been so surely growing into my heart, I leaped from the saddle and tore my way through the people to the house.

"It was Annie, poor girl, bruised and bleeding, her face and dress torn from struggling. They were gathered round her with white faces, and, oh, with what terrible patience they were trying to gain from her fluttering lips the name of her murderer. They made way for me and I knelt at her side. She was beyond my skill, and my will merged with theirs. One thought was in our minds.

"Who?" I asked.

"Her eyes half opened, 'That black—' She fell back into my arms dead.

"We turned and looked at each other. The mother had broken down and was weeping, but the face of the father was like iron.

"'It is enough,'" he said; 'Jube has disappeared.' He went to the door and said to the expectant crowd, 'She is dead.'

"I heard the angry roar without swelling up like the noise of a flood, and then I heard the sudden movement of many feet as the men separated into searching parties, and laying the dead girl back upon her couch, I took my rifle and went out to join them.

"As if by intuition the knowledge had passed among the men that Jube Benson had disappeared, and he, by common consent, was to be the object of our search. Fully a dozen of the citizens had seen him hastening toward the woods and noted his skulking air, but as he had grinned in his old good-natured way they had, at the time, thought nothing of it. Now, however, the diabolical reason of his slyness was apparent. He had been shrewd enough to disarm suspicion, and by now was far away. Even Mrs. Daly, who was visiting with a neighbour, had seen him stepping out by a back way, and had said with a laugh, 'I reckon that black rascal's a-running off somewhere.' Oh, if she had only known.

"'To the woods! To the woods!' that was the cry, and away we went, each with the determination not to shoot, but to bring the culprit alive into town, and then to deal with him as his crime deserved.

"I cannot describe the feelings I experienced as I went out that night to beat the woods for this human tiger. My heart smouldered within me like a coal, and I went forward under the impulse of a will that was half my own, half some more malignant power's. My throat throbbed drily, but water nor whiskey would not have quenched my thirst. The thought has come to me since that now I could interpret the panther's desire for blood and sympathise with it, but then I thought nothing. I simply went forward, and watched, watched with burning eyes for a familiar form that I had looked for as often before with such different emotions.

"Luck or ill-luck, which you will, was with our party, and just as dawn was graying the sky, we came upon our quarry crouched in the corner of a fence. It was only half light, and we might have passed, but my eyes had caught sight of him, and I raised the cry. We levelled our guns and he rose and came toward us.

"'I t'ought you wa'n't gwine see me,' he said sullenly, 'I didn't mean no harm.'

"'Harm!'

"Some of the men took the word up with oaths, others were ominously silent.

"We gathered around him like hungry beasts, and I began to see terror dawning in his eyes. He turned to me, 'I's moughty glad you's hyeah, doc,' he said, 'you ain't gwine let 'em whup me.'

"'Whip you, you hound,' I said, 'I'm going to see you hanged,' and in the excess of my passion I struck him full on the mouth. He made a motion as if to resent the blow against even such great odds, but controlled himself.

"'W'y, doctah,' he exclaimed in the saddest voice I have ever heard, 'w'y, doctah! I ain't stole nuffin' o' yo'n, an' I was comin' back. I only run off to see my gal, Lucy, ovah to de Centah.'

"'You lie!' I said, and my hands were busy helping the others bind him upon a horse. Why did I do it? I don't know. A false education, I reckon, one false from the beginning. I saw his black face glooming there in the half light, and I could only think of him as a monster. It's tradition. At first I was told that the black man would catch me, and when I got over that, they taught me that the devil was black, and when I had recovered from the sickness of that belief, here were Jube and his fellows with faces of menacing blackness. There was only one conclusion: This black man stood for all the powers of evil, the result of whose machinations had been gathering in my mind from childhood up. But this has nothing to do with what happened.

"After firing a few shots to announce our capture, we rode back into town with Jube. The ingathering parties from all directions met us as we made our way up to the house. All was very quiet and orderly. There was no doubt that it was as the papers would have said, a gathering of the best citizens. It was a gathering of stern, determined men, bent on a terrible vengeance.

"We took Jube into the house, into the room where the corpse lay. At sight of it, he gave a scream like an animal's and his face went the colour of storm-blown water. This was enough to condemn him. We divined, rather than heard, his cry of 'Miss Ann, Miss Ann, oh, my God, doc, you don't t'ink I done it?'

"Hungry hands were ready. We hurried him out into the yard. A rope was ready. A tree was at hand. Well, that part was the least of it, save that Hiram Daly stepped aside to let me be the first to pull upon the rope. It was lax at first. Then it tightened, and I felt the quivering soft weight resist my muscles. Other hands joined, and Jube swung off his feet.

"No one was masked. We knew each other. Not even the culprit's face was covered, and the last I remember of him as he went into the air was a look of sad reproach that will remain with me until I meet him face to face again.

"We were tying the end of the rope to a tree, where the dead man might hang as a warning to his fellows, when a terrible cry chilled us to the marrow.

"'Cut 'im down, cut 'im down, he ain't guilty. We got de one. Cut him down, fu' Gawd's sake. Here's de man, we foun' him hidin' in de barn!'

"Jube's brother, Ben, and another Negro, came rushing toward us, half dragging, half carrying a miserable-looking wretch between them. Someone cut the rope and Jube dropped lifeless to the ground.

"'Oh, my Gawd, he's daid, he's daid!' wailed the brother, but with blazing eyes he brought his captive into the centre of the group, and we saw in the full light the scratched face of Tom Skinner—the worst white ruffian in the town—but the face we saw was not as we were accustomed to see it, merely smeared with dirt. It was blackened to imitate a Negro's.

"God forgive me; I could not wait to try to resuscitate Jube. I knew he was already past help, so I rushed into the house and to the dead girl's side. In the excitement they had not yet washed or laid her out. Carefully, carefully, I searched underneath her broken finger nails. There was skin there. I took it out, the little curled pieces, and went with it to my office.

"There, determinedly, I examined it under a powerful glass, and read my own doom. It was the skin of a white man, and in it were embedded strands of short, brown hair or beard.

"How I went out to tell the waiting crowd I do not know, for something kept crying in my ears, 'Blood guilty! Blood guilty!'

"The men went away stricken into silence and awe. The new prisoner attempted neither denial nor plea. When they were gone I would have helped Ben carry his brother in, but he waved me away fiercely, 'You he'ped murder my brothah, you dat was *his* frien', go 'way, go 'way! I'll tek him home myse'f.' I could only respect his wish, and he and his comrade took up the dead man and between them bore him up the street on which the sun was now shining full.

"I saw the few men who had not skulked indoors uncover as they passed, and I—I—stood there between the two murdered ones, while all the while something in my ears kept crying, 'Blood guilty! Blood guilty!'"

The doctor's head dropped into his hands and he sat for some time in silence, which was broken by neither of the men, then he rose, saying, "Gentlemen, that was my last lynching."

1904

An Ante-Bellum Sermon

We is gathahed hyeah, my brothahs,
    In dis howlin' wildaness,
Fu' to speak some words of comfo't
    To each othah in distress.
An' we chooses fu' ouah subjic'   5
    Dis—we'll 'splain it by an' by;
"An' de Lawd said, 'Moses, Moses,'
    An' de man said, 'Hyeah am I.'"

Now ole Pher'oh, down in Egypt,
    Was de wuss man evah bo'n,   10
An' he had de Hebrew chillun
    Down dah wukin' in his co'n;
'T well de Lawd got tiahed o' his foolin',
    An' sez he: "I'll let him know—
Look hyeah, Moses, go tell Pher'oh   15
    Fu' to let dem chillun go."

"An' ef he refuse to do it,
    I will make him rue de houah,
Fu' I'll empty down on Egypt
    All de vials of my powah."   20

Yes, he did—an' Pher'oh's ahmy
    Was n't wuth a ha'f a dime;
Fu' de Lawd will he'p his chillun,
    You kin trust him evah time.

An' yo' enemies may 'sail you
    In de back an' in de front;
But de Lawd is all aroun' you,
    Fu' to ba' de battle's brunt.
Dey kin fo'ge yo' chains an' shackles
F'om de mountains to de sea;
    But de Lawd will sen' some Moses
    Fu' to set his chillun free.

An' de Ian' shall hyeah his thundah,
    Lak a blas' f'om Gab'el's ho'n,
Fu' de Lawd of hosts is mighty
    When he girds his ahmor on.
But fu' feah some one mistakes me,
    I will pause right hyeah to say,
    Dat I'm still a-preachin' ancient,
I ain't talkin' 'bout to-day.

But I tell you, fellah christuns,
    Things 'll happen mighty strange;
Now, de Lawd done dis fu' Isrul,
    An' his ways don't nevah change,
An' de love he showed to Isrul
    Was n't all on Isrul spent;
Now don't run an' tell yo' mastahs
    Dat I's preachin' discontent.

'Cause I is n't; I'se a-judgin'
    Bible people by deir ac's;
I'se a-givin' you de Scriptuah,
    I'se a-handin' you de fac's.
Cose ole Pher'oh b'lieved in slav'ry,
    But de Lawd he let him see,
Dat de people he put bref in,—
    Evah mothah's son was free.

An' dahs othahs thinks lak Pher'oh,
    But dey calls de Scriptuah liar,
Fu' de Bible says "a servant
    Is a-worthy of his hire."
An' you cain't git roun' nor thoo dat,
    An' you cain't git ovah it,
Fu' whatevah place you git in,
    Dis hyeah Bible too 'll fit.

25

30

35

40

45

50

55

60

So you see de Lawd's intention, 65
   Evah sence de worl' began,
Was dat His almighty freedom
   Should belong to evah man,
But I think it would be bettah,
   Ef I'd pause agin to say, 70
Dat I'm talkin' 'bout ouah freedom
   In a Bibleistic way.
But de Moses is a-comin',
   An' he's comin', suah and fas'
We kin hyeah his feet a-trompin', 75
   We kin hyeah his trumpit blas'.
But I want to wa'n you people,
   Don't you git too brigity;
An' don't you git to braggin'
   'Bout dese things, you wait an' see. 80

But when Moses wif his powah
   Comes an' sets us chillun free,
We will praise de gracious Mastah
   Dat has gin us liberty;
An' we'll shout ouah halleluyahs, 85
   On dat mighty reck'nin' day,
When we'se reco'nised ez citiz'—
   Huh uh! Chillun, let us pray!

1896

JACK LONDON
1876–1916

Jack London enjoyed having his photo taken. His archive at the Huntington Library includes hundreds of his photographs, and many are of him. Anyone who gazes at his likeness might wonder *which* London the photo happened to arrest in that one second of a short but complex life. At the time of his death in 1916, when he was only 40 years old, London was already America's best-selling writer, and his work has been translated into over 100 languages. While we have his two semiautobiographical accounts, *Martin Eden* (1909) and *John Barleycorn: Alcoholic Memoirs* (1913), not to mention his photographs, letters, and countless biographies, "Jack London" is a character unto himself. At times, the narratives of his life masquerade as sensational fiction, but what consistently and indisputably emerges is his identity as working class—at first as a working-class laborer and then as a working writer whose fiction and nonfiction capture the dramatic action and labor of survival.

Jack London was born in January of 1876, America's centennial year, amid a burgeoning industrial economy and the height of American literary realism. His parents, Flora Wellman and William Henry Chaney, were living in San Francisco by common-law marriage. When Wellman refused to get an abortion, Chaney left her before their child was born (coincidentally, he made his living advising couples on childrearing by reading their horoscopes). Wellman married John London, a Civil War veteran, when Jack was nine months old. Jack was perhaps most bonded with his stepsister, Eliza London, and his neighbor, Mrs. Prentiss, a former slave who then worked as a wet nurse in Oakland, California. From ages ten to fifteen, he worked physically demanding jobs to support his family. After working eighteen-hour days packing pickles into jars, at fifteen he quit school and borrowed three hundred dollars from Mrs. Prentiss to buy his first boat, the *Razzle Dazzle*. He became an oyster pirate, stealing from company-owned beds to sell in San Francisco Bay docks. From here on, London's biography is dotted with names of vessels on which he would travel throughout his life—each marking a crucial phase of his life and writing career. Before he was seventeen, he boarded the *Sophia Sutherland* to hunt seals in the North Pacific. After his seven-month voyage, London wrote "A Typhoon Off the Coast of Japan" (1893), which won first place and twenty-five dollars in a writing contest sponsored by the *San Francisco Morning Call*. He worked briefly for the Oakland Electric Railway, but the grueling labor in the power plant soon inspired a very different experience with the railway: as a member of Deserting Coxey's Army, he rode the rails from California to Washington, D.C., on a protest march for unemployed workers in the United States. He was eventually arrested for vagrancy in New York. By the time he returned home, he was committed to learning and writing, and breezed through two years of high school in two months. Already influenced by Charles Darwin and Herbert Spencer, he moved on to Marx, Kant, and Nietzsche. He joined a local branch of the Socialist Party, and earned the nickname "Boy Socialist." Years later, in 1901 and then again in 1905, he would run for mayor of Oakland on the Socialist party's ticket. "South of the Slot" (1909)[1] notably reflects London's socialist politics, his visceral experiences with the divisions of labor, and his knowledge of the ever-widening gap between privileged and working classes.

After just one year at the University of California, Berkeley, London took off again in 1897, this time as a miner in the Alaskan Gold Rush. Readers of London's Northland tales, including *The Call of the Wild* (1903) and *White Fang* (1906), will surely perceive the influence that London's time in the unforgiving Klondike had on his writing. He sold *The Call of the Wild* to his editor George Brett at Macmillan for a flat fee of $2,000. Even though it sold millions of copies, London made no royalties. However, the $2,000 plus $700 from the *Saturday Evening Post* for serial rights was enough to purchase a

---

[1]"South of the Slot" was first published in the *Saturday Evening Post* in May of 1909. It later appeared in the collection *The Strength of the Strong* (Macmillan, 1914).

sloop for his sailboat. Soon thereafter, he planned a southland voyage on his custom ship the *Snark*. With a month of bad luck—and bad planning—behind them, London and his meager crew finally reached Honolulu and docked at Pearl Harbor. This was the beginning of nearly two years traveling in the South Pacific, which would be one of the most fulfilling and productive periods of his life. He continued to write 1,000 words a day while traveling; he photographed and illustrated for travel magazines and wrote essays and travel narratives, including *The Cruise of the Snark* (1911), which also partially funded their expedition. One of the best-known stories inspired by his visits to Kalaupapa leper colony on Molokai is "Koolau the Leper" (1909)[2]. His stories from these southland experiences convey the intrusion of Euro-Americans and the subsequent effects on Hawaiian indigenous cultures. Although London is best known for his fiction, he also left behind an extensive archive of essays and photographs from his time as a war correspondent during the Russo-Japanese war, his essays about the slums of London's East End, which inspired *People of the Abyss* (1903), and his coverage of the San Francisco earthquake for *Collier's*. This work, combined with his photographs, fiction, and essays of and about the South Pacific, distinguish Jack London as a cultural producer *and* critic.

Shortly before his death, London discovered the work of Carl Jung, which had particular resonance while his health steadily declined. His last writing combined Jungian archetypes with his own understanding of Polynesian myth. London died at his ranch in the Sonoma Valley from complications related to kidney failure, though some have argued that it was a self-induced morphine overdose. His ashes were buried at his ranch, along with an ilima lei from his friends in Hawaii. The coincidence of his birth with the centennial is worth noting again, since he died not only a national figure, but also a figure *of* America with its teeming contradictions and aspirations.

Kara Thompson
College of William and Mary

PRIMARY WORKS

The Call of the Wild, 1903; *The People of the Abyss*, 1903; *The Sea-Wolf*, 1904; *The Road*, 1907; *The Iron Heel*, 1908; *Martin Eden*, 1909; *The Valley of the Moon*, 1913; *John Barleycorn*, 1913; *Novels, Stories and Social Writings*, ed. Donald Pizer, 2 vols., 1982; *The Letters of Jack London*, ed. Earle Labor et al., 3 vols., 1988; *The Complete Short Stories of Jack London*, ed. Earle Labor et al., 1993; *No Mentor but Myself: A Collection of Articles, Essays, Reviews, and Letters on Writing and Writers*, ed. Dale L. Walker and Jeanne Campbell Reesman, 1999.

---

[2]"Koolau the Leper" was first published in the *Pacific Monthly* in December, 1909. It later appeared in a collection of six stories, *The House of Pride* (Macmillan, 1912). The title story, "The House of Pride" and the collection itself incited controversy among white elites and missionaries in Hawaii who disapproved of London's working-class politics, his depictions of Euro-American colonialism, and his somewhat daring confrontation with the topic of leprosy.

South of the Slot[1]

Old San Francisco, which is the San Francisco of only the other day, the day before the Earthquake, was divided midway by the Slot. The Slot was an iron crack that ran along the center of Market street, and from the Slot arose the burr of the ceaseless, endless cable that was hitched at will to the cars it dragged up and down. In truth, there were two slots, but in the quick grammar of the West time was saved by calling them, and much more that they stood for, "The Slot." North of the Slot were the theaters, hotels, and shopping district, the banks and the staid, respectable business houses. South of the Slot were the factories, slums, laundries, machine-shops, boiler works, and the abodes of the working class.

The Slot was the metaphor that expressed the class cleavage of Society, and no man crossed this metaphor, back and forth, more successfully than Freddie Drummond. He made a practice of living in both worlds, and in both worlds he lived signally well. Freddie Drummond was a professor in the Sociology Department of the University of California, and it was as a professor of sociology that he first crossed over the Slot, lived for six months in the great labor-ghetto, and wrote "The Unskilled Laborer"—a book that was hailed everywhere as an able contribution to the literature of progress, and as a splendid reply to the literature of discontent. Politically and economically it was nothing if not orthodox. Presidents of great railway systems bought whole editions of it to give to their employees. The Manufacturers' Association alone distributed fifty thousand copies of it. In a way, it was almost as immoral as the far-famed and notorious "Message to Garcia,"[2] while in its pernicious preachment of thrift and content it ran "Mrs. Wiggs of the Cabbage Patch"[3] a close second.

At first, Freddie Drummond found it monstrously difficult to get along among the working people. He was not used to their ways, and they certainly were not used to his. They were suspicious. He had no antecedents. He could talk of no previous jobs. His hands were soft. His extraordinary politeness was ominous. His first idea of the rôle he would play was that of a free and independent American who chose to work with his hands and no explanations given. But it wouldn't do, as he quickly discovered. At the beginning they accepted him, very provisionally, as a freak. A little later, as he began to know his way about better, he insensibly drifted into the rôle that would work—namely, he was a man who had seen better days, very much better days, but who was down in his luck, though, to be sure, only temporarily.

---

[1]"South of the Slot" was first published in the *Saturday Evening Post* in May of 1909. It later appeared in the collection *The Strength of the Strong* (Macmillan, 1914).

[2]A didactic essay by Elbert Hubbard (1856–1915) preaching to employees the virtues of obedience and efficiency.

[3]One of the most popular novels by Alice Caldwell Hegan Rice (1870–1942), *Mrs. Wiggs of the Cabbage Patch* (1901), features a widow whose husband has died of drink. She sustains herself and her many children with the refrain, "Everything in the world comes right if we jes' wait long enough."

He learned many things, and generalized much and often erroneously, all of which can be found in the pages of "The Unskilled Laborer." He saved himself, however, after the sane and conservative manner of his kind, by labeling his generalizations as "tentative." One of his first experiences was in the great Wilmax Cannery, where he was put on piece-work making small packing cases. A box factory supplied the parts, and all Freddie Drummond had to do was to fit the parts into a form and drive in the wire nails with a light hammer.

It was not skilled labor, but it was piece-work. The ordinary laborers in the cannery got a dollar and a half per day. Freddie Drummond found the other men on the same job with him jogging along and earning a dollar and seventy-five cents a day. By the third day he was able to earn the same. But he was ambitious. He did not care to jog along and, being unusually able and fit, on the fourth day earned two dollars. The next day, having keyed himself up to an exhausting high-tension, he earned two dollars and a half. His fellow workers favored him with scowls and black looks, and made remarks, slangily witty and which he did not understand, about sucking up to the boss and pace-making and holding her down when the rains set in. He was astonished at their malingering on piece-work, generalized about the inherent laziness of the unskilled laborer, and proceeded next day to hammer out three dollars' worth of boxes.

And that night, coming out of the cannery, he was interviewed by his fellow workmen, who were very angry and incoherently slangy. He failed to comprehend the motive behind their action. The action itself was strenuous. When he refused to ease down his pace and bleated about freedom of contract, independent Americanism, and the dignity of toil, they proceeded to spoil his pace-making ability. It was a fierce battle, for Drummond was a large man and an athlete, but the crowd finally jumped on his ribs, walked on his face, and stamped on his fingers, so that it was only after lying in bed for a week that he was able to get up and look for another job. All of which is duly narrated in that first book of his, in the chapter entitled "The Tyranny of Labor."

A little later, in another department of the Wilmax Cannery, lumping as a fruit-distributor among the women, he essayed to carry two boxes of fruit at a time, and was promptly reproached by the other fruit-lumpers. It was palpable malingering; but he was there, he decided, not to change conditions, but to observe. So he lumped one box thereafter, and so well did he study the art of shirking that he wrote a special chapter on it, with the last several paragraphs devoted to tentative generalizations.

In those six months he worked at many jobs and developed into a very good imitation of a genuine worker. He was a natural linguist, and he kept notebooks, making a scientific study of the workers' slang or argot, until he could talk quite intelligibly. This language also enabled him more intimately to follow their mental processes, and thereby to gather much data for a projected chapter in some future book which he planned to entitle "Synthesis of Working-Class Psychology."

Before he arose to the surface from that first plunge into the under-world he discovered that he was a good actor and demonstrated the plastic-ity of his nature. He was himself astonished at his own fluidity. Once having mastered the language and conquered numerous fastidious qualms, he found that he could flow into any nook of working-class life and fit it so snugly as to feel comfortably at home. As he said, in the preface to his sec-ond book, "The Toiler," he endeavored really to know the working people, and the only possible way to achieve this was to work beside them, eat their food, sleep in their beds, be amused with their amusements, think their thoughts, and feel their feelings.

He was not a deep thinker. He had no faith in new theories. All his norms and criteria were conventional. His Thesis, on the French Revolution, was noteworthy in college annals, not merely for its painstaking and volumi-nous accuracy, but for the fact that it was the dryest, deadest, most formal, and most orthodox screed ever written on the subject. He was a very re-served man, and his natural inhibition was large in quantity and steel-like in quality. He had but few friends. He was too undemonstrative, too frigid. He had no vices, nor had anyone ever discovered any temptations. Tobacco he detested, beer he abhorred, and he was never known to drink anything stronger than an occasional light wine at dinner.

When a freshman he had been baptized "Ice-Box" by his warmer-blooded fellows. As a member of the faculty he was known as "Cold-Storage." He had but one grief, and that was "Freddie." He had earned it when he played full-back on the 'Varsity eleven, and his formal soul had never succeeded in living it down. "Freddie" he would ever be, except officially, and through nightmare vistas he looked into a future when his world would speak of him as "Old Freddie."

For he was very young to be a Doctor of Sociology, only twenty-seven, and he looked younger. In appearance and atmosphere he was a strapping big college man, smooth-faced and easy-mannered, clean and simple and wholesome, with a known record of being a splendid athlete and an implied vast possession of cold culture of the inhibited sort. He never talked shop out of class and committee rooms, except later on, when his books showered him with distasteful public notice and he yielded to the extent of reading occasional papers before certain literary and economic societies.

He did everything right—too right; and in dress and comportment was inevitably correct. Not that he was a dandy. Far from it. He was a college man, in dress and carriage as like as a pea to the type that of late years is being so generously turned out of our institutions of higher learning. His handshake was satisfyingly strong and stiff. His blue eyes were coldly blue and convincingly sincere. His voice, firm and masculine, clean and crisp of enunciation, was pleasant to the ear. The one drawback to Freddie Drum-mond was his inhibition. He never unbent. In his football days, the higher the tension of the game, the cooler he grew. He was noted as a boxer, but he was regarded as an automaton, with the inhuman precision of a machine judging distance and timing blows, guarding, blocking, and stalling. He was rarely punished himself, while he rarely punished an opponent. He was too clever and too controlled to permit himself to put a pound more weight into a punch than he intended. With him it was a matter of exercise. It kept him fit.

As time went by, Freddie Drummond found himself more frequently crossing the Slot and losing himself in South of Market. His summer and winter holidays were spent there, and, whether it was a week or a week-end, he found the time spent there to be valuable and enjoyable. And there was so much material to be gathered. His third book, "Mass and Master," became a text-book in the American universities; and almost before he knew it, he was at work on a fourth one, "The Fallacy of the Inefficient."

Somewhere in his make-up there was a strange twist or quirk. Perhaps it was a recoil from his environment and training, or from the tempered seed of his ancestors, who had been bookmen generation preceding generation; but at any rate, he found enjoyment in being down in the working-class world. In his own world he was "Cold-Storage," but down below he was "Big" Bill Totts, who could drink and smoke, and slang and fight, and be an all-around favorite. Everybody liked Bill, and more than one working girl made love to him. At first he had been merely a good actor, but as time went on, simulation became second nature. He no longer played a part, and he loved sausages, sausages and bacon, than which, in his own proper sphere, there was nothing more loathsome in the way of food.

From doing the thing for the need's sake, he came to doing the thing for the thing's sake. He found himself regretting as the time drew near for him to go back to his lecture-room and his inhibition. And he often found himself waiting with anticipation for the dreamy time to pass when he could cross the Slot and cut loose and play the devil. He was not wicked, but as "Big" Bill Totts he did a myriad things that Freddie Drummond would never have been permitted to do. Moreover, Freddie Drummond never would have wanted to do them. That was the strangest part of his discovery. Freddie Drummond and Bill Totts were two totally different creatures. The desires and tastes and impulses of each ran counter to the other's. Bill Totts could shirk at a job with clear conscience, while Freddie Drummond condemned shirking as vicious, criminal, and un-American, and devoted whole chapters to condemnation of the vice. Freddie Drummond did not care for dancing, but Bill Totts never missed the nights at the various dancing clubs, such as The Magnolia, The Western Star, and The Elite; while he won a massive silver cup, standing thirty inches high, for being the best-sustained character at the Butchers and Meat Workers' annual grand masked ball. And Bill Totts liked the girls and the girls liked him, while Freddie Drummond enjoyed playing the ascetic in this particular, was open in his opposition to equal suffrage, and cynically bitter in his secret condemnation of coeducation.

Freddie Drummond changed his manners with his dress, and without effort. When he entered the obscure little room used for his transformation scenes, he carried himself just a bit too stiffly. He was too erect, his shoulders were an inch too far back, while his face was grave, almost harsh, and practically expressionless. But when he emerged in Bill Totts's clothes he was another creature. Bill Totts did not slouch, but somehow his whole form limbered up and became graceful. The very sound of the voice was changed, and the laugh was loud and hearty, while loose speech and an occasional oath were as a matter of course on his lips. Also, Bill Totts was a trifle inclined to late hours, and at times, in saloons, to be good-naturedly bellicose with other workmen. Then, too, at Sunday picnics or when coming home from the show, either arm betrayed a practiced familiarity in stealing around girls' waists, while he displayed a wit keen and delightful in the flirtatious badinage that was expected of a good fellow in his class.

So thoroughly was Bill Totts himself, so thoroughly a workman, a genuine denizen of South of the Slot, that he was as class-conscious as the average of his kind, and his hatred for a scab even exceeded that of the average loyal union man. During the Water Front Strike, Freddie Drummond was somehow able to stand apart from the unique combination, and, coldly critical, watch Bill Totts hilariously slug scab longshoremen. For Bill Totts was a dues-paying member of the Longshoremen Union and had a right to be indignant with the usurpers of his job. "Big" Bill Totts was so very big, and so very able, that it was "Big" Bill to the front when trouble was brewing. From acting outraged feelings, Freddie Drummond, in the rôle of his other self, came to experience genuine outrage, and it was only when he returned to the classic atmosphere of the university that he was able, sanely and conservatively, to generalize upon his underworld experiences and put them down on paper as a trained sociologist should. That Bill Totts lacked the perspective to raise him above class-consciousness, Freddie Drummond clearly saw. But Bill Totts could not see it. When he saw a scab taking his job away, he saw red at the same time, and little else did he see. It was Freddie Drummond, irreproachably clothed and comported, seated at his study desk or facing his class in "Sociology 17," who saw Bill Totts, and all around Bill Totts, and all around the whole scab and union-labor problem and its relation to the economic welfare of the United States in the struggle for the world market. Bill Totts really wasn't able to see beyond the next meal and the prize-fight the following night at the Gaiety Athletic Club.

It was while gathering material for "Women and Work" that Freddie received his first warning of the danger he was in. He was too successful at living in both worlds. This strange dualism he had developed was after all very unstable, and, as he sat in his study and meditated, he saw that it could not endure. It was really a transition stage, and if he persisted he saw that he would inevitably have to drop one world or the other. He could not continue in both. And as he looked at the row of volumes that graced the upper shelf of his revolving book-case, his volumes, beginning with his Thesis and ending with "Women and Work," he decided that that was the world he would hold to and stick by. Bill Totts had served his purpose, but he had become a too dangerous accomplice. Bill Totts would have to cease.

Freddie Drummond's fright was due to Mary Condon, President of the International Glove Workers' Union No. 974. He had seen her, first, from the spectators' gallery, at the annual convention of the Northwest Federation of Labor, and he had seen her through Bill Totts' eyes, and that individual had been most favorably impressed by her. She was not Freddie Drummond's sort at all. What if she were a royal-bodied woman, graceful and sinewy as a panther, with amazing black eyes that could fill with fire or laughter-love, as the mood might dictate? He detested women with a too exuberant vitality and a lack of ... well, of inhibition. Freddie Drummond accepted the doctrine of evolution because it was quite universally accepted by college men, and he flatly believed that man had climbed up the ladder of life out of the weltering muck and mess of lower and monstrous organic things. But he was a trifle ashamed of this genealogy, and preferred not to think of it. Wherefore, probably, he practiced his iron inhibition and preached it to others, and preferred women of his own type, who could shake free of this bestial and regrettable ancestral line and by discipline and control emphasize the wideness of the gulf that separated them from what their dim forbears had been.

Bill Totts had none of these considerations. He had liked Mary Condon from the moment his eyes first rested on her in the convention hall, and he had made it a point, then and there, to find out who she was. The next time he met her, and quite by accident, was when he was driving an express wagon for Pat Morrissey. It was in a lodging house in Mission Street, where he had been called to take a trunk into storage. The landlady's daughter had called him and led him to the little bedroom, the occupant of which, a glove-maker, had just been removed to hospital. But Bill did not know this. He stooped, up-ended the trunk, which was a large one, got it on his shoulder, and struggled to his feet with his back toward the open door. At that moment he heard a woman's voice.

"Belong to the union?" was the question asked.

"Aw, what's it to you?" he retorted. "Run along now, an' git outa my way. I wanta turn round."

The next he knew, big as he was, he was whirled half around and sent reeling backward, the trunk overbalancing him, till he fetched up with a crash against the wall. He started to swear, but at the same instant found himself looking into Mary Condon's flashing, angry eyes.

"Of course I b'long to the union," he said. "I was only kiddin' you."

"Where's your card?" she demanded in business-like tones.

"In my pocket. But I can't git it out now. This trunk's too damn heavy. Come on down to the wagon an' I'll show it to you."

"Put that trunk down," was the command.

"What for? I got a card, I'm tellin' you."

"Put it down, that's all. No scab's going to handle that trunk. You ought to be ashamed of yourself, you big coward, scabbing on honest men. Why don't you join the union and be a man?"

Mary Condon's color had left her face, and it was apparent that she was in a rage.

"To think of a big man like you turning traitor to his class. I suppose you're aching to join the militia for a chance to shoot down union drivers the next strike. You may belong to the militia already, for that matter. You're the sort—"

"Hold on, now, that's too much!" Bill dropped the trunk to the floor with a bang, straightened up, and thrust his hand into his inside coat pocket. "I told you I was only kiddin'. There, look at that."

It was a union card properly enough.

"All right, take it along," Mary Condon said. "And the next time don't kid."

Her face relaxed as she noticed the ease with which he got the big trunk to his shoulder, and her eyes glowed as they glanced over the graceful massiveness of the man. But Bill did not see that. He was too busy with the trunk.

The next time he saw Mary Condon was during the Laundry Strike. The Laundry Workers, but recently organized, were green at the business, and had petitioned Mary Condon to engineer the strike. Freddie Drummond had had an inkling of what was coming, and had sent Bill Totts to join the union and investigate. Bill's job was in the wash-room, and the men had been called out first, that morning, in order to stiffen the courage of the girls; and Bill chanced to be near the door to the mangle room when Mary Condon started to enter. The superintendent, who was both large and stout, barred her way. He wasn't going to have his girls called out, and he'd teach her a lesson to mind her own business. And as Mary tried to squeeze past him he thrust her back with a fat hand on her shoulder. She glanced around and saw Bill.

"Here you, Mr. Totts," she called. "Lend a hand. I want to get in."

Bill experienced a startle of warm surprise. She had remembered his name from his union card. The next moment the superintendent had been plucked from the doorway raving about rights under the law, and the girls were deserting their machines. During the rest of that short and successful strike, Bill constituted himself Mary Condon's henchman and messenger, and when it was over returned to the University to be Freddie Drummond and to wonder what Bill Totts could see in such a woman.

Freddie Drummond was entirely safe, but Bill had fallen in love. There was no getting away from the fact of it, and it was this fact that had given Freddie Drummond his warning. Well, he had done his work, and his adventures could cease. There was no need for him to cross the Slot again. All but the last three chapters of his latest, "Labor Tactics and Strategy," was finished, and he had sufficient material on hand adequately to supply those chapters.

Another conclusion he arrived at, was that in order to sheet-anchor himself as Freddie Drummond, closer ties and relations in his own social nook were necessary. It was time that he was married, anyway, and he was fully aware that if Freddie Drummond didn't get married, Bill Totts assuredly would, and the complications were too awful to contemplate. And so, enters Catherine Van Vorst. She was a college woman herself, and her father, the one wealthy member of the faculty, was the head of the Philosophy Department as well. It would be a wise marriage from every standpoint, Freddie Drummond concluded when the engagement was consummated and announced. In appearance cold and reserved, aristocratic and wholesomely conservative, Catherine Van Vorst, though warm in her way, possessed an inhibition equal to Drummond's.

All seemed well with him, but Freddie Drummond could not quite shake off the call of the underworld, the lure of the free and open, of the unhampered, irresponsible life South of the Slot. As the time of his marriage approached, he felt that he had indeed sowed wild oats, and he felt, moreover, what a good thing it would be if he could have but one wild fling more, play the good fellow and the wastrel one last time, ere he settled down to gray lecture-rooms and sober matrimony. And, further to tempt him, the very last chapter of "Labor Tactics and Strategy" remained unwritten for lack of a trifle more of essential data which he had neglected to gather.

So Freddie Drummond went down for the last time as Bill Totts, got his data, and, unfortunately, encountered Mary Condon. Once more installed in his study, it was not a pleasant thing to look back upon. It made his warning doubly imperative. Bill Totts had behaved abominably. Not only had he met Mary Condon at the Central Labor Council, but he had stopped in at a chophouse with her, on the way home, and treated her to oysters. And before they parted at her door, his arms had been about her, and he had kissed her on the lips and kissed her repeatedly. And her last words in his ear, words uttered softly with a catchy sob in the throat that was nothing more nor less than a love cry, were "Bill . . . dear, dear Bill."

Freddie Drummond shuddered at the recollection. He saw the pit yawning for him. He was not by nature a polygamist, and he was appalled at the possibilities of the situation. It would have to be put an end to, and it would end in one only of two ways: either he must become wholly Bill Totts and be married to Mary Condon, or he must remain wholly Freddie Drummond and be married to Catherine Van Vorst. Otherwise, his conduct would be beneath contempt and horrible.

In the several months that followed, San Francisco was torn with labor strife. The unions and the employers' associations had locked horns with a determination that looked as if they intended to settle the matter, one way or the other, for all time. But Freddie Drummond corrected proofs, lectured classes, and did not budge. He devoted himself to Catherine Van Vorst, and day by day found more to respect and admire in her—nay, even to love in her. The Street Car Strike tempted him, but not so severely as he would have expected; and the great Meat Strike came on and left him cold. The ghost of Bill Totts had been successfully laid, and Freddie Drummond with rejuvenescent zeal tackled a brochure, long-planned, on the topic of "diminishing returns."

The wedding was two weeks off, when, one afternoon, in San Francisco, Catherine Van Vorst picked him up and whisked him away to see a Boys' Club, recently instituted by the settlement workers with whom she was interested. It was her brother's machine, but they were alone with the exception of the chauffeur. At the junction with Kearny Street, Market and Geary Streets intersect like the sides of a sharp-angled letter "V." They, in the auto, were coming down Market with the intention of negotiating the sharp apex and going up Geary. But they did not know what was coming down Geary, timed by fate to meet them at the apex. While aware from the papers that the Meat Strike was on and that it was an exceedingly bitter one, all thought of it at that moment was farthest from Freddie Drummond's mind. Was he not seated beside Catherine? And, besides, he was carefully expositing to her his views on settlement work—views that Bill Totts' adventures had played a part in formulating.

Coming down Geary Street were six meat wagons. Beside each scab driver sat a policeman. Front and rear, and along each side of this procession, marched a protecting escort of one hundred police. Behind the police rear guard, at a respectful distance, was an orderly but vociferous mob, several blocks in length, that congested the street from sidewalk to sidewalk. The Beef Trust was making an effort to supply the hotels, and, incidentally, to begin the breaking of the strike. The St. Francis had already been supplied, at a cost of many broken windows and broken heads, and the expedition was marching to the relief of the Palace Hotel.

All unwitting, Drummond sat beside Catherine, talking settlement work, as the auto, honking methodically and dodging traffic, swung in a wide curve to get around the apex. A big coal wagon, loaded with lump coal and drawn by four huge horses, just debouching from Kearny Street as though to turn down Market, blocked their way. The driver of the wagon seemed undecided, and the chauffeur, running slow but disregarding some shouted warning from the crossing policemen, swerved the auto to the left, violating the traffic rules, in order to pass in front of the wagon.

At that moment Freddie Drummond discontinued his conversation. Nor did he resume it again, for the situation was developing with the rapidity of a transformation scene. He heard the roar of the mob at the rear, and caught a glimpse of the helmeted police and the lurching meat wagons. At the same moment, laying on his whip and standing up to his task, the coal driver rushed horses and wagon squarely in front of the advancing procession, pulled the horses up sharply, and put on the big brake. Then he made his lines fast to the brake-handle and sat down with the air of one who had stopped to stay. The auto had been brought to a stop, too, by his big panting leaders which had jammed against it.

Before the chauffeur could back clear, an old Irishman, driving a rickety express wagon and lashing his one horse to a gallop, had locked wheels with the auto. Drummond recognized both horse and wagon, for he had driven them often himself. The Irishman was Pat Morrissey. On the other side a brewery wagon was locking with the coal wagon, and an east-bound Kearny-

Street car, wildly clanging its gong, the motorman shouting defiance at the crossing policeman, was dashing forward to complete the blockade. And wagon after wagon was locking and blocking and adding to the confusion. The meat wagons halted. The police were trapped. The roar at the rear increased as the mob came on to the attack, while the vanguard of the police charged the obstructing wagons.

"We're in for it," Drummond remarked coolly to Catherine.

"Yes," she nodded, with equal coolness. "What savages they are."

His admiration for her doubled on itself. She was indeed his sort. He would have been satisfied with her even if she had screamed and clung to him, but this—this was magnificent. She sat in that storm center as calmly as if it had been no more than a block of carriages at the opera.

The police were struggling to clear a passage. The driver of the coal wagon, a big man in shirt sleeves, lighted a pipe and sat smoking. He glanced down complacently at a captain of police who was raving and cursing at him, and his only acknowledgment was a shrug of the shoulders. From the rear arose the rat-tat-tat of clubs on heads and a pandemonium of cursing, yelling, and shouting. A violent accession of noise proclaimed that the mob had broken through and was dragging a scab from a wagon. The police captain reinforced from his vanguard, and the mob at the rear was repelled. Meanwhile, window after window in the high office building on the right had been opened, and the class-conscious clerks were raining a shower of office furniture down on the heads of police and scabs. Wastebaskets, ink-bottles, paperweights, typewriters—anything and everything that came to hand was filling the air.

A policeman, under orders from his captain, clambered to the lofty seat of the coal wagon to arrest the driver. And the driver, rising leisurely and peacefully to meet him, suddenly crumpled him in his arms and threw him down on top of the captain. The driver was a young giant, and when he climbed on top his load and poised a lump of coal in both hands, a policeman, who was just scaling the wagon from the side, let go and dropped back to earth. The captain ordered half a dozen of his men to take the wagon. The teamster, scrambling over the load from side to side, beat them down with huge lumps of coal.

The crowd on the sidewalks and the teamsters on the locked wagons roared encouragement and their own delight. The motorman, smashing helmets with his controller bar, was beaten into insensibility and dragged from his platform. The captain of police, beside himself at the repulse of his men, led the next assault on the coal wagon. A score of police were swarming up the tall-sided fortress. But the teamster multiplied himself. At times there were six or eight policemen rolling on the pavement and under the wagon. Engaged in repulsing an attack on the rear end of his fortress, the teamster turned about to see the captain just in the act of stepping on to the seat from the front end. He was still in the air and in most unstable equilibrium, when the teamster hurled a thirty-pound lump of coal. It caught the captain fairly on the chest, and he went over backward, striking on a wheeler's back, tumbling on to the ground, and jamming against the rear wheel of the auto.

Catherine thought he was dead, but he picked himself up and charged back. She reached out her gloved hand and patted the flank of the snorting, quivering horse. But Drummond did not notice the action. He had eyes for nothing save the battle of the coal wagon, while somewhere in his complicated psychology, one Bill Totts was heaving and straining in an effort to come to life. Drummond believed in law and order and the maintenance of the established, but this riotous savage within him would have none of it. Then, if ever, did Freddie Drummond call upon his iron inhibition to save him. But it is written that the house divided against itself must fall. And Freddie Drummond found that he had divided all the will and force of him with Bill Totts, and between them the entity that constituted the pair of them was being wrenched in twain.

Freddie Drummond sat in the auto, quite composed, alongside Catherine Van Vorst; but looking out of Freddie Drummond's eyes was Bill Totts, and somewhere behind those eyes, battling for the control of their mutual body, were Freddie Drummond, the sane and conservative sociologist, and Bill Totts, the class-conscious and bellicose union workingman. It was Bill Totts, looking out of those eyes, who saw the inevitable end of the battle on the coal wagon. He saw a policeman gain the top of the load, a second, and a third. They lurched clumsily on the loose footing, but their long riot-clubs were out and swinging. One blow caught the teamster on the head. A second he dodged, receiving it on the shoulder. For him the game was plainly up. He dashed in suddenly, clutched two policemen in his arms, and hurled himself a prisoner to the pavement, his hold never relaxing on his two captors.

Catherine Van Vorst was sick and faint at sight of the blood and brutal fighting. But her qualms were vanquished by the sensational and most unexpected happening that followed. The man beside her emitted an unearthly and uncultured yell and rose to his feet. She saw him spring over the front seat, leap to the broad rump of the wheeler, and from there gain the wagon. His onslaught was like a whirlwind. Before the bewildered officer on top the load could guess the errand of this conventionally clad but excited-seeming gentleman, he was the recipient of a punch that arched him back through the air to the pavement. A kick in the face led an ascending policeman to follow his example. A rush of three more gained the top and locked with Bill Totts in a gigantic clinch, during which his scalp was opened up by a club, and coat, vest, and half his starched shirt were torn from him. But the three policemen were flung wide and far, and Bill Totts, raining down lumps of coal, held the fort.

The captain led gallantly to the attack, but was bowled over by a chunk of coal that burst on his head in black baptism. The need of the police was to break the blockade in front before the mob could break in at the rear, and Bill Totts' need was to hold the wagon till the mob did break through. So the battle of the coal went on.

The crowd had recognized its champion. "Big" Bill, as usual, had come to the front, and Catherine Van Vorst was bewildered by the cries of "Bill! O you Bill!" that arose on every hand. Pat Morrissey, on his wagon seat, was jumping and screaming in an ecstasy, "Eat 'em, Bill! Eat 'em! Eat 'em alive!" From the sidewalk she heard a woman's voice cry out, "Look out, Bill—front end!" Bill took the warning and with well-directed coal cleaned the front end of the wagon of assailants. Catherine Van Vorst turned her head and saw on the curb of the sidewalk a woman with vivid coloring and flashing black eyes who was staring with all her soul at the man who had been Freddie Drummond a few minutes before.

The windows of the office building became vociferous with applause. A fresh shower of office chairs and filing cabinets descended. The mob had broken through on one side the line of wagons, and was advancing, each segregated policeman the center of a fighting group. The scabs were torn from their seats, the traces of the horses cut, and the frightened animals put in flight. Many policemen crawled under the coal wagon for safety, while the loose horses, with here and there a policeman on their backs or struggling at their heads to hold them, surged across the sidewalk opposite the jam and broke into Market Street.

Catherine Van Vorst heard the woman's voice calling in warning. She was back on the curb again, and crying out:

"Beat it, Bill! Now's your time! Beat it!"

The police for the moment had been swept away. Bill Totts leaped to the pavement and made his way to the woman on the sidewalk. Catherine Van Vorst saw her throw her arms around him and kiss him on the lips; and Catherine Van Vorst watched him curiously as he went on down the sidewalk, one arm around the woman, both talking and laughing, and he with a volubility and abandon she could never have dreamed possible.

The police were back again and clearing the jam while waiting for reinforcements and new drivers and horses. The mob had done its work and was scattering, and Catherine Van Vorst, still watching, could see the man she had known as Freddie Drummond. He towered a head above the crowd. His arm was still about the woman. And she in the motorcar, watching, saw the pair cross Market Street, cross the Slot, and disappear down Third Street into the labor ghetto.

In the years that followed no more lectures were given in the University of California by one Freddie Drummond, and no more books on economics and the labor question appeared over the name of Frederick A. Drummond. On the other hand there arose a new labor leader, William Totts by name. He it was who married Mary Condon, President of the International Glove Workers' Union No. 974; and he it was who called the notorious Cooks and Waiters' Strike, which, before its successful termination, brought out with it scores of other unions, among which, of the more remotely allied, were the Chicken Pickers and the Undertakers.

1909

Koolau the Leper[1]

"Because we are sick they take away our liberty. We have obeyed the law. We have done no wrong. And yet they would put us in prison. Molokai is a prison.[2] That you know. Niuli, there, his sister was sent to Molokai seven years ago. He has not seen her since. Nor will he ever see her. She must stay there until she dies. This is not her will. It is not Niuli's will. It is the will of the white men who rule the land. And who are these white men?

"We know. We have it from our fathers and our fathers' fathers. They came like lambs, speaking softly. Well might they speak softly, for we were many and strong, and all the islands were ours. As I say, they spoke softly. They were of two kinds. The one kind asked our permission, our gracious permission, to preach to us the word of God. The other kind asked our permission, our gracious permission, to trade with us. That was the beginning. To-day all the islands are theirs, all the land, all the cattle—everything is theirs. They that preached the word of God and they that preached the word of Rum have foregathered and become great chiefs. They live like kings in houses of many rooms, with multitudes of servants to care for them. They who had nothing have everything, and if you, or I, or any Kanaka[3] be hungry, they sneer and say, 'Well, why don't you work? There are the plantations.'"

Koolau paused. He raised one hand, and with gnarled and twisted fingers lifted up the blazing wreath of hibiscus that crowned his black hair. The moonlight bathed the scene in silver. It was a night of peace, though those who sat about him and listened had all the seeming of battle-wrecks. Their faces were leonine. Here a space yawned in a face where should have been a nose, and there an arm-stump showed where a hand had rotted off. They were men and women beyond the pale, the thirty of them, for upon them had been placed the mark of the beast.

They sat, flower-garlanded, in the perfumed, luminous night, and their lips made uncouth noises and their throats rasped approval of Koolau's speech. They were creatures who once had been men and women. But they were men and women no longer. They were monsters—in face and form grotesque caricatures of everything human. They were hideously maimed and distorted, and had the seeming of creatures that had been racked in millenniums of hell. Their hands, when they possessed them, were like harpy-claws. Their faces were the misfits and slips, crushed and bruised by some mad god at play in the machinery of life. Here and there were features which the mad god had smeared half away, and one woman wept scalding

---

[1]"Koolau the Leper" was first published in the *Pacific Monthly* in December, 1909. It later appeared in a collection of six stories, *The House of Pride* (Macmillan, 1912). The title story, "The House of Pride," and the collection itself incited controversy among white elites and missionaries in Hawai'i, who disapproved of London's working-class politics, his depictions of Euro–American colonialism, and his somewhat daring confrontation with the topic of leprosy.

[2]Molokai is a Hawaiian island that served as a colony for victims of leprosy starting in the 1860s.

[3]Hawaiian: person or man.

tears from twin pits of horror, where her eyes once had been. Some were in pain and groaned from their chests. Others coughed, making sounds like the tearing of tissue. Two were idiots, more like huge apes marred in the making, until even an ape were an angel. They mowed and gibbered in the moonlight, under crowns of drooping, golden blossoms. One, whose bloated ear-lobe flapped like a fan upon his shoulder, caught up a gorgeous flower of orange and scarlet and with it decorated the monstrous ear that flip-flapped with his every movement.

And over these things Koolau was king. And this was his kingdom,—a flower-throttled gorge, with beetling cliffs and crags, from which floated the blattings of wild goats. On three sides the grim walls rose, festooned in fantastic draperies of tropic vegetation and pierced by cave-entrances—the rocky lairs of Koolau's subjects. On the fourth side the earth fell away into a tremendous abyss, and, far below, could be seen the summits of lesser peaks and crags, at whose bases foamed and rumbled the Pacific surge. In fine weather a boat could land on the rocky beach that marked the entrance of Kalalau Valley, but the weather must be very fine. And a cool-headed mountaineer might climb from the beach to the head of Kalalau Valley, to this pocket among the peaks where Koolau ruled; but such a mountaineer must be very cool of head, and he must know the wild-goat trails as well. The marvel was that the mass of human wreckage that constituted Koolau's people should have been able to drag its helpless misery over the giddy goat-trails to this inaccessible spot.

"Brothers," Koolau began.

But one of the mowing, apelike travesties emitted a wild shriek of madness, and Koolau waited while the shrill cachination was tossed back and forth among the rocky walls and echoed distantly through the pulseless night.

"Brothers, is it not strange? Ours was the land, and behold, the land is not ours. What did these preachers of the word of God and the word of Rum give us for the land? Have you received one dollar, as much as one dollar, any one of you, for the land? Yet it is theirs, and in return they tell us we can go to work on the land, their land, and that what we produce by our toil shall be theirs. Yet in the old days we did not have to work. Also, when we are sick, they take away our freedom."

"Who brought the sickness, Koolau?" demanded Kiloliana, a lean and wiry man with a face so like a laughing faun's that one might expect to see the cloven hoofs under him. They were cloven, it was true, but the cleavages were great ulcers and livid putrefactions. Yet this was Kiloliana, the most daring climber of them all, the man who knew every goat-trail and who had led Koolau and his wretched followers into the recesses of Kalalau.

"Ay, well questioned," Koolau answered. "Because we would not work the miles of sugar-cane where once our horses pastured, they brought the Chinese slaves from over seas. And with them came the Chinese sickness—that which we suffer from and because of which they would imprison us on Molokai. We were born on Kauai. We have been to the other islands, some here and some there, to Oahu, to Maui, to Hawaii,[4] to Honolulu. Yet always did we come back to Kauai. Why did we come back? There must be a reason. Because we love Kauai. We were born here. Here we have lived. And here shall we die—unless—unless—there be weak hearts amongst us. Such we do not want. They are fit for Molokai. And if there be such, let them not remain. To-morrow the soldiers land on the shore. Let the weak hearts go down to them. They will be sent swiftly to Molokai. As for us, we shall stay and fight. But know that we will not die. We have rifles. You know the narrow trails where men must creep, one by one. I, alone, Koolau, who was once a cowboy on Niihau, can hold the trail against a thousand men. Here is Kapalei, who was once a judge over men and a man with honor, but who is now a hunted rat, like you and me. Hear him. He is wise."

Kapalei arose. Once he had been a judge. He had gone to college at Punahou.[5] He had sat at meat with lords and chiefs and the high representatives of alien powers who protected the interests of traders and missionaries. Such had been Kapalei. But now, as Koolau had said, he was a hunted rat, a creature outside the law, sunk so deep in the mire of human horror that he was above the law as well as beneath it. His face was featureless, save for gaping orifices and for the lidless eyes that burned under hairless brows.

"Let us not make trouble," he began. "We ask to be left alone. But if they do not leave us alone, then is the trouble theirs, and the penalty. My fingers are gone, as you see." He held up his stumps of hands that all might see. "Yet have I the joint of one thumb left, and it can pull a trigger as firmly as did its lost neighbor in the old days. We love Kauai. Let us live here, or die here, but do not let us go to the prison of Molokai. The sickness is not ours. We have not sinned. The men who preached the word of God and the word of Rum brought the sickness with the coolie slaves who work the stolen land. I have been a judge. I know the law and the justice, and I say to you it is unjust to steal a man's land, to make that man sick with the Chinese sickness, and then to put that man in prison for life."

"Life is short, and the days are filled with pain," said Koolau. "Let us drink and dance and be happy as we can."

From one of the rocky lairs calabashes were produced and passed around. The calabashes were filled with the fierce distillation of the root of the *ti*-plant;[6] and as the liquid fire coursed through them and mounted to their brains, they forgot that they had once been men and women, for they were men and women once more. The woman who wept scalding tears from open eye-pits was indeed a woman apulse with life as she plucked the strings of an *ukulele* and lifted her voice in a barbaric love-call such as might have come from the dark forest-depths of the primeval world. The air tingled with her cry, softly imperious and seductive. Upon a mat, timing his rhythm to the woman's song, Kiloliana danced. It was unmistakable. Love

[4]Hawaiian islands.
[5]A university in Honolulu.
[6]A flowering tropical bush.

danced in all his movements, and, next, dancing with him on the mat, was a woman whose heavy hips and generous breast gave the lie to her disease-corroded face. It was a dance of the living dead, for in their disintegrating bodies life still loved and longed. Ever the woman whose sightless eyes ran scalding tears chanted her love-cry, ever the dancers danced of love in the warm night, and ever the calabashes went around till in all their brains were maggots crawling of memory and desire. And with the woman on the mat danced a slender maid whose face was beautiful and unmarred, but whose twisted arms that rose and fell marked the disease's ravage. And the two idiots, gibbering and mouthing strange noises, danced apart, grotesque, fantastic, travestying love as they themselves had been travestied by life.

But the woman's love-cry broke midway, the calabashes were lowered, and the dancers ceased, as all gazed into the abyss above the sea, where a rocket flared like a wan phantom through the moonlit air.

"It is the soldiers," said Koolau. "Tomorrow there will be fighting. It is well to sleep and be prepared."

The lepers obeyed, crawling away to their lairs in the cliff, until only Koolau remained, sitting motionless in the moon-light, his rifle across his knees, as he gazed far down to the boats landing on the beach.

The far head of Kalalau Valley had been well chosen as a refuge. Except Kiloliana, who knew back-trails up the precipitous walls, no man could win to the gorge save by advancing across a knife-edged ridge. This passage was a hundred yards in length. At best, it was a scant twelve inches wide. On either side yawned the abyss. A slip, and to right or left the man would fall to his death. But once across he would find himself in an earthly paradise. A sea of vegetation laved the landscape, pouring its green billows from wall to wall, dripping from the cliff-lips in great vine-masses, and flinging a spray of ferns and air-plants into the multitudinous crevices. During the many months of Koolau's rule, he and his followers had fought with this vegetable sea. The choking jungle, with its riot of blossoms, had been driven back from the bananas, oranges, and mangoes that grew wild. In little clearings grew the wild arrowroot; on stone terraces, filled with soil scrapings, were the *taro* patches and the melons;[7] and in every open space where the sunshine penetrated, were *papaia* trees burdened with their golden fruit.[8]

Koolau had been driven to this refuge from the lower valley by the beach. And if he were driven from it in turn, he knew of gorges among the jumbled peaks of the inner fastness where he could lead his subjects and live. And now he lay with his rifle beside him, peering down through a tangled screen of foliage at the soldiers on the beach. He noted that they had large guns with them, from which the sunshine flashed as from mirrors. The knife-edged passage lay directly before him. Crawling upward along the trail that led to it he could see tiny specks of men. He knew they were not

---

[7]Taro is a starchy tuber that was a traditional staple crop in the Hawaiian islands.   [8]A variation of papaya, a tropical fruit.

the soldiers, but the police. When they failed, then the soldiers would enter the game.

He affectionately rubbed a twisted hand along his rifle barrel and made sure that the sights were clean. He had learned to shoot as a wild-cattle hunter on Niihau, and on that island his skill as a marksman was unforgotten. As the toiling specks of men grew nearer and larger, he estimated the range, judged the deflection of the wind that swept at right angles across the line of fire, and calculated the chances of overshooting marks that were so far below his level. But he did not shoot. Not until they reached the beginning of the passage did he make his presence known. He did not disclose himself, but spoke from the thicket.

"What do you want?" he demanded.

"We want Koolau, the leper," answered the man who led the native police, himself a blue-eyed American.

"You must go back," Koolau said.

He knew the man, a deputy sheriff, for it was by him that he had been harried out of Niihau, across Kauai, to Kalalau Valley, and out of the valley to the gorge.

"Who are you?" the sheriff asked.

"I am Koolau, the leper," was the reply.

"Then come out. We want you. Dead or alive, there is a thousand dollars on your head. You cannot escape."

Koolau laughed aloud in the thicket.

"Come out!" the sheriff commanded, and was answered by silence.

He conferred with the police, and Koolau saw that they were preparing to rush him.

"Koolau," the sheriff called. "Koolau, I am coming across to get you."

"Then look first and well about you at the sun and sea and sky, for it will be the last time you behold them."

"That's all right, Koolau," the sheriff said soothingly. "I know you're a dead shot. But you won't shoot me. I have never done you any wrong."

Koolau grunted in the thicket.

"I say, you know, I've never done you any wrong, have I?" the sheriff persisted.

"You do me wrong when you try to put me in prison," was the reply. "And you do me wrong when you try for the thousand dollars on my head. If you will live, stay where you are."

"I've got to come across and get you. I'm sorry. But it is my duty."

"You will die before you get across."

The sheriff was no coward. Yet was he undecided. He gazed into the gulf on either side, and ran his eyes along the knife-edge he must travel. Then he made up his mind.

"Koolau," he called.

But the thicket remained silent.

"Koolau, don't shoot. I am coming."

The sheriff turned, gave some orders to the police, then started on his perilous way. He advanced slowly. It was like walking a tight rope. He had nothing to lean upon but the air. The lava rock crumbled under his feet, and on either side the dislodged fragments pitched downward through the depths. The sun blazed upon him, and his face was wet with sweat. Still he advanced, until the halfway point was reached.

"Stop!" Koolau commanded from the thicket. "One more step and I shoot."

The sheriff halted, swaying for balance as he stood poised above the void. His face was pale, but his eyes were determined. He licked his dry lips before he spoke.

"Koolau, you won't shoot me. I know you won't."

He started once more. The bullet whirled him half about. On his face was an expression of querulous surprise as he reeled to the fall. He tried to save himself by throwing his body across the knife-edge; but at that moment he knew death. The next moment the knife-edge was vacant. Then came the rush, five policemen, in single file, with superb steadiness, running along the knife-edge. At the same instant the rest of the posse opened fire on the thicket. It was madness. Five times Koolau pulled the trigger, so rapidly that his shots constituted a rattle. Changing his position and crouching low under the bullets that were biting and singing through the bushes, he peered out. Four of the police had followed the sheriff. The fifth lay across the knife-edge, still alive. On the farther side, no longer firing, were the surviving police. On the naked rock there was no hope for them. Before they could clamber down Koolau could have picked off the last man. But he did not fire, and, after a conference, one of them took off a white undershirt and waved it as a flag. Followed by another, he advanced along the knife-edge to their wounded comrade. Koolau gave no sign, but watched them slowly withdraw and become specks as they descended into the lower valley.

Two hours later, from another thicket, Koolau watched a body of police trying to make the ascent from the opposite side of the valley. He saw the wild goats flee before them as they climbed higher and higher, until he doubted his judgment and sent for Kiloliana who crawled in beside him.

"No, there is no way," said Kiloliana.

"The goats?" Koolau questioned.

"They come over from the next valley, but they cannot pass to this. There is no way. Those men are not wiser than goats. They may fall to their deaths. Let us watch."

"They are brave men," said Koolau. "Let us watch."

Side by side they lay among the morning-glories, with the yellow blossoms of the *hau* dropping upon them from overhead,[9] watching the motes of men toil upward, till the thing happened, and three of them, slipping, rolling, sliding, dashed over a cliff-lip and fell sheer half a thousand feet.

Kiloliana chuckled.

[9]Hau is a type of hibiscus tree.

"We will be bothered no more," he said.

"They have war guns," Koolau made answer."The soldiers have not yet spoken."

In the drowsy afternoon, most of the lepers lay in their rock dens asleep. Koolau, his rifle on his knees, fresh-cleaned and ready, dozed in the entrance to his own den. The maid with the twisted arm lay below in the thicket and kept watch on the knife-edge passage. Suddenly Koolau was startled wide awake by the sound of an explosion on the beach. The next instant the atmosphere was incredibly rent asunder. The terrible sound frightened him. It was as if all the gods had caught the envelope of the sky in their hands and were ripping it apart as a woman rips apart a sheet of cotton cloth. But it was such an immense ripping, growing swiftly nearer. Koolau glanced up apprehensively, as if expecting to see the thing. Then high up on the cliff overhead the shell burst in a fountain of black smoke. The rock was shattered, the fragments falling to the foot of the cliff.

Koolau passed his hand across his sweaty brow. He was terribly shaken. He had had no experience with shell-fire, and this was more dreadful than anything he had imagined.

"One," said Kapahei, suddenly bethinking himself to keep count.

A second and a third shell flew screaming over the top of the wall, bursting beyond view. Kapahei methodically kept the count. The lepers crowded into the open space before the caves. At first they were frightened, but as the shells continued their flight overhead the leper folk became reassured and began to admire the spectacle. The two idiots shrieked with delight, prancing wild antics as each air-tormenting shell went by. Koolau began to recover his confidence. No damage was being done. Evidently they could not aim such large missiles at such long range with the precision of a rifle.

But a change came over the situation. The shells began to fall short. One burst below in the thicket by the knife-edge. Koolau remembered the maid who lay there on watch, and ran down to see. The smoke was still rising from the bushes when he crawled in. He was astounded. The branches were splintered and broken. Where the girl had lain was a hole in the ground. The girl herself was in shattered fragments. The shell had burst right on her.

First peering out to make sure no soldiers were attempting the passage, Koolau started back on the run for the caves. All the time the shells were moaning, whining, screaming by, and the valley was rumbling and reverberating with the explosions. As he came in sight of the caves, he saw the two idiots cavorting about, clutching each other's hands with their stumps of fingers. Even as he ran, Koolau saw a spout of black smoke rise from the ground, near to the idiots. They were flung apart bodily by the explosion. One lay motionless, but the other was dragging himself by his hands toward the cave. His legs trailed out helplessly behind him, while the blood was pouring from his body. He seemed bathed in blood, and as he crawled he cried like a little dog. The rest of the lepers, with the exception of Kapahei, had fled into the caves.

"Seventeen," said Kapahei. "Eighteen," he added.

This last shell had fairly entered into one of the caves. The explosion caused all the caves to empty. But from the particular cave no one emerged. Koolau crept in through the pungent, acrid smoke. Four bodies, frightfully mangled, lay about. One of them was the sightless woman whose tears till now had never ceased.

Outside, Koolau found his people in a panic and already beginning to climb the goat trail that led out of the gorge and on among the jumbled heights and chasms. The wounded idiot, whining feebly and dragging himself along on the ground by his hands, was trying to follow. But at the first pitch of the wall his helplessness overcame him and he fell back.

"It would be better to kill him," said Koolau to Kapahei, who still sat in the same place.

"Twenty-two," Kapahei answered. "Yes, it would be a wise thing to kill him. Twenty-three—twenty-four."

The idiot whined sharply when he saw the rifle leveled at him. Koolau hesitated, then lowered the gun.

"It is a hard thing to do," he said.

"You are a fool, twenty-six, twenty-seven," said Kapahei. "Let me show you."

He arose and, with a heavy fragment of rock in his hand, approached the wounded thing. As he lifted his arm to strike, a shell burst full upon him, relieving him of the necessity of the act and at the same time putting an end to his count.

Koolau was alone in the gorge. He watched the last of his people drag their crippled bodies over the brow of the height and disappear. Then he turned and went down to the thicket where the maid had been killed. The shell-fire still continued, but he remained; for far below he could see the soldiers climbing up. A shell burst twenty feet away. Flattening himself into the earth, he heard the rush of the fragments above his body. A shower of *hau* blossoms rained upon him. He lifted his head to peer down the trail, and sighed. He was very much afraid. Bullets from rifles would not have worried him, but this shell-fire was abominable. Each time a shell shrieked by he shivered and crouched; but each time he lifted his head again to watch the trail.

At last the shells ceased. This, he reasoned, was because the soldiers were drawing near. They crept along the trail in single file, and he tried to count them until he lost track. At any rate, there were a hundred or so of them—all come after Koolau the leper. He felt a fleeting prod of pride. With war guns and rifles, police and soldiers, they came for him, and he was only one man, a crippled wreck of a man at that. They offered a thousand dollars for him, dead or alive. In all his life he had never possessed that much money. The thought was a bitter one. Kapahei had been right. He, Koolau, had done no wrong. Because the *haoles* wanted labor with which to work the stolen land,[10] they had brought in the Chinese coolies, and with them had

[10]*Haole* is Hawaiian for "white person."

come the sickness. And now, because he had caught the sickness, he was worth a thousand dollars—but not to himself. It was his worthless carcass, rotten with disease or dead from a bursting shell, that was worth all that money.

When the soldiers reached the knife-edged passage, he was prompted to warn them. But his gaze fell upon the body of the murdered maid, and he kept silent. When six had ventured on the knife-edge, he opened fire. Nor did he cease when the knife-edge was bare. He emptied his magazine, reloaded, and emptied it again. He kept on shooting. All his wrongs were blazing in his brain, and he was in a fury of vengeance. All down the goat trail the soldiers were firing, and though they lay flat and sought to shelter themselves in the shallow inequalities of the surface, they were exposed marks to him. Bullets whistled and thudded about him, and an occasional ricochet sang sharply through the air. One bullet ploughed a crease through his scalp, and a second burned across his shoulder-blade without breaking the skin.

It was a massacre, in which one man did the killing. The soldiers began to retreat, helping along their wounded. As Koolau picked them off he became aware of the smell of burnt meat. He glanced about him at first, and then discovered that it was his own hands. The heat of the rifle was doing it. The leprosy had destroyed most of the nerves in his hands. Though his flesh burned and he smelled it, there was no sensation.

He lay in the thicket, smiling, until he remembered the war guns. Without doubt they would open up on him again, and this time upon the very thicket from which he had inflicted the damage. Scarcely had he changed his position to a nook behind a small shoulder of the wall where he had noted that no shells fell, than the bombardment recommenced. He counted the shells. Sixty more were thrown into the gorge before the warguns ceased. The tiny area was pitted with their explosions, until it seemed impossible that any creature could have survived. So the soldiers thought, for, under the burning afternoon sun, they climbed the goat trail again. And again the knife-edged passage was disputed, and again they fell back to the beach.

For two days longer Koolau held the passage, though the soldiers contented themselves with flinging shells into his retreat. Then Pahau, a leper boy, came to the top of the wall at the back of the gorge and shouted down to him that Kiloliana, hunting goats that they might eat, had been killed by a fall, and that the women were frightened and knew not what to do. Koolau called the boy down and left him with a spare gun with which to guard the passage. Koolau found his people disheartened. The majority of them were too helpless to forage food for themselves under such forbidding circumstances, and all were starving. He selected two women and a man who were not too far gone with the disease, and sent them back to the gorge to bring up food and mats. The rest he cheered and consoled until even the weakest took a hand in building rough shelters for themselves.

But those he had dispatched for food did not return, and he started back for the gorge. As he came out on the brow of the wall, half a dozen rifles cracked. A bullet tore through the fleshy part of his shoulder, and his cheek was cut by a sliver of rock where a second bullet smashed against the cliff. In the moment that this happened, and he leaped back, he saw that the gorge was alive with soldiers. His own people had betrayed him. The shell-fire had been too terrible, and they had preferred the prison of Molokai.

Koolau dropped back and unslung one of his heavy cartridge-belts. Lying among the rocks, he allowed the head and shoulders of the first soldier to rise clearly into view before pulling trigger. Twice his happened, and then, after some delay, in place of a head and shoulders a white flag was thrust above the edge of the wall.

"What do you want?" he demanded.

"I want you, if you are Koolau the leper," came the answer.

Koolau forget where he was, forgot everything, as he lay and marvelled at the strange persistence of these *haoles* who would have their will though the sky fell in. Aye, they would have their will over all men and all things, even though they died in getting it. He could not but admire them, too, what of that will in them that was stronger than life and that bent all things to their bidding. He was convinced of the hopelessness of his struggle. There was no gainsaying that terrible will of the *haoles*. Though he killed a thousand, yet would they rise like the sands of the sea and come upon him, ever more and more. They never knew when they were beaten. That was their fault and their virtue. It was where his own kind lacked. He could see, now, how the handful of the preachers of God and the preachers of Rum had conquered the land. It was because—

"Well, what have you got to say? Will you come with me?"

It was the voice of the invisible man under the white flag. There he was, like any *haole*, driving straight toward the end determined.

"Let us talk," said Koolau.

The man's head and shoulders arose, then his whole body. He was a smooth-faced, blue-eyed youngster of twenty-five, slender and natty in his captain's uniform. He advanced until halted, then seated himself a dozen feet away:—

"You are a brave man," said Koolau wonderingly. "I could kill you like a fly."

"No, you couldn't," was the answer.

"Why not?"

"Because you are a man, Koolau, though a bad one. I know your story. You kill fairly."

Koolau grunted, but was secretly pleased.

"What have you done with my people?" he demanded. "The boy, the two women, and the man?"

"They gave themselves up, as I have now come for you to do."

Koolau laughed incredulously.

"I am a free man," he announced. "I have done no wrong. All I ask is to be left alone. I have lived free, and I shall die free. I will never give myself up."

"Then your people are wiser than you," answered the young captain. "Look—they are coming now."

Koolau turned and watched the remnant of his band approach. Groaning and sighing, a ghastly procession, it dragged its wretchedness past. It was given to Koolau to taste a deeper bitterness, for they hurled imprecations and insults at him as they went by; and the panting hag who brought up the rear halted, and with skinny, harpy-claws extended, shaking her snarling death's head from side to side, she laid a curse upon him. One by one they dropped over the lip-edge and surrendered to the hiding soldiers.

"You can go now," said Koolau to the captain. "I will never give myself up. That is my last word. Good-by."

The captain slipped over the cliff to his soldiers. The next moment, and without a flag of truce, he hoisted his hat on his scabbard, and Koolau's bullet tore through it. That afternoon they shelled him out from the beach, and as he retreated into the high inaccessible pockets beyond, the soldiers followed him.

For six weeks they hunted him from pocket to pocket, over the volcanic peaks and along the goat trails. When he hid in the lantana jungle,[11] they formed lines of beaters, and through lantana jungle and guava scrub they drove him like a rabbit. But ever he turned and doubled and eluded. There was no cornering him. When pressed too closely, his sure rifle held them back and they carried their wounded down the goat trails to the beach. There were times when they did the shooting as his brown body showed for a moment through the under-brush. Once, five of them caught him on an exposed goat trail between pockets. They emptied their rifles at him as he limped and climbed along his dizzy way. Afterward they found blood-stains and knew that he was wounded. At the end of six weeks they gave up. The soldiers and police returned to Honolulu, and Kalalau Valley was left to him for his own, though head-hunters ventured after him from time to time and to their own undoing.

Two years later, and for the last time, Koolau crawled unto a thicket and lay down among the *ti*-leaves and wild ginger blossoms. Free he had lived, and free he was dying. A slight drizzle of rain began to fall, and he drew a ragged blanket about the distorted wreck of his limbs. His body was covered with an oilskin coat. Across his chest he laid his Mauser rifle,[12] lingering affectionately for a moment to wipe the dampness from the barrel. The hand with which he wiped had no fingers left upon it with which to pull the trigger.

He closed his eyes, for, from the weakness in his body and the fuzzy turmoil in his brain, he knew that his end was near. Like a wild animal he had crept into hiding to die. Half-conscious, aimless and wandering, he lived back in his life to his early manhood on Niihau. As life faded and the drip of the rain grew dim in his ears, it seemed to him that he was once more in the thick of the horse-breaking, with raw colts rearing and bucking under him, his stirrups tied together beneath, or charging madly about the breaking corral and driving the helping cowboys over the rails. The next instant,

---

[11]Family of flowering tropical plants.   [12]German infantry rifle.

and with seeming naturalness, he found himself pursuing the wild bulls of the upland pastures, roping them and leading them down to the valleys. Again the sweat and dust of the branding pen stung his eyes and bit his nostrils.

All his lusty, whole-bodied youth was his, until the sharp pangs of impending dissolution brought him back. He lifted his monstrous hands and gazed at them in wonder. But how? Why? Why should the wholeness of that wild youth of his change to this? Then he remembered, and once again, and for a moment, he was Koolau, the leper. His eyelids fluttered wearily down and the drip of the rain ceased in his ears. A prolonged trembling set up in his body. This, too, ceased. He half-lifted his head, but it fell back. Then his eyes opened, and did not close. His last thought was of his Mauser, and he pressed it against his chest with his folded, fingerless hands.

1908

ACKNOWLEDGMENTS

African American Folktales. "Animal Tales: Who Ate Up the Butter?," "Animal Tales: Fox and Rabbit in the Well," "John and Old Marster: Baby in the Crib," "John and Old Marster: John Steals a Pig and a Sheep," "John and Old Marster: Talking Bones," and "John and Old Marster: Old Boss Wants into Heaven," from *American Negro Folktales* by Richard M. Dorson, Fawcett Publications, 1967, pp. 68–71, 97–98, 138, 138–139, 147–148, 158–161. Used by permission of Hilliard Lyons Trust Company LLC, Trustee, on behalf of the author. "Animal Tales: The Signifying Monkey," from *Deep Down in the Jungle* by Roger D. Abrahams. Reprinted by permission of Transaction Publishers Inc. "Conjure Stories: Two Tales from Eatonville, Florida," from *Hoodoo in America* by Zora Hurston, *Journal of American Folk-Lore* 44, no. 174 (October–December 1931): 404–405. Published by the University of Illinois Press for the American Folklore Society. "Memories of Slavery: Malitis," told by Mrs. Josie Jordan, in B. A. Botkin, ed., *Lay My Burden Down: A Folk History of Slavery* (Chicago: U of Chicago P, 1945): pp. 4–5. This volume contains excerpts from the Slave Narrative Collection of the Federal Writers' Project, collected during the 1930s. "Memories of Slavery: The Flying Africans," from *Drums and Shadows: Survival Studies among the Georgia Coastal Negroes* (Athens: Univeristy of Georgia press, 1940): pp. 78–79, 150–151.

Mary Austin. Excerpts from *Earth Horizon* by Mary Austin. Copyright © 1932 by Mary Austin. Copyright © renewed 1960 by School of American Research. Reprinted by permission of Houghton Mifflin Harcourt Publishing Company. All rights reserved.

Charles Waddell Chesnutt. "Journal," from *The Journals of Charles W. Chesnutt* by Charles Waddell Chesnutt, ed. Richard H. Brodhead. Copyright © 1993 Duke University Press.

Corridos. "Kiansis I (Kansas I)," "Gregorio Cortez (Gregorio Cortez)," "Jacinto Treviño (Jacinto Treviño)," "Hijo Desobediente (The Disobedient Son)," and "Corrido de César Chávez (Ballad of César Chávez)," from *A Texas-Mexican Cancioñero*, translated by Americo Paredes (1976). Reprinted by permission of the author. "Recordando al President (Remembering the President)," from *A Texas-Mexican Cancioñero*, translated by Americo Paredes (1976), and from Dan William Dickey, *The Kennedy Corridos: A Study of the Ballads of a Mexican American Hero* (Austin: Center for Mexican American Studies, University of Texas at Austin, 1978). Reprinted by permission.

Edith Maud Eaton. "In the Land of the Free" and "The Wisdom of the New," from *Island: Poetry and History of Chinese Immigrants on Angel Island, 1910–1940*, edited by Him Mark Lai, Genny Lim, and Judy Yung (published by HOC DOI). Reprinted by permission of the University of Washington Press.

Sadakichi Hartmann. "Cathedral Sacrilege." Reprinted by permission of Marigold Linton.

José Martí. "Our America," from *Our America* by José Martí (Monthly Review Press), pp. 84–94. Used by permission.

Victoria Earle Matthews. "The Value of Race Literature," from *The New Negro*, edited by Henry Louis Gates Jr. © 2007 by Henry Louis Gates Jr. and Gene Andrew Jarrett. Published by Princeton University Press. Reprinted by permission of Princeton University Press.

Index of Authors, Titles, and First Lines of Poems

LIST OF AUTHORS

Adams, Henry
African American Folktales
Alcott, Louisa May
Aldrich, Thomas Bailey
Anonymous in the New York World
Antin, Mary
Austin, Mary

Bierce, Ambrose
Bonnin, Gertrude

Cable, George Washington
Cahan, Abraham
Capetillo, Luisa
Chesnutt, Charles Waddell
Chopin, Kate
Clemens, Samuel Langhorne (Mark Twain)
Comfort, Anna Manning
Cooper, Anna Julia
Corridos
Crane, Stephen

De Veyra, M. P.
Dunbar, Paul Laurence
Dunbar-Nelson, Alice
Dunne, Finley Peter

Eastman, Charles Alexander
Eastman, Elaine Goodale
Eaton, Edith Maud

Foote, Julia A. J.
Freeman, Mary E. Wilkins

Galán, Carlos F.
Garland, Hamlin
Ghost Dance Songs
Gilman, Charlotte Perkins
Grady, Henry W.
Grass, John
Guiney, Louise Imogen

Harper, Frances Ellen Watkins
Harris, Joel Chandler
Hartmann, Sadakichi
Hopkins, Pauline Elizabeth
Howells, William Dean

James, Henry
Jewett, Sarah Orne
Jewett, Sophie
Johnson, E. Pauline

Kalaw, Maximo M.
King, Grace
Kipling, Rudyard

Lazarus, Emma
London, Jack
Lopez, Sixto

Martí, José
Matthews, Victoria Earle
McKinley, William
Menken, Adah
Miller, Kelly
Moulton, Louise Chandler

Nast, Thomas
Noguchi, Yone
Norris, Frank

Oskison, John Milton

Page, Thomas Nelson
Palaneapope
Peraza, N. Bolet
Piatt, Sarah Morgan Bryan
Posey, Alexander Lawrence

Quezon, Manuel L.
Quintero de Joseph, Maria Guadalupe
    Gutierrez

Ramirez, Sara Estela
Red Cloud
Reese, Lizette Woodworth
Riley, James Whitcomb
Robinson, Rowland E.
Ruiz de Burton, María Amparo

Santayana, George
Serra, Rafael
Sinclair, Upton
Sitting Bull
Spofford, Harriet Prescott
Standing Bear

Thaxter, Celia
The Filipino Students' Magazine
The Women's Auxiliary of the Anti-
    Imperialist League
Thomas, Edith
Tourgée, Albion W.
Turning Hawk, Captain Sword, Spotted
    Horse, and American Horse
Two Moons